MW01617374

CINCINNATI SILVER

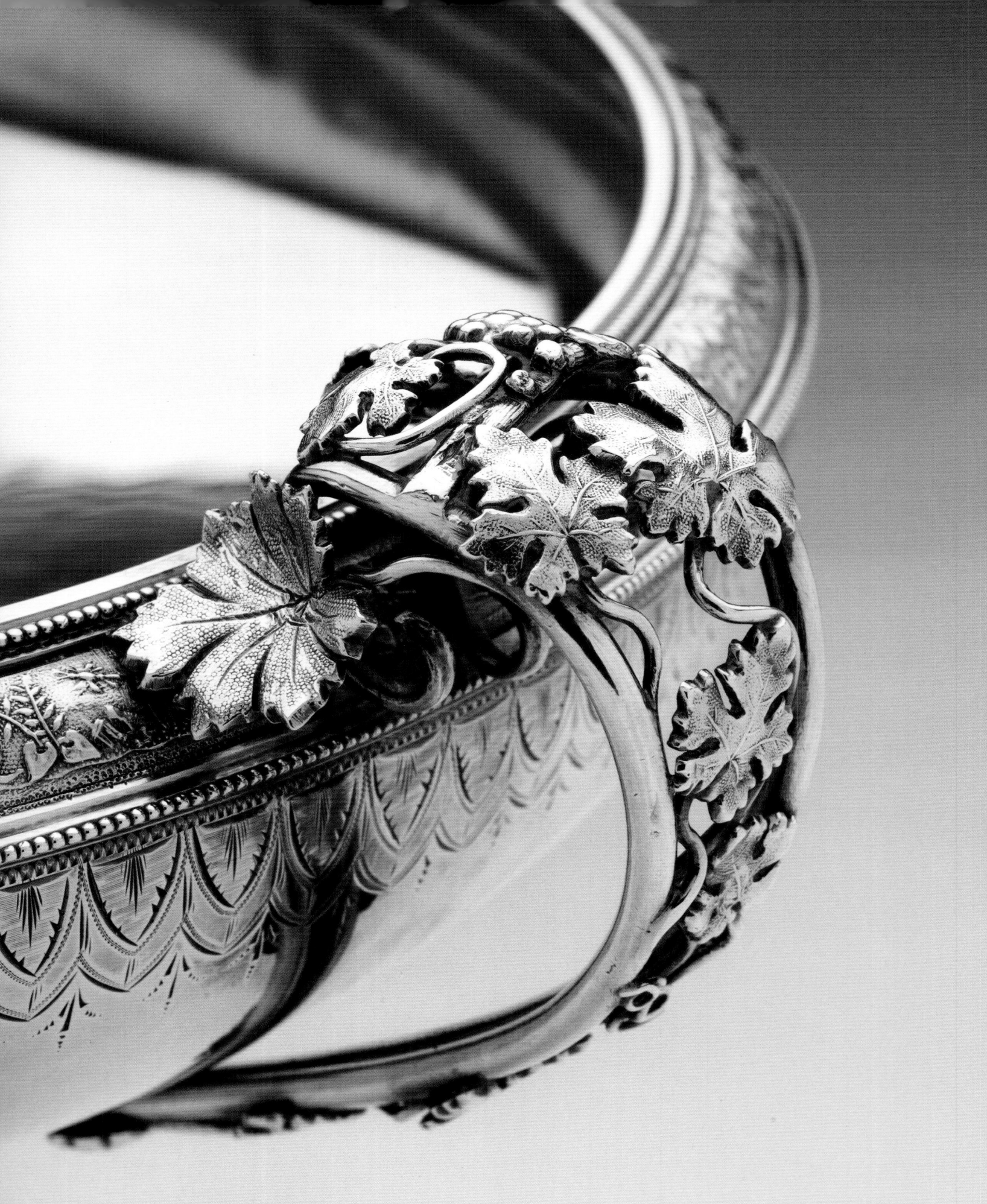

CINCINNATI SILVER

1788–1940

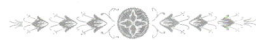

AMY MILLER DEHAN

WITH CONTRIBUTIONS BY JANET C. HAARTZ AND NORA KOHL

CINCINNATI ART MUSEUM
In association with
D GILES LIMITED, LONDON

2014

cincinnati ✳ art museum

g

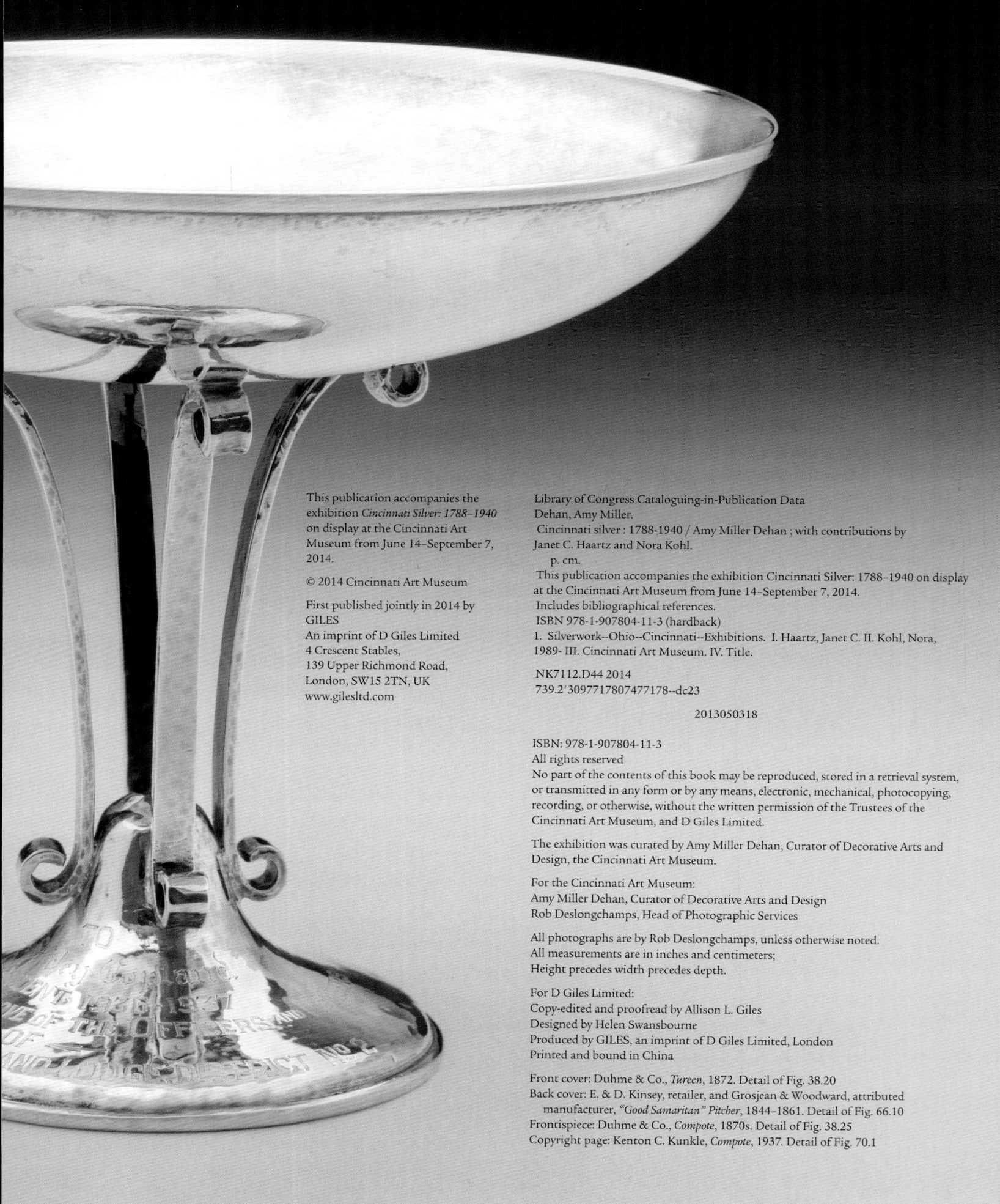

This publication accompanies the exhibition *Cincinnati Silver: 1788–1940* on display at the Cincinnati Art Museum from June 14–September 7, 2014.

© 2014 Cincinnati Art Museum

First published jointly in 2014 by GILES
An imprint of D Giles Limited
4 Crescent Stables,
139 Upper Richmond Road,
London, SW15 2TN, UK
www.gilesltd.com

Library of Congress Cataloguing-in-Publication Data
Dehan, Amy Miller.
 Cincinnati silver : 1788-1940 / Amy Miller Dehan ; with contributions by Janet C. Haartz and Nora Kohl.
    p. cm.
 This publication accompanies the exhibition Cincinnati Silver: 1788–1940 on display at the Cincinnati Art Museum from June 14–September 7, 2014.
 Includes bibliographical references.
 ISBN 978-1-907804-11-3 (hardback)
 1. Silverwork--Ohio--Cincinnati--Exhibitions. I. Haartz, Janet C. II. Kohl, Nora, 1989- III. Cincinnati Art Museum. IV. Title.

 NK7112.D44 2014
 739.2′3097717807477178--dc23

                    2013050318

ISBN: 978-1-907804-11-3
All rights reserved
No part of the contents of this book may be reproduced, stored in a retrieval system, or transmitted in any form or by any means, electronic, mechanical, photocopying, recording, or otherwise, without the written permission of the Trustees of the Cincinnati Art Museum, and D Giles Limited.

The exhibition was curated by Amy Miller Dehan, Curator of Decorative Arts and Design, the Cincinnati Art Museum.

For the Cincinnati Art Museum:
Amy Miller Dehan, Curator of Decorative Arts and Design
Rob Deslongchamps, Head of Photographic Services

All photographs are by Rob Deslongchamps, unless otherwise noted.
All measurements are in inches and centimeters;
Height precedes width precedes depth.

For D Giles Limited:
Copy-edited and proofread by Allison L. Giles
Designed by Helen Swansbourne
Produced by GILES, an imprint of D Giles Limited, London
Printed and bound in China

Front cover: Duhme & Co., *Tureen*, 1872. Detail of Fig. 38.20
Back cover: E. & D. Kinsey, retailer, and Grosjean & Woodward, attributed manufacturer, *"Good Samaritan" Pitcher*, 1844–1861. Detail of Fig. 66.10
Frontispiece: Duhme & Co., *Compote*, 1870s. Detail of Fig. 38.25
Copyright page: Kenton C. Kunkle, *Compote*, 1937. Detail of Fig. 70.1

CONTENTS

The Cincinnati Art Museum wishes to thank the following for making the exhibition *Cincinnati Silver: 1788–1940*, and this publication possible:

SPONSORS

The Duveneck Association of the Cincinnati Art Museum
National Endowment for the Arts
Cambridge Charitable Foundation, in memory of Charles H. Randolph
Marcia and Ron Joseph
Ohio Historical Decorative Arts Association
Lee Cown Tour Group Fund

LENDERS

The Cincinnati Museum Center
The Glendower Mansion, Warren County Historical Society
Bradley S. Karoleff, Coins + LLC
Lauren Stanley Silver
Ann Duhme Newstedt Phelps
Irene and Daniel Randolph
Jerome and Virginia Redfearn
Ronald T. Vance
and several anonymous lenders

The Cincinnati Art Museum gratefully acknowledges the generous operating support provided by:

ArtsWave
Ohio Arts Council
The City of Cincinnati
and our Members

DIRECTOR'S FOREWORD

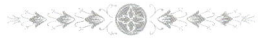

ONE THING THAT sets Cincinnati apart from most other Midwestern cities is the breadth and quality of art-making in many different media from the early decades of the 19th century onward. This is true in silver. Before 1850, there were more silversmiths, jewelers, watch makers, and clock makers working in Cincinnati than in any other city in the Midwest. The Cincinnati Art Museum has, since its inception, acted as the anchor for this astonishing and continued outpouring of disciplined creativity. Prompted by the recent concentration on our city and its artistic heritage in the permanent exhibition galleries of *The Cincinnati Wing: The Story of Art in the Queen City* (opened 2003), and by the scholarship and indefatigable research of our Curator of Decorative Arts and Design, Amy Dehan, the collection of Cincinnati silver and an understanding of the local trade became one of the Decorative Arts and Design department's primary goals.

Over the last decade, through purchase and donation, our collection of local silver has quadrupled and now numbers over five hundred pieces. We are proud to say that this collection is the largest public collection of its kind, equal in depth, breadth, and importance to the Art Museum's other well-known and published Cincinnati collections. It contains elegantly designed and skillfully wrought tea sets, water pitchers, loving cups, and other wares ranging from the beginning of the city's silversmithing trade, established by 1795,

through the Art Deco period. Examples by major makers and members of the trade like the Best family (active 1802–1830s), the Kinsey family (active 1834–1882), the McGrew family (active 1817–1888), and Duhme & Co. and its related firms (1842–about 1928) are represented, as well as works by more obscure makers like Joseph G. Joseph (active 1834–1846), Robert Sturm (active 1890–1932), and Kenton C. Kunkle (active 1898–1941).

Through the development and examination of this collection as a whole, and through extensive archival research, we are, for the first time, beginning to understand the particulars of the local trade (the migration patterns and education of local smiths, choice production and distribution systems, and popular stylistic trends), and, what is perhaps most important, the position and significance of the local trade within the broader history of American silver. We are also coming to understand how the designs and forms in this medium fit into the overall picture of art-making in Cincinnati and the surrounding region. This book and the accompanying exhibition present and celebrate the beauty and history of the silver wares both made and used over the course of centuries in our fair Queen City.

AARON BETSKY

OPPOSITE: Duhme & Co., *Footed Bowl,* 1880s. Detail of Fig. 38.33

CURATOR'S ACKNOWLEDGMENTS

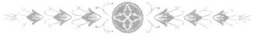

A PROJECT LIKE THIS is not the work of one, but the work of many. First and foremost, I would like to thank the late Elizabeth Beckman for her indispensible book, *An In-depth Study of the Cincinnati Silversmiths, Jewelers, Watch and Clockmakers Through 1850, Also Listing the More Prominent Men in These Trades from 1851 until 1900,* published in 1975. This has been, and will continue to be, a "bible" for many of us, and it is from her superlative study that this current project dares to grow.

Over the course of nearly a decade, the Cincinnati Art Museum's collection of local silver and related material has quadrupled in size, promoting and delivering new elements of scholarship on this subject. I am forever grateful for the fervor and generosity of recent donors such as James Randolph Hillard, M.D. and Aingeal Grehan; Mr. and Mrs. Charles Fleischmann III; Drs. James and Betty Sutherland; Mrs. Jane Sikes Hageman; Lee Cowan and the Lee Cowan Tour Group; Dr. James and Sheri Swinehart; Kathleen Sturm Puls; Corrine Lawson Pennington Coler; Charles Cleves; Mimi Morgan; Dr. James and Susan Widder; Dr. Michael Sze; Edward J. Requardt; the family of Charles H. (Randy) Randolph; Phillip C. and Whitney Rowe Long; Michele Sandler; and the Cincinnati Decorative Arts Society.

This effort also drew great benefit from those who were willing to lend works from their collections for inclusion in the book and/or exhibition. In addition to the individuals and institutions listed on page 6, I wish to thank Mr. Samuel Baughman Craig. I am also indebted to the gracious collectors who allowed me to view their collections, and to the descendants of those silversmiths treated here who generously shared family papers and reminiscences.

Anita Ellis, Deputy Director of Collections, advocated for this project during the development of the Art Museum's *Cincinnati Wing* (2003), and has been a great mentor and source of encouragement throughout. Thank you, Anita. Former director Timothy Rub and current director Aaron Betsky also recognized the need for this scholarship and endorsed my pursuit of this endeavor. The completion of this undertaking, which seemed endless and completely overwhelming at times, is largely due to my colleague and co-author Dr. Janet C. Haartz and her tireless efforts. Over the last ten years, when other projects demanded my attention, Dr. Haartz kept this one moving forward. I am deeply indebted to her, and grateful for her enthusiasm, insights and patient friendship. The Henry Luce Foundation provided essential funding for research. I am especially grateful for the work of Luce Foundation Curatorial Assistants Anne Buening, Marissa Hershon and Maureen McLaughlin, who spent hours tirelessly searching period documents and dredging up wonderful bits of information to bring the men and objects herein to life. During the final year of this project, I would not have survived without the help of my ever-dependable and astute curatorial assistant, Nora Kohl. Ms. Kohl performed a great deal of research, proofing, and fact-checking. She tracked and gathered all photography, and kept everything beautifully organized. The contributions of past interns and volunteers, Debra Godsoe, Leah Daniels, Emily Everhart, Michelle Frederick, and the late Jean Clendening, also deserve high recognition. Kristin Spangenberg, Curator of Prints, shared several relevant newspaper articles that she located during her own work. The late Môna Chapin, former librarian, and Galina Lewandowicz, current head librarian at the Art Museum's Mary R. Schiff Library and Archives, and their staff, were indispensable, keeping us supplied with much-needed references and garnering inter-library loans from around the world.

The Art Museum is blessed with an extremely dedicated, generous, and talented staff. It is a family that I am proud to be part of. Special thanks go to former administrative assistants, Kirstie Craven and Jade Sams, and our current administrative assistants, Linda Pieper and Terri Weiler, for helping with the less-than-glamorous but imperative budget and project details. Rob Deslongchamps, Head of Photographic Services, captured the beauty and the life of the objects contained in these pages with grace and good humor. Megan Emery, former Associate Conservator of Objects, and her staff and volunteers, including Elizabeth Allaire, Becky Linhardt, Kendall Trotter, and Mark Allen, worked diligently to keep all of the silver polished and looking its best for photography and the exhibition. Chief Conservator Serena Urry lent her abilities in treating portraits borrowed for the show. The talented Danelle Cheney provided the digital rendering of marks for which we did not have photography. Susan Hudson, Director of Collections and Exhibition Management, ably kept all aspects of the exhibition in line, and Jay Pattison, Chief Registrar, and Jennifer Eckman, Assistant Registrar, lent their expertise in accommodating loans for photography and exhibition. Exhibition Designer Chrystal Roggenkamp created the imaginative design for the show. Kim Flora, Chief Preparator, and her team of miracle-workers skillfully created all casework and mounts and carefully installed all of the work. PB+J and coordinator Greg Lutz produced all exhibition labels and graphics.

Colleagues and friends close to home and across the country who generously lent their support and expertise include Anne Shepherd, Laura Chase, Linda Bailey, Barbara Dawson, and other members of the reference staff at the Cincinnati Historical Society Library and Archives; Linda Kocis and the reference staff at the Public Library of Cincinnati and Hamilton County; Lynley Culpepper of the Warren County Historical Society; R. G. Dun & Co. collection specialists at the Harvard Business School; Pat Medert of the Ross County Historical Society; Edward Elsner, North County Library System, Oswego, New York; Justin White, Oswego County Records Center, New York; Leslie Jacobs, Clermont County Public Library; John LaMont at the Seattle Library; the Western Reserve Historical Society; Vicky Przekurat; Jeanette Levesque; Cliff Thies, Director of The Rising Sun Historical Society; Janet Wareham, Washington County Historical Society of Pennsylvania; Michael R. Averdick; David Conzett, Curator of History Collections, The Cincinnati Museum Center; Andrew Richmond, Garth's Auction; Wesley C. Cowan, Cowan's Auction; silversmith Ubaldo Vitali; Don Fennimore, Curator Emeritus, Winterthur Museum; Ann K. Wagner, Associate Curator of Decorative Arts, Winterthur Museum; Scott Erbes, Director of Collections and Exhibitions and Curator of Decorative Arts and Design at The Speed Art Museum; Ryan Grover at the Biggs Museum of American Art; John Stuart Gordon, Assistant Curator of American Decorative Arts, Yale University Art Gallery; Dean Lahikainen, Curator of American Decorative Arts, Peabody Essex Museum; Jerome Redfearn; Clifton Anderson; Ron Vance; and independent curator Christopher Busta-Peck.

Certainly, without the generous sponsorship and support of the organizations recognized on page 6, this book and the accompanying exhibition would not have been possible.

D Giles Limited of London produced this beautiful book, and I am thankful to Managing Director Dan Giles, Production Manager Sarah McLaughlin, designer Helen Swansbourne, Editorial Managers Magda Nakassis and Pat Barylski, and editor Allison L. Giles for their careful oversight and guidance.

And finally, I would like to thank my family. My parents and my husband's parents have been a constant source of encouragement and understanding, and have stepped in whenever and wherever I've needed them. Above all, my very patient, supportive and loving husband Brian cheerfully took over all parental and household duties on countless nights and weekends, and my sweet daughters Audrey and Caitlyn were forgiving of my absences and met me with much needed hugs, kisses and silliness when I reappeared. I dedicate my work to you.

AMY MILLER DEHAN

INTRODUCTION

❖

AMY MILLER DEHAN

IN CONTRAST TO THE Queen City's production in ceramics and furniture, Cincinnati's silver industry has gone, for the most part, unrecognized. Elizabeth Beckman's *An In-depth Study of the Cincinnati Silversmiths, Jewelers, Watch and Clockmakers Through 1850* (1975) represents the sole, major contribution to scholarship on this subject until now. While her study includes a list of participants in the industry between 1851 and 1900, it does not fully address this era—a time when the American silver industry began to soar, and ultimately achieved world dominance. The current project, in turn, seeks an understanding of Cincinnati's place in and contribution to this rising industry. Spanning the time from Cincinnati's founding in 1788 through the 1940s, it has revealed notable achievements regionally and nationally, demonstrating that Cincinnati was an important center for silver, excelling in this artistic endeavor as it did in so many others.

Beckman's research was the great stepping-stone from which this research began. In our attempt to update her work with the additional information that has come to light, and to develop a better understanding of the nature, growth, decline, and significance of the long-standing local industry, we tried to focus only on those individuals and firms expressly involved in the silver industry. This was an especially difficult task as the areas of manufacture and trade in silver, watches, clocks, and jewelry have always been so intertwined.

We also tried to determine who was making silver, as opposed to retailing it. The question of authorship when it comes to silver can be a sticky one, and can, in some cases, be impossible to fully resolve. The business arrangements between jobbers and journeymen, and independent merchant-producers who ran their own shops and practiced a combination of making and retailing were complex and are not always reflected in the stamps found on the back or bottom of a piece of silver. In some cases, guarded assertions about making and retailing have been made when enough strong information or evidence was present. But, in many cases, sufficient documentation is still lacking. As Ian M.G. Quimby points out in his essay on silver authorship, "As with modern products, the name attached to a product does not always signify the manufacturer . . . the so-called maker's stamp should be viewed as a sort of trademark—rather than as an artist's signature."[1] Quimby goes on to remind us that stamps were traditionally applied "to assure accountability and recourse in the event of fraud. Thus, whether the silversmith actually made the piece was less important than the implicit guarantee offered by his stamp."[2]

For this study, which began almost ten years ago, Cincinnati city directories were a vital point of departure. We began our work by searching, page by page, through the directories (before digitization!), starting with the first edition (1819) and continuing through 1910. Later editions were consulted on a case-by-case basis. The data collected from the directories included the names, addresses, partnership details, and preferred business listings of those associated with the trade. We also consulted other primary sources including extant marked silver, newspapers, trade journals, diaries, inventories, invoices, federal non-population censuses and credit reports. Our findings were pared and refined to focus on those for whom evidence of silver making or selling was found. Details about these individuals and firms were then fleshed out through information gleaned from other primary sources (birth, death, burial, military, marriage, estate, travel and immigration records, and federal censuses) and secondary sources (other publications on regional silver, genealogical records, local histories). Combined, these sources provided insight on manufacturing, selling, and purchasing trends, and soon a larger view of the local silver, watch, clock, and jewelry industry's importance on a regional and national scale emerged.

We recognize that a primary reliance on city directories poses its own set of problems.[3] As noted by the publisher of Cincinnati's 1849/50 City Directory, incorrect or partial information was often given. Canvassers reported that a wife did not often know the business of her husband, or could not give the correct spelling of his name, and that workmen and boys in manufactories and shops could not provide the most accurate information. As a result, individuals were listed over the years with multiple variants of surname, given name, or both. Omissions of individuals and firms could have occurred for a variety of reasons, including relocation to an address outside the city limits or the decision of individuals not to subscribe to the directory. The absence of directory listings for Jacob Deterly is explained in his January 1, 1825 diary entry; "This day received the Cincinnati Directory which was promised to subscribers at 75 cents, but demanded 1 DOLLAR!! May I never again loose [sic] my reason or mental faculties to lend my name to assist an infamous, swindling book publisher. Twice have I been imposed on!"[4]

Difficulties in separating those who were working or dealing in silver from those who were not were compounded by the fact that the headings used to describe the specialties of businessmen, firms, and institutions in the business listings in the back of most directories changed from year to year. In some years, silversmiths or silver manufacturers were listed separately, and in others, they were lumped into broad categories that included manufacturers and dealers in jewelry, watches, clocks, plated ware, and fancy goods. Pinpointing an individual or a firm's working address could be a challenge, as it was difficult to determine if a change in address represented relocation, a change in street name, or an arbitrary change in the building's street number. As the city grew, some street names were changed. For example, Western Row, so named because it was on the western edge of the city, became Central Avenue in 1860. Because there were no official house numbers before 1853, numbers were self-assigned and could change at random from year to year. During the early years, the most accurate addresses were descriptive, such as "northwest corner of Fourth and Main Streets." Although official numbers were assigned according to the new street numbering rules of 1853, addresses continued to be subject to ambiguity; for example, the Carlisle Building, southwest corner of Fourth and Walnut, and 51 West Fourth Street represented the same address and were used interchangeably in directories and newspaper advertisements. In 1895, alterations were made to the street numbering system again, changing not only the numbering on both east-west and north-south streets, but also directing that the demarcation of "East" or "West" would run from Vine Street instead of Main Street. As a result, an address at 175 Vine was suddenly 419 Vine, and 24 West Fourth Street became 18 East Fourth.

The main body of this book consists of two essays that address the local silver industry during the period between 1788 and 1865, and then between 1865 and 1940, and the biographies and business details of 518 silversmiths and firms between 1788 (the year of Cincinnati's founding) and 1940 (when our last independent silversmiths were working). These biographies are divided into two sections. Those silversmiths and firms for whom extant, marked silver is known are addressed in the section titled *Cincinnati Silversmiths and Firms with Known Wares*. Those who played a role in the trade but for whom extant, marked silver is not known are addressed in *Appendix A*.[5] The biographies in both sections are arranged alphabetically. Those for individuals are ordered alphabetically by surname. When known, life dates are given and followed by working or active dates for the individual's activities in Cincinnati. In the event that an individual or firm is addressed elsewhere in the book, the name of that person or firm is set in bold text. All quotations are literal. Spelling, punctuation and grammar are portrayed as in the original source. When photography of marks was not available, marks were hand-rendered or described within the text of an entry. Renderings were created from images of marks published in other books, on the internet, or as part of eBay auction listings. *Appendix B* lists all Cincinnati silver in the permanent collection of the Cincinnati Art Museum at the time of this publication. Images of silver from this collection illustrate this book.

This body of work has provided numerous insights, revealing previously unknown makers, and additional information on styles, production methods, and distribution systems for those makers who have long been identified. Undoubtedly, some silversmiths, firms, pieces of information, and extant marked silver wares have slipped by us. Nevertheless, we hope that this volume will prove valuable to those interested in Cincinnati silver and to future researchers. We anticipate the new information and scholarship that this study might encourage.

1. Ian M.G. Quimby with Dianne Johnson, *American Silver at Winterthur*, Winterthur, DE: Henry Francis DuPont Winterthur Museum, 1995, 17.
2. Ibid.
3. "Preface," 1849/50 Cincinnati City Directory, 3–4.
4. Jacob Deterly, *"Remarks" of Jacob Deterly: diary from 1819 to 1848; life in southern Ohio: Cincinnati, Marietta, Athens* (transcribed and indexed by Madge Hubbard and Opal Saffell), Seattle: Northwest Lineage Researcher, 1972, 2:3.
5. Exceptions were made for Celadon Symmes and Jacob Deterly who are addressed in the section entitled *Silversmiths and Firms with Known Wares*. Despite the fact that silver marked by these men has not been found, the significant roles they played in the trade warranted a more thorough treatment of their lives and contributions.

OPPOSITE: **Duhme & Co.**, *Tureen*, 1870s.
Detail of Fig. 38.22

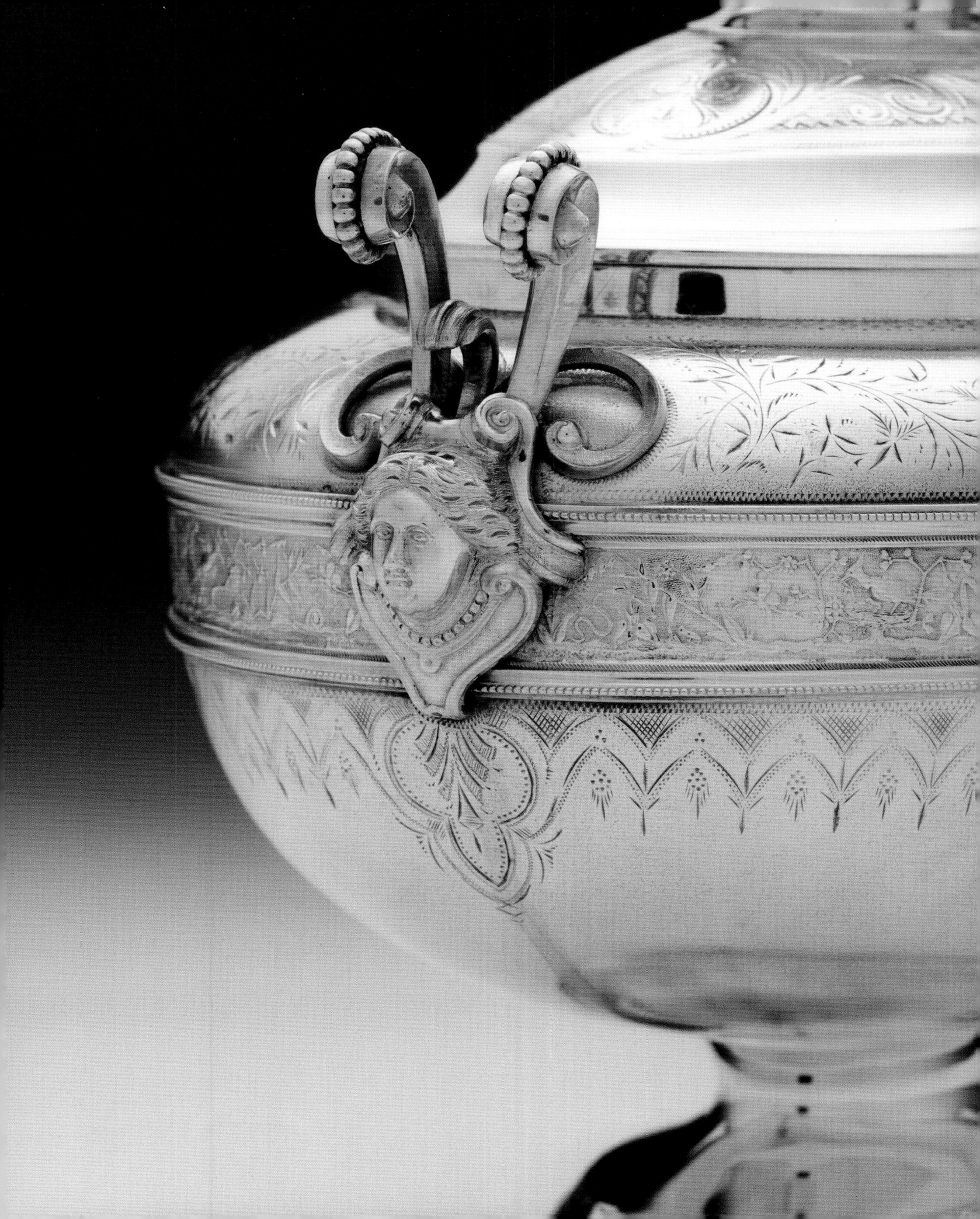

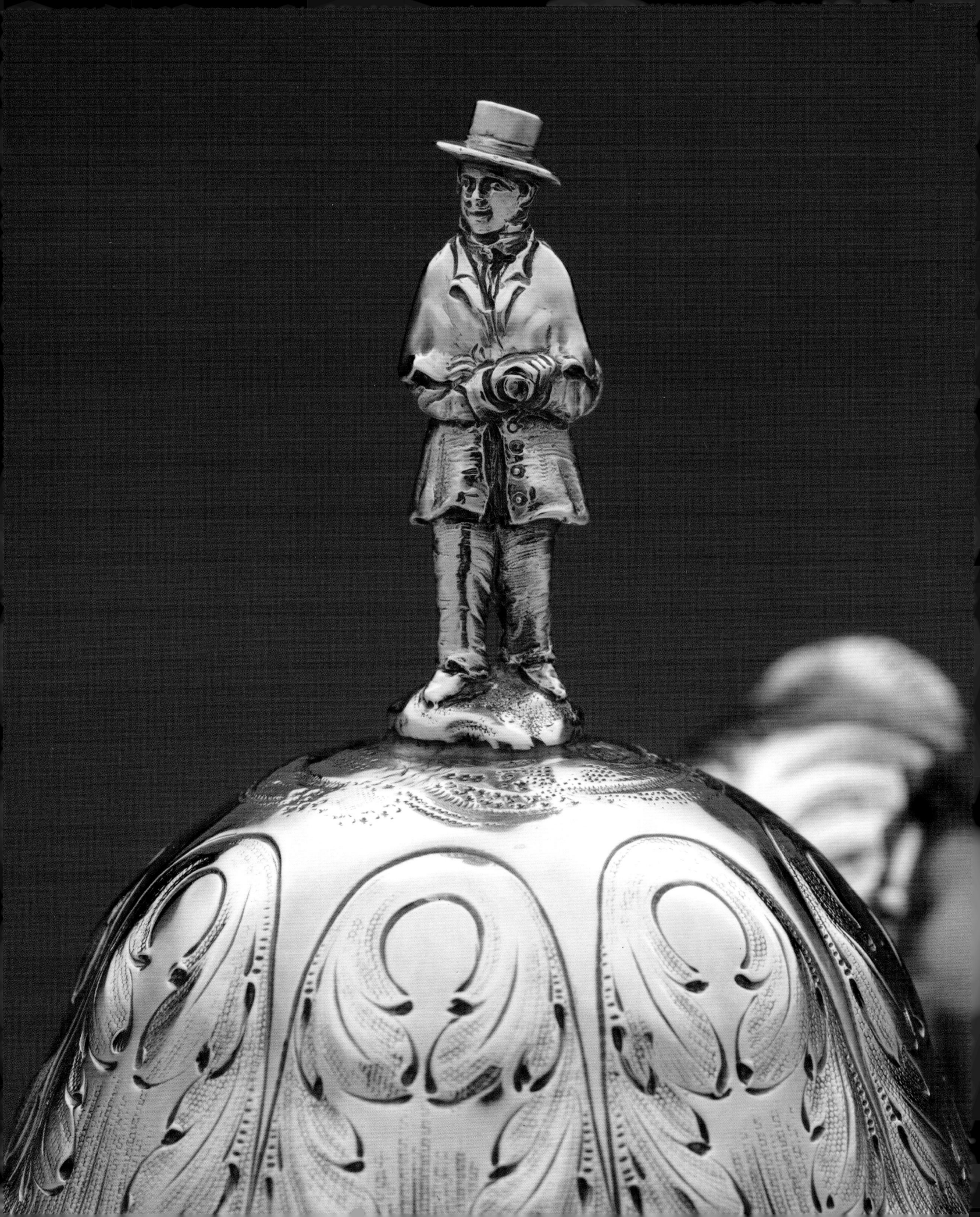

ESTABLISHMENT AND GROWTH
1788–1865

AMY MILLER DEHAN

CELADON SYMMES, reported to have been Cincinnati's first silversmith, established his business in about 1789, only a year after the city's founding.[1] A set of jeweler's tools and a pewter spoon mold owned by Symmes remain (figs. 137.1, 137.2), but silver marked by him is unknown. Considering the rough, nascent state of Cincinnati at this time—a small outpost on the frontier with but a handful of settlers—it is not difficult to imagine why his business was short-lived. The demand for luxury goods like silver in the burgeoning town and its hinterlands would have been trumped by the need for basic utilitarian implements. Trained silversmiths who found themselves in Cincinnati during its first decades would have adapted their practices to provide wares in other less-valuable metals. But Cincinnati, with its prime location along the Ohio River, quickly grew and matured. In 1793, the name and occupation of John Whitesides, silversmith, appears in the books of Cincinnati merchants Smith & Findlay.[2] Details of Whiteside's practice and location remain a mystery. The supplies that he bought do not relate to his trade, and, alas, no silver with his mark is known.

By 1795, General Anthony Wayne had defeated the Native Americans in the area at the Battle of Fallen Timber (1794), and the Treaty of Fort Greenville had ceded Ohio to the United States, opening it for increased settlement. That year, the city boasted a population of about 500.[3] In December 1795 Isaac Van Nuys and John Smith advertised their metal-smithing business, promising the highest prices for "old copper, brass, &c. &c." which they would melt and fashion into new and needed articles.[4] The city continued to mature, and soon both Van Nuys and Smith were advertising as silversmiths, goldsmiths, and watch makers.

By 1800, the city's population had increased to about 750, and surrounding areas registered more than 14,000 inhabitants (fig. E1.1).[5] Cincinnati's wealth had grown in stride with its populace, and that year, General John S. Gano ordered six large, silver tablespoons from Van Nuys for the sum of $19.75—a costly and rare commission for this time.[6] Cincinnati became a "depot" for commodities and settlers from the East. In 1796, an English traveler marveled at the amount of stores "for supplying other Western points," and declared the city "a place of great business."[7] Three silversmiths served the city of 960 people in 1805.[8]

The city's earliest smiths, like Symmes and Van Nuys, were part of an initial band of settlers who arrived from New Jersey. The first of foreign birth, arriving as early as 1802, were members of the Best

OPPOSITE: **Beggs & Smith,** *Tea & Coffee Service,* c. 1850.
Detail of Fig. 9.2

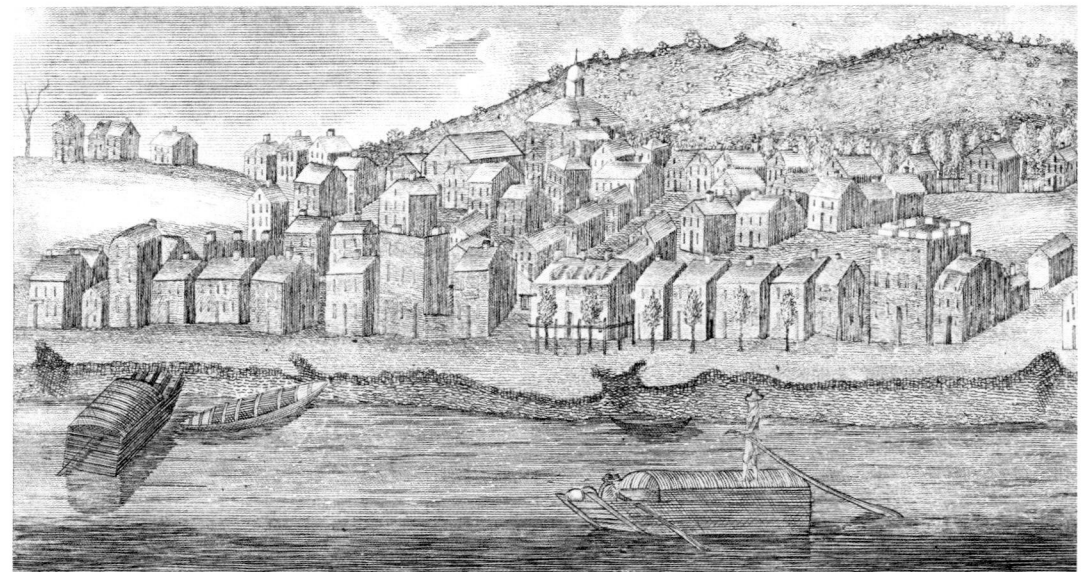

FIG. E1.1: Jervis Cutler, *A View of Cincinnati on the Ohio*, 1812, engraving, 3 × 5 in. (7.6 × 12.8 cm), from *A Topographical Description of the State of Ohio . . .*, Boston: Charles Williams; J Belcher, Printer, 1812, facing 42

family from England. Seeking freedom from the British crown, the Bests came to Cincinnati by way of Philadelphia, over land to Pittsburgh, and down river by keel boat. The city's promising location and growth made it an attractive place for the Bests and for subsequent silversmiths. In 1810, Daniel Drake wrote that "by far the greatest number" of the city's inhabitants were mechanics, and in 1803, Thomas Carter wrote of the great opportunities for artisans and laborers, stating, "mechanics here can make their fortunes in four or five years."[9]

While the 1869 rendering of Samuel Best's 1802 establishment at Front and Walnut Streets (fig. E1.2) may not be wholly accurate, it does represent the type of arrangement that the earliest smiths maintained.[10] Initially, single dwellings would have served as both home and work place. A small area would have been dedicated to living quarters, a front area would have served for the display and sale of goods, and a closed, back area would have safeguarded raw materials and tools, and contained the heat and dirt generated by a forge and workshop. In 1816, the shop of Robert Best & Co. was described in a notice for sale as "well calculated for a mercantile establishment, having an excellent store room in front, with an accompting [accounting] room adjoining . . . a good situation for either a Blacksmith or Cooper's Shop."[11] In 1821, Jacob Deterly wrote of preparing his Main Street shop for operation by whitewashing the walls, installing shelving, and jack-planing the counter.[12] Most of the city's earliest establishments for the making and/or selling of silver, watches, clocks, and jewelry were located within the blocks surrounding Main and Front Streets—the hub of early mercantile activity.

During this era, local shops consisted of one or two master craftsmen and, in some cases, one or two young apprentices or journeymen.[13] Partnerships were short-lived—a reflection of the transient character of early Cincinnati and the struggles to establish a successful business in a new, developing town. Those early master silversmiths who established themselves in Cincinnati intended to expand the trade by engaging apprentices. Early advertisements gave preference to boys "of the country" between the ages of 14 and 16 who were deemed "honest," "sober," "active," and "from respectable connexions [*sic*]."[14] An apprentice's family may have paid a premium, as was common in other localities, for the privilege of his apprenticeship, or as security against loss, embezzlement, or even desertion.[15] In 1811, Philip Price advertised a six-cent reward for a runaway apprentice of "about 20 years of age."[16] These apprenticeships, when served in full, probably lasted about five years.[17] Several local masters, like Luke Kent, Sr. and Alexander McGrew, passed the knowledge and skills of their art down through their families, creating multi-generational, long-standing establishments.

Unable to remain busy or profitable through the production of silver alone, these early smiths pursued related trades in order to increase their value within the commercial community. Symmes may have been a silversmith by trade, but his spoon mold tells us that he produced more common, less expensive pewter utensils. It was not unusual for silversmiths to also work as whitesmiths (tin and copper workers), as illustrated by Van Nuys and Smith. French plated spoons marked by Van Nuys (fig. 142.2) speak to the desire for luxury goods (e.g. silver), whilst acknowledging their limited practicality and affordability on the frontier.[18] Printing was also a common pursuit. Both Van Nuys and Samuel Best served as printers for the Treasury and local banks. The most common trades allied with those of the silversmith throughout the period were watch, clock, jewelry, and spectacle making. The manufacture of guns and scientific devices, and, of course, engraving, repair work, and the retail of a wide variety of ready-made goods procured elsewhere, like cutlery, music boxes, musical instruments, and other fancy goods, were also popular sidelines. Most silversmiths rounded out their stock by retailing silver made by others, and it was not uncommon for them to mark these retailed wares with their own stamps, thus muddying the waters of authorship. Unrelated side pursuits such as farming and land speculation were also means of supplementing incomes. Due to the value of the raw material silversmiths worked with and safeguarded, they were generally regarded as leaders and upstanding citizens of their community. As you will see throughout the biographies of those included in this book, many held public, civic and military offices.

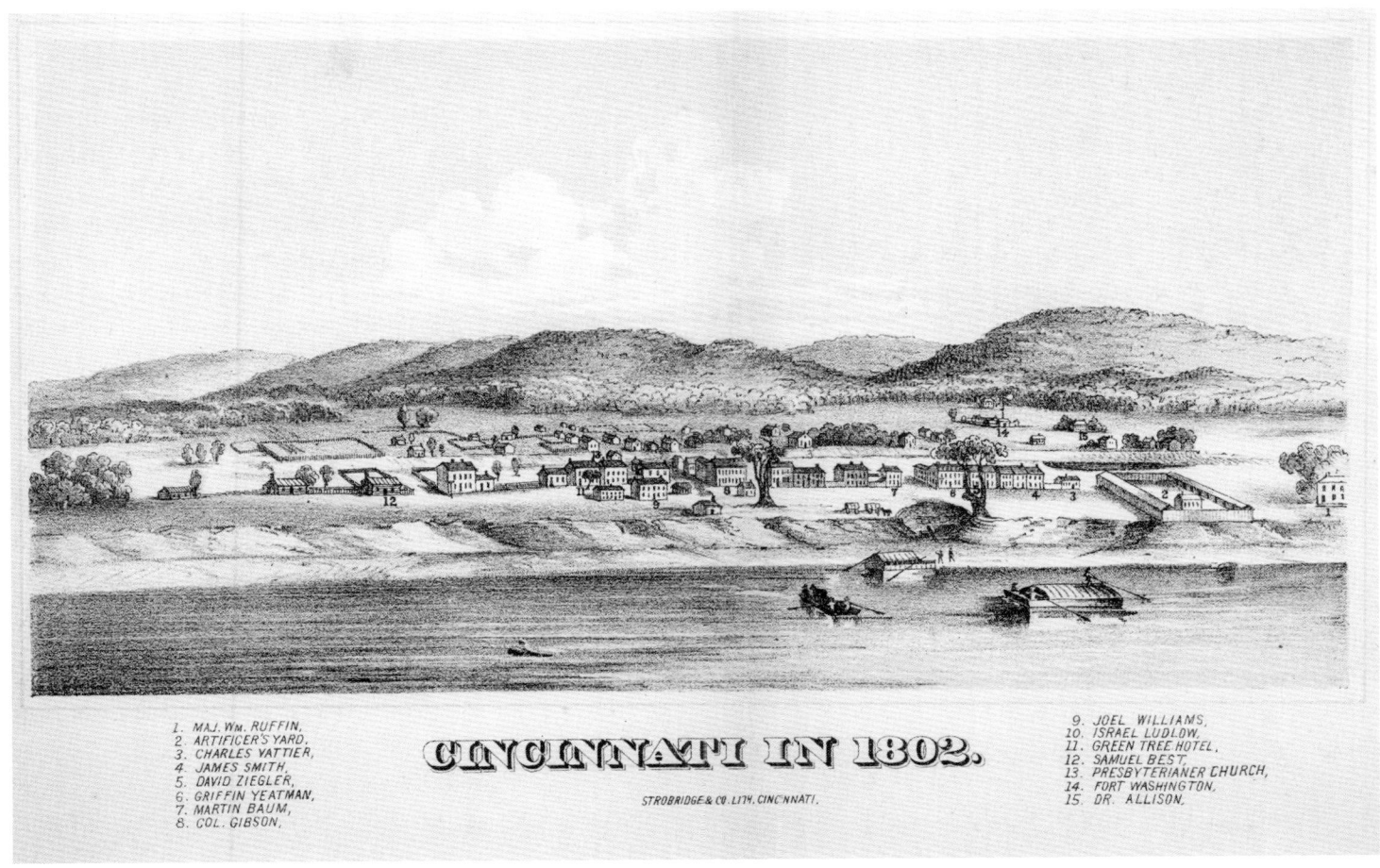

1. MAJ. Wm. RUFFIN,
2. ARTIFICER'S YARD,
3. CHARLES VATTIER,
4. JAMES SMITH,
5. DAVID ZIEGLER,
6. GRIFFIN YEATMAN,
7. MARTIN BAUM,
8. COL. GIBSON,
9. JOEL WILLIAMS,
10. ISRAEL LUDLOW,
11. GREEN TREE HOTEL,
12. SAMUEL BEST,
13. PRESBYTERIANER CHURCH,
14. FORT WASHINGTON,
15. DR. ALLISON,

CINCINNATI IN 1802.

STROBRIDGE & CO. LITH. CINCINNATI.

FIG. E1.2: *Cincinnati in 1802*, from George E. Stevens, *The City of Cincinnati: A Summary of Its Attractions, Advantages, Institutions and Internal Improvements, with A Statement of Its Public Charities*, Cincinnati: George S. Blanchard & Co., 1869

At this time, a smith's material came from either melting coins (particularly Spanish-American silver dollars) or older silver objects considered to be out of fashion.[19] The term "coin silver" derives from the practice of using coinage. The standard of coin silver usually fell between .892 and .900 parts silver to alloy, as opposed to sterling which was .925 parts silver. The practice of marking wares "COIN" or "PURE COIN" did not come into use in Cincinnati until the 1840s and 1850s. The sterling standard was not in general use in the United States until about 1860, although, interestingly, Robert Best & Co. advertised their silver wares as "warranted to be of Sterling silver" in 1815.[20]

Once the coin was melted, it was hammered or rolled into sheets that the smith used to create various forms by hand raising, or through the use of swages—shaped dies or forms that the metal was hammered into or over in order to achieve a particular form. Handles, finials, legs, spouts and the like were cast in sand or metal molds. Tools and dies were considerable investments. Many would have been made by the smith or his apprentice. By and large, the earliest hollowware lacks milled bands of ornament, but by the 1820s these and other fittings like finials, feet, and handles, could be purchased from specialized suppliers. Later, when small shops grew into large, mechanized factories, many of these milled bands and fittings were produced in-house. Roller dies for forming flatware were not in common use until 1840, when William Gale's 1826 patent of this process expired.[21]

Finished wares were marked with the full or abbreviated name of the firm or individual smith, and sometimes with an indication of the city where they were made, using an iron die that was either made or purchased by the smith. In 1853, C.F. Hall's Engraving Rooms in Cincinnati advertised "steel stamps for silversmiths" and "jewelry and silver plate marking for the trade."[22] Unfortunately, no system of dating was applied, so today, silver is dated either by style, by the active dates of the individual or firm that marked it, or through engraved inscriptions that include a date. All silver (and gold), regardless of whether it was hollow or flatware, was referred to, in these early days, as "plate." The origin of this term, which was largely abandoned when electroplated goods became popular in the 1840s, is still debated.

The most popular form made throughout this early period was the most versatile of utensils: the spoon. The earliest examples, dating from between about 1800 and 1815, have downturned oval handles (fig. 16.2), coffin-shaped handles (fig. 12.2), or handles with a shape that falls between the traditional coffin and fiddle styles (figs. 16.3, 142.2). Between about 1815 and 1830, a broad fiddle shape dominated (fig. 16.8, 22.1, 125.2), and around 1840, spoons with tipped, exaggerated fiddle handles and pointed shoulders came into favor (fig. 66.15)—a shape distinctly identifiable with Cincinnati and produced here into the 1890s. Other popular forms made during this period included ladles, tongs, mugs, and beakers. Tea and coffee pots, creamers, sugars, goblets, and forks were made but were only affordable to those with great wealth.[23]

Between 1810 and 1820, the city's population grew from 2,540 to 9,602.[24] Despite the hardships created by the War of 1812, the city continued to prosper, and silversmiths continued to arrive from New Jersey, Maryland, Pennsylvania, Virginia, England, and France. The rising cost of eastern goods encouraged local manufacturing. In 1815, Cincinnati chronicler Daniel Drake noted that "stills, tea kettles and other vessels of copper, with a great variety of tin ware, are made in abundance . . . many different articles of jewelry, and silverware of every sort—after the most fashionable models and handsomely *enchased* are manufactured . . . clocks of every kind are made, and watches repaired."[25] That same year, Samuel Best was issued a formal license (fig. 16.5) to make silverware, liable to duty, issued by the Collector of Revenue for the first Collection District of Ohio.[26] In 1819, there were nine silver shops employing 22 workmen.[27]

With the increase in people and prosperity, Cincinnati grew in refinement. Gorham Worth, a Connecticut native, recalls a dinner held between 1817 and 1821 hosted by Cincinnati merchant David Kilgour, whose elegant home features prominently in the painting, *The Steamboat George Washington and View of the Ohio River* (fig. E1.3): " . . . I have never seen anything east of the mountains to be compared to the luxuries of that table! The costly dinner service, –the splendid cut glass,–the rich wines . . ."[28] Silversmiths took note of this new wealth and increased the variety of goods they offered. Those wares that were not made locally were bought in the East or

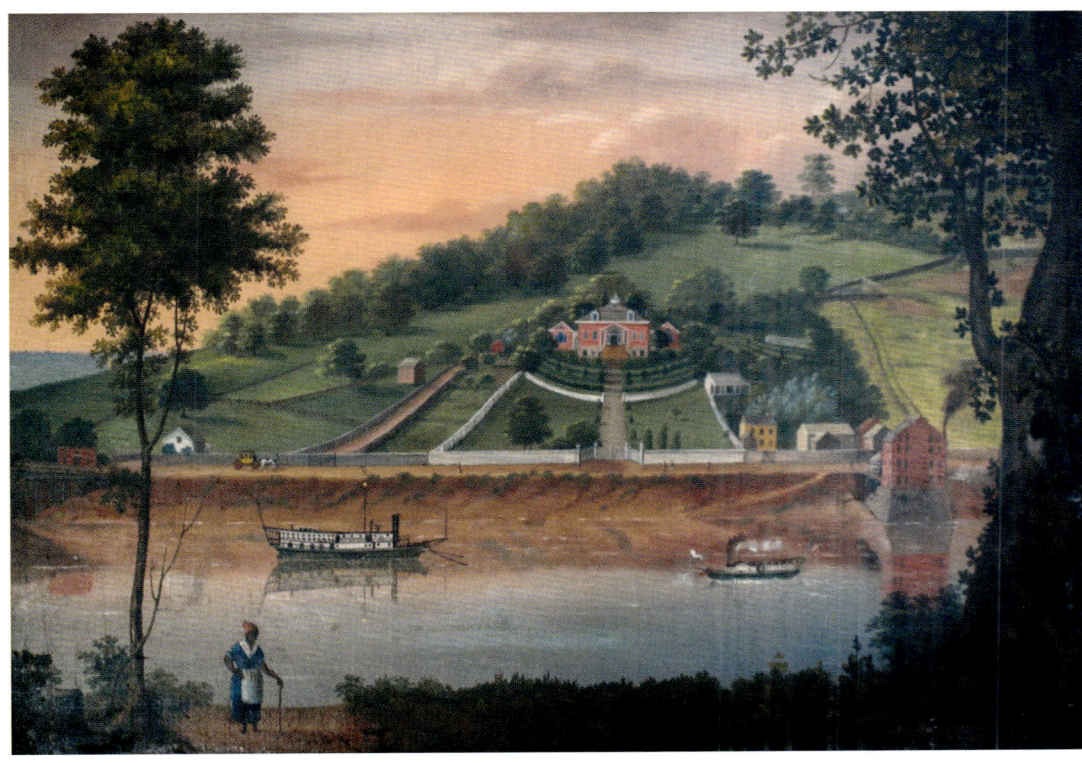

FIG. E1.3: Artist unknown, *The Steamboat George Washington and View of the Ohio River,* 1816, oil on canvas, Private Collection

imported and received through New York, Philadelphia, Baltimore, and later, New Orleans.[29] The influence of these goods on those made in Cincinnati during this period is evident.

In the three years following the War of 1812, Cincinnati's trade with the East and South expanded dramatically.[30] In 1820, a system of canals to improve connections between the East and areas west of the Allegheny Mountains was under construction, and the successful journey of the steamboat *Enterprise,* in 1815, up the Mississippi and Ohio Rivers from New Orleans to Pittsburgh, was the forerunner of what became fleets of steamboats on inland waters, opening trade upriver and east. Wares crafted in Cincinnati found their way into the states bordering the Ohio and Mississippi Rivers.[31]

In the 1820s, silversmiths from Maine, Rhode Island, Vermont, and Switzerland were among those who established themselves in the local business. Seven silversmith shops with 17 hands and a yearly production of $8,600 were recorded in 1826.[32] As local manufacturing and industry grew, the Ohio Mechanics' Institute, founded in 1828, supported these smiths and their fellow mechanics by providing classes, a large library, and exhibitions that promoted western manufactures throughout the region.[33] Silversmith Alexander McGrew served as one of its directors in 1834.[34]

The city had swelled to 24,831 people by 1830, and its population nearly doubled in the following decade, reaching 46,382 in 1840.[35] The 1830s saw the largest influx of individuals active in the silver, jewelry, watch, and clock trade to date, largely from New England, but also from the District of Columbia, Virginia, and Maryland. Those of foreign birth continued to come from England, but also from Germany. This period marked the beginnings of the city's large Germanic population. New arrivals explicitly advertising as silver manufacturers included William and Archibald Cooper; Allen, Rhodes & Co. from New England; Edward Kinsey of Wales; Abraham Palmer of Pennsylvania; Pulaski Scovil, formerly of Connecticut and New York; and George A. Stinger, born in Washington, DC and trained in Baltimore. Most operated as both retailers and wholesalers. An advertisement published by Allen, Rhodes & Co. noted, "country dealers constantly supplied."[36] Wares made during this period followed the Neoclassical style that was popular in the East, and the small shops that made them were still powered by hand. Steam power was in local use after 1812, but the first mention of a steam-powered silver manufactory does not appear until 1864.[37]

Charles Frederic Goss noted that in 1836, "with the exception of Pittsburgh, there is no city in the West or the South that, in its

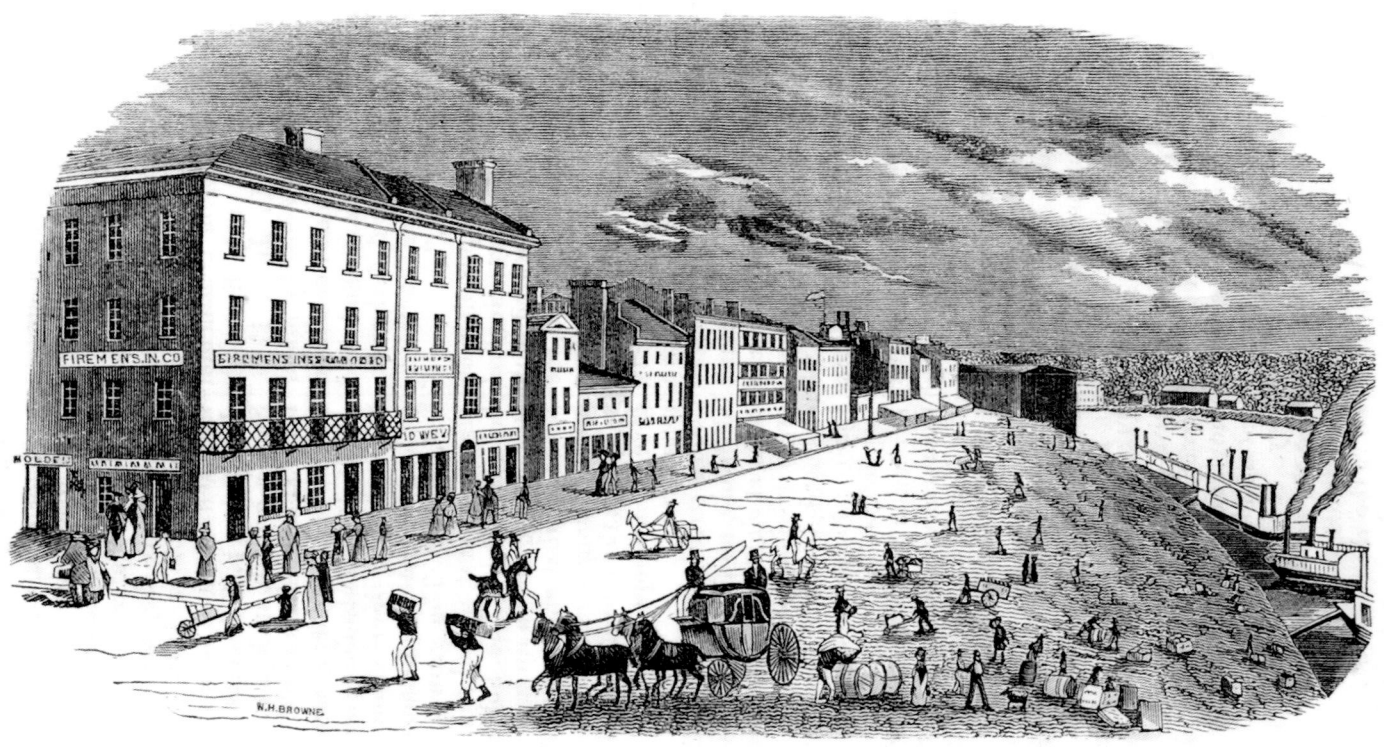

FIG. E1.4: *Cincinnati Landing*, 1848, hand-colored wood-engraving, 3½ × 6¼ in. (8.9 × 15.9 cm), CAM, Gift of the Altrusa Club of Cincinnati, 1966.118

manufactures and manufacturing capacity, bears any approach to Cincinnati and her associate towns."[38] The Panic of 1837 affected some of the local smiths and related tradesmen between 1837 and 1840, but most of those who had established themselves in the 1830s remained in business for fifteen years or longer.

In 1838, the Ohio Mechanics' Institute inaugurated their annual fairs, which encouraged entries of silver wares. Edward Kinsey and Abraham Palmer were the first smiths to participate in what would become a major catalyst for the advancement and promotion of Cincinnati's industrial arts. These fairs intended "to bring before the people specimens of the products of home industry that both the merchant and the consumer may see, at one view, the variety and quality of our manufactures," and later evolved into the grand Cincinnati Industrial Expositions held between 1870 and 1888.[39]

The national and local economy improved dramatically in the 1840s and 1850s, and the city at large experienced its most impressive growth in immigration and industrialization (fig. E1.4). As observed by historian Walter Stix Glazer, "during the seven decades prior to the Civil War no other American city experienced such a spectacular rise, and few entertained such splendid ambitions for

future growth and greatness."[40] Between 1840 and 1850, the population grew by 150% to reach 115,438, despite the 1849–1850 cholera epidemic, which claimed the lives of 4,832 people, more than 4% of the city's population.[41] In the following decade, the population increased to 161,044.[42] By 1860, Cincinnati was the fifth largest city in the nation and the second largest manufacturing city—second only to Philadelphia (fig. E1.5).[43] In 1841, the value of the silverware produced in the city was $56,600, and by 1851, there were five silversmith, goldsmith, and silver plating establishments producing $90,000 worth of silver.[44] In 1859, five shops employing fifty hands were producing $110,000 worth of silverware.[45] These five shops are not named, but based on evidence of manufacturing activities discovered in objects, advertisements and other documents, they included E. & D. Kinsey, Palmer & Owen, George Stinger, and C. & J. Vanhouten. The fifth shop may have been that of Samuel T. Carley who manufactured jewelry and exhibited "silver ornaments" at the 1850 Mechanics' Institute Fair. During this time, in addition to Main Street (fig. E1.6), the areas of Fourth Street (east of Main Street) (fig. E1.7); Fifth Street; and the West End (Linn Street and Western Row) became localized centers for trade.[46]

The sharp increase in silver production was encouraged by the

Tariff of 1842, championed by Senator Henry Clay. Intended to deter foreign competition, the Tariff placed a 30% ad valorem tax on imported silverware, making it less attractive to American buyers. The tax, also levied on other products, was to be paid in silver or gold, making silver coinage, the silversmith's raw material, more readily available. The discovery in 1859 of the Comstock Lode, the first major discovery of silver ore in the United States, also increased the availability of silver, making it affordable to a greater range of patrons.

In 1858, E. & D. Kinsey was "said to do the largest [silver] manufacturing business in the West."[47] Their goods, like the wares of their local contemporaries, traveled west and southwest, most likely by boat and railroad. As more efficient means of transportation increased, Cincinnati's manufacturers and dealers made

frequent trips to Philadelphia, Baltimore, and New York, and much of the locally-made silver remained in step with the styles popular in these cities. Spanning the 1840s and 1860s, these styles included Rococo, Gothic and Renaissance revivals. Inspiration also came from foreign design sources observed in imported wares, design books, and works exhibited in World Fairs. Edward Kinsey and Herman Duhme traveled to several venues in Europe in 1851, including the Great Exhibition of the Works of Industry of All Nations in London, and David Kinsey attended the *Exposition Universelle* in Paris in 1855.[48]

With the advent of the Civil War, activities in the silver trade slowed. Many of Cincinnati's silver manufacturers and retailers went to war, and a severe economic depression befell the city between 1861 and the early months of 1863.[49] A newspaper notice

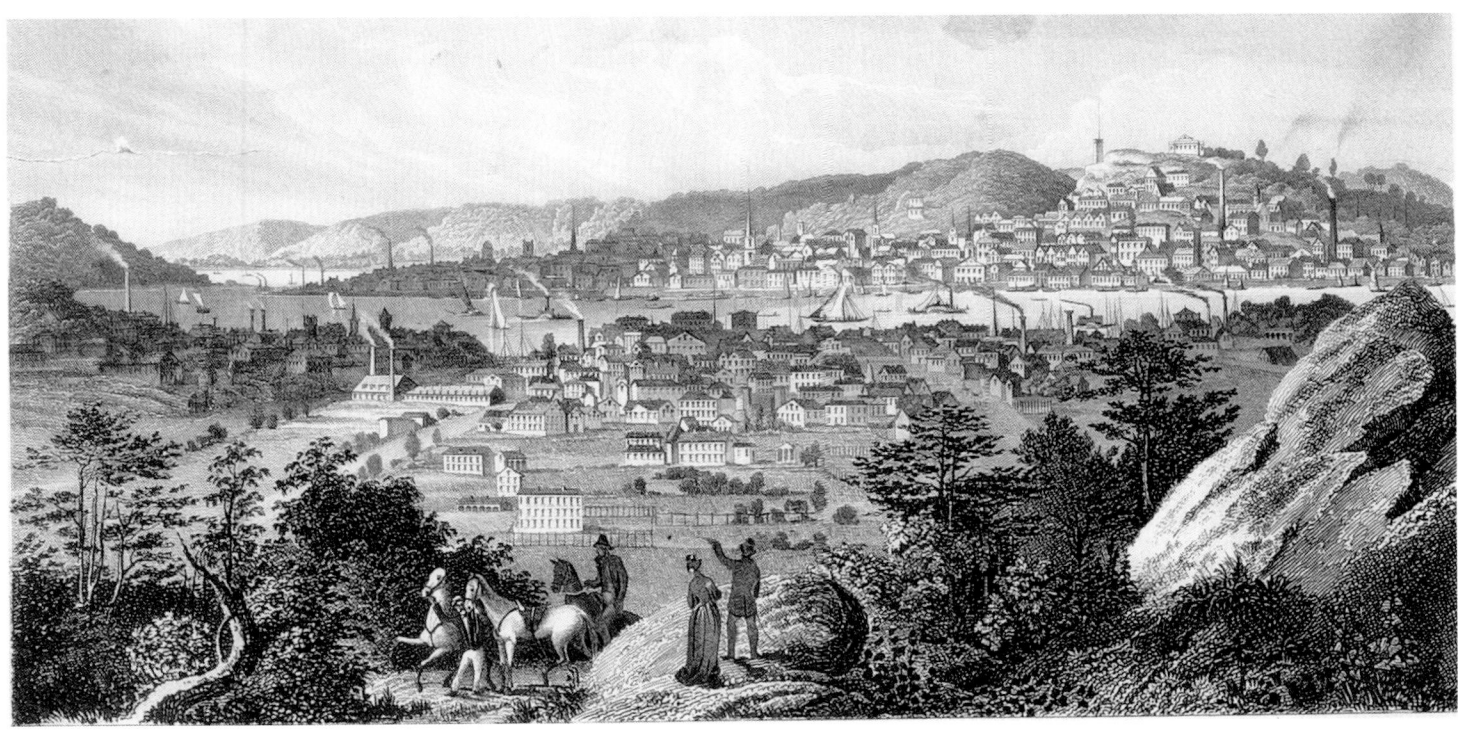

FIG. E1.5: *Birds-eye View of Cincinnati*, c. 1840–1850, engraving, 2⅜ × 6¾ in. (6 × 17.1 cm), CAM, X1944.2

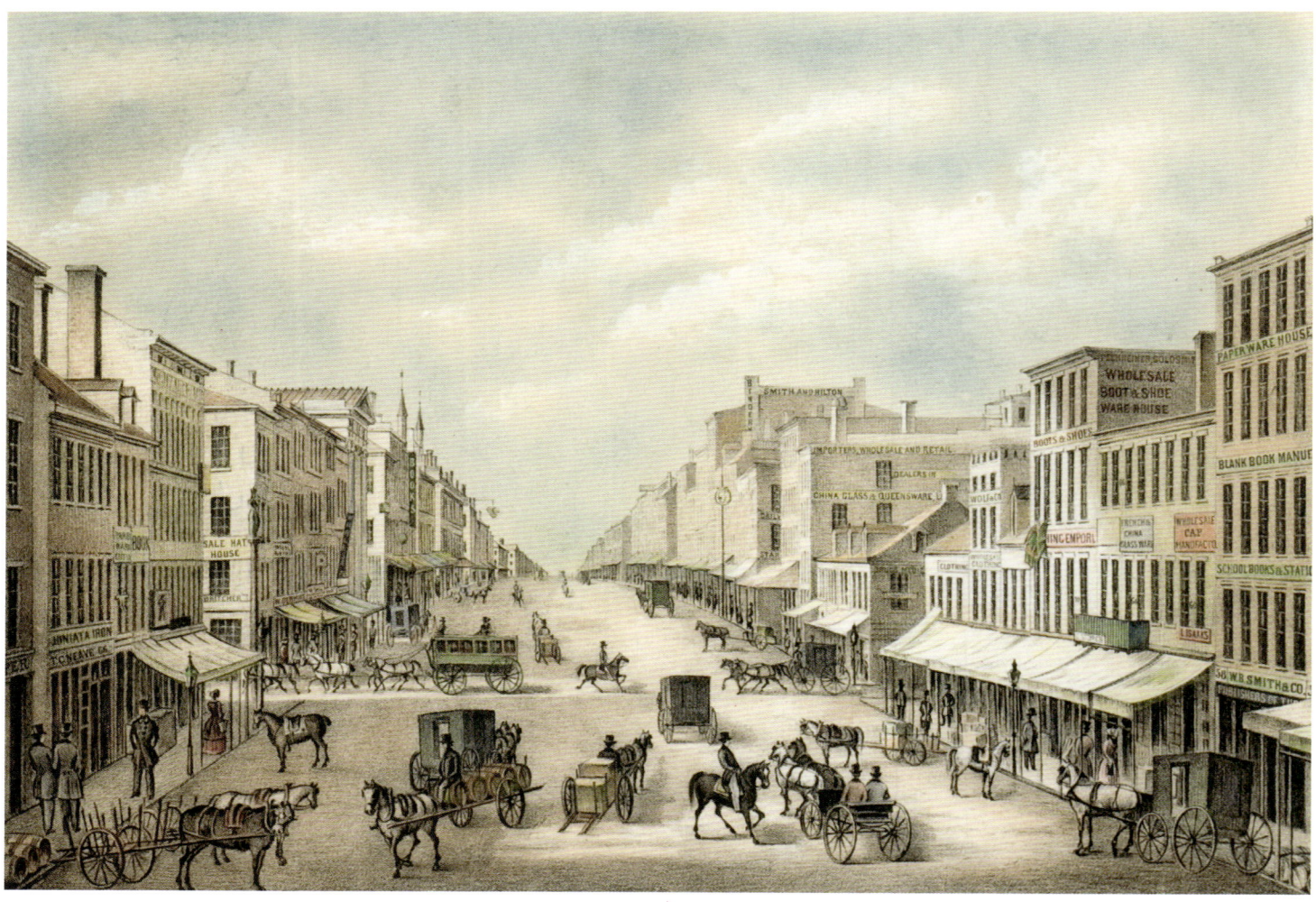

FIG. E1.6: Otto Onken (American, b. c. 1815, d. 1897), printer, *Main Street Between Second and Fifth*, 1850, color lithograph, 6½ × 11 in. (16.5 × 27.9 cm), CAM, Bequest of Herbert Greer French, 1943.647

published during this era states, "Silver change has become so scarce that shop-keepers and small dealers find it difficult to supply themselves with an amount sufficient to supply their customers. The saloon-keepers especially, it is said, suffer from a want of change."[50] Cincinnati's considerable trade with the South ceased, and debts owed by southern merchants went unpaid.[51] Many local mercantile firms went bankrupt, and a number of manufacturers were forced to cease or curtail operations. Silver manufacturers C. & J. Vanhouten shuttered their doors in 1862, after Charles Vanhouten left to serve in the Union Army. Other manufactories

altered their activities to support the war effort. Duhme & Co. reportedly manufactured bullets and pontoon bridges.[52] The city was an important organization center for the military during the war, and silver retailers such as H.P. Elias and Samuel Hatch, a clerk at Duhme & Co., left their posts to become sutlers, or peddlers who followed army camps and sold provisions to the troops. They earned considerable money doing so.[53] The Civil War created both hardship and opportunity. Cincinnati's silver trade had taken root, and it would continue to evolve, profit, and gain national recognition in the period following the War.

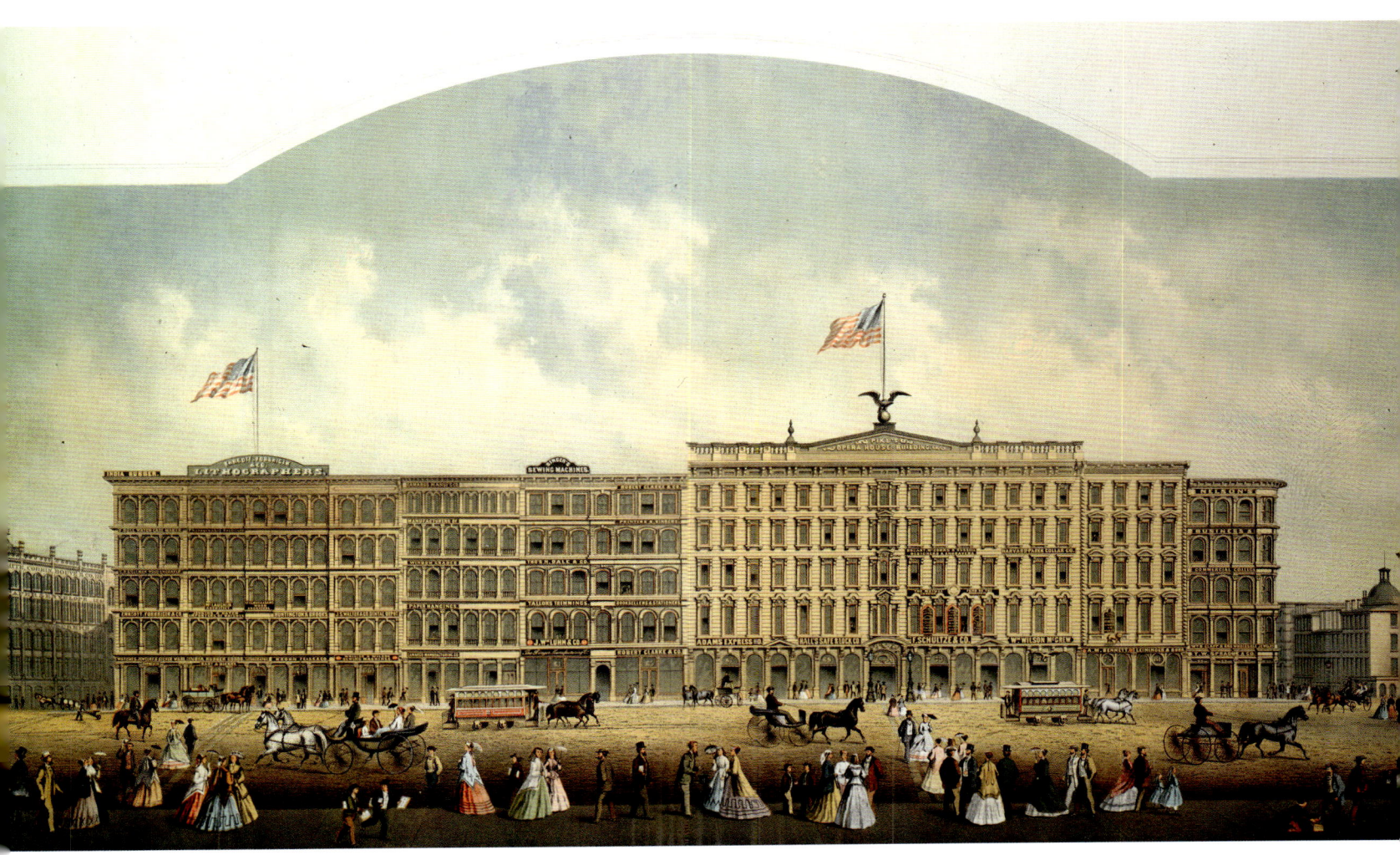

FIG. E1.7: Ehrgott, Forbriger and Company (American, estab. 1856, closed 1869), *South Side of Fourth Street, Between Walnut and Vine*, c. 1867, lithograph, The Cincinnati Historical Society, Gift of P.W. Schath, 1958

1. John Adams Vinton, *The Symmes Memorial*, Boston: David Clapp & Son, 1873, 92; Rhea Mansfield Knittle, *Early Ohio Silversmiths and Pewterers, 1787–1847*, Cleveland: The Calvert-Hatch Co., 1943, 26.

2. Torrence papers, Cincinnati Historical Society, box 56, folder 3, 134.

3. Richard C. Wade, *The Urban Frontier: The Rise of Western Cities, 1790–1830*, Urbana and Chicago: University of Illinois Press, 1996, 54.

4. Advertisement, *Centinel of the North-Western Territory*, December 19, 1795.

5. 1819 Cincinnati City Directory, 29; Wade, *The Urban Frontier*, 26.

6. John S. Gano manuscripts, Cincinnati Historical Society, box 2, ledger 1787–1802, 41.

7. S.B. Nelson and J.M. Runk, *History of Cincinnati and Hamilton County, Ohio: Their Past and Present*, Cincinnati: S.B. Nelson & Co., 1894, 1:63.

8. 1853 Cincinnati City Directory, 12.

9. Daniel Drake, *Notices Concerning Cincinnati*, Cincinnati: Printed for the author, at the press of John W. Browne, 1810, 3; C.E. Cabot, "The Carters in Early Ohio. A Glimpse of Cincinnati in Its First Quarter Century," *The New England Magazine* (May 1899): 350.

10. When compared to Israel Ludlow's 1802 plan of the town, the placement of Best's log house in the rendering published in 1869 appears to be too far west. For Ludlow's plan see *Record of the distribution and sale of lots in the town of Losantiville (now Cincinnati) 1789*, Cincinnati: R. Clark, 1870.

11. Advertisement (fig. 14.2), *Western Spy*, April 26, 1816, 3.

12. Jacob Deterly, *"Remarks" of Jacob Deterly: diary from 1819 to 1848; life in southern Ohio: Cincinnati, Marietta, Athens* (transcribed and indexed by Madge Hubbard and Opal Saffell), Seattle: Northwest Lineage Researcher, 1972, 1:16.

13. A journeyman was someone who had completed an apprenticeship but was not yet deemed a master of his trade.

14. Advertisements: *Western Spy*, June 12, 1805, reproduced in Beckman, 140; *Western Spy*, September 23, 1806, reproduced in Beckman, 19; *Western Spy*, January 1, 1806, 3, col. 4; *Western Spy*, July 22, 1806; *Western Spy*, June 3, 1807, reproduced in Beckman, 16; *Western Spy*, February 18, 1815, reproduced in Beckman, 13.

15. For more on the early American silver apprenticeship structure see Catherine B. Hollan, "Baltimore Apprenticeships in Silversmithing and Its Related Branches," Jennifer Goldsborough, *Silver in Maryland*, Baltimore: Maryland Historical Society, 1983, 38.

16. Notice, *Western Spy*, November 16, 1811.

17. In the absence of formal records, newspaper advertisements are currently the only source of information about such arrangements in Cincinnati.

18. French plate, a process of plating copper with thin sheets of silver leaf, was used by French platers beginning in the early 18th century. Early on, and continuing throughout Cincinnati's history, there was a desire for metal wares that offered a less expensive alternative to silver. Robert Best, Seymour & Williston, Woodruff & Deterly, and George Sullivan advertised the sale of plated ware as early as 1815. In the 1820s and 1830s, Alexander McGrew and Peleg Collins were among those selling Britannia—metal ware created with a pewter alloy, typically containing 90% tin, 8% antimony, and 2% copper. Later, local manufacturers such as Homan Manufacturing Company (est. 1847–1941) and Queen City Silver Co., Inc. (circa 1888–1949) created plated goods for the American mass market.

19. Silver was not mined commercially in the United States until the 1850s.

20. Joseph P. Brady, "An American Coin Silver Primer," *Silver Magazine* (January/February 2002): 12–17; Advertisement, *Western Spy*, February 18, 1815, reproduced in Beckman, 13; Robert Best's reference to sterling surely grew out of experience in his native England, where sterling had been the standard for centuries.

21. Charles Venable, *Silver in America: A Century of Splendor*, New York: Harry N. Abrams Inc., 1995, 20.

22. 1853 Cincinnati City Directory, 204.

23. As late as 1835, forks were confined to the wealthy, see "Silver and Silver Plate," *Harper's New Monthly Magazine* (September 1868): 437.

24. Charles Greve, *Centennial History of Cincinnati and Its Representative Citizens*, Chicago: Biographical Publishing Co., 1904, 1:684.

25. Daniel Drake, *Natural and Statistical View, or Picture of Cincinnati and Miami Country*, Cincinnati: Looker & Wallace, 1815, 143.

26. John J. Rowe Collection, Cincinnati Historical Society, box 2, vol. 3, verso of page 65.

27. Benjamin Drake and Edward D. Mansfield, *Cincinnati in 1826*, Cincinnati: Morgan, Lodge & Fisher, 1827, 64.

28. "Reprint of 'Recollections of Cincinnati' by Gorham A. Worth," *Quarterly Publication of the Historical and Philosophical Society of Ohio* 9, no. 2 & 3 (April–July): 38, Cincinnati: Abingdon Press, 1916; The Cincinnati Art Museum collection contains the front hall from Kilgour's home, *Kilgour Hallway*, Museum Purchase, 1955.526.

29. Deterly, *"Remarks,"* 2:26–29; Rev. Charles Frederic Goss, *Cincinnati: The Queen City, 1788–1912*, Cincinnati: The S.J. Clarke Publishing Co., 1912, 2:331; Drake, *Natural and Statistical View*, 148; Drake and Mansfield, *Cincinnati in 1826*, 76.

30. Goss, *Cincinnati: The Queen City*, 330.

31. Ibid.

32. John W. Leonard, *The Centennial Review of Cincinnati: one hundred years of progress in commerce, manufactures, the professions, and in social and municipal life*, Cincinnati: J.M. Elstner, 1888, 67; Drake and Mansfield, *Cincinnati in 1826*, 64.

33. Charles Cist, *Cincinnati in 1841: Its Early Annals and Future Prospects*, Cincinnati: E. Morgan, 1841, 128–131.

34. 1834 Cincinnati City Directory.

35. Greve, *Centennial History of Cincinnati*, 684.

36. Advertisement, *Cincinnati Daily Gazette*, August 30, 1834, reproduced in Beckman, 117.

37. In 1812, a nine-story steam mill was built on the Cincinnati river bank. It housed areas for manufacturing flour, receiving wool and cotton machinery, a flax-seed oil mill, a fulling mill, etc.; Drake, *Natural and Statistical View*, 137–138; David Kinsey's "Steam Silver-Ware Manufactory" is advertised in the *Cincinnati Enquirer*, May 13, 1864, 1.

38. Goss, *Cincinnati: The Queen City*, 227.

39. John B. Chamberlin, *A Century of Cincinnati*, Cincinnati: Williams & Co., 1888, lxx.

40. Walter Stix Glazer, *Cincinnati in 1840, The Social and Functional Organization of an Urban Community during the Pre-Civil War Period*, Columbus: Ohio State University Press, 1999, 7–8.

41. Charles Cist, *Sketches and Statistics of Cincinnati in 1851*, Cincinnati: William H. Moore & Co., 1851, 45.

42. Greve, *Centennial History of Cincinnati*, 684.

43. Charles Cist, *Sketches and Statistics of Cincinnati in 1859*, Cincinnati: Moore, Wilstach, Keys, 1859, 240; Glazer, *Cincinnati in 1840*, 7.

44. *41st and 42nd Annual Report of the Cincinnati Chamber of Commerce and Merchants' Exchange, for Two Commercial Years, Ending August 31, 1890*, Cincinnati: The Ohio Valley Co. Printers, 1891, 2:16; Cist, *Sketches and Statistics of Cincinnati in 1851*, 238.

45. Cist, *Sketches and Statistics in Cincinnati in 1859*, 330, 343.

46. By the 1860s, Western Row had been renamed Central Avenue.

47. Ohio, Vol. 2, p. 228, R.G. Dun & Co. Collection, Baker Library, Harvard Business School.

48. "Edward Kinsey" in National Archives and Records Administration (NARA), Washington DC, *Passport Applications, 1795–1905*, ARC Identifier 566612/MLR Number A1 508, NARA series M1372, roll 36; Herman Duhme, *U.S. Passport Applications, 1795–1925* [online database], Provo, Utah: Ancestry.com Operations, Inc., 2007; Greve, *Centennial History of Cincinnati*, 491; "News by the Mails," *The New York Times*, July 20, 1855; "David Kinsey" in National Archives and Records Administration (NARA), Washington DC, *Passport Applications, 1795–1905*, roll 78.

49. Those in the silver trade who went to war include Philip Louis Reese, Thomas Lovell, James F. Rhodes,

William Michie, Jr., James C. Michie, E.E. Isbell, George D. Parks, Theodore Aspinwall, son of Chauncey B. Aspinwall, Charles Vanhouten, Charles S. Kinsey, son of David Kinsey, Robert H. Palmer, son of Abraham Palmer, John H. Pigman, Joseph Stinger, son of George Stinger, Ezekial Shott, and William T. Ryland. Of these, Aspinwall, Ryland, and Vanhouten died in action. For more on the Civil War's effect on Cincinnati, see Steven J. Ross, *Workers On the Edge: Work, Leisure and Politics in Industrializing Cincinnati, 1788–1890*, New York: Columbia University Press, 1985, 193–196.

50. *Cincinnati Enquirer*, June 29, 1862, 2.

51. *Annual Statement of the Commerce of Cincinnati, for the Commercial Year, Ending August 31, 1861, Reported to the Chamber of Commerce, by William Smith, Superintendent of the Merchants' Exchange*, Cincinnati: Gazette Co., 1861, 5.

52. Louis Leonard Tucker, *Cincinnati During the Civil War, Issue 9 of Publications of the Ohio Civil War Centennial Commission*, Columbus: Ohio State University Press for the Ohio Historical Society, 1962, 19; John Roger Newstedt and Charles von D. Knighton, *A Cincinnati Saga: The McNicoll-Duhme Connection: A History of Two Families Intertwined in the Early Days of the City from 1804 to the Present with Embellishments and A Measure of Astonishment*, unpublished manuscript, 1996, 48, facsimile, Cincinnati Art Museum, Decorative Arts & Design Department, Duhme & Co. files.

53. Ohio, Vol. 6, p. 123, R.G. Dun & Co. Collection; Ohio, Vol. 3, p. 240, R.G. Dun & Co. Collection.

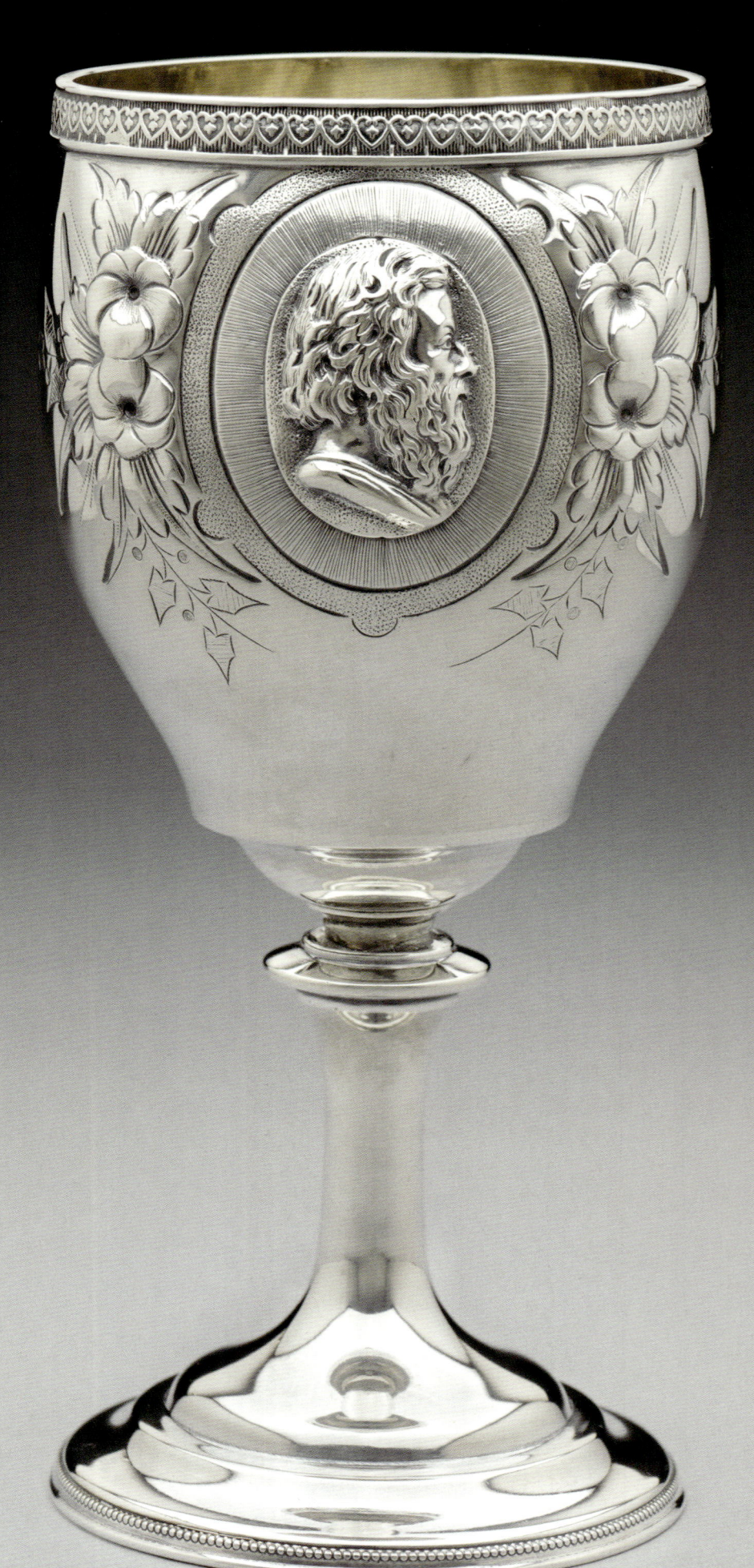

ADJUSTMENT, HEYDAY, AND DECLINE
1865–1940

⊰⊱◈⊰⊱

AMY MILLER DEHAN

FOLLOWING THE Civil War, the American silver industry, including that in Cincinnati, continued to change and advance. Adjustments that began to take hold in the 1840s continued into the 1860s. Workshops transformed in size and scale. E. & D. Kinsey's Fifth Street workshop employed 15 hands in 1850.[1] A shop of this size was considered large, and the Kinseys' was the largest on record in Cincinnati for size and production at this time.[2] As the years passed, and staff and production continued to increase, more silver manufacturers maintained separate addresses for living and working. Palmer & Owen employed three hands in 1851 and appear to have had a separate workshop, as did George Stinger who employed five hands in his jewelry, watch-making, and silversmithing business.[3] Duhme & Co. employed 25 to 30 hands in their silver-making department by 1868.[4] Throughout the industry, the transformation from a few master craftsmen working in one small shop to bands of specialized artisans working in large factories continued, and was nearly complete by 1870.[5]

New machines, tools and processes, powered by steam and hand, allowed for greater production, efficiency, and uniformity in work, but also led to a new subdivision and specialization of labor. Roller and drop presses allowed for the production of flatware and hollowware blanks that were then further shaped, finished, embellished, and polished. Stamped out blanks, or shells, for vessels were placed on metal lathes and "spun up" (as opposed to hand-raising) around wood or steel forms called chucks (fig. E2.2). This process, called spinning, was patented in 1834 by William Crossman and was in popular use by the 1850s. Multi-part or sectional chucks that collapsed for removal, introduced in the 1870s, allowed for the creation of more complex forms. In Cincinnati, this growth and change in the trade was supported by independent entities like M. R. Conway, a manufacturer of silversmith and jewelry machinery, and by the Cincinnati Bureau of Design and Engraving that worked "exclusively for the trade." Both advertised in the 1879 Cincinnati City Directory and were located in very close proximity to Duhme & Co.[6]

Silver workers, in the context of a large shop, assumed specialized skills and roles such as designer, pattern maker, die cutter, molder, stamper, spinner, chaser, embosser, engraver, plater, burnisher, and polisher.[7] Work was made in "batch production," meaning that similar types of wares were created in stages, passing

OPPOSITE: FIG. E2.1: Duhme & Co., *Goblet*, 1860s, parcel gilt silver, H. 7½ in. (19.1 cm), CAM, Museum Purchase with funds provided by Mr. and Mrs. Charles Fleischmann III, 2005.49. Mark 38.7

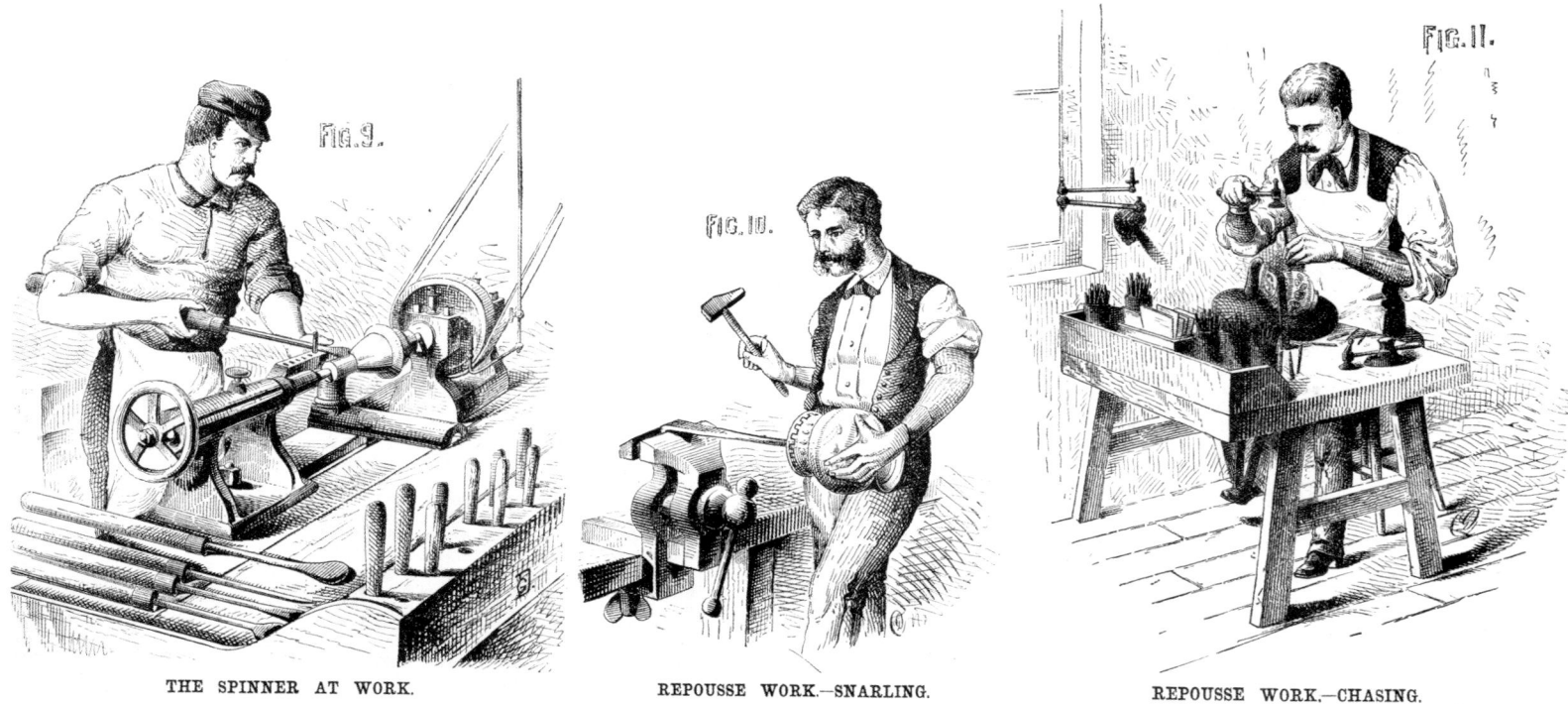

FIG. E2.2: *The Spinner at Work*; *Repoussé Work—Snarling*; *Repoussé Work—Chasing*, from "The Manufacture of Silverware," *Scientific American* 36, no. 19 (May 12, 1877): 290

from one stage and specialized worker to the next, until complete (figs. E2.2, E2.3).

With this specialization of labor, the nature of training in the trade also changed. Lengthy apprenticeships that encompassed all aspects of the trade were often replaced by shorter courses that focused on only one or two aspects. In 1869, it was reported that "about twenty intelligent boys, sons of jewelers and silversmiths" were "learning at [Herman Duhme's] establishment."[8] Other opportunities for education were available at the University of Cincinnati's School of Design (established in 1869, and later known as the Art Academy of Cincinnati). There, a special course of study for "engraving on metals" was offered as early as 1873.[9] It is probable that this course focused primarily on the engraving of plates for printmaking, although Charles Goetheim, who was noted as an "engraver of metals at Duhme & Co." in the School of Design's student list for the 1877/78 academic year, exhibited engraved silverware of his own design at the school's annual exhibition in 1876.[10] Others in the 1877/78 student list included Charles Neubauer, "watch case engraver"; Emil Rehse, "engraver on metals"; William Thorburn, "jeweler"; and Charles Wilms, "jeweler."[11] In 1874, a description of the school's ornamental design

course stated that students would learn "how to treat ornamentation as applied to wall decorations, paper hanging, metal work, stone, wood, etc."[12] Emil Rehse's silver cup was shown under the category of ornamental design in the school's 1875 annual exhibition.[13] Similar classes were probably offered at the Ohio Mechanics' Institute, but records of its curriculum prior to 1900 were unavailable at the time of this publication.

After Edward Kinsey's retirement from E. & D. Kinsey, his brother David Kinsey continued to operate their large silver manufactory under his own name. In May 1864 his factory was advertised as steam-powered.[14] Reportedly, the first American silver manufacturer to install steam-powered drop presses was John Gorham, Kinsey's much larger eastern competitor.[15] Both firms were making silver wares from coin and bullion at this time. Kinsey

OPPOSITE: FIG. E2.3: "The Manufacture of Silverware," *Scientific American* 36, no. 19 (May 12, 1877): 290: (1) melting; (2) flattening silver into sheets; (3) flatware blanks; (4) flatware roller die; (5) flatware blank with formed handle; (6) die stamping with drop press; (7) polishing; (8) finished pitcher of spun segments with die-rolled ornament and cast handle

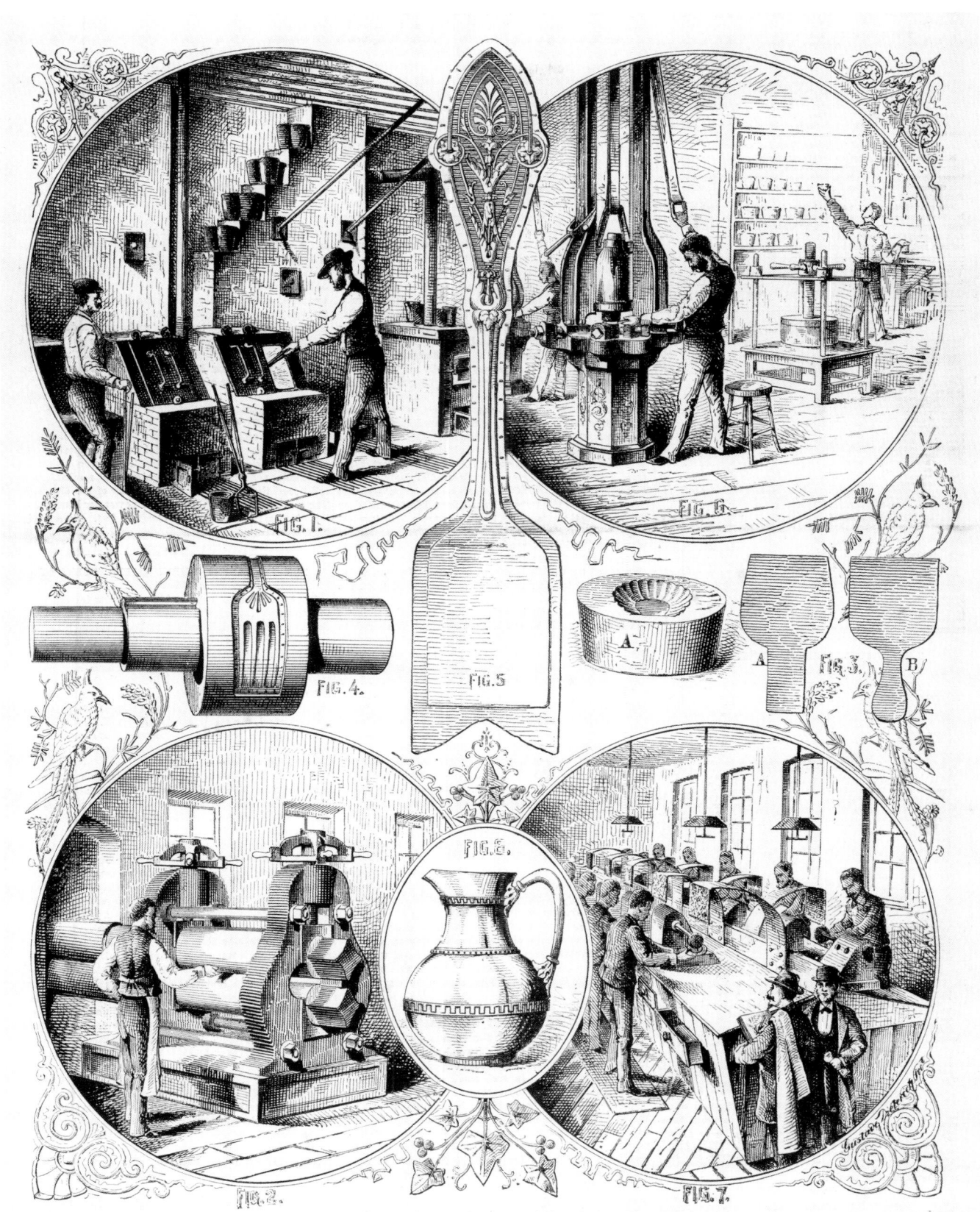

THE MANUFACTURE OF SILVERWARE.—(See page 290.)

was noted to be one of the largest consumers of bar metal in the West.[16] While the source of his material is unknown, it is probable that, like Gorham, he was acquiring it through Wall Street coin and bullion dealers and arranging for its delivery to Cincinnati by express train, or purchasing it through local banks.[17] In 1870, Kinsey reported a staff of nine and a year's production valued at $67,000.[18] He was surpassed in output by both Duhme & Co., whose staff of over 160 produced $250,000 worth of product, and John B. Morris whose staff of three produced "watch fobs, silver spoons, etc." valued at $142,800.[19] However, the ratio of silverware to other types of goods produced by Duhme & Co. and John B. Morris is not documented.[20]

Duhme & Co. began manufacturing silver around 1866. They were, by far, the largest silver and jewelry manufacturer in the city.[21] Descriptions of their manufactory tell us that machinery and steam power were "used in every department and utilized to do the work of hundreds," that they utilized silver in ingot and coin form, and that their factory was broken into different departments, with manufacturing in the basement (to support the operation of drop presses and other high impact machines) and finishing on an upper floor.[22] Like other American houses of this size, they hired foreign talent, boasting that 14 different nationalities were represented on their staff.[23] A number of these came from northern and central Europe, including Justus Kruckemeyer (b. Germany) who headed the firm's silver department; Herman Franz Serodino (b. Germany) and Wenzel Partl (b. Austria) who were foremen of the gold department; silversmith Theodore Neuhaus, Sr. (b. Germany), who had previously worked for the Kinseys; his son Theodore Jr., who eventually served as superintendent of the silver manufacturing department; and Charles F. Goettheim (b. Cincinnati to German immigrants), one of the firm's principal designers. Across the trade, it was generally felt that the presence and influence of foreign skilled workers prompted innovation in design, improved craftsmanship, and lent a certain worldly and fashionable distinction to a firm's reputation.

In 1874, Clemens Oskamp joined the ranks of Cincinnati silver manufacturers when he acquired the silverware manufactory of Francis A. Bunnell (1830–1896) of Syracuse, New York. Oskamp moved the works, including Bunnell's patterns and dies, to Cincinnati.[24] There, "the newest and most perfect machinery and devices" enabled him "to turn out patterns of workmanship of the most exquisite and beautiful finish."[25] He primarily made flatware, but also went on to produce jewelry. In 1880, he reported a staff of 33 producing $30,000 worth of wares. Again, the ratio of silver to jewelry represented in this number is not known.

With the 1859 discovery of the Comstock Lode of silver ore in Nevada—the first major discovery of silver in the United States—America became the largest producer of silver in the world. The price of bullion dropped, making silver affordable to the middle class for the first time. It was thought, in 1868, that there was more silver owned and in daily use in the United States than anywhere else in the world.[26] As small craftsmen's shops developed into large factories, silversmiths were no longer dealing directly with their customers. Manufacturers sold to wholesale dealers, or jobbers, who then sold to retailers, who sold to the public.

The Kinseys, Duhme & Co., and Oskamp all maintained salesrooms for both public and wholesale trade. Their sales to other local trade retailers were especially strong. In 1878, Sidney Maxwell stated, "it speaks well for our manufactures that two-thirds of the solid silver sold here is of our own production."[27] In the 1860s, most of the stores that sold silver were situated around the following areas: Main Street, Fourth Street east of Vine Street, Fifth Street, the West End (Linn Street and Central Avenue), and Over-the-Rhine, an area north of the Miami and Erie Canal, characterized by its concentration of German immigrants.[28] These areas, with the exception of Main Street, continued as centers for the trade into the 1870s. In the 1880s, Fifth Street gained more prominence, and in the 1890s and 1900s, most of the silver trade that had not scattered elsewhere throughout the city was focused in the central business district, around Fourth Street east of Vine Street, and Fifth Street.

Traveling salesmen took stock, which included wares of their firm's own manufacture as well as imports and ready-mades bought in the East or abroad, to distant, wide-spread locales. Each of the firms sold their own silver alongside silver wares produced by eastern makers, and a variety of fancy goods that included jewelry and watches (also, in some cases, of their own make), clocks,

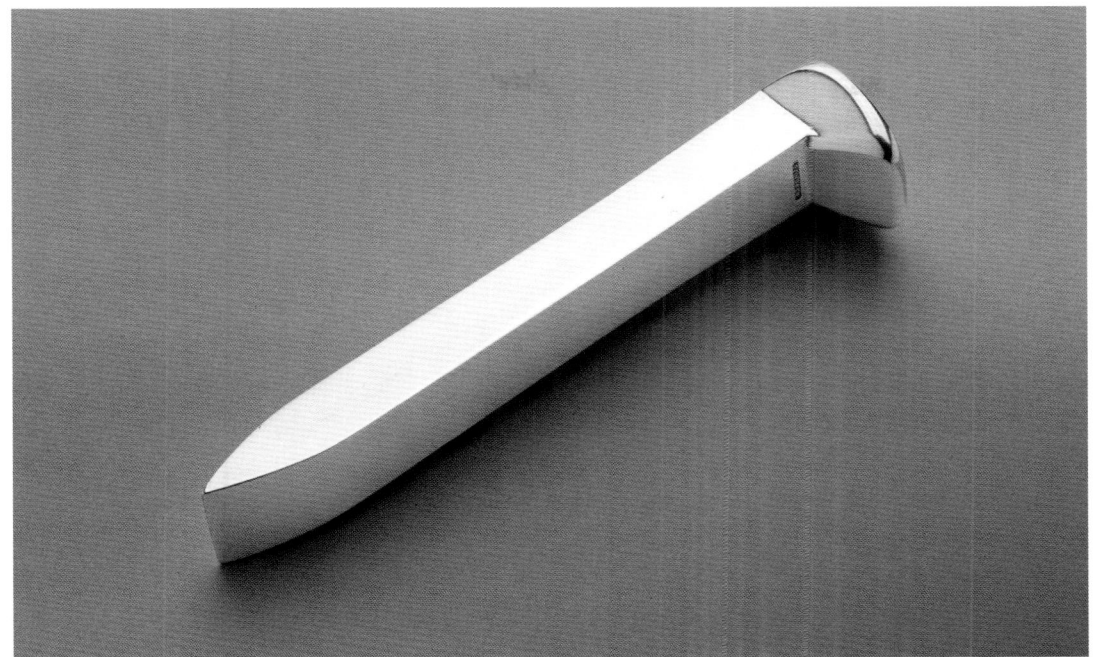

FIG. E2.4: Duhme & Co., *Spike*, 1879–1880, L. 5½ in. (14 cm), CAM, Gift of the Trustees of the Southern Railroad, 1884.309. Mark 38.16. In an attempt to recover lost trade with the South following the Civil War, the city of Cincinnati underwrote and built the Cincinnati Southern Railway. This spike was made to commemorate the laying of the last rail of the railway that still runs between Cincinnati and Chattanooga, Tennessee.

bronzes, stationery, ceramics, glass, and other types of bric-a-brac. In addition to sending goods out through salesmen, the firms also encouraged western and southern retailers to travel to Cincinnati to stock up, rather than make the long trip east. Cincinnati's central location was fundamental to its manufacturers' success, as by 1869, there were direct railroad lines between Cincinnati and Baltimore, Philadelphia, New York, Toledo, Chicago, St. Louis, Louisville, and Lexington (fig. E2.4).[29] Silver manufacturers continued to advertise in local and regional newspapers and city directories, and with the founding of the national trade journal *The Jewelers' Circular* (later known as *The Jewelers' Circular and Horological Review*), they were able to promote themselves across the country. Additional publicity was generated through the manufacture and display of large presentation pieces at the well-attended Cincinnati Industrial Expositions held between 1870 and 1888, and eventually through the production of sales catalogues.

Business in Cincinnati was humming until the Panic of 1873 precipitated by a fall in demand for silver internationally as Germany and the United States switched to a currency system backed solely by gold. This change depressed the price of silver, and created high interest rates and shortages of currency across the United States and abroad. While the nation's silver manufacturers could buy silver at the lowest prices, the strain on capital resources reduced production. Cincinnati weathered the Panic better than other cities. Its banks and most businesses remained intact; however sales and production of manufactures, across the board,

were down over $16 million.[30] The resulting downturn led to the failure of silver manufacturer John B. Morris in 1875, as well as several retailers. David Kinsey died in 1874, and while his heirs continued the business of retailing silver and other goods, it is unclear whether they continued to operate the silverware manufactory. Regardless, they were never able to bring the business back to its former height. In 1880, the capital invested and value of products reported by Duhme & Co. had not changed from that reported in 1870, although the size of their staff and, naturally, the value of their raw material had decreased.[31] The Panic forced surviving businesses to become more calculating and efficient. This was true nationwide, and following this period, the entire silver industry was represented by a few firms in New York City, Syracuse, southern New England, and Baltimore.[32] In Cincinnati, Duhme & Co. was the only firm that could compete with these companies in terms of output and quality. Clemens Oskamp did not enter into the production of silver until 1874. Like Duhme & Co., his interests were diversified in both jewelry and silver, and his foray into silver flatware manufacturing came through the opportunity to buy an already well-established, active business, complete with tools, dies, and machinery. While Oskamp was successful, he did not operate on a scale comparable to that of Duhme.

Beginning around 1870, and continuing through the turn of the century, American silver, as aptly stated by Dorothy T. Rainwater, "was subject to a bewildering welter of styles."[33] It is disappointing on many levels that the institutional records of Duhme & Co. do not survive. They might have afforded an inventory of the books, drawings, and perhaps even objects in the company's design library—the inspirational sources for their designers. Extant silver underscores their cognizance of the varied fashions and styles that were both affordable for and popular with their clientele. Principal styles explored by the firm, and reflected in the eastern wares sold by Cincinnati retailers during this period, include revivals of the Classical, Gothic, and Colonial styles as well as those that embraced the aesthetics of Japan, the Orient, and the English Aesthetic Movement. Quite often, one design simultaneously combined several different styles and influences. It is this eclectic mix, popular in the last quarter of the 19th century, that identifies some of the most ambitious and whacky pieces of the Victorian era.

The local preference for sterling silver appeared in the late 1860s. The 1877 City Directory lists Harmon Winslow, a former employee of the Kinseys, as a silversmith and an assayer. This represents the only known local advertisement for assay work. While Cincinnati did not have a formal assay system, most makers were working in sterling silver by this time and would have been testing their wares regularly to ensure that their materials met the sterling standard. Larger firms would have employed an assayer, whereas smaller firms would have presumably sought out individuals like Winslow. In 1896, Ohio passed legislation that declared that anyone selling silver marked as sterling, or in a box marked sterling, which did not prove to be sterling, would be guilty of a misdemeanor.[34]

In time, the city's interests within the broad trade category of silver, clocks, watches, and jewelry focused more on jewelry, a sizeable and growing local enterprise since before the Civil War. Cincinnati's Board of Trade reported that in 1881, there were 47 establishments active in the manufacture of jewelry and silverware.[35] At this time, only Duhme & Co. and Clemens Oskamp are known to have been producing silver, and both manufactured jewelry as well. This calculation did not include the large number of wholesale and retail jewelry dealers in the city. By 1892, it was avowed that "there were more jewelry stores in this city for the population than any other city in the country."[36] By 1919, the city was ranked the third largest jewelry trade center in the United States, with 432 large manufacturing houses, over 100 retail stores, and countless other supply houses, watch factories, diamond dealers, and related operations.[37] Its stature as such was credited (as was most of Cincinnati's industrial and commercial growth and vitality) to its location. Cincinnati was "the city most easily and quickly reached by mail and express from a large and rich portion of the country."[38] A significant number of these jewelry stores retailed silver of local and eastern manufacture alongside their wide range of goods, establishing themselves as competitors of the local manufacturing retailers.

Among the most notable Cincinnati wholesale and retail jewelry establishments who sold significant quantities of silver were Clemens Hellebush, William Wilson McGrew, E.E. Isbell, Frank Herschede, A. & J. Plaut, Michie Bros., George Herman Newstedt, Oskamp, Nolting & Co., The Clemens Oskamp Co., Joseph S. Voss & Son, Albert Brothers, the Schwabs, and Loring Andrews. Most of these firms marked the silver that they sold with their own name, adding to confusion about authorship. While some sold locally manufactured wares, they also sold a great deal of silver produced elsewhere. The silver wares sold with the greatest zeal in the local market included those of Frank M. Whiting Co., Whiting Mfg. Co., Wood & Hughes, Reed & Barton, Dominick & Haff, Towle Mfg. Co., George W. Shiebler, Peter Krider, and William B. Durgin Co. Gorham Mfg. Co. maintained an especially strong market in the Midwest and was sold heavily by many of the Cincinnati firms, including Duhme & Co. Gorham's relationship with William Wilson McGrew was particularly strong, as evidenced not only by the amount of their silver bearing his retail mark, but also in their willingness to allow him to exhibit some of their greatest World Fair pieces in his displays at the Cincinnati Industrial Expositions. After 1915, Loring Andrews became an authorized dealer of S. Kirk & Son of Baltimore.

Cincinnati's last large stronghold in the manufacture of silver, Duhme & Co., began to crumble shortly after the death of founder Herman Duhme in 1888. By 1893, a year marked by yet another serious economic recession, the firm had curtailed manufacturing, and in July 1895 it closed its wholesale operations to focus solely on retail. Bankruptcy proceedings began in 1896. After its fall, the Duhme Manufacturing Co., the Herman Keck Manufacturing Co.,

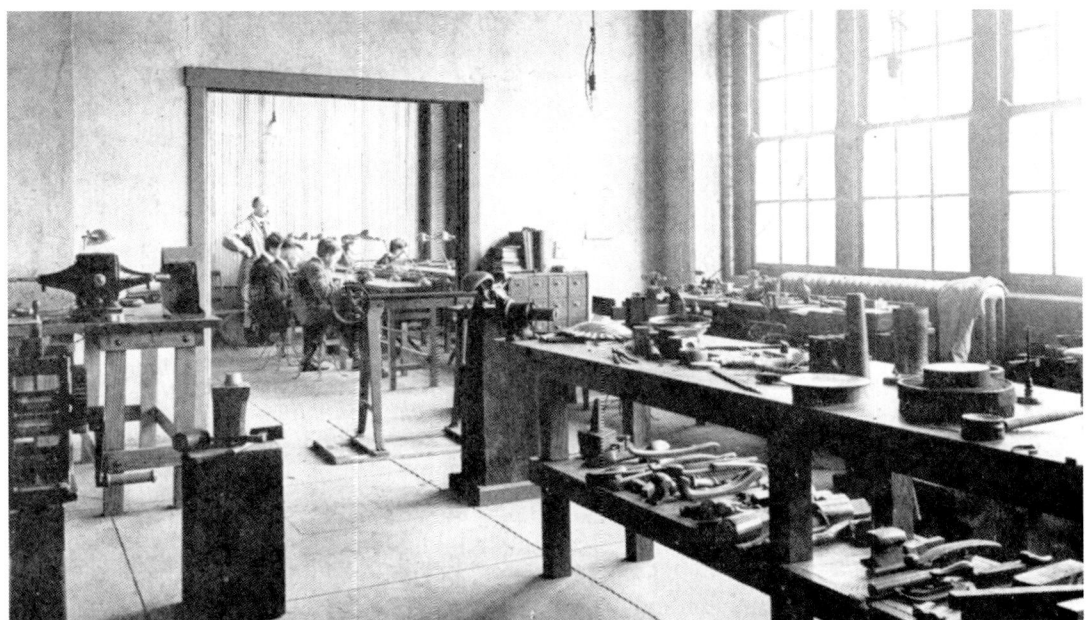

FIG. E2.5: Silver and jewelry classroom from the 1917 *Ohio Mechanics' Institute Catalogue*, School Curriculum Records, 74, Courtesy of University of Cincinnati Archives and Rare Books Library

various firms headed by Theodore Neuhaus, Jr. (former superintendent of Duhme's silver manufacturing department), and O.E. Bell's Cincinnati Silver Company sprang up, but all were only modestly successful and short-lived. Large-scale silver manufacturing in Cincinnati was over.

There was a return to small shop activity and hand crafting in accordance with the ideals of the American Arts and Crafts Movement (circa 1890–1920). Local smiths who were part of this movement include Robert Sturm and Kenton C. Kunkle. Both men earned a living through their work for the local jewelry trade, but extant wares (and in the case of Sturm, sample books) tell us that they crafted fine silver pieces on commission. Ideologies of the Arts and Crafts Movement encouraged artists to work in multiple media. In 1907, the Art Academy of Cincinnati offered a special class for enameling on metals, and from 1909 to 1921, Anna Riis taught a course in metal and leather work.[39] Cincinnati artists such as M. Louise McLaughlin, Maria Longworth Nichols Storer, E.T. Hurley, and Benn Pitman extended their artistic endeavors to explore metals such as copper, tin, and brass. While they employed techniques also used to work silver, and may have worked in the metal, there is, to date, no evidence to suggest that they did.

In September 1916, through the support of Cincinnati's Wholesale Jewelry Manufacturers and Jobbers Association, a silversmith and jewelry program was introduced at the Ohio Mechanics' Institute.[40] The four-year program was established to afford young men the opportunity to "learn modeling and designing and fit themselves as artisan-jewelers," offering "prac-

tical training in design and construction of jewelry and silverware of all kinds."[41] Theodore Hanford Pond (1873–1923), a nationally recognized Arts and Crafts silversmith who had established similar departments at the Maryland Institute in Baltimore, the Mechanics' Institute in Rochester, New York, and the Rhode Island School of Design in Providence, was hired to direct the program. Two workshops (fig. E2.5) provided space for the instruction of up to fifty pupils.[42] The description of the program's silversmith course notes, "The shop work in this course offers practical training in the raising and hammering of hollow ware in copper, brass and silver, forging flatware such as spoons, forks, knives, etc., and the decoration of wares of all kinds with piercing, carving, chasing, engraving and enameling."[43] The program was short-lived. Pond did not appear in city directories after 1917, and information about the program did not appear in subsequent annual catalogues of the Mechanics' Institute. Any interaction between Pond and Cincinnati's later known silversmiths—Sturm, Kunkle, or Joseph Julius Tressel—is unknown. Tressel was primarily a metal plater and repairer, but extant silver and copper wares in the Arts and Crafts style, made between 1925 and the late 1940s, attest to his activities as a designer and craftsmen. In addition to an apprenticeship and studies at the Art Academy of Cincinnati, Tressel earned a certificate in chemistry at the Ohio Mechanics' Institute in 1919.[44] The work of these men marks the end of this study, as by this time most American silver production was carried on by a few large firms centered in the Northeast.

1. 1850 Federal Non-Population Census Schedules, Products of Industry, Schedule 4, Hamilton County, Ohio.

2. Charles Venable, *Silver in America: A Century of Splendor*, New York: Harry N. Abrams Inc., 1995, 22.

3. Charles Cist, *Sketches and Statistics of Cincinnati in 1851*, Cincinnati: William H. Moore & Co., 1851, 188; 1850 Federal Non-Population Census Schedules, Hamilton County, Ohio.

4. Ohio, Vol. 3, p. 98, R.G. Dun & Co. Collection, Baker Library, Harvard Business School.

5. For more on the transition of small shop to manufactory, see Stephen Victor's essay, "From the Shop to the Manufactory, Silver and Industry, 1800–1970," in Barbara McLean Ward and Gerald W.R. Ward (eds.), *Silver in American Life*, New York: American Federation of the Arts, 1979. Also see Venable, *Silver in America*, chapters 1 and 4.

6. 1879 Cincinnati City Directory; Conway was located on the same corner as Duhme (probably the same building), and the Bureau was only a block away on the southwest corner of Fifth and Walnut Streets.

7. For more on the production of both flatware and hollowware at this time, see "The Manufacture of Silverware," *Scientific American* 36, no. 19 (May 12, 1877): 290.

8. "Progress in the Decorative Arts: The Manufacture of Gold and Silverware in the West," *Cincinnati Enquirer*, May 18, 1869, 3.

9. *School of Design of the University of Cincinnati, Course of Instruction, Rules &c. Adopted by the Board of Directors, December 19, 1872*, Cincinnati: J.R. Mills & Co., 1873, 5.

10. *Catalogue of the University of Cincinnati for the Academic Year 1877–'8*, Cincinnati: Office of the University, 1877, 100; *Catalogue of the 8th Annual Exhibition of the School of Design of the University of Cincinnati, June 1876*,
Cincinnati: A.H. Pugh, 1876, 40.

11. *Catalogue of the University of Cincinnati for the Academic Year 1877–'8*, 100–104.

12. *Catalogue of the University of Cincinnati for the Academic Year 1874*, Cincinnati: Office of the University, 1874, 26.

13. *Catalogue of the 7th Annual Exhibition of the School of Design of the University of Cincinnati, June 1875*, Cincinnati: A.H. Pugh, 1875, 40.

14. David Kinsey's "Steam Silver-Ware Manufactory" is advertised in the *Cincinnati Enquirer*, May 13, 1864, 1.

15. Charles H. Carpenter, *Gorham Silver, 1831–1981*, New York: Dodd, Mead & Co., 1982, 48.

16. "Great Industrial Exposition, The Closing Days," *Cincinnati Enquirer*, October 19, 1870, 3.

17. For a discussion of buying bullion and coin at this time, see "Silver and Silver Plate," *Harper's New Monthly Magazine* (September 1868): 438–440.

18. 1870 Federal Non-Population Census Schedules, Products of Industry, Schedule 4, Hamilton County, Ohio.

19. Ibid.

20. Morris was also a manufacturer of watch cases. Little is known about the silver he produced. Spoons with his mark are very rare. 1870 Federal Non-Population Census Schedules, Hamilton County, Ohio.

21. During the 1850s and early 1860s, the employer identified with most of the silversmiths, silver polishers, etc. through city directory searches was E. & D. Kinsey (later David Kinsey). This changed in the later 1860s when Duhme & Co. employed the larger number.

22. M. Joblin, *Cincinnati Past and Present or, Its Industrial History, As Exhibited In the Life-Labors of Its Leading Men*, Cincinnati: Elm Street Printing Co., 1872, 32–38; John W. Leonard, *The Centennial Review of Cincinnati: one hunderd years of progress in commerce, manufactures, the professions, and in
social and municipal life*, Cincinnati: J.M. Elstner, 1888, 67; "On the Road," *Jewelers' Circular and Horological Review* (July 1888): 44.

23. "Holiday Goods and Holiday Presents," *Cincinnati Enquirer*, December 20, 1869, 8; Joblin, *Cincinnati Past and Present*, 32–38.

24. R. David Ives, "Francis A. Bunnell and His Successor Clemens Oskamp," *Silver Magazine* (November/December 1991): 13.

25. D. J. Kenny, "Clemens Oskamp," *Illustrated Cincinnati: A Pictorial Handbook*, Cincinnati: G.E. Stevens, 1875, 396.

26. "Silver and Silver Plate," 434.

27. Sidney D. Maxwell, *The Manufactures of Cincinnati . . .* , Cincinnati: R. Clarke & Company, 1878, 26.

28. By the 1860s, Western Row had been renamed Central Avenue.

29. George E. Stevens, *The Queen City in 1869*, Cincinnati: George S. Blanchard & Co., 1869, 86.

30. E.H. Austerlitz, *Cincinnati, from 1800 to 1875, A Condensed History of Cincinnati Combined with Exposition Guide for 1875, Fully Illustrated, together with a description of pictures and works of art, exhibited at the Cincinnati Industrial Exposition, 1875*, Cincinnati: Bloch & Co., 1875, 106.

31. 1880 Federal Non-Population Census Schedules, Products of Industry, Schedule 4, Hamilton County, Ohio.

32. Venable, *Silver in America*, 22.

33. Dorothy T. Rainwater, Gorham Manufacturing Company, Unger Brothers, *Sterling silver hollowware [sic]: tea and coffee service, pitchers and ewers, bookmarks, ash trays, candelabra, salts and papers, desk sets and dressing sets, berry bowls, napkin rings, cups, tea balls and bells, trays, flasks, match safes*, Princeton, NJ: Pyne Press, 1973, 12.

34. "The Circular's Sterling Silver Bill Now a Law in Ohio," *JCHR* (March 4, 1896): 23.

35. Albert N. Marquis (ed.), *The Industries of Cincinnati*, Cincinnati: A.N.
Marquis & Co., 1883, 60–64.

36. "Jewelry Failure," *Cincinnati Enquirer*, April 24, 1892, 9.

37. "Cincinnatti [sic], Fifty years have seen a remarkable growth in the distributing center of the Jewelry Trade of the South City now Greatest Inland Diamond Market," *JCHR* (February 5, 1919): 393.

38. Ibid.

39. 1907–1921 Art Academy of Cincinnati catalogues, Mary R. Schiff Library and Archives, Cincinnati Art Museum.

40. "Works of the Jewelry Classes at the Ohio Mechanics' Institute at Cincinnati, O.," *JCHR* (July 18, 1917): 1; "School for Artisans Opened at Ohio Mechanics' Institute," *The Cincinnatian: Official Organ of the Cincinnati Chamber of Commerce* (November 27, 1916): 6; Enrollment records for the program could not be found.

41. Ibid.; *General Bulletin of the Ohio Mechanics' Institute (Annual Catalogue), Cincinnati, 1917–1918*, Cincinnati: Ohio Mechanics' Institute, 1917, 73–75, University of Cincinnati Archives and Rare Books Library, box 35.

42. Ibid.; Work by Pond is rare, however examples in silver and copper have been documented. *Vase*, circa 1910, copper, The Minneapolis Art Institute, The Modernism Collection, Gift of Norwest Bank Minnesota, 98.276.159; "A Server by Theodore Hanford Pond," http://www.smpub.com/ubb/Forum 17/HTML/000382.html.

43. General Bulletin of the Ohio Mechanics' Institute, 1917; Advertisements for the course appeared in the *Cincinnati Enquirer* on June 17, 1917, 8, and on August 19, 1917, 7.

44. "Artist in Metal is 81: Recalls 25-Cent Weekly Pay," *Cincinnati Times Star*, February 24, 1956, 40; Art Academy of Cincinnati card file, Mary R. Schiff Library and Archives.

OPPOSITE: **Duhme & Co.,** *Salad Spoon and Fork*, c. 1880s. Detail of Fig. 38.40

OVERLEAF: **Duhme & Co.,** *Tea and Coffee Service*, late 1870s–1880s. Fig. 38.36

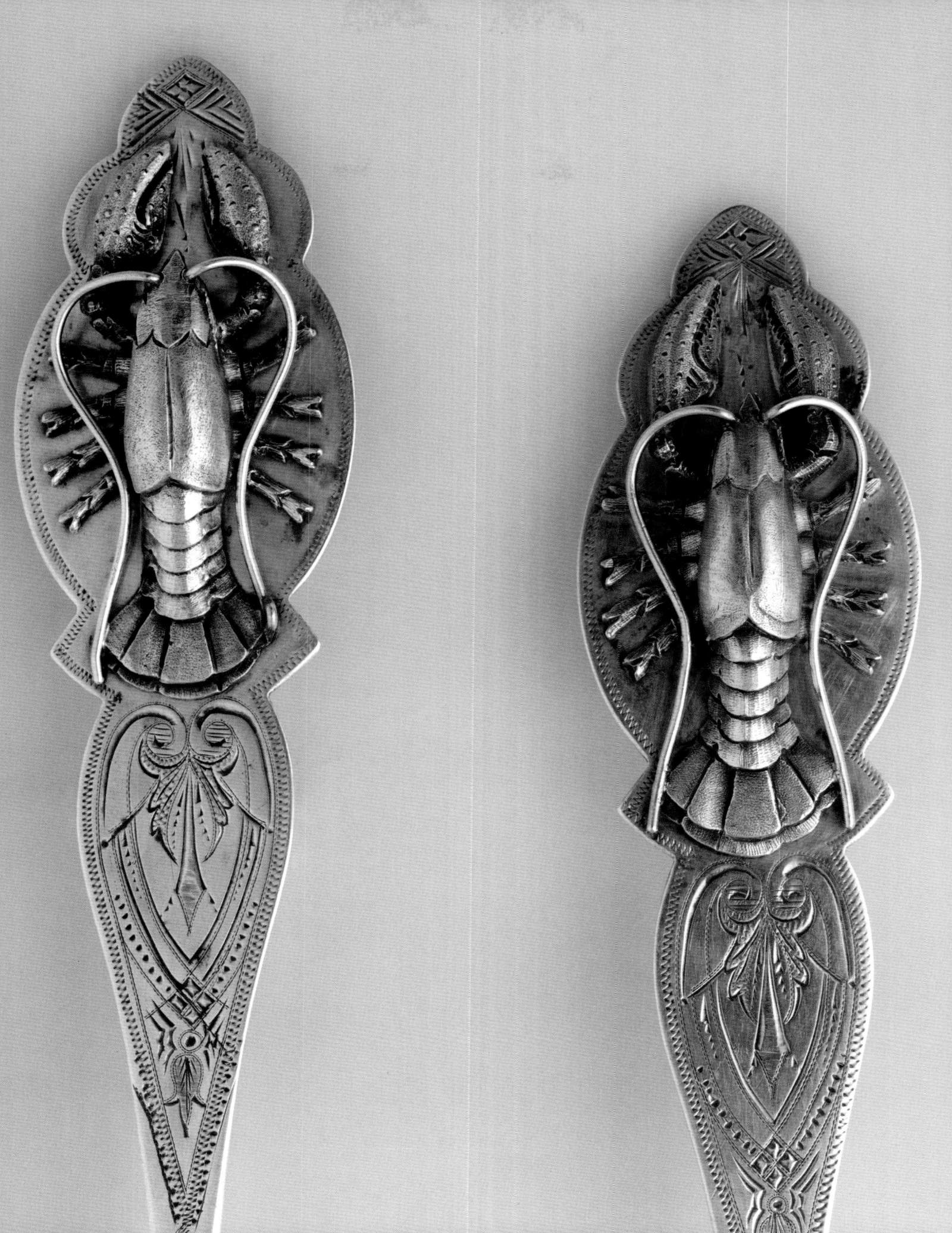

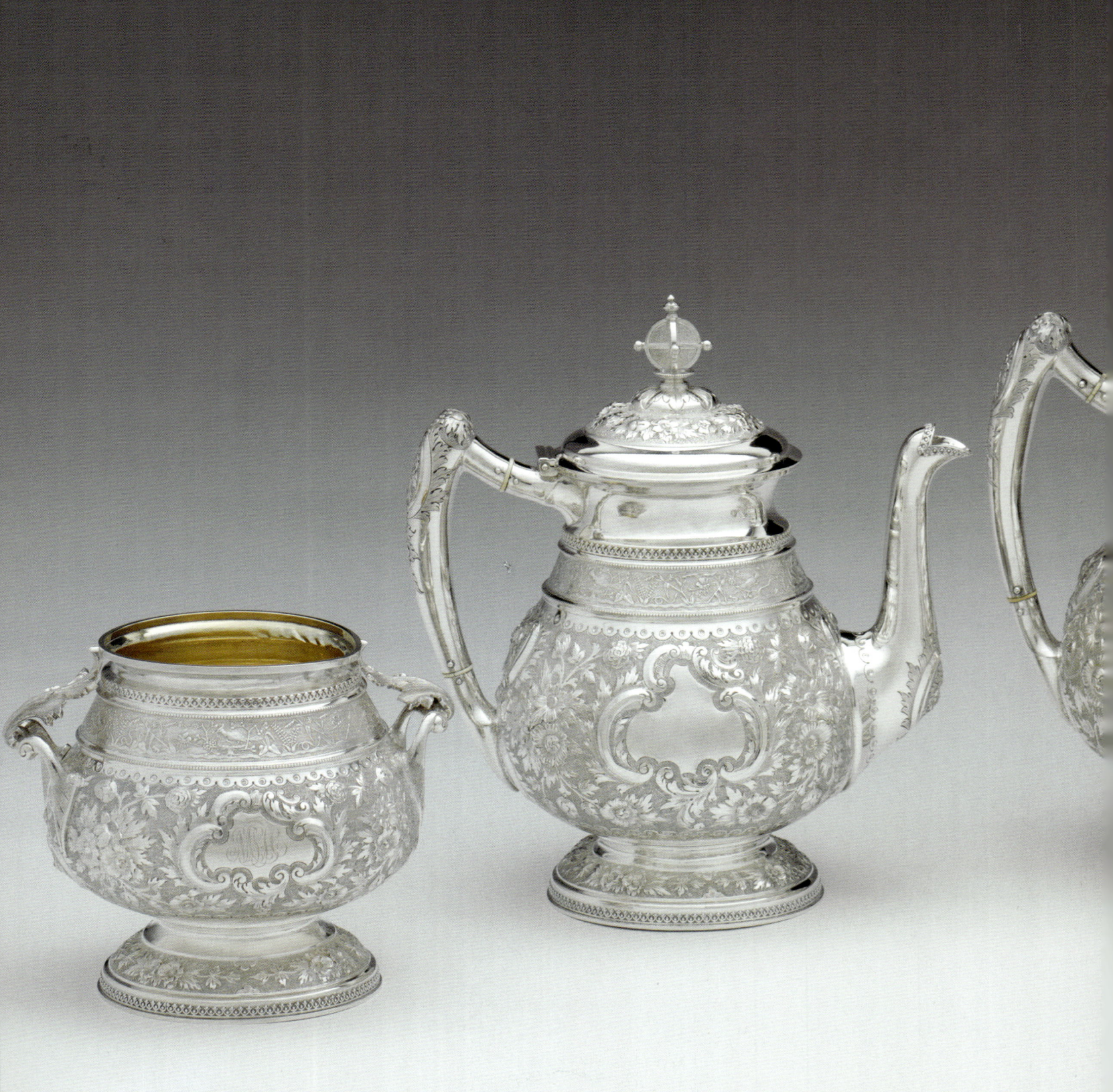

CINCINNATI SILVERSMITHS AND FIRMS WITH KNOWN WARES

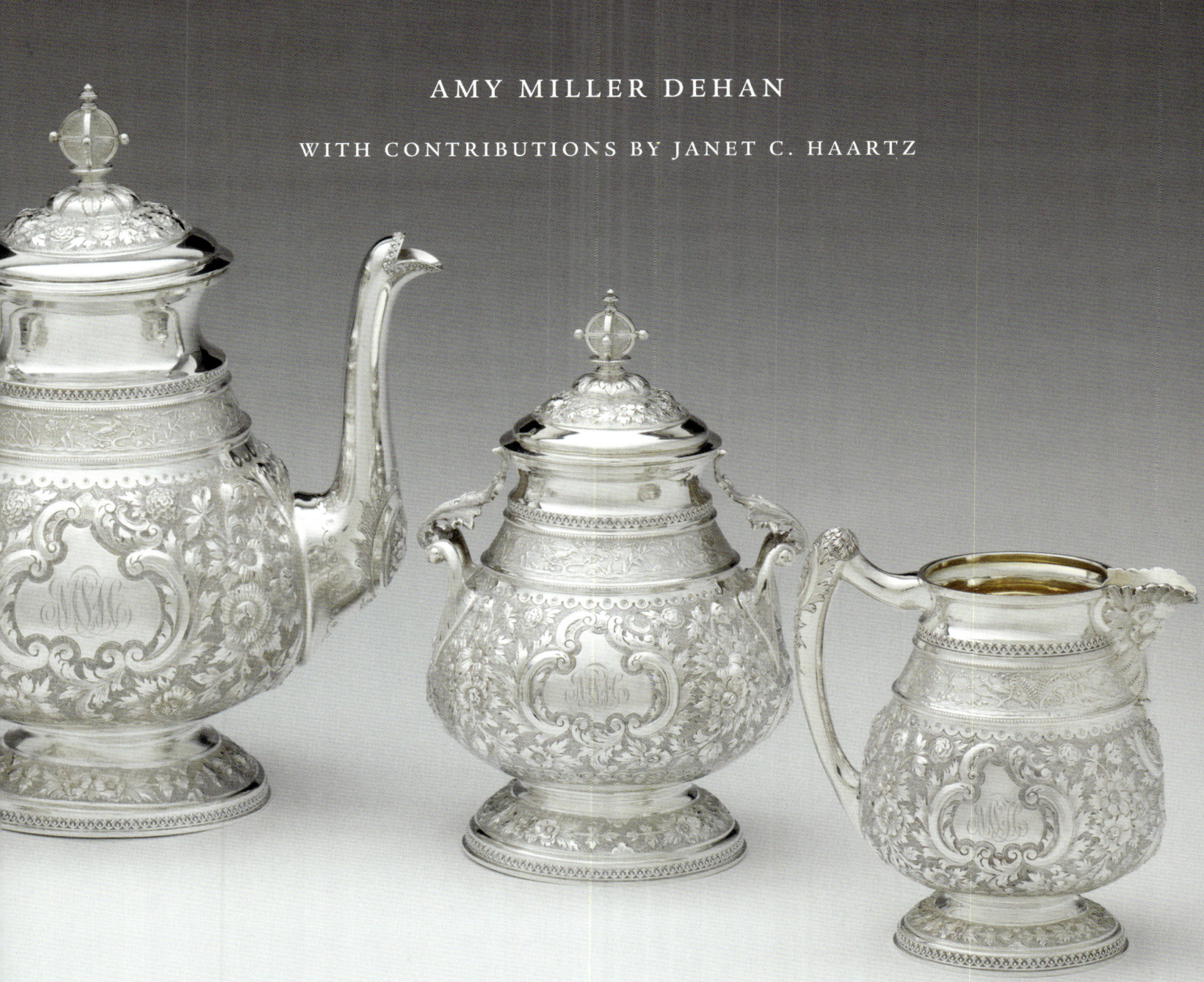

AMY MILLER DEHAN

WITH CONTRIBUTIONS BY JANET C. HAARTZ

1. ALLEN & RHODES

1833–1834

This firm was established when **Pulaski Scovil** sold his interest in **C. Allen & Co.** (his partnership with **Caleb Allen, Jr.**) to **Thomas F. Rhodes** in June 1833.[1] Rhodes and Allen were both from Providence, Rhode Island, the center of a growing jewelry industry. The two men would have surely known one another prior to arriving in Cincinnati—Rhodes by 1832, and Allen by 1833.

Nothing is known of Rhodes' or Allen's training. Both listed their occupation as jeweler in the 1834 Cincinnati City Directory, and in April of that year they published an advertisement for two apprentices to the jewelry business, and two to the manufacturing of silverware.[2] This suggests that one or both principals possessed skills in these areas of the business that they were willing to teach.

On June 17, 1833, Allen & Rhodes announced that they would "manufacture and keep for sale an extensive assortment of JEWELRY," at "36 Lower Market Street, up stairs."[3] Among the wares recently received from New York and Philadelphia were "Gold and silver Lever English and French Watches, gold chains; coral, jett and fillagree [*sic*] Ear Rings and Pins, fine Cutlery [and] a general assortment of Fancy goods, &c."[4] In August 1834 the firm evolved into **Allen, Rhodes & Co.** when John G. Anthony (fig. 117.1), the brother-in-law of Rhodes, joined the firm.[5] It was not until the establishment of Allen, Rhodes & Co. that there was an increased emphasis on advertising the partners' role as silver manufacturers.

The mark of this firm has been found on spoons with fiddle handles and either rounded or pointed shoulders.[6]

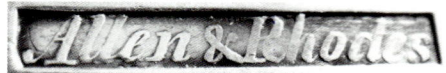

MARK 1.1

1. Advertisement, *Cincinnati Daily Gazette*, June 17, 1833, reproduced in Beckman, 121.
2. Advertisement, *Cincinnati Daily Gazette*, April 18, 1834, reproduced in Beckman, 1.
3. Advertisement, *Cincinnati Daily Gazette*, June 17, 1833, reproduced in Beckman, 1.
4. Ibid.
5. Advertisement, *Cincinnati Daily Gazette*, September 6, 1834, reproduced in Beckman, 117; John Gould Anthony married Ann Whiting Rhodes on October 16,

1832. Ann Whiting, Thomas Frederick, and James Fenner were the children of Thomas and Lydia (Keene) Rhodes of Providence; *Memorial Biographies of The New England Historical Genealogical Society, Towne Memorial Fund*, vol. 7, *1871–1880*, Boston: The New England Historical Genealogical Society, 1907, 266.
6. Allen & Rhodes, eBay listings and private collections, Cincinnati silver binders, Cincinnati Art Museum.

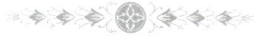

2. ALLEN, RHODES & CO.

1834–1836

In August 1834 John G. Anthony (1804–1877, fig. 117.1), brother-in-law of **Thomas F. Rhodes**, joined the firm of **Allen & Rhodes**, creating Allen, Rhodes & Co.[1] Soon after, they advertised under the headline, "SILVER PLATE"—a term derived from English usage that was at this time used to describe goods made of silver, rather than those plated with a layer of silver. The advertisement announces that the firm was "prepared to execute all orders for Silver Plate, Coffee and Tea setts [*sic*],–Goblets, Mugs, Tumblers, Dessert Knives, Forks, Communion setts [*sic*], &c. made to order." It also stated that they kept on hand "A large supply of Table, Desserts [*sic*], Tea, Cream, Salt, and Mustard spoons, Sugar Tongs, Soup Ladles, Tumblers, Butter and Dessert Knives, which they warrant equal to coin." An indication of their distribution system is provided in the statement, "country dealers constantly supplied."[2] No address is given in this advertisement, but it is assumed that the firm continued to operate at the former stand of Allen & Rhodes on Lower Market Street until sometime prior to February 1835, when they advertised their receipt of a new "assortment of superior accordions with instruction books" at 34 Main Street, on the northeast corner of Main and Second Streets.[3] Their advertisement in the

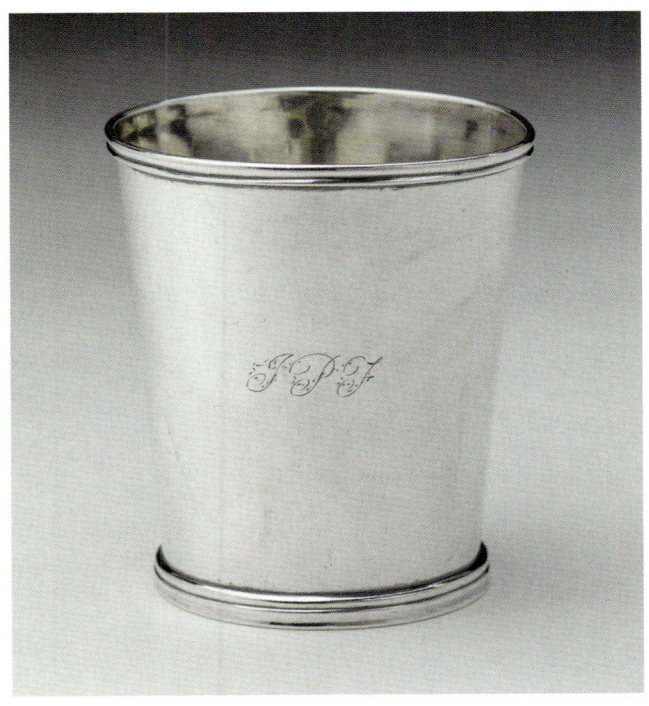

FIG. 2.1: Allen, Rhodes & Co., *Beaker*, 1834–1836,
H. 3⅜ in. (8.6 cm), Diam. 3⅛ in. (7.9 cm), CAM, Museum
Purchase: John S. Conner Fund, 2009.159

1836/37 City Directory proclaimed, "MANUFACTURE SILVER
PLATE AND JEWELRY, AND KEEP FOR SALE, At wholesale, only
Watches, Cutlery and Fancy Goods: Also A LARGE ASSORTMENT
OF WATCH-MAKER'S TOOLS, And watch materials."[4] The firm
dissolved later that year, as Rhodes and Anthony ran an advertise-
ment for their own firm (**Rhodes & Anthony**) in October 1836,
and **Caleb Allen, Jr.** ran one for his subsequent firm, **C. Allen &
Co.**, in the 1837 *Western Address Directory*.[5]

According to their advertisements, Allen, Rhodes & Co.
produced some of the silver that they sold. Mark 2.1 has been
found on a beaker (fig. 2.1); a salt spoon with fiddle handle, pointed
shoulders, and shell bowl; and a serving spoon with fiddle handle
and rounded shoulders. Mark 2.2 has been observed on a spoon
and ladle with fiddle handles. The spoon has pointed shoulders,
and the ladle has rounded shoulders.[6]

MARK 2.1

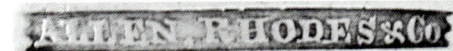

MARK 2.2

1. Advertisement, *Cincinnati Daily
   Gazette*, September 6, 1834,
   reproduced in Beckman, 117; 1836/37
   Cincinnati City Directory; John
   Gould Anthony married Ann Whiting
   Rhodes on October 16, 1832. Ann
   Whiting, Thomas Frederick, and
   James Fenner were the children of
   Thomas and Lydia (Keene) Rhodes of
   Providence. *Memorial Biographies of The
   New England Historical Genealogical
   Society, Towne Memorial Fund*, vol. 7,
   1871–1880, Boston: The New England
   Historical Genealogical Society, 1907,
   266.
2. Advertisement, *Cincinnati Daily
   Gazette*, August 30, 1834, reproduced
   in Beckman, 117.
3. Advertisement, *Cincinnati Daily
   Gazette*, March 6, 1835, 3; 1836/37
   Cincinnati City Directory.
4. Advertisement, 1836/37 Cincinnati
   City Directory, reproduced in
   Beckman, 2.
5. Advertisement, *Cincinnati Daily
   Gazette*, October 8, 1836, reproduced
   in Beckman, 6; Advertisement,
   Western Address Directory, 1837, 327.
   The information for this directory
   would have been collected in late
   1836.
6. Allen, Rhodes & Co., eBay listings
   and private collections, Cincinnati
   silver binders, Cincinnati Art
   Museum.

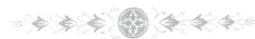

3. C. ALLEN & CO.

1833, 1836–1840/1841

There were two firms that went by the name of C. Allen & Co. The first
was a short-lived partnership between **Caleb Allen, Jr.** and **Pulaski
Scovil** that ended in June 1833. The announcement of the firm's
dissolution is the first record of both Allen and Scovil in Cincinnati.[1]

The second firm of this name was established by Caleb Allen, Jr.
and his brother, **William Allen** in 1836.[2] They advertised as

"MANUFACTURERS OF SILVER WARE & JEWELLERY [*sic*]
AND JOBBERS IN WATCH TOOLS, MATERIALS, AND FANCY
GOODS" at 21 Main Street, "4 doors from Front St."[3] In the
1839/40 City Directory, they advertised as "MANUFACTURERS
OF JEWELRY, DEALERS in Clocks, Watches, Watch-tools and
Materials, and FANCY GOODS GENERALLY" on the northeast

corner of Main and Columbia Streets. There were no directories printed in 1841, and in 1842 there is no listing for the firm. Rather, William is listed alone, as a silversmith working at the old stand, and only a residential address is published for Caleb.[4]

The marks of C. Allen & Co. have been observed on spoons with fiddle handles and pointed or rounded shoulders.[5]

1. Advertisement, *Cincinnati Daily Gazette*, June 17, 1833, reproduced in Beckman, 121.
2. Advertisement, W.G. Lyford, *The Western Address Directory*, Baltimore: Jos. Robinson, 1837, 327; Information for this directory would have been collected in late 1836.
3. Advertisement, W.G. Lyford, *The Western Address Directory*.
4. 1842 Cincinnati City Directory.
5. C. Allen & Co., eBay listings and private collections, Cincinnati silver binders, Cincinnati Art Museum.

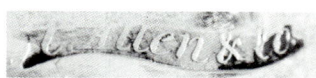

MARK 3.1

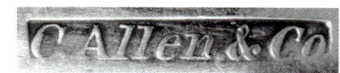

MARK 3.2

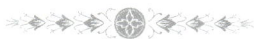

4. LORING ANDREWS & CO.
1895[1]–1903

THE LORING ANDREWS CO.
1903–1959

LORING ANDREWS & RATTERMAN, INC.
1959–1965

NEWSTEDT-LORING ANDREWS
1965–present

Loring Andrews (1856–1921) was born in Cincinnati on March 20, 1856, to Maria Zuemar (1835–1910) and David B. Andrews (1822–1863).[2] His father, born in Ireland, was a "manufacturer and dealer in watches, clocks, jewelry, gold and silverware" from 1848 to at least 1861.[3] Loring was only seven years old when his father died, and too young to be his apprentice. By 1873, he was working as a clerk in the shop of **William Wilson McGrew**, and when McGrew sold his business to **E.E. Isbell & Co.** in 1875, Andrews continued there as a clerk.[4] A special correspondent traveling in 1888 for *The Jewelers' Circular and Horological Review* noted that Andrews, Mr. Isbell's assistant, was an authority on pottery.[5] When E.E. Isbell & Co. dissolved in 1895, Andrews took over the business. With the

backing of the heirs of Thomas Gaff, Isbell's deceased partner, the firm of Loring Andrews & Co. was established.[6] Initially, the firm operated at 107 and 109 East Fourth Street, near Walnut Street. In 1900, the firm expanded, leasing the store that adjoined it on Fourth Street. An arch was cut through the buildings' shared wall to enlarge the salesroom in order "to display their new large pieces of bric-a-brac and art goods."[7] The firm's new address was 105 and 107 East Fourth Street.[8]

Loring Andrews & Co. manufactured and dealt in jewelry, sold and repaired watches and clocks, and dealt in imported and domestic ceramics, glass, and silver (fig. 4.1).[9] There is no evidence to suggest that the firm manufactured any of the silver that it sold.

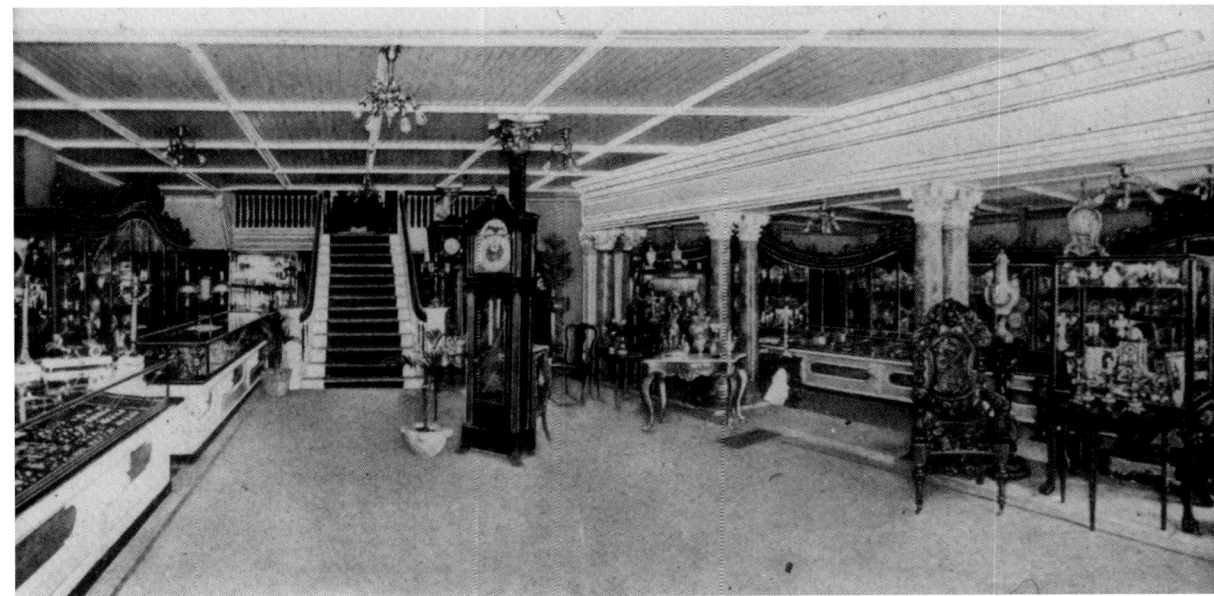

FIG. 4.1: *Loring Andrews & Co., 105 and 107 East Fourth Street*, Cincinnati History Slide Collection, Public Library of Cincinnati and Hamilton County

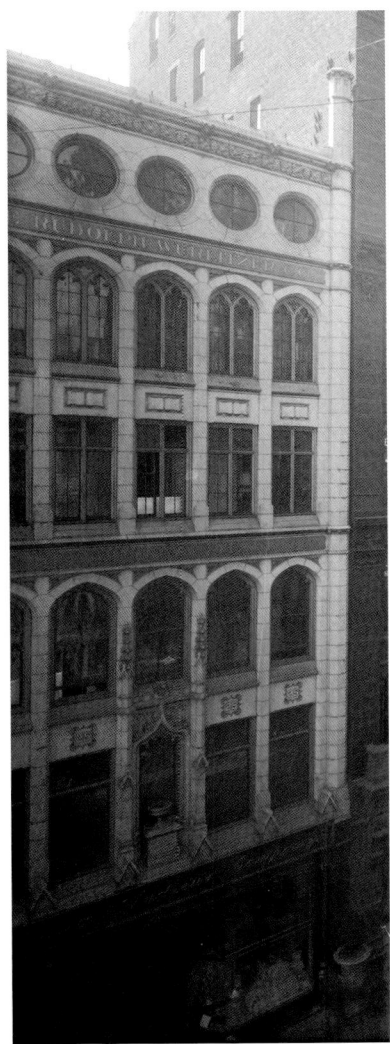

FIG. 4.2: Rombach & Groene, (American, estab. 1884, closed after 1960), *View of Southside of Fourth Street Between Walnut and Main*, March 1st, 1916, glass negative, SC#296, Cincinnati Historical Society Library. This building housed The Loring Andrews Co. and Rudolph Wurlitzer Co.

Andrews made yearly trips to Europe, usually during the summer months, to buy stock for the busy fall retail season.[10] In 1896, a description of the firm's display windows read, "Besides the magnificent silver pieces they show, they add fine porcelains, and in one window display unique mugs and tobacco jars in college colors."[11] In 1898, they were noted for their display of ceramics and metalwork by Maria Longworth Nichols Storer, founder of the Rookwood Pottery Co., whose goods they also exhibited and sold.[12] Later in its history, the firm touted an array of contemporary and antique wares ranging from bronze sculptures and Royal Copenhagen porcelain to Lalique glass and Russian icons.[13]

The firm incorporated as The Loring Andrews Co. on June 10, 1903, with a capital stock of $150,000.[14] Willard W. Howe, a member of the Gaff family, became president and Loring Andrews served as vice president. Other stockholders included Edward J. Morris, William Henry Williamson, and Morrison R. Waite.[15] The firm leased new quarters at 117 and 119 East Fourth Street (fig. 4.2), as the building where it had previously resided was to be torn down for the construction of a new skyscraper.[16] It was duly noted that while The Loring Andrews Co. had previously occupied four floors, its new home would yield additional space, "owing to the extreme length of the building."[17]

In December, the firm lost many goods that it had just received from the Custom House when several feet of coping from the neighboring nine-story St. Paul Building (111 East Fourth Street) "fell with a crash through the skylight" of Andrews' store. "The pieces struck a table of imported glass and fancy lamps of rare type, and narrowly missed some shoppers who were in the vicinity."[18]

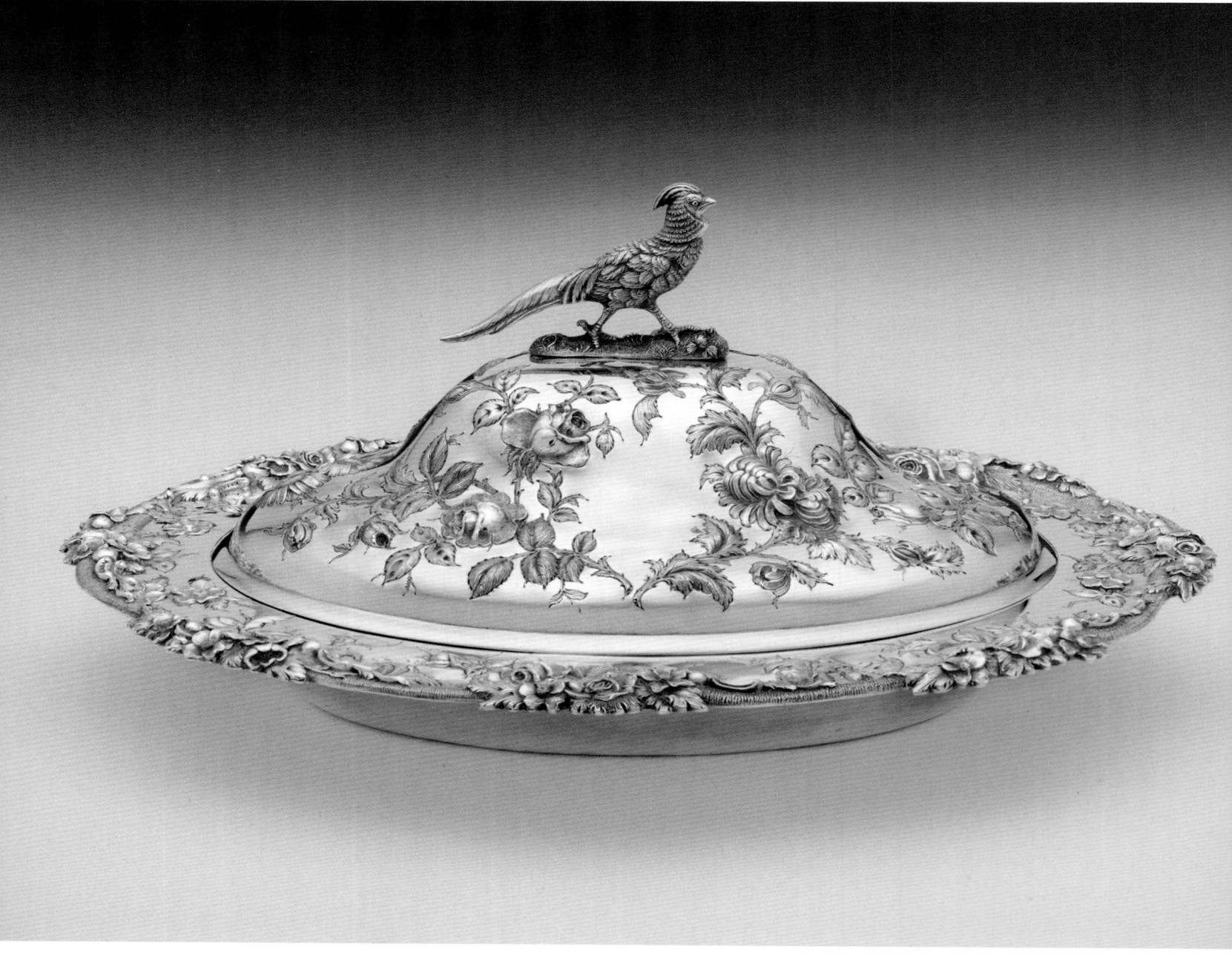

FIG. 4.3: Loring Andrews & Co., retailer, Jacobi & Jenkins, manufacturer, (estab. c. 1894, closed 1903), *Covered Vegetable Dish*, c. 1895–1903, 6½ × 14 × 11⅜ in. (16.5 × 35.6 × 28.9 cm), CAM, From the Collection of Mrs. Frank L. Wright II, 2001.1a–b

The following year, damages to the firm's jewelry factory and a loss of stock totaling approximately $45,000 were sustained due to a fire started in a neighboring building.[19] All losses were covered by insurance, however, and business did not slow. In September 1910 the firm exhibited at the Ohio Valley Exposition in Cincinnati's Music Hall.[20] Their display, "made up of a large collection of rare and costly articles in jewelry and silverware, together with a handsome display of Rookwood pottery, was considered one of the favorite exhibits."[21]

In the spring of 1911, the firm's neighboring tenants, the Rudolph Wurlitzer Company, negotiated the long-term lease of their own premises and those currently leased by The Loring

Andrews Co.[22] Wurlitzer offered the jewelry firm the option to sublet for a five-year term, or vacate by June. Loring Andrews stockholders did not wish to sublet for more than a year, and so decided to dissolve the firm and sell off its stock. Rumor had it that Andrews would go to New York and open shop there. The community was outraged at the potential loss of the store, and "at this critical moment unhoped-for allies appeared in several of the most prominent society women of Cincinnati, who bought large blocks of stock to preserve the firm."[23] The stock, belonging to Willard and Charles Howe, was purchased by Mrs. A. Howard Hinkle, Mrs. Dan Holmes, Mrs. Mary Emery, Mrs. W.P. Anderson, Mrs. Larz Anderson, and Miss Mary Hanna. The ladies negotiated to renew the firm's lease at its East Fourth Street location, and appointed gentlemen to the board of directors to represent them. Loring Andrews became president of the firm, and newly appointed board members included R.C. Anderson (whose efforts were credited with saving the store), A. Clifford Shinkle, George W. Warrington, Charles Livingood, Vachel W. Anderson, Charles P. Taft, and J.M. Hutton. Remaining members of the old board were William H. Williamson, who resumed his position as secretary and treasurer, and H.T. Howe and C.G. Howe of Aurora, Indiana. The capital stock of the firm at this time totaled $120,600.[24] Andrews died on August 24, 1921.[25] A. Clifford Shinkle became president of the firm, and A.F. Chapman was appointed vice president.[26] In 1931, Shinkle resigned and was succeeded by E.W. Edwards.[27]

Throughout its long history, The Loring Andrews Co. served some of the most prominent citizens of Cincinnati. In 1901, Charles P. Taft purchased $53,600 worth of jewelry at the firm, including an 88½ karat diamond necklace, and a strand of 211 pearls.[28] In 1906, Congressman Nicholas Longworth presented his new bride, Alice Roosevelt, with a "handsome diamond necklace" designed and manufactured by The Loring Andrews Co. Its stones "set in most artistic mountings were of perfect match and about three-fourths of a carat each."[29]

Extant silver sold and marked by the firm includes flatware and hollowware manufactured by William B. Durgin Co. (Concord, New Hampshire), A.G. Schultz & Co. (Baltimore), Jacobi & Jenkins (Baltimore), Frank W. Smith Silver Co. (Gardner, Massachusetts), Frank M. Whiting Co. (North Attleboro, Massachusetts), Lebkuecher & Co. (Newark, New Jersey), Dominick & Haff (New York City), Gorham Mfg. Co. (Providence, Rhode Island), R. Wallace & Sons (Wallingford, Connecticut), Goodnow & Jenks (Boston), and George Jensen of Denmark.[30] The firm became an authorized dealer of silver by S. Kirk & Son (Baltimore) sometime after 1915.[31] Most of the manufacturers selling wares at wholesale to Loring Andrews would have added the name of the Loring Andrews firm (stamped, incuse, in uppercase letters) to the pieces before shipping them to Cincinnati. This saved the retailer an extra step, allowing the firm to unpack the wares and put them directly in their display cases, and it helps to explain the profusion of different versions of the Loring Andrews mark. Support for this notion is found in the fact that many of the Kirk-produced wares are stamped with the Loring Andrews name and the misspelled "Cincinatti," and that the mark on the Jacobi & Jenkins covered vegetable dish (fig. 4.3, mark 4.1) has an unnecessary comma.

In November 1954 The Loring Andrews Co. was purchased by Gordon Lang, owner of Spaulding and Co., Chicago jewelers and silversmiths.[32] Two years later, the store relocated to 27 West Fourth Street.[33] By 1959, still under the leadership of Lang, the firm had merged with Ratterman, Inc., another prominent jewelry store, and became Loring Andrews & Ratterman, Inc.[34] In 1965, it merged with **Newstedt's**, successor of the firm **George H. Newstedt**.[35] This merger was likely precipitated by the loss of Newstedt's long-time location at the northwest corner of Fourth and Race Streets to urban renewal. Newstedt-Loring Andrews operated at 27 West Fourth Street until 1992.[36] In 1969, the firm opened a second, suburban location in Hyde Park.[37] In 1989, the Hyde Park store closed and was moved to Kenwood Towne Center where it operated until 1996.[38] The business then returned to Hyde Park Square in 1994, where it continues to operate as a jewelry store on Erie Avenue.[39]

MARK 4.1

1. Later histories suggest that the Loring Andrews firms can trace their beginnings back to 1805, when **Alexander McGrew** purportedly opened shop. An 1805 establishment date for McGrew cannot, to date, be documented. These histories trace Loring Andrews' roots back through **E.E. Isbell** who bought out **William Wilson McGrew**, who succeeded **Wilson McGrew**, who succeeded **Alexander McGrew**. For the purpose of this study, 1895, the date that Loring Andrews & Co. was established by Loring Andrews and the Gaff Estate is used.

2. 1860 Federal Census, Cincinnati, Hamilton, Ohio; Loring Andrews, David B. Andrews, Maria Z. Andrews, burial records, Spring Grove Cemetery, Cincinnati, Ohio.

3. 1848–1861 Cincinnati City Directories; Beckman, 5.

4. 1873–1895 Cincinnati City Directories.

5. "On the Road," *Jewelers' Circular and Horological Review* (July 1888): 44.

6. 1896–1898 Cincinnati City Directories; Beginning in the 1899 City Directory, the Gaff estate and its manager Thomas T. Gaff, as well as Mrs. Rachael S. Gaff and Willard Warren Howe (also a Gaff family member through his mother Vianna Ballou Gaff) are listed as associates of Loring Andrews & Co.; "William Ward Gaff," *Twenty-fifth Anniversary Report of the Secretary of the Class of 1881 of Harvard College*, Boston: Harvard College, 1906, 190.

7. "Cincinnati," *JCHR* (May 9, 1900): 42; "Cincinnati," *JCHR* (July 18, 1900): 34; "Cincinnati," *JCHR* (August 15, 1900): 45; "Cincinnati," *JCHR* (October 3, 1900): 44; "Cincinnati," *JCHR* (October 17, 1900): 55.

8. 1899 Cincinnati City Directory.

9. Loring Andrews & Co. were included in the business directory listings for "clocks, bronzes and Paris fancy articles," "clocks and regulators," "silver ware," and "watches, clocks and jewelry" between 1895 and 1910. In 1896 and 1897 they were also included under the listings for "silver manufacturers"; When the company was incorporated in 1903, it was stated that they would manufacture and deal in jewelry.

"Cincinnati," *JCHR* (June 17, 1903): 60.

10. "Cincinnati," *JCHR* (August 25, 1897): 32; "Cincinnati," *JCHR* (July 13, 1898): 27; "Cincinnati," *JCHR* (July 13, 1898): 30; "Transatlantic Voyagers," *JCHR* (September 6, 1900): 41; "Transatlantic Voyagers," *JCHR* (June 4, 1902): 44; "Cincinnati," *JCHR* (June 4, 1902): 56; "Cincinnati," *JCHR* (May 27, 1903): 62; "Cincinnati," *JCHR* (June 15, 1904): 60; "Transatlantic Voyagers," *JCHR* (May 24, 1905): 68; "Cincinnati," *JCHR* (May 22, 1907): 61; "Cincinnati," *JCHR* (October 7, 1908): 99; "Cincinnati," *JCHR* (November 3, 1909): 97.

11. "Cincinnati," *JCHR* (December 16, 1896): 22.

12. "Cincinnati," *JCHR* (March 30, 1898): 38; "Cincinnati," *JCHR* (December 5, 1900): 49; In 1904, The Loring Andrews Co. displayed the wares that Rookwood was preparing to send the World Fair in St. Louis. "Cincinnati," *JCHR* (April 13, 1904): 63.

13. "The Week in Art Circles," *Cincinnati Enquirer*, September 26, 1937, 4, col. 7.

14. Typewritten history dated 1940, Cincinnati Art Museum, Decorative Arts & Design Department, Loring Andrews & Co. research file; "Cincinnati," *JCHR* (June 17, 1903): 60.

15. Ibid.; William Henry Williamson had managed the office work of E.E. Isbell & Co. since 1893, and continued in that capacity when Andrews took over the business. "William Henry Williamson," *Harvard College, Class of 1875, Secretary's Report, No. VIII (1875–1905)*, Cambridge, MA: Harvard University, 1905, 96.

16. "Cincinnati," *JCHR* (February 11, 1903): 59–60; "Cincinnati," *JCHR* (June 16, 1903): 60; "Real Estate and Building," *Cincinnati Enquirer*, February 6, 1903, 8.

17. Ibid.

18. "Cincinnati," *JCHR* (December 23, 1903): 56.

19. "Fire at Cincinnati Causes Severe Loss to Two Prominent Jewelry Concerns," *JCHR* (November 23, 1904); "Fire Losses of the John Holland Gold Pen Co. and the Loring Andrews Co.," *JCHR* (November 30, 1904): 38.

20. "Jewelry Exhibits at Ohio Valley Exposition at Cincinnati," *JCHR* (September 28, 1910): 75.

21. Ibid.

22. "Real Estate and Building," *Cincinnati Enquirer*, March 15, 1911, 10; "Real Estate and Building," *Cincinnati Enquirer*, March 16, 1911, 11; "Wealthy Women," *Cincinnati Enquirer*, March 19, 1911, 16; "Cincinnati," *JCHR* (March 22, 1911): 95; "Men and Matters," *Cincinnati Enquirer*, March 25, 1911, 5.

23. "Cincinnati," *JCHR* (March 22, 1911): 95.

24. "Cincinnati," *JCHR* (March 25, 1911): 95; "Wealthy Women," March 16, 1911.

25. Unmarried, Loring Andrews lived with his mother until her death, and with his cousin and heir Clifford E. Blagg (1870–1923). He was a member of the Queen City Club, Business Men's Club, and Cincinnati Country Club. "Loring Andrews Dead," *JCHR* (September 6, 1921): 81; Death notice, *Cincinnati Enquirer*, August 26, 1921, 7; Burial records, Spring Grove Cemetery.

26. Typewritten history dated 1940, Cincinnati Art Museum.

27. Ibid.

28. Invoice, facsimile, Cincinnati Art Museum, Decorative Arts & Design Department, Loring Andrews research file.

29. "Cincinnati," *JCHR* (February 28, 1906): 68.

30. Loring Andrews, eBay listings and private collections, Cincinnati silver binders, Cincinnati Art Museum.

31. "In 1911, [Kirk] company directors began discussing the concept of selling their goods at wholesale prices to authorized dealers, but it was not until 1915 that this method of national distribution began." Descriptive Summary: "Samuel Kirk & Son, Inc. Papers, 1834–1979," *Maryland Historical Society*, http://www.mdhs.org/library/Mss/ms002720.html, accessed December 23, 2008; A copy of the 1935 sales catalogue *Sterling silverware by Kirk, America's oldest silversmiths, Samuel Kirk & Son, Inc.: Baltimore, Maryland* imprinted with The Loring Andrews Co. name and address on the cover sold on eBay in May 2012. Printed for the use of

Loring Andrews customers, this catalogue indicates that Andrews was an authorized dealer of Kirk silver. eBay listing, facsimile, Cincinnati Art Museum, Decorative Arts & Design Department, Loring Andrews research file.

32. "A New Setting for An Old Business," *JCHR* (August 1956): 107; "Loring Andrews Traces History Back 155 Years," *Cincinnati Enquirer*, January 30, 1961, 12; 1953–1958 Cincinnati City Directories.

33. "A New Setting for An Old Business," (August 1956); Loring Andrews press release, n.d., Cincinnati Art Museum, Decorative Arts & Design Department, Loring Andrews research file.

34. 1959–1964 Cincinnati City Directories; "Loring Andrews Traces History Back 155 Years," January 30, 1961.

35. 1965 Cincinnati City Directory.

36. "After 191 years, jeweler to close," *Cincinnati Post*, April 12, 1996; 1965–1992 Cincinnati City Directories.

37. "After 191 years, jeweler to close," April 12, 1996. 1969–1989 Cincinnati City Directories; Stan Kittle, current president of Newstedt-Loring Andrews, to Janet Haartz, telephone conversation, July 24, 2013, Cincinnati Art Museum, Loring Andrews & Co. research file.

38. "After 191 years, jeweler to close," April 12, 1996; Stan Kittle to Janet Haartz, July 24, 2013.

39. Ibid.; 2013 Cincinnati City Directory.

5. CHARLES ASMANN

1831–1906, w. 1858–1906

Charles Asmann was born September 29, 1831, in Prussia, where he learned his trade.[1] He emigrated to the United States in 1853 or 1854, and appears in the 1858 Cincinnati City Directory as a watch maker working at 474 Race Street.[2] He does not appear in the city's directories for the following two years, but in 1861 he is listed as a watch maker just across the river in Covington, Kentucky.[3] During this time, Asmann worked for the Kentucky silversmith George W. McDannold (1801–1865), whose business he bought in 1863.[4] Asmann spent the remainder of his career working in Covington. There, he advertised as a "watchmaker and jeweler, dealer in clocks, jewelry, silver and plated ware."[5] His marks have been documented on exaggerated, tipped fiddle handled spoons and ladles which are very similar, if not identical, to forms associated with **E. & D. Kinsey**, suggesting that as a dealer, he acquired most of his silver wares from nearby manufacturers.[6] George W. McDannold appears to have bought stock from the Kinseys as well.[7]

Asmann died on August 10, 1906.[8] He and his wife Emma (nee Albrecht, b. about 1842 in Saxony, m. 1856, d. 1890) had at least eight known children, all born in Kentucky: George (b. about 1858); Henry (b. about 1860); Anna (b. about 1861); Charles (b. about 1863); Amelia (b. about 1865); Laura (b. about 1867); Emma (b. about 1875); and Minnie (b. about 1878).[9] Charles Asmann passed his trade on to his children. Charles Jr., George, and Henry worked as watch makers for a time, and Emma and Minnie worked as gold and gold leaf cutters.[10] Charles' brother, William Asmann (d. 1870) was an engraver at **Duhme & Co.**[11]

1. *Biographical Encyclopedia of Kentucky of the Dead and Living Men of the Nineteenth Century*, Cincinnati: J.M. Armstrong, 1878, 212; 1870, 1880, and 1900 Federal Censuses, Covington, Kenton, Kentucky; Ancestry.com, *Kentucky Death Records, 1852–1953* [online database], Provo, Utah: Ancestry.com Operations Inc., 2007; Marquis Boultinghouse, *Silversmiths, Jewelers, Watch and Clock Makers of Kentucky, 1785–1900*, Lexington, KY: M. Boultinghouse, 1980, 34. All future references to Boultinghouse in this catalogue are to this book.
2. The 1900 Federal Census indicates that Asmann immigrated in 1853, while the *Biographical Encyclopedia of Kentucky* states that he immigrated in 1854; Immigration records could not be located.
3. 1861 Cincinnati City Directory (Covington section); The same year, Charles' brother William Asmann, an engraver, is boarding with Charles.
4. *Biographical Encyclopedia of Kentucky*, 212.
5. 1867 Cincinnati City Directory (Covington section).

6. C. Asmann, eBay listings and private collections, Cincinnati silver binders, Cincinnati Art Museum.
7. A beaker bears the marks of both E. & D. Kinsey and George W. McDannold. *Beaker*, Cincinnati Art Museum, Museum Purchase: John S. Conner Endowment, 2005.24.
8. Ancestry.com, *Kentucky Death Records, 1852–1953* [online database], Provo, Utah: Ancestry.com Operations Inc., 2007.
9. *Biographical Encyclopedia of Kentucky*, 212; Ancestry.com, *Kentucky Death Records, 1852–1953*; 1870, 1880, and 1900 Federal Censuses, Covington, Kenton, Kentucky.
10. Michael R. Averdick, *A Directory of Silversmiths, Jewelers, Watch and Clock Makers and Related Trades of Covington and Newport, Kentucky & Vicinity, 1833–1900*, Covington, KY: 829 Willard Street Press, 2002, 6.
11. William Asmann committed suicide in his brother's store in May 1870. "Suicide," *Cincinnati Enquirer*, May 2, 1870, 7.

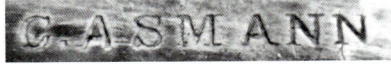

MARK 5.1

C.ASMANN

MARK 5.2

6. CHAUNCEY BUTLER ASPINWALL

1802–1882, w. 1846–1882

Chauncey B. Aspinwall was born April 30, 1802, in Lebanon, New Hampshire, the youngest of ten children born to Hannah Conant (1756–1823) and Zalmon Aspinwall (1741–1824).[1] Details of his training as a jeweler and watch maker are undocumented, but it is likely that he trained with an older brother, either Zalmon or Horatio. Zalmon (1783–1814) was a silversmith and watch maker, and a partner with John Jones (Jones & Aspinwall) in Boston from 1809–1810.[2] Horatio G. (1794–1825) was a jeweler in Lebanon, New Hampshire.[3]

By 1829, Chauncey Aspinwall was working as a jeweler in Oswego, New York where he was a partner with Edward Griffing in the firm of Aspinwall & Griffing from 1831 to 1834.[4] A teaspoon in the collection of the Yale University Art Gallery (fig. 6.1) bears the mark of C.B. Aspinwall & Company of Oswego (mark 6.1) and is dated circa 1830.[5] Aspinwall remained in Oswego through 1844, but had arrived in Cincinnati by 1846 when he first appears in the city directory as a watch maker.[6]

From 1848 until 1855, Aspinwall carried on a retail trade as a jeweler and watch maker near his residence at John and Betts Streets in what was then the northwest area of Cincinnati.[7] In 1853, he entered into a short-lived partnership in a jewelry store on Western Row (now Central Avenue) with Andrew A. Eyster (**Aspinwall & Eyster**) but by 1855, he was again working alone as

a jeweler.[8] Aspinwall apparently abandoned the jewelry and watch-making trades from 1856 to 1864. City directories from those years list his occupation as agent (patent rights, real estate, claim, or pension) and/or collector. Aspinwall was again listed as a watch maker in 1865 and 1866.[9] However, his jewelry firm is listed as a loan office in 1868, indicating that he had not entirely given up this other business pursuit.[10]

In 1867, Aspinwall became the principal of C.B. Aspinwall & Co. and moved to a more prominent address on Fourth Street.[11] Although the firm advertised in the directories' business listings for watches, jewelry, and silverware through 1881, no silver marked by the firm and characteristic of that era has been documented.[12] Chauncey's son, William Henry, an engraver and jeweler, worked at the firm until his death in October 1869.[13] Aspinwall's son-in-law, Alonzo F. Bean, was listed as a partner in the firm in 1873; he was simultaneously the proprietor of A.F. Bean & Co. which sold wooden and willow wares at the same address.[14]

Aspinwall married Sarah Whitely (1805–1864) in Utica, New York.[15] They were the parents of seven children, all of whom were born in New York: John Zalmon (1827–1829), **Edward G.** (1829–1850), Horace Zalmon (1831–1867), **William Henry** (1834–1869), Theodore Hubbard (1836–1837), **Theodore Hubbard** (1839–1864), and Mary Whitely (b. 1844).[16] Three of their sons followed

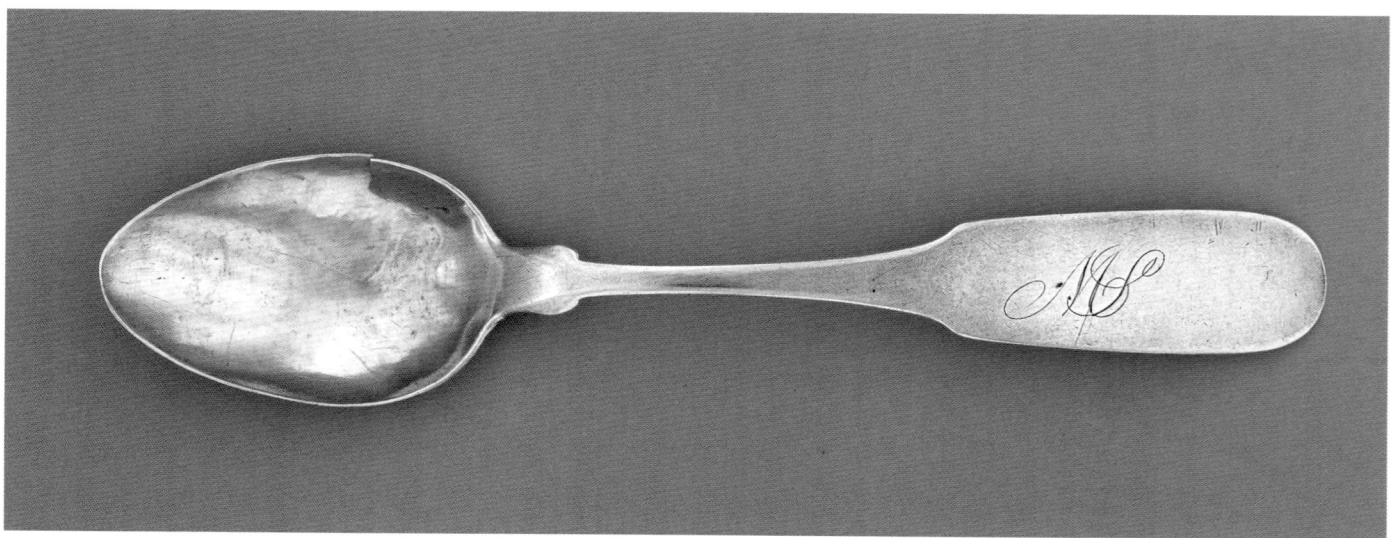

FIG. 6.1: C.B. Aspinwall and Company, *Teaspoon*, c. 1830, L. 5¹³⁄₁₆ in. (14.7 cm), Yale University Art Gallery, Gift of Phillip K. Kossack, 1989.56.3

their father into the jewelry and watch making trades, but, sadly, their careers were cut short by premature death. Edward's occupation was given as watch maker and jeweler when he died of consumption in 1850.[17] William Henry, as noted, worked at C.B. Aspinwall & Co.[18] Theodore was a watch maker and jeweler, working in Cincinnati for **Edward H. Hill** in 1859 and 1860, prior to enlisting for service in the Union Army during the Civil War.[19] He died in action.[20] Chauncey B. Aspinwall continued working well into his 79th year. He died in December 1882 at his daughter's home in Madeira and is buried in Spring Grove Cemetery with his wife Sarah and sons Edward, William, and Horace.[21]

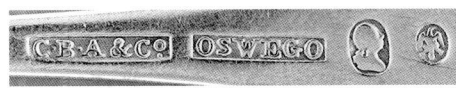

MARK 6.1

1. Algernon Aikin Aspinwall, *Aspinwall Genealogy*, Rutland, VT: The Tuttle Co., 1901, 58, 84, 87.
2. Louise Belden's *Marks of American Silversmiths* (Charlottesville: University Press of Virginia, 1980) is cited as a source in Wm. Erik Voss, *American Silversmiths*, http://freepages.genealogy.rootsweb. ancestry.com/~silversmiths/makers/ silversmiths. Although Voss credits the senior Zalmon (1741–1824) as the silversmith and Jones' partner, it is unlikely that a man of 59 years who had been living and working as a farmer in Lebanon, NH for many years (1783 to at least 1802) would be a silversmith in Boston in 1809. The *Aspinwall Genealogy* (p. 84) records that Zalmon (1783 – 1814) went to Boston "as a young man and engaged in business there" but does not specify his occupation.
3. Aspinwall, *Aspinwall Genealogy*, 86.
4. John C. Churchill (ed.), *Landmarks of Oswego County, New York*, Syracuse, NY: D. Mason, 1895, 320; Advertisement of dissolution dated October 1834, published in *Oswego Palladium*, November 18, 1835, 4; Information from Oswego journals was kindly provided by Edward Elsner, Librarian, Oswego Public Library; Aspinwall & Griffing advertised in 1831 and 1832 per George Barton Cutten, *The Silversmiths, Watchmakers and Jewelers of The State of New York Outside of New York City*, Hamilton, NY: privately printed, 1939, cited in Beckman, 6.
5. The only published documentation found for C.B. Aspinwall & Co. in Oswego was an advertisement in which the firm is given as the Oswego agent for the "Kingston Packet," a shipping firm operating on Lake Erie between Kingston, Ontario, Canada, and Oswego. Advertisement, *Kingston Chronicle Gazette*, June 29, 1833, 1.
6. 1840 Federal Census, West Oswego, Oswego, NY; 1850 Federal Census, Cincinnati, Hamilton, Ohio reports daughter Mary W. was born in New York in 1844; 1846 Cincinnati City Directory, Appendix Containing Corrections and Additions, Subsequent to the Preparation of the Alphabetical List, 407.
7. 1848–1855 Cincinnati City Directories; The occupations listed in federal census records for Aspinwall reflect those found in the directories. In 1850, his occupation is given as "jeweler"; in 1860, as "agent"; in 1870, as "keeps retail jewelry store & watchmaker"; and in 1880, as "jeweler." 1850, 1860, 1870, 1880 Federal Censuses, Cincinnati, Hamilton, Ohio.
8. 1853–1855 Cincinnati City Directories.
9. 1855, 1866 Cincinnati City Directories.
10. 1858 Cincinnati City Directory; In 1859, Aspinwall was one of three trustees for the 11th District Public School in Cincinnati, the only record found of Aspinwall's activities other than his trade and businesses. 1859 Cincinnati City Directory, 313.
11. 1867 Cincinnati City Directory.
12. 1867–1881 Cincinnati City Directories.
13. 1867–1869 Cincinnati City Directories; Aspinwall, *Aspinwall Genealogy*, 86.
14. 1873–1875 Cincinnati City Directories.
15. Aspinwall, *Aspinwall Genealogy*, 87.
16. Ibid.; 1850 Federal Census, Cincinnati, Hamilton, Ohio; Burial records, Spring Grove Cemetery, Cincinnati, Ohio; Burial records, Fifth Ward Cemetery, Oswego, NY. Cemetery records kindly provided by Justin White, Oswego County Records Center, Oswego, NY.
17. Edward G. Aspinwall, burial record, Spring Grove Cemetery.
18. 1868, 1869 Cincinnati City Directories.
19. 1859, 1860 Cincinnati City Directories; 1860 Federal Census, Cincinnati, Hamilton, Ohio; Aspinwall, *Aspinwall Genealogy*, 87.
20. Aspinwall, *Aspinwall Genealogy*, 87.
21. Burial records, Spring Grove Cemetery.

7. JOHN BALLENGER

1850–1902, w. 1878–1879

Ballenger, who was of Irish descent, was born in June 1850.[1] His obituary states that he was a native of Ohio, and was initially connected with the jewelry business of R. Albert before going into business for himself.[2] The first known record of Ballenger in Cincinnati comes by way of a November 1877 newspaper mention that he was visiting the city with his bride.[3] In 1878, he appears in the Cincinnati City Directory as a watch maker boarding at 48 West Ninth Street, and in 1879 he is listed as a watch maker living at 246 Plum Street and later at 252 West Fourth Street.[4] By 1880, he had relocated to Maysville, Kentucky where he spent the remainder of his career and became "one of the best known jewelers in northeast Kentucky."[5] Diamonds, watches, clocks, jewelry, sterling silver, bronzes, art pottery, and novelties are among the goods listed in an 1894 advertisement.[6] In 1897, onyx tables, bric-a-brac, game sets, cut glass, and lamps were added to his list of specialties.[7] Ballenger traveled to Cincinnati often, presumably to buy stock. An 1886 newspaper notation reads, "J. Ballenger, the jeweler, has been at Cincinnati several days on a business trip. His customers and the public can expect something new and nobby [chic or smart] in the jewelry line."[8] His mark has been observed on tipped, exaggerated fiddle handle flatware (fig. 7.1), as well as on examples in **Duhme & Co.**'s "No. 1" (circa 1869) flatware pattern. The similarity between Ballenger's mark and Duhme & Co.'s mark 38.9 adds further support to the notion that Duhme & Co. supplied Ballenger with silver wares.

Ballenger died suddenly of pneumonia at his residence at Second and Woods Streets in Maysville on January 16, 1902.[9] He was survived by his wife, Allie Bascom Ballenger, whom he had married between 1880 and 1900.[10]

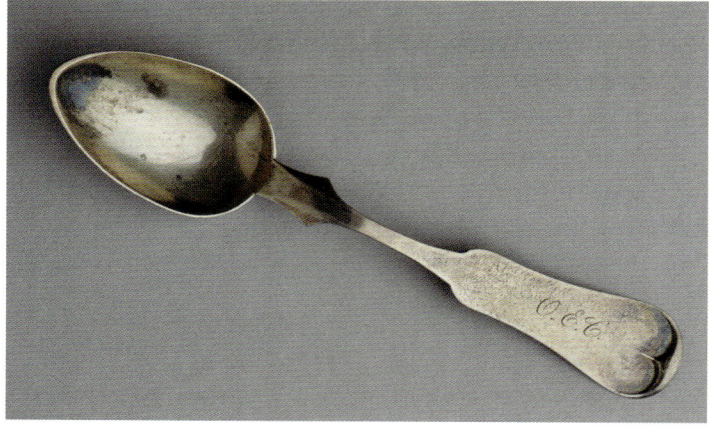

FIG. 7.1: John Ballenger, *Spoon*, c. 1870s, L.5¾ in. (14.6 cm), Courtesy Winterthur Museum, Gift of Vincent H. Beckman in memory of Elizabeth Desloge Beckman, 1984.0005.344.001

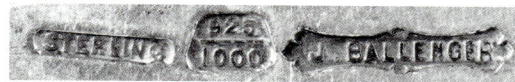

MARK 7.1

1. In the 1880 Census, Ballenger's birth place is recorded as Ireland but in 1900, it is recorded as Ohio. 1880 and 1900 Federal Censuses, Maysville, Mason, Kentucky; He was a member of the Scottish Rite Masons. *Daily Evening Bulletin* (Maysville, KY), February 21, 1889.
2. "Mr. John Ballenger," *Daily Evening Bulletin* (Maysville, KY), January 16, 1902; There is no record for "R. Albert" in Cincinnati and he does not appear in Boultinghouse. Edward & Louis H. Albert, wholesale jewelers in Cincinnati, were not active until the 1890s.
3. "City Personals," *Cincinnati Enquirer*, November 16, 1877, 8.
4. In the 1879 City Directory, he is originally listed at 246 Plum, but then in the "Alterations, Removals, &c." section of the directory, his home address is given as 252 West Fourth.
5. 1880 Federal Census, Maysville, Mason, Kentucky; "Mr. John Ballenger," *Daily Evening Bulletin* (Maysville, KY), January 16, 1902.

6. Advertisement, *Daily Evening Bulletin* (Maysville, KY), September, n.d., 1894.
7. Advertisement, *Daily Public Ledger* (Maysville, KY), September 30, 1897, 1.
8. "Personal," *Daily Evening Bulletin* (Maysville, KY), August 4, 1886. Ballenger's other trips to Cincinnati are documented in *Daily Evening Bulletin* (Maysville, KY), February 21, 1889, and in "Maysville," *Cincinnati Enquirer*, September 13, 1891, 23.
9. "Mr. John Ballenger," *Daily Evening Bulletin* (Maysville, KY), January 16, 1902; "Grim Reaper," *Cincinnati Enquirer*, January 17, 1902, 2.
10. 1880 and 1900 Federal Censuses, Maysville, Mason, Kentucky; Ballenger had been married earlier, as noted in "City Personals," *Cincinnati Enquirer*, November 16, 1877, 8. In the 1880 census, he was boarding with Emily (aged 60) and Allie (aged 31) Pearce. It is possible that the Allie he married was Allie Pearce.

8. JOHN J. BANGS

about 1809–1870, w. 1829

John Bangs was born in Maine around 1809.[1] He is listed in the 1829 Cincinnati City Directory as a silversmith boarding at D. Kautz's. Details of his business in the Queen City are unknown. By 1837, he was advertising in Maumee, a small town in northwestern Ohio, in the watches and jewelry business.[2] Bangs moved on to Chillicothe, arriving there as early as 1839, where he advertised his watchmaking and jewelry partnership with **Edward Pell Pratt** in the *Scioto Gazette*.[3] This partnership dissolved in May 1840, and he opened his own shop in Chillicothe where he was in business until his death in late December 1870.[4] An appraisal of Bangs' estate provides an inventory of his Chillicothe stock, which included jewelry, watches, 47 pieces of silverware, 26 pieces of plated ware, plated spoons, 146 pairs of spectacles, musical instruments, watch and jewelry findings and tools, and lathes.[5] An account of funds owed by the estate includes invoices from L. & W. Herzog Co., "importers of watches, manufacturers and dealers in jewelry" on Nassau Street in New York, and John Thompson & Co. on Broadway in New York which dealt in "jewelry, real and imitation hair and fancy goods."[6] These invoices suggest that much of Bangs' business was in the retail of goods made by others. While items relative to jewelry and watches are specified in the invoices, silver wares are not. However, his mark has been found on a beaker, also marked by Wood & Hughes (New York City), indicating that they were one of his suppliers.[7]

Bangs married Hannah Augusta Williams, born about 1820 in Canada, on May 17, 1846, in Chillicothe. She was a milliner.[8] They had six children: Florence, Harry S., John W., Mary Alice (Alice), Anna V. (Viola), and Park S.[9] At Bangs' death, "1 sett [*sic*] Silver Ware" is enumerated by appraisers as Hannah's property and separate from her husband's estate.[10]

Hollowware and flatware marked by John J. Bangs are known, yet it is uncertain whether any of these pieces were marked during his short tenure in Cincinnati. The aforementioned beaker which also bears the mark of Wood & Hughes, and a ladle with a tipped fiddle handle and rounded shoulders and London hallmarks for 1832 are struck with an incuse "J. J. BANGS." A beaker, a pair of tongs with shell terminals, and a spoon with a tipped fiddle handle and rounded shoulders are known to bear mark 8.1. A watch with John J. Bangs' insignia printed on the enclosed watch paper and dated 1842 has also been documented.[11]

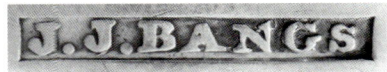

MARK 8.1

1. 1850, 1860, 1870 Federal Censuses, Chillicothe, Ross, Ohio.
2. Advertisement, *Maumee Express*, September 22, 1837, 3; Business Directory, *Maumee Express*, 1837, http://www.heritagepursuit.com /Lucas/LucasTownshipWaynesville -921.html, accessed December 13, 2004.
3. Advertisement, *Scioto Gazette*, May 23, 1839, cited in Beckman, 7; Notice of partnership dissolution, *Scioto Gazette*, May 20, 1840, cited in Beckman, 8.
4. Beckman, 8; 1850, 1860, 1870 Federal Censuses, Chillicothe, Ross, Ohio; Invoice for funeral notice from the *Scioto Gazette*, January 9, 1872, facsimile, Cincinnati Art Museum, Decorative Arts & Design Department, John J. Bangs research file.
5. Appraisal of estate, facsimile, Cincinnati Art Museum, Decorative Arts & Design Department, John J. Bangs research file.
6. Estate settlement papers, facsimile, John J. Bangs research file.
7. John J. Bangs, eBay listings and private collections, Cincinnati silver binders, Cincinnati Art Museum.
8. Article of Agreement, estate settlement papers, facsimile, John J. Bangs research file.
9. 1850, 1860, 1870 Federal Censuses, Chillicothe, Ross, Ohio; Ancestry.com, *Ross County, Ohio Marriage Records* [online database], Provo, Utah: The Generations Network Inc., 2004; Last Will and Testament of John J. Bangs, facsimile, John J. Bangs research file.
10. Order to Appraise Estate, facsimile, John J. Bangs research file. The silverware is qualified in the document as an article that the widow "brought with her at the time of marriage, or came to her by bequest, or was purchased with her money afterwards."
11. John J. Bangs, eBay listings and private collections, Cincinnati Art Museum.

9. BEGGS & SMITH

1848–1862

In 1848, **Joseph P. Beggs** and **Harry R. Smith** joined assets, $4,000 and $3,000 respectively, to establish the firm of Beggs & Smith at 14 West Fourth Street.[1] In city directories, the firm was listed under the business category of "jewelry, silverware, &c."[2] An elaborate advertisement from 1853 (fig. 9.1) indicates that they dealt in watches, diamonds, jewelry and kept "a general assortment of fine silver, Forks, Spoons, Cups, Pitchers, Tea Sets etc." in stock as well. In 1857, they were "thought to do the heaviest business in their line," but most, if not all of their silver was acquired from eastern manufacturers.[3] Extant silver bearing manufacturer marks in addition to the retail marks of Beggs & Smith provide information on the firm's suppliers, who included Grosjean & Woodward (New York City), John R. Wendt (New York City), and James Dixon & Sons (London).[4]

By August 1859 Smith had purchased Beggs' interest in the firm, and **Charles Boerner** and **Jackson Slane**, longtime employees of the house, became partners. They continued to operate as Beggs & Smith.[5] A December advertisement announced, "having refitted their store, [they] have filled it with the most extensive assortment of FINE GOLD & SILVER WATCHES, SILVER WARE, FINE JEWELRY, AND FANCY GOODS, Ever brought to the Western country. These goods are NEW, selected by one of their firm, just returned from New York—many articles of direct importation from Europe."[6] Business was slow, however, and the firm was soon unable to pay its creditors.[7] By March 31, 1862, Jackson Slane withdrew his interest in the firm. Beggs & Smith dissolved, and the remaining partners continued in business as **Smith & Boerner**.[8]

An elaborate tea and coffee service (fig.9.2) bears the Beggs & Smith mark alongside an unidentified group of pseudo hallmarks (mark 9.1).[9] This service was commissioned for and presented to the English-born Fenton Lawson (1808–1853), who made Cincinnati his lifelong home. Lawson was instrumental in forming Cincinnati's Independent Fire Engine and Hose Company (est. 1830), arranging for the purchase of two engines and a hose reel from Philadelphia.[10] These firefighting implements, nicknamed the "Pilot," "Rover," and "Water Witch" respectively, are portrayed in the elaborate, chased firefighting scenes that decorate the bodies of each piece in the service. Lawson served as head of the fire company for over a decade. Upon his retirement in 1850, he received this remarkable tea and coffee service at a public meeting at Melodeon Hall on Walnut Street.[11] The coffee pot bears the inscription, "To Fenton Lawson from the Cincinnati Independent Fire Engine and Hose Company, Pilots, Rovers and Witches, September, 1850." The specific details portrayed in the service's decoration suggest that it was embellished in Cincinnati, perhaps by an engraver at Beggs & Smith.

Beggs & Smith's marks have been documented on various forms of flatware, including examples with die-pressed designs, and those with tipped, exaggerated fiddle handles. They have also been seen on tongs with claw terminals, beakers, mugs (fig. 9.3), tea and coffee services, and water pitchers.[12] In some cases, these

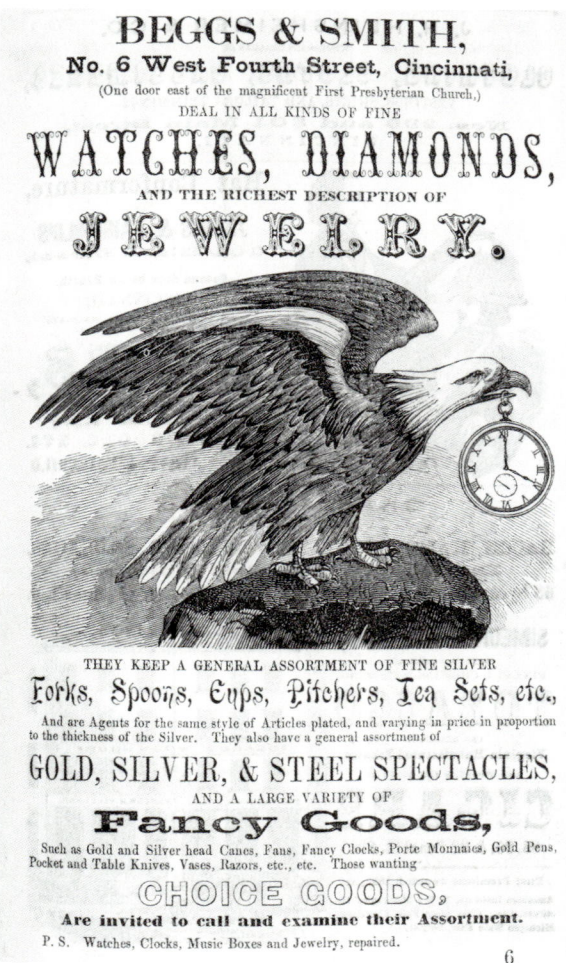

FIG. 9.1: Advertisement, *W.W. Reilly & Co.'s Ohio State Business Directory 1853–4*, Cincinnati: Morgan & Overend, 1853, 81

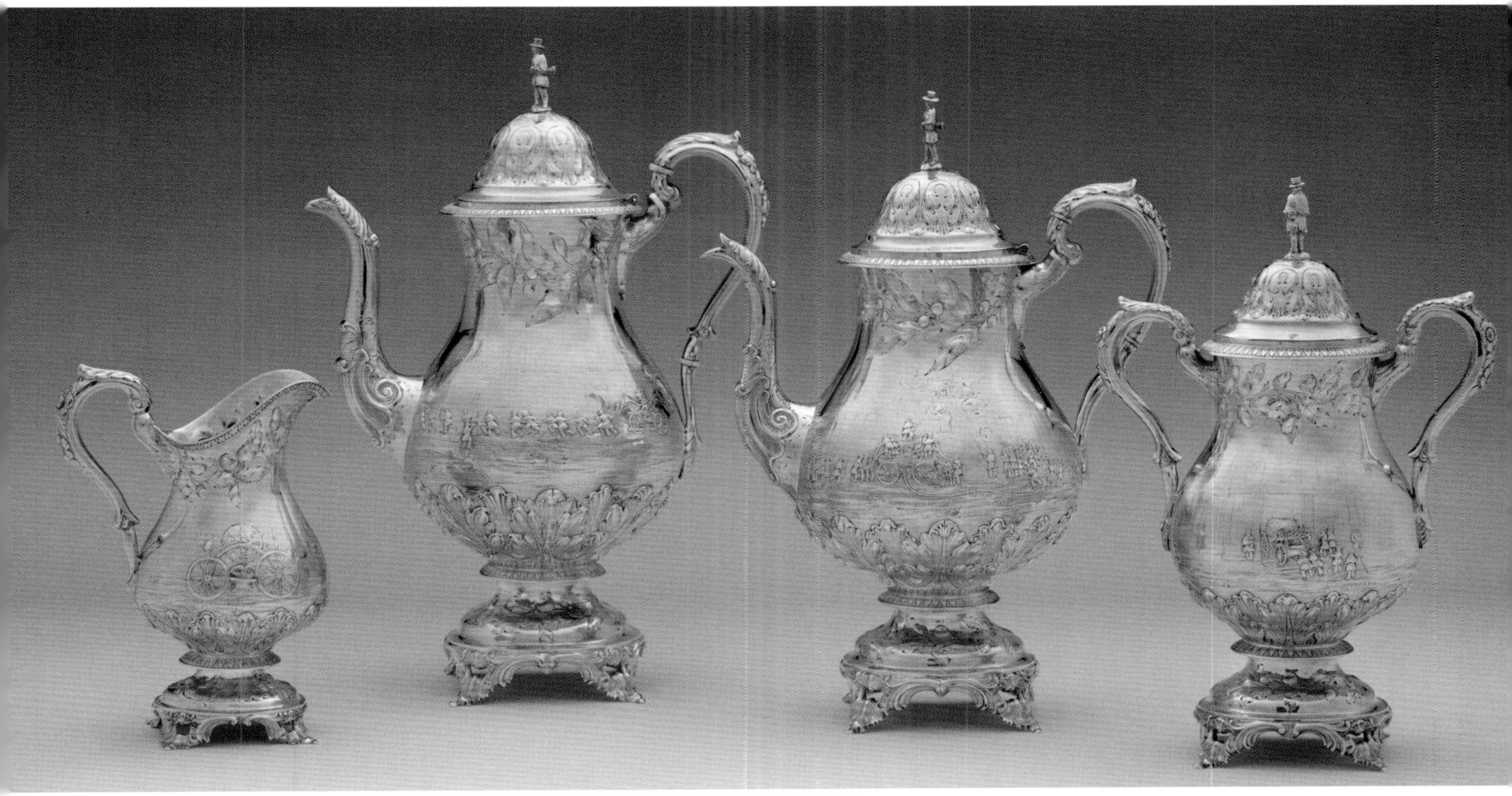

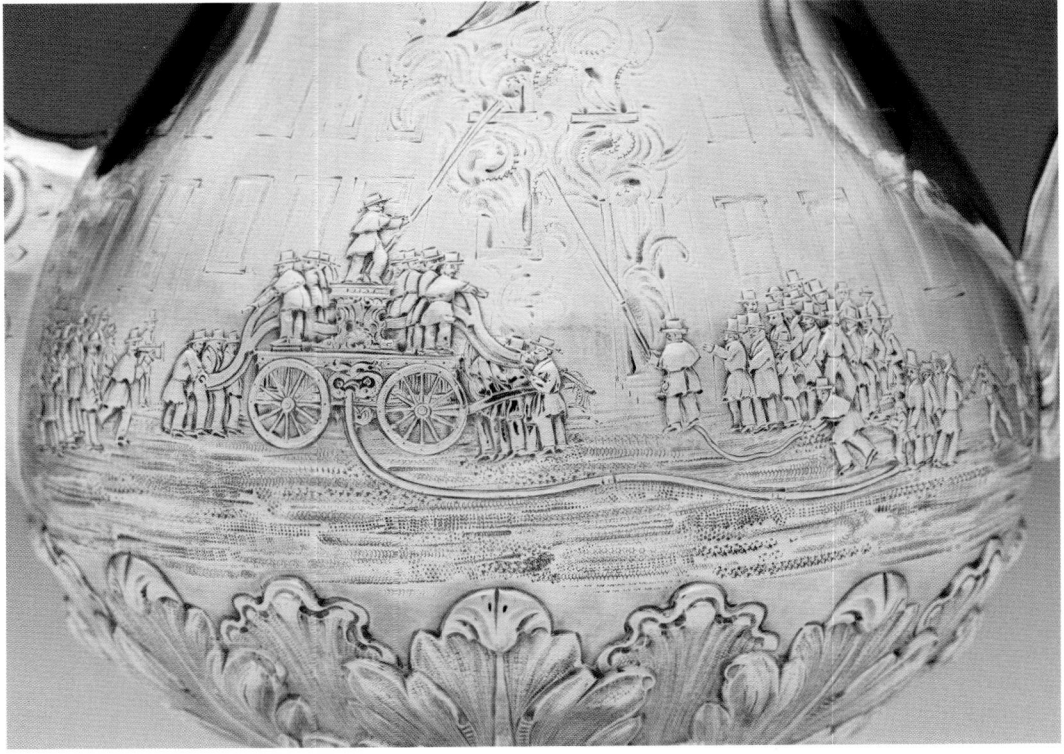

FIG. 9.2: Beggs & Smith,
Tea & Coffee Service, c. 1850,
coffee pot: 16 × 11 in. (40.6 × 27.9 cm),
teapot: 15 × 10½ in. (38.1 × 26.7 cm),
sugar: 7¾ × 6¼ in. (19.7 × 15.9 cm),
creamer: 7¾ × 6½ in. (19.7 × 16.5 cm),
CAM, Gift of Corinne Lawson
Pennington Coler in honor of her great,
great, great grandfather, Fenton Lawson
(1808–1853), 2006.109a–e

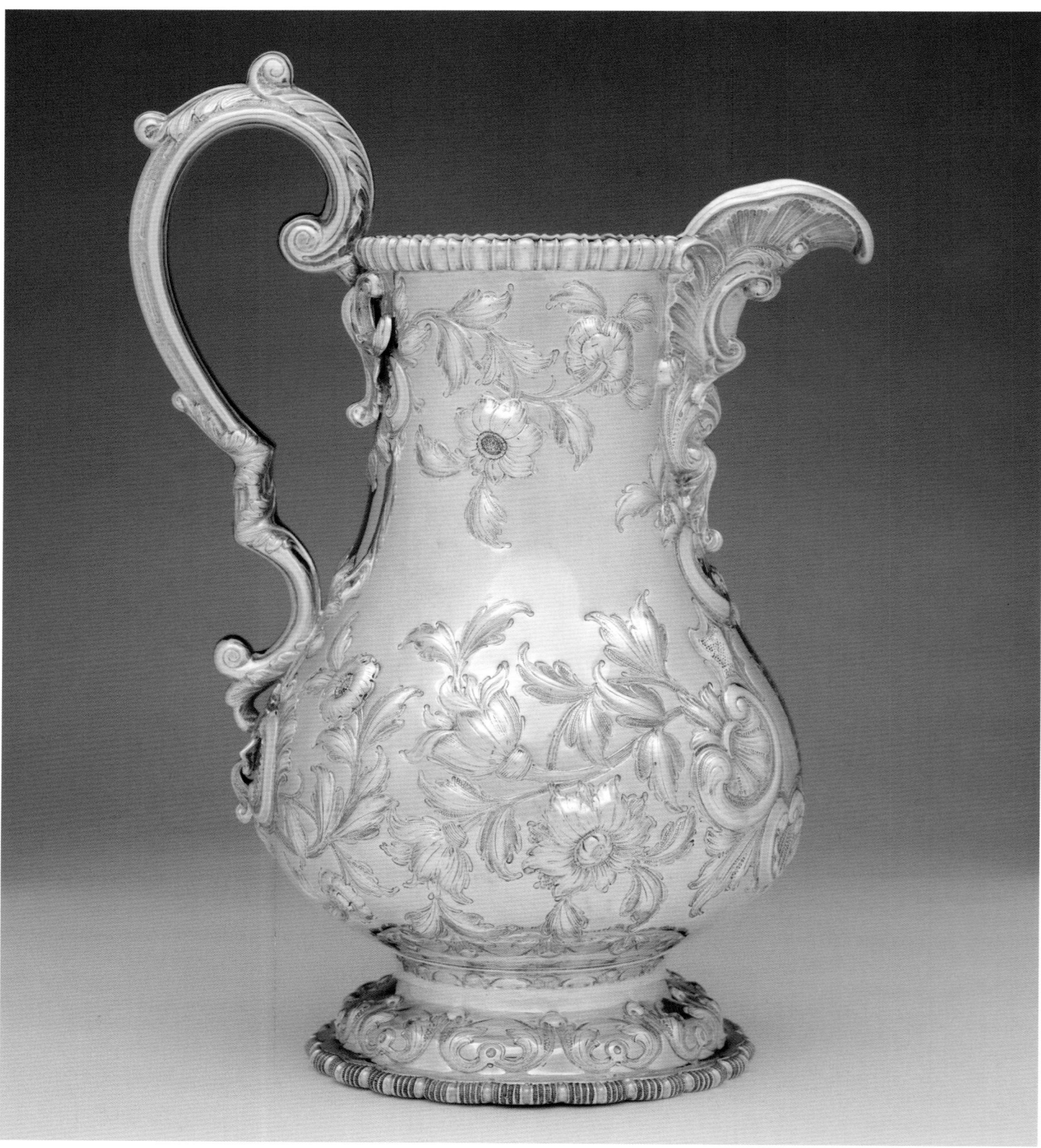

FIG. 9.4: Beggs & Smith, retailer, and Grosjean & Woodward, manufacturer, *Pitcher*, c. 1859, H. 11¾ in. (29.8 cm), CAM, Gift of Ellen G. Rionda, 1959.88. Inscription: "To Saml. N. Pike, Esq. in token of the Respect Esteem and Affection of Jos. Tilney, Wm. M. Fleiss, Geo. Simmonds, George Kidd, Cin, December 25th, 1859."

marks appear alone, and in other cases they are accompanied by the manufactory mark of other firms, as in the case of the pitcher in fig. 9.4, which bears mark 9.2. An incuse "B & S" mark, stamped on four die-pressed spoons, has been attributed to the firm. Spoons of the same pattern (Whiting Mfg. Co.'s "Le Cordon" pattern [1850]) that bear the mark of Smith & Boerner give merit to this attribution.[13]

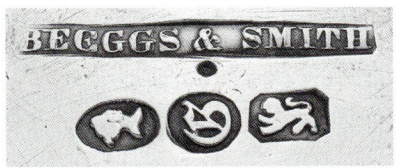

MARK 9.1

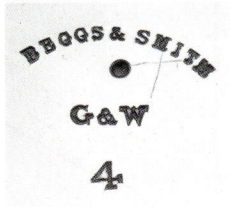

MARK 9.2

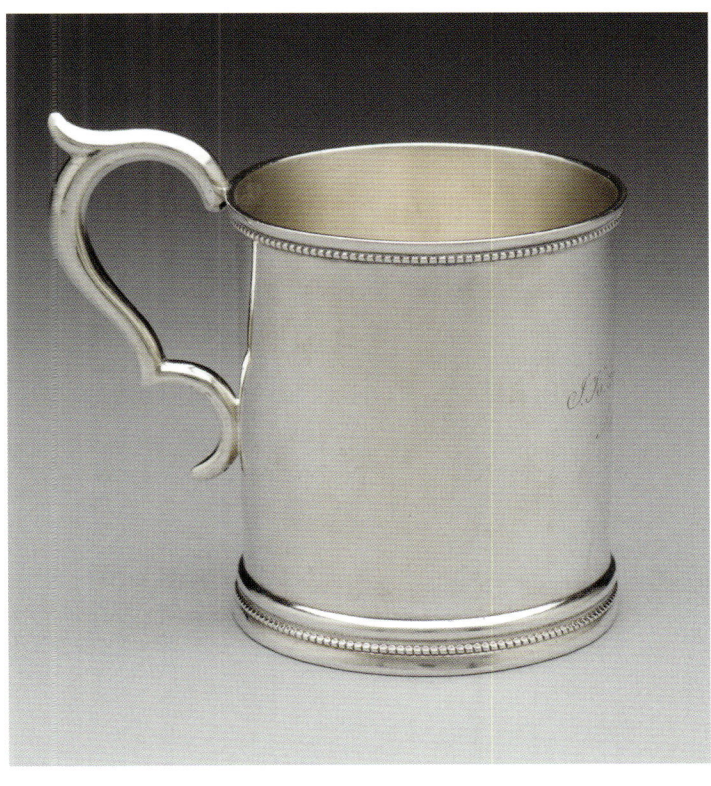

FIG. 9.3: Beggs & Smith, *Mug*, c. 1855, 3½ × 3⅞ in. (8.9 × 9.8 cm), CAM, Gift of James Randolph Hillard, M.D. and Aingeal Grehan, 2007.184. Inscription: "J.K. Smith Butler March 16, 1855." Marked: BEGGS & SMITH in rectangular cartouche, struck over a "D"

1. Ohio, Vol. 1, p. 96, R.G. Dun & Co. Collection, Baker Library, Harvard Business School; After 1853, the firm was located at 6 West Fourth Street, "one door east of the 1st Presbyterian Church." The change in street number may not indicate a change of location. In 1853, street addresses were standardized for the first time. Prior to that, there were no official street numbers, and people often designated their own numbers. Prices current files, Cincinnati Historical Society, box 1, folder 23; 1853–1861 Cincinnati City Directories.
2. 1849/50–1860 Cincinnati City Directories.
3. Ohio, Vol. 3, p. 12, R.G. Dun & Co. Collection.
4. Beggs & Smith, eBay listings and private collections, Cincinnati silver

binders, Cincinnati Art Museum; *Pitcher*, Grosjean & Woodward, manufacturer, Beggs & Smith, retailer, Cincinnati Art Museum, 1959.88; *Tray*, James Dixon & Sons, manufacturer, Beggs & Smith, retailer, Cincinnati Art Museum, 2006.110; Beggs & Smith is recorded in the order ledgers of James Dixon & Sons, "Letters from America: James Dixon & Sons and the American Market, 1853–1863," *Silver Studies* (2006): 112.
5. Ohio, Vol. 3, p. 12, R.G. Dun & Co. Collection.
6. Advertisement, *Cincinnati Enquirer*, December 20, 1859, 2.
7. Ohio, Vol. 3, p. 12, R.G. Dun & Co. Collection.
8. Ibid.
9. Although the unidentified set of hallmarks has been attributed by Dr.

John R. McGrew and Hollis French to Francis W. Cooper, silversmith, 102 Reade Street, New York City, active circa 1840–51, this attribution is probably erroneous. In a telephone conversation with Dr. McGrew (November 8, 2006), he explained that he had based his attribution on an attribution made previously by Hollis French, who is now deceased. Dr. McGrew suspected that French read the middle character as a "C" rather than a "G." The set of hallmarks in question has also appeared on pieces marked by Palmer & Newcomb (active circa 1850, location unknown) and Seymour Hoyt (active circa 1817–1850, New York City). John R. McGrew, *Manufacturers' Marks on American Coin Silver*, Hanover, PA: Argyros Publications, 2004.

10. Charles Greve, *Centennial History of Cincinnati and Its Representative Citizens*, Chicago: Biographical Publishing Co., 1904, 1:516.
11. Rev. Charles Frederic Goss, *Cincinnati: The Queen City, 1788–1912*, Cincinnati: The S.J. Clarke Publishing Co., 1912, 4:161–2.
12. Beggs & Smith, eBay listings and private collections, Cincinnati Art Museum; *Tongs*, Elizabeth Beckman Collection, Cincinnati Museum Center.
13. Beggs & Smith, eBay listings and private collections, Cincinnati Art Museum.

10. J.P. BEGGS & CO.

1842–1843

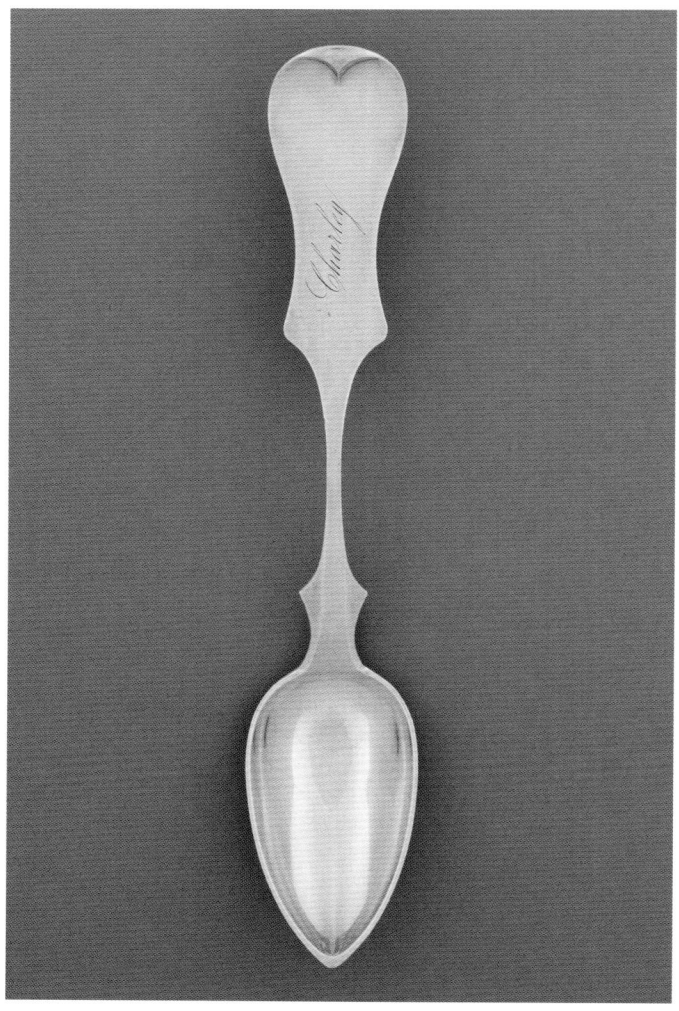

FIG. 10.1: J.P. Beggs & Co., *Tablespoon*, 1842–1843, L. 7¼ in. (18.4 cm), CAM, Bequest of Fanny Bryce Lehmer, 1936.788

In May 1841 **Wilson McGrew** announced that he was "leaving his books and accounts with Joseph P. Beggs" who had worked with him as a watch maker since 1839.[1] Beggs continued business at McGrew's stand on Main Street, between Third and Fourth Streets, as J.P. Beggs & Co.[2] Beggs' partners were never named, but it is possible that McGrew kept a hand in his old business and represented the "& Co.," as by April of 1843, McGrew had returned to Cincinnati and the firm of **McGrew & Beggs** was formed.[3]

Joseph P. Beggs was born in Pennsylvania around 1808, and "learned his trade as a jeweler at a time when the first duties of an apprentice was to beat spoons out of silver coin."[4] He was working in Pittsburgh, in 1829, as part of Wallace & Beggs, clock makers and watch makers.[5] By 1836, he had arrived in Cincinnati, where he is listed in the city directory as a watch maker. In 1850 his occupation was given as silversmith, yet in the 1860 Federal Census he is described as a merchant, in the 1870 Federal Census as "sells jewelery," and in city directories between 1868 and 1871 as a clerk.

There are no known advertisements or accounts that describe the stock or business focus of the short-lived J.P. Beggs & Co. firm. Extant wares bearing mark 10.1 include spoons with fiddle handles and pointed shoulders; spoons with tipped, exaggerated fiddle handles and pointed shoulders (fig. 10.1); a salt spoon with scalloped bowl and tipped, exaggerated fiddle handle; and a creamer and sugar (fig.10.2).[6] It is unclear whether Beggs manufactured any of his wares. A spoon in a private collection bears an unidentified Midwestern manufacturer's mark in the shape of an eagle's head (upside-down in the included image, mark 10.2), indicating that at least some of the wares bearing the firm's stamp were only retailed by the firm.[7]

Following Beggs' involvement in McGrew & Beggs (1843–1848), and **Beggs & Smith** (1848–1859), he was listed in Cincinnati city directories only five times between 1860 and 1871. In each of those years, he was included only in the alphabetical listings, and not in the business sections as he had been from 1842 through 1859. Information about his occupation is not included in the listings until 1868, when he is enumerated as a clerk at the address corresponding to the shop of **William Wilson McGrew**—the son and heir of Wilson McGrew, Beggs' former partner. From 1869 to 1871, Beggs lived in Covington, Kentucky, and was employed as a clerk at 6 West Fourth Street, the address of the firm owned by his partner in the 1850s, Harry R. Smith (**Harry R. Smith & Co.**).

Joseph P. Beggs and his wife Mary (b. about 1825, Pennsylvania) had at least four children, all born in Ohio: Carter C. (b. about 1848); Henry (or Harry) C. (b. 1851); Sarah (or Sallie) C. (b. about 1855); and Joseph P. (b. about 1862).[8] By 1873, Beggs had returned to Pittsburgh, were he lived with his son Carter C. Beggs, an oil broker.[9] By 1880, J.P. Beggs and his wife and their two youngest children were living in Oil City, a small town in northwestern Pennsylvania where the first commercial oil well in the United States was established. Beggs' occupation was given as "oil producer" in the 1880 Census, and his son Carter C. was recorded in Pittsburgh working as an "oil dealer." Beggs died in Pittsburgh on December 9, 1884, and is buried there at the Homewood Cemetery.[10]

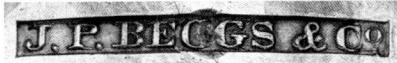

MARK 10.1

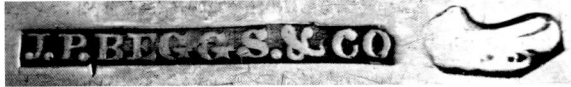

MARK 10.2

1. "Last Notice," *Cincinnati Daily Gazette*, May 20, 1841, reproduced in Beckman, 94; 1839/40 Cincinnati City Directory; Both McGrew and Beggs were born in Pennsylvania, and likely knew each other before arriving in Cincinnati. The reason for McGrew's departure is unknown.
2. 1842, 1843 Cincinnati City Directories.
3. Ohio, Vol. 1, p. 71, R.G. Dun & Co. Collection, Baker Library, Harvard Business School; Advertisement, *Cincinnati Daily Gazette*, September 10, 1843, reproduced in Beckman, 8; While J.P. Beggs & Co. is listed in the 1844 City Directory, it is probable that this information was collected in 1843, just prior to the formation of McGrew & Beggs.
4. Information gleaned from the federal census listings vary. In 1850, his birth year is given as about 1808, in 1860, as about 1817, in 1870, and 1880, as about 1806. 1850 Federal Census, Cincinnati, Hamilton, Ohio; 1860 Federal Census, Yonkers, Westchester, New York; 1870 Federal Census, Covington, Kenton, Kentucky; 1880 Federal Census, Oil City, Venango, Pennsylvania; "Death of an Old Cincinnatian," *Cincinnati Enquirer*, December 11, 1884, 4.
5. Beckman cites an advertisement that ran in the *Pittsburgh Gazette*, December 28, 1829. Beckman, 8; A spoon struck by Wallace & Beggs is in the collection of the University of Kansas' Spencer Museum of Art, 1928.3624.
6. J.P. Beggs & Co., eBay listings and private collections, Cincinnati silver binders, Cincinnati Art Museum.
7. Ibid.; John R. McGrew, *Manufacturers' Marks on American Coin Silver*, Hanover, PA: Argyros Publications, 2004, 111.
8. 1850 Federal Census, Cincinnati, Hamilton, Ohio; 1860 Federal Census, Yonkers, Westchester, New York; 1870 Federal Census, Covington, Kenton, Kentucky; 1880 Federal Census, Oil City, Venango, Pennsylvania.
9. 1873–1884 Pittsburgh City Directories.
10. "Death of an Old Cincinnatian," December 11, 1884.

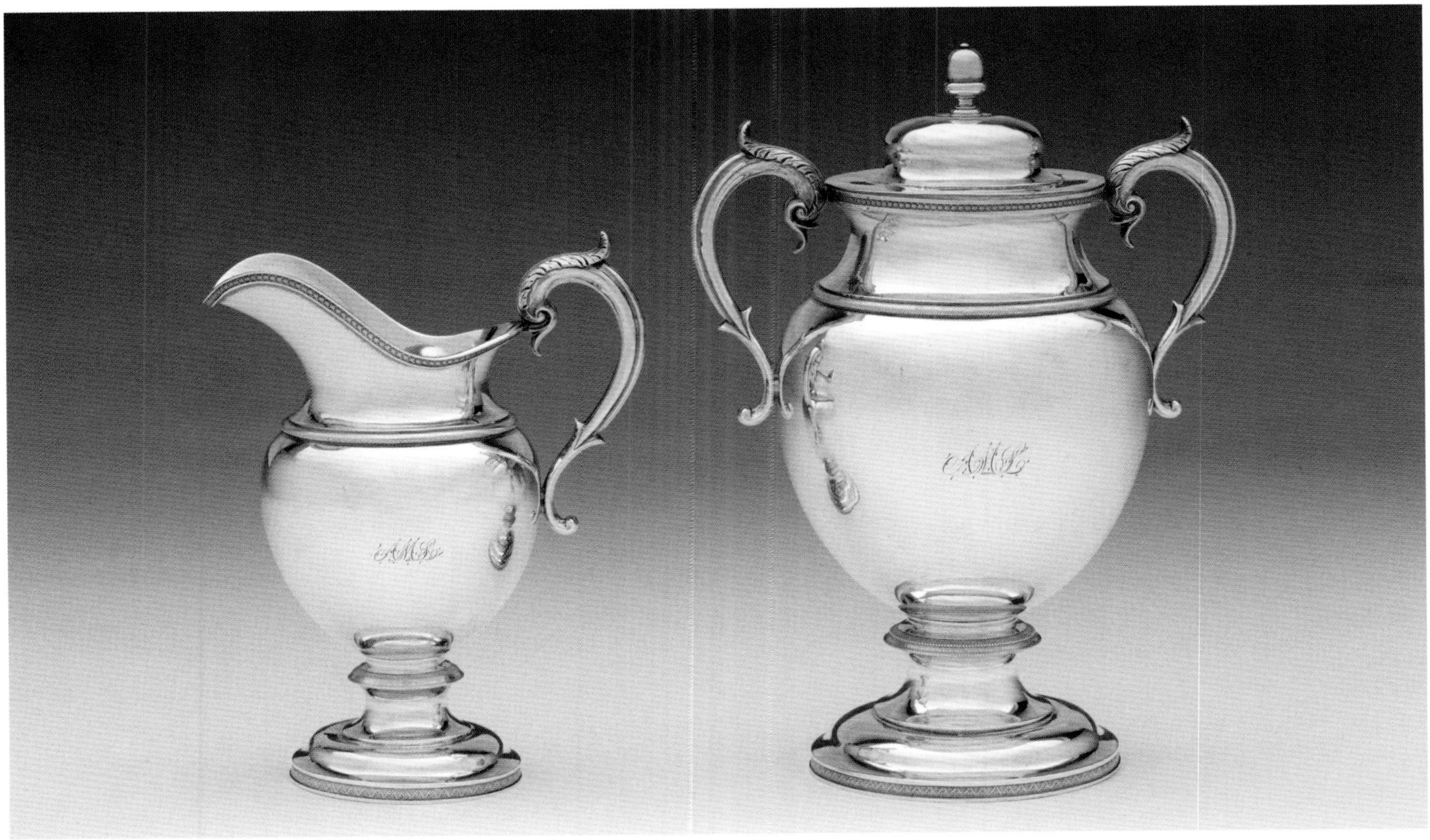

FIG. 10.2: J.P. Beggs & Co., *Creamer and Sugar*, 1842–1843, creamer: 7⅝ × 5⅞ × 3⁹⁄₁₆ in. (19.4 × 14.9 × 9cm), sugar: 10½ × 7½ × 5 in. (26.7 × 19.1 × 12.7 cm), CAM, Gift of Mr. and Mrs. Charles Fleischmann III, 2005.19–20a–b

11. O.E. BELL & CO.

1891–1895

THE O.E. BELL CO.

1895–1900

Orpheus Edmund Bell was born in June 1862 to Sarah Melinda Pettijohn (1837–1921) and Joseph E. Bell (1829–1869), a farmer in Brown County, Ohio.[1] After his father's death, O.E. Bell's mother married Methodist minister G.E. McLaughlin, and the family moved to Clinton County, Ohio.[2] Bell first appears in Cincinnati city directories in 1888 as a dealer in stoves, but by 1890 he had changed profession and was manager at the Elgin Jewelry Company, located in the Carlisle Building at 51 West Fourth Street.[3] The following year, he worked briefly as a traveling salesman for the firm of **Oskamp, Nolting & Co.** before launching O.E. Bell & Co. on Fourth St.[4]

O.E. Bell & Co. (later known as The O.E. Bell Co.) was both a wholesale and manufacturing firm. They bought jewelry, clocks, and watch movements and cases directly from manufacturers to sell to retailers. In addition, they manufactured watch cases through their subsidiary The Bell Watch Case Co. (est. 1895), and sterling and silver-plated novelty wares through their subsidiary The Cincinnati Silver Co. (est. 1895). Their goods were marketed through catalogues and circulars, and through their extensive network of traveling salesmen, believed to be "a larger traveling source than any similar concern in the west."[5] In addition to trade in the northeastern, southwestern, and central states, by 1896, they were trading in Mexico and Australia.[6]

On July 1, 1895, the firm was incorporated as a stock company, and its name was changed to The O.E. Bell Co. Orpheus E. Bell, William Addis Corre, James Ernst, and Albert G. Corre were its incorporators. At this time, it was noted that the firm would increase its stock and its territory, and it was reported that "the rooms they now occupy are being remodeled and refurnished in modern style."[7] The firm's capital stock was reported at $30,000, to be sold in $100 shares.[8]

Prior to 1895, the silver and silver-plated novelty wares sold by the firm were almost certainly made by other manufacturers.[9] It was not until June 1895 that The O.E. Bell Co. began to promote their own line of manufactured silver and plated wares: "The O.E. Bell Co. have received their first output of silver tea sets, butter dishes and trays. They are in several designs and satin finished and are attractive and low in price."[10] In July 1895 it was reported that

the company was "getting their silver factory into shape to supply the trade with Fall goods."[11] Later that summer, circulars were printed to advertise these wares, and salesmen carried "new samples of silver plated ware made by this house."[12] In an interview in August, O.E. Bell said, "In silverware [we] are creating a market for the best grades [ie. sterling], and the trade seem to agree that in plated ware the best is the cheapest."[13]

Of the silverwork produced by the company, two items received particular attention in the leading trade journal. In July 1897 it was noted that the firm had completed "a very handsome silver bowling prize for the Covington Club," which stood nineteen inches high.[14] And, in 1898, they were commissioned to make a souvenir spoon celebrating the 32nd encampment of the Grand Army of the Republic held in Cincinnati that fall. Made in all grades (sterling and plated), the bowl of the spoon featured the Garfield monument with the number of the encampment, and the GAR monogram appeared in a shield at the top of the bowl. A view of the city's suspension bridge adorned the top of the handle, the word "Cincinnati" ran the length of the handle, and the back of the handle boasted a furled American flag.[15]

Recently documented sterling silver wares bearing the bell-shaped mark associated with the firm include an egg cup and a powder jar.[16] The company's mark echoed the shape of the sign erected outside its building in February 1894: "a five foot bell, gold-leafed and lettered in black."[17] A bell was also carved into the stone arch above the entry to O.E. Bell's grand house in Norwood, Ohio.[18]

In the summer of 1896, the firm secured a four-story building at 412 Vine Street, and moved their factory and stock there. The first floor served as the office, the second as the shipping department, the third floor was dedicated to the manufacture of leather novelties (belts and such with silver mounts) and repairs, and the fourth for the manufacture of silver novelties, "which the company began last year with good success."[19] It was also noted that they had engaged "a well known man who was at the head of a one time big jewelry concern in Cincinnati" to take charge of the factory, "which will engage in the manufacture of jewelry, do all kinds of repair work and do ordered work."[20] The firm continued to be very successful. In December, the firm had "increased their capital to $50,000, an increase of $20,000 over the original corporate stock."[21]

The Bell subsidiary, The Cincinnati Silver Co., does not appear in city directories after 1898. In 1897, both it and **The Carlisle-Osborne Silver Co.** moved from locations in the Carlisle Building to 412 Vine Street. It is likely that The Carlisle-Osborne Silver Co. enveloped The Cincinnati Silver Co. and became yet another Bell subsidiary.[22] In February 1900 it was reported that Bell had completed a deal for the incorporation of the Bell Watch Case Co. "under the laws of New Jersey" with a capital stock of $250,000, and that the new company would succeed the Ohio company of the same name and assume the business of The O.E. Bell Co. The headquarters and factory of the company were moved to Mansfield, Ohio.[23] By 1902, the watch case manufactory had been purchased by the North American Watch Company, and by 1910, Orpheus Bell had relocated to Philadelphia, where he was involved in the manufacturing and selling of automobiles.[24] By 1930, he was living in Washington, DC.[25] He died there on June 8, 1951, and is interred at the Fort Lincoln Cemetery in Brentwood, Maryland.[26]

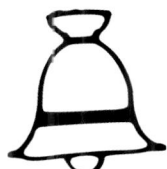

MARK 11.1

1. 1860 Federal Census, Washington, Brown, Ohio; 1880 Federal Census, Clarke, Clinton, Ohio; Livengood Family Tree, Ancestry.com, http://trees.ancestry.com/tree/7132283/person/-354342524, accessed October 31, 2012.

2. 1880 Federal Census, Clarke, Clinton, Ohio.

3. 1888–1890 Cincinnati City Directories; The Elgin Jewelry Company was listed in Cincinnati city directories for one year only (1890), in the business section, under the category of importers, manufacturers and wholesale dealers in watches, jewelry, &c. Bell may have been in Cincinnati earlier than 1888. He lived in Norwood, a suburb of Cincinnati that was not included in Cincinnati city directories at that time. He was probably included in the 1890 Cincinnati City Directory, despite his residential address, because he was an upper-level employee of a Cincinnati firm.

4. 1891 Cincinnati City Directory; In the 1891 Directory, Bell is listed as an affiliate of Oskamp, Nolting & Co. in the alphabetical listings. His firm, O.E. Bell & Co., is not included in the alphabetical listings, but appears in the business listings and in the section for alterations, omissions, removals, etc. This suggests that Bell was a salesmen when the data for the alphabetical listings were collected, but had organized the firm by the time the data for the business listings and alterations were collected. This anomaly has been observed in other cases. In the 1891 City Directory, the address of Bell's firm is given as 59 West Fourth Street. This may be a misprint, as the 1892–1896 directories give the firm's address as 51 West Fourth Street, the Carlisle Building.

5. "Cincinnati," *Jewelers' Circular and Horological Review* (October 16, 1895): 35; In various mentions throughout the *JCHR*, it is noted that salesmen for O.E. Bell & Co. were covering Texas, Oklahoma, Indiana, Missouri, Kansas, and Illinois. For a complete record of mentions for O.E. Bell & Co. and its subsidiaries in the *JCHR*, see O.E. Bell & Co. research file, Decorative Arts & Design Department, Cincinnati Art Museum.

6. "Cincinnati," *JCHR* (October 28, 1896): 22; "Cincinnati," *JCHR* (August 25, 1897): 32.

7. "Cincinnati," *JCHR* (May 29, 1895): 24; "Cincinnati," *JCHR* (June 12, 1895): 26.

8. "Cincinnati," *JCHR* (June 12, 1895): 26.

9. Advertisement, *JCHR* (July 18, 1894): 23; Advertisement, *JCHR* (November 28, 1894): 51; "Cincinnati," *JCHR* (November 28, 1894): 55.

10. "Cincinnati," *JCHR* (June 12, 1895): 26.

11. "Cincinnati," *JCHR* (July 10, 1895): 24.

12. "Trade Gossip," *JCHR* (August 21, 1895): 21, 30; "Trade Gossip," *JCHR* (October 23, 1895): 29; Advertisement, *JCHR* (November 20, 1895): 35.

13. "All Cincinnati Jobbers Expect a Prosperous Fall," *JCHR* (August 21, 1895): 11.

14. "Cincinnati," *JCHR* (July 14, 1897): 24.

15. "Cincinnati," *JCHR* (June 1, 1898): 31; "Cincinnati," *JCHR* (July 13, 1898): 30.

16. Many firms used marks that incorporated a bell. The mark that we attribute to The O.E. Bell Co. is the one identified in Dorothy T. Rainwater & Martin and Collette Fuller, *Encyclopedia of American Silver Marks*, Atglen, PA: Schiffer, 2004, 27; Plated wares produced by The Cincinnati Silver Co. are marked with a circular stamp with "CINCINNATI SILVER CO. CINTI. O." in the outer ring of the stamp, and an image of a bell and "QUADRUPLE SILVER" in the center. See Rainwater, *Silver Marks*, 45. Rainwater gives the date of The Cincinnati Silver Co. as 1892–circa 1900, but the firm was established in 1895 and does not appear in city directories until 1896; O.E. Bell & Co., eBay listings and private collections, Cincinnati silver binders, Cincinnati Art Museum.

17. "Cincinnati," *JCHR* (February 21, 1894): 21; Advertisement, *JCHR* (July 18, 1894): 23.

18. "Cincinnati," *JCHR* (September 26, 1894): 55.

19. "Cincinnati," *JCHR* (June 24, 1896): 26.

20. "Cincinnati," *JCHR* (July 15, 1896): 24; Searches in Cincinnati city directories did not reveal the identity of this "well known man."

21. "Cincinnati," *JCHR* (December 30, 1896): 22.

22. Other subsidiaries may have included The American Watch Club and Walker-Edmunds Co., as J.B. Walker was manager of both, and an officer of The O.E. Bell Co. in 1899 and 1900.

23. "Fact and Fancies," *Cincinnati Enquirer*, February 5, 1900, 5; "Cincinnati," *JCHR* (August 9, 1899): 40; "Cincinnati," *JCHR* (April 18, 1900): 40; "Cincinnati," *JCHR* (May 9, 1900): 12; "Mansfield O., Decided Upon as the Home of the Bell Watch Case Co.," *JCHR* (August 30, 1899): 22; In 1900, The Bell Watch Case Co. general offices were moved to Chicago. A factory for watch movements was established by Bell in Appleton, Wisconsin; "Cincinnati," *JCHR* (October 3, 1900): 42–43.

24. "Bell Watch Case Co.," *National Association of Watch and Clock Collectors message board*, http:/mb.nawcc.org/showwiki.php?title=Bell_Watch_Case_Co, accessed October 31, 2012; 1910 and 1920 Federal Censuses, Philadelphia, Philadelphia, Pennsylvania; Notice of dissolution of Baker-Bell Motor Co., *Automobile Trade Journal*, February 1, 1916, 121.

25. 1930 and 1940 Federal Censuses, Washington, Washington, District of Columbia.

26. Orpheus Edmund Bell, death notice, *The Washington Post*, June 9, 1951.

12. BEST & DETERLY

1812–1813

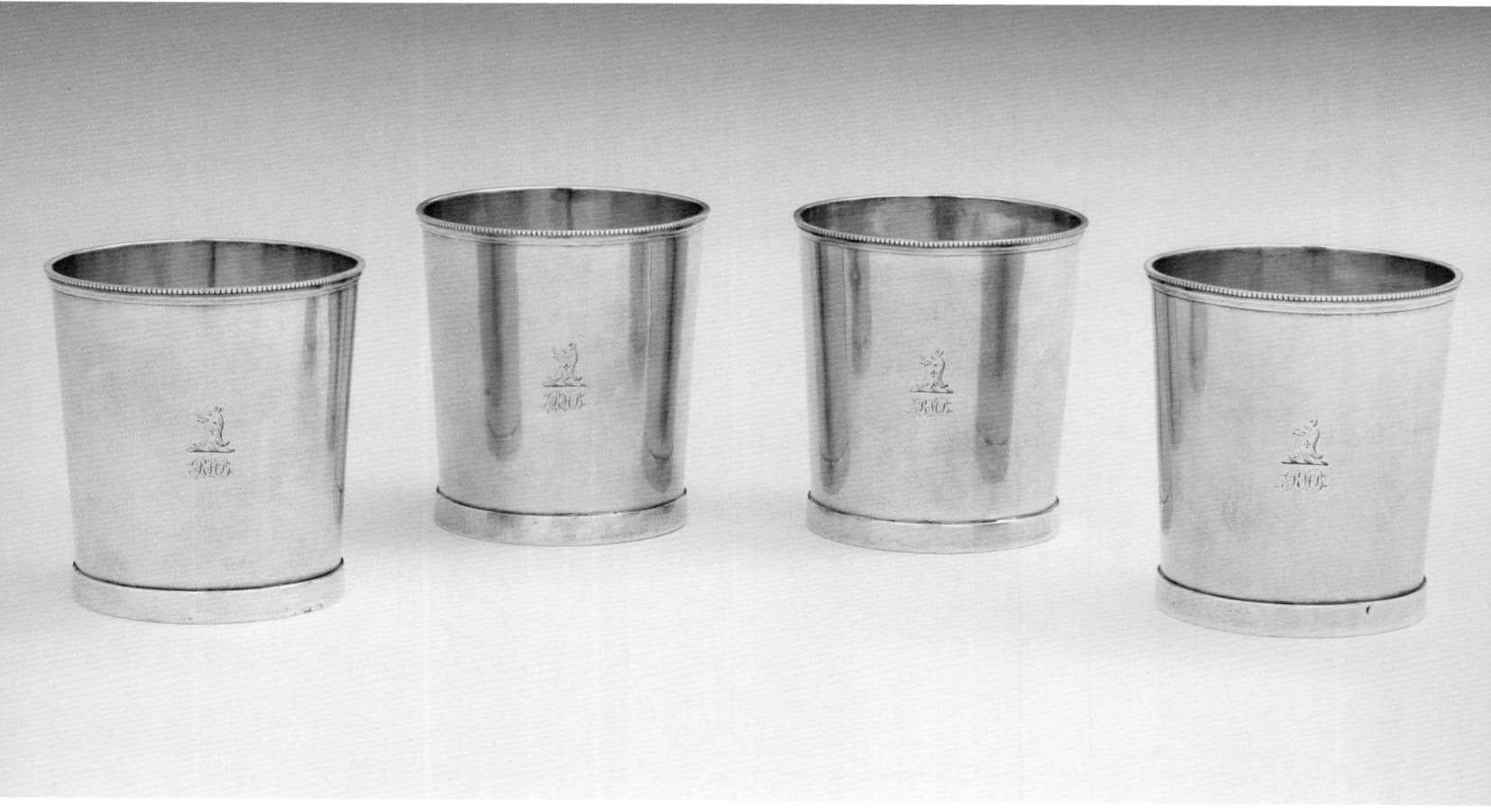

FIG. 12.1: Best & Deterly, *Set of Beakers*, 1812–1813, 3¼ × 3 in. (8.3 × 7.6 cm), CAM, Gift of Doctors James and Betty Sutherland, 2002.49a–d

Robert Best and **Jacob Deterly** joined company on November 7, 1812, conducting business on Main Street, "next door to I.C. Barker & Co.'s Drugstore," "four doors from Front Street."[1] The two men advertised as watch and clock makers, jewelers, and silversmiths. Their inaugural advertisement states that "They choose rather to recommend themselves to the public by the execution of their work, and attention to business, than by a pompous advertisement, and doubt not of giving general satisfaction to those who favour [sic] them with their patronage."[2] Their stated willingness to give "the highest price . . . for old gold, silver, copper, brass and pewter" indicates that they were indeed melting down material and manufacturing their own wares.[3] Their advertisement for "2 or 3 APPRENTICES (from 10 to 14 years of age)" suggests that their

shop was large enough to accommodate at least five craftsmen.[4] In July 1813 they published an apology (fig. 12.3) explaining that since their establishment, their attention had been dominated by making molds and other equipment for the army, and therefore, they had been obliged to hand all watch repairing to journeymen, yielding some unsatisfactory results. They assured customers that they now would turn their attention to these matters and make good on all poor repairs.[5] They also advertised the recent receipt of superior European manufactured materials for watches from Philadelphia, an assortment of "the best and most fashionable Jewelry," and silverware including "Soup or Milk Ladles—Cream or Jelly Spoons—Table, Desert [sic], Tea, Mustard and Salt do. [spoons]—Sugar Tongs—Tumblers—Saddle Mounting, &c. &c. all which they

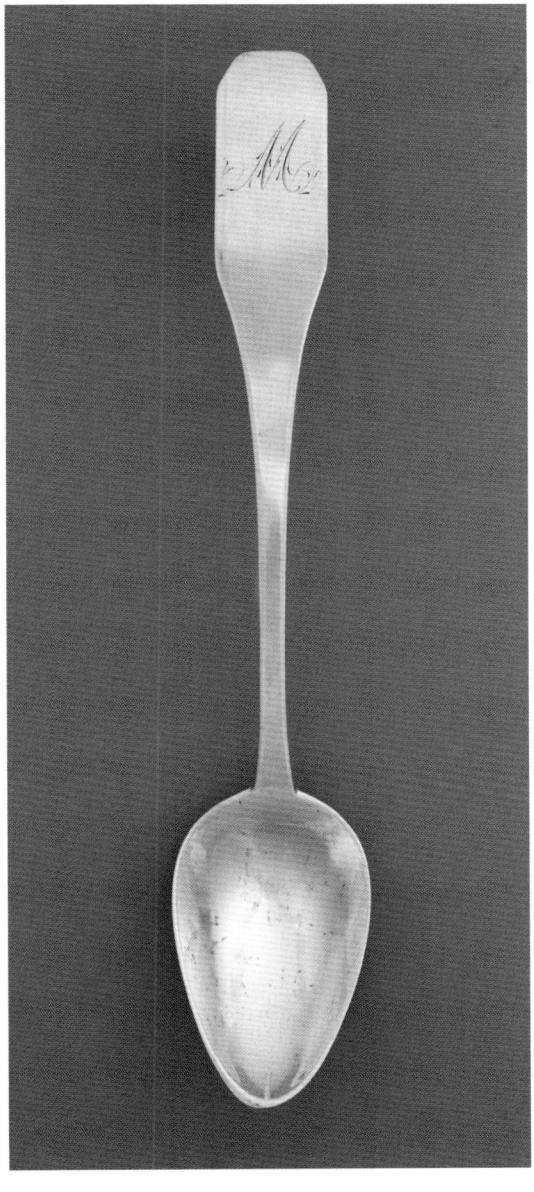

FIG. 12.2: Best & Deterly, *Tablespoon*, 1812–1813, L. 9½ in. (24.1 cm), CAM, Gift of John S. Conner, 1910.210

Cincinnati, July 31st, 1813.   52 3w.

BEST & DETERLY,

WATCH & CLOCK MAKERS,

JEWELLERS, SILVERSMITHS, &c

MAIN STREET, FOUR DOORS FROM FRONT STREET,

CINCINNATI,

GRATEFULLY acknowledge all past favors.— They beg leave to offer an apology for the too great cause of complaint they have given to some of their customers; since their commencement a considerable portion of their time has been spent in making moulds and other equipments for the army, they were therefore obliged to commit the Watch repairing to the hands of Journeymen, and now are convinced of the injury done thereby, to their customers, as well as their reputation; they assure those who may in future favor them, with their custom, that they will wholly attend to that branch themselves, as they are convinced they can thereby give perfect satisfaction, both in the performance of their Watches, as well as the price.

Those who have had Watches repaired at their shop which do not perform well are assured that they will with pleasure correct any fault occasioned by the neglect of their workmen gratis.

They have lately received from Philadelphia a very extensive assortment of the best European manufactured materials for Watches, &c.

They likewise have on hand, and intend keeping a general assortment of the best and most fashionable Jewelry.

Also, Silver ware, amongst which are the following articles, Soup or Milk Ladles—Cream or Jelly Spoons—Table, Desert, Tea, Mustard and Salt do—Sugar Tongs—Tumblers—Saddle Mounting, &c. &c. all which they will sell as low as they can be purchased in the western country.

N. B. The highest price in cash will be given for old Gold, Silver, Copper Brass & Pewter.

Cincinnati, July 31st, 1813.   51 3m

FIG. 12.3: Advertisement, *Western Spy*, July 31, 1813

will sell as low as they can be purchased in the Western country."[6] The partnership was dissolved "by mutual consent" on September 27, 1813, and it is stated that Deterly planned to leave Cincinnati soon after.[7]

The mark of this firm (mark 12.1) has been documented on a set of four beakers (fig. 12.1) and a tablespoon with a coffin-shaped handle (fig. 12.2).

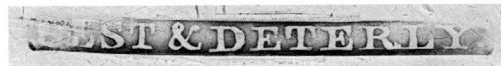

MARK 12.1

1. Advertisement, *Liberty Hall*, November 7, 1812, reproduced in Beckman, 12.
2. Ibid.
3. Ibid.
4. Ibid.
5. Advertisement, *Western Spy*, July 31, 1813.
6. Ibid.
7. Advertisement, *Western Spy*, September 27, 1813, reproduced in Beckman, 13.

13. BEST & SON

circa 1820s–1830s

Coin silver spoons with exaggerated fiddle handles and pointed shoulders stamped Best & Son are known.[1] These spoons were most likely marked by **Thomas Best, Jr.**'s son, Henry (1804–1873), and his son Edwin (1839–1928) who worked in Dayton, Ohio.[2] Henry was working as a jeweler and gunsmith in Dayton by 1824, and later taught these skills to his son, Edwin.

1. Garth's Auction, *May 23, 2009 Americana Catalog featuring the Third Annual Ohio Valley Auction*, Delaware, Ohio: Garth's Auction, 2009, lot 81; Best & Son, eBay listings and private collections, Cincinnati silver binders, Cincinnati Art Museum.
2. Jane Sikes, "The Best Family," *The Magazine Antiques* (July 1974): 123; Advertisement, *Dayton Journal and Advertiser*, October 4, 1831, 3; For more on the Best family and their involvement in the jewelry and silver trade in Dayton, refer to Augustus Waldo Drury, *History of the City of Dayton and Montgomery County, Ohio*, Cincinnati: The S.J. Clarke Publishing Co., 1909, 2:575–576; Edwin joined his father in partnership in 1860, and they used the mark "H. Best & Son."

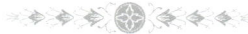

MARK 13.1

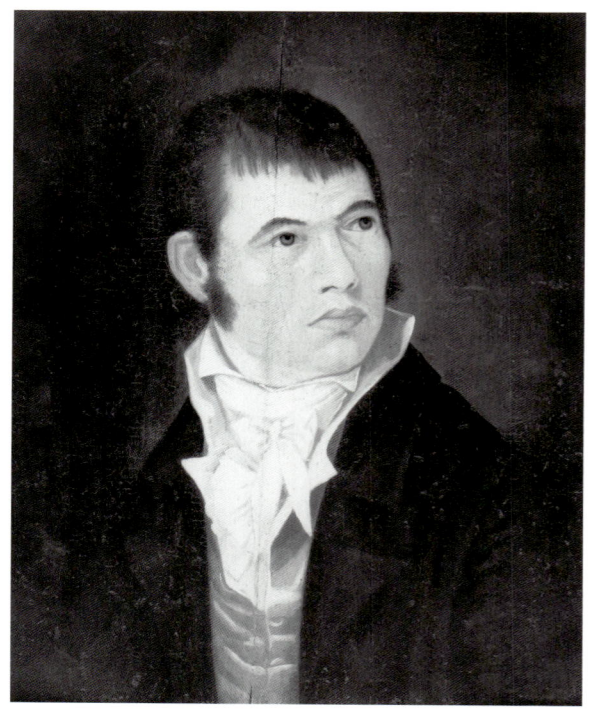

14. ROBERT BEST

1790–1830, w. 1811–1819

Robert Best (fig. 14.1) was born on January 12, 1790, in Ilminster, Somerset, England, the third and youngest son of **Thomas Best, Sr.** and Sarah Greenham.[1] He arrived in the United States on September 25, 1801, with his parents, his brother **Thomas Jr.**, Thomas' wife, and his cousin Henry.[2] In a biographical sketch of 1831, it is noted that Robert "never went to school but three months," and that he learned the watch, clock making and silver trade at his father's knee. During his apprenticeship it is said that he devoted all his time to the study of *Chamber's Cyclopaedia*, a foreshadowing of his proclivity for science.[3] Once he became an established craftsman and businessman, it was noted that "he was distinguished for taste, and had an accurate and comprehensive knowledge of every chemical art connected with metallurgy," and "as a watch maker he was equally remarkable for his acquaintance with the principals of horology; like Rittenhouse, having scientifically studied the mechanism of clocks, watches and chronometers, which the majority of artists look at only with the eye of empiricism."[4]

Robert probably came to Cincinnati with his parents around 1803. By twenty years of age he was a member of the third company of the Cincinnati Militia, third division.[5] He opened his first shop in Hamilton, Butler County, Ohio, about 30 miles north of Cincinnati, in March 1811, advertising his services as a watch and

FIG. 14.1: John James Audubon (American, b. 1785, d. 1851), *Portrait of Robert Best*, c. 1820, oil on wood panel, 22 × 19½ in. (55.9 × 49.5 cm), present location unknown

clock maker, silversmith and jeweler.[6] By July 1812, Best had returned to Cincinnati, where he became involved in a series of short-lived partnerships of the type that characterize the early days of the silver trade in Cincinnati. He first partnered with his brother **Samuel** in a shop on Main Street. This arrangement lasted about five months, ending in November when Samuel left the partnership and Robert continued business at the Main Street location with **Jacob Deterly**.[7] Ten months later, **Enos Woodruff** purchased Deterly's share of the firm, and the firm of **Best & Woodruff** continued business on Main Street.[8]

In 1815, Jacob Deterly returned as a partner, and the firm advertised as **R. Best & Co.**, suggesting Robert as owner of the majority interest. In February, the firm announced the relocation of their shop to "the centre of the three Brick Houses lately erected on Main, between Columbia and lower Market streets."[9] An extensive description of their services and stock suggests that the capital invested in their business was significant. Of great interest in the announcement is the addition of "HOLLOW WARE MAKING and manufacturing of all kinds of PLATED WARE," and the unusually early emphasis given to sterling versus coin in the statement "SILVERWARE of every description, (warranted to be Sterling silver)."[10] Despite this claim, there is no known silver marked by Robert Best & Co. that is also marked as sterling. A subsequent announcement (fig. 14.2) regarding the sale of a house and lot on Main Street "where R. Best & Co. now do business" indicates that Best was the owner of the firm's shop.[11] The house was described as "in every respect well calculated for a mercantile establishment having an excellent storeroom in front with an accompting [accounting] room adjoining," and noted in a subsequent advertisement as "a good situation for either a Blacksmith or Cooper's Shop" with a lot, extending "190 feet to a 20 foot alley."[12]

In May 1817 Robert resumed business with his brother Samuel on Main Street, "a few doors below the United States' Branch Bank."[13] Notice of the dissolution of this partnership was submitted on September 11, 1818 (fig. 16.6).[14] Working on his own, Robert continued to tout silver (fig. 14.3), and special attention was also given to the fact that his apprentices now had permission to make kaleidoscopes.[15]

Ever interested in science, in 1819, Robert accepted the position of manager of Cincinnati's Western Museum—an institution dedicated to collecting and understanding the natural history of the Western Territory. He sold his silver, watch, clock, and jewelry business to Seymour, Williston & Benson, and shortly thereafter embarked on several expeditions to collect specimens for the new

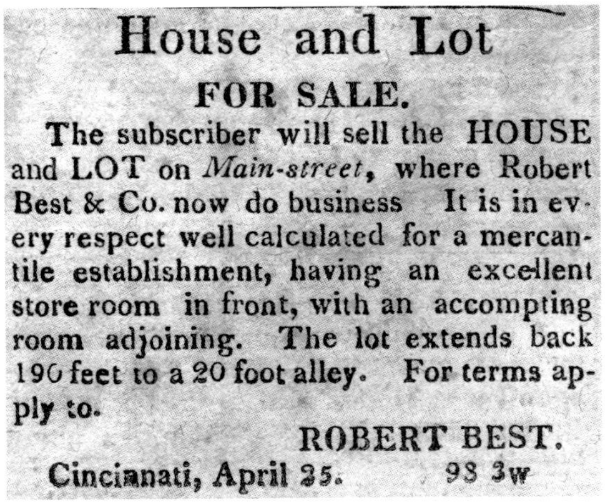

FIG. 14.2: Advertisement, *Western Spy*, April 26, 1816, 3

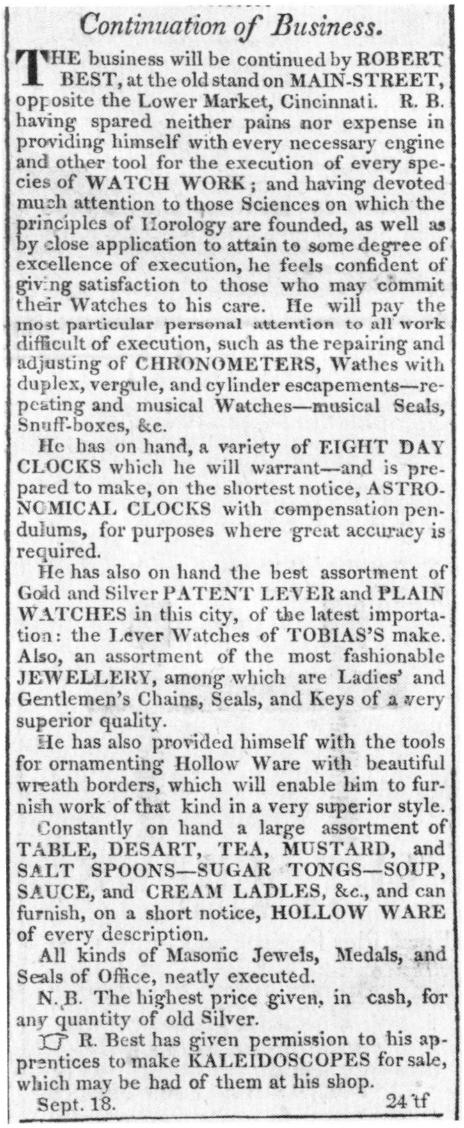

FIG. 14.3: Advertisement, *Western Spy*, October 3, 1818, 3

museum.[16] After the departure of the museum's first curator, John James Audubon (1785-1851), in 1820, Robert was named curator.[17] But his salaries for this position, and his position as assistant to the professor of chemistry at the Medical College of Ohio were evidently not enough to sustain him, and an advertisement of that year announced his willingness to repair "all kinds of philosophical and mathematical instruments—all the higher order of *Time Keepers*, and in short, every species of delicate and *Complicated Machinery*."[18] He continued to advertise these services, without any mention of silver work, until the spring of 1823, when he moved to Lexington, Kentucky where he was named Assistant Professor of Chemistry at Transylvania University, and specialized in pharmaceutical chemistry.[19] When not tending to his professional duties, Best read and attended lectures, and in 1826, he became a licensed physician and surgeon.[20] But his life ended prematurely in 1830 at the age of 40. His funeral was held on September 29th.[21] It is said that Best had been in poor health and a state of melancholy for several years, the latter triggered by the accidental drowning of his only son, Samuel, age 10, in the Ohio River in 1820.[22] In addition to a son, Robert and his wife Rachel Wooley had four daughters: Amanda (1813-1845), Emma May (b. 1818), Clara Cornetta (b. 1825), and Elizabeth (circa 1828-1852).[23]

A salt shovel (fig. 14.4) with a broad fiddle handle bearing Robert Best's mark (mark 14.1) is known. A second mark, similar to the one shown here, but inside a cartouche with serrated edges, has been reported, but not seen in recent years.[24]

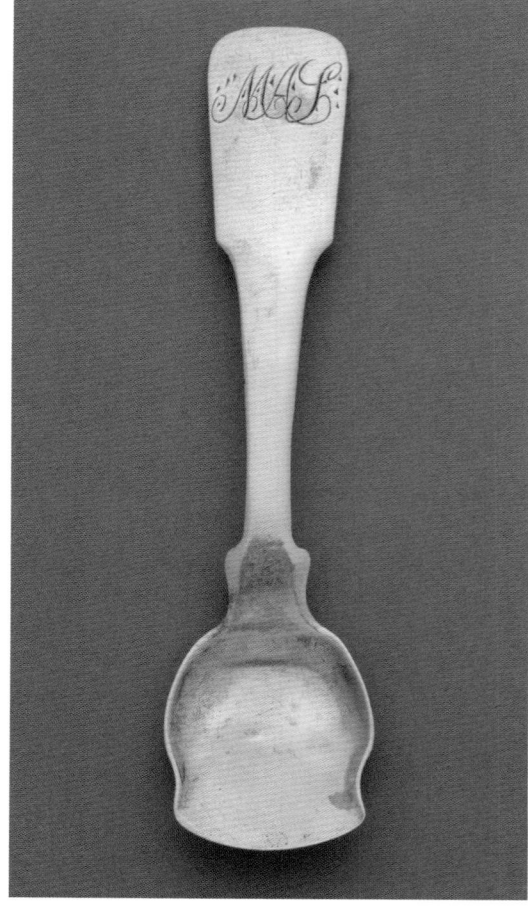

FIG. 14.4: Robert Best, *Salt Shovel*, c. 1812–1819, L. 3⅜ in. (8.6 cm), CAM, Gift of Mrs. Jane Sikes Hageman, 2002.83

R.BEST

MARK 14.1

1. Mrs. Wilbur Shuey, "The Best Family," May 2, 1969, Cincinnati Art Museum, curatorial file 1966.1175.
2. Samuel Best Diary, Mary R. Schiff Library and Archives, Cincinnati Art Museum.
3. Daniel Drake MD and James C. Findlay MD (eds.), *The Western Journal of Medical and Physical Sciences*, Cincinnati, E. Deming, 1831, 4:612.
4. Ibid.
5. "Roll of the 3rd Company of Cincinnati Militia 3d of May 1810," *Quarterly Publication of the Historical and Philosophical Society, 1918–1920*, vols. 13–15, Cincinnati: Historical and Philosophical Society of Ohio, 1921, 125; "A roll of the third company in third battalion of the 1st brigade," September 29, 1810, Torrence papers,

Cincinnati Historical Society, box 51, folder 4, 49.
6. Advertisement, *Liberty Hall*, March 20, 1811, reproduced in Beckman, 12.
7. Advertisement, *Western Spy*, July 4, 1812, reproduced in Beckman, 16; Advertisement, *Liberty Hall*, November 7, 1812, reproduced in Beckman, 12.
8. Advertisement, *Western Spy*, September 27, 1813, reproduced in Beckman, 13.
9. Advertisement, *Western Spy*, February 18, 1815, reproduced in Beckman, 13.
10. Ibid.
11. Advertisement, *Western Spy*, April 26, 1816, 3; Advertisement, *Liberty Hall*, May 5, 1817, reproduced in Beckman, 17.
12. Ibid.
13. Advertisement, *Liberty Hall*, May 5,

1817, reproduced in Beckman, 17.
14. "Dissolution of Partnership," *Western Spy*, September 26, 1818, 3 (fig. 16.6).
15. Announcement, *Western Spy*, October 3, 1818, 3.
16. Advertisement, *Cincinnati Inquisitor and Advertiser*, August 31, 1819, reproduced in Beckman, 14. This advertisement also ran in the *Western Spy*, September 4, 1819; Jacob Deterly, *"Remarks" of Jacob Deterly: diary from 1819 to 1848; life in southern Ohio: Cincinnati, Marietta, Athens* (transcribed and indexed by Madge Hubbard and Opal Saffell), Seattle: Northwest Lineage Researcher, 1972, December 1, 1819 entry; A. Septuagenarian, "Historical Sketches–No. III." *Genius of the West* 4, no. 7 (July 1855): 193–197.
17. Drake and Findlay, *Western Journal*, 613; John James Audubon, Lucy Green Bakewell Audubon, Robert William Buchanan, *The Life of John James Audubon*, New York: G.P. Putnam & Son, 1869, 58; Henry A.

Ford and Mrs. Kate B. Ford, *History of Cincinnati, Ohio*, Cleveland: L.A. Williams, 1881, 372.
18. Drake and Findlay, *Western Journal*, 613; Ford, *History of Cincinnati*, 372; Advertisement, *Liberty Hall*, December 30, 1820, reproduced in Beckman, 14.
19. *Liberty Hall*, February 17, 1823; "Transylvania University Medical Department," *Frankfurt Argus*, May 21, 1824, 3.
20. Charles Greve, *Centennial History of Cincinnati and Its Representative Citizens*, Chicago: Biographical Publishing Co., 1904, 1:609; Drake and Findlay, *Western Journal*, 613.
21. James M. Duff, *Duffs Funeral Notices Scrap Book: 1806–1807*, Lexington: Lexington Public Library, 2002, reproduced in Boultinghouse, 65.
22. Death notice, *Western Spy*, (n.d), reproduced in Beckman, 14.
23. Shuey, "The Best Family," 1969; Boultinghouse, 66.
24. Beckman, 15.

15. R. BEST & CO.

1815–1817

By 1815, **Jacob Deterly** had purchased an interest in **Best & Woodruff**'s Main Street shop to form R. Best & Co., a "Watch and Clock making, Jeweller [*sic*] and Silversmith business."[1] In February 1815 the firm advertised the relocation of their business to "the centre one of the three Brick Houses lately erected on Main, between Columbia and lower Market streets."[2] With combined capital and an expanded shop, the firm offered a wide variety of goods, including watches, eight-day clocks, mourning and fancy jewelry, tortoise-shell combs, and other accessories.

Of particular interest to this study is their announcement of "having added the HOLLOW WARE making and manufacturing all kinds of PLATED WARE."[3] They advertised "SILVER WARE of every description (warranted Sterling silver) which they will sell as low as can be purchased in any part of the U. States: consisting of the following articles, viz: all kinds of *Urns, Coffee and Tea Pots, Sugar and Slop Bowls, Cream Ewers, Pitchers, Goblets, Tumblers, Salt Cellars, Casters, Soup and Sauce Ladles, Cream and Mustard Spoons, Salt and Marrow do. [Spoons], Table and Dessert & Tea do. [Spoons]*, of the three

last mentioned articles they have constantly on hand from 50 to 100 setts [*sic*] of various patterns."[4] To offer a variety of patterns in table, dessert, and tea spoons hints at the scale of the firm's involvement in silver. It is especially interesting that they were warranting, at this early date, that their silver was of sterling standard. Use and knowledge of the term surely came from the partners' associations with the silver trade in England. It is doubtful that the firm would have had access to silver of the sterling standard, as most of their material would have come from circulating coinage, and there was no uniform testing or monitoring of the fineness of silver in America until the 1850s. There are no known works by this firm that are marked as sterling.

Extant silver bearing the mark of this firm reflects the variety of goods offered in their advertisements. Both the construction and design of the work suggest that R. Best & Co. could have been manufacturing much of what they sold. The following types of wares have been found with their mark: spectacles (fig. 15.1); tongs; beakers (fig. 15.2); and dessert, serving and tablespoons (fig. 15.3).[5]

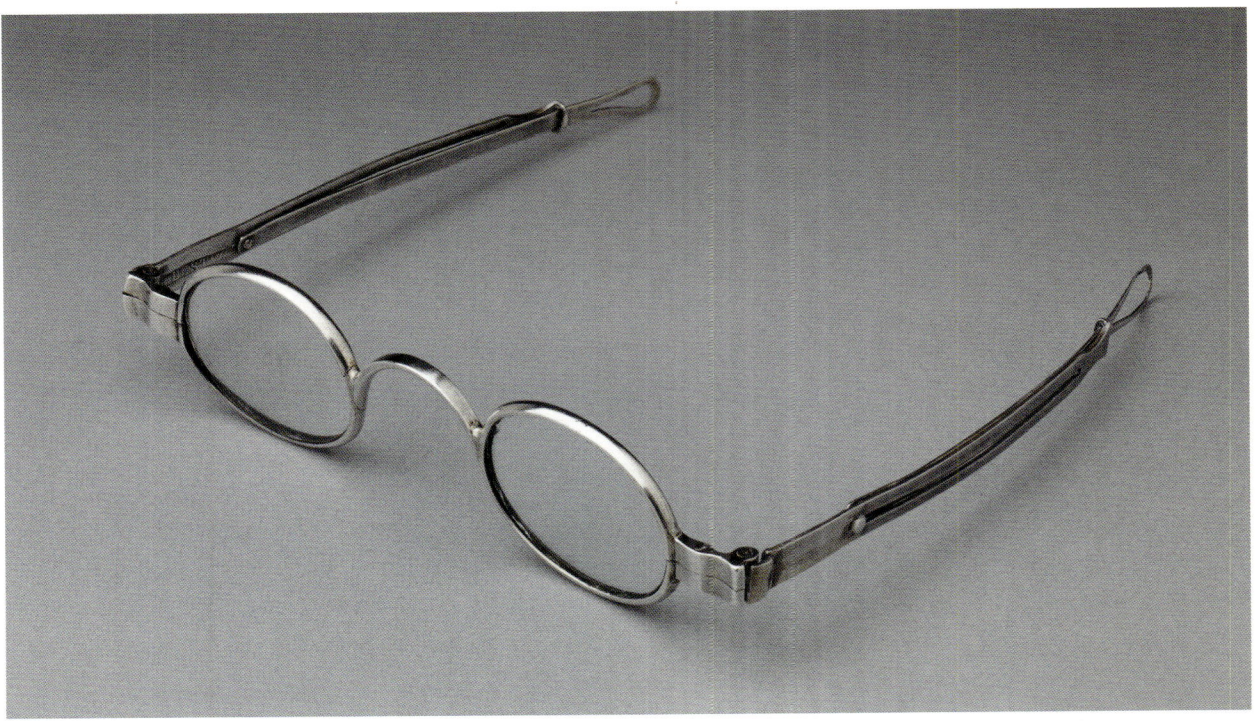

FIG. 15.1: R. Best & Co., *Spectacles*, 1815–1817, bridge: 1 in. (2.54 cm), lens: 1 × 1 15/16 in. (3.5 × 4.9 cm), temple range of length: 4¼ to 7 in. (10.8 to 17.8 cm), CAM, Anonymous Gift, 2002.8a–b

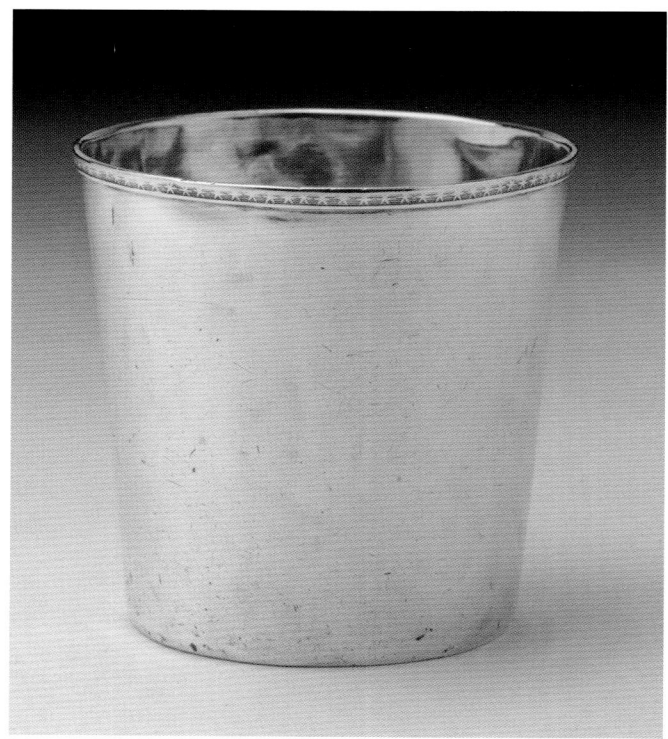

FIG. 15.2: R. Best & Co., *Beaker*, 1815–1817, 3⅛ × 3 × 2½ in.
(7.9 × 7.6 × 6.4 cm), CAM, Museum Purchase: Gift of Harry
G. Friedman, by exchange, 2001.2

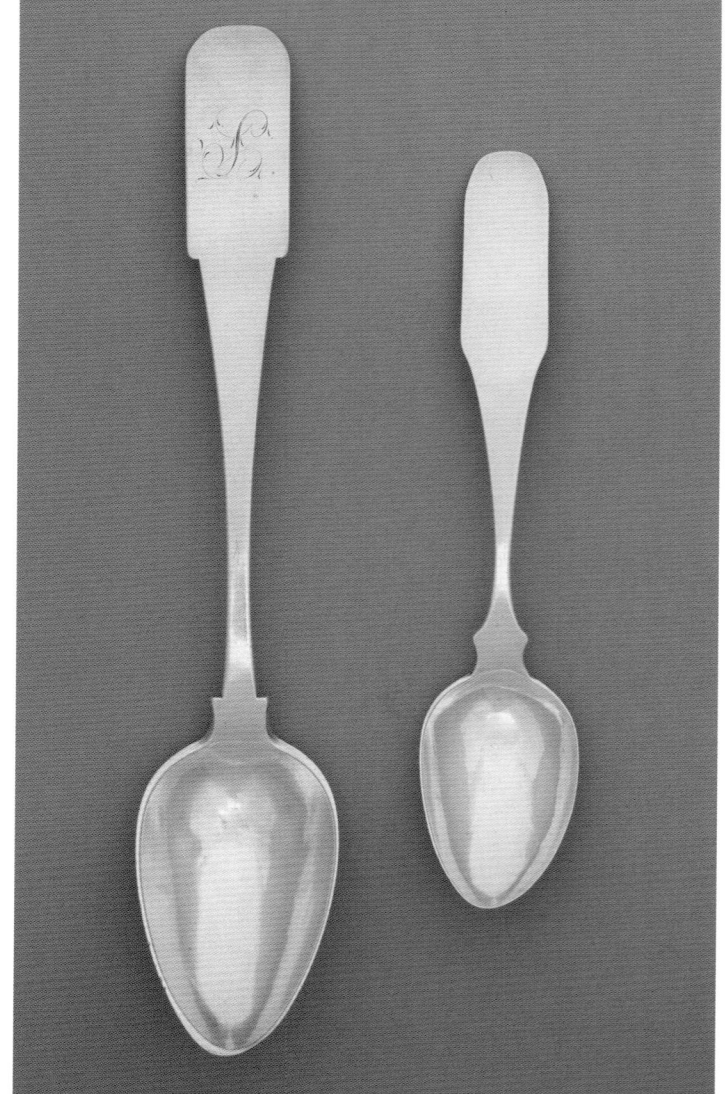

FIG. 15.3: R. Best & Co., *Dessert Spoon*, 1815–1817, L. 6⅞ in.
(17.5 cm), CAM, Gift of Dr. Suzanne A. Beutler, 1983.202;
R. Best & Co., *Serving Spoon*, 1815–1817, L. 9⅜ in. (23.8 cm),
CAM, Anonymous Gift, 2002.7

R. Best & Co. offered "an extensive assortment of PLATED WARE, CONSISTING OF Men and Women's Stirrup Irons, Bridle bits, Spurs, Martingale Hooks, &c."[6] Their dedication to this aspect of the business is evident in their offer to "give constant employ to 2 or 3 Boys from 14 to 16 years of age, who can come well recommended as apprentices to the Plating business."[7] The firm's activities in silver plating originated during the partnership of Best & Woodruff. Woodruff was a plater and brought this expertise to the partnership.[8] Plated wares bearing the mark of R. Best & Co. are unknown.

R. Best & Co. was dissolved "by mutual consent" on April 28, 1817.[9] Robert went on to partner with his brother **Samuel Best**, and **Woodruff & Deterly** continued at the Main Street address.

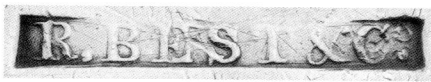

MARK 15.1

1. Advertisement, *Western Spy*, February 18, 1815, reproduced in Beckman, 13.
2. Ibid.
3. Ibid.
4. Ibid.
5. Robert Best & Co., eBay listings and private collections, Cincinnati silver binders, Cincinnati Art Museum.
6. Advertisement, *Western Spy*, February 18, 1815.
7. Ibid.
8. There are no records to suggest that Robert Best or Jacob Deterly were producing plated silver prior to their involvement with Enos Woodruff.
9. Advertisement, *Liberty Hall*, May 16, 1817, 1.

16. SAMUEL BEST

1776–1859, W. 1802–1818

Samuel Best, born May 17, 1776, in Ilminster, Somerset, England, was the eldest son of watch and clock maker **Thomas Best, Sr.** and Sarah Greenham (1755–1828).[1] Samuel was a silversmith, watch and clock maker, jeweler and engraver.[2] He likely acquired these skills in his father's Ilminster shop; an 1817 advertisement boasts that he had "learnt and followed the Watchmaking Business many years in Europe."[3] Samuel Best's diary and day book (fig. 16.1) survive. Written when he was approximately nineteen years old, a March 2, 1795, entry reads, "I made the first 2 Quart tea kettle," and four years later on November 9, 1799, he records, "Gave my first Order to Butler Brothers, Birmingham for Coffin Plates, &c., Hinges, &c. &c."[4] In an advertisement prior to his emigration to America, Best is described as "Ironmonger and Cutler," and his prosperity as such can be assumed by the fact that he owned his own dwelling house, which he advertised to sell at auction on Monday, August 3, 1801.[5]

Samuel expected to leave England from Bristol with the rest of his family on the Philadelphia-bound vessel *The Roebuck* in August of 1801, but he was held back.

> "On account of a suspicion of my being a mechanic and an objection arising at the custom house to me taking out some tools and utensils contrary to law, I was prevented from accompanying my friends—but

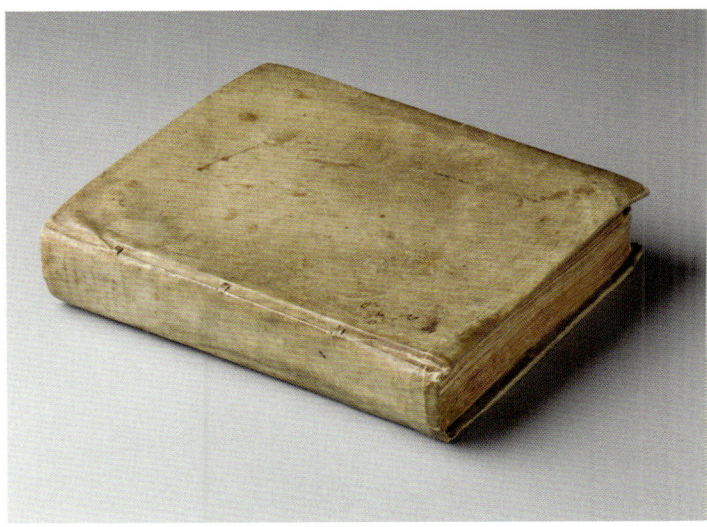

FIG. 16.1: *Samuel Best Diary 1791–1799, and Account Book 1809–1812*, Mary R. Schiff Library and Archives, CAM, Gift of Doris Dupraz

through Mr. Wm. Bower's interests—I was assisted in to pass at the custom house at Bristol by Wm. Cornelius Fry, glass bottle manufacturer, Old Market, and got a passage in the *Brutus*, Captn. John Bunce, to Philadelphia. The vessel was the property of Mr. John Warder, merchant of that city. We departed from Mud Dock in the city of Bristol on Sunday morning the sixth of September 1801 at 6 o'clock p.m. . . . We arrived at Philadelphia on Thursday the 15th of October. Some part of the goods were forwarded to Pittsburgh prior to my arrival and all the party, beside my father [and] mother . . . who procured employment in the vicinity of Philadelphia were gone forward to Pittsburgh."[6]

Samuel recorded leaving for Pittsburgh with his belongings on November 6, and arriving there, "after a fatiguing journey" on November 23, 1801. Shortly thereafter, on December 1st, he left Pittsburgh by boat (probably keel boat), traveling down the Ohio River. He notes that he, his brother **Thomas Best, Jr.**, and his cousin Henry Best "proceeded down without any material hinderance [sic] till we got on Grape Island."[7]

> "In the morning after we got in the water about knee deep and with levers we hove her off the gravel after about one hour's hard work and proceeded till within about 40 miles off Wheeland [sic, Wheeling] where we engaged with one Cuppy to pilot us to Wheeling for 3 dollars, after which we came on by ourselves till we fell in with a large Orleans Boat belonging to Creton, Glass, etc. to whom we lashed ourselves and proceeded on to Limestone [Maysville, Kentucky] very agreeably. We passed Killikanic Creek on the 15th of December and arrived at Limestone the next evening. On the 17th Thomas and myself set out for Bourbon [Paris, Kentucky] at which place we arrived on Saturday evening following. . . . On Wednesday 30th December [1801] I worked for the first time at the watch business for one [Thomas] Philips at Bourbon . . ."[8]

The Scottish-born silversmith Thomas Philips (1774–1843) is believed to have arrived in Lexington as early as 1795. He maintained a shop on High Street south of the Public Square.[9] Samuel's sojourn there was short-lived.

By 1802, Best had settled in Cincinnati and set up shop at the northwest corner of Front and Walnut Streets.[10] The earliest documented piece of silver marked by a member of the Best family following their arrival in America, is a teaspoon (fig. 16.2) stamped "S & T. Best." (mark 16.1).[11] Discovered during excavations at the Piqua, Ohio home of Colonel John Johnston, the spoon bears the monogram JRJ and is believed to have commemorated Johnston's

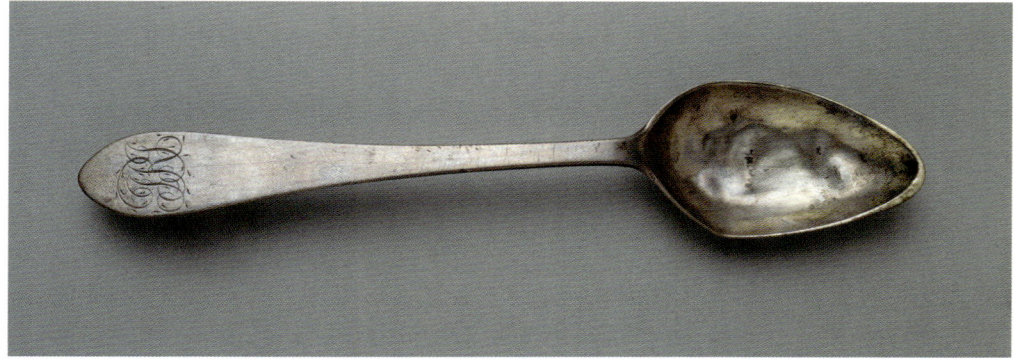

FIG. 16.2: S. & T. Best, *Teaspoon*, about 1802, L. 5½ in. (14 cm), Courtesy of the Ohio Historical Society, H80910

marriage to his wife Rebecca in July 1802.[12] It is not clear whether this is the mark Samuel employed when working with his father, Thomas Sr., or his brother, Thomas Jr.

On December 13, 1804, Samuel married Eunice Winkley (d. 1820), whose father Joseph Windecker Winkley of Rotterdam, Holland, had emigrated before the American Revolution.[13] Coin silver spoons engraved "ESB" for Eunice and Samuel Best were created to mark their union (fig.16.3). Eunice bore Samuel five children: Samuel (1807–1840), Robert (d. before 1854), Eliza (1805–1822), Irene (b. about 1817, d. before 1857), and Edwin (b. about 1820).[14]

By February 1805 Samuel was advertising in the *Western Spy* as a "Clock & Watch Maker, Silver-Smith, &c, next door to Mr. Anderson's tavern, Front Street."[15] In this advertisement, he "returns his greatful [sic] acknowledgements to his friends, and the public in general for their past favors" and "hopes by strict attention in point of execution and punctuality, to meet their future support." After a mention of clock glasses kept on hand, the realities of frontier living and trading prove evident when he offers "a liberal price" in cash for "good country sugar."[16] An invoice (fig. 16.4) for work completed for James Findlay between April 17, 1805, and June 20, 1806, demonstrates the variety of Best's work.[17]

Samuel advertised for apprentices in 1806 and 1807. In January 1806 he solicited for "AN HONEST SOBER active boy of 14 or 15 years of age, wanted as an apprentice to the Clock and Watch making & Silver-smith's business," noting that "A boy from the country would be preferred," and he ran a similar advertisement in July.[18] A third appeal appeared in June 1807. Reformed in tone and preference, it reads, "TO PARENTS & GUARDIANS: *"Children like tender Osiers take the bow, As first they're fashioned, so they grow."* WANTED immediately, a Boy from respectable connexions [sic] of

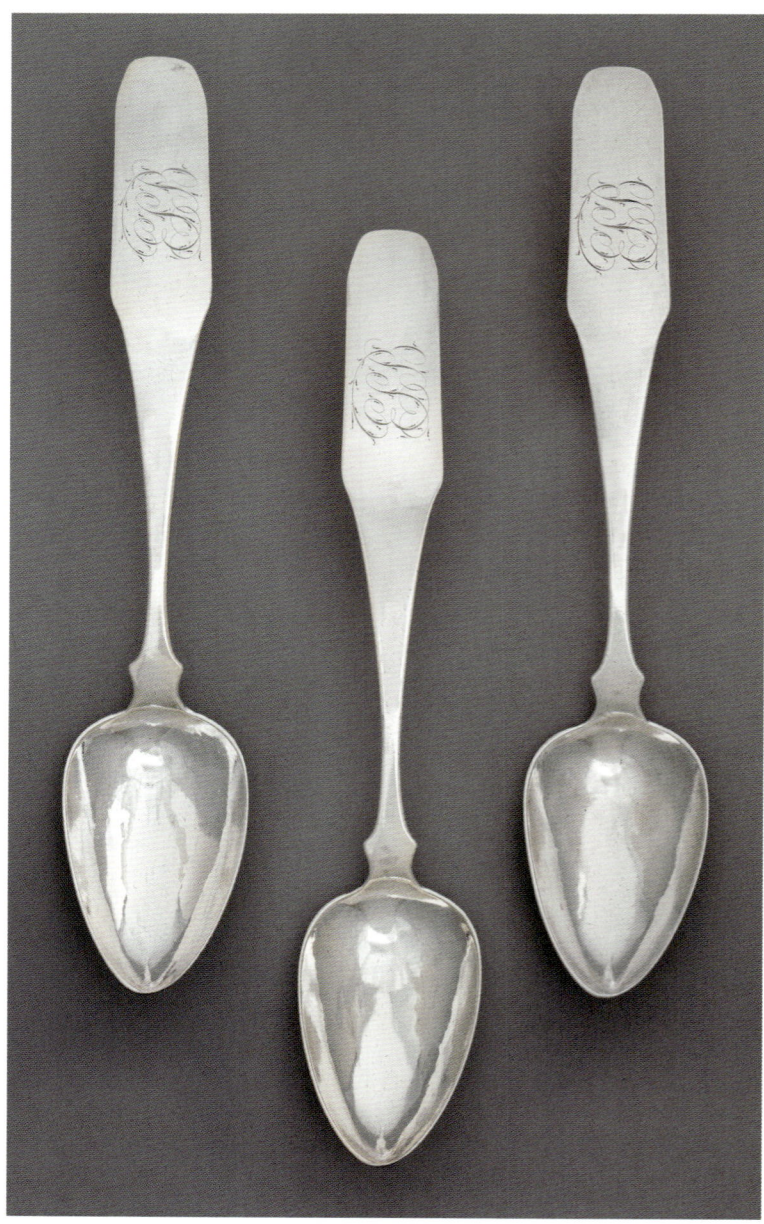

FIG. 16.3: Samuel Best, *Tablespoons*, 1804, L. 9½ in. (24.1 cm), CAM, Gift of Doris Dupraz, 1969.537-538, 1991.1

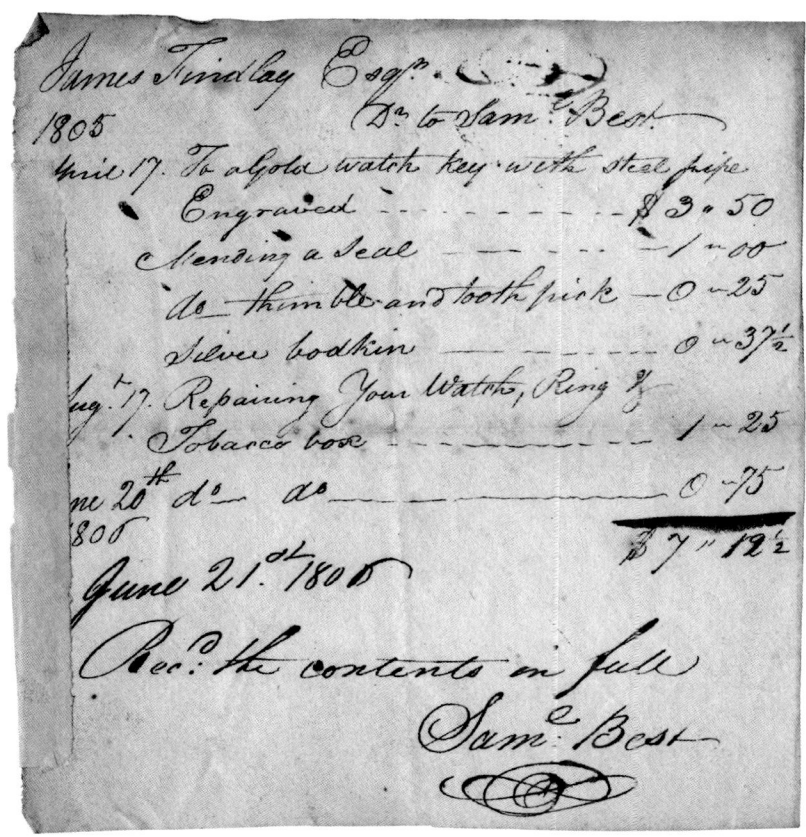

FIG. 16.4: Samuel Best, Invoice to
James Findlay, June 16, 1806, Torrence
papers, Cincinnati Historical Society,
box 33

about 14 or 15 years of age, as an apprentice to the CLOCK AND WATCH MAKING and SILVERSMITH'S business."[19]

Best's advertisements tapered off between 1808 and 1812, yet his diary contains an impressive list of clients—over 300—from October 2, 1809, to February 20, 1811, for whom he repaired and cleaned French and English watches and clocks. His list concludes on February 20, 1811, with the boldly rendered notations, "AMEN" and "FINIS cum Fis . . . [illeg.]" But an extant bill for clock and watch work completed for Dr. James Findlay, dated December 21, 1811, indicates that his business continued.[20] Samuel had become part of the Third Company in the Cincinnati Battalion of the 1st Brigade and 1st Division under Captain George P. Torrence as early as May 1810, and served through October 1811, but there is no record of his participation in the War of 1812.[21]

In June 1812 an account of the work of Henry Wallace (about 1788–1818) appears in Best's diary. This account begins on June 19th, indicating an order for three sets of tea spoons for Samuel Best.[22] A running list of his work, ranging from the making and repair of soup spoons to sword scabbards, continues into July, after which time dates are no longer provided. At the end of the account, the total owed Henry Wallace for his work on 38 jobs was $71.11½. Wallace, who was probably a journeyman working in Best's shop,

was later the partner of **Isaac Paxton** in Hamilton, Ohio. He died at the age of 30 and is buried with Paxton and his wife (the sister of **Isaac Van Nuys**), and their family in Hamilton.[23]

In July 1812 Samuel partnered with his younger brother Robert, who had just closed shop in Hamilton, Ohio. They commenced business on "Main Street; in the store lately occupied by Jacob Baymiller, next door to T. C. Barker & Co.'s Drug Store."[24] The announcement of their partnership promises that the new firm will keep "a constant supply of the most fashionable *Jewelry & Silverwork, Watch Chains, Keys and Seals—Dirks &c.—Clocks and Time Pieces of the best material & workmanship warranted—Pad, Chest, Desk, Drawer and small Furniture Locks fitted with Keys,*" and "Litherland, Whiteside & Co's PATENT LEVER WATCHES, for sale." But by November, the partnership had dissolved.[25]

Not long after, Samuel resumed business at his old stand at Front and Walnut, and in an advertisement of January 18, 1814, apologizes, "Having for the last 18 months, been much engaged in engraving and printing for the Banks, he has not been able to pay that attention to matters more immediately within the scope of his business."[26] By 1814, Cincinnati had three banks, and the city's population had doubled within five years to over 5,000.[27] As the city developed in size and commerce, it also grew in cultural

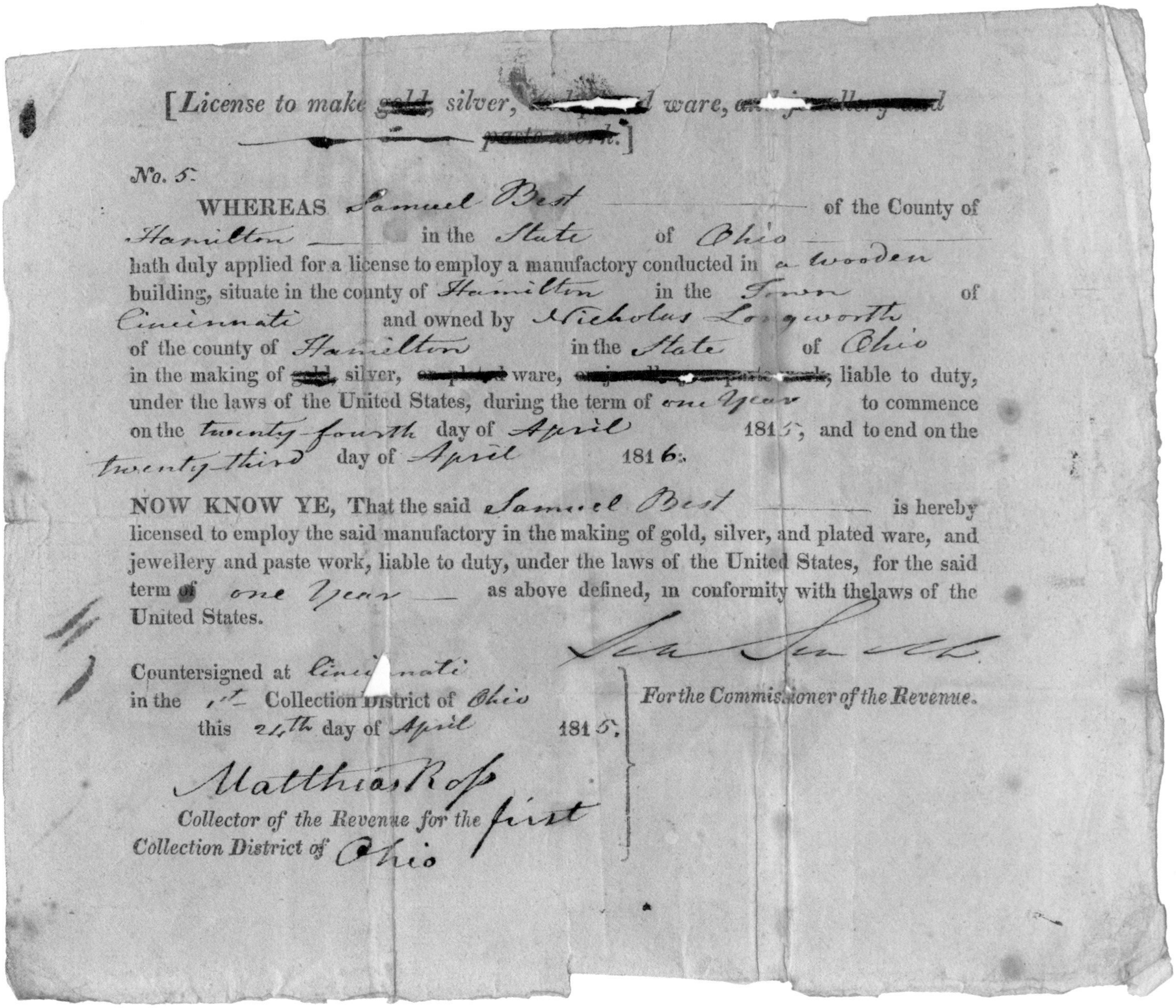

[License to make gold, silver, ~~plated~~ ware, ~~jewellery and paste work.~~]

No. 5.

WHEREAS *Samuel Best* ——————— of the County of *Hamilton* ——— in the *State* of *Ohio* hath duly applied for a license to employ a manufactory conducted in *a wooden* building, situate in the county of *Hamilton* in the *Town* of *Cincinnati* and owned by *Nicholas Longworth* of the county of *Hamilton* in the *State* of *Ohio* in the making of ~~gold~~ silver, ~~plated~~ ware, ~~jewellery and paste work,~~ liable to duty, under the laws of the United States, during the term of *one Year* to commence on the *twenty-fourth* day of *April* 181*5*, and to end on the *twenty-third* day of *April* 181*6*.

NOW KNOW YE, That the said *Samuel Best* ——— is hereby licensed to employ the said manufactory in the making of gold, silver, and plated ware, and jewellery and paste work, liable to duty, under the laws of the United States, for the said term of *one Year* as above defined, in conformity with the laws of the United States.

Countersigned at *Cincinnati*
in the *1st* Collection District of *Ohio*   *For the Commissioner of the Revenue.*
this *24*th day of *April* 181*5*.

Matthias Ross
Collector of the Revenue for the *first*
Collection District of *Ohio*

FIG. 16.5: *United States Licence to make silverware*, April 24, 1815, John J. Rowe Collection, Cincinnati Historical Society

refinement. Recognizing and surely benefitting from this growth and vitality, Samuel Best invested in a large and varied stock of luxury commodities, advertising "Silver Tumblers and Rummers, Milk and Soup Ladlers [*sic*], Sauce and Cream do. [ladlers], Mustard, Marrow, Table and Tea Spoons, Sugar Tongs, etc., Also Swords, Dirks, Mounting for Belts and other Military Equipment, Clocks, Watch Seals and Keys together with Saddle mounting of every description, Silver or Plated."[28] It is fair to assume that much of this silver was of Best's own manufacture, as a license to make silverware, liable to duty, was issued to him on April 24, 1815, by the collector of revenue for the first collection district of Ohio (fig. 16.5).[29]

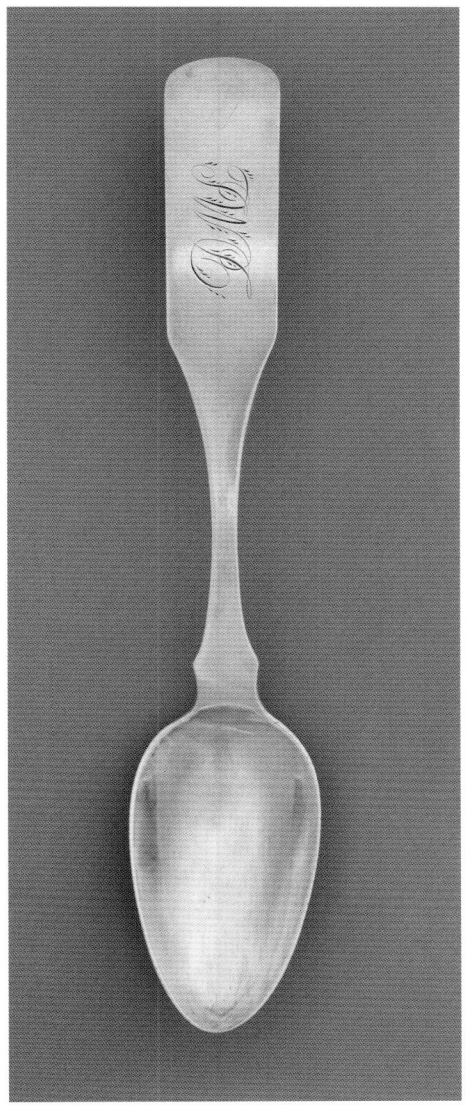

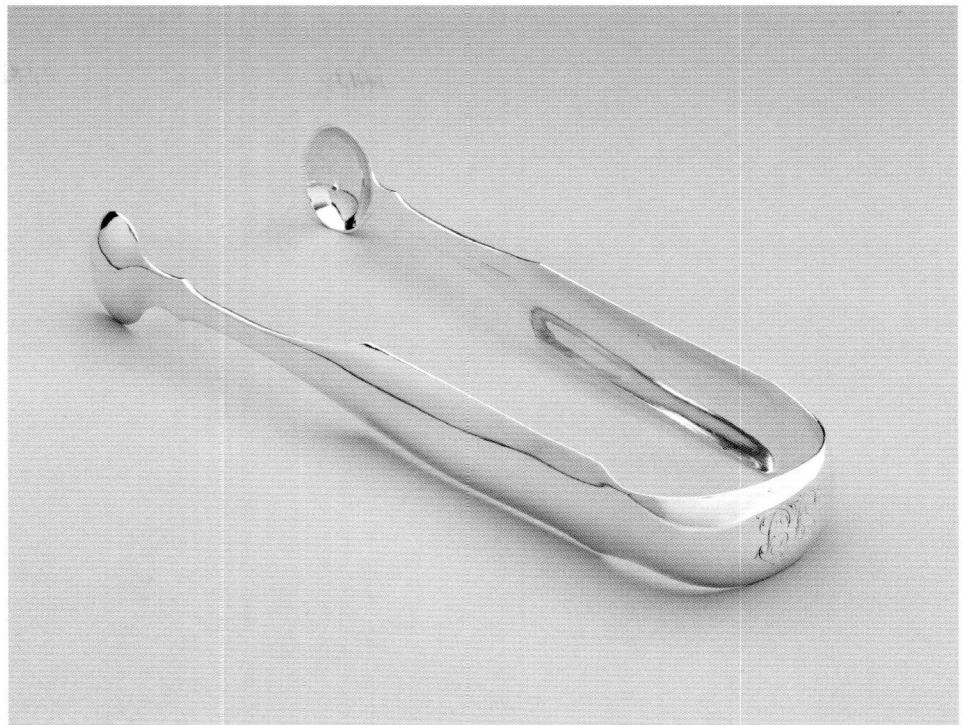

FIG. 16.7: Samuel Best, *Sugar Tongs*, 1802–1818, L. 6⅛ in. (15.6 cm), CAM, Museum Purchase, 1962.118

FIG. 16.8: Samuel Best, *Tablespoon*, 1802–1818, L. 8⅝ in. (21.9 cm), CAM, Given by Elizabeth M. and Annie W. Anderson in memory of their mother, Mrs. Buckner W. Anderson, 1969.734

By May 1817 Samuel and his younger brother Robert reunited as business partners on "Main street, a few doors below the United States' Branch Bank," advertising as "WATCH AND CLOCK MAKERS, JEWELLERS [*sic*], SILVERSMITHS, ENGRAVERS, &c."[30] A continued emphasis on silver is seen in their advertisement of "Jewellery [*sic*] and Silver Ware of every description," noting that "as the beauty of the latter depends much on the style of engraving, they trust, the manner in which they can execute that part of the work, will be an inducement for Ladies and Gentlemen, who may want articles of that kind, to favor them with their custom."[31] This partnership, like the last, was short-lived. An announcement of its dissolution as of September 11, 1818, appeared in the *Western Spy* (fig. 16.6), indicating that Robert would continue business at the stand, and settle all existing accounts.

Dissolution of Partnership.

THE partnership of SAMUEL & ROBERT BEST, is this day dissolved by mutual consent : All persons having accounts with them are requested to call on Robert Best, who is authorised to settle the same.

SAMUEL & ROBERT BEST.
Cincinnati, Sept. 11th, 1818.

FIG. 16.6: "Dissolution of Partnership," *Western Spy*, September 26, 1818, 3

It was not long after this that Samuel left for Rising Sun, Indiana. He was enticed, perhaps, by a call like the one published by the town's founder, John James, in August 1814 that offered "great encouragement to mechanics who wish to become settlers" in this new community on the west bank of the Ohio River, about 40 miles south of Cincinnati.[32] Samuel spent the remainder of his life in Rising Sun, and continued practicing his trade there. His will, written in 1854, notes that he had a shop "on the corner of the street and alley in Lot number One Hundred and Nine . . . the shop where I keep my jewelry store and usually work when in health . . ."[33] In 1828, he married Sarah Green who bore him four children: Alfred, Octavius Washington, Scipius, and Lucinda, and in 1849 he married his third wife, Mary Crouch, who had a son from a previous marriage.[34] Samuel died on November 22, 1859, at the age of 83.[35]

Judging from what is known about Best, his accounts, and his extant works, he was the most prolific of all of the Best family silversmiths. His success can also be estimated by the considerable assets he owned during and at the end of his life, including: a farm in Boone County, Kentucky "consisting of about sixty-seven acres" which he later sold for $2,500; two lots; a house; his shop and adjoining buildings; a "Drug Store property"; and a "barber shop" property in Rising Sun.[36]

Silver sugar tongs (fig. 16.7), a beaker, spoons with coffin-shaped handles, and broad fiddle-handled spoons with pointed shoulders (fig. 16.8) that bear the mark of Samuel Best are known, as well as tall-case clocks.[37]

A gold bracelet of hand-wrought, solid square links with a ruby and pearl clasp was given to the Cincinnati Art Museum in 1990 by a descendant of Samuel Best who maintained that the bracelet was Samuel's own handiwork, "a betrothal present to the lady after his wife."[38] The bracelet bears no marks that distinguish it as Samuel's work. However, he did advertise as a jeweler who worked in gold, and his will notes a jewelry lathe amongst his belongings.[39]

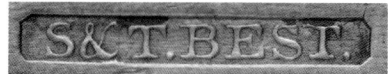

MARK 16.1

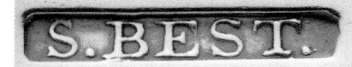

MARK 16.2

1. Burial marker, Rising Sun, Indiana, photograph in Sikes papers, Mary R. Schiff Library and Archives, Cincinnati Art Museum, record group 14, series 1, box 14, folder 5; 1850 Federal Census, Rising Sun, Indiana, roll M432_163, p. 301B, image 23; Samuel Best file, Ohio County Historical Society, Rising Sun, Indiana.

2. He advertises as all of these in the *Western Spy*, July 4, 1812, reproduced in Beckman, 16.

3. Advertisement, *Liberty Hall*, May 5, 1817, reproduced in Beckman, 17.

4. Samuel Best Diary, Mary R. Schiff Library and Archives, Cincinnati Art Museum.

5. Announcement of property sale, unmarked newspaper clipping, Best family files, Warren County Historical Society, Lebanon, Ohio, cited in Sikes papers, Mary R. Schiff Library and Archives, record group 14, series 8, box 1.

6. A later newspaper account notes that the Best family left England to escape the rule of the monarchy, who had ruled that no mechanics were permitted to emigrate to America, and that they had had to smuggle their tools through the custom house, and secure the aid of a Quaker friend to make an oath that they were not mechanics. "Robert Best Lewis," *Rising Sun Times*, 1897, Samuel Best file, Ohio County Historical Society; Samuel Best Diary, Mary R. Schiff Library and Archives; The passenger and immigration list cites Best's arrival in Philadelphia on October 17, 1801, however his diary gives the date as October 15, 1801. Ancestry.com *Passenger Lists of Vessels Arriving at Philadelphia, Pennsylvania, 1800–1882* [online database], Provo, Utah: Ancestry.com Operations Inc., 2003.

7. Grape Island is a 45-acre island on the Ohio River in Pleasants County, West Virginia, just off the shore from the communities of Grape Island and Spring Run. Little is known about Henry Best, cousin of Samuel, Thomas, and Robert. According to Samuel's diary, he found work on December 30, 1801, with one Allentrap in Bourbon (now Paris), Kentucky. There is a receipt issued in Cincinnati and dated February 1, 1805, for $10.81 paid by John S. Gano to Henry Best. John S. Gano manuscripts, Cincinnati Historical Society.

8. Samuel Best Diary, Mary R. Schiff Library and Archives.

9. Boultinghouse, 216.

10. Charles Greve, *Centennial History of Cincinnati and Its Representative Citizens*, Chicago: Biographical Publishing Co., 1904, 414; The 1869 engraving of Cincinnati in 1802 does not likely show the actual cabin that Samuel Best lived in, nor the accurate location of his dwelling (fig. E1.2).

11. *Spoon*, Ohio Historical Society, call no. H 80910.

12. John Johnston (1775–1861) was born in Ireland and immigrated to the United States at the age of 11. As a young man, Johnston served under General Anthony Wayne in the Northwest Territory. In 1802, he married Rebecca Robinson of Philadelphia in Lancaster, Ohio. Yates Publishing, *U.S. and International Marriage Records, 1560–1900* [online database], Provo, Utah: Ancestry.com Operations Inc., 2004. That same year, President Thomas Jefferson appointed Johnston to be the Indian Agent at the trading agency in Fort Wayne, Indiana Territory. From 1811 until 1829, Johnston served as the agent at the newly established agency at Piqua, Ohio. The Ohio Historical Society maintains his Piqua home as an historic site.

13. Marriage announcement, *Liberty Hall*, December 25, 1804, 3; Mrs. Wilbur Shuey, "The Best Family," May 2, 1969, Cincinnati Art Museum, curatorial file 1966.1175; An October 9, 1820 entry in Jacob Deterly's diary notes, "Sam'l Best's wife died." Jacob Deterly, *"Remarks" of Jacob Deterly: diary from 1819 to 1848; life in southern Ohio: Cincinnati, Marietta, Athens* (transcribed and indexed by Madge Hubbard and Opal Saffell), Seattle: Northwest Lineage Researcher, 1972, 2:33; "Robert Best Lewis," *Rising Sun Times*, 1897, Samuel Best file, Ohio County Historical Society.

14. Shuey, "The Best Family," 1969; Hand-written notes, Samuel Best file, Ohio County Historical Society; Sons

Samuel and Robert had died by the time Samuel's will was written. Samuel Best, will dated June 19, 1854, Ohio County Historical Society; Samuel Best, Jr. advertised the manufacture of tin and sheet iron ware in Rising Sun, in 1834. Advertisement, *Rising Sun Times*, November 29, 1834.

15. Advertisement, *Western Spy*, February 13, 1805, reproduced in Beckman, 16.

16. Ibid.

17. Torrence papers, Cincinnati Historical Society, box 33, folder 31–45.

18. Advertisement, *Western Spy*, January 1, 1806, 3, col. 4; Advertisement, *Western Spy*, July 22, 1806.

19. Advertisement, *Western Spy*, June 3, 1807, reproduced in Beckman, 16.

20. Torrence papers, Cincinnati Historical Society, box 33, folder 46–66.

21. Torrence papers, Cincinnati Historical Society, box 51, folder 4, 49.

22. Neither city directories, census nor tax data show a Henry Wallace in Cincinnati at this time, suggesting that he was not independent, but rather working for Best. There was a land grant issued for military service in Ohio to a Henry Wallace, assignee of soldier John Crowder, on April 10, 1810, but there is no evidence to conclude that it is the same Henry Wallace as our subject. Ancestry.com, *U.S. War Bounty land Warrants, 1789–1858 record for John Crowder*.

23. Wallace died on August 14, 1818, and is buried in Greenwood Cemetery, Hamilton, Ohio. Correspondence between Harold G. Miller and Marjorie Burress, Sikes papers, Mary R. Schiff Library and Archives, record group 14, series 1, box 6, file 3.

24. Advertisement, *Western Spy*, July 4, 1812, reproduced in Beckman, 16.

25. Advertisement, *Liberty Hall*, November 7, 1812, reproduced in Beckman, 12.

26. Advertisement, *Western Spy*, January 18, 1814, reproduced in Beckman, 17; A letter from J. J. Hayden, lawyer and executor of Samuel Best's estate, written to Nicholas Longworth on February 25, 1861, references a bank note—"one of the first Bank Bills issued in Cincinnati, Jan'y 15, 1810"—that was engraved by Best. John J. Rowe Collection, Cincinnati Historical Society, box 1, folder 7, 92–93; The aforementioned bank note could have been engraved for the Miami Exporting Co., which established a banking office known as the "Miami Bank " in 1807, or the Farmers' and Mechanics' Bank, whose charter was obtained by Nicholas Longworth in 1811.

27. Rev. Charles Frederic Goss, *Cincinnati: The Queen City, 1788–1912*, Cincinnati: The S.J. Clarke Publishing Co., 1912, 173.

28. Advertisement, *Western Spy*, January 18, 1814, reproduced in Beckman, 17.

29. John J. Rowe Collection, box 2, vol. 3, verso of page 65.

30. Advertisement, *Liberty Hall*, May 5, 1817, reproduced in Beckman, 17.

31. Ibid.

32. Samuel Best does not appear in Cincinnati's 1819 City Directory; Unmarked newspaper clipping, Sikes papers, Mary R. Schiff Library and Archives; John James registered the town of Rising Sun in 1816. In 1817, it was believed to have had 30 or 40 dwelling houses.

33. Samuel Best, will.

34. While some family documents mention a daughter Lenora, Samuel Best's will mentions a daughter named Lucinda. It is possible that Lucinda and Lenora are one and the same; Shuey, "The Best Family," 1969; Family history provided by Emma Hilkey, granddaughter of Thomas Best, Jr., to William Hamilton, Best family files, Warren County Historical Society; Ancestry.com, *Indiana Marriage Collection, 1800–1941* [online database], Provo, Utah: Ancestry.com Operations Inc., 2005.

35. Photograph of Samuel Best's grave marker, Sikes papers, Mary R. Schiff Library and Archives, record group 14, series 1, box 14, folder 5; Samuel Best file, Ohio County Historical Society.

36. Samuel Best, will.

37. Samuel Best, eBay listings and private collections, Cincinnati silver binders, Cincinnati Art Museum; *Tongs*, Cincinnati Art Museum, 1962.118; *Spoons*, Cincinnati Art Museum, 1969.537, 1969.538, 1969.734, 1991.1; The Samuel Best tall-case clock in the Cincinnati Art Museum's collection (1966.1175) may be the clock that was made for Mr. John Wood, and later passed down to his grandsons William O. and John C. Davie. The Museum's clock matches descriptions of the clock made for Wood in that the case has inlaid designs and the map on the face indicates India and Asia as "Tartary" and Australia as "New Holland." Conteur (Edwin Henderson), "Manufacture and Sale of Jewelry in Cincinnati During Preceding Century," *Cincinnati Enquirer*, October 23, 1923. Another clock, made for Casper Hopple in 1814, is imaged and cited in Jane Sikes, "The Best Family," *The Magazine Antiques* (July 1974): 127. This clock also features the use of "Tartary" and "New Holland."

38. Correspondence from Doris Dupraz, Samuel Best research file, Cincinnati Art Museum.

39. Advertisement, *Western Spy*, July 4, 1812, reproduced in Beckman, 16; Advertisement, *Liberty Hall*, May 5, 1817, reproduced in Beckman, 17; Samuel Best, will.

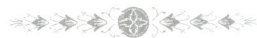

17. THOMAS BEST, SR.

1747–1813, w. 1803–1813

Thomas Best (fig. 17.1) was born in Somerset, England, in the Parish of Kingsbury Episcopi, a village and civil parish on the River Parrett, near Martock.[1] Prior to his emigration to America, he worked in Ilminster, Somerset, as a clock and watch maker—a trade that he passed on to all three of his sons, **Samuel**, **Thomas**, and **Robert**.[2] The details of Thomas' own apprenticeship and work in England are all but unknown, with the exception of a notation in Samuel's diary indicating that his father had created the dial, or clock face, at Whitelackington Church, one mile northeast of Ilminster, on November 2, 1793, and a later reminiscence of his (and his family's) consummate mechanical skill and ingenuity as "workers in gold and silver, cutlers, makers of surgical, mathematical and musical instruments."[3]

Thomas' success as a mechanic and businessman is presumed, as he possessed the means to relocate his family (three sons, a daughter-in-law, two daughters, a son-in-law, and his wife, Sarah Greenham [fig. 17.2]) to America.[4] The detailed account of his dwelling house—"pleasantly situated on Strawberry Bank,"— and its contents that appears in an auction announcement posted just before his journey to America also suggests prosperity. Listed among the articles to be sold on July 31, 1801, are "Pewter and Brass; Mahogany and other Tables; Chairs, China and Glass; Feather Beds and Bedsteads; Bureau and Bookcase; Pictures, a variety of Books . . . Kitchen Furniture; Brewing Utensils; empty Casks; A compleat [sic] Chamber Organ with Mahogany Case and stand; Microscopes and Magnifying Glasses; a collection of Tools

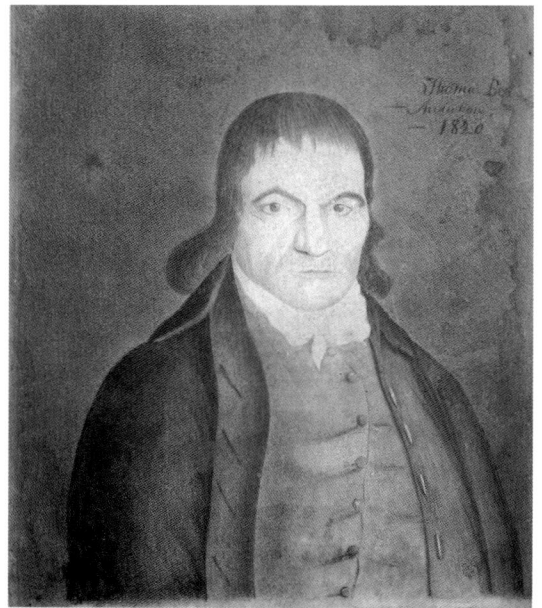

FIG. 17.1: John James Audubon (1785–1851), *Thomas Best*, 1820, black chalk, touched with neutral wash on paper, 11⅝ × 10¹⁄₁₆ in. (29.5 × 25.56 cm), Museum of Fine Arts, Boston, Gift of Maxim Karolik for the M. and M. Karolik Collection of American Watercolors and Drawings, 1800–1875, 52.1563. Photograph © [2014] Museum of Fine Arts, Boston

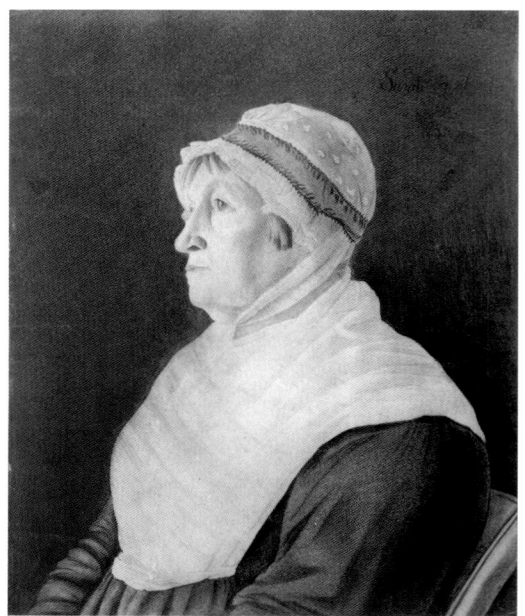

FIG. 17.2: John James Audubon (1785–1851), *Sarah Best*, 1820, graphite and black chalk on paper, possibly touched with a neutral wash, 11⅝ × 9⁹⁄₁₆ in. (29.5 × 24.29 cm), Museum of Fine Arts, Boston, Gift of Maxim Karolik for the M. and M. Karolik Collection of American Watercolors and Drawings, 1800–1875, 52.1564. Photograph © [2014] Museum of Fine Arts, Boston

in the Clock and Watch Business, and various other Articles too numerous to insert."[5]

The family reportedly left England to escape the rule of the monarchy.[6] On August 17, 1801, Thomas and his family (apart from his son Samuel, who was briefly detained by customs officials) set sail from Bristol on the Philadelphia-owned and bound vessel *The Roebuck* with Captain Bernard Raser, carrying five beds and bedding, one tool chest, four chests, eight boxes of wearing apparel, seven barrels of bread and seven guns.[7] After a little over a month's journey, they docked at Philadelphia on the evening of September 25, 1801.[8] Both Thomas and his wife Sarah found work there, although the nature of their employment is unknown.[9]

By 1803, Thomas and Sarah had settled (probably with their youngest son Robert) in Cincinnati, where they joined sons Samuel and Thomas Jr.[10] Thomas Sr. would have been about 56 years old when they arrived. There are no accounts of his work or practice in Cincinnati, other than a mention that he was building a grand organ at the time of his death. The organ had a case featuring the head of Apollo which was allegedly sculpted by the revered Cincinnati artist Hiram Powers.[11] Best died in Cincinnati on May 13, 1813, following a short illness.[12] His obituary (fig. 17.3) indicates that he was a Mason and that he had been, for several

years, a respected inhabitant of Cincinnati. "A numerous concourse of his fellow citizens attended the corpse to the grave," and it is remarked that "Nature had endowed him with a strong mind, and a penetrating judgment, which, joined to his habitual industry, displayed an eminent share of ingenuity."[13] A later account written in 1831, describes Thomas as "a man with strong and philosophical intellect," but poor, implying that Thomas may not have been as successful in America as he had been in

DIED at an advanced age, on Thursday the 13th inst. after a short illness, *THOMAS BEST*, a native of Somersetshire, in England, and for several years a respected inhabitant of this town. Nature had endowed him with a strong mind, and a penetrating judgment, which, joined to his habitual industry, displayed an eminent share of ingenuity.

He was buried with the honours of Masonry, and, besides the brethren of the Craft, a numerous concourse of his fellow citizens, attended the corpse to the grave.

FIG. 17.3: Obituary, *Western Spy* 3, no. 42, May 22, 1813

England.[14] In the twilight of his career, Thomas may have moved to Cincinnati, not to pursue his own success, but to be near to and supportive of his sons who were pursuing the family trade. His widow, Sarah subsequently moved to Lebanon, Ohio to be near her daughters, Ann and Sarah, and her son Thomas. She died there on October 24, 1828.[15]

Fiddle-handled spoons marked T. Best (mark 17.1) are known, however, it is impossible to determine if they represent the work of Thomas Best, Sr. in Philadelphia or Cincinnati, or if they were produced by his son, Thomas, who worked primarily in Cincinnati, and Lebanon, Ohio.[16]

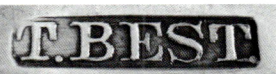

MARK 17.1

1. Mrs. Wilbur Shuey, "The Best Family," May 2, 1969, Cincinnati Art Museum, curatorial file 1966.1175. Details regarding Thomas Best's birthplace are noted in this document as having come from the back of his portrait miniature. The whereabouts of the miniature are unknown.

2. Announcement of property sale, unmarked newspaper clipping, Best family files, Warren County Historical Society, Lebanon, Ohio.

3. Samuel Best Diary, Mary R. Schiff Library and Archives, Cincinnati Art Museum; "Robert Best Lewis," *Rising Sun Times*, 1897, Samuel Best file, Ohio County Historical Society, Rising Sun, Indiana.

4. Samuel Best Diary, Mary R. Schiff Library and Archives; Thomas married Sarah Greenham (1755–1828) in 1775. Their children were Samuel (1776–1859), Thomas (1781–1844), Ann (b. 1778), Sarah (b. 1788), and Robert (1790–1830). Yates Publishing, *U.S. and International Marriage Records, 1560–1900* [online database], Provo, Utah: Ancestry.com Operations Inc., 2004.

5. Announcement of property sale, Best family files, Warren County Historical Society.

6. "Robert Best Lewis," 1897.

7. Ancestry.com, *Philadelphia Passenger Lists, 1800–1945* [online database], Provo, Utah: Ancestry.com Operations Inc., 2006.

8. Samuel Best Diary, Mary R. Schiff Library and Archives.

9. Ibid.; Neither Thomas, Sarah, nor their son Robert appears in Philadelphia city directories between 1800 and 1803.

10. Daniel Drake, MD and James C. Findlay, MD (eds.), *The Western Journal of the Medical and Physical Sciences*, Cincinnati: E. Deming, 1831, 4:612.

11. "Robert Best Lewis," 1897.

12. Obituary, *Western Spy*, May 22, 1813.

13. Ibid.

14. Drake and Findlay, *Western Journal*, 612.

15. Obituary, *Western Spy*, October 24, 1828, 1.

16. T. Best, Cincinnati silver binders, Cincinnati Art Museum; A tall-case clock, described as late 18th century and marked by Thomas Best of London could possibly be the work of our subject, but evidence of his presence in London has yet to be found. *Clock*, "Clocks and Barometers," Bonham's, Knightsbridge, London, May 18, 2010, lot 327.

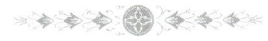

18. THOMAS BEST, JR.

1781–1844, w. 1806 or earlier–1807

Thomas Best (fig. 18.1) was born on August 21, 1781, in Ilminster, Somerset, England. He was the second son of **Thomas Best, Sr.** and Sarah Greenham.[1] We know little of his youth, with the exception that he broke his thigh playing in the churchyard on June 17, 1795, and that in 1799, he returned from an expedition, nature unknown, to Holland.[2] Thomas learned the skills required for watch and clock making, silversmithing and jewelry making in the shop of his father, with whom he and his wife Margaret Mannly (fig. 18.2) immigrated to America, docking in Philadelphia on September 25, 1801.[3] After Thomas' brother **Samuel** arrived in Philadelphia in October 1801, the brothers and their cousin Henry traveled with their belongings and stocks across land to Pittsburgh and then by keel boat to Bourbon (now Paris), Kentucky, arriving there in late December 1801. On December 31, Thomas Jr. found work "at the tinplate working at one Batterton in Bourbon."[4]

It is possible that Thomas moved on to Cincinnati as early as 1802, if he, not his father, was Samuel Best's partner in producing the spoons marked "S. & T. Best," for Colonel John and Rachel Johnston (fig. 16.2, mark 16.1).[5] Thomas is found in Cincinnati public records in March 1806, when he and his partner **Isaac Van Nuys** (Van Nuys & Best) purchased a lot on the north side of Market Street (later Pearl Street) from Charles and Pamela Vattier for $400.[6] In September, Van Nuys & Best ran an advertisement for "A small active LAD, about 14, or 15 years of age, as an apprentice to the Clock and Watch making, Silver–Smith & Jewelry business."[7] On June 5, 1807, the announcement was made that the partnership was dissolved and that all accounts could be settled with Best, who would continue in the firm's shop on Sycamore Street.[8]

By 1808, Thomas and his wife had moved to Lebanon, Ohio where he continued working in the clock, watch, jewelry, and silver business, advertising "an elegant assortment of Jewelry, Silver Ware, Steel and Gilt Watch chains, seals, keys, &c."[9] He is also remembered as a maker of "drums, buttons, etc." for the soldiers of the War of 1812.[10] His wife established a shop "under the sign of the golden bonnet" where she made silk and straw bonnets and hats.[11] Thomas continued to work in Lebanon until his death in

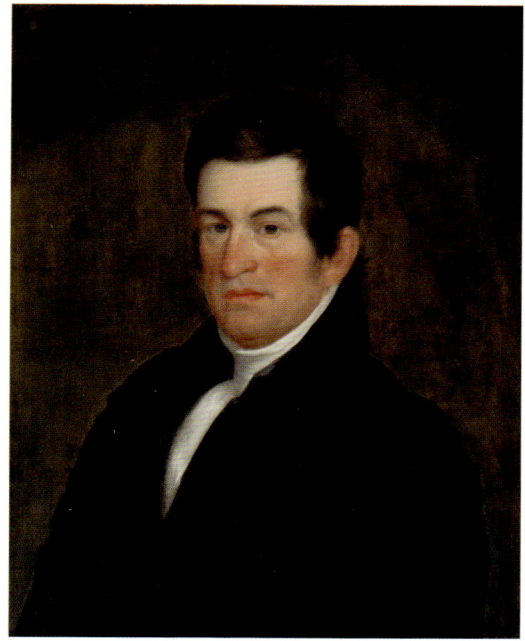

FIG. 18.1: Horace Harding (1794–1857), *Thomas Best*, 1830, oil on canvas, 26¾ × 21 in. (67.9 × 53.3 cm), Glendower Mansion, Warren County Historical Society

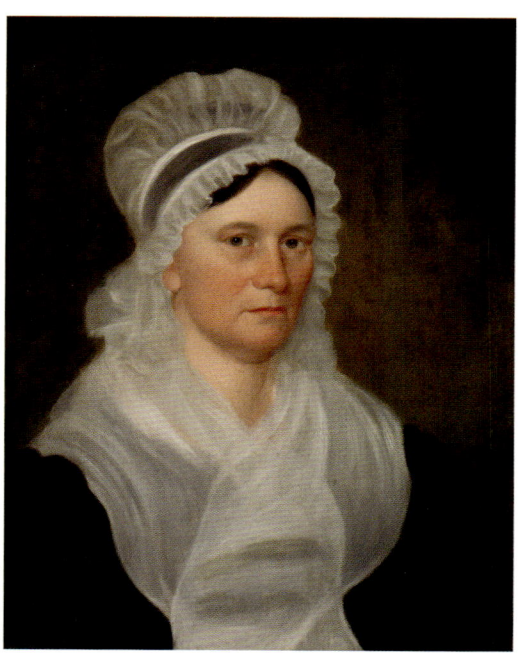

FIG. 18.2: Horace Harding (1794–1857), *Margaret Mannly Best*, 1830, oil on canvas, 26¾ × 21 in. (67.9 × 53.3 cm), Glendower Mansion, Warren County Historical Society

1844.[12] His son Henry (1804–1873) became a jeweler and gunsmith in Dayton in 1824, and he in turn passed the trade on to his son Edwin (1839–1928).[13]

Early fiddle-handled spoons marked T. Best are known, however it is impossible to determine if they represent the work of Thomas Best, Jr. or his father.[14] It is likely that coin silver spoons bearing the mark **Best & Son** are the work of Thomas Jr.'s son and grandson.[15]

A clock, now in Ohio's Warren County Historical Society collection, is attributed to Thomas Best, Jr.[16]

Silver stamped "Best & Dover" may be associated with Thomas Jr. and his nephews Thomas (b. 1801) and Samuel Best Dover (b. 1802), sons of Ann Best and James Dover, however, no proof of this connection has been found.[17]

1. Mrs. Wilbur Shuey, "The Best Family," May 2, 1969, Cincinnati Art Museum, curatorial file 1966.1175.
2. Samuel Best Diary, Mary R. Schiff Library and Archives, Cincinnati Art Museum.
3. Margaret was born in Ilminster, Somerset, England, in 1783. She died in Paducah, Kentucky, in 1858. Shuey, "The Best Family" 1969; Samuel Best Diary, Mary R. Schiff Library and Archives.
4. Samuel Best Diary, Mary R. Schiff Library and Archives.
5. *Spoon*, Ohio Historical Society, call no. H 80910, (fig. 16.2, mark 16.1); Sikes papers, Mary R. Schiff Library and Archives, record group 14, series 13, box 1.
6. Correspondence between Marjorie Burress and Harold G. Miller, September 30, 1989, Sikes papers, Mary R. Schiff Library and Archives,

record group 14, series 1, box 6, folder 3; *Hamilton County Deed Book G1*, 10; This property was mortgaged to Vattier the same day, for the same amount. *Hamilton County Deed Book D1*, 206. Vattier, of Le Havre, moved west with General St. Clair's army. He amassed a fortune dealing in real estate. In 1813, Best and Van Nuys sold this property, bought in 1806, to Andrew Hopple for $700. *Hamilton County Deed Book L1*, 188. By this time, Best was in Warren County (Lebanon) and Van Nuys was in Butler County, according to notarial examinations associated with the transfer.
7. Advertisement, *Western Spy*, September 23, 1806, reproduced in Beckman, 19.
8. Advertisement, *Western Spy*, June 5, 1807, reproduced in Beckman, 20.
9. Best's advertisement in the *Western Star* (Lebanon, Ohio) on October 5,

1822, thanks the public for their support for "upwards of fourteen years," indicating that he arrived there around 1808. In previous instances, Best's advertisements in the *Western Star* on June 9 and August 4, 1808, were cited as evidence that he was in Lebanon by 1808. However, these advertisements could not be located, possibly due to a transcription error in the dates; Advertisement, *Western Star*, August 19, 1826, 4.
10. Augustus Waldo Drury, *History of the City of Dayton and Montgomery County, Ohio*, Cincinnati: The S.J. Clarke Publishing Co., 1909, 2:57.
11. Advertisement, *Western Star*, August 19, 1826, 4; Advertisement, *Western Star*, September 2, 1826, 4.
12. Drury, *History of the City of Dayton*, 575.
13. Jane Sikes, "The Best Family," *The Magazine Antiques* (July 1974): 123; Advertisement, *Dayton Journal and

Advertiser*, October 4, 1831, 3; Drury, *History of the City of Dayton*, 575–576.
14. Thomas Best, eBay listings and private collections, Cincinnati silver binders, Cincinnati Art Museum.
15. Garth's Auction, *May 23, 2009 Americana Catalog featuring the Third Annual Ohio Valley Auction*, Delaware, Ohio: Garth's Auction, 2009, lot 81; Best & Son, eBay listings and private collections, Cincinnati silver binders, Cincinnati Art Museum.
16. Columbus Museum of Art, *Made in Ohio: Furniture 1788–1888*, Columbus: Columbus Museum of Art, 1984, 68–69. The support for this attribution is unclear.
17. Shuey, "The Best Family," 1969; Best & Dover, eBay listings and private collections, Cincinnati silver binders, Cincinnati Art Museum.

19. SOLOMON RAPHAEL BIESENTHAL

1829–1903, w. 1850–1856

Solomon (Salo) Biesenthal was born in Germany on March 26, 1829.[1] He departed from the port of Hamburg on the *George Washington* and arrived in New York with his wife, Rosalie (1818–1907), his daughter Julia (1845–1922), and five chests on August 24, 1848.[2] He and his family first appear in Cincinnati in the 1850 Federal Census. His son, Raphael, is listed as 8 months old and born in Ohio, suggesting that they had established themselves in Cincinnati by 1849.[3] Between 1851 and 1856, Solomon appeared in Cincinnati city directories as a jeweler and watch maker, listed under the business category of "jewelry, silverware, watches &c.," working at 242 West Sixth Street (where he also probably lived), and in 1856 at 252 West Fifth Street.[4] An unfavorable report from R.G. Dun & Co. credit reporters in November 1856 explains why he left Cincinnati: "Was in the jewelry and swindling business—has cleared out. Was associated with a band of thieves whose plunder he received and sold. He turned state's evidence and thus escaped, is regarded here as unmitigated scoundrel."[5]

Biesenthal relocated to Louisville, Kentucky, appearing in the city's 1859/60 Directory as a watch maker and jeweler. He lived and worked there until at least 1900.[6] In 1870, he reported a capital investment of $2,000, two employees earning wages of $600 a year, and a production of 53 watches, 215 spectacles, 80 rings, and 50 spoons.[7] One of his employees was his son, Raphael (Ralph).[8] Solomon died on June 16, 1903, and is buried in The Temple Cemetery in Louisville.[9]

The mark (mark 19.1) of Solomon Raphael Biesenthal has been found on spoons with both tipped fiddle and tipped exaggerated fiddle-shaped handles with rounded or pointed shoulders.[10]

S R.BI ES ENTHAL.

MARK 19.1

1. This date is inscribed on Biesenthal's burial marker in The Temple Cemetery, Louisville, Kentucky. However, his immigration record and the 1850 Federal Census suggest a birth year of 1819, and records kept by the Herman Meyer & Son funeral home indicate a birth date of March 25, 1824. His birthplace is given in various sources as Poland, Germany, and Prussia; Burial marker, The Temple Cemetery, Louisville, Kentucky, www.meyerfuneral.com/cemetery /TheTemple/stones/A6,10,5 /Biesenthal,SolomonR1903.jpg; Funeral record, The Temple Cemetery, Louisville, Kentucky; 1850 Federal Census, Cincinnati, Hamilton, Ohio; 1880 and 1900 Federal Censuses, Louisville, Jefferson, Kentucky; Ancestry.com, *New York Passenger Lists, 1820–1957* [online database], Provo, Utah: Ancestry.com Operations Inc., 2010.

2. Ancestry.com, *New York Passenger Lists, 1820–1957.*
3. 1850 Federal Census, Cincinnati, Hamilton, Ohio.
4. 1851/52, 1853, 1855, 1856 Cincinnati City Directories.
5. Ohio, Vol. 2, p. 295, R.G. Dun & Co. Collection, Baker Library, Harvard Business School.
6. Boultinghouse, 67; 1870, 1880, 1900 Federal Censuses, Louisville, Jefferson, Kentucky.
7. 1870 Manufacturing Census, Louisville, as reported in Boultinghouse, 67.
8. 1869 Louisville City Directory; 1870 Louisville City Directory; 1900 Federal Census, Louisville, Jefferson, Kentucky.
9. Burial marker, The Temple Cemetery, Louisville, Kentucky.
10. S.R. Biesenthal, eBay listings and private collections, Cincinnati silver binders, Cincinnati Art Museum.

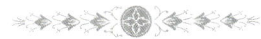

20. HENRY BLISS

1808–1862, w. 1849–1862

Henry Bliss was born on August 6, 1808, in Springfield, Massachusetts, to Jacob Bliss (1763–1829) and Mary Collins (1765–1854).[1] He was in Cincinnati and working as a clerk in the shop of **Nathan L. Hazen** (157 Main Street) by 1849, while boarding at the Broadway Hotel.[2] Hazen (b. 1809) and Bliss were both born in Massachusetts—in cities about 35 miles apart—thus it is possible that they knew one another prior to arriving in Cincinnati. In 1851,

when Hazen died suddenly, Bliss purchased most of his stock.[3] With Hazen's widow, Hannah Jeanette Twitchell, as a silent partner, Bliss continued in business at Hazen's stand.[4] He ran advertisements for "Watches, Jewelry and Silver Ware" in city directories between 1853 and 1858.[5] Credit reporters evaluated his business as fair and his means as little, and noted that he was careless about paperwork and often late for payments.[6] By about 1856, he had wed Hazen's widow, who provided most of Bliss' financial means through her inherited $10,000 life insurance policy and property in Texas.[7]

In April 1858 Bliss was "trying to sell out for the purpose of superintending a retail concern which **Duhme & Co.** intended to open," and much of his stock was purchased by **William C. Swift**.[8] The following year, Bliss was employed at Duhme & Co., but soon left to establish a liquor store with C.A. Smith.[9] Unfortunately, Smith died shortly after their venture had started.[10] In 1860, census records report the value of Bliss' personal estate at $300. The value of his wife's personal estate is not provided.[11] In 1861, he was working as a jeweler at 103 Broadway.[12] He died on June 15, 1862, survived by his wife and two of their children, Henry (about 1856–1899) and Emma (b. 1859).[13]

It is doubtful that Bliss manufactured any of the silverware that he sold. Mark 20.1 has been documented on several tipped, exaggerated fiddle-handled spoons with pointed shoulders (fig. 20.1). "H. BLISS.," stamped incuse, has been observed on a salt ladle with a die pressed handle in a fiddle threaded pattern and rounded shoulders.[14] There were at least two other silversmiths by the name of Henry (Henri) Bliss: one who worked in New Orleans and died in September 1830, and another who worked in Bennington, Vermont, around 1875–1880.[15] They are not to be confused with our subject.

MARK 20.1

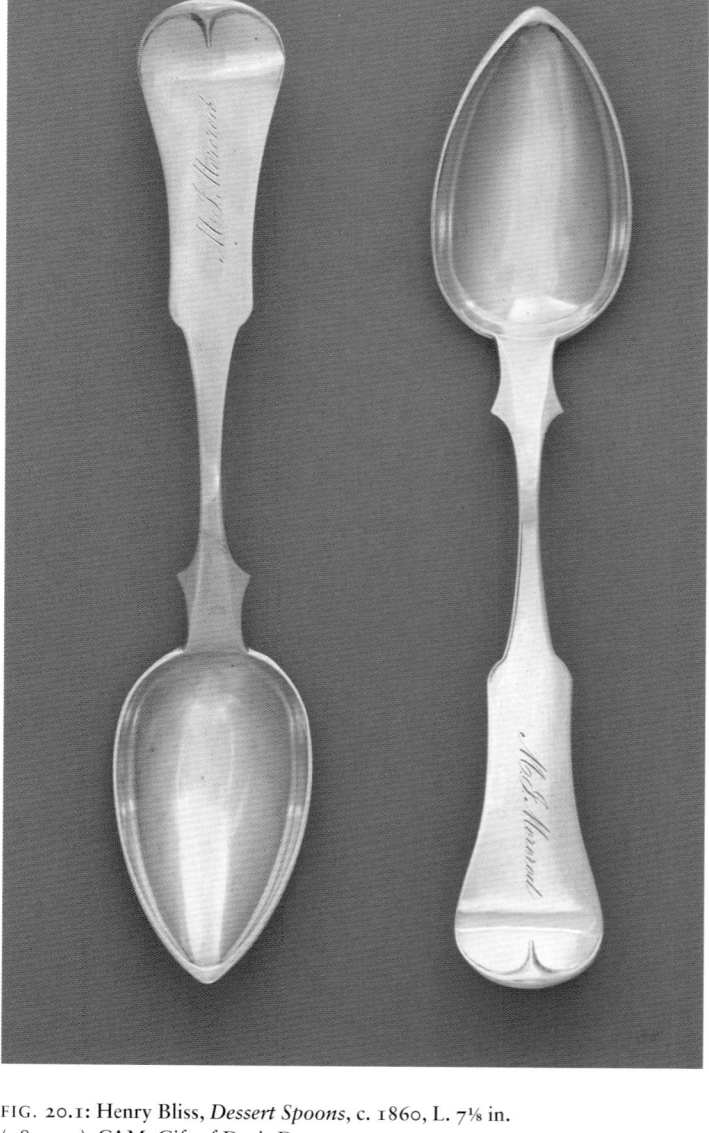

FIG. 20.1: Henry Bliss, *Dessert Spoons*, c. 1860, L. 7⅛ in. (18.1 cm), CAM, Gift of Doris Dupraz, 1991.3.1–2

1. Wagner, Schwarzentrub, Koehly & McCoy Family Tree, Ancestry.com, accessed September 27, 2012; Death notice, *Centinel of Freedom* (Newark, NJ), July 1, 1862, 3.
2. 1849/50 Cincinnati City Directory; It is likely that Bliss spent some time in Newark, NJ before arriving in Cincinnati, as his death notice appears in a Newark newspaper and notes Bliss as "formerly of this city." Death notice, *Centinel of Freedom*, July 1, 1862.
3. There are reportedly dinner forks with the marks of both Hazen and Bliss in the collection of the Peabody Essex Museum, Salem, MA. Dean Lahikainen, Curator, Peabody Essex

Museum, to Amy Dehan, telephone conversation, 2012.
4. Ohio, Vol. 1, p. 295, R.G. Dun & Co. Collection, Baker Library, Harvard Business School.
5. Advertisement, 1853 Cincinnati Business Directory, reproduced in Beckman, 23; Advertisements were published in the Cincinnati city directories in 1855 (page 144), 1856 (page 128), 1857 (page 146), and 1858 (page 58).
6. Ohio, Vol. 1, p. 295, R.G. Dun & Co. Collection.
7. Ohio, Vol. 3, p. 258, R.G. Dun & Co. Collection.
8. Ibid.
9. 1859 Cincinnati City Directory; Ohio,

Vol. 3, p. 263, R.G. Dun & Co. Collection.
10. Ibid.
11. 1860 Federal Census, Cincinnati, Hamilton, Ohio.
12. 1861 Cincinnati City Directory.
13. Ohio, Vol. 3, p. 263, R.G. Dun & Co. Collection; Death notice, *Centinel of Freedom*, July 1, 1862; Toni Eyvonne Beacraft, "Descendants of Charles, Generation No. 30, family tree," familytreemaker.genealogy.com; Hannah Jeanette and Henry Jr. are buried in Spring Grove Cemetery, Cincinnati, Ohio with members of the Hazen family. Henry Bliss appears to be buried in Springfield Cemetery, Hampden County, Massachusetts.

Burial records, Spring Grove Cemetery, Cincinnati, Ohio; "Henry Bliss," *Find A Grave*, www.findagrave.com, accessed November 5, 2012.
14. Henry Bliss, eBay listings and private collections, Cincinnati silver binders, Cincinnati Art Museum.
15. *Crescent City Silver*, New Orleans: Historic New Orleans Collection, 1980, 82; Wm. Erik Voss, "Henri O. Bliss," *American Silversmiths*, http://freepages.genealogy.rootsweb.com/~silversmiths/makers/silversmiths.

21. CHRISTIAN F. BROCKMAN[1]

1814–1898, w. 1839–1857

Christian Frederic Brockman was born in Hanover, Germany, the son of Ernst Brockman (1773–1854).[2] He had arrived in Cincinnati by May 25, 1839, when he advertised in the *Cincinnati Advertiser & Journal* as a "watch and clock maker" on Main Street between Sixth and Seventh Streets, stating that he repaired watches and jewelry "at the shortest notice."[3] When he relocated to Main Street between Seventh and Eighth Streets in 1848, he added silverware and jewelry to his stock, advertising in the category for "Jewelry, Silver Ware, Watches, etc." in the Cincinnati Business Directory. An illustrated advertisement in the 1850/51 City Directory trumpeted, "WATCH MAKER, AND DEALER IN SILVER WARE, JEWELRY, &C.," and added, "Also, Engraving Done."[4] Brockman's occupation, given in the alphabetical section of the city directories, was "watchmaker" until 1849/50 when "jeweler" was used; in 1857, he was a "silversmith and jeweler." The R.G. Dun & Co. credit reports for the years Brockman was in Cincinnati indicate that he was "industrious" and a "good business man."[5] In February 1858 Brockman sold the business to Adolph Stutz, who had worked for him since 1856, and moved with his family to a farm near Lynchburg in Clinton County, Ohio where he lived until his death in 1898.[6]

Silver spoons marked "F. Brockman" (mark 21.1) with tipped, exaggerated fiddle handles and pointed shoulders have been documented.[7] This was most likely the mark used by C.F. Brockman: not only did he advertise as a dealer in silverware, but he was also listed as Frederic Brockman in some of the early city directories.

Brockman and his wife, Margaret Meunthe Brockman (1823–1908), were the parents of eight daughters: Louisa, Amelia, Emma, Dorothy, Dorethea, Anna, Tina, and Alice.[8]

MARK 21.1

1. A number of variants for both Brockman's given and surname are found in census and city directory listings of the era. There were two brothers working in Cincinnati: Christian Frederic, a watch maker and silversmith, and Christian E., who was a china and glass dealer. In other cases, where there were two brothers who had the same first name but different middle names, the first names that they used were not always consistent. C.F. Brockman appears as Christian, Charles and Frederic in various primary records. Variants observed in the spelling of his surname are Brockmann, Brockman, Broakman, and Brookman. Brockman is used here, based on wares attributed to C.F. Brockman that are punched "F. BROCKMAN".
2. C F. Brockman, burial record, Spring Grove Cemetery, Cincinnati, Ohio; 1860, 1870, 1880 Federal Censuses, Clark, Clinton, Ohio; Ernst Brockman's burial record indicates his place of death as "Ohio River, near Evansville." Ernst Brockman, burial record, Spring Grove Cemetery.
3. Advertisement, *Cincinnati Advertiser & Journal*, 1839, reproduced in Beckman, 25. Notations included in the advertisement indicate that it was first run on May 25 and would continue to run for a year.
4. Advertisement, 1850/51 Cincinnati City Directory, 59, reproduced in Beckman, 25.
5. Ohio, Vol. 1, p. 89, R.G. Dun & Co. Collection, Baker Library, Harvard Business School.
6. Ibid.; 1860, 1870, 1880 Federal Censuses, Clark, Clinton, Ohio; C.F. Brockman, burial record.
7. Beckman, 25; *Teaspoon*, Elizabeth Beckman Collection, Cincinnati Museum Center.
8. Burial records, Spring Grove Cemetery; 1860, 1870, 1880 Federal Censuses, Clark, Clinton, Ohio.

22. JOSEPH BUDD

b. circa 1800, w. 1836

Joseph Budd was listed as a watch maker on the east side of Main Street, between Seventh and Eighth Streets for one year, 1836.[1] Budd was born in New Jersey around 1800, and worked in Mount Holly and Pemberton before coming to Hamilton, Ohio, around 1830.[2] He was listed there as a silversmith and clock maker with a shop on the north side of the public square in 1833. He reportedly sold out in 1842.[3] He might well be the New Jersey-born silversmith, J.M. Budd, living in Columbus, Ohio, recorded in the 1850 Federal Census, and he was likely the father of Major Joseph L. Budd (1834–1922), a Civil War veteran and merchant who lived in Lebanon, Hamilton, and Cincinnati.[4]

While in Hamilton, Budd created at least one tall-case clock.[5] Marks 22.1 and 22.2 have been found on spoons and ladles with fiddle handles and rounded shoulders (fig. 22.1). Spoons bearing mark 22.1 have, on occasion, also been marked with an eagle with down-turned wings, facing left, in a square cartouche (mark 22.3); a leaf; or a butterfly-shaped mark.[6] These are manufacturers' marks. The eagle may have been the manufacturing mark for either **Edward Kinsey** or **Pulaski Scovil**. The leaf is unidentified, and the butterfly-shaped mark has strong ties to someone working in Philadelphia.[7]

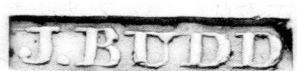

MARK 22.1

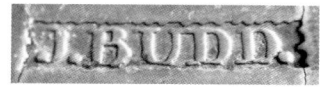

MARK 22.2

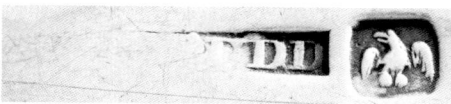

MARK 22.3

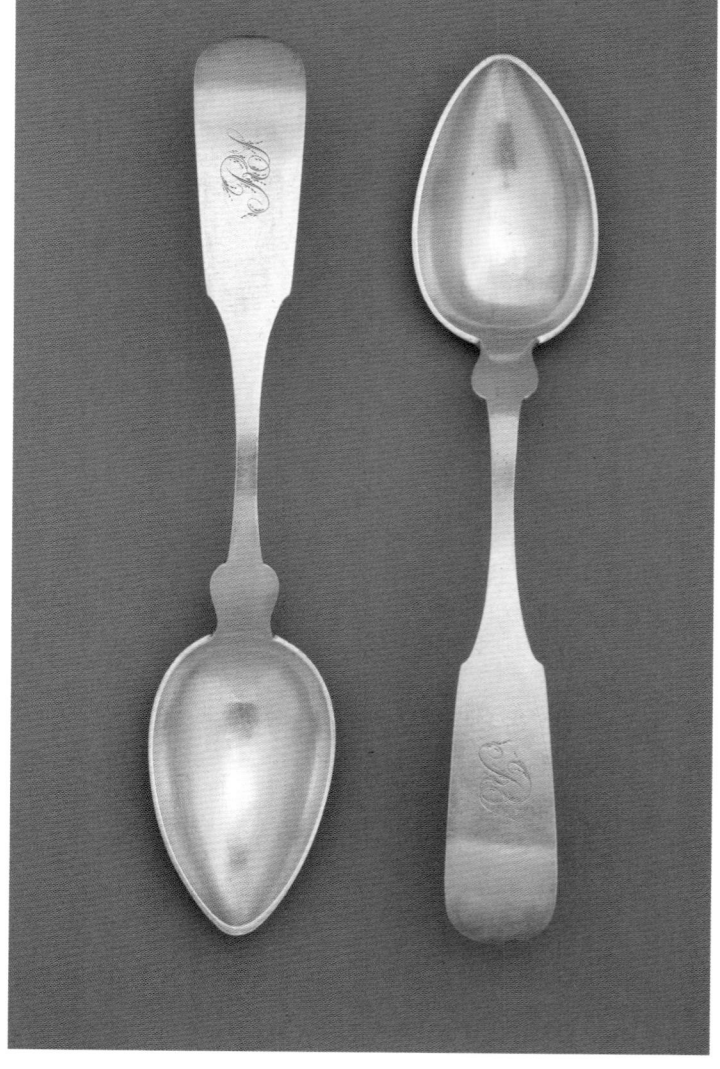

FIG. 22.1: J. Budd, *Pair of Tablespoons*, c. 1830s, Private Collection

1. 1836/37 Cincinnati City Directory.
2. William E. Drost, *Clocks and Watches of New Jersey*, Elizabeth, New Jersey: Engineering Publishers, 1966, 49.
3. James W. Gibbs, *Buckeye Horology: A Review of Ohio Clock and Watch Makers*, Columbia, PA: The Art Crafters Printing Co., 1971, 2.
4. 1850 Federal Census, Columbus, Franklin, Ohio; There is a Joseph Budd, born in Pennsylvania, living in Clermont County, Ohio, in 1860 and 1870, who is buried with his wife, Charlotte, in Spring Grove Cemetery. His occupation is recorded as farmer. This man probably has no relation to our subject. 1860 and 1870 Federal Censuses, Pierce, Clermont, Ohio; Burial records, Spring Grove Cemetery, Cincinnati, Ohio; Major Budd's death certificate indicates that he was born in Mt. Holly, New Jersey to Joseph Budd and Mary Downs. Arne Trelvik, "Biographies with Warren County Connections," *The USGenWeb Project*, http://www.rootsweb.ancestry.com /~ohwarren/military/cwb.htm#Budd.
5. Gibbs, *Buckeye Horology*, 2.
6. Joseph Budd, eBay listings and private collections, Cincinnati silver binders, Cincinnati Art Museum.
7. John R. McGrew, *Manufacturers' Marks on American Coin Silver*, Hanover, PA: Argyros Publications, 2004, 98, 140.

23. SAMUEL T. CARLEY

1810–1898, w. 1836–1865

Born in New York, Samuel T. Carley worked in New York City between 1832 and 1835 where he was listed in city directories as both a jeweler and a merchant.[1] Carley's obituary states that he arrived in Cincinnati in 1836.[2] This is supported by the fact that he appears as a partner in the firm Rhodes, Anthony & Carley (also known as **Rhodes, Anthony & Co.**) in the 1837 *Western Address Directory*, which was likely prepared for publication in late 1836.[3] This partnership had disbanded by 1839, as Carley listed independently as a jewelry manufacturer working on the north side of Fourth Street, between Main and Sycamore, in the 1839/40 City Directory. Two years later, he moved to Third Street between Main and Walnut.[4]

Carley's partnership with **William Owen** was established by 1846, when the directory includes **Owen & Carley**, watch makers, at 135 Main Street. By 1849, their partnership had dissolved, and Carley had joined jeweler Henry Wray in S.T. Carley & Co. Described in directory listings as manufacturing jewelers, they operated on the north side of Baker Street between Walnut and Vine until 1851, when they moved to 150 Walnut Street, five doors south of Fourth Street.[5] In the 1850 Products of Industry Census, they reported as silversmiths and jewelers with $2,000 of capital, who employed a maximum of 12 hands, paid $480 in wages that year, and used $3,600 worth (or 240 ounces) of gold and $500 worth of precious stones to produce a product (including jobbing and repairing) worth $3,000.[6] Their only known advertisement notes, "Diamonds Set in the Newest Styles, And every variety of Jewelry made to order."[7] In 1850, the firm exhibited "silver ornaments" at the Mechanics' Institute Annual Fair, and in 1851, the firm employed watch maker Edward Solomon.[8] S.T. Carley & Co. had dissolved by 1853, when Owen and Wray list independently in the city directory.

Carley continued as a manufacturing jeweler at 148 Walnut Street.[9] In 1856, he moved to the southwest corner of Fourth and Main Streets, where he continued until his retirement from the business in 1865.[10] According to census records, in 1860, he was living in Millcreek Township with an estimated $2,000 in real estate and $1,000 in personal property, and in 1870, he was farming in Clermont County with $6,000 in real estate and $800 in personal property.[11] He died April 13, 1898, in Mount Holly, Clermont County, at the age of 82, and was remembered in his obituary as the first jeweler to recognize the beauty of pearls found in the Miami River, and to send them to the East.[12] He was a serious collector of fossils and a principal member of the Western Academy of Natural Sciences.[13]

Carley's wife Mary was born in New York and died on February 7, 1891.[14] The Carleys are buried at the Odd Fellows Cemetery in Amelia, Ohio.[15] They had at least seven children: Eliza, Susan, William S., Oliver, Edwin, Mary O., and Samuel Thane.[16]

Throughout his long career, Carley's focus on the manufacture and retail of jewelry is evident in city directory listings, in the occupation descriptions of those he employed, and in the sentiments shared in his obituary. Beginning in 1840, Carley employed **A. Falize** (b. 1811), a Belgian jeweler who may well have been a member of the Falize dynasty of Parisian jewelers.[17] Falize boarded with Carley until 1846.[18] John Heil, a jeweler, also boarded, and presumably worked with Carley, in 1843 and 1844.[19] Other employees included **Fedor Ruppiler** and **Herman Serodino**.[20]

Evidence of Carley's participation in the local silver trade is found in spoons with fiddle handles and pointed shoulders, and in a mustard ladle with an exaggerated tipped fiddle handle and pointed shoulders bearing his mark (mark 23.1).[21] While this mark uses only the Carley surname, it is believed, based on the forms of the flatware, that this is Samuel T. Carley's mark. While Carley may have been producing silver jewelry, the silver flatware bearing his mark was most likely produced elsewhere and merely retailed in his shop.

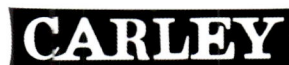

MARK 23.1

1. Samuel T. Carley's grave marker, Odd Fellows Cemetery, Amelia, Ohio; 1850, 1860 Federal Censuses, Millcreek, Hamilton, Ohio; 1870, 1880 Federal Censuses, Monroe, Clermont, Ohio; Paul Von Khrum, *Silversmiths of New York City*, New York: Von Khrum, 1978, 25.

2. "The Death of Samuel T. Carley," *Jewelers' Circular and Horological Review* 8 (March 3, 1898): 1.

3. Advertisement, *Western Address Directory*, 1837, 328; Carley is also mentioned in a published endorsement by Rhodes, Anthony & Carley for Wm. T. Anderson's chemical powder, used for polishing silver. Advertisement, *Cincinnati Daily Gazette*, February 8, 1837.

4. 1842 Cincinnati City Directory. In his 1842 directory listing, Carley is described as a manufacturer of jewelry.

5. 1849/50, 1850/51, 1851/52 Cincinnati City Directories; Advertisement, *Gray's Cincinnati Business Mirror and City Advertiser, 1851–1852*, reproduced in Beckman, 26; Wray was boarding with Carley in 1849.

6. 1850 Federal Non-Population Census Schedules, Products of Industry, Schedule 4, Hamilton County, Ohio.

7. Advertisement, *Gray's Cincinnati Business Mirror and City Advertiser, 1851–1852*, reproduced in Beckman, 26.

8. Ohio Mechanics' Institute, *Board of Directors' Minute Book 1840–1969*, vol. 1, *December 1840–August 1854*, University of Cincinnati Archives and Rare Books Library, 88; *Report of the Committee of the Tenth Exhibition of the Ohio Mechanics' Institute*, Cincinnati: Marshall & Langtry, 1850, 26; 1851/52 Cincinnati City Directory.

9. 1853 Cincinnati City Directory.

10. 1856–1865 Cincinnati City Directories; Beginning in 1859, the city directories note that Carley occupies the upstairs of this building.

11. 1860 Federal Census, Millcreek, Hamilton, Ohio; 1870 Federal Census, Batavia, Clermont, Ohio.

12. "The Death of Samuel T. Carley" (March 3, 1898).

13. John P. Foote, *The Schools of Cincinnati, and Its Vicinity*, Cincinnati: C.F. Bradley & Co., 1855, 59; Henry A. Ford and Mrs. Kate B. Ford, *History of Cincinnati, Ohio*, Cleveland: L.A. Williams, 1881, 230–231.

14. Death notice, *The Clermont Sun*, http://www.rootsweb.ancestry.com /˜ohclecgs/newsletter/obituarys.html; 1850 Federal Census, Cincinnati, Hamilton, Ohio.

15. Samuel Thomas Carley, *Find A Grave*, http://www.findagrave.com/cgi -bin/fg.cgi?page=gr&GRid=4415470.

16. 1850 Federal Census, Cincinnati, Hamilton, Ohio; 1860 Federal

Census, Millcreek, Hamilton, Ohio; 1870, 1880 Federal Censuses, Monroe, Clermont, Ohio.

17. There are many variations for Falize's first name (Alexander, Arsine, Arséne) in historical records. Only once, in the 1846 Cincinnati City Directory, does his name appear as Alexander, the given name cited in both Beckman and Boultinghouse. Due to this ambiguity, A. Falize is used for this study. Falize arrived in New York from Le Havre, France in October 1837. In 1842, he opened a shop in Lexington, Kentucky, with W. Eaves. For more on the House of Falize in Paris, see Katherine Purcell, *Falize: A Dynasty of Jewelers*, New York: Thames and Hudson, 1999; 1840–1846 Cincinnati City Directories; Ancestry.com, *New York Passenger Lists,*

1820–1957 [online database], Provo, Utah: Ancestry.com Operations Inc., 2010; Boultinghouse, 110; Katherine Purcell to Janet Haartz, correspondence, June 13, 2011, Cincinnati Art Museum, A. Falize research file.

18. 1843, 1844, 1846 Cincinnati City Directories. By 1849, when the next directory was published, Falize appears to have left Cincinnati.

19. 1843, 1844 Cincinnati City Directories.

20. 1853–1859 Cincinnati City Directories.

21. Samuel T. Carley, eBay listings and private collections, Cincinnati silver binders, Cincinnati Art Museum; Beckman, 27, 29.

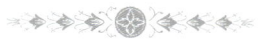

24. PETER CAZELLES

b. circa 1787,[1] w. 1815–1825

Peter Cazelles, a Roman Catholic from Bordeaux, France began his apprenticeship, which was to last five years, with Louis Poncet in Baltimore, Maryland on September 23, 1803.[2] Tax records place him in Cincinnati by 1810.[3] In 1814, he provided music for performers at the Shellbark Theatre on Main Street, and in January 1815 he married Clarissa Mennessier, daughter of Francis and Mary Mennessier.[4] On July 28, 1815, Cazelles announced his return from Baltimore and the opening of his shop on Main Street, "next door to Mr. Philips' book-store on the hill." He detailed his holding of fashionable jewelry and "Silver Soup Ladles, Do. Table, Desert [sic] and Tea-spoons, Do. Sugar Tongs and Mustard do."[5] In 1817, Cazelles' household included himself, two women over 21 (Clarissa, and probably his mother-in-law), a male child (his son), and a girl between 12 and 21 (probably a servant).[6] In June of that year, he advertised his receipt from Boston of "A GENERAL ASSORTMENT OF Jewellery [sic] and Silver Ware" available at low prices at his new stand, "the brick building on Upper Market near the corner of Main street."[7] In September, the Cazelles and Mary Mennessier sold lot 109 Main Street for $1,900 to John Sutherland.[8] Cazelles was listed as a silversmith at 112 Main Street

in 1819, and **Jacob Deterly** records a house fire at the Cazelles' on February 22, 1821, noting that it was "extinguished without destroying the whole building."[9] The 1825 City Directory lists Cazelles as a silversmith and a jeweler at 113 Main Street, and in June of that year he advertised as a "WATCH MAKER, SILVER SMITH AND JEWELLER" offering an "elegant assortment of the most fashionable JEWELRY AND SILVER WARE" with the highest prices given for old gold and silver.[10] But not long after, Cazelles was declared insane by the Court of Common Pleas, and fellow French émigré Joseph Dorfeuille, naturalist and director of the Western Museum, was appointed his guardian.[11] Dorfeuille announced the closing of Cazelles' business in September.[12] We do not know what became of Cazelles or his family.

The mark of Peter Cazelles (mark 24.1) has been found on spoons with fiddle handles and pointed shoulders.[13]

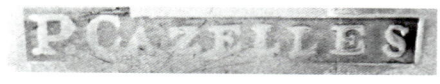

MARK 24.1

1. Jennifer Faulds Goldsborough, *Silver in Maryland*, Baltimore: Maryland Historical Society, 1983, 246.
2. Apprentice records show that Cazelles' father was "living and now in France" when Cazelles began his apprenticeship with Poncet, a silversmith, goldsmith and jeweler who worked in Baltimore between 1800 and 1822. Poncet was likely part of the fourth wave of French immigrants who came to work in Baltimore around 1793. J. Hall Pleasants and Howard Sill, *Maryland Silversmiths, 1715–1830*, Baltimore: Lord Baltimore Press, 1930, 79–80, 169–170, 276; Rev. John H. Lamott, *History of the Archdiocese of Cincinnati, 1821–1921*, New York: F. Pustet, 1921, 37; V.F. O'Daniel, "The Centenary of Ohio's Oldest Catholic Church (1818–1918)," *The Catholic Historical Review* 4, no. 1 (April 1918): 31.
3. Ronald V. Jackson, Accelerated Indexing Systems, comp., *Ohio Censuses, 1790–1890* [online database], Provo, Utah: The Generations Network Inc., 1999.
4. Beckman, 27; Charles Greve, *Centennial History of Cincinnati and Its Representative Citizens*, Chicago: Biographical Publishing Co., 1904, 1:468; Sikes papers, Mary R. Schiff Library and Archives, Cincinnati Art Museum, record group 14, series 1, box 7, file 2.
5. Advertisement, *Liberty Hall*, July 28, 1815, reproduced in Beckman, 27.
6. 1817 Hamilton County Tax List included in Ronald V. Jackson, Accelerated Indexing Systems, comp., *Ohio Censuses, 1790–1890*; Beckman, 27; Sikes papers, Mary R. Schiff Library and Archives, record group 14, series 1, box 7, file 2.
7. Advertisement, *Liberty Hall*, June 18, 1817, reproduced in Beckman, 28.
8. Beckman, 27, cites Virginia Ray Cummins' book on Hamilton County Court Records as a source and uses the spelling "Sutherland." Jane Sikes uses the spelling "Sunderland." Sikes papers, Mary R. Schiff Library and Archives, record group 14, series 1, box 7, file 2.
9. Jacob Deterly, *"Remarks" of Jacob Deterly: diary from 1819 to 1848; life in southern Ohio: Cincinnati, Marietta, Athens* (transcribed and indexed by Madge Hubbard and Opal Saffell), Seattle: Northwest Lineage Researcher, 1972, 1:12.
10. Advertisement, *West Union Village Register*, June 1825, reproduced in Beckman, 28.
11. Guardianship appointment dated August 31, 1825, Probate Court Journal Entries (1791–1837), vol. 2, page 339, Hamilton County Probate Court; Beckman, 28.
12. Advertisement, *Cincinnati Advertiser*, September 8, 1825, reproduced in Beckman, 28.
13. Peter Cazelles, eBay listings and private collections, Cincinnati silver binders, Cincinnati Art Museum.

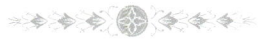

25. STEPHEN D. CHOATE

1814–1861,[1] w. 1836–1840

Stephen Decatur Choate was born in Delaware.[2] He appears in Cincinnati city directories for the first time in 1836, listed as a silversmith living at Cyrus Coffin's boarding house.[3] The next city directory was not printed until 1839, when Choate is recorded as a silversmith working at the shop of **Joseph Draper**.[4] It is likely that Choate came to Cincinnati to work with Draper who had also come from Delaware. Choate's tenure in Cincinnati was brief. He relocated to Louisville, appearing in its city directories from 1841 to 1852.[5] Choate's advertisement in the 1852 Louisville City Directory bills his establishment as a lamp store, but also notes that he is a dealer in watches, jewelry, lamp glasses, fancy goods, and most importantly to this study, a "manufacturer of silver ware, &c."[6] Census records from 1860 list him as a watch maker in Shelby County, Kentucky.[7] Choate's wife, Anne V. Roberts, was a native of Wales, and his five known children, Harrison, Elizabeth A., Edward, Robert, and Louis, were all born in Kentucky after 1840.[8] **Robert W. Choate**, who was living with Stephen D. Choate's family in 1850, and who advertised as a watch maker and jeweler in Louisville, is presumed to be the older brother of our subject.[9] Stephen D. Choate is buried in Grove Hill Cemetery in Shelbyville, Kentucky.[10]

At the time of this study, the only known silver marked by Choate are spoons and a counterstruck coin. The spoons, with rounded shoulders and tipped fiddle handles, bear incuse stamps reading, "S.D. CHOATE / 5 STREET / LOUISVILLE" or "S.D. CHOATE LOUISVILLE." The counterstruck 1834 dime, used as a form of advertising, reads "S. D. CHOATE / SILVERSMITH / LOUISVILLE."[11]

1. Stephen Decatur Choate, *Find A Grave*, www.findagrave.com; Stephen Decatur Choate, burial record, www.grovehillcemetery.net.
2. Ibid.; Goodwin Family Tree, www.ancestry.com; Lynda Jones Family Tree, www.ancestry.com; 1850 Federal Census, Louisville District 3, Jefferson, Kentucky; 1860 Federal Census, District 1, Shelby, Kentucky; 1839/40 Cincinnati City Directory.
3. 1836/37 Cincinnati City Directory.
4. 1839/40 Cincinnati City Directory.
5. Boultinghouse, 87.
6. Boultinghouse, 88.
7. 1850 Federal Census, District 1, Shelby, Kentucky.
8. 1850 Federal Census, Louisville District 3, Jefferson, Kentucky; 1860 Federal Census, District 1, Shelby, Kentucky; Betty R. Darnell, "Jefferson County, Kentucky, Recorded Births, 1852–1901," *Louisville Metro Archives*, http://www.louisvilleky.gov/NR/rdonlyres/E4E78EA7-3617-465B-805A-7B78F5AD267A/0/JeffCoBirths.pdf, 42.
9. Boultinghouse, 87–88.
10. Stephen Decatur Choate, *Find A Grave*, www.findagrave.com; Stephen Decatur Choate, burial record, www.grovehillcemetery.net.
11. Stephen Choate, eBay listings and private collections, Cincinnati silver binders, Cincinnati Art Museum.

26. FRANCIS CLARK

b. about 1800, w. 1846–1850

Francis Clark, his wife Martha (b. about 1805), and his first son James (b. about 1838) were all born in New Jersey.[1] The family may have been in Cincinnati by 1843, as Clark's second son, Francis is recorded as born in Ohio that year.[2] Credit reporters note that Clark came from New York, but specifics about his training and career prior to his arrival in Cincinnati are not yet known.[3] Between February and October 1846, he and **James F. Rhodes** formed F. Clark & Co.[4] Rhodes was reported to have "no cap[ital], but good connexions [*sic*]," and to be a jeweler by trade.[5] It is probable that Clark was the capitalist, and perhaps the bookkeeper (as noted in the 1846 City Directory), while Rhodes managed the firm's stock, which was noted as good.[6] When the short-lived firm dissolved in the fall, Clark continued in business alone.[7] There was no city directory published in 1847, but in the 1848/49 Cincinnati Business Directory, Clark is listed as working at 103 Main Street (third door above Third Street), under the heading of "Jewelry, Watches and Silver Ware Stores and Manufacturers."[8] As early as November 1848 he was running advertisements in Sandusky, Ohio for his Cincinnati firm.[9] Closer to home, in December of that year, he advertised under the headline of "Jewelry," and heralded his inventory as a "splendid stock of rich Goods, embracing a full assortment of Watches and Jewelry recently selected with much care and taste."[10] The advertisement continued, "Besides Watches and Jewelry, he offers a great variety of Silver Goods, embracing—Spoons, Forks, Cups, &c.," and also plated wares. In the 1849/50 City Directory he listed as a jeweler, but in October 1849 he announced that he was closing his business and offering "for sale at cost his entire stock of Goods."[11] His closure was also advertised in northern Ohio.[12] The 1850 Federal Census enumerates his occupation as silversmith, but the 1850/51 City Directory lists him as a clerk, working for his former partner, James F. Rhodes, who had taken over Clark's business.[13] Clark could not be found in Cincinnati city directories or census listings after 1850. He does not appear to be affiliated with the F.H. Clark active in Tennessee or Georgia.[14]

Spoons with tipped, exaggerated fiddle handles and pointed shoulders that bear marks 26.1 and 26.2 are known.[15] The illustrated teaspoon (fig. 26.1), struck with mark 26.1, matches, in form and in its engraving, "Carlisle," a set of five teaspoons marked by **E. & D. Kinsey** (fig. 66.15). It is unclear whether mark 26.2 was used by Francis Clark or **Patrick F. Clark**.[16] Both Francis and Patrick F. Clark were active in Cincinnati around the same time. Any relation between the two is unknown. Francis Clark was primarily a retailer who bought stock from silver manufacturers, some local, and stamped it with his name.

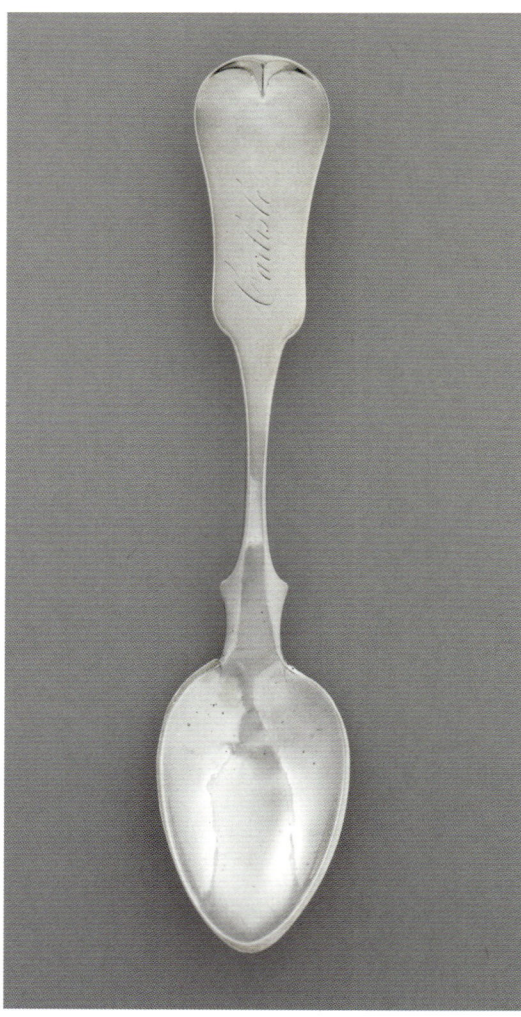

FIG. 26.1: Francis Clark, *Teaspoon*, 1848–1850, L. 6⅛ in. (15.6 cm), CAM, Given by Elizabeth M. and Annie W. Anderson in memory of their mother, Mrs. Buckner W. Anderson, 1969.739. Inscription: "Carlisle" for George and Sarah Carlisle, married 1828. George Carlisle (1797–1863) was one of Cincinnati's pioneer bankers and businessmen.

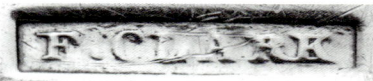

MARK 26.1

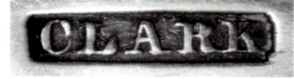

MARK 26.2

1. 1850 Federal Census, Cincinnati, Hamilton, Ohio.
2. Ibid.; The 1842, 1843, and 1844 Cincinnati City Directories include a Francis B. Clark, grocer, boarding at Mrs. L. Floyd's, and the 1845 Cincinnati City Directory includes an F. Clark, bookkeeper, boarding at Mrs. L. Floyd's. This may or may not be our subject.
3. Ohio, Vol. 1, p. 141, R.G. Dun & Co. Collection, Baker Library, Harvard Business School.
4. Ibid.
5. Ibid.
6. Ibid.
7. Ibid.
8. 1848/49 Cincinnati Business Directory; Advertisement, *Cist's Weekly Advertiser*, December 3, 1848, reproduced in Beckman, 29.
9. Advertisement, *Daily Sanduskian*, November 8, 1848, 2. This advertisement ran almost daily between November 6, 1848, and October 27, 1849.
10. Advertisement, *Cist's Weekly Advertiser*, December 3, 1848.
11. Advertisement, *Daily Cincinnati Commercial*, October 29, 1849, reproduced in Beckman, 29.
12. Advertisement, *Daily Sanduskian*, October 30, 1849, 2. This advertisement ran almost daily between October 29 and November 10, 1849.
13. Dun reporters state "Jas F. Rhodes succeeds C. & R. [Clark & Rhodes]." However, there is no known documentation, to date, including marked wares, which support the notion that the firm was ever known as Clark & Rhodes. Ohio, Vol. 1, p. 141, R.G. Dun & Co. Collection.
14. Boultinghouse, 89; Stephen G.C. Ensko, *American Silversmiths and Their Marks*, New York: Dover Publications, 1983, 37; Ralph M. Kovel, *Kovel's American Silver Marks*, New York: Crown Publishers, circa 1989, 74.
15. Francis Clark, eBay listings and private collections, Cincinnati silver binders, Cincinnati Art Museum.
16. Voss attributes mark 26.2 to Levi Clark (1801–1875) of Connecticut. However, its appearance on a spoon in a typical Cincinnati shape suggests a Cincinnati attribution. Wm. Erik Voss, *American Silversmiths*, http://freepages.genealogy.rootsweb.ancestry.com/~silversmiths/makers/silversmiths.

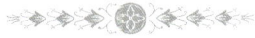

27. PATRICK F. CLARK

w. 1846–1851

Patrick F. Clark first appears in Cincinnati in 1846 as a silversmith, boarding with Abraham Hanna on Seventh Street between Plum and Western Row.[1] When the next city directory was published in 1849, he was listed as a silversmith on the west side of Plum Street, between Ann and Mason Streets.[2] Clark does not appear in the 1850/51 City Directory, but is listed on the south side of Third Street, between Smith and Park, in the 1851/52 edition.[3] After that, he disappears from city records. It is possible that our subject is the same Patrick F. Clark recorded in the 1842–43, 1851–54, and 1866 Philadelphia city directories as a silversmith and coppersmith.[4] There is also record of a P.F. Clark in Pittsburgh in 1874.[5]

Spoons with narrow, shoulderless stems and ball-shaped terminals—a popular design during the 1840s and 1850s—have been documented with the mark of P.F. Clark (mark 27.1).[6] It is unclear whether the mark "CLARK" in a rectangular cartouche (see **Francis Clark**, mark 26.2), found on spoons with tipped, exaggerated fiddle handles and pointed shoulders, was employed by Patrick F. Clark or Francis Clark.

1. 1846 Cincinnati City Directory.
2. 1849/50 Cincinnati City Directory.
3. 1851/52 Cincinnati City Directory.
4. The following listings are found in Philadelphia City Directories: 1842: P. F. Clark, silversmith, 158½ Cherry; 1843: Patrick F. Clark, silversmith, rear 44 South Third Street; 1851–1854: Pat. Clark, coppersmith, 1 Myer's Ct.; 1866: Patrick Clark, coppersmith, 2121 Filbert.
5. 1874 Pittsburgh City Directory: P.F. Clark, silversmith, 84 Robinson St.
6. Similar spoons have been noted with the mark of **E. & D. Kinsey**. P.F. Clark, eBay listings and private collections, Cincinnati silver binders, Cincinnati Art Museum.

P. F. CLARK

MARK 27.1

28. RICHARD CLAYTON

1807–1877, w. 1834–1858

Richard Clayton first appeared in Cincinnati in 1834, listing in the city directory as a clock and watch maker. He arrived with considerable means, as he purportedly built the five-story building near the Public Landing at the southeast corner of Sycamore and Second Streets that was home to his business and his later concerns until at least 1871.[1] Clayton was born in England and nothing is known of his lineage, training, or life prior to his arrival in Cincinnati, except that he had developed a passion for hot-air ballooning in his native land.[2] His shop was often referred to as Clayton's Balloon Store, as in addition to conducting his watch, jewelry, and fancy goods business, he was reported to have made balloons as well.[3] In the 1840 City Directory he advertised as both a watch maker and an aeronaut.

Clayton's first and most famous voyage, in his *Star of the West* balloon, "the first ever constructed West of the Mountains," occurred on April 8, 1835.[4] Known in international press coverage as "Clayton's Ascent" and memorialized in the illustrated bandbox and storage jug (figs. 28.1 and 28.2), the journey began in Cincinnati—Clayton launched his balloon from an amphitheatre on Court Street (between Race and Elm Streets)—and ended in Monroe County, Virginia, today known as Clayton, West Virginia. Clayton set a distance record, traveling 350 miles in nine and a half hours.[5] Along the way, once an altitude of a mile had been reached, he dropped a 20-pound dog in a basket which landed safely by way of a parachute.[6] In total, Clayton is believed to have made about 30 balloon voyages, his last known flight taken in 1844.[7] None were as remarkable as his first, but he is credited with undertaking the first air-mail delivery in 1835. Clayton sold tickets to his launches at 50 cents per person, but he did not make money in this endeavor.[8]

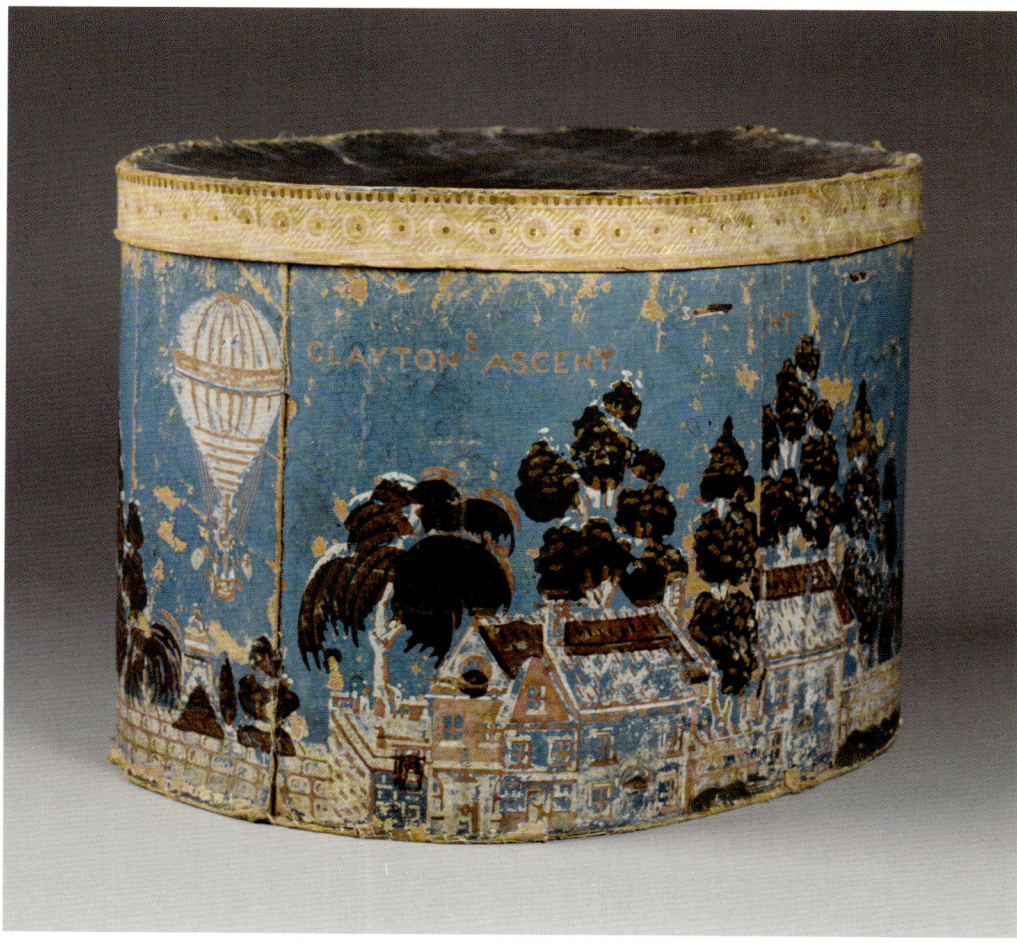

FIG. 28.1: *Bandbox: Clayton's Ascent,* c. 1835–1850, pasteboard, wallpaper, newspaper and string, 13 × 15 × 18½ in. (33 × 38.1 × 47 cm), CAM, Gift of Jim and Sheri Swinehart, 2013.23a–b

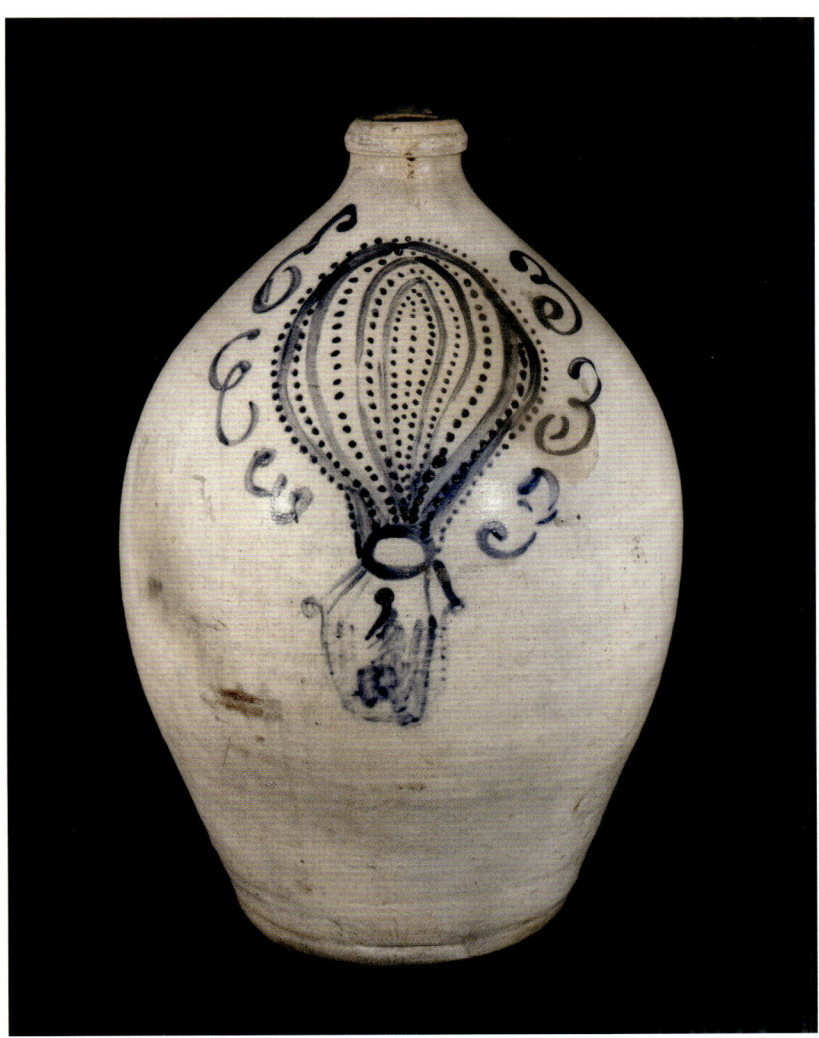

FIG. 28.2: *Jug*, c. 1835–1850, stoneware, H. 16 in. (40.6 cm), Frank and Barbara Pollack, American Antiques & Art, Highland Park, Illinois

WATCHMAKER. 555

CLAYTON'S
Wholesale House for Gold and Silver
WATCHES,
JEWELRY, WATCH MATERIALS, TOOLS, &c.

All articles in the above line sold at New York and Philadelphia prices. An immense saving to Watch Makers and Dealers in Jewelry to purchase at this establishment, for the expense of travelling east, the loss of time, and the great risk of getting goods out safe will be entirely saved.

Watch Materials and Tools will be sold from twenty-five to fifty per cent. lower than they have ever been sold in the western country. Lunet Glasses, (warranted the best imported,) such as have been selling here at $9 50, will be sold at $7 50. Also, the best Quelet Mainsprings fifty per cent. reduced in price, and a similar reduction in the price of almost every article.

The above statement may appear to some as a mere business puff, but R. C. assures the public that if any persons who have lately purchased east, (goods such as are above described) will show him their bills, that he will supply them with the same kind at precisely the same prices.

He would also respectfully invite those friends who have hitherto favoured him with their patronage, and the public in general, to call and see his goods, particularly his Gold and Silver Watches, (for a better and more splendid assortment cannot be found west of the mountains,) consisting of

M. J. Tobias' best Gold Levers, cased in various ways;

and Levers of other eminent makers; and a variety of Ladies' Gold Watches, with lever and cylinder escapements. A fine assortment of Silver Ware Plated Goods, Brittania Ware, &c.

☞ *Store on the Southeast corner of Sycamore and Second streets, commonly called Clayton's Balloon Store.*

FIG. 28.3: Advertisement, *Robinson & Jones' Cincinnati Directory for 1846*, Cincinnati: Robinson & Jones, 1846, 555

Clayton's business advertisements often included images of hot-air balloons, and in 1846, he ran the extensive advertisement seen here (fig. 28.3), which provides the earliest indication of Clayton as a wholesaler and dealer in silverware. Other advertisements tell us that "the Atlantic Steamers 'Europa' and 'Canada', [on] every trip that they have made within the last six months, have brought large supplies of watches directed to R. Clayton," and that his business, largely dependent on jewelers of the western states who could buy from him at "15 to 25 percent less than the like sold in the wholesale stores of New York," was so "immense" that he employed 12 men as salesmen and assistants.[9] Credit reports validate the growth and success of Clayton's business, assessing his worth, including "heavy" holdings in real estate, as $30,000 in 1852.[10] Clayton was known to have traveled "much

through Europe" and was distinguished by maintaining a cash-only business.[11]

In January 1843 Clayton married Jane Jenkins, and in March 1844 he wed Mary Ann Jenkins, presumably the sister of his first wife. His only daughter, Charlotte (b. about 1845) was "educated and brought up by her two aunts, Fanny and Martha Jenkins," suggesting that her mother died prematurely.[12] **Henry Jenkins**, Clayton's brother-in-law, began working with Clayton around 1847.[13] In 1853, Clayton transferred his interest in the jewelry department to Jenkins and retained interest solely in the watch and clock trade.[14] Jenkins occupied the first floor of Clayton's building and Clayton worked on the second floor. Acting as manager of Clayton's portion of the business, Jenkins was charged no rent and had access to Clayton's employees as needed.[15] William O'Hara and

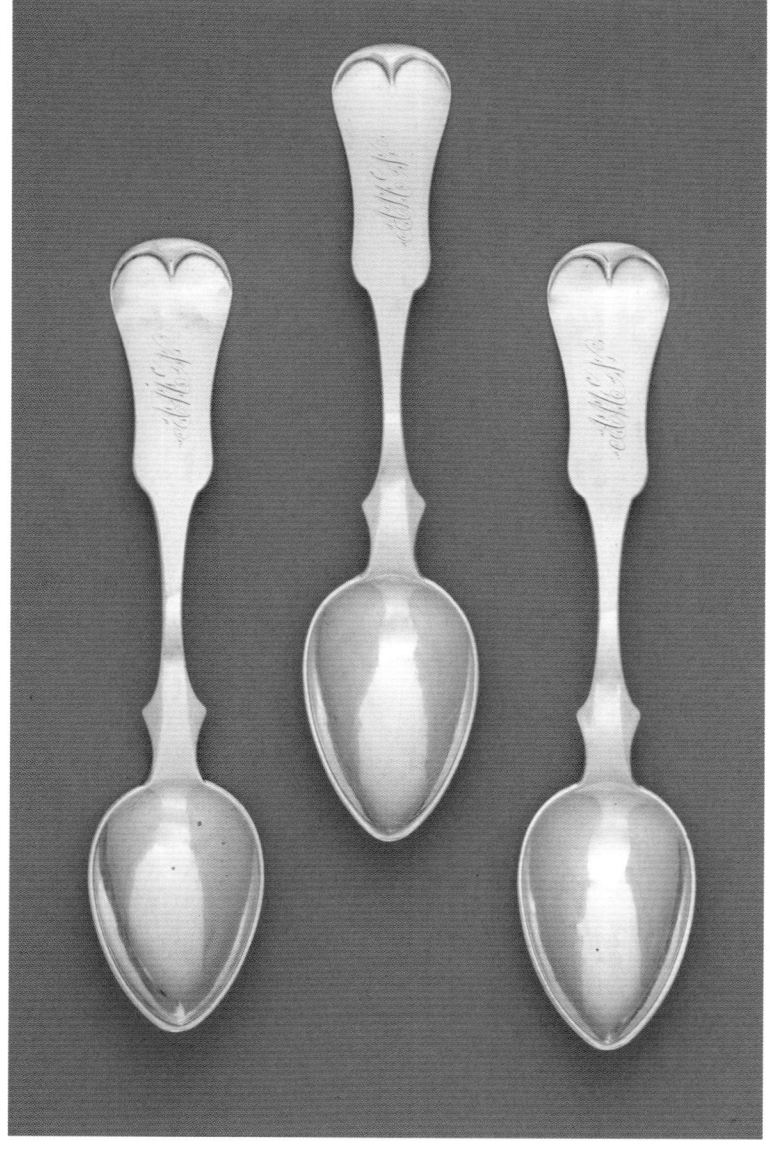

FIG. 28.4: Richard Clayton, *Teaspoons*, c. 1850, L. 6 in. (15.2 cm), CAM, Museum Purchase: John S. Conner Fund, 2012.4a–c

his nephew **Edward J. Hughes**; **William H. Gayle**; **John B. Morris**; watch makers **Frederick W. Marmet**, **M. C. Motch** and **Garret T. Dorland**; and **Frederick Anton Dassell**, a jeweler, were among Clayton's employees.[16] By December 1858 Clayton had reportedly sold his remaining interest in the business to Jenkins who continued at the same location as H. Jenkins & Co. with partners John B. Morris, and George B. Harting.[17]

Census records from 1860 report Clayton as a retired merchant living in Ludlow, Kentucky, with $75,000 in real estate and $25,000 in personal property.[18] In 1854, he had purchased Somerset Hall, a large Federal style mansion in Ludlow,

constructed in 1832, sited high on a hill, facing the Ohio River.[19] Jenkins continued to use Clayton's name in advertising, and it is thought that Clayton maintained some interest in the business.[20] One can speculate that Clayton's temporary retirement may have been brought on by health issues, as an R.G. Dun report of March 1861 notes that Clayton is "still out of business—at times is more or less mentally deranged."[21] Not long after this, Jenkins sold the business to Morris and Harting, and Clayton traveled east with Jenkins to meet with creditors.[22] Harting died soon afterwards and Morris continued in business under his own name, although Clayton was believed to have had a controlling interest over Morris and the firm.[23] The 1862 City Directory indicates that Clayton was boarding at the Broadway Hotel, which suggests that he was then living in Cincinnati on a part-time basis. In 1863, Morris advertised as "Successor to R. Clayton, Importer and Dealer in Watches, Jewelry, Silver Ware, Watch-Makers' Tools and Materials, Watch Glasses, Clocks, Regulators, &c." at Sycamore and Second Streets where he continued in business until relocating to Walnut Street around 1870.[24]

Clayton's will was composed in Brooklyn, New York, in September 1874.[25] His reasons for relocating to New York are unknown. Clayton died there on February 19, 1877, and is buried in Green Wood Cemetery.[26] His estate, at the time of his death, was estimated at $100,000.[27]

Known silver forms bearing mark 28.1 or the incuse stamp "R. CLAYTON." include teaspoons (fig. 28.4), tablespoons, serving spoons, ladles and sugar shovels, all with pointed shoulders, and tipped, exaggerated fiddle handles. A ladle, in a private collection, bears mark 28.2 which includes a shield-breasted eagle, facing left, in a square cartouche. This eagle is likely the manufactory mark of **Edward Kinsey**.[28] The incuse stamp, "CLAYTON" has been documented on a master butter knife with a threaded, fiddle handle.[29] Mark 28.3 has been found on a teaspoon with a slightly exaggerated fiddle handle and pointed shoulders.[30] It is not believed that Clayton made any of the silver bearing his marks.

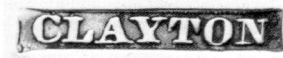

MARK 28.1

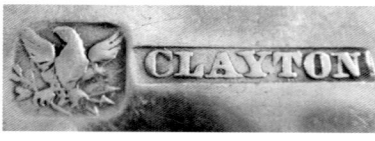

MARK 28.2

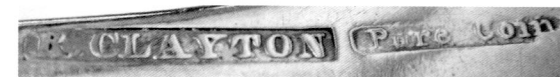

MARK 28.3

1. The address is given as 26 Sycamore in the 1853 Cincinnati Directory; 1834–1871 Cincinnati City Directories; Ohio, Vol. 1, p. 90, R.G. Dun & Co. Collection, Baker Library, Harvard Business School.

2. 1860 Federal Census, Ludlow, Kenton, Kentucky; Obituary, *Cincinnati Commercial Tribune*, February 22, 1877; For more information on Clayton's career as an aeronaut, see Maurer Maurer, "Richard Clayton: Aeronaut," *Bulletin of the Historical and Philosophical Society of Ohio* 13 (April 1955): 142-150, and the primary sources cited therein.

3. Advertisement, 1846 Cincinnati City Directory, 555; Ohio, Vol. 1, p. 90, R.G. Dun & Co. Collection.

4. Advertisement, *Cincinnati Republican*, March 25, 1835, reproduced in Beckman, 30.

5. Ibid.; "Richard Clayton: Aeronaut" (April 1955).

6. "Richard Clayton: Aeronaut" (April 1955).

7. "Clayton, The Aeronaut," *Ohio State Journal*, November 24, 1841; "Aerial Voyaging," *Vermont Journal*, June 27,

1844; R.G. Dun credit reporters cite that he had made 50 ascensions by 1847, but this cannot be documented. Ohio, Vol. 1, p. 90, R.G. Dun & Co. Collection.

8. "Richard Clayton: Aeronaut" (April 1955); "Mr. Clayton's Second Ascension," *Cincinnati Advertiser*, May 9, 1835, reproduced in Beckman, 31; Ohio, Vol. 1, p. 90, R.G. Dun & Co. Collection.

9. Advertisement, *Cincinnati Enquirer*, January 1, 1850, 9; Advertisement, *Cincinnati Enquirer*, January 5, 1850, 2.

10. Ohio, Vol. 1, p. 90, R.G. Dun & Co. Collection.

11. Clayton is noted on a passenger list in 1860, traveling from Liverpool to New York. Ancestry.com, *New York Passenger Lists, 1820–1957* [online database], Provo, Utah: Ancestry.com Operations Inc., 2010; Ohio, Vol. 1, p. 90, R.G. Dun & Co. Collection; Advertisement, *Cincinnati Daily Gazette*, 1846, reproduced in Beckman, 33.

12. Hamilton County marriage records, Hamilton County Probate Records, vol. A 11, 91; Hamilton County

marriage records, vol. A 12, 391; Beckman, 34; 1860 Federal Census, Ludlow, Kenton, Kentucky; The Jenkins sisters were born in Ireland, as per the 1860 Federal Census.

13. Ohio, Vol. 1, p. 433, R.G. Dun & Co. Collection.

14. Ibid.

15. Ibid.

16. Ohio, Vol. 1, p. 128, R.G. Dun & Co. Collection; Ohio, Vol. 2, p. 31, R.G. Dun & Co. Collection; 1856 Cincinnati City Directory; Ohio, Vol. 1, p. 428, R.G. Dun & Co. Collection.

17. Ohio, Vol. 1, p. 90, R.G. Dun & Co. Collection.

18. 1860 Federal Census, Ludlow, Kenton, Kentucky.

19. Kenton County Public Library, "Genealogy," *Somerset Hall*, http://www.kenton.lib.ky.us /genealogy/history/ludlow/article.cf m?ID=109.

20. 1863–1865 Cincinnati City Directories.

21. Ohio, Vol. 1, p. 90, R.G. Dun & Co. Collection.

22. Ohio, Vol. 1, pp. 132, 148, R.G. Dun & Co. Collection.

23. Ohio, Vol. 1, p. 428, R.G. Dun & Co. Collection.

24. 1863–1870 Cincinnati City Directories; Advertisement, *Cincinnati Enquirer*, October 27, 1870.

25. Richard Clayton, will dated September 19, 1874, proved February 27, 1877, New York, King's County Estate Files, 1866–1923, https://famil-ysearch.org/pal:/MM9.1./N7LJ-92Q.

26. Richard Clayton, will; Richard Clayton, burial record, Green Wood Cemetery, Brooklyn, New York, http://www.green-wood.com /burial_results/index.php.

27. Richard Clayton, will.

28. John R. McGrew, *Manufacturers' Marks on American Coin Silver*, Hanover, PA: Argyros Publications, 2004, 98.

29. Richard Clayton, eBay listings and private collections, Cincinnati silver binders, Cincinnati Art Museum.

30. *Teaspoon*, Elizabeth Beckman Collection, Cincinnati Museum Center.

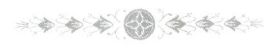

29. PELEG COLLINS

b. 1798, w. 1825–1850

Peleg Collins was born in 1798, in Foster, Providence County, Rhode Island, to Quaker parents, Beriah Collins (1772–1864) and Alice Fish (b. 1773).[1] It is presumed that he learned his trade in the Northeast. A reminiscence of 1889 notes that his father was a jeweler.[2] Prior to working in Cincinnati at 166 Main Street in 1825, he was a clock and watch maker, and jeweler, in Coventry, Rhode Island.[3]

In February 1829 Collins entered into partnership with Samuel A.M. Shipp in the clock, jewelry and watch-making business, operating at 44 Main.[4] A mention in employee **Jacob Deterly**'s diary of Collins' return from the East in April 1832 indicates that part of **Shipp & Collins**' business was retail.[5] By 1834, the partnership had dissolved, as both men ran their own advertisements, Shipp at 53 Main Street and Collins at 117 Main Street, in an April edition of the *Cincinnati Daily Gazette*.[6] Shipp's store was robbed in November 1834, and he announced his retirement the following January.[7] He sold his remaining stock to Collins who continued business at 53 Main Street, offered "a handsome assortment of

Watches (all descriptions,) Jewelry, fancy goods, Plated and Britannia Ware, Clocks, Silver Ware, &c. &c.," and listed as a watch maker and silversmith in city directories.[8] Watch maker Harry R. Smith (see **Harry R. Smith & Co.**) was boarding with Collins, and probably working with him between 1842 and 1844.[9]

In 1841, Collins became director of the Bank of Cincinnati, and it was likely this position that enabled him to come to the aid of fellow jeweler, watch maker and fancy goods retailer **Nathan L. Hazen** in 1843.[10] Hazen had assumed too much debt and placed his property in Collins' hands until he could recover, at which time he took Collins in as a partner.[11] **Hazen & Collins** advertised as watch makers, silversmiths, and jewelers on Main Street, offering "All kinds of Silver Ware made to order."[12] However, both men appear to have been primarily retailers, a fact which suggests that they were probably acting as agents when it came to taking requests for silver made to order. Their partnership ended in January 1847.[13]

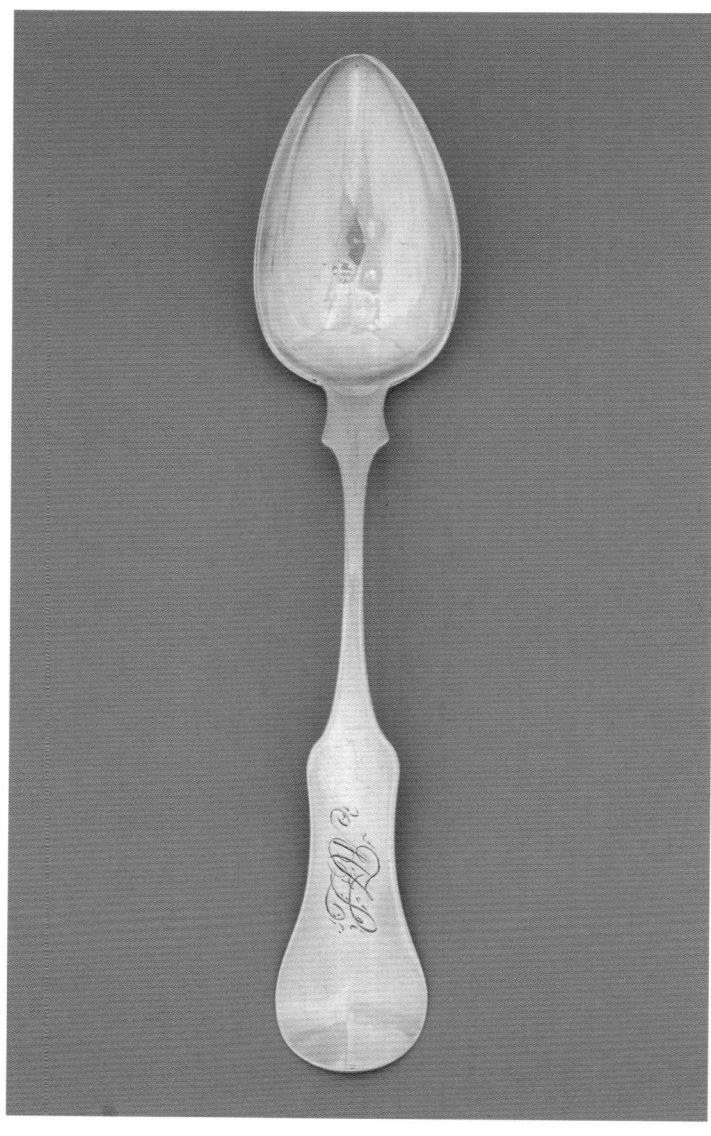

FIG. 29.1: Peleg Collins, *Tablespoon*, c. 1840–1850, L. 8¾ in. (22.2 cm), CAM, Given by Elizabeth M. and Annie W. Anderson in memory of their mother, Mrs. Buckner W. Anderson, 1969.733

In 1848, Collins was reported to have capital worth $900.[14] In March, he ran an advertisement illustrated with the image of a large ship that announced his return from the East with a bounty of goods.[15] R.G. Dun & Co. credit reporters note that he had traveled to Philadelphia, bought largely on credit, then returned to Cincinnati and sold the goods to his son, Charles E. Collins, "a swindler." Peleg then "decamped for St. Louis and now laughs at his creditors refusing to say anything."[16] Nothing is known of Peleg Collins' activities in St. Louis, but he soon returned to Cincinnati,

and was listed in 1849 as a jeweler at Fifth Street, between Elm and Plum.[17] Charles ran an advertisement in November 1849 for his watch, jewelry and silverware business at 121 Main Street.[18] Peleg retired from the business in 1850.[19] That year, he appears in federal census records twice.[20] In August, he is listed in Cincinnati as a silversmith, living with his family (wife Mary, Charles Edwin, b. 1825, and Harriet, b. about 1831), and in November, he is recorded living alone in Sacramento, and "eating house" is given as his occupation.[21] In 1866, he appears on a voter register as a jeweler in Los Angeles, and in the 1870 Census he is listed there as a farmer. His family is not listed with him.[22]

Mark 29.1 has been observed on spoons with fiddle handles and pointed shoulders as well as those with tipped, exaggerated fiddle handles and pointed shoulders (fig. 29.1). A sugar shell with a tipped fiddle handle and no shoulders has been documented with the mark "COLLINS" in a rectangular cartouche and "PURE COIN [pellet]" in a separate rectangular cartouche.[23]

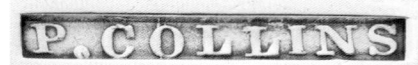

MARK 29.1

1. Ken and Shirley Hoxie, "Fifth Generation," *Descendants of Lodowick Hauksie (Hoxy, Hoxsie, Hoxy)*, http://freepages.genealogy.rootsweb.ancestry.com/~hoxieschenck/Hoxie_10_08_06/b26131.htm, accessed September 23, 2011; The death certificate of Peleg Collins' son, Charles Edwin, indicates Peleg's birthplace as Taunton, Massachusetts, but all other known sources indicate Rhode Island. Death certificate, Charles E. Collins, New York City Department of Records and Information Services, New York, NY; Silversmith Arnold Collins was working in Newport, Rhode Island in 1735, but we do not know if he was related to our subject. Paul J. and Mary-Louise Fredyma, *A Directory of Rhode Island Silversmiths and Their Marks*, Hanover, NH: Fredyma, 1972, 4.

2. "A Romantic Story. How Fortune Came to Deserted Children After Many Years," *Cleveland Plain Dealer*, January 18, 1889, 3.

3. Collins is listed as a watch maker in the 1825 Cincinnati City Directory.

Elizabeth Beckman cites that Collins is listed in Cincinnati in the 1820 Federal Census. The only Collins reported in this census in Cincinnati is George Collins, between 16 and 25 years of age, engaged in manufacturing. Details of his occupation are not available. 1820 Federal Census, Cincinnati, Hamilton, Ohio; Evidence of Collins' work in Coventry is found in a watch paper, private collection, see Wm. Erik Voss, "Peleg Collins," *American Silversmiths*, http://freepages.genealogy.rootsweb.ancestry.com/~silversmiths/makers/silversmiths/247514.htm.

4. Partnership noted on February 3, 1829, Jacob Deterly, *"Remarks" of Jacob Deterly: diary from 1819 to 1848; life in southern Ohio: Cincinnati, Marietta, Athens* (transcribed and indexed by Madge Hubbard and Opal Saffell), Seattle: Northwest Lineage Researcher, 1972, 2:37; Advertisement, 1829 Cincinnati City Directory, reproduced Beckman, 126. Beckman indicates that this advertisement for Shipp & Collins

appeared in the 1828 City Directory, but in fact it appeared in 1829. A directory was not published in 1828.

5. Deterly, *"Remarks,"* 2:67.
6. Advertisement, *Cincinnati Daily Gazette*, April 3, 1834, reproduced in Beckman, 35.
7. Deterly, *"Remarks,"* 2:103.
8. Ibid.; Advertisement, *Cincinnati Daily Gazette*, January 17, 1835, reproduced in Beckman, 126; Advertisement, *Cincinnati Daily Gazette*, March 14, 1835, reproduced in Beckman, 36; 1834, 1836/37, 1839/40, 1842 Cincinnati City Directories.
9. 1842–44 Cincinnati City Directories.
10. *Journal of the Senate of the State of Ohio*, vol. 40, Columbus: S. Medary, 1842, 225.
11. Ohio, Vol. 1, p. 89, R.G. Dun & Co. Collection, Baker Library, Harvard Business School.
12. 1843, 1844, 1846 Cincinnati City Directories; Advertisement, *Kimball & James' Business Directory for the Mississippi Valley*, 1844, reproduced in Beckman, 36; Advertisement,

Cincinnati Daily Gazette, December 17, 1846, reproduced in Beckman, 65. Ohio, Vol. 1, p. 86, R.G. Dun & Co. Collection.
13. Ohio, Vol. 1, p. 89, R.G. Dun & Co. Collection.
14. Ohio, Vol. 1, pp. 90, 249, R.G. Dun & Co. Collection.
15. Advertisement, *Cincinnati Daily Gazette*, March 14, 1848, reproduced in Beckman, 36.
16. Ohio, Vol. 1, pp. 90, 249, R.G. Dun & Co. Collection; "Death Notice," *Jewelers' Circular and Horological Review* 23 (September 21, 1891): 86.
17. 1849/50 Cincinnati City Directory. The 1848/49 Cincinnati Business Directory did not include Collins.
18. Beckman, 36.
19. "Death Notice, Charles E. Collins," *JCHR* (September 21, 1891).
20. 1850 Federal Census, Cincinnati, Hamilton, Ohio. 1850 Federal Census, Sacramento, Sacramento, California.
21. Ibid.; Beckman, in error, gives Peleg's wife's name as Nancy. The mother of

Charles Edwin Collins is listed on his birth certificate as Mary S. Collins. Federal census information supports this. Charles Edwin, who frequently went by C.E., is listed as a silversmith in the same household as his parents in the 1850 Census. An Edwin Collins, silversmith, (presumably Charles Edwin) is listed as boarding at P. Collins' in the 1843, 1844, and 1846 Cincinnati City Directories. In 1860 Federal Census records, C.E. Collins is listed as a watch maker in San Francisco, married to Catherine E. In 1870 Census records, he is listed in New York as a manufacturing jeweler, married to Hattie (b. 1850 in Connecticut). On April 18, 1872, he and his wife Hattie A. Tomlinson applied for passports in the state of New York. In a notice of his death, he is described as a "large acquaintance among the jewelers of this city [New York]" who retired from the business in 1882, and lived afterward in New Orleans most of the time. He died of heart disease at 51 East 20th Street on

August 27, 1891. There are no known works of silver bearing his mark; Death certificate, Charles E. Collins; "Death Notice," (September 21, 1891); Ancestry.com, *U.S. Passport Applications, 1795–1905* [online database], Provo, Utah: Ancestry.com Operations Inc., 2007; Ohio, Vol. 1, pp. 13, 90, 190, 249, R.G. Dun & Co. Collection.
22. Ancestry.com, *California, Voters Registers 1866–1898* [online database], Provo, Utah: Ancestry.com Operations Inc., 2011; 1870 Federal Census, Los Angeles, Los Angeles, California; A sordid tale involving Peleg and Mary Collins and their daughter Harriet was published in 1889, but its veracity could not be proven. "A Romantic Story. How Fortune Came to Deserted Children After Many Years," January 18, 1889.
23. Peleg Collins, eBay listings and private collections, Cincinnati silver binders, Cincinnati Art Museum; Beckman, 15, 36.

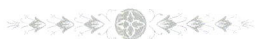

30. ARCHIBALD COOPER

w. 1836–1837

Archibald Cooper appeared in the 1836/37 Cincinnati City Directory, as a gold and silversmith boarding at William Borland's with William Cooper (presumably his brother), and working at Coopers & Saulnier's silverware manufactory (see **William Cooper**). After the dissolution of Coopers & Saulnier in the last half of February 1836, Archibald became William's partner in **W. & A. Cooper**.[1] In late 1837, the Coopers relocated to Louisville, Kentucky, and were listed in that city's 1838 Directory as silversmiths. It appears that Archibald spent the remainder of his career in Kentucky. In August 1842 he married Eliza Murray in Caldwell County, Kentucky.[2] His absence from Louisville directories between 1844 and 1847 might be explained by military service, or it is possible that he was minding the branch business that the Coopers maintained in Frankfort, Kentucky.[3] In 1848, Archibald reappeared in the Louisville city directory as a silversmith boarding at the Bowles House.[4] An A.S. Cooper, presumably our subject, is listed as a watch maker, boarding on the west side of Fourth between Green and Walnut, in 1858.[5] He does not appear in subsequent Louisville directories.

Spoons with fiddle handles and pointed shoulders have been found with mark 30.1. A sauce ladle of the same form bears mark 30.2 which could have been used by either Archibald or William Cooper.[6] The scarcity of marked works associated with William and Archibald Cooper suggests that most of the silver they produced was stamped and sold by someone else.

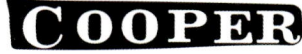

MARK 30.1   MARK 30.2

1. Dissolution notice, *Daily Evening Post*, February 22, 1836.
2. Ila Earle Fowler, comp., *Kentucky Pioneers and Their Descendants*, Frankfort, KY: Daughters of Colonial Wars, 1950, 316.
3. Boultinghouse states that Archibald Cooper served in the Mexican

American War. Boultinghouse, 92. Records of Cooper's military service could not be located by this author.
4. 1848 Louisville City Directory, 44.
5. 1858/59 Louisville City Directory, 46.
6. Archibald Cooper, eBay listings and private collections, Cincinnati silver binders, Cincinnati Art Museum.

31. W. & A. COOPER

w. 1836–1837

William and **Archibald Cooper**, presumably brothers, entered into partnership after the dissolution of Coopers & Saulnier on February 22, 1836.[1] That same day, they ran an advertisement for their silverware manufactory on Walnut, between Second and Pearl Streets.[2] An advertisement, identical in wording but with the added rendering of a teapot, ran two days later (fig. 31.1).[3] This advertisement also appeared, on occasion, with drawings of an assortment of silver (fig. 31.2). By 1838, the Coopers had relocated to Louisville, appearing in the city directory there. They continued business in Louisville until at least 1844.[4] By February 11, 1842, they had established a second branch of their business in Frankfort, Kentucky, advertising, "some fine specimens of their SILVERWORK and DRAWINGS," in addition to the types of wares such as jewelry, fancy goods, Britannia ware, and cutlery that they dealt in.[5]

Considering their roles as designers and manufacturers of silver, it is presumed that the Coopers sold much of what they made to others involved in the local and regional silver trade, who in turn marked the Coopers' wares with their own names. Known, extant wares bearing the marks of W. & A. Cooper include spoons and ladles with fiddle handles and rounded shoulders, butter knives, beakers, a covered pitcher (fig. 31.3), and a salver.[6] Their mark (mark 31.1) is occasionally accompanied by the stamp "Pure Coin" in a rectangular cartouche, by "CIN. O." in a rectangular cartouche, or by incuse floral flourishes stamped at either end of the mark.

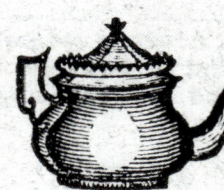

FIG. 31.1: Advertisement, *Cincinnati Daily Gazette,* February 24, 1836, 2

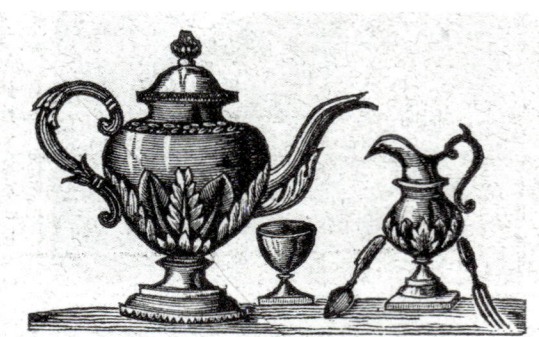

FIG. 31.2: Advertisement, *Cincinnati Daily Gazette,* March 26, 1836, 3

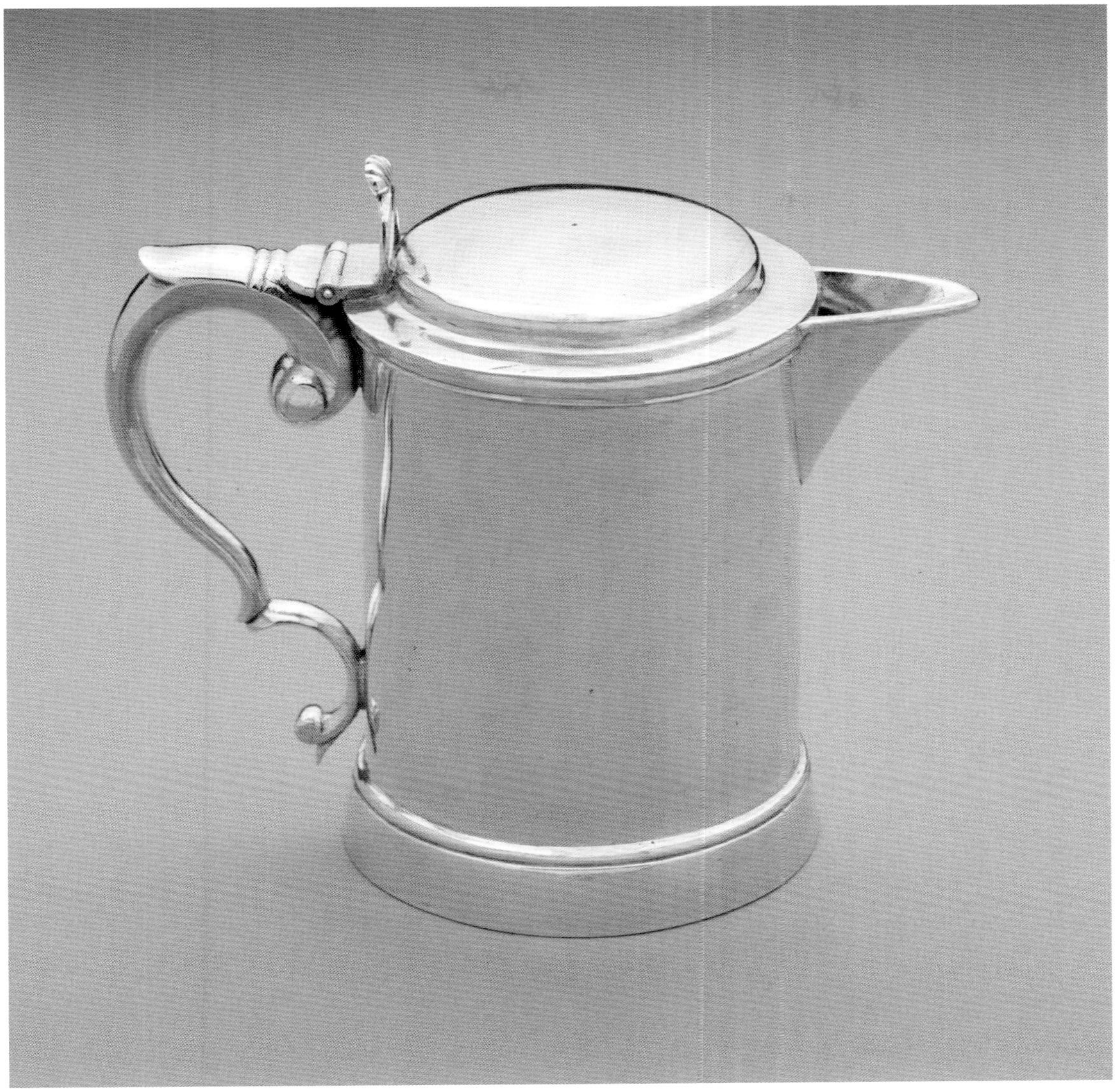

FIG. 31.3: W. & A. Cooper, *Covered Pitcher*, 1836–1837, 4½ × 5 in. (11.4 × 12.7 cm), CAM, Museum Purchase with funds provided by Mr. and Mrs. Charles Fleischmann III, 2005.43

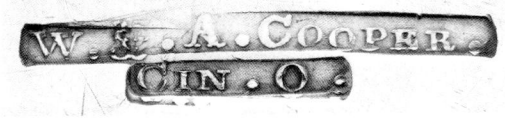

MARK 31.1

1. Dissolution notice, *Daily Evening Post*, February 22, 1836.
2. Advertisement, *Daily Evening Post*, February 22, 1836.
3. Advertisement, *Cincinnati Daily Gazette*, February 24, 1836, 2.
4. Boultinghouse, 92; The 1844 Louisville City Directory lists Butler Bryant as an employee of W. & A. Cooper, indicating that they were still in business.
5. Boultinghouse, 92; Advertisement, *The Commonwealth* (Frankfort, KY), February 11, 1842.
6. W. & A. Cooper, eBay listings and private collections, Cincinnati silver binders, Cincinnati Art Museum; *Salver* and *Pair of Beakers*, Museum of Fine Arts, Houston, *Southern Silver: An Exhibition of Silver made in the South prior to 1860*, Houston: Museum of Fine Arts, 1968, catalogue nos. E-3-A, E-3-B; *Tablespoon*, Speed Art Museum, Louisville, Kentucky, 1988.1.15.1.

32. WILLIAM COOPER

w. 1835–1837, 1846

William Cooper's first appearance in Cincinnati is made in an August 1835 advertisement for his silverware manufactory on Walnut Street, between Second and Pearl Streets.[1] In the advertisement, Cooper states that he "MANUFACTURES to order, [and] also keeps for sale, wholesale and retail, SILVER WARE Of all kinds, warranted equal to Spanish Dollars; among which are the following articles of the newest fashions, viz: TEA SETTS [sic], TABLE, DESERT [sic], & TEA SPOONS, of different patterns, MUGS, TUMBLERS, GOBLETS, &c, FORKS, FRUIT AND BUTTER KNIVES." Cooper's history or training prior to reaching Cincinnati is uncertain. A William Cooper (b. 1807) was engaged as an apprentice to Richard Mason & Sons, silver platers in Baltimore, Maryland, on June 28, 1822.[2] Although it is likely, we cannot be sure that this William Cooper is the same as our subject. In the 1836/37 Cincinnati City Directory, William Cooper is listed as a gold and silversmith.

Between mid August 1835 and early February 1836, William and **Archibald Cooper**, presumably brothers, entered into business with W.H. Saulnier.[3] The firm of Coopers & Saulnier operated at William Cooper's previous Walnut Street location, and their advertisement from February 10, 1836, was almost identical to William's of August 1835, with the exception that silver combs were added to the list of wares available.[4] This partnership did not last long. On February 22, 1836, the men announced their dissolution.[5]

William and Archibald continued as **W. & A. Cooper** in the same location until relocating to Louisville in late 1837. Both appear in the 1838 Louisville City Directory as silversmiths working at 72 West Main Street, and they continued business in Louisville at least through 1844.[6]

In September 1846 William returned to Cincinnati. He does not appear in city directory listings that year, but he advertised his silverware manufactory in the *Cincinnati Daily Gazette* as accessible from Third Street, "in the court adjoining Franklin Bank."[7] No city directory was published in 1847, and William's manufactory does not appear in the 1848/49 Cincinnati Business Directory, therefore it is plausible that the William Cooper in Spring Grove Cemetery records, born December 29, 1809, in Baltimore, deceased July 29, 1847, from consumption, might be William Cooper, our subject.[8]

A ladle with a fiddle handle and pointed shoulders has been observed with William Cooper's mark (mark 32.1).[9] A sauce ladle of the same form has been documented with a mark using only the surname Cooper (see **Archibald Cooper**, mark 30.2). This mark could have been used by either one of the Cooper brothers. The scarcity of marked works associated with William and Archibald Cooper suggests that most of the silver they produced was stamped and retailed by someone else.

MARK. 32.1

1. Advertisement, *Daily Evening Post*, August 14, 1835, reproduced in Beckman, 38.
2. Jennifer Faulds Goldsborough, *Silver in Maryland*, Baltimore: Maryland Historical Society, 1983, 247.
3. Nothing is known about W.H. Saulnier. He was not included in the alphabetical listings in the Cincinnati City Directory for 1836/37.
4. The 1836/37 Cincinnati City Directory lists the firm as Coopers & Saulnier. Listings for both William and Archibald indicate that they were both working at the firm; Advertisement, *Daily Evening Post*, February 10, 1836, reproduced in Beckman, 39.
5. Dissolution notice, *Daily Evening Post*, February 22, 1836.
6. Boultinghouse, 92; The 1844 Louisville City Directory lists Butler Bryant as an employee of W. & A. Cooper, indicating that they were still in business.
7. Advertisement, *Cincinnati Daily Gazette*, September 7, 1846, reproduced in Beckman, 39. The Franklin branch of the State Bank of Ohio was located on Third Street between Main and Walnut.
8. Burial records, Spring Grove Cemetery, Cincinnati, Ohio.
9. William Cooper, eBay listings and private collections, Cincinnati silver binders, Cincinnati Art Museum.

33. JACOB DETERLY

1786–1848, w. 1812–1834

Born in Maryland on March 16, 1786, Jacob Deterly was the son of Saxon-born Johann Ludwig Deterly (1739-1795) and Mary Elizabeth Keither (1741-1804).[1] The first record of Deterly in Cincinnati, a deed to **Harmon Long**, is dated April 10, 1807.[2] On September 29, 1810, and May 2, 1811, Deterly is listed in the battalion muster for Cincinnati's third company in the third battalion of the first brigade under the direction of Captain George P. Torrence.[3]

The details of Deterly's apprenticeship are unknown, and little is known about his activities between 1807 and 1812. The earliest known article bearing his name is a set of clockworks for a tall-case clock dated 1812.[4] On November 7, 1812, Deterly and **Robert Best** formed **Best & Deterly**, operating a shop on Main Street where they advertised as watch and clock makers, jewelers and silversmiths.[5] The partnership ended on September 27, 1813, with an announcement that Deterly planned to leave Cincinnati.[6] The reason for his departure is still a matter of speculation. It is possible that he went to Louisville for a short time to help establish E. Ayers & Co. (1813-1820), a firm managed by Elias Ayers whose "& Co." represented the interests of Deterly and **Enos Woodruff**.[7] In January or early February 1815, Deterly joined Robert Best and Enos Woodruff to form **Robert Best & Co.**, a firm that lasted until the spring of 1817, when Best left the partnership. The remaining partners formed **Woodruff & Deterly**, which operated until February 1, 1821.[8]

Jacob Deterly maintained a diary in which he recorded events from his life, and from the lives of his associates and neighbors between October 1819 and May 1841.[9] This diary is one of the precious few documents relevant to the Cincinnati silver trade that remains, allowing us a glimpse of how the early trade and its craftsmen operated. Deterly does not specifically mention any silver, jewelry, clocks, or watches that he worked on, but he does allude to his work in general and mentions other wares, perhaps because they were different from the types of objects he normally made. On April 25, 1821, he notes, "made a pair of large hand bellows being the first I ever made." The very next day he writes about the completion of a hydrometer for Mr. Harvey [sic], presumably the English-born rectifier and distiller Arthur Harvie.[10] In November, he writes of graduating a thermometer and engraving a scale for the brewer Davis Embree.[11]

After the dissolution of Woodruff & Deterly in February 1821, Deterly presumably worked alone at 18 Market Street.[12] By October 17, 1821, he was renting at 92 Main Street.[13] He writes, the "room was found in a damnable pickle—white wash'd the walls, put up shelving and jack-planed the counter. Done it all myself." About a week later, on October 25, he "open'd the ware and began to regulate everything."[14] But on February 15, 1822, he received notice that the shop was no longer available to let, and by May 30 he had rented 2½ Front Street for $100 a year, and again began whitewashing and unpacking his stock.[15] In the 1825 Cincinnati Directory, he lists as a clock and watch maker.[16] The lack of subsequent directory listings for Deterly is explained in his January 1, 1825 entry, "This day received the Cincinnati Directory which was promised to subscribers at 75 cents, but demanded 1 DOLLAR!! May I never again loose [sic] my reason or mental faculties to lend my name to assist an infamous, swindling book publisher. Twice have I been imposed on!"[17]

In January 1826 Deterly again received notice that the lease on his shop was about to be terminated.[18] Yet, he seems to have remained at Front Street until moving into the shop of Samuel A. M. Shipp on October 7, 1826.[19] Shipp and Deterly's friendship can be traced as far back as 1819, when Deterly records that he became very ill on Christmas day and was "waited on by the good self of S.A.M. Shipp."[20] Evidence for an arrangement between Shipp and Woodruff & Deterly can be found in 1824 diary entries that refer to a $25 debt owed to Shipp for his services to the firm.[21] Shipp and Deterly's later collaboration appears to have commenced on September 22, 1826, when Deterly notes having advanced Shipp $500, part of stock for their "connexion [sic] in business."[22] Three days later, Shipp embarked on a trip to New York to buy "jewellery [sic], military goods and so forth."[23] A reasonable portion of the men's merchandise came from the East, notably New York, Philadelphia, and Baltimore, as there are several notations of Shipp's trips there to buy stock.[24] A September 1827 advertisement indicates that they were operating under Shipp's name in a brick house at 44 Main Street.[25] A March 15, 1828 advertisement for Shipp's business reads, "Having permanently engaged Mr. Jacob Deterly, who is well known as a first rate workman, and Mr. C. B. McCullough to attend entirely to the repairing of watches, he [Shipp] confidently hopes to give general satisfaction in that branch of his business."[26]

In July 1828 Deterly traveled by steamboat to Marietta, Ohio, the home of his brother Michael (1782-1860), where he stayed for about nineteen days.[27] Shortly thereafter he was summoned to pay $3,000 owed by Woodruff & Deterly to Samuel Hildeburn of Philadelphia.[28] A month later he took inventory of his present stock, and on November 1, 1828, he sold his interest in that stock to Shipp for cash, which he presumably used to pay the Hildeburn debt.[29]

On April 20, 1829, Deterly noted that he had set up his bench to work at his brother's house in Marietta, but he returned to Cincinnati in intervals until 1834 to work in the shop of **Shipp & Collins**, while also working at the shop of Marietta watch maker D.B. Anderson.[30] In 1838, he began paying installments for the purchase of a farm in Rome Township, Athens County, Ohio, where he resided from May 14, 1841, until his death on February 10, 1846.[31] Amos Miller, the husband of his niece Louisa (1807–1882), remembered Deterly as "an honest man, a scholar and a gentleman," noting that Deterly had spent his last years studying mathematics and astronomy.[32]

There are no known examples of silver bearing the mark of Jacob Deterly, yet there are examples marked by the firms he was associated with, including Robert Best & Co., Woodruff & Deterly, and Shipp & Collins. He lists in the city directory as a silversmith when paired with Enos Woodruff, and we know that his various firms advertised the sale of silver wares, and the purchase of old silver and other metals for melting. An 1836 diary entry indicates

his outlay of $52.06 for the purchase of old silver in Marietta.[33] A diary entry from October 13, 1828, notes how fashionable hickory canes are, many mounted with silver heads. "One in particular," he writes, "is to be mounted with a gold head in style, which is intended to be presented to Gen'l Andrew Jackson."[34] Whether or not this referred to something that he was creating or just observing, we do not know.

There is clear evidence that Deterly focused his efforts on the making and repair of clocks, watches, and other mechanical devices: the aforementioned 1812 clockworks, an 1823 diary entry that observed his discontent with other Cincinnati Main-Street watch repairers who saw fault in Deterly for selling below standard bill prices, and his employ by both Shipp and Anderson as a watch repairer. Additional evidence is found in an 1830 diary entry that details Dr. Locke's request for Deterly to return to Cincinnati to make an orrery, a mechanical model of the solar system, and the 1831 entry that mentions the repair of a theodolite, a surveying instrument with a rotating telescope for measuring horizontal and vertical angles. Deterly is included here because of his involvement in the early trade and because the observations and records found in his diary are of great importance in their revelation of so many aspects of the early Cincinnati silver trade.

1. Beckman, 40; 1825 Cincinnati City Directory; Jacob Deterly, "Remarks" of Jacob Deterly: diary from 1819 to 1848; life in southern Ohio: Cincinnati, Marietta, Athens (transcribed and indexed by Madge Hubbard and Opal Saffell), Seattle: Northwest Lineage Researcher, 1972, 1:15; It is unclear whether Johann Ludwig Deterly was the same person as Johann Jacob Dieterle who arrived in Philadelphia in 1774. Gale Research, Passenger and Immigration Lists Index, 1500s–1900s [online database], Provo, Utah: Ancestry.com Operations Inc., 2010.
2. Ruth Bowers and Anita Short, Gateway to the West, Baltimore: Genealogical Publishing Co., Inc., 1989, 1:575.
3. "Roll of the 3rd Company of Cincinnati Militia 29th of September 1810," Quarterly Publication of the Historical and Philosophical Society, 1918–1920, vols. 13–15, Cincinnati: Historical and Philosophical Society

of Ohio, 1921, 127; "Roll of the 3rd Company of Cincinnati Militia 2nd of May 1811," Quarterly Publication of the Historical and Philosophical Society, 1918–1920, vols. 13–15, Cincinnati: Historical and Philosophical Society of Ohio, 1921, 128.
4. This clock is in a private collection. Jacob Deterly research file, Cincinnati Art Museum, Decorative Arts & Design Department.
5. Advertisement, Liberty Hall, November 7, 1812, reproduced in Beckman, 12.
6. Advertisement, Western Spy, September 27, 1813, reproduced in Beckman, 13.
7. Boultinghouse, 35; Deterly, "Remarks," 1:6–7.
8. Advertisement, Liberty Hall, May 5, 1817, 3, reproduced in Beckman, 17; Advertisement, Western Spy, April 7, 1821, reproduced in Beckman, 43.
9. The whereabouts of the original diary are unknown; Deterly, "Remarks," 15.
10. Deterly, "Remarks," 1:14; 1825

Cincinnati City Directory.
11. Deterly, "Remarks," 1:16; 1819 Cincinnati City Directory.
12. Deterly's diary notes that he began renting a room there from Col. F. Carr on May 17, 1821. Deterly, "Remarks," 1:14.
13. Deterly, "Remarks," 1:16.
14. Ibid.
15. Deterly, "Remarks," 1:18–19.
16. 1825 Cincinnati City Directory.
17. Deterly, "Remarks," 2:3.
18. Deterly, "Remarks," 2:14.
19. Deterly, "Remarks," 2:20.
20. Deterly, "Remarks," 1:5.
21. Deterly, "Remarks," 1:39.
22. Deterly, "Remarks," 2:20.
23. Ibid.
24. Deterly, "Remarks," 2:26–29.
25. Advertisement, Saturday Evening Chronicle, September 29, 1827; Deterly, "Remarks," 2:26–27.
26. Advertisement, Saturday Evening Chronicle, March 15, 1828, reproduced in Beckman, 125.

27. Deterly, "Remarks," 2:31–34.
28. Ibid.
29. Ibid.
30. Deterly, "Remarks," 2:39–152; Deterly evidently had a change of heart about D.B. Anderson, as a diary entry on June 12, 1824, notes that Anderson had visited Cincinnati for five or six weeks with the intention of establishing a stand there. A few days before Anderson left, Deterly says that he attempted to hoax the locals into believing that he was the inventor and maker of his timepieces, which had been made by a Scotsman who worked with Anderson in Marietta the previous fall. Deterly, "Remarks," 1:42.
31. Deterly, "Remarks," 2:129–152.
32. Deterly, "Remarks," Addendum, dated February 10, 1848; Louisa was the daughter of Jacob Deterly's brother Michael.
33. Deterly, "Remarks," 2:119.
34. Deterly, "Remarks," 2:33.

34. HENRY A. DODT

1860–1907, w. 1883–1906

Henry A. Dodt was born in Cincinnati to German immigrants Maria "Mary" A. (1820–1884) and Bernard H. Dodt. (b. about 1819).[1] His father was a wagon maker.[2] Henry learned the watch-making trade from the local watch maker and jeweler William Deters, (1849–1911, w. 1878–1911).[3] By 1883, Dodt had opened his own shop in the Emery Arcade, an "attractive and artistic store" stocked with jewelry, diamonds, "watches, clocks & etc."[4] A preserve spoon bearing his retailer mark (mark 34.1) alongside the mark of Wendell Manufacturing Co. (Chicago) indicates that silver ware was also part of his line.[5]

In 1906, because of failing health, Dodt sold out to his partner Adolph Schmidt (1870–1913) who continued business at the Arcade.[6] Dodt died on April 8, 1907, at his home in Walnut Hills.[7] He is buried at St. John's German Catholic Cemetery in the Cincinnati neighborhood of St. Bernard.[8] Dodt and his wife Wilhelmina "Minnie" Overbeck (b. 1864, m. 1886) had five children: Clara (1887–1920), Clemens H. (b. 1890), Henry A.L. (b.1891), Eugene E. (b. 1896), and Eleanor (b. 1902).[9]

H.A.DODT

MARK 34.1

1. 1850, 1880 Federal Censuses, Cincinnati, Hamilton, Ohio; Maria A. Dodt, death record, Cincinnati Health Department, University of Cincinnati Archives and Rare Books Library, http://hdl.handle.net /2374.UC/442088.
2. 1850 Federal Census, Cincinnati, Hamilton, Ohio.
3. "Death of Henry A. Dodt," *Jewelers' Circular and Horological Review* (April 17, 1907): 51; Deters is listed in city directories as a watch maker and jeweler. There is no extant evidence to suggest that he dealt in silver. 1869–1911 Cincinnati City Directories; William Deters, death record, Cincinnati Health Department, http://hdl.handle.net/2374.UC/2157 59.
4. John W. Leonard, *The Centennial Review of Cincinnati: one hundred years of progress in commerce, manufactures, the professions, and in social and municipal life*, Cincinnati: J.M. Elstner, 1888, 69.
5. H.A. Dodt, eBay listings and private collections, Cincinnati silver binders, Cincinnati Art Museum. To date, no other examples marked by Dodt have been identified.
6. "Death of Henry A. Dodt" (April 17, 1907); Schmidt resided with Dodt and his family from the late 1880s until his marriage in 1898. He was an orphan, and it is likely that he apprenticed with Dodt; 1880 Federal Census, Bond Hill, Hamilton, Ohio; 1900 Federal Census, Cincinnati, Hamilton, Ohio; 1887–1898 Cincinnati City Directories; Marriage record, Hamilton County Probate

Records, vol. 138, 409, http://www .probatect.org/CourtRecordsArchive /bukmarriages.aspx; "Dismissed is the Cross-Petition and Interpleader of Harmeyer in Life Insurance Suit," *Cincinnati Enquirer*, December 18, 1913.
7. Henry A. Dodt, death record, Cincinnati Health Department, http://hdl.handle.net/2374.UC/2566 08. This record provides a death date of May 8, 1907, but this is likely a transcription error, as Dodt's death notice in *JCHR* cites April 8.
8. Ibid.
9. 1900 Federal Census, Cincinnati, Hamilton, Ohio; Henry A. Dodt, death notice, *Cincinnati Enquirer*, April 10, 1907, 7; Marriage record, Hamilton County Probate Records, vol. 100, 123, http://www.probatect.org/CourtReco rdsArchive/bukmarriages.aspx; [Clara] Dodt, birth record, Cincinnati Health Department, University of Cincinnati Archives and Rare Books Library, http://hdl.handle.net/2374.UC/4635 94; Clemens H. Dodt, birth record, Cincinnati Health Department, http://hdl.handle.net/2374.UC/4264 00; Henry A. L. Dodt, birth record, Cincinnati Health Department, http://hdl.handle.net/2374.UC/4349 36; Eugene E. Dodt, birth record, Cincinnati Health Department, http://hdl.handle.net/2374.UC/2903 10; Eleanor Dodt, birth record, Cincinnati Health Department, http://hdl.handle.net/2374.UC /280467.

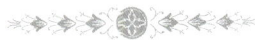

35. GARRET T. DORLAND

1829–1892, w. 1853–1881

Garret T. Dorland was born in Fredericksburg, Holmes County, Ohio, on November 22, 1829. He was the son of Mary Moore (1785–1869) and James Dorland (1781–1858).[1] Garret T. Dorland is first recorded in Cincinnati in 1853, as a watch maker working at 36 Sycamore, the address of **Richard Clayton**'s shop, and boarding at the Merchant's Hotel.[2] By 1855, he was clerking for William O'Hara, "importer of watches, jewelry, etc." and a former

Clayton employee.[3] Dorland continued to work for O'Hara after the establishment of Hughes & O'Hara in 1856.[4] Operating at 19 Main Street, this firm advertised the sale of jewelry, watches and silverware until its dissolution in September 1857 when the partnership of **Hughes & Dorland** was established.[5]

After the failure and dissolution of Hughes & Dorland in the latter half of 1860, Dorland continued in business alone at the

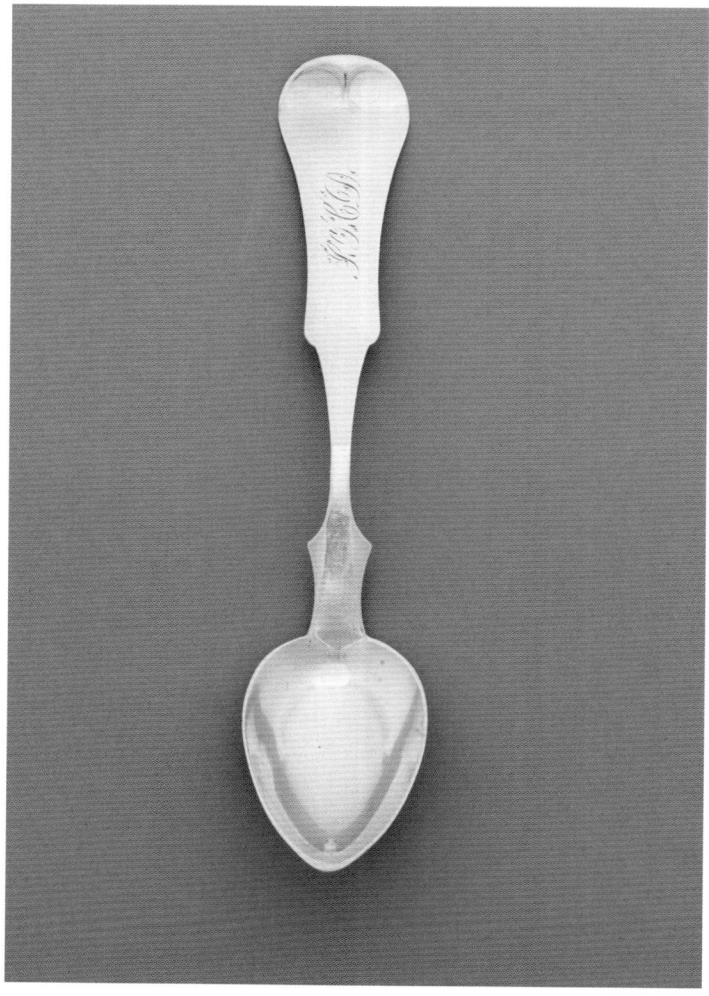

FIG. 35.1: Garret Dorland, *Teaspoon*, 1853–1881, L. 5¾ in. (14.6 cm), CAM, Museum Purchase: John S. Conner Fund, 2012.13

firm's former location on the northwest corner of Main and Pearl Streets.[6] In 1872, he relocated to 48 West Fourth Street.[7] Accounts describe Dorland as a wholesale jeweler, and in 1863, he advertised "watches, jewelry, watchmakers' tools, watch-glasses and materials," an indication of his primary business focus and training.[8] When thieves broke into his store in 1867, they reportedly absconded with gold pens, opera glasses, silver butter knives, and watch chains, unable to access the gold watches and chains locked in his safe.[9] Much of Dorland's stock came from the East, although he did patronize some local suppliers.[10] In 1869, an advertisement for holiday presents that could be purchased at his store noted silverware and silver-plated ware.[11] Spoons with tipped, exaggerated fiddle handles and pointed shoulders (fig. 35.1) have been, so far, the only silver found to bear his mark (mark 35.1).[12] These, based on their shape, were made locally, but surely not by Dorland.

Dorland struggled as a businessman, failing and settling with creditors again and again. Credit reporters noted that he lived too extravagantly for a man of his means. While they cited that he had "made a good deal of money during the [Civil] war," details of how the money was earned are not provided. His worth was estimated, at its highest point in 1867, to be between $8,000 and $10,000.[13] For the 1870 Products of Industry Census, he reported $500 of capital, two employees that earned a combined $1,500 in wages per year, and the use of $2,000 worth of material to produce product valued at $11,600.[14] In 1878, he again filed for bankruptcy with liabilities reported at $20,000, and by June 1879 he was advertising the auction of his remaining stock.[15]

Dorland took in his son, Harry Edward Dorland (1854–1927), and Samuel Duncan as partners at about this time, and operated as G.T. Dorland & Co.[16] Duncan had contributed $5,000, inherited from his mother, to the concern.[17] But Dorland's business skills had not improved, and by July 1881 the firm had failed.[18] By 1883, Dorland had moved to Pueblo, Colorado.[19] In 1885, he is recorded as a boarder at Pueblo's Laclede Hotel. His occupation is given as capitalist.[20] Dorland died in Pueblo on March 23, 1892, from kidney disease. His obituary notes that he had been running Pueblo's Fifth Avenue Hotel prior to his death. Dorland was a member of the Cincinnati Knights Templar and the First Presbyterian Church. He is buried in Spring Grove Cemetery, Cincinnati.[21]

Dorland and his wife Eliza Virginia Royse (1832–1918) were married in Cincinnati on November 22, 1853.[22] They had at least seven children: Harry Edward, Charles Eugene (1856–1858), Laura "Kitty" C. (b. 1858), Fanny "Louie" (b. 1860), Myra Augusta (1862–1864), a stillborn child (b. 1865), and May (adopted, b. 1870).[23] Dorland was married to a second wife, Julia (b. about 1835), by 1885.[24]

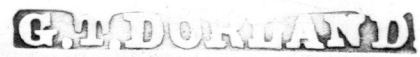

MARK 35.1

1. 1880 Federal Census, Cincinnati, Hamilton, Ohio; John Dorland Cremer, *Records of The Dorland Family in America*, Washington, DC: Byron S. Adams, 1898, 206–211; "The Late G.T. Dorland," *Cincinnati Enquirer*, March 30, 1892, 8; James Dorland's occupation is unknown. It is not specified in the 1850 Federal Census, Salt Creek Township, Wayne County, Ohio.
2. 1853 Cincinnati City Directory.
3. 1855 Cincinnati City Directory.
4. Edward J. Hughes (formerly associated with Richard Clayton) was O'Hara's uncle; Ohio, Vol. 2, p. 31, R.G. Dun & Co. Collection, Baker Library, Harvard Business School.

5. 1857 Cincinnati City Directory; Notice of dissolution, *Cincinnati Enquirer*, September 3, 1857, 2.

6. 1861 Cincinnati City Directory; Ohio, Vol. 2, p. 66–67, R.G. Dun & Co. Collection

7. Ohio, Vol. 2, pp. 66–67, R.G. Dun & Co. Collection; 1872 Cincinnati City Directory.

8. Advertisement, *Cincinnati Enquirer*, September 7, 1863, 2; "Narrow Escape From Death," *Cincinnati Enquirer*, December 28, 1863, 2.

9. "Heavy Robbery of Jewelry," *Cincinnati Enquirer*, February 21, 1867, 2.

10. Ohio, Vol. 2, p. 66, R.G. Dun & Co. Collection; Ohio, Vol. 7, p. 119, R.G. Dun & Co. Collection.

11. Advertisement, *Cincinnati Enquirer*, December 20, 1869, 8.

12. Garret T. Dorland, eBay listings and private collections, Cincinnati silver binders, Cincinnati Art Museum.

13. Notice of assignment, *Cincinnati Enquirer*, June 13, 1861, 1; Ohio, Vol. 2, p. 66, R.G. Dun & Co. Collection; Ohio, Vol. 7, pp. 119–120, 149, R.G. Dun & Co. Collection; A description of Dorland's daughter Laura (Kitty)'s wedding indicates that the Dorlands belonged to the prominent social circle of Cincinnati, and that no expense was spared on this occasion. "Beightler–Dorland," *Cincinnati Enquirer*, March 5, 1880, 4.

14. 1870 Federal Non-Population Census Schedules, Products of Industry, Schedule 4, Hamilton County, Ohio.

15. Ohio, Vol. 7, pp. 119–120, 149, R.G. Dun & Co. Collection.

16. Ohio, Vol. 7, p. 454, R.G. Dun & Co. Collection; Harry Dorland was working for his father by 1873; 1873–1879 Cincinnati City Directories.

17. Ohio, Vol. 7, p. 454, R.G. Dun & Co. Collection.

18. Ibid.; Advertisement, *Cincinnati Enquirer*, December 21, 1880, 8; Advertisement, *Cincinnati Enquirer*, August 19, 1881, 8.

19. Notice, *Cincinnati Enquirer*, August 12, 1883, 14.

20. 1885 Colorado State Census, Pueblo, Colorado.

21. Death notice, *Cincinnati Enquirer*, March 26, 1892, 5; Garret T. Dorland, burial record, Spring Grove Cemetery, Cincinnati, Ohio.

22. Marriage record, Hamilton County Probate Records, vol. B5, 155, http://www.probatect.org/Court RecordsArchive/bukmarriages.aspx; Cremer, *Records of The Dorland Family*, 211; "The Late G.T. Dorland," March 30, 1892, 8; Eliza V. Dorland, burial marker, Masonic Home Cemetery, Springfield, Ohio, *Find A Grave*, http://www.findagrave.com/cgi-bin/fg.cgi?page=gr&GSln=Dorland&GSfn=eliza&GSbyrel=all&GSdyrel=all&GSob=n&GRid=22610504&df=all&.

23. "The Late G.T. Dorland," March 30, 1892, 8; Burial records, Spring Grove Cemetery, Cincinnati, Ohio.

24. 1885 Colorado State Census, Pueblo, Colorado.

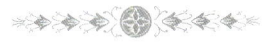

36. JOSEPH DRAPER

1801–1864, w. 1834–1856

Joseph Draper was born near Trowbridge, England, and came to the United States with his father when he was about nine years old.[1] Draper's eulogy notes that shortly after their arrival, Joseph's father boarded a boat to return to England to retrieve his wife and other children, but drowned just before the ship reached England. Alone, the young Draper apprenticed himself to a silversmith in Wilmington, Delaware.[2] In 1826, he acquired the silversmithing firm of Henry J. Pepper (1790–1853) in Wilmington, and in May of the following year, he advertised in the *American Watchman* that he would "manufacture and keep constantly for sale, silver spectacles, Table and Tea Spoons . . . ."[3] But by early February 1832 the silversmith and jeweler had announced his departure in the *Delaware Journal*.[4]

Draper may have been in Cincinnati by mid to late 1832, but does not appear in city directories until 1834, when he advertised as a silversmith on Fourth Street, between Main and Walnut.[5] By this time, he had married Martha Inskip (about 1810–1891), who bore him his first child, Martha, around 1833 in Ohio.[6] In 1836, Draper relocated his shop to Main Street, between Third and Fourth Streets, and then moved back to Fourth Street around 1849, consistently advertising as a silversmith, watch maker or jeweler.[7] In 1847, he noted that in addition to Masonic clothing, supplies and jewels, he also kept on hand "Gold and

Silver Watches, Chains, Keys, Breast Pins, Rings, Spectacles, Pencils and Silver Ware, of all descriptions" and that "Clocks, Watches, Music Boxes, [would be] cleaned and repaired in the best manner."[8]

Credit reports from 1844 through 1857 describe Draper as an honest, economical, well-respected business man. In fact, one exuberant report proclaimed, "he is one of the best men south of Mason & Dixon's Line."[9] His stock was valued at around $3,000 during this time, and he owned considerable real estate.[10] In 1850, the Products of Industry Census indicated that he had $1,100 invested in capital, employed two hands, paid an average of $80 a month in wages, and worked with $1,000 worth of gold and $500 worth of silver to produce product (including jobbing and repairing) valued at $3,000.[11] In 1856, Draper sold his business to **Henry P. Elias**, his long-time assistant.[12] In addition to Elias, Draper employed several others, suggesting the size and output of his shop to be considerable. These employees included watch maker Joseph B. Boyd from New York between 1840 and about 1844; silversmith **Stephen D. Choate** of Delaware, about 1840; silversmith **William D. Dunlevy**, about 1840; silver finisher Frederick Gerstecker of Germany, about 1840; silversmith **Edward J. Reis** from Maryland, about 1840; and burnisher Mary Hoffman, about 1837. Based on like addresses given in city directory listings,

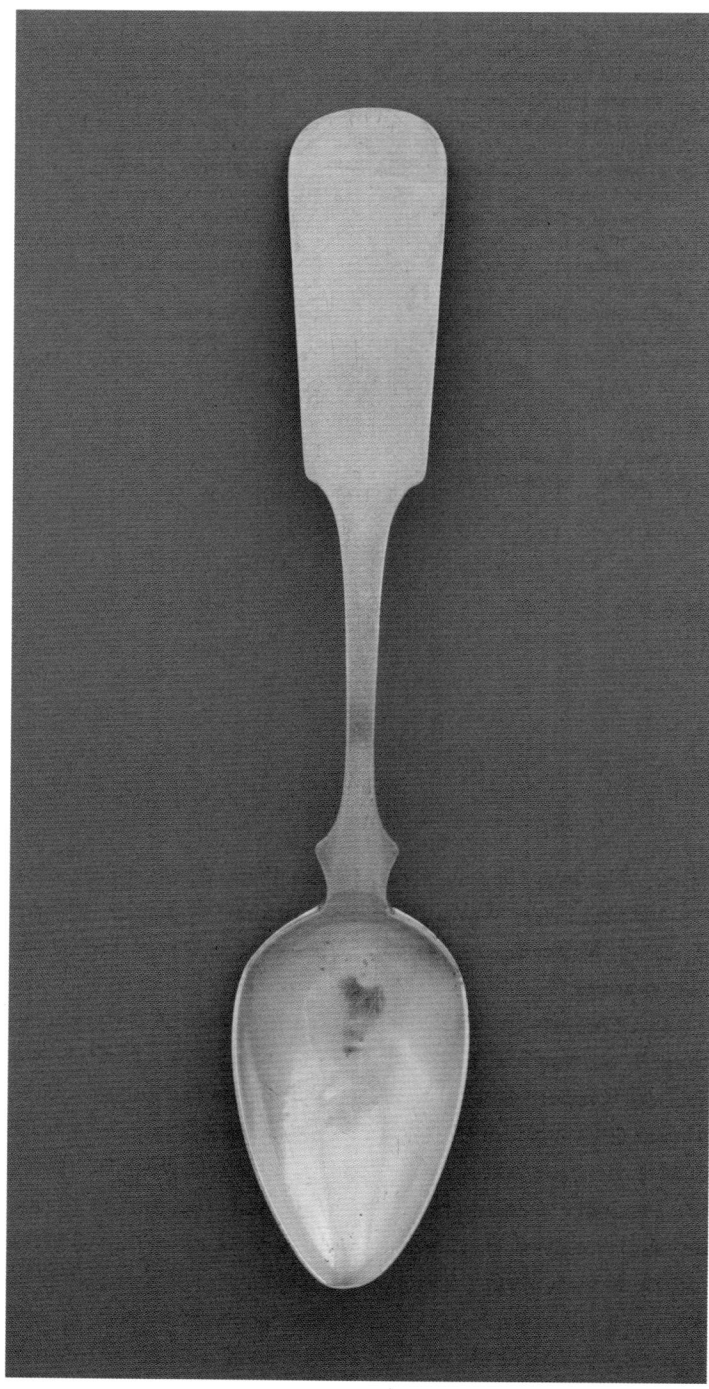

FIG. 36.1: Joseph Draper, *Serving Spoon*, c. 1830, 8⅝ in. (21.9 cm), Private Collection

he also probably employed watch maker Reese C. Evans, about 1853; and **William R. Evans**, about 1844–1846.[13]

After Draper's retirement from the silver trade, he served as an officer and president of the Queen City Fire and Marine Insurance Company.[14] A significant figure in the community, he was a long-time member of Ninth Street Baptist Church (for whom he made two communion cups), a Mason, director of one of the local banks, a trustee of the Cincinnati College of Medicine and Surgery, director of the City Infirmary, and an original stockholder of the Cincinnati and Covington Suspension Bridge Co.[15] Draper died on November 16, 1864, and at that time owned several parcels of land in Covington, Kentuck, and a home in Cincinnati.[16]

A wide variety of silver marked by Draper exists. Chatelaines, beakers, tongs, ladles, and spoons of various sizes with fiddle (fig. 36.1) or exaggerated fiddle handles and pointed shoulders are known to bear mark 36.1. Mark 36.2 has been documented on tablespoons with fiddle handles and pointed shoulders. Mark 36.3 is known on double-handled, baluster-shaped communion cups, spectacles and tablespoons, and mark 36.4 has been seen on a pressed pattern spoon (circa 1850s), and a miniature spoon with exaggerated fiddle handle and pointed shoulders.[17] It bears noting that there was a silversmith also named Joseph Draper active in Kentucky in 1850, b. about 1825. Therefore, mark 36.4 might belong to him, rather than to our subject.[18]

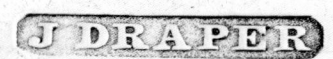

MARK 36.1

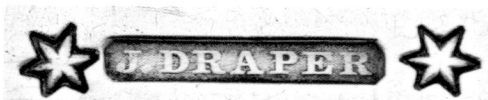

MARK 36.2

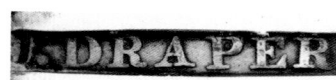

MARK 36.3

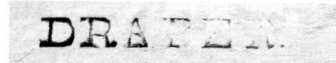

MARK 36.4

1. *Proceedings of the Memorial Associations, Eulogies at Music Hall and Biographical Sketches of Many Distinguished Citizens of Cincinnati*, vol. 1, Cincinnati: A.E. Jones, 1881, 142; Joseph Draper, burial record, Spring Grove Cemetery, Cincinnati, Ohio.

2. *Proceedings of the Memorial Associations*, Jones, 142–144. The identity of this silversmith is unknown.

3. Donald L. Fennimore, *Delaware Silver: the Col. Kenneth P. and Regina I. Brown Collection*, Dover, DE: Biggs Museum of American Art, 2008, 54.

4. Beckman, 45.

5. There were no Cincinnati city directories published in 1832 or 1833. An advertisement for Draper's successor, Henry P. Elias, states that Draper established himself in 1832. Advertisement, *Cincinnati Daily Gazette*, October 16, 1869.

6. Joseph's wife Martha was born in England, the daughter of John C. and Martha Inskip. The Drapers had ten children: Martha (b. about 1833), Anna (b. about 1835), Edward Washington (1837–1838), Louisa (b about 1838), Harrisonia (b. about 1842), John (1844–1911), Margaret (1848–1848), Elizabeth (1849–1850), Sarah (1851–1851), and George W. (1853–1895). 1850 Federal Census, Cincinnati, Hamilton, Ohio; Burial records, Spring Grove Cemetery, Cincinnati, Ohio; Joseph Draper, will dated November 1864, proved November 22, 1864, box 18, case 8945, University of Cincinnati Archives and Rare Books Library.

7. 1836–1849 Cincinnati City Directories. Remarks included in the account of Draper in *Proceedings of the Memorial Associations* indicate that Draper was the first manufacturer of silverware in Cincinnati and the first jeweler on West Fourth Street. This is incorrect.

8. Advertisement, *Cincinnati Daily Commercial*, June 30, 1847.

9. Ohio, Vol. 1, p. 86, R.G. Dun & Co. Collection, Baker Library, Harvard Business School.

10. Ibid.; In the 1860 Federal Census, Cincinnati, Hamilton, Ohio, the value of Draper's real estate is given as $15,000. His personal estate is valued at $1,300.

11. 1850 Federal Non-Population Census Schedules, Products of Industry, Schedule 4, Hamilton County, Ohio.

12. Ohio, Vol. 2, p. 217, R.G. Dun & Co. Collection; In August 1861 Draper returned to the business, overseeing it until October 1862 while Elias was presumably working as a sutler. Ohio, Vol. 5, p. 51, R. G. Dun & Co. Collection.

13. 1837–1853 Cincinnati City Directories; Advertisement, *Daily Evening Post*, June 9, 1837, reproduced in Beckman, 47, mentions burnisher Mary Hoffman. In the 1846 City Directory, William R. Evans is listed as Robert Evans.

14. 1861 Cincinnati City Directory; 1860 Federal Census, Cincinnati, Hamilton, Ohio.

15. *Proceedings of the Memorial Associations*, Jones, 142–144; *Communion Cups*, Cowan's Auction, Cincinnati, June 23, 2007, lot 283.

16. Joseph Draper, will; Joseph Draper, burial record.

17. Joseph Draper, eBay listings and private collections, Cincinnati silver binders, Cincinnati Art Museum; Fennimore, *Delaware Silver*, 54–60.

18. Boultinghouse, 100; Fennimore, *Delaware Silver*, 54–60.

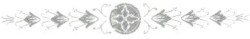

37. FREDERICK DROZ

w. 1822–1831

Frederick Droz, of Switzerland, first appears in Cincinnati in 1822, advertising in May at 11 Lower Market Street as a watch and clock maker and jeweler, paying the highest prices for old gold and silver.[1] In 1825, his shop was located at 243 Main Street, and then in 1829 and 1831 he was listed at the corner of Main and Seventh Streets.[2] He does not appear in directory listings after 1831.

A Frederick Humbert Droz who worked in Cleveland as a watch maker, jeweler and a practitioner of the alternative therapy known as Baunscheidtism, came to the United States from Germany in 1852.[3] A relationship between him and the Cincinnati Droz has not been elucidated.

The mark of Frederick Droz (mark 37.1) has been observed on a spoon with a fiddle-shaped handle.[4]

1. Advertisement, *Western Spy and Literary Gazette*, May 18, 1822, reproduced in Beckman, 48; 1825 Cincinnati City Directory; Beckman indicates that Droz was listed in the 1819 Directory as a silversmith working at the corner of Seventh and Main Streets, but this could not be found.

2. 1825, 1829, 1831 Cincinnati City Directories. In 1829, he lists as a silversmith and all other years as a watch maker.

3. 1861, 1865, 1878, 1884, 1886 Cleveland City Directories; Ancestry.com. *U.S. Naturalization Records Indexes, 1794–1995* [online database], Provo, Utah: Ancestry.com Operations Inc., 2007.

4. F. Droz, eBay listings and private collections, Cincinnati silver binders, Cincinnati Art Museum.

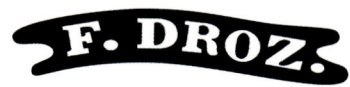

MARK 37.1

38. DUHME & CO.

1843–1893

THE DUHME COMPANY

1893–1897

THE DUHME JEWELRY CO.

1897–1910

THE DUHME MANUFACTURING CO.

1898

DUHME BROS. & CO.

1898–1905

DUHME BROS.

1905–about 1928

Duhme & Co. was the largest, most productive and successful firm in the history of Cincinnati's silver industry. It and its successive firms operated for over 80 years, and in the last half of the 19th century, Duhme & Co. was a serious competitor of the Eastern firms of Tiffany & Co., Gorham Mfg. Co., Whiting Mfg. Co., and others. The firm's founder, Johann Hermann Gerhard Duhme, later known as Herman G. Duhme (fig. 38.1) was born in Osnabruck, Hanover, Germany on June 14, 1819, to Herman H. and Margaret Duhme.[1] In 1834, Herman H. Duhme led his family and a large party of Hanoverians to America. They set sail from Bremen in July and arrived in New York in September.[2] Traveling across land and by river, the group settled in Springfield, Ohio, where the young Herman G. Duhme went to work with Griffith Foos (1772–1859), founder of Springfield, farmer, and former tavern and oil-mill operator.[3]

The Early Years

In 1838, Herman G. relocated to Cincinnati to join his brother Henry H. Duhme (1814–1874) in work at Charles (Karl) Wolff's dry goods store on Fifth, between Walnut and Vine Streets.[4] By 1839, Herman G. was employed at Lewis H. Wellman's dry goods shop on the north side of Fifth, also between Walnut and Vine.[5]

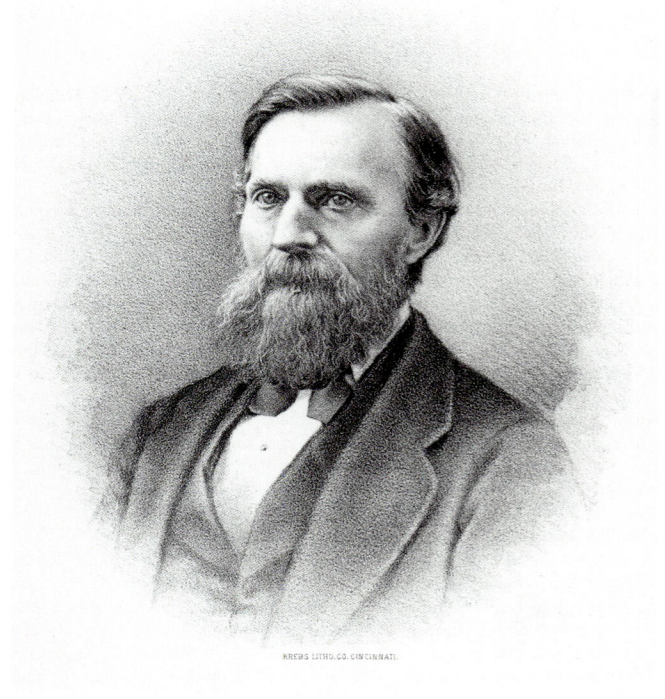

FIG. 38.1: Engraved image of Herman G. Duhme from Van Armin Tenner, *Cincinnati Sonst Und Jetzt*, Cincinnati: Druck van Mecklenborg & Rosentahl, 1878, 41

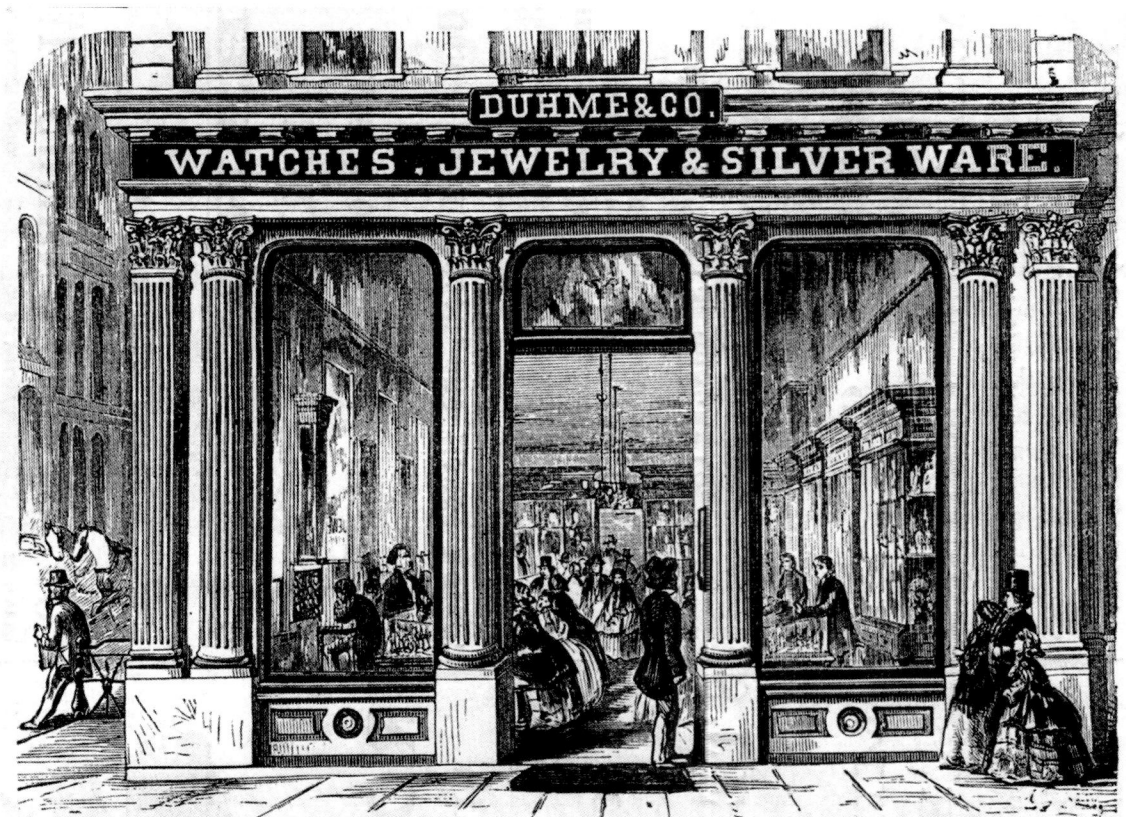

FIG. 38.2: Duhme & Co., Carlisle Building, from *The New World in 1859*, New York: H. Bailliere, 1859, facing 75

Regarded as an "industrious and frugal" man, Herman G. worked and saved enough capital to buy a small amount of stock in New York and opened his own business as a dealer in "watch tools and materials, jewelry, fine cutlery and fancy goods" on Fourth Street (5 West Fourth Street), between Main and Vine Street by 1842.[6] When Herman G.'s brother John H. Duhme (b. about 1816) joined the business in 1843, the firm became Duhme & Co.[7] In 1848, the firm was taxed on $10,000 and was conducting "a large flourishing business."[8] By late 1849, they had relocated to 130 Main Street, in the Commercial Bank Building, between Third and Fourth Streets, opposite the Masonic temple.[9] Their advertisement in the 1850/51 City Directory lists "CLOCKS, WATCHES, JEWELRY, WATCH-MAKERS' TOOLS AND MATERIALS . . . Gold, Silver and Common Spectacles; Gold and Silver Pencils; Spectacle Glasses; Percussion Caps; Revolving Pistols; Razors; Knives; Scissors; Dentists' Files; Toys, &c., &c." as goods that were "constantly on hand."[10]

In 1851, Herman G. Duhme traveled to London to attend the Great Exhibition of the Works of Industry of All Nations, held between May 1 and October 15, 1851.[11] He and his brother Henry H. had purchased a farm in Delhi Township, Ohio, in 1846, where they established expansive vineyards for the production of Catawba wine.[12] Specimens of their wine were entered at the Great Exhibition.[13] During his sojourn, Herman G. visited the leading manufacturers in his line in England, France, Germany, and Switzerland, to make arrangements to import their products, and to conduct research to help in the development and expansion of his own business.

By 1852, Herman G. Duhme had established a second retail business under the management of James H. Cook in St. Louis, Missouri.[14] In a letter from Cook, written to Duhme and dated February 4, 1852, Cook states that "business at present is extremely dull . . . the prospects for continuing business here are not flattering and I am of the opinion that we had better close it up this spring as I do not think it will pay to continue on."[15] Cook requested a small amount of jewelry, and returned the following wares to Cincinnati by Livingston Express: bar gold, California gold, silver spoons, silver cases, and silver goblets. This represents the earliest documented mention of silver table wares in association with the firm. These were most likely wares retailed, and not made, by the firm.

Despite the nationwide economic crisis from 1857 to the start of the Civil War, Duhme & Co. grew. Employees **Louis Phillipus Muller**, **Samuel Hatch**, and **Albert C. Pratt** were enumerated as principals of the firm by 1857.[16] But an R.G. Dun & Co. credit report notes that Muller, Hatch and Pratt, "young men who have been in the house a long time . . . tho' their names appear in the firm are not partners, having only an interest for services in lieu of salary."[17] In the summer of 1858, Duhme & Co. relocated to the Carlisle Building on the southwest corner of Fourth and Walnut Streets (fig. 38.2).[18] The retail department, located in the front part of their store, was supervised by **Henry Bliss**. Among the stocked wares and services listed in an August advertisement were "silver and silver plated ware," jewelry, watches, spectacles, gold pens,

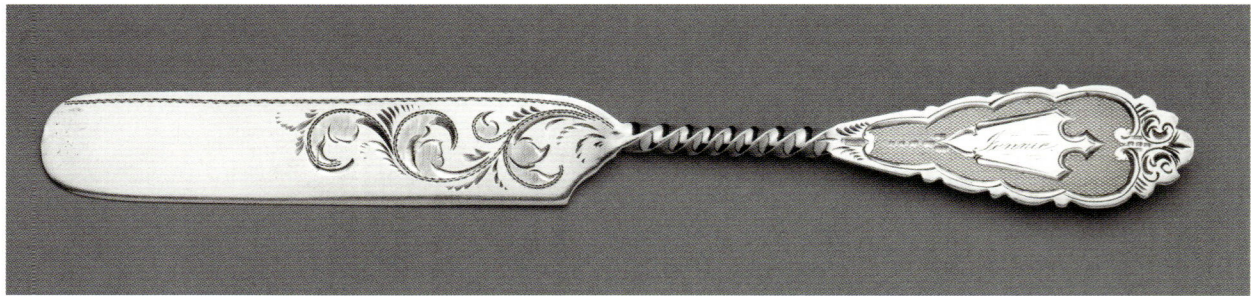

FIG. 38.3: Henry H. Duhme, *Knife*, c. 1863, L. 6⅜ in. (16.2 cm), CAM, Museum Purchase: John S. Conner Fund, 2011.8. Mark 38.18

watch glasses, tools and materials for jobbing and watch repairs.[19] In 1859, "silver ware" was included for the first time in the firm's city directory listing, and a December advertisement enumerates that in addition to watches and jewelry, their stock included: "Spoons and Fancy Articles of Silver, Silver Napkin Rings, Fruit Knives and Silver Card Cases. Silverware of all kinds in great variety, and all other articles in the Jewelry Line just received."[20] An advertisement from 1861 notes that they were retailing "Gorham Table Plate" and offering "Sterling Silver Table Ware, a great variety of new and elegant designs."[21] Double-marked silver (those pieces with both Duhme & Co. marks and the marks of other manufacturers) indicate that throughout its history, Duhme & Co. also dealt in silver made by Dominick & Haff (New York City); William B. Durgin Co. (Concord, New Hampshire); Reed & Barton (Taunton, Massachusetts); Whiting Mfg. Co. (North Attleboro, Massachusetts); George W. Shiebler (New York City); Frank M. Whiting Co. (North Attleboro, Massachusetts); and R. Wallace & Sons (Wallingford, Connecticut).[22]

The 1860s

Based on what little evidence and documentation exists, Duhme probably did not begin to manufacture its own silverware, at least on a large scale, until the early 1860s, after its move to the Carlisle Building.[23] The 1862 City Directory is the first in which we find a silversmith, **Justus Kruckemeyer**, employed at Duhme, in addition to jewelers, bookkeepers and salesmen.[24] A reminiscence published in 1923 recalls that Kruckemeyer was "at the head of the silversmithing department," and that **Herman Franz Serodino** succeeded **Wenzel Partl** as foreman of the gold department.[25] Further support for the notion that the firm had some manufacturing capabilities by this time comes with the report that during the Civil War they made bullets and pontoon bridges.[26]

Duhme & Co.'s involvement in manufacturing most likely began with jewelry and then moved into silver table and novelty

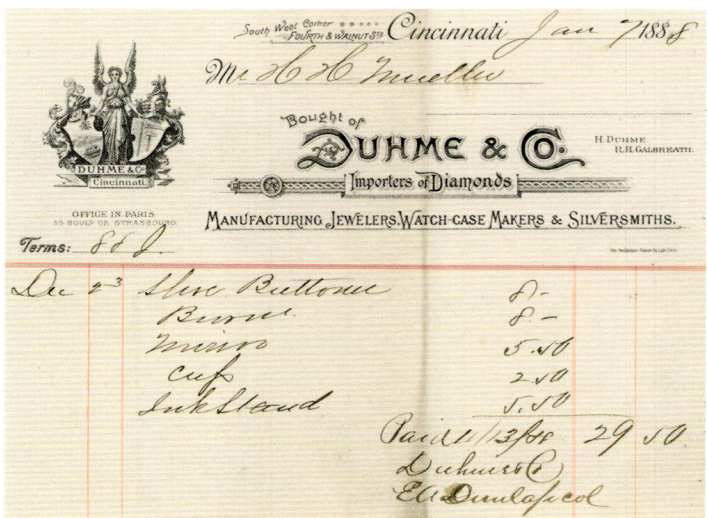

FIG. 38.4: Duhme & Co., *Billhead*, 1888, Courtesy of Irene and Daniel Randolph. This billhead notes the partnership of Duhme and Galbreath which lasted until Duhme's death in August 1888.

wares. In 1862, they advertised "to corporations, societies, clubs and individuals–Solid gold, solid silver premium plate, medals, badges, emblematic pins or jewels, of any description made promptly to order . . . by Duhme & Co., Silversmiths and Jewelers."[27] It was not until 1866 that they listed in city directories as manufacturers of silverware, and the first known published advertisement noting their manufacture of coin silver did not appear until the spring of 1867.[28]

Complaints against Duhme from creditors began to mount in 1859.[29] In 1857, Herman G. Duhme's first wife Mary Ann McNichol, who had brought considerable wealth to the marriage through her father, Peter McNichol, applied for a divorce that was not finalized until 1859.[30] Under considerable duress, Herman G. sold his stock to his brother Henry H. Duhme in February 1861 to secure debts owed to Henry H. and other parties, and Duhme & Co. remained in Henry H.'s name until March of 1867.[31] A butter knife (fig. 38.3) from this period, struck, incuse, on the blade with "H. H. Duhme," could have been retailed at Duhme & Co. or in Henry H.'s dry goods store.

In April 1864 Herman G. Duhme married Mary C. Galbreath, the ex-wife of his first wife Mary Ann McNichol's brother.[32] Around 1868, Duhme took his former employee and new brother-in-law **Robert Harvey Galbreath** in as partner (fig. 38.4).[33] Galbreath's father, James, had been a successful manufacturer of axes and other tools. Whether or not R.H. Galbreath was responsible for the firm's increased activities in manufacturing at this time is unknown. However, it was this new focus in Duhme's business approach that turned the company around and led to its success as the most prolific and profitable jewelry and silver firm in Cincinnati.

In late December 1867 reports noted that Duhme's "stock of sterling silver comprises everything new and beautiful in that line."[34] "The largest stock of silver cups and goblets, some plain, others highly decorated and lined with gold" (fig. 38.5) were recognized as "peculiarly attractive and exceedingly suitable for New Years gifts," and their patterns of "twist-handle knives, forks, spoons &c. in silver" were deemed "exceedingly handsome."[35] The following year, it was noted that "from their own Silver Factory, they have Solid Silver Tea Sets, Salvers, Butter Dishes, Ladles, Spoons, Forks, &c., &c., of Sterling and Coin Silver."[36] Credit reporters remarked that Duhme did "the largest business in their line here, manufacturing considerable silver plate, employing 25 to 30 hands," and that they were estimated to be worth $100,000.[37]

An account from the era reads:

The facilities for manufacturing enjoyed by this house, enables them to at all times keep a large stock of the most desirable goods on hand. This is one of the largest manufacturing jewelry establishments in the country. All the machinery and apparatus required for turning the crude material into the most beautiful articles of ornament and use are set up in their large building where about 80 hands are kept constantly employed. Amongst these hands are some of the best gold and silversmiths in the country. In the basement of the building, we watched, with great interest, the bars of gold and silver going through all the different stages of manufacture. The finishing rooms in the upper stories of the building look like so many beehives. Some are at work on salt spoons, which are the smallest articles made; others on napkin rings; others on tea sets and so on up to the most elaborately finished urns, punchbowls, etc. Here mostly all of the different articles manufactured can be seen going through some of the many processes required before they are finished for the salesroom.[38]

In March 1868 Herman G. wrote to his sons Herman Jr. (1851–1923) and Frank (1854–1920), who were studying in Switzerland: "Our business is tolerable good, but most of our people say it is very dull with them. . . . Uncle Henty [*sic*, Henry H.] is going to give up the [dry goods] business."[39] Eight months later, Herman G. wrote to his sons, "We number about 115 persons in the store and factory, and all [have] more to do than we can conceivably

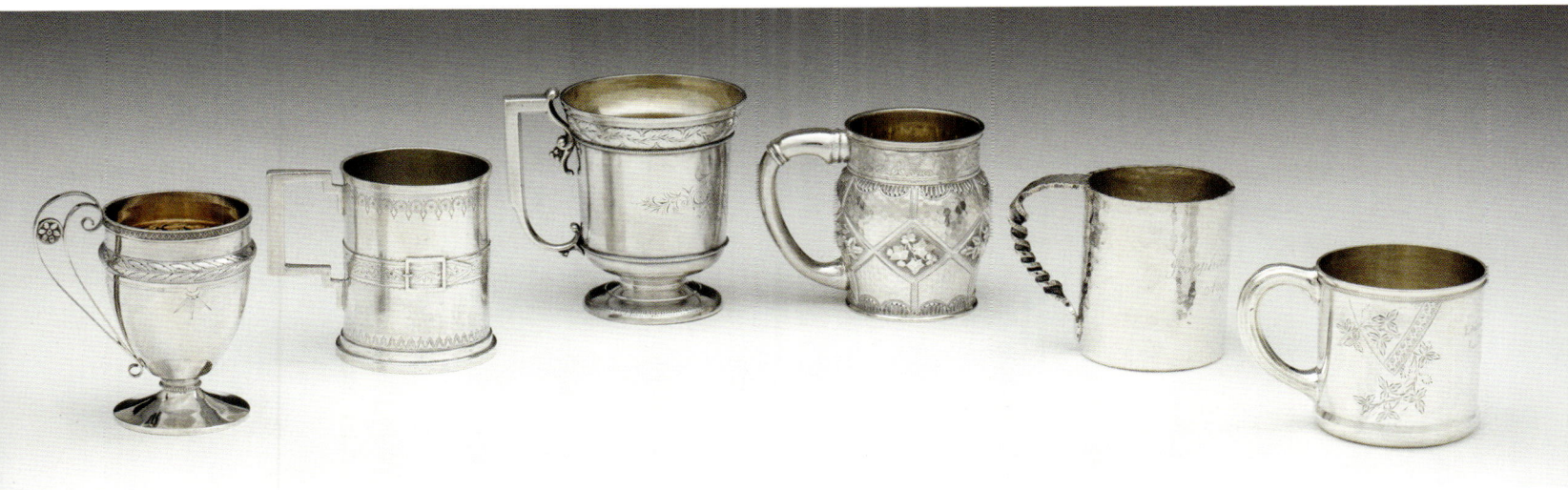

FIG. 38.5: (L to R) Duhme & Co., *Cup*, c. 1875, parcel gilt silver, 4⅜ × 4⅛ in. (11.1 × 10.5 cm), CAM, Gift of James Randolph Hillard, M.D. and Aingeal Grehan, 2007.170. Inscription: Leo / Jany 1st 1875. Mark 38.7; Duhme & Co., *Mug*, 1870s, 3¾ × 4⅛ in. (9.5 × 10.5 cm), CAM, Gift of James Randolph Hillard, M.D. and Aingeal Grehan, 2007.171. Inscription: Jennie Williams. Mark 38.7; Duhme & Co., *Cup*, c. 1865, parcel gilt silver, 4⅜ × 4⅝ in. (11.1 × 11.7 cm), CAM, Gift of James Randolph Hillard, M.D. and Aingeal Grehan, 2007.172. Inscription: M.W.R. / FROM / E.R. Mark 38.7; Duhme & Co., *Mug*, c. 1880, parcel gilt silver, 3⅝ × 4⅝ in. (9.2 × 11.7 cm), CAM, Gift of James Randolph Hillard, M.D. and Aingeal Grehan, 2007.174. Mark 38.9; Duhme & Co., *Mug*, c. 1881, 3¼ × 4¼ in. (8.3 × 10.8 cm), CAM, Gift of James Randolph Hillard, M.D. and Aingeal Grehan, 2007.111. Inscription: Josephine Arthur Rohrer / August 14th. 1881. Mark 38.10; Duhme & Co., *Mug*, c. 1887, 3 × 3¹⁄₁₆ in. (7.6 × 7.8 cm), CAM, Bequest of Edmund Kerper, 1959.33. Inscription: Edmund Mooney Kerper. / 1st Anniversary. Nov. 27th. 1887 / FROM / J.E.M. Mark 38.10

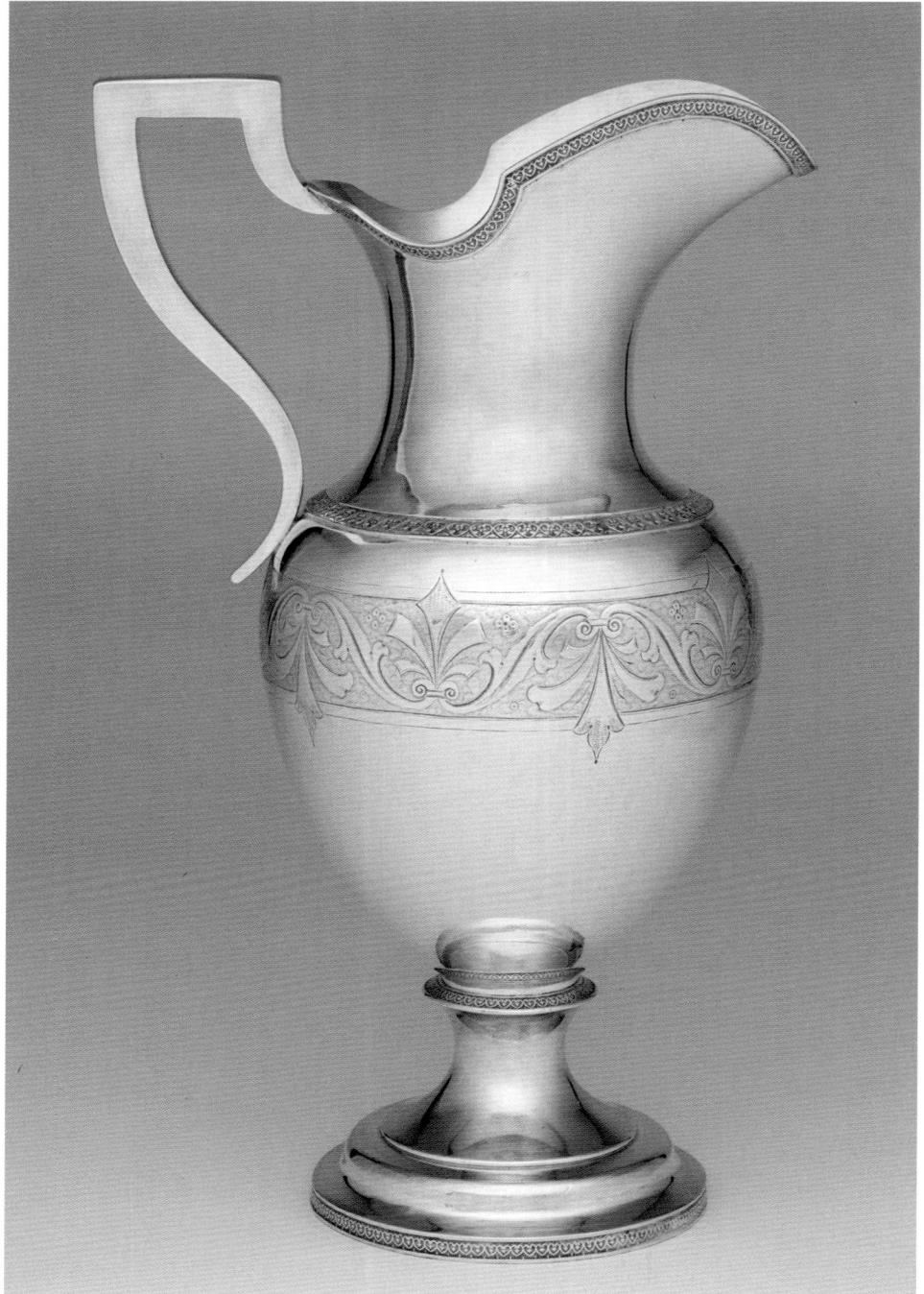

FIG. 38.6: Duhme & Co., *Ewer*, 1860s, H. 14¾ in. (37.5 cm), W. 9 in. (22.29 cm), CAM, Museum Purchase with funds provided by Mr. and Mrs. Charles Fleischmann III, 2005.69. Mark 38.7

accomplish. Business is pretty good. Our store looks well, and it will be a very pleasant place for you when you return. You will be able to sell goods right off."[40] Between May 1, 1868, and April 30, 1869, the gross sales of the store amounted to $467,201.[41]

Further descriptions of the manufactory, its processes, and its staff were provided in an extensive article in May 1869, explaining, "when articles of silverware are specially ordered, the designer goes to work and supplies the model. For the general articles of use and [those] intended for the salesroom, he merely pleases himself."[42] Most articles were "made from bars of silver or coins melted down in the establishment," and using "suitable machines . . . not only in the manufacture of knives, forks, spoons, etc., but also in the embossing and engraving of these and similar articles, and a mug, a napkin ring or a pitcher is turned out as rapidly and as certainly

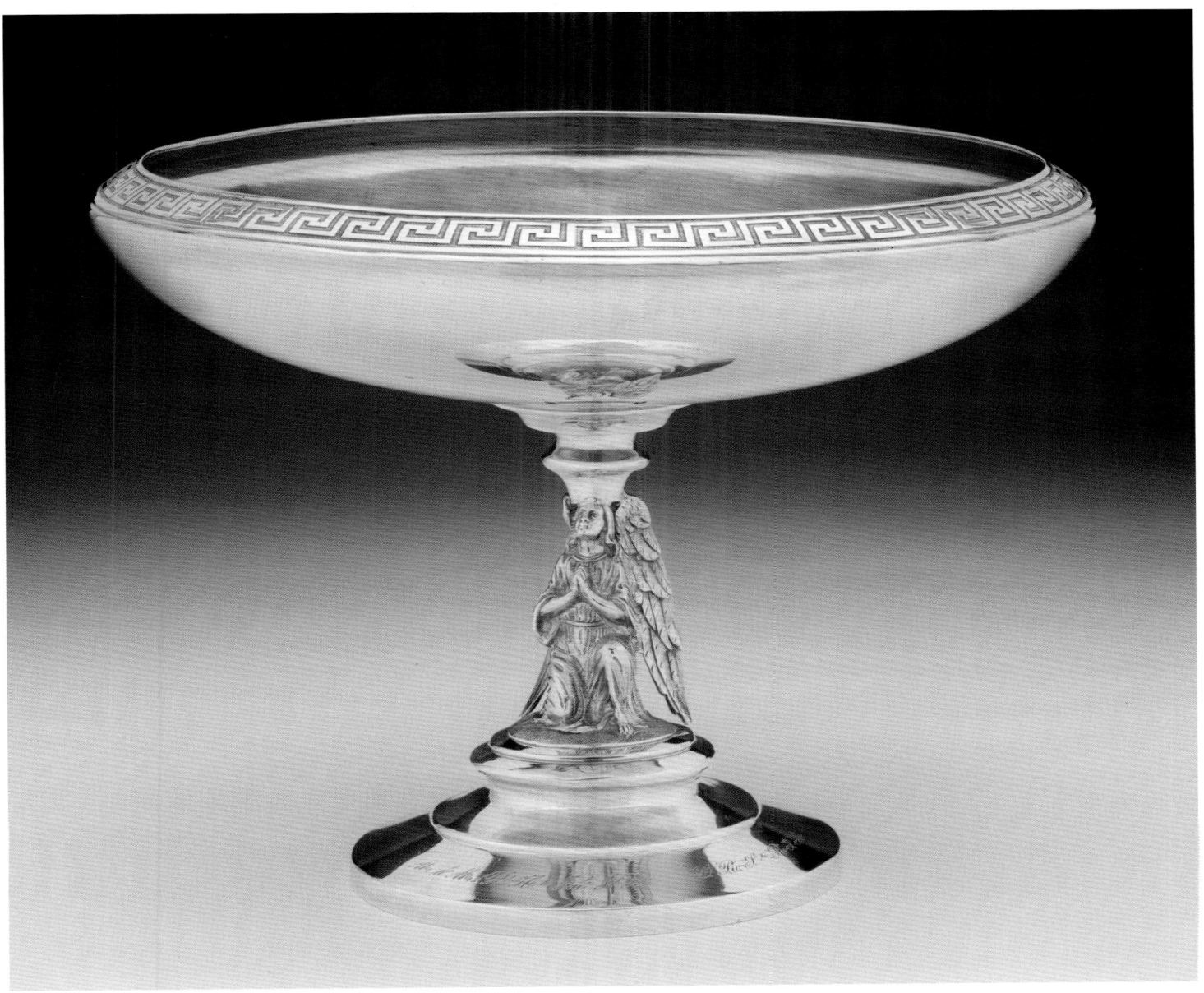

FIG. 38.7: Duhme & Co., *Compote*, 1860s, H. 8¾ in. (22.2 cm), Diam. 12⅛ in. (30.8 cm), CAM, Gift of Joan S. Reis, 1985.174.
Inscriptions: Mr. & Mrs. Ph. H. to J. & J. R.; L. R. S. To R. J. R. Mark 38.7

as if it were of tin or iron." "Not less than from 125 to 150 experienced hands are daily employed on the fine metals and in the art of setting diamonds and precious stones," and about twenty apprentices, "sons of jewelers and silversmiths" were reported. Among the firm's employees, it was said that fourteen different nationalities were represented. Elsewhere, it was noted that every piece of silver carried the stamp of the manufacturer, and that steam power was "used in every department and utilized to do the work of hundreds."[43] The 1870 Product of Industry Census reported that Duhme had $100,000 of capital invested, employed

162 employees (140 male, 10 female, and 12 youth), paid $135,000 in wages that year, and utilized one steam engine, $50,000 worth of silver, $50,000 worth of gold, and $200 of miscellaneous material to create a product valued at $250,000.[44]

During the 1860s, much of the coin silver produced by Duhme was fashioned in the Classical Revival style (figs. 38.6, 38. 7, 38.8). The earliest flatware patterns offered by the firm were the simple, tipped, exaggerated fiddle pattern (in production through the 1880s) and a pattern referred to by collectors and researchers as "Duhme No. 1" (circa 1869) (fig. 38.9).[45] Variations of the "fancy"

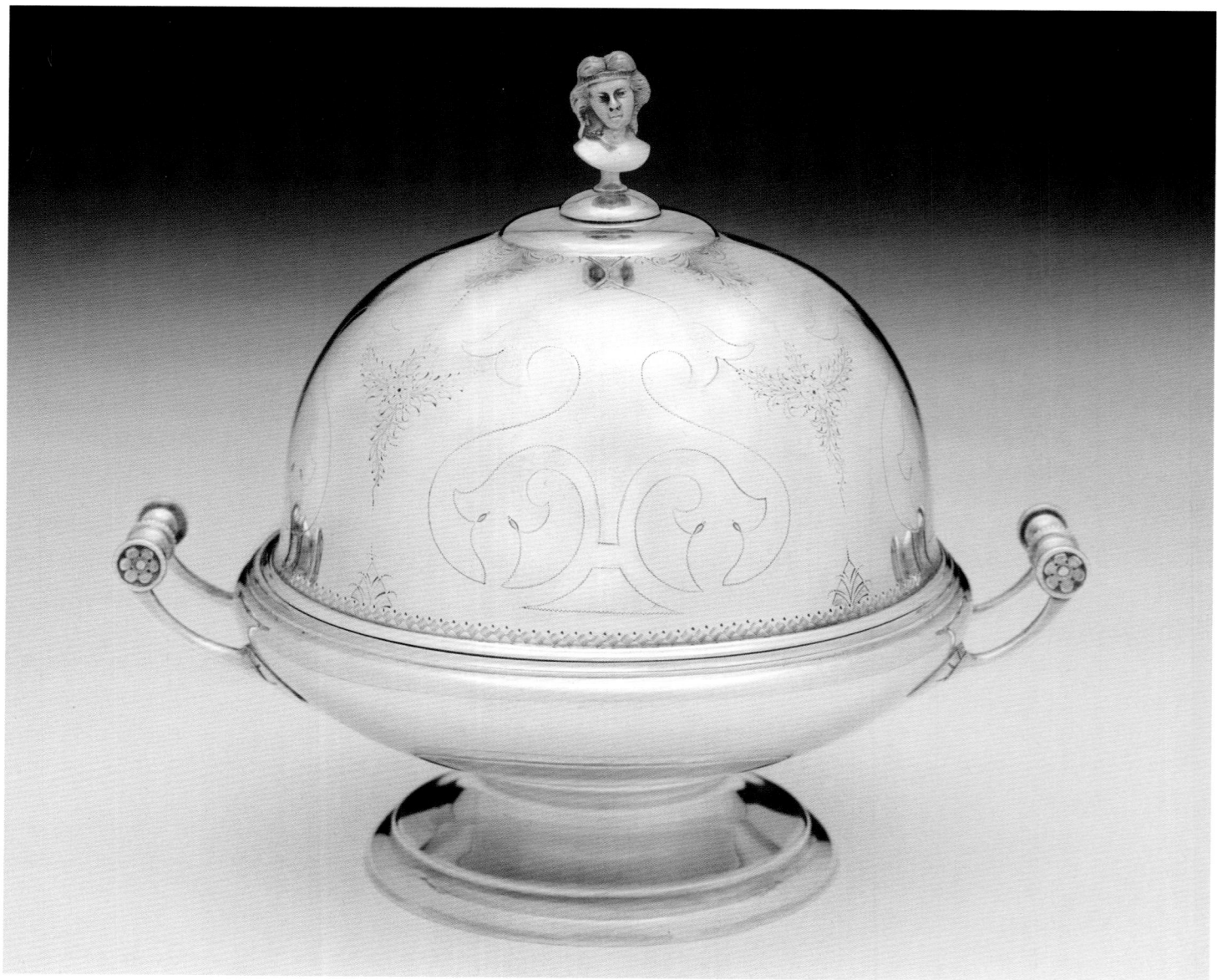

FIG. 38.8: Duhme & Co., *Butter Dish*, 1860s, H. 7½ in. (19.1 cm), Diam. 8½ in. (21.6 cm), CAM, Museum Purchase with funds provided by Mr. and Mrs. Charles Fleischmann III, 2005.67a–b. Marks 38.2 and 38.7. The bust finial of this butter dish is similar to that used in Gorham Mfg. Co.'s bust pattern, introduced circa 1867.

fiddle handle, as seen in "No. 1", were also offered, usually with bright-cut engraving and/or twist stems (fig. 38.10). Duhme's applied medallion pattern was one of the many medallion patterns offered by American silver firms such as Wood & Hughes, Gorham Mfg. Co., and George W. Shiebler.[46] Produced with a variety of male and female Classical heads, wares with these medallions included hollowware (fig. E2.1, 38.11, 38.12) and flatware in full table service and in smaller gift sets of serving flatware (fig. 38.13). This pattern's popularity continued into the 1880s.[47] The unidentified

Neoclassical die-pressed patterns in figs. 38.14 and 38.15 also bear Duhme & Co. marks.[48] Flatware with three-dimensional cast finials in the form of a child in Classical drape also likely appeared in the 1860s (fig. 38.16). Wares in the Gothic Revival style demonstrated in an elegant bachelor's tea service (fig. 38.17), and in the Rococo Revival style, such as steer and stag head flatware (figs. 38.18, 38.19), were other Duhme creations of the era.[49] Marks 38.1 through 38.7 were commonly used throughout the 1860s.[50]

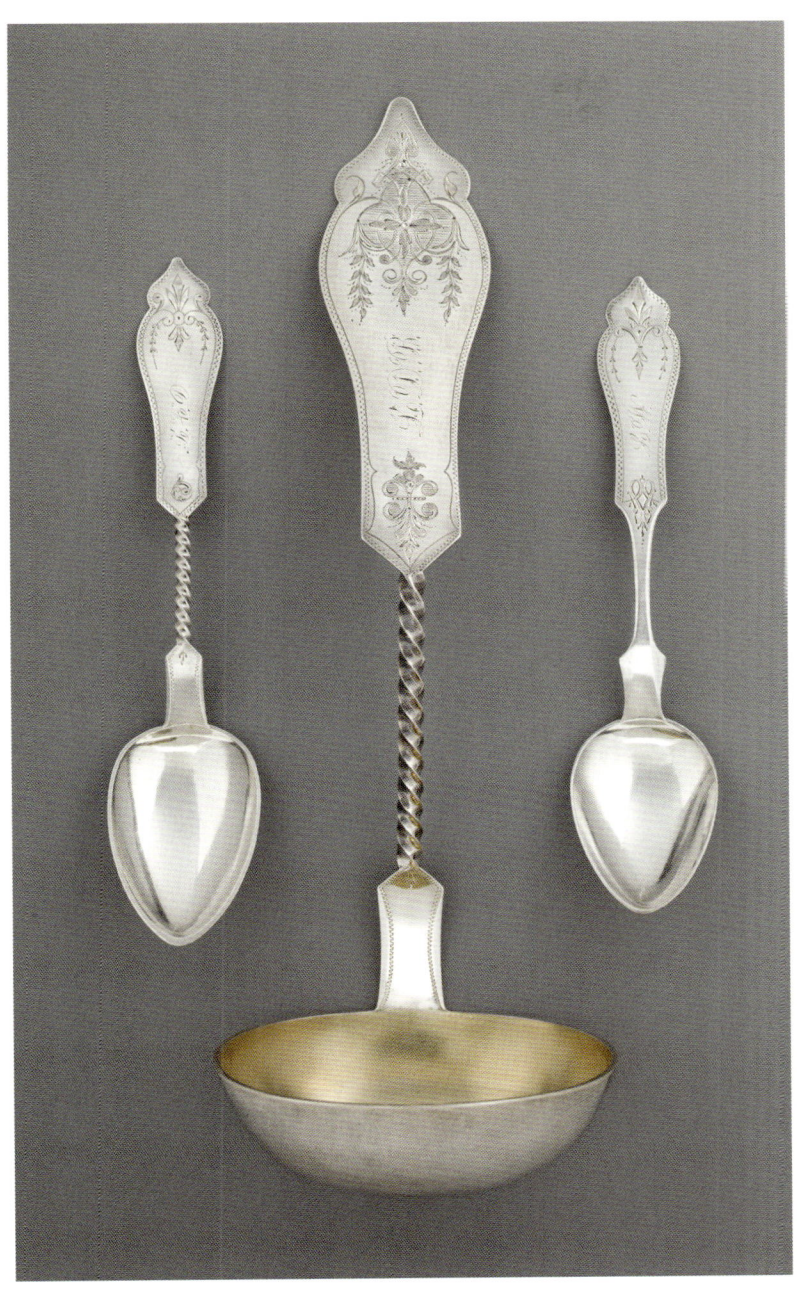

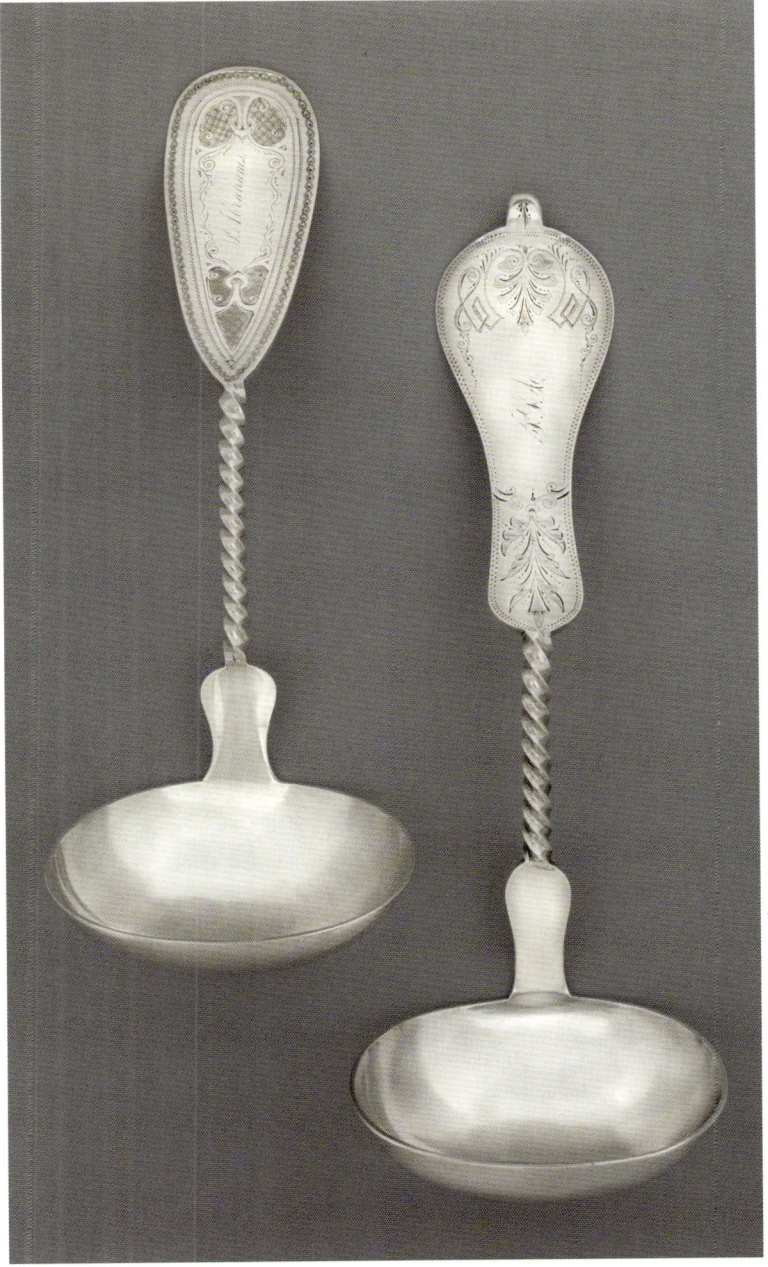

FIG. 38.9: Duhme & Co., *Serving Spoon*, "No. 1" pattern, c. 1870, L. 8⅜ in. (21.3 cm), CAM, Gift of Dr. Suzanne A. Beutler, 1983.214. Mark 38.7; Duhme & Co., *Ladle*, "No. 1" pattern, c. 1870, parcel gilt silver, L. 13 in. (33.3 cm), CAM, Gift of James Randolph Hillard, M.D. and Aingeal Grehan, 2007.133. Mark 38.3; Duhme & Co., *Soup Spoon*, "No. 1" pattern, c. 1870, L. 7¾ in. (19.7 cm), CAM, Gift of Rose Wallace Kumler, 1964.95. Mark 38.3

FIG. 38.10: Duhme & Co., *Ladle*, c. 1865, L. 12¼ in. (30.8 cm), CAM, Gift of James Randolph Hillard, M.D. and Aingeal Grehan, 2007.136. Mark 38.1; Duhme & Co., *Ladle*, c. 1870, L. 13 in. (33.3 cm), CAM, Gift of James Randolph Hillard, M.D. and Aingeal Grehan, 2007.135. Mark 38.3

FIG. 38.11: Duhme & Co., *Cruet Stand*,
c. 1880, H. 15 in. (38.1 cm), Diam. 8 in.
(20.3 cm), CAM, Museum Purchase with
funds provided by Mr. and Mrs. Charles
Fleischmann III, 2005.68. Inscription:
From S. T. Hauser to his Sister Theodosia
M. Knight, Montana. Mark 38.7

OPPOSITE: FIG. 38.12: Duhme & Co.,
Cruet Stand, c. 1880, H. 13¾ in. (34.9 cm),
Diam. 8¾ in. (22.2 cm), CAM, Gift of
James Randolph Hillard, M.D. and Aingeal
Grehan, 2007.124a–h. Inscription: from
S.T. Hauser to his Sister E. H. Barbour.
Mark 38.7

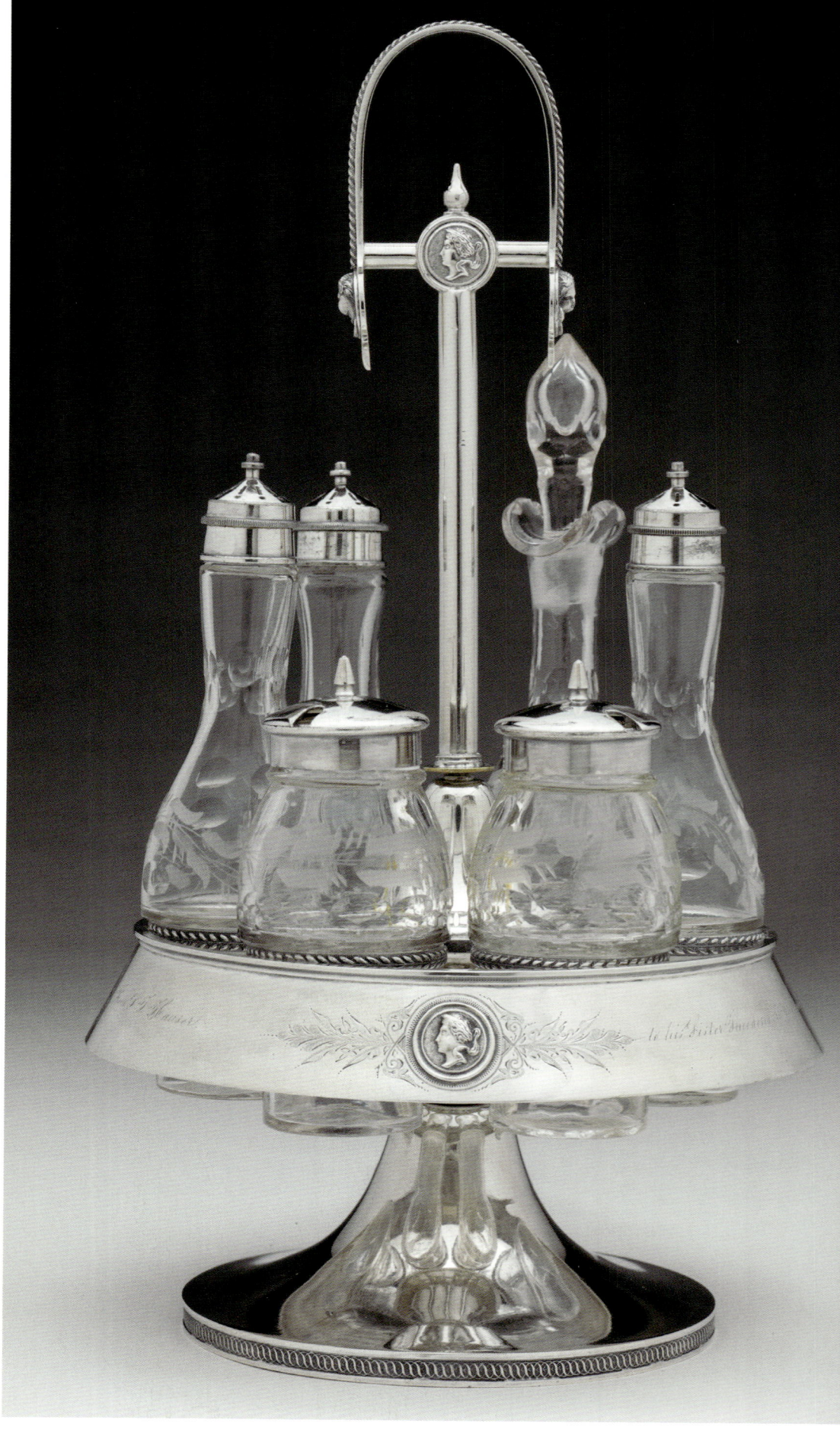

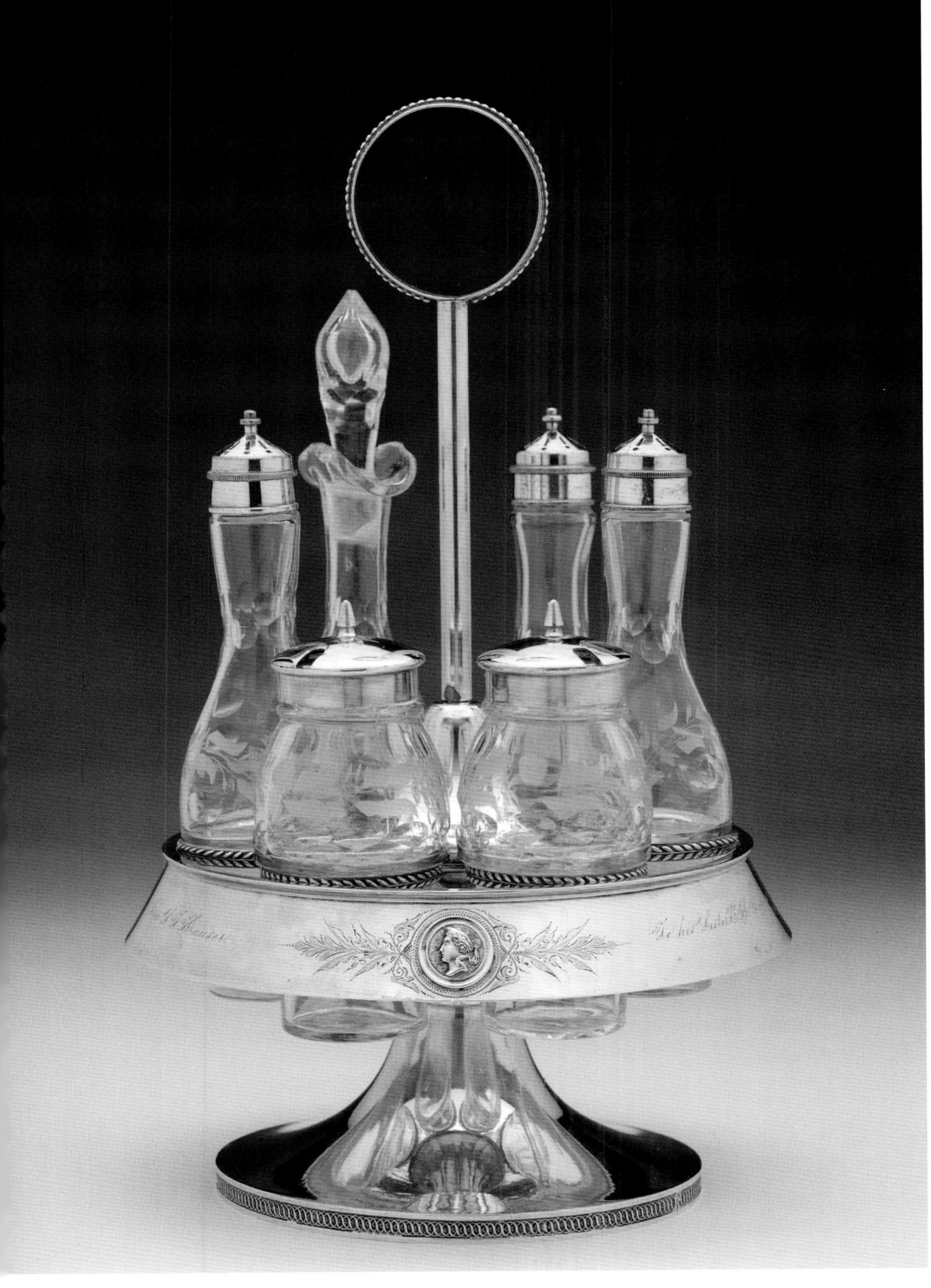

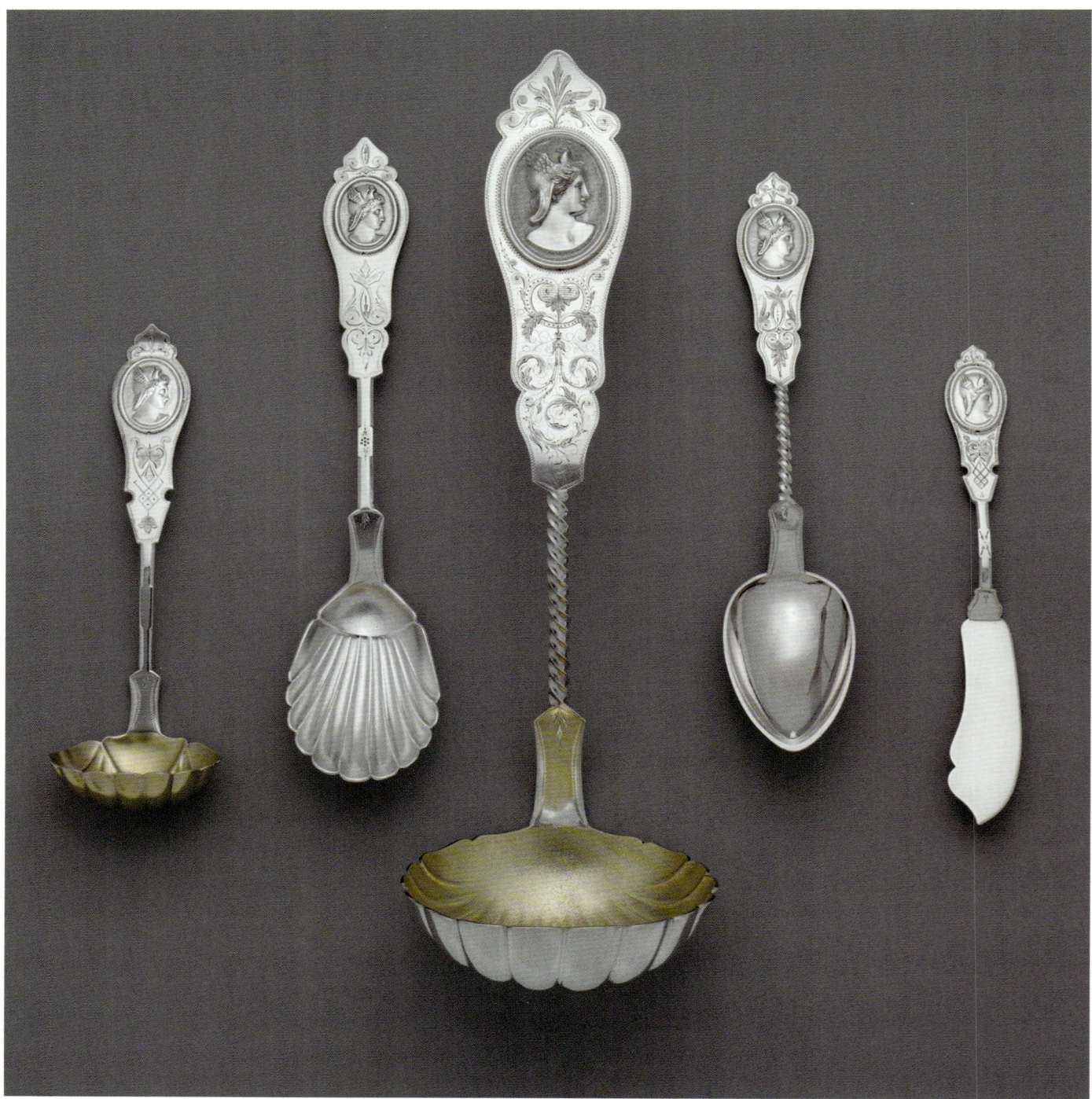

FIG. 38.13: (L to R) Duhme & Co., *Ladle*, 1860s, parcel gilt silver, L. 8¼ in. (21 cm), CAM, Gift of James Randolph Hillard, M.D. and Aingeal Grehan, 2007.131. Mark 38.7; Duhme & Co., *Serving Spoon*, 1860s, L. 9⅝ in. (24.4 cm), CAM, Gift of James Randolph Hillard, M.D. and Aingeal Grehan, 2007.147. Mark 38.7; Duhme & Co., *Ladle*, 1860s, parcel gilt silver, L. 12¾ in. (32.4 cm), CAM, Gift of James Randolph Hillard, M.D. and Aingeal Grehan, 2007.144. Mark 38.7; Duhme & Co., *Serving Spoon*, 1860s, L. 8⅝ in. (21.9 cm), CAM, Gift of Dorothy Krug Newstedt, 1975.267. Mark 38.3; Duhme & Co., *Knife*, 1860s, L. 7 in. (17.8 cm), CAM, Gift of James Randolph Hillard, M.D. and Aingeal Grehan, 2007.157. Mark 38.7

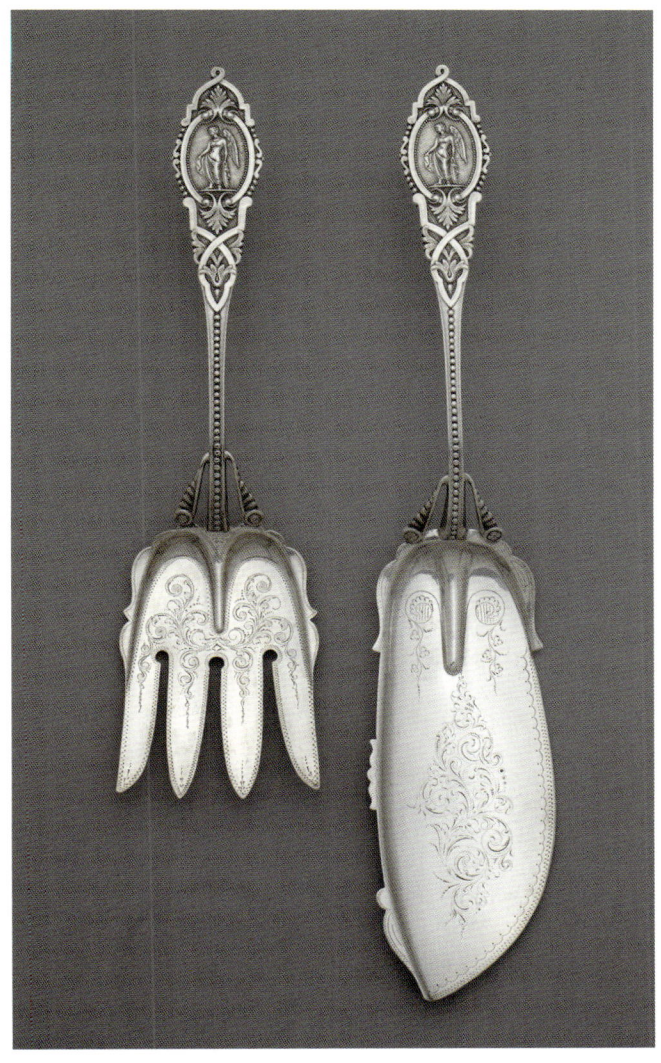

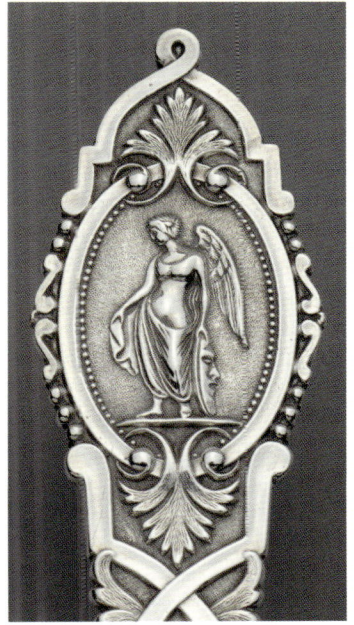

LEFT AND ABOVE: FIG. 38.14: Duhme & Co., *Fish Serving Set*, c. 1865, fork: L. 9⅞ in. (25.1 cm), knife: L. 12⅜ in. (31.4 cm), CAM, Gift of James Randolph Hillard, M.D. and Aingeal Grehan, 2007.158a–b. Mark 38.7

BELOW AND RIGHT: FIG. 38.15: Duhme & Co., *Knife*, c. 1865, parcel gilt silver, L. 12⅜ in. (31.4 cm), CAM, Gift of James Randolph Hillard, M.D. and Aingeal Grehan, 2007.167. Mark 38.7

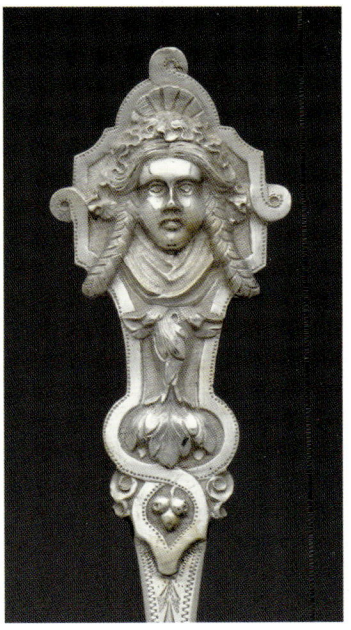

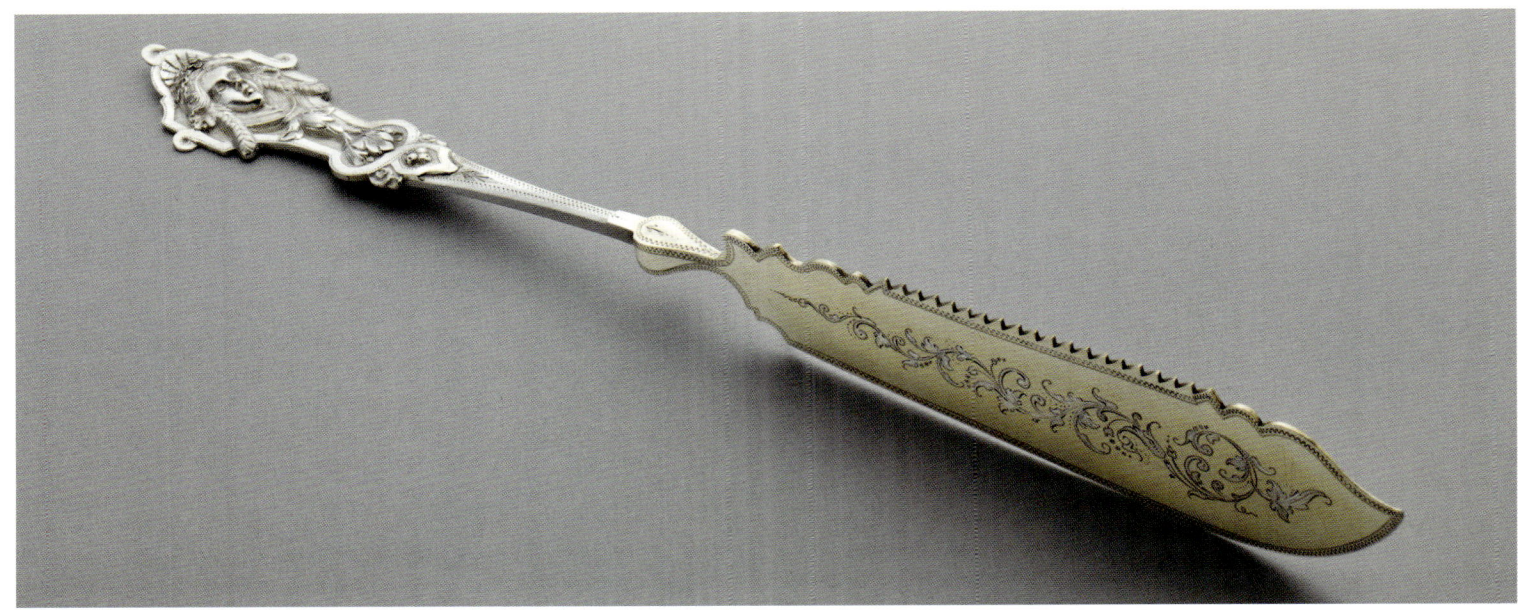

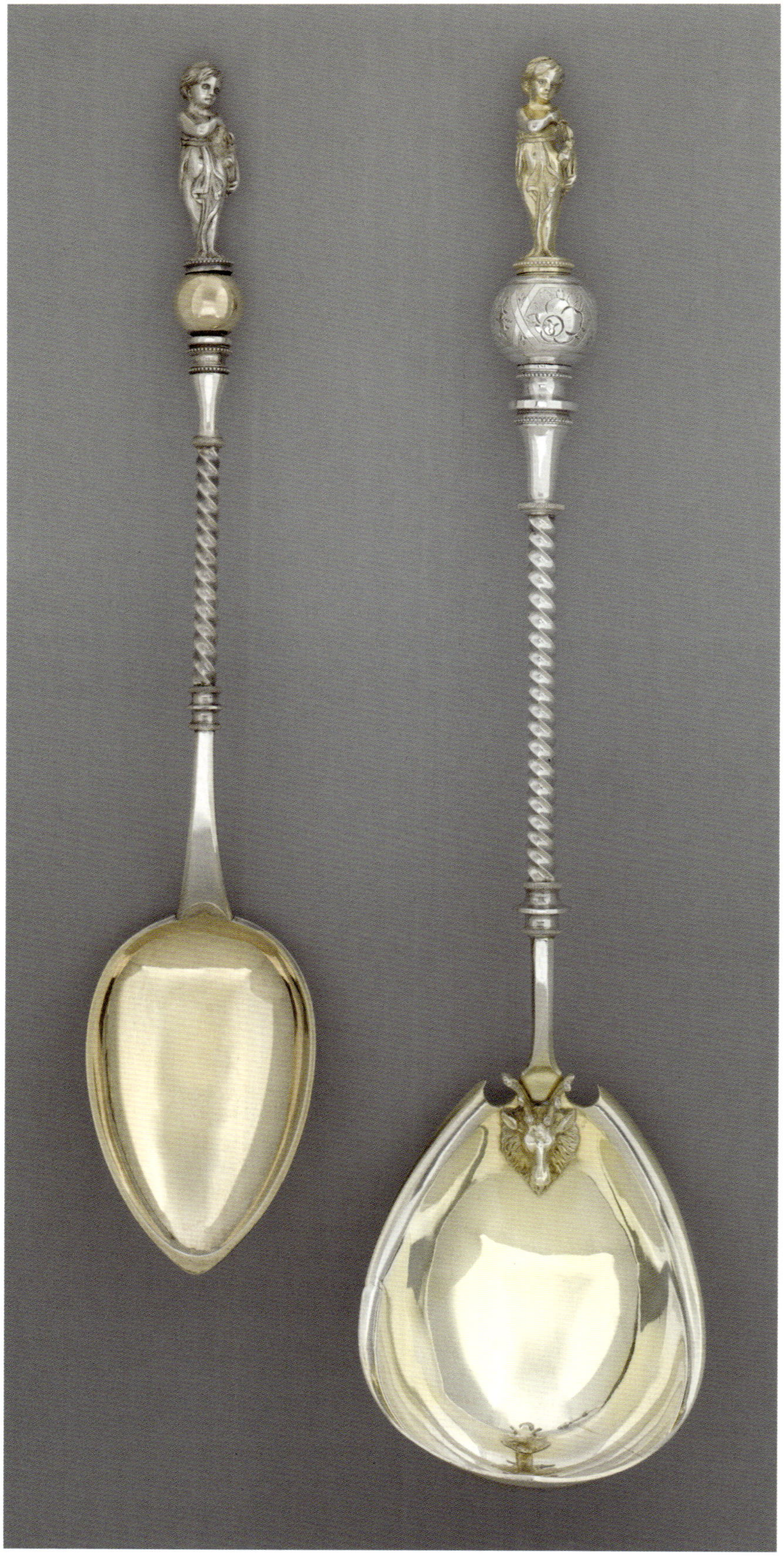

FIG. 38.16: Duhme & Co., *Serving Spoon*, 1860s, parcel gilt silver, L. 13½ in. (34.3 cm), CAM, Museum Purchase with funds provided by Mr. and Mrs. Charles Fleischmann III, 2005.66. Mark 38.7 and an incuse 5-pointed star; Duhme & Co., *Ladle*, 1860s, parcel gilt silver, L. 15 in. (39.4 cm), CAM, Gift of Mr. and Mrs. Charles Fleischmann III, 2005.23. Mark 38.7

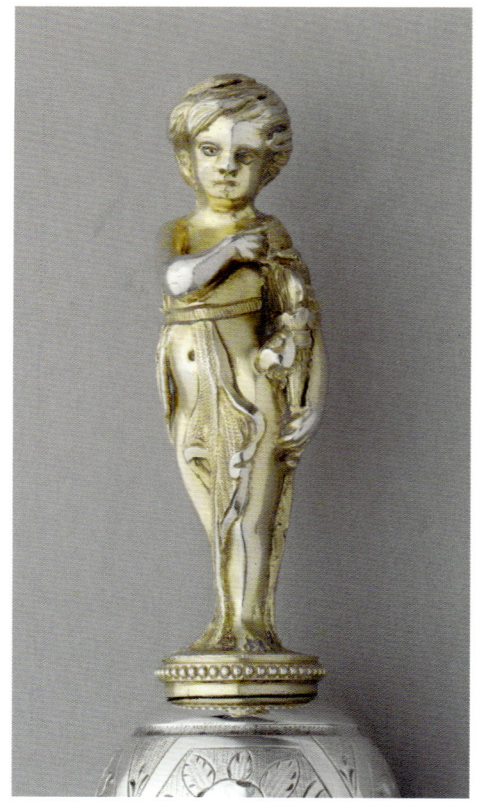

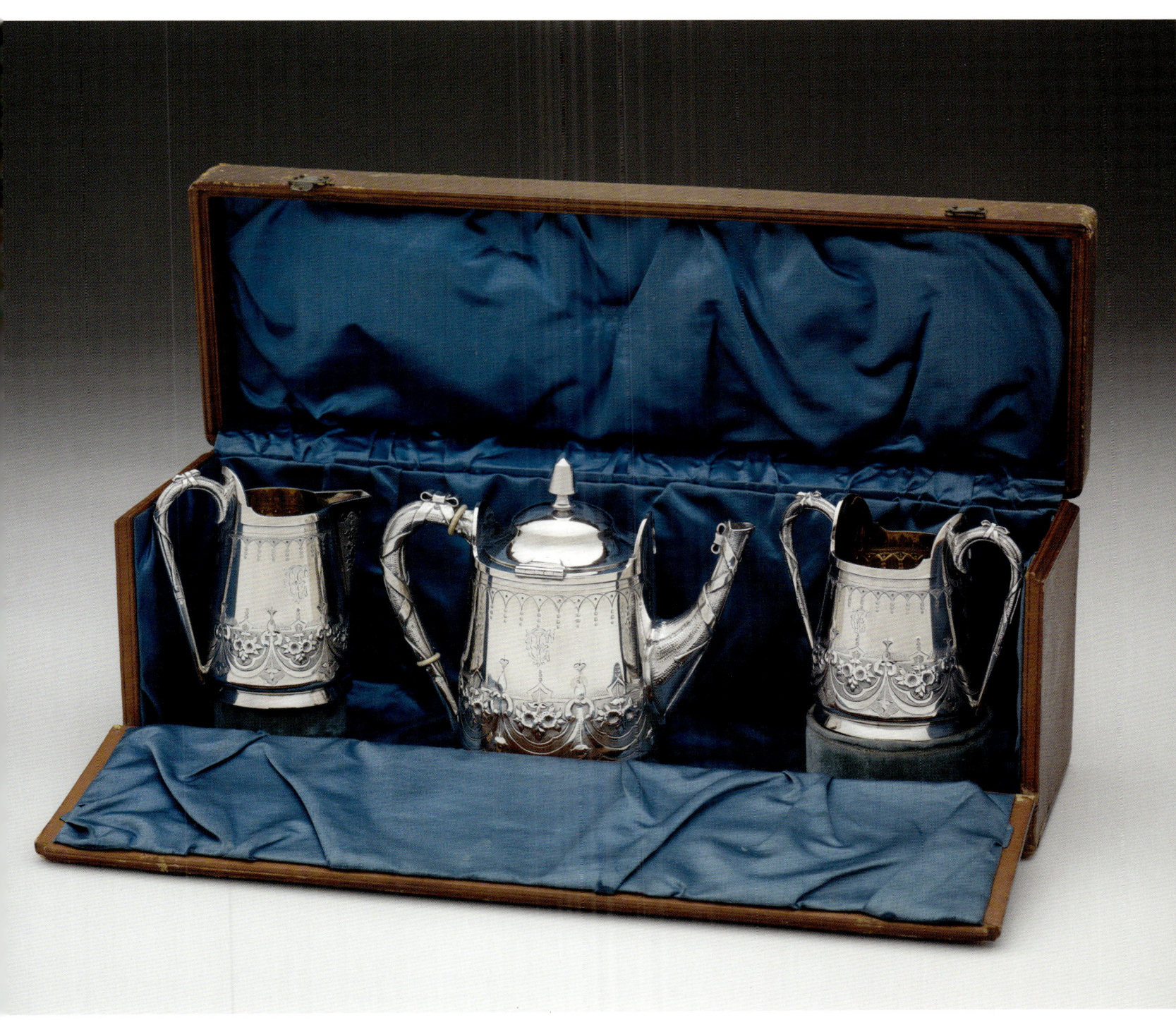

FIG. 38.17: Duhme & Co., *Tea Service with Presentation Case*, 1860s, parcel
gilt silver, leather, modern fabric, creamer: 4¼ × 4¼ in. (10.8 × 10.8 cm), teapot:
5½ × 6¾ × 3⅞ in. (14 × 17.1 × 9.8 cm), sugar: 4 × 5 in. (10.2 × 12.7 cm),
presentation case: 6 × 16 × 5 in. (15.2 × 40.6 × 12.7 cm), CAM, Museum
Purchase with funds provided by Mr. and Mrs. Charles Fleischmann III,
2005.12a–d. Mark 38.7

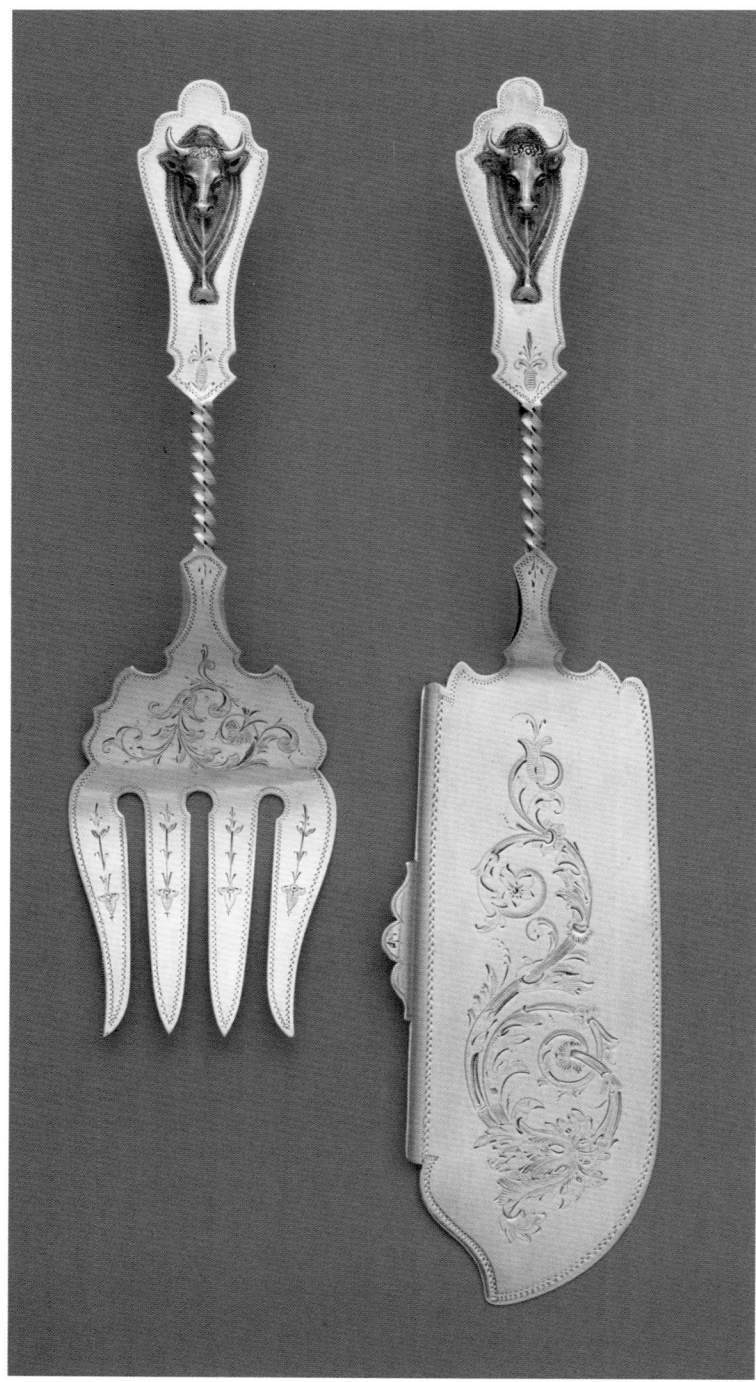

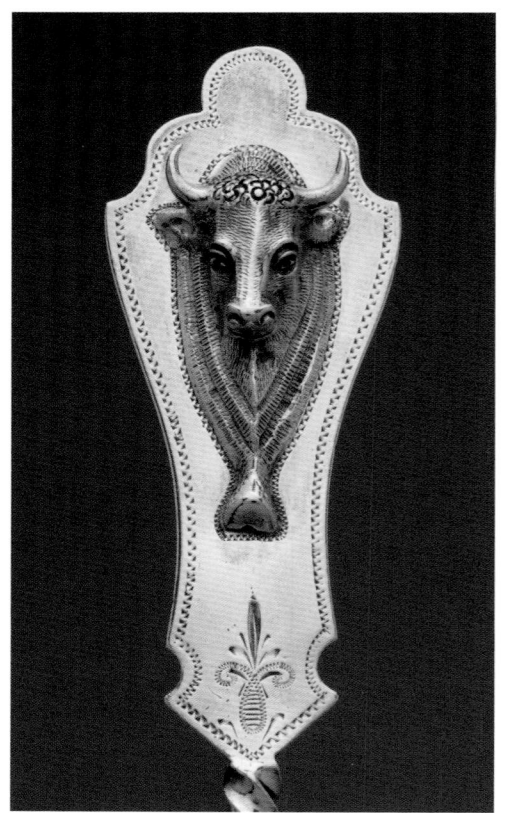

Detail of Fig. 38.18

FIG. 38.18: Duhme & Co., *Fish Serving Set*, 1860s, fork: L. 9 in. (22.9 cm), knife: L. 11⅝ in. (29.5 cm), CAM, Gift of James Randolph Hillard, M.D. and Aingeal Grehan, 2007.159a–b. Mark 38.7

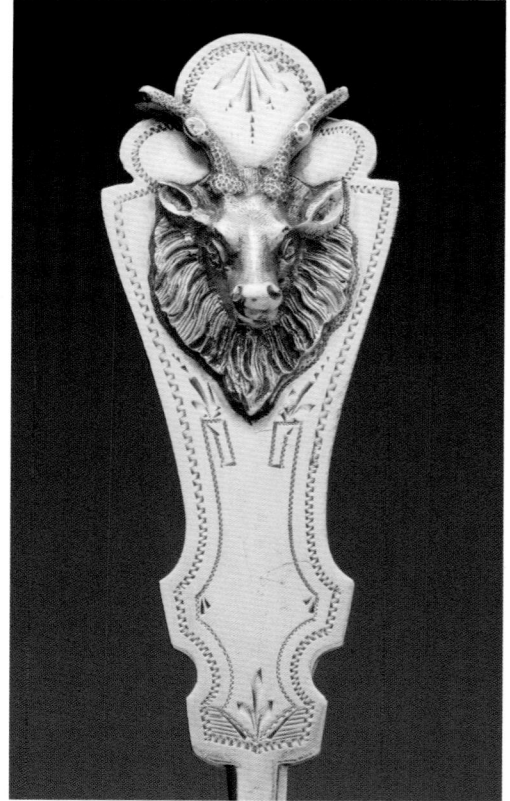

Detail of Fig. 38.19

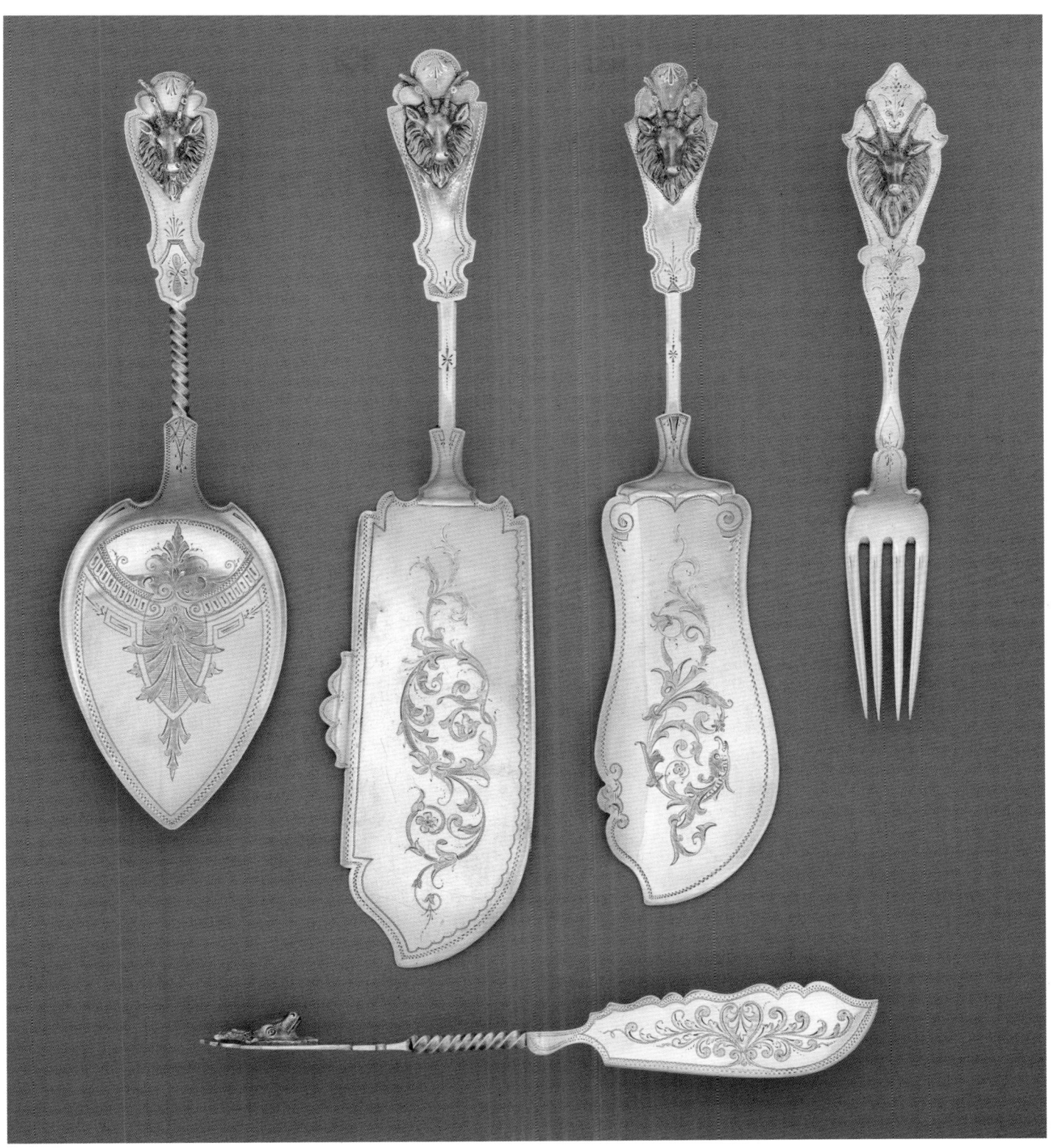

FIG. 38.19: (L to R) Duhme & Co., *Pastry Server*, 1860s, L. 9½ in. (12.1 cm), CAM, Gift of James Randolph Hillard, M.D. and Aingeal Grehan, 2007. 155.
Mark 38.7; Duhme & Co., *Fish Slice*, 1860s, L. 12 in. (30.5 cm), CAM, Museum Purchase with funds provided by Mr. and Mrs. Charles Fleischmann III, 2005.73.
Mark 38.7; Duhme & Co., *Fish Slice*, 1860s, L. 11 in. (27.9 cm), CAM, Museum Purchase with funds provided by Mr. and Mrs. Charles Fleischmann III, 2005.70.
Mark 38.7; Duhme & Co., *Dinner Fork*, 1860s, L. 8⅝ in. (21.9 cm), CAM, Gift of Dr. Suzanne A. Beutler, 1983.200. Marks 38.7 and 38.2; (bottom) Duhme &
Co., *Knife*, c. 1865, L. 8¾ in. (22.2 cm), CAM, Gift of James Randolph Hillard, M.D. and Aingeal Grehan, 2007.154. Mark 38.7

The 1870s

Duhme & Co.'s business continued to grow and thrive throughout the 1870s.[51] **Emmett W. Ankeny**, who had worked at Duhme since 1864, or earlier, became a partner in the firm in 1870.[52] His obituary notes that he was manager of the wholesale room which had been established by 1871, and was located in the rear of the basement, on the same floor where the silver was melted, processed, and manufactured.[53] In 1871, the firm began to manufacture gold and silver watch cases, eventually buying out Francis Doll (b. about 1825, d. 1871), who had established the first watch case factory in the West.[54]

Duhme & Co. was one of two entrants (**David Kinsey** was the other) in the class of solid silverware at the first Cincinnati Industrial Exposition in 1870.[55] Duhme's display, "a case of solid silver ware of the most elaborate and chaste designs, consisting of tureens, baskets, water pitcher, urn, forks, spoon, ladles, etc.," received first prize. Exposition officials deemed the workmanship to be "of the very highest order" and the "beauty of design and executions of detail" incomparable with anything else in the whole exhibition. Kinsey's wares, "not so elaborate in design [as Duhme's]," were described, in turn, as "of a class coming more within the reach of the less wealthy but more numerous class of people, who prefer solid silver plate to the cheaper plated article and yet could not afford the costly though beautiful ware previously mentioned in this report." Duhme's wares were also commended for the fact that they were all the work of western artisans.

In 1871, Duhme & Co. competed in the Cincinnati Industrial Exposition's silverware division against **William Wilson McGrew** and against Joseph Steinau & Co., a wholesale firm that manufactured and dealt in jewelry and plated silver wares.[56] Little is known about the material displayed, although it can be inferred through McGrew and Steinau & Co.'s participation that the division was broadened to include retailed and plated wares. McGrew took the first premium. However, that same year, Duhme was awarded an important commission from a Boston man, who "after examining all the patterns in Boston and New York stores" asked the firm to create a silver ladle with gilt bowl to commemorate the visit of Grand Duke Alexis of Russia.[57]

Duhme's competition in the 1872 Cincinnati Industrial Exposition included **William Owen & Co.**, Gorham Mfg. Co. (shown in William Wilson McGrew's display), and **John B. Morris**. Gorham's monumental *Hiawatha's Boat Centerpiece* (fig. 80.1) secured top prize for McGrew, but visitors to Duhme's display were wooed by a monumental tureen (fig. 38.20) featuring beautiful engraved designs, ram head handles and a cast finial in the shape of a wading bird.[58] The tureen is engraved on the underside: "Designed & Manufactured by Herman Duhme of Duhme & Co. For Cincinnati Exposition 1872." Herman was an entrepreneur and manager, never a designer or silversmith. However, he was justly proud of this piece that was produced under his supervision.

Despite the hardships felt across the country in 1873, Duhme made a come-back and won first prize at that year's Industrial Exposition, defeating William Wilson McGrew, their sole competitor in the division of silverware.[59] A December 1873 advertisement boasts, "During the Panic [of 1873], the gold and silver works of Duhme & Co. were not closed, the Importations of the House did not cease, nor were its Purchases for Cash interrupted. The result is a very large collection of useful and elegant articles."[60] Aside from silver, the firm carried "gold plate, . . . gold and silver plated goods, electroplated goods, gilt and ormolu work for the table . . . personal decorations of various kinds, jewelry containing precious stones, etc., besides a miscellaneous assortment of goods; many of which would come under the designation of hardware goods as readily under that of jewelry . . . French bronzes, clocks, candelabra, etc. . . ."[61]

In 1874, Duhme & Co.'s Industrial Exposition display was in the Main Hall, directly across the aisle from the exhibits of **H.R. Smith & Co.** and **Clemens Oskamp** who entered plated ware.[62] Duhme took home the premium for solid silverware and gold and silver watch cases. Judges noted, "The display of goods by this firm are of their own design and manufacture and are deserving of special notice. In elegance of design, and perfect finish, they are unexcelled, and show the advanced position attained by the mechanic in this special line."[63]

Again, Duhme & Co. won the highest prize for solid silverware at the 1875 Cincinnati Industrial Exposition, where they exhibited "Solid Silverware, Gold Jewelry, Watch Cases, Ornamental Articles, Fine Silverware, Table Cutlery, etc."[64] The firm's only competitor was Clemens Oskamp.[65] A major commission that year included a 100-piece silver service presented to Peter Gibson, owner of the Gibson House hotel, in recognition for his services in protecting and managing the Mount Carbon estate in Kanawha Valley, West Virginia, for several years. The gift included a casket of 87 pieces of table silver, a soup tureen, a cake basket with filigree open work, fruit and berry dishes, a hot water urn and tea set, and a caster. The large, covered pieces were "capped by a silver dove's nest, with two charming little doves, having golden ruffles at their necks, billing and cooing, and fluttering their soft wings in mutual pleasure."[66] The tureens in figs. 38.21 and 38.22 may represent similar designs. A silver service presented to Colonel Sidney D. Maxwell, on the occasion of his marriage, by the Pork Packers Association, for which he served as secretary, represented another well-reported commission that year.[67]

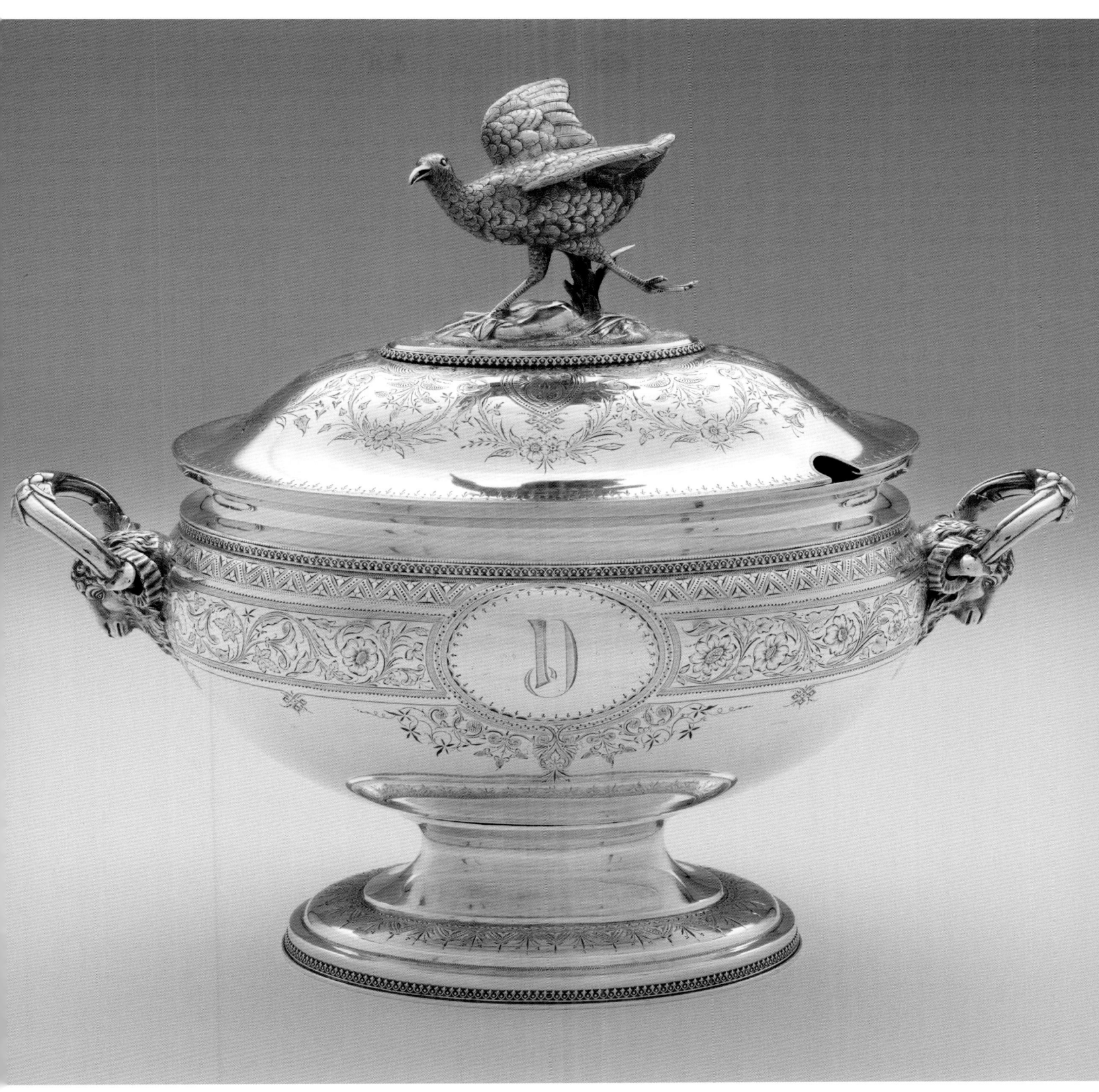

FIG. 38.20: Duhme & Co., *Tureen*, 1872, 14 × 11¼ × 9 in. (35.6 × 28.6 × 22.9 cm), Collection of Anne Duhme Newstedt Phelps.
Inscription: Designed & Manufactured by Herman Duhme of Duhme & Co. For Cincinnati Exposition 1872. Marks 38.2 and 38.7

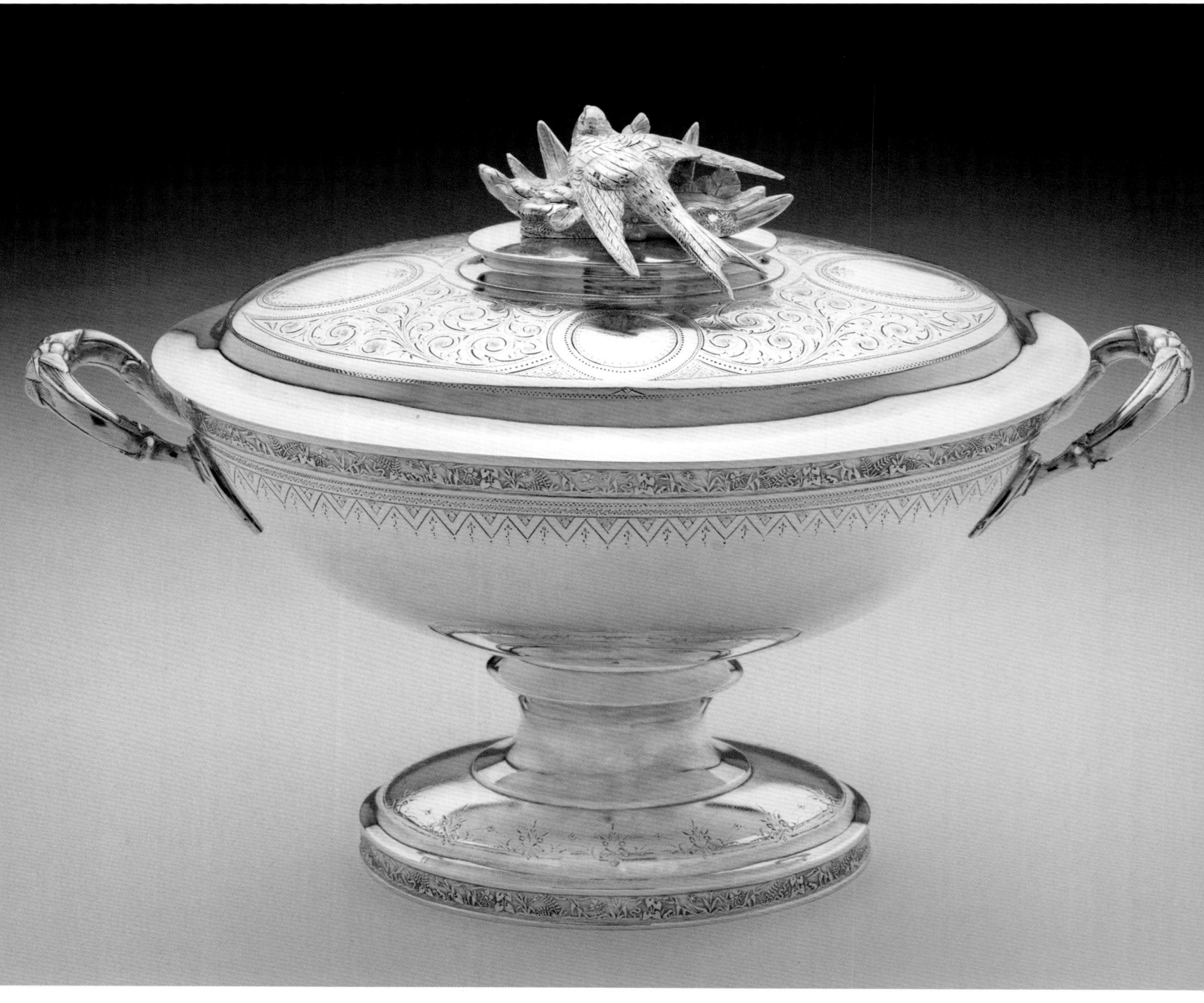

FIG. 38.21: Duhme & Co., *Tureen*, 1870s, 8½ × 13 × 7¼ in. (21.6 × 33 × 18.4 cm), CAM, Museum Purchase: John S. Connor Endowment, Mark P. Herschede Endowment, and Dwight J. Thomson Endowment, 1999.207. Marks 38.2 and 38.7

An 1878 promotional flier cites the presence of a Duhme & Co. office in Paris at 35 Boulevard de Strasbourg.[68] Little is known about this venture. It is possible that it was a short-lived retail venue established to coincide with the occasion of the 1878 *Exposition Universelle*.[69] In 1879, Duhme's competition at the

Cincinnati Industrial Exposition was **E.E. Isbell & Co.** Judges noted, "As a general display where all are creditable, and while in some special articles others may excel, we think, all things considered, Messrs. Duhme & Co. have the best, and to whom we recommend a premium."[70]

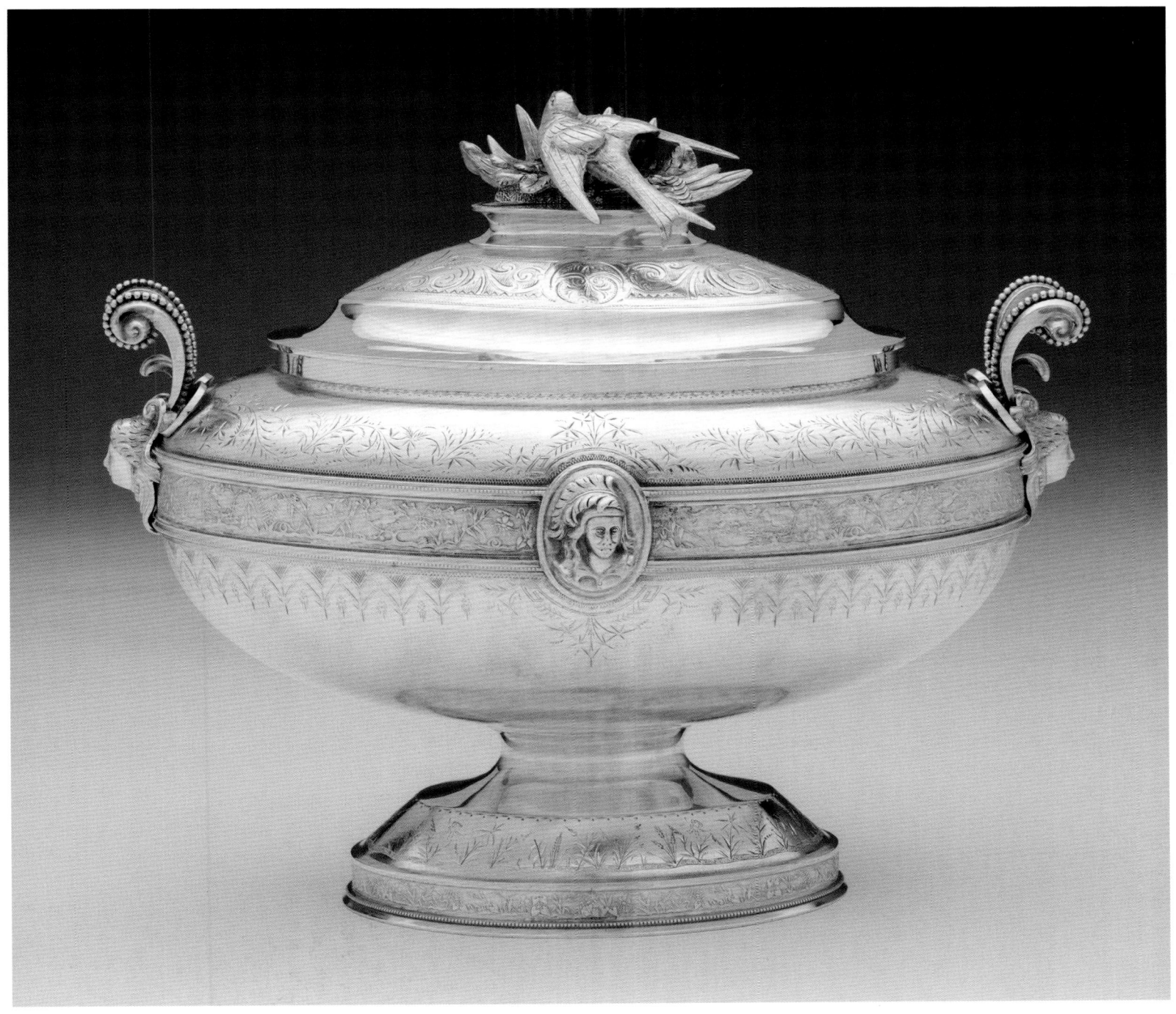

FIG. 38.22: Duhme & Co., *Tureen*, 1870s, 10½ × 12¼ × 8½ in. (26.7 × 31.1 × 21.6 cm), CAM, Museum Purchase: Gloria W. Thomson Fund for Decorative Arts, 2013.74a–b. Marks 38.2 and 38.7

Throughout the 1870s, Duhme & Co. continued to stay abreast of popular fashions and worked in both coin and sterling. While Classically-inspired, bright-cut, and Rococo Revival works continued to remain popular in Duhme's line during the first part of the decade (figs. 38.23, 38.24, 38.25, 38.26), the firm also dabbled in the Egyptian Revival style and concentrated on the Aesthetic Movement style as the decade continued (figs. 38.21, 38.22, 38.27, 38.28).[71] The unidentified pattern of the ice-cream server and spoons in fig. 38.28, with egret and snake, is exotically-inspired, and foreshadows the firm's interest in Japonisme.

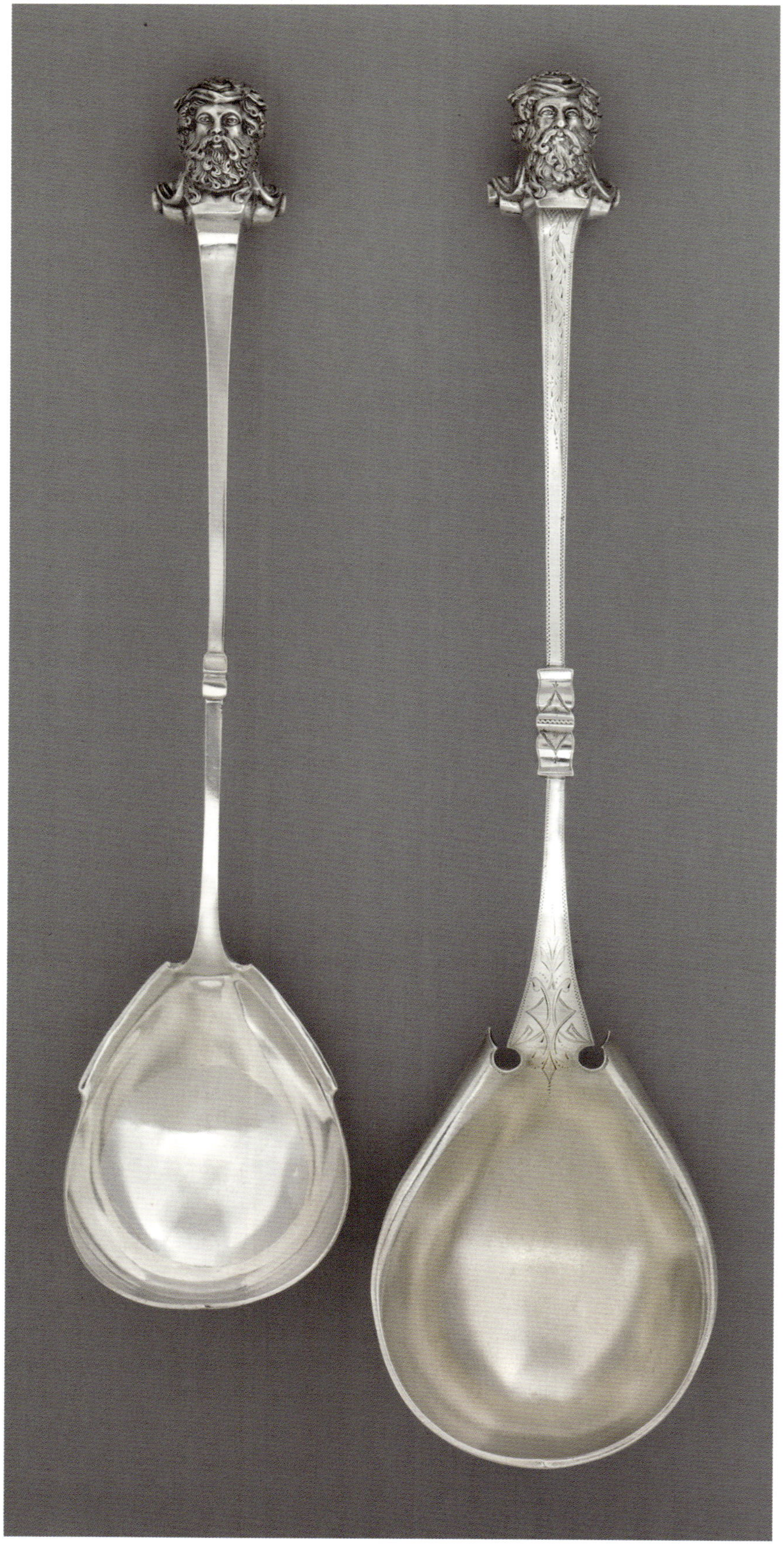

FIG. 38.23: Duhme & Co., *Ladle*, 1870s, L. 13 in. (33 cm), CAM, Museum Purchase with funds provided by Mr. and Mrs. Charles Fleischmann III, 2005.65. Mark 38.7; Duhme & Co., *Ladle*, c. 1874, L. 14⅝ in. (37.1 cm), CAM, Gift of James Randolph Hillard, M.D. and Aingeal Grehan, 2007.143. Mark 38.3

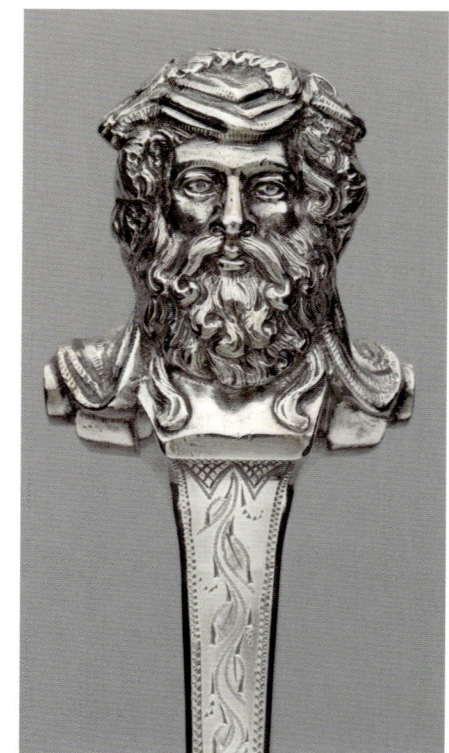

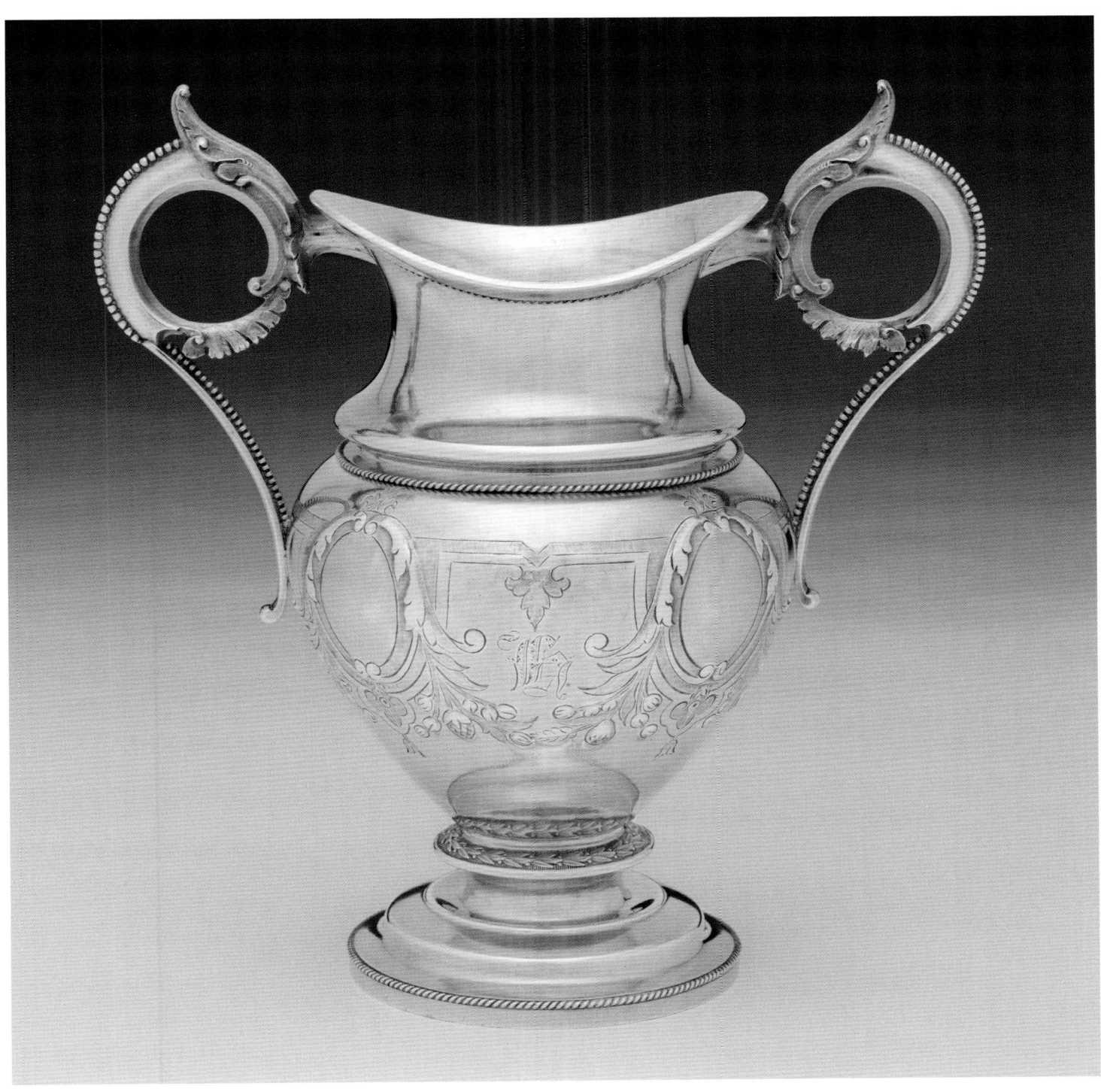

FIG. 38.24: Duhme & Co., *Vase*, 1870s, H. 8 in. (20.3 cm), W. 8 in. (20.3 cm), CAM, Gift of James Randolph Hillard, M.D. and Aingeal Grehan, 2007.120. Marks 38.2 and 38.7

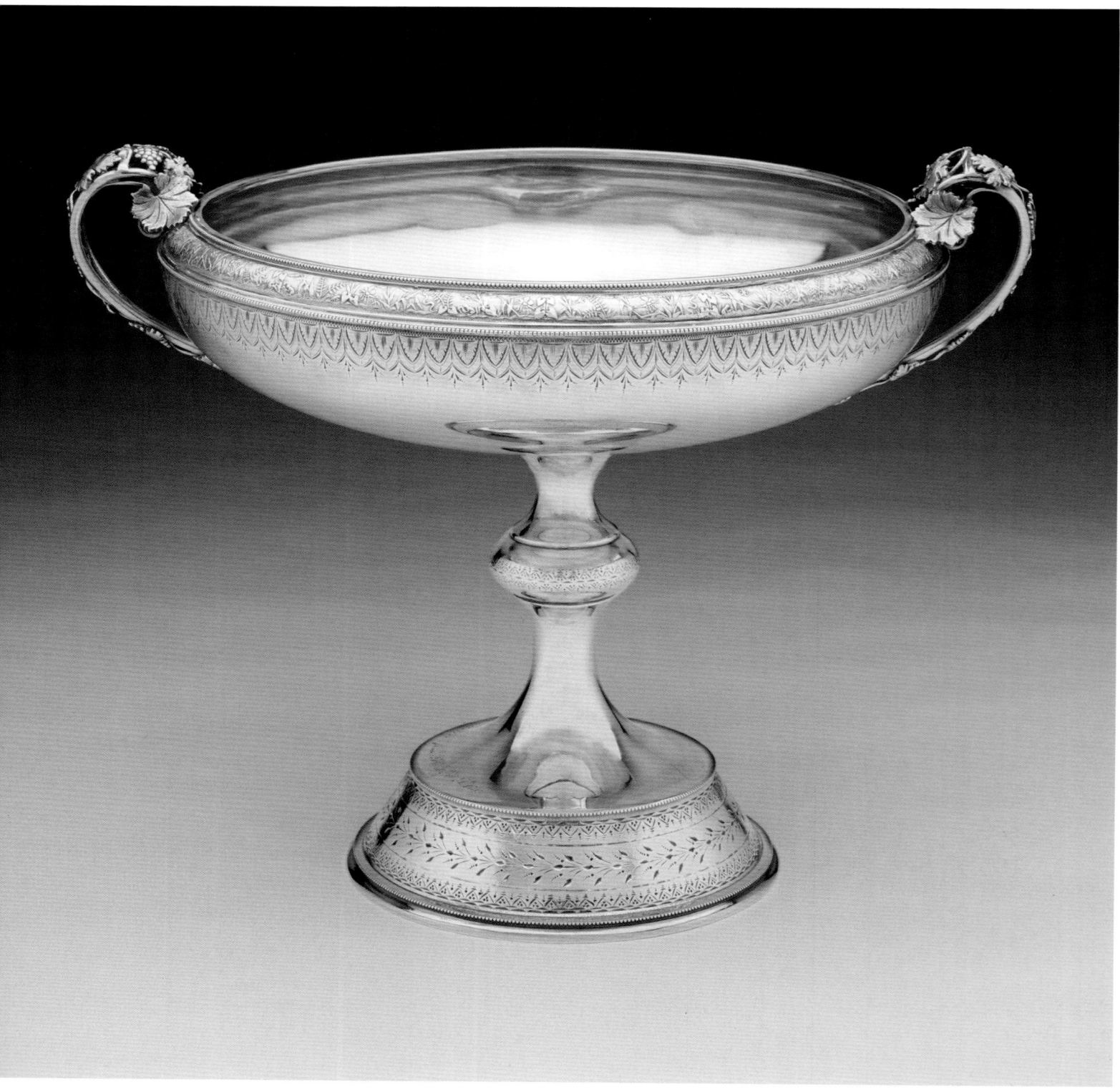

FIG. 38.25: Duhme & Co., *Compote*, 1870s, H. 8¾ in. (22.2 cm),
W. 11¼ in. (28.6 cm), CAM, Gift of James Randolph Hillard, M.D.
and Aingeal Grehan, 2007.119. Mark 38.7

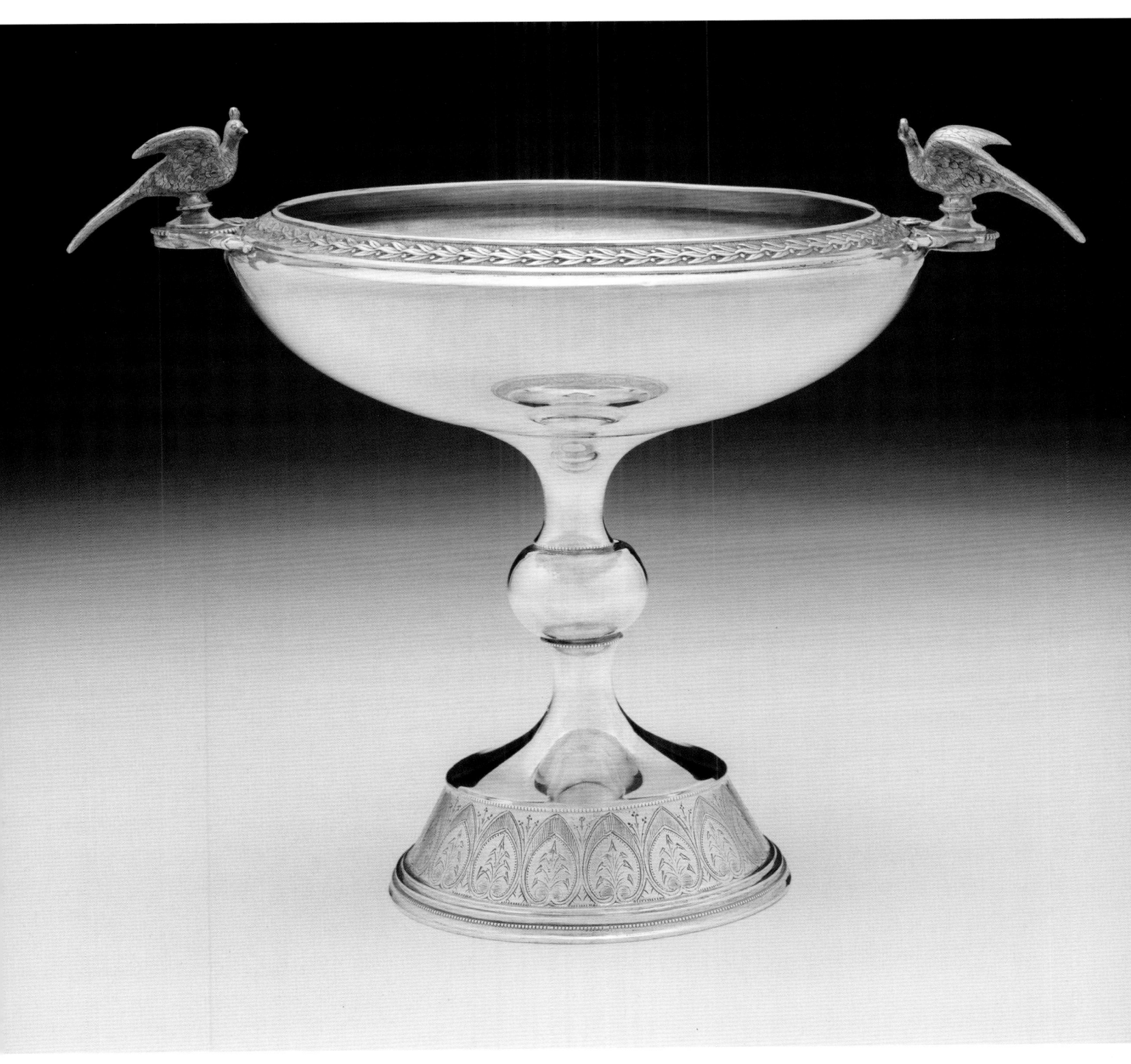

FIG. 38.26: Duhme & Co., *Compote*, 1870s, H. 10¼ in. (26 cm),
W. 13⅞ in. (35.3 cm), CAM, Gift of James Randolph Hillard, M.D.
and Aingeal Grehan, 2007.199. Marks 38.2 and 38.7

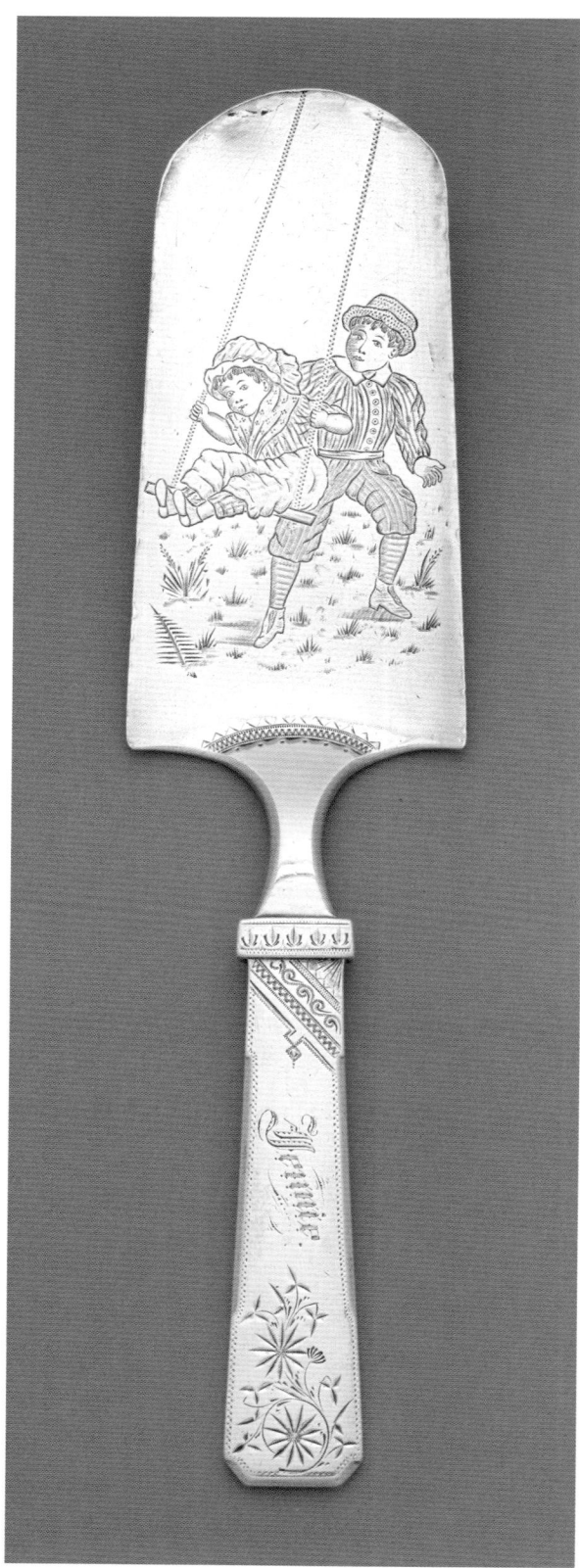

A die-rolled border incorporating stylized plants, insects, and snakes (fig. 38.29) that appears over and over in Duhme & Co.'s hollowware (figs. 38.21, 38.22, 38.25, 38.34, 38.36) was also developed during this period. **Charles Goettheim**, later remembered as Duhme's chief designer, may have been employed by Duhme as early as 1873.[72] He is credited with designing much of the work produced by Duhme until he left the company in 1889. Marks observed on pieces from the 1870s include 38.1 through 38.5, and 38.7 through 38.9.[73]

In 1878, Duhme & Co. released the following statement: "In view of the fact that a marked change has developed during the past year, as regards styles and values of Jewelry, Silverware, and art objects generally, we wish to announce to our old patrons, and to the general public that we are promptly conforming to the new condition . . . As the demand increases for special designs that are unique, and at the same time inexpensive, both in gold and silver, we are directing the efforts of our designers and artificers in such a manner as to meet the demand; and in our salesrooms may now be found a collection of attractive articles, original in design and execution."[74] This "marked change" undoubtedly references the Bland-Allison Act, passed February 28, 1878, which re-instituted the bimetallic monetary policy of the United States by requiring a set amount of silver to be purchased by the U.S. government and circulated as silver dollars. This reversed the demonetization of

FIG. 38.27: Duhme & Co., *Pastry Server*, c. 1875, L. 8½ in. (21.6 cm), CAM, Gift of James Randolph Hillard, M.D. and Aingeal Grehan, 2007.166. Mark 38.11

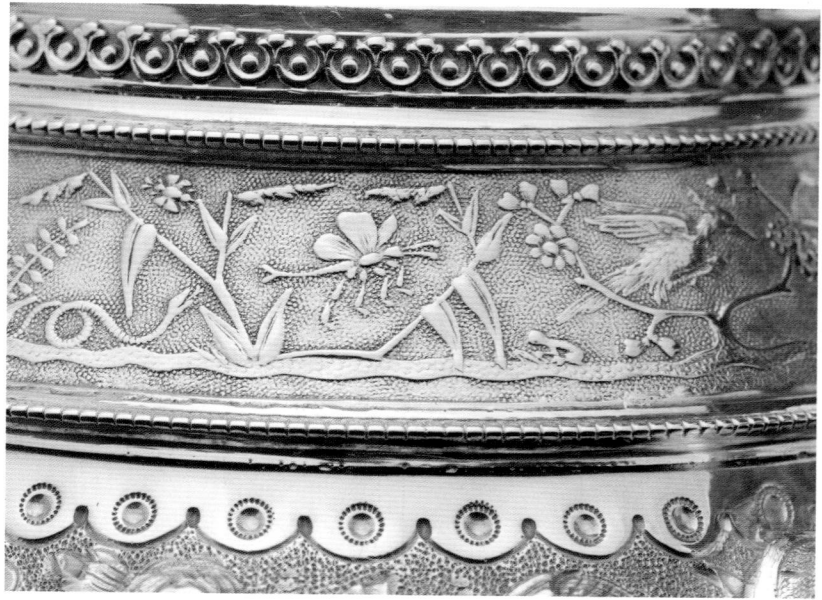

FIG. 38.29: Detail, Duhme & Co., *Sugar Bowl from Tea and Coffee Service* (fig. 38.36), late 1870s–1880s, 8 × 5½ × 5 in. (20.3 × 14 × 12.7 cm), CAM, Gift of Dr. and Mrs. James L. Hecht, 1984.202 a–b

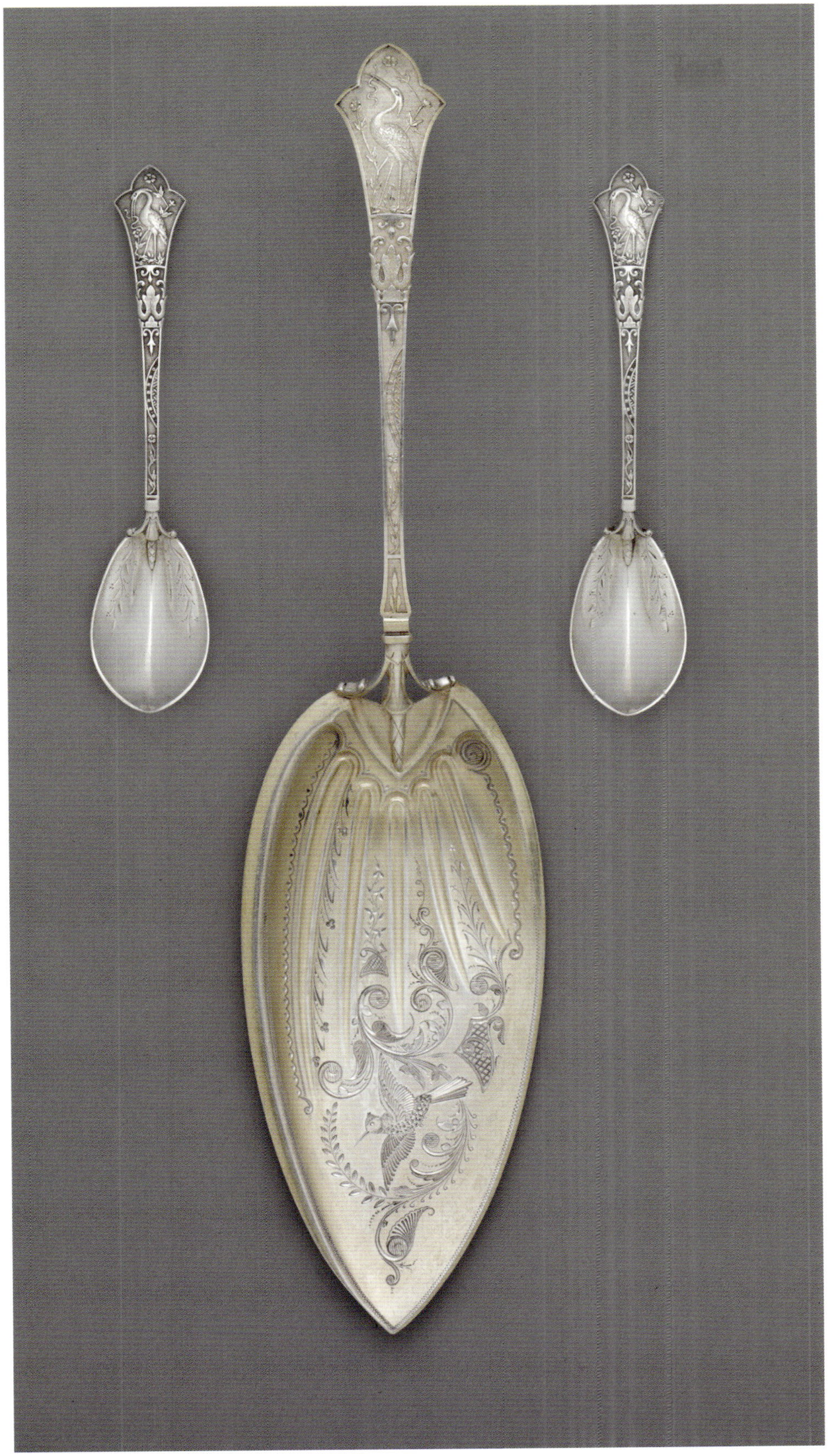

FIG. 38.28: Duhme & Co., *Ice Cream
Server*, 1870s, parcel gilt silver, L. 13⅞ in.
(35.2 cm), CAM, Gift of James Randolph
Hillard, M.D. and Aingeal Grehan,
2007.145. Mark 38.3; Duhme & Co.,
Pair of Ice Cream Spoons, 1870s, L. 6 in.
(15.2 cm), CAM, Gift of James Randolph
Hillard, M.D. and Aingeal Grehan,
2007.146a–b. Mark 38.7

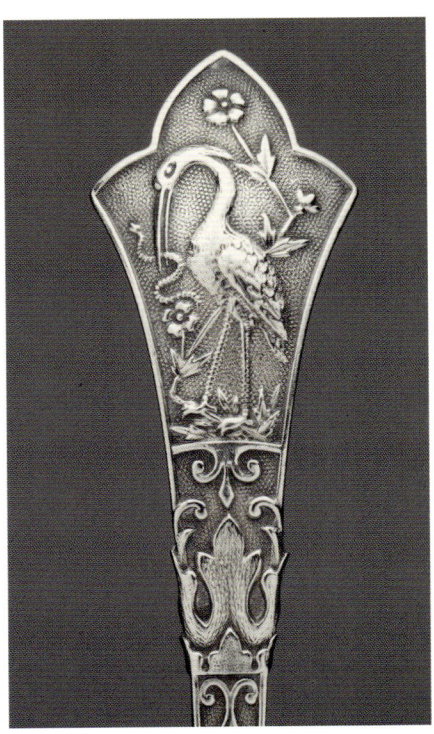

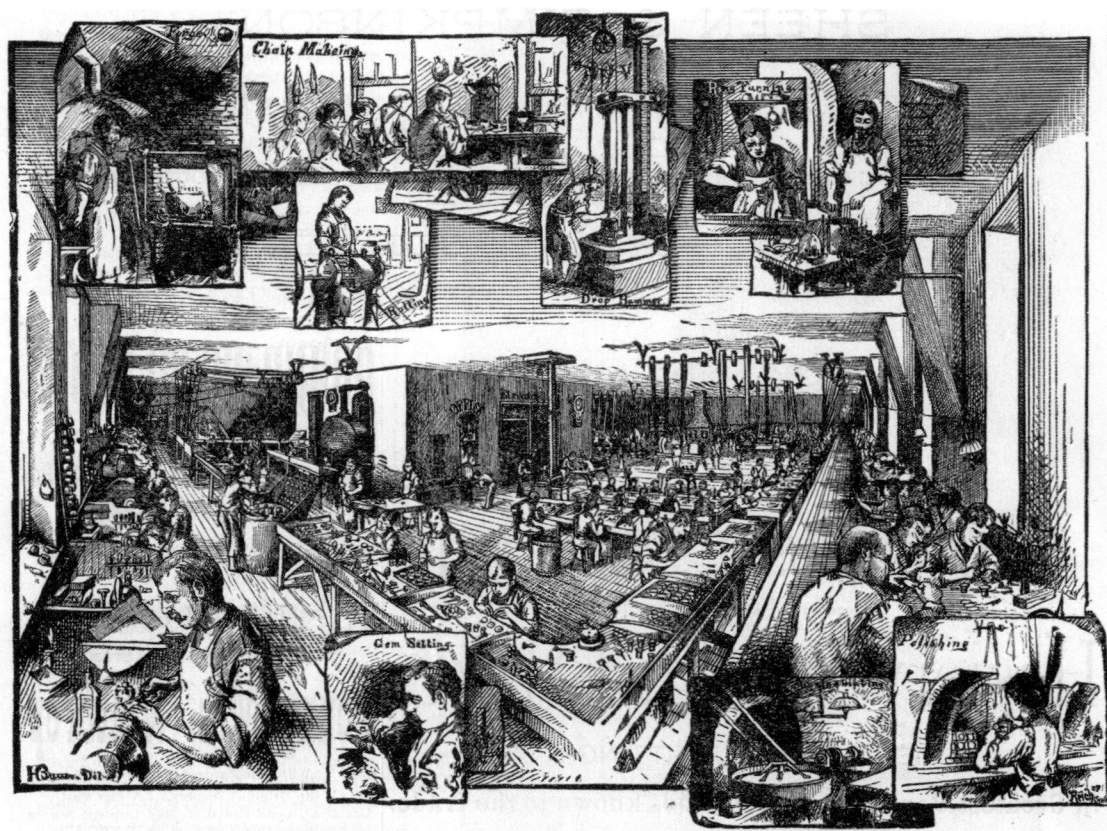

SCENE IN THE GOLDSMITH SHOPS OF DUHME & CO., CARLISLE BUILDING, FOURTH & WALNUT STS.

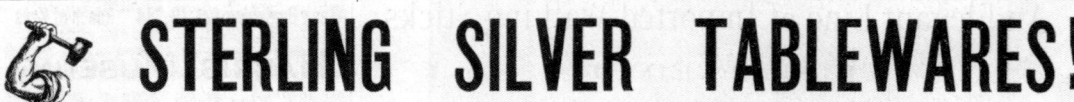

STERLING SILVER TABLEWARES!

All Silverwares made by **DUHME & CO.** bear the mark ⟨STERLING⟩ ⟨925/1000⟩ ⟨DUHME&CO⟩ and are guaranteed **925/1000 Fine,** the standard for English sterling.

DUHME & CO. are among the few prominent manufacturers of Sterling Silverwares in the United States who do not produce rolled or machine-made wares, their entire product being hand-made, hand-engraved and hand-burnished, by which processes, only, can the best results be realized.

Fourteen styles of Spoons and Forks, complete lines of larger pieces, also chests of Silver, constantly in stock or made to order, at

DUHME & CO. - Fourth and Walnut.

FIG. 38.30: Advertisement, *The Cincinnati Graphic*, October 11, 1884, 16

silver and the adoption of the gold standard that had occurred with the passage of the Coinage Act of 1873. When this act was passed, silver was no longer purchased by the government for coinage and was, therefore, more readily available. This lowered the value and price of silver. For this reason those in the mining and silversmithing industry supported the country's return to bimetallic currency. Ironically, the reintroduction of silver into the country's currency system with the Bland-Allison Act led to further economic disruption, as the price of silver was subject to radical fluctuation driven by the discovery of silver throughout the West

at this time. In an effort to encourage customers, despite these fluctuations, Duhme's marketing approach pushed the merit and value of their unique designs and skillful craftsmanship.

This emphasis on original design and execution, along with the advent of reform movements like the Aesthetic Movement and the Arts and Crafts Movement, explain why Duhme & Co. ceased to emphasize the modernity of their mechanized factory and their innovative equipment as they had in the 1860s and 1870s. Beginning in the late 1870s, Duhme & Co. promoted the idea that their wares were all hand-made—a claim that does not find support

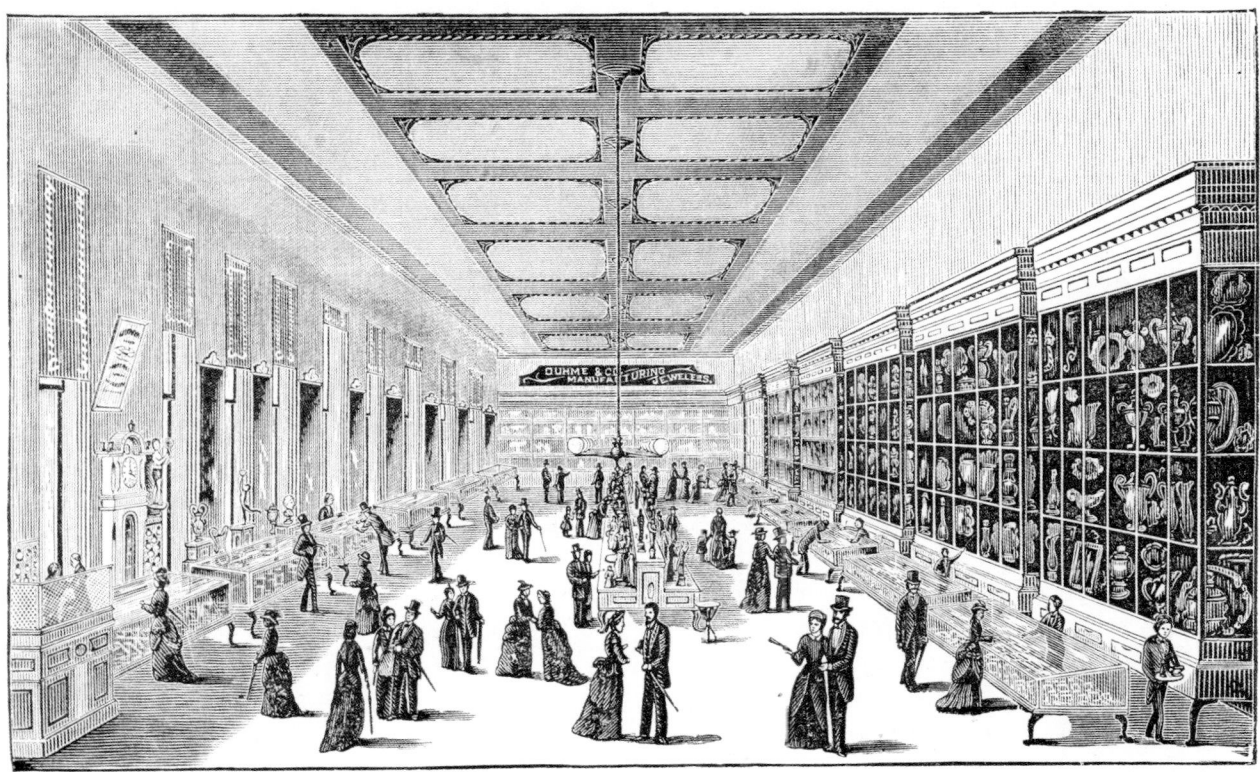

INTERIOR VIEW OF DUHME & CO.'S

FIG. 38.31: *Duhme & Co.*, from Daniel J. Kenny, *Illustrated Cincinnati: A Pictorial Handbook*, Cincinnati: G.E. Stevens, 1875

in the combination of hand and machine production techniques (spinning, die-pressing, casting, etc.) observed in their extant wares from this time.[75] As early as 1879, it was reported that "All their flat silver and gold wares, which embrace everything except the table sets, are made by hand and hammered out. This method is preferred to the rolling process as securing better work, the artificer being by this means enabled more readily to detect flaws and imperfections. For the same reason no hot work is allowed, but everything is wrought and cut."[76] An illustrated 1884 advertisement in *The Cincinnati Graphic* (fig. 38.30) portrays men producing wares in various stages in different shops within the large manufactory.[77] At the bottom of the advertisement, the image of a raised hand holding a hammer furthers this idea of hand production. The advertisement asserts that Duhme & Co. is "among the few manufacturers of Sterling Silverware in the U.S. who do not produce rolled or machine-made wares, their entire product being hand-made, hand-engraved and hand-burnished, by which processes, only, can the best result be achieved."[78] However, the illustration clearly shows roller machines and drop hammers in use. The only machines mentioned in promotional materials during this era are those that aided the completion of decorative finish work: "The manufacturing departments are equipped with the most approved devices to aid in the delicate processes, which include engine turning, etching, enameling, etc."[79]

The 1880s

In the 1880s, Duhme & Co. was still regarded as "one of the largest in their business."[80] They occupied two large stores in the Carlisle Building (fig. 38.31), each with a frontage of 25 feet and extending back at least 100 feet, and "finished inside with cherry and black walnut (natural finish)."[81] The firm continued to use the basement for manufacturing, another upper floor for finishing work, and the main floor for sales—one store for retail sales, and the other for wholesale and the display of "French clocks, bronzes, pottery, cut glass and novelties in rich, fancy goods."[82] In the 1880 Products of Industry Census, they reported $100,000 of capital invested, 150 employees (100 men, 15 women, and 35 youth and children), payment of $78,000 a year in wages, and the use of $78,000 worth of material to produce a product valued at $250,000.[83] While their capital and value of product had not

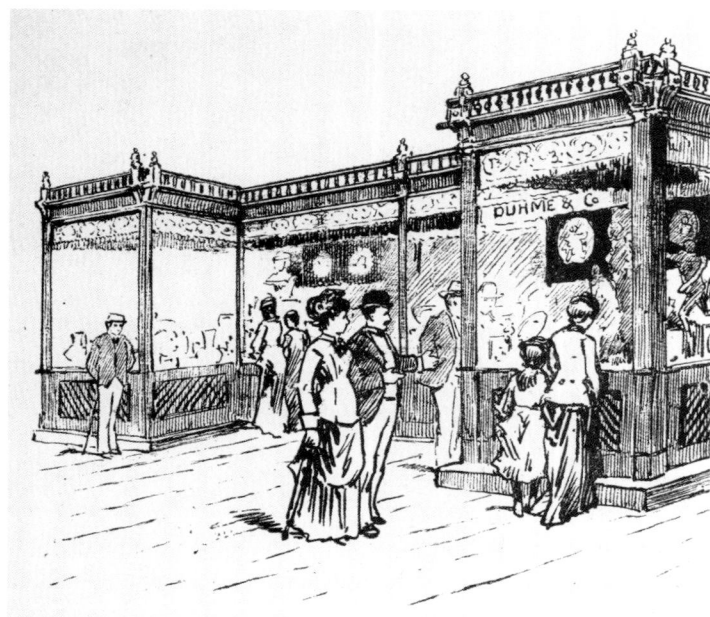

FIG. 38.32: *Duhme & Co.'s Exposition Display,* from Clara de Vere, *The Exhibition Sketchbook: Notes of the Cincinnati Exposition of 1881,* Cincinnati: Weisbrodt & Co., 1881

changed since their report in 1870, the size of their staff and the value of their material had decreased, a demonstration of the effects of the financial Panic of 1873.

The firm had no competition in the class for silverware at the 1880 Industrial Exposition.[84] The following year, R.H. Galbreath served as president of the Cincinnati Industrial Exposition Association and chairman of the Committee on Fine Arts, and Duhme's display in the Main Hall earned a gold medal (fig. 38.32).[85] Again, they were the sole exhibitors of solid silverware. A visitor to the fair wrote, their "cases are arranged with consummate taste; the lining of the back is fluted ecru silk with a dull red frieze wrought in an art design of red and gold. Within is a fortune in art silver—unique in design, exquisite in appliqués of gold and silver, with curious hints of age. Each piece seems to have a story of its own."[86] Of great interest is the juror's comment: "We call special attention to the beaten Silverware, which, in point of design and *color* is unrivaled."[87] This, paired with the observation of "appliqués of gold and silver," suggest that the firm displayed examples of mixed metal wares, possibly in the Japanese style with hand-hammered surfaces, as suggested by "beaten silver" (fig. 38.33). Mixed metal work by Duhme has yet to be documented.

On November 22, 1880, friends of the outgoing Cincinnati mayor Charles Jacob, Jr. (1834–1913) presented him with a beautifully engraved water set made by Duhme & Co. (fig. 38.34). Another important commission came from New York City for a

complete set of silver "ordered for a bridal present to be given on the occasion of the marriage of one of the Goodhart family" in October 1882.[88] The set consisted of "one hundred and nineteen pieces of solid silver and twenty nine pieces of the finest English cutlery with pearl handles and silver holsters." The pattern of the flatware was described as having "a superb but chaste decoration called diamond art and the initials of the future owner in handsome lettering."[89] The soup ladle was "of convenient and beautiful design, and the gold lining to the larger pieces like a golden veil over the silver." With great pride, the report went so far as to say that "when the bride opens this box she will be assured that she has reached that containing a present unequaled among all her gifts."[90]

The firm continued as the only exhibitors of solid silver wares at the 1882, 1883, and 1884 Industrial Expositions.[91] Their display at the last Cincinnati Industrial Exposition in 1888 was described as " . . . one of the handsomest and most elaborate collections of curios ever gathered together in one cabinet. Decorated fire screens and small cabinets, gorgeous vases, bronze statuary, silver designs, both useful and ornamental, toilet cases, punch bowls, etc. . . . The visitor, who sees much to admire in the illuminated cards and other advertising daubs common in all exhibitions, see nothing in particular to admire in this Duhme collection. The connoisseur in fine art, the person who would prefer the work of Rosa Bonheur to that of the favorite in *Judge* or in *Puck,* gives the Duhme exhibit pause every time."[92]

In 1884, Herman G. Duhme's son Frank became a partner in the firm, and in August 1885, the firm reported, "things are stale, flat and unprofitable . . . Prospects for fall trade are so mixed it's hard to say . . . Both the wholesale and retail departments are dull, yet now is a time when we don't expect much. We are however making arrangements for a good big fall trade, whether it comes or not."[93] Following Herman G. Duhme's unexpected death on August 23, 1888, in St. Clair, Michigan, the firm was reorganized.[94] Herman G.'s widow, Mary Galbreath Duhme, became the majority owner, and the firm was managed by her brother, R.H. Galbreath, and Herman's son Frank and nephew Charles H. Duhme (1855–1906).[95] Galbreath continued to oversee the retail department and imports, Charles H. Duhme looked over the wholesale department and Frank managed the finances.[96] It was noted that two traveling salesmen looked after the trade in the South and West, and Duhme & Co.'s "branch establishment at Kansas City, managed by Mr. W.F. Wilmes, takes care of the business west of the Mississippi River."[97] A large wholesale trade was reported in Ohio, Indiana, Kentucky, Illinois, West Virginia, Missouri, and Kansas, and while references to mail order catalogues were noted, none, to date, are known.[98] The silverware department around this time employed

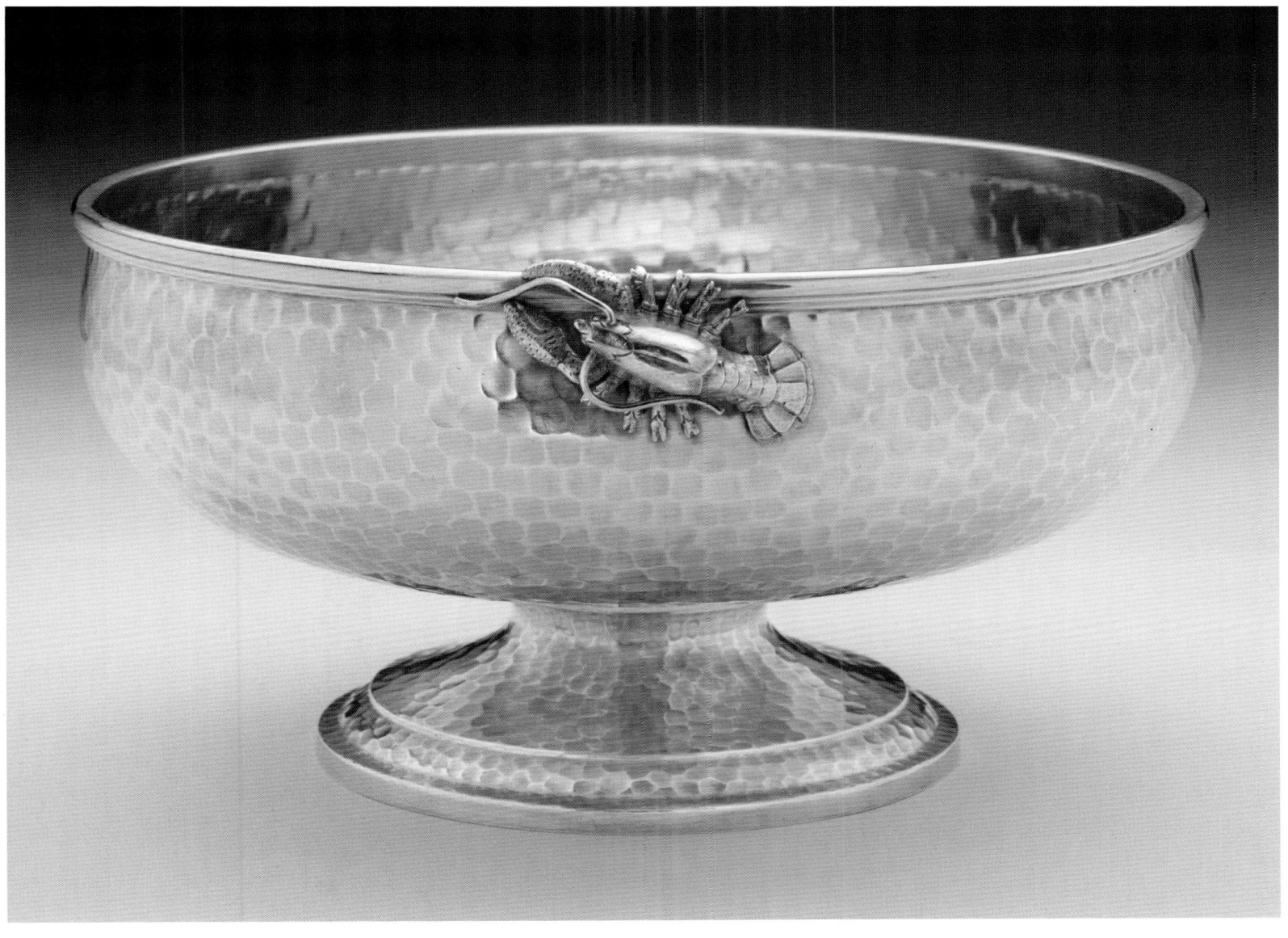

FIG. 38.33: Duhme & Co., *Footed Bowl*, 1880s, 4¼ × 8¾ in. (10.8 × 22.2 cm), CAM, Museum Purchase, 2000.156. Mark 38.9

30 hands, the gold jewelry department 45, the watch case department 60 hands, and the watch repairing department ten hands. About 25 clerks and assistants were employed in the store.[99]

By the 1880s, Duhme was working primarily in sterling as opposed to coin silver, and in 1882, claimed "fourteen styles of spoons and forks, complete lines or larger pieces" to offer.[100] They continued to work in the Aesthetic Movement style (figs. 38.34, 38.35, 38.36, 38.37). Certainly influenced by Tiffany & Co.'s highly-acclaimed display of Japanesque metalwork at the 1878 Paris World's Fair, Duhme's line of Japanese-inspired silver grew. Their new hammer-textured medallion flatware combined Japanese-inspired decoration with a Neoclassical theme—a uniquely Victorian approach—and was very well received (fig. 38.38, 38.39). This was a full line pattern and featured over ten different male and female figure heads from Classical mythology.[101] Forms with applied lobsters and sea creatures are more strictly Japanesque (figs. 38.33, 38.40), while the footed bowl in fig. 38.41 is a more subtle example.[102] The firm explored very florid styles during this decade as well (fig. 38.42). Their engraved "Lily" pattern (fig. 38.43) closely recalls Joseph Seymour's "Lily" pattern (1884), and their flatware pattern that is sometimes referred to as "Duhme No. 3" (fig. 38.44) is similar to Dominick & Haff's "Rococo" (1888).[103]

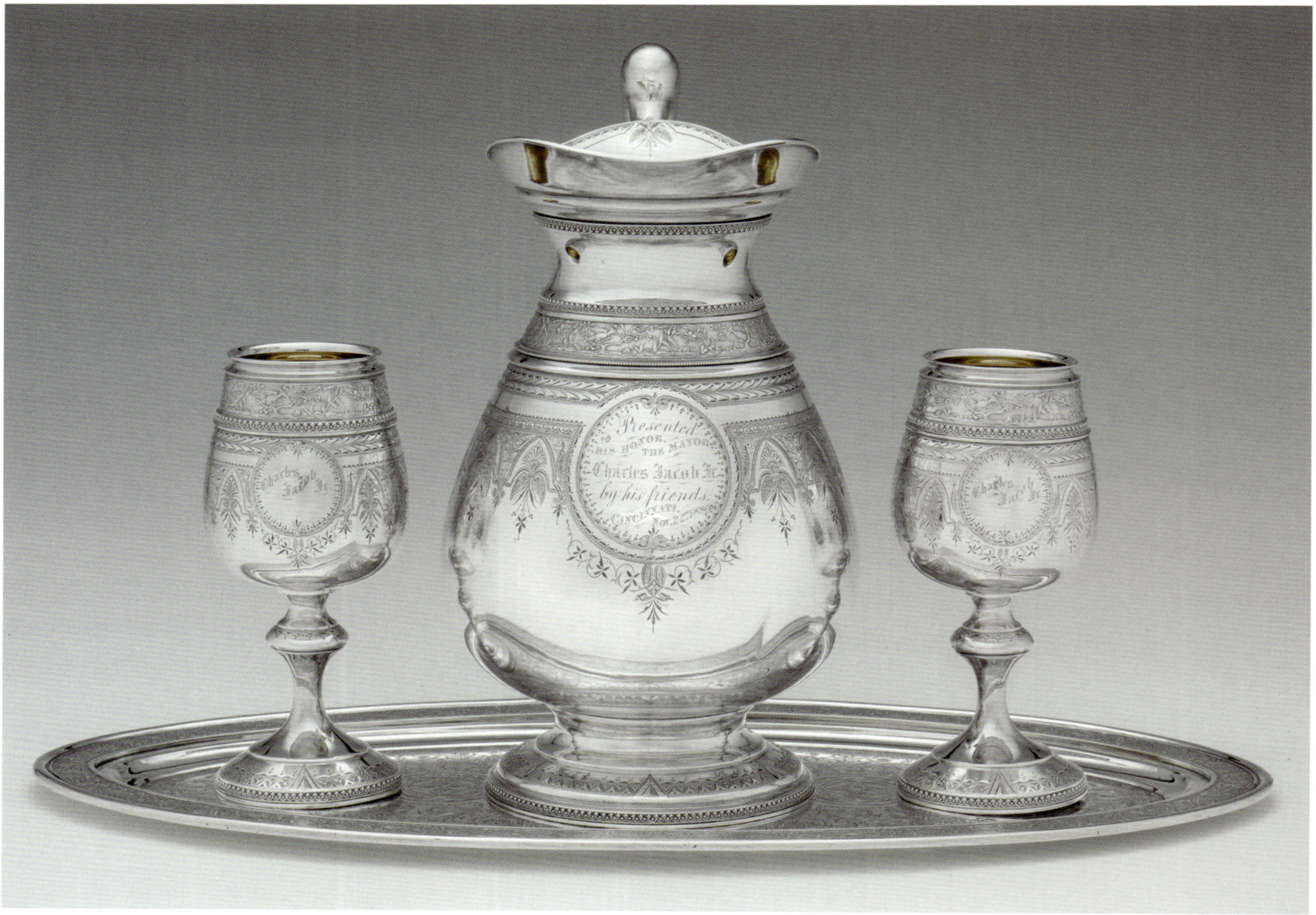

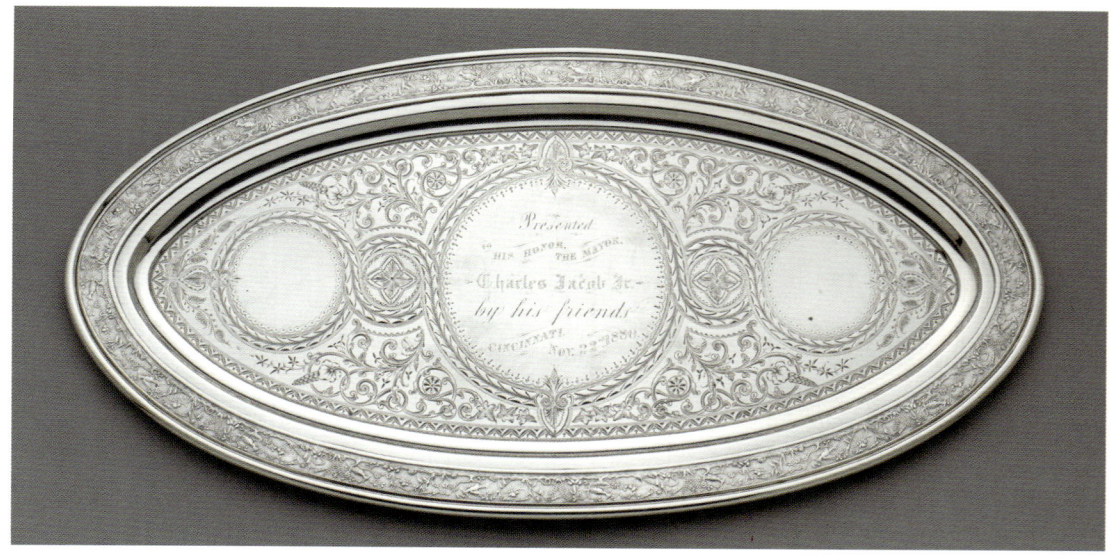

FIG. 38.34: Duhme & Co., *Mayoral
Presentation Set*, 1880, parcel gilt silver,
tray: 22 × 10⅛ in. (50.8 × 25.7 cm),
pitcher: 11⅞ × 7 in. (30.2 × 17.8 cm),
goblets: 7¼ × 3½ in. (18.4 × 8.9 cm),
Collection of Anne Duhme Newstedt
Phelps. Inscription: Presented TO HIS
HONOR THE MAYOR, Charles Jacob,
Jr. by his friends, CINCINNATI, NOV.
22, 1880. Marks 38.2 and 38.3

Their "Dresden" pattern (fig. 38.45), advertised by this name in Duhme's 1898/99 Holiday Shopping List, was probably introduced in the late 1880s.[104] At least three other florid, die-pressed patterns that incorporate "Duhme & Co." in the tool used to stamp the design for the reverse of the spoon have been identified, but are not illustrated here. One has a handle with lush shell, C-scroll and foliate designs, and an irregular-shaped reserve near the tip of the handle for engraving.[105] A second pattern features swirling, dense floral elements with an oval reserve, and a third pattern incorporates scrolling lines, pearling, and a shield-shaped reserve.[106] The firm's "Cupid" pattern, also from this period, combines a tipped handle, winged child's head, and irregular Rococo-style reserve, and was advertised by this name in Duhme's 1898/99 Holiday Shopping List.[107] Marks used during the 1880s include 38.3, 38.4, and 38.7 through 38.13.[108] Mark 38.11 was reproduced in the firm's advertisements as early as 1881.[109]

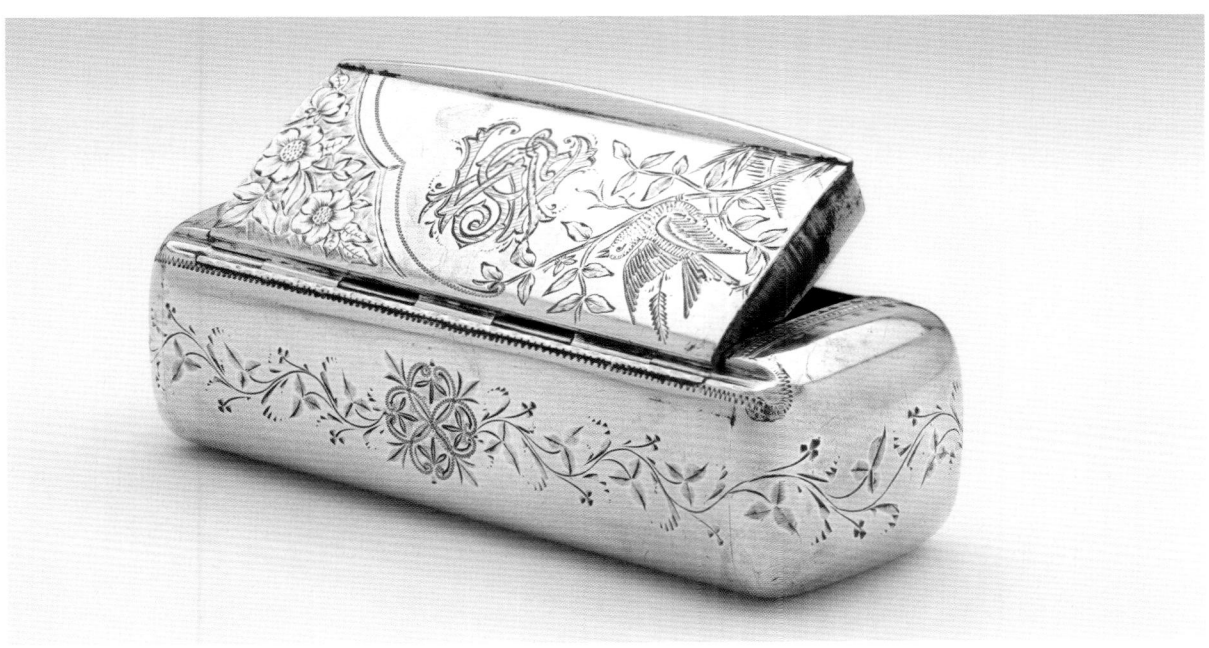

FIG. 38.35: Duhme & Co., *Snuff Box*, c. 1882, 1 × 3¾ × 1 in. (2.7 × 9.5 × 2.7 cm), CAM, Gift of the Estate of Margaret Mayberry Clark, 1965.217. Inscription: Co. S.V. Mayberry / Chief Dep'ty of the Treasurers of Hamilton Co. O. / 1862 1882 / From the Clerks Aug. Settlement 1882. Monogram: SVM. Mark 38.10

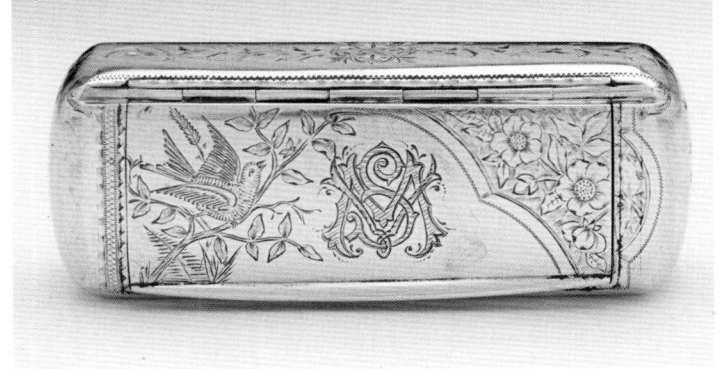

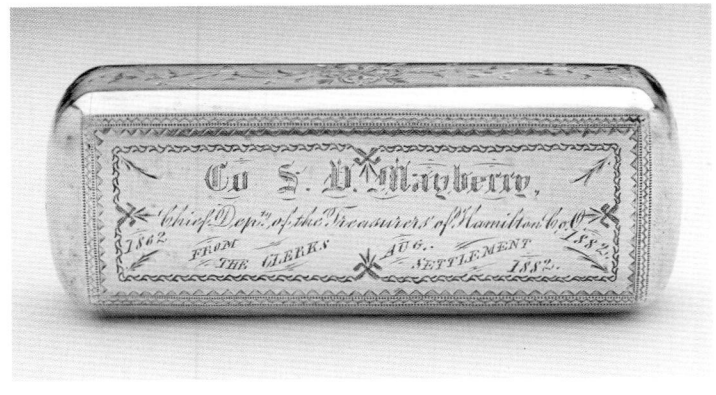

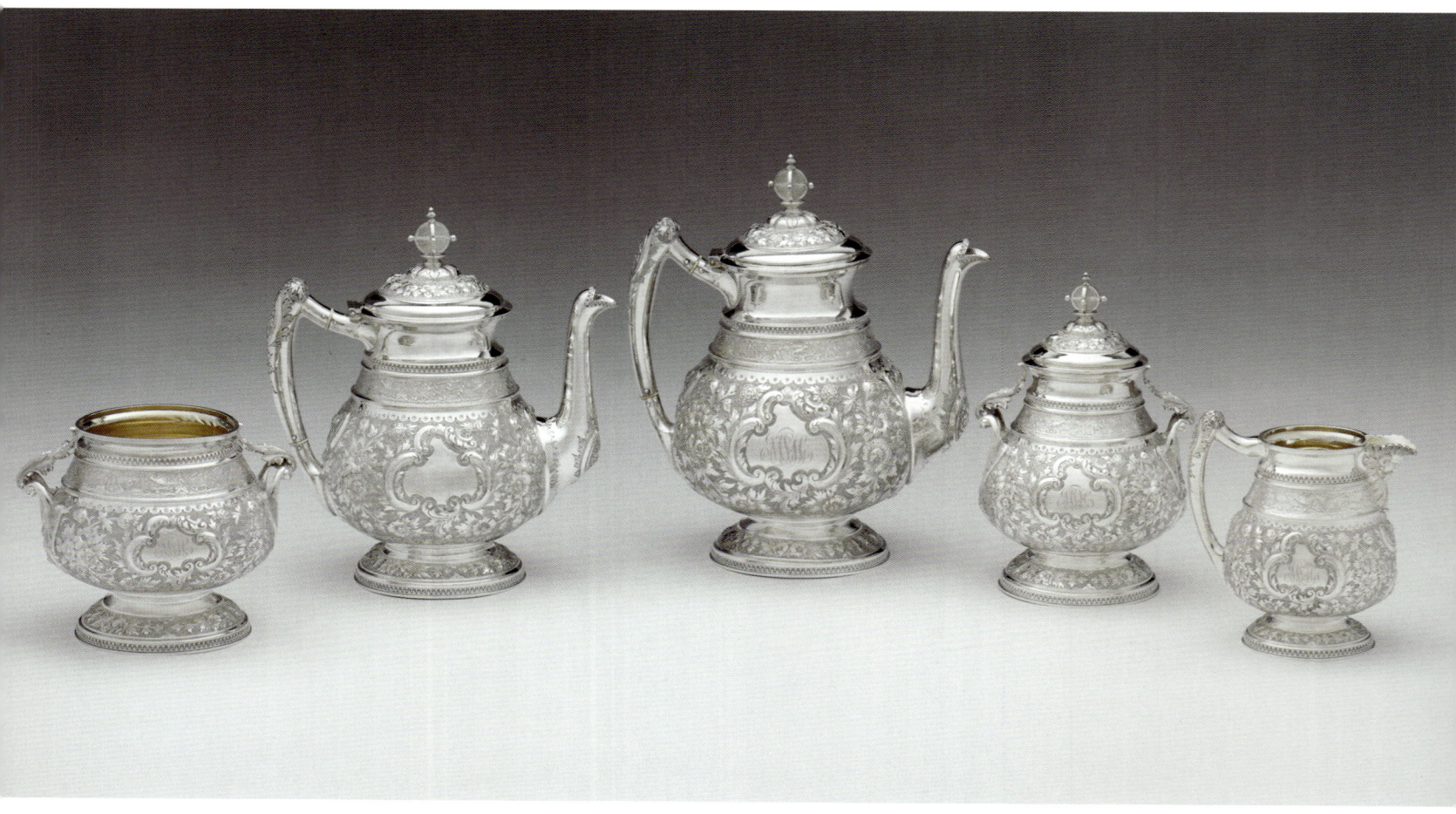

FIG. 38.36: Duhme & Co., *Tea and Coffee Service*, late 1870s–1880s, parcel gilt silver, waste bowl: 5¼ × 6½ × 5½ in. (13.3 × 16.5 × 14 cm), teapot: 9¼ × 8½ × 5⅝ in. (23.5 × 21.6 × 14.3 cm), coffee pot: 10½ × 9 × 6¼ in. (26.7 × 22.9 × 15.9 cm), sugar bowl: 8 × 5½ × 5 in. (20.3 × 14 × 12.7 cm), creamer: 5¼ × 5¼ × 5 in. (13.3 × 13.3 × 12.7 cm), CAM, Gift of Dr. and Mrs. James L. Hecht, 1984.198–202. Marks 38.2 and 38.7

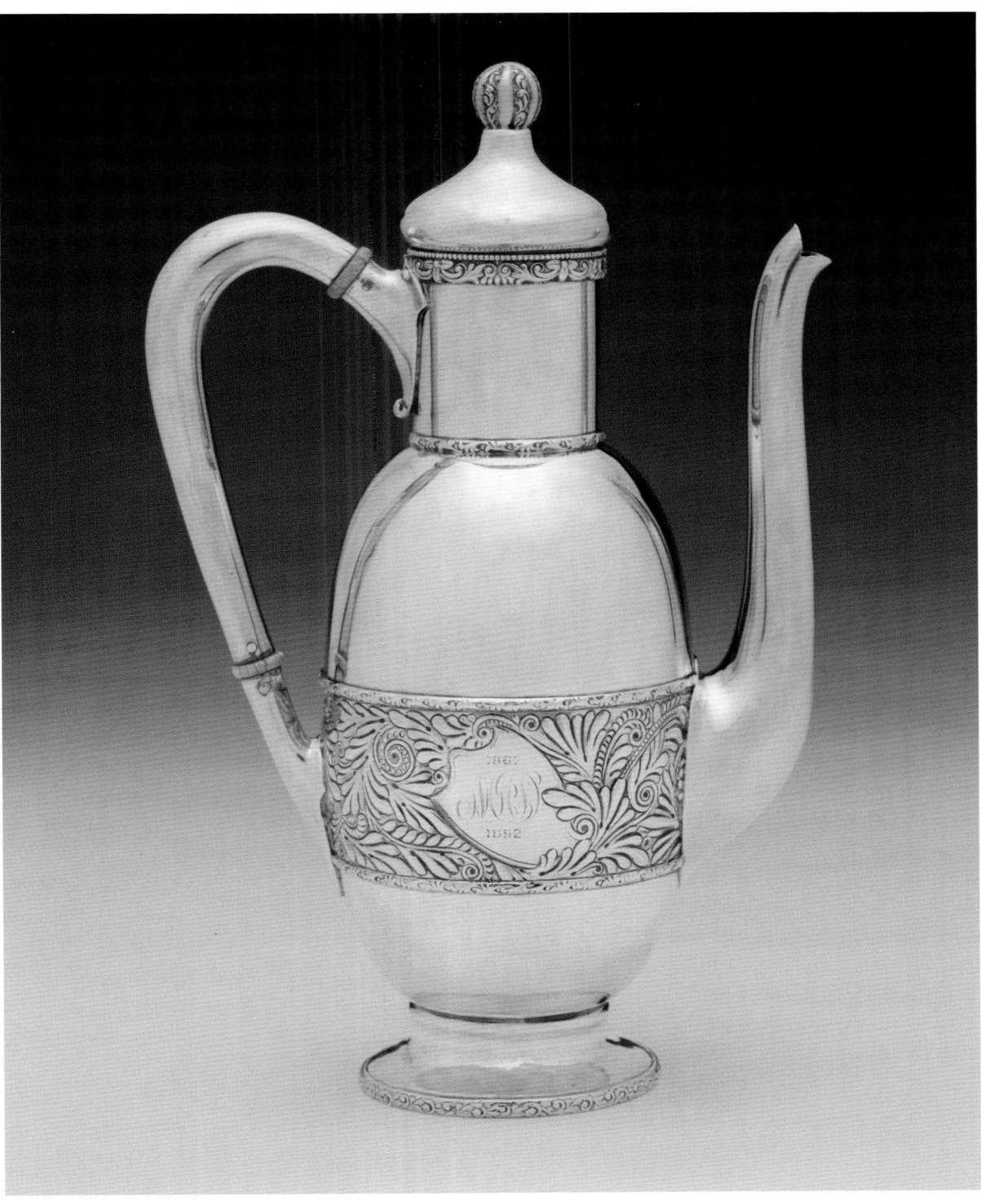

FIG. 38.37: Duhme & Co., *Coffee Pot*, c. 1892, H. 9¼ in. (23.5 cm), W. 6¼ in. (15.9 cm), CAM, Gift of James Randolph Hillard, M.D. and Aingeal Grehan, 2007.118. Inscription: 1867 MAD 1892. Mark 38.10

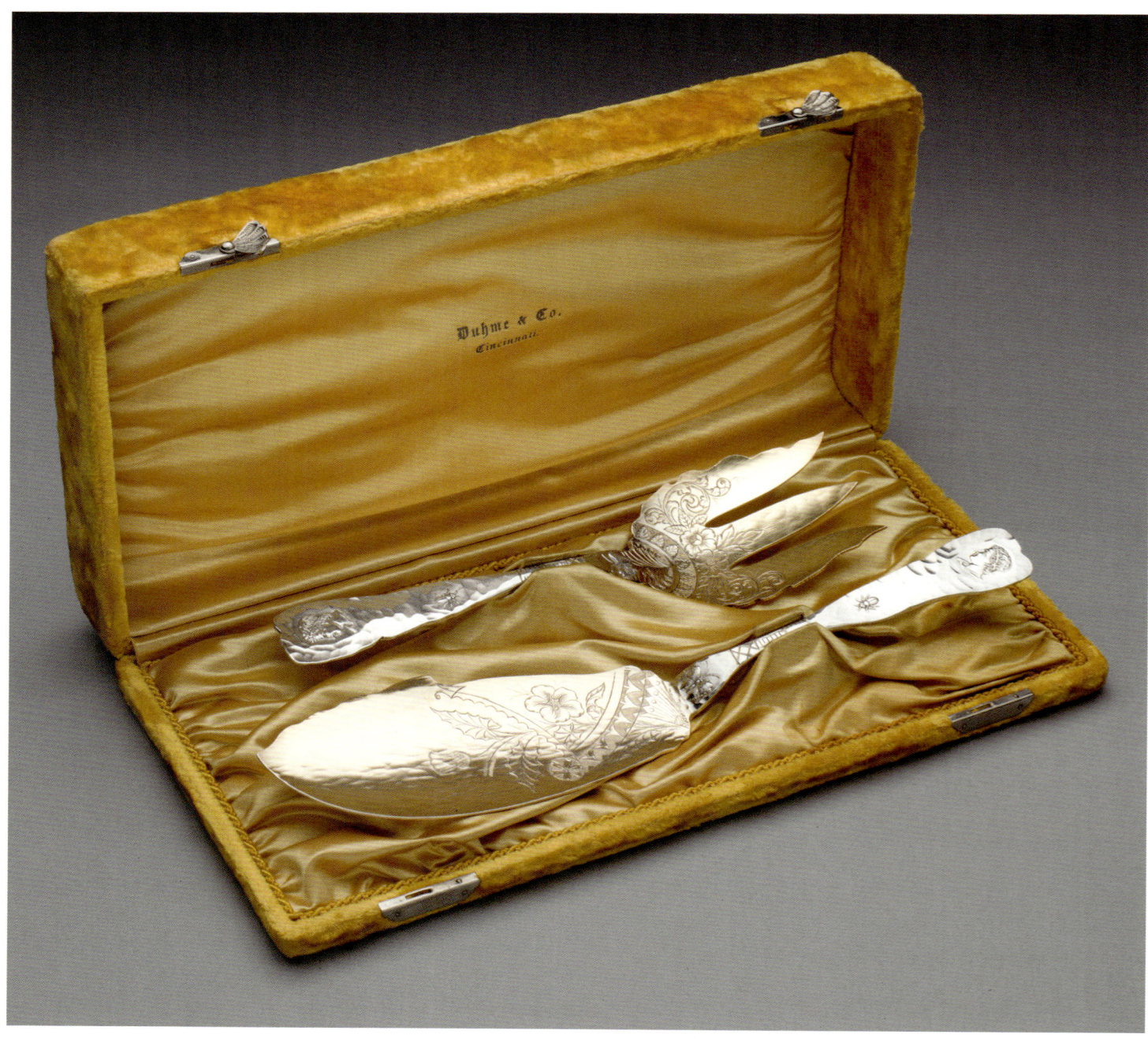

FIG. 38.38: Duhme & Co., *Fish Serving Set*, c. 1887, parcel gilt silver,
slice: L. 12⁹⁄₁₆ in. (31.9 cm), fork: L. 9¾ in. (24.8 cm), CAM, Gift of
Dorothy Krug Newstedt, 1975.266a–c. Mark 38.13

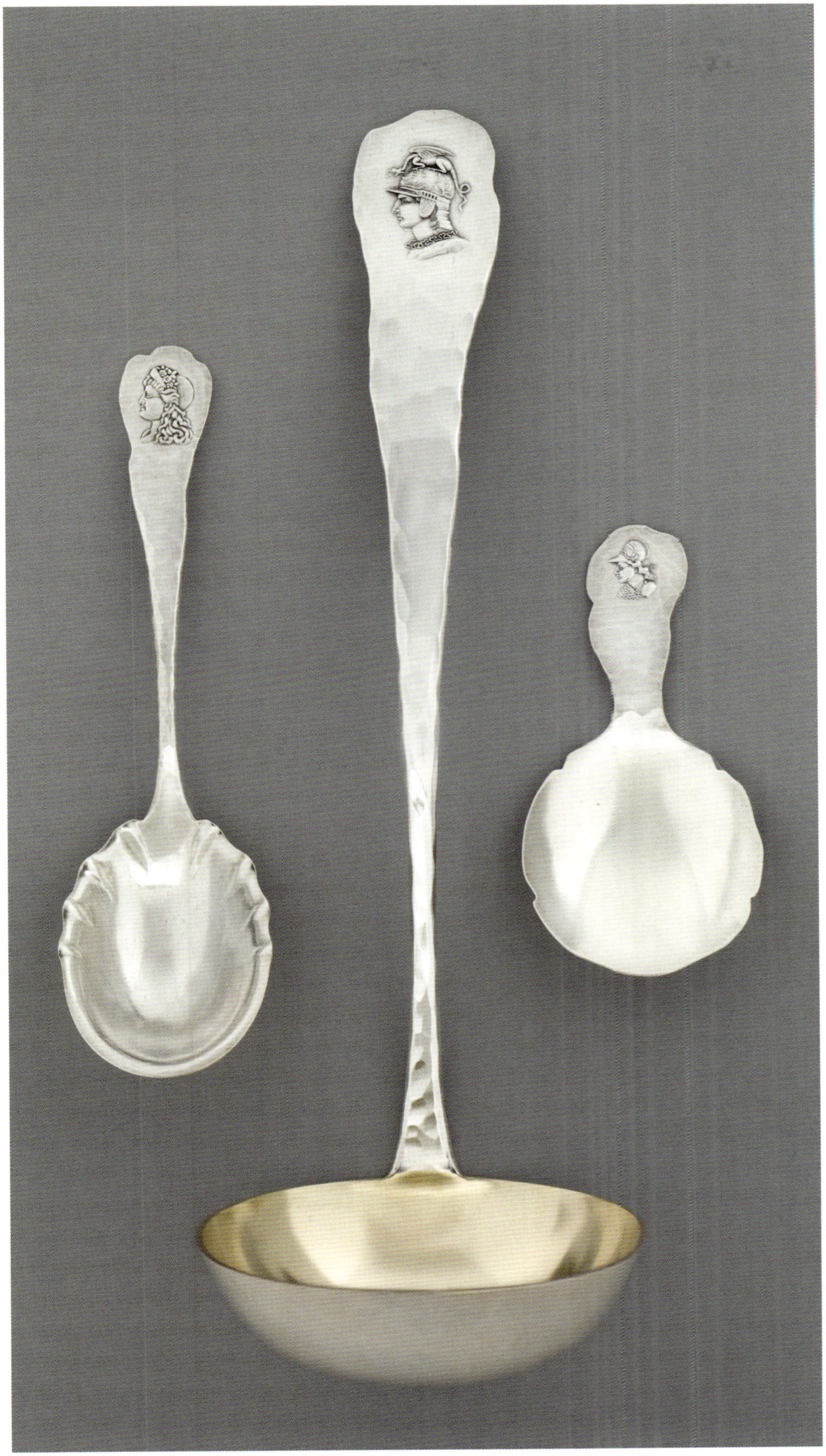

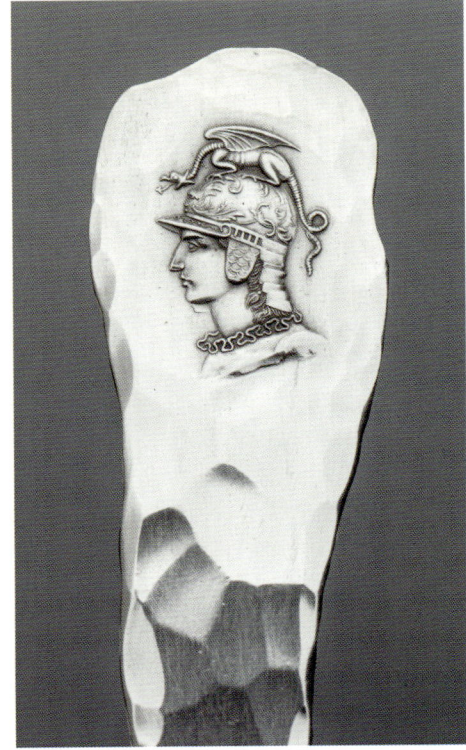

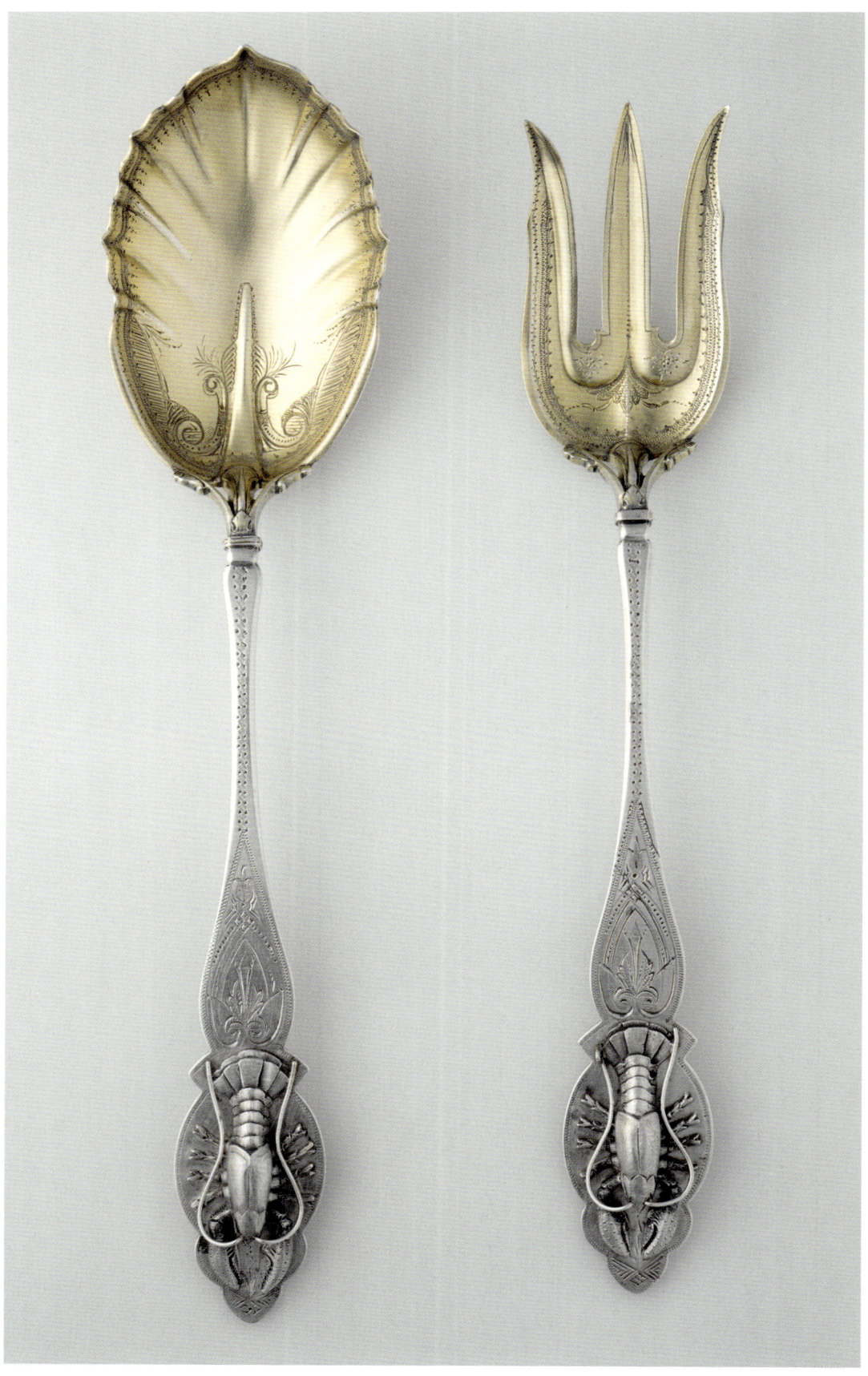

FIG. 38.40: Duhme & Co., *Salad Spoon and Fork*, c. 1880s, parcel gilt silver, spoon: L. 12 in. (30.5 cm), fork: L. 11 in. (27.9 cm), CAM, Gift of James Randolph Hillard, M.D. and Aingeal Grehan, 2007.121a–b. Mark 38.3

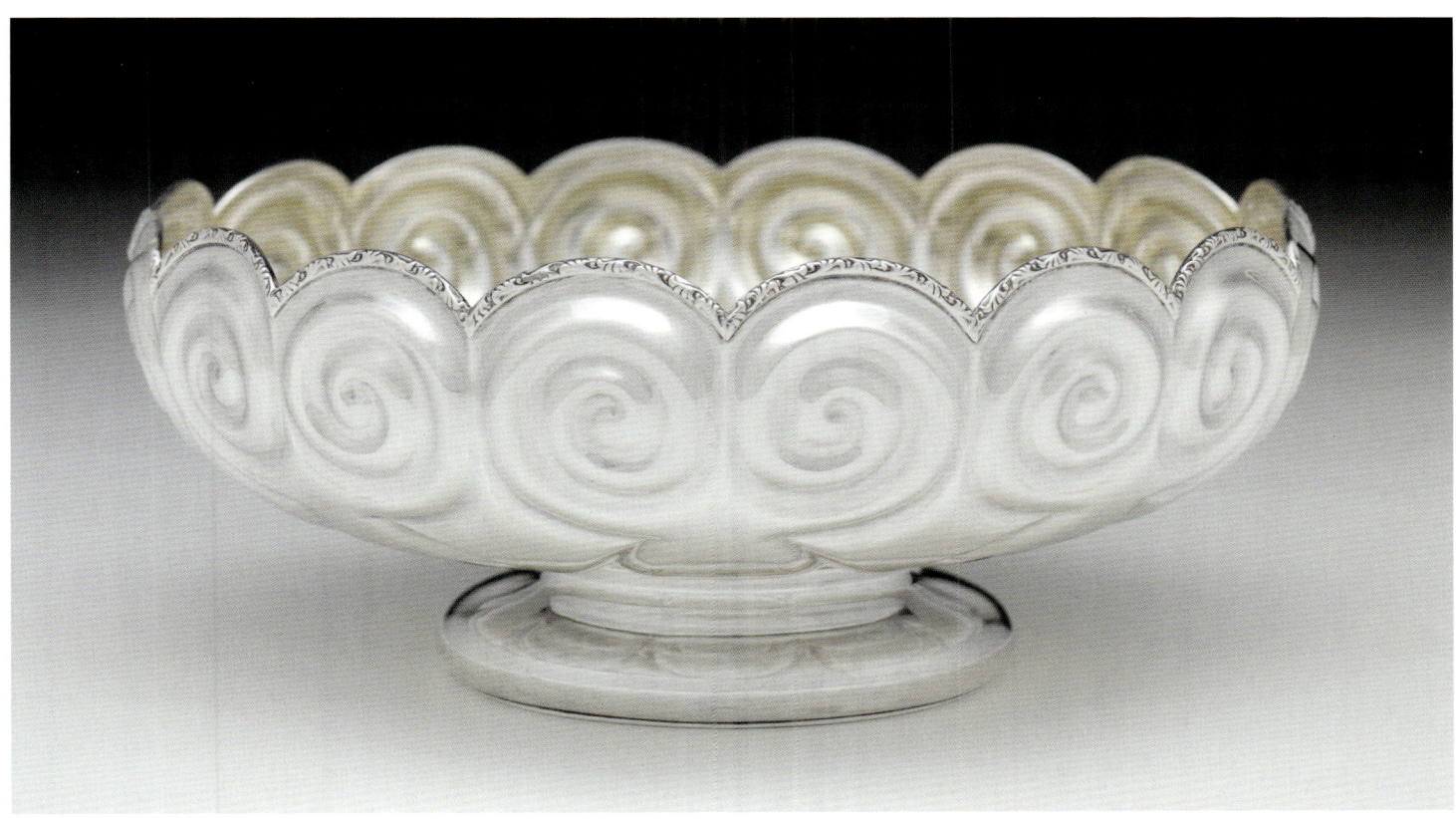

FIG. 38.41: Duhme & Co., *Footed Bowl*, 1880s, H. 3½ in. (3.5 cm),
Diam. 8 in. (20.3 cm), CAM, Museum Purchase with funds provided
by Mr. and Mrs. Charles Fleischmann III, 2005.57. Mark 38.10

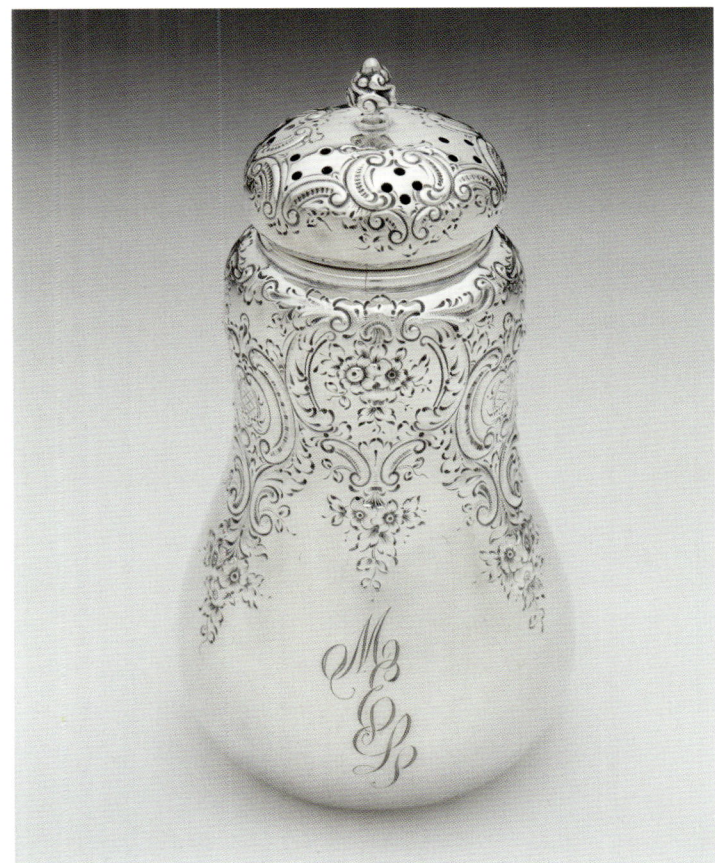

FIG. 38.42: Duhme & Co.,
Sugar Shaker, 1880s, H. 5¾ in.
(14.6 cm), Diam. 3 in. (7.6 cm),
Museum Purchase with funds
provided by Mr. and Mrs.
Charles Fleischmann III,
2005.63a–b. Mark 38.7

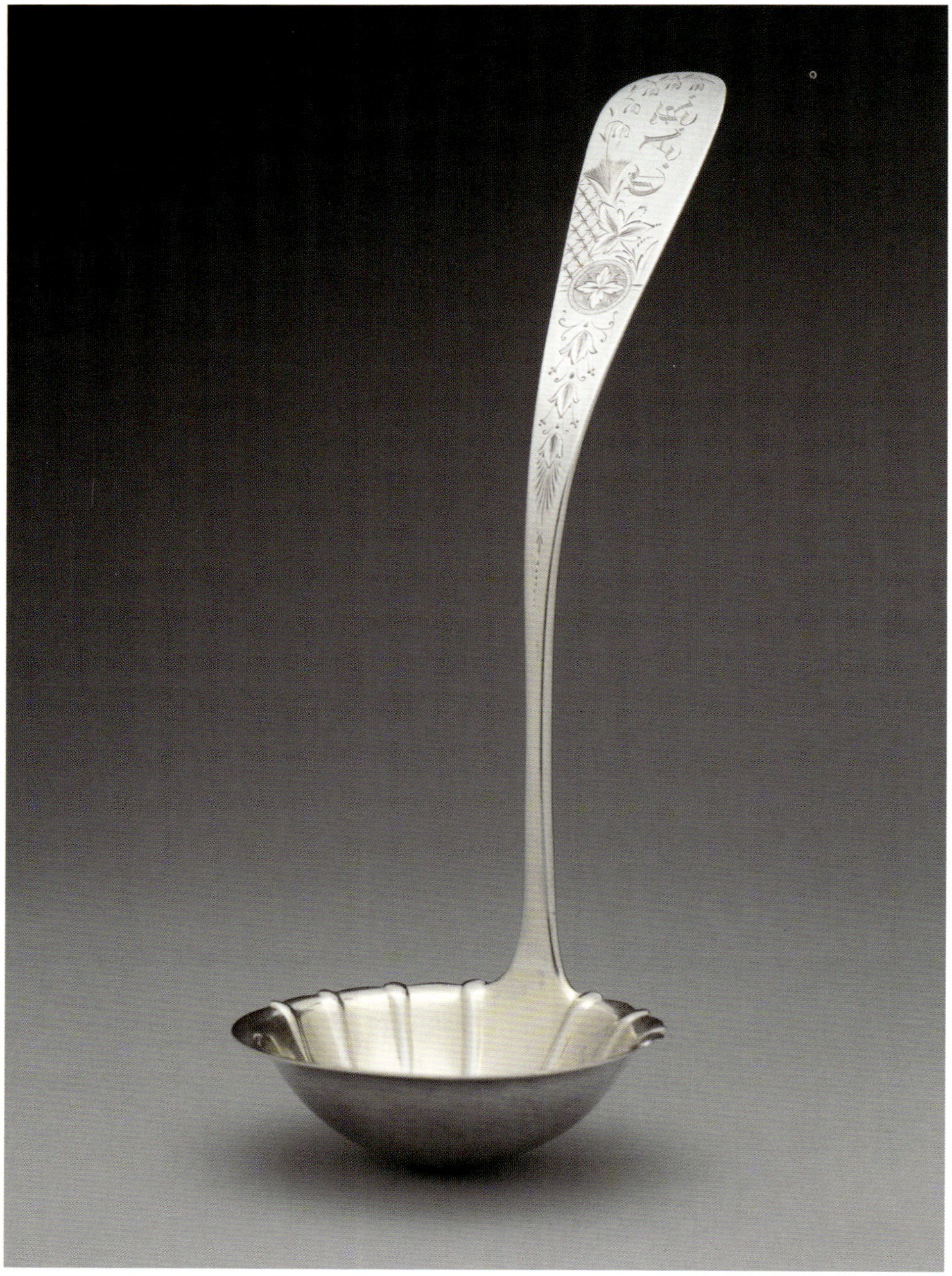

FIG. 38.43: Duhme & Co., *Ladle*, "Lily"
pattern, 1880s, L. 10¾ in. (27.6 cm), CAM,
Gift of James Randolph Hillard, M.D. and
Aingeal Grehan, 2007.139. Mark 38.11

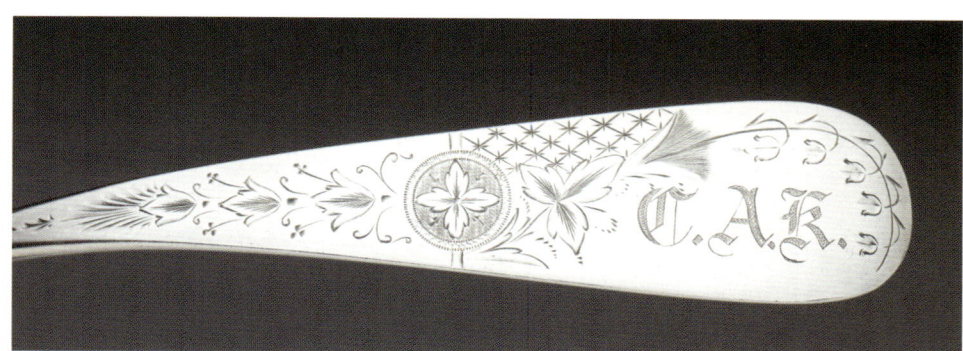

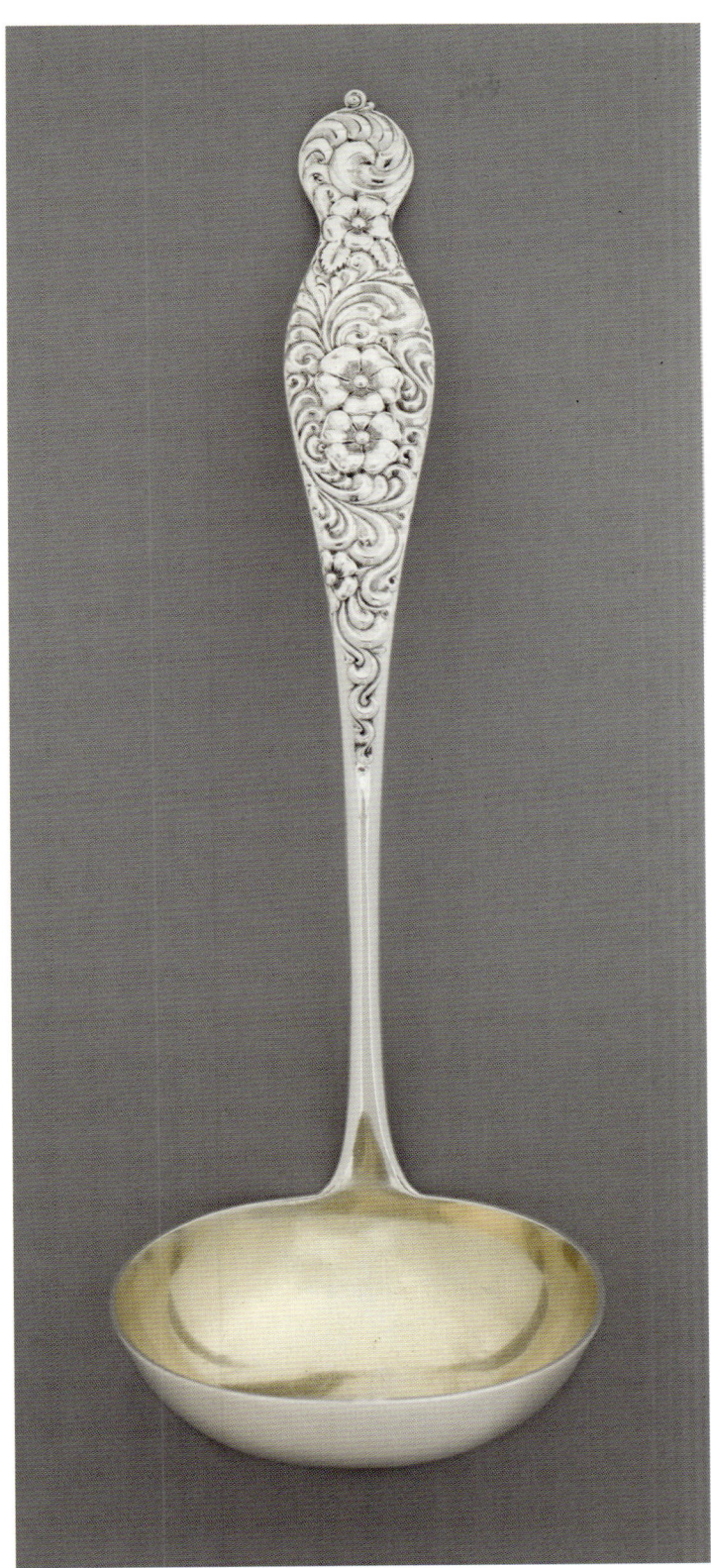

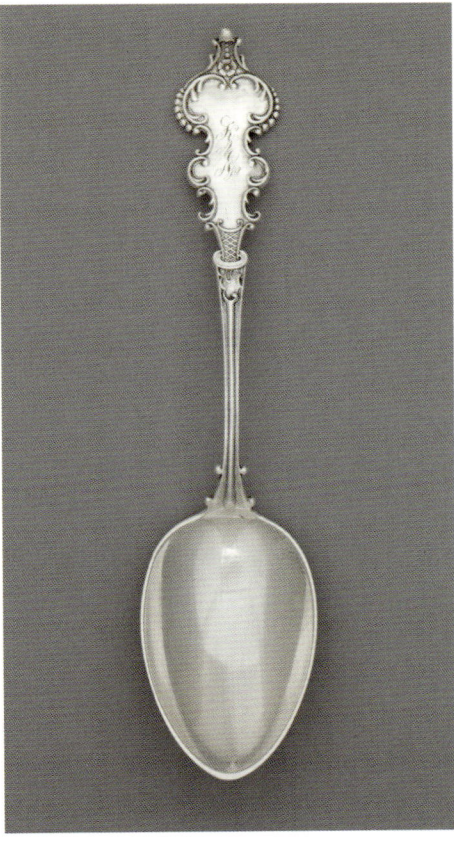

FIG. 38.45: Duhme & Co., *Teaspoon*, "Dresden" pattern, c. 1890, L. 5⁹⁄₁₆, (14.1 cm), CAM, Gift in memory of Charles H. (Randy) Randolph, DDS, from his wife, children and grandchildren, 2011.289. Mark was incorporated into die press for pattern, DUHME & CO (STERLING)

FIG. 38.44: Duhme & Co., *Ladle*, "No. 3" pattern, c. 1890, parcel gilt silver, 12½ in. (31.8 cm), CAM, Gift in memory of Charles H. (Randy) Randolph, DDS, from his wife, children and grandchildren, 2011.290. Mark was incorporated into die press for pattern, DUHME & Co., in an oblong cartouche with tapered ends

The Final Years

Some time prior to 1891, Duhme introduced aluminum spoons. A report from April of that year stated that "when they began to make some of the aluminum spoons, they thought the fad would be short lived, but they are constantly besieged for them. They do not care to make large quantities as that would interfere with their regular factory work, and they would rather sell their solid silver in which there is more profit."[110] By June, they had "added four new [silver] spoons to their great variety."[111] These may have been souvenir spoons, as it is known that Duhme & Co. introduced a Cincinnati Art Museum spoon and a Fort Washington Spoon that year.[112] In 1891, the annual product of jewelry and silverware in Cincinnati was $1,741,000, and Duhme & Co. was noted for holding "a commanding position among the industrial and mercantile institutions of the country."[113] Beginning in 1890, Theodore Neuhaus, Jr. (see **Theodore Neuhaus & Co.**) was superintendent of Duhme's silver flatware manufacturing department, and in January 1892 **Frank Kramer** was noted as the department's foreman.[114] However, in February 1893 the firm announced the relocation of its silver factory to a top floor of the Carlisle Building in order to remodel the basement for a silver plate and materials department "to supply demand."[115] This relocation of the silver manufactory to a top floor—a highly unsuitable location for drop presses—suggests that much of the heavy machinery used to make silver had been abandoned, and that the manufacturing of silver now pursued by the firm was minimal.[116] Several silver commissions received between the May 1893 and July 1897 are noted in the newspapers, but it is likely that most were only brokered and perhaps engraved by Duhme.[117]

During this period, the firm's sales in silver seem to have tapered. Several of its die-stamped patterns introduced in the 1880s bear dated engravings from the 1890s. This, and 1890s advertisements for the "Dresden" pattern, indicate the firm's reliance on old designs. Souvenir spoons continued to be popular, including small spoons, advertised as souvenirs for children, with a raised wishbone design.[118] Duhme & Co. marks used during this period include 38.10, 38.14, and 38.15.[119]

In April 1893 Duhme & Co. became The Duhme Company when it was incorporated by R.H. Galbreath, Charlotte Duhme, Frank Duhme, Franklin Ives, and E.H. Kleinschmidt. The capital stock was $400,000 and sold in single shares of $100. Its certificate of incorporation stated that the business of the company would be "the manufacturing of gold and silver ware, jewelry and watch cases, and the transacting of a general jewelry business."[120] But the Panic of 1893 had by this time set in and there were soon rumors that the business was in trouble.[121] In early May, The Duhme Company had

plans to exhibit at the World's Columbian Exposition in Chicago, but by the end of the month, they had dropped out.[122] In August, the firm announced that they would "start up neither their watch case nor silverware factories, until the silver question is settled."[123] The "silver question" referred to the continued debate over whether the country's coinage and monetary policy should be based solely on gold, or on both gold and silver.[124] The Duhme Company is not known to have manufactured any silver after this time. Wares, mostly flatware, with the incuse marks of The Duhme Company are rare, the most common marks being "DUHME" and "THE DUHME COMPANY." Of these wares, the majority have been observed also to bear the manufacturing marks of Gorham Mfg. Co., Dominick & Haff, Bigelow Kennard & Co. (Boston), or Landers, Frary & Clark (New Britain, Connecticut).

In March 1894 The Duhme Company reduced its staff by eight salesmen, and cut all salaries, including that of the president of the firm, by ten percent.[125] Charles H. Duhme was appointed president of the firm, in the hope that he could right the company, but it was too late.[126] In July 1895 the firm announced the closure of its wholesale business so that it could concentrate exclusively on its retail operation.[127] E. & J. Swigart, who specialized in jewelers' supplies and materials, bought the entire material department and Charles H. Ankeny (1844–1908), who had been in charge of the wholesale department since 1891, returned to Lafayette, Indiana, where he would continue the business of C.H. Ankeny & Co.[128] The firm had, without doubt, abandoned the manufacturing of silver and gold ware by this time, as alleged by Frank and Herman Duhme when they filed a petition for the appointment of a receiver for The Duhme Company and the dissolution of the firm in December 1896.[129] The brothers, who then owned one-fifth of the business, contended that the company could not be profitable as managed by the majority stock owners who barred them from participating in management. They claimed that the business had been conducted at a loss since The Duhme Company's incorporation, an assertion that eventually proved to be true. The brothers also revealed that R.H. Galbreath, their step-mother Mary C. Galbreath Duhme, and their step-sister Charlotte Duhme Eustis, had concealed losses and declared a fictitious dividend, which was later cancelled to avoid a forced receivership by law. Ultimately, the firm was required to declare bankruptcy on March 5, 1897.[130] Their assets amounted to $104,521.16 while their liabilities totaled $170,397.97.[131] Gorham and Dominick & Haff were among their creditors. The firm's failure was estimated to be one of the largest in Cincinnati that year.[132]

On May 4, 1897, the remaining assets of the company were purchased by Lucille Constance Elstun Duhme and Mary Caroline

Mazzone Duhme (acting on behalf of their husbands, Frank and Herman Duhme) with the assistance of Herman Keck, Jr. and his brother Oscar (see the **Herman Keck Manufacturing Co.**), who had been buying out other troubled jewelry firms.[133] The business continued as The Duhme Jewelry Co. at the firm's previous location in the Carlisle Building. Herman Duhme appeared in the 1898 City Directory as superintendent, and Frank Duhme was listed as manager. R.H. Galbreath was listed as general manager. However, the Kecks controlled the firm.

On January 22, 1898, the Duhme Manufacturing Co. was incorporated with a capital stock of $100,000 by Herman and Frank Duhme, Oscar and Herman Keck, and Theodore Neuhaus.[134] One report states that they were "makers of sterling silverware" with a factory at the corner of Fourth and Walnut (the Carlisle Building), while another states the purpose of the company was to "deal in gold and silverware, clocks, watches, and jewelry of all kind." At the same time, Neuhaus, Lakin & Co., another concern in which the Kecks were heavily involved, moved into the Carlisle Building as well to "begin manufacturing silver."[135]

Discord between the Kecks and the Duhme family grew, and in May 1898 relations were severed when Herman Duhme gave Oscar Keck "a thrashing for various insults of longstanding."[136] By June, the Duhme brothers were seeking a location for their own enterprise.[137] In July, they leased space at 37 and 39 East Fourth Street, near Walnut Street, in the Harrison Building and founded Duhme Bros. & Co. Situated next door to Pike's Opera House, they were just a handful of stores west of Keck's firm which resided in the location that Duhme & Co. had occupied since 1859.[138] Partners of the firm were the wives of Herman and Frank Duhme, and Emily J. Galbreath, wife of R.H. Galbreath.[139]

Duhme Bros. & Co. advertised in directories as "Dealers in Watches, Jewelry, Diamonds, Silverware, Fancy Goods, etc."[140] In 1901, the 85-foot deep Duhme Bros. & Co. store, with fixtures of cherry, was described as "solid, from front to rear, with magnificent wall cases . . . ablaze with silver, cut glass and fine art pieces."[141] Between 1900 and 1902, the firm reported receiving orders for chests of silver for wedding presents; a silver trowel presented by the Cincinnati Commercial Club to Jacob G. Schmidlapp, president of Union Savings Bank and Trust Co., for the laying of the cornerstone of the bank's new skyscraper; and a "10-inch gold lined loving cup of exquisite design" for a presentation by employees of Roger Brown & Co., a Cincinnati pig iron firm.[142] A loving cup with horn handles, in the Cincinnati Art Museum collection, is not marked by the firm, but features the engraved inscription: "Presented by Duhme Bros. & Co. Cincinnati to Landford C. Carpenter, Sweepstakes for best Horse Mare or Gelding shown in

harness at Abdallah Park Cynthiana, Ky. 1900."[143] Duhme Bros. & Co. probably did not make any of this silver, as they were primarily retailers. No silver bearing the mark of Duhme Bros. & Co. is currently known.

In February 1903 Pike's Opera House, next door to Duhme Bros. & Co, caught fire (fig. 38.46).[144] The shop of Duhme Bros. & Co was completely gutted by flames, and the loss was estimated at $40,000. During the fire, efforts were made to save the silverware, bric-a-brac and other items from their wall cases, and a few wagon loads of stock were removed to City Hall before the fire became too intense. Duhme descendants recall that Herman and his sons ran down to the store to rescue the safe that contained their records, but the safety and current whereabouts of these records are still unknown.[145] The firm's machinery, type unknown, was reportedly spared from the fire, as it was across the street from their store.[146] Following the fire, the firm relocated to the Boyland Building, 138 and 140 East Fourth Street, and in doing so were able to host all of their departments under one roof.[147] But the firm continued to struggle.

In August 1903, receivers were appointed for the firm, and it was found to have liabilities of $50,745.72.[148] Nonetheless, the company effected a settlement with their creditors and re-opened their store at 138 Fourth Street in December 1903, enlarging it in January 1904.[149] It was around this time that R.H. Galbreath left and reunited with the Kecks, for whom he worked until moving to New York in 1905.[150] By the end of March 1904 the Court of Common Pleas had ordered the sale of Duhme Bros. & Co.'s chattel

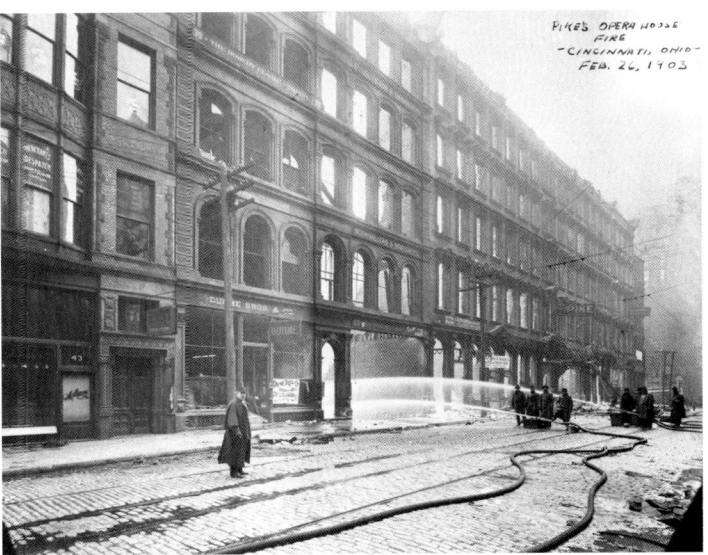

FIG. 38.46: *Duhme Bros. & Co. storefront after Pike's Opera House Fire,* February 26, 1903, negative B-80-031, Cincinnati Historical Society

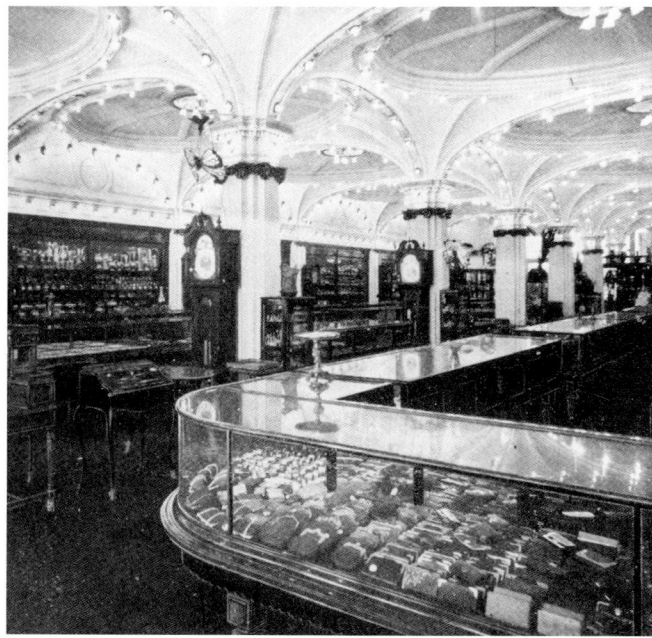

FIG. 38.47: *Duhme Jewelry Co.*, from Charles Gilbert Hall, *The Cincinnati Southern Railway: a History: a complete and concise history of the events attending the building and operation of the road*, Cincinnati: The McDonald Press, 1902, 174

property.[151] Among the goods sold at auction were "Tea Sets, Loving Cups, Bowls, Fruit Dishes, Bon Bon Dishes, Water Pitchers, Spoons and Forks, Knifes." The firm's largest creditors were "eastern firms who sell to all of the rest of the jewelers [in Cincinnati]."[152] Their stock and fixtures were purchased by local businessman, George Halm, for $24,075. He made arrangements for the store to reopen in its former place of business under the management of Frank and Herman Duhme.[153] But by November, the brothers announced that they had "other interests in view," and would retire permanently from the jewelry business. A six-week long auction followed and the firm officially closed in January 1905.[154] Just six months later, the business reopened as Duhme Bros., dealers in jewelry and musical instruments, on Madison Avenue in Covington, Kentucky, and was operated by the grandsons of John H. Duhme (Herman G. Duhme's brother), John Herman Duhme (1881–1947) and Charles Edwin Duhme (1882–1966).[155] The brothers were associates until at least 1928. After this, only John Herman continued as a jeweler on Madison with subsequent moves to Eighth Street and later to Pike Street, where he worked until at least 1945.[156]

After the Duhmes and the Kecks split in 1898, the Kecks continued to run The Duhme Jewelry Co., which functioned as the retail branch of the Herman Keck Manufacturing Co. which, in turn, had absorbed the Duhme Manufacturing Co. Herman Keck, Jr. was president, Oscar Keck was secretary and treasurer, and R.H.

Galbreath served as manager.[157] The Duhme Jewelry Co. boasted $300,000 in stock, versus the $28,000 in stock held by Duhme Bros. & Co., and in June 1899 Keck sued Duhme Bros. & Co. over the use of the Duhme name, asserting that customers would confuse the two firms and obtain the wrong impression about his store. The courts ruled in favor of Duhme Bros. & Co., allowing them to keep their name.[158] In October 1899 labor unrest over shop rules led to a strike by about 50 of Keck's engravers, silversmiths, and polishers.[159] In late 1900, the firm moved to new, larger head-quarters, "brightly illuminated with incandescent lamps," at 19–25 West Fourth Street, between Vine and Race Streets (fig. 38.47).[160] In addition to manufacturing and selling jewelry, silver, and clocks, the firm carried on a large business in diamonds and maintained its own diamond cutting plant.[161] Employees included R.H. Galbreath, **Herbert Townsend Kent** (son of **Luke Kent, Jr.**), Fred Hellebush (son of **Clemens Hellebush**), and E.E. Isbell.[162] After Herman Keck, Jr.'s death in 1906, Oscar Keck became president of The Duhme Jewelry Co. and the Herman Keck Manufacturing Co.[163] A victim of the Panic of 1907, Oscar Keck was soon under the pressure of creditors.[164] In an attempt to avoid bankruptcy, he held an auction sale of the stock of The Duhme Jewelry Co. which ran from October 1908 to January 1909.[165] But the proceeds were not enough to bring his firms out of debt, and the courts, acting on the behalf of eastern creditors who charged Keck as "incompetent and unfit to control the company," appointed a receiver for the two firms whose affairs were deemed "so interwoven that such action was deemed necessary."[166] Among the companies' largest creditors were Gorham for $1,776.20; R. Blackington & Co. (North Attleboro, Massachusetts) for $2,657.90; and R. Wallace & Sons for $1,342.51.[167] Silver marked by The Duhme Jewelry Co. has also been found with the manufacturer marks of Howard Sterling Co. (Providence, Rhode Island); Ferd, Fuchs & Bros. (New York City); Whiting Mfg. Co. (Providence, Rhode Island); and Frank M. Whiting Co. (North Attleboro, Massachusetts).[168] After a long, complex, scandal-ridden court battle, the firms were declared insolvent.[169] A receiver's sale was held in December 1909 and a final sale held on June 14, 1910, including machinery, fixtures, silverware, bric-a-brac, jewelry, and loose and mounted stones, closed down both businesses.[170]

Wares marked with incuse variations of "THE DUHME JEWELRY CO." include flatware and hollowware.[171] Wares observed with the incuse mark "THE DUHME MFG CO." are rare. To date, only hollowware, such as the Turkish coffee pot in fig. 38.48, has been noted with this mark.[172] No silver bearing the mark of the Herman Keck Manufacturing Co. has been documented during the course of this study.

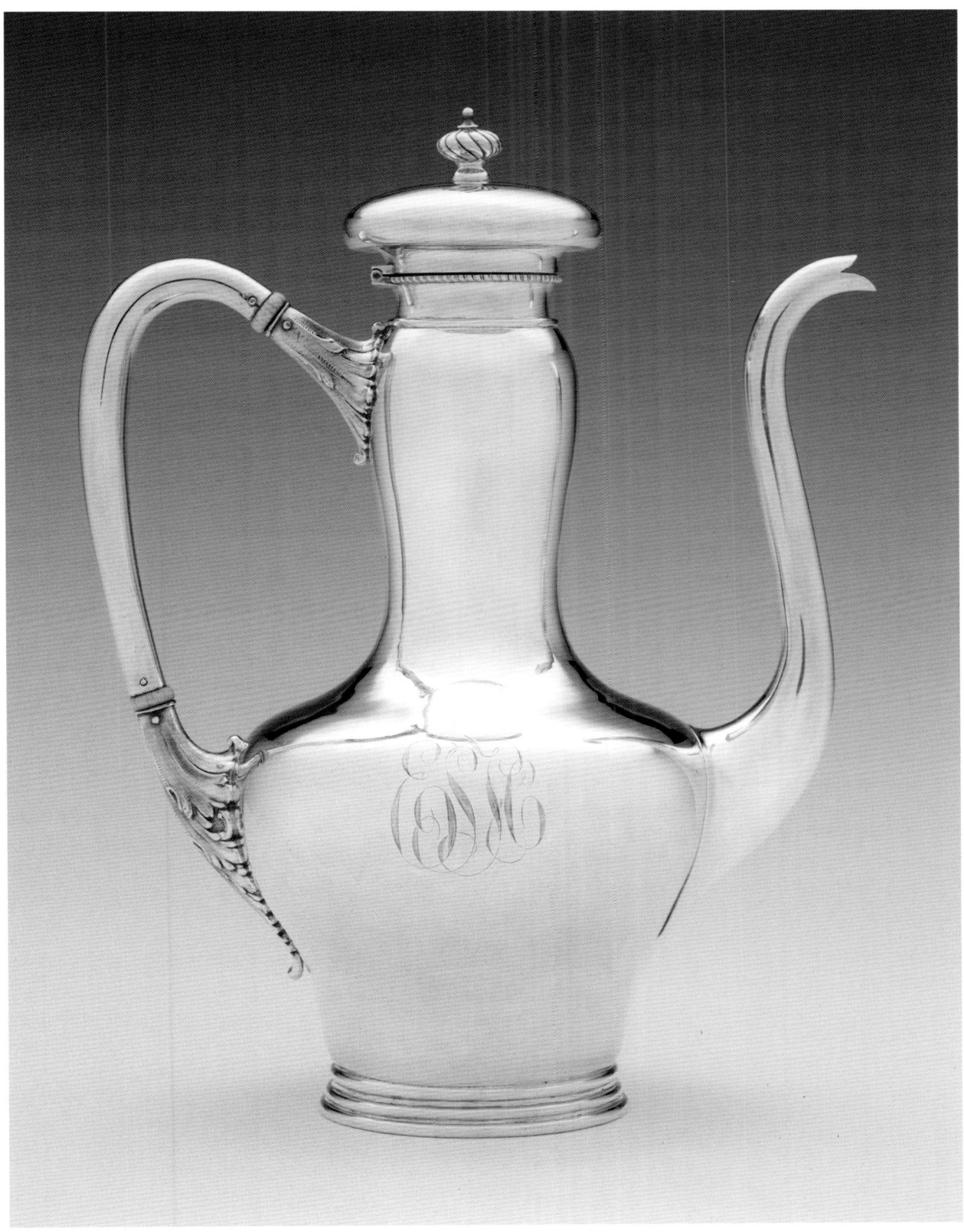

FIG. 38.48: Duhme Manufacturing Co., *Turkish Coffee Pot*,
1898, H. 11⅜ in. (28.9 cm), W. 8¾ in. (22.2 cm),
CAM, Museum Purchase, 2000.157. Mark 38.17

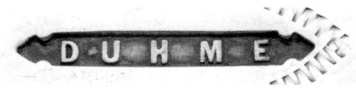

MARK 38.1

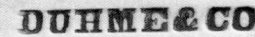

MARK 38.7

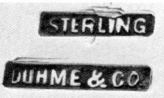

MARK 38.13

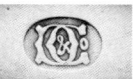

MARK 38.2

STERLING $\frac{925}{1000}$ DUHME & CO.

MARK 38.8

STERLING DUHME & CO. CINCINNATI.

MARK 38.14

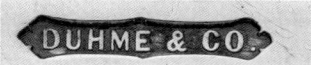

MARK 38.3

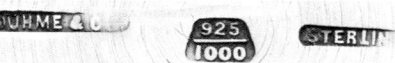

MARK 38.9

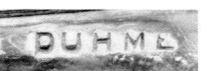

MARK 38.15

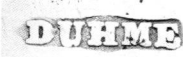

MARK 38.4

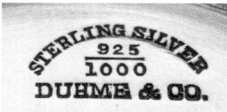

MARK 38.10

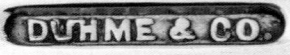

MARK 38.16

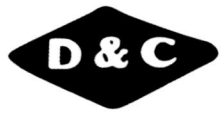

MARK 38.5

MARK 38.11

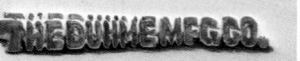

MARK 38.17

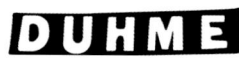

MARK 38.6

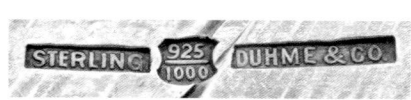

MARK 38.12

MARK 38.18

1. John Roger Newstedt and Charles von D. Knighton, *A Cincinnati Saga: The McNicoll-Duhme Connection: A History of Two Families intertwined in the Early Days of the City from 1804 to the Present with Embellishments and A Measure of Astonishment*, unpublished manuscript, 1996, facsimile, Cincinnati Art Museum, Decorative Arts & Design Department, Duhme & Co. files; M. Joblin, *Cincinnati Past and Present: or, Its Industrial History, As Exhibited in the Life-Labors of Its Leading Men*, Cincinnati: Elm Street Printing Co., 1872, 326; Charles Robson, *Biographical Encyclopedia of Ohio of the Nineteenth Century*, Cincinnati: Galaxy Publishing Co., 1876, 51; Albert N. Marquis (ed.), *The Industries of Cincinnati . . .* , Cincinnati: A.N Marquis & Co., 1883, 105.

2. Newstedt and Knighton, *A Cincinnati Saga*, 37–39; While some references say that they sailed on the *Great Western*, this could not be substantiated at the time of this publication.

3. Charles Greve, *Centennial History of Cincinnati and Its Representative Citizens*, Chicago: Biographical Publishing Co., 1904, 2:491; Robson, *Biographical Encyclopedia*, 51; Newstedt and Knighton, *A Cincinnati Saga*, 37–39; Paul W. Schanher, "Springfield's Saga Continues," *Springfield History*, blogspot, July 28, 2010, http://springfieldhistory. blogspot.com/2010/07/springfields-saga-continues.html; Griffith Foos, Ferncliff Cemetery, Springfield, Ohio, *Find A Grave*, www.findagrave.com.

4. Henry H. Duhme is listed in Cincinnati city directories as both Henry H. and Herman H. In other places he is referred to as Herman Heinrich. For the purpose of this study, he is referred to as Henry H. Duhme; John W. Leonard, *The Centennial Review of Cincinnati: one hundred years of progress in commerce, manufactures, the professions, and in social and municipal life*, Cincinnati: J.M. Elstner, 1888, 67; Newstedt and Knighton, *A Cincinnati Saga*, 39–40; Henry H. Duhme eventually purchased Wolff's business.

5. 1839/40 Cincinnati City Directory. The information for this directory would have been collected in 1839.

6. Advertisement, 1842 Cincinnati City Directory, 247, reproduced in Beckman, 50; Joblin, *Cincinnati Past and Present*, 326–328; Marquis, *The Industries of Cincinnati*, 105; Ohio, Vol. 1, p. 176, R.G. Dun & Co. Collection, Baker Library, Harvard Business School.

7. 1844 Cincinnati City Directory; Ohio, Vol. 1, p. 176, R.G. Dun & Co. Collection.

8. Ohio, Vol. 1, p. 176, R.G. Dun & Co. Collection.

9. 1849/50 Cincinnati City Directory; Joblin, *Cincinnati Past and Present*, 326–328.

10. 1850/51 Cincinnati City Directory, 67.

11. Greve, *Centennial History of Cincinnati*, 2:491; "Herman Duhme" in Ancestry.com, *U.S. Passport Applications, 1795–1925* [online database], Provo, Utah: Ancestry.com Operations Inc., 2007.

12. Newstedt and Knighton, *A Cincinnati Saga*, 42.

13. *Official Catalogue of the Great Exhibition of the Works of Industry of All Nations*, London: Spicer Brothers, 1851, 184.

14. Norman Mack, *Missouri's Silver Age: Silversmiths of the 1800s*, Carbondale, IL: Southern Illinois University Press, 2005, 40. Mack reports silver marked "Duhme St. Louis." At the time of publication, no silver with this mark could be documented.

15. Facsimile of letter from J.H. Cook to H. Duhme, St. Louis to Cincinnati, February 4, 1852, provided by Dr. James Randolph Hillard.

16. Samuel Hatch and Albert C. Pratt are listed as principals in the 1857 and 1858 Cincinnati City Directories. Louis P. Muller is listed as a principal in the city directories from 1856 to 1858.

17. Ohio, Vol. 3, p. 5, R.G. Dun & Co. Collection; Pratt left in 1859. Ohio Vol. 3, p. 15, R.G. Dun & Co. Collection.

18. 1859 Cincinnati City Directory; Ohio, Vol. 3, p. 5, R.G. Dun & Co. Collection.

19. Advertisement, *Cincinnati Enquirer*, August 11, 1858, 3.

20. 1859 Cincinnati City Directory; Advertisement, *Cincinnati Enquirer*, December 20, 1859, 2.

21. Advertisement, *Cincinnati Commercial Tribune*, August 13, 1861, 5; Throughout their tenure, Duhme sold silver plate from manufacturers that included Gorham, Wilcox, and Rogers & Bro.; Advertisement, *Cincinnati Enquirer*, May 9, 1870, 5; Advertisement, *Cincinnati Enquirer*, July 18, 1874, 8; Advertisement, *Cincinnati Daily Gazette*, December 18, 1876, 8.

22. Duhme & Co., eBay listings and private collections, Cincinnati silver binders, Cincinnati Art Museum.

23. In 1888, John William Leonard states that a manufacturing department was added in the early 1860s. Maurice Joblin, writing in 1872, also implies that manufacturing did not start until the 1860s. Leonard, *Centennial Review of Cincinnati*, 67; Joblin, *Cincinnati Past and Present*, 326–328

24. There may have been other silversmiths working at the firm prior to this, or at the same time as Kruckemeyer, who were not included in city directory listings. Kruckemeyer appears in city directories as a silversmith at Duhme's from 1862–64 and 1867–70, and from 1871–88, as a foreman silversmith. Other silversmiths who were listed in Cincinnati city directories as working at Duhme & Co. were: J.W. Engbersen (1869–1871), Theodore Neuhaus, Sr. (1866–1874); Henry Alms (1870); Theo. Biltz (1870, 1871, 1874); Herman Mirenfeld (1870); Adam Peterman (1870); Adam Rieder (1870, 1883); John Telthester (1871); Wm. Theuerkauf (1878–1882); and William H. Willis (1876–1893).

25. "Manufacture and Sale of Jewelry in Cincinnati During Preceding Century," *Cincinnati Enquirer*, October 23, 1923.

26. Louis Leonard Tucker, *Cincinnati During the Civil War, Issue 9 of Publications of the Ohio Civil War Centennial Commission*, Columbus: Ohio State University Press for the Ohio Historical Society, 1962, 19; Newstedt and Knighton, *A Cincinnati Saga*, 1996, 48.

27. Advertisement, *Cincinnati Enquirer*, March 13, 1862, 2.

28. 1866 Cincinnati City Directory; Advertisement, *Cincinnati Enquirer*, April 22, 1867, 2; "Local Notices," *Cincinnati Enquirer*, June 7, 1867, 2; In 1866, Duhme reportedly "manufactured" 180 pieces of silverware, "consisting of tea urns, tea sets, ice pitchers, goblets, salvers, etc. all gotten up and finished at heavy expense and in a manner highly creditable to their manufacturers" as premiums that were awarded at the National Tobacco Fair, held in Cincinnati. However, from the report, it is not completely clear whether Duhme was the manufacturer or simply the supplier of the premiums. "The National Tobacco Fair," *Cincinnati Enquirer*, July 12, 1866, 2; The silver tea service donated to the Tobacco Fair in 1870 was more likely of Duhme's own manufacture. "The Tobacco Fair," *Cincinnati Enquirer*, August 2, 1870, 8; "Local Notices," *Cincinnati Enquirer*, June 7, 1867, 2; Also see a notice for silver coin wanted by Duhme & Co. in "Local Notices," *Cincinnati Enquirer*, August 1, 1867, 2.

29. Ohio, Vol. 3, p. 15, R.G. Dun & Co. Collection.

30. Herman G. Duhme and Mary Ann McNicholl married in April 1847 and had two sons, Herman Jr. and Frank. Greve, *Centennial History of Cincinnati*, 2:492; "Law Report: Common Pleas," *Cincinnati Enquirer*, February 27, 1859, 2.

31. Ohio, Vol. 3, p. 5, R.G. Dun & Co. Collection; Ohio, Vol. 3, p. 15, R.G. Dun & Co. Collection; Ohio, Vol. 3, p. 98, R.G. Dun & Co. Collection; Ohio, Vol. 4, p. 49, R.G. Dun & Co. Collection; Henry H. Duhme continued to run his dry goods store on Fifth Street at this time; 1865 and 1866 Cincinnati City Directories.

32. Marriage record, cited by Newstedt and Knighton, *A Cincinnati Saga*, 46; Greve, *Centennial History of Cincinnati*, 2:492. Herman G. Duhme and Mary C. Galbreath had two children: Charlotte "Lottie" and Albert.

33. Newstedt and Knighton, *A Cincinnati Saga*, 47; Galbreath had worked at Duhme & Co. as a salesman in 1861. Ohio, Vol. 3, p. 98, R.G. Dun & Co. Collection; 1861-1905 Cincinnati City Directories.

34. "City Features," *Cincinnati Daily Gazette*, December 30, 1867, 1.

35. Ibid.

36. Advertisement, *Cincinnati Daily Gazette*, December 16, 1868, 2.

37. Ohio, Vol. 3, p. 98, R.G. Dun & Co. Collection; Duhme was never known to have manufactured plated ware. "Plate" here is used as a generic term to describe metalwork, not plated silver.

38. "City Features," *Cincinnati Daily Gazette*, December 30, 1867, 1.

39. Letter from Herman G. Duhme to sons Herman and Frank, Cincinnati to Neuchatel, March 18, 1868, courtesy of Charles von D. Knighton.

40. Letter from Herman G. Duhme to sons Frank and Herman, Cincinnati to Neuchatel, November 5, 1868, courtesy of Charles von D. Knighton; Also see "Great Preparations for New Year's Day," *Cincinnati Enquirer*, December 29, 1869, 8.

41. "Progress in the Decorative Arts: The Manufacture of Gold and Silverware in the West: A Visit to Duhme & Co.'s," *Cincinnati Enquirer*, May 18, 1869, 3.

42. "Progress in the Decorative Arts: The Manufacture of Gold and Silverware in the West," May 18, 1869. Another description of the firm's works can be found in "Great Jewelers of the West," *Cincinnati Enquirer*, June 8, 1872, 8. Therein, it is noted that Mexican coins were melted into bars.

43. "Holiday Goods and Holiday Presents," *Cincinnati Enquirer*, December 20, 1869, 8; Joblin, *Cincinnati Past and Present*, 32–38.

44. 1870 Federal Non-Population Census Schedules, Products of Industry, Schedule 4, Hamilton County, Ohio.

45. The absence of records for Duhme &

Co. leaves us without any indication of how the patterns were referred to or named by the firm.

46. D. Albert Soeffing, *Silver Medallion Flatware*, New York, NY: New Books Inc., 1988; Duhme's medallion is often referred to as "Linthioum," but the origin of this name is unknown.

47. Pieces from this pattern have been documented with dated inscriptions between 1868 and 1883. Duhme & Co., eBay listings and private collections, Cincinnati Art Museum.

48. The pattern of the fish serving knife and fork, 2007.158 a–b, is similar to John R. Wendt's "Apollo" (1856).

49. Stag head flatware was also made by Gorham Mfg. Co., Albert Coles, Newell Harding, George Sharp, and John Cook. William P. Hood, Jr., John R. Olson, Charles S. Curb, "Monarch of the Dining Room: Stag Head Flatware," *Silver Magazine* (May/June 2006): 30–39.

50. Duhme & Co., eBay listings and private collections, Cincinnati Art Museum; Marks 1–4 were used on flatware and hollowware. In the course of the study, mark 2 was always used with another Duhme mark, and never appears alone. Mark 5 is rare and has appeared most often on flatware. Mark 6 appears mostly on flatware. Mark 7 with or without a period after "CO," appears on flatware and hollowware, and was used on wares manufactured by Duhme as well as those only retailed by the firm.

51. In 1904, Greve wrote, "it is a fact that the value of the dust and sweepings from its workrooms is more in one year than the whole original capital invested." This overzealous comment likely came from the statement made by a Duhme employee and published in the *Cincinnati Enquirer* in 1871: "We get three to four thousand dollars a year for our dust and sweepings." Greve, *Centennial History of Cincinnati*, 2:491; "A Walk Among the Gold and Silver Working Machinery," *Cincinnati Enquirer*, December 16, 1871, 4.

52. Newstedt and Knighton, *A Cincinnati Saga*, 47; According to his obituary, Ankeny began work at Duhme's in 1862, although he is not listed in city directories as an employee there until 1864. "The Late Emmett W. Ankeny," *Cincinnati Enquirer*, March 30, 1874, 8.

53. "Art in the Exposition, The Silversmith and the Goldsmith, Nature Immortalized in Metal, Messrs. Duhme & Co.'s Display," *Cincinnati Enquirer*, October 7, 1871, 8; D.J. Kenny, *Cincinnati Illustrated: A Pictorial Guide*, Cincinnati: Robert Clarke & Co., 1879, 115.

54. "Watches and Clocks," *Jewelers'*

Circular and Horological Review (October 1889): 86; Doll was born in Wurttemberg, Germany. He worked in Cincinnati as a watch maker between 1850 and 1871, when he died from small pox. 1850 Federal Census, Cincinnati, Hamilton, Ohio; 1850–1872 Cincinnati City Directories; Frank Doll, death record, Cincinnati Health Department, University of Cincinnati Archives and Rare Books Library, http://hdl.handle.net/2374.UC/595766.

55. *Report of the General Committee of the Cincinnati Industrial Exposition, held in Cincinnati, under the auspices of the Ohio Mechanics' Institute, Board of Trade, and Chamber of Commerce, from September 21st to October 22nd, 1870*, Cincinnati: General Committee of the Cincinnati Industrial Exposition, 1870, 279.

56. *Report of the General Committee of the Cincinnati Industrial Exposition, held in Cincinnati, under the auspices of the Ohio Mechanics' Institute, Board of Trade, and Chamber of Commerce*, Cincinnati: General Committee of the Cincinnati Industrial Exposition, 1871, 143; "Art in the Exposition, The Silversmith and the Goldsmith, Nature Immortalized in Metal, Messrs. Duhme & Co.'s Display," October 7, 1871; Listings for Jos. Steinau & Co. appear in Cincinnati City Directories between 1870 and 1883.

57. "Alexis and Western Art," *Cincinnati Enquirer*, December 14, 1871, 8.

58. *Report of the Board of Commissioners of the Cincinnati Industrial Exposition, held in Cincinnati, under the auspices of the Board of Trade, Ohio Mechanics' Institute and Chamber of Commerce*, Cincinnati: General Committee of the Industrial Exposition, 1872, 161; John James Audubon's *The Birds of America; From Original Drawings by John James Audubon*, published in 1840–43 may have been a possible design source. This bird bears a resemblance to the Virginia rail and the king rail, however, it is most likely an artistic invention.

59. *Report of the Board of Commissioners of the Cincinnati Industrial Exposition, held in Cincinnati, under the auspices of the Board of Trade, Ohio Mechanics' Institute, and Chamber of Commerce*, Cincinnati: General Committee of the Industrial Exposition, 1873, 187; "The Useful and the Beautiful at the Cincinnati Exposition. Silver and Jewelry," *Cincinnati Daily Gazette*, September 26, 1873, n.p.

60. Joblin, *Cincinnati Past and Present*, 326–328; Marquis, *The Industries of Cincinnati* 105; "Great Jewelers of the West," *Cincinnati Enquirer*, June 8, 1872, 8; Advertisement, *Cincinnati*

Daily Gazette, December 23, 1873, 1; A reminiscence records that their business that year amounted to $800,000, but this is not substantiated in the R.G. Dun & Co. report, which states that the house was believed to be worth between $150,000 and $200,000 that year; Conteur (Edwin Henderson), "Manufacture and Sale of Jewelry in Cincinnati During Preceding Century," October 23, 1923; Ohio, Vol. 3, p. 1, R.G. Dun & Co. Collection.

61. D.J. Kenny, *Illustrated Cincinnati: A Pictorial Handbook*, Cincinnati: G.E. Stevens, 1875, 145.

62. D.J. Kenny, *Kenny's Cincinnati Exposition Guide and Catalogue of the Fine Arts Department, containing the name and address of every exhibitor at the Fifth Cincinnati Industrial Exposition of 1874*, Cincinnati: Cincinnati Gazette Co., 1874, 73–75; *Report of the Board of Commissioners of the Cincinnati Industrial Exposition, held in Cincinnati, under the auspices of the Board of Trade, Chamber of Commerce, and Ohio Mechanics' Institute from September 2nd to October 3rd, 1874*, Cincinnati: General Committee of the Industrial Exposition, 1874, 252–253.

63. *Report of the Board of Commissioners of the Cincinnati Industrial Exposition, 1874*, 252–253.

64. E.H. Austerlitz, *Cincinnati, from 1800 to 1875, A Condensed History of Cincinnati Combined with Exposition Guide for 1875, Fully Illustrated, together with a description of pictures and works of art, exhibited at the Cincinnati Industrial Exposition, 1875*, Cincinnati: Bloch & Co., 1875, 30.

65. *Report of the Board of Commissioners of the Cincinnati Industrial Exposition, held in Cincinnati, under the auspices of the Board of Trade, Chamber of Commerce, and Ohio Mechanics' Institute from September 8th to October 9th, 1875*, Cincinnati: General Committee of the Industrial Exposition, 1875, 325; Austerlitz, *Cincinnati, from 1800 to 1875*, 30–31.

66. "Rich Gifts from Noble Donors." *Cincinnati Enquirer*, June 16, 1875, 8; Peter Gibson was a Scottish immigrant, born on October 20, 1802, who immigrated to America in 1831; "Death of Peter Gibson," *Cincinnati Enquirer*, July 27, 1884, 12.

67. Notice, *Cincinnati Enquirer*, July 8, 1875, 8; "Colonel S.D. Maxwell," *Cincinnati Enquirer*, June 30, 1875, 5; Maxwell was also the superintendent of the Chamber of Commerce.

68. Duhme & Co., advertising flyer, Ephemera Collection, Business and Industry, Cincinnati Historical Society.

69. No documentation of Duhme's

participation in the *Exposition Universelle* has been found.

70. *Report of the Board of Commissioners of the Cincinnati Industrial Exposition, held in Cincinnati, under the auspices of the Chamber of Commerce, Board of Trade, and Ohio Mechanics' Institute from September 10th to October 11th, 1879*, Cincinnati: General Committee of the Industrial Exposition, 1879, 308.

71. Flatware bearing a "D & C" in a diamond shaped cartouche with handles that feature two cast variations on an Egyptian head have been attributed to Duhme & Co. Some of these pieces also bear the incuse mark of E. Jaccard & Co. Other researchers have attributed the pieces to John Wendt of New York. This line appears to have been limited. To date, only serving pieces have been seen by this author. Makers with similar patterns issued in the late 1860s or early 1870s include Gorham, Albert Coles, and Wood & Hughes. William P. Hood, Jr., John R. Olson, Charles S. Curb, "American Silver Flatware in the Egyptian Revival Style, Part Two," *Silver Magazine* (July/August, 2003): 20–27.

72. Conteur, "Manufacture and Sale of Jewelry in Cincinnati During The Preceding Century," October 23, 1923; Between 1873 and 1883, Goettheim was listed in Cincinnati city directories as an engraver. From 1883 to 1889, his occupation was given as designer or engraver (or both) at Duhme's.

73. Duhme & Co., eBay listings and private collections, Cincinnati Art Museum; Mark 9 was used on flatware and hollowware.

74. Duhme & Co., advertising flyer, Ephemera Collection, Cincinnati Historical Society.

75. James Randolph Hillard, M.D., Benjamin Randolph, John Roger Newstedt, M.D., Charles Knighton, "Duhme & Company of Cincinnati, Part I: New Insights into the Manufacturer and Its Flatware," *Silver Magazine*, (September/October 1997): 20.

76. Kenny, *Cincinnati Illustrated*, as quoted in Beckman.

77. The lower part of this advertisement, without the manufactory illustration was published in the *Cincinnati Daily Gazette*, February 16, 1882, 8.

78. Advertisement, *The Cincinnati Graphic*, October 11, 1884, 16.

79. Marquis, *The Industries of Cincinnati*, 105.

80. Ohio, Vol. 11, p. 317, R.G. Dun & Co. Collection.

81. "On the Road," *JCHR* (July 1888): 44.

82. Leonard, *Centennial Review of Cincinnati*, 67; "On the Road," *JCHR*

(July 1888): 44; Duhme became the city agent for Rookwood Pottery in 1881, and "Mr. Morris or Mr. Galbreath of Duhme & Co. came to the pottery regularly each month to select the wares to sell at the store in Cincinnati." When Duhme & Co. went under, they owed Rookwood Pottery $1,500. Herbert Peck, *The Book of Rookwood Pottery*, New York: Crown Publishers, 1968, 55; Minutes, Directors' Meeting, The Rookwood Pottery Co., May 1, 1897, 32 and February 16, 1898, 33.

83. 1880 Federal Non-Population Census Schedules, Products of Industry, Schedule 4, Hamilton County, Ohio. Greve reports a staff of 300 in 1904, yet this, in comparison to the census data and the firm's standing in the latter part of the decade, seems high. Greve, *Centennial History of Cincinnati*, 2:492.

84. *Report of the Board of Commissioners of the Eighth Cincinnati Industrial Exposition, held in Cincinnati, under the auspices of the Chamber of Commerce, Board of Trade, and Ohio Mechanics' Institute from September 8 to October 9, 1880*, Cincinnati: Board of the Industrial Exposition, 1880, 192–193.

85. "Trade Gossip," *JCHR* (August 1881): 188.

86. Clara de Vere, *The Exhibition Sketchbook: Notes of the Cincinnati Exposition of 1881*, Cincinnati: Weisbrodt & Co., 1881.

87. *Report of the Board of Commissioners of the Ninth Cincinnati Industrial Exposition, held in Cincinnati, under the auspices of the Chamber of Commerce, Board of Trade, and Ohio Mechanics' Institute from September 7 to October 8, 1881*, Cincinnati: Board of the Industrial Exposition, 1881, 176–177.

88. "Artistic Silverware," *Cincinnati Commercial Tribune*, October 31, 1882, 4.

89. The term "diamond art" may refer to bright-cut engraving.

90. "Artistic Silverware," October 31, 1882.

91. *Report of the Board of Commissioners of the Tenth Cincinnati Industrial Exposition, held in Cincinnati, under the auspices of the Chamber of Commerce, Board of Trade, and Ohio Mechanics' Institute from September 6 to October 7, 1882*, Cincinnati: Board of the Industrial Exposition, 1882, 174–175; *Report of the Board of Commissioners of the Eleventh Cincinnati Industrial Exposition, held in Cincinnati, under the auspices of the Chamber of Commerce, Board of Trade, and Ohio Mechanics' Institute from September 5 to October 6, 1883*, Cincinnati: Board of the Industrial Exposition, 1883, 154–155; *Report of the Board of*

Commissioners of the Twelfth Cincinnati Industrial Exposition, held in Cincinnati, under the auspices of the Chamber of Commerce, Board of Trade, and Ohio Mechanics' Institute from September 3 to October 4, 1884, Cincinnati: Board of the Industrial Exposition, 1884, 149–150; *Official Guide of the Centennial Exposition of the Ohio Valley and Central States*, Cincinnati: John F.C. Mullen, 1888, 98.

92. "Cincinnati," *JCHR* (September 1888): 76.

93. Newstedt and Knighton, *A Cincinnati Saga*, 55; "How's Business," *Cincinnati Enquirer*, August 1, 1885, 4.

94. Greve, *Centennial History of Cincinnati*, 2:491; "Trade Gossip," *JCHR* (September 1888): 103; Burial records, Spring Grove Cemetery, Cincinnati, Ohio; Duhme was remembered in the *JCHR* as "a capable, intelligent, enterprising and pushing man, devoting himself to the best interest of the business and strenuous at all times for that which he recognized to be right." He was a member of the Cincinnati Board of Trade between 1870–1884, and a member of the First Congregational Church of Cincinnati (Unitarian) and the Natural History Society; George Augustine Thayer, *First Congregational Church of Cincinnati (Unitarian): A History*, 1917, 47; "Natural History Society," *Cincinnati Enquirer*, July 12, 1871, 4.

95. "Trade Gossip," *JCHR* (October 1888): 115; Charles H. Duhme was the son of Henry H. Duhme; Charles H. Duhme, burial record, Spring Grove Cemetery.

96. "On the Road," *JCHR* (July 1888): 44.

97. Ibid.; Further information about this "branch establishment" at Kansas City could not be found. William Frederick Wilmes (1858–1912) was documented as an affiliate of Bauman-Massa Jewelry Co. (est. 1882) in Missouri in 1899. "St. Louis," *JCHR* (July 19, 1899): 35; William Frederick Wilmes, burial marker, Platte City Cemetery, Missouri, *Find A Grave*, findagrave.com.

98. Hillard et al., "Duhme & Company of Cincinnati, Part I: New Insights into the Manufacturer and Its Flatware," 20; Leonard, *Centennial Review of Cincinnati*, 67; *The City of Cincinnati and its Resources*, Cincinnati: Cincinnati Times Star Co., 1891, 118.

99. Leonard, *Centennial Review of Cincinnati*, 67; A report in November states that 200 Duhme employees participated in a parade to celebrate Jeweler's Day. "Cincinnati," *JCHR* (November 1888): 95; In 1889, it was reported that the firm "employ about 65 men and turn out about

5,000 [watch] cases a year, principally fine cases, of which they make a specialty. The factory is in the same building as their store, on the corner of Fourth and Walnut." "Watches and Clocks," *JCHR* (October 1889): 86.

100. Advertisement, *Cincinnati Daily Gazette*, February 15, 1882, 8.

101. Duhme, eBay listings and private collections, Cincinnati Art Museum; Soeffing, *Silver Medallion Flatware*.

102. Pressed glass in this pattern, often referred to as "snail," was also produced during this era.

103. Duhme, eBay listings and private collections, Cincinnati Art Museum.

104. Photocopy (source unknown) of the 1898/99 Holiday Shopping List published by The Duhme Jewelry Company, Cincinnati Art Museum, Decorative Arts & Design Department, Duhme & Co. research file. A December 6 1898 advertisement in the *Cincinnati Enquirer*, page 5, says, "Send for our Holiday Shopping List, containing many valuable suggestions."

105. Duhme, eBay listings and private collections, Cincinnati Art Museum

106. Ibid.; The pattern with swirling lines, pearling and shield-shaped reserve is identified as "Duhme No. 4," introduced in 1890, in Tere Hagan, *Sterling Flatware: An Identification and Value Guide*, Gas City, IN: L-W Book Sales, 1999, 4.

107. Duhme, eBay listings and private collections, Cincinnati Art Museum; Photocopy (source unknown) of the 1898/99 Holiday Shopping List published by The Duhme Jewelry Company, Duhme & Co. research file.

108. To date, mark 10 has been observed on holloware only.

109. Advertisement, *Cincinnati Enquirer*, November 16, 1881, 8.

110. "Cincinnati," *JCHR* (April 13, 1891): 33.

111. "Cincinnati," *JCHR* (June 24, 1891): n.p.

112. "Cincinnati," *JCHR* (May 27, 1891): 24; "Cincinnati," *JCHR* (September 2, 1891): 25; In 1893, the firm debuted their "Cincinnatian Columbian Seal Spoon" which featured a view of Cincinnati with five bridges, wharves, steamer and hilltops. "Cincinnati," *JCHR* (May 3, 1893): 28; Advertisement, Charles F. McLean, *A Book about the Zoo: A Superbly Illustrated Descriptive Guide to the Zoological Garden of Cincinnati*, Cincinnati: Cohen & Co. Printers, 1893, n.p.

113. *The City of Cincinnati and its Resources*, 118.

114. Neuhaus' role as superintendent at Duhme is noted in the 1890–1897 Cincinnati City Directories; Kramer

is noted as foreman in a report on Duhme's sale of spoons in *JCHR* (January 18, 1893): 31. It is not clear when he was appointed foreman.

115. "Cincinnati," *JCHR* (February 22, 1893): n.p; "Cincinnati," *JCHR* (March 8, 1893): 20.

116. This notion is also supported by the fact that the last city directory listing that associates Kramer with Duhme appears in 1893.

117. In May 1893 the firm "completed an order for a Cincinnati coaching club in the shape of a fine sterling pitcher, with the word 'Roamer,' the club name, in raised gold, which begins with the stock of a whip and ends with the lash in a flourish." "Cincinnati," *JCHR* (May 10, 1893): 45; In June 1893 there was a dispute over an unpaid bill for a silver water service purchased by the Ohio Senate and presented to the outgoing Lieutenant Governor Harris. "An Unpaid Bill," *Cincinnati Enquirer*, June 18, 1893, 5; The loving cup to be presented to Major McKinley on October 3, 1896, by the employees of Mauser Mfg. Co., NY was displayed in Duhme's window in September. "Cincinnati," *JCHR* (September 30, 1896): 24; In 1897, a loving cup for ex-Mayor Caldwell on retiring from office was "made and designed by Duhme Co. and was perfectly plain except for the inscriptions which covered the three sides. On one side was the city seal with the motto "Jucta Juvant," on another the seal of the State and inscription of presentation, and on the last, the motto of the famous Piccadilly Club, 'Speak well of the town you live in: spend your money at home.'" "Cincinnati," *JCHR* (July 14, 1897): 24. This loving cup survives in a private collection.

118. Advertisement, *Cincinnati Enquirer*, December 6, 1898, 5; Duhme & Co., eBay listings and private collections, Cincinnati silver binders, Cincinnati Art Museum.

119. Duhme & Co., eBay listings and private collections, Cincinnati Art Museum; Mark 38.14 was only observed on the small "wishbone" spoons, and mark 38.15, observed on flat and holloware, could have been utilized by Duhme & Co., The Duhme Company, or The Duhme Jewelry Co.

120. "Duhme & Co. Incorporated as the Duhme Co.," *JCHR* (April 26, 1893): 15; "Receiver: For the Duhme Company Asked for in Petition Filed Yesterday," *Cincinnati Enquirer*, December 29, 1896. The firm was still occasionally referred to as Duhme & Co. in advertisements and in the *Jewelers' Circular and Horological Review* throughout the 1890s and later.

121. "A Digest of Duhme & Co.'s Statement Refuting Rumors," *JCHR* (June 21, 1893): 11; "Mr. (Charles H.) Ankeny is anxious to refute this rumor," "Cincinnati," *JCHR* (September 6, 1893): 28.

122. Duhme was shown on a map of exhibitors at the World's Fair in "Ground Plan of Section N, Devoted to Jewelry and Kindred Lines," *JCHR* (May 8, 1893): 27. But by May 31, they had been replaced on this map by Dirskin Silver Filigree. "Arrangement and Condition of Exhibits in the American Jewelry Section," *JCHR* (May 31, 1893): 25.

123. "Cincinnati," *JCHR* (August 30, 1893): 26.

124. At this time, there was a movement to repeal the Sherman Silver Purchase Act (1890), which mandated the amount of silver to be purchased by the government and used for coinage. The repeal of the act meant that the government did not have to buy as much silver, and therefore its value would decrease. The Act was repealed in the autumn of 1893, and gold became the currency standard.

125. "Cincinnati," *JCHR* (March 14, 1894): 25.

126. 1895 Cincinnati City Directory; Newstedt and Knighton, *A Cincinnati Saga*, 73; In July 1888 Charles H. Duhme was in charge of the wholesale department. "On the Road," *JCHR* (July 1888): 44.

127. "Cincinnati," *JCHR* (July 17, 1895): 24; A large silver loving cup trophy, containing 62 ounces of silver was, according to a newspaper account, manufactured for the October 1895 *Enquirer* Regatta by The Duhme Company at a cost of $200. However, it is likely, considering the state of the firm at this time, that the trophy was made elsewhere and brokered by The Duhme Company It is pictured in "Splendid Trophy," *Cincinnati Enquirer*, October 1, 1895, 9.

128. Charles H. Ankeny and Emmett W. Ankeny were brothers. Charles began working at Duhme & Co. after the Civil War. In 1893, he was president of the Cincinnati Wholesale Jewelers' Association. "Prospects for the Trade," *JCHR* (September 6, 1893): 11; "Cincinnati," *JCHR* (July 17, 1895): 24; "The Cincinnati Jewelers' Association Elect Their Officers," *JCHR* (March 4, 1891): 19; "The Career of the Late Charles H. Ankeny, Lafayette, Ind.," *JCHR* (October 14, 1908): 71; Richard P. DeHart, *Past and Present of Tippecanoe County Indiana*, Indianapolis: B.R. Bowen & Co., 1909, 543–544. Another effort to improve business was the addition of a sales and

sample room for Howard Bicycles for which Duhme became agents. This line was abandoned after a year. "Cincinnati," *JCHR* (February 19, 1896): 28; "Cincinnati," *JCHR* (March 25, 1896): n.p.; "Cincinnati," *JCHR* (April 29, 1896): 12; "Cincinnati," *JCHR* (April 8, 1896): 27; "The Bicycle as a Jeweler's Side Line," *JCHR* (May 27, 1896): 6; "Cincinnati," *JCHR* (February 17, 1897): 28.

129. "Receiver For the Duhme Company Asked For in a Petition Filed Yesterday," *Cincinnati Enquirer*, December 19, 1896, 10; "Explained. That Alleged Dividend Said To Have Been Declared by the Duhme Company," *Cincinnati Enquirer*, December 30, 1896, 10; "A Receiver Wanted for the Duhme Co.," *JCHR* (December 30, 1896): 14; "An Application for Receiver for the Duhme Co.," *JCHR* (January 6, 1897): 29; "Status of Affairs of the Duhme Co.," *JCHR* (January 13, 1897): 31; "The Duhme Co. Obtain an Extension from Their Creditors," *JCHR* (January 20, 1897): 20; "The Duhme Co. Make Changes to Cut Down Expenses," *JCHR* (February 3, 1897): 17; *The Court Index*, Official Paper of the Hamilton County Courts, December 29, 1896, December 30, 1896, January 5, 1897, January 6, 1897, January 11, 1897, March 6, 1897; Newstedt and Knighton, *A Cincinnati Saga*, 78–84

130. In an effort to cut expenses in February 1897, The Duhme Company only renewed rent for one storefront and made alterations to the interior of the show room. "The Duhme Co. Make Changes to Cut Down Expenses" (February 3, 1897).

131. "Succumbed to Financial Pressure. The Duhme Company Makes an Assignment," *Cincinnati Enquirer*, March 6, 1897, 16; *The Court Index*, Official Paper of the Hamilton County Courts, April 19, 1897, 1, March 6, 1897, 1, June 5, 1897, 1, June 11, 1897, 1, January 3, 1898, January 8, 1899; "The Assignment of the Duhme Co.," *JCHR* (March 10, 1897): 20; "Status of the Affairs of the Duhme Co.," *JCHR* (March 17, 1897): 25; "Cincinnati," *JCHR* (April 14, 1897): 24; "Cincinnati," *JCHR* (April 28, 1897): 26; "Bids for the Duhme Co. Stock, Fixtures and Machinery," *JCHR* (May 5, 1897): 15; "Duhme Co.'s Debts $66,000 Ahead of Their Assets," *JCHR* (April 21, 1897): 14; "Report of the Committee of Creditors of the Duhme Co.," *JCHR* (April 14, 1897): 18.

132. The other failure cited in comparison was that of Henry Probasco. *The Court Index*, Official Paper of the Hamilton County

Courts, January 3, 1898, 1.

133. *The Court Index*, Official Paper of the Hamilton County Courts, May 1, 1897, and May 4, 1897. The report of May 4 indicates that the business was to resume as Duhme & Co., but Duhme & Co. never appears in city directories after 1893. Rather, in 1897, the firm is listed in the city directory as The Duhme Jewlery Co.; 1898 Cincinnati City Directory; "Duhme Fixtures Sold," *Cincinnati Enquirer*, May 4, 1897, 5; Mr. Remme, previously foreman of Duhme watch case factory, established the Queen City Watch Case Co. and bought Duhme's principal tools. "Cincinnati," *JCHR* (February 2, 1898): 56; Perhaps it was a claim to build confidence, but in May 1897 it was reported that the mines opened by Frank and Herman Duhme in New Mexico in 1896 were "found to be far richer than thought," with "enough copper to make a fortune, besides other precious metals." "Cincinnati," *JCHR* (May 26, 1897): 26; Lucille Elstun Duhme eventually divorced Frank Duhme and married Charles Whipple Hickock of the Gorham Mfg. Co. "Cincinnati," *JCHR* (July 6, 1904): 48; In September 1897 The Duhme Jewelry Co. re-leased the room they had given up in February and added a stationery department and enlarged their pottery and bric-a-brac department. "Cincinnati," *JCHR* (September 22, 1897): 33; "Cincinnati," *JCHR* (November 3, 1897): 38.

134. "Duhme Manufacturing Co.," *Cincinnati Enquirer*, January 23, 1898, 16; "Duhme Company of Cincinnati Incorporated at Columbus," *Cincinnati Enquirer*, January 23, 1898, 30.

135. "Facts and Fancies," *Cincinnati Enquirer*, January 21, 1898, 5; Notice, *JCHR* (January, 26, 1898); Silver marked by Neuhaus, Lakin & Co. has not yet been documented.

136. "Resented Insulting Remark. Herman Duhme Gives Oscar Keck a Thrashing," *Cincinnati Enquirer*, May 3, 1898, 8.

137. "Cincinnati," *JCHR* (June 8, 1898): 28; It was rumored that they had made "overtures to buy out the [Clemens] Hellebush store," but this did not come to pass. "Cincinnati," *JCHR* (June 15, 1898): 20; "Cincinnati," *JCHR* (July 13, 1898): 30.

138. Duhme Bros. & Co. occupied the first floor and basement. "Herman and Frank Duhme Lease a Store," *JCHR* (July 27, 1898): 20; 1899–1904 Cincinnati City Directories; "The Cincinnati Fire," *JCHR* (March 4, 1903): 32.

139. *The Court Index*, Official Paper of the Hamilton County Courts, June 3, 1899; "Reciever Asked for Duhme Bros.," *Cincinnati Enquirer*, August 26, 1903, 5.

140. 1899, 1900, 1902, 1903 Cincinnati City Directories; Gold watch cases marked by Duhme Bros. & Co. have been observed. Hillard et al., "Duhme & Company of Cincinnati, Part I: New Insights into the Manufacturer and Its Flatware," 21.

141. "Retail Merchandising and Hints to Jewelers," *JCHR* (June 5, 1901): 59.

142. "Cincinnati," *JCHR* (April 25, 1900): 44; "Cincinnati," *JCHR* (May 2, 1900): 44; "Cincinnati," *JCHR* (December 31, 1902): 58.

143. *Loving Cup*, circa 1900, Cincinnati Art Museum, Gift of James Randolph Hillard, M.D. and Aingeal Grehan, 2007.187. It is stamped, on the bottom, incuse: "STERLING 925-1000 Fine 10025." The brothers were involved in harness racing and were breeders of trotting horses at their farm in Woodlawn, Ohio (now a suburb of Cincinnati). *Catalogue of Trotting Stock belonging to H. & F. Duhme*, Cincinnati: Wm. A. Webb & Sons, Printers, 1887.

144. "The Cincinnati Fire" (March 4, 1903); "Cincinnati," *JCHR* (March 11, 1903): 38; "Cincinnati," *JCHR* (March 18, 1903): 60; "Cincinnati," *JCHR* (March 25, 1903): 57.

145. Newstedt and Knighton, *A Cincinnati Saga*, 84; There are no known extant corporate records for any of the Duhme firms.

146. "Cincinnati," *JCHR* (May 13, 1903): 69. It is not clear exactly what type of machinery was located across the street and why. The firm's watch-making works were listed as damaged by the fire, indicating that they must have been in the same location as the store.

147. Details of the various departments at Duhme Bros. are unknown; "Cincinnati," *JCHR* (March 25, 1903): 57; "Cincinnati," *JCHR* (April 8, 1903): 52; "Receiver Asked for Duhme Bros.," *Cincinnati Enquirer*, August 26, 1903.

148. "Receivers Appointed for Duhme & Co., Cincinnati, O.," *JCHR* (September 2, 1903): 72; "Cincinnati," *JCHR* (September 30, 1903): 74; "Cincinnati," *JCHR* (October 21, 1903): 74; Frank Duhme was also going through a divorce at this time. See "Receiver Asked for Duhme Bros.," August 26, 1903.

149. "Cincinnati," *JCHR* (December 16, 1903): n.p.; "Cincinnati," *JCHR* (January 13, 1904): 56.

150. Newstedt and Knighton, *A Cincinnati Saga*, 84; Galbreath took a position with Tiffany & Co. in 1905. He

returned to Cincinnati around 1909, but then went to New York again in 1910, and died there on September 1, 1915. Robert Galbreath, burial record, Spring Grove Cemetery; "Cincinnati," *JCHR* (September 20, 1905).

151. "Sale of the Business of Duhme Bros. & Co.," *JCHR* (March 30, 1904): 31; "Cincinnati," *JCHR* (April 20, 1904): 62; "Cincinnati," *JCHR* (April 27, 1904): 64.

152. "Cincinnati," *JCHR* (April 20, 1904): 62.

153. "Cincinnati," *JCHR* (May 4, 1904): 65.

154. "Cincinnati," *JCHR* (November 16, 1904): 72; "Duhme Bros., Cincinnati, O., Finally Wind Up Their Business," *JCHR* (January 11, 1905): 40; "Cincinnati," *JCHR* (June 7, 1905): 58; An article in the *Cincinnati Enquirer*, January 24, 1905, page 9, states that Frank Duhme was "connected with a Colorado oil company that will probably take him to the field of operations," and that Herman was "interested in a company growing bananas in Honduras."

155. "Cincinnati," *JCHR* (June 28, 1905): 58; 1904/05–1938/39 Covington, KY City Directories; "Duhme Bros. in Covington," *JCHR* (January 11, 1922): 57; *The Purchaser's Guide to the Musical Industries*, Englewood, NJ: Music Trades Corporation, 1945, 236.

156. 1904/05–1945 Covington, KY City Directories; Ancestry.com, *Kentucky, Death Records, 1852–1953* [online database], Provo, Utah: Ancestry.com Operations Inc., 2007.

157. 1899 Cincinnati City Directory.

158. *The Court Index*, Official Paper of the Hamilton County Courts, June 3, 1899, and June 5, 1899, 1.

159. "Silversmiths of H. Keck Jewelry Co. Strike Because of Discharge of a Fellow Workman – Over Fifty Men Out," *Cincinnati Enquirer*, October 27, 1899, 7; "Local Trade Unions," *Cincinnati Enquirer*, October 30, 1899, 10; "Keck Strike Settled," *Cincinnati Enquirer*, October 31, 1899, 5.

160. "Forced Sale," *Cincinnati Enquirer*, September 28, 1900, 7; "Cincinnati," *JCHR* (February 20, 1901): 48; 1901 Cincinnati City Directory.

161. "Cincinnati," *JCHR* (July 8, 1903): 56; "Cincinnati," *JCHR* (April 20, 1904): 62.

162. "Cincinnati," *JCHR* (December 16, 1903): n.p.; "Cincinnati," *JCHR* (February 21, 1906): 68; "Cincinnati," *JCHR* (December 21, 1904): 55; "Cincinnati," *JCHR* (April 5, 1905): 64. Also see Cincinnati city directories.

163. 1907 Cincinnati City Directory.

164. In January 1909 the Whiting Mfg. Co. had filed suit against The Duhme Jewelry Co. for $268. "New Suits Filed," *Cincinnati Enquirer*, June 8, 1909, 13.

165. "Cincinnati," *JCHR* (October 7, 1908): 99; "Cincinnati," *JCHR* (January 13, 1909): 36.

166. "Receiver Appointed for the Herman Keck Mfg. Co. and Duhme Jewelry Co. in Proceedings Brought by Creditors," *JCHR* (February 10, 1909): 65.

167. "United States Court Asked To Confirm Report of Bankruptcy Referee, Which Finds Herman Keck Mfg. Co., Cincinnati, to be Insolvent," *JCHR* (November 17, 1909): 73.

168. The Duhme Jewelry Co., eBay listings and private collections, Cincinnati Art Museum.

169. "Receiver in Charge of Herman Keck Mfg. Co.," *JCHR* (February 17, 1909): 59; "Cincinnati," *JCHR* (February 24, 1909): 83; "Receiver of Keck and Duhme Companies Get Back Diamonds," *JCHR* (March 17, 1909): 61; "Herman Keck Manufacturing Co. Files Answers to Creditors' Petitions and Asks That Bankruptcy Proceedings be Dismissed," *JCHR* (March 31, 1909): 71; "Affairs of Herman Keck Manufacturing Company and Duhme Jewelry Company, Cincinnati, Ohio," *JCHR* (April 1909); "Hearings in Bankruptcy Proceedings Against Herman Keck Mfg. Co. Stayed Pending Negotiations for Settlement," *JCHR* (April 21, 1909): 69; "Cincinnati," *JCHR* (May 12, 1909): 84; "Cincinnati," *JCHR* (May 26, 1909): 84; "Court Denies Motion to Sell Assets of Duhme Jewelry Co. – Examination in Keck Case Resumed," *JCHR* (June 2, 1909): 61; "United States Court Asked To Confirm Report of Bankruptcy Referee, Which Finds Herman Keck Mfg. Co., Cincinnati, to be Insolvent," *JCHR* (November 17, 1909): 73; "Cincinnati," *JCHR* (January 5, 1910): 81; "Proceedings in the Bankruptcy of the Herman Keck Mfg. Co. and the Duhme Jewelry Co.," *JCHR* (March 2, 1910): 79; "Further Developments in the Bankruptcy Proceedings Against the Keck and Duhme Companies," *JCHR* (March 16, 1910): 73; "Full Abstract of Cincinnati Courts' Decision That Keck and Duhme Companies Were One Concern," *JCHR* (June 8, 1910): 76; "Kecks Abandon Appeal from Court's Decision on Keck and Duhme Bankruptcy Case and Litigation is Settled," *JCHR* (August 17, 1910): 79.

170. "Cincinnati," *JCHR* (December 15, 1909): 88; "Trustee of Keck & Duhme Companies Sells Assets— Bond to Stop Sale Was Not Filed," *JCHR* (June 22, 1910): 75.

171. The Duhme Jewelry Co., eBay listings and private collections, Cincinnati Art Museum.

172. Duhme Mfg. Co., eBay listings and private collections, Cincinnati Art Museum.

39. WILLIAM TURNER EAVES

1809–1895, w. 1836–1842

Born in England, William Eaves arrived in New York from Liverpool on July 8, 1833.[1] He was in a short-lived partnership with **James H. Martin**, (Eaves & Martin, jewelers) in 1836, and continued to work as a jeweler in Cincinnati until 1842.[2] Eaves and A. Falize (see **Samuel T. Carley**) advertised in 1842 that they had opened a shop in Lexington, Kentucky, to "manufacture all kinds of jewelry, silverware and do engraving."[3] The city directories of St. Louis, Missouri, list Eaves as a silversmith from 1845–48, and in 1849, he was in partnership with Abraham Herbel in St Louis.[4] By 1860, Eaves had moved to Sacramento, California, working as a jeweler as part of the firm Eaves & Nye.[5] Eaves was working in Storey County, Nevada, by 1865.[6] The 1870 Census gives his occupation as a manufacturing jeweler.[7] He had returned to Sacramento by 1876, and died there in 1895.[8]

Silver marked by Eaves from the St. Louis partnership of Eaves & Herbel and from the Sacramento firm of Eaves & Nye is known.[9] The St. Louis (Eaves & Herbel) and Sacramento (Eaves & Nye) spoons are of "a style peculiar to the Midwest" with an exaggerated fiddle handle that is characteristic of flatware manufactured by the **E. & D. Kinsey** and **David Kinsey** firms of Cincinnati.[10] Silver marked by Eaves that can be firmly attributed to his time in Cincinnati has not been documented.

1. Ancestry.com, *New York Passenger Lists, 1820–1957* [online database], Provo, Utah: Ancestry.com Operations Inc., 2010.
2. 1836/37, 1839/40, 1842 Cincinnati City Directories.
3. Boultinghouse, 105.
4. Norman Mack, *Missouri's Silver Age: Silversmiths of the 1800s*, Carbondale, IL: Southern Illinois University Press, 2005, 58; Edgar W. Morse, *Silver in the Golden State*, Oakland, CA: The Oakland Museum History Department, 1986, 3.
5. 1860 Federal Census, Sacramento, Sacramento, California; Morse, *Silver in the Golden State*, 3. Morse does not include the given name for Nye. He was probably the Emanuel Nye who lived next door to Eaves, as per the 1860 Census.
6. Ancestry.com, *U.S. IRS Tax Assessment Lists, 1862–1918* [online database], Provo, Utah: Ancestry.com Operations Inc., 2008.
7. 1870 Federal Census, Gold Hill, Storey County, Nevada.
8. Ancestry.com, *California, Voter Registers, 1866–1898* [online database], Provo, Utah: Ancestry.com Operations Inc., 2011; Ancestry.com, *California, San Francisco Area Funeral Home Records, 1895–1985* [online database], Provo, Utah: Ancestry.com Operations Inc., 2010.
9. Lynne E. Springer and Deborah J. Binder, *St. Louis Silversmiths*, St. Louis, MO: The Saint Louis Art Museum, 1980, 25; Morse, *Silver in the Golden State*, 3.
10. Mack, *Missouri's Silver Age*, 57–58; Morse, *Silver in the Golden State*, 3.

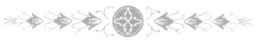

40. HENRY P. ELIAS

circa 1832–1882, w. 1853–1868

Henry P. Elias was born in Wales in about 1832, to John and Elizabeth (Betsey) Elias.[1] The family immigrated to America in 1836 on the ship *John Jay*.[2] By 1850, John Elias was a farmer near Gallipolis, Ohio, and Henry was in Cincinnati, boarding with **Joseph Draper**, and his occupation was noted as "apple dealer."[3] Between 1853 and 1856, Elias was an assistant at Joseph Draper's shop, working as a watch maker or jeweler.[4] In July 1856 Elias bought the business from Draper, and changed the firm's name to Henry P. Elias.[5]

For the first few years, the business prospered. Credit reports through 1860 describe Elias as "favorably thot [*sic*] of by the trade," reliable and honest.[6] During those years, Elias vigorously promoted the business, even to the point of placing an advertisement in a trade catalogue for dentists' materials.[7] The silver-plated tea set, two gold-headed canes, two silver-plated castors, and set of Masonic jewels that he submitted to the Ohio Mechanics' Institute Exhibition in 1858, were deemed by the judges to be "articles of fine manufacture, and beautiful design."[8] However, in the business downturn following the onset of the Civil War, credit reports of 1861 indicate that Elias was "hard pressed," noting "his success will depend much on improvement of the times."[9] In August 1861 Joseph Draper stepped in and ran the business until October 1862.[10] During this time, Elias was likely working as a sutler, or army camp follower who peddled provisions to the troops. It was noted that he made considerable money this way.[11]

By 1867, business had improved. Elias was relying on his younger brothers William and **Richard Elias** to operate the store while he and a partner, George Davidson, opened the St. James Hotel.[12] The jewelry firm's name was changed to H.P. Elias and Brothers, and Elias was reported to be devoting his efforts to the hotel, buying his partner's share in February 1868.[13] In 1869, the St. James Hotel was described as the only hotel on the "fashionable promenade" of Fourth Street; its facilities were "admirable," and it had "gained friends rapidly under the popular management of Henry P. Elias, Esq."[14] Elias sold the jewelry firm to his brother Richard in August 1869, and in January 1870 he sold the hotel to J.J. McGrath and left Cincinnati.[15]

By the time of the 1880 Census, Henry P. Elias had returned to Gallipolis, Ohio, and was living with his sister Jane's family; his occupation was given as "farmer."[16] He died in Mason County, West Virginia, on August 30, 1882, bequeathing two tracts of farmland to Jane.[17]

Silver flatware marked by Elias includes a butter spreader with twist stem and engraved handle and blade, and a salt spoon with shell-shaped bowl and tipped exaggerated fiddle handle. Both are marked on the reverse with an incuse "H. P. ELIAS." A teaspoon with a tipped, exaggerated fiddle handle bears mark 40.1.[18] Most, if not all, of the wares marked by Elias were retailed, and not made, by him.

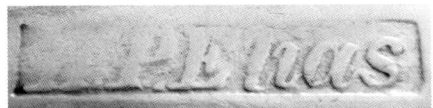

MARK 40.1

1. Recorded birth years for Henry Elias vary between 1830 and 1838. The most probable year was 1832, the year given in his immigration record, the 1850 Federal Census, and the R.G. Dun & Co. reports; Ancestry.com, *New York Passenger and Immigration Lists, 1820–1850* [online database], Provo, Utah: Ancestry.com Operations Inc., 2003; 1850 Federal Census, Cincinnati, Hamilton, Ohio; Ohio, Vol. 2, p. 217, R.G. Dun & Co. Collection, Baker Library, Harvard Business School.

2. Ancestry.com, *New York Passenger and Immigration Lists, 1820–1850*. The ship manifest lists the parents, Henry (age 4), Jane (age 2), and John (age 6 months).

3. 1850 Federal Census, Gallipolis, Gallia, Ohio. Four more children were born to the Elias family in Ohio: Ellis "Eli" (b. about 1838), William M. "Moses" (b. about 1839), Richard (b. about 1843), and Ellen (b. about 1845).

4. 1853, 1855, 1856 Cincinnati City Directories.

5. Ohio, Vol. 2, p. 217, R.G. Dun & Co. Collection.

6. Ibid.

7. H.P. Elias, eBay listings and private collections, Cincinnati silver binders, Cincinnati Art Museum.

8. *Report of the Sixteenth Exhibition of the Ohio Mechanics' Institute, held in Cincinnati, From September 6 to October 2, 1858*, Cincinnati: Ohio Mechanics' Institute, 1858, 83–84. Elias was listed as a wholesale dealer in watches and jewelry in the *Universal Masonic Lodge Director of 1860*. Amy Armstrong, compiler, *Worldwide Masonic Directory, 1860* [online database], Provo, Utah: The Generations Network Inc., 2001.

9. Ohio, Vol. 2, p. 217, R.G. Dun & Co. Collection.

10. Ohio, Vol. 5, p. 51, R.G. Dun & Co. Collection.

11. Ohio, Vol. 6, p. 123, R.G. Dun & Co. Collection.

12. 1867 Cincinnati City Directory; Ohio, Vol. 6, p. 123, R.G. Dun & Co. Collection.

13. Ibid.

14. George E. Stevens, *The City of Cincinnati: A Summary of Its Attractions, Advantages, Institutions and Internal Improvements*, Cincinnati: George S. Blanchard & Co., 1869, 22.

15. Ohio, Vol. 6, p. 123, R.G. Dun & Co. Collection; "St. James Hotel – A Change," *Cincinnati Enquirer*, January 6, 1870, 5.

16. 1880 Federal Census, Gallipolis, Gallia, Ohio.

17. Ancestry.com, *West Virginia, Deaths Index 1853–1973* [online database], Provo, Utah: Ancestry.com Operations Inc., 2011; The two tracts of farmland subsequently became the subject of a court suit which rose to the Supreme Court of Appeals of West Virginia. Alfred Caldwell, *Reports of Cases Argued and Determined in the Supreme Court of Appeals of West Virginia*, vol. XXVII, 1885–6, 578–581.

18. H.P. Elias, eBay listings and private collections.

41. WILLIAM R. EVANS

1820–1860, w. 1844–1860

William R. Evans was born in Wales on February 15, 1820.[1] He was likely the son of Eleanor and William M. Evans (1792–1863), a watch and clock maker active in Cincinnati between 1849 and 1863.[2] William R. Evans first appears in Cincinnati in 1844, when he is listed in the city directory as a silversmith working on Main Street between Third and Fourth Streets—near or at the same location as **William Allen** and **Joseph Draper**. It is probable that he was working with Draper, as in 1846, a Robert Evans (probably a city directory transcription error for William R.) was working at Draper's, and later, in 1853, William's older brother, Rees, was also employed by Draper.[3]

By 1848, William R. Evans and his family were living in Covington, Kentucky, just across the river from Cincinnati.[4] There, he worked as a silversmith, jeweler, and "dealer in watches and fancy articles."[5] In 1850, his real estate was valued at $2,000, and in 1851, he purchased the Covington jewelry store of William Gallup on Scott Street, between Fifth and Sixth Streets.[6] In 1855, a notice stated that "owing to ill health" he was leaving the jewelry business and offering his goods for low prices.[7] Another notice decreed that he was leaving his unfinished business in the hands of George W. McDannold.[8] But by July 1856 Evans had returned, announcing that "after suffering a severe spell of the Western Fever during the last 12 months, he is now entirely cured of it," and that he was preparing a store on Madison Street, east side, between Fifth and Sixth Streets.[9] An advertisement from 1858 indicates that he was retailing jewelry bought in New York.[10] Evans remained in business until his death on July 12, 1860.[11] His widow, Elizabeth L. (b. Wales, 1825–1860), ran the business until her death in November.[12]

Evans and his wife had six children for whom records were found: Miles (b. about 1847), Rees (1848–1851), Charlotte (1849–1851), Mary Jane "Jennie" (1852–1853), Alice (b. about 1854), and Susan (b. about 1859).[13] William R. Evans was an active member of the Masonic Lodge and his funeral services were held at the Fourth Street Presbyterian Church.[14]

Known wares stamped with an incuse "W. R. EVANS" include beakers and a ladle with a tipped, exaggerated fiddle handle and pointed shoulders. Mark 41.1 has been found on spoons with tipped, exaggerated fiddle handles and pointed shoulders.[15] Marquis Boultinghouse records mark 41.2 in his book on Kentucky silver.[16]

MARK 41.1

W.R.EVANS

MARK 41.2

1. William R. Evans, burial marker, Linden Grove Cemetery, Covington, Kentucky; 1850, 1860 Federal Censuses, Covington, Kenton, Kentucky; Immigration records could not be found.
2. William M. Evans, burial record, Spring Grove Cemetery, Cincinnati, Ohio; 1849–1863 Cincinnati City Directories. Eleanor and William M. Evans had several children: Sarah J. (b. about 1830), Gwynne E. (b. about 1837), and Edward W. (b. about 1839); Edward W. Evans worked with his father at the firm William M. Evans & Son, specializing in watches and clocks, in 1863. 1863 Cincinnati City Directory; 1850 and1860 Federal Censuses, Cincinnati, Hamilton, Ohio. William M. Evans was also likely the father of Rees C. Evans (d. 1868), who is confirmed as William R. Evans' older brother. Rees C. Evans, burial record, Spring Grove Cemetery.
3. 1846, 1853 Cincinnati City Directories; There is no other directory entry or census record for a watch maker named Robert Evans in Cincinnati. To further support the idea that Robert Evans was William R., the entry in question cited Robert as working for James [sic] Draper.
4. William's son Rees was born in Kentucky in 1848; 1850 Federal Census; Rees Evans, death notice, Covington Journal, June 14, 1851, 2.
5. Advertisement, Covington Journal, June 14, 1851, 1. Among the articles listed are spectacles, pistols, Masonic regalia, and gold pens.
6. 1850 Federal Census; Advertisement, Covington Journal, March 22, 1851, 2; Covington Journal, June 14, 1851, 1; 1855 Cincinnati City Directory;

Michael R. Averdick, *A Directory of Silversmiths, Jewelers, Watch and Clock Makers and Related Trades of Covington and Newport, Kentucky & Vicinity 1833–1900*, Covington, KY: 829 Willard Street Press, 2002, 24.
7. Advertisement, Covington Journal, October 6, 1855, 3.
8. Advertisement, Covington Journal, January 12, 1856, 3. This advertisement appears to have been placed in October 1855.
9. Advertisement, Covington Journal, July 26, 1856, 2.
10. Covington Journal, April 7, 1858, reproduced in Averdick, 24, 2; Also see advertisement, "A Rare Chance for Jewelry," Covington Journal, July 14, 1860, 4.
11. William R. Evans, death notice, Covington Journal, July 14, 1860, 3.
12. 1861 Cincinnati City Directory, Covington listings; Elizabeth Evans, burial marker, Linden Grove Cemetery.
13. 1850 and 1860 Federal Censuses, Covington, Kenton, Kentucky; Rees Evans, death notice, June 14, 1851; Mary Jane Evans, death notice, Covington Journal, December 10, 1853, 2; Charlotte Evans, death notice, Covington Journal, June 14, 1851; Rees Evans, burial marker, Linden Grove Cemetery; Jennie Evans, burial marker, Linden Grove Cemetery.
14. "Masonic Funeral," Covington Journal, July 14, 1860, 2; Covington Journal, July 21, 1860, 2.
15. William R. Evans, eBay listings and private collections, Cincinnati silver binders, Cincinnati Art Museum.
16. Boultinghouse, 300.

42. HYMAN WOLF FRANKENSTEIN[1]

1849–1908, w. 1873–1906

H.W. Frankenstein, as he was known, was born in Königsberg, Prussia, in October 1849.[2] He came to the United States in 1870, and was established in Cincinnati by 1872.[3] He first appeared in Cincinnati city directories in 1873, listing as a jeweler at 275 Central Avenue, between Seventh and Eighth Streets.[4] His first years in business were shaky, at best. In January 1874 credit reporters noted that he was of "fair reputation, [but] not in fair financial condition."[5] By November, his concern was owned by **Clemens Oskamp** and reporters warned, "[he] should get credit from no one else. Everything covered by chattel mortgage."[6] In February 1875 Frankenstein partnered with Peter W. Coyle, a watch maker and jeweler who appeared in Cincinnati directories between 1862 and 1881.[7] Their firm, Frankenstein & Coyle, owned by Oskamp, was short-lived, dissolving by March 2, 1875.[8] Frankenstein continued on Central Avenue, operating under his name with the backing of Oskamp, but failed in December.[9] By June 1876 he had settled with creditors and was back in business.[10]

In December 1876 Frankenstein advertised another sale: "Jewelry, &c. NOT SELLING OUT, But as I am going into the manufacture of Jewelry at the same place, I will offer my entire stock of Gold and Silver Watches, fine and medium Jewelry, Solid Silver and Plated Ware, Clocks, &c., regardless of cost or value."[11] By September 1877 he had joined with Gustave Fuchs, "a practical jeweler and diamond setter, but a man of no means," to form Frankenstein & Fuchs, but their partnership had terminated by November.[12] Frankenstein continued in business as H.W. Frankenstein & Co., but continued to struggle.[13] In the 1880 Product of Industry Census, he reported as a jeweler and watch and clock manufacturer with $500 capital and four employees (two men, one woman and one youth) who worked ten hours a day. His skilled employees were paid $2 in wages per day, and his unskilled

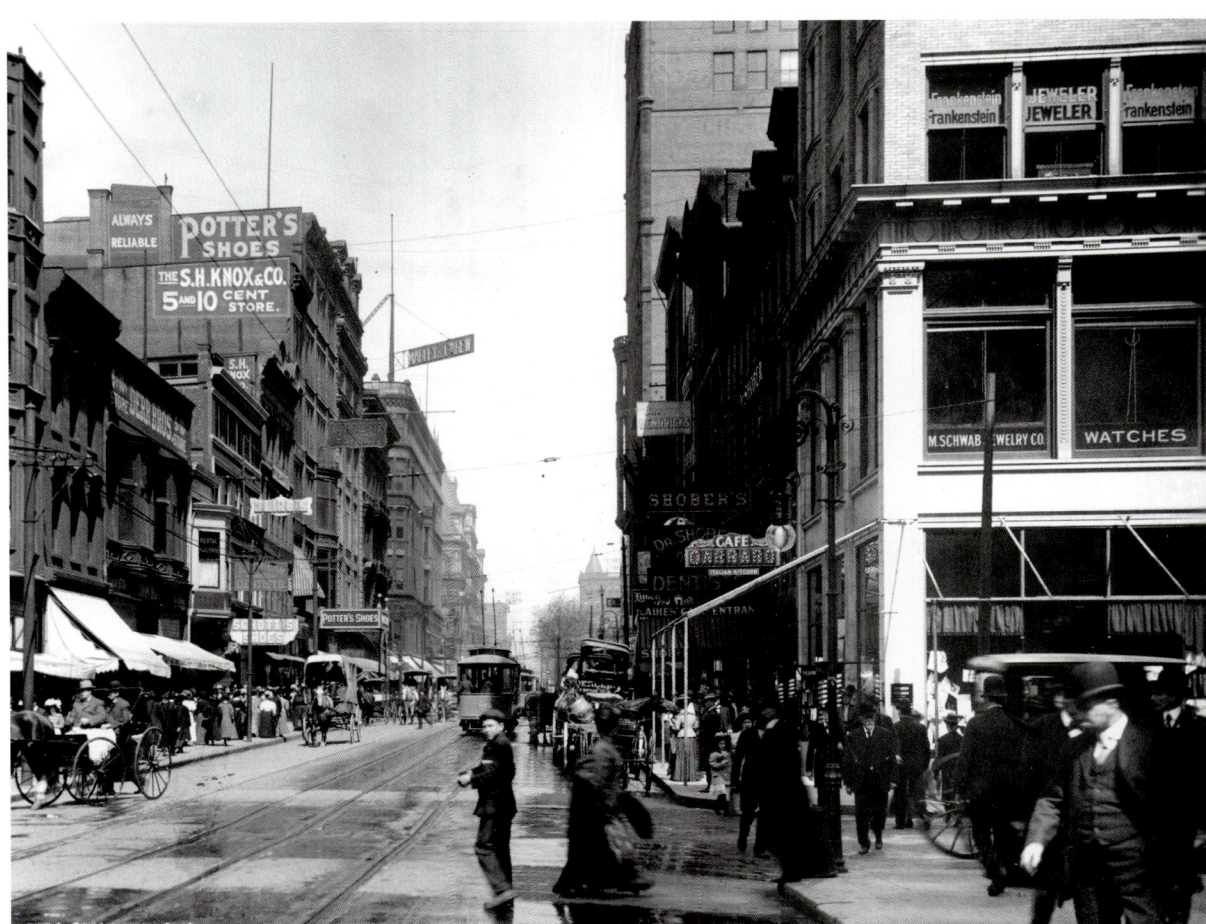

FIG. 42.1: *Building at Fifth and Race Streets*, looking east on Fifth Street, SC#STR-5th-040, Cincinnati Historical Society

workers took home $.35 a day. Between June 1, 1879, and May 31, 1880, he paid $740 in wages, and his shop utilized $150 worth of material to produce product valued at $2,000.[14] In 1883, he made the following statement, which credit reporters considered "rather sanguine": a capital of $7,000; a stock of $6,000; book accounts of $2,000 with liabilities of $1,300; and $2,000 of insurance. However, what appears to have been a significant improvement in standing did not bring him confidence in the trade.[15]

In 1886, Frankenstein began advertising the sale of goods on installment.[16] An entertaining advertisement in 1887 states, "During the Past Month 100 Boys promised their mothers not to SMOKE, and saved their 50c per week and bought a watch of the Frankenstein Installment Co., 150 Men indulged in ONE GLASS OF BEER less per day and bought a watch of the FRANKENSTEIN INSTALLMENT CO. 100 Young Ladies ate LESS CANDY and bought a watch of the FRANKENSTEIN INSTALLMENT CO. FOLLOW THEIR EXAMPLE."[17] "Clocks, Jewelry, Silverware, Rogers' Table, Fancy Goods, &c." were also "sold on small weekly payments."[18] In 1888, Frankenstein expanded with additional locations at 311 and 313 Central Avenue and 227 West Ninth Street, and he began to offer home furnishings on installment.[19] By October 1891 he offered cloaks and clothing for sale, and had opened a fourth location in Hamilton, Ohio, by December 1892.[20]

Frankenstein failed in May 1893 when business went stagnant, a situation recognized, in part, as a reaction to the repeal of the Sherman silver law and the extraordinarily rainy weather. The fact that Frankenstein held no assets above his liabilities was also to blame.[21] A final statement recorded liabilities of $40,000 and assets of $25,000.[22]

Between 1893 and 1894, he served as manager of the Atlas Jewelry Company at 176 Race Street, and was operating as a jeweler in the Carew Building in 1895.[23] In 1896, he established The Frankenstein Co., wholesale jewelers and watch and diamond sellers on installment, at 17 Emery Arcade.[24] The firm's name changed to Frankenstein Co. in 1899, when he sold his stock in order to pursue the wholesale jewelers' supply business.[25] Frankenstein retired from the business in 1906, due to his declining health. His wife, Clara Frank Frankenstein (1853–1929), and son, Eli G. Frankenstein (b. 1881), ran the business as the Frankenstein Jewelry Co. in the Andrews Building, on the southeast corner of Fifth and Race Streets (fig.42.1), until it went under in 1907.[26] H.W. Frankenstein died on June 11, 1908, and was buried in Walnut Hills United Jewish Cemetery.[27] He and Clara had ten children for whom records were found: Samuel (1874–1879); Stella (b. 1877), who married William Andress; Lotta (b. 1879); Eli G.; Mamie (b. 1883); Irene (b. 1885); Alfred J. (b. 1887); Herbert A. (b. 1890); Pauline (b. 1892); and William Phillip (1896–1972).[28]

Frankenstein's mark (mark 42.1) has been found on a tablespoon with a tipped, exaggerated fiddle handle and pointed shoulders.[29] Pocket watches marked with his name have also been documented.[30] There is no evidence to suggest that he made any of the silver that bears his name.

MARK 42.1

1. H.W. Frankenstein's full name appears in Mamie Frankenstein, birth record, Cincinnati Health Department, University of Cincinnati Archives and Rare Books Library, http://hdl.handle.net /2374.UC/493463.
2. 1900 Federal Census, Cincinnati, Hamilton, Ohio; Mamie Frankenstein, birth record.
3. 1900 Federal Census, Cincinnati, Hamilton, Ohio; Frankenstein's 1886 City Directory listing notes that his business was established in 1872, however a later advertisement in the Cincinnati Enquirer, February 7, 1892, 8, indicates that his business was established on October 13, 1871.
4. 1873 Cincinnati City Directory; Advertisement, Cincinnati Enquirer, May 1, 1887, 8.
5. Ohio, Vol. 10, p. 157, R.G. Dun &

Co. Collection, Baker Library, Harvard Business School.
6. Ibid.
7. Ibid.
8. Ibid.
9. Ibid.
10. Ibid.
11. Advertisement, Cincinnati Enquirer, December 17, 1876, 1.
12. Ohio, Vol. 10, p. 157, R.G. Dun & Co. Collection; Gustave Fuchs later changed his name to Gustave Fox and was active as a manufacturing jeweler in Cincinnati between 1876 and 1925. Also see Advertisement, Cincinnati Enquirer, December 14, 1876, 8.
13. Ibid.
14. 1880 Federal Non-Population Census Schedules, Products of Industry, Schedule 4, Hamilton County, Ohio.

15. Ohio, Vol. 10, p. 165, R.G. Dun & Co. Collection.
16. 1886 Cincinnati City Directory.
17. Advertisement, Cincinnati Enquirer, May 1, 1887, 8.
18. Ibid.
19. Advertisement, Cincinnati Enquirer, April 22, 1888, 6.
20. Advertisement, Cincinnati Enquirer, February 7, 1892, 8; Advertisement, Hamilton Daily Democrat, December 28, 1892, 2.
21. "Big Failure. An Installment House Assigns, With Heavy Liabilities—Dull Trade the Given Cause," Cincinnati Enquirer, May 2, 1893, 9.
22. "Another Cincinnati Failure," The Stark County Democrat (Canton, OH), May 4, 1893, 1.
23. 1893, 1894, 1895 Cincinnati City Directories.
24. 1896–1906 Cincinnati City

Directories; Advertisement, Cincinnati Enquirer, November 20, 1898, 3.
25. "Cincinnati," Jewelers' Circular and Horological Review (July 5, 1899): 29.
26. Frankenstein's death record notes he suffered from "diabetes mellitus" for two years. Hyman W. Frankenstein, death record, Cincinnati Health Department, University of Cincinnati Archives and Rare Books Library, http://hdl.handle.net /2374.UC/218608; "Jewelry Firm Forced to the Wall," Cincinnati Enquirer, November 9, 1907, 16; 1900 Federal Census, Cincinnati, Hamilton, Ohio; Clara Frank Frankenstein, burial record, Jewish Cemeteries of Greater Cincinnati, www.jcemcin.org.
27. Hyman Frankenstein, burial record, Jewish Cemeteries of Greater Cincinnati.

28. 1880, 1900, and 1910 Federal Censuses, Cincinnati, Hamilton, Ohio; Samuel Frankenstein, death record, Cincinnati Health Department, http://hdl.handle.net/2374.UC/575 689; Samuel Frankenstein, burial record, Jewish Cemeteries of Greater Cincinnati; Samuel Frankenstein, death notice, *Cincinnati Enquirer*, May

17, 1879, 5; Lotta Frankenstein, birth record, Cincinnati Health Department, http://hdl.handle.net/2374.UC/574 746; Elisa Frankenstein, birth record, Cincinnati Health Department, http://hdl.handle.net/2374.UC/480 653; Mamie Frankenstein, birth record; Alfred Frankenstein, birth record, Cincinnati Health

Department, http://hdl.handle.net/2374.UC/463889; Pauline Frankenstein, birth record, Cincinnati Health Department, http://hdl.handle.net/2374.UC/345766; Wm. Phillip Frankenstein, birth record, Cincinnati Health Department, http://hdl.handle.net/2374.UC/292 341; William Frankenstein, burial

record, Jewish Cemeteries of Greater Cincinnati.
29. *Tablespoon*, Elizabeth Beckman Collection, Cincinnati Museum Center.
30. H.W. Frankenstein, eBay listings and private collections, Cincinnati silver binders, Cincinnati Art Museum.

43. HENRY FRANKLIN

about 1819[1]–1868, w. 1856–1862

Henry Franklin was born in Kalisz (Kalisch), Poland.[2] He was active in Cincinnati by 1846, working as a hat maker and retailer, first as Henry Franklin & Co., and later with Lazarus Isaacs (Isaacs & Franklin) until their failure around 1855.[3] In 1856, he joined his brother-in-law, Henry Beatus who advertised as a jeweler (Henry Beatus & Co.) at 53 Public Landing.[4] At the time, Franklin was noted as having considerable money and real estate, but was not trusted by credit reporters who regarded him as "unscrupulous and dishonest," and noted that he had "defrauded his creditors" when his previous business had failed.[5] In 1857, Henry Beatus & Co became known as Beatus & Franklin, and advertised as wholesale and retail dealers in watches and jewelry on the northeast corner of Main and Second Streets.[6] In March of that year, they relocated to 48 Main (between Second and Third Streets) and were doing a large business, but were still regarded with caution by credit reporters.[7] By March 1859 Beatus & Franklin had failed and were sued for numerous debts.[8] Franklin had partnered with Leo Frank who had been in the clothing business, by July.[9] Franklin & Frank advertised as manufacturers and dealers in jewelry at 48 Main, but by January 1861 Franklin was again in trouble with creditors and the partnership dissolved. Franklin sold his business to Nathan Morris, but it was suspected that this was merely a ploy to keep creditors at bay.[10] In 1862, Franklin was listed in the city directory without note of occupation, working at 78 Main Street—the same working address of Henry Beatus, whose name was included under the business listings for "watches, jewelry and silver ware."[11] Subsequent city directories included Franklin, but do not provide his occupation or a working address. He died on December 24, 1868

and is buried in the Walnut Hills Jewish Cemetery in Cincinnati, with his wife Fannie (b. Germany, about 1812, d. 1892).[12]

Spoons bearing mark 43.1 may be associated with Henry Franklin. These spoons share the tipped, exaggerated fiddle handle and pointed shoulder seen so often in Cincinnati. Franklin almost certainly bought them from a local manufacturer (like **E. & D. Kinsey**) and stamped them with his own mark.[13]

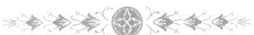

MARK 43.1

1. The 1850 Census indicates that he was born about 1810. From his age at death (49) given on his burial marker, he was born about 1819. 1850 Federal Census, Cincinnati, Hamilton, Ohio; Henry Franklin, burial marker, Walnut Hills Jewish Cemetery, Cincinnati, Ohio, www.jcemcin.org.
2. Burial marker, Walnut Hills Jewish Cemetery.
3. 1846, 1849/50, 1850/51, 1853, 1855 Cincinnati City Directories.
4. 1856 Cincinnati City Directory; Ohio, Vol. 2, p. 244, R.G. Dun & Co. Collection, Baker Library, Harvard Business School.
5. Ohio, Vol. 2, p. 244, R.G. Dun & Co. Collection.
6. 1857 Cincinnati City Directory.
7. Ohio, Vol. 2, p. 244, R.G. Dun & Co. Collection.
8. Ohio, Vol. 2, p. 250, R.G. Dun & Co. Collection.
9. Ibid.
10. Ibid.
11. 1862 Cincinnati City Directory.
12. Burial markers, Walnut Hills Jewish Cemetery.
13. H. Franklin, eBay listings and private collections, Cincinnati silver binders, Cincinnati Art Museum.

44. WILLIAM FURSTE[1]

1827–1904, w. 1857–1901

William Furste was born in Germany in October 1827.[2] He arrived in Baltimore in May 1854 from Bremen, Germany, on the *Blucher*.[3] He was in Cincinnati by 1857, when he first appeared as a silversmith in the city directory, and in October of that year he married Julia Lowe, another German immigrant.[4] Over the next 44 years, he worked as a silversmith in Cincinnati. Census records list his occupation as (journeyman) silversmith, as do city directory listings.[5] He worked as a silversmith for **E. & D. Kinsey** and **David Kinsey** from 1857 through at least 1868.[6] Directory listings after that time do not indicate where he was employed, as only his home address is given. Furste periodically advertised in the business directory sections for "silversmiths" from 1883 through 1901, so he may have had his own workshop. However, works marked by him are not seen often. Known spoons and ladles struck with mark 44.1 have tipped, exaggerated fiddle handles and pointed shoulders.[7]

Census records indicate that William and Julia Furste were the parents of three children: Henry (b. 1858), Lina (b. 1864), and Laura (b. 1868).[8] Julia died in October 1896 and William married the widow Magdalena Kloeckler in January 1902.[9] William Furste died in Cincinnati in August 1904.[10]

1. There are many spelling variants for Furste's name found in city directory and census records: Turste, Firsti, Ferste, Fuerste, Furst, Furste, and Forister. Furste is used here based on the subject's mark.
2. William Fuerste [*sic*], burial record, Spring Grove Cemetery, Cincinnati, Ohio; 1900 Federal Census, Cincinnati, Hamilton, Ohio
3. Ancestry.com, *Baltimore Passenger and Immigration Lists, 1820–1872* [online database], Provo, Utah: Ancestry.com Operations Inc., 2004; 1900 Federal Census, Cincinnati, Hamilton, Ohio.
4. Marriage record, Hamilton County Probate Records, vol. B15, 269.
5. 1870, 1880, 1900 Federal Censuses, Cincinnati, Hamilton, Ohio; 1857–1901 Cincinnati City Directories.
6. 1857–1868 Cincinnati City Directories.
7. *Tablespoon*, Elizabeth Beckman Collection, Cincinnati Museum Center; William Furste, eBay listings and private collections, Cincinnati silver binders, Cincinnati Art Museum.
8. Julia Fuerste [*sic*], burial record, Spring Grove Cemetery; 1870, 1880 Federal Censuses, Cincinnati, Hamilton, Ohio.
9. Marriage record, Hamilton County Probate Records, vol. 157, 137.
10. William Fuerste [*sic*], burial record, Spring Grove Cemetery.

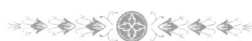

MARK 44.1

45. DAVID GOLDSMITH

w. circa 1840

The 1839/40 Cincinnati Directory lists David Goldsmith, a German jeweler, residing on Race Street, between Front and Columbia Streets. Very little is known about Goldsmith and his business. Beginning in 1835 and continuing into the 1880s, there are several records of a David Goldsmith in the Cincinnati area, but these likely refer to more than one man of the same name. Nothing has thus far been uncovered to enable any of these records to be positively identified with our subject. On June 7, 1835, a David Goldsmith married Syltha Crosley in Cincinnati.[1]

In 1838, a David Goldsmith was among a group of citizens who supported the Home for the Jewish Aged and Infirm of Cincinnati.[2] In 1840, the census recorded a David Goldsmith living in Columbia Township (not far outside downtown Cincinnati), who was between 30 and 40 years of age, living with one female of the same age range, and one boy between the ages of 10 and 15.[3] Cincinnati directories between 1842 and 1844 list a David Goldsmith at the corner of Symmes and Pike, but no occupation is given, and in 1850, a David Goldsmith, painter, is listed on the west side of Bank Alley between Third and Fourth Streets.[4] Surveys of New York silversmiths list a David Goldsmith working in Troy, New York, around 1840, and in New York City between 1846 and 1850.[5]

Spoons with fiddle handles and rounded shoulders have been documented with mark 45.1.[6]

D.GOLDSMITH.

MARK 45.1

1. Ancestry.com, *Marriage records, Hamilton County, Ohio* [online database], Provo, Utah: Ancestry.com Operations Inc., 2005.
2. Rev. Charles Frederic Goss, *Cincinnati: The Queen City, 1788–1912*, Cincinnati: The S.J. Clarke Publishing Co., 1912, 2:48.
3. 1840 Federal Census, Columbia, Hamilton, Ohio.
4. 1840, 1843, 1844, 1850/51 Cincinnati City Directories. The 1850 Federal Census, Cincinnati, Hamilton, Ohio indicates that the painter named David Goldsmith was married to a woman named Ann.
5. Paul Von Khrum, *Silversmiths of New York City*, New York: Von Khrum, 1978, 25; *New York State Silversmiths*, Eggertsville, NY: The Darling Foundation of New York State, 1964, 87; The 1850 Federal Census, New York Ward 13, New York, New York, enumerates a German jeweler, David Goldsmith, b. about 1809, married to Henrietta with six children all born in New York between 1837 and 1849; The 1850 Federal Census, New York Ward 6, New York, New York, lists another David Goldsmith, jeweler, b. 1814 in Germany, married to Sarah, with three children, all born in New York between 1845 and 1849.
6. David Goldsmith, eBay listings and private collections, Cincinnati silver binders, Cincinnati Art Museum.

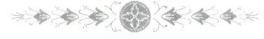

46. NATHAN LORD HAZEN

1809–1851, w. 1831–1851

Nathan Hazen was born in 1809, in Worthington, Massachusetts. He was the son of Nathan Hazen (1763-1847) and Phoebe Starkweather (1771-1856), both fourth-generation Americans born in New London, Connecticut.[1] Hazen's sister Emily (1795-1852) married Chauncey Johnson (1798-1854), a silversmith in Albany, New York, who trained Hazen in the trade.[2] In 1829 and 1830, Hazen worked in Troy, New York.[3]

Hazen appears in Cincinnati in 1831, boarding at the Broadway Hotel and selling watches, jewelry, and fancy goods under Letton's Museum at the corner of Main and Fourth Streets.[4] During his tenure in Cincinnati, he remained near this location at Main and Fourth Streets, working at 143 Main and later 157 Main.[5] An advertisement from May 1831 features a long list of items available at Hazen's stand, including "silver, table, tea, desert [*sic*] and cream spoons and sugar tongs."[6] While he is noted as a jeweler and a watch maker in various directory listings, it is probable that most of his business was in the repair of clocks and watches and the retailing of goods rather than in manufacturing.[7] Hazen advertised often, and in March 1838 announced that he had just returned from the East with "one of the most Admirable assortments of Watches, Jewelry and Fancy Articles that he has ever offered to the Public."[8]

In March 1832 **Jacob Deterly** records that Horace P. Woodbridge went to work in Hazen & Garner's shop.[9] Little is known about Hazen's partnership with the watch maker and silversmith **John Garner**. It can be assumed that it was brief, as Garner did not appear in the Cincinnati Directory for 1831 and died in 1832.[10] In 1840, **Thomas Conway**, a watch maker from Maryland was employed by Hazen, and in 1843, Hazen and **Peleg Collins** formed **Hazen & Collins**.[11] An R.G. Dun & Co. reporter observed that in 1841, Hazen became "much involved," placed his property in the hands of Collins, and after "extricating himself from embarrassments" took Collins in as a partner.[12] Credit reporters also noted that Hazen lived well and was "the most flashy man in the city," postulating, "he may die suddenly."[13] His extravagant lifestyle continued after his four-year partnership with Collins dissolved, and it was again noted that he was making money but did not seem to save much.[14] Between 1847 and 1850, reporters wrote, "Keeps a showy store, but v[ery] extravag[an]t – does perhaps as lar[ge] a bus[iness] as any in the city of the kind."[15] An illustrated and lengthy advertisement published in May 1847 supports this observation.[16] Therein, Hazen announced his return, again, from the eastern cities with "a large and splendid assortment of Watches, Jewelry and Fancy Goods." Among the dozens of types of wares listed are silver and plated ware, "Heavy Silver Spoons, Forks, 3 sizes, & Butter Knives, Threaded pattern; all kinds of Silver Ware made to order; Silver Plated Castors; Cake Baskets; Candlesticks; Snuffers and Trays; Dixon & Son's Britannia Ware,

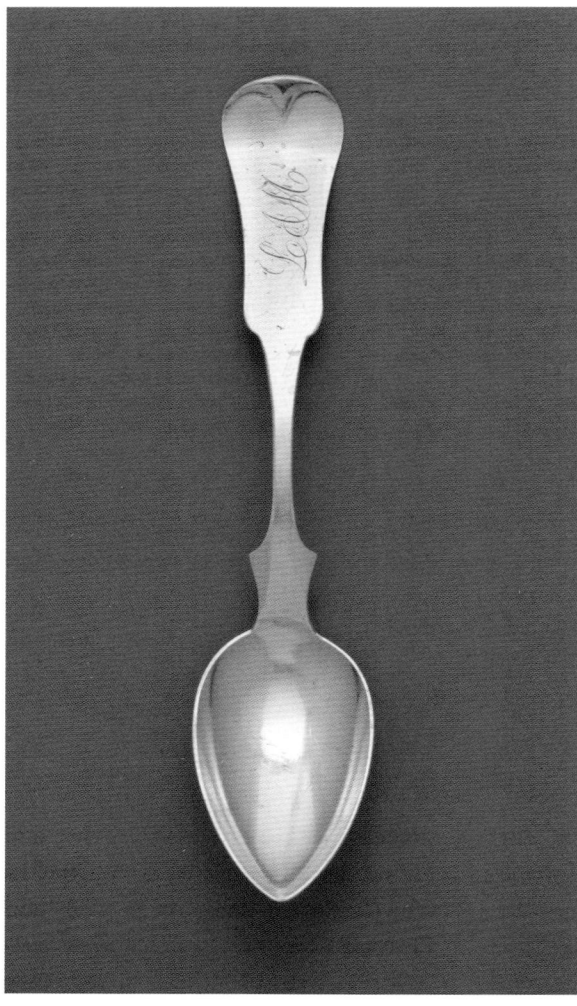

FIG. 46.1: Nathan L. Hazen, *Teaspoon*, c. 1840–1851, L. 6⅛ in. (15.6 cm), CAM, Gift of Dr. Suzanne A. Beutler, 1983.198

&c." It is said that his store was the first in Cincinnati to feature plate glass show windows.[17]

By 1851, Hazen appears to have become more responsible and thrifty, yet his improved credit and business was marred by the theft of $5,000 of his property in July of 1851.[18] In December of that year, he died of apoplexy.[19] **Henry Bliss** who had clerked at Hazen's shop since at least 1849, purchased the remainder of his stock and continued the business, acting as an agent for Hazen's widow, Hannah Jeannette Twichell (1813–1891) whom he would later marry.[20] Hannah received $10,000 in life insurance funds when Hazen died, as well as property in Texas.[21]

It is uncertain whether Hazen made any of the silver that bears his marks. A mug and spoons with tipped, exaggerated fiddle handles and pointed shoulders have been found with mark 46.1. Mark 46.2 has been documented on spoons of the same shape (fig. 46.1), as well as tongs with claw terminals, a mug, and two large ewers. The ewers were presented as trophies to former Ohio Governor Allen Trimble (1783–1870). The ewer presented in 1835 (fig. 46.2) was awarded by the Hamilton County Agricultural Society for Trimble's horse, Tariff, purportedly named after the protective tariffs promoted by Trimble's friend Henry Clay. These tariffs on imported goods encouraged domestic industries. In fact, Clay's Tariff of 1842 was instrumental in the success of the country's silversmiths. The second ewer (fig. 46.3) was awarded in 1838 for Trimble's horse, Hazelwood, judged "best 2 year old" by the Miami Valley Agricultural Society. Mark 46.3 has been found on spoons with fiddle handles and beakers, including one with an inscription dated 1838. It has also been found on spoons with fiddle handles that are embellished with an embossed basket of flowers and that also bear the mark of New York City jewelers G. Tillotson & Co. (active 1829–30).[22]

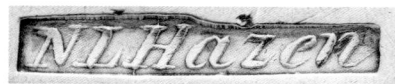

MARK 46.1

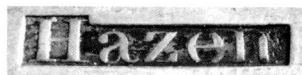

MARK 46.2

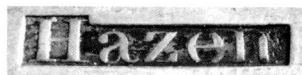

MARK 46.3

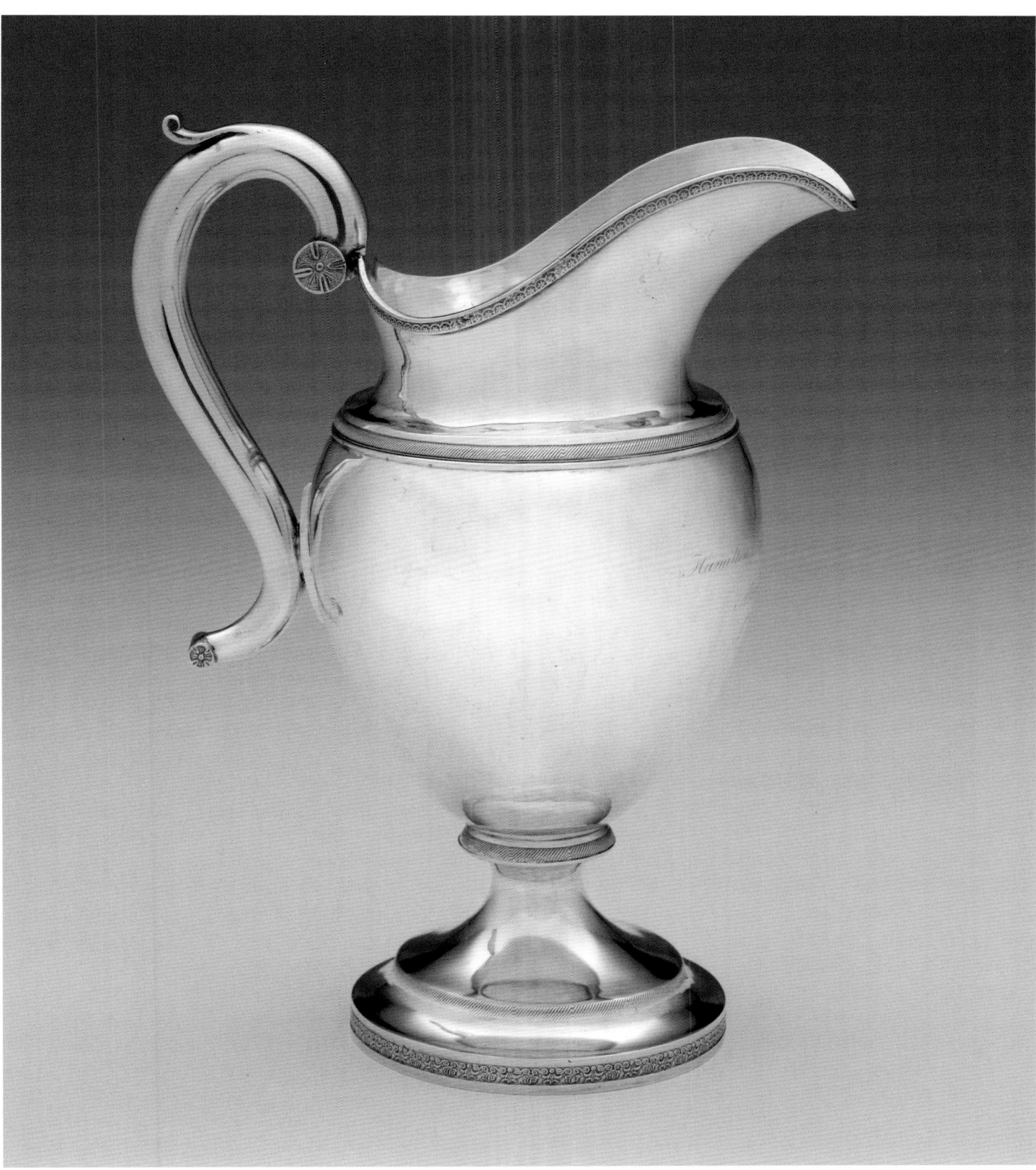

FIG. 46.2: Nathan L. Hazen, *Ewer*, 1835, 10¼ × 7¾ in. (26 × 19.7 cm),
Private Collection. Inscription: Awarded by the Hamilton County
Agricultural Society to Allen Trimble for his horse Tariff 1835

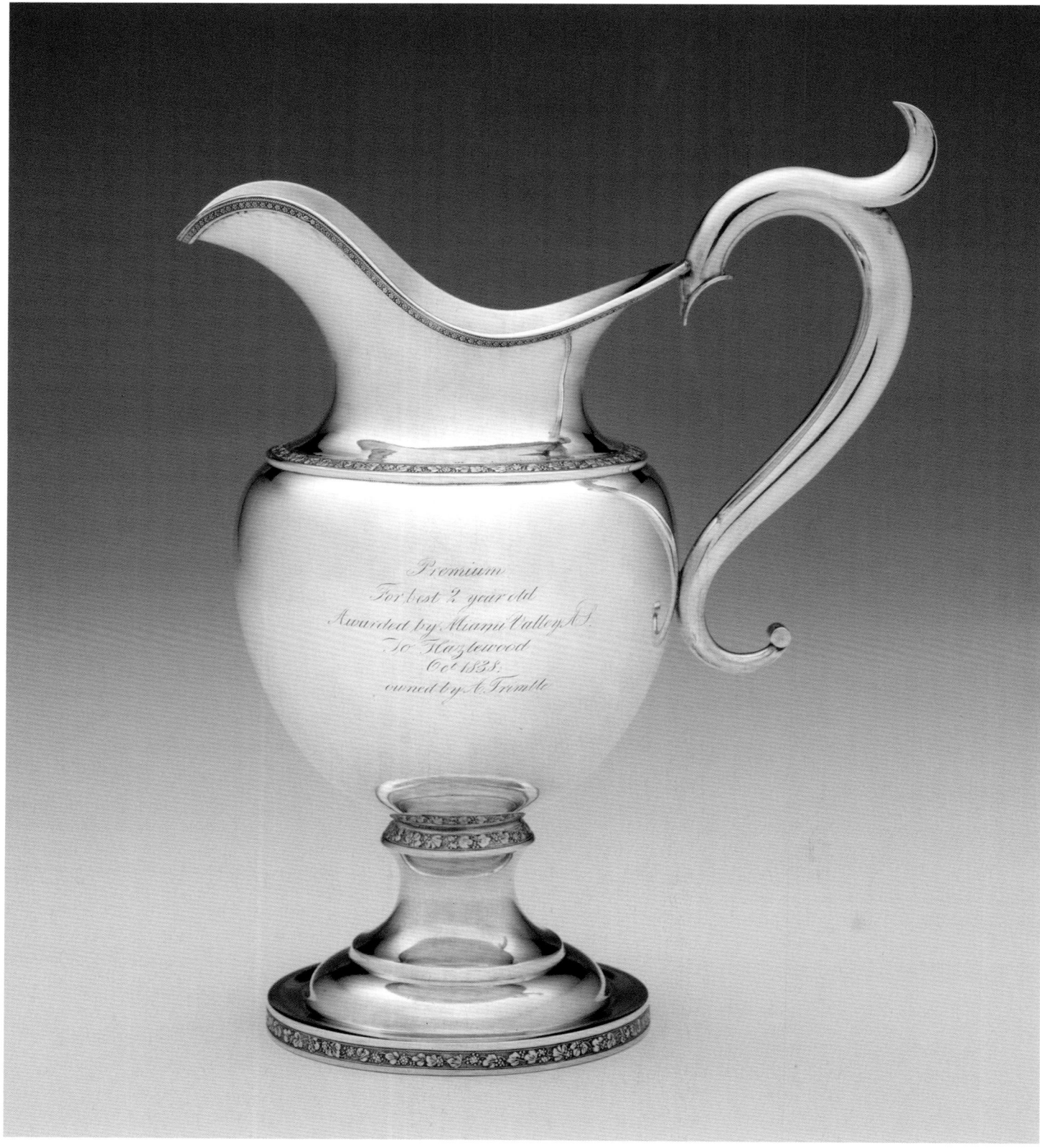

FIG. 46.3: Nathan L. Hazen, *Ewer*, 1838, 10¼ × 8¼ in. (26 × 21 cm), Private
Collection. Inscription: Premium For best 2 year old Awarded by Miami Valley
A.S. To Hazelwood Oct. 1838 owned by A. Trimble

1. Nathan L. Hazen, burial record, Spring Grove Cemetery, Cincinnati, Ohio; Family Tree, http://trees.ancestry.com/tree /23315051/family.

2. Wm. Erik Voss, "Chauncey Johnson," *American Silversmiths*, http://freepages.genealogy.rootsweb. ancestry.com/~silversmiths/makers/ silversmiths/202400.htm, accessed August 16, 2012; *Descendants of Edward Hazen*, http://www.genealogy.com/users/h /a/z/Walter-Eugene-Hazen/GENE1 -0077.html, accessed August 16, 2012.

3. Hazen appeared in Troy directories 1829–1830. *New York State Silversmiths*, Eggertsville, NY: The Darling Foundation of New York State, 1964, 98; George Barton Cutten, *The Silversmiths, Watchmakers and Jewelers of The State of New York Outside of New York City*, Hamilton, NY: privately printed, 1939, 33.

4. 1831 Cincinnati City Directory. Ralph Letton's museum occupied the second and third stories of a

brick building at Main and Fourth Streets. It featured an automated organ with animated wax figure band, bird and animal specimens, minerals, mammoth bones, Indian antiquities, and portraits of early Cincinnatians. Mary Sayre Haverstock et. al., *Artists in Ohio, 1787–1900: A Biographical Dictionary*, Kent, Ohio: Kent State University Press, 2000, 521; Charles Greve, *Centennial History of Cincinnati and Its Representative Citizens*, Chicago: Biographical Publishing Co., 1904, 1:643.

5. Before 1853, there were no official street numbers, therefore this change may not reflect a move, but rather a change in a self-assigned street number.

6. Advertisement, *Cincinnati Daily Gazette*, May 7, 1831, reproduced in Beckman, 64.

7. 1831, 1834, 1836/37, 1839/40, 1842 Cincinnati City Directories; Advertisement, W.G. Lyford, *The Western Address Directory*, Baltimore: Jos. Robinson, 1837, 327.

8. Advertisement, *Liberty Hall*, March 12, 1838, reproduced Beckman, 64.

9. Jacob Deterly, *"Remarks" of Jacob Deterly: diary from 1819 to 1848; life in southern Ohio: Cincinnati, Marietta, Athens* (transcribed and indexed by Madge Hubbard and Opal Saffell), Seattle: Northwest Lineage Researcher, 1972, 2:67.

10. 1829, 1831 Cincinnati City Directories; Isaac Covalt, *Cemetery Records of the Methodist Episcopal Church*, Cincinnati, m85, microfilm 59, roll 2, Cincinnati Historical Society.

11. 1839/1840 Cincinnati City Directory; Ohio, Vol. 1, p. 89, R.G. Dun & Co. Collection, Baker Library, Harvard Business School.

12. Ohio, Vol. 1, p. 89, R.G. Dun & Co. Collection.

13. Ibid.

14. Ibid.

15. Ibid.

16. Advertisement, *Cist's Daily Advertiser*, May 14, 1847, reproduced in Beckman, 65.

17. *Descendants of Edward Hazen*.

18. Ohio, Vol. 3, p. 258, R.G. Dun & Co. Collection.

19. Nathan L. Hazen, burial record.

20. 1849/50 Cincinnati City Directory; Ohio, Vol. 1, p. 295, R.G. Dun & Co. Collection; Ohio, Vol. 3, p. 258, R.G. Dun & Co. Collection; Hannah J. Bliss, death record, Cincinnati Health Department, University of Cincinnati Archives and Rare Books Library, http://hdl.handle.net /2374.UC/340456.

21. Ohio, Vol. 3, p. 258, R.G. Dun & Co. Collection.

22. Nathan L. Hazen, eBay listings and private collections, Cincinnati silver binders, Cincinnati Art Museum; Catherine Hollister, comp., *Manhattan New York City Directory: 1829–30* [online database], Provo, Utah: Ancestry.com Operations Inc., 2002; It is possible that the spoons embossed with baskets and flowers were old stock that Hazen brought to Cincinnati from New York.

47. HAZEN & COLLINS

1843–1847

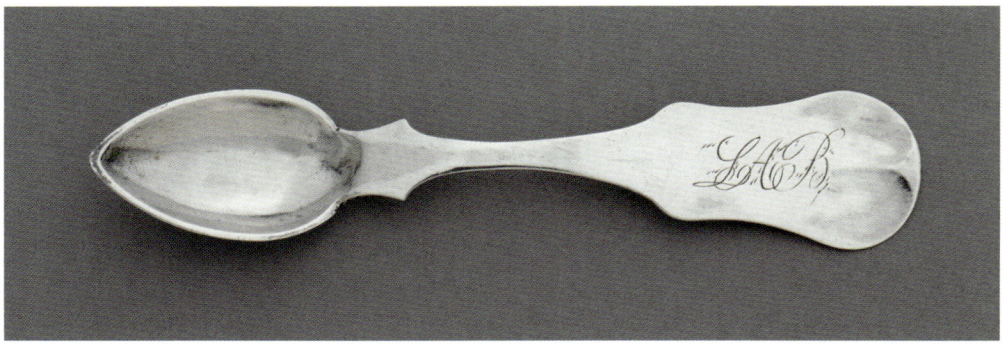

FIG. 47.1: Hazen & Collins, *Spoon*, 1843–1847,
L. 3⅜ in. (8.6 cm), CAM, x1981.14

Former New Englanders **Nathan Lord Hazen** and **Peleg Collins** formed a partnership in 1843. Reportedly, Hazen had run into financial debt in 1841, and sought out Collins, then director of the Bank of Cincinnati, to aid his recovery.[1] Hazen turned his property over to Collins, and once Hazen had recovered, Hazen took Collins on as a partner. Their firm advertised as dealers in watches, jewelry, and fancy goods, and provided related repair work.[2] Although they advertised "Silver Forks, Spoons, Butter Knives, &c., threaded and plain" and "All kinds of Silver Ware made to order," these were reported to come from "importers and manufacturers" in the East.[3] The firm was in business on Main Street, three doors above Fourth Street, until the partnership ended in January 1847.[4]

Their mark (mark 47.1), sometimes supplemented by "CINCINNATI" in a rectangular cartouche and a shield-breasted eagle facing left, has been documented on spoons and ladles with tipped, exaggerated fiddle handles and pointed shoulders (fig. 47.1), and on a pitcher (fig. 47.2).[5] The eagle is likely the manufactory mark of **Edward Kinsey**.[6]

1. *Journal of the Senate of the State of Ohio*, vol. 40, Columbus: S. Medary, 1842, 225; Ohio, Vol. 1, p. 89, R.G. Dun & Co. Collection, Baker Library, Harvard Business School.
2. Advertisement, 1843 Cincinnati City Directory, n.p., advertising section at back of book.
3. Advertisement, *Cincinnati Daily Gazette*, December 17, 1846, reproduced in Beckman, 65; Advertisement, *Cincinnati Enquirer*, November 18, 1843, 1; Advertisement, *Cincinnati Enquirer*, December 23, 1844, 4; Advertisement, *Cincinnati Enquirer*, January 6, 1845, 4; Advertisement, *Cincinnati Enquirer*, March 8, 1845, 3; Advertisement, *Cincinnati Enquirer*, June 13, 1845, 1.
4. Ohio, Vol. 1, p. 89, R.G. Dun & Co. Collection; Notice of dissolution, *Cincinnati Enquirer*, January 27, 1847, 2; The street number for the firm varies in the advertisements cited above as street numbers were not standardized or set at this time. The address found in the city directories most frequently is "Main between Fourth and Fifth."
5. Hazen & Collins, eBay listings and private collections, Cincinnati silver binders, Cincinnati Art Museum; *Spoon*, Cincinnati Art Museum, x1981.14; *Pitcher*, Cincinnati Art Museum, 2005.74.
6. John R. McGrew, *Manufacturers' Marks on American Coin Silver*, Hanover, PA: Argyros Publications, 2004, 98.

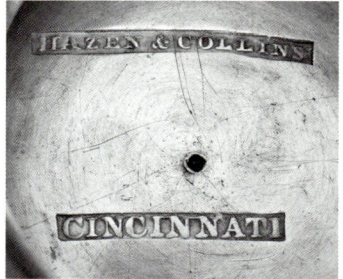

MARK 47.1

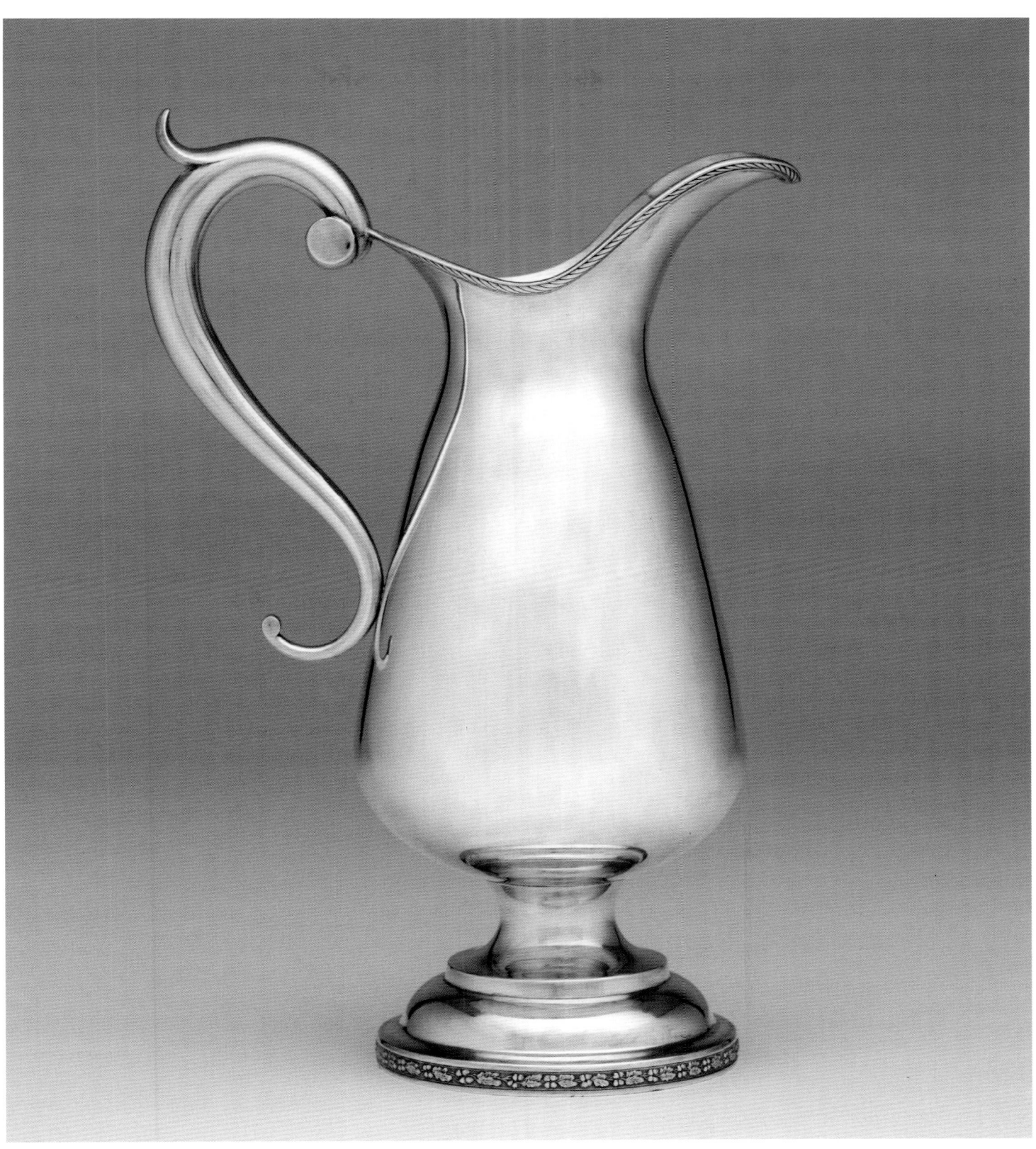

FIG. 47.2: Hazen & Collins, *Ewer*, 1843–1847, 9⅝ × 7⅛ in.
(24.5 × 18.1 cm), CAM, Museum Purchase with funds
provided by Mr. and Mrs. Charles Fleischmann III, 2005.74

48. CLEMENS HELLEBUSH

1832–1893, w. 1851–1893

CLEMENS HELLEBUSH (THE FIRM)

1866–1895

THE HELLEBUSH CO.

1896–1900

Clemens Hellebush (fig. 48.1), born December 18, 1832, in north-western Germany, near Damme, was the son of Elizabeth and Hermann Hellebush, a school teacher.[1] He came to America in 1848.[2] His brother, Bernard Henry Francis "Frank" Hellebush, had already emigrated and settled in Cincinnati where he taught school. Clemens joined him as a pupil and assistant teacher.[3] Although Clemens had been groomed to be a school teacher, his interests were mercantile. At the age of 17, he became a clerk at Cincinnati's Storch & Co., importers of French, German, and English fancy goods and toys, and he later worked as a clerk in the dry goods house of James LeBoutillier on Fourth Street.[4] Around 1851, he entered the house of jeweler **Theodore Oskamp**. When Oskamp died in 1854, his brother, **Clemens Oskamp**, offered Hellebush an interest in the business. In 1860, Hellebush, who lived in Covington, Kentucky, (across the Ohio River from Cincinnati) reported $10,000 worth of real estate and a personal estate worth $500.[5] He fulfilled two five-year contracts with Oskamp before he opened his own wholesale jewelry house at the northeast corner of Pearl and Main Streets in 1866.[6]

Hellebush began his business as a jobber, or wholesaler, of American and European watches, watch materials, jewelry, silver, and fancy goods, but eventually grew to become a retailer and jewelry manufacturer.[7] Reports on his credit were always very favorable. They noted that his business was profitable, his character was of the finest, and that his worth was growing.[8] In 1875, he was a member of the Cincinnati Board of Trade, and in 1876, his total worth, including real estate, was estimated at $200,000 or more. Sales in his store were reported to have amounted to $325,000— making him one of the largest and most successful concerns in the city.[9]

It was about this time that he moved to a large home on five acres of land in the Walnut Hills area of Cincinnati.[10] On May 8, 1855, he had wed Lucia Elizabeth Specker (b. Germany, about 1838–1906), sister of the proprietors of Specker Brothers, a very large wholesale dry goods firm on Pearl Street.[11] Hellebush and his wife were the parents of 13 children: Franciska "Frances"(b. 1856, married C.C. Rickenhoff); Amelia Clara (b. about 1857); Edward (b. about 1859); Matilda (b. about 1861, married F.W.A Bietmann); Clemens (b. about 1862); Alphonse (b. about 1865); Joseph (about 1865–1904); Clara (b. 1869, married Almos Emminger); Lillie May (1870–1896); Frederick (b. about 1872); Eleanore (b. about 1873); Antoinette (b. about 1877, married Frank L. Ratterman); and Charles Kearns (1879–1971).[12]

In 1879, Hellebush relocated his shop to the Pike Opera House Building, at 77 West Fourth Street.[13] According to the 1880 Products of Industry Census, he had $8,000 of capital invested in the business, employed 12 hands (including two women) whose combined yearly compensation was $5,000, and used $1,500 of material and power harnessed from the Ohio River to produce $15,000 worth of product that year.[14] His new shop was described as "a large store about 25 by 150 feet deep with black walnut fixtures." The side cases, noted by a reporter as the largest he had ever seen in any store in the country, had "handsomely carved frames with French plate glass, 11 feet long," and were "well stocked with all the latest goods."[15]

In 1883, credit reporters remarked that Hellebush thoroughly understood the business, was among the wealthiest jewelers in the city, and was in all, considered worth $300,000.[16] By 1885, he had developed a method for making imitation marble and had organized the United States Clock Case Company, later known as the U.S. Patent Marble Clock Case Co.[17] And, in 1886, he became the first president of the Cincinnati Wholesale Jewelers' Association, whose "object was the attainment of harmony of action and mutual confidence among local dealers, as well as the protection and the promotion of the general welfare of the trade" in Cincinnati.[18]

Hellebush made frequent trips east to purchase merchandise, and handled "a large stock of all goods in his line, of both American and foreign make, his importations being brought direct from the most celebrated European manufacturers."[19] He

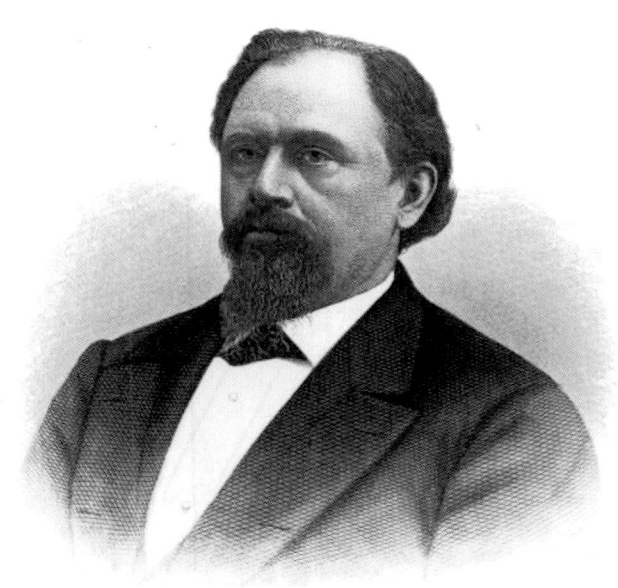

FIG. 48.1: Clemens Hellebush, from Charles Robson, *Biographical Encyclopedia of Ohio of the Nineteenth Century*, Cincinnati: Galaxy Publishing Co., 1876, opposite page 238

aired his disregard for traveling agents and jewelry catalogues, in the 1870s and 1880s, citing his reliance on "strict integrity and honorable dealing as the best advertisement," but he eventually employed both.[20]

Hellebush carried a notable line of silver for his patrons. He reportedly maintained "effective arrangements with the manufacturers by which he monopolizes his own specialties in articles of jewelry, silver and plated ware; so that the same patterns cannot be found in any other house."[21] He kept "a full line of Gorham silverware and Reed & Barton's plated ware," and "his magnificent show-cases—the finest in the country—[were] fairly ablaze with these goods, in every variety of graceful and artistic design."[22] Whiting Mfg. Co. also provided some of the wares that bear Hellebush's retail mark.[23] In August 1891 among the foreign goods bought by Hellebush was "a most unique lot of silver."[24] While Hellebush employed "a large number of first-class jewelers who manufacture[d] to [Hellebush's] own taste and design the greater portion of his domestic goods, and who [completed] work to order, such as setting diamonds, and also solid gold and silver work," his attention appears to have been focused on the clock, watch, and jewelry end of the trade rather than on silver flatware and hollowware.[25]

Notable silver sales and commissions of the firm that were cited in the trade journals included "a complete outfit of silver of about 30 pieces" ordered by Mayor John B. Mosby in 1891; a silver water service and chest of silver valued at $1,000 to be presented to the master mechanic of the Kentucky Central Railroad by its employees in 1893; and an order of silver for the Phoenix Club in 1894.[26]

In 1892, Mayor Mosby formed a committee to raise $10,000 for the purchase of a grand silver service for the new naval cruiser *Cincinnati*. The contract to furnish the silver was won by Hellebush, who had competed against the bids of **Duhme & Co.**, Clemens Oskamp, **Frank Herschede**, **A. & J. Plaut**, and **Oskamp, Nolting & Co.** The service consisted of eight pieces: a punch bowl weighing 555 ounces; an ice bowl weighing 69 ounces; fish dish, 72 ounces; meat dish, 64 ounces; two fruit dishes, 204 ounces; and a pair of ice tongs. It was produced by Dominick & Haff, and was displayed in the window of the Hellebush store with great fanfare before its presentation in July 1895.[27] It is currently on loan from the U.S. Department of the Navy to the Public Library of Cincinnati and Hamilton County.[28]

Extant silver flatware and hollowware marked by the firm illustrate the wide variety of forms and styles popular during the firm's lengthy tenure. They range from simple spoons with tipped, exaggerated fiddle handles to high style Victorian flatware (including Whiting's "Hyperion" [1888]) and wares with hammered surface textures from the Arts and Crafts period. Marks used by the firm include mark 48.1, as well as the incuse marks, "C.H.," "CLEMENS HELLEBUSH CINCINNATI," and "CLEMENS HELLEBUSH."[29]

Eventually, Hellebush's sons, Clemens Jr., Alphonse, Joseph, and Frederick became involved in the business.[30] By 1888, the elder Clemens Hellebush managed the business and was in charge of the diamond department, while Clemens Jr. was in charge of the retail department, assisted by **William Wilson McGrew**. The wholesale department was run by A.B. Clark, and two traveling salesmen kept the firm well represented in the South and the West.[31] In 1891, an art room with "picturesque statuettes and other art pieces" was added, and the wholesale department was enlarged.[32]

Clemens Hellebush died on January 17, 1893, reportedly leaving an estate worth $400,000 to $500,000.[33] However, it was soon revealed that he had accumulated much debt. His son, Clemens Jr., went to New York and called a meeting of his father's creditors. His father's liabilities for merchandise were comparatively small, but there were large cash liabilities as Hellebush had always made a point of paying his debts for merchandise but often had to borrow largely to do so. With liabilities totaling $420,840 and assets at

$356,343, Hellebush Jr. hoped that a settlement could be approved or arrangements could be made that would allow him and his brothers to continue to run the business with the financial support of their mother and friends.[34] The creditors appointed a committee to travel to Cincinnati to examine the firm's affairs, and Hellebush's sons continued to run the business, but they were unable to restore its solvency.[35] In 1895, it was reported that the estate owed $300,000 to the bankrupt Commercial Bank. Hellebush had begun to bank there around 1883, and around 1890 his loan requests had increased exponentially. Fearing a collapse of the Commercial Bank, other banks, and the Hellebush estate, the bank officer continued to lend to Hellebush Sr. and later to Clemens Hellebush, Jr. in the hope that they could turn things around. But that did not happen. After a lengthy court battle, a settlement was reached between the Hellebush estate and the bank. The estate paid the bank $60,000 and released the real estate dower of Hellebush's widow, which included the Hellebush homestead. The store remained the property of the Hellebush family, and business continued. Alphonse Hellebush and his mother, Lucia, bought the store's stock for $59,764 cash, removing the store from possession of the estate and allowing the store to regain good credit so that new stock could be bought. The remainder of the $60,000 was raised through the sale of book accounts and real estate, and by the sale at auction in November 1895 of old merchandise that Alphonse had purchased.[36]

On St. Patrick's Day 1896, the new Hellebush store opened several doors east of its previous home. Located at 45 East Fourth Street, the firm continued in its jobbing and retail business. Elaborately decorated, the new store had fixtures of cherry wood with brass ornaments. Large plate-glass mirrors embellished the side walls in the front part of the store, creating a reception hall for the ladies with large, upholstered settees. "Arranged in true Metropolitan style," the new house operated as The Hellebush Co.[37] But by February 1900 it had failed, owing large debts to eastern creditors.[38] Unable to effect a settlement, the stock was purchased by Clemens Hellebush, Jr., and eventually sold at auction in October. The firm was officially out of business by January 9, 1901.[39]

MARK 48.1

1. Charles Robson, *Biographical Encyclopedia of Ohio of the Nineteenth Century*, Cincinnati: Galaxy Publishing Co., 1876, 538. Hellebush's birthplace is given as "Boeringhausen, near Damme, in the southern part of the Grand Duchy of Oldenberg."
2. Gale Research, *Passenger and Immigration Lists Index, 1500s–1900s*, [online database], Provo, Utah: Ancestry.com Operations Inc., 2010.
3. Robson, *Biographical Encyclopedia*, 538; William H. Perrin, J. H. Battle, "Prof. B.H.F. Hellebusch [sic]," *Kentucky: A History of the State*, Louisville, KY: F.A. Battey, 1887, 814.
4. Robson, *Biographical Encyclopedia*, 538; 1849/50 Cincinnati City Directory.
5. 1860 Federal Census, Covington, Kenton, Kentucky.
6. John W. Leonard, *The Centennial Review of Cincinnati: one hundred years of progress in commerce, manufactures, the professions, and in social and municipal life*, Cincinnati: J.M. Elstner, 1888, 67; Ohio, Vol. 6, p. 193, R.G. Dun & Co. Collection, Baker Library, Harvard Business School; Robson, *Biographical Encyclopedia*, 538; 1866 Cincinnati City Directory.
7. Advertisement, 1870 Cincinnati

Business Directory, 283; Advertisement, *Cincinnati of To-Day: Progress and Prospects of the Great Queen City of the West, Its Commerce and Industries, A Historical and Descriptive Glance*, Cincinnati: Travellers Protective Association of America, 1892, 41.
8. Ohio, Vol. 6, p. 193, R.G. Dun & Co. Collection; Ohio, Vol. 6, p. 305, R.G. Dun & Co. Collection; Ohio, Vol. 3, p. 398, R.G. Dun & Co. Collection; Ohio, Vol. 6, p. 441, R.G. Dun & Co. Collection.
9. Ohio, Vol. 6, p. 193, R.G. Dun & Co. Collection; *Annual and . . . Statistical Report of the Cincinnati Board of Trade and Transportation*, vol. 3, Cincinnati: Board of Trade and Transportation, 1875, 22; Robson, *Biographical Encyclopedia*, 538.
10. Robson, *Biographical Encyclopedia*, 538.
11. Ibid.; Clemens Hellebush, will dated October 28, 1892, proved January 23, 1893, vol. 57, p. 555, Hamilton County Registry of Probate, Cincinnati, Ohio; "It is Ended," *Cincinnati Enquirer*, January 18, 1893, 4; Clemens Hellebush, death record, Cincinnati Health Department, University of Cincinnati Archives and Rare Books Library,

http://hdl.handle.net/2374.UC/346575; "Cincinnati," *Jewellers' Circular and Horological Review* (March 28, 1906): 64.
12. Clemens Hellebush, will; "It is Ended," January 18, 1893; Joseph Hellebush, death notice, *Cincinnati Enquirer*, September 1, 1904, 7; 1860 and 1870 Federal Censuses, Covington, Kenton, Kentucky; 1880 Federal Census, Cincinnati, Hamilton, Ohio; Marriage record, Clara Hellebush to Almos Emminger, Hamilton County Probate Records, vol. 174, 326, http://www.probatect.org/CourtRecordsArchive/bukmarriages.aspx; "Random Notes," *Cincinnati Enquirer*, June 27, 1909, B4.
13. 1879 Cincinnati City Directory; Leonard, *Centennial Review of Cincinnati*, 67.
14. 1870 Federal Non-Population Census Schedules, Products of Industry, Schedule 4, Hamilton County, Ohio.
15. "On the Road," *JCHR* (July 1888): 44.
16. Ohio, Vol. 6, p. 441, R.G. Dun & Co. Collection.
17. 1885 Cincinnati City Directory; The office and the factory of this firm were located at 46 and 48

Melancthon Street, and Clemens Hellebush, Jr. acted as manager and treasurer; Untitled, *JCHR* (July 1885): 191; Clemens Hellebush. 1887. Mold for Clock-Cases. US Patent 369,337, filed August 12, 1886, and issued September 6, 1887; Leonard, *Centennial Review of Cincinnati*, 67; Advertisement, *JCHR* (November 1888): n.p.
18. "Father Time Keepers," *Cincinnati Enquirer*, January 14, 1886, 4; "Our Cincinnati Correspondence," *JCHR* (February 1886).
19. *The Industries of Cincinnati . . .* , Albert N. Marquis (ed.), Cincinnati: A.N. Marquis & Co., 1883, 138.
20. Robson, *Biographical Encyclopedia*, 538; "On the Road," *JCHR* (December 1883): 369; "Cincinnati," *JCHR* (November 16, 1892): 34; "A Drummer's Doings," *Cincinnati Enquirer*, December 15, 1881, 4.
21. Robson, *Biographical Encyclopedia*, 538.
22. Marquis, *The Industries of Cincinnati*, 138.
23. Clemens Hellebush, eBay listings and private collections, Cincinnati silver binders, Cincinnati Art Museum.
24. "Cincinnati," *JCHR* (August 12, 1891): 34.

25. Robson, *Biographical Encyclopedia*, 538.

26. "Cincinnati," *JCHR* (April 22, 1891): 24; "Cincinnati," *JCHR* (April 16, 1893): 36; "Cincinnati," *JCHR* (November 7, 1894): 34.

27. "One Hundred Committeemen to Raise the Cincinnati's Silver Service Fund," *Cincinnati Enquirer*, November 19, 1892, 9; "The 'Cincinnati'. The Silver Service Fund Might," *Cincinnati Enquirer*, January 9, 1893, 8; "Artistic Bits," *Cincinnati Enquirer*, September 7, 1894, 4; "Silver Service," *Cincinnati Enquirer*, April 2, 1895, 10; "Free Silver. The Elegant Silver For the Cruiser Cincinnati To Be Presented To-Day," *Cincinnati Enquirer*, July 17, 1895, 1; "In Keeping With the Handsome Ship," *Cincinnati Enquirer*, July 18, 1895, 9; "Cincinnati's Silver Service," *The New York Times*, July 18, 1895; "The Cincinnati's Lost Silver," *The New York Times*, April 10, 1901.

28. The U.S.S. *Cincinnati* was dismantled in 1921.

29. Clemens Hellebush, eBay listings and private collections, Cincinnati Art Museum.

30. "Demise of Clemens Hellebush," *JCHR* (January 5, 1893): 16.

31. "On the Road," *JCHR* (July 1888): 44.

32. "Cincinnati," *JCHR* (November 4, 1891): 31; "Cincinnati," *JCHR* (November 11, 1891): 31.

33. Clemens Hellebush, death record; "Divided Equally. The Hellebush Estate," *Cincinnati Enquirer*, January 24, 1893, 7.

34. "Clemens Hellebush, Jr. Calls a Meeting of his Father's Creditors," *JCHR* (February 22, 1893): 24.

35. "Men and Things," *Cincinnati Enquirer*, February 25, 1893, 4.

36. "The Clemens Hellebush Estate Owes $300,000 to an Insolvent Bank," *JCHR* (April 10, 1895): 10; "Two Deeds From Clemens Hellebush to the Commercial Bank Filed," *JCHR* (April 24, 1895): 27; "Cincinnati," *JCHR* (May 1, 1895): 28; "Cincinnati," *JCHR* (May 15, 1895): 28; "The Settlement of the Commercial Bank and the Hellebush Estate," *JCHR* (May 29, 1895): 11; "A Petition Suit on Behalf of Clemens and Lucia Hellebush," *JCHR* (June 19, 1895): 12; "Cincinnati," *JCHR* (June 26, 1895): 26; "The Hellebush Estate," *Cincinnati Enquirer*, July 9, 1895, 9; "Cincinnati," *JCHR* (August 7, 1895): 30; "Petition to Remove the Executors of the Hellebush Estate," *JCHR* (August 21, 1895): 14; "A Contest About Hellebush Deeds," *Cincinnati Enquirer*, June 14, 1895, 12; "Deeds That Were Absolute," *Cincinnati Enquirer*, August 29, 1895, 9; "Figures in the Hellebush Debt," *Cincinnati Enquirer*, September 10, 1895, 9; "At Last. Hellebush Estate Debt to the Defunct Commercial Bank Settled," *Cincinnati Enquirer*, September 7, 1895, 16; "The Hellebush Compromise," *Cincinnati Enquirer*, October 18, 1895, 12; "Second Hellebush Failure," *JCHR* (February 21, 1900): 20; "Cincinnati," *JCHR* (May 26, 1897): 26; "Cincinnati," *JCHR* (July 14, 1897): 24; Auction notice, *Cincinnati Enquirer*, November 11, 1895, 8.

37. 1896 Cincinnati City Directory; "Cincinnati," *JCHR* (January 1, 1896): 24; "Cincinnati," *JCHR* (January 29, 1896): 12; "Cincinnati," *JCHR* (March 18, 1896): 27; "Cincinnati," *JCHR* (March 25, 1896).

38. "Second Hellebush Failure," (February 21, 1900); "The Outlook of the Business of Clemens Hellebush," *JCHR* (March 28, 1900): 17; "Cincinnati," *JCHR* (April 11, 1900): 41; "Dull Trade And Pressures of Creditors Cause Hellebush Jewelry Firm To Make An Assignment," *Cincinnati Enquirer*, February 15, 1900, 5.

39. "Cincinnati," *JCHR* (June 6, 1900): 40; "Cincinnati," *JCHR* (July 18, 1900): 34; "Cincinnati," *JCHR* (September 19, 1900): 53; "Cincinnati," *JCHR* (October 3, 1900): 44; "Cincinnati," *JCHR* (October 10, 1900): 53; "The Passing of the Historic Hellebush Jewelry House," *JCHR* (January 9, 1901): 19.

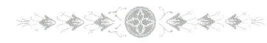

49. FRANK HERSCHEDE

1857–1922, w. 1872–1922

THE FRANK HERSCHEDE CO.

1905–1964

HERSCHEDE JEWELERS

1965–1996

Frank Herschede was born in Cincinnati in 1857.[1] He was one of six children born to German immigrants Mary Linneman (1829–1885) and Johann (John) Herschede (1813–1875), who worked as a finisher in a foundry.[2] As a young man, Frank was in the employ of watch maker Charles Cook.[3] In September 1877, with an advance of $100,000 from his widowed mother, "a certain jobber stocked him up," and he established a well-appointed store, specializing in watches, diamonds, jewelry, and silverware in the Emery Arcade, between Vine and Race Streets.[4] The Emery Arcade ran from the Emery Hotel to Race Street, one block west. An arcade covered by glass, it included many shops and services. By 1882, Herschede had also become the proprietor of the National Jewelry Co., located in the Arcade, and it was reported that he carried a large stock in both stores.[5] In 1885, Herschede moved his jewelry store to 179 Vine, at the corner of Vine and the Arcade, and in March 1896 he announced that he would move to Fourth Street (24 East Fourth Street).[6] The Fourth Street location was lavish with an inlaid mosaic floor and frescoed ceilings, and it allowed more space for the

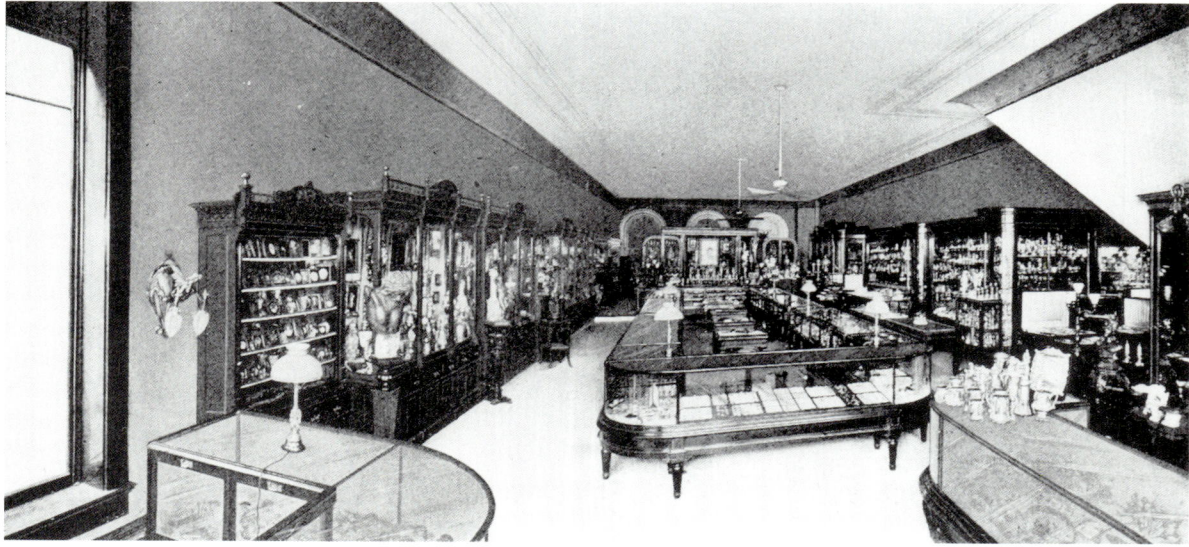

FIG. 49.1: The Frank Herschede Co., from George W. Engelhardt, *Cincinnati: The Queen City*, Cincinnati: G.W. Engelhardt, 1901, 211

bric-a-brac department and the fine hall clocks that Herschede had begun to sell with great success in 1885 (fig. 49.1). "The magnificent display of table silver loaned by the leading makers of this country" attracted great attention at the store's reopening.[7]

Herschede maintained a sizeable and active silver department, but there is no evidence to support the notion that his firm produced any of the silver that bears its marks. Herschede's travels to buy stock in the East were frequently noted, and several extant wares bear Herschede marks accompanied by the marks of the following manufacturers: Frank M. Whiting Co.; Reed & Barton (Taunton, Massachusetts); Dominick & Haff (New York City); Graff, Wash & Dunn (New York City); Meriden (Meriden, Connecticut); Redlich & Co. (New York City); Towle Mfg. Co. (Newburyport, Massachusetts); Roger Williams Silver Co. (Providence, Rhode Island); and George W. Shiebler (New York City).[8] Herschede also maintained an affiliation with Gorham Mfg. Co. (Providence, Rhode Island), brokering a cigar cabinet that was proclaimed "the handsomest in the world" for presentation to Mr. Fleischmann, mayor of Cincinnati, in 1900.[9] Herschede also secured the sponsorship of Gorham for a large and impressive display of silver, including significant 18th-century European examples, for the 1910 Ohio Valley Exposition.[10] Many trophies, fair premiums, and presentation pieces were provided by Herschede.[11] One example is the loving cup presented in 1904 to William Stanhope Rowe, president of the 1st National Bank of Cincinnati (fig. 49.2). It is marked by Herschede (mark 49.1) and George W. Shiebler & Co. A beaker (fig. 49.3) bears mark 49.2.

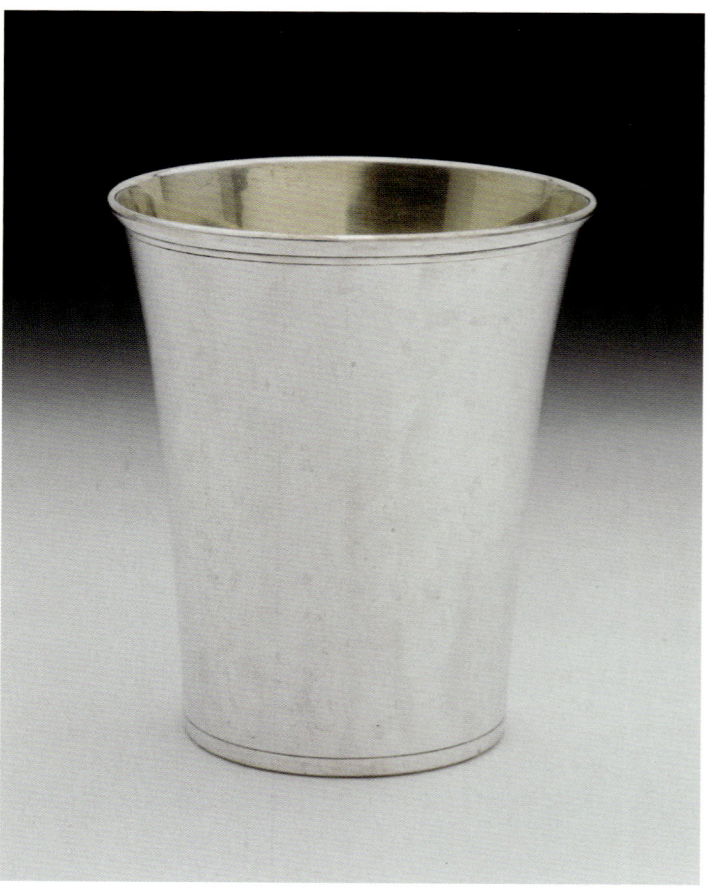

FIG. 49.3: The Frank Herschede Co., *Beaker*, c. 1906, 4½ × 4 in. (11.4 × 10.2 cm), CAM, Museum Purchase with funds provided by Mr. and Mrs. Charles Fleischmann III, 2005.53

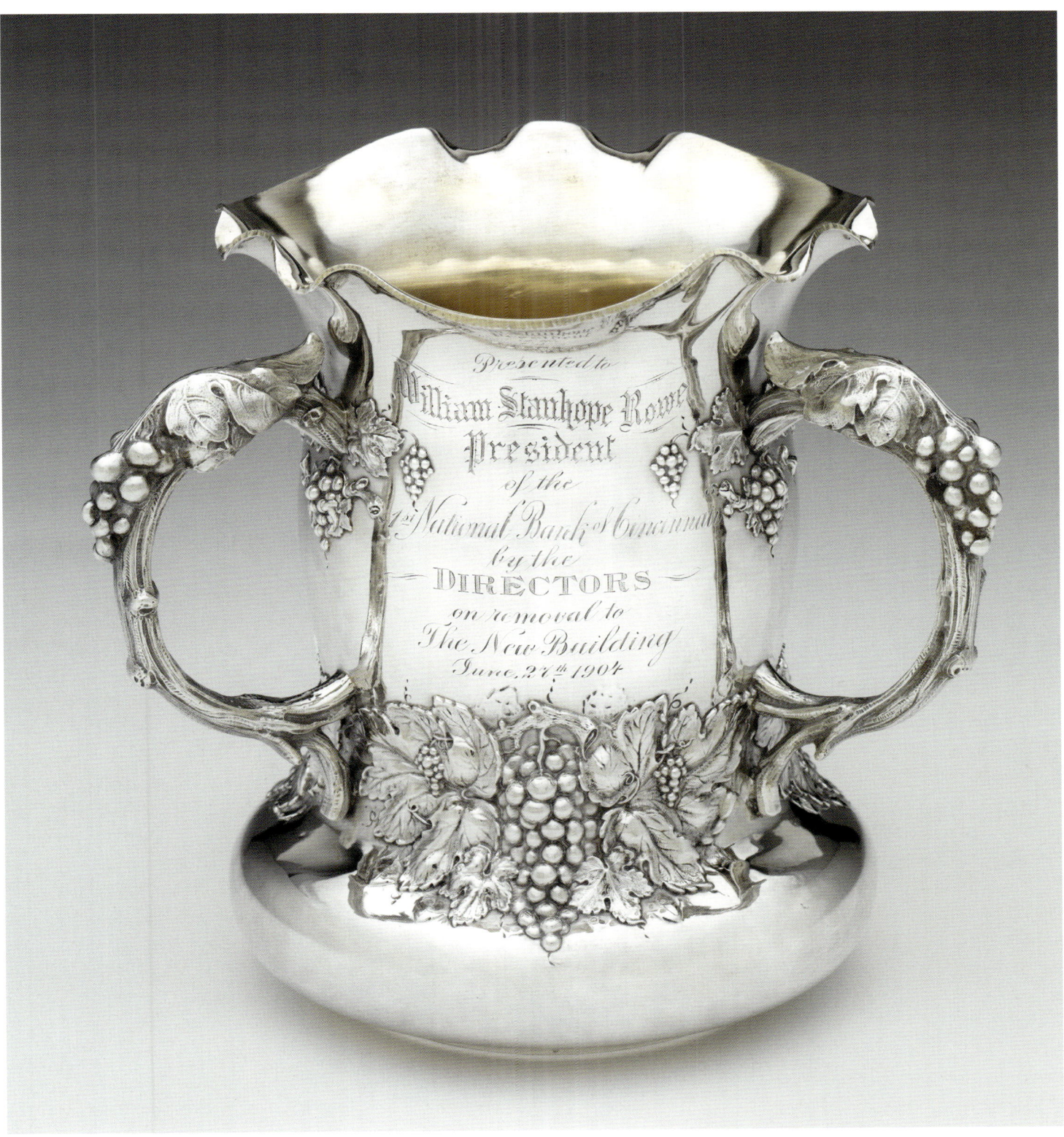

FIG. 49.2: Frank Herschede, retailer, and George W. Shiebler & Co., manufacturer, (estab. 1876, closed 1915), *Loving Cup*, 1904, 9½ × 10 in. (24.1 × 25.4 cm), CAM, Gift of Phillip C. and Whitney Rowe Long, 2002.118. Inscription: Presented to William Stanhope Rowe President of the 1st National Bank of Cincinnati by the DIRECTORS on removal to The New Building June 27th 1904. Engraved on the bottom with list of Directors' names: HENRY C. URNER / RICHARD DYMOND / JOSEPH RAWSON / ALBERT H. MITCHELL / JULIUS FREIBURG / JAMES J. HOOKER / CHARLES S. HARRISON / JAMES C. ERNST

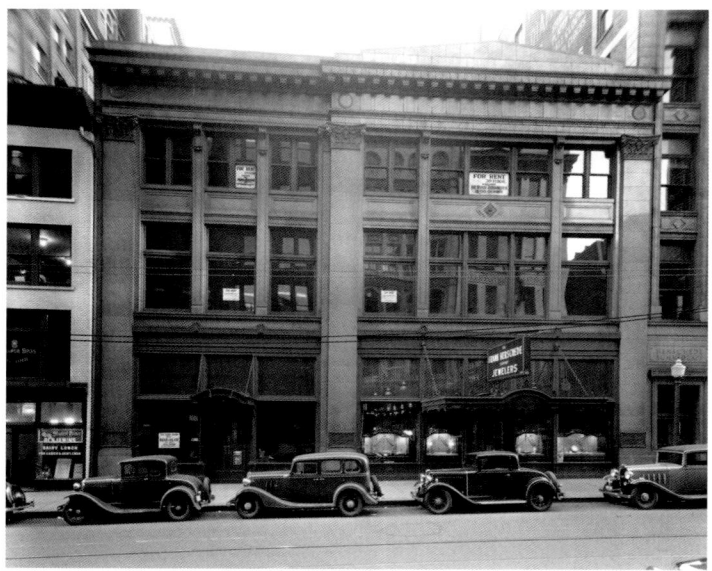

FIG. 49.4: The Frank Herschede Co., SC#156-187, box 2, Hannaford Collection, Cincinnati Historical Society

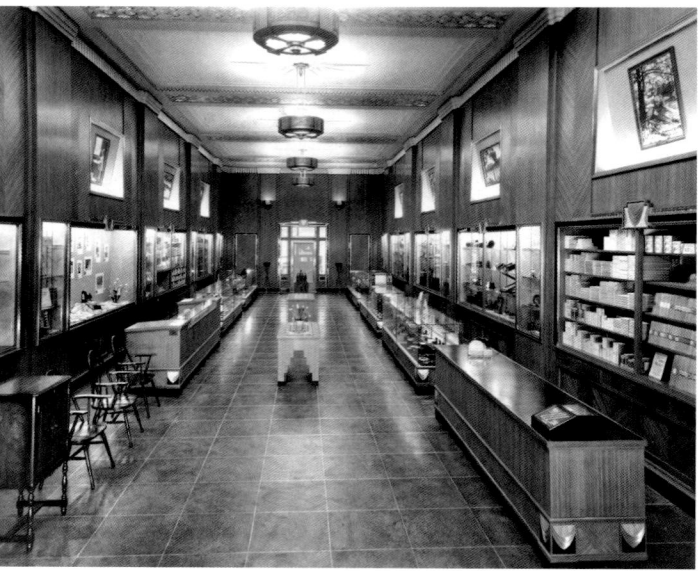

FIG. 49.5: The Frank Herschede Co., SC#156-187, box 2, Hannaford Collection, Cincinnati Historical Society

Other silverware—both flat and hollow wares—have been found with the incuse stamps of "FRANK HERSCHEDE, CIN.," "FRANK HERSCHEDE CO.," and "THE FRANK HERSCHEDE CO."[12]

In March 1906 the company announced that it had added a new factory that enabled it to design and manufacture all of its jewelry.[13] Prior to that, it had secured commissions to make various presentation medals and the "Bishop's Cross, one of the most magnificent order designs executed this season [1900]."[14] The installation of a new "silver plating outfit" was noted in 1908.[15]

Herschede maintained one of the most elegant and well-stocked luxury goods stores of the era, and, as such, several burglaries mark the firm's long history. The most notable incidents occurred in 1910 and 1930. On January 31, 1910, would-be thieves used nitroglycerine in an attempt to blow up the store's safe. While they did not escape with any merchandise, the blast did create over $2,000 worth of damage, including the destruction of several pieces of fine silver in the firm's window display.[16] In February 1930 robbers, believed to be Chicago gangsters, drilled through the 8-12-inch concrete walls and floors of several vaults with drills, acetylene torches and dynamite, and cut their way through the safe's 10-inch thick steel walls. They left with over $250,000 worth of jewelry.[17]

Over time, Herschede built up an extremely successful trade in hall clocks. In January 1903 The Herschede Hall Clock Company was incorporated with a capital stock of $150,000. The company leased a large building at Plum and Canal Streets, and employed over 100 hands for the manufacture of hall clocks.[18] The firm's display at the 1904 World's Fair in St. Louis consisted of hall clocks only.[19] In 1959, the clock company purchased the Rookwood Pottery Co. (1880–) and moved to Starksville, Mississippi, in 1960.[20]

In June 1905, with a capital of $250,000, Herschede incorporated his jewelry, silver, and fancy goods business as a stock company. The new concern was known as The Frank Herschede Co. Frank Herschede became president; J. Fred Kramer (former director of the silver department) became vice president; and Frank's son Edward became secretary and treasurer. Charles W. Lucius and **Charles L. Mudge** were on the board of directors.[21]

The Frank Herschede Co. relocated in November 1921 to 124 East Fourth Street, one block east of its previous location, in a building that it constructed and owned (fig. 49.4). Engraved invitations were sent to thousands of Cincinnatians. The new store was 185 feet deep and 40 feet wide at the front, and 60 feet wide in the center. The walls and ceilings were decorated in an Italian Renaissance style with Wedgwood medallions, and a marble stairway led to a mezzanine, used by staff. The store was built without support columns, allowing for an unobstructed view from the front to the back of the store, and the manner in which the space was lit made counter lights unnecessary, and obliterated any shadows. The fixtures, cases and furniture were of solid mahogany.[22]

Frank Herschede died in Rochester, Minnesota, on September 17, 1922, following surgery at the Mayo Clinic.[23] Herschede and his wife, German-born Lisetta "Sadie" Ratterman (1856-1950), had married in 1879.[24] They had ten children for whom records are known: Frank (1879–1880); Edward Frederick (1880–1951); Clara E. (b. 1882); Lawrence Bernard (1884–1966); Walter John (1885–1964); Alfred Theodore (1887–1948); Adele (b. 1889); Helen H. (1893–1984); Adelide E. (1894–1962); and Mildred M. (1899–1984).[25] Following Frank Herschede's death, his son Edward assumed the presidency of The Frank Herschede Co.[26] Charles W. Lucius became vice president, and Frank's son Lawrence B. Herschede became secretary and treasurer. In 1939, the store moved to 8 West Fourth Street.[27] Edward Herschede retired in 1946, and Lawrence Herschede took his place as president.[23] Frank's widow, Sadie, became vice president, and Mark F. Herschede (1917–1991), Lawrence's son, became secretary and treasurer.[29] In 1955, Lawrence became chairman of the board, and Mark became president.[30] By 1961, in addition to its downtown location, the firm had added locations in suburban Cincinnati, in Hyde Park, Kenwood Plaza, and Tri-County Shopping Center.[3-] The firm was known as Herschede Jewelers in 1965.[32] Mark

Herschede retired in 1987, and his wife Joan stepped in.[33] The downtown store closed in October 1995 due to declining sales, and the company went out of business when its Hyde Park store closed around 1996.[34]

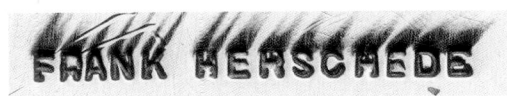

MARK 49.1

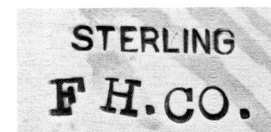

MARK 49.2

1. 1870 and 1900 Federal Censuses, Cincinnati, Hamilton, Ohio; "Jeweler Expires in Minnesota," *Cincinnati Enquirer*, September 19, 1922, 20.
2. Mary Herschede, death record, Cincinnati Health Department, University of Cincinnati Archives and Rare Books Library, http://hdl.handle.net/2374.UC/443185; John Herschede, death record, Cincinnati Health Department, http://hdl.handle.net/2374.UC/610578; 1870 Federal Census, Cincinnati, Hamilton, Ohio; Frank's younger brother Anthony is listed in Cincinnati city directories beginning in 1877. His occupation was initially given as watch maker. He worked for or with Frank from 1880–82. After that, he had his own store in the Emery Arcade and on Main Street from 1883–1918.
3. 1873 Cincinnati City Directory; Ohio, Vol. 11, p. 149, R.G. Dun & Co. Collection, Baker Library, Harvard Business School.
4. An engraved tablet on the side of the marble stairway of Herschede's location opened in December 1921 indicates that Herschede founded his business on June 15, 1877. "Well Known Jewelry Firm of Cincinnati, O., Complete Their New Store," *Jewelers' Circular and Horological Review* (December 28, 1921). The R.G. Dun & Co. records cite September. Ohio, Vol. 11, p. 149, R.G. Dun & Co. Collection.
5. Ohio, Vol. 11, p. 149, R.G. Dun & Co. Collection.
6. 1885 Cincinnati City Directory; "Cincinnati," *JCHR* (March 18, 1896); "Cincinnati," *JCHR* (May 13, 1896): 24.
7. "Cincinnati," *JCHR* (July 1, 1896): 26.
8. "Cincinnati," *JCHR* (February 17, 1897): 28; "Cincinnati," *JCHR* (April 21, 1897): 26; "Cincinnati," *JCHR* (April 6, 1898): 35; "Cincinnati," *JCHR* (June 20, 1900): 44; Frank Herschede, eBay listings and private collections, Cincinnati silver binders, Cincinnati Art Museum.
9. "The Handsomest Cigar Cabinet in the World," *JCHR* (October 17, 1900): 1.
10. "Jewelry Exhibits at Ohio Valley Exposition at Cincinnati," *JCHR* (September 28, 1910): 75; "Artistic Work of Silver and Goldsmiths to be Shown at Exposition," *Cincinnati Enquirer*, May 5, 1910, 5.
11. "Cincinnati," *JCHR* (July 29, 1903): 61; "Cincinnati," *JCHR* (May 1, 1907): 87; "Cincinnati," *JCHR* (June 19, 1907): 90; "Cincinnati," *JCHR* (February 2, 1910): 183. This article states that the trophies were furnished by "various silversmiths of New York"; "Cincinnati," *JCHR* (May 31, 1911): 99; "Cincinnati," *JCHR* (August 9, 1911): 111; "The Enquirer Handicap Trophy For 1919," *Cincinnati Enquirer*, June 13, 1919, 7; Frank Herschede, eBay listings and private collections, Cincinnati Art Museum.
12. Frank Herschede, eBay listings and private collection, Cincinnati Art Museum.
13. "Cincinnati," *JCHR* (March 21, 1906): 67; "Cincinnati," *JCHR* (April 18, 1906): 69.
14. "Cincinnati," *JCHR* (June 15, 1898): 20; "Cincinnati," *JCHR* (September 12, 1900): 51; This cross was commissioned for the consecration of Mark Henry Moeller as Catholic Bishop. "GRANDEUR: And Pomp Unsurpassed Mark Henry Moeller's Consecration as a Bishop," *Cincinnati Enquirer*, August 26, 1900, 16.
15. "Cincinnati," *JCHR* (December 2, 1908): 95; The firm's plating rooms were located above the showroom on the second floor. "Cincinnati," *JCHR* (December 18, 1912): 87.
16. "Unsolved, Is Explosion Mystery," *Cincinnati Enquirer*, February 2, 1910, 4. "Mysterious Explosion Does Great Damage to Store of Frank Herschede Co., Cincinnati, O." *JCHR* (February 9, 1910): 67.
17. Précis for the Frank Herschede Co. records, Cincinnati Historical Society, mss 987.
18. "Cincinnati," *JCHR* (January 7, 1903): 56; "The Organization of the Herschede Hall Clock Co. Celebrated by a Banquet," *JCHR* (January 14, 1903): 42; "Cincinnati," *JCHR* (January 14, 1903): 56; "The Herschede Hall Clock Co.'s Factory," *JCHR* (May 27, 1903): 90.
19. Advertisement (with image), *JCHR* (September 21, 1904): 41; "World's Fair Notes," *JCHR* (July 27, 1904): 31.
20. Robert H. Herschede, obituary, *Cincinnati Enquirer*, August 9, 2007, B4.
21. "Cincinnati," *JCHR* (June 7, 1905): 58; "Cincinnati," *JCHR* (June 21, 1905): 60; "Cincinnati," *JCHR* (June 28, 1905): 58.
22. "Well Known Jewelry Firm of Cincinnati, O. Complete Their New Store," *JCHR* (December 28, 1921).
23. "Jeweler Expires in Minnesota," September 19, 1922; Ancestry.com, *Minnesota, Death Index, 1908–2002* [online database], Provo, Utah: Ancestry.com Operations Inc., 2001.
24. 1900 Federal Census, Cincinnati, Hamilton, Ohio.
25. 1880, 1900, 1910, 1920 Federal Censuses, Cincinnati, Hamilton, Ohio; "Jeweler Expires in Minnesota," September 19, 1922; Burial records, Cincinnati Catholic Cemetery Society, http://www.cccsohio.org/search-burial-records.html.
26. 1925 Cincinnati City Directory.
27. 1940 Cincinnati City Directory.
28. 1947 Cincinnati City Directory.
29. Ibid.; Mark P. Herschede, burial record, Spring Grove Cemetery, Cincinnati, Ohio.
30. 1955 Cincinnati City Directory.
31. 1961 Cincinnati City Directory.
32. 1967 Cincinnati City Directory.
33. Précis for the Frank Herschede Co. records.
34. Ibid.

50. EDWARD H. HILL

1812–1878, w. 1840–1873

Edward H. Hill was born on December 3, 1812, in Alexandria, Virginia, and had arrived in Cincinnati by 1839, when he was employed as a watch maker at **John Owen**'s shop on Main Street, between Third and Fourth Streets.[1] A city directory was not published for 1841, and in the 1842 edition, Hill does not appear. However, credit reporters note that he took over the business of **Joseph G. Joseph**, the silversmith and spectacle and mathematical instrument maker, who worked on Main Street between Third and Fourth, in 1842.[2] Hill is listed as a watch maker in the 1843 and 1844 city directories working at 175 Main and boarding with J.W. Logan, whose partner in the tobacco business Logan & Hill was Samuel V. Hill, a possible relative of Edward H. Hill.[3]

By 1844, Edward H. Hill was married, and listing in the business section of the city directory under the classification of "Watchmakers and Silversmiths."[4] He was estimated to be worth $1,500, and his business was reportedly in "good standing, doing well, and getting along prudently."[5] By 1846, he was working at 155 Main Street.[6] He was able to purchase a house on Seventh Street between Mound and Cutter Streets for himself and his young family in 1847.[7] That same year, he advertised new watches and jewelry "just received from the Eastern cities by Express" as well as "silver and plated spoons" (fig. 50.1).[8] In 1848, he advertised in the business directory under the category of "Jewelry, Watches, Silver Ware Stores and Manufacturers," and he paid taxes on $2,500 of revenue.[9] By 1850, census records note that the value of his real estate was $4,500 and in February 1851 he was reported to maintain fair capital and business.[10] This favorable description of his business was repeated by credit reporters until 1856, when their assessment of his business further improved, and they noted that he was making money, owned valuable real estate, and was estimated to be worth $20,000.[11] Between 1856 and 1857, he moved to 103 Main, the former address of **James F. Rhodes**.[12] Hill's fortune soon turned; notice of his unpaid debts came in the spring of 1860, and he relocated to 14 West Fourth Street, near Main Street, "to command a better class of trade."[13] The following year, he was noted to have a "quiet business" and to have "paid all he owed."[14]

In 1862, Hill partnered with John Bexell (b. about 1827, w. 1858–1869), a Swede who had arrived in the United States in 1853 and had settled in Cincinnati by 1858 after working in Hamilton, Ohio.[15] Operating under the name of Bexell and Hill, the new partners practiced at Hill's previous location at 103 Main Street. But by 1863, the partnership had dissolved, and both men were

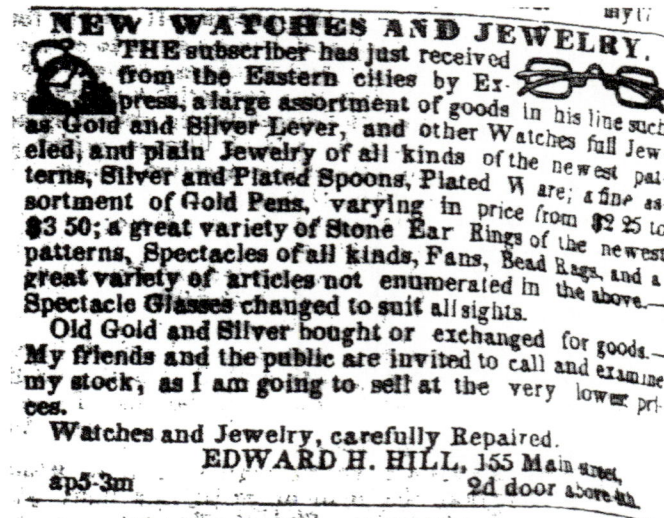

FIG. 50.1: Advertisement, *Cincinnati Daily Commercial*, June 29, 1847

working independently.[16] There is no known silver bearing the mark of this short-lived firm.

Hill continued in business at 103 Main. In 1870, census records report Hill as a watch maker with $8,000 of real estate and a personal estate valued at $3,000.[17] That same year, he reported in the Products of Industry Census as a jobber and "repairer of watches and &c." with $300 worth of capital invested. He had employed three hands (two males and one youth) and paid wages of $1,500 that year, utilizing hand power and $300 worth of springs and glasses to produce $3,000 worth of product.[18] He appears in city directories under the business heading of "Watches, Jewelry and Silver Ware" and "Watches, Clocks and Jewelry" through 1873.

Edward H. Hill died on October 20, 1878, in Hillsboro, Highland County, Ohio.[19] He and his wife Pauline G. Hill (b. about 1826, Pennsylvania) had eight children, all born in Ohio: Edward H. (1844–1850), who died of cholera; John J. (b. about 1847); Samuel V. (b. about 1849); Annie S. (b. about 1851); Edward H. (b. about 1853); William (b. about 1856); Leonard (b. about 1860); and Walter (b. about 1863).[20]

Teaspoons, tablespoons, and dessert spoons with tipped, exaggerated fiddle handles and pointed shoulders (fig. 50.2) have been found with mark 50.1. Two soup ladles, a mustard ladle, and a dessert spoon with pressed pattern (fig. 50.2) have been found with mark 50.2. The eagle is likely the manufacturing mark of **Edward Kinsey** or **Pulaski Scovil**.[21] A teaspoon in a derivation of the olive pattern has been found with an incuse, "E. H. HILL."[22] Hill probably did not manufacture any of the silver wares that he sold.

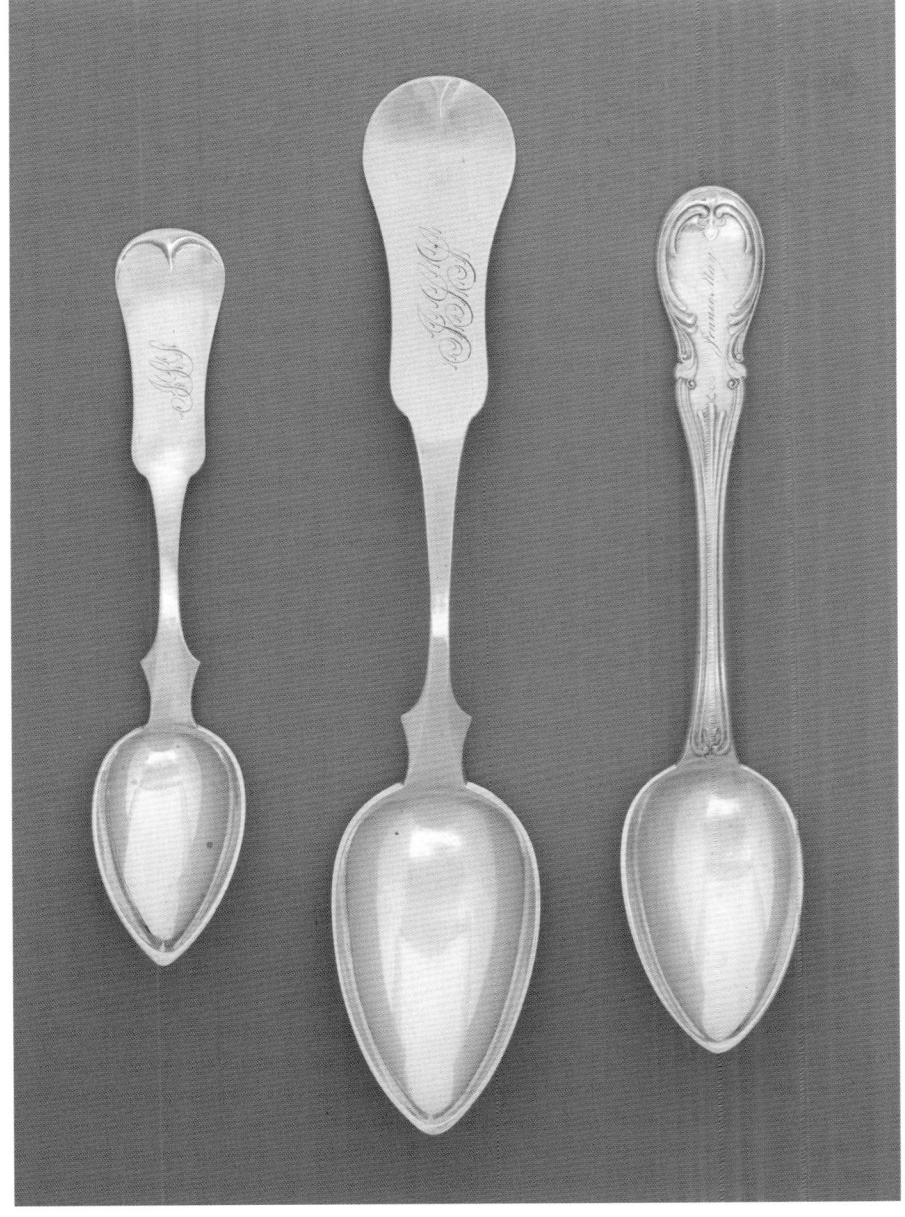

FIG. 50.2: Edward H. Hill, *Teaspoon*, 1840–1873, L. 6⅛ in. (15.5 cm), CAM, Given by Mimi Morgan in memory of her mother, Miriam Katherine Vandervort Morgan, 2013.2; Edward H. Hill, *Tablespoon*, 1840–1873, L. 8⅞ in. (22.5 cm), CAM, Given by Mimi Morgan in memory of her mother, Miriam Katherine Vandervort Morgan, 2013.1; Edward H. Hill, *Dessert Spoon*, 1840–1873, L. 7½ in. (19 cm), CAM, Given by Mimi Morgan in memory of her mother, Miriam Katherine Vandervort Morgan, 2013.3

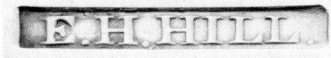

MARK 50.1

MARK 50.2

1. E.H. Hill, burial record, Spring Grove Cemetery, Cincinnati, Ohio; 1839/40 Cincinnati City Directory; 1850, 1860 Federal Censuses, Cincinnati, Hamilton, Ohio.
2. Ohio, Vol. 1, p. 90, R.G. Dun & Co. Collection, Baker Library, Harvard Business School.
3. 1843, 1844 Cincinnati City Directories; Samuel V. Hill appears in Cincinnati city directories as early as 1829. His occupation, early on, is given as carpenter. In the 1839/40 Cincinnati City Directory, his birthplace is given as DC which at that time included Alexandria, VA, Edward H. Hill's birthplace.
4. Marriage record, Hamilton County

Probate Records, vol. A12, page 102, http://www.probatect.org /CourtRecordsArchive /bukmarriages.aspx.
5. Ohio, Vol. 1, p. 90, R.G. Dun & Co. Collection.
6. 1846 Cincinnati City Directory.
7. Ohio, Vol. 1, p. 90, R.G. Dun & Co. Collection.
8. Advertisement, *Cincinnati Daily Commercial*, June 29, 1847.
9. 1848/49 Cincinnati Business Directory; Ohio, Vol. 1, p. 90, R.G. Dun & Co. Collection.
10. 1850 Federal Census, Cincinnati, Hamilton, Ohio; Ohio, Vol. 1, p. 90, R.G. Dun & Co. Collection.
11. Ohio, Vol. 1, p. 90, R.G. Dun & Co.

Collection.
12. 1856, 1857 Cincinnati City Directories.
13. Ohio, Vol. 1, p. 90, R.G. Dun & Co. Collection.
14. Ibid.
15. 1858 Cincinnati City Directory; Ancestry.com, *Boston Passenger and Crew List, 1820–1943* [online database], Provo, Utah: Ancestry.com Operations Inc., 2006; Ohio, Vol. 1, p. 90, R.G. Dun & Co. Collection.
16. 1863 Cincinnati City Directory.
17. 1870 Federal Census, Cincinnati, Hamilton, Ohio.
18. 1870 Federal Non-Population Census Schedules, Products of

Industry, Schedule 4, Hamilton County, Ohio.
19. E.H. Hill, burial record.
20. Ibid., 1850, 1860, 1870 Federal Censuses, Cincinnati, Hamilton, Ohio; Edward H. Hill (1844–1850), burial record, Spring Grove Cemetery, Cincinnati, Ohio.
21. John R. McGrew, *Manufacturers' Marks on American Coin Silver*, Hanover, PA: Argyros Publications, 2004, 99.
22. E.H. Hill, eBay listings and private collections, Cincinnati silver binders, Cincinnati Art Museum.

51. HENRY RALPH HOLMAN

1832–1913, w. 1855–1857

Henry R. Holman was born in Wilbraham, Massachusetts, on June 12, 1832, to John and Elizabeth Holman.[1] In 1850, at the age of 17, he was boarding and possibly apprenticing with watch maker Charles C. Coleman (b. about 1820) in Worcester, Massachusetts.[2] Holman had arrived in Cincinnati by 1855, and was listed as a watch maker at 182 Barr Street.[3] In 1856 and 1857, he was noted in city directories as a watch maker working at 103 Main Street, which was the address of **James F. Rhodes** in 1856, and of **Edward H. Hill** in 1857. He was not included in subsequent Cincinnati city directories, and by 1860, he had relocated to Kansas City, Missouri, where he continued to work as a watch maker and jeweler.[4] He married Carrie A. Churchill (1836–1905) and they had five children.[5] Three lived past infancy: C. Maud (b. about 1860), Charles Henderson (b. 1862), and Frederick R. (b. 1863).[6] By 1880, the family had moved to Denver, Colorado, where Holman and his son Charles Henderson worked as jewelers.[7] In 1895, Henry, Carrie and Frederick were in Sioux City, Iowa, where Henry continued to work as a jeweler until his death on August 5, 1913.[8]

The marks of Henry R. Holman have been documented on spoons with tipped, exaggerated fiddle handles and pointed shoulders.[9] The form of the spoons is typical of Cincinnati, but they cannot be documented with certainty to his time in the city. The significance of the hot air balloon mark is unknown.[10] It is probably a yet-to-be-identified manufacturer's mark. Tablespoons in the Missouri Historical Society's collection with tipped, slightly exaggerated fiddle handles and rounded shoulders bear the incuse stamps: "H.R. HOLMAN & CO." and "KANSAS CITY."[11]

H.R.HOLMAN.COIN

MARK 51.1

H.R.HOLMAN.

MARK 51.2

1. Ancestry.com, *Massachusetts, Town Records, 1620–1988* [online database], Provo, Utah: Ancestry.com Operations Inc., 2011.
2. 1850 Federal Census, Worcester Ward 7, Worcester, Massachusetts.
3. 1855 Cincinnati City Directory
4. 1860 and 1870 Federal Censuses, Kansas City, Jackson, Missouri.
5. The Holmans were practicing Episcopalians. Kansas City Chapter of the Daughters of the American Revolution (ed.), *Vital Historical Records of Jackson County, Missouri 1826–1876*, Kansas City, MO: Lowell Press, 1933, 152, 302; Norman Mack, *Missouri's Silver Age: Silversmiths of the 1800s*, Carbondale, IL: Southern Illinois University Press, 2005, 32; Ancestry.com, *Iowa State Census Collection, 1836–1925* [online database], Provo, Utah: Ancestry.com Operations Inc., 2007; "Mrs. H. R. Holman," grave record, *Work Projects Administration, 1930s Graves Registration Survey*, http://iowawpagraves.org /view.php?id=1032866.
6. 1870 Federal Census, Kansas City, Jackson, Missouri; 1880 Federal Census, Denver, Arapahoe, Colorado; 1900 Federal Census, Sioux City, Woodbury, Iowa; Another son, Frederick Augustus Holman, died at the age of two years and eleven days; *Vital Historical Records*, Kansas City, 152, 202; Mack, *Missouri's Silver Age*, 82; Charles Henderson Holman eventually became a doctor, practicing in New York City; *Universities and Their Sons: New York University, Its History, Influence, Equipment and Characteristics*, Boston: R. Herndon Company, 1903, 311.
7. 1880 Federal Census, Denver, Arapahoe, Colorado.
8. Ancestry.com, *Iowa State Census Collection, 1836–1925* [online database], Provo, Utah: Ancestry.com Operations Inc., 2007; 1900 Federal Census, Sioux City, Woodbury, Iowa; "Henry R. Holman," grave record, *Work Projects Administration, 1930s Graves Registration Survey*, http://iowaw-pagraves.org/view.php?id=1032866. In the transcription of the survey, Henry's death and birth dates are transposed, and his death year is incorrectly reported as 1932.
9. Henry R. Holman, eBay listings and private collections, Cincinnati silver binders, Cincinnati Art Museum.
10. There is no known connection between Holman and **Richard Clayton**, Cincinnati's hot-air balloonist and watch maker.
11. Mack, *Missouri's Silver Age*, 82.

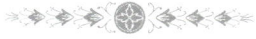

52. HENRY VICTOR HORTON

1804–1871, w. 1836–1855

Henry Victor Horton was born on August 22, 1804, in Union Village, Washington County, New York, the son of Jonathan K. Horton (1777–1848) and Elizabeth Tice (about 1781–1858).[1] Henry V. Horton's father was a descendant of Barnabus Horton (b. 1591, Morley, Leicestershire, England, d. 1686, Southampton, Long Island) and a member of the New York State Assembly. His mother, of Dutch descent, was the daughter of Jan Johanes Tice and Catrina Van Tassel.[2] Henry V. Horton was christened in the

Reformed Dutch Church, Greenwich, Washington County, New York in March 1814.[3] Nothing is known about his training.

Horton married Sophia Matilda Dougherty (b. 1812, Manilus, New York, d. 1891, Cincinnati) on December 25, 1829, and had arrived in Cincinnati by 1836, when he advertised in the city's directory as a watch maker on Fifth Street, between Vine and Race.[4] City directories were not published in 1837 or 1838, but in November of 1839 Horton ran an advertisement announcing the commencement of his business in "WATCHES, JEWELRY and SILVER WARE . . . in the store lately occupied by **T. W. McMurphey**, on the west side of Main, between Fourth and Fifth streets, where he will keep a general assortment of Goods in his line. Particular care and attention will be given to the repairing of all the different kinds of Watches, Clocks, Time-Pieces, &c."[5] The 1839/40 City Directory contains a large advertisement with a pocket watch illustration, reading, "H. V. HORTON, WATCH MAKER, SILVERSMITH, and JEWELLER, 189, Main street, between Fourth and Fifth, CINCINNATI, Brittannia-ware [sic] Fancy Goods, Clocks, Watches, Jewelry, &c."[6] In 1842, 1843, and 1844, Horton is listed as a watch maker in city directories. The address of his employ is not given and it is likely that he had closed his Main Street shop and was, during this period, working for someone else. In August 1844 he advertised that he had "resumed the Clock and Watch repairing business and can hereafter be found on the West side of Main, 3 doors below Fourth."[7] The advertisement continues, "He flatters himself that 20 years experience in his business, nearly half of which has been spent in this city, warrants him in looking for a share of public patronage," thus suggesting that his career began around 1824.

Between September 1845 and February 1846, Horton was a junior partner in the fancy goods store C. & W.H. Allen (see **William Allen**).[8] Credit reporters assessed Horton, at this time, as "poor, but honest and attentive to business" and recommended him credit only for small sums.[9] In the 1846 Cincinnati City Directory he was listed as a watch maker on the west side of Plum, above Ninth Street. By 1848, he had relocated to Louisville, Kentucky, where he worked as a jeweler at Fifth and Walnut Streets for a short while.[10] In 1849, he reappears in Cincinnati directories as a manufacturer of emblems for the Order of the Sons of Temperance, working at 24 West Fourth Street and living on the west side of Elm between Ninth and William Streets. In May 1845 Horton had founded the Ohio division of the Order, and it was his dedication to the cause of "reclaiming the fallen," not his dealings in watches, silver, and jewelry, for which he is most remembered.[11]

Between 1850 and 1853, Horton is absent from published Cincinnati directories, and does not reappear until 1855, when he is listed as a watch maker at 147 Bayler. It is possible that he was in New York during this time, as his daughter, Maria J. (also known as Ida), was reportedly born in Union Village, New York, on August 3, 1850. Horton's Cincinnati directory listing in 1855 marks the last time that his occupation is given as watch maker. In 1856, his occupation is not listed in the directory, yet we know that he was appointed an inspector by the Ohio Senate.[12] Subsequent directories indicate that he was working as a canal inspector (1857), canal boat inspector (1858), insurance agent and agent for Lillie's Burglar and Fireproof Safe and Bank Locks (1859), a canal collector (1860), a real estate agent (1862), employee of commercial brokers S.F. Cary & Co. (1863, 1864), and as Grand Scribe of the Sons of Temperance (1869, 1870). He reported as a publisher (probably for the Sons of Temperance) in the 1870 Census.[13]

In 1860, Horton was living in Millcreek Township, Hamilton County, with real estate valued at $2,000 and a personal estate valued at $100.[14] Ten years later, he was living in Miami Township, Hamilton County, with real estate valued at $5,000 and a personal estate valued at $1,000.[15] He died on January 3, 1871, after a long illness and is buried with his wife at Spring Grove Cemetery.[16] He was a member of the Fifth Presbyterian Church in Cincinnati, and he and his wife had eight children: Lewis V. (b. 1834), Elizabeth T. (b. 1836), Alonzo C. (b. 1838), Angeline G. (b. 1841), Harry K. (b. 1842), Thomas C. (b. 1848), Maria J. (Ida) (b. 1850), and Samuel C. (b. 1855). All but Maria were born in Ohio.[17]

Henry V. Horton used two incuse stamps, "H. V. HORTON" and "HORTON." These have been observed on fiddle-handled spoons with rounded shoulders. One of these spoons also bears a set of three pseudo hallmarks (a star, an acorn, and a capital D—all in square cartouches).[18] These manufacturer marks likely belong to a maker from New York (possibly Troy), who has yet to be identified.[19] All information suggests that Horton's focus was watch making and repair, and that he likely purchased and retailed the silver, jewelry, and other goods that he advertised.

1. Unless otherwise cited, all biographical information comes from Charles Robson, *Biographical Encyclopedia of Ohio of the Nineteenth Century*, Cincinnati: Galaxy Publishing Co., 1876, 436-438; *Tombstone Inscriptions in Greenwich, NY Cemetery*, http://www.rootsweb.ancestry.com/~nywashin/TombH.htm.

2. *Van Tassel & Allied Lines Generation Four*, http://www.vantassell.net/genealogy/gen4.htm.

3. "New York Births and Christenings, 1640-1962," *FamilySearch* https://familysearch.org/pal:/MM9.1.1/FDPX-HVM.

4. The biographical entry on Henry's son, Alonzo C. Horton, included in S.B. Nelson and J.M Runk, *History of Cincinnati and Hamilton County, Ohio: Their Past and Present*, Cincinnati: S.B. Nelson & Co., 1894, 1:874, indicates that Henry V. Horton arrived in Cincinnati in 1830. He does not appear in the 1831 Cincinnati City

Directory. The entry on Henry Victor Horton in the *Biographical Encyclopedia* indicates that Horton did not arrive in Cincinnati until November 1834. If this is true, Horton arrived in this city too late to be included in the 1834 Cincinnati City Directory. There was no edition of the city directory published in 1835.

5. Advertisement, *Cincinnati Daily Gazette*, November 12, 1839, reproduced in Beckman, 69.

6. Advertisement, 1839/40 Cincinnati City Directory, 518, reproduced in Beckman, 69.

7. In the 1842 Cincinnati City Directory, his address is given as Vine between Ninth and Court, and in 1843 and 1844, his address is given as Court between Elm and Plum; Advertisement, *Cincinnati Daily Gazette*, August 30, 1844, reproduced in Beckman, 69.

8. Ohio, Vol. 1, p. 56, R.G. Dun & Co. Collection, Baker Library, Harvard Business School.

9. Ibid.

10. There were no Cincinnati city directories published in 1847 or 1848; Beckman, 70.

11. Robson, *Biographical Encyclopedia*, 437.

12. "Ohio Legislature," *Cleveland Plain Dealer*, January 30, 1856, 2.

13. 1857–1870 Cincinnati City Directories; 1870 Federal Census, Miami, Hamilton, Ohio.

14. 1860 Federal Census, Millcreek, Hamilton, Ohio.

15. 1870 Federal Census, Miami, Hamilton, Ohio.

16. Obituary, *Cincinnati Enquirer*, January 4, 1871, 4; Burial records, Spring Grove Cemetery, Cincinnati, Ohio.

17. Robson, *Biographical Encyclopedia*, 436; 1860 and 1870 Federal Censuses.

18. Henry V. Horton, eBay listings and private collections, Cincinnati silver binders, Cincinnati Art Museum.

19. John R. McGrew, *Manufacturers' Marks on American Coin Silver*, Hanover, PA: Argyros Publications, 2004, 21.

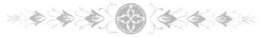

53. HUGHES & DORLAND

1857–1860

Edward J. Hughes (1824–1900) and **Garret T. Dorland** first worked together in the shop of **Richard Clayton**.[1] Hughes left Clayton in 1855, when Clayton's promises of partnership did not come to fruition, and established the firm of Hughes & O'Hara with his nephew, William O'Hara.[2] Dorland worked for the firm, and when O'Hara left in September 1857, he became partner. The firm of Hughes & Dorland conducted business at 19 Main Street in the Madison House Building and advertised as importers of watches and jewelry.[3] They were largely wholesalers. An 1858 advertisement solicited "Peddlers, Country Merchants and all other Dealers in Watches and Jewelry" to call on them for "the largest and cheapest assortment of watches and jewelry ever brought to Cincinnati," and continues, "These goods were bought for cash, and have just arrived by express."[4]

On February 22, 1859, the firm opened a retail location at 151 Walnut Street, three doors below Fourth Street.[5] To mark the occasion "they entertained their friends and the public in the most hospitable and generous style," and it was remarked that "if their mercantile popularity can be in any way measured by their personal, as shown yesterday, their fortune may be considered already made." The goods, "large, varied and entirely new," were reportedly selected from the best manufacturers in the United States and Europe, and their window displayed a Parisian clock, "representing birds flitting about in the foliage of a house, which appear so natural that one expects every moment to hear them sing." Requiring winding but once a year, it was said to be exact to

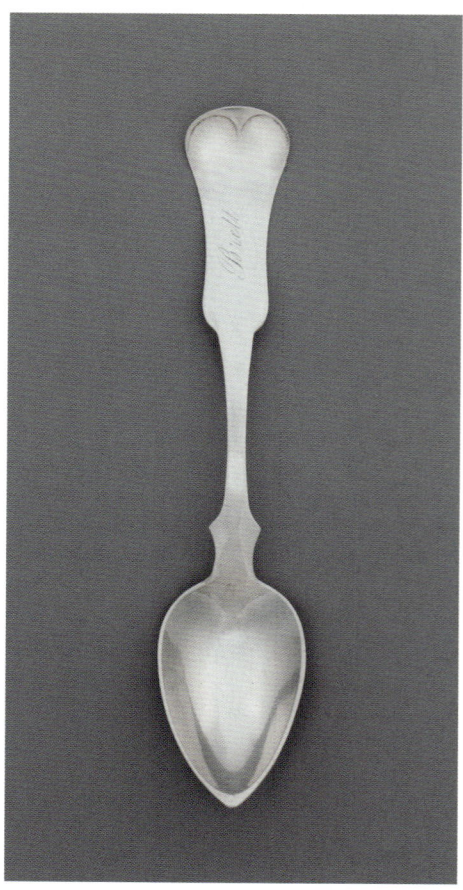

FIG. 53.1: Hughes & Dorland, *Teaspoon*, 1857–1860, L. 6¼ in. (15.9 cm), CAM, Museum Purchase: John S. Conner Fund, 2012.53

the smallest fraction of a second.[6] But the firm's mercantile popularity and acumen did not prove strong. By October, they were in trouble with creditors, and a year later, in October 1860, they dissolved. Each partner assumed his responsibility for the firm's debts and their stock was divided equally. Much of it, reportedly, was purchased by **Adolph Witt**, who had taken over Hughes & Dorland's old stand at 19 Main Street. Witt had worked with Hughes and Dorland as a watch maker since their days with Richard Clayton, and had continued working with them through the tenures of Hughes & O'Hara and Hughes & Dorland.[7]

The mark of Hughes & Dorland (mark 53.1) has been documented on spoons with tipped, exaggerated fiddle handles and pointed shoulders (fig. 53.1).[8] These were not made by the firm, but, based on their form, purchased from a local manufacturer.

![Mark 53.1 — HUGHES & DORLAND]

MARK 53.1

1. Hughes was born in Ireland and worked in St. Louis as a dry goods merchant before arriving in Cincinnati. The 1870 Federal Census documents him and his family in Rockville, Indiana, where he was working as a retailer of men's dry goods. In 1880, he was living in Parsons, Kansas, and working as a fancy goods dealer. Ohio, Vol. 2, p. 67, R.G. Dun & Co. Collection, Baker Library, Harvard Business School; Burial marker, Middletown Historical Pioneer Cemetery, Middletown, Butler County, Ohio, *Find A Grave*, www.findagrave.com; 1860 Federal Census, Cincinnati, Hamilton, Ohio; 1870 Federal Census, Rockville, Parke, Indiana; 1880 Federal Census, Parson, Labette, Kansas.
2. Ohio, Vol. 2, p. 31, R.G. Dun & Co. Collection.
3. 1855–1857 Cincinnati City Directories; Notice of dissolution, *Cincinnati Enquirer*, September 3, 1857, 2; Advertisement, *Cincinnati Enquirer*, February 3, 1858, 3.
4. Advertisement, *Cincinnati Enquirer*, April 20, 1858, 2.
5. Advertisement, *Cincinnati Enquirer*, February 23, 1859, 2; Their 1860 City Directory listing indicates that they maintained their wholesale location on Main (Main and Pearl), and a retail store on Walnut.
6. "New Jewelry Store–Opening of Hughes & Dorland's Establishment," *Cincinnati Enquirer*, February 23, 1859, 2.
7. Ohio, Vol. 2, p. 67, R.G. Dun & Co. Collection; 1853–1860 Cincinnati City Directories.
8. Hughes & Dorland, eBay listings and private collections, Cincinnati silver binders, Cincinnati Art Museum.

54. HUNTINGTON & LABOYTEAUX

1850–1856

The firm Huntington & LaBoyteaux was established in early 1850 at 5 West Fourth Street by **William Coit Huntington**, who had been a silversmith, watch maker and jeweler in Cincinnati since 1846, and **Isaac N. LaBoyteaux**, whose training in the trade is unknown.[1] From 1851 through 1853, R.G. Dun & Co. credit reports for the firm were very positive, indicating that business was increasing, the firm's credit was good, and they were "steadily making money."[2] In 1853, they built a large, new shop at 119 Main Street, between Third and Fourth Streets, where they advertised as "Importers of WATCHES and dealers in JEWELRY, SILVER WARE, GOLD PENS, AND FANCY ARTICLES."[3] The firm continued to prosper; the 1855 R.G. Dun & Co. reports indicate that the firm was "well-established," with good credit and good capital.[4] An 1855 advertisement for their wholesale business included notice that they were also manufacturing and selling "a full assortment of Silver, German Silver and Wood Counter Show Cases, suitable for Jewellers [sic], Stationers, Druggists, Fancy goods dealers, etc." from ware rooms in the basement of the shop at 119 Main.[5] When Huntington's brothers Albert W. and John C. joined the firm in February 1856, the name was changed to **Huntington Brothers & Co.** With the publication of the 1857 Cincinnati City Directory, Isaac LaBoyteaux was no longer listed as an associate of the firm.

Spoons with tipped, exaggerated fiddle handles have been found with mark 54.1.[6]

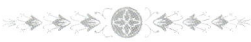

MARK 54.1

1. Ohio, Vol. 1, p. 170, R.G. Dun & Co. Collection, Baker Library, Harvard Business School; 1850/51 Cincinnati City Directory.
2. Ohio, Vol. 1, p. 170, R.G. Dun & Co. Collection.
3. Ibid.; *W.W. Reilly & Co.'s Ohio State Business Directory for 1853–54*, Cincinnati: Morgan & Overend, 1853, 46.
4. Ohio, Vol. 1, p. 170, R.G. Dun & Co. Collection.
5. 1855 Cincinnati City Directory, 144.
6. Huntington & LaBoyteaux, eBay listings and private collections, Cincinnati silver binders, Cincinnati Art Museum.

55. HUNTINGTON BROTHERS & CO.

1856–1868

The six youngest sons of Erastus Huntington (1769–1846)—Albert Williams (1816–1879), Henry Dwight (1817–1884), John Caldwell (1819–1887), William Coit (1821–1904), Frederick Gilbert (1826–1905), and Horace (b. 1828)—moved from Norwich, Connecticut, to Cincinnati between 1844 and 1849.[1] With the exception of **William Coit Huntington**, a silversmith and watch maker, the brothers were proprietors of successful wholesale and retail firms dealing in crockery, china, glassware, and fancy and house furnishing goods.

Huntington Brothers & Co. was formed in February 1856 when the firm John C. Huntington & Co. (John and Albert, proprietors) joined William at his large and "fine" store at 119 Main.[2] The new firm combined the china, glass, and Queensware offerings of John C. Huntington & Co. with the jewelry, silver, and fancy goods trade of **Huntington & LaBoyteaux**.[3] The firm's vast offerings included silver wares, of which they were undoubtedly retailers, not manufacturers. They exhibited a "Large case of (plated) Silver Ware" at the 1858 Ohio Mechanics' Institute Fair which the Committee on Awards judged as "Good; but too late for premium."[4] Extant coin silver flatware, including tablespoons, a ladle, and a butter knife with tipped, exaggerated fiddle handles and pointed shoulders bear mark 55.1.[5] This mark has been attributed to the silversmiths William and John Huntington who "In spite of the busy schedule in their real estate operations could have collaborated in a silversmith shop while they were both in Marion, Alabama" between 1839 and 1842.[6] However, the form, typically associated with Cincinnati, and the documented existence of a firm bearing a name identical to the mark indicate that the mark can reliably be attributed to the Cincinnati firm. An incuse mark, "HUNTINGTON BROS & CO" [no punctuation], has been documented on a die-stamped dessert spoon in Gorham Mfg. Co.'s "Josephine" (1855) pattern.[7]

In 1864, John withdrew from Huntington Brothers, but continued a china, glass, Queensware, and house furnishings business at the same address under the name of John C. Huntington & Co. with Orceneth Fisher Tice (**Tice & Huntington**).[8] Charles L. F. Huntington (1841–1926), a nephew who had started working at Huntington Brothers in 1863, was associated with the new firm, while Albert and William continued the wholesale business as Huntington Brothers & Co. through 1868.[9] By 1870, Albert, a wealthy "retired merchant," had returned to Norwich.[10]

HUNTINGTON BROS & CO

MARK 55.1

1. *The Huntington Family in America, 1633 to 1915*, Hartford, CT: Huntington Family Association, 1915, 436; Burial records, Spring Grove Cemetery, Cincinnati, Ohio; 1844–1849/50 Cincinnati City Directories.
2. Ohio, Vol. 1, p. 170, R.G. Dun & Co. Collection, Baker Library, Harvard Business School; 1857–1868 Cincinnati City Directories.
3. 1857–1864 Cincinnati City Directories.
4. *Report of the Sixteenth Exhibition of the Ohio Mechanics' Institute*, Cincinnati: Ohio Mechanics' Institute, 1858, 58.
5. William Johnston Hogan, *Huntington Silversmiths 1763–1885*, Durham, NC: Sir Walter Press, 1977, 54–55; Huntington Brothers & Co., eBay

listings and private collections, Cincinnati silver binders, Cincinnati Art Museum.
6. Hogan, *Huntington Silversmiths*, 54–55.
7. Huntington Brothers & Co., eBay listings and private collections, Cincinnati Art Museum; Noel D. Turner, *American Silver Flatware 1837–1910*, San Diego, CA: A.S. Barnes & Co., 1972, 99, 372.
8. 1865 Cincinnati City Directory.
9. Charles L.F. was the son of Joseph Hyde Huntington (1811–1865), an older brother who remained in Norwich, CT; 1864–1868 Cincinnati City Directories.
10. 1870 Federal Census, Norwich, New London, Connecticut.

56. WILLIAM COIT HUNTINGTON

1821–1904, w. 1846–about 1868[1]

William, the son of Sarah Williams and Erastus Huntington, was born in Norwich, Connecticut in 1821.[2] Although no record of his training has been found, he probably apprenticed with the silversmith, watch maker and jeweler Edward Coit, who worked in Norwich from 1825 to 1860.[3] In 1846, William followed his brothers Henry D. and John C. to Cincinnati, setting up shop at 123 Main Street between Third and Fourth Streets as a watch maker, silversmith, and jeweler.[4] Over the next four years, he published numerous advertisements in local newspapers. One of the earliest and most frequently published advertisements stated that he was a "MANUFACTURER OF JEWELRY AND SILVER WARE and dealer in Clocks, Watches, Musical Instruments, Fancy Goods, &c."[5] Another, headed "SILVER WARE," noted that he had on hand and was manufacturing to order silverware of all descriptions, and also noted, "1000 grams of Old Silver wanted in exchange for goods in any line."[6] Other advertisements featured "WATCHES, JEWELRY, &C," and announced that Huntington had "just received from the East, a fresh supply of Goods in his line," followed by a long list of goods including pens, silk purses, music boxes, card cases, and even violin and guitar strings.[7]

Extant coin silver flatware, including teaspoons and a mustard ladle with tipped, exaggerated fiddle handles and pointed shoulders, bear mark 56.1. The form, typical of flatware associated with Cincinnati in the mid-19th century, and the shared similarity of the style of letters used in this mark and the **Huntington & LaBoyteaux** mark, support the attribution of the mark to William C. Huntington. Although the mark has also been attributed to Richard Huntington, it is more likely that he used the mark "Huntington" with italicized letters in an irregular rectangular cartouche.[8] The marks "W.H." in a rectangular cartouche and "W. HUNTINGTON" in a serrated rectangular cartouche can be firmly attributed to the silversmith William Huntington who worked in North Carolina in the 1820s.[9]

In 1850, Cincinnati's William Huntington joined forces first with **Isaac N. LaBoyteaux** to form **Huntington & LaBoyteaux**, and between 1856 and 1868 he and his brothers operated as **Huntington Brothers & Co.** Thereafter, he pursued a variety of business interests, although he returned to the fancy goods trade briefly between 1873 and 1876 in the firm W. C. Huntington & Co. with his youngest brother, Horace (b. 1828). The firm specialized in the import and sale of china, glass, Queensware, lamps, and home furnishings.[10] William's major efforts after 1868 were directed at various real estate ventures including the subdivision and development of a tract of land in Mount Auburn, which was at that time outside but near the city limits, and development in the village of College Hill. Huntington had moved to that area in 1867 to an "elegant homestead and farm" not far from the residence of his former partner, Isaac LaBoyteaux.[11] Described as a "site of unusual beauty" on the edge of the hill looking over the valley, the farm comprised 60 acres.[12] By 1900, biographical references to William C. Huntington noted only "real estate" as his occupation.[13] He died in Asheville, North Carolina, on April 10, 1904, and was buried in Cincinnati's Spring Grove Cemetery.[14]

William married Mary Elizabeth Johnston (b. about 1829–1857) on September 2, 1851.[15] Children born to them were Samuel Johnston (1853–1891), Sarah Williams (1854–1942), and Mary Elizabeth (1857–1860).[16] In 1862, he married Mary Henderson Lindsly (1827–1863) in Greenwich, Connecticut. He married Sarah Louise Monroe (b. 1842) in Medway, Massachusetts, in 1874.[17] They were the parents of two sons, LeBaron Monroe (1875–after 1940) and Albert Tracy (b. 1878.)[18]

HUNTINGTON

MARK 56.1

1. *The Huntington Family in America, 1633 to 1915*, Hartford, CT: Huntington Family Association, 1915, 436; Wm. C. Huntington, burial record, Spring Grove Cemetery, Cincinnati, Ohio.
2. Wm. C. Huntington, burial record.
3. Wm. Erik Voss, "Edward Coit," *American Silversmiths*, http://freepages.genealogy.rootsweb.ancestry.com/~silversmiths/makers/silversmiths/tageightnames2.htm. The Huntington family includes many Coits but a relationship between Edward Coit and William's family was not elucidated.
4. Advertisement, *Cincinnati Enquirer*, September 23, 1846, 1; 1846 Cincinnati City Directory.
5. Advertisement, *Cincinnati Enquirer*, September 23, 1846, 1. This advertisement was repeated until at least January 16, 1850, 1.
6. Advertisement, *Cincinnati Enquirer*, November 19, 1846, 3:3.
7. Advertisement, *Cincinnati Daily Commercial*, June 29, 1847. Between September 1846 and January 1850, Huntington published more than 90 advertisements in the *Cincinnati Enquirer*, most of which were duplicates of earlier advertisements. Some unique examples include those on October 27, 1846, 3:4; November 11, 1846, 3:3; August 30, 1847, 3:2; and September 14, 1848, 4:1.
8. The silversmith Richard Huntington (1786–1855), who was also born in Norwich, CT, worked in Utica, NY 1823–55. Wm. Erik Voss, "Richard Huntington," *American Silversmiths*, http://freepages.genealogy.rootsweb.ancestry.com/~silversmiths/makers/silversmiths/96753.htm. Both marks are attributed to the Utica silversmith in Stephen G.C. Ensko, *American Silversmiths and their Marks*, New York: Dover Publications, 1983, 187.
9. William Johnston Hogan, *Huntington Silversmiths 1763–1885*, Durham, NC: Sir Walter Press, 1977, 42–48.

10. 1873–1876 Cincinnati City Directories; Horace took over the firm in 1877, and by 1878, had expanded it to a second location in the Emery Arcade. He was the first in Cincinnati to sell pottery made by the pioneering Cincinnati ceramist, Louise McLaughlin. See Anita J. Ellis, *The Ceramic Career of M. Louise McLaughlin*, Athens, OH: Ohio University Press, 2003, 64.

11. Lewis M. Hosea, *Cincinnati Superior Court Decisions*, "Albert H. Chatfield v. The City of Cincinnati," Cincinnati: The W.H. Anderson Co, Law Publishers, 1907, 48–59; Robert D. Handley & William Disney, *Reprint of Ohio Cases Published in America Law Record 1872–1887*, "Edward Sargent, Executor, etc. v. James W. Sibley" [Hamilton District Court, 1884], Norwalk, OH: The Laning Printing Co, 1897, 13:33–38; D.J. Kenny, *Illustrated Cincinnati: A Pictorial Handbook*, Cincinnati: G.E. Stevens, 1875, 329; William also served as President of the Cincinnati Safety Lamp Co. from 1878–1880, and he was proprietor of the Cincinnati Glue and Paste Co. between 1887 and 1890; 1878–1900 Cincinnati City Directories.

12. Sidney D. Maxwell, *Suburbs of Cincinnati: Sketches*, Cincinnati: G.E. Stevens & Co, 1870, 62; Kenny, *Illustrated Cincinnati*, 327.

13. *The Huntington Family in America*, 443; *New England Society of Cincinnati Yearbook: Officers and Members*, Cincinnati: the society, 1902, 31.

14. Wm. C. Huntington, burial record.

15. *The Huntington Family in America*, 442.

16. Ibid.; 1860 Federal Census, Cincinnati Ward 14, Hamilton, Ohio; 1870 Federal Census, Mill Creek, Hamilton, Ohio; 1880 Federal Census, College Hill, Hamilton, Ohio; Burial records, Spring Grove Cemetery, Cincinnati, Ohio.

17. Ancestry.com, *Massachusetts, Town and Vital Records, 1620–1988* [online database], Provo, Utah: Ancestry.com Operations Inc., 2011.

18. *The Huntington Family in America* 442; Burial records, Spring Grove Cemetery; 1880 Federal Census, College Hill, Hamilton, Ohio.

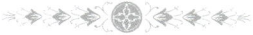

57. E.E. ISBELL & CO.

1875–1895

In January 1875 **William Wilson McGrew**'s business was declared insolvent. When his assets were sold, his former employee Everett E. Isbell (1838–1917) and Isbell's partner Thomas Gaff (1808–1884) purchased the balance of his stock for $10,000, and established their concern at McGrew's former shop at 58 West Fourth Street, on the north side of the street, between Walnut and Vine Streets (fig. 57.1).[1]

Everett E. Isbell was born in New York to Harriet and Charles B. Isbell.[2] He was a Civil War veteran and first appeared in Cincinnati city directories in 1861 as a watch maker, boarding on Elm Street.[3] During his early years in the city, he worked for jeweler Adolphe Lohde (active 1859–1864) in 1863, and for the jewelry firm Jandorf & Nordlinger (active 1864–1865) in 1864. Between 1868 and 1875, he was employed by McGrew as a clerk and a watch maker.[4] Isbell's partner Thomas Gaff was a wealthy, Scottish-born distiller from Aurora, Indiana.[5]

In April 1875 E.E. Isbell & Co. advertised that they would offer McGrew's former stock "far below their original cost, preparatory to restocking with all the new and elegant goods in our line," and noted, "the present stock consists mainly of watches, choice articles of jewelry, solid silver and plated ware, including Gorham and Sheffield manufacture."[6] By 1888, their business was flourishing. A correspondent reporting for *The Jewelers' Circular and Horological Review* described E.E. Isbell & Co. as the second largest retail jewelry store in Cincinnati. He reported: "They have a handsome store well stocked with rich, elegant goods and Mr. Isbell is called the art

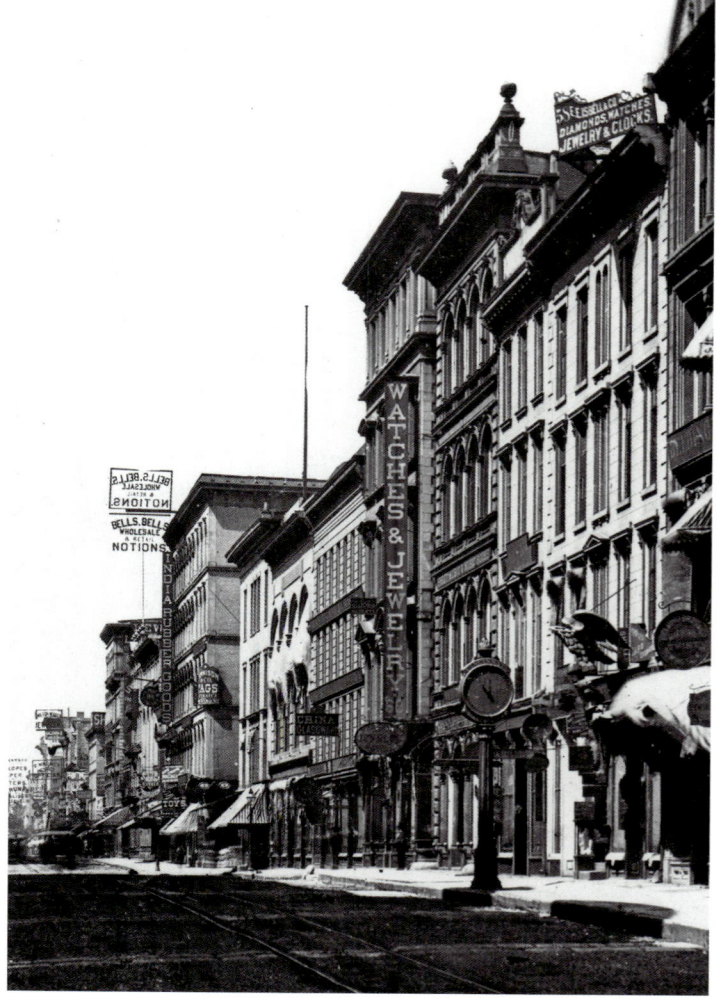

FIG. 57.1: *Fourth Street, looking west from Walnut, 1878*, Cincinnati History Slide Collection, The Public Library of Cincinnati and Hamilton County

jeweler of Cincinnati. They have not as large a store or stock as some others, but none will deny they have a beautiful stock of well selected novelties, second to none in the city. Their stock comprises fancy gems, jewelry, cut-glass, silver, lamps, leather goods, and they are the Cincinnati agents for the sale of [wares by] the Kezonta Pottery Company."[7] While E.E. Isbell & Co. touted their stock of sterling silver in many of their advertisements (fig. 57.2), there is no evidence to suggest that they manufactured any of the silver that they sold (figs. 57.3, 57.4).[8] Almost all of the silver flatware and hollowware documented with E.E. Isbell & Co.'s marks (marks 57.1 and 57.2) also bear the marks of manufacturers which include the International Silver Company (Meriden, Connecticut), Dominick & Haff (New York City), Peter L. Krider (Philadelphia), Frank M. Whiting Co. (North Attleboro, Massachusetts), William Wilson & Son (Philadelphia), Towle Mfg. Co. (Newburyport, Massachusetts), and George W. Shiebler & Co. (New York City).[9]

WATCHES, DIAMONDS, FASHIONABLE JEWELRY,

SOLID STERLING SILVER WARE,

Fine French Clocks and Bronzes, Fine Foreign Fancy Goods, &c.
Fine Corals and Cameos, Pearl and Ivory Handle Knives,
Plated Table Ware, Tea Setts, &c.

The Pantoscopic Eye Glasses and Spectacles.
BOUGHT FOR CASH.
LOWEST PRICES WARRANTED.
REPAIRING OF ALL KINDS.

E. E. ISBELL,
JEWELERS,   58 W. FOURTH ST.

FIG. 57.2: Advertisement from E.H. Austerlitz, *Cincinnati, from 1800 to 1875, A Condensed History of Cincinnati Combined with Exposition Guide for 1875 . . .*, Cincinnati: Bloch & Co., 1875

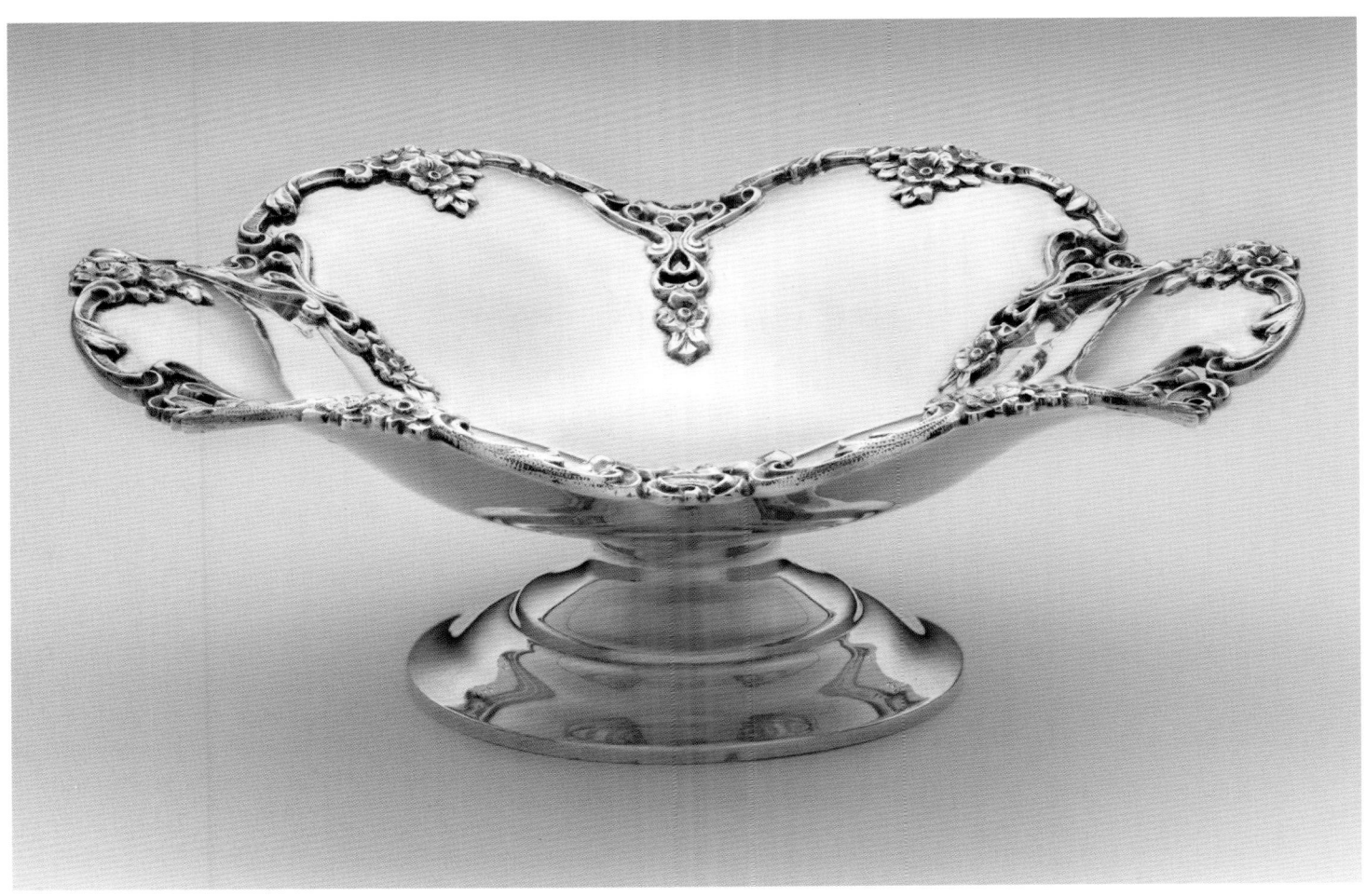

FIG. 57.3: E.E. Isbell & Co., *Footed Bowl*, 1875–1895, 2½ × 7 in. (6.4 × 17.8 cm), CAM, Museum Purchase with funds provided by Mr. and Mrs. Charles Fleischmann III, 2005.44

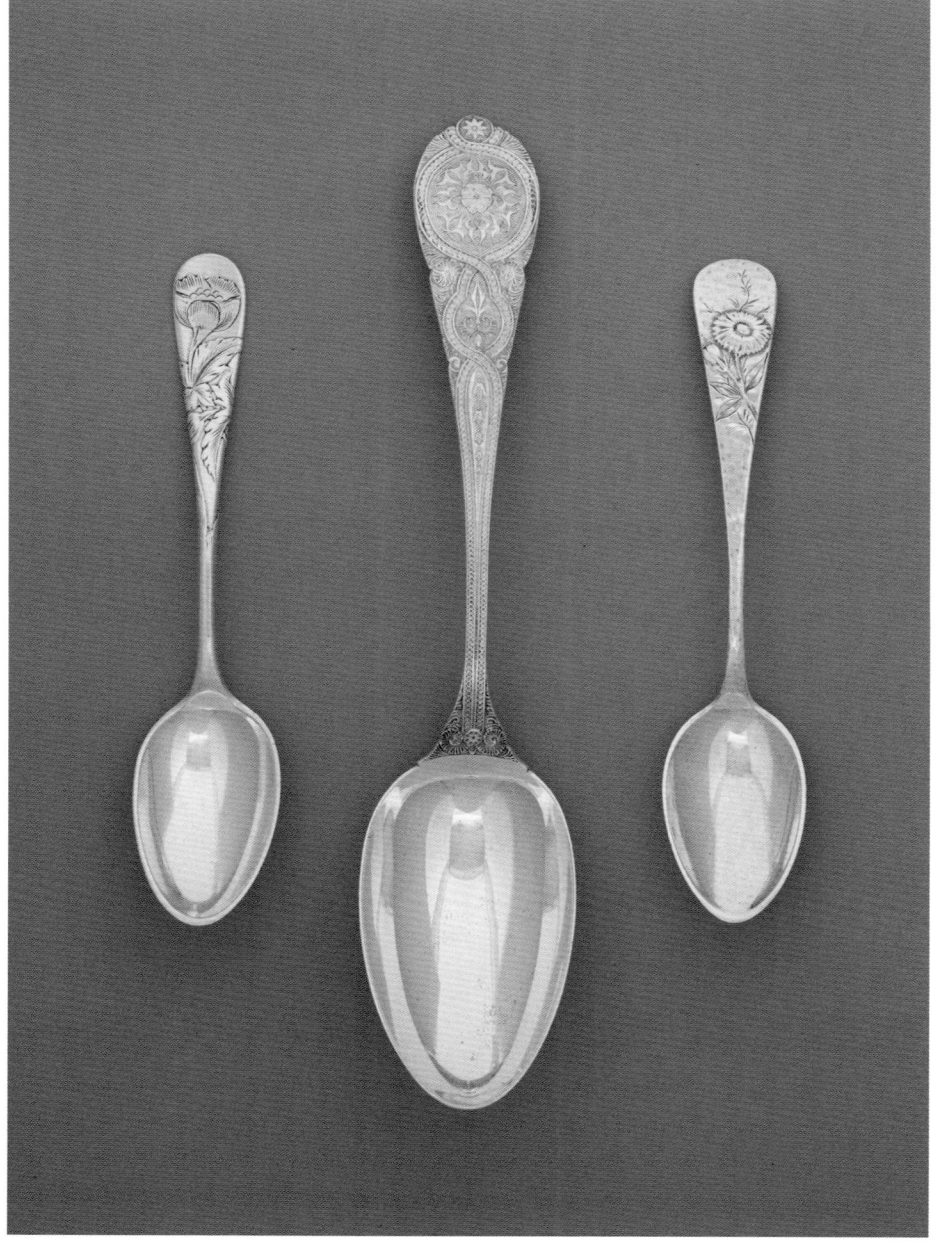

FIG. 57.4: E.E. Isbell & Co., *Teaspoon*, 1875–1895, L. 5¹⁵⁄₁₆ in. (15.1 cm), CAM, Given by Elizabeth M. and Annie W. Anderson in memory of their mother, Mrs. Buckner W. Anderson, 1969.751; E.E. Isbell & Co., *Tablespoon*, 1875–1895, L. 8¾ in. (22.2 cm), CAM, Gift of Louise Eastman Warrington, 1975.75; E.E. Isbell & Co., retailer, Gorham Mfg. Co. (estab. 1831), manufacturer, *Teaspoon*, c. 1888, L. 5½ in. (14 cm), CAM, Bequest of Fanny Bryce Lehmer, 1936.773

After Gaff's death in 1884, Isbell continued to run the business with financial backing from Gaff's estate. The firm was taken over by longtime employee Loring Andrews, and became **Loring Andrews & Co.** in 1895.[10] Isbell subsequently worked as a salesman at Loring Andrews & Co and for **The Duhme Jewelry Co.**[11] He had one son, Norton E. Isbell, who was noted as traveling in Central America at the time of Isbell's death in April 1917.[12]

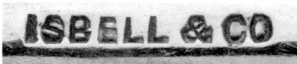

MARK 57.1

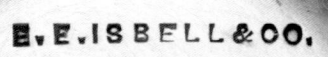

MARK 57.2

1. Ohio, Vol. 4, p. 43, R.G. Dun & Co. Collection, Baker Library, Harvard Business School; Ohio, Vol. 10, p. 355, R.G. Dun & Co. Collection; E.H. Austerlitz, *Cincinnati, from 1800 to 1875, A Condensed History of Cincinnati Combined with Exposition Guide for 1875, Fully Illustrated, together with a description of pictures and works of art, exhibited at the Cincinnati Industrial Exposition, 1875,* Cincinnati: Bloch & Co., 1875, 173 and advertisement on un-numbered page; In 1895, address numbers were standardized, and 58 West Fourth Street became 32 East Fourth Street; 1895 Cincinnati City Directory.

2. Everett E. Isbell, burial record, Spring Grove Cemetery, Cincinnati, Ohio; 1900 Federal Census, Evanston, Hamilton, Ohio.

3. "Funeral of Everett E. Isbell, Jeweler, Is To Be Held," *Cincinnati Enquirer,* April 21, 1917, 10.

4. 1861–1875 Cincinnati City Directories.

5. Ohio, Vol. 10, p. 355, R.G. Dun & Co. Collection; "Thomas Gaff," *Find A Grave,* www.findagrave.com, accessed November 2, 2012.

6. Advertisement, *Cincinnati Enquirer,* April 25, 1875, 8.

7. "On the Road," *Jewelers' Circular and Horological Review* (July 1888): 44.

8. Advertisement, *Cincinnati Commercial Tribune,* December 10, 1876, 5. This advertisement calls special attention to their "stock of Sterling Silver in REPOUSSE or QUEEN ANNE."; The loving cup presented by the stockholders of the M&M Insurance Co. to their director Robert Hosea, furnished by E.E. Isbell & Co., was likely manufactured elsewhere and sold and engraved by E.E. Isbell.

"Cincinnati," *JCHR* (April 17, 1895): 30.

9. E.E. Isbell & Co., eBay listings and private collections, Cincinnati silver binders, Cincinnati Art Museum.

10. 1884–1895 Cincinnati City Directories.

11. 1896–1910 Cincinnati City Directories. Isbell worked for Loring Andrews & Co. from 1896–1897 and 1909–1916, and for The Duhme Jewelry Co. from 1898–1908.

12. "Funeral of Everett E. Isbell, Jeweler, Is To Be Held," April 21, 1917.

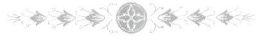

58. JANDORF & MAYER

1869–1874

This firm was established in 1869 by Pfeiffer Jandorf (about 1833–1914) and Leopold D. Mayer (1837–1895).[1] Jandorf, born in Hengstfeld, Germany, was the son of Rufen Lippmann Jandorf (1805–1833) and Baesle (Bessy) Feldenheimer (1807–1866).[2] He came to the United States in 1852, and was in Cincinnati by 1864 when he partnered with David Nordlinger (b. 1841, Germany) in the jewelry firm Jandorf & Nordlinger (active 1864–1865) located at 54 West Fourth Street.[3] Jandorf & Nordlinger dissolved in May 1865, and it was noted that Jandorf, alone, was authorized to use the name of the firm in liquidation.[4] By 1866, Jandorf had joined Louis Friedman, previously of Baltimore, to create Friedman & Jandorf (active 1866), a firm listed in the city directory under the business heading of "Watches, Clocks & Jewelry."[5] They continued to operate at 54 West Fourth Street, and by 1867, Max Nathan and Leopold D. Mayer had joined the firm to create the wholesale jewelry business of Nathan, Friedman & Co. (active 1867).[6] Mayer was born in 1837 in Besançon, France and arrived in America in 1864.[7] He made his first appearance in Cincinnati city directories in 1859, working at the northwest corner of Fourth and Sycamore Streets and listed under the business heading of "Jewelry, Silverware, Watches, &c."[8] By 1868, Friedman appears to have left, and the firm became Nathan, Jandorf & Mayer (active 1868–1869).[9] When Nathan withdrew in June 1869, Jandorf & Mayer continued at the Fourth Street stand in the wholesale business.[10]

R.G. Dun & Co. reported that Nathan, who had been in the liquor business prior to entering the wholesale jewelry trade in 1853, had been the capitalist of Nathan, Jandorf & Mayer, and,

therefore, there was little confidence in Jandorf & Mayer's solvency.[11] A report of sales made by Cincinnati wholesalers between the period of May 1, 1869, and April 30, 1870, indicated that Jandorf & Mayer had collected $110,837, but by January 1871 they were in serious debt with creditors.[12] With liabilities of $40,000, their assets were sold to Mayer's brother for $35,000, a price that was reportedly two-thirds of the firm's appraised value.[13] After settling with creditors, paying 40 cents on the dollar, Jandorf & Mayer, having "skillfully managed" their failure, under "suspicious circumstances," reportedly "came out ahead in finances but with the loss of character as business men and impaired credit."[14]

The firm continued in the wholesale business, and in June 1871 opened a new retail store, with great fanfare, at 58 West Fourth Street, the former site of the Grover & Baker Sewing Machine Company (fig. 58.1). While they billed themselves as "one of the oldest and most reliable" firms in the city, credit reporters remained wary. An extensive description of the new store tells us that there were "single plate windows, set in a handsome bronzed and gilt framework of iron" and that the room was 100 feet deep by 20 feet wide. In addition to the French clocks, bronzes, paintings, mirrors, jewelry, and watches offered, there were "three magnificently carved walnut cases for the display of silverware in sets and single pieces." Jandorf & Mayer claimed a specialty of the goods manufactured by Gorham Mfg. Co. and Whiting Mfg. Co.[15] While they certainly bought from eastern houses, they also bought stock made closer to home. Works bearing their mark (mark 58.1) are rare, and the few pieces documented are typical Cincinnati forms—spoons with

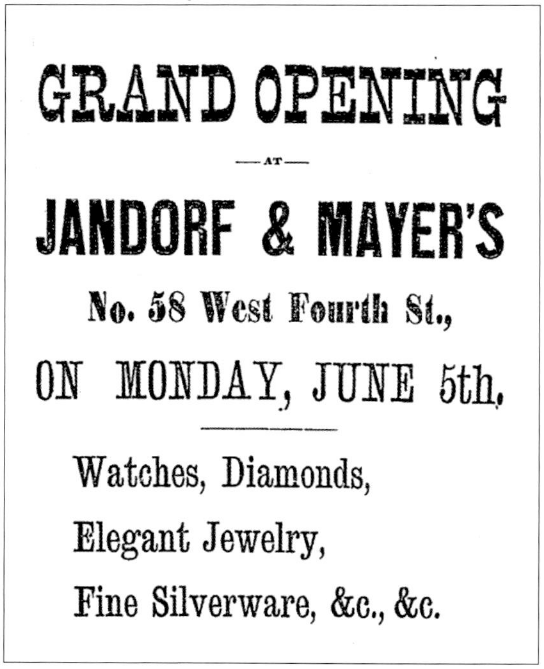

GRAND OPENING

—AT—

JANDORF & MAYER'S

No. 58 West Fourth St.,

ON MONDAY, JUNE 5th.

Watches, Diamonds,

Elegant Jewelry,

Fine Silverware, &c., &c.

FIG. 58.1: Advertisement, *Cincinnati Enquirer*, June 4, 1871, 5

pointed shoulders and tipped, exaggerated fiddle handles.[16] Their reputation in the trade was so poor that it is unlikely that they could buy much in the East, as many of the houses there refused to extend them credit.[17] In 1873, the firm was listed at 122 West Fourth Street, and by January 1874 they had failed again. All of their stock and fixtures were sold, and the firm was dissolved by mutual consent.[18]

By 1879, Pfeiffer Jandorf was in New York City.[19] He worked as a jeweler on Broadway with his brothers, Charles and Abraham, until 1892, when they all became bicycle dealers.[20] He and his wife, Rachael (1846–1917, nee Shineberg) had seven children for whom records were found: Lewis, Harry, Blanche, Clarence, Grace, Elsie, and Sadie.[21] Pfeiffer Jandorf died on March 14, 1914.[22] By 1880, Leopold Mayer had relocated to Chicago, where he worked as a cigar dealer.[23] He and his wife, Emma (b. about 1843), had five children for whom records were found: Leopold, Julia, Christina, Edgar, and Eugene. Leopold Mayer died on June 2, 1895, in Chicago from a tumor on the lung. He is buried in Cincinnati in the Walnut Hills Jewish Cemetery.[24]

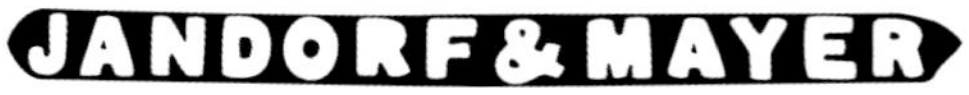

JANDORF & MAYER

MARK 58.1

1. Leo D. Mayer, death certificate, "Illinois, Cook County, Deaths, 1878–1922," index and images, *FamilySearch*, https://familysearch.org/pal:/MM9.1.1/N7KM-V3L, accessed January 14, 2013; Pfeiffer Jandorf, 1900 Federal Census, Manhattan, New York, New York; Pfeifer Jandorf, death index result, www.italiangen.org/NYCDeathresults.asp?kind=wcb&Esurname=Jandorf&Efirst=Pfeifer&StartYear=&, accessed January 31, 2013; Ohio, Vol. 7, p. 48, R.G. Dun & Co. Collection, Baker Library, Harvard Business School; 1868, 1869 Cincinnati City Directories; Pfeiffer Jandorf's name is given as Philip Jandorf in the 1910 Federal Census, Manhattan, New York, New York. There are variants in the spelling of Pfeiffer's first name (Pfeifer, Philip, Pfieffer, etc.) in various sources.

2. Pfeiffer Jandorf's birthdates are given as 1835 in the 1900 Federal Census, Manhattan, New York, New York, as about 1837 in the 1870 Federal Census, Hamilton, Cincinnati, Ohio, and as December 11, 1833, in Allan T. Hirsch, Jr., "Feldenheimer Family Tree," http://www.ahirsh.com/pdfs

/FELDENHEIMER_TREE.pdf, accessed January 31, 2013. Information regarding his birthplace and parents comes from Allan T. Hirsh, Jr.

3. Gale Research, *Passenger and Immigration Lists Index, 1500s–1900s* [online database], Provo, Utah: Ancestry.com Operations Inc., 2010. Collected from "Jewish Emigration From Wurttemberg (1848–1855)," *American Jewish Historical Society* 41, no. 3 (March 1952): 253–268 (Appendix 1); In 1864 and 1865, Jandorf & Nordlinger advertised under the business categories of "Jewelry Manufacturers," "Jewelry, Silverware, Watches, &c.," and "Importers and Wholesale Dealers in Watches, Jewelry & Silverware"; 1864, 1865 Cincinnati City Directories.

4. Dissolution of partnership, *Cincinnati Enquirer*, May 26, 1865, 4.

5. 1866 Cincinnati City Directory; **E.E. Isbell** was employed as a clerk at this address in 1866. Louis Friedman was listed in the 1860 Baltimore City Directory as an affiliate of May, Brother & Co., which dealt in imported watch makers' articles.

6. Max Nathan first appeared in city directories in 1853 as a wholesale

dealer in jewelry, watches etc. He was later a partner in the same line of business with Morris Escales (Nathan & Escales, active 1856–60, and Nathan, Escales & Co., active 1860); 1853–1860 Cincinnati City Directories.

7. Leon D. (Leo) Mayer, burial record, Jewish Cemeteries of Greater Cincinnati, jcemcin.org, accessed January 31, 2013; Ancestry.com, *New York Passenger List, 1820–1957* [online database], Provo, Utah: Ancestry.com Operations Inc., 2010.

8. Mayer is not included in the 1864 or 1865 City Directories, but in 1866 he is noted as a partner in a saloon with Henry Fox.

9. 1868, 1869 Cincinnati City Directories.

10. Ohio, Vol. 7, p. 48, R.G. Dun & Co. Collection.

11. Ibid.

12. "Our Financial Basis: The Wholesale Dealers of Cincinnati," *Cincinnati Enquirer*, May 26, 1870, 8; Ohio, Vol. 7, p. 48, R.G. Dun & Co. Collection.

13. Ohio, Vol. 7, p. 48, R.G. Dun & Co. Collection. The identity of Mayer's brother is not known.

14. Ibid.

15. "A Magnificent Establishment: Opening of Jandorf & Mayer's New

Jewelry Store," *Cincinnati Enquirer*, June 4, 1871, 8.

16. Jandorf & Mayer, eBay listings and private collections, Cincinnati silver binders, Cincinnati Art Museum.

17. Ohio, Vol. 7, p. 55, R.G. Dun & Co. Collection.

18. Ibid.; "Assignment," *Cincinnati Enquirer*, January 6, 1874, 8.

19. 1879 New York City Directory.

20. 1879–1894 New York City Directories; 1900 Federal Census, Manhattan, New York, New York.

21. Allan T. Hirsch, Jr., "Feldenheimer Family Tree"; 1870 Federal Census, Cincinnati, Hamilton, Ohio; 1900 and 1910 Federal Censuses, Manhattan, New York, New York.

22. Pfeifer Jandorf, death index result, www.italiangen.org.

23. 1880 Federal Census, Chicago, Cook, Illinois; Leopold D. Mayer's death record indicates that he had been in Chicago since 1875; 1875–1892 Chicago City Directories.

24. Leo D. Mayer, death certificate, "Illinois, Cook County, Deaths, 1878–1922."; Leon [*sic*] D. Mayer, burial marker, Walnut Hills Jewish Cemetery, www.jcemcin.org.

59. JOSEPH G. JOSEPH

1801–1873, w. 1834 or earlier–1846

According to the 1839/40 City Directory, which included the places of nativity of those listed, Joseph was born at sea, on the Atlantic Ocean.[1] Later records indicate that he was "Hebrew," born in Exeter, England, on February 12, 1801.[2] His whereabouts prior to his arrival in Cincinnati and the details of his training are unknown. Joseph may have been in Cincinnati as early as 1831, as a J. Joseph is listed as a petitioner for the establishment of a Grand Lodge for the Independent Order of Odd Fellows that year.[3] Just a year later, **Jacob Deterly** records his payment of a dollar's balance to "Mr. Joseph" on a music box.[4] As Joseph later advertised the sale of a variety of goods, including surveying instruments, it is possible that the music box could have been purchased from him.[5]

The first listing for Joseph G. Joseph, a watch maker on Main Street between Third and Fourth Streets, appears in the 1834 City Directory. An advertisement from 1835 describes Joseph as a "watch and spectacle maker" at 154 Main Street, "opposite the U. S. Bank."[6] In 1836, he listed as an optician and jeweler at 169 Main Street, "four doors above the steeple church and nearly opposite the Dennison's Hotel." A large, elaborately illustrated advertisement touts his "old established spectacle store," and describes Joseph as an optician, jeweler, silversmith, and watch and clock maker. While special attention is given to spectacles of all kinds, he also advertises "day and night Telescopes, and spy Glasses, Surveyors Compasses, and Chains, Mathematical and drawing instruments, Brewers, Bath, and Botanical Thermometers, . . . Ladies and Gentlemen's gold and Silver, Lever, Horizontal, Vertical and Plain Watches, Gold Watch and Neck Chains, Seals, Keys, Ear and Finger Rings, Broaches, Pins, Silver Tea, Table, Soup and Cream Spoons of all descriptions; and every other article in his vocation," and promises "The highest price given to Gold and

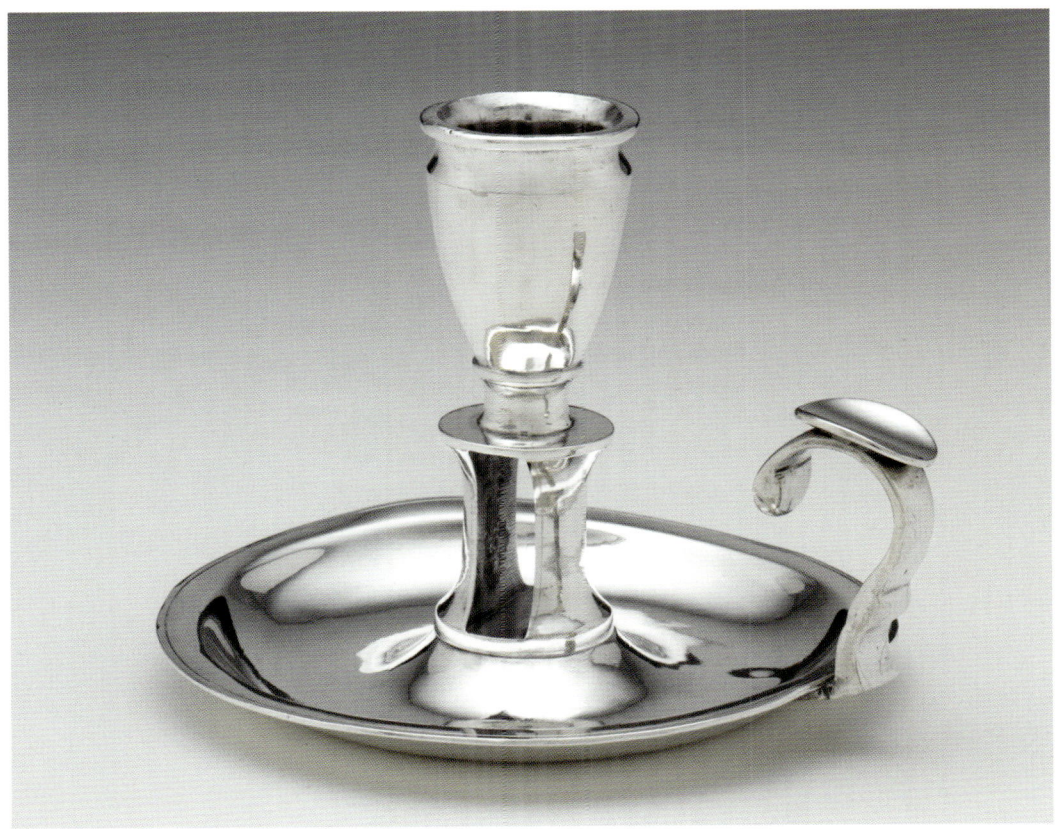

FIG. 59.1: Joseph Joseph, *Chamberstick*, 1834–1846, 4 × 5⅜ in. (10.2 × 13.7 cm), CAM, Museum Purchase with funds provided by Mr. and Mrs. Charles Fleischmann III, 2005.45

Silver."[7] Joseph was at 169 Main Street, "opposite the Gazette Office," from at least February 1837 to August 1838, when he relocated to 141 Main Street, "one door from 4th [Street]."[8] He likely traveled back to England once, if not twice, as his daughter Esther is reportedly born there around 1836, and a Joseph Joseph, watch maker, born in 1801, is recorded as arriving in New York City from Liverpool on the *Westchester* on September 1, 1838.[9] In 1842, our subject listed as a silversmith at Elm Street between Front and Second Streets.[10] R.G. Dun & Co. credit reports indicate that he sold his business to **Edward H. Hill** that year.[11]

In 1843 and 1844, Joseph appears in the directories as a silversmith at Front between Vine and Race Streets, in 1846, as a clerk at the same location, and between 1849, 1850, and 1851, as a clothier and jewelry store owner at 49 Front Street between Sycamore and Broadway.[12] He is listed intermittently in city directories from 1852 to 1867 as associated with show cases, as a jeweler, and as a clerk.[13] In the 1860 Census his occupation is recorded as trader, and in 1870, it was noted that he was infirm.[14] He died on January 14, 1873, at his last residence, 137 Gest Street, and is buried at the Adath Israel Cemetery in Cincinnati in Price Hill.[15] He and his English-born wife, Rachel (1815–1898), had seven known children: Esther (b. about 1836), Mark (b. about 1844), Henry (b. about 1847), Moses (b. about 1851), Sally (b. about 1852) Brina (Brinie) (b. about 1854), and Rebecca (1856–1873).[16]

Both of Joseph's known marks (marks 59.1 and 59.2) have appeared on spoons and ladles with fiddle handles and pointed shoulders. The banner included in mark 59.1 features a misspelling of Cincinnati. This mark was used without the "Cincinnatti" [*sic*] banner on some spoons, a chamberstick [fig. 59.1] and tongs with shell terminals.[17]

In 1852, a J.G. Joseph dealing in hydrometers, barometers, thermometers, telescopes, microscopes, and spectacles advertised at 56 King Street East in Toronto, Canada. Hollowware and flatware bearing the incuse marks "J.G. JOSEPH & CO." and "TORONTO." have been documented. There is no known connection between this J.G. Joseph and our subject.[18]

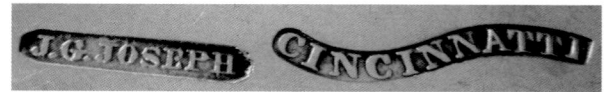

MARK 59.1

MARK 59.2

1. 1839/40 Cincinnati City Directory.
2. Joseph Joseph, death record, *1865–1875 Cincinnati Birth and Death Records*, University of Cincinnati; Burial records, Jewish Cemeteries of Greater Cincinnati, www.jcemcin.org.
3. Theodore A. Ross, *Odd Fellowship: Its History and Manual*, New York: M.W. Hazen Co., 1890, ch. 3.
4. Jacob Deterly, *"Remarks" of Jacob Deterly: diary from 1819 to 1848; life in southern Ohio: Cincinnati, Marietta, Athens* (transcribed and indexed by Madge Hubbard and Opal Saffell), Seattle: Northwest Lineage Researcher, 1972, 2:65.
5. Advertisement, 1839/40 Cincinnati City Directory, 9, reproduced in Beckman, 76.
6. Advertisement, *Cincinnati Daily Gazette*, February 6, 1835, 1.

7. Advertisement, 1836/37 Cincinnati City Directory, front not paginated. A similar advertisement appeared in *Liberty Hall*, June 21, 1836, reproduced in Beckman, 74.
8. Advertisement, *Cincinnati Daily Gazette*, May 8, 1837; Advertisement, *Cincinnati Daily Gazette*, February 9, 1837; Advertisement, *Cincinnati Daily Gazette*, May 25, 1837; In "Old Established Store," *Cincinnati Daily Gazette*, August 21, 1838, Joseph's new address is given as 141 Main Street. In the 1840 Cincinnati City Directory, the address is given as 140 Main.
9. 1860 Federal Census, Cincinnati, Hamilton, Ohio; Ancestry.com, *New York Passenger Lists, 1820–1897* [online database], Provo, Utah: Ancestry.com Operations Inc., 2010.
10. 1842 Cincinnati City Directory.

11. Ohio, Vol. 1, p. 90, R.G. Dun & Co. Collection, Baker Library, Harvard Business School.
12. 1843, 1844, 1846, 1849/50, 1850/51 Cincinnati City Directories.
13. 1852, 1853, 1855, 1856, 1859–1862, 1864–1869 Cincinnati City Directories.
14. 1860 and 1870 Federal Census, Cincinnati, Hamilton, Ohio.
15. Joseph Joseph death record; Burial records, Jewish Cemeteries of Greater Cincinnati.
16. Rachel Joseph, death record, *1896–1899 Cincinnati Birth and Death Records*, University of Cincinnati; 1860 and 1870 Federal Censuses, Cincinnati, Hamilton, Ohio; Rebecca Joseph, death record, *1865–1875 Cincinnati Birth and Death Records*, University of Cincinnati; Rachel and Rebecca are buried at the Montefiore

Jewish Cemetery in Price Hill, Cincinnati.
17. Joseph G. Joseph, eBay listings and private collections, Cincinnati silver binders, Cincinnati Art Museum.
18. Advertisement, *The Canadian Journal: A repertory of Industry, Science and Art and a record of the proceedings of The Canadian Institute*, Toronto: Hugh Scobie, October 1852, back cover. York University Libraries, Clara Thomas Archives & Special Collections, Sheldon and Judy Godfrey Collection, F0435, Accession 2006-057/002 (07); Joseph G. Joseph, eBay listings and private collections, Cincinnati Art Museum.

60. KENT & MICHIE

1869–1878

Luke Kent, Jr. and **William Michie, Jr.**'s involvement began as early as 1856, when Michie was listed as a clerk in Luke Kent's store.[1] Both were surely trained by their fathers who were active in the local trade. Michie became Luke Kent's partner when Luke Kent & Co. (fig. 60.1) was established in 1865.[2] It was not until November 1869 that the firm became known as **Kent & Michie**.[3] Reports and knowledge of Michie's standing indicate that Kent was the capitalist.[4] Operating in the Galt House Building at the southwest corner of Sixth and Main Streets, the men continued in the line of business advertised by Luke Kent & Co.: jewelers and opticians, dealing in watches, jewelry, opera and spy glasses, stereoscopes, clocks, silver and plated ware, spectacles, optical goods and stereoscopic views (fig. 60.2).[5]

The 1870 Products of Industry Census reports that Kent & Michie employed three men—two males (the proprietors) and one youth (likely an apprentice)—, paid a total of $1,000 in wages a year, held working material described as "springs, silver &c." valued at $300, and produced a year's worth of product valued at $2,500. Their capital for the year was estimated at $200.[6] Credit reporters

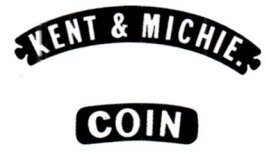

FIG. 60.2: Advertisement, *Cincinnati Daily Gazette,* December 13, 1869, 5

deemed them to be "honest and reliable," "very safe and responsible," and profitable.[7]

In November 1874 the firm was estimated to be worth $50,000, but by February 1875 a close examination of their books revealed that neither partner maintained real estate in their name. All of Kent's property had been transferred to his wife, often an indication of financial difficulty.[8] In December 1877 the firm's capital was estimated at about $15,000, and in April 1878 the firm was dissolved by mutual consent.[9] Despite being hard-pressed for money, Kent settled with Michie and continued in business alone.[10] Michie joined his brothers in **Michie, Jeweler** at 178 West Fourth Street.[11]

There are two known marks used by Kent & Michie. An Elgin pocket watch bears mark 60.1. Butter knives and spoons with tipped, exaggerated fiddle handles and pointed shoulders have been documented with mark 60.2.[12]

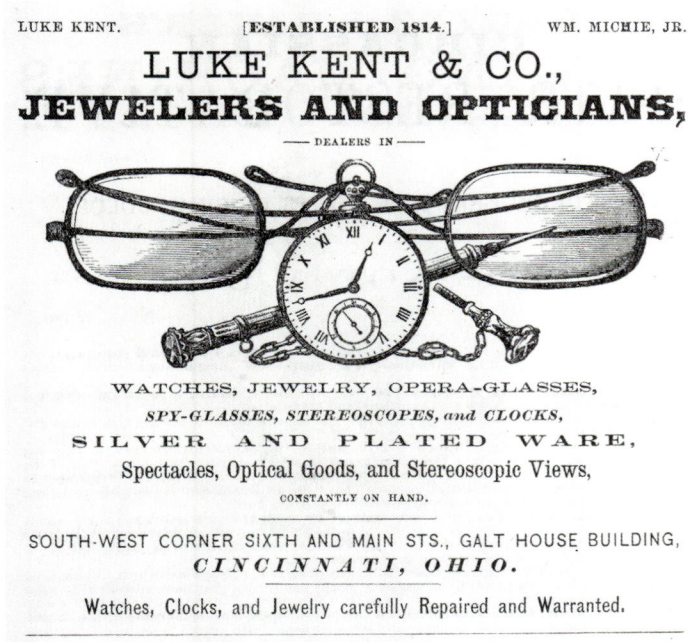

FIG. 60.1: Advertisement, *Minutes of the Cincinnati Annual Conference of the Methodist Episcopal Church, for the year 1866,* Cincinnati: Methodist Book Concern, 1866, 773

MARK 60.1

MARK 60.2

1. 1856 Cincinnati City Directory; A notice of Michie's dissolution of partnership with Kent, published in 1878, says that Michie had been with the firm for about 27 years, which would mean that he joined the firm in about 1852.

2. 1858, 1859, 1865 Cincinnati City Directories; Advertisement, *Minutes of the Cincinnati Annual Conference of the Methodist Episcopal Church, for the year 1866*, Cincinnati: Methodist Book Concern, 1866, 773; Announcement, *Cincinnati Daily Gazette*, December 23, 1868, 2; Dun does not report the partnership and name change of Luke Kent & Co.

until March 23, 1867. Ohio, Vol. 1, p. 13, R.G. Dun & Co. Collection, Baker Library, Harvard Business School.

3. Ohio, Vol. 1, p. 13, R.G. Dun & Co. Collection; 1870 Cincinnati City Directory.

4. Ibid.

5. Advertisement, *Cincinnati Daily Gazette*, December 13, 1869, 5. Other advertisements for Luke Kent & Co. appeared in the *Cincinnati Daily Gazette* in December 24, 1867, 2; December 21, 1868, 1; and December 30, 1868, 1; Other advertisements for Kent & Michie appeared in the *Cincinnati Enquirer*

on December 17, 1869, 8; December 24, 1869, 5 and 8; and December 29, 1869, 8.

6. 1870 Federal Non-Population Census Schedules, Products of Industry, Schedule 4, Hamilton County, Ohio.

7. Ohio, Vol. 4, p. 335, R.G. Dun & Co. Collection.

8. Ibid.; A notice in the *Cincinnati Enquirer*, February 10, 1875, indicates that the proprietor of the Galt House, William E. Marsh, had begun suits to evict Kent & Michie from the building due to a dispute with Thomas J. Jones who had sublet the space to Kent & Michie. The

eviction of Kent & Michie from the Galt House does not appear to have occurred.

9. Ohio, Vol. 4, p. 388, R.G. Dun & Co. Collection; Notice of dissolution, *Cincinnati Commercial Tribune*, April 11, 1878, 8.

10. Ohio, Vol. 4, p. 388, R.G. Dun & Co. Collection.

11. Notice of dissolution, *Cincinnati Commercial Tribune*, April 11, 1878, 8; 1878 Cincinnati City Directory.

12. Kent & Michie, eBay listings and private collections, Cincinnati silver binders, Cincinnati Art Museum.

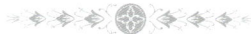

61. LUKE KENT, SR.

about 1771–1842,[1] w. 1813 or earlier–1842

Luke Kent, Sr. (fig. 61.1) was born in Portsmouth, England.[2] Details of his arrival in the United States are unknown, but his earliest Cincinnati advertisement as a watch and clock maker, published in July 1813, notes "his long experience at the city of Washington [D.C.]" prior to his establishment on the east side of Main Street, between Fourth and Fifth Streets, "on the hill opposite the courthouse, where he will carry on the business in all its branches."[3] An 1810 tax list suggests that Kent held interests in Hamilton County at that time.[4] Recollections from his eulogy state that he traveled from Washington, DC "over the mountains by wagon to Marietta, and then by flatboat to Cincinnati."[5] Kent arrived with his wife, Elizabeth Douglas Kent (1783–1841), who is listed in the 1812–1813 membership roster for Cincinnati's First Methodist Episcopal Church, and two young children, Martha (b. 1811) and **Luke Kent, Jr.** (1812–1895).[6] The Kents had at least nine children: Martha, Luke Jr., William, Mary, Elizabeth, **Thomas** (1815–1880), John Wesley (b. 1817), Asbury (1820–1859), and Alfred (b. about 1825).[7] The Cincinnati enterprise established by Luke Kent, Sr. was continued by two subsequent generations, establishing the Kents in the local silver trade for almost eighty years.

In city directories, Luke Kent, Sr. is listed alternately as a silversmith, watch and clock maker, and jeweler, a reflection of his pledge to carry on the business in all branches. His shop stayed central to Main Street. As street numbers were not standardized before 1853, and were, prior to that, arbitrarily assigned and

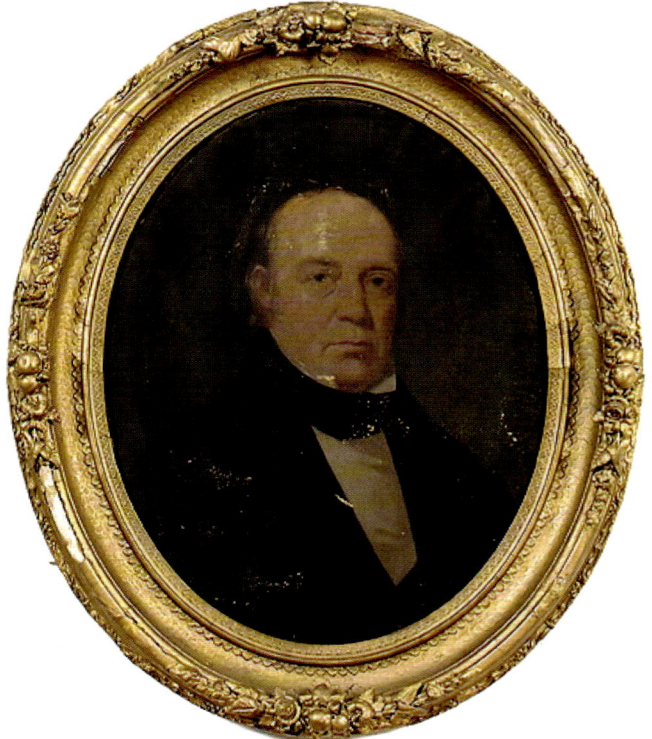

FIG. 61.1: *Luke Kent, Sr.*, oil on canvas, Courtesy of Jerome Redfearn, Photograph courtesy of Cowan's Auction

adjusted, it is difficult to ascertain if all of the early variations in his address represent moves. Around 1817, he relocated from the east side of Main Street to the west side, below Allen's Drug Store; in 1819, he lists at 185 Main Street; and in 1825, at 193 Main.[8] In 1829, he is listed on Main between Fourth and Fifth Streets (probably near his original location); in 1831 and 1834, he is on Main between Fifth and Sixth Streets; and in 1836, he is at 216 Main.[9]

Little is known about the size and production of Kent's shop. In 1829, he employed Abraham A. Allen as a watch maker, and Luke Kent, Jr. trained in the shop, beginning at age sixteen.[10] In 1838, the father and son jointly purchased a home and lot on Fifth Street, and in 1840, they became business partners, advertising as Luke Kent & Son at 210 Main Street.[11] Luke Kent, Sr. died on May 8, 1842.[12] Eulogized as an "open-hearted, genial old gentleman" involved in the "Radical Methodist Church," he bequeathed to his son Luke, "all the tools and materials of the watchmaking and jewelry business, remaining on hand at [his] death," as well as the right and title to the house and business that the men had jointly occupied on Main Street.[13]

A fair amount of silver marked "L. KENT" or "LUKE KENT," struck incuse or inside a cartouche (marks 61.1, 61.2, and 61.3), has been documented. However, it is often unclear if this silver was marked by Luke Kent, Sr. or Luke Kent, Jr. Earlier forms bearing versions of these marks are more readily attributed to Luke Kent, Sr., while spoons with exaggerated fiddle handles (a form that came into favor in the 1840s, and which have been found with all three of the illustrated marks) are more easily attributed to the younger Luke Kent. In addition to spoons (fig. 61.2) and ladles, a pair of tongs, bearing mark 61.2, has been documented.[14]

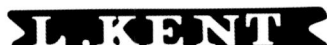

MARK 61.1

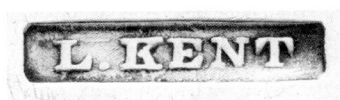

MARK 61.2

LUKE KENT

MARK 61.3

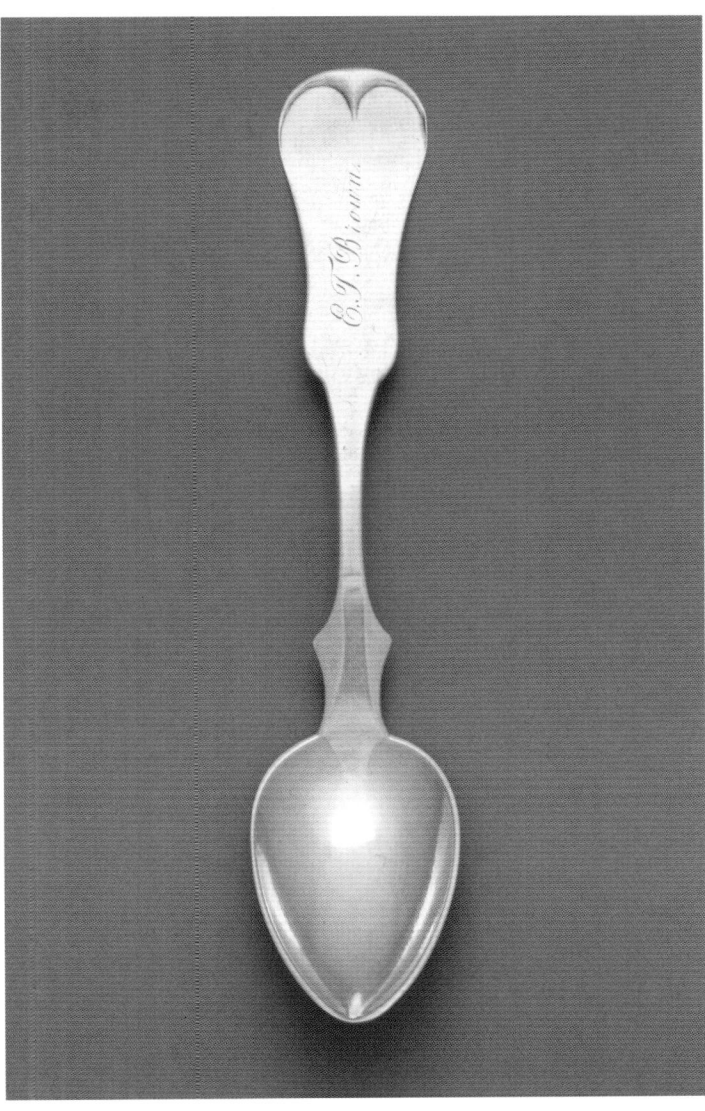

FIG. 61.2: Luke Kent, Sr. or Jr., *Teaspoon*, c. 1840–1860, L. 6¼ in. (15.9 cm), CAM, Anonymous Gift, 2011.29

1. Luke Kent (Sr.), burial record, Spring Grove Cemetery, Cincinnati, Ohio.
2. *In Memoriam, Cincinnati, 1881: Containing Proceedings of the Memorial Associations, Eulogies at Music Hall and Biographical Sketches of Many Distinguished Citizens of Cincinnati*, vol. 1, Cincinnati: A.E. Jones, 1881, 193; 1825 Cincinnati City Directory.
3. Advertisement, *Liberty Hall*, July 19, 1813, reproduced in Beckman, 77; *Proceedings of the Memorial Associations*, Jones, 193; Rev. Charles Frederic Goss, *Cincinnati: The Queen City, 1788–1912*, Cincinnati: The S.J. Clarke Publishing Co., 1912, 3:96;

Luke Kent, Sr. does not appear in *A Century of Alexandria, District of Columbia, & Georgetown Silver 1750–1850*, Washington DC: Corcoran Gallery of Art, 1966.
4. Ronald V. Jackson, Accelerated Indexing Systems, comp., *Ohio Censuses, 1790–1890* [online database], Provo, Utah: Ancestry.com Operations Inc., 1999.
5. *Proceedings of the Memorial Associations*, 193; A commemorative plate inside a tall-case clock given to the Cincinnati Art Museum by Luke Kent, Sr.'s grandson, Walter W. Kent, recalls that Kent Sr. came to

Cincinnati by flatboat on his way from Washington, DC via Pittsburgh, landing in Cincinnati at Broadway. *Clock*, Cincinnati Art Museum, 1940.989.

6. Burial records, Spring Grove Cemetery; Marie Dickore, "The Old Stone Church: First Methodist Episcopal Church in Cincinnati, Ohio," *Bulletin of the Historical and Philosophical Society of Ohio* 17 (October 1959): 305–311. The membership record covered the period between October 1, 1812, and December 25, 1813.

7. Luke Kent, Sr., will filed May 25, 1842, box 4, University of Cincinnati Archives and Rare Books Library; Burial records, Spring Grove Cemetery; Baptism records, Methodist Episcopal Church, Cincinnati, Cincinnati Historical Society, mss QM592, vol. 7; Martha married Marson Allen, Mary married David Disney, Elizabeth married James M. Lyon, and Thomas was most probably the watch maker who listed in the 1836/37, 1839/40, and 1844 Cincinnati City Directories; *Old Woodward, A Memorial Relating to*

Woodward High School, 1831–1836 and Woodward College, 1836–1851 in the City of Cincinnati, Cincinnati: 'Old Woodward' Club, 1884, 211–212.

8. *Proceedings of the Memorial Associations*, 193; 1819, 1825 Cincinnati City Directories; An address for Allen's Drug Store could not be found in city directories.

9. 1829, 1831, 1834, 1836/37 Cincinnati City Directories.

10. *Proceedings of the Memorial Associations*, 193; 1829 Cincinnati City Directory. Allen appears once in city directories, and no further information is

known about him.

11. Luke Kent, Jr., will filed July 26, 1895, box 106, case 42745, University of Cincinnati Archives and Rare Books Library; 1840, 1842 Cincinnati City Directories.

12. Luke Kent (Sr.), burial record.

13. *Proceedings of the Memorial Associations*, 193; Luke Kent, Sr., will.

14. Luke Kent, eBay listings and private collections; Cincinnati silver binders, Cincinnati Art Museum.

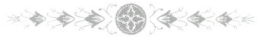

62. LUKE KENT, JR.

1812–1895, w. circa 1830–1880

Luke Kent, Jr. (fig. 62.1) was born in Washington, DC and came to Cincinnati with his parents Elizabeth Douglas and **Luke Kent, Sr.** in 1813.[1] He trained in his father's shop on Main Street, and listed himself as a silversmith, watch maker, and jeweler there in the 1834 and 1836/37 city directories.[2] In 1840, Luke Kent & Son was established at 210 Main Street, and in 1842, following Kent Sr.'s death, Kent Jr. inherited all of his father's tools, materials, and the business.[3] He continued the business under his name on Main Street, between Fifth and Sixth Streets.[4]

In 1856, Kent's business was reported to be strong, and he was noted to be of good character and habit, honest, and attentive to his business. At this time he was estimated to own about $20,000 in real estate and to be employing four or five men, with no mortgages on his property.[5] In following years, his business continued to be well-rated by the R.G. Dun & Co. credit reporting agency, who estimated his worth at $25,000 in 1864.[6]

One of Kent's known employees was **William Michie, Jr.**, who was first enumerated as a clerk at the store in 1856.[7] Michie appears to have worked there as a watch maker through 1865, when he was noted in the city directory as Kent's partner in Luke Kent & Co.[8] Silver and plated ware were among the variety of goods the firm offered, but it is unlikely that Kent or Michie were producing these wares. In January 1867 Edward Clopper, a local merchant and friend of the Kents, reportedly acquired an eight-day clock for ten dollars from Luke Kent, Jr., described as having "an absurdly ornate black-walnut case whose pendulum carries a mirror in the form of a four-pointed star."[9]

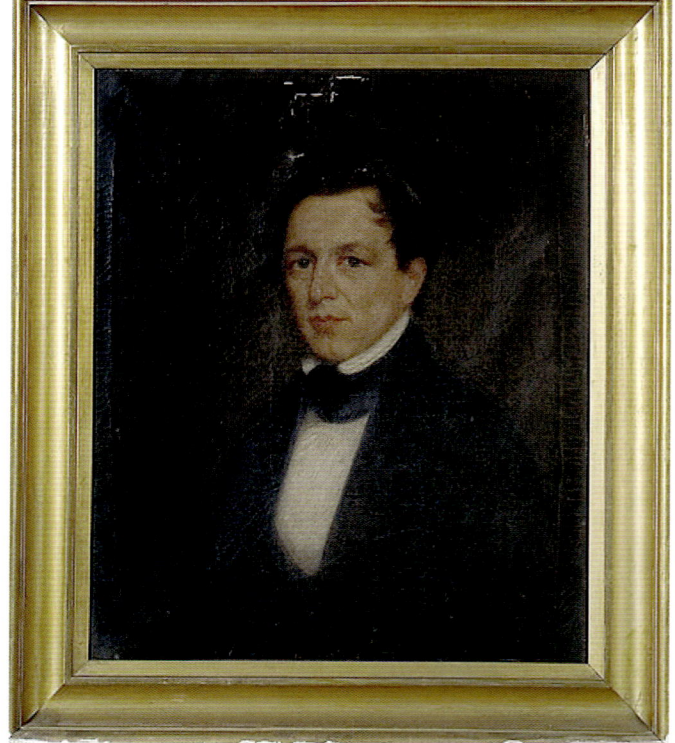

FIG. 62.1: *Portrait of Luke Kent, Jr.*, oil on canvas, Courtesy of Jerome Redfearn, Photograph courtesy of Cowan's Auction

In 1869, the firm changed its name to **Kent & Michie**.[10] Michie is described as a "very nice man of modest means" by R.G. Dun & Co., and the business continued to do well with Kent's estimated worth rising to $50,000 in November 1874. But by February 1875 the business appeared to be struggling and all of Kent's property had been transferred to his wife, Adeline Ernst.[11] Adeline (1823–1896) was the sister of Kent's first wife, Amelia Mary Ernst (d. 1837).[12] The sisters were daughters of the well-to-do horticulturist and abolitionist Andrew H. Ernst (1796–1860).[13] Subsequent reports note a decrease in the firm's capital, and in April 1878 Kent and Michie dissolved by mutual consent and Kent continued in business alone.[14]

As part of the dissolution with Michie, Kent was forced to borrow against his wife's property in order to settle, and thus became indebted to her. He struggled throughout the next year. Credit reporters noted, "his location is no longer a good one and [he] must move," and he was sued by the Dueber Watch Case Manufactory.[15] To settle his debt of $1,300 to his wife, he turned the business and all of his stock over to his son **Herbert Townsend Kent** in August 1879.[16]

By 1880, H.T. Kent, as he was known, had relocated the business to a more prominent and spacious location at 58 West Fifth Street on Fountain Square, where he advertised as Kent's, Jeweler and Optician, offering "Bargains in Diamonds, Watches, Jewelry, Spectacles, Solid Silver and Plated Ware" from leading manufacturers (fig. 62.2).[17] Luke Kent, Jr. worked there "repairing old watches and suiting all eyes with glasses."[18] In August 1891 the failure of H.T. Kent and the family business, which had spanned over three-quarters of a century, was noted in *The Jewelers' Circular and Horological Review*. Kent's stock was assessed at $4,100 with liabilities of $6,100, and his goods were sold at auction.[19] It was disclosed that wares "were sometimes sold at sacrifice prices in order to raise money; [and] that nearly $2,000 worth of goods were taken out of the store a day or two before the assignment and returned to parties in New York, and that property was transferred by the assignor to his wife, whom he married only in April last."[20] In his assignment, H.T. Kent made preferences to family members including his mother, Adeline, to whom he was the most indebted at $1,540.[21] "The sympathy of the local trade are with him," it was noted, "as he was popular with everybody."[22] He went on to work as a salesman with **Duhme & Co.** and eventually entered the real estate business.[23]

In his later years, Luke Kent, Jr. served as an officer at Trinity Methodist Episcopal Church.[24] Kent was the father of eleven children. With his first wife Amelia, he had Amelia E. (1837–1845, died of measles), and with Adeline he had Luke (1841, lived three months), Edmund (b. about 1843), Ella (b. 1841, lived one day),

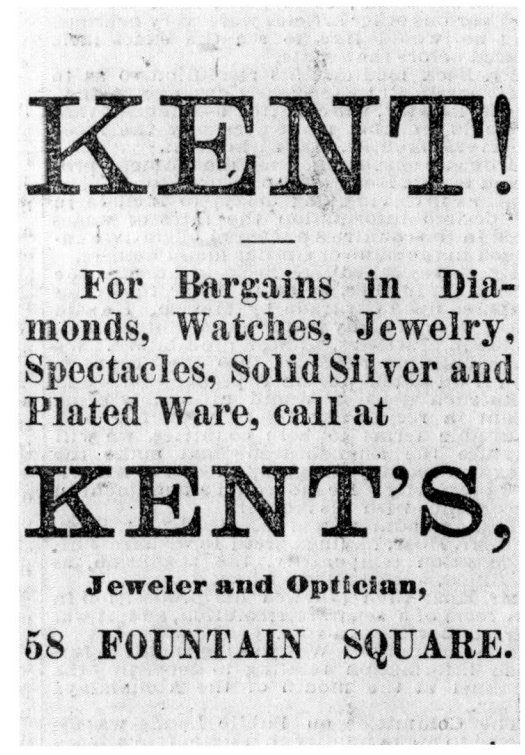

FIG. 62.2: Advertisement, *Cincinnati Enquirer*, December 22, 1881, 8

Charles Woodward (1846–1847, died of scarlet fever), Andrew H. Ernst (b. about 1854), Amelia E. "Lillian" (1850–1940), Herbert Townsend (1856–1918), Otis (b. about 1858), John (1868, stillborn), and Walter W. (1868–1936).[25] It is noted that during the summer of 1863, he and his eldest son (probably Edmund) crossed the river into Kentucky to defend Cincinnati during Morgan's Raid.[26] Luke and Adeline Kent maintained a residence on Ninth Street, deeded to Amelia E. in 1872.[27] Luke Kent, Jr. died on May 29, 1895.[28] His cause of death was recorded as atrophy of the brain and marasmus (emaciation). Adeline died on September 25, 1896.[29] They are buried at Spring Grove Cemetery.[30] Adeline's estate was valued at $52,300 in 1896.[31]

For an illustration of marks associated with Luke Kent, Jr., see the biography of Luke Kent, Sr.

1. Kent's burial record indicates that he was born in Georgetown. An 1810 tax record indicates that Kent's father may have been in Hamilton County, or at least owned interests there by that time. Luke Kent (Jr.), burial record, Spring Grove Cemetery, Cincinnati, Ohio; *In Memoriam, Cincinnati, 1881: Containing Proceedings of the Memorial Associations, Eulogies at Music Hall and Biographical Sketches of Many Distinguished Citizens of Cincinnati*, vol. 1, Cincinnati: A.E. Jones, 1881, 193; Ronald V. Jackson, Accelerated Indexing Systems, comp., *Ohio Censuses, 1790–1890*, [online database], Provo, Utah: Ancestry.com Operations Inc., 1999 (1810 Hamilton County Tax List).

2. *Proceedings of the Memorial Associations*, Jones, 193.

3. 1839/40, 1842 Cincinnati City Directories; Luke Kent, Sr., will filed May 25, 1842, box 4, University of Cincinnati Archives and Rare Books Library.

4. 1844, 1846, 1848/49, 1849/50, 1850/51, 1851/52, 1853 Cincinnati City Directories; The addresses given in the directories from 1834 through 1879 (210, 234, 238, 240 Main Street, Main between Fifth and Sixth Street, and southwest corner of Sixth and Main Streets) are probably all the same address. At this time, the street numbers of buildings were designated by their owners and could change at any time; Ohio, Vol. 1, p. 91, R.G. Dun & Co. Collection, Baker Library, Harvard Business School; Advertisement, *Minutes of the Cincinnati Annual Conference of the Methodist Episcopal Church, for the year 1861*, Cincinnati: Methodist Book Concern, R.P. Thompson, 1861.

5. Ohio, Vol. 1, p. 91, R.G. Dun & Co. Collection.

6. Ohio, Vol. 1, p. 13, R.G. Dun & Co. Collection.

7. 1856 Cincinnati City Directory.

8. 1858, 1859, 1865 Cincinnati City Directories; Advertisement, *Minutes of the Cincinnati Annual Conference of the Methodist Episcopal Church, for the year 1866*, Cincinnati: Methodist Book Concern, 1866, 773; Dun does not report the partnership and name change of Luke Kent & Co. until March 23, 1867. Ohio, Vol. 1, p. 13, R.G. Dun & Co. Collection.

9. Edward Nicholas Clopper, *An American Family*, Cincinnati: Standard Printing and Publishing Co., 1950, 542. The current location of this clock is unknown.

10. Ohio, Vol. 1, p. 13, R.G. Dun & Co. Collection; 1870 Cincinnati City Directory.

11. Ohio, Vol. 4, p. 335, R.G. Dun & Co. Collection; Luke Kent married Amelia Mary Ernst on August 28, 1836. Marriage record, Hamilton County Probate Records, vol. 6, page 5, http://www.probatect.org /CourtRecordsArchive /bukmarriages.aspx.

12. Samuel Atkins Eliot, *Biographical History of Massachusetts: Biographies and Autobiographies of the Leading Men in the State*, vol. 5, Boston: Massachusetts Biographical Society, 1914, n.p., George Alexander Otis Ernst entry; Burial records, Spring Grove Cemetery, Cincinnati, Ohio; Adeline Ernst Kent obituary, *Laura Slade Scrapbook*, Cincinnati Historical Society, mss 9SX631, vol. 1, p. 57.

13. Ibid.

14. Ohio, Vol. 4, p. 388, R.G. Dun & Co. Collection.

15. Ohio, Vol. 4, p. 396, R.G. Dun & Co. Collection.

16. Ibid.

17. John W. Leonard, *The Centennial Review of Cincinnati: one hundred years of progress in commerce, manufactures, the professions, and in social and municipal life*, Cincinnati: J.M. Elstner, 1888, 69; Advertisement, *Cincinnati Enquirer*, December 22, 1881, 8; Other advertisements that include lists of the goods offered for sale at H.T. Kent's appeared in the *Cincinnati Enquirer* on December 6, 1879, 12; March 16, 1880, 8; April 13, 1880, 11; November 6, 1880, 12; December 14, 1880, 10; and in the *Cincinnati Commercial Tribune* on December 11, 1879, 8; December 24, 1880, 8; and December 18, 1881, 12.

18. Advertisement, *Cincinnati Enquirer*, October 27, 1880, 5.

19. "Cincinnati," *Jewelers' Circular and Horological Review* 23, no. 4 (August 26, 1891): 8, 33.

20. "Cincinnati," *JCHR* 23, no. 7 (September 16, 1891): 25.

21. "Cincinnati," *JCHR* 23, no. 4 (August 26, 1891): 8.

22. "Cincinnati," *JCHR* 23, no. 4 (August 26, 1891): 8, 33.

23. Rev. Charles Frederic Goss, *Cincinnati: The Queen City, 1788–1912*, Cincinnati: The S.J. Clarke Publishing Co., 1912, 3:96.

24. S.B. Nelson and J.M Runk, *History of Cincinnati and Hamilton County, Ohio: Their Past and Present*, Cincinnati: S.B. Nelson & Co., 1894, 201.

25. Burial records, Spring Grove Cemetery, Cincinnati, Ohio; 1850, 1860, 1870, 1880 Federal Censuses, Cincinnati, Hamilton, Ohio; Clopper, *An American Family*, 132–133.

26. Clopper, *An American Family*, 523.

27. Adeline E. Kent, will filed October 5, 1896, box 112, case 44365, University of Cincinnati Archives and Rare Books Library.

28. Luke Kent (Jr.), death record, Health Department, University of Cincinnati Archives and Rare Books Library, http://hdl.handle.net/2374.UC/638 866.

29. Burial records, Spring Grove Cemetery.

30. Ibid.

31. Adeline Ernst Kent obituary, *Laura Slade Scrapbook*.

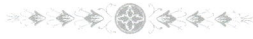

63. WILLIAM H. KIMBERLY

w. 1825–1828

The first record of William H. Kimberly's presence in Cincinnati comes in 1825, when he lists in the city directory as an instrument and truss-maker from Maryland doing business at 58 Main Street.[1] Confirmation of his activities in silver appears in November 1827, when he advertises his return "from the eastern cities, where he has been engaged for some time," and the recommencement of his business at its new location on Sycamore Street, between Front and Columbia. Emphasis is given to his ability to make "Surgical Instruments, Penknives, &c." and trusses (belts for hernia treatment), but it is also noted that "He will also carry on the SILVERSMITH AND JEWELLERY [sic] BUSINESS, at the same place, where gentlemen and ladies can have all kinds of work done in the neatest manner."[2]

Kimberly was likely the son of William Kimberly (about 1768–1821) and Elizabeth Webb (b. 1783).[3] William Kimberly, Sr. was a silversmith and jewelry manufacturer in New York City from 1790 to 1804.[4] In 1804, Kimberly Sr. moved to Baltimore, where he continued to manufacture and sell silverware until his death.[5] When Kimberly Sr. died, he left his tools to his eldest son, William.[6] This may explain the addition of silversmith and jewelry activities mentioned in the younger William Kimberly's 1827 advertisement.

William H. Kimberly is not listed in the 1829 Cincinnati City Directory (the first directory published after the 1825 edition). It is presumed that he left Cincinnati in 1828. He is later found in the 1842 St. Louis City Directory, listed as a watch maker.[7] Three fiddle-handled teaspoons with mark 63.1 reside in the Missouri Historical Society collection.[8] A relationship between our subject and William H. Kimberly (1821–1898), a Baltimore-born merchant active in Virginia, could not be determined.[9]

MARK 63.1

1. 1825 Cincinnati City Directory.
2. Advertisement, *Cincinnati Chronicle and Literary Gazette*, November 15, 1827, 3.
3. Wm. Erik Voss, *American Silversmiths*, http://freepages.genealogy.rootsweb.com/~silversmiths/makers/silversmiths; J. Hall Pleasants and Howard Sill, *Maryland Silversmiths, 1715–1830*, Baltimore: Lord

Baltimore Press, 1930, 144; William H. Kimberly's birth year is given as 1804 without citation in Norman Mack, *Missouri's Silver Age: Silversmiths of the 1800s*, Carbondale IL: Southern Illinois University Press, 2005, 101.
4. Stephen G.C. Ensko, *American Silversmiths and Their Marks*, Southampton, NY: Cracker Barrel Press, 1937, 80; Advertisement, *Daily*

Advertiser, June 10, 1794, 2; Advertisement, *Daily Advertiser*, June 18, 1794, 1; Advertisement, *Daily Advertiser*, September 22, 1795, 1; Advertisement, *Columbian Gazetteer*, September 29, 1794, 4; Advertisement, *Daily Advertiser*, October 11, 1794, 1; Advertisement, *Daily Advertiser*, October 6, 1796, 1; Advertisement, *Mercantile Advertiser*, April 11, 1800, 3.
5. Baltimore Museum of Art, *Eighteenth and Nineteenth Century Maryland Silver in the Collection of the Baltimore Art Museum*, Baltimore: Baltimore Museum of Art, 1975, 187.
6. Mack, *Missouri's Silver Age*, 101; Pleasants and Sill, *Maryland Silversmiths*, 144.
7. 1842 St. Louis City Directory.

8. Mack, *Missouri's Silver Age*, 101. Mack asserts that one of these spoons is also marked "St. Louis," but reference photographs and correspondence with Anne Woodhouse, Missouri History Museum Library and Research Center, confirmed that none of them was marked in this way. For correspondence and photographs see Cincinnati Art Museum, Decorative Arts & Design Department, W.H. Kimberly research file.
9. "Death of W.H. Kimberly," *The Washington Post*, August 15, 1898, 3.

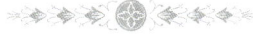

64. DAVID KINSEY

1819–1874, w. 1839–1874

David Kinsey (fig. 64.1) was born in Wales on October 18, 1819, to Ann and **Thomas Kinsey**.[1] The brother of **Edward Kinsey**, he was eight months old when he arrived in New York with his family on June 21, 1820.[2] The Kinseys settled briefly in New Jersey before moving to the Cincinnati area around 1834.[3] David would have learned the trade from his father and his older brother Edward. He is listed as a silversmith working at Edward Kinsey's silver manufactory in the 1839/40 Cincinnati City Directory, and in March of 1843, Edward sold his "whole stock" to David, for unknown reasons, and David continued the business at Edward's old stand at the northwest corner of Walnut and Sixth Streets.[4]

That year, he submitted one case of silverware to the Ohio Mechanics' Institute Fair, comprising silver-headed canes; suspender buckles; castors; pitchers; cups; soup, gravy, and cream ladles; butter knives; sugar tongs; table, tea and dessert spoons; salt and mustard spoons; and large gravy spoons that were "admired for their richness."[5]

It was not long before Edward returned to the business, re-establishing himself by July 1843, and the brothers formed the partnership of **E. & D. Kinsey** in 1844.[6] Five years later, in 1849, David went west, over land "where the Indian roamed, and where the ax of the pioneer had not been heard," in search of gold. He returned to Cincinnati without success in 1850 via the Isthmus of

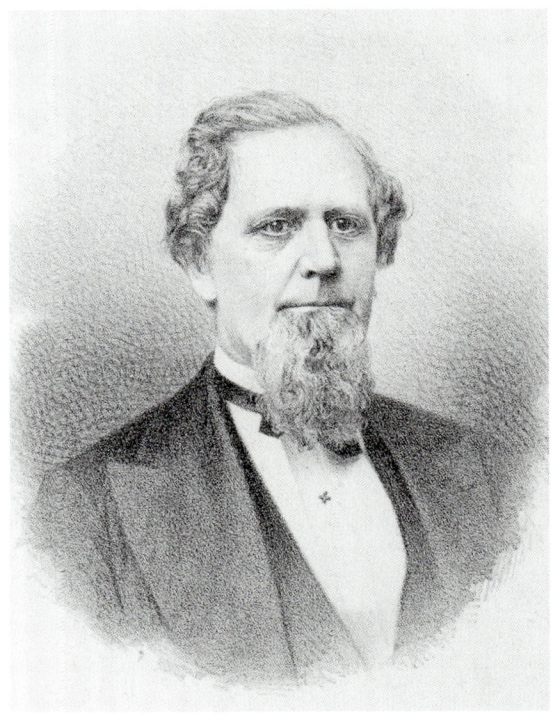

FIG. 64.1: David Kinsey, from W.J. Comley and W. D'Eggville, *Ohio: The Future Great State*, Cincinnati and Cleveland: Comley Brothers Manufacturing and Publishing Company, 1875, 223

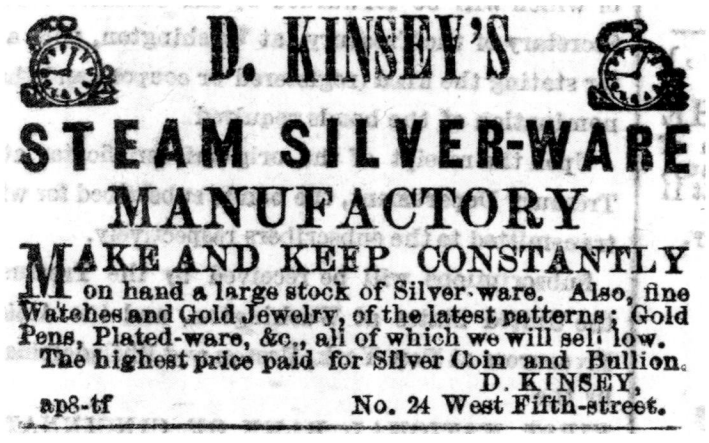

Panama, and it was on this return trip that he contracted the disease, described in burial records as a disease of the lungs, that would eventually end his life.[7]

David married Julia Ann Pocock (b. 1820, Terre Haute, Indiana, d. 1903) in 1843. Julia was the sister of Edward's wife, Temperance.[8] David and Julia had five children: **Charles Stanley**; Willie (1845–1848); Amelia (1848–1850); **Edward W.**; and **Louis A. Kinsey**.[9] In 1850, David, Julia, and their first son Charles were living with Edward Kinsey's family, but by 1857, they had their own home at 374 West Fourth Street with one German servant.[10] David's real estate was valued at $8,000 and the worth of his personal estate was estimated at $500 in 1860.[11]

After Edward's retirement in 1861, David continued the business alone under his own name. An 1864 R.G. Dun & Co. credit report indicates that he was doing well, had "ample means" and a stock worth about $25,750.[12] An advertisement published that year for "D. KINSEY'S Steam Silver-Ware MANUFACTORY" (fig. 64.2) provides the first mention of Kinsey's use of steam power, yet it is possible that the Kinseys were using it even earlier. The advertisement also provides details regarding the firm's assortment of stock and its use of raw material (coin and bullion). David's business continued to fare well. In October 1866 R.G. Dun & Co. reported him as "independent, better off than any in the trade, doing a splendid business."[13] The following year, they reported that he owned plenty of real estate and was worth about $75,000.[14]

In 1870, Kinsey displayed "water pitchers, goblets, snuff boxes, baskets, spoons, forks, etc., all of 'sterling' quality" at the first annual Cincinnati Industrial Exposition.[15] His only competitor in

the silverware class, **Duhme & Co.**, was awarded the first premium. The *Cincinnati Enquirer* reported on Kinsey's display:

> Near the Entrance of the Fine Art Hall is a splendid display of solid silverware, comprising a full service, from the extensive manufactory of D. Kinsey, No. 24 West Fifth Street. The service is of new and elegant original design, very heavy, and is made from bar metal, of which this house is one of the largest consumers of the West. Probably no Western manufactory has originated so many new and popular patterns of silverware as the house of D. Kinsey.... It is the oldest silverware manufactory in the West, as well as one of the most prominent, having maintained a leading position for nearly half a century. Its goods have always been noted for their superiority, both in beauty and design, quality of material and character of manufacture. Mr. Kinsey is also an extensive importer of fine watches, jewelry, &c. of which he presents a large stock at low prices.[16]

In the 1870 Products of Industry Census, the firm reported capital of $30,000; a staff of nine (eight males and one youth) whose annual wages totaled $6,000; and that they had worked 40,000 ounces of silver valued at $50,000 plus $10,000 worth of other materials with one steam engine to produce a total product valued at $67,000.[17] David's sons, Charles, Edward, and Louis all worked at the firm at one point or another.[18]

In 1872, David moved his business to 28 West Fourth Street.[19] His will was written on April 16, 1873, and he died on March 27, 1874, at age 55, of "disease of the heart and lungs."[20] His will directed that a monument costing between $1,500 and $2,500 be erected upon his lot in Spring Grove Cemetery; that $5,000 and all household furnishings and personal property in his dwelling house and all stock and interest in the Royer Wheel Co., at which his son Louis A. Kinsey had been a clerk in the early 1870s, go to his wife Julia Ann Kinsey; that his sons Edward W. and Louis each receive real and/or personal property valued at $30,000; and that after all payment had been made, each of his sons, Charles, Edward and Louis receive one-third of the remainder of the estate.[21] The total value of his estate was estimated at $200,000.[22]

Edward W. Kinsey assumed management of the silver manufactory after his father's death. R.G. Dun reporters were not optimistic, reporting, "He is not a very good business man and his success is a matter of some doubt."[23] In January 1875 Edward sold his interest in the business to his brother Louis and **John B. Callahan**, who had been employed by the Kinseys since 1866. They continued as **D. Kinsey & Co.**[24]

David Kinsey's manufactory produced and retailed a range of different forms in coin and sterling silver, and employed a number of different marks. Mark 64.1 has been observed on a tea service (fig. 64.3); beakers (fig. 64.4), one of which was awarded as a premium in

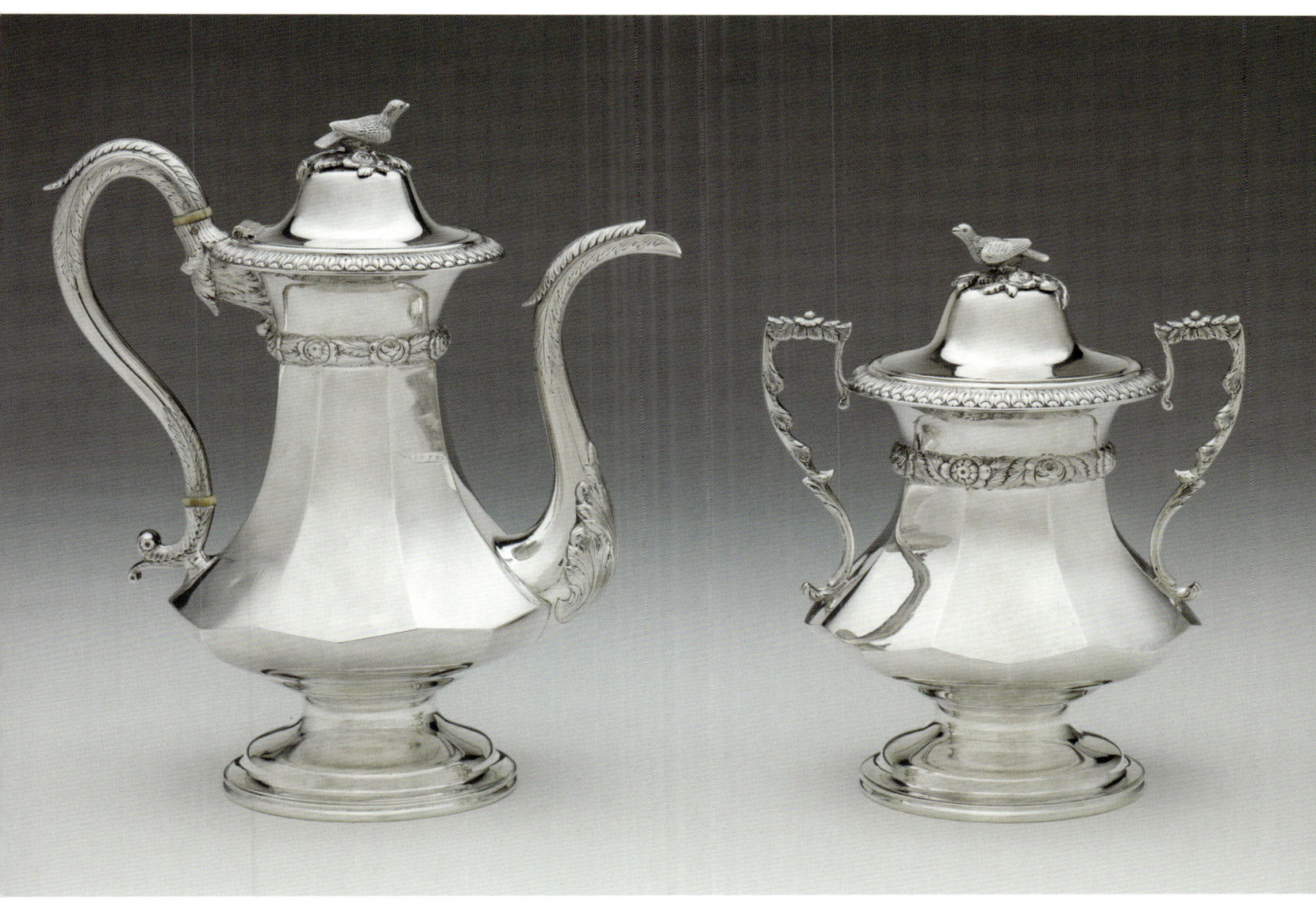

FIG. 64.3: David Kinsey, *Tea Service* (photographed without *Creamer*), 1861–1874, teapot: 12 × 11¼ in. (30.5 × 28.5 cm), sugar, 10 × 8 in. (25.4 × 20.3 cm), CAM, Gift of Mr. and Mrs. Charles Fleischmann III, 2009.143a–d

1869; a mug that also bears the mark of Wood & Hughes (New York City); a ladle and sugar shell with tipped, exaggerated fiddle handles and pointed shoulders; and a serving spoon with scalloped bowl, twist stem, and fancy fiddle handle with all-over engraved decoration. This mark has also been observed on flatware in three die-pressed patterns that were also sold by E. & D. Kinsey: the tipped, fiddle thread pattern; the unidentified pattern seen in the ladle in fig. 66.7; "Dew Drop" (1860) manufactured by George W. Shiebler; and a variant of the "Olive" pattern with a beaded border. The incuse "DAVID KINSEY" stamp has been documented on beakers; spoons with pointed shoulders and tipped, exaggerated fiddle handles; and spoons with fancy

fiddle handles and twist stems, similar to Duhme & Co.'s "No. 1" (circa 1869). Mark 64.2 has been documented on a butter knife and spoons with tipped, exaggerated fiddle handles and pointed shoulders; a ladle of the same form but with all-over engraved decoration; and spoons with fancy fiddle handles with bright cut decoration and twist stems, similar to Duhme & Co.'s "No. 1." Mark 64.3 was stamped on spoons with tipped, exaggerated fiddle handles and pointed shoulders (fig. 64.5), some embellished with all-over engraving on the bowl and the handle. Mark 64.4, possibly David Kinsey's earliest mark, has been documented on a pair of salt spoons with early fiddle handles and pointed shoulders.[25]

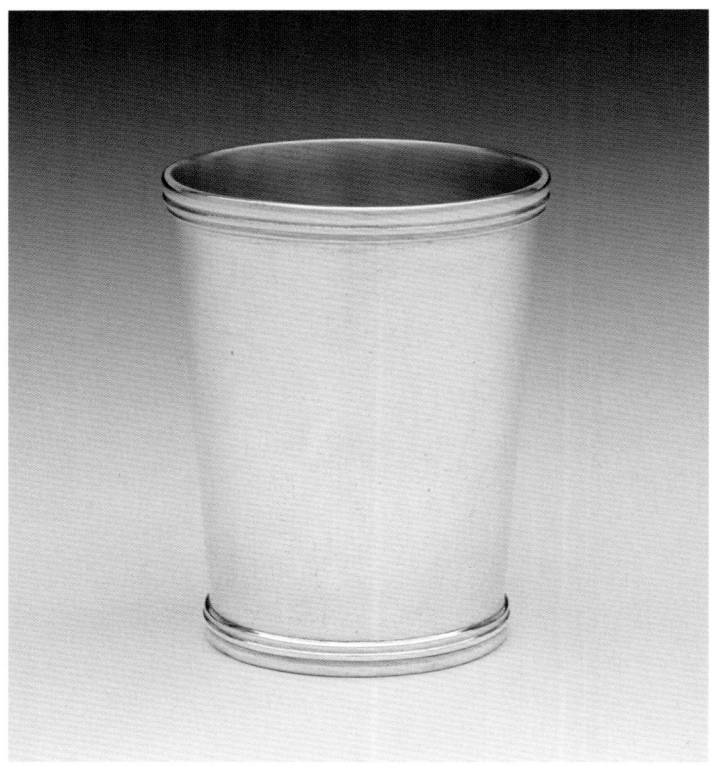

FIG. 64.4: David Kinsey, *Beaker*, 1861–1874, H. 4 in. (10.2 cm), CAM, Gift of John S. Conner, 1910.382

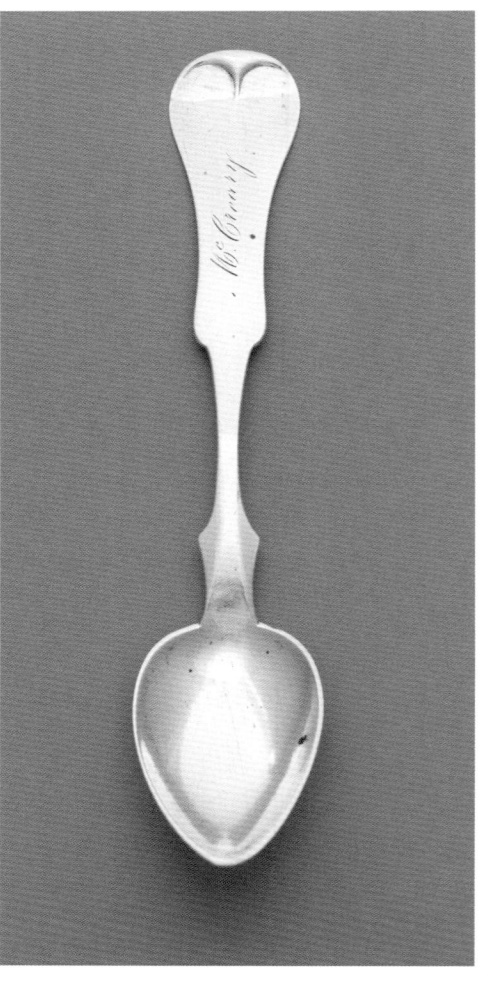

FIG. 64.5: David Kinsey, *Teaspoon*, 1861–1874, L. 6 in. (15.2 cm), CAM, Museum Purchase: John S. Conner Fund, 2012.14. Inscription: McCreary

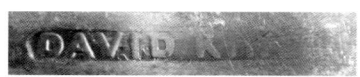

MARK 64.1

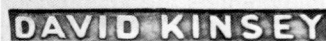

MARK 64.2

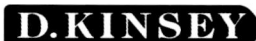

MARK 64.3

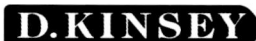

MARK 64.4

1. David Kinsey, burial record, Spring Grove Cemetery, Cincinnati, Ohio; William J. Comley and W. D'Eggville, *Ohio: The Future Great State*, Cincinnati and Cleveland: Comley Brothers Manufacturing and Publishing Co., 1875, 222.

2. Ancestry.com, *New York Passenger Lists, 1820–1957* [online database], Provo, Utah: Ancestry.com Operations Inc., 2010. The children of Thomas and Ann listed on the passenger list are Jane (20), Lydia (16), Stephen (18), Hannah (12), Evan (10), Edward (8), Betsy (6), Charles (4), and David (infant).

3. Comley and D'Eggville, *Ohio: The Future Great State*, 222; The 1850 Federal Census gives the birthplace of Edward and David as New Jersey;

Edward Kinsey appears in the Campbell County, Kentucky, tax list of 1833. Thomas Kenzey [*sic*] is included in the Kenton County, Kentucky tax lists in 1834 and 1835; Michael R. Averdick, *A Directory of Silversmiths, Jewelers, Watch and Clock Makers and Related Trades of Covington and Newport, Kentucky & Vicinity 1833–1900*, Covington, KY: 829 Willard Street Press, 2002, 36.

4. Advertisement, *Cincinnati Daily Gazette*, March 2, 1843, reproduced in Beckman, 81.

5. "Mechanics' Fair," *Cincinnati Enquirer*, June 26, 1843, 2; "Mechanics' Fair," *Cincinnati Enquirer*, June 28, 1843: 2.

6. Advertisement, *Cincinnati Daily Gazette*, January 24, 1844,

reproduced in Beckman, 86.

7. Comley and D'Eggville, *Ohio: The Future Great State*, 222.

8. Julia A. Kinsey, burial record, Spring Grove Cemetery; Comley and D'Eggville, *Ohio: The Future Great State*, 222.

9. Burial records, Spring Grove Cemetery; Charles S. Kinsey was listed in the 1865 Cincinnati City Directory as a silversmith working at E. & D. Kinsey. It is likely that he apprenticed with his father. In the 1860 Federal Census, he is listed as a clerk, probably for E. & D. Kinsey. Between 1866 and 1885, he worked as a surveyor or in some other capacity associated with civil engineering. Louis A. Kinsey was listed in the 1871 Cincinnati City

Directory as a silversmith working at the D. Kinsey firm. He surely apprenticed with his father. He left in 1872, to serve as a clerk and then a bookkeeper at the Royer Wheel Co., a manufacturer of wheel hubs and spokes.

10. 1850 and 1860 Federal Censuses, Cincinnati, Hamilton, Ohio; 1857–1861 Cincinnati City Directories.

11. 1850 Federal Census, Cincinnati, Hamilton, Ohio; 1860 Federal Census, Cincinnati, Hamilton, Ohio; Thomas L. Byram, *The Genealogy of Nine Early Families in the Ohio River Valley*, Brooklyn, NY: 405

Westminster Road Press, 1969, 57.

12. Ohio, Vol. 2, p. 228, R.G. Dun & Co. Collection, Baker Library, Harvard Business School.

13. Ohio, Vol. 2, p. 228, R.G. Dun & Co Collection.

14. Ibid.

15. *Report of the General Committee of the Cincinnati Industrial Exposition, held in Cincinnati, under the auspices of the Ohio Mechanics' Institute, Board of Trade, and Chamber of Commerce, From September 21st to October 22nd, 1870*, Cincinnati: General Committee of the Cincinnati Industrial Exposition, 1870, 279.

16. "Great Industrial Exposition, The Closing Days," *Cincinnati Enquirer*, October 19, 1870, 3

17. 1870 Federal Non-Population Census Schedules, Products of Industry, Schedule 4, Hamilton County, Ohio.

18. 1860 and 1870 Federal Censuses, Cincinnati, Hamilton, Ohio. 1865–1873 Cincinnati City Directories.

19. 1872 Cincinnati City Directory.

20. David Kinsey, will dated April 16, 1873, proved April 2, 1874, vol. 2, p. 381, Hamilton County Registry of Probate, Cincinnati, Ohio; David Kinsey, burial record; Death notice,

Cincinnati Enquirer, March 31, 1874, 5.

21. David Kinsey, will.

22. Ohio, Vol. 10, p. 342, R.G. Dun & Co. Collection.

23. Ibid.

24. Advertisement, *Cincinnati Times Star*, January 27, 1875, 4; Ohio, Vol. 10, p. 289, R.G. Dun & Co. Collection.

25. David Kinsey, eBay listings and private collections, Cincinnati silver binders, Cincinnati Art Museum.

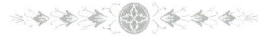

65. D. KINSEY & CO.

1875–1879

After **David Kinsey**'s death in 1874, his son **Edward W. Kinsey** (1851–1913) assumed management of his father's business at 28 West Fourth Street.[1] In January 1875 he sold his interest in the business to his brother **Louis A. Kinsey** (1854–1928) and **John B. Callahan** (1849–1921), an employee of the Kinseys since 1866, and the name of the firm became D. Kinsey & Co. (fig. 65.1).[2] Kinsey and Callahan had a "capital of $32,000 equally divided."[3] Initially, the credit reporters of R.G. Dun & Co. noted the firm with favor, but eventually their perspective changed. In June 1877 reporters noted that the firm was carrying on a limited business, and that it was doubtful that they were making any money. By October of that year, Callahan had withdrawn as partner, although he continued to work there.[4] Louis continued in business alone as D. Kinsey & Co.[5] In September 1878 R.G. Dun reporters observed, he "has not kept up the business as his father did and is doing so little business that it is considered only a question of time with him . . . Parties who first courted his trade and sold him freely now give him the 'go by' altogether . . . It is also reported that he plays euchre for money which fact does not tend to strengthen confidence in him."[6] In March 1879 Louis Kinsey leased a store in the Johnson Building at the corner of Fifth and Walnut Streets, and began to sell his old stock, some of which had been owned by his father, at auction.[7] By the end of the month, he had changed the name of his firm to **L.A. Kinsey**.[8]

Extant silver bearing mark 65.1 includes master butter knives, and spoons of various sizes with modified fancy fiddle handles

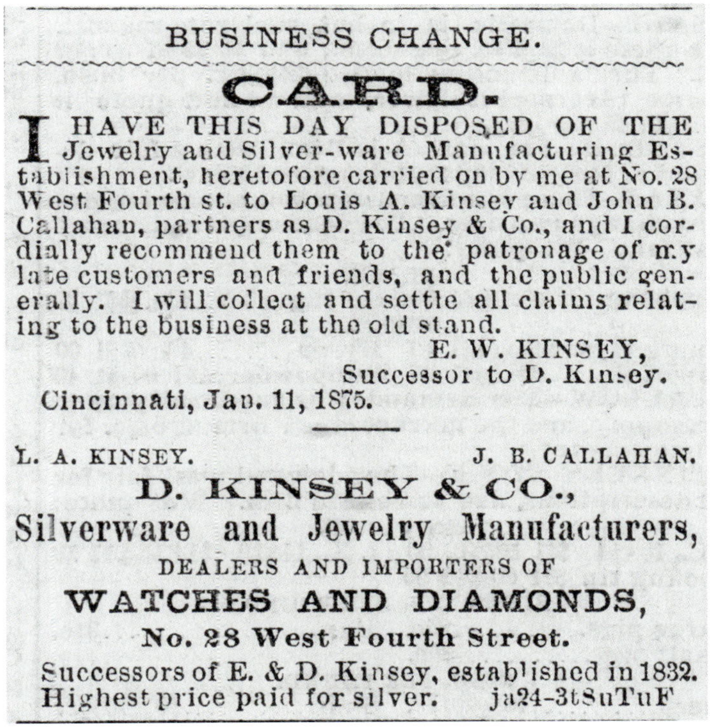

BUSINESS CHANGE.

CARD.

I HAVE THIS DAY DISPOSED OF THE Jewelry and Silver-ware Manufacturing Establishment, heretofore carried on by me at No. 28 West Fourth st. to Louis A. Kinsey and John B. Callahan, partners as D. Kinsey & Co., and I cordially recommend them to the patronage of my late customers and friends, and the public generally. I will collect and settle all claims relating to the business at the old stand.

E. W. KINSEY,
Successor to D. Kinsey.

Cincinnati, Jan. 11, 1875.

L. A. KINSEY.　　　　　　　　J. B. CALLAHAN.

D. KINSEY & CO.,
Silverware and Jewelry Manufacturers,
DEALERS AND IMPORTERS OF
WATCHES AND DIAMONDS,
No. 28 West Fourth Street.

Successors of E. & D. Kinsey, established in 1832.
Highest price paid for silver.　　ja24-3t8uTuF

FIG. 65.1: "Business Change," *Cincinnati Enquirer*, January 26, 1875, 5

with bright cut decoration and twist stems, similar to **Duhme & Co.**'s "No. 1" (circa 1869). One documented master butter knife in this style has a wonderful, engraved river bank scene with a boat on the blade. Spoons with tipped, exaggerated fiddle handles and pointed shoulders have also been observed with mark 65.1. An incuse "D. KINSEY & CO." mark has also been observed on flatware in the aforementioned styles.[9] In addition to any silver of his or his late father's manufacture, Louis was retailing the work of others. It is doubtful that the manufactory was still in operation under Edward W. Kinsey or Louis A. Kinsey.

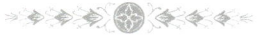

MARK 65.1

1. 1900 Federal Census, Los Angeles, Los Angeles, California; Death date published in *California Decisions: The Official Organ of the Supreme Court of the State of California*, vol. 55, *January–June, 1918*, San Francisco: The Recorder Printing and Publishing Company, 1918, 647–650; Ohio, Vol. 10, p. 289, R.G. Dun & Co. Collection, Baker Library, Harvard Business School.

2. 1866–1874 Cincinnati City Directories; Advertisement, *Cincinnati Times Star*, January 27, 1875, 4; Ohio, Vol. 10, p. 289, R.G. Dun & Co. Collection.

3. Ohio, Vol. 10, p. 289, R.G. Dun & Co. Collection.

4. Ibid.

5. Ibid.

6. Ibid.; Credit reporters also note that an old friend of his father's "Middleton of NY" was backing Louis A. Kinsey. The identity of "Middleton of NY" has yet to be discovered.

7. Ohio, Vol. 10, p. 289, R.G. Dun & Co. Collection.

8. Ibid.

9. David Kinsey & Co., eBay listings and private collections, Cincinnati silver binders, Cincinnati Art Museum.

66. E. & D. KINSEY

1844–1861

Brothers **Edward** and **David Kinsey** formed the E. & D. Kinsey silverware manufactory in January 1844.[1] The Kinseys' shop was on the northwest corner of Sixth and Walnut Streets, Edward's former stand, until about 1850, when it moved to 32 West Fifth Street, between Main and Walnut Streets, near the Fifth Street Market.[2] Edward and David both resided in the quarters above their shop, until David moved to a home on Fourth Street in 1857.[3] An image of their Fifth Street establishment is found in a depiction of Abraham Lincoln's pre-election visit to Cincinnati in 1859 (fig. 66.1). Lincoln spoke at 8 o'clock in the evening on September 17 to an assembled crowd from the second-story, iron balcony of the Kinseys' building.[4]

The range of goods that E. & D. Kinsey made and offered for wholesale and retail sale is enumerated in an 1844 advertisement (fig. 66.2). A later advertisement indicates that they also imported fine watches, jewelry, and Sheffield plate.[5] The scope of their production and distribution is noteworthy. Their wares were going west and southwest, and evidence suggests that a great deal of their work, especially flatware, was sold and marked by other silversmiths and retailers in Cincinnati and its surrounding areas.

The 1850 Products of Industry Census indicates that the firm employed a staff of 16 (13 males and 3 females—females were often employed as burnishers) and that they had $5,000 worth of capital invested.[6] They had utilized $25,000 worth of silver that year to create product valued at $35,000, and they were, by far, the largest and most profitable Cincinnati firm in the silver, jewelry, watch, and clock making category reporting that year.[7] In 1851, credit reporters noted: "doing a large business" and "are getting wealthy very fast." In 1858, the firm was "said to do the largest manufacturing business in the West; perfectly good and have made money notwithstanding the times."[8]

The Kinseys advertised and exhibited their wares often. In 1850, they entered "specimens of silver ware" at the Ohio State Fair and the Ohio Mechanics' Institute (OMI) Fair, both held in Cincinnati.[9] They were frequent exhibitors at the OMI Fair, and won a silver medal in 1854, when the judges reported, "the samples of silverware presented by Messrs. E. & D. Kinsey, fully sustains the high reputation they have already won. The elegance of form and the splendor of finish of the various articles in their collection were admired by thousands during the exhibition."[10] Four years later,

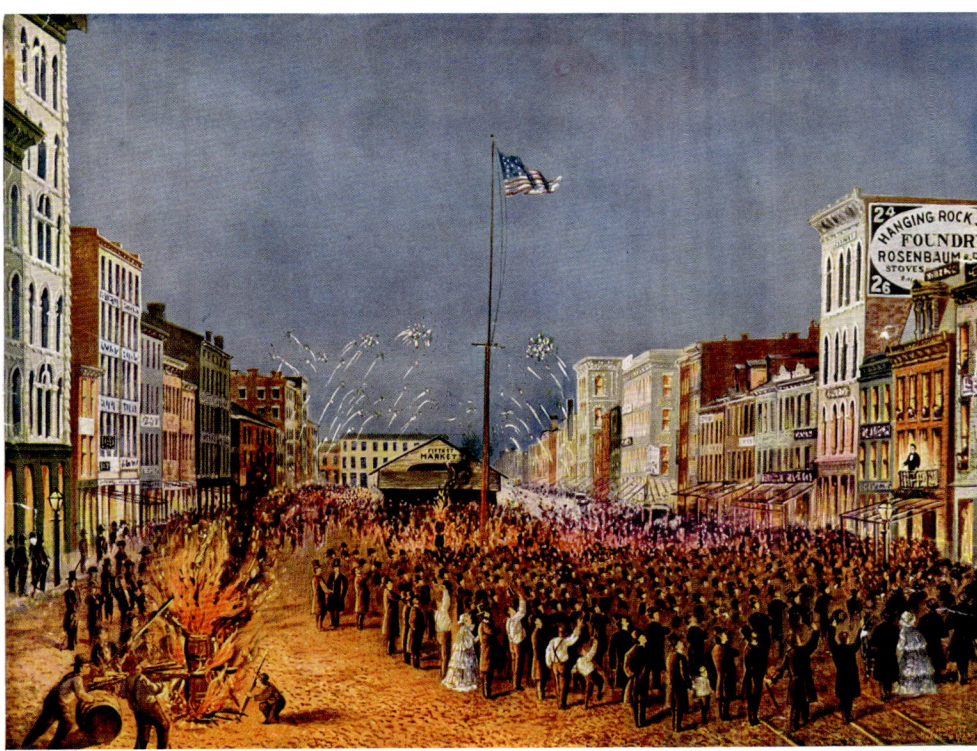

FIG. 66.1: Traxel & Mas, *Lincoln in Cincinnati Speaking from Balcony at No. 32 West Fifth Street, now Goverment Square, September 17, 1859*, lithograph, Photo & Print Collection, Cincinnati Museum Center

SILVER WARE MANUFACTORY,
Corner 6th and Walnut sts.

THE subscribers being associated together under the firm of E. & D. KINSEY, would respectfully inform their friends and the public generally, that they will continue to carry on the business in all its various branches, at the above old and well established stand, where all orders in their line will be thankfully received.

Among the articles generally made at this establishment, we would mention the following: Table, Tea and Dessert Spoons, of the most fashionable patterns; Soup, Gravy, and Cream Ladles; Table and Dessert Forks; Onyx, Agate, and Pearl handled Butter Knives; Silver and Gold Spectacles, a good assortment of which is kept constantly on hand, and for sale wholesale and retail.

We are prepared to make to order at the shortest notice Presentation, and other Plate, of any style or pattern that may be required, and will warrant the material and workmanship to be of the very best quality.

Being both practical workmen, and having had 10 years experience in business in this city, we hope to merit at least a share of public patronage.

E. KINSEY,
D. KINSEY.

jan 24

FIG. 66.2: Advertisement, *Daily Cincinnati Gazette*, January 24, 1844

they exhibited a "large case of silverware" described by the award committee as "beautifully executed and of appropriate pattern," but entered too late to receive a prize.[11]

Edward Kinsey traveled abroad in 1851 to England, Belgium, Germany, France, and Switzerland.[12] While in London, he most certainly attended the Great Exhibition of the Works of Industry of All Nations, held in Hyde Park from May to October. Tokens (fig. 66.3) that advertise the Kinseys' manufactory on one side, bear an

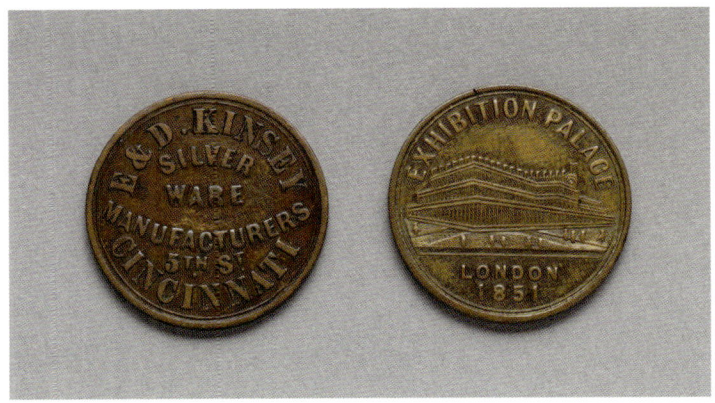

FIG. 56.3: E. & D. Kinsey, *Great Exhibition Tokens*, Courtesy of Irene and Daniel Randolph

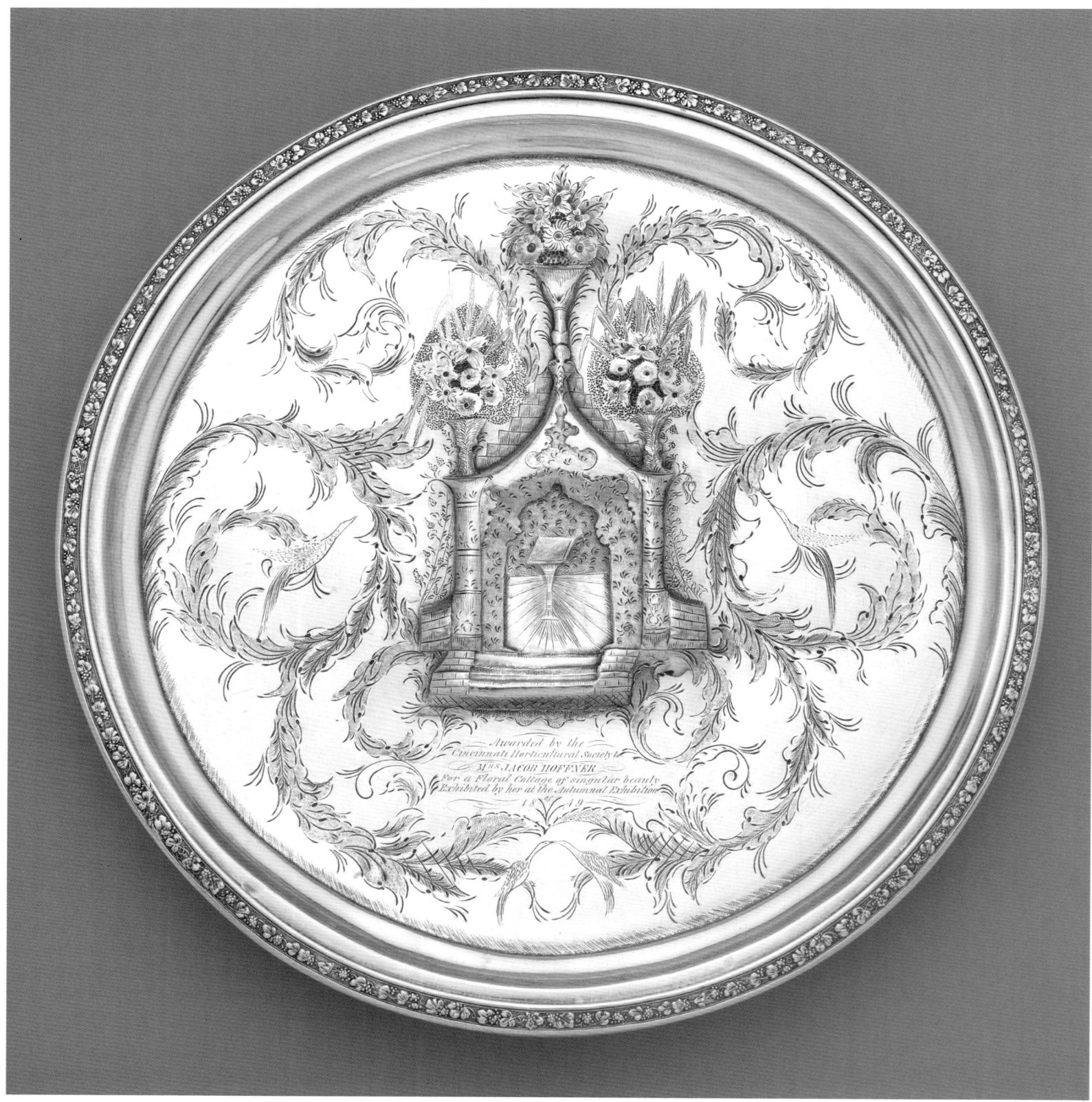

FIG. 66.4: E. & D. Kinsey, *Salver*, 1849, 1¼ × 10⁵⁄₁₆ in. (3.2 × 26.2 cm), CAM, Museum Purchase: Lee Cowan Group Art Purchase Fund, 2003.158. Inscription: Awarded by the Cincinnati Horticultural Society To MRS. JACOB HOFFNER For a Floral Cottage of Singular Beauty Exhibited by her at the Autumnal Exhibition of 1849

image of the London exhibition palace in 1851 on the reverse. However, evidence that the Kinseys exhibited at the Great Exhibition could not be found.[13] The tokens were likely used as store cards, promoting the firm and implying that the Kinseys were aware of the latest fashions and techniques introduced at The Great Exhibition.[14] In 1855, David traveled to Paris, most likely to attend the *Exposition Universelle*, a world fair held on the Champs-Elysées from May to November.[15] In August 1859 Edward returned to Europe, traveling to Paris and London with his daughter Eugenia.[15]

As noted in their earliest advertisement, the firm was "prepared to make to order at the shortest notice Presentation and other Plate."[17] We know of several such orders through written accounts and extant silver. In 1845, they were commissioned to make a pitcher, standing 13 inches high and 20 inches in circumference, that was "Presented to the Hon. James Kilbourne by the friends of the Eclectic Medical Institute of Cincinnati, in consideration of his able and efficient support of the cause of Medical Reformation."[18] Another pitcher, described as "one of the most beautiful and magnificent silver pitchers that could be produced . . . of antique model, with slight chasing of the borders and handle," was made by the firm and presented to Mr. Salmon P. Chase "from the colored people of Cincinnati, for his various services in behalf of the oppressed and particularly for his eloquent advocacy of the rights of man in the case of Samuel Watson who was claimed as a fugitive slave, Feb. 12, 1845."[19] A pitcher of "nearly two quarts capacity, of elegant design and finish" was made for Captain W.C. Trumbour, clerk of the Walnut Street House and given to him upon his leave by the House's boarders in 1853.[20] And, on March 17, 1853, an impressive pitcher measuring 17 inches high, with an inverted pear-shaped body covered in chased and engraved decoration of leaves, sunflowers, and pineapples, resting on a square plinth base with paw feet was "Presented to J.D. Taylor For his patriotic and manly efforts in support of the American system of common schools."[21]

The firm's marks have been found on various forms, mostly beakers and pitchers, presented at agricultural fairs, as well as a wonderfully unique salver (fig. 66.4) that was presented to Mrs. Jacob Hoffner by the Cincinnati Horticultural Society for her "floral cottage of singular beauty, exhibited at the Autumnal Exhibition in 1849."[22] Its repoussé and chased decoration include a folly-like shrine bedecked with flowers and containing an open book on a pedestal. Delicate scrolling leaves and birds of paradise surround the shrine. This decoration was, no doubt, meant to recall the cottage that it celebrated, which is described in a contemporary account as:

. . . about six feet square, and with the two steps of ascent, about 8 or 9 feet high. It was formed of lattice and wire work, in which . . . climbing vines were so skillfully interwoven as to cover it entirely . . . . At each corner of the cottage was a marble statue (about three feet high), each representing one of the four seasons. Two lambs sculpted in marble, lay one on each side of the steps leading into the cottage, and in the interior were a chair and table; on the latter was a globe of gold-fish, above which hung a rare and curious orchid . . . . The chair (and sometimes another) was occasionally occupied by a beautiful child, who dispensed bouquets of flowers to such as made suitable application for them.[23]

Known church silver produced by E. & D. Kinsey includes a pair of chalices (engraved with the date 1850) and a wine ewer (engraved 1858) for the Swedenborgian First New Jerusalem Society, and a two-handled cup for the Ninth Street Baptist Church (circa 1850).[24] The cup was designed to match an earlier cup made for the church and marked by **Joseph Draper**.[25]

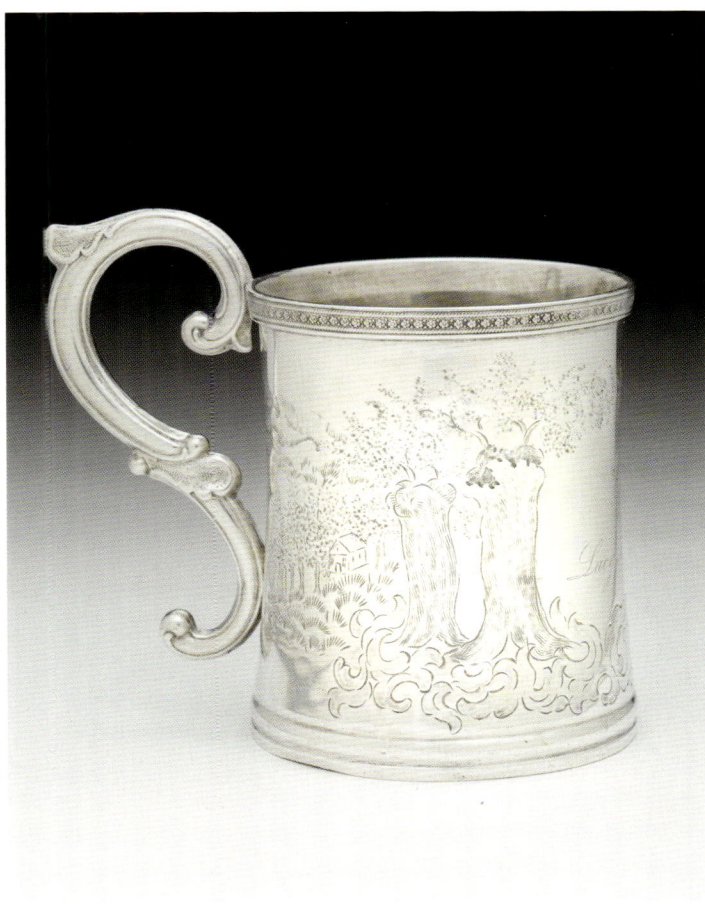

FIG. 66.5: E. & D. Kinsey, *Mug*, 1844–1861, 3¼ × 4¼ × 2¾ in. (8.3 × 10.8 × 7 cm), Bequest of Virginia H. Irwin, 1956.401. Inscription: G I to Lucy Ann Burdsal

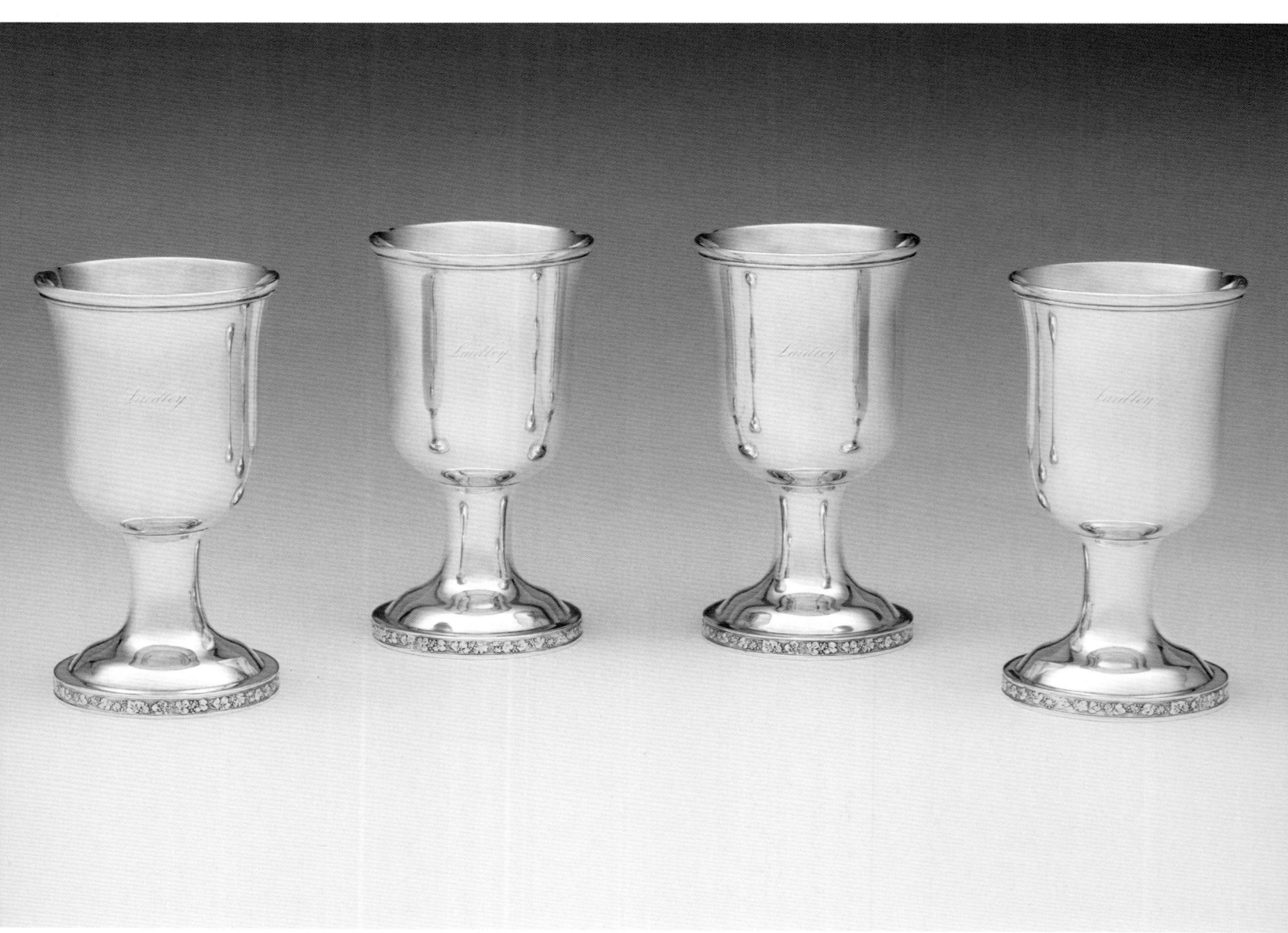

FIG. 66.6: E. & D. Kinsey, *Set of Goblets*, 1844–1861, 5⅝ × 3 in. (14.3 × 7.6 cm), Private Collection. Inscription: Laidley

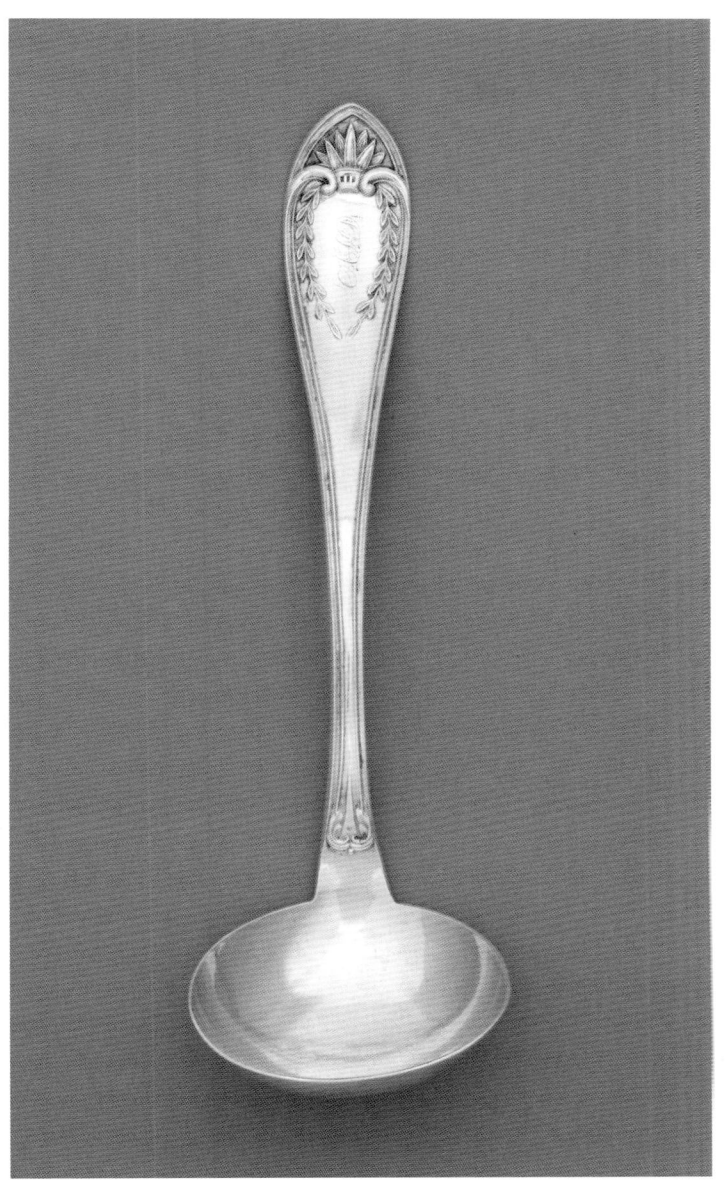

FIG. 66.7: E. & D. Kinsey, *Ladle*, 1844–1861, L. 7⅜ in. (18.7 cm),
CAM, Gift of Dr. Suzanne A. Beutler, 1983.207

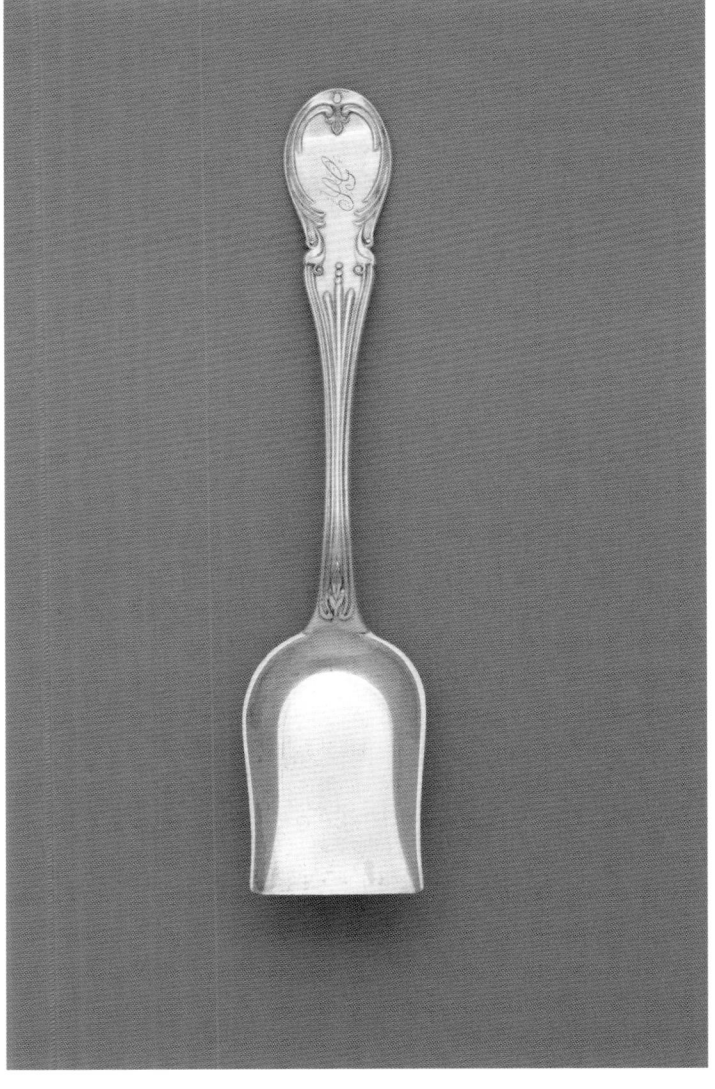

FIG. 66.8: E. & D. Kinsey, *Sugar Shovel*, 1844–1861, L. 6 in. (15.2 cm),
CAM, Gift of John S. Conner, 1910.192

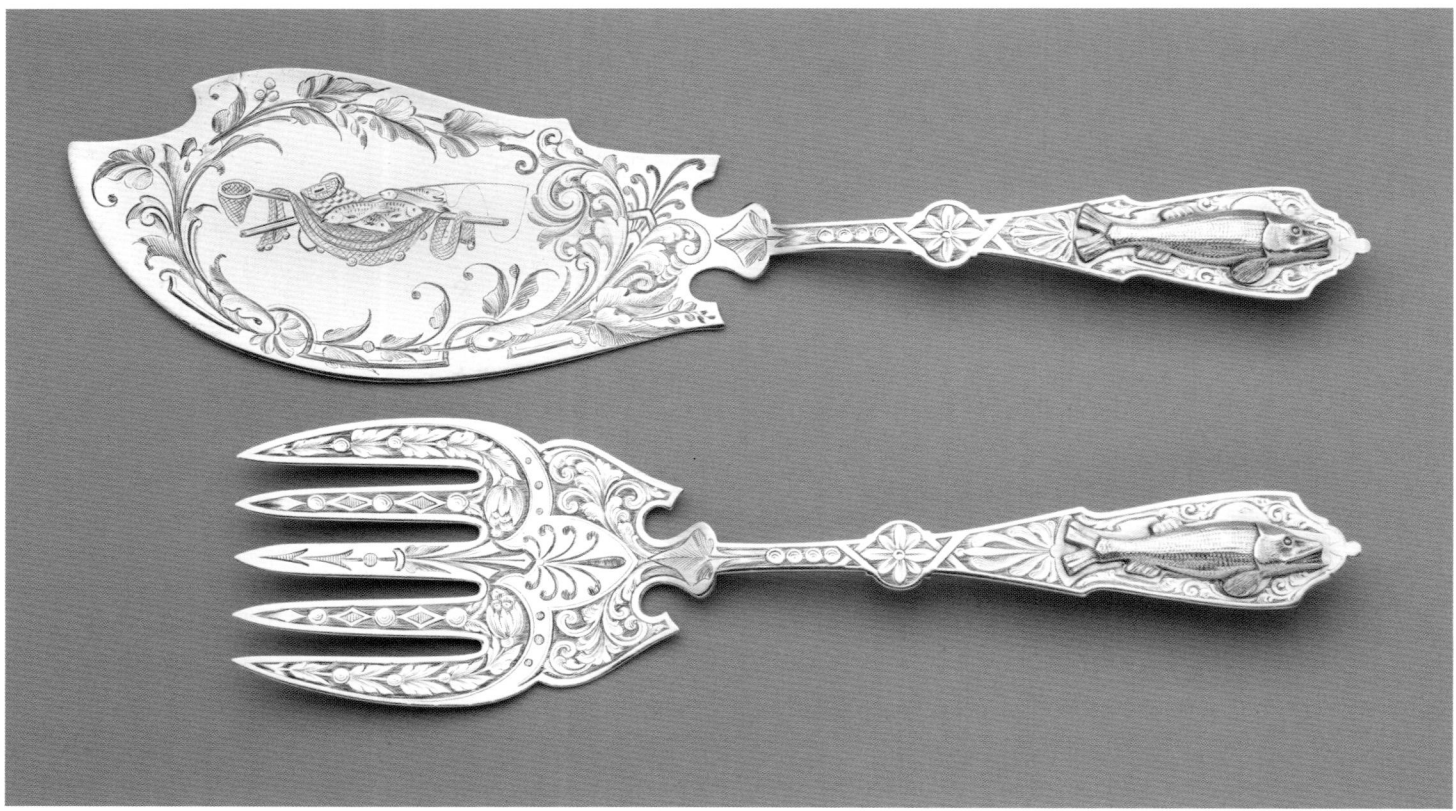

FIG. 66.9: E. & D. Kinsey, *Fish Set*, 1844–1861, Beckman Collection, Cincinnati Museum Center

Without question, the firm of E. & D. Kinsey was the largest and most important silver producer in the Midwest leading up to the Civil War. At least 25 men who are addressed in Appendix A worked at E. & D. Kinsey, and there were surely more who have gone undiscovered. The sheer amount of silver existing with their mark also attests to their productivity and success. In 1861, Edward retired, and David continued the business in his own name.

The firm used a number of different marks during their history. Based on extant ware with dated, engraved inscriptions, mark 66.1 was used during the time that Edward and David Kinsey were partners.[26] The various forms known with this mark include beakers, presentation pitchers, mugs (fig. 66.5), goblets (fig. 66.6), and flatware with tipped, exaggerated fiddle handles and pointed shoulders. Flatware in this design with mark 66.1 has also been documented with a second mark—the shield-breasted, left-facing eagle with upturned wings believed to have been a manufacturing mark used by Edward Kinsey (fig. 67.3).[27] A master butter knife with exaggerated fiddle handle and twist stem, covered in engraved decoration that includes a river bank scene on the blade has also been observed with mark 66.1, as well as flatware in at least five die-pressed

patterns: a tipped, fiddle thread pattern; the pattern of the ladle observed in fig. 66.7; "Dew Drop" (1860) produced by George W. Shiebler; the pattern of the sugar shovel in fig. 66.8; and a variant of the "Olive" pattern with a beaded border.[28] Mark 66.2 , observed on a pair of salt spoons with fiddle handles and pointed shoulders, is rarely found.

The aforementioned chalices made for the First New Jerusalem Society, a mug, and the Hoffner salver (fig. 66.4) all bear mark 66.3. Mark 66.4 appears on a number of works, many of which bear dated inscriptions that place them between 1854 and 1858. This mark may have been used largely for goods that were bought and retailed by the Kinseys. A group of related objects with mark 66.4 suggests that the Kinseys were customers of Grosjean & Woodward (New York).[29] Wares with this mark include a fish set (fig. 66.9), pitchers (including fig. 66.10), tea and coffee services (including fig. 66.11), mugs with repoussé chased decoration in the Rococo Revival style, beakers, salvers, and the abovementioned wine ewer for the First New Jerusalem Society.[30] Mark 66.5 is not found often. It has been documented on a tea and coffee service, and a hot-water urn, both in the Rococo Revival style.[31]

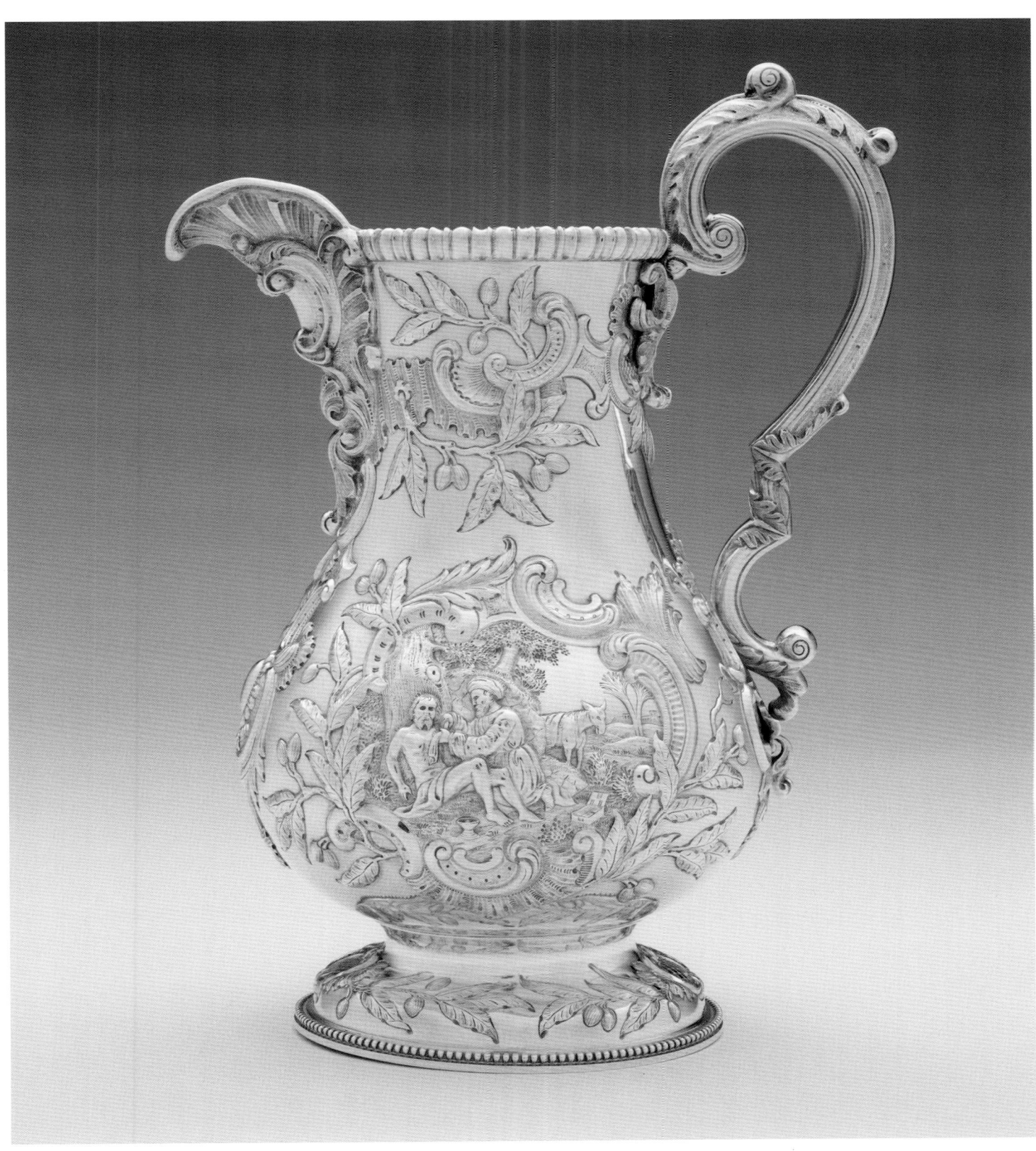

FIG. 66.10: E. & D. Kinsey, retailer, and Grosjean & Woodward,
attributed manufacturer, *"Good Samaritan" Pitcher*, 1844–1861,
11¹³⁄₁₆ × 9 × 6¼ in. (30 × 22.9 × 15.9 cm), CAM, Museum Purchase, 2000.158

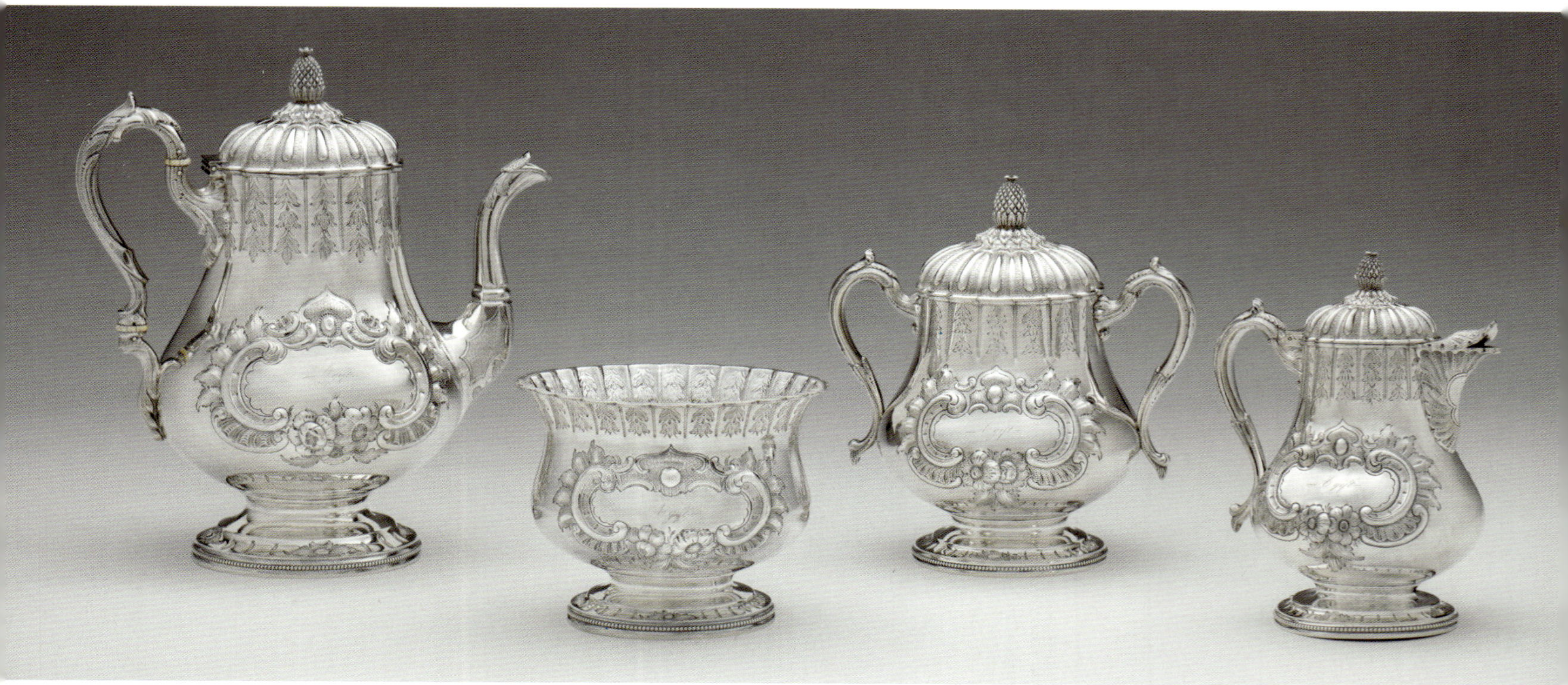

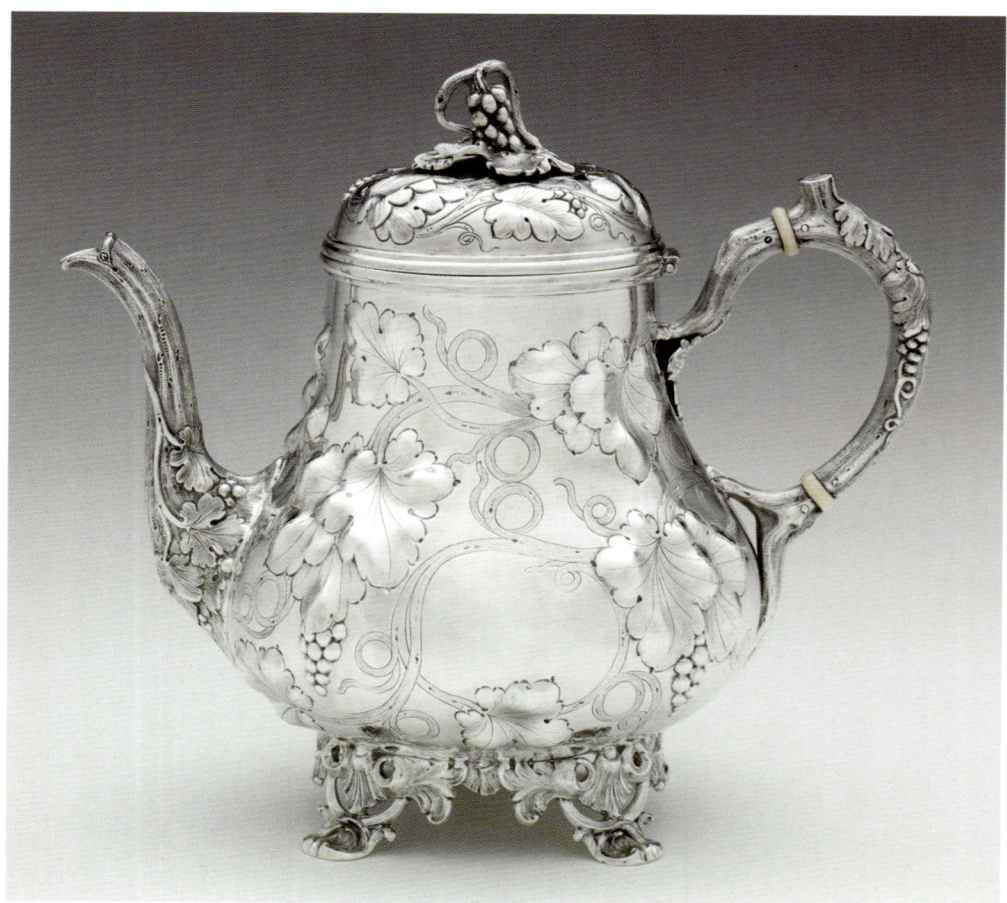

FIG. 66.11: E. & D. Kinsey, *Coffee Pot, Waste Bowl, Sugar, and Creamer,* 1844–1861, coffee pot: 11 × 10½ in. (27.9 × 26.7 cm), waste bowl: 4¾ × 6 in. (12.1 × 15.2 cm), sugar 8⅛ × 8 × 6 in. (20.6 × 20.3 × 15.2 cm), creamer: 7½ × 6 in. (19.1 × 15.2 cm), CAM, Gift of Mr. and Mrs. Charles Fleischmann III, 2005.22a–b, 2007.5a–c

FIG. 66.12: E. & D. Kinsey, *Teapot,* 1844–1861, 9⅛ × 10½ in. (23.2 × 26.7 cm), CAM, Gift of James Randolph Hillard, M.D. and Aingeal Grehan, 2007.195

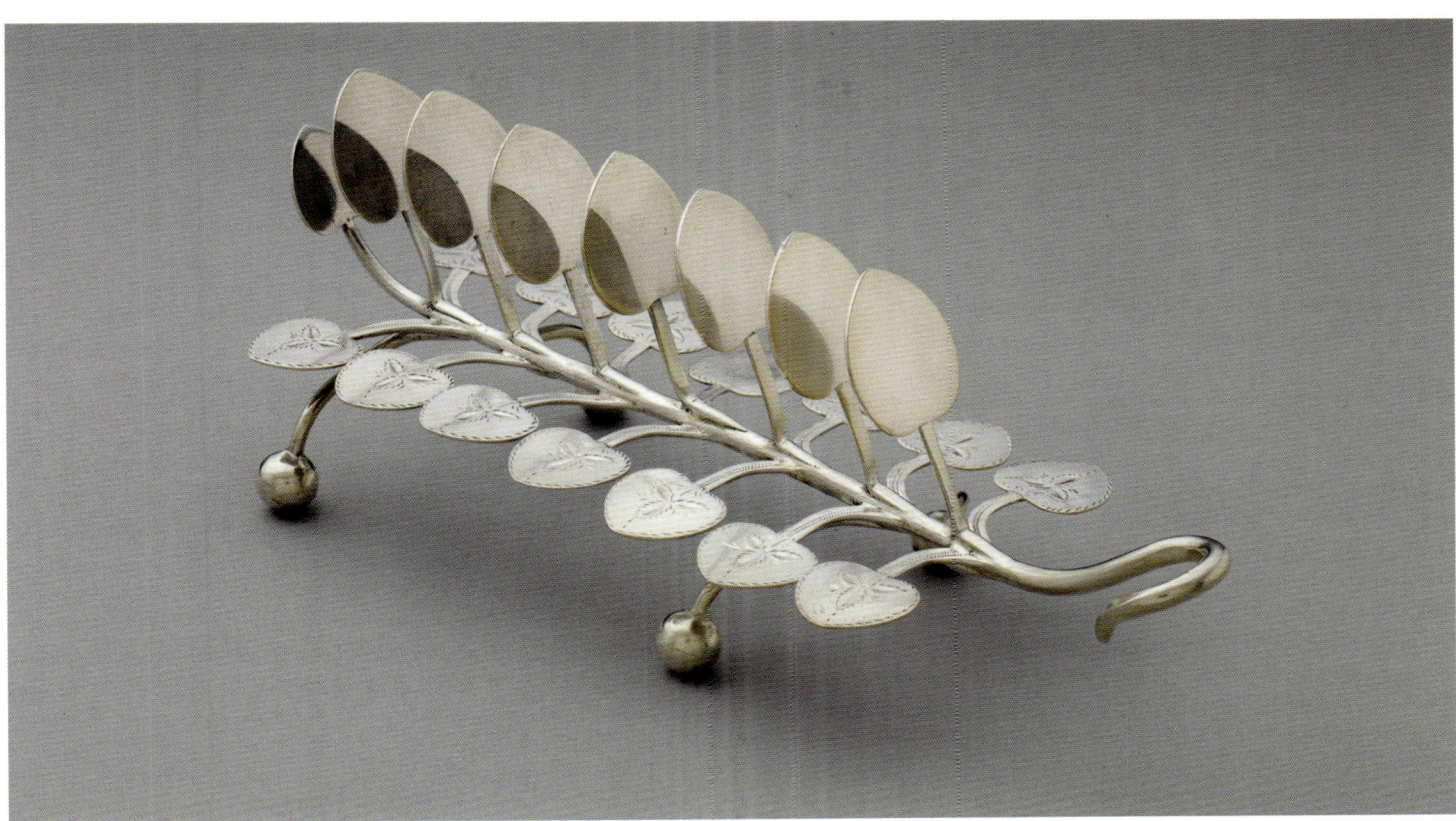

FIG. 66.13: E. & D. Kinsey, *Toast Rack*,
1844–1861, 3 × 3 × 8 in. (7.6 × 7.6 × 20.3 cm),
CAM, Gift of Mr. and Mrs. Charles
Fleischmann III, 2009.1

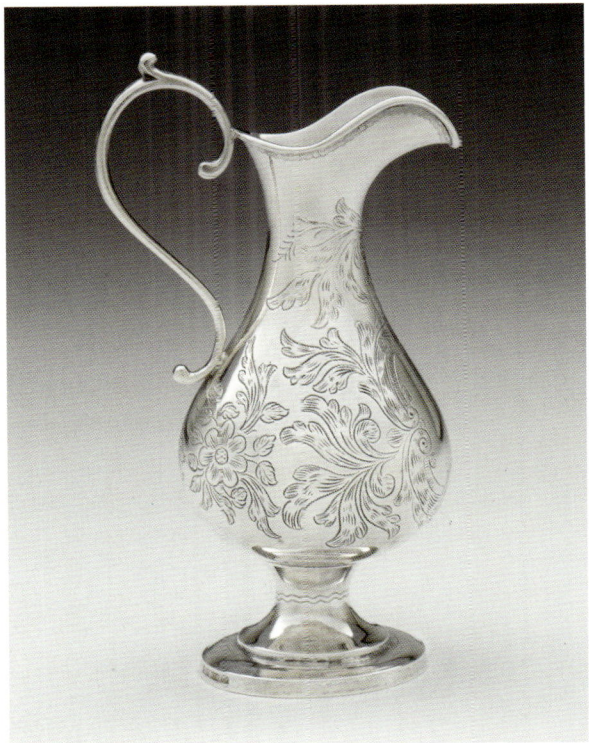

FIG. 66.14: E. & D. Kinsey, *Miniature Ewer*,
1844–1861, 5½ × 3⅛ in. (14 × 7.9 cm), Private Collection

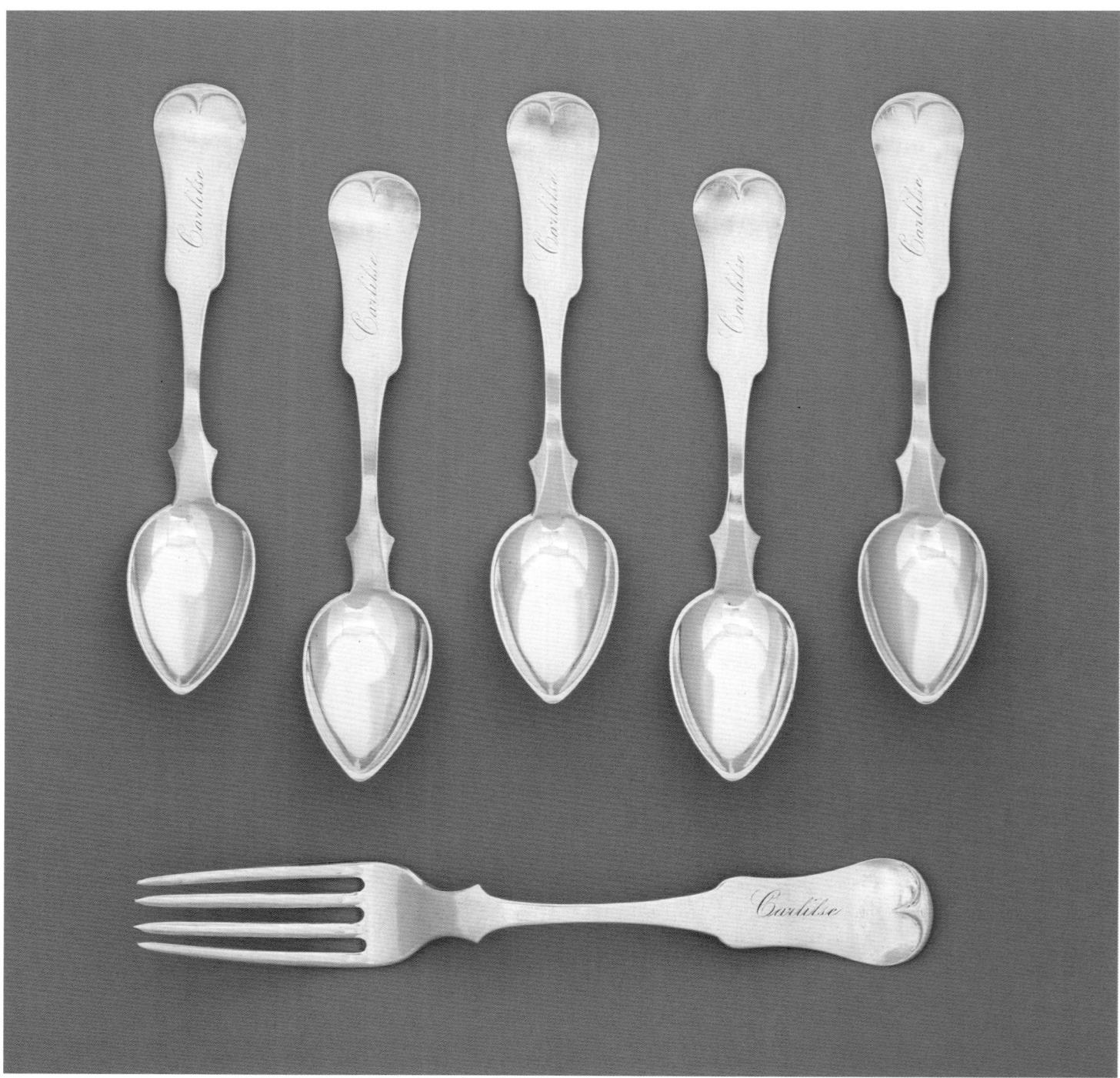

FIG. 66.15: E. & D. Kinsey, *Teapoons*, 1844–1861, L. 6⅛ in. (15.6 cm), CAM, Given by Elizabeth M. and Annie W. Anderson in memory of their mother, Mrs. Buckner W. Anderson, 1969.740–745; E. & D. Kinsey, *Dessert Fork*, 1844–1861, L. 7¹¹⁄₁₆ in. (19.5 cm), Given by Elizabeth M. and Annie W. Anderson in memory of their mother, Mrs. Buckner W. Anderson, 1969.745. Inscription: Carlisle. This flatware belonged to George and Sarah Carlisle, married 1828. George Carlisle (1797–1863) was one of Cincinnati's pioneer bankers and businessmen.

Mark 66.6 is occasionally accompanied by "CINCINNATI," in a rectangular cartouche, and/or one of two eagles: the shield-breasted, left-facing eagle associated with Edward Kinsey (fig. 67.3), or the left-facing eagle (without a shielded breast) that is associated with either Edward Kinsey or **Pulaski Scovil** (fig. 67.4).[32] It is, by far, the mark that is seen the most today. Works with dated inscriptions place this mark in use between approximately 1853 and 1855, although it is possible that this punch could have been used before or after these dates. It has been documented on a teapot (fig. 66.12), toast rack (fig. 66.13), the two-handled cup made for the Ninth Street Baptist Church, the presentation ewer for J.D. Taylor, a vinaigrette, chatelaine, mugs, cream pitchers, beakers, and both full size and miniature ewers (fig. 66.14). It also appears frequently on flatware, particularly examples with the tipped, exaggerated fiddle handles and pointed shoulders (fig. 66.15). This form, with its strongly

defined tip at the pinnacle of the handle, must have been produced by the thousands, as it was retailed by many of the regional silversmiths working during this era. Spoons with tipped, fiddle handles (without the exaggeration) and rounded shoulders; spoons with round shafts and ball finials; forks in a die-pressed fiddle thread and shell pattern; serving flatware in multiple variations of the exaggerated fiddle handle with all-over engraved decoration, with or without twist stems; and tongs with shell or claw terminals have also been found with this mark. Other individuals or firms whose marks appear alongside mark 66.6 include Phillip Zoellner (Portsmouth, Ohio, 1855–circa 1860), Butler & McCarthey (Philadelphia, circa 1869), J.E. Caldwell & Co. (Philadelphia, 1848–present), and Geissler & Delang (Evansville, Indiana, circa 1869).[33] A threaded fiddle butter knife has been documented with mark 66.7.[34]

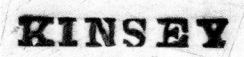

MARK. 66.1

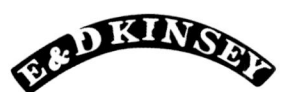

MARK. 66.4

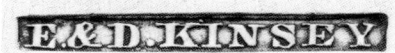

MARK. 66.6

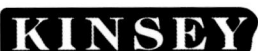

MARK. 66.2

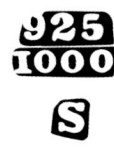

MARK. 66.5

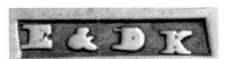

MARK. 66.7

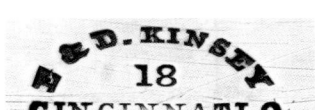

MARK. 66.3

1. Edward Kinsey had opened a silverware manufactory by June 1836. Advertisement, *Cincinnati Daily Gazette*, June 13, 1836, reproduced in Beckman, 84; Advertisement, 1839/40 Cincinnati City Directory, 39, reproduced in Beckman, 85; Advertisement, *Cincinnati Daily Gazette*, January 24, 1844, reproduced in Beckman, 86.

2. 1844–1861 Cincinnati City Directories; Between 1842 and 1844, city directories list the Kinseys' address as the corner of Seventh and Walnut Streets. Advertisements from this time indicated that their shop was at the northwest corner of Walnut and Sixth Streets, indicating

that the address in the directories was a misprint. In 1853, house numbers were changed throughout the city. This accounts for the change in the Kinseys' address in 1853 from 32 West Fifth to 24 West Fifth Street.

3. 1850 and 1860 Federal Censuses, Cincinnati, Hamilton, Ohio; 1857–1861 Cincinnati City Directories.

4. Daniel Mark Epstein, *The Lincolns: Portrait of A Marriage*, New York: Ballantine Books, 2008, 239; Gene D. Lewis (ed.), "Lincoln's Cincinnati Speech of 1859," *Bulletin of The Cincinnati Historical Society* 23, no. 3 (July 1965): 149.

5. *W.W. Reilly & Co.'s Ohio State Business*

Directory for 1853–54, Cincinnati: Morgan & Overend, 1853, 1:36.

6. 1850 Federal Non-Population Census Schedules, Products of Industry, Schedule 4, Hamilton County, Ohio.

7. Ibid.

8. Ohio, Vol. 1, p. 90, Vol. 2, p. 228, R.G. Dun & Co. Collection, Baker Library, Harvard Business School.

9. *Fifth Annual Report of the Board of Agriculture of the State of Ohio, to the Forty-Ninth General Assembly, for the year 1850*, Columbus: S. Medary, 1851, 631; Ohio Mechanics' Institute, *Board of Directors' Minute Book 1840–1969*, vol. 1, *December 1840–August 1854*, University of

Cincinnati Archives and Rare Books Library, 87–88.

10. *Report of the Thirteenth Annual Exhibition of the Ohio Mechanics' Institute*, Cincinnati: Ohio Mechanics' Institute, 1854, 45, 55.

11. *Report of the Sixteenth Exhibition of the Ohio Mechanics' Institute*, Cincinnati: Ohio Mechanics' Institute, 1858, 83.

12. "Edward Kinsey" in National Archives and Records Administration (NARA), Washington DC, *Passport Applications, 1795–1905*, ARC Identifier 566612/MLR Number A1 508, NARA series M1372, roll 36, roll 78.

13. Leonard Forrer, *Biographical Dictionary Of Medallists*, London:

Spink & Son Ltd., 1909, 4:667; David E. Schenkman (ed.), *A Survey of American Trade Tokens*, Lawrence, MA: Quarterman Publications, Inc., 1975, 130–131.

14. Innovators themselves, the Kinseys applied for a patent for an improved mode of stopping bottles and cans in 1852, which entailed "providing the mouth of bottles and cans with a cylindrical or other shaped tube made of silver, tin, or other metals or substances"; Edward and David Kinsey. Improvement in bottle stoppers. US Patent 9407, issued Nov. 16, 1852.

15. "News by the Mails," *The New York Times*, July 20, 1855. Evidence that the Kinseys exhibited at the fair could not be found.

16. "Edward Kinsey" in NARA, *Passport Applications, 1795–1905*, roll 95.

17. Advertisement, *Cincinnati Daily Gazette*, January 24, 1844, reproduced in Beckman, 86.

18. Payne Kenyon Kilbourne, *The Family Memorial. A History and Genealogy of the Kilbourn Family in the United States and Canada From the Year 1635 to the Present Time . . .*, Hartford: Brown & Parsons, 1845, 117; *Ohio Statesman* (Columbus, OH), April 4, 1845, 914.

19. "Chase and the Equalizations of Whites and Blacks," *Cincinnati Enquirer*, August 11, 1857, 2; This pitcher is now in the collection of the Cincinnati Museum Center. Ironically, in the latter half of the 1830s, Edward Kinsey was part of a group of men who sought to secure relations between Cincinnati and the South by silencing Cincinnati abolitionists. In August 1836 he was one of many who stormed and dismantled the abolitionist printing shop, the *Philanthropist*. During this event, he was reportedly shot in the hip and the leg with pigeon shot.

"Mobs—Effects of Abolitionism— Destruction of Property—Bloodshed," *The Louisville Daily Journal*, August 4, 1836, 2; Sally Griffith, "A Proper Spirit of Enterprise: The Booster Ethos and Resistance to Abolitionism in Jacksonian Cincinnati," *Trading Cultures: The Worlds of Western Merchants, Essays on Authority, Objectivity, and Evidence*, Turnhout, Belgium: Brepols, 2001, 243.

20. "Honors to Whom Honors are Due," *Cincinnati Enquirer*, August 3, 1853, 3; Multiple spellings were found in the historical record for Trumbour, including Trumpbour and Trumpbower.

21. Pitcher, "The American Scene: Furniture, Paintings, and Folk Art," Cowan's, October 9, 2010, lot 339.

22. E. & D. Kinsey, eBay listings and private collections, Cincinnati silver binders, Cincinnati Art Museum; *Report of the autumnal exhibition of the Cincinnati Horticultural Society on the 26, 27, 28, & 29, September 1849*, Cincinnati : Gazette Office, 1849, 4–5.

23. *Report of the autumnal exhibition of the Cincinnati Horticultural Society on the 26, 27, 28, & 29, September 1849*, Cincinnati : Gazette Office, 1849, 4–5.

24. Kinsey, ebay listings and private collections, Cincinnati Art Museum.

25. *Two-Handled Cups*, circa 1850, private collection. A fourth cup of the same form, engraved 1880, was made in silver plate for the Ninth Street Baptist Church. The maker of the silver-plated cup is unknown. Information courtesy of Clifton Anderson.

26. Documented pieces with this mark date between 1856 and 1861. Kinsey, ebay listings and private collections, Cincinnati Art Museum.

27. John R. McGrew, *Manufacturers' Marks on American Coin Silver*,

Hanover, PA: Argyros Publications, 2004, 98.

28. Tere Hagan, *Sterling Flatware: An Identification and Value Guide*, Gas City, IN: L-W Book Sales, 1999, 17; Kinsey, ebay listings and private collections, Cincinnati Art Museum; David Kinsey's mark was later seen on flatware in all of these patterns, except for the pattern seen in the sugar shovel, 1910.192 (fig. 66.8).

29. A mug bears mark 66.4 alongside the mark of Grosjean & Woodward. A pitcher (1959.88, fig. 9.4) marked by Beggs & Smith, and Grosjean & Woodward shares remarkable similarities with three other pitchers: the *"Good Samaritan" Pitcher* (2001.158, fig. 66.10) marked by E. & D. Kinsey; a pitcher at the Speed Museum of Art that is marked by E. & D. Kinsey (Speed Museum of Art, 2004.10); and a pitcher marked by Tiffany & Co., illustrated in Charles H. Carpenter with Mary Grace Carpenter, *Tiffany Silver*, New York: Dodd, Mead, 1978, 71. Tiffany was known to have retailed the goods of Grosjean & Woodward (as well as those made by Wood & Hughes) in the 1850s, see Carpenter, *Tiffany Silver*, 246–247. Additionally, a pitcher with an engraved inscription including the year 1857 that sold at Neal Auction Co., December 6 and 7, 2003, lot 485, had an incised Tiffany & Co. mark overstruck with E. & D. Kinsey's mark 4. This suggests that Tiffany and the Kinseys shared a common manufacturing source for some of their retailed wares.

30. E. & D. Kinsey, eBay listings and private collections, Cincinnati Art Museum; A beaker, Cincinnati Art Museum, Gift of Mr. and Mrs. Charles Fleischmann III, 2005.24, is struck with mark 66.4 and the mark

of George W. McDannold, who was active in Covington, Kentucky, between 1850 and 1863. Boultinghouse notes that the "McDANNOLD" mark, the latest of the three marks employed by the smith, has been found overstruck on the "E. & D. KINSEY" mark. This suggests that McDannold purchased silver wholesale from the Kinseys and then resold it. It is believed that after **Charles Asmann** bought out McDannold's business in 1861, he continued to buy from the Kinseys. Boultinghouse, 196; A salver, Cincinnati Art Museum, Museum Purchase with funds provided by Mr. and Mrs. Charles Fleischmann III, 2005.46, is also struck with mark 66.4.

31. These wares also share similarities with designs marked by Grosjean & Woodward; E. & D. Kinsey, eBay listings and private collections, Cincinnati Art Museum.

32. McGrew, *Manufacturers' Marks*, 98–99; E. & D. Kinsey, eBay listings and private collections, Cincinnati Art Museum.

33. Although he does not appear in Cincinnati city directory listings, Zoellner, a native of Germany, is said to have been working in Cincinnati between 1853 and 1855. It is possible that he could have worked for the Kinseys, but proof of this cannot be found. *Portsmouth, Ohio 1898 in pictures and information*, http://www.theportsmouthinfo.com/page /6596/Portsmouth-, accessed May 25, 2013; E. & D. Kinsey, eBay listings and private collections, Cincinnati Art Museum.

34. E. & D. Kinsey, ebay listings and private collections, Cincinnati Art Museum.

67. EDWARD KINSEY

1810–1865, w. 1834–1861[1]

Edward Kinsey, son of Ann and **Thomas Kinsey** was born in Wales. Thomas, Ann, and their nine children, including Edward, came to America on *The Lady Gallatin* which left Liverpool, England, and arrived in New York on June 21, 1820.[2] The family settled briefly in New Jersey before arriving in Newport, Campbell County, Kentucky, just across the Ohio River from Cincinnati, by 1833.[3]

Edward Kinsey surely learned the silversmithing trade from his father, Thomas. Although Thomas' occupation is given as farmer on *The Lady Gallatin* passenger list, the 1850 and 1860 Federal Censuses indicate that he was a silversmith and jeweler, noting in 1860, that at age 87, he lived with Edward and worked every day.[4] No silver bearing his mark is known.

Edward is believed to have been the earliest silversmith working in the Newport, Kentucky area.[5] He appears in the 1834 Newport City Directory as a silversmith boarding at the Newport Hotel, on the corner of York and Front Streets. He was likely in business with **Pulaski Scovil** (**Scovil & Kinsey**) at this time. By 1836, he had moved across the river, and was listed in the Cincinnati City Directory as a silversmith residing on Fourth Street near Race Street.[6] In June, he ran an advertisement for his silver manufactory at the corner of Walnut and Third Streets, where he announced that he "manufactures to order, and offers for sale, Silver Ware of all kinds, warranted equal to Spanish dollars, among which are TEA AND COFFEE SETTS [*sic*], Soup Ladles, Table, Dessert and Tea Spoons, Mugs, Tumblers and Goblets, Candle Sticks, Forks, Fruit and Butter Knives, together with every article in his line . . . furnished to order, at short notice, wholesale or retail."[7] Two years later, in February 1838 Kinsey announced that he had relocated his manufactory to the corner of Sixth and Walnut.[8]

Edward's entries in the First Annual Ohio Mechanics' Institute Fair (1838) provide another snapshot of the types of wares he produced. Edward, who entered "one silver pitcher, sugar tongs, table and tea spoons, tumblers, and knives," and **Abraham Palmer**, were the only silversmiths who participated.[9] The Fair committee reported, "The subscribers, having examined the specimens of silver ware, exhibited by Mr. E. Kinsey . . . adjudge, that Mr. Kinsey is entitled to a certificate for the skill in workmanship and the good taste displayed in the form and fashion of his articles."[10] The following year, he participated in the fair under the category of "miscellaneous articles" and took third prize. Entries of cotton yarn and spun silk took first and second prize. The judges noted that "The Silver Ware manufactured by E. Kinsey is beautiful and well finished. The forms are neat and in good taste, and the whole are creditable to the workman."[11] In 1842, the Mechanics' Institute appointed Edward as a judge for the class of goods that included silver ware.[12]

The fact that Kinsey's business survived the Panic of 1839 is testament to his business acumen and production. An 1840 advertisement read, "not withstanding hard times he [Kinsey] still continues the manufacture of silver."[13] By that year, there were at least six men working at his firm: **Caleb Harris**, **Thomas Johnston**, **Ebenezer Mayle**, **John Pigman**, **Ephraim E. Shepard**, and Edward's brother **David Kinsey**.[14]

For unexplained reasons, Edward sold his "whole stock" to his brother David in March 1843.[15] But by July, he had recommenced business and announced his intention to continue the manufacturing of silverware "in all its various branches" at his old stand, "where he has lately been introduced to the manufacture of Gold and Silver Spectacles, which will be furnished to dealers and others at prices to correspond with the times" (fig. 67.1). In the same advertisement, he solicited agricultural societies to submit their orders for premiums and prizes.[16]

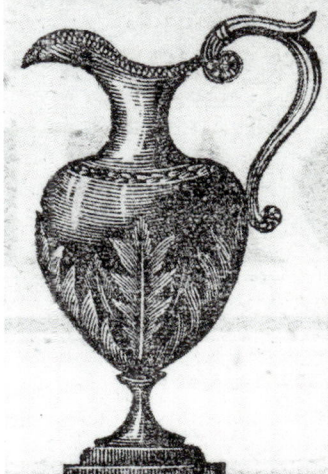

FIG. 67.1: Advertisement, *Cincinnati Daily Gazette*, July 8, 1843, 2

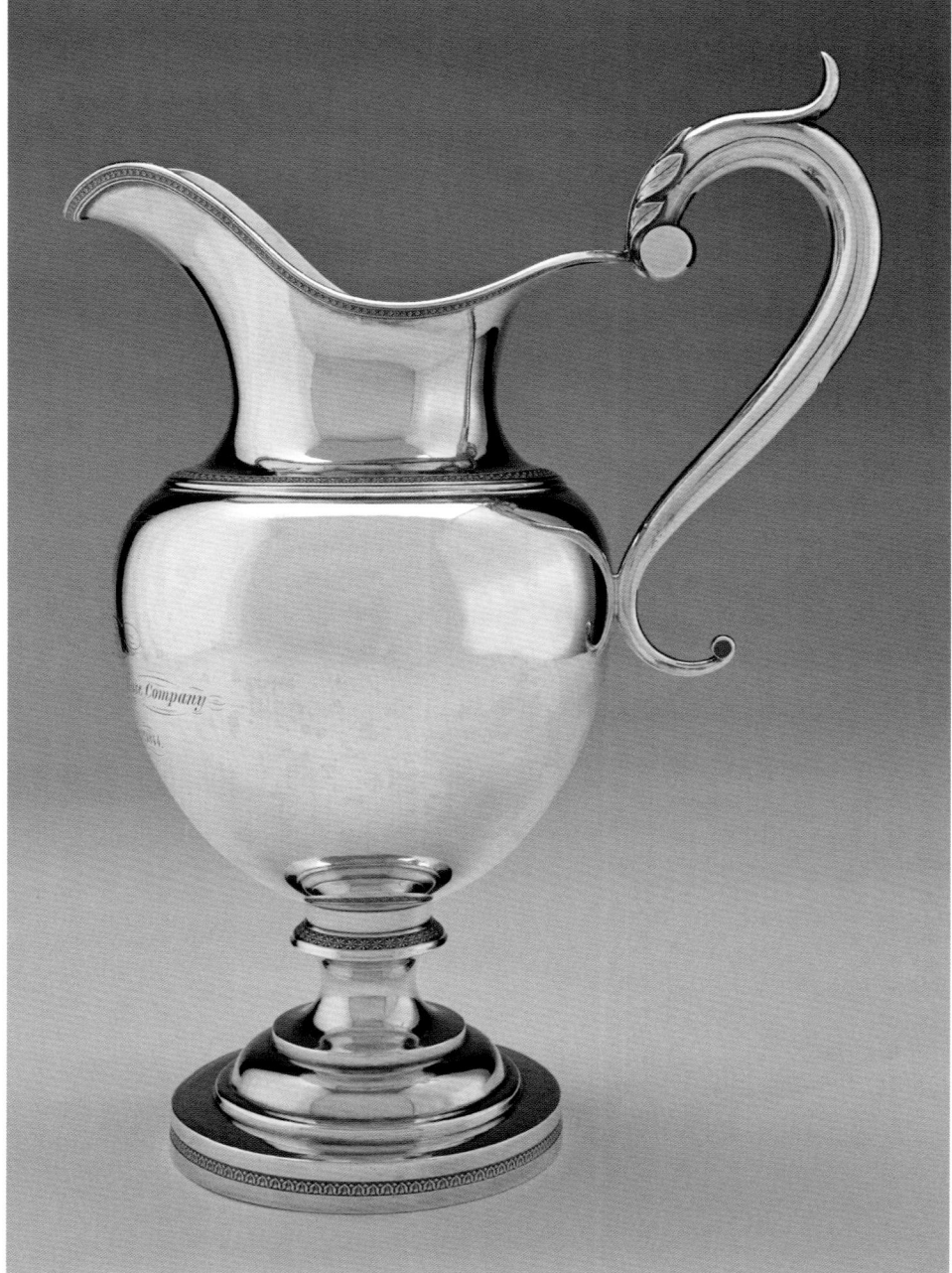

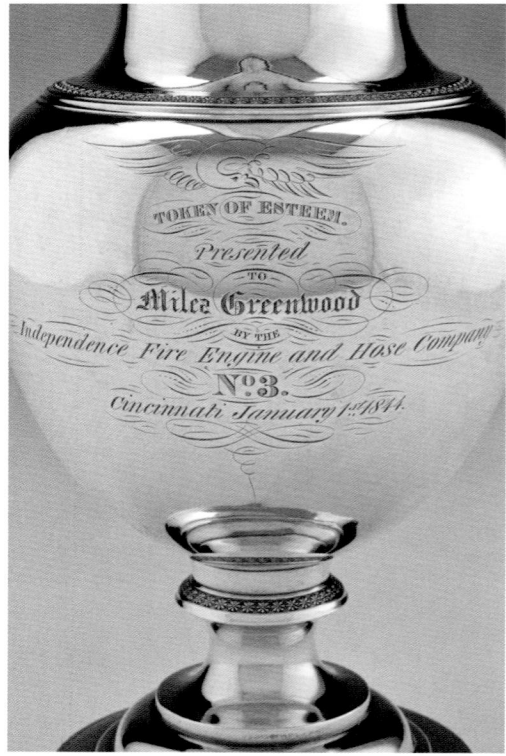

FIG. 67.2: Edward Kinsey, *Ewer*, 1843, Courtesy of a Greenwood descendent, Photograph © [2013] Ognen Borissov. Inscription: TOKEN OF ESTEEM. Presented TO Miles Greenwood BY THE Independence Fire Engine and Hose Company No. 3. Cincinnati January 1st 1844

Detail of Fig. 67.2

That year, Edward created a large two-quart presentation ewer (fig. 67.2), commissioned by the Independence Fire Engine and Hose Company No. 3, for presentation to Miles Greenwood (1807–1885) on January 1, 1844. Greenwood, born in New Jersey, had come to Cincinnati and established the Eagle Ironworks, the largest foundry of its kind in the West. He was a founder of the Ohio Mechanics' Institute and president of the volunteer Independence Fire Engine and Hose Company No. 3. He purchased uniforms and equipment for the company and paid its volunteer firemen out of his own pocket before organizing the first paid fire department in Cincinnati in 1852. The Neoclassical design of the ewer is similar to the ewer in Kinsey's illustrated advertisements, and to other ewers with his mark.[17] The milled band of arches at the foot is frequently spotted on Kinsey wares. The ewer bears mark 67.2 and an inscription at the base that reads, "Edwd. Kinsey, Maker"—a possible indicator of Kinsey's esteem for Greenwood and/or his pride in this particularly fine piece. The engraved, calligraphic eagle, above the presentation inscription,

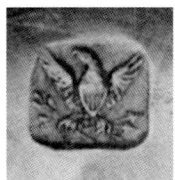

FIG. 67.3: Detail, E. & D. Kinsey, *Ewer*, from Elizabeth Beckman, *An In-depth Study of the Cincinnati Silversmiths . . .*, Cincinnati: BB & Co., 1975, 87

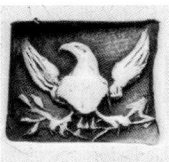

FIG. 67.4: Detail, Edward H. Hill, *Tablespoon*, 1840–1873, L. 8⅞ in. (22.5 cm), CAM, Given by Mimi Morgan in memory of her mother, Miriam Katherine Vandervort Morgan, 2013.1

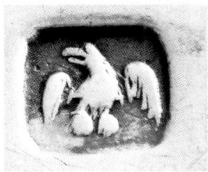

FIG. 67.5: Detail, J. Budd, *Tablespoon*, Private Collection

possibly executed by an in-house engraver, is especially lyrical and fitting for this piece. This ewer is the only dated piece of Edward Kinsey silver known at this time.

In January 1844 Edward and David Kinsey created **E. & D. Kinsey**, a prosperous and prolific manufacturing firm.[18] In 1850, Edward reported owning $10,000 worth of real estate and a personal estate of $15,000.[19] His wealth grew with the business which was worth between $60,000 and $70,000 in February 1860.[20] He retired in 1861, and lived the remainder of his life at 152 Broadway.[21]

The physical description of Edward Kinsey from an 1851 passport application describes him as 5'7" tall, with dark brown eyes, dark brown hair, and light complexion.[22] His character was consistently lauded by credit reporters who noted him as "an honest, prudent man and a skillfull [*sic*] workman . . . industrious, economical and prompt."[23]

Edward married Temperance H. Pocock (b. about 1820, Indiana) on December 29, 1840.[24] Temperance was the daughter of Rebecca Hartman and Salem Pocock (b. 1784, Baltimore, Maryland). Her sister, Julia Ann, married Edward's brother David. Temperance was a physician, possibly the first woman physician in Cincinnati.[25] She and Edward had three children: Eugenia V. (1841–1862), Catherine V. (1847–1849), and Edward D. (1848–1850).[26] It is presumed that the family was Methodist, as several members were buried at the Methodists' Wesleyan Cemetery and later moved to Spring Grove Cemetery.[27]

Edward Kinsey died on October 18, 1865, from apoplexy of the brain.[28] His will, written in March 1855, instructed that Temperance receive $12,000, "justly her due, I having realized the above amount from her father's estate."[29] The balance of his estate was to be "equally divided between my wife and daughter Eugenia except that my executrice herein after named is to pay over to my aged father $3,000 per anum during his lifetime . . . " At the time of Edward's death, only his wife survived him.

Edward Kinsey produced a large amount of coin silver in a variety of forms, as evidenced by the many pieces that survive today. He sold his wares to the general public as well as to other silversmiths, watch makers, and jewelers on a wholesale basis. In some instances, Edward Kinsey's mark 67.1 appears with the marks of **Willey & Blaksley** (fig. 67.10) and **Scovil & Co.**[30]

Three different eagle marks occasionally appear alongside Kinsey's marks: a shield-breasted eagle, facing left, with upturned wings and talons clutching olive branches on the left side and arrows on the right side, in a square cartouche (fig. 67.3); a left-facing eagle with upturned wings that also clutches olive branches and arrows, one arrow pointed upward at a severe angle (fig. 67.4); or a left-facing eagle with down-turned wings in a square cartouche (fig. 67.5).

John R. McGrew asserts that the shield-breasted eagle with upturned wings (fig. 67.3) was Edward Kinsey's manufacturing mark.[31] This appears to be true, as this eagle mark has been observed on works stamped by firms active in the mid 1830s to the early 1860s, including F. H. Clark & Co. (Memphis), **Hazen & Collins**, **Palmer & Smith**, **Richard Clayton**, **Bushnell Willey**, and even E. & D. Kinsey, but Edward was the only silver manufacturer among them who was active by the mid 1830s.[32]

The left-facing eagle with upturned wings whose breast is not shielded (fig. 67.4), was documented on a piece retailed by the St. Louis jeweler E. Mead (w. 1837–50).[33] For this reason, it is referred to by John R. McGrew as the "St. Louis Eagle."[34] It has also been observed on a work by D.B. Miller, possibly of Boston, working around 1850; a spoon marked by **E.H. Hill**; a ladle marked by Palmer & Smith; a ladle marked by E. & D. Kinsey; and a beaker that features both Edward Kinsey's mark 67.1 and

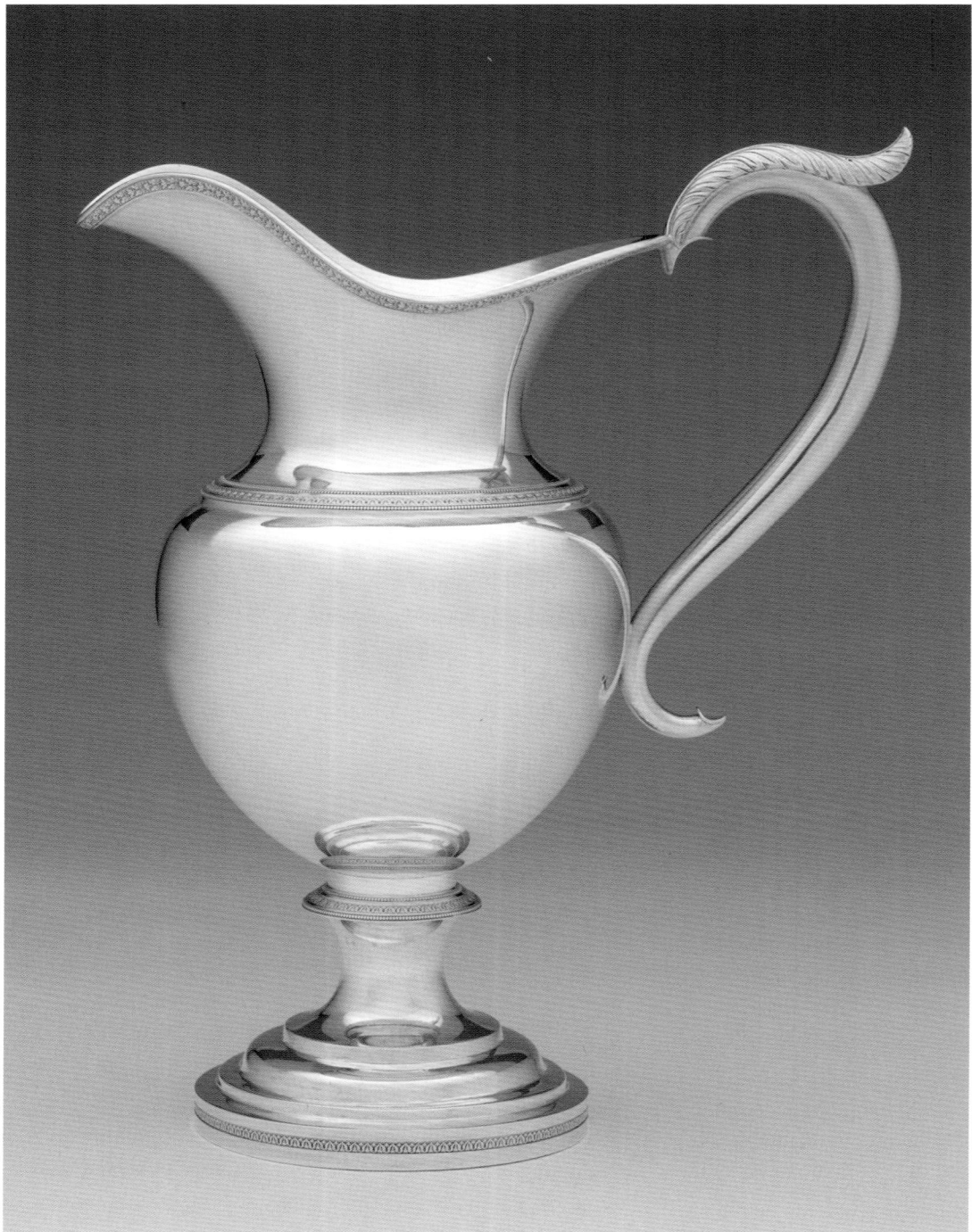

FIG. 67.6: Edward Kinsey, *Ewer*, 1834–1844, 13¾ × 11¼ × 6¼ in. (34.9 × 28.6 × 15.9 cm), CAM, Museum Purchase, 1907.194

Scovil & Co.'s mark 122.1.[35] Among these firms and individuals, Kinsey and Pulaski Scovil are the only known silver manufacturers. This suggests that this eagle is connected to one or both of them.

The left-facing eagle with down-turned wings (fig. 67.5), referred to by John R. McGrew as the "Ohio eagle," may also be associated with Edward Kinsey and/or Pulaski Scovil.[36] It appears on wares with Edward Kinsey's marks 67.1 and 67.2, as well as on wares marked by other firms or individuals active in the region during the 1830s: Willey & Blaksley; Scovil, Willey & Co.; and **J. Budd**.[37] Again, among these, only Kinsey and Pulaski Scovil were known to have manufactured silver.

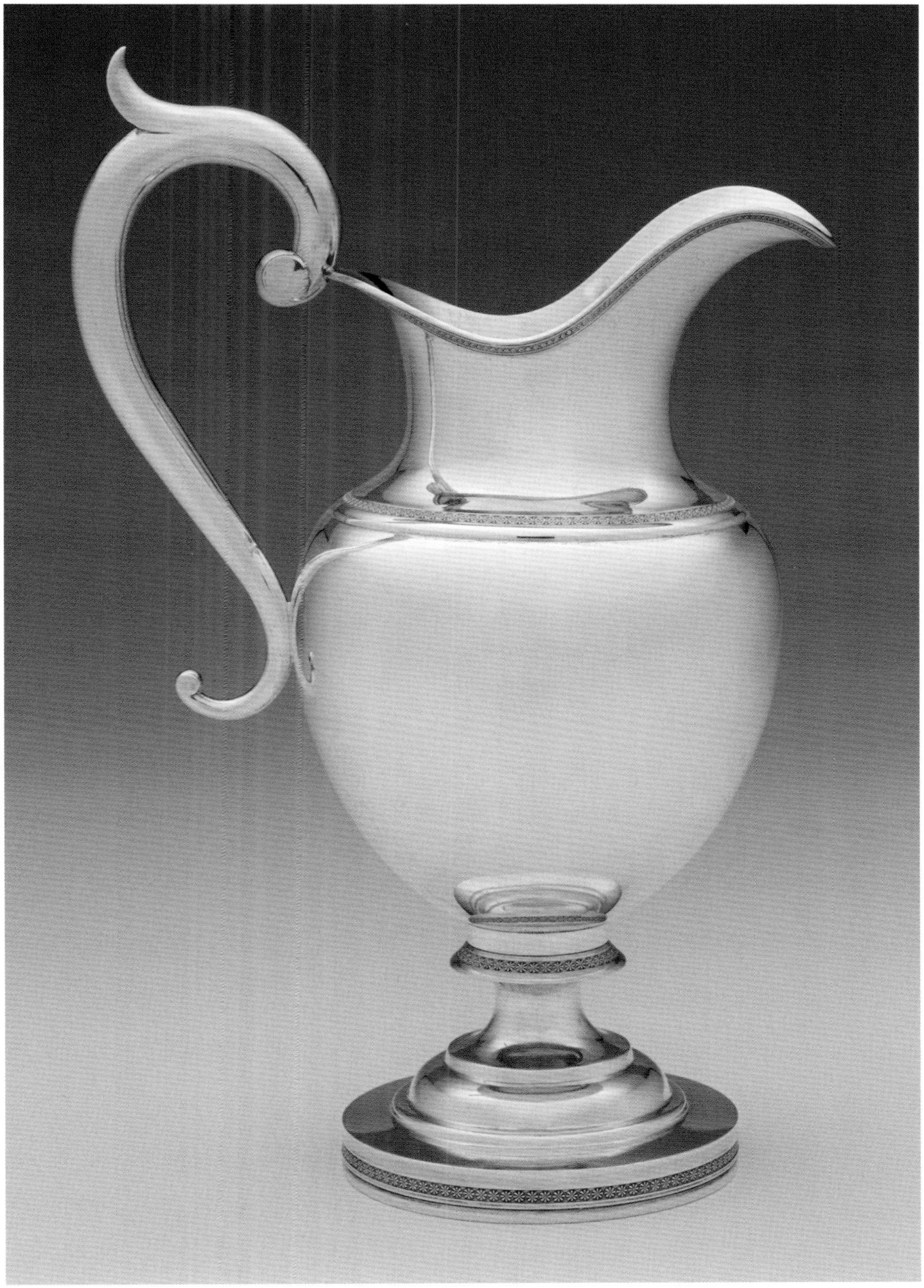

FIG. 67.7: Edward Kinsey, *Ewer*, 1834–1844, 14¹¹⁄₁₆ × 9¹¹⁄₁₆ in. (37.3 × 24.6 cm), Private Collection

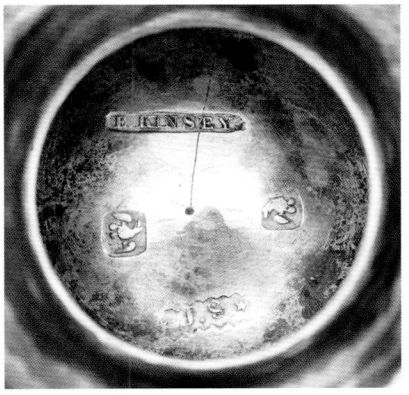

Detail of Fig. 67.7

Kinsey's mark 67.1 has also been observed alongside "CINCINNATI" in a rectangular or banner-shaped cartouche. Forms observed with mark 67.1 include ewers (figs. 67.6 and 67.7); a coffee pot (fig. 67.8); covered sugar bowls (fig. 67.9); creamers (fig. 67.10); beakers; tongs with shell or claw terminals; and spoons and ladles with fiddle handles and pointed or rounded shoulders.[38] Mark 67.2 has been documented on presentation ewers, including the aforementioned Miles Greenwood ewer (fig. 67.2), and on spoons and ladles with fiddle or tipped, exaggerated fiddle handles and pointed shoulders.[39] A third mark, "Edward Kinsey" in a rectangular cartouche was noted by Elizabeth Beckman, but has not been seen in recent years.[40]

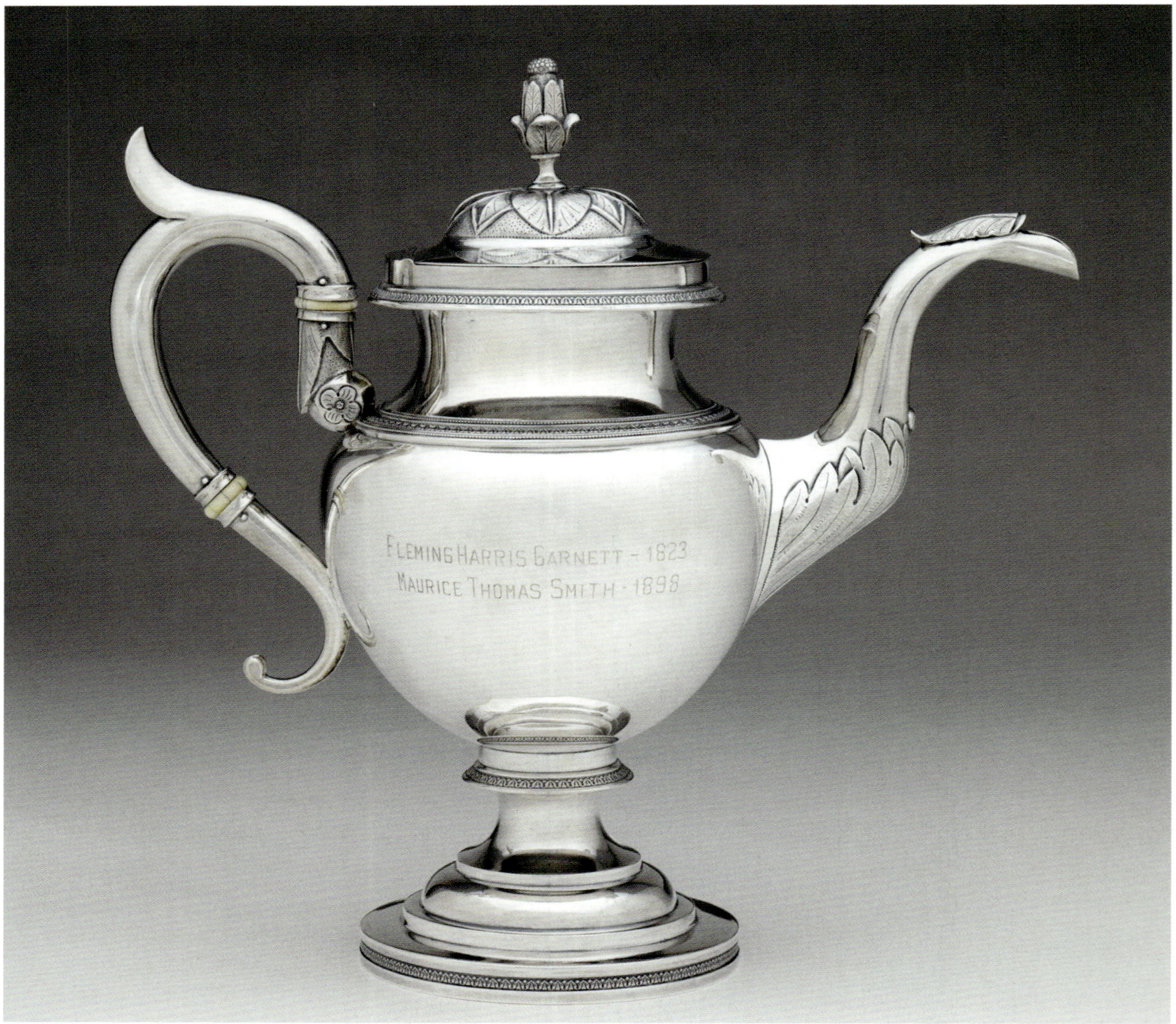

FIG. 67.8: Edward Kinsey, *Coffee Pot*, 1834–1844, 12 × 12¾ in. (30.5 × 32.4 cm), CAM,
Museum Purchase with funds provided by Mr. and Mrs. Charles Fleischmann III, 2005.35.
Inscription: FLEMING HARRIS GARNETT - 1823 / MAURICE THOMAS SMITH - 1898

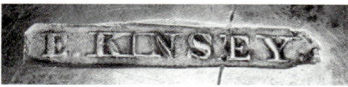

MARK 67.1

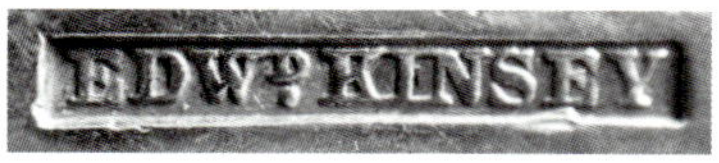

MARK 67.2

1. A billhead from the firm of **L.A. Kinsey**, a legacy firm of Edward Kinsey, E. & D. Kinsey, and David Kinsey, states that the Kinsey businesses were established in 1832. "Great Industrial Exposition, The Closing Days," *Cincinnati Enquirer*, October 19, 1870, 3, states the same. Documentation that Edward Kinsey was working locally by 1832 could not be found. An advertisement for E. & D. Kinsey which appeared in the *Cincinnati Daily Gazette*, January 24, 1844, notes that they had "10 years experience in business in this city," reproduced in Beckman, 86; 1834 Newport, Kentucky City Directory.

2. Ancestry.com, *New York Passenger Lists, 1820–1957* [online database], Provo, Utah: Ancestry.com Operations Inc., 2010. The children of Thomas and Ann listed on the passenger list are Jane (20), Lydia (16), Stephen (18), Hannah (12), Evan (10), Edward (8), Betsy (6), Charles (4), and David (infant).

3. William J. Comley and W. D'Eggville, *Ohio: The Future Great State*, Cincinnati and Cleveland: Comley Brothers Manufacturing and Publishing Co., 1875, 222; The 1850 Federal Census gives the birthplace of Edward and David as New Jersey; Edward Kinsey appears in the Campbell County tax list of 1833. Thomas Kenzey [sic] is included in the Kenton County tax lists of 1834 and 1835. Michael R. Averdick, *A Directory of Silversmiths, Jewelers, Watch and Clock Makers and Related Trades of Covington and Newport, Kentucky & Vicinity, 1833–1900*, Covington, KY: 829 Willard Street Press, 2002, 36.

4. 1850 and 1860 Federal Censuses, Cincinnati Ward 2, Hamilton, Ohio.

5. Averdick, *Directory of Silversmiths*, 36.

6. 1836/37 Cincinnati City Directory.

7. Advertisement, *Cincinnati Daily Gazette*, June 13, 1836, reproduced in Beckman, 84. See also Advertisement, *Cincinnati Daily Gazette*, January 23, 1838, 3; W.G. Lyford, *Western Address Directory*, Baltimore: Jos. Robinson, 1837, 327.

8. Advertisement, *Cincinnati Daily Gazette*, February 2, 1838, 2, reproduced in Beckman, 84.

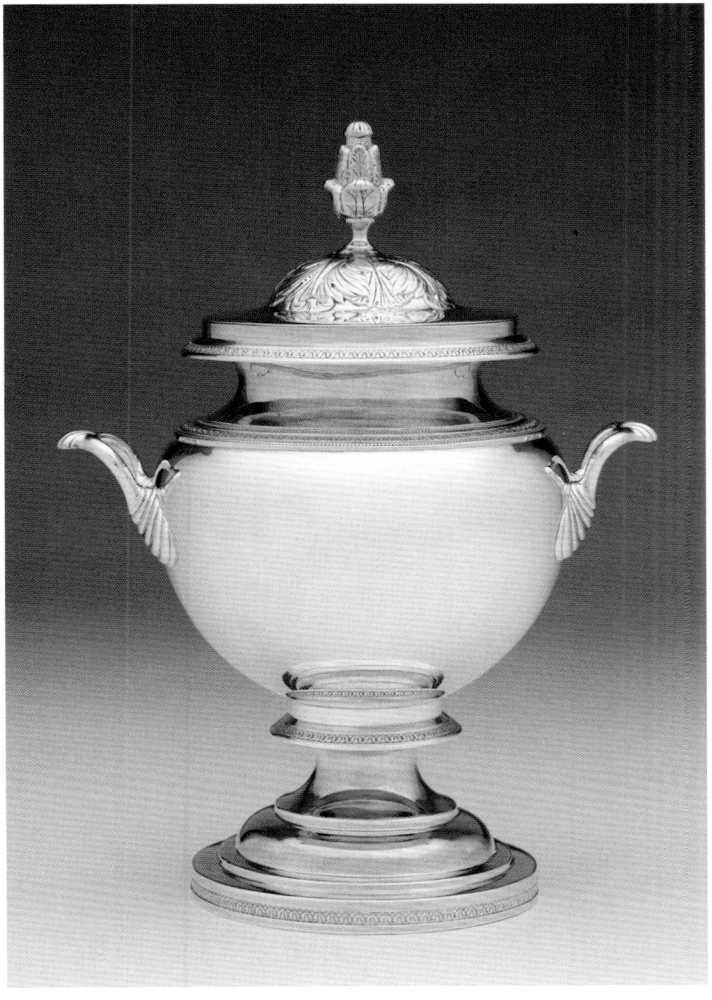

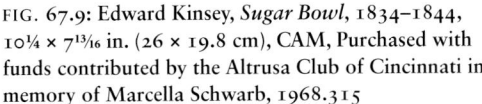

FIG. 67.9: Edward Kinsey, *Sugar Bowl*, 1834–1844, 10¼ × 7¹³⁄₁₆ in. (26 × 19.8 cm), CAM, Purchased with funds contributed by the Altrusa Club of Cincinnati in memory of Marcella Schwarb, 1968.315

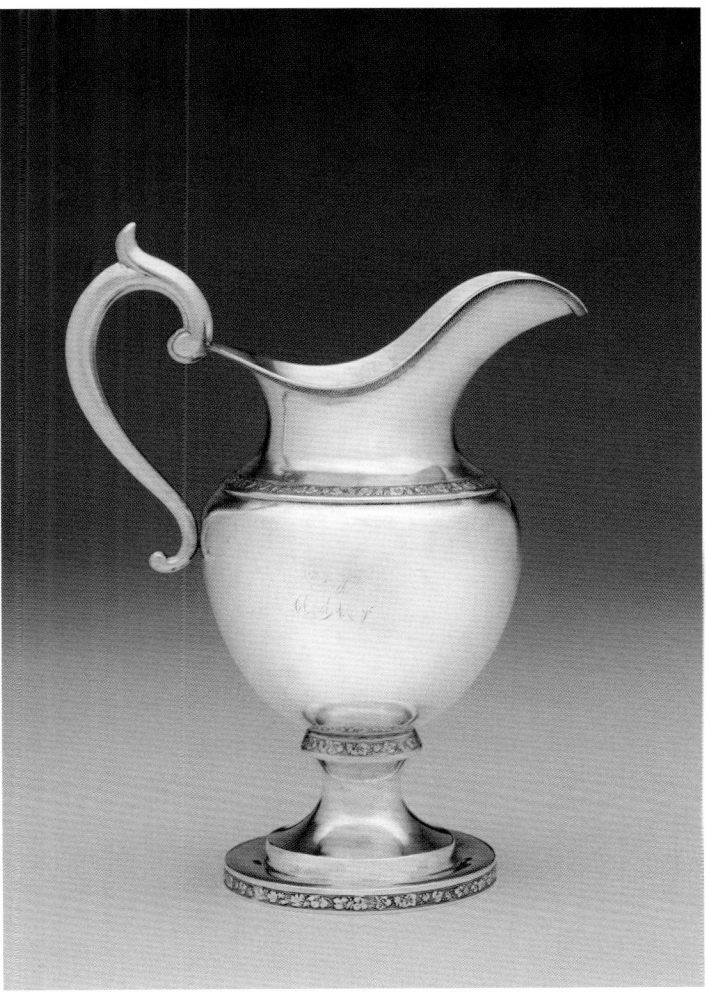

FIG. 67.10: Edward Kinsey, and Willey & Blaksley, *Creamer*, c. 1840, 8⅜ × 6⁵⁄₁₆ × 4 in. (21.3 × 16 × 10.2 cm), CAM, Museum Purchase with funds provided by Mr. and Mrs. Charles Fleischmann III, 2005.47. Inscription: EK.

9. *Report of the First Annual Fair of the Ohio Mechanics' Institute*, Cincinnati: Ohio Mechanics' Institute, 1838.
10. Ibid.
11. *Proceedings of the Second Annual Fair of the Ohio Mechanics' Institute*, Cincinnati: R.P. Brooks, 1839, 19.
12. Advertisement, "Ohio Mechanics' Institute," *Cincinnati Enquirer*, June 21, 1842, 3.
13. Advertisement, *Cincinnati Daily Gazette*, August 26, 1840.
14. Each of these men was noted in the 1839/40 Cincinnati City Directory as a "silversmith at E. Kinsey's."
15. Advertisement, *Cincinnati Daily Gazette*, March 2, 1843, reproduced in Beckman, 81.
16. Advertisement, *Cincinnati Daily Gazette*, July 8, 1843, 2.
17. Ibid.; Similar ewers include one in the Cincinnati Art Museum, Museum Purchase, 1907.194 (fig. 67.6), one in a private collection, and the one published in Beckman, 86.
18. Advertisement, *Cincinnati Daily Gazette*, January 24, 1844, reproduced in Beckman, 86.
19. 1850 Federal Census, Cincinnati, Hamilton, Ohio.
20. Ohio, Vol. 2, p. 228, R.G. Dun & Co. Collection, Baker Library, Harvard Business School.
21. 1862–1865 Cincinnati City Directories; Ohio, Vol. 2, p. 228, R.G. Dun & Co. Collection.
22. "Edward Kinsey" in National Archives and Records Administration (NARA), Washington DC, *Passport Applications, 1795–1905*, ARC Identifier 566612/MLR Number A1 508, NARA Series M1372, roll 36; "Edward Kinsey" in NARA, *Passport Applications, 1795–1905*, roll 78; Edward traveled to Europe again in August 1859, with his daughter Eugenia. They went to Paris and London. "Edward Kinsey" in NARA, *Passport Applications, 1795–1905*, roll 95.
23. Ohio, Vol. 1, p. 90, R.G. Dun & Co. Collection.
24. Wm. Erik Voss, "Edward Kinsey," http://freepages.genealogy.rootsweb. ancestry.com/~silversmiths/makers/silversmiths/96284.htm; Thomas L.
Byram, *The Genealogy of Nine Early Families in the Ohio River Valley*, Brooklyn, NY: 405 Westminster Road Press, 1969, 57.
25. 1858–1863 Cincinnati City Directories; Temperance does not appear in the Cincinnati Directory after 1863. She is believed to have married a Dr. Keckler after Edward's death in 1865; Byram, *Nine Early Families*, 57; Jack Thomas Hutchinson, *Leaves from the Tree, an American Heritage: a History of the Ancestral Families of Robert Bone Hutchinson and Jack Thomas Hutchinson*, Decorah, IA: Anundsen Publishing Co., 1989, 238.
26. Eugenia V. Kinsey, Catherine V. Kinsey, Edward Kinsey, burial

records, Spring Grove Cemetery, Cincinnati, Ohio; 1850 Federal Census, Cincinnati, Hamilton, Ohio; Beckman, 86.

27. Eugenia V. Kinsey, Catherine V. Kinsey, Edward Kinsey, burial records.

28. Edward Kinsey, burial record.

29. Edward Kinsey, will dated October 24, 1865, box 8, case 9755, University of Cincinnati Archives and Rare Books Library.

30. A beaker has been documented with Edward Kinsey's mark 67.1, a left-facing eagle (described by John R. McGrew as the "St. Louis Eagle," fig. 67.4), and the mark of Scovil & Co. A

cream pitcher (fig. 67.10) bears mark 67.1 alongside the mark of Willey & Blaksley; Edward Kinsey, eBay listings and private collections, Cincinnati silver binders, Cincinnati Art Museum; John R. McGrew, *Manufacturers' Marks on American Coin Silver*, Hanover, PA: Argyros Publications, 2004, 98; *Cream Pitcher*, Cincinnati Art Museum, Museum Purchase with funds provided by Mr. and Mrs. Charles Fleischmann III, 2005.47.

31. McGrew, *Manufacturers' Marks*, 98.

32. eBay listings and private collections, Cincinnati silver binders, Cincinnati Art Museum.

33. McGrew, *Manufacturers' Marks*, 2004, 98.

34. Ibid.

35. Stephen G.C. Ensko, "D.B. Miller," *American Silversmiths and Their Marks*, New York: Dover Publications, 1948, 167; *Tablespoon*, Cincinnati Art Museum, Given by Mimi Morgan in memory of her mother, Miriam Katherine Vandervort Morgan, 2013.1; The beaker is in a private collection.

36. McGrew, *Manufacturers' Marks*, 99.

37. eBay listings and private collections, Cincinnati Art Museum; A large ewer in a private collection bears Edward Kinsey's mark 1, plus two

stamps of the eagle with downturned wings, and a partially illegible mark that appears to be a "J. S." or "U.S." followed by a star, in a serrated cartouche.

38. Edward Kinsey, eBay listings and private collections, Cincinnati Art Museum.

39. Another ewer with this mark and the left-facing, shield-breasted eagle with upturned wings is pictured in Beckman, 86–87; Edward Kinsey, eBay listings and private collections, Cincinnati Art Museum.

40. Beckman, 87.

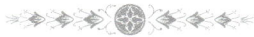

68. LOUIS A. KINSEY

1854–1928[1], w. 1871–1882

Louis Adeptus Kinsey was born in Ohio, the son of **David Kinsey** and Julia Ann Pocock.[2] He apprenticed with his father, and was first listed in Cincinnati city directories as a silversmith, working at his father's firm, in 1871. He left in 1872 to serve as a clerk, then book-keeper at the Royer Wheel Co., a local manufacturer of wheel hubs and spokes.[3] In January 1875, with **John B. Callahan**, he purchased his older brother **Edward W. Kinsey**'s share of the family business and renamed the firm **D. Kinsey & Co.**[4] In March 1879 Kinsey (now operating alone) relocated the fledgling firm from 28 West Fourth Street to the Johnston Building at the southwest corner of Fifth and Walnut Streets, and changed the concern's name to L.A. Kinsey.[5] While credit reporters believed that the new location might improve his business prospects, it did not.[6] By June 1880 the indebted Louis had sold out to his mother, Julia A. Kinsey.[7] The firm then listed as "J. A. Kinsey" in city directories and advertised as "Kinsey's."[8] Louis continued to work there as manager and bookkeeper until the firm's closure in April 1882.[9] An account of the close-out auction reads, ". . . it is a matter of great regret to Mr. Kinsey's legion of friends and old-time patrons that he is now forced, by reason of failing health, to close out his business entirely, and seek a less confining occupation."[10] In 1880, Julia reported as a watch and clock repairer in the Products of Industry Census, with $1,000 capital in the business, two employees, and a product worth $2,500.[11]

An 1879 advertisement (fig. 68.1) for L.A. Kinsey "Silversmith and Jeweler" provides a description of stock, and an invoice for a

purchase made by a Mrs. Maloney, dated May 4, 1880, indicates that she was able to buy a tea set, butter dish and sugar spoon for $37.00 from the establishment.[12] Louis may have been operating the manu-factory, as an advertisement from 1881 (fig. 68.2) suggests that during the period that Julia owned the business, it was still active. If this is true, it was likely operating on a much smaller scale.[13] Extant silver with the mark of L.A. Kinsey (mark 68.1) includes flat-ware in the "Arabesque" pattern (1875) by Whiting Mfg. Co. (New York City). L.A. Kinsey's mark has also been seen on spoons with tipped, exaggerated fiddle handles.[14]

Louis and his wife, Charlotte "Lottie" A. Elliot (1854–1942), had at least three children: a stillborn infant (b. 1875); Elliot D. (1877–1878); and Albert (b. 1879).[15] Between 1887 and 1891, Louis was employed as a cashier for F.A. Bradley, a Cincinnati broker in commodities and stocks.[16] By 1898, he had his own business (L.A. Kinsey Co.) as a commodity and stock broker in Indianapolis, Indiana, with subsidiary offices in Cincinnati and Fort Wayne, Indiana.[17] According to the society columns of the *Indianapolis Star*, Louis and Lottie had moved to Chicago by 1908.[18] The 1920 Federal Census gives their address as Sheridan Drive, situated in what is still an affluent area north of the Chicago city center, and lists Louis' occupation as a real estate salesman.[19] Louis died on July 30, 1928, and is buried in Chicago's Rosehill Cemetery.[20] Julia died in Indianapolis in 1903.[21]

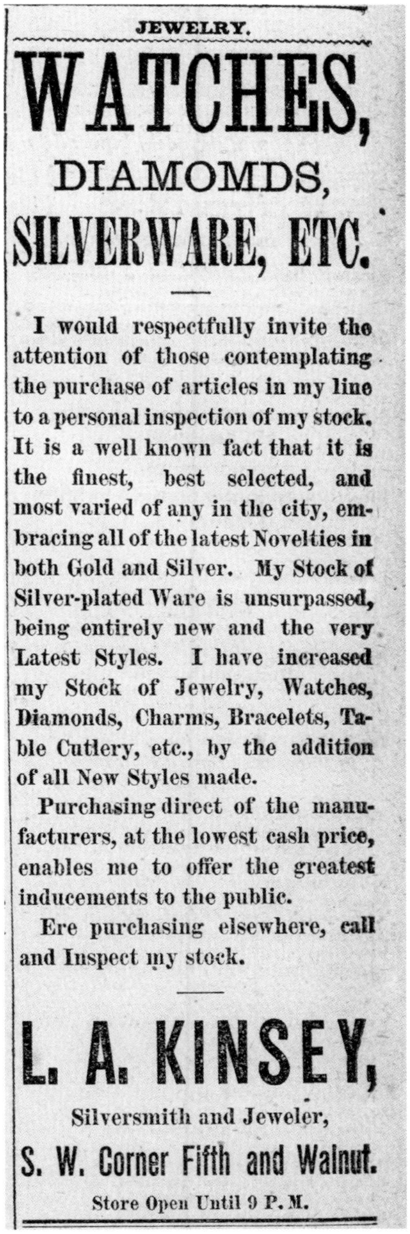

FIG. 68.1: Advertisement, *Cincinnati Enquirer*, December 8, 1879, 8

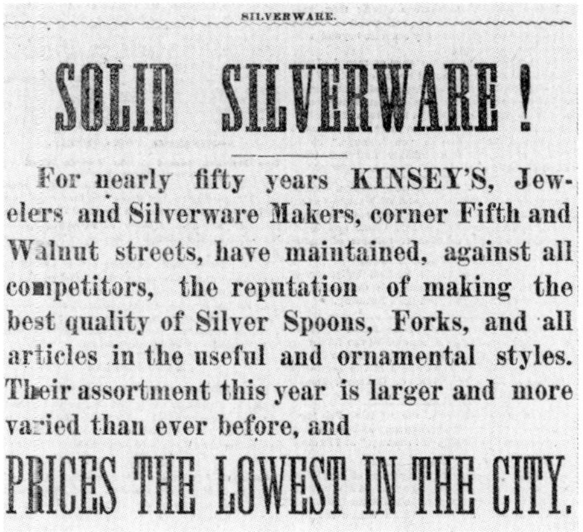

MARK 68.1

FIG. 68.2: Advertisement, *Cincinnati Commercial Tribune*, December 11, 1881, 5

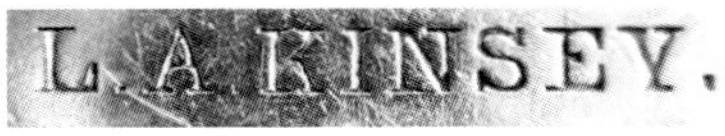

1. Louis A. Kinsey's birth date is given as July 1854 in the 1900 Federal Census, Indianapolis, Marion, Indiana. In the 1860 and 1880 Federal Censuses, Cincinnati, Hamilton, Ohio, his birth date is given as about 1854. His death record cites August 26, 1853. Louis Adeptus Kinsey, death record, Ancestry.com, *Illinois, Deaths and Stillbirths Index, 1916–1947* [online database], Provo, Utah: Ancestry.com Operations Inc., 2011.

2. 1860 Federal Census, Cincinnati Ward 6, Hamilton, Ohio; 1900 Federal Census, Indianapolis, Marion, Indiana; Louis Adeptus Kinsey, death record.

3. 1872, 1873 Cincinnati City Directories.

4. Advertisement, *Cincinnati Times Star*, January 27, 1875, 4; Ohio, Vol. 10, p. 289, R.G. Dun & Co. Collection, Baker Library, Harvard Business School.

5. Callahan left the partnership in October 1877, but continued to work there until 1882. 1877–1882 Cincinnati City Directories; Ohio, Vol. 10, p. 289, R.G. Dun & Co. Collection.

6. Ohio, Vol. 10, p. 405, R.G. Dun & Co. Collection.

7. Ibid.

8. 1881, 1882 Cincinnati City Directories; Advertisement, *Cincinnati Commercial Tribune*, December 11, 1881, 5; Advertisement, *Cincinnati Commercial Tribune*, December 18, 1881, 16.

9. Ohio, Vol. 10, pp. 405, 434, R.G. Dun & Co. Collection; 1881, 1882 Cincinnati City Directories; "Retiring from Business," *Cincinnati Enquirer*, April 16, 1882, 8; "Clearing-Out Sale," *Cincinnati Enquirer*, April 19, 1882, 5.

10. "A Lifetime Will Not Insure a Better Chance Than Kinsey's Jewelry Auction Sale—Specimens of Sale," *Cincinnati Enquirer*, April 23, 1882, 4.

11. 1880 Federal Non-Population Census Schedules, Products of Industry, Schedule 4, Hamilton County, Ohio.

12. Advertisement, *Cincinnati Enquirer*, December 8, 1879, 12; Invoice, Prices current files, Cincinnati Historical Society, box 2, folder 4.

13. Advertisement, *Cincinnati Commercial Tribune*, December 11, 1881, 5.

14. L.A. Kinsey, eBay listings and private collections, Cincinnati silver binders, Cincinnati Art Museum.

15. Charlotte A. Kinsey, death record, Ancestry.com, *Illinois, Deaths and Stillbirths Index, 1916–1947*; 1880 Federal Census, Cincinnati, Hamilton, Ohio; 1900 Federal Census, Indianapolis, Marion, Indiana; Burial records, Spring Grove Cemetery, Cincinnati, Ohio; Albert was living in Buffalo, New York, in 1920. 1920 Federal Census, Buffalo Ward 25, Erie, New York.

16. 1879–1891 Cincinnati City Directories.

17. 1898 Cincinnati City Directory; "The Market Report," *Fort Wayne News*, June 7, 1899, 5; "The Market Report," *Fort Wayne News*, June 15, 1899, 8; "L.A. Kinsey & Co.," advertisement, *Cincinnati Enquirer*, September 24, 1899, 11.

18. *Indianapolis Star*, October 11, 1908, 11.

19. 1920 Federal Census, Chicago Ward 25, Cook, Illinois.

20. Louis Adeptus Kinsey, death record.

21. Julia A. Kinsey, burial record, Spring Grove Cemetery.

69. HENRY KORF

1825–1912, w. 1851–about 1900

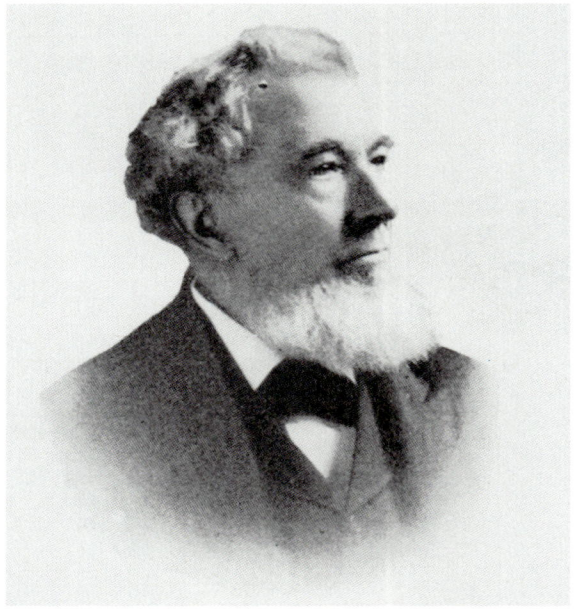

FIG. 69.1: Henry Korf, from George W. Engelhardt, *Cincinnati: The Queen City*, Cincinnati: G.W. Engelhardt, 1901, 209

Henry Korf (fig. 69.1) was born in Germany to Gertrude Thie and Henry Korf on November 23, 1825.[1] He came to the United States and was in Cincinnati by 1850, when he was enumerated in the census as a watch maker living in the same household as **Theodore Oskamp**.[2] In 1851, he was listed in the city directory as a watch maker at Oskamp's shop at 62 Main Street.[3] Korf opened his own shop in 1852 at 369 Main Street (near the corner of Ninth and Main Streets).[4] In late 1872 or early 1873, he moved to 277 Main Street (between Sixth and Seventh Streets), where he remained for the rest of his career.[5] While the focus of Korf's business was watches and jewelry, he did, like most jewelers of the era, deal in silver wares.[6] None of this silver was likely of his manufacture.

Korf's business started small, but had grown substantially by the 1880s. In 1860, credit reporters estimated that he was worth $3,000, and noted that he was conducting a very small business, and therefore only eligible for small amounts of credit. Ten years later, his standing had not changed.[7] In 1870, he reported that he had $300 of capital invested in his jewelry business, and that he had four employees (two men and two youths) whose total wages for one year were $1,300. Using hand-powered equipment and $300 worth of watch trimmings, they produced product valued at $3,000.[8]

However, by 1878, he was believed to be worth $50,000, and was noted by credit reporters as a "responsible man and good for all he may order."[9] In 1880, he reported a capital investment of $8,000, and four employees whose total wages for one year were $2,496. Utilizing $700 worth of material, they produced product valued at $14,400.[10]

Korf retired around 1900, and his sons George and Henry, Jr. continued to run the business.[11] After their father's death in 1912, Henry Korf, Jr. managed the firm. In 1919 Henry, Jr. explained "We handled a great deal of plated goods 50 years ago, but owing to the entrance of the department stores in that line, the retail jeweler has almost eliminated what was once one of his big stocks."[12] The jewelry store moved to the Schmidt Building on Sixth Street between 1925 and 1926, and relocated to 431 Main Street between 1944 and 1945, where it operated until it closed under the management of John Tebbe in 1962.[13]

Henry Korf, Sr. resided in the Cincinnati suburb of Walnut Hills for most of his life. He died there on May 23, 1912, and was buried in Calvary Cemetery, associated with St. Francis De Sales Church.[14] He was preceded in death by his wife, Mary (1834–1911).[15] Mary and Henry had three known children: Henry Jr. (1855–1932), Mary (b. 1857), and George (1859–1912).[16]

Spoons with tipped, exaggerated fiddle handles and pointed shoulders have been found with Henry Korf's mark (mark 69.1).[17]

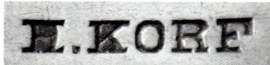

MARK 69.1

1. Henry Korf, death record, "Ohio, Deaths, 1908–1953," index and images, *FamilySearch.org;* Korf's birthdate is recorded as November 21, 1825, in Clifford Neal Smith's *Early Nineteenth Century German Settlers in Ohio (Mainly Cincinnati and Environs), Kentucky, and Other States,* McNeal, AZ: Westland Publications, 1991, 38.
2. 1850 Federal Census, Cincinnati, Hamilton, Ohio; Both Korf's death notice and a later biography state that he started in business in Cincinnati in 1849. "Death of Henry Korf, Sr.," *Jewelers' Circular and* *Horological Review* (May 29, 1912): 86; George W. Engelhardt, *Cincinnati: The Queen City,* Cincinnati: George W. Engelhardt Co., 1901, 209; Our subject may be the same person as "H.C. Korf," age 21, listed in passenger and immigration lists as arriving in New York from Bremen on the *New York* on June 16, 1841. Ancestry.com, *New York Passenger and Immigration Lists, 1820–1850* [online database], Provo, Utah: Ancestry.com Operations Inc., 2003; Korf's immigration date is given as 1849 in Smith's *Early Nineteenth Century German Settlers,* 38.

3. 1851/52 Cincinnati City Directory.
4. "Henry Korf," *JCHR* (February 5, 1919): 395; 1853–1866 Cincinnati City Directories.
5. 1873–1912 Cincinnati City Directories; In 1895, when the city streets were renumbered, 277 Main became 625 Main; "Henry Korf" (February 5, 1919).
6. Engelhardt, *Cincinnati: The Queen City*, 209; *Leading Manufacturers and Merchants of Cincinnati and Environs*, Cincinnati: International Publishing Co., 1886, 173.
7. Ohio, Vol. 2, p. 192, R.G. Dun & Co. Collection, Baker Library, Harvard Business School.
8. 1860, 1870 Federal Non-Population Census Schedules, Products of Industry, Schedule 4, Hamilton County, Ohio.
9. Estimates of Korf's worth also included real estate. Ohio, Vol. 2, p. 192, R.G. Dun & Co. Collection; Ohio, Vol. 11, p. 208, R.G. Dun & Co. Collection.
10. 1880 Federal Non-Population Census Schedules, Products of Industry, Schedule 4, Hamilton County, Ohio.
11. Henry Korf, death record; "Death of Henry Korf, Sr." (May 29, 1912); Henry Korf, Jr. appeared in the 1880 census as a silver plater, boarding with Louise Homan. In 1881, he was granted a U.S. patent (251,250) for his improvements to the cushioning of the bottom of table hollowware to avoid scratching tables, etc.
12. "Henry Korf" (February 5, 1919).
13. 1920–1962 Cincinnati City Directories; Following the death of Henry Korf, Jr., city directory listings indicate that the store was run by Julian F. Hakman between 1932 and at least 1938. In 1940, it appears that John Tebbe became manager.
14. "Death of Henry Korf, Sr." (May 29, 1912).
15. 1900 Federal Census, Cincinnati, Hamilton, Ohio; Ancestry.com and Ohio Department of Health, *Ohio, Deaths, 1908–1932* [online database], Provo, Utah: Ancestry.com Operations Inc., 2010.
16. 1860, 1870, 1880, 1900, 1910 Federal Censuses, Cincinnati, Hamilton, Ohio; Ancestry.com and Ohio Department of Health, *Ohio, Deaths, 1908–1932*; Death record, Henry Korf, Jr., "Ohio, Deaths, 1908–1953," index and images, *FamilySearch.org*.
17. Henry Korf, eBay listings and private collections, Cincinnati silver binders, Cincinnati Art Museum.

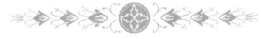

70. KENTON C. KUNKLE

1861–1941, w. 1898–1941

Kenton Clark Kunkle was born on August 28, 1861, in Ohio to Matilda (1837–1919) and Charles Kunkle (1831–1883), a journeyman wagon maker and farmer.[1] At the age of eight, Kenton and his family were living in Union Township in Warren County, Ohio, about 30 miles northeast of Cincinnati, and when he was 18, the family was living in Deerfield Township, about 25 miles northeast of Cincinnati. Nothing is known of Kenton's training.

Kenton appeared in Cincinnati in 1898, working as a molder.[2] The following year, he was working as a metal spinner (forming metal on a lathe) at the **Herman Keck Manufacturing Co.**, and in 1900 he continued to work for Keck at **The Duhme Jewelry Co.** while living in Bellevue, Kentucky, just across the river from Cincinnati.[3] By 1901, Kunkle had joined **William Engbersen** and **Robert Sturm** to form Engbersen, Sturm & Co. (1900–1904), which operated at 230 Longworth, but by the time the 1902 City Directory was published, he had returned to The Duhme Jewelry Co., where he was employed until about 1905.[4] In 1906, he listed in the directory as a silversmith working in the Lion Building on the southeast corner of Elm and Fifth Streets (434 Elm)—a location that housed numerous jewelry, watch, and metalworking businesses, including William Engbersen & Co., The Dorst Co., **Theodore Neuhaus & Co.**, Gruen Watch Case Company, and The Queen City Watch Case Manufacturing Company. He worked at this location until his death.[5] The 1910 Census indicates that he worked as a silversmith for the jewelry industry, and the 1920 Census enumerates that he worked as a silversmith for a jewelry factory. No information about his employers is provided.[6] Kunkle continued to reside in Bellevue until about 1920, when he moved to Deer Park, Sycamore Township, about 15 miles northeast of downtown Cincinnati.[7] He died on February 18, 1941.[8]

Kunkle is the last known individual enumerated as a silversmith in Cincinnati city directories. His last listing appears in the 1941 edition. A sterling, hand-wrought, Art Deco compote (fig. 70.1) featuring an applied medallion with menorah in the center of the bowl (fig. 70.2) is the only known work by Kunkle. It was created for presentation by the local chapter of B'nai Brith, an international Jewish service organization, to their president, A. Shirley Copland, in 1937.

Kenton C. Kunkle married Carrie Steddom (b. Ohio, 1868–1946) around 1888.[9] Records were found for three of their children: Edith Kay (Mrs. Ralph Simcox, 1890–1979); Clarence A. (1893–1901); and Charles W. (1897–1908).[10]

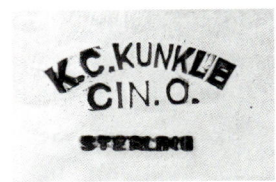

MARK 70.1

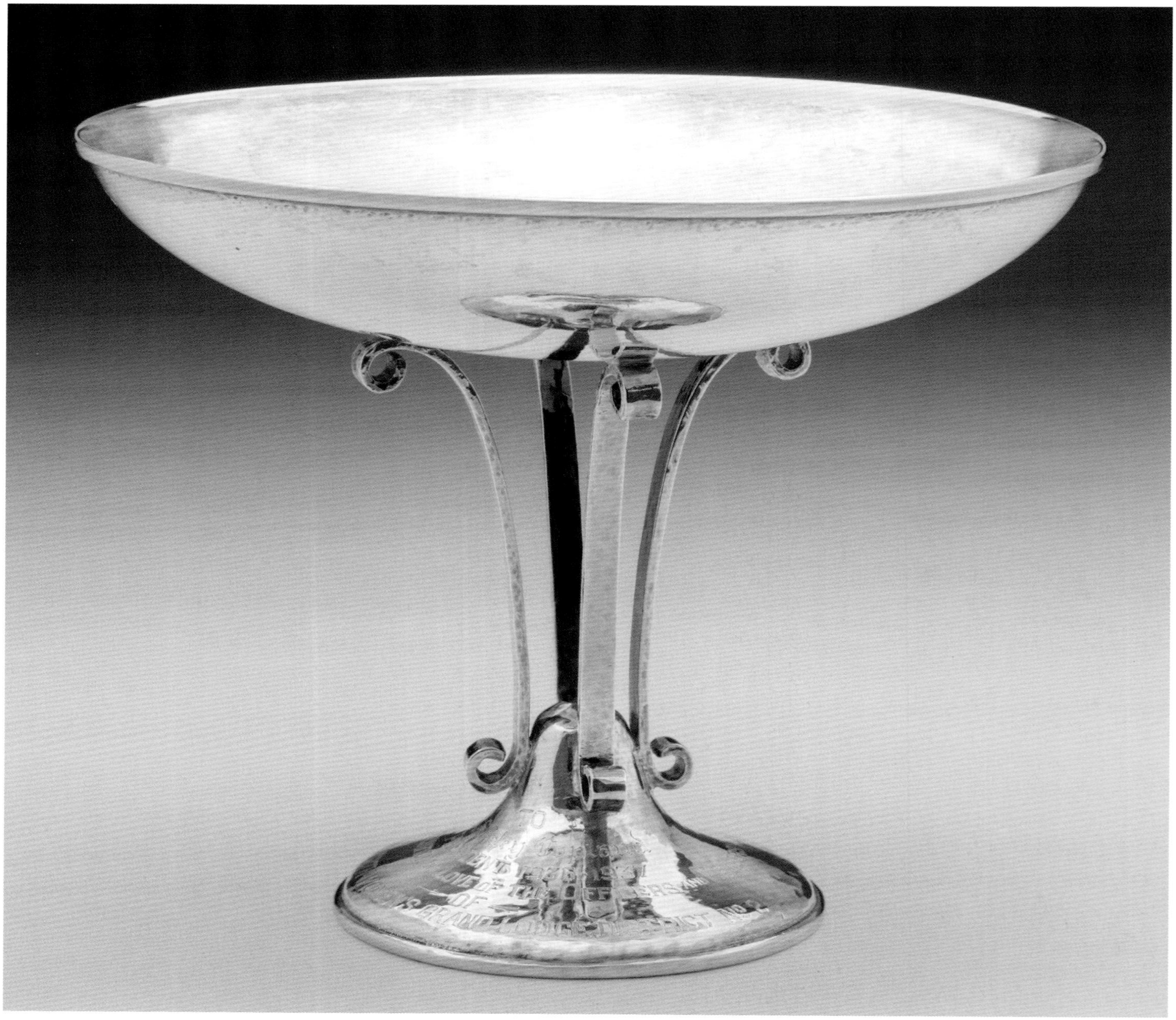

FIG. 70.1: Kenton C. Kunkle, *Compote*, 1937, 5 × 7½ in. (15.2 × 19.1 cm), CAM, Museum Purchase: John S. Conner Fund, 2005.7.
Inscription: TO A. SHIRLEY COPLAND PRESIDENT 1936–1937 WITH APPRECIATION AND LOVE OF THE OFFICERS AND
MEMBERS OF B'NAI B'RITH WOMEN'S GRAND LODGE, DISTRICT NO 2

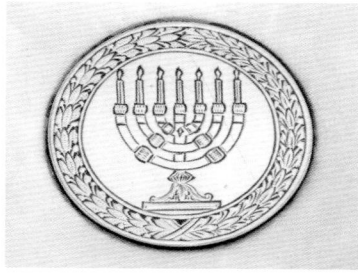

FIG. 70.2:
**Kenton C. Kunkle,
Compote, 1937.
Detail of fig. 70.1**

1. 1870 Federal Census, Union Township, Warren, Ohio; 1880 Federal Census, Deerfield Township, Warren, Ohio; 1900 Federal Census, Bellevue, Campbell, Kentucky. The 1870 Federal Census gives the birthplace of Kenton C. Kunkle as Pennsylvania while all other census data give his birthplace as Ohio; Grave marker, Lebanon Cemetery, Warren County, Ohio.
2. 1898 Cincinnati City Directory. Before this time, he does not appear in city directories in Covington, Newport, Dayton, Bellevue, or Ludlow, Kentucky.
3. 1899, 1900 Cincinnati City Directories; Keck had taken over The Duhme Jewelry Co. by this time.

4. 1901–1906 Cincinnati City Directories.

5. 1906–1941 Cincinnati City Directories.

6. 1910 Federal Census, Bellevue, Campbell, Kentucky; 1920 Federal Census, Sycamore, Hamilton, Ohio.

7. 1916/17 and 1918/19 Covington & Newport Directory; 1920 Federal Census, Sycamore, Hamilton, Ohio.

8. Ancestry.com and Ohio Department of Health, *Ohio Deaths, 1908–1932, 1938–1944, and 1958–2002* [online database], Provo, Utah: The

Generations Network Inc., 2006; Death notice, K. Clark Kunkle, *Kentucky Post*, February 19, 1941, 6.

9. Estate records, Hamilton County Probate Court; 1900, 1910 Federal Censuses, Bellevue, Campbell, Kentucky.

10. Estate records, Hamilton County Probate Court; 1900 Federal Census, Bellevue, Campbell, Kentucky; Death notice, K. Clark Kunkle, February 19, 1941; Grave markers, Lebanon Cemetery, Warren County, Ohio.

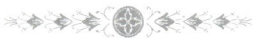

71. HERMAN LANGE

about 1844–1940, w. 1887–1921

HERMAN LANGE (THE FIRM)

1887–1934

LANGE JEWELER

1935–1961

GRASSMUCK & LANGE

1962–2007

Herman Lange (fig. 71.1) was born in Lobsens, Prussia, around 1844.[1] He immigrated to the United States on the steamer *Allemannia*, which left Hamburg, Germany, and arrived in New York on May 7, 1868.[2] R.G. Dun & Co. credit reports note a Herman Lange, previously working in Paris, Kentucky, who opened a small watch and jewelry concern and who also retailed tobacco and cigars, in Cincinnati on Fourth and John Streets in the last months of 1871. But by May 1872 his shop had closed.[3] It is unclear if this was our Herman Lange, but it is certain that our subject was in Dallas, Texas, in the 1870s, and was working as a jeweler in Maysville, Kentucky, from at least the late part of 1879 to 1886.[4] Lange was included in the 1887 Cincinnati City Directory as a jeweler with a shop at 17 Emery Arcade, on the corner of Arcade and Vine Streets.

An advertisement from 1909 indicates that among the variety of jewelry and clocks that he carried, he also kept "the grandest stock of Silverwares, Sterling Silver, and Quadruple Plate."[5] Lange did not make any of the silver that he retailed. He made frequent trips east to buy stock, and extant silver bearing Lange's marks, plus manufacturer marks, tell us that his suppliers included Towle Mfg.

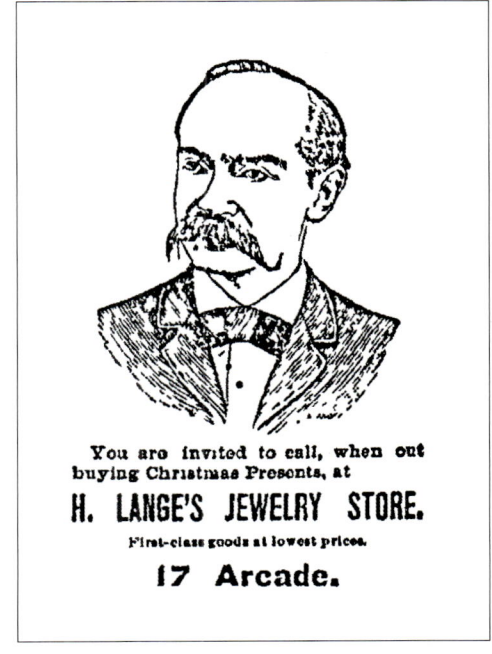

FIG. 71.1: Herman Lange, *Cincinnati Commercial Tribune*, December 15, 1889, 5

Co. (Newburyport, Massachusetts), George W. Shiebler & Co. (New York City), Mechanics Sterling Company (Attleboro, Massachusetts), and Gorham Mfg. Co. (Providence, Rhode Island).[6] Spoons marked by Lange in Duhme & Co.'s "No. 1" (circa 1869) pattern indicate that he also had local suppliers. Flatware marked by Lange ranges from examples in the simple, earlier tipped, fiddle pattern to those with more elaborate die-pressed patterns produced later in the 19th century. Several souvenir spoons have been noted with an incuse "H. LANGE", and a gold wedding band bears this mark in a rectangular cartouche.[7] Mark 71.1 has been documented on spoons with tipped, fiddle handles and rounded shoulders and spoons with tipped, exaggerated fiddle handles with pointed shoulders.[8]

By April 1892 Lange had incurred at least $5,000 worth of debt.[9] The cause of Lange's trouble was reported to be dull business, blamed on the fact that "there were more jewelry stores in this city for the population than any other city in the country" and "in part to the weather."[10] In July, Lange offered to pay his creditors 25% of his debts, and all court costs and attorney fees.[11] In March 1893 a "grand auction sale of the stock of Herman Lange" was announced.[12] Lange recovered and continued in business.

Around 1873, Lange married Elise Sachs (1849–1926), daughter of Ruka Rice and M.W. Sachs.[13] They had four children: Louis (1874–1953); Morris (1876–1962); Sidney (b. 1879), a physician; and Theresa (b. 1883), who married Eugene Saenger.[14] Louis and

Morris followed in their father's footsteps. By 1900, Louis was working as a jeweler for **A.G. Schwab & Bro.**, and in 1901, he married A.G. Schwab's daughter, Rubie.[15] Morris had joined his father in business by 1910, and when Herman retired around 1921, Morris took charge.[16] The firm of Herman Lange was included in city directories until 1935, when the name of business, still under Morris' management, was changed to Lange Jeweler.[17] Morris presumably ran the firm until shortly before his death. By 1962, Louis B. Grassmuck was president, and the name of the firm, which continued to operate on Vine Street, became Grassmuck & Lange Jewelers, Inc.[18] Around 1970, William F. Grassmuck became president and he ran the business until the firm's closure in 2007.[19]

Herman Lange died in St. Petersburg, Florida in 1940.[20] He was a long-time visitor to Florida and at the end of his life spent his summers and winters there. At almost 90 years old, he was noted for his rigorous morning routine: evolutions on the parallel bars on the Pancoast beach, "under wraps" in his overcoat.[21] "Give me 10 more years—or a warmer day—and I'll be through with this preliminary training and ready to take off my overcoat and show you a few things in earnest," he told a local newspaper reporter.[22]

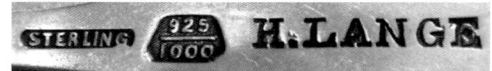

MARK 71.1

1. Lange's 1912 passport application gives his birthdate as March 10, 1844. The 1900 Federal Census, Cincinnati, Hamilton, Ohio records his birthdate as April 1843. Ancestry.com, *U.S. Passport Applications, 1795–1925* [online database], Provo, Utah: Ancestry.com Operations Inc., 2007.

2. Manifest of Passengers, Steamer *Allemannia*, www.immigrantships.net/v7/1800v7/allemannia18680507 01.html, accessed January 7, 2013.

3. Ohio, Vol. 9, p. 141, R.G. Dun & Co. Collection, Baker Library, Harvard Business School.

4. Two of Lange's sons were born in Texas: Louis, b. 1874, and Morris, b. 1876; 1880 Federal Census, Maysville, Mason, Kentucky. Louis gave his birth place as Dallas, Texas, in his marriage record, Hamilton County Probate Records, vol. 153, 33, http://www.probatect.org/CourtRecordsArchive

/bukmarriages.aspx; Boultinghouse, 326; Lange advertised as a jeweler on Second Street in Polk's Directories (Maysville, KY) of 1879/80 and 1887/88; 1880 Federal Census, Maysville, Mason, Kentucky. Two of Lange's children were born in Kentucky: Sidney, b. 1879, and Theresa, b. 1883; 1900 Federal Census, Cincinnati, Hamilton, Ohio; Herman Lange was naturalized as a citizen of the United States in Maysville, Kentucky, in 1882. Ancestry.com, *U.S. Passport Applications, 1795–1925*.

5. Advertisement, *Cincinnati Enquirer*, April 24, 1909, 8.

6. "Out-of-Town jewelers registered in New York," *Jewelers' Circular and Horological Review* (August 12, 1891): 22; Herman Lange, eBay listings and private collections, Cincinnati silver binders, Cincinnati Art Museum.

7. Herman Lange, eBay listings and private collections, Cincinnati Art Museum.

8. Ibid.

9. "Jewelry Failure," *Cincinnati Enquirer*, April 24, 1892, 9; "Herman Lange's Assignment," *Public Ledger* (Maysville, KY), April 25, 1892, 1.

10. Ibid.

11. "Settlement," *Cincinnati Enquirer*, July 28, 1892, 4.

12. Advertisement, *Cincinnati Enquirer*, March 31, 1893, 5.

13. Elise Lange, death record, "Ohio Deaths, 1908–1953," index and images, *FamilySearch*, www.familysearch.org/pal:/MM9.1.1/X8JF-RBW, accessed January 8, 2013; "Random Notes," *Cincinnati Enquirer*, April 19, 1908, B4.

14. 1900 Federal Census, Cincinnati, Hamilton, Ohio.

15. 1900 Cincinnati City Directory; Marriage record, Hamilton County Probate Records, vol. 153, 33, http://www.probatect.org/CourtRecordsArchive/bukmarriages.aspx; "Social Affairs," *Cincinnati Enquirer*, June 6, 1901, 7.

16. 1910–1935 Cincinnati City Directories.

17. 1900, 1910, 1920, 1930 Federal Censuses, Cincinnati, Hamilton, Ohio; 1910–1935 Cincinnati City Directories; The location of the store changed around 1931 from 425 Vine Street to 435 Vine Street, where it operated until its closure. In some years, the firm was referred to in the directories as Lange The Jeweler.

18. 1962 Cincinnati City Directory.

19. 1970–2007 Cincinnati City Directories; "Longtime Jewelers Leave Downtown, Citing Decline of Shoppers," *Cincinnati Enquirer*, June 6, 2007, A9.

20. Herman Lange, obituary, *The Evening Independent* (St. Petersburg, FL), March 19, 1940, 4.

21. "Nonagenarian Beach Visitor Chins Himself, Herman Lange of Cincinnati Wears Topcoat for Daily Acrobatic Workout," *The Miami News*, February 18, 1934, 8.

22. Ibid.

72. J. LANGE & BRO.

1860–1881

Julius Lange (b. about 1831–1889) and his brother, Louis (1835–1920), were born in Germany. Sons of Louis and Catherine Lange, they came to the United States in the 1850s.[1] Julius made his first appearance in Cincinnati city directories in 1860, advertising under the business heading of "Jewelry, Silver Ware, Watches &c.," and operating at 190 West Fifth Street. The following year, he and Louis advertised as J. Lange & Bro., located at 52 West Fourth Street.[2] Their firm appeared under the business heading of "Jewelry Manufacturers" and, in subsequent years, it also appeared under the headings of "Watch Manufacturers," "Jewelry, Silver Ware, Watches &c.," and "Watches, Clocks, Jewelry, &c." In 1880 and 1882, they were also included under the business listings for silver and silver-plated ware.

R.G. Dun & Co. credit reports from March 1860 note that the Langes had just established their firm, "call[ed] themselves diamond cutters and jewelers," and had $1,200 of capital invested in the business.[3] They started out small, but by 1868, the brothers were noted as doing a "good business in finer grades of jewelry," and as "good businessmen, deemed reliable, and in good home credit, though they buy little here." Their means were estimated between $25,000 to $30,000, and "considered sufficient for their business."[4] In 1870, the firm reported in the Federal Non-Population Census as manufacturers of jewelry, with $500 of capital invested. They employed two hands (one male and one youth) whose yearly wages totalled $150, and used $600 worth of gold, $200 worth of silver, and $100 worth of other materials to produce $2,500 worth of jewelry that year.[5]

There is no evidence to suggest that J. Lange & Bro. were manufacturing silver, although it was part of their line. Spoons and ladles with tipped, exaggerated fiddle handles and pointed shoulders have been found with mark 72.1. Mark 72.2 appears on later, more elaborate die-pressed patterned flatware that is also marked by the manufacturers Wood & Hughes (New York City), Gorham Mfg. Co. (Providence, Rhode Island), and George W. Shiebler & Co. (New York City).[6]

In June 1881 Julius Lange announced that he and his wife were leaving for New York, spending the summer in Saratoga, and then setting sail for Europe in September, "to be gone for six months or perhaps for several years." When they returned, they made their permanent home in New York City.[7] Prior to leaving Cincinnati, Julius and his wife Marie (1848–1924, b. Massachusetts, nee Courcelles) lived on Dayton Street, an area on the west end of Cincinnati that was home to many of the era's wealthiest merchants, pork packers, and brewers.[8] Julius and Marie had two daughters, Julia (1879–1968) and Pauline (b. circa 1886).[9] Julius died in Manhattan on October 5, 1889.[10]

Louis continued the business under his name at the same location until late 1884 or early 1885.[11] Credit reporters noted that he was reticent about his affairs, but estimated to be worth as much as $15,000.[12] He married Louisa Barkholz (1843–1928), daughter of Louise Geiler and Frederick Barkholz.[13] They had five children for whom records were found: Laura (1860–1932); Adele (1863–1919); Louise "Lulu" (1866–1941); Blanche (1869–1946); and Frederick (1871–1872).[14] The family resided in the Hartwell neighborhood of Cincinnati, north of downtown.[15] Louis Lange died on December 12, 1920.[16]

J.LANGE & BRO

MARK 72.1

MARK 72.2

1. Louis Lange, burial record, Spring Grove Cemetery, Cincinnati, Ohio; A passport application for Louis Lange gives his immigration year as 1854. The 1900 Federal Census reports Louis Lange's immigration date as 1854, the 1910 Census as 1856, and the 1920 Census as 1851. A Louis Lange with the occupation of "smith" is included in a passenger list for the *Adolphine* departing from Bremen and arriving in New York on January 19, 1852, but his birth date is given as about 1832. Ancestry.com, *U.S. Passport Applications, 1795–1925* [online database], Provo, Utah: Ancestry.com Operations Inc., 2007; Ancestry.com, *New York Passenger Lists, 1820–1957* [online database], Provo: Utah: Ancestry.com Operations Inc., 2010; 1860, 1870, 1880 Federal Censuses, Cincinnati, Hamilton, Ohio; 1900 and 1910 Federal Censuses, Springfield, Hamilton, Ohio; 1920 Federal Census, Cincinnati, Hamilton, Ohio.
2. 1861–1882 Cincinnati City Directories.
3. Ohio, Vol. 4, p. 184, R.G. Dun & Co. Collection, Baker Library, Harvard Business School.
4. Ibid.
5. 1870 Federal Non-Population Census Schedules, Products of Industry, Schedule 4, Hamilton County, Ohio.
6. J. Lange & Bro., eBay listings and private collections, Cincinnati silver binders, Cincinnati Art Museum.

7. "Cincinnati Loses a Merchant," *Cincinnati Enquirer*, June 15, 1881, 4.

8. Marie T. Lange, obituary, *The New York Times*, November 3, 1924, 17; Marriage announcement, "Wenig-Lange," *The New York Times*, April 11, 1906; "City Personals," *Cincinnati Enquirer*, September 30, 1878, 8; "City Personals," *Cincinnati Enquirer*, April 24, 1879, 4; "New Year Calls," *Cincinnati Enquirer*, January 1, 1878, 8; 1880 Federal Census, Cincinnati,

Hamilton, Ohio; "A Double Birthday Party," *Cincinnati Enquirer*, December 28, 1880, 5; Marie T. Lange, obituary, November 3, 1924.

9. Julia's married name was Wenig, and Pauline's married name was Kuhn. Marie T. Lange, obituary, November 3, 1924; Marriage announcement, "Wenig-Lange," April 11, 1906.

10. Julius Lange, death index result, certificate number 31715, Manhattan, soundex L520,

http://www.italiangen.org/NYCDeathresults.asp?kind=exact&Esurname=Lange&Efirst=Julius&StartYear=&EndYear=&B1=Submit, accessed January 9, 2013.

11. 1882–1885 Cincinnati City Directories; Ohio, Vol. 4, p. 81, R.G. Dun & Co. Collection.

12. Ohio, Vol. 4, p. 81, R.G. Dun & Co. Collection.

13. Louisa Lange, burial record, Spring Grove Cemetery.

14. Burial records, Spring Grove Cemetery; 1880 and 1920 Federal Censuses, Cincinnati, Hamilton, Ohio; 1900 and 1910 Federal Censuses, Springfield, Hamilton, Ohio.

15. "Hartwell," *Cincinnati Enquirer*, January 27, 1884; 1900 and 1910 Federal Censuses, Springfield, Hamilton, Ohio; 1920 Federal Census, Cincinnati, Hamilton, Ohio.

16. Louis Lange, burial record.

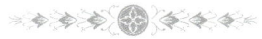

73. JONAS LEVY

b. about 1799[1]–1884, w. 1819–1836, 1838–around 1839/40

Jonas Levy, born Menachem Levy, came from Exeter, England, and arrived in Cincinnati in June 1819.[2] With **Joseph Jonas**, he was part of the first Jewish services of worship held in Cincinnati that fall, and was ordained as a shohet (a ritual slaughterer of animals according to Jewish dietary law) for Cincinnati's pioneer Jewish community in 1823.[3] He was also part of the first Jewish congregation, Bene Israel, formed in 1824.[4] When the 1825 City Directory was published (the next issue following the 1819 edition), he listed as a watch maker and silversmith on Lower Market Street.[5] In October 1829 a large advertisement announced his new establishment, J. Levy & Co., opticians, jewelers, silversmiths, watch and clock makers, at 154 Main Street opposite the U.S. Bank between Third and Fourth Streets.[6] Levy's partners in this establishment are unknown. The notice underscores his optometry line, emphasizing Levy's "many years experience and practice with the first Opticians in Europe," and makes mention of jewelry and watches. His directory listing for 1831 indicates that in addition to his jeweler's shop on Main Street, he was also running a clothing store on Front Street between Main and Sycamore and at 31½ Lower Market Street. Levy resided on Second Street, between Broadway and Sycamore. In the next issue of the city directory (1834) he listed as a jeweler working on Main Street between Front and Second Street. Between 1836 and 1838, Levy appeared in New York City directories, advertising as a jeweler at 140 Bowery.[7] By January 1838 he had returned to Cincinnati and established an auction and commission business at 3 Lower Market Street, "3 doors east of Main," where he offered a "splendid assortment of Dry Goods and Fancy Articles, just received from New York . . . Also—A large quantity of Gold and

Silver Watches, Silver Plated Ware, and most kinds of choice jewelry."[8] His last listing in Cincinnati appeared in the 1839/40 City Directory.

By 1841, Levy had moved to Arkansas where he reported in the 1850 Federal Census as a silversmith in Little Rock with real estate valued at $5,000.[9] By 1855, he was working in Memphis, Tennessee, where the 1860 Census lists him as a watch maker with a personal estate valued at $500.[10] His wife Rebecca (b. Delaware, about 1814) maintained a personal estate valued at $1,000.[11] The Levys had eleven known children: Frances (b. about 1832/1836), Manuel (b. about 1833), E.A. (b. about 1837), Esther (b. about 1836/37), Sarah (b. about 1838), Leon (b. about 1840), Sallie (b. about 1842), Ellen and Emma (b. about 1845), Simeon (b. about. 1846), and William (b. about. 1850).[12] Jonas Levy eventually returned to Exeter, England, where he died on February 19, 1884. He is buried at the Exeter Jewish Cemetery.[13]

In advertisements, directory listings, and census records, Levy's activities as a watch maker, optometrist and jeweler receive the greatest emphasis. It is doubtful that he produced any of the silver bearing his mark (mark 73.1). To date, a pair of tongs with shell terminals, and fiddle-handled spoons with rounded shoulders are known.[14] None of these can be documented specifically to his time in Cincinnati.

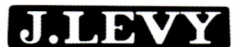

MARK 73.1

1. The 1850 Federal Census lists Jonas Levy as 51 years of age (b. about 1799). He is reported as 52 years of age (b. about 1808) in the 1860 Federal Census, Cincinnati, Hamilton, Ohio. Since he arrived in Cincinnati in 1819, a birth year closer to 1799 seems most probable. 1850 Federal Census, Little Rock, Pulaski, Arkansas; 1860 Federal Census, Memphis Ward 6, Shelby, Tennessee.

2. "R. Solomon Hirschel," *Jewish Quarterly Review*, vol. 10, 1919–1920, London: Macmillan & Co. Ltd, 487; Appendix IX, *Jewish Quarterly Review*, vol. 11, 1920–1921, London: Macmillan & Co. Ltd, 356; Joseph Jonas, "The Jews in Cincinnati," *The Occident and American Jewish Advocate* 1, no. 11 (February 1844) http://www.jewish-history.com /Occident/volume1/feb1844 /ohio.html; There was a Barnet and Jonas Levi operating a jewelry store

in Connersville, IN, around 1821, but there is no evidence to suggest that our subject and this Jonas Levi were the same person. *History of Fayette County, Indiana*, Chicago: Warner, Beers & Co., 1885, 137.

3. Charles Greve, *Centennial History of Cincinnati and Its Representative Citizens*, Chicago: Biographical Publishing Co., 1904, 940; Rev. Charles Frederic Goss, *Cincinnati, The Queen City, 1788–1912*, Cincinnati: The S.J. Clarke Publishing Co., 1912, 2:34; "R. Solomon Hirschel," *Jewish Quarterly Review*, 487.

4. Greve, *Centennial History of Cincinnati*, 940; Goss, *Cincinnati, The Queen City*, 2:34.

5. 1825 Cincinnati City Directory.

6. Advertisement, *National Republican*, October 26, 1829, reproduced in Beckman, 89.

7. *New York State Silversmiths*, Eggertsville, NY: The Darling Foundation, 1964, 118; Paul Von

Khrum, *Silversmiths of New York City*, New York: Von Khrum, 1978, 80. Levy's daughter Esther was born around 1836/37 in New York; 1850 Federal Census, Little Rock, Pulaski, Arkansas; 1860 Federal Census, Memphis Ward 6, Shelby, Tennessee.

8. Advertisement, *Cincinnati Daily Gazette*, January 11, 1838, reproduced in Beckman, 89.

9. Martin Very, appellant, v. Jonas Levy, United States Supreme Court Report, 54 U.S. 345; 1850 Federal Census, Little Rock, Pulaski, Arkansas. His children, Ellen, Emma, Simeon and William were all born in Arkansas; Levy owned a 16 year old female black slave according to the 1850 Federal Census Slave Schedules. In the 1860 Federal Census, a Cornelia Levy (age 24) is listed at the end of the Levy household listing and a one year-old Lallinas is listed under Cornelia. It is possible that Cornelia was Levy's

slave and Lallinas was her son.

10. Benjamin Hubbard Caldwell, *Tennessee Silversmiths*, Winston-Salem: Museum of Early Southern Decorative Arts, 1988, 121.

11. 1860 Federal Census, Memphis Ward 6, Shelby, Tennessee; In the 1850 Federal Census, Rebecca is reported as 39 years old (b. about 1811). In the 1860 Federal Census, she is reported as 44 years old (b. about 1816).

12. 1850 Federal Census, Little Rock, Pulaski, Arkansas; 1860 Federal Census, Memphis Ward 6, Shelby, Tennessee.

13. Jonas Levy (Jonah b. Menachem), *Cemeteryscribes.com*, http://www.cemeteryscribes.com/ getperson.php?personID=I5147&tree =Cemeteries.

14. Jonas Levy, eBay listings and private collections, Cincinnati silver binders, Cincinnati Art Museum.

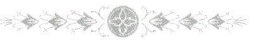

74. THOMAS LOVELL

1839/40–1904, w. 1855–1904

Thomas Lovell was born around 1840 in Ireland, and immigrated to the United States in 1854.[1] He is first documented in Cincinnati in 1855, working as a clerk for David B. Andrews (see **Loring Andrews & Co.**), from whom he learned the jewelry business.[2] In December 1858 Andrews, who had fallen into debt, sold much of his stock to Lovell and Peter W. Coyle (d. 1883).[3] Lovell opened shop at the northwest corner of Fifth and Race Streets, and was enumerated as a jeweler and a watch maker in city directory listings between 1856 and 1904. Over his long career, credit reporters consistently regarded him as "honest and cautious," declaring that he was in good credit and "doing business in a modest way and considered safe for all business wants."[4] He owned at least two houses, one at the corner of Betts and Baymiller Streets and the other on George Street, between Mound and Cutter Streets, and between 1874 and 1880, his net worth was estimated between $20,000 and $30,000.[5]

While the focus of his business seems to have been the sale of watches, clocks, and jewelry, he occasionally billed himself as a silversmith in advertisements, and was often listed under the business category of "silver ware" in city directories. An 1875 advertisement in a northern Kentucky newspaper gives precedence to his stock of jewelry, watches, and clocks, but also mentions the availability of "solid silver and the best quality of Triple Plated Ware," and in 1876, a Cincinnati advertisement was dedicated to his "Sterling Silver TEA and TABLE SPOONS at figures beyond competition."[6]

In 1880, Lovell reported his business as watch and clock repairing. He had $200 of capital invested, and kept one employee at $625 per year in wages. The material he used was valued at $250 and the value of his product was $1,400.[7] In the spring of 1891, Lovell relocated his store to 149 West Fifth Street, "where he swung a sign that shows he will wholesale and retail."[8] The new fixtures in his store were oak—all the cases, tables, desks, and chairs were "of the latest design"—and he had purchased "a complete new stock."[9] Late in 1894, Lovell relocated again to his final shop at 428 Race, which was in the Emery Arcade.[10]

After suffering for two years with a serious illness, Lovell announced in November 1904 that he planned to retire and to close out his business with an auction sale.[11] He died on December 28, 1904, before he was able to do so.[12] His funeral was held at the

Holy Family Church, in the Cincinnati suburb of Price Hill, and he was buried in St. Joseph's Cemetery.[13] Lovell's wife, Matilda Coyle (b. Ireland), immigrated in 1860 and they were married by 1862, when Thomas registered for the Civil War draft. They had no children.[14]

Several of Lovell's commissions—all associated with the Roman Catholic Church—were noted in newspapers and trade journals of the day. In 1882, he furnished a silver ice-water pitcher, tray, and goblet that was presented as a silver jubilee gift to Bishop William Henry Elder.[15] In 1904, he provided "a special order, a sterling silver, gold-plated crown, studded with 75 of the finest quality brilliants," to be presented by the St. Joseph Sisters of Charity to the St. Joseph Catholic Church, and "a fine piece of workmanship in the shape of a sterling silver, gold plated crown studded with 111 fine rhinestones," to be presented to the St. Peter's Cathedral at Eighth and Plum Streets.[16]

Extant silver marked by Thomas Lovell is rare. To date, his mark (mark 74.1) has been documented on spoons with tipped, exaggerated fiddle handles and pointed shoulders.[17]

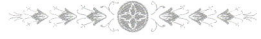

MARK 74.1

1. 1900 Federal Census, Cincinnati, Hamilton, Ohio; Death notice, *Jewelers' Circular and Horological Review* (January 4, 1905): 41; Thomas Lovell, death record, Cincinnati Health Department, University of Cincinnati Archives and Rare Books Library, http://hdl.handle.net /2374UC/238741; Conflicting information about Lovell's arrival in the United States appears in "Hotel Gossip," *Cincinnati Enquirer*, November 20, 1898, 2. There, it is noted that "Lovell came to Cincinnati in 1847, a lad of 11, with his father and mother, sisters and brother, from near Heathfield, Ballycastle, Province of Connaught, Ireland."

2. 1855 Cincinnati City Directory; Ohio, Vol. 4, p. 139, R.G. Dun & Co. Collection, Baker Library, Harvard Business School; Death notice (January 4, 1905): 41.

3. Ohio, Vol. 1, p. 326, R.G. Dun & Co. Collection; Ohio, Vol. 4, p. 139, R.G. Dun & Co. Collection; Peter W. Coyle, death notice, *Cincinnati Enquirer*, June 15, 1883, 5.

4. Ohio, Vol. 4, p. 139, R.G. Dun & Co. Collection.

5. Ohio, Vol. 4, p. 138–139, R.G. Dun & Co. Collection.

6. Advertisement, *Ludlow Reporter* (KY), July 31, 1875, 3, reproduced in Michael R. Averdick, *A Directory of Silversmiths, Jewelers, Watch and Clock Makers and Related Trades of Covington and Newport, Kentucky & Vicinity, 1833–1900*, Covington, KY: 829 Willard Street Press, 2002, 44; Advertisement, *Cincinnati Commercial Tribune*, December 17, 1876, 5.

7. 1880 Federal Non-Population Census Schedules, Products of Industry, Schedule 4, Hamilton County, Ohio.

8. Notice, *JCHR* (March 25, 1891): 29.

9. Notice, *JCHR* (May 27, 1891): 33.

10. 1895–1904 Cincinnati City Directories; Death notice (January 4, 1905): 41.

11. Notice, *JCHR* (November 23, 1904): 68.

12. Thomas Lovell, death record.

13. Death notice (January 4, 1905): 41.

14. In the 1900 Census, Matilda's birthdate is given as 1855, and it is recorded that she and Thomas had been married for 30 years. Her birthdate is likely a transcription error, as it would mean that she had married by age five; 1900 Federal Census, Cincinnati, Hamilton, Ohio; Ancestry.com, *U.S. Civil War Draft Registration Records, 1863–1865* [online database], Provo, Utah: Ancestry.com Operations, Inc., 2010; "Fifteen Years Ago: The Glass Wedding of Mr. and Mrs. Thomas Lovell," *Cincinnati Enquirer*, September 19, 1877, 8.

15. "Silver Jubilee of Bishop Elder," *Cincinnati Daily Gazette*, May 4, 1882, 4.

16. Notice, *JCHR*, (August 17, 1904): 59; Notice, *JCHR*, (October 19, 1904): 74; Representatives of St. Peter in Chains Cathedral and St. Joseph Catholic Church, when contacted during this project, had no knowledge of the crowns.

17. Thomas Lovell, eBay listings and private collections, Cincinnati silver binders, Cincinnati Art Museum.

75. FREDERICK W. MARMET

1832–1891, w. about 1857–1884

Frederick W. Marmet was born on October 1, 1832, in Hamm, Westphalia, Germany, the son of Clara Niehaus and William F. Marmet.[1] William, a physician, brought his family to the United States in 1849, when Frederick was about 17 years old.[2] They had settled in Cincinnati by August 1850.[3] Frederick's first listing in the Cincinnati city directories occurs in 1857, when he is enumerated as a watch maker working on the southeast corner of Second and Sycamore Streets—the location of **Richard Clayton**'s firm. The following year, he was listed as a dealer in watches, jewelry, etc. at 61 Broadway.[4] Marmet continued to work on Broadway for the duration of his career.[5] In 1860, census takers noted the value of his personal estate was $2,000.[6] By 1870, this had grown to an estimated $6,000.[7] Credit reporters consistently noted that Frederick's business was small, thus a significant portion of his worth likely came from his family and his wife's family. Frederick married Marie (Mary) Weyland (1846–1899), daughter of Susanna (1824–1887) and Peter Weyland (1821–1875), a prominent and wealthy brewer.[8] In 1885, about the time that Frederick retired from the business, he and his wife received a significant settlement from Peter Weyland's estate.[9] Frederick died on December 4, 1891, from injuries sustained when he jumped from a buggy.[10] He and his wife had four known children: P.W. (1865–1866), Otto (b. about 1867), Susanna (1869–1904), and Mary (1871–1943).[11]

Frederick W. Marmet was a watch maker and a merchant of jewelry and other fancy goods. Silver bearing his mark was likely produced and bought from local manufacturers. To date, his stamp (mark 75.1), has been documented on a pair of teaspoons with tipped, exaggerated fiddle handles and pointed shoulders.[12]

F.W. MARMET

MARK 75.1

1. 1850, 1860 Federal Censuses, Cincinnati, Hamilton, Ohio; Charles Greve, "Otto Marmet," *Centennial History of Cincinnati and Its Representative Citizens*, Chicago: Biographical Publishing Co., 1904, 2:435–436; "Frederick W. Marmet," grave marker, Spring Grove Cemetery, Cincinnati, Ohio.
2. Gale Research, *Passenger and Immigration Lists Index, 1500s–1900s* [online database], Provo, Utah: Ancestry.com Operations Inc., 2010.
3. 1850 Federal Census, Cincinnati, Hamilton, Ohio.
4. 1858 Cincinnati City Directory.
5. Beginning in 1861, city directories enumerate Marmet's address as 65 Broadway, however it is likely that this was the same location as 61 Broadway. During this time, street numbers were not standardized, they were arbitrarily assigned or self-designated, and could easily change. Standardization of street numbers was implemented in 1853, but not everyone complied immediately.
6. 1860 Federal Census, Cincinnati, Hamilton, Ohio.
7. 1870 Federal Census, Cincinnati, Hamilton, Ohio.
8. Ohio, Vol. 9, p. 118, R.G. Dun & Co. Collection, Baker Library, Harvard Business School; Marmet's father was a successful physician, and his brothers were prominent and successful businessmen. Greve, "Otto Marmet," 435–436; "Death's Dart Strikes Down Mr. Florence Marmet in the Prime of Life," *Cincinnati Enquirer*, November 15, 1887, 8; *Reprint of Ohio Cases Published in the Weekly Law Bulletin*, vols. 10–17, "Catherine Jung et al. v. Susanna Wesland et al.," Norwalk, OH: The American Publishers Co., 1899, 485–498; "Marie Marmet," grave marker, Spring Grove Cemetery; Burial records, Spring Grove Cemetery.
9. *Reprint of Ohio Cases*, "Catherine Jung et al. v. Susanna Wesland et al.," 485–498; Ohio, Vol. 9, p. 118, R.G. Dun & Co. Collection.
10. "F. W. Marmet," death record, Cincinnati Health Department, University of Cincinnati Archives and Rare Books Library, http://hdl.handle.net/23744.UC/62 4999; Frederick W. Marmet, death notice, *Cincinnati Enquirer*, September 7, 1891, 8.
11. 1870, 1880 Federal Censuses, Cincinnati, Hamilton, Ohio; Burial records, Spring Grove Cemetery.
12. Marmet, eBay listings and private collections, Cincinnati silver binders, Cincinnati Art Museum.

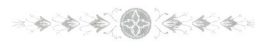

76. JAMES H. MARTIN

about 1814–1890, w.1836–1853

James Martin was born around 1814, probably in Rhode Island.[1] By January 1836 he had arrived in Cincinnati and partnered with **William T. Eaves** to create the jewelry manufactory Eaves & Martin.[2] Five years later, he joined **John Owen** to form Martin & Owen, manufacturers of spectacles and jewelry.[3] This partnership was short-lived, as the 1842 City Directory indicates that he was working alone as a jeweler on Third Street between Walnut and Vine Streets. A year later, he listed as a watch maker and jeweler on Main Street, between Third and Fourth Streets.[4] Martin moved to the south side of Fourth Street between Plum and Western Row in 1846.[5] A directory was not published in 1847, and he did not appear in the 1848/49 Cincinnati Business Directory. By 1849, he had partnered with J.C. Schooley to form Martin & Schooley, a real estate and loan broker firm, and in the 1850 Federal Census he reported his occupation as an agent.[6]

In the 1851/52 City Directory, Martin was listed as a gold and silverware manufacturer working on the north side of Sixth Street, between Walnut and Vine Streets. In March 1853 credit reporters noted that he had maintained a small store, in a small way, for several years, and had just taken a new store (at 183 Main Street). His credit was reported as "not strong" and his means were estimated at about $1,500.[7] Later that year, it was reported that he "made a fraudulent failure" and was "worthless."[8] He was listed at 206 Court Street with no mention of an occupation in 1855 and 1856, and from 1857 to at least 1885, he was in the real estate business.[9]

James and his wife Jane (b. 1814, Orange County, New York) moved to Decatur, Illinois where he died on April 24, 1890, and she died on May 4, 1897.[10] Both were buried in Cincinnati. They had at least three children: John E. (b. about 1837), Elizabeth (b. about 1839), and Charles G. (b. about 1843).[11]

James H. Martin's mark (mark 76.1) has been observed on a sauce ladle and on a dessert spoon with exaggerated fiddle handles and pointed shoulders.[12]

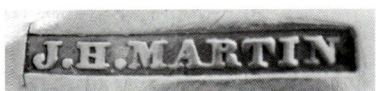

MARK 76.1

1. 1850, 1870, and 1880 Federal Censuses, Cincinnati, Hamilton, Ohio; James H. Martin, burial record, Spring Grove Cemetery, Cincinnati, Ohio. Martin's place of birth is given as Rhode Island in the 1850 and 1870 Censuses, as Massachusetts in the 1880 Census, and as New York in his death record. He is almost certainly misrepresented as G.H. Martin, a jeweler, born in Rhode Island, in the 1839/40 Cincinnati City Directory.

2. Advertisement, *Cincinnati Daily Gazette*, January 4, 1836, reproduced in Beckman, 90.

3. Advertisement, reproduced in Beckman, 90, and cited as from the *Daily Times*, October 20, 1841.

4. 1843, 1844 Cincinnati City Directories; This was the same area where **Wilson McGrew**, **Owen & Read**, and others had shops. He could have been working for one of them or simply working in the vicinity.

5. 1846 Cincinnati City Directory.

6. 1849/1850 Cincinnati City Directory; 1850 Federal Census, Cincinnati, Hamilton, Ohio.

7. Ohio, Vol. 1, p. 182, R.G. Dun & Co. Collection, Baker Library, Harvard Business School; 1853 Cincinnati City Directory.

8. Ohio, Vol. 1, p. 182, R.G. Dun & Co. Collection.

9. 1855, 1856, 1857–1885 Cincinnati City Directories; Martin does not appear in the Cincinnati city directories after 1885.

10. Burial records, Spring Grove Cemetery.

11. 1850, 1870, 1880 Federal Censuses, Cincinnati, Hamilton, Ohio.

12. Beckman, 91; James H. Martin, eBay listings and private collections, Cincinnati silver binders, Cincinnati Art Museum.

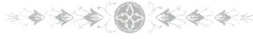

77. McGREW & BEGGS

1843–1848

On April 21, 1843, **Wilson McGrew** and his former associate Joseph P. Beggs (see **J.P.Beggs & Co.**) established the firm of McGrew & Beggs.[1] Both men were born in Pennsylvania and could have known one another prior to their arrival in Cincinnati. McGrew, who had reportedly inherited $20,000, furnished most of the capital.[2] In September, the firm advertised that they had "just received (in addition to their stock of Watches and Jewelry) a splendid assortment of Plated Goods, of superior quality and entirely new patterns, consisting of fine . . . Baskets, Candlesticks and Branches, large and small Waiters, with feet, . . . Also Silver Forks, threaded pattern, with a general assortment of Silver Ware of our own manufacture, warranted."[3] Their willingness to pay the highest prices for old silver was also noted.[4] In addition to advertising as "dealers in watches, jewelry, silver ware and fancy goods," they also offered watch, clock, and jewelry repair services.[5] They conducted business at the shop formerly run by McGrew on Main Street, between Third and Fourth Streets.[6] After the firm's dissolution in March 1848, McGrew continued business on his own, and Beggs partnered with Harry R. Smith to form **Beggs & Smith**.[7]

Silver struck with the mark of McGrew & Beggs (mark 77.1) includes spoons of various sizes with either fiddle handles or tipped, exaggerated fiddle handles and pointed shoulders (fig. 77.1); and spoons and forks in a fiddle thread pattern.[8]

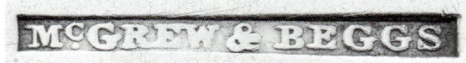

MARK 77.1

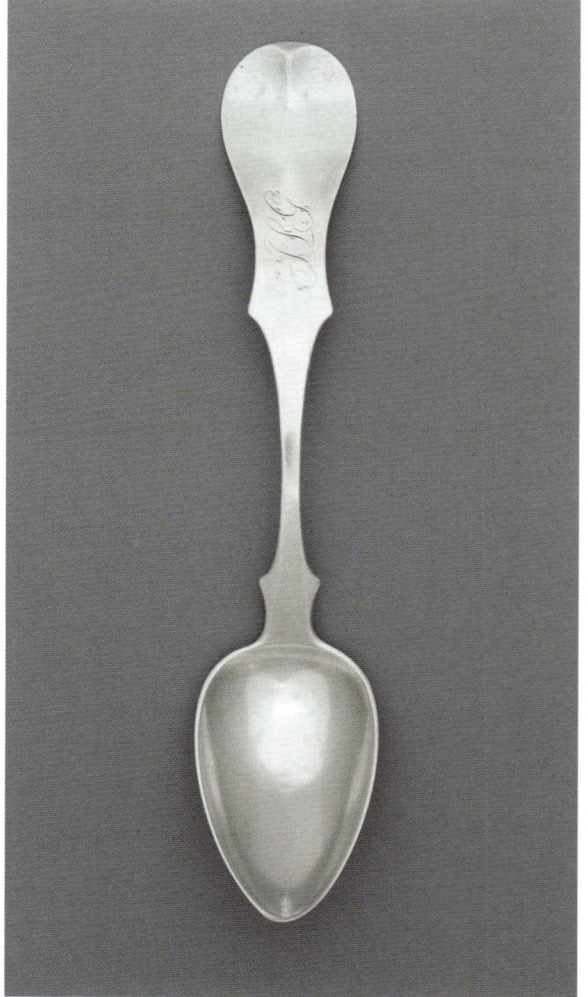

FIG. 77.1: McGrew & Beggs, *Tablespoon*, 1843–1848, L. 8¹¹⁄₁₆ in. (22 cm), Museum Purchase: John S. Conner Fund, 2013.11

1. Ohio, Vol. 1, p. 71, R.G. Dun & Co. Collection, Baker Library, Harvard Business School.

2. Ibid.; Wilson McGrew likely received money from **Alexander McGrew** just prior to Alexander McGrew's death. Wilson is not enumerated in the will of Alexander McGrew as one of Alexander's children whose care and guardianship of person and property was left to his wife, but he was a witness to the will, along with J.P. Beggs. Alexander McGrew's will was written on April 20, 1843, just

one day before the establishment of McGrew & Beggs. Alexander McGrew, will dated April 20, 1843, proved May 15, 1843, vol. 2, p. 381, Hamilton County Registry of Probate, Cincinnati, Ohio.

3. Advertisement, *Cincinnati Daily Gazette*, September 10, 1843, reproduced in Beckman, 8.

4. Ibid.

5. *Kimball & James' Business Directory for the Mississippi valley, 1844 including . . . Pittsburg, Beaver, Steubenville, Wheeling Portsmouth, Maysville, Cincinnati,*

Lawrenceburg, Madison, Louisville, St. Louis, Memphis, Vicksburg, Natchez, New Orleans: with a brief notice of the discovery and occupation of the Mississippi valley, and a historical and statistical sketch of the principal cities above mentioned, Cincinnati: Kendall & Barnard, 1844, [n.p.], reproduced in Beckman, 94.

6. Their street number is not given in the 1844 Cincinnati City Directory, but their advertisement in the 1844 *Kimball & James' Business Directory* gives their address as 157 Main

Street. This may be a misprint, as McGrew's previous shop was located at 159 Main which was given as 137 Main in 1846. 1844, 1846 Cincinnati City Directories; *Kimball & James' Business Directory*, [n.p.], reproduced in Beckman, 94.

7. Ohio, Vol. 1, p. 71, R.G. Dun & Co. Collection.

8. McGrew & Beggs, eBay listings and private collections, Cincinnati silver binders, Cincinnati Art Museum.

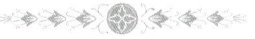

78. ALEXANDER McGREW

about 1775–1843, w. 1817–1836

Alexander McGrew was born around 1775 in Williamsport, Washington County, Pennsylvania (now known as Monongahela, Washington County), possibly to Martha Kirk (b. 1730) and Alexander McGrew (b. Ireland 1727–1781).[1] He remained in Washington County until at least 1809.[2] He may have stayed briefly in Henry County, Kentucky before settling in Cincinnati, where he married Aurelia Heywood (1793–1820), daughter of Thomas Heywood of Cincinnati, on September 3, 1811.[3]

The first indication of McGrew's business activities in the city appears in April 1817 when he advertises with **Joseph Jonas** as McGrew & Jonas.[4] Jonas was "immediately from London" and had been educated in watch finishing.[5] Nothing is known about McGrew's training. McGrew & Jonas advertised as "Clock and Watchmakers and Silversmith and Jewellers [*sic*]" with a shop on Main Street, one door above the Post Office.[6] In August 1818 they announced the procurement of new stock via the *James Monroe* from Liverpool (fig. 78.1). Special emphasis was given to watches and jewelry, but it was stated, "they are also now able to furnish Tea Sets and Hollow Ware, Of all descriptions, and newest fashions; having engaged first rate workmen from New York and Philadelphia." Wares marked by their firm are unknown. When the partnership ended in May 1819, McGrew continued on his own, listing in the city directory as a silversmith at McGrew & Jonas' old stand (159 Main Street, between Third and Fourth Streets), and living in the rear of the shop.[7] His relationship with Joseph Jonas, who also continued independently in the trade, must have remained amicable, for in 1823, McGrew opened his back room to a group of fourteen Cincinnatians, including Jonas, to use as a Jewish Synagogue.[8]

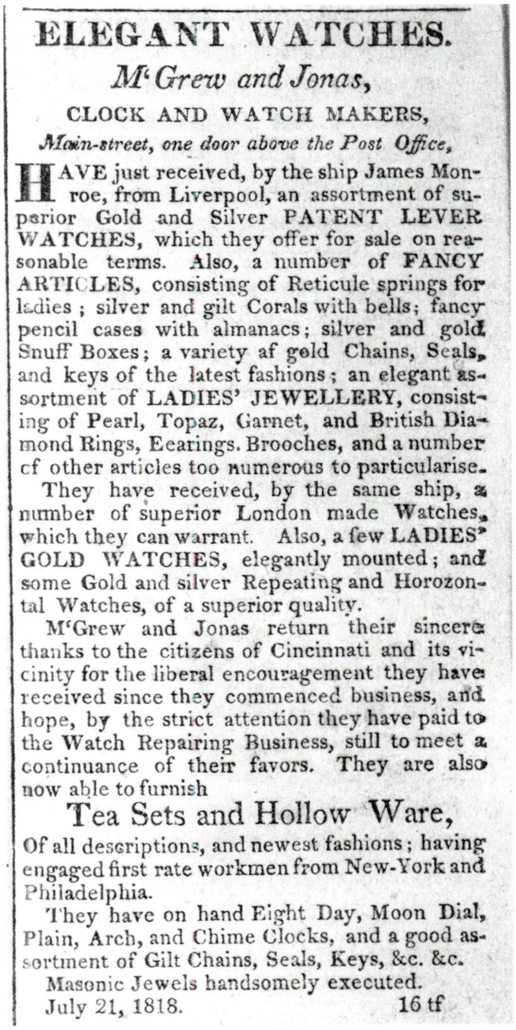

ELEGANT WATCHES.

M'Grew and Jonas,

CLOCK AND WATCH MAKERS,

Main-street, one door above the Post Office,

HAVE just received, by the ship James Monroe, from Liverpool, an assortment of superior Gold and Silver PATENT LEVER WATCHES, which they offer for sale on reasonable terms. Also, a number of FANCY ARTICLES, consisting of Reticule springs for ladies; silver and gilt Corals with bells; fancy pencil cases with almanacs; silver and gold Snuff Boxes; a variety of gold Chains, Seals, and keys of the latest fashions; an elegant assortment of LADIES' JEWELLERY, consisting of Pearl, Topaz, Garnet, and British Diamond Rings, Earings. Brooches, and a number of other articles too numerous to particularise.

They have received, by the same ship, a number of superior London made Watches, which they can warrant. Also, a few LADIES' GOLD WATCHES, elegantly mounted; and some Gold and silver Repeating and Horozontal Watches, of a superior quality.

M'Grew and Jonas return their sincere thanks to the citizens of Cincinnati and its vicinity for the liberal encouragement they have received since they commenced business, and hope, by the strict attention they have paid to the Watch Repairing Business, still to meet a continuance of their favors. They are also now able to furnish

Tea Sets and Hollow Ware,

Of all descriptions, and newest fashions; having engaged first rate workmen from New-York and Philadelphia.

They have on hand Eight Day, Moon Dial, Plain, Arch, and Chime Clocks, and a good assortment of Gilt Chains, Seals, Keys, &c. &c.

Masonic Jewels handsomely executed.

July 21, 1818.   16 tf

FIG. 78.1: Advertisement, *Western Spy*, August 1, 1818, 2

McGrew listed in Cincinnati city directories up until his retirement in 1836, with his occupation given as either a silversmith or a watch maker.[9] His advertisement in November 1827 (fig. 78.2) reveals the breadth of his stock.[10] Aside from watches, spectacles and thimbles, wares made from silver are curiously absent from this impressive list. If he made any silver, his stock was likely supplemented by silver that was made and purchased elsewhere. A May 1829 advertisement reads, "The undersigned has just returned from N. [New] York, and now offers goods in his line of superior quality at the lowest prices."[11] By this time, it appears that McGrew had opened a second location on Front Street between the Cincinnati Hotel and Sycamore Street.[12] Again, a list of wide-ranging goods ensues with no mention of silver (except for silver double- and single-eyed spectacles) until the very bottom of the advertisement: "N.B. One splendid Silver Tea Sett [sic]." Unfortunately, no silver tea sets marked by Alexander McGrew are known today. Evidently, McGrew also offered the service of engraving, as Salmon P. Chase recalls taking his newborn daughter's bracelet to McGrew's shop in 1835 to have it engraved with her name. Chase notes that "by accident, however, the jeweler did not execute my order, and my dear Kitty [Chase's wife], seeing the bracelet returned unmarked never knew that I had complied with her request."[13]

Reports on the strength of McGrew's business are not available, but a sense of his standing can be discerned through the following information. In 1828, he had the means to own a farm, which he advertised for sale or rent, and which is described as "lying on the Ohio river, six miles below Cincinnati, on the Ohio side" with a situation "well calculated for the cultivation of the Vine."[14] And, in recollections published by his son Robert, McGrew is remembered as a "moneyed" man.[15]

McGrew's enterprising spirit is also evident in his involvement in the development of railroads in the Midwest. In 1830, he was appointed to a committee to explore the development of a railroad that would further Cincinnati's economic development and national standing, and in 1832, he was an incorporator of The Cincinnati and St. Louis Railroad Co. This railroad was never realized, but its surveyed route would later become part of the Ohio and Mississippi Railroad.[16] In 1834 McGrew served as a director of the Ohio Mechanics' Institute (est. 1828).[17] In 1835 McGrew was appointed to the Board of Internal Improvements, a committee designed to coordinate a multitude of civic enrichment projects, including several proposals for railroads, and he was awarded a patent for his idea of using compressed air to propel railroad cars, boats and other vehicles.[18]

In January 1836 McGrew announced his retirement, stating that "he embraces the occasion of his withdrawing from business, to return his acknowledgements for the liberal patronage bestowed upon him, and respectfully recommending [sic] his successor [Wilson McGrew] (who remains in the old stand) to the consideration and favors of his friends and the public."[19] The training of **Wilson McGrew**, likely Alexander's nephew, in the family business had begun prior to 1825, when Wilson was listed as a silversmith working in Alexander's shop on Main Street.[20]

In the 1839/40 Cincinnati City Directory, Alexander is listed as a farmer, boarding at Pearl Street House. Presumably, he was farming in the outskirts of the city, possibly at the location offered

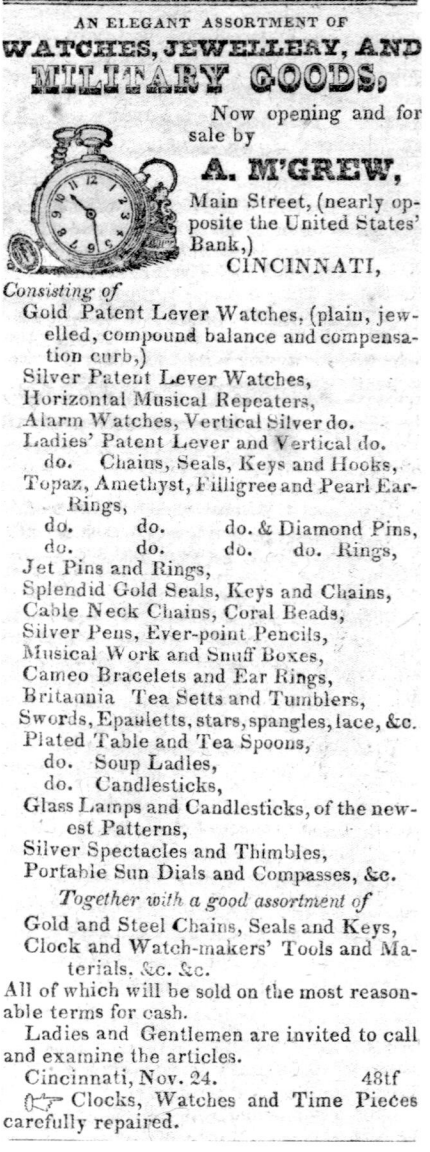

FIG. 78.2: Advertisement, *Saturday Evening Chronicle*, November 24, 1827, 3

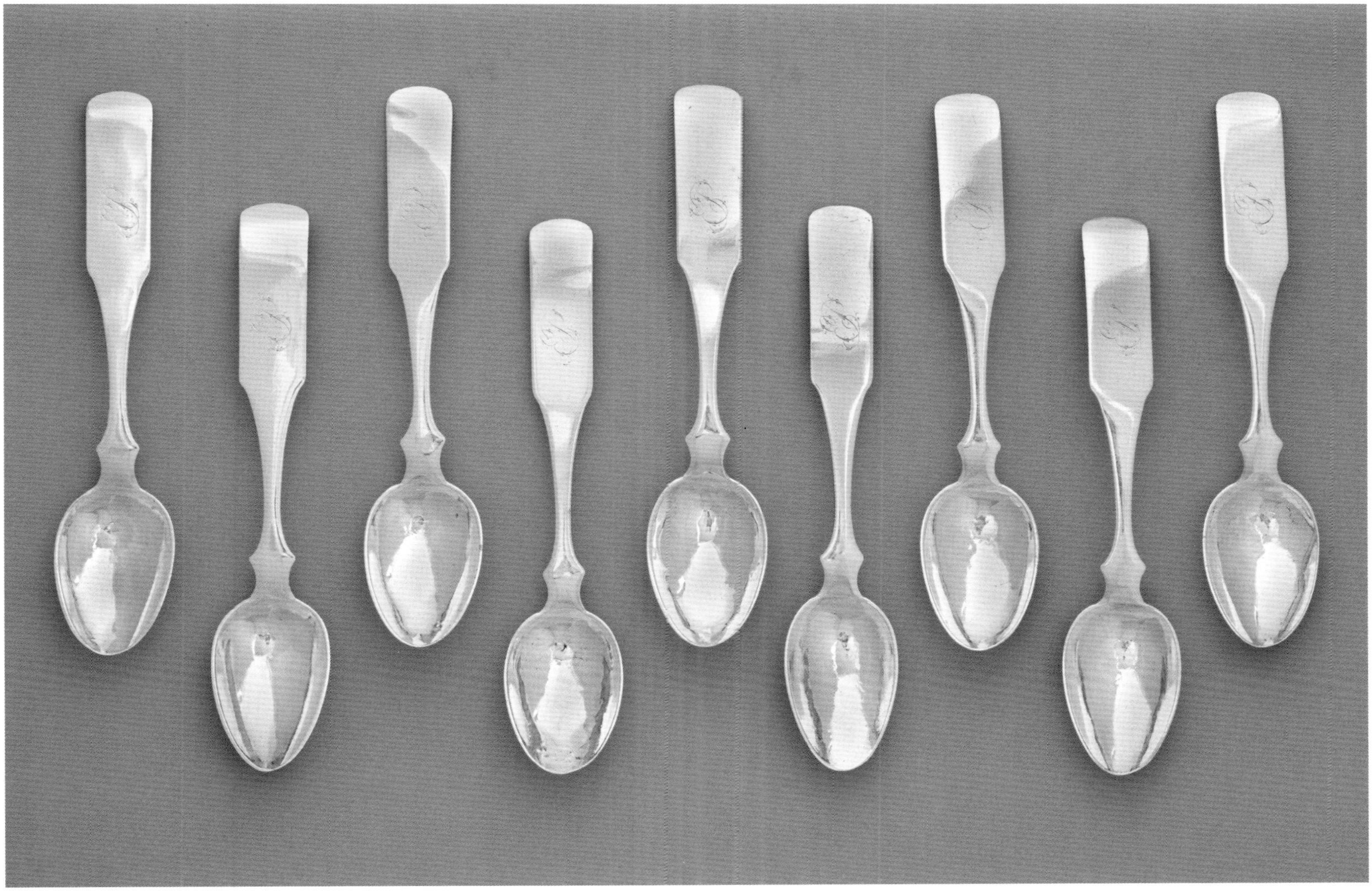

FIG. 78.3: Alexander McGrew, *Set of Teaspoons*, 1817–1819,
L. 5¾ in. (14.6 cm), CAM, Museum Purchase, 1962.109–117

for rent in 1828, and boarding when he had business in town.[21] McGrew remained active during his retirement. In 1842, he applied for another patent for the improved construction of windmills.[22]

Alexander McGrew's last will and testament was written on April 20, 1843.[23] He died five days later.[24] At the time of his death, he was survived by his wife, Caroliana Carter Hall, and at least five children: Alexander M., William R., Robert J., Amelia M., and Caroline E[25] Three previous wives and a daughter preceded him in death.[26]

Teaspoons (fig. 78. 3), serving spoons, and salt spoons, all with fiddle handles, have been found with Alexander McGrew's mark (mark 78.1). A tall-case clock, whose dial bears McGrew's name, is also known.[27]

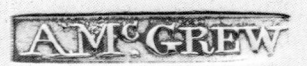

MARK 78.1

1. Alexander McGrew, OneWorld Tree, Ancestry.com, http://trees.ancestry .com/owt/person.aspx?pid=4412567 &st=3, accessed February 12, 2013; 1825 Cincinnati City Directory. His age is given as 55 (b. about 1788) in his death notice, *Cincinnati Daily Gazette*, April 26, 1843, 2.
2. On June 5, 1809, his plea for the return of a strayed horse was published in the *Washington Reporter*.

"Washington Reporter News 1809," http://www.pa-roots.org/data/read .php?819,374470, accessed December 8, 2011; An Alexander McGrew appears in the 1810 Census for Nottingham Township, Washington County, Pennsylvania, http://www.rootsweb.ancestry.com /˜pawashin/census/1810 /nottingham-twp_orig-names.html.
3. Alexander McGrew, 1810 Census,

Henry County, Kentucky. Alexander's sister Hannah McGrew (1774–1818) was married to John Simmons (1771–1846) in Henry County, Kentucky, in 1793. She may have been living in Cincinnati about 1799 when son Benjamin Simmons was born. McGrew-Simmons marriage record found in Edmund West, comp. *Family Data Collection - Marriages* [online database], Provo, Utah: Ancestry.com Operations Inc., 2001; Benjamin Simmons birthplace found in Edmund West, comp. *Family Data Collection - Births* [online database], Provo, Utah: Ancestry.com Operations Inc., 2001; Heywood-McGrew marriage announcement, *Western Spy*, September 14, 1811; Heywood-McGrew marriage announcement, *Washington Reporter*, September 3, 1811. In Washington County sources, Aurelia's name is published as Acrelia. She is buried with her family at the Kepper Cemetery, Miami County, Ohio. http://www.thetroyhistorical society.org/cemetery/kepper _cemetery.html, accessed June 5, 2013.

4. Later histories, particularly of **Loring Andrews & Co.**, which trace the Andrews firm's history back to Alexander McGrew, state that McGrew established his Cincinnati business in 1805 (possibly on Water Street), but this has not been documented; Advertisement, *Western Spy*, April 14, 1817, reproduced in Beckman, 91.

5. Advertisement, *Western Spy*, April 14, 1817, reproduced in Beckman, 91.

6. Ibid.

7. Advertisement, *Inquisitor and Cincinnati Advertiser*, May 17, 1819, reproduced in Beckman, 92; 1819 Cincinnati City Directory.

8. Jonathan D. Sarna and Nancy H. Klein, *The Jews of Cincinnati*, Cincinnati: Center for the American Jewish Experience, Hebrew Union College – Jewish Institute of Religion, 1989, 32.

9. 1819-1834 Cincinnati City Directories. There was no directory published in 1835, and in the 1836/37 edition there is no occupation listed for McGrew.

10. Advertisement, *Saturday Evening Chronicle*, November 24, 1827, 3. This advertisement ran again on November 24, 1828, in the *Saturday Evening Chronicle*.

11. Advertisement, *Cincinnati Daily Gazette*, May 21, 1829, reproduced in Beckman, 92.

12. Ibid.

13. John Nivens (ed.), *The Salmon P. Chase Papers*, vol. 1, *Journals 1829–1872*, Kent, OH: Kent State University Press, 1993, 87. Chase was a lawyer who would later become an Ohio Senator, Ohio Governor, U.S. Secretary of the Treasury and ultimately the Chief Justice of the U.S. Supreme Court.

14. Advertisement, *Saturday Evening Chronicle*, March 15, 1828.

15. "Talk of the Town," *Cincinnati Enquirer*, January 25, 1902, 16.

16. Ibid.

17. 1834 Cincinnati City Directory; John P. Foote, *The Schools of Cincinnati, and Its Vicinity*, Cincinnati: C.F. Bradley & Co., 1855, 11.

18. William A. Taylor, *Ohio Statesmen and Annals of Progress*, Columbus: The Westbote Co., 1899, 1:155; Charles Greve, *Centennial History of Cincinnati and Its Representative Citizens*, Chicago: Biographical Publishing Co., 1904, 1:589; Sally Griffith, "A Proper Spirit of Enterprise: The Booster Ethos and Resistance to Abolitionism in Jacksonian Cincinnati," *Trading Cultures: The Worlds of Western Merchants, Essays on Authority, Objectivity, and Evidence*, Turnhout, Belgium: Brepols, 2001, 243; "Talk of the Town," January 25, 1902; Edmund Ruffin (ed.), *The Farmers' Register*, Petersburg, VA: Edward Ruffin, 1836, 3:595–596; Alexander McGrew. 1835. Air, Condensed, For Propelling Boats, Cars, &c. US Patent X9199, issued Oct. 27, 1835.

19. Advertisement, *Cincinnati Daily Gazette*, January 25, 1836, reproduced in Beckman, 92.

20. 1825 Cincinnati City Directory; Genealogical research to date could not confirm the exact relation between Alexander and Wilson. Wilson is not named in Alexander's will, but is a witness to it. Wilson's father's name is given as William in Wilson's burial record, Spring Grove Cemetery, Cincinnati, Ohio. This could not be verified. See McGrew genealogy file, Decorative Arts & Design Department, Cincinnati Art Museum.

21. McGrew owned a building on Front Street between Sycamore and Broadway, which was damaged by fire in 1840. *Daily Chronicle*, March 31, 1840.

22. Alexander McGrew. 1842.

23. Improvement in Windmills. US Patent 2746, issued Aug. 2, 1842.

24. Alexander McGrew, will dated April 20, 1843, proved May 15, 1843, vol. 2, p. 381, Hamilton County Registry of Probate, Cincinnati, Ohio.

25. Alexander McGrew, death notice, *Cincinnati Daily Gazette*, April 26, 1843, 2.

26. Alexander McGrew, will; Caroliana was the daughter of Elizabeth L. Colston and Dr. Benjamin H. Hall. John Frederick Dorman, *Virginia Revolutionary Pension Applications*, Washington, DC: J.F. Dorman, 1975, 21:57.

27. In 1820, McGrew's wife Aurelia died, and in 1822 he married Alvira L. Fisher (d. 1824), daughter of Brownlow and Elizabeth Fisher of New Jersey, who bore him a daughter Aurelia Elizabeth (1822–1823). His third wife was Margaret Amelia Osborne (b. about 1794, d. 1834); Beckman, 91; Alvira L. McGrew, Aurelia E. McGrew and Margaret A. McGrew, burial records, Spring Grove Cemetery; Marriage record for Alexander and Alvira, Hamilton County Probate Records, vol. 2, 46, http://www.probatect .org/CourtRecordsArchive /bukmarriages.aspx; Margaret A. McGrew, death notice, *Cincinnati Daily Gazette*, September 6, 1834, 2.

28. Alexander McGrew, eBay listings and private collections, Cincinnati silver binders, Cincinnati Art Museum; *Teaspoons* (pair), Yale University Art Gallery, Gift of Alan R. Kossack, 1994.87.106.1–2; *Tall-case clock*, Garth's Auctioneers & Appraisers, November 23 & 24, 2007, lot 720.

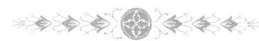

79. W. McGrew & Son

1854–1858

William Wilson McGrew, described by credit reporters as a "quiet young man of good character and habits, but [with] no means," had joined his father **Wilson McGrew** in the business by March 1854.[1] Their firm, W. McGrew & Son, had relocated from 187 Main to the southwest corner of Fourth and Main Streets by 1856, and advertised as "Manufacturers and Importers of WATCHES, JEWELRY, SILVER AND PLATED WARE, AT WHOLESALE and RETAIL."[2] By January 1856 Wilson's health had declined so that

he was no longer able to attend to the business. Credit reporters noted that William Wilson, "peculiarly adapted to the trade," was managing the firm and was "remarkably industrious."[3] By July 1857 Wilson was mentally incompetent.[4] In September, William Wilson advertised his return from the East with "one of the finest stocks of Watches, Jewelry and Silver Ware ever brought to this city," but by October 1857 he was in serious debt.[5] In April 1858, after settling with creditors, William Wilson McGrew continued in business, under his own name, at the old stand, paying $2,000 a year in rent.[6]

Most, if not all, of the silver that W. McGrew & Son marked was retailed, not made, by them. Spoons with tipped, exaggerated fiddle handles and pointed shoulders have been identified with mark 79.1.[7] Flatware in Gorham's "Josephine" (1855) and Henry Hebbard's "Grecian" (circa 1857) patterns have been documented with an incuse "W. McGREW & SON" mark.[8]

1. Ohio, Vol. 1, p. 71, R.G. Dun & Co. Collection, Baker Library, Harvard Business School.
2. 1856 Cincinnati City Directory; Advertisement, *Cincinnati Enquirer*, April 30, 1857, 1.
3. Ohio, Vol. 2, p. 32, R.G. Dun & Co. Collection.
4. Ibid.
5. Advertisement, *Cincinnati Enquirer*, September 2, 1857, 3; Ohio, Vol. 2, p. 32, R.G. Dun & Co. Collection.
6. Ohio, Vol. 4, p. 38, R.G. Dun & Co. Collection.
7. W. McGrew & Son, eBay listings and private collections, Cincinnati silver binders, Cincinnati Art Museum; *Dessert Spoon*, Winterthur Museum, Gift of William J. Flather, 1990.0098.
8. W. McGrew & Son, eBay listings and private collections, Cincinnati Art Museum.

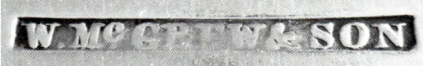

MARK 79.1

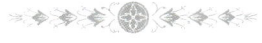

80. WILLIAM WILSON McGREW
1833–1893, w. 1853 or earlier–1892

William Wilson McGrew was born in Cincinnati on March 8, 1833, son of Sarah Gallagher McGrew and **Wilson McGrew**.[1] He reportedly left college at age seventeen to enter his father's store, where he learned the silver, jewelry, and watch maker's trade.[2] By 1853, he was working there as a salesman, and between 1854 and 1858, the business operated as **W. McGrew & Son**.[3] In April 1858, following the decline of his father's health and the failure of W. McGrew & Son, William Wilson McGrew commenced business under his own name at the southwest corner of Fourth and Main Streets.[4] Noted "as a quiet young man of good character and habits," "peculiarly adapted to the trade," and "remarkably industrious," R.G. Dun & Co. credit reporters predicted that McGrew would turn the business around, thanks to "a good run of old substantial customers" and his "excellent location."[5] Despite keeping a well stocked store that carried all types of jewelry, fancy goods, silver, and Sheffield plated wares, McGrew struggled.[6] In April 1862 credit reporters noted that "for some time past he has been very hard up and frequently protested but with [the] indulgence of creditors has managed to keep his head above water."[7]

In December the following year, McGrew moved his shop to 56 West Fourth Street, between Walnut and Vine Streets, investing $7,000 in the fitting up of his new store, soon regarded as "the finest establishment in the city."[8] His business flourished and he was again in good circumstances with creditors.[9] By 1867, he had built a grand house in Glendale, 20 miles north of Cincinnati, which cost about $50,000, and his total worth was estimated to be $100,000.[10] In September of that year, he relocated his business again. On opening night, the store at 77 West Fourth Street in Pike's Opera Building (fig. E1.7) "was thronged with people of taste." The show room, measuring 128 by 33 feet, featured counters of white marble with Lisbon panels and Irish black marble bases. Cases of French plate glass held jewelry, and the floor was of black and white marble tiles. The ceiling was frescoed.[11] Later descriptions of the store elaborate on the silver displays noting that "upon either side [of the showroom] the white, gleaming silver shines, cast into almost every shape," and that "most of the sterling silverware is put up in cases lined with different colored satins and velvets, and neatly stamped inside, in gold letters, with the name and mark of the house."[12] His display of silver epergnes was regarded as especially grand.[13] A very boastful 1868 holiday advertisement extolling the virtues of McGrew's varied and rich stock proclaimed it to "exceed the wonders of Aladdin's palace a thousand times over," and noted that "Paris, Vienna, London and all the great capitals of Europe have contributed some of their finest wares, to swell the show."[14]

Most of McGrew's stock was bought in the eastern cities, where he maintained special relationships with two of the largest houses, Gorham Mfg. Co. and Whiting Mfg. Co.[15] Advertisements from 1871 tout Gorham's sterling and plated wares in "all their newest

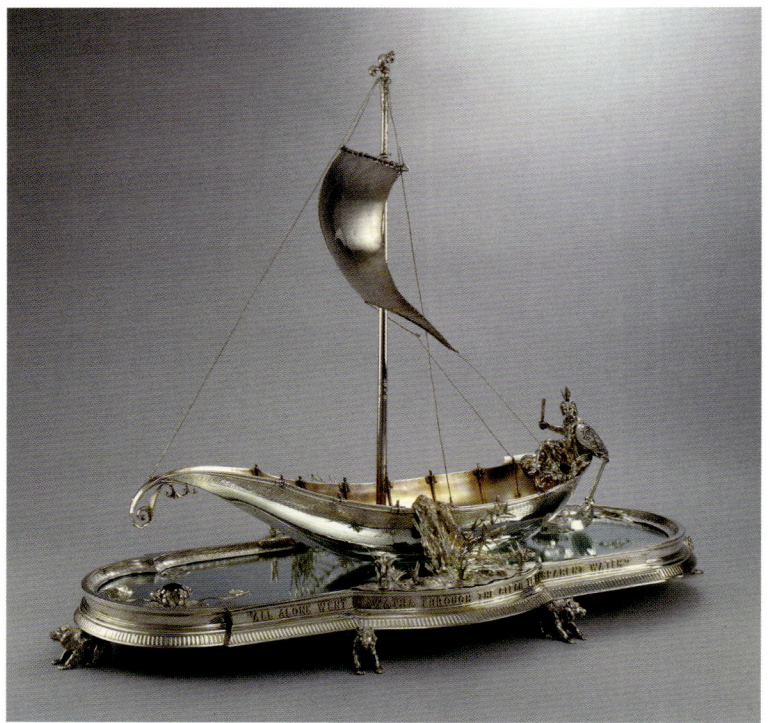

FIG. 80.1: Gorham Mfg. Co. (estab. 1831), *Hiawatha's Boat Centerpiece*, 1871, silver with gilding, 34 × 44½ × 19 in. (83.4 × 113 × 48.3 cm), Photo by Bruce White, copyright **White House Historical Association: 674**

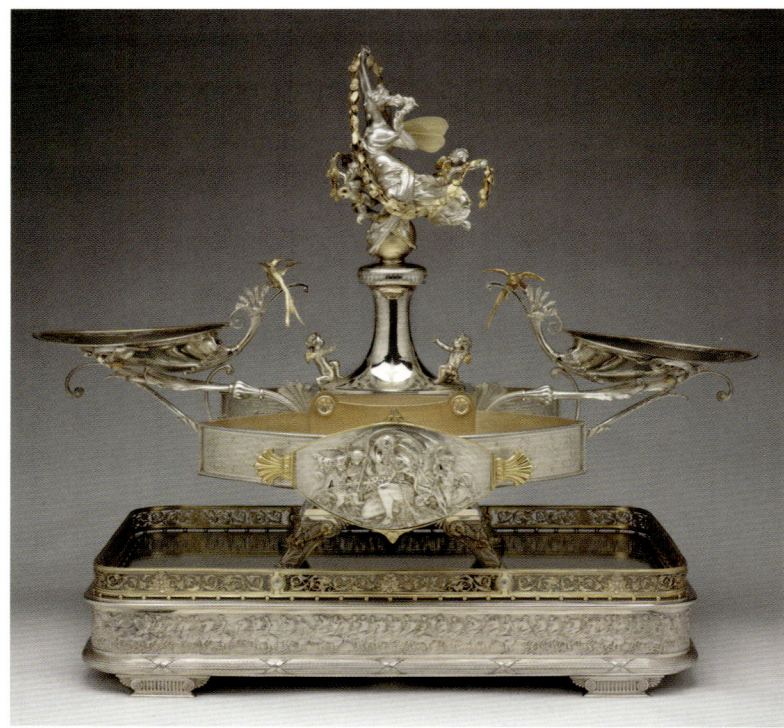

FIG. 80.2: Thomas Pairpoint, designer, Gorham Mfg. Co. (estab. 1831), *Neptune Epergne*, 1876, silver with gilding, 26 × 36 × 21½ in. (66 × 91.4 × 54.6 cm), The Gorham Collection, RISD Museum, Gift of Textron Inc., 1991.126.80

and choicest productions in Dinner, Tea, and Dessert Services" as one of the great and "unequaled" features of McGrew's.[16] Although he occasionally billed himself as a jeweler and silversmith, there is no evidence to suggest that McGrew ever manufactured any of the silver that he sold.[17] He did, however, employ jewelers and watch makers who would have done some setting and repair work.[18] In the 1870 Products of Industry Census, he reported that in the jobbing and repairing of jewelry he had invested $500 capital, and employed three hands (two men and one youth) who utilized $500 of "misc. material to generate $5,000 worth of repairs, &c."[19]

When the Irish troops of the 10th Ohio Volunteer Infantry regiment sought a medal to honor their former leader Brigadier General William Haines Lytle (1826–1863), they solicited McGrew, who furnished them with the Maltese cross presented to Lytle on August 9, 1863. The cross was made of gold, with a large emerald surrounded by diamonds at its center. The perimeter of the cross was also set with stones. "Attached to the cross was a silver shield and pin by which it was fastened to the breast."[20] It is not clear whether McGrew made the cross. He advertised a stock of loose gemstones and employed men who would have been capable of creating the piece, but he also dealt heavily with eastern jewelers.[21]

Silver was an important part of McGrew's line. In 1869, he displayed a specimen of silver weighing at least six ounces from the celebrated Ebersole mine in Nevada.[22] He also furnished "a massive solid silver salver with an urn, huge as it was elegant and costly" for presentation by the congregation of the Central Presbyterian Church to their minister, the Rev. Dr. Oscar A. Hills and his new bride.[23] And, "silver table ware and choice sets of service of most artistic designs" were amongst the articles offered for holiday gift giving.[24]

McGrew's name appears on the prize medals awarded for the first Cincinnati Industrial Exposition in 1870, alongside the name of designer Anthony C. Paquet (1814–1882), suggesting that the die was made in McGrew's shop.[25] While he did not exhibit any of his wares that year, he made a grand showing the following year, competing against **Duhme & Co.** and Joseph Steinau & Co., manufacturers and wholesale dealers in jewelry and plated silver wares.[26] Little is known about the material displayed, although it can be inferred through McGrew's and Steinau & Co.'s participation that the silverware division was broadened to include retailed and plated wares. McGrew won first prize, a silver medal, and was recognized by judges for his efforts in teaching "how silver may be applied to domestic purposes." His display, according to one report, "was one which divided the attention of visitors with [the] Power Hall and deservedly so. It was neat, elegant and large." It featured everything from dinner forks and spoons to the "beautiful trifles with which men of taste love to adorn their dwellings."[27] His display may have won him the honor of furnishing the "elegant silver tea service" presented to Alfred Traber Goshorn, president of the Industrial Exposition's General Committee, at the closing of the fair.[28]

In 1872, as the national economy began to weaken, McGrew's business followed suit. He arranged compromises with his creditors, sold large portions of his stock at discount prices, and relocated to 58 West Fourth Street, a location deemed "equally good as the old and likely to remain so for some time to come."[29] Despite his struggles, his "friends among the manufacturers" continued to offer their assistance, and in an attempt to bolster his business, he made his most ambitious display to date at the 1872 Cincinnati Industrial Exposition when he exhibited Gorham's *Hiawatha's Boat Centerpiece* (fig. 80.1).[30] Inspired by Henry Wadsworth Longfellow's poem, *Hiawatha,* the gold and silver centerpiece, made in 1871, measured almost three feet high and four feet long.[31] Its sale price was $3,000, and a writer for the *Cincinnati Daily Gazette* remarked that it was "one of the most magnificent objects ever placed in any exposition," and that it was "rarely to be seen without the presence of a host of admirers."[32] Other works in McGrew's display included "a gondola berry dish in the shape of an iceberg in solid sterling silver, also a magnificent tea set, chased in full relief, two beautiful vases in oxidized silver . . . a collection of snow berry and berry and preserve spoons in gold and silver; a Japanese combination [or mixed metal] ladle . . . a bread knife and plate of uncommon fine workmanship . . . a magnificent cheese dish and ice bowl and tongs . . . [and] some beautiful cake baskets."[33]

Despite this, McGrew's business continued to suffer. Again in 1873, the centerpiece of his display at the Cincinnati Industrial Exposition was a large and impressive piece by Gorham, the *Neptune Epergne and Plateau,* (fig. 80.2) priced at $4,000.[34] His booth also featured another grand epergne with a central female figure holding a basket; a "fox and grape punch bowl"; a leaf-shaped cake basket with a lily of the valley stalk and flower-shaped handle; and boxed sets of flatware.[35] But his impressive displays were not enough to save him. By January 1875 he had accumulated $89,433 in liabilities and was forced to make an assignment "in consequence of the general depression in commercial circles."[36] In February, 25 of his New York creditors (including Whiting, Gorham, and the Meriden Britannia Company) filed statements with the United States District Court to force him into bankruptcy.[37] McGrew's stock and store fittings were purchased in

April by his former employee E.E. Isbell and Thomas Gaff (**E.E. Isbell & Co.**) for $10,000 and promptly sold at deeply discounted prices.[38] E.E. Isbell & Co. then restocked and began operation at McGrew's former store.

McGrew, released of his debts through bankruptcy and bolstered with the $10,000 from Isbell and Gaff, relocated to 152 West Fourth Street, near Elm Street (fig. 80.3) and resumed business with a light stock.[39] In August 1877 he filed again for bankruptcy. His stock was sold at auction in November, and he went to work in the retail department of **Clemens Oskamp**.[40] McGrew died on January 1, 1893, of heart failure. Services were held at Christ Church (Episcopal) in Glendale.[41]

McGrew's first marriage to Eliza Dodsworth (1835-1870) took place on October 6, 1856.[42] Records for eight of their children have been found: William Wilson, Jr. (1861-1888), Charles E. (about 1864-1892), Sallie, Mary, Carrie, Alice, Agnes, and Eliza.[43] In 1873, McGrew married Clara D. Carroll (d. 1924), an affluent widow from Chicago who spent much of her private fortune in the attempt to right her new husband's floundering business.[44] They

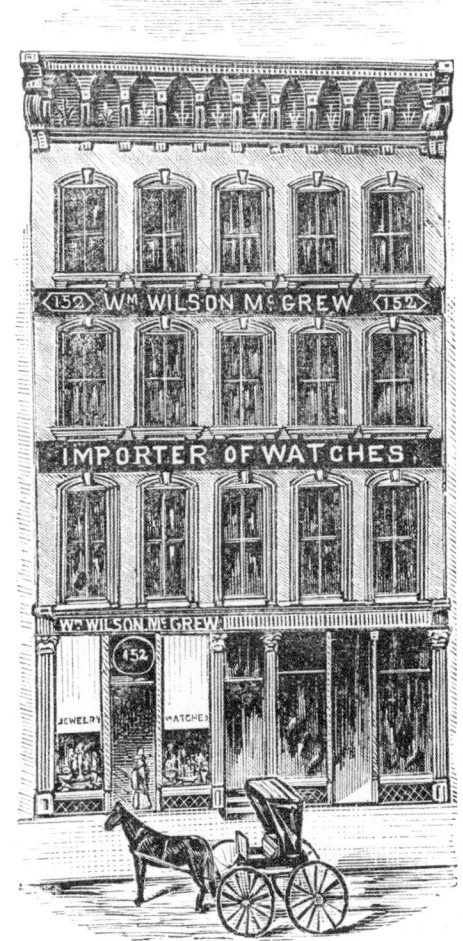

FIG. 80.3: William W. McGrew's store on West Fourth between Race and Elm from Daniel J. Kenny, *Illustrated Cincinnati: A Pictorial Handbook,* Cincinnati: G.E. Stevens, 1875, 163

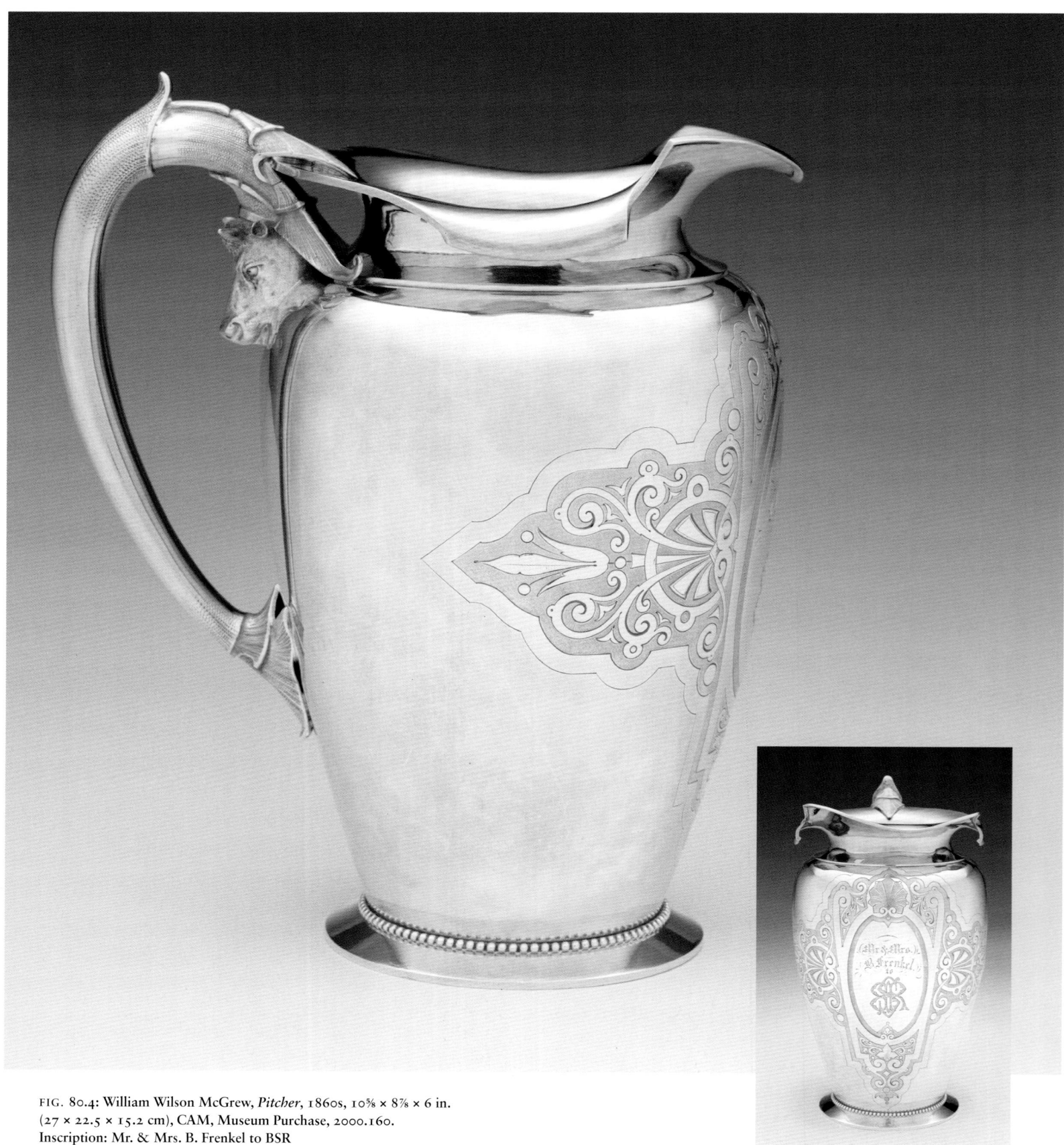

FIG. 80.4: William Wilson McGrew, *Pitcher*, 1860s, 10⅝ × 8⅞ × 6 in.
(27 × 22.5 × 15.2 cm), CAM, Museum Purchase, 2000.160.
Inscription: Mr. & Mrs. B. Frenkel to BSR

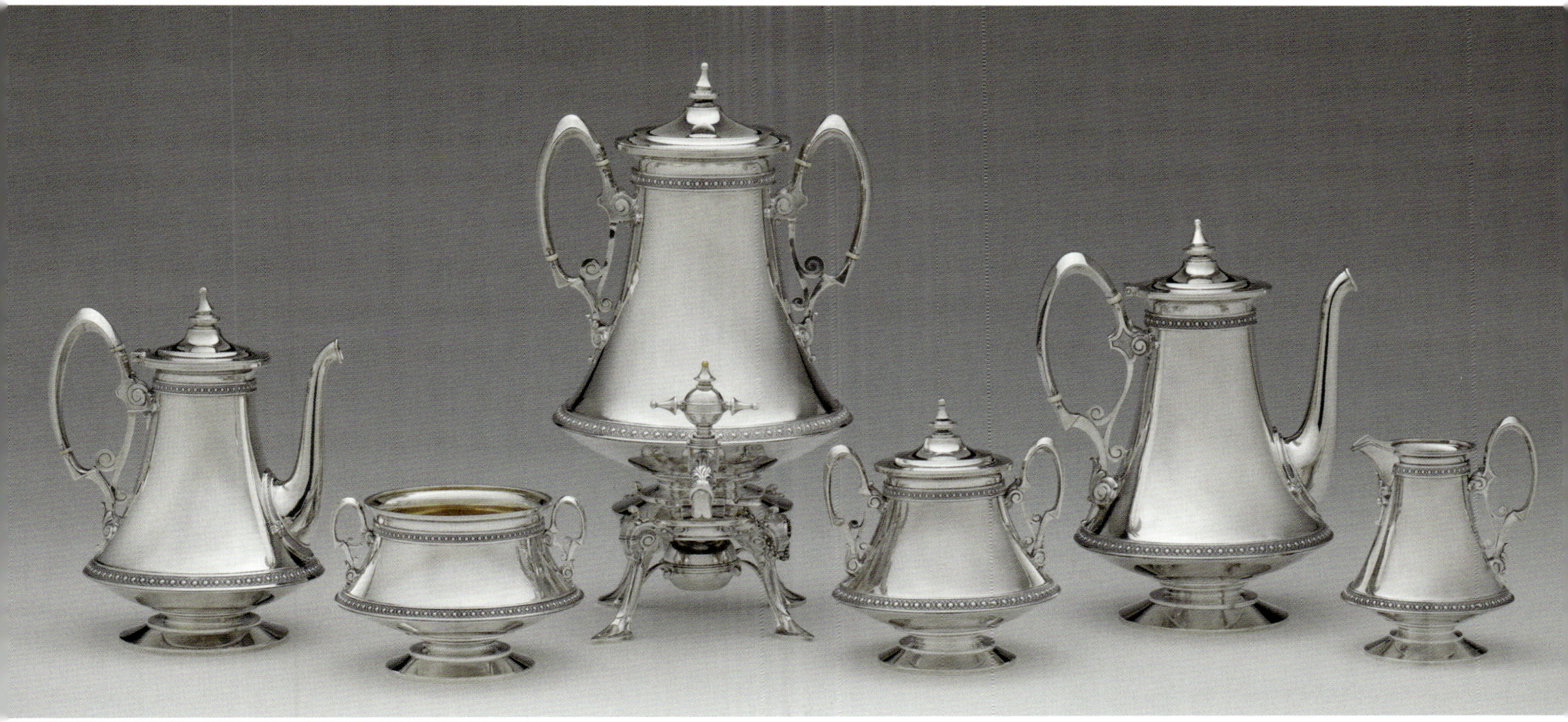

FIG. 80.5: William Wilson McGrew, *Tea and Coffee Service*, c. 1856, coffee pot: 10½ × 8⅜ × 6⅜ in. (26.7 × 21.3 × 16.2 cm), teapot: 9 × 7½ × 6 in. (22.9 × 19.1 × 15.2 cm), hot water urn: 14 × 7½ × 11¼ in. (35.6 × 19 × 28.6 cm), creamer: 5¹³⁄₁₆ × 4⅞ × 4⅛ in. (14.8 × 12.4 × 10.5 cm), sugar bowl: 6½ × 5¾ × 5½ in. (16.5 × 14.6 × 14 cm), waste bowl: 4¹³⁄₁₆ × 6 × 5¹³⁄₁₆ in. (12.2 × 15.2 × 14.8 cm), CAM, Museum Purchase, 2000.161a–f

had six children: Clarence W., Stanley E., Nora, Clara J. (1881–1893), Norman, and Helen (about 1885-1966).[45]

Silver struck with mark 80.1 includes flatware in the "Mask" (1859) and "Grecian" (1862) patterns of Henry Hebbard; in "Josephine" (1855) by Gorham; and in "Fan" (1864) by Wood & Hughes. A goblet with the mark of Peter L. Krider (Philadelphia) and a handsome pitcher also feature this mark.[46] The pitcher (fig. 80.4) was a gift to the possessor(s) of the monogram "BSR" from Mr. and Mrs. Benedict Frenkel. Mr. Frenkel, a member of Cincinnati's Jewish community, was active in the clothing business. The head of a bull, applied under the pitcher's handle is of special note. The bull, sometimes associated with the sacrifices made to gain repentance and reconciliation with God, is a fitting motif for this pitcher, as water and wine have also been considered spiritual purifiers. Mark 80.2 has been observed on wares manufactured by Gorham, including a mug, a collapsible cup, salts, and flatware in the following patterns: "Beaded" (1855); "Cottage" (1861); "Medallion" (1864); "Ionic" (1865); and "Rosette" (1868).[47] A tea and coffee service (fig. 80.5), cup (fig. 80.6), and flatware in John R. Wendt & Co.'s "Medallion" (1862) and "Apollo" (1865)

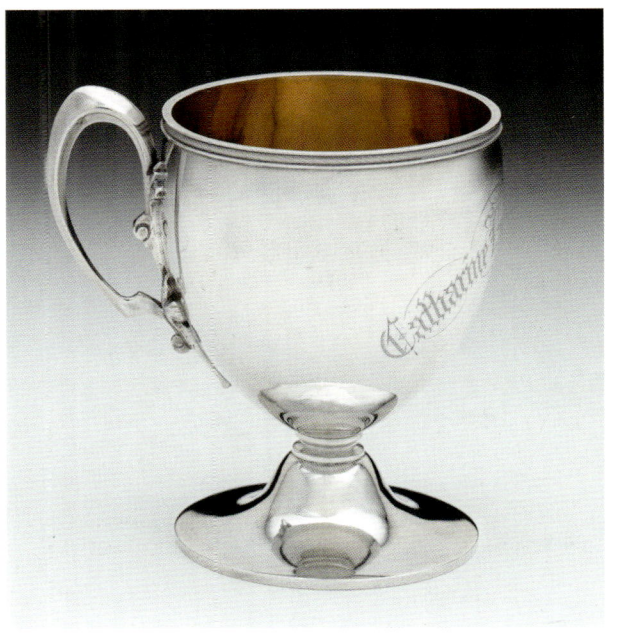

FIG. 80.6: William Wilson McGrew, *Cup*, c. 1869, 4 × 3⅝ × 2¾ in. (10.2 × 9.2 × 7 cm), CAM, Gift of Jane Hageman, 2000.159. Inscription: Catherine Longworth Anderson Aug 2nd 1869

patterns have been documented with mark 80.3.[48] Spoons with tipped, exaggerated fiddle handles and pointed shoulders, including a salt spoon with scalloped bowl, have been seen with mark 80.4.[49] Mark 80.5 appears on a mug with a presentation inscription dated 1871.[50]

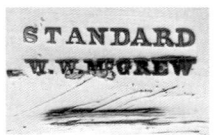

MARK 80.1

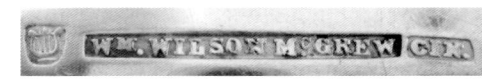

MARK 80.4

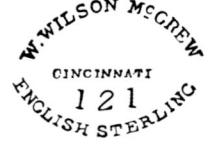

MARK 80.2

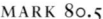

MARK 80.5

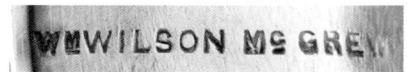

MARK 80.3

1. William W. McGrew, burial record, Spring Grove Cemetery, Cincinnati, Ohio. This burial record lists William W. McGrew's father as William, in error. We know from various accounts and documents that his father was Wilson McGrew; "Wm. Wilson McGrew: A Brief Sketch of a Career Identified with Cincinnati," undated news clipping, *Laura Slade Scrapbook*, Cincinnati Historical Society, vol. 2, 1889(?)–1904.
2. "Wm. Wilson McGrew: A Brief Sketch of a Career Identified with Cincinnati," undated news clipping, *Laura Slade Scrapbook*.
3. 1853–1858 Cincinnati City Directories; Ohio, Vol. 1, p. 71, R.G. Dun & Co. Collection, Baker Library, Harvard Business School.
4. Ohio, Vol. 4, p. 38, R.G. Dun & Co. Collection.
5. Ohio, Vol. 2, p. 32, R.G. Dun & Co. Collection; Ohio, Vol. 1, p. 71, R.G. Dun & Co. Collection; Ohio, Vol. 4, p. 38, R.G. Dun & Co. Collection.
6. "Silver and Gems," *Cincinnati Enquirer*, July 1, 1860, 2; Ohio, Vol. 4, p. 38, R.G. Dun & Co. Collection.
7. Ohio, Vol. 4, p. 38, R.G. Dun & Co. Collection.
8. Ibid.; 1864–1867 Cincinnati City Directories.
9. Ohio, Vol. 4, p. 38, R.G. Dun & Co. Collection.
10. Ibid.
11. "McGrew's New Jewelry Establishment," *Cincinnati Enquirer*, September 18, 1867, 2.
12. "Wm. Wilson McGrew," *Cincinnati Enquirer*, October 6, 1871, 8;

"Christmas," *Cincinnati Daily Gazette*, December 20, 1871, 1.
13. Ibid.
14. "Jewelry. McGrew." *Cincinnati Daily Gazette*, December 21, 1868, 1. Also see Advertisement, *Cincinnati Enquirer*, November 1, 1867, 2; Advertisement, *Cincinnati Daily Gazette*, December 16, 1867, 2.
15. Advertisement, *Cincinnati Daily Gazette*, December 17, 1868, 2; Advertisement, *Cincinnati Enquirer*, December 19, 1868, 5; Advertisement, *Cincinnati Enquirer*, June 16, 1870, 5; "Christmas," December 20, 1871; "United States Courts: Wm. Wilson McGrew's Liabilities," *Cincinnati Enquirer*, February 11, 1875, 8.
16. "Christmas," December 20, 1871; "The Standard of Silver," *Cincinnati Times-Star*, December 21, 1871, 2.
17. Advertisement, 1871 Cincinnati City Directory, 847; Advertisement, *Cincinnati Daily Gazette*, October 30, 1872, 4.
18. Employees of William Wilson McGrew included **Jackson Slane**, from about 1864 to 1869, and **William Day**, from about 1864 to 1869, both eventually of **Slane & Day**. Other employees included **Joseph P. Beggs** in 1868, **E.E. Isbell**, from 1868 to 1875, and around 1872, Horace A. Comstock from Dayton, an apprentice who eventually became a manufacturing jeweler in Indiana; 1864–1875 Cincinnati City Directories; Jacob Piatt Dunn, *Indiana and Indianans, A History of the Aboriginal and Territorial Indiana and the Century of Statehood*,

Chicago and New York: The American Historical Society, 1919, 4:1,566.
19. 1870 Federal Non-Population Census Schedules, Products of Industry, Schedule 4, Hamilton County, Ohio.
20. "What A Fighting Democrat Thinks," *Albany Evening Journal*, October 8, 1863, 2.
21. There are unsubstantiated references to Tiffany & Co. as the manufacturer of this medal, which is now in the collection of The Cincinnati Museum Center.
22. "City Matters," *Cincinnati Enquirer*, July 14, 1869.
23. "Silver Service Presentation," *Cincinnati Enquirer*, November 5, 1869, 8.
24. "W. Wilson McGrew," *Cincinnati Enquirer*, December 21, 1869, 8; See also "Christmas," *Cincinnati Daily Gazette*, December 21, 1872, 2. This advertisement notes various types of flatware in boxed gift sets.
25. Gerald W.R. Ward and Barbara McLean Ward (eds.), *Silver in American Life: Selections from the Mabel Brady Garvan and Other Collections at Yale University*, New York: American Federation of the Arts, 1979, 60–61, cat. 18; In 1871, the exposition commissioners purchased new 64mm and 44mm medals made from new dies created by Krider & Biddle of Philadelphia. Paquet's design remained, but details were improved and the year was no longer part of the die, but rather engraved. Richard B. Dusterberg, "Cincinnati, Mother of Expositions," *The*

American Numismatic Society Journal 20:4 [United States]: Token & Medal Society, 1980, 12.
26. *Report of the General Committee of the Cincinnati Industrial Exposition, held in Cincinnati, under the auspices of the Ohio Mechanics' Institute, Board of Trade, and Chamber of Commerce*, Cincinnati: General Committee of the Cincinnati Industrial Exposition, 1871, 143; "Art in the Exposition, The Silversmith and the Goldsmith, Nature Immortalized in Metal, Messrs. Duhme & Co's Display," *Cincinnati Enquirer*, October 7, 1871, 8.
27. Ibid.; "Wm. Wilson McGrew," October 6, 1871, 8; Advertisement, *Cincinnati Enquirer*, October 5, 1871, 5.
28. "The Exposition, Closing Scenes Last Night," *Cincinnati Enquirer*, October 8, 1871, 8; Goshorn was later appointed the first director of the Cincinnati Art Museum.
29. Ohio, Vol. 4, p. 41, R.G. Dun & Co. Collection; Advertisement, *Cincinnati Enquirer*, August 22, 1872, 8.
30. Ohio, Vol. 4, p. 38, R.G. Dun & Co. Collection; "Exposition Items. Description of the Great Industrial Exposition of 1872," *Cincinnati Daily Gazette*, September 9, 1872, 2.
31. The centerpiece was also shown at the Philadelphia Centennial Exposition in 1876 where it was acquired by Mrs. Ulysses S. Grant for the White House; Charles H. Carpenter, *Gorham Silver, 1831–1981*, New York: Dodd, Mead & Co., 1982, 74–76.
32. "Exposition Items. Description of

the Great Industrial Exposition of 1872," September 9, 1872.

33. Ibid.

34. The description of the epergne exhibited matches the *Neptune Epergne and Plateau* (fig. 80.2). It was also shown at the 1876 Philadelphia Centennial Exposition and was part of the 740-piece dining service commissioned by Colonel Henry Jewett Furber of Chicago; "The Useful and the Beautiful at the Cincinnati Exposition. Silver and Jewelry," *Cincinnati Daily Gazette*, September 26, 1873, n.p.; *Report of the General Committee of the Cincinnati Industrial Exposition, held in Cincinnati under the auspices of the Board of Trade, Ohio Mechanics' Institute and Chamber of Commerce from September 3rd to October 4th, 1873*, Cincinnati: General Committee of the Cincinnati Industrial Exposition, 1873, 186.

35. "The Useful and the Beautiful at the Cincinnati Exposition. Silver and Jewelry" September 26, 1873.

36. 1875 Cincinnati City Directory; D.J. Kenny, *Illustrated Cincinnati: A Pictorial Handbook*, Cincinnati: G.E. Stevens, 1875, 163; Ohio, Vol. 4, p. 43, R.G. Dun & Co. Collection; "Assignment of William Wilson McGrew," *Cincinnati Enquirer*, January 3, 1875, 1.

37. Ohio, Vol. 4, p. 43, R.G. Dun & Co. Collection; "United States Courts: Wm. Wilson McGrew's Liabilities," February 11, 1875.

38. Ohio, Vol. 4, p. 43, R.G. Dun & Co. Collection; Ohio, Vol. 10, p. 355, R.G. Dun & Co. Collection; "Watches, Jewelry, &c., Special Inducements," *Cincinnati Enquirer*, April 22, 1875, 8.

39. 1875 Cincinnati City Directory; Kenny, *Illustrated Cincinnati*, 163; Ohio, Vol. 4, p. 42, R.G. Dun & Co. Collection.

40. "Correspondence, Cincinnati Letter," *Jeweler, Silversmith and Watchmaker* (September 1877): 9; Ohio, Vol. 4, p. 42, R.G. Dun & Co. Collection; "On the Road [From Our Special Correspondent], Cincinnati, O.," *Jewelers' Circular and Horological Review* 6 (July 1888): n.p.; 1878, 1879 Cincinnati City Directories.

41. Wm. Wilson McGrew, burial record; "Very Sudden Was the Death of William Wilson McGrew, at Glendale," *Cincinnati Enquirer*, January 2, 1893, 4.

42. Eliza McGrew, burial record, Spring Grove Cemetery; "Wm. Wilson McGrew: A Brief Sketch of a Career Identified with Cincinnati," undated news clipping, *Laura Slade Scrapbook*; Wm. Wilson McGrew obituary, *Laura Slade Scrapbook*.

43. Wm. Wilson McGrew, Jr., Charles E. McGrew, burial records, Spring Grove Cemetery; William Wilson McGrew, probate record dated January 10, 1893, application book 52, p. 72, Hamilton County Registry of Probate, Cincinnati, Ohio; Sallie McGrew, marriage notice, *Cincinnati Daily Gazette*, February 8, 1874, 5.

44. "The McGrew-Carroll Wedding Which Surprised Glendale Twenty Years Ago . . .," *Cincinnati Enquirer*, March 27, 1893, 4; William Wilson McGrew, probate record; Wm. Wilson McGrew obituary, *Laura Slade Scrapbook*; Clara D. McGrew, death notice, *The New York Times*, February 6, 1924, 19.

45. William Wilson McGrew probate record; Clara J. McGrew, burial record, Spring Grove Cemetery; Helen McGrew was a recognized operatic soprano who performed under the stage name of Helen Stanley. In William Wilson McGrew's probate record, she is identified mistakenly as his son. "Ex-Opera Star, Helen Stanley, Dead at 82," *The Morning Record*, Meriden, CT, November 26, 1966, 2; "Cincinnati Girl Had Triumphed in German Opera," *The Gazette Times*, Pittsburgh, PA, September 17, 1911, 11.

46. William Wilson McGrew, eBay listings and private collections, Cincinnati silver binders, Cincinnati Art Museum.

47. Ibid.; *Pair of Salts*, Cincinnati Art Museum, Museum Purchase with funds provided by Mr. and Mrs. Charles Fleischmann III, 2005.52.

48. William Wilson McGrew, eBay listings and private collections, Cincinnati Art Museum; *Mug*, Cincinnati Art Museum, Gift of Jane Hageman, 2000.159.

49. William Wilson McGrew, eBay listings and private collections, Cincinnati Art Museum; Several of these are also struck with a harp in a conforming cartouche.

50. William Wilson McGrew, eBay listings and private collections, Cincinnati Art Museum.

81. WILSON McGREW

1800–1859, w. 1825–1856

Wilson McGrew was born on January 22, 1800, in Pennsylvania.[1] He is listed in Cincinnati as a silversmith working at the shop of **Alexander McGrew**, who was most likely his uncle, in 1825.[2] In 1829, Wilson was listed as a watch maker, in 1831, as a silversmith, and in 1834, as a clerk, still under the employ of Alexander.[3] In 1834, noted as "one of our most respectable jewelers, a gentleman who is well known in this city and highly respected," Wilson fell victim to a political joke gone awry when he was persuaded to alter and gild 25-cent pieces to look like half eagles ($5 gold coins produced between 1795 and 1929) "in order to have a laugh" at the Democratic supporters of President Andrew Jackson. McGrew was prosecuted for counterfeiting, but was ultimately pardoned by the Mayor.[4]

On January 25, 1836, Alexander McGrew published notice that he "had disposed of his entire stock in trade in *the Watch and Jewelry business* to *Wilson McGrew*."[5] Wilson continued at Alexander's former stand at 159 Main Street, between Third and Fourth Streets.[6] In September 1840 Wilson advertised his "return from the Eastern cities" with a new, large and varied stock.[7] The advertisement also ran in Maysville and Lexington, Kentucky, and among the goods promoted were "silver Spectacles, Pencils and Thimbles. Also silver Tea setts [*sic*], plated ware consisting of Candlesticks and branches, Waiters, Baskets, &c; new and beautiful patterns [of] Brittania [*sic*] ware; [and] table Cutlery." Not long after, on November 13th, a robbery took place, and Wilson lost goods valued between $18,000 and $20,000.[8] Among the articles taken was McGrew's pocket and account book, but the crooks, "finding nothing in them that they could make available had the impudence to carry them to the owner's residence, between three and four squares from the store, and thrust them under his gate."[9]

In May 1841 McGrew gave notice that he was leaving his books and accounts with **Joseph P. Beggs**, who had also come to Cincinnati from southwestern Pennsylvania, and who had been employed by McGrew since 1839.[10] McGrew did not appear in the 1842 or 1843 Cincinnati city directories, and Beggs took over McGrew's stand, operating as **J. P. Beggs & Co.**[11] It is possible that it was during this time that McGrew was involved in a partnership in Louisville, in a hardware firm known as McGrew & Stewart.[12] Credit reporters noted that while McGrew was confined for paralysis, Stewart "gambled and stole some $70,000 [worth of] property."[13] McGrew closed the business and paid up his debt. Back in Cincinnati, Beggs' partner(s) in J.P. Beggs & Co. were never

published, and it is assumed that McGrew, keeping a hand in his old business, represented the "& Co."[14]

By April 1843 McGrew had returned to Cincinnati, and the partnership of **McGrew & Beggs** was established.[15] Credit reporters note that McGrew furnished most of the capital in the firm of McGrew & Beggs, as he had inherited $20,000.[16] This money may have been received from Alexander McGrew just before his death. Although Wilson is not enumerated in Alexander's will, he and J.P. Beggs signed the will as witnesses.[17] The will was written on April 20, 1843, just one day before the establishment of McGrew & Beggs. By March 1848 the partnership had dissolved, and McGrew was reportedly worth at least $15,000 after paying his debts, and "continued doing business and making money."[18] In September of that year, he donated a $300 sidereal clock to Cincinnati's observatory.[19]

In August 1850 McGrew announced that he had just returned from another buying trip in the East, and had "every variety of Watches, Jewelry and Fancy Goods" to offer, including "Silver, Plated, and Brittania [*sic*] Ware, Table and Pocket Cutlery."[20] In February 1851 McGrew's store was robbed again, this time at a loss of "about $12,000 worth of goods."[21] But McGrew carried on, and Salmon P. Chase, who was then a United States Senator, went to McGrew's to buy his daughter a "beautiful silver goblet" engraved with her name in 1853.[22]

By March 1854, Wilson's son, **William Wilson McGrew** (1833–1893), had formally joined the business, and the firm's name was changed to **W. McGrew & Son**.[23] By January 1856, Wilson's health was in serious decline, and credit reporters noted that William Wilson was running the business.[24] Wilson was mentally incompetent by July 1857, and by October the business was in serious debt.[25] After settling with creditors, William Wilson continued business at the old stand under his own name, William Wilson McGrew.[26]

Wilson McGrew and his workmen may have produced a small amount of the silver that bears his mark, but it is believed that he was largely retailing the work of other smiths. Mark 81.1 has been found on fiddle-handled spoons with either rounded or pointed shoulders; various types of flatware with tipped, exaggerated fiddle handles and pointed shoulders (fig. 81.1); tongs with shell terminals; a salver; and a mug with an eight-paneled body with repoussé work.[27] Mark 81.2 appears on a beaker in the Winterthur Museum collection.[28] Flatware with this mark includes examples in an oval-

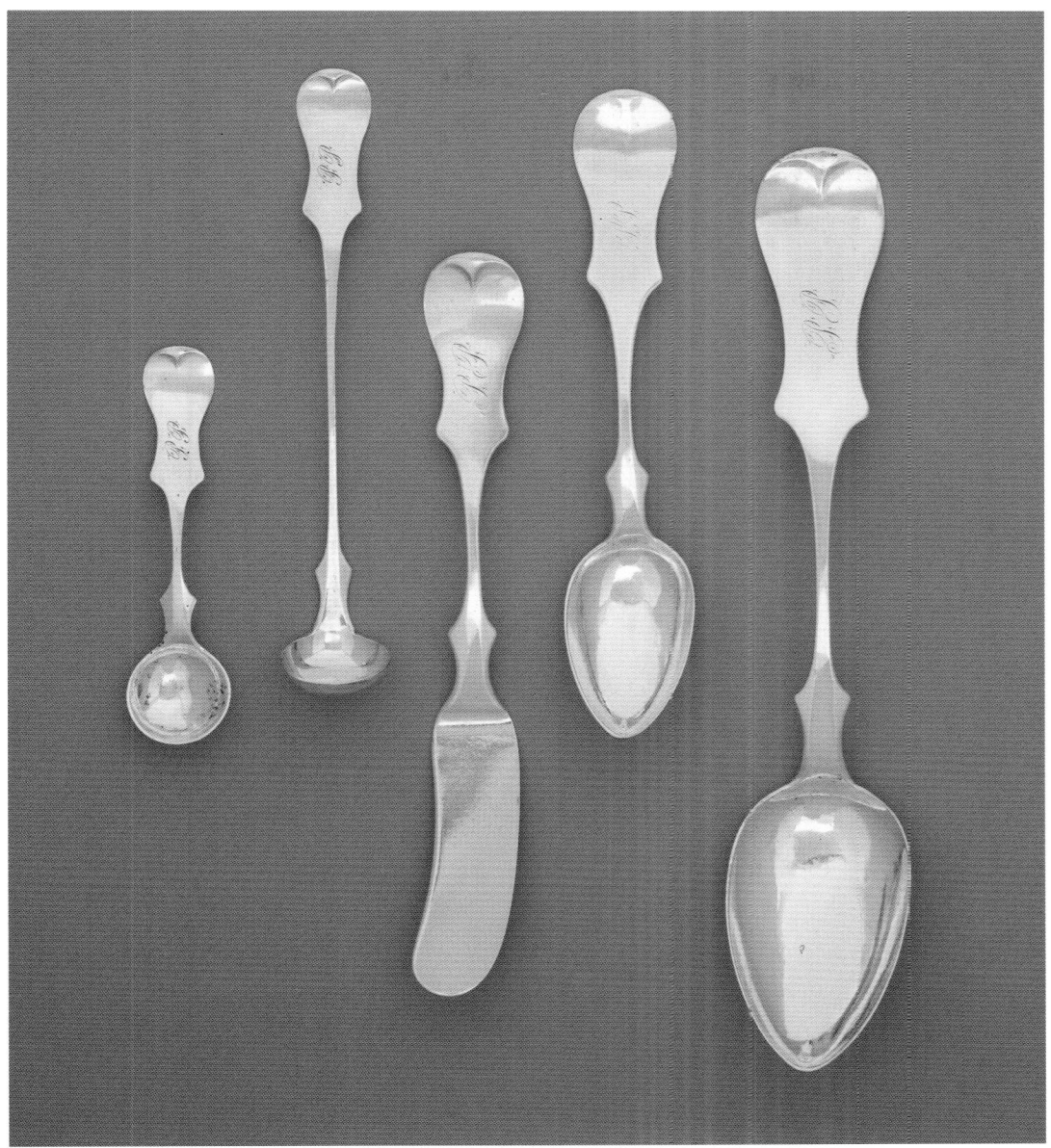

FIG. 81.1: (L to R) Wilson McGrew, *Salt Spoon*, c. 1840–1856, L. 3½ in. (8.9 cm), Museum Purchase, 1962.84; Wilson McGrew, *Condiment Ladle*, c. 1840–1856, L. 5⅝ in. (14.3 cm), Museum Purchase, 1962.86; Wilson McGrew, *Butter Knife*, c. 1840–1856, L. 6⅝ in. (16.8 cm), Museum Purchase. 1962.87; Wilson McGrew, *Teaspoon*, c. 1840–1856, L. 5⅞ in. (14.9 cm), Museum Purchase, 1962.104; Wilson McGrew, *Tablespoon*, c. 1840–1856, L. 8¼ in. (21 cm), Museum Purchase, 1962.83

threaded pattern (fig. 81.2); forks in the "Morning Glory" (1852) pattern by Henry Hebbard & Co. (New York City, circa 1847–1869); and flatware in "Oriental" (1855) and "Honeysuckle" (1837) (fig. 81.3) by the New York designer John Polhemus.[29] Beakers (fig. 81.4) have been found with mark 81.3.[30] An incuse, "W. McGREW CIN CIN NAT," has been documented on a plated, covered tureen marked by H. Wilkinson & Co. of Sheffield, England.[31]

Wilson McGrew died on May 31, 1859.[32] His first wife, Sarah Gallagher McGrew (1807–1836), bore him three children: William Wilson; Sallie (b. about 1834); and Marshall (1836–1875).[33] Wilson married his first wife's sister, Margaret Gallagher Powell (1811–1845), after a steamboat explosion in 1838 killed her husband.[34] He and Margaret had one child, Ross W. McGrew (1845–1846).[35] McGrew seems to have been a member of the Presbyterian church in Cincinnati, as many family members were initially interred there, and then moved to Spring Grove Cemetery around 1858.

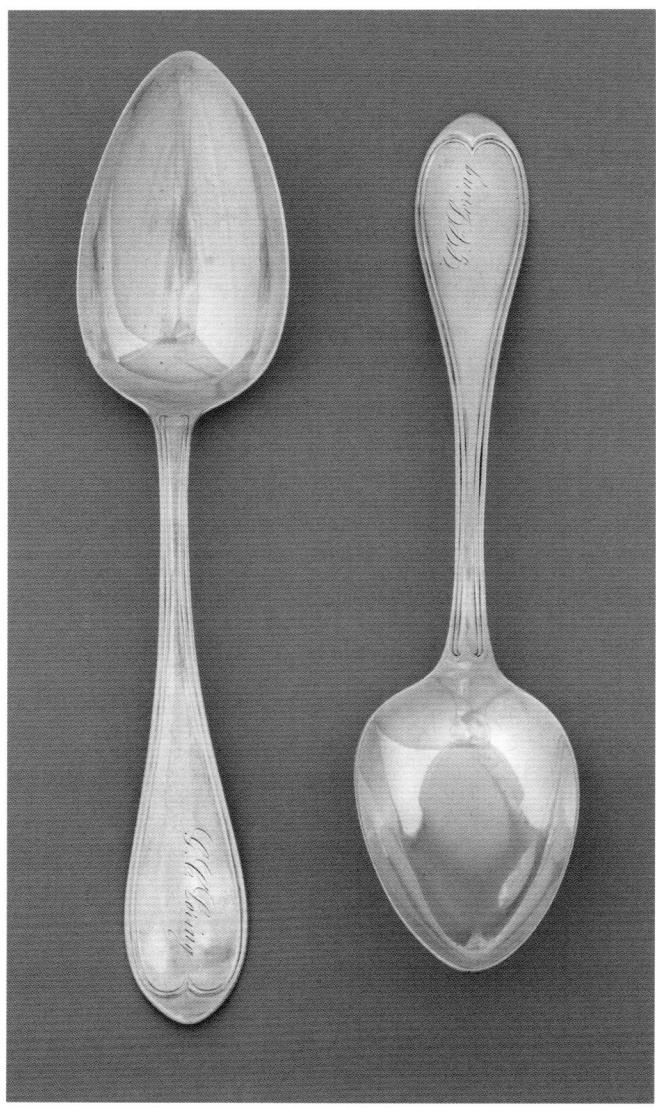

FIG. 81.2: Wilson McGrew, *Tablespoons*, 1836–1856, L. 8³⁄₁₆ in. (20.8 cm), CAM, Given by Elizabeth M. and Annie W. Anderson in memory of their mother, Mrs. Buckner W. Anderson, 1969.735–736. Inscription: G.C. Loring

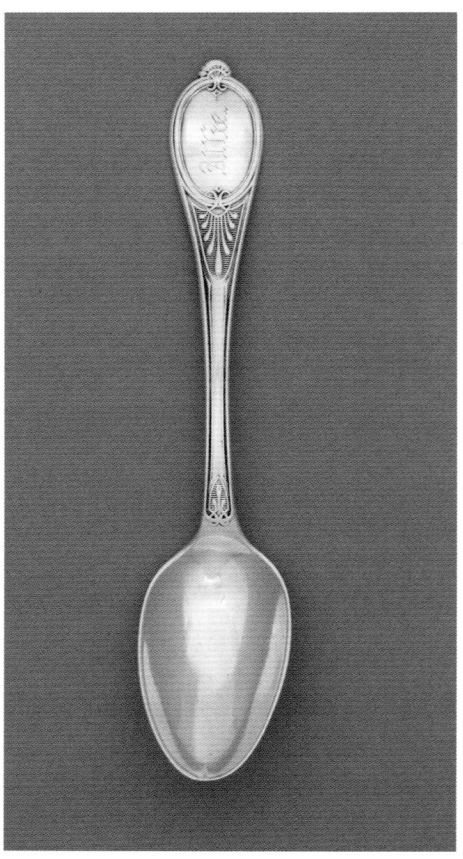

FIG. 81.3: Wilson McGrew, retailer, John Polhemus, manufacturer, (New York, c. 1811–1877), *Teaspoon*, "Honeysuckle" pattern, 1837–1856, L. 5⅞ in. (14.9 cm), CAM, Gift of Dr. Suzanne A. Beutler, 1983.199. Inscription: Allie

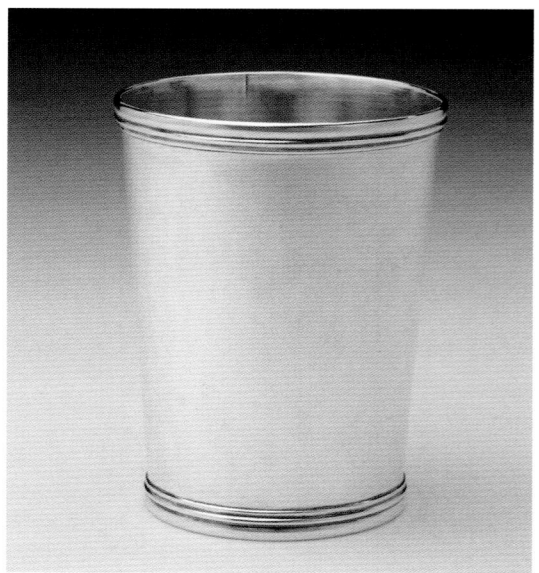

FIG. 81.4: Wilson McGrew, *Beaker*, 1836–1856, 4⅜ × 3⅛ in. (11.1 × 7.9 cm), CAM, Museum Purchase with funds provided by Mr. and Mrs. Charles Fleischmann III, 2005.51

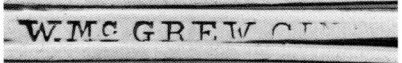

W. McGREW

MARK 81.1   MARK 81.3

MARK 81.2

1. Wilson McGrew, burial record, Spring Grove Cemetery, Cincinnati, Ohio.

2. 1825 Cincinnati City Directory; Genealogical research to date could not confirm the exact relationship between Alexander and Wilson. Wilson is not named in Alexander's will, but is a witness to it. Wilson's father's name is given as William in Wilson's burial record. See McGrew genealogy file, Cincinnati Art Museum, Decorative Arts & Design Department.

3. 1829, 1831, 1834 Cincinnati City Directories.

4. "Golden Humbug," *Niles' Weekly Register*, September 27, 1834, 47; "Conspiracy," *Republican Banner*, December 16, 1834, 1.

5. Advertisement, *Cincinnati Daily Gazette*, January 25, 1836, reproduced in Beckman, 92.

6. In 1846, 159 Main was renumbered as 137 Main. 1846 Cincinnati City Directory.

7. "Watches, Jewelry, and Silverware," *Cincinnati Daily Gazette*, September 15, 1840, reproduced in Beckman, 94. This advertisement appeared in the same newspaper on October 9, 1840, 4.

8. "Great Burglary and Robbery," *The Evening Post* (New York), November 24, 1840, n.p.

9. Ibid.

10. 1839/40 Cincinnati City Directory; "Last Notice," *Cincinnati Daily Gazette*, May 20, 1841, reproduced in Beckman, 94.

11. 1842, 1843 Cincinnati City Directories.

12. Ohio, Vol. 2, p. 32, R.G. Dun & Co. Collection, Baker Library, Harvard Business School.

13. Ibid.

14. R.G. Dun & Co. reporters infer that McGrew was simultaneously engaged in the hardware business in Louisville and the jewelry business in Cincinnati. Ohio, Vol. 2, p. 32, R.G. Dun & Co. Collection.

15. Ohio, Vol. 1, p. 71, R.G. Dun & Co. Collection.

16. Ibid.

17. Alexander McGrew, will dated April 20, 1843, proved May 15, 1843, vol. 2, p. 381, Hamilton County Registry of Probate, Cincinnati, Ohio.

18. Ohio, Vol. 1, p. 71, R.G. Dun & Co. Collection.

19. "Observatory Clock," *Sandusky Clarion*, September 11, 1848.

20. Advertisement, *Cincinnati Enquirer*, August 30, 1850, 4.

21. Ohio, Vol. 1, p. 71, R.G. Dun & Co. Collection.

22. Chase had previously patronized Alexander McGrew. His daughter Kate was a friend and schoolmate of Wilson's daughter Sallie in New York. James P. McClure, Peg A. Lampheir, Erika M. Kreger (eds.), *"Spur Up Your Pegasus": Family Letters of Salmon, Kate and Nettie Chase, 1844–1873*, Kent, OH: Kent State University Press, circa 2009.

23. Ohio, Vol. 1, p. 71, R.G. Dun & Co. Collection.

24. Ohio, Vol. 2, p. 32, R.G. Dun & Co. Collection.

25. Advertisement, *Cincinnati Enquirer*, September 2, 1857, 3; Ohio, Vol. 2, p. 32, R.G. Dun & Co. Collection.

26. Ohio, Vol. 4, p. 38, R.G. Dun & Co. Collection.

27. W. McGrew, eBay listings and private collections, Cincinnati silver binders, Cincinnati Art Museum; *Salt Spoon*, Cincinnati Art Museum, Gift of John S. Conner, 1910.178; *Soup Spoons, Salt Spoons, Condiment Ladle, Butter Knives*, and *Teaspoons*, Cincinnati Art Museum, Museum Purchase, 1962.79–108; *Tongs*, Elizabeth Beckman Collection, Cincinnati Museum Center.

28. *Beaker*, Winterthur Museum, Bequest of Henry Francis du Pont, 1970.1079.

29. W. McGrew, eBay listings and private collections, Cincinnati Art Museum; *Teaspoon*, Cincinnati Art Museum, Gift of Dr. Suzanne A. Beutler, 1983.199; A sugar shell in the oval-threaded pattern has three journeyman marks that have not yet been identified.

30. W. McGrew, eBay listings and private collections, Cincinnati Art Museum; *Beaker*, Cincinnati Art Museum, Museum Purchase, funds provided by Mr. and Mrs. Charles Fleischmann III, 2005.51.

31. W. McGrew, eBay listings and private collections, Cincinnati Art Museum.

32. Wilson McGrew, burial record; Death notice, Wilson McGrew, *Cincinnati Daily Gazette*, June 1, 1859.

33. Sarah G. McGrew, burial record, Spring Grove Cemetery; Marshall McGrew, burial record, Spring Grove Cemetery; McClure, Lampheir, Kreger, *"Spur Up Your Pegasus,"* n.p.; Sally married a Dr. E. Williams, and at the time of Wilson's death, lived in Naples, Italy. Wm. Wilson McGrew obituary, *Laura Slade Scrapbook*, Cincinnati Historical Society, vol. 2, 1889 (?)–1904.

34. Margaret R. McGrew, burial record, Spring Grove Cemetery; "From the Cincinnati Whig, Extra, Cincinnati, April 25, 8 o'clock, P.M. Most Awful Steamboat Accident. Loss of 125 Lives," *Hudson River Chronicle*, May 8, 1838, 1.

35. Ross W. McGrew, burial record, Spring Grove Cemetery.

82. DENNIS McHENRY, JR.

b. about 1799, w. 1832–1851

Dennis McHenry, Jr. was born around 1799, the son of Dennis McHenry, Sr. (about 1751–1831).[1] On April 9, 1814, he was apprenticed to James Webb, a goldsmith and jeweler in Baltimore, Maryland, and worked in that city, at least until 1830, when he was appointed assayer.[2] McHenry appeared in Cincinnati's 1831 City Directory, boarding at John Hanley's, with no occupation details provided. In 1832, he partnered with **Thomas A. Conway**, also formerly of Baltimore, to form **Conway & McHenry**, a jewelry, watch making, and silver firm that lasted less than two years.[3] McHenry continued at the firm's stand on Main Street between Third and Fourth Streets until at least 1836, when he was listed as a silversmith on Fourth Street, between Main and Walnut.[4] In 1839 he was listed as a silversmith working at **Palmer & Hanks**, jewelers and silversmiths on Main Street.[5] The census data for 1840 indicates that he was married with one male child under the age of five.[6] By November 1842 McHenry had gone bankrupt, as a notice in the newspaper called for him, and a list of others, to deliver his assets to an appointed assignee.[7] He continued to appear in city directories, through 1850, as a silversmith and jeweler working on Vine Street between Seventh and Eighth Streets.[8] McHenry is last recorded in Cincinnati in the 1851/52 City Directory as a jeweler working on the south side of Fourth Street between Elm and Plum Streets.[9]

A spoon with an exaggerated fiddle handle, stamped "D. McHENRY" in a rectangular cartouche has been documented.[10]

1. Jennifer Faulds Goldsborough, *Silver in Maryland*, Baltimore: Maryland Historical Society, 1983, 269; No birth records could be found for McHenry. According to the 1850 Federal Census, Cincinnati, Hamilton, Ohio, he was born in 1815. This is an obvious transcription error when considered with the documentation of his Baltimore apprenticeship and work history; Dennis McHenry, Sr., death notice, *Baltimore Patriot*, December 18, 1831, 3.
2. Goldsborough, *Silver in Maryland*, 269; In 1829, McHenry was elected to the Baltimore City Council. "Tenth Ward Election," *Baltimore Patriot*, March 19, 1829, 68; In September 1829 he was appointed assayer of Baltimore. Notice, *Baltimore Gazette and Daily Advertiser*, September 21, 1829, 3.
3. Advertisement, *Cincinnati Daily Gazette*, May 1, 1832, reproduced in Beckman, 96; Dissolution of Partnership, *Cincinnati Whig*, February 10, 1834, reproduced in Beckman, 97.
4. Advertisement, *Cincinnati Whig*, February 10, 1834, reproduced in Beckman, 97; 1836/37 Cincinnati City Directory.
5. 1839/40 Cincinnati City Directories.
6. 1840 Federal Census, Cincinnati, Hamilton, Ohio.
7. Advertisement, *Cincinnati Enquirer*, January 20, 1843. This notice was originally submitted on November 22, 1842.
8. 1842, 1843, 1844, 1846, 1849/50 Cincinnati City Directories.
9. 1851/52 Cincinnati City Directory.
10. Dennis McHenry, eBay listings and private collections, Cincinnati silver binders, Cincinnati Art Museum.

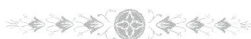

83. THEODORE W. McMURPHEY[1]

1814–1848, w. 1839–1844

Theodore W. McMurphey was the son of Mary A. and Robert McMurphey.[2] He was born in Middletown, Delaware, on November 10, 1814.[3] Theodore appears in Cincinnati city directories for the first time in the 1839/40 edition, alongside his brother Samuel (1818–1847), whose occupation is not given, and his brother **Albert**, a silversmith boarding at **Abraham Palmer**'s. Theodore is listed as a silversmith and watch maker on the west side of Main between Fourth and Fifth Streets, a location in the vicinity of **Palmer & Hanks**' shop at 127 Main as well as the shop of **Nathan L. Hazen** at 143 Main.[4] There are no known details regarding the McMurphey brothers' training. In 1842, Theodore was listed as a clerk boarding at his mother's, with his brother Samuel.[5] He is listed in this way until the publication of the 1846 Cincinnati Business Directory, when he is enumerated as a bank broker.[6] Theodore died of consumption on October 5, 1848.[7] He and his family are buried at Spring Grove Cemetery. Theodore and his wife Mary Bennett (1821–1912) had two children: Susan (1846–1922) and Theodore W. (1848–1913).[8]

A teaspoon with fiddle handle and pointed shoulders (fig. 83.1) has been found to bear the mark (mark 83.1) believed to have been used by Theodore W. McMurphey.

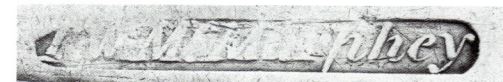

MARK. 83.1

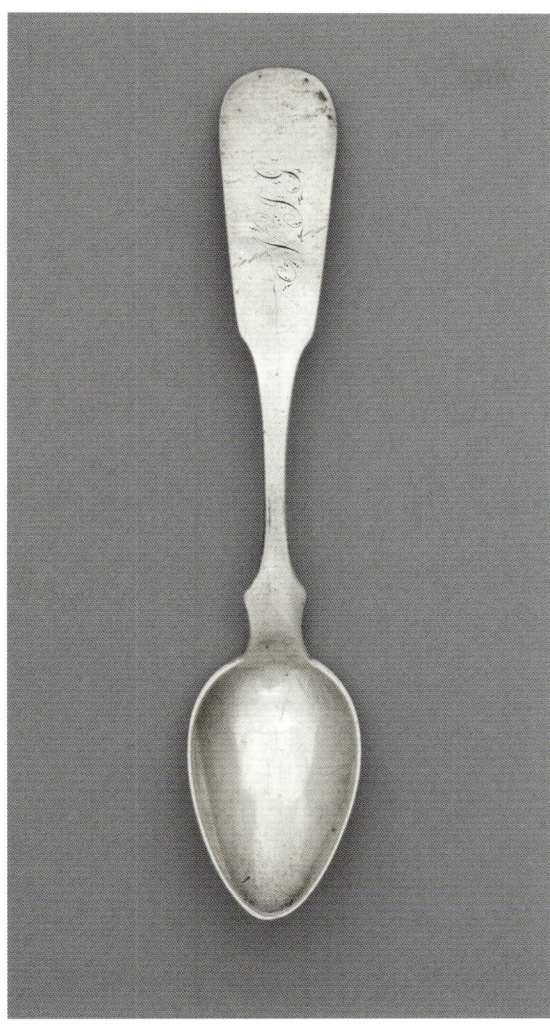

FIG. 83.1: Theodore McMurphey, *Teaspoon*, 1839–1842, L. 5½ in. (14 cm), CAM, Museum Purchase: John S. Conner Fund, 2012.52

1. The subject's surname is spelled "McMurphy" in most historical records, including his last will and testament, the 1840 Federal Census, Cincinnati City Directory listings, and Spring Grove Burial records. The mark attributed to the subject is spelled "McMurphey," and his widow is listed with this spelling variant in the 1900 Federal Census. Based on the mark, McMurphey will be used here. The 1839/40 Cincinnati City Directory publishes the subject's middle initial as B, but all other records found were for Theodore W.
2. Theodore W. McMurphy, burial record, Spring Grove Cemetery, Cincinnati, Ohio.
3. Ibid. The subject's burial record indicates that he was born in Middletown, MD, but all other records, including the 1839/40 Cincinnati City Directory, census records, and the burial record for his brother, Samuel, indicate that the correct birthplace was Middletown, DE. Samuel McMurphy, burial record, Spring Grove Cemetery.
4. 1839/40 Cincinnati City Directory.
5. In the 1842 Cincinnati City Directory, Mrs. Mary A. McMurphy is listed at Centre, between Race and

Elm Streets. Mary A. McMurphy is listed as Theodore's mother on his burial record.
6. Samuel had also changed occupations. He was working as an accountant and boarding with Theodore. Presumably, both brothers were working at City Bank. 1846 Cincinnati City Directory.
7. Samuel also died of consumption in January 1847. Theodore W. McMurphy, Samuel McMurphy, burial records; Theodore W. McMurphy, will dated October 5, 1848, proved October 11, 1848, vol. 8, p. 133, Hamilton County Registry of Probate, Cincinnati, Ohio.
8. Mary was the daughter of Robert Bennett and Eleanor Burch. She was born in England and emigrated in 1831. The 1900 Federal Census gives her birth date as September 1822 but her burial record specifies September 24, 1821. Mary McMurphy, Theodore W. (son of subject), Susan McMurphy, burial records, Spring Grove Cemetery; 1860 Federal Census, Cincinnati, Hamilton, Ohio; 1900 Federal Census, Cincinnati, Hamilton, Ohio.

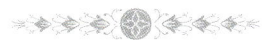

84. MICHIE BROS.

1883–1917

In late 1883, **William Michie, Jr.** (1837–1915) and his brother Henry Bliss Michie (1855–1919) formed Michie Bros.[1] The firm operated at 178 West Fourth Street, the address of their former establishment, **Michie, Jeweler**. Their brother James C. Michie (see **W. & J.C. Michie**) continued to work at the firm, but was not listed as a principal. In 1883, he was appointed postmaster of Covington,

Kentucky and by 1887, had left the jewelry business to become an insurance agent.[2]

Henry Bliss Michie was born after his family immigrated to the United States and settled in Ohio.[3] He was named for **Henry Bliss**, the employer of his father, William Michie, Sr. (see **W. & J.C. Michie**). Henry Bliss Michie first appeared in city directories in

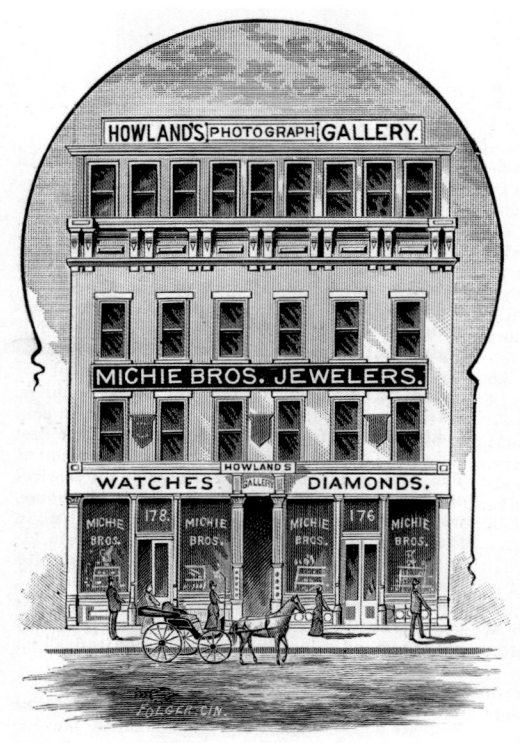

FIG. 84.1: Michie Bros., from John William Leonard, *The Centennial Review of Cincinnati: One Hundred Years of Progress . . .* , Cincinnati: J.M. Elstner, 1888, 68

"attained commanding proportions," and owed its success to "the thorough and systematic methods for which the concern is justly noted."[11] In 1895, street numbers were changed city-wide, and Michie's address became 212 West Fourth Street.[12] William Michie, Jr. appears to have retired from the business due to poor health in the latter part of 1914.[13] He died in January 1915.[14] Henry B. Michie assumed control of the firm, and at the end of 1917, "disposed of the business."[15] He died on December 15, 1919, leaving his widow, Della (1860–1924), and six children: Mary (1883–1967), Anne (1884–1951), Margaret (1886–1966), Delia Ruth (1891–1979), Alice (b. 1893), and William H. (1901–1966).[16]

Michie Bros. probably did not make any of the silver that they sold. Mark 84.1 was used by the firm between 1885 and 1888, based on its appearance on identifiable patterns introduced by Michie Bros.' suppliers during that time. However, it is possible that this mark could also have been used earlier, by Michie, Jeweler. Silver documented with this mark includes a butter knife with pointed shoulders and a tipped, exaggerated fiddle handle (a Cincinnati form that was introduced in the 1840s and produced into the last

1874, working as a clerk at William A. McCall & Co., a firm specializing in hardware and cutlery.[4] He joined his brothers in Michie, Jeweler in 1878.[5] The firm became Michie Bros., and credit reporters noted that Henry was a "responsible man" but had added no capital to the business.[6]

Michie Bros. were jewelry manufacturers and wholesale and retail dealers in watches, clocks, diamonds, and jewelry. They maintained a factory at 2 Home Street where they produced jewelry that included "Masonic, I.O.O.F., Knights of Pythias and all Society jewels, rings and decorations."[7] The factory, "provided with all the requisite facilities and appliances," gave employment to "a large force of the most experienced workmen and artisans known to the business of diamond setting, making, engraving and enameling society jewels and decorations and repairing fine gold jewelry." The watch repair department was a "special feature of the house."[8] Michie Bros.' showroom at 178 West Fourth Street (fig. 84.1) displayed a "magnificent stock of diamonds, watches, jewelry, silver and plated ware, etc."[9] An advertisement from 1885 (fig. 84.2) lists many of the various silver forms that the company offered.[10] In 1891, it was stated that while the business started small, it had

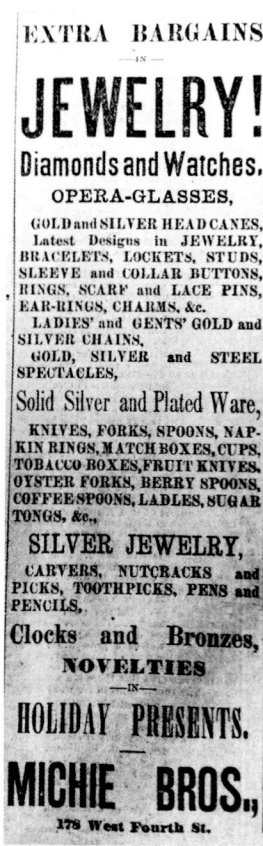

FIG. 84.2: Advertisement, *Cincinnati Commercial Tribune*, December 20, 1885, 9

quarter of the 19th century). It has been observed on flatware in Joseph Seymour & Co.'s "No. 5" (circa 1885) pattern; Towle Mfg. Co.'s "Lily" (1888) and "Pomona" (1887) patterns; Dominick and Haff's "Rococo" (1888) pattern; and a pattern similar to **Duhme & Co.**'s "No. 1" (circa 1869).[17] Flatware and hollowware struck with the incuse "MICHIE BROS." (mark 84.2, sometimes accompanied by an incuse "CINCINNATI") include a vase with ruby glass liner; souvenir spoons; dinner knives with mother of pearl handles; and flatware in the following patterns: Dominick & Haff's "Renaissance" (1894), "Trianon" (1885), and "Grape" (1895); Gorham's "Chantilly" (1895); Reed & Barton's "La Reine" (1893), "Hepplewhite" (1907), and "Les Six Fleurs" (1901); and Towle Mfg. Co.'s "Rustic" (1895) and "Old Colonial" (1895).[18]

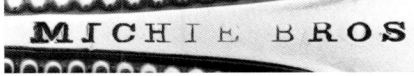

MARK 84.1

MARK 84.2

1. 1884 Cincinnati City Directory.
2. 1887 Cincinnati City Directory.
3. Henry B. Michie, burial record, Spring Grove Cemetery, Cincinnati, Ohio.
4. 1874 Cincinnati City Directory; 1880 Federal Census, Miami, Clermont, Ohio.
5. 1878 Cincinnati City Directory.
6. Ohio, Vol. 4, p. 391, R.G. Dun & Co. Collection, Baker Library, Harvard Business School.
7. John W. Leonard, *The Centennial Review of Cincinnati. one hundred years of progress in commerce, manufactures, the professions, and in social and municipal life*, Cincinnati: J.M. Elstner, 1888, 68.
8. *The City of Cincinnati and its Resources*, Cincinnati, OH: Cincinnati Times Star Co., 1891, 119.
9. Ibid.
10. Advertisement, *Cincinnati Commercial Tribune*, December 20, 1885, 9.
11. *The City of Cincinnati and its Resources*, 119.
12. 1895 Cincinnati City Directory.
13. 1915 Cincinnati City Directory; Death notice, *Cincinnati Enquirer*, January 17, 1915.
14. William Michie, burial record, Spring Grove Cemetery.
15. "Henry B. Michie Dies," *Cincinnati Enquirer*, December 16, 1919, 9.
16. 1900 Federal Census, Cincinnati, Hamilton, Ohio; Henry B. Michie, Anne M. Witt, Margaret Lahke, William H. Michie, Della H. Michie, burial records, Spring Grove Cemetery; "Henry B. Michie Dies," December 16, 1919; *Michie's Abroad*, independently published, circa 1907, Library of Congress collection.
17. Michie Bros., eBay listings and private collections, Cincinnati silver binders, Cincinnati Art Museum; Tere Hagan, *Sterling Flatware: An Identification and Value Guide*, Gas City, IN: L-W Book Sales, 2004, 221.
18. Michie Bros., eBay listings and private collections, Cincinnati Art Museum.

85. MICHIE, JEWELER

1878–1883

When James C. Michie (see **W. & J.C. Michie**) became indebted to creditors in late 1877, his brother, **William Michie, Jr.**, left the firm of **Kent & Michie** and came to his aid, purchasing the business.[1] William, James, and their brother Henry Bliss Michie (see **Michie Bros.**) then formed "Michie, Jeweler." They advertised as manufacturing, wholesale, and retail jewelers, and repairers of fine watches and continued at James C. Michie's former stand at 178 West Fourth Street.[2] William Jr. was the principal while James worked in the background and Henry worked as a clerk.[3] According to credit reports, they did a small business. They had no more than $4,000 invested in the business, and generally bought for cash so that they were not forced to ask favors from anyone.[4] In advertisements and city directory listings, the firm's name was given successively as "Michie, The Jeweler," "Michie, Jeweler," and "Michie."[5]

Solid silver and plated wares were almost always listed among the wares they sold, which included diamonds, watches, jewelry, opera glasses, gold and silver headed canes, spectacles, and other fancy novelties.[6] It is not believed that the firm manufactured any of the silver that it sold. The firm may have used the incuse stamp "MICHIE" to mark its wares (see Michie Bros., mark 84.1): it is seen on flatware patterns introduced by the 1870s, such as the tipped, exaggerated fiddle handle, and on a pattern similar to **Duhme & Co.**'s "No. 1" (circa 1869).[7] But it is important to note that both of these patterns remained popular and were made into the 1890s. Other silver wares documented with this mark are in patterns introduced after the active dates of "Michie, The Jeweler." By late 1883, the firm name had changed to Michie Bros.

1. Ohio, Vol. 4, p. 388, R.G. Dun & Co. Collection, Baker Library, Harvard Business School; Notice of dissolution, *Cincinnati Commercial Tribune*, April 11, 1878, 8.
2. 1878 Cincinnati City Directory; Advertisement, *Cincinnati Daily Gazette*, December 15, 1880, 10; Henry B. Michie, burial record, Spring Grove Cemetery, Cincinnati, Ohio.
3. 1878–1883 Cincinnati City Directories; Ohio, Vol. 4, p. 390, R.G. Dun & Co. Collection.
4. Ohio, Vol. 4, p. 390, R.G. Dun & Co. Collection.
5. In city directories, the firm listed as "Michie, The Jeweler" in 1878, as "Michie, Jeweler" in 1879 and 1880, and as "Michie" between 1881 and 1883.
6. Advertisement, *Cincinnati Daily Gazette*, December 11, 1880, 14; Advertisement, *Cincinnati Commercial Tribune*, December 12, 1880, 8; Advertisement, *Cincinnati Daily Gazette*, December 15, 1880, 10; Advertisement, *Cincinnati Commercial Tribune*, December 18, 1881, 12; Advertisement, *Cincinnati Daily Gazette*, December 21, 1881, 2;
   Advertisement, *Cincinnati Daily Gazette*, December 13, 1882, 8; Advertisement, *Cincinnati Daily Gazette*, December 18, 1882, 10.
7. Michie Jeweler, eBay listings and private collections, Cincinnati silver binders, Cincinnati Art Museum.

86. WILLIAM MICHIE, JR.

1837–1915, w. 1856–1915

William Michie, Jr. was born in Dundee, Scotland, on February 8, 1837, the son of Ann Dick Smith (1817–1891) and watch maker William Michie, Sr. (b. circa 1808–1877, see **W. & J.C. Michie**).[1] The family sailed from Liverpool to New York and had settled in Newport, Kentucky, near Cincinnati in September 1843.[2] William Jr. first appeared in the Cincinnati city directory in 1856, working as a clerk at the shop of **Luke Kent, Jr.** He continued there as a watch maker, leaving briefly to serve in the Union army in the Civil War, until the establishment of **Kent & Michie** in November 1869.[3] When his brother James C. Michie (see W. & J.C. Michie) became indebted to creditors, William came to his aid by purchasing the business, and the firm of Kent & Michie was dissolved by mutual consent in April 1878.[4] William continued the business at 178 West Fourth Street as "**Michie, Jeweler**," with the assistance of his brothers James C. and Henry B (see **Michie Bros.**).[5] William Jr. was the principal while James worked in the background, and Henry worked as a clerk.[6] By late 1883, the brothers renamed the firm Michie Bros.[7]

Teaspoons made by William B. Durgin Co. (Concord, New Hampshire, and Providence, Rhode Island) in their "Honeysuckle" (1886) pattern, have been observed with mark 86.1.[8] There is no known time when William Michie, Jr. worked independently. These teaspoons were made and retailed during the life-time of the Michie Bros. firm. It is possible that the rarity of this mark can be explained by the chance that an order for Durgin's "Honeysuckle" flatware was placed by William Michie, Jr. on behalf of Michie Bros., and Durgin mistakenly marked them with his name, instead of the Michie Bros. name. There is no evidence to suggest that Michie Bros. made any of the silver wares that they sold.

William and his wife, Margaret Lange (1839–1926) had no children.[9] He died on January 16, 1915, and they are both buried in Spring Grove Cemetery in Cincinnati.[10]

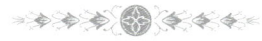

MARK 86.1

1. 1870 and 1900 Federal Censuses, Cincinnati, Hamilton, Ohio; "Death of Wm. Michie, Sr.," *Cincinnati Enquirer*, January 29, 1877, 8; William Michie, Jr., passport application, Ancestry.com, *U.S. Passport Applications, 1795–1925* [online database], Provo, Utah: Ancestry.com Operations Inc., 2007; *Michie's Abroad*, independently published, circa 1907, Library of Congress collection.
2. William Michie, Jr., passport application, *U.S. Passport Applications, 1795–1925*.
3. Ohio, Vol. 1, p. 13, R.G. Dun & Co. Collection, Baker Library, Harvard Business School; United States National Archives, *Civil War Service Records* [online database], Provo, Utah: MyFamily.com Inc., 1999.
4. Ohio, Vol. 4, p. 388, R.G. Dun & Co. Collection; Notice of dissolution, *Cincinnati Commercial Tribune*, April 11, 1878, 8.
5. 1878 Cincinnati City Directory.
6. 1878–1883 Cincinnati City Directories; Ohio, Vol. 4, p. 390, R.G. Dun & Co. Collection.
7. 1884–1919 Cincinnati City Directories.
8. William Michie, eBay listings and private collections, Cincinnati silver binders, Cincinnati Art Museum; Tere Hagan, *Sterling Flatware: An Identification and Value Guide*, Gas City, IN: L-W Book Sales, 2004, 81.
9. 1900, 1910 Federal Censuses, Cincinnati, Hamilton, Ohio.
10. Death notice, *Cincinnati Enquirer*, January 17, 1915, 5; William Michie, Margaret L. Michie, burial records, Spring Grove Cemetery, Cincinnati, Ohio.

87. W. & J.C. MICHIE

1867–1875

This firm was established in 1867 by William Michie, Sr. (b. circa 1808–1877) and his son, James C. Michie (1841–1901).[1] William Michie, Sr. was born in Brechin, Scotland, to Ann Williamson (d. 1845) and William Michie (1764–1860), a blacksmith.[2] He learned the watch making trade at Montrose and was in business in Brechin and Dundee, Scotland, before he and his wife Ann Dick Smith (1817–1891), and their family set sail from Liverpool and arrived in the United States in 1843.[3] They settled near Cincinnati, in Newport, Kentucky, soon afterwards. By 1849, William Michie, Sr. was employed as a watch repairer at the shop of **Nathan L. Hazen**, and he continued to work there after **Henry Bliss** took over the business in 1853.[4] Both Michie and Hazen moved to **Duhme & Co.** in 1859, where Michie, known to those in the local trade as "Daddy" Michie, served as head watch maker.[5]

Michie's son, James C. Michie was born on July 29, 1841, in Dundee, Scotland.[6] His earliest exposure to the trade surely came through his father; however, he may also have acquired skills under the tutelage of **Luke Kent, Jr.**, for whom he worked as a watch maker beginning in 1858, or possibly earlier.[7] The 1860 Census lists James C. Michie as a silversmith in Xenia, Ohio.[8] While he appears in Cincinnati city directories as a watch maker living in Cincinnati in 1861 and 1862, no working address is given. Between 1863 and 1865, James C. Michie left Cincinnati to serve in the Union Army where he rose from private to captain during the Civil War.[9] When he returned to Cincinnati, he found employment at Duhme & Co.[10]

In December 1867 William Michie, Sr. and James C. Michie left Duhme & Co. and formed W. & J.C. Michie, "Jewelers and Dealers in

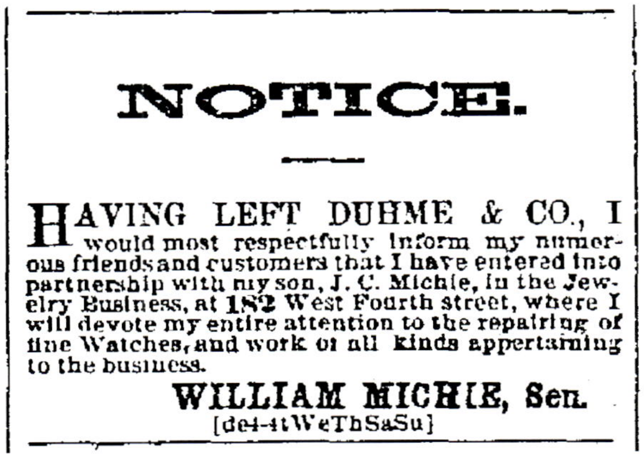

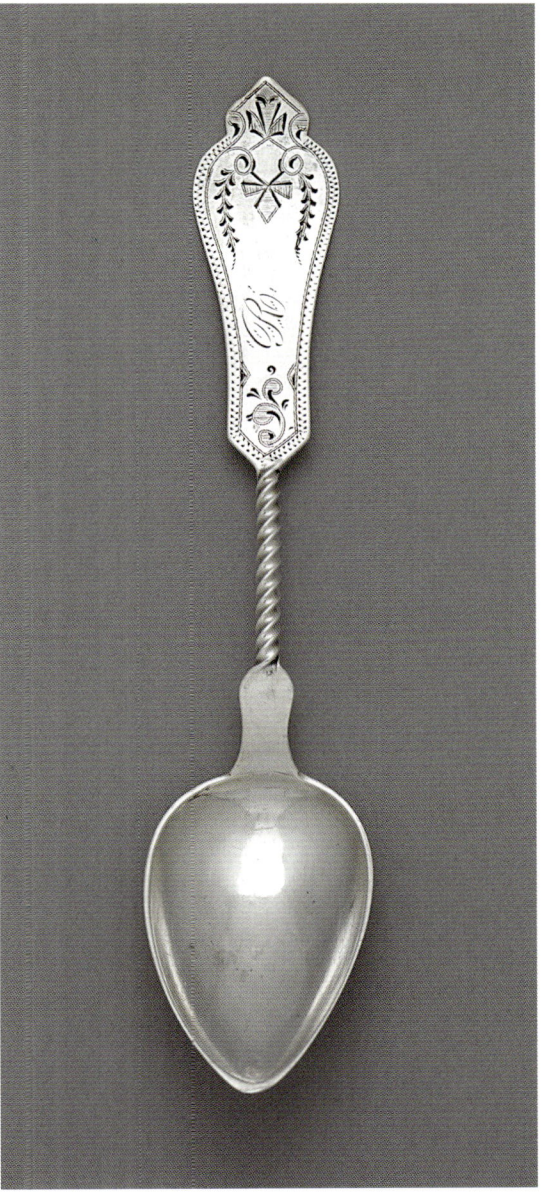

FIG. 87.2: W. & J.C. Michie, *Teaspoon*, 1867–1875, L. 5⅞ in. (14.9 cm), CAM, Gift of Charles Cleves, 2011.25

NOTICE.

HAVING LEFT DUHME & CO., I would most respectfully inform my numerous friends and customers that I have entered into partnership with my son, J. C. Michie, in the Jewelry Business, at 182 West Fourth street, where I will devote my entire attention to the repairing of fine Watches, and work of all kinds appertaining to the business.

WILLIAM MICHIE, Sen.
[de4-4tWeThSaSu]

FIG. 87.1: Notice, *Cincinnati Enquirer*, December 7, 1867, 2

Fine Watches, Silver & Plated Ware," at 182 West Fourth Street (fig. 87.1).[11] By 1869, they they were located at 178 West Fourth Street, and were described by R.G. Dun & Co. credit reporters as "good workmen" who were "highly respected as very honorable," "industrious and attentive to business."[12] Their means were estimated as small, between $3,000 and $4,000, and it was noted that most of their stock was supplied by Duhme & Co., "with whom they have all the credit they want."[13] The Michies were primarily watch makers, and probably did not make any of the silver that they sold. Given their prior relationship with Duhme & Co., it is not surprising that they were retailers of wares from that house. The W. & J.C. Michie mark (mark 87.1) has been found on a sugar shell with scalloped bowl, pointed shoulders, and tipped, exaggerated fiddle handle, as well as a teaspoon in Duhme's "No. 1" (circa 1869) pattern (fig. 87.2).[14]

William Michie, Sr. appears to have withdrawn his controlling interest in the firm sometime in 1875, as directories published in 1876 and 1877 indicate James C. Michie as the successor to W. & J.C. Michie. However, William Michie, Sr. remained somewhat involved, giving "his whole attention" to watch repairing until his sudden death on January 28, 1877.[15] He and his wife Ann had at least nine children: **William Jr.** (1837–1915); Colonel Peter Smith (1839–1901), a professor at West Point; James Carey (1841–1901); Thomas Smith (1845–1882); Alexander (1847–1865); Simon Ross (1849–1850); Anna W. (1852–1937); Henry Bliss (1855–1919); and Mary (1857–1865).[16] In addition to James C., both William Jr. and Henry Bliss Michie were also involved in the watch, jewelry, and silver trade (see **Michie, Jeweler** and **Michie Bros.**).

In December 1877, deep in debt to creditors, James C. sold out to his brother, William Michie, Jr., formerly of **Kent & Michie**.[17] William Jr., with the assistance of James C. and Henry Bliss Michie, went on to create the firm known as Michie, Jeweler, which evolved into Michie Bros. in 1883.[18] James C. Michie was appointed Postmaster in Covington, Kentucky that year, and between 1887 and 1889, he was listed in city directories as an insurance agent.[19] Subsequently, he moved to Dayton, Ohio where he was appointed Commissary of Subsistence for the Central Branch National Home for disabled volunteer soliders.[20] He died in Dayton on October 20, 1901.[21] He and his wife, Eliza Stevenson (b. circa 1843, England, d. 1922) had two daughters: Lizzie (1873–1874) and May (1874–1906).[22]

MARK 87.1

1. Notice, *Cincinnati Enquirer*, December 7, 1867, 2; Co-partnership notice, *Cincinnati Enquirer*, December 4, 1867, 2; 1868 Cincinnati City Directory.

2. 1870 Federal Census, Cincinnati, Hamilton, Ohio; "Death of Wm. Michie, Sr." *Cincinnati Enquirer*, January 29, 1877, 8; William Michie, Sr.'s father went to Brechin in about 1804–05 and worked as a blacksmith at the East Mill for over 50 years. He traveled to the United States about 1858 "at the solicitation of his son" and died in Cincinnati in 1860; *Michie's Abroad*, independently published, circa 1907, Library of Congress collection.

3. Ancestry.com, *Passenger and Immigration Lists Index, 1500s–1900s* [online database], Provo, Utah: Ancestry.com Operations Inc., 2010. Original data: William P. Filby (ed.), *Passenger and Immigration Lists Index, 1500s–1900s*, Farmington Hills, MI: Gale Research, 2010; "Death of Capt. James C. Michie," *Jewelers' Circular and Horological Review* (November 13, 1901): 28; William Michie, Jr., passport application, Ancestry.com, *U.S. Passport Applications, 1795–1925* [online database], Provo, Utah: Ancestry.com Operations Inc., 2007; *Michie's Abroad*, 19–20.

4. 1849/50 and 1853 Cincinnati City Directories.

5. 1859 Cincinnati City Directory; Conteur (Edwin Henderson), "Manufacture and Sale of Jewelry in Cincinnati During Preceding Century," *Cincinnati Enquirer*, October 23, 1923.

6. Capt. Jas. C. Michie, burial record, Spring Grove Cemetery, Cincinnati, Ohio; "Death of Capt. James C. Michie" (November 13, 1901).

7. James C. Michie's obituary indicates that he trained with Luke Kent. It is likely that he learned the trade from both his father and Kent; 1856–1877 Cincinnati City Directories.

8. 1860 Federal Census, Xenia, Greene, Ohio.

9. "Death of Capt. James C. Michie" (November 13, 1901); American Civil War Soldiers Record, James C. Michie, Historical Data Systems, comp.

American Civil War Soldiers [online database], Provo, Utah: MyFamily.com Inc., 1999; *Michie's Abroad*.

10. 1866 Cincinnati City Directory.

11. Notice, *Cincinnati Enquirer*, December 7, 1867, 2; Co-partnership notice, December 4, 1867; 1868 Cincinnati City Directory.

12. 1869 Cincinnati City Directory; Ohio, Vol. 7, p. 113, R.G. Dun & Co. Collection, Baker Library, Harvard Business School.

13. Ohio, Vol. 7, p. 113, R.G. Dun & Co. Collection.

14. Tere Hagan, *Sterling Flatware: An Identification and Value Guide*, Gas City, IN: L-W Book Sales, 1999, 3; W. & J.C. Michie, eBay listings and private collections, Cincinnati silver binders, Cincinnati Art Museum.

15. Advertisement, 1876 Cincinnati City Directory, 674; Advertisement, 1877 Cincinnati City Directory, 694; "Death of Wm. Michie, Sr." January 29, 1877.

16. Henry B. Michie, William Michie, James C. Michie, Anna Schneider, burial records, Spring Grove Cemetery; Cincinnati City Directories; Alexander Michie, death notice, *Cincinnati Enquirer*, June 9, 1865, 2; Peter Smith Michie, *Find A Grave*, www.findagrave.com; *Michie's Abroad*.

17. Ohio, Vol. 7, p. 287, R.G. Dun & Co. Collection.

18. 1878, 1884 Cincinnati City Directories.

19. Michael R. Averdick, *A Directory of Silversmiths, Jewelers, Watch and Clock Makers and Related Trades of Covington and Newport, Kentucky & Vicinity, 1833–1900*, Covington, KY: 829 Willard Street Press, 2002, 48; *Michie's Abroad*; 1887–1889 Cincinnati City Directories.

20. *Michie's Abroad*.

21. Capt. Jas. C. Michie, burial record.

22. 1870 Federal Census, Cincinnati, Hamilton, Ohio; Lizzie Michie, burial record, Spring Grove Cemetery; Mary [sic] M. Herdliska, burial record, Spring Grove Cemetery; "Died in Philadelphia, Mrs. Charles Herdliska, Well Known Here, Passed Away Yesterday," *Cincinnati Enquirer*, May 21, 1906, 10; *Michie's Abroad*.

88. JOHN B. MORRIS

1836–1903, w. 1856–1879

John B. Morris (fig. 88. 1) was born in Tralee, Ireland, to Ann Parker (1811–1872) and John Morris (b. about 1805–1861).[1] The family came to the United States in the 1840s, possibly passing through Pennsylvania, before settling in Covington, Kentucky.[2] Morris apprenticed with watch maker **Richard Clayton**.[3] He became a partner with **Henry Jenkins** and George B. Harting in H. Jenkins & Co., when Clayton sold his business to his former employees in the latter part of 1858.[4] They continued business at his stand on the southeast corner of Second and Sycamore Streets. In 1861, Jenkins sold his interest in the firm to his partners, who continued briefly as Morris & Harting until Harting's death in 1862.[5] After that, Morris ran the business under his own name at the same site, advertising as "Successor of R. Clayton" and "Importer and Dealer in Watches, Jewelry, Silver Ware, Watch-Makers' Tools and Materials, Watch Glasses, Clocks, Regulators, &c."[6]

In the 1870 Products of Industry Census, Morris reported as a "dealer in jewelry, watches, and manufacturer of watch cases and silver spoons." Prior to this, Morris is not known to have advertised as a silversmith or silver manufacturer in city directories or elsewhere. For the year ending June 1, 1870, he reported a capital investment of $16,500, three employees who were paid a total of $1,875 wages, and the use of $15,000 worth of gold (750 ounces) and $20,000 worth of silver (13,000 ounces) to make watch cases and silver spoons valued at $142,800.[7]

However, by October 1870 Morris was in financial trouble and reportedly made a trip east to settle with creditors. His debt was believed to be $20,000 while his net worth (which did not include property kept in his wife's name) was estimated at $10,000.[8] In 1871, he moved his store to 168 Walnut Street.[9] By 1872, it was thought that his condition was improving, but in January 1875 credit reporters noted that he was "not in very good standing with the majority of the trade."[10] He failed again that year, and in December 1876 credit reporters remarked, "[he] has been in business some time but has not been very fortunate."[11] In 1879, he sold out to his largest creditor, Henry Gremmel of New York and left his other creditors "in the lurch."[12] By 1880, he was in the lock manufacturing business (Morris Sash Lock Manufacturing Co.) and later established the Eagle Iron Foundry & Machine Works and The John B. Morris Foundry Company, in which he achieved greater success.[13]

Morris married Helen McGregor (1840–1905) of Cincinnati.[14] They had four known children: William Henry (1858–1868); John

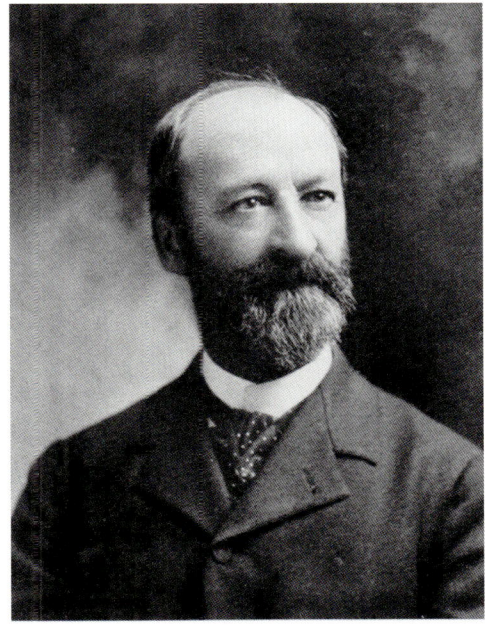

FIG. 88.1: John B. Morris, from Charles Greve, *Centennial History of Cincinnati and Its Representative Citizens*, Chicago: Biographical Publishing Company, 2:814

A. (1861–1874); George McGregor (b. 1870); and Helen Aloise (1872–1874).[15] John B. Morris was a Mason, a member of the Knights of Pythias, an Episcopalian, and a Republican.[16] He died of pneumonia on March 6, 1903, and is buried with his family in Spring Grove Cemetery.[17]

Morris' mark (mark 88.1) has been found on spoons with tipped, exaggerated fiddle handles and pointed shoulders.[18]

J.B.MORRIS

MARK 88.1

1. Charles Greve, *Centennial History of Cincinnati and Its Representative Citizens*, Chicago: Biographical Publishing Co., 1904, 2:815; Burial records, Spring Grove Cemetery, Cincinnati, Ohio; John B. Morris' father is listed as a laborer in the 1850 Federal Census, Covington, Kenton, Kentucky.

2. There is conflicting information about the Morris family's immigration date. The 1850 Federal Census places the family in Covington, KY. Ann and John Morris' second youngest child, George, is recorded as born in Pennsylvania around 1848. Their youngest child, Robert, about six months old, is noted as born in Kentucky, placing them there by mid-1849. Margaret, seven, is listed as the last child born in Ireland, which places the family in Ireland until 1843. Based on this, they came to the United States between

1843 and 1848. The 1900 Census says that Morris arrived in the United States in 1845. Greve's biography states that John B. Morris was six when he came to Cincinnati, indicating that the family settled in the city in 1842. This is probably incorrect; 1900 Federal Census, Cincinnati, Hamilton, Ohio; Greve, *Centennial History of Cincinnati*, 2:815.

3. Greve, *Centennial History of Cincinnati*, 2:815; 1856, 1857, 1859 Cincinnati City Directories; Ohio, Vol. 1, p. 428, R.G. Dun & Co. Collection, Baker Library, Harvard Business School.

4. Ohio, Vol. 1, p. 90, R.G. Dun & Co. Collection; 1860, 1861 Cincinnati City Directories.

5. Ohio, Vol. 1, pp. 132, 148, R.G. Dun & Co. Collection.

6. 1863 Cincinnati City Directory.

7. 1870 Federal Non-Population Census Schedules, Products of Industry,

Schedule 4, Hamilton County, Ohio; According to city directories, Louis Stichtenoth, a jeweler, worked at the southeast corner of Second and Sycamore Streets between 1856 and 1871.

8. Ohio, Vol. 1, p. 198, R.G. Dun & Co. Collection.

9. 1872 Cincinnati City Directory.

10. Ohio, Vol. 1, p. 198, R.G. Dun & Co. Collection.

11. Ibid.

12. Ohio, Vol. 6, p. 342, R.G. Dun & Co. Collection.

13. Greve, *Centennial History of Cincinnati* 2:816; 1880-1902 Cincinnati City Directories; Morris was the successor of Miles Greenwood, founder of the Eagle Ironworks. *Eagle Iron Foundry & Machine Works, John B. Morris & Co., Successors of Miles Greenwood . . .*, Cincinnati: John B. Morris & Co., 1888.

14. Burial records, Spring Grove Cemetery; Helen's father, George McGregor, was a lock manufacturer working at 175 Race Street in 1870. He may have led John B. Morris into this line of business. George McGregor lived with his daughter and son-in-law from at least 1860 until his death in 1895; Cincinnati City Directories; 1860 Federal Census, Cincinnati, Hamilton, Ohio.

15. 1860, 1870, 1880, 1900 Federal Censuses, Cincinnati, Hamilton, Ohio; Burial records, Spring Grove Cemetery.

16. Greve, *Centennial History of Cincinnati* 2:816.

17. Burial records, Spring Grove Cemetery.

18. John B. Morris, eBay listings and private collections, Cincinnati silver binders, Cincinnati Art Museum; Elizabeth Beckman collection, Cincinnati Museum Center.

89. MICHAEL C. MOTCH

1837–1899, w. 1857

Michael Charles Motch was born in Cincinnati in 1837. His parents, Henry, a carpenter, and Appolonia Motch, were Catholic, Alsatian immigrants.[1] Michael C. Motch was listed in the 1857 City Directory as a watch maker at the southeast corner of Second and Sycamore Streets, the site of **Richard Clayton**'s business.[2] This is the only year that he is known to have worked in Cincinnati proper. He spent the remainder of his career just across the Ohio River in Covington, Kentucky where he established a jewelry business (M.C. Motch) with his younger brother, John, on Madison Avenue.[3] It is very likely that Motch had Cincinnati patrons. His primary business was that of a watch maker and jeweler, and he probably did not make any of the silver bearing his mark. Spoons with mark 89.1 feature tipped, exaggerated fiddle handles and pointed shoulders—a form identified with Cincinnati, and likely made by manufacturers there.[4]

Michael C. Motch married Mary Goetz (1842–1916). They had five known children: Cora (b. 1865); Arthur E. (1867–1935); Lulu (b. 1871); Edwin (b. 1875); and Stanley (b. 1877).[5] Michael C. Motch died on January 1, 1899, and is buried in Cincinnati.[6] The business he established was carried on by his family and is still in operation today in the same building, 613 Madison Avenue, Covington, Kentucky.[7]

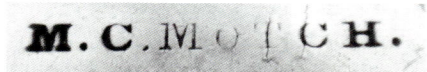

MARK 89.1

1. Burial records, Spring Grove Cemetery, Cincinnati, Ohio; Ancestry.com, *Kentucky, Death Records, 1852–1953* [online database], Provo, Utah: Ancestry.com Operations, Inc., 2007; 1850 Federal Census, Cincinnati, Hamilton, Ohio; Karl Lietzenmayer, "M.C. Motch, Jewelers, A Kentucky Centennial Company," *Bulletin of the Kenton County Historical Society*, May/June 2011.

2. It is probable that Motch apprenticed with the watch maker Richard Clayton.

3. For more on M.C. Motch's activities in Kentucky, see Michael R. Averdick, *A Directory of Silversmiths, Jewelers, Watch and Clock Makers and Related Trades of Covington and Newport, Kentucky & Vicinity, 1833–1900*, Covington, KY: 829 Willard Street Press, 2002, 50–54. See also Boultinghouse, 207–208.

4. M.C. Motch, eBay listings and private collections, Cincinnati silver binders, Cincinnati Art Museum.

5. Lietzenmayer, "M.C. Motch, Jewelers, A Kentucky Centennial Company," May/June 2011; Michael C. Motch, burial record, Spring Grove Cemetery.

6. Burial records, Spring Grove Cemetery; Ancestry.com, *Kentucky, Death Records, 1852–1953* [online database], Provo, Utah: Ancestry.com Operations, Inc., 2007.

7. The building was designed by James W. McLaughlin, Cincinnati's most prominent architect at the time; Lietzenmayer, "M.C. Motch, Jewelers, A Kentucky Centennial Company," May/June 2011.

90. SAMUEL MUSGROVE

b. 1800, w. 1820–1840

Musgrove was born in Kentucky in 1800, most likely one of ten children born to Elizabeth Moore (1772–post 1860) and Cuthbert Musgrove (circa 1770–post 1860) of Virginia.[1] Our first reference to Samuel in Cincinnati appears in **Jacob Deterly**'s diary, when Deterly writes "**Abner Sotcher** & Saml. Musgrove have commenced plating" on March 7, 1820—a partnership that had dissolved by April 7th.[2] Details of Musgrove's training are unknown, however, we can surmise that he had knowledge of metalworking by way of his plating activities with Sotcher; through a Deterly diary entry indicating that **James Phillips** had returned to learn the silversmithing business from Samuel Musgrove in May 1827; and through his recurring listings as a silversmith in city directories and censuses.[3]

We cannot be certain where Musgrove's shop was until 1834, when his business address is given as Post Office Alley, between Third and Fourth Streets.[4] There are no known advertisements for Musgrove's business. In August 1831 Deterly notes that someone had attempted to sell Musgrove the silver breast-plate that had been attached to the coffin of David Kilgour, one of Cincinnati's most prominent settlers.[5] The 1839/40 City Directory indicates that **Rodolpho Cox** of Virginia was employed as a silversmith at Musgrove's shop.[6]

Musgrove does not appear in Cincinnati directories after 1840. By August 1850, perhaps as early as 1847, he was in Larue County, Kentucky, with his wife Eliza (b. about 1811, Ohio) and their seven children.[7] By 1853, he had relocated to Nashville, Tennessee, where he continued to practice his trade, appearing under the categories of "silversmiths and platers," and "watchmakers and jewelers" in business listings. In 1860, he listed as a "gold and silver manufacturer."[8]

Early fiddle-handled spoons with rounded shoulders and a pair of tongs stamped with an incuse "S. MUSGROVE" are known. Mark 90.1 has been found on a fiddle-handled spoon with rounded shoulders, and tipped, fiddle-handled spoons with rounded shoulders.[9]

MARK 90.1

1. 1839/40 Cincinnati City Directory; 1850 Federal Census, Hamiltons, Larue, Kentucky; R. Musgrove, "Total Musgrove Family Tree," Ancestry.com, http://trees.ancestry.com/tree/663798 3/family?cfpid=-1257228779; Richard Graham Musgrove, *The American Family Musgrove*, Houston: ArGee, 1993, 636; Benjamin Hubbard Caldwell, *Tennessee Silversmiths*, Winston-Salem: Museum of Early Southern Decorative Arts, 1988, 132; Cuthbert Musgrove had emigrated from Scotland to Virginia, and then settled in Kentucky. G.D. Gardner, "A Glimmer from the Past: Art of the Silversmiths in Hardin County," *Bits and Pieces of Hardin County History* 26, no. 4 (Winter 2008), Elizabethtown, KY: Hardin County Historical Society.
2. Jacob Deterly, "Remarks" of Jacob Deterly: *diary from 1819 to 1848; life in southern Ohio: Cincinnati, Marietta, Athens* (transcribed and indexed by Madge Hubbard and Opal Saffell), Seattle: Northwest Lineage Researcher, 1972, 1:6–7.
3. Deterly, "Remarks," 2:24; 1831, 1834, 1836/37, 1839/40 Cincinnati City Directories; 1850 Federal Census, Hamiltons, Larue, Kentucky.
4. 1834 Cincinnati City Directory.
5. Deterly, "Remarks," 2:61.
6. 1839/40 Cincinnati City Directory.
7. 1850 Federal Census, Hamiltons, Larue, Kentucky; There are multiple marriage records for Samuel Musgove, but it is unclear if all of these records pertain to the subject of this entry. On September 20, 1825, a Samuel Musgrove married Elizabeth Kenny in Caldwell County, Kentucky, see *Kentucky Pioneers and Their Descendants*, Kentucky: Daughters of the Colonial Wars, 1950, 291. On May 15, 1828, Jacob Deterly records Musgrove's marriage to an unnamed girl from Cincinnati. Deterly, "Remarks," 2:20. A marriage license was issued to Samuel Musgrove and Elizabeth Reed on April 6, 1829, in Mason County, Kentucky, see *Kentucky Pioneers and Their Descendants*, 160. In 1830, there is an Ohio marriage record for Samuel Musgrove (b. 1791, Virginia) and Mary Parish (b. 1799, Maryland), but a later record from Kentucky Court Order Book 45 (Circuit Clerk's Office) dated November 1849 notes, ". . . Samuel Musgrove and Elizabeth his wife . . . are not now inhabitants of this Commonwealth." Yates Publishing, *U.S. and International Marriage Records, 1560–1900* [online database], Provo, Utah: Ancestry.com Operations Inc., 2004. *Kentucky Pioneers and Their Descendants*, 156; Boultinghouse, 209; Gardner, "A Glimmer from the Past," (Winter 2008).
8. Caldwell, *Tennessee Silversmiths*, 132; John Paul Campbell, *The South Business Directory and General Commercial Advertiser*, Charleston, SC: Steam Power Press of Walker & James, 1854; Musgrove may have moved elsewhere by 1860, or died, as he and his family are not found in Nashville in the 1860 Federal Census.
9. Samuel Musgrove, eBay listings and private collections, Cincinnati silver binders, Cincinnati Art Museum; Caldwell, *Tennessee Silversmiths*, 133.

91. NATHAN & LEVY

1860–1863

The firm of Nathan & Levy had formed by July 18, 1860, when Morris Escales withdrew from the wholesale jewelry firm of Nathan, Escales & Co. (active 1860).[1] The remaining partners, Max Nathan (d. 1895) and Joseph Levy (b. about 1825) were brothers-in-law, and continued the business at 100 Walnut Street, between Pearl and Third Streets.[2] Earlier credit reports for the firm of Nathan & Escales (1855–1859), as the firm was known prior to Levy's involvement in January 1859, indicate that they had no store, but rather sold stock to peddlers from the second story of a building on Main Street.[3] The firm of Nathan & Levy may have operated in a similar fashion. There are no known newspaper advertisements for the firm. An advertisement published in the 1860–61 *Ohio State Gazetteer and Business Directory* described the firm as "Wholesale Dealers in Jewelry, Silver and Plated Ware."[4] The Nathan & Levy partnership had dissolved by September 23, 1863.[5] Levy went into the wholesale and retail clothing business with his brother, and Nathan joined the firm of Rubens & Nathan (1864–1866), "Jobbers of English, Swiss & American Watches, Jewelry, Spectacles, &c."[6]

Teaspoons and tablespoons with tipped, exaggerated fiddle handles and pointed shoulders have been documented with mark 91.1.[7]

MARK 91.1

1. Ohio, Vol. 3, p. 145, R.G. Dun & Co. Collection, Baker Library, Harvard Business School; 1860 Cincinnati City Directory.
2. Ohio, Vol. 3, p. 145, R.G. Dun & Co. Collection; 1861–1863 Cincinnati City Directories; Max Nathan, burial record, Schachnus Cemetery, Cincinnati, Ohio, jcemcin.org; 1860 Federal Census, Cincinnati Ward 14, Hamilton, Ohio; Joseph Levy married Babette Nathan (d. 1865) on December 20, 1858. Marriage record, Hamilton County Probate Records, vol. 18, 217, http://www.probatect.org/CourtRecordsArchive/bukmarriages.aspx; Babette Levy, burial record, Walnut Hills Jewish Cemetery, jcemcin.org; George Hawes, comp., *Ohio State Gazetteer and Business Directory for 1860–'61*, Indianapolis, IN: George W. Hawes, 1860, 153.
3. Ohio, Vol. 1, p. 407, R.G. Dun & Co. Collection.
4. Hawes, *Ohio State Gazetteer*, 153.
5. Ohio, Vol. 3, p. 145, R.G. Dun & Co. Collection.
6. Ohio, Vol. 5, p. 202, R.G. Dun & Co. Collection; 1864–1866 Cincinnati City Directories.
7. *Teaspoon*, Elizabeth Beckman Collection, Cincinnati Museum Center; Nathan & Levy, eBay listings and private collections, Cincinnati silver binders, Cincinnati Art Museum.

92. THEODORE NEUHAUS, JR.

1867–1937, w. 1881–1925

THEODORE NEUHAUS & CO.

1899–1911

THEODORE NEUHAUS COMPANY

1911–1913

NEUHAUS MANUFACTURING COMPANY

1914, 1921–1925

Theodore Neuhaus, Jr. (1867-1937, fig. 92.1) was born in Cincinnati.[1] He undoubtedly apprenticed with his father, **Theodore Neuhaus, Sr.** (1838-1885) who had worked with **E. & D. Kinsey**, **David Kinsey** and **Duhme & Co.** Theodore Neuhaus, Jr. made his first appearance in city directories in 1881, listing as a watch maker.[2] By 1884, he was working at Duhme & Co. as a clerk and a salesman, and beginning in 1890, he was superintendent of Duhme's silver manufacturing department.[3] He continued to serve in this capacity until the spring of 1897, when **The Duhme Company** declared bankruptcy and the firm was reorganized to form **The Duhme Jewelry Co.**[4]

In May 1897 Neuhaus Jr. announced that his new enterprise, The Neuhaus Manufacturing Company, had been incorporated for $25,000 and would be located at the Custom House Square.[5] It would be the "the only plant of this kind in the West for the manufacture of wares in solid silver and rich gold jewelry."[6] Neuhaus advertised that he had commandeered all of the skilled mechanics at the old Duhme firm, which at one time employed 125 men in its factory, as well as the firm's dies and patterns.[7] Patrons who had ordered goods from these dies, patterns, etc. were promised that they could continue to acquire them through him.[8]

In August 1897 the firm's name was published as Neuhaus, Lakin & Co., and it was announced that they had added another floor to their factory, enabling them to extend their business.[9] The jeweler John M. Lakin was Neuhaus' partner.[10] Five days later, the newspaper announced that Oscar Trounstine (b. 1863) had joined the concern and would manage its financial office.[11] Although the firm was listed in the 1898 City Directory (published in June 1898) as Neuhaus, Trounstine & Co., it was organized into a stock company under the name Neuhaus, Lakin & Co. in January 1898,

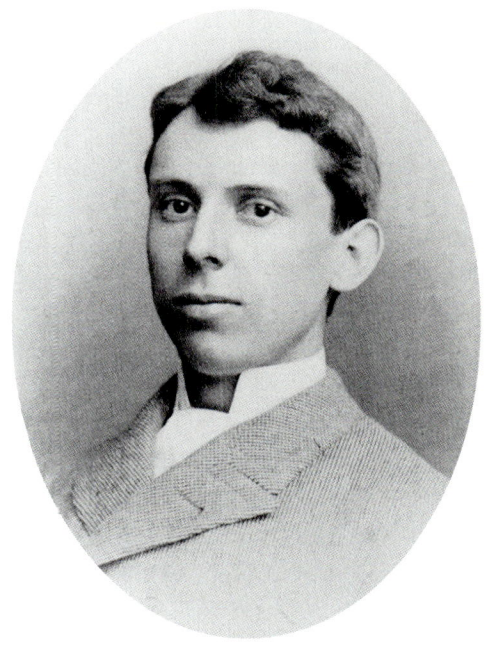

FIG. 92.1: Theodore Neuhaus, from Benjamin La Bree, *Notable Men of Cincinnati at the Beginning of the 20th Century*, Louisville, KY: Geo G. Fetter Co., 1904, 171

and was reported to be relocating its works to the plant formerly occupied by Duhme & Co. in the Carlisle Building at Fourth and Walnut Streets. The point was made that Neuhaus, Lakin & Co.'s manufacturing business "will be kept entirely separate from the retail business of The Duhme Jewelry Co." The new firm aspired to "engage in the manufacture of silver and gold articles on a larger scale' so that "a home institution may turn out the work and get all the business that belongs in Cincinnati instead of local jewelers being compelled to go East for it."[12]

The nature of the relationship between the Duhme firm operated by Herman Keck, Jr. and the Neuhaus firm remains hazy. Just days after Neuhaus, Lakin & Co. announced their incorporation in January 1898, the Duhme Manufacturing Co. was incorporated, and it, too, was to operate in the Carlisle Building.[13] One newspaper report notes the Duhme Manufacturing Co. as "makers of sterling silver" while the other says that the "purpose of the organization is to deal in gold and silverware, clocks, watches and jewelry."[14] Incorporators of the Duhme Manufacturing Co. were Herman and Frank Duhme, Oscar and **Herman Keck**, and Theodore Neuhaus, Jr.[15] In turn, Herman Keck, Jr. was a principal stockholder in the new Neuhaus firm.[16]

In February 1898 it was announced that Neuhaus Jr. had withdrawn from the Duhme concern and would form a partnership with Oscar Trounstine.[17] Lakin's role, if any, is unknown. Neuhaus and Trounstine were to open their business at the northwest corner of Fifth and Vine Streets, over Foreman's shoe store, and would soon be traveling to New York to purchase machinery so that their factory could be up and running by the end of the month. However, the 1899 City Directory lists only the firm of Theodore Neuhaus & Co., operating in the Lion Building (434 Elm Street) at the southeast corner of Fifth and Elm Streets; Trounstine's involvement, if any, is unclear.[18]

The firm advertised as "Manufacturers of SPECIAL JEWELRY, SILVERWARE, all grades of BADGES, MEDALS, CLASS PINS, and SOCIETY EMBLEMS."[19] Drawings were promised to be "cheerfully submitted."[20] They made "gold work in badge and pin designs a specialty."[21] They received large orders for school pins, and held accounts to produce medals and jewelry for the Independent Order of Odd Fellows, National Cash Register Company in Dayton, Peters Cartridge Co., Cincinnati Fall Festival Association, the Elks, Grand Army of the Republic, Laundrymen's Association, Cincinnati Police, and International Fox Hunters.[22] Neuhaus was well regarded for his designs. In 1901, he was preparing "an elaborately illustrated catalogue of medals, badges, and class pins."[23] The designs were his own and represented months of labor.[24] He reportedly kept a 10 × 12 inch scrap book of several hundred pages, collecting all of the new and unique designs published in various trade journals which served as a "valuable fund of ideas for the designer and manufacturer."[25] His work was so admired that in 1904, he reportedly received "some very flattering offers from an important Paris jewelry concern" to join them in business.[26] He was appointed to design and create the 24-karat gold jewel to be presented to President Roosevelt on his visit to the 1902 Cincinnati

Fall Festival, and the official badge of the 1904 St. Louis World's Fair, where he served as a juror for the gold and silver jewelry, stationery, and watch making department.[27]

In December 1900 Neuhaus reported that his firm was "one of the most progressive manufacturing concerns of the west. No matter what a thing costs, if it will facilitate their business or increase their trade, it is immediately introduced. It is a model factory."[28] In 1901, he boasted that his firm had "made pieces in silver and gold for houses in various parts of the country as far west as the Pacific Coast."[29] Neuhaus designed and supplied loving cups, silver prizes, and souvenirs for The Fleischmann Company, Latonia Association, Cincinnati Gun Club, Peters Cartridge Co., and the Aero Club of America balloon race.[30] The firm also added silver mounts to loving cups created by The Rookwood Pottery Company.[31]

Commissions illustrating the sophistication of the firm's work include a silver loving cup for a golden wedding anniversary, "chased in gold with the portraits of the couple in gold relief"; the Cincinnati Trophy for the Latonia horse races; and the Jacob Baiter retirement cup.[32] Neuhaus won the competition for the design of a loving cup that would be presented to the winner of the two-year old five-and-a-half furlong sprint at the Latonia Race in 1902, and produced identical versions of the cup for subsequent races.[33] The cup, weighing 100 ounces, was donated by the Hon. Julius Fleischmann, mayor of Cincinnati. Featured on the front page of *The Jewelers' Circular and Horological Review,* the cup boasted "beautiful modeling and rich chasing." The front panel of the silver cup featured a horse head surrounded by a horse shoe, both cast in solid gold. The three handles took the form of corn stalks, and the base was cast to suggest oats.

The Baiter Cup was presented by The Fleischmann Company and family to Jacob P. Baiter upon his retirement in 1910, after 35 years of service to the Fleischmann firm.[34] It was 18½ inches tall and 10 inches wide. Made of 14-karat gold, it had three handles. Between the handles, there was a portrait in relief of Mr. Baiter; his monogram with forget-me-knots in relief; and a "hand wrought palm of oak leaves, symbolical of long life and purity" with a presentation inscription. The cup rested on a solid green marble base, and reportedly cost over $2,500.[35]

Extant silver by the firm is rare. Much of it was likely sold to retailers who impressed it with their own marks. This may be especially true if there was a collaboration between Neuhaus' firm and the late Duhme firms. A pin presented to an employee of the National Cash Register Company; a silver match safe in the shape of a loaf of bread, made for The Fleischmann Company; and a set of silver bread plates have been documented recently.[36] The bread plates bear mark 92.1.

In May 1911 bankruptcy proceeding were initiated against Theodore Neuhaus & Co.[37] It was reported that the insolvency of the firm had come as a surprise to Charles Theye (1858–1941), who had been handling the manufacturing end of the business, while Neuhaus was overseeing financial matters.[38] The only reason given for the failure was lack of business. The firm attempted to regain its footing by incorporating as the Theodore Neuhaus Company and raising new capital, but this was unsuccessful.[39] The firm settled with its creditors at 33⅓ percent, and Neuhaus' wife was forced to mortgage her home to pay the debts. The firm was reorganized as the Theodore Neuhaus Company.[40]

In 1914, the firm listed in city directories as Neuhaus Manufacturing Co., operating in the Butler Building, on the south side of Sixth Street between Vine and Race Streets (15 West Sixth).[41] The firm was not listed in the 1915 City Directory, and in 1916, Theodore Neuhaus, Jr. was listed as a sales agent for The Dorst Company, local manufacturing jewelers. Between 1917 and 1920, Neuhaus was a special representative and sales manager for the Gustave Fox Company, another Cincinnati manufacturing jeweler.[42] The 1921 and 1922 City Directories indicate that Neuhaus Jr and the Neuhaus Manufacturing Company were active again and working in room 210 in the Commercial Tribune Building (528 Walnut), but Neuhaus Jr. filed a voluntary petition for bankruptcy on October 17, 1922.[43] His largest creditors were Abel Bros. & Co. (New York), Gorham Mfg. Co. (Providence, Rhode Island), and the Gustave Fox Company (Cincinnati). The firm appears to have revived in 1924, but is not listed after 1925.[44]

Theodore Neuhaus, Jr. was married to Elizabeth Ann Dunham (b. 1872).[45] He fathered at least three children: Elizabeth Frances (b. 1896), David Culy (b. 1898), and Theodore Addison (b. 1905).[46] Theodore Neuhaus, Jr. died on February 3, 1937.[47] He is buried in the Walnut Hills Cemetery in Cincinnati.[48]

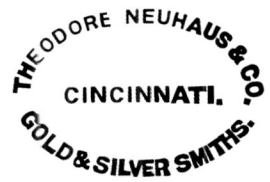

MARK 92.1

1. Theodore Neuhaus, "Ohio, Deaths, 1908–1953," index and images, *FamilySearch*, https://familysearch.org/pal:/MM9.1/XZD2-KBZ, accessed January 3, 2013.
2. 1881 Cincinnati City Directory.
3. 1884–1897 Cincinnati City Directories.
4. 1897, 1898 Cincinnati City Directories.
5. Advertisement, "The Neuhaus Mfg. Co.," *Cincinnati Enquirer*, May 23, 1897, 20.
6. Ibid.
7. Ibid.; There is no extant evidence to suggest that the Neuhaus firm made wares using the Duhme dies, patterns, etc.
8. Ibid.
9. "Cincinnati," *Jewelers' Circular and Horological Review* (August 25, 1897): 32.
10. 1898 Cincinnati City Directory; Lakin was previously a salesman at Duhme & Co., and at The Duhme Company; 1890–1896 Cincinnati City Directories.
11. "Facts and Fancies," *Cincinnati Enquirer*, August 30, 1897, 4; Trounstine was born in Ohio to Rebecca and Abraham Trounstine, both of German descent. His father was a clothier; 1800, 1900 Federal Censuses, Cincinnati, Hamilton, Ohio.
12. "Facts and Fancies," *Cincinnati Enquirer*, January 21, 1898, 5.

13. "Duhme Manufacturing Co.," *Cincinnati Enquirer*, January 23, 1898, 16; "Duhme Company," *Cincinnati Enquirer*, January 23, 1898, 30.
14. Ibid.
15. Ibid.
16. "Facts and Fancies," *Cincinnati Enquirer*, January 21, 1898, 5.
17. "Men and Matters," *Cincinnati Enquirer*, February 6, 1898, 4; "Facts and Fancies," *Cincinnati Enquirer*, February 19, 1898, 4; 1898 Cincinnati City Directory.
18. 1899 Cincinnati City Directory; A 1911 report in the *Jewelers' Circular and Horological Review* says that Trounstine withdrew from the firm in 1899, however, another report published in the same journal in 1901 infers that he was still part of the firm; "Cincinnati," *JCHR* (June 26, 1901): 50; "Theodore Neuhaus & Co., Cincinnati, O., Offer Creditors a Settlement at 25 Per Cent," *JCHR* (May 17, 1911): 83.
19. Advertisement, *JCHR* (November 4, 1903): 76.
20. Ibid.
21. "Cincinnati," *JCHR* (November 21, 1900): 55.
22. See the following "Cincinnati" columns in the *JCHR*: May 16, 1900, 38; June 6, 1900, 20; July 4, 1900, 39; September 12, 1900, 52; October 3, 1900, 44; November 21, 1900, 55; February 20, 1901, 49; August 21, 1901, 52; October 23, 1901, 72;

October 30, 1901, 71; December 18, 1901, 51; April 2, 1902, 58; April 23, 1902, 60; August 6, 1902, 55; August 27, 1902, 67; September 3, 1902, 67; September 17, 1902, 71; October 1, 1902, 69; December 3, 1902, 64; May 20, 1903, 64; and March 16, 1904, 70; "Men and Matters," *Cincinnati Enquirer*, April 10, 1902, 7; "Victory of Cincinnati. Theodore Neuhaus & Co. Receive the Contract To Make the Beautiful Jewels To Be Worn By the Elks in July." *Cincinnati Enquirer*, March 6, 1904, A8.
23. "Cincinnati," *JCHR* (February 6, 1901): 75.
24. Ibid.
25. Ibid.
26. "Cincinnati," *JCHR* (September 11, 1904): 72.
27. "President Roosevelt's Jewel," *Cincinnati Enquirer*, August 31, 1902, 3; "Cincinnati," *JCHR* (September 10, 1902): 69; "Cincinnati," *JCHR* (December 16, 1903): 57; "Cincinnati," *JCHR* (September 7, 1904): 70.
28. "Trade Gossip," *JCHR* (December 26, 1900): 44.
29. "Cincinnati," *JCHR* (August 28, 1901): 58.
30. Neuhaus produced 1,500 silver match boxes in the shape of bread loaves for The Fleischmann Co. "Cincinnati," *JCHR* (August 27, 1902): 67; Theodore Neuhaus & Co., eBay listings and private collections,

Cincinnati silver binders, Cincinnati Art Museum; "Cincinnati," *JCHR* (November 18, 1903): 69; "Cincinnati," *JCHR* (March 23, 1904): 60; "Balloons To Race in This City," *Cincinnati Enquirer*, September 17, 1907, 12.
31. "Men and Matters," *Cincinnati Enquirer*, October 4, 1899, 7; "Cincinnati," *JCHR* (April 30, 1902): 59.
32. "Cincinnati," *JCHR* (August 28, 1901): 58; "Cincinnati," *JCHR* (May 14, 1903): 59; "A Notable Racing Trophy," *JCHR* (July 2, 1902); "Testimonial For Former Cincinnatian," *Cincinnati Enquirer*, February 27, 1910, 13.
33. "A Notable Racing Trophy," (July 2, 1902); "Cincinnati," *JCHR* (June 8, 1904): 65; "Cincinnati," *JCHR* (July 13, 1904): 52.
34. "Testimonial For Former Cincinnatian," February 27, 1910.
35. Ibid.; Mr. Baiter purchased a large loving cup in the East Indian style from Tiffany & Co., who had featured it in their display at the 1893 Columbian Exposition, and presented it to Mr. Fleischmann and his wife in honor of their 25th wedding anniversary in 1894; Amy Miller Dehan, "Tiffany's Tiger Hunt Loving Cup," *The Magazine Antiques* 169, no. 3 (March 2006): 64–71; *Loving Cup*, 1893, Cincinnati Art Museum, Gift of

Mr. and Mrs. Charles Fleischmann III, 2004.9.

36. Theodore Neuhaus & Co., eBay listings and private collections, Cincinnati silver binders, Cincinnati Art Museum.

37. "Theodore Neuhaus & Co., Cincinnati, O., Offer Creditors a Settlement at 25 Per Cent" (May 17, 1911); "Creditors File Bankruptcy Petition Against Theo. Neuhaus & Co., Cincinnati, Who Offered Settlement at 25 Cents," *JCHR* (May 24, 1911): 73; "Cincinnati," *JCHR* (May 31, 1911): 99; "Cincinnati," *JCHR* (June 14, 1911): 97.

38. Theye's occupation is given as jeweler (1900), manufacturing jeweler (1910), and enameler and wholesale jeweler (1920) in the 1900, 1910, and 1920 Federal Censuses, Cincinnati, Hamilton, Ohio; Charles Theye, burial record, Spring Grove Cemetery, Cincinnati, Ohio; "Men and Matters," *Cincinnati Enquirer*, April 15, 1911, 12; "Cincinnati," *JCHR* (April 19, 1911): 98.

39. "Men and Matters," *Cincinnati Enquirer*, April 15, 1911, 12; "Cincinnati," *JCHR* (April 19, 1911): 98.

40. "Cincinnati," *JCHR* (June 28, 1911): 100; "Cincinnati," *JCHR* (July 19, 1911): 97; "Cincinnati," *JCHR* (January 24, 1912): 106b.

41. "Men and Matters," *Cincinnati Enquirer*, December 7, 1913, 31; 1914 Cincinnati City Directory.

42. 1917–1920 Cincinnati City Directories.

43. "Manufacturing Jeweler Bankrupt," *Cincinnati Enquirer*, October 18, 1922, 11.

44. 1924, 1925 Cincinnati City Directories.

45. 1900 Federal Census, Cincinnati, Hamilton, Ohio; Elizabeth is not buried with Theodore Neuhaus, Jr. at Spring Grove Cemetery. His death record states that his wife, at his time of death was Florence Kelly. This suggests that he may have remarried. "Ohio, Deaths, 1908–1953," index and images, *FamilySearch*, https://familysearch.org/pal://MM9.1/XZD2-KBZ, accessed January 3,

2013; Ancestry.com, *Ohio, Births and Christening Index, 1800–1962* [online database], Provo, Utah: Ancestry.com Operations Inc., 2011.

46. "Ohio, Deaths, 1908–1953," index and images, *FamilySearch*; Ancestry.com, *Ohio, Births and Christening Index, 1800–1962*; "Cincinnati," *JCHR*, (May 31, 1905): 60.

47. "Ohio, Deaths, 1908–1953"; Ancestry.com, *Ohio, Births and Christening Index, 1800–1962*.

48. Theadore [*sic*] Neuhaus, burial record, http://www.walnuthills cemetery.org/Genealogy_Search.php, accessed January 3, 2013.

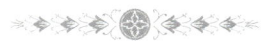

93. GEORGE HERMAN NEWSTEDT

1875–1953, w. 1889–1953

THE GEORGE H. NEWSTEDT CO.

1923–1942

GEORGE H. NEWSTEDT & CO.

1943–1956

NEWSTEDT'S

1958–1965

NEWSTEDT-LORING ANDREWS

1965–present

George H. Newstedt (fig. 93.1) was born on February 13, 1875, in Syke, Germany, about 14 miles south of Bremen, to Matilda Behne and Dietrich Nüstedt, a brewer.[1] In 1889, at age fourteen, he sailed to New York from Bremen on the *Elbe*.[2] His maternal uncle, Christian Johann Frederick Bene (Behne), had preceded him and was a partner in the wholesale jewelry business of Bene and Lindenberg (later Bene, Lindenberg & Co.) in Cincinnati, with Simon Lindenberg and Simon Sommers.[3] George was also preceded by his older brothers, August (1873–1961) who had arrived in 1885 and settled in Cincinnati, and William (1871–1920) who lived in Chicago.[4] George's formal education ended when he left Germany.[5] He worked for his uncle, after settling in Cincinnati, and eventually for Benjamin Greenwald, manager and later president of the American Watch & Jewelry Company.[6] Initially, Newstedt swept the floor and slept on a cot in the back of Greenwald's store, but by 1894, he had worked his way up to secretary and treasurer of the

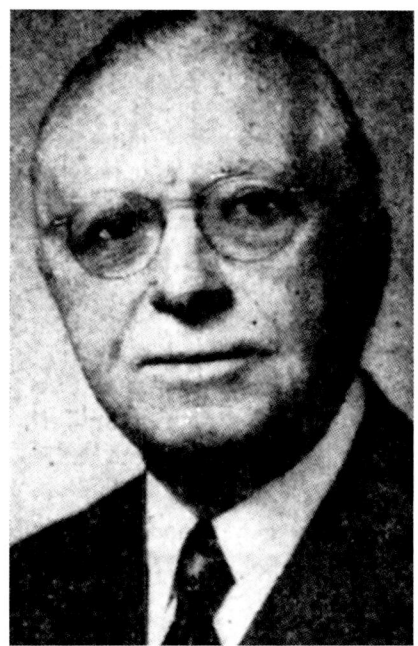

FIG. 93.1: George H. Newstedt, Obituary, *Cincinnati Enquirer*, February 23, 1953, 1

American Watch & Jewelry Company.[7] He continued there until September 1900 when he opened his own shop at 434 Walnut, across from the Gibson Hotel.[8] After a trip to the East to buy stock, he was set up to retail diamonds, watches, clocks and jewelry.[9] In 1901, the building housing the shop was purchased by The Cincinnati Traction Company who wished to demolish it. After a long court battle, a compromise was made. The Cincinnati Traction Company gave Newstedt $7,500 cash and he vacated the premises, moving to 404 Walnut Street.[10] In the fall of 1905, Newstedt relocated again, moving to the northwest corner of Fourth and Race Streets.[11] The new store (fig. 93.2) was opened on September 5. "The stock, most of it new for the opening, was shown to a good advantage in rich, up-to-date mahogany and plate glass cases," and "wall cases resting against daintily tinted blue walls gave a tone and rich appearance in keeping with the fine stock displayed."[12]

In addition to dealing in diamonds, jewelry, watches, and clocks, Newstedt also sold cut glass and sterling and plated silver, and offered watch and clock repair services.[13] Most, if not all of his stock was procured in the East or in Europe.[14] There is no evidence to suggest that the firm produced any of the silver wares that it sold. A variety of flatware and hollowware forms have been found with stamped, incuse marks that include "G. H. NEWSTEDT," "GEORGE H. NEWSTEDT," and later "GEO. H. NEWSTEDT C̲o̲ CIN'TI, O." However, most of these wares also bear the marks of their manufacturers, including Reed & Barton (Taunton,

Massachusetts) and Towle Mfg. Co. (Newburyport, Massachusetts).[15] An account of a 1904 robbery of Newstedt's store notes that during the break-in, "silver bowls and pitchers were turned upside down and many articles thrown upon the floor," and "a silver candelabra was twisted out of shape."[16]

In 1900, George H. Newstedt married Ann Tudor (1880–1954), daughter of Anna Jones and Hugh Tudor, founder of Tudor Boiler Works.[17] They had three children: Elizabeth (1904–1992), who married Clair S. Hall, Jr.; Virginia (1905–1969), who wed Herbert F. Kreimer; and Tudor (1913–1973), who eventually joined his father

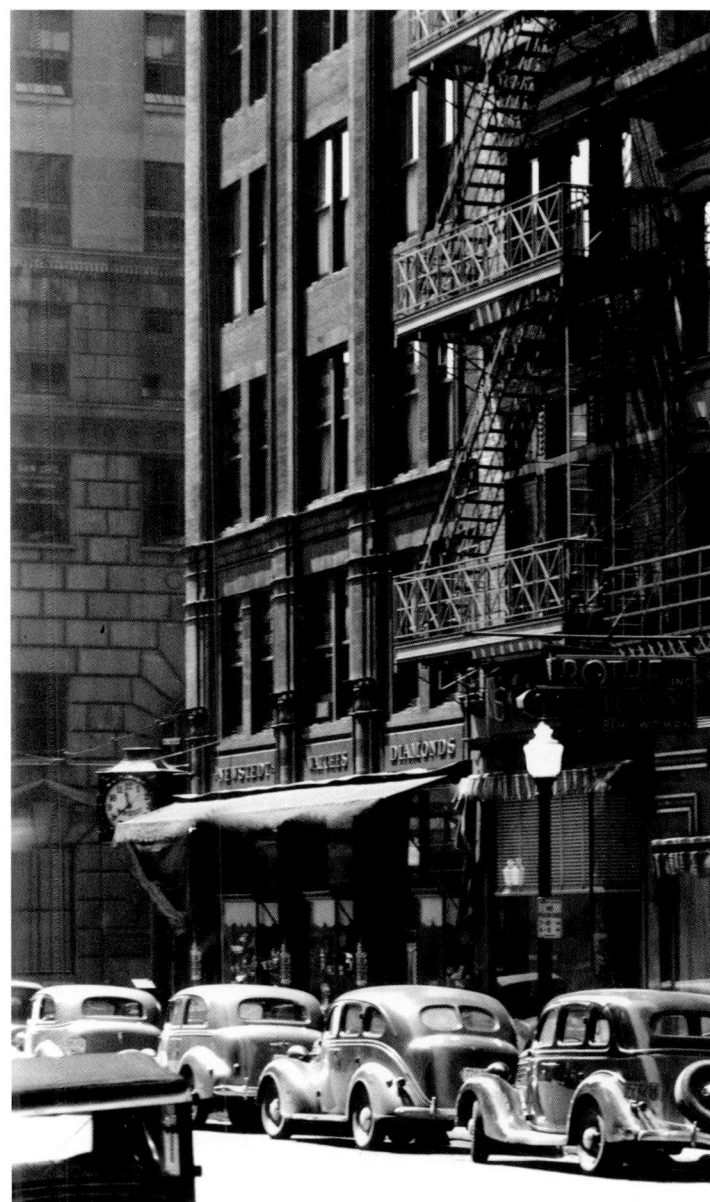

FIG. 93.2: Newstedt's, northwest corner of Fourth and Race, SC#156-246, Cincinnati Historical Society

in the family business.[18] The family lived in the Cincinnati neighborhood of Hyde Park. In addition to his activities as a successful retailer, Newstedt was a prize-winning golfer and a member of the Queen City Club, Rotary Club, Masonic Lodge, and Cincinnati Retail Jewelers' Association.[19]

The name of Newstedt's firm changed to The George H. Newstedt Co. around 1923.[20] In 1943, Newstedt's son Tudor was listed as a co-proprietor and the firm was listed as George H. Newstedt & Co.[21] Following George Newstedt's death in February 1953, business was continued by Tudor Newstedt until 1956.[22] Around 1958, city directories indicate another change in name and management, when the firm became known as Newstedt's and was operated by George Newstedt's daughter, Elizabeth N. Hall.[23] In 1965, the firm merged with Loring Andrews & Ratterman, Inc., successor to **The Loring Andrews Co.**[24] This merger was most likely initiated by the loss of Newstedt's long-time location on the northwest corner of Fourth and Race Streets to urban renewal. Newstedt-Loring Andrews operated at 27 West Fourth Street until 1992.[25] In 1969, the firm opened a suburban location in Hyde Park, and later another in Kenwood Towne Center, where it operated until 1996.[26] The business continues to operate as a jewelry store on Erie Avenue in Hyde Park Square.[27]

1. Family reminiscence, George H. Newstedt research file, Cincinnati Art Museum, Decorative Arts & Design Department; George H. Newstedt, burial record, Spring Grove Cemetery, Cincinnati, Ohio.
2. Ancestry.com, *New York Passenger Lists, 1820–1957* [online database], Provo, Utah: Ancestry.com Operations Inc., 2010; Ancestry.com, *U.S. Passport Applications, 1795–1925* [online database], Provo, Utah: Ancestry.com Operations Inc., 2007.
3. Family reminiscence, George H. Newstedt research file; 1878–1903 Cincinnati City Directories.
4. Family reminiscence, George H. Newstedt research file. Ancestry.com, *New York Passenger Lists, 1820–1957*; 1878–1903 Cincinnati City Directories; August Newstedt married Anna Duhme (1876–1946), granddaughter of Herman G. Duhme, founder of Duhme & Co., and daughter of Herman Duhme (1851–1923). August Newstedt, Anna Newstedt, burial records, Spring Grove Cemetery; August Newstedt worked for Bene & Lindberg, see "Cincinnati," *Jewelers' Circular and Horological Review* (March 6, 1901): 51. In the 1920 Federal Census, Cincinnati, Hamilton, Ohio, his occupation is given as dealer in wholesale jewelry.
5. 1940 Federal Census, Cincinnati, Hamilton, Ohio; Family reminiscence, George H. Newstedt research file.
6. Family reminiscence, George H. Newstedt research file; George Newstedt, obituary, *Cincinnati Enquirer*, February 23, 1953; 1891–1905 Cincinnati City Directories; The American Watch & Jewelry Co. was located at the northeast corner of Fourth and Plum Streets (1891–1896), and later at the southeast corner of Race and Longworth Streets (1897–1905).
7. Family reminiscence, George H. Newstedt research file; 1894–1898 Cincinnati City Directories.
8. George Newstedt, obituary, February 23, 1953; 1901 Cincinnati City Directory; "Cincinnati," *JCHR* (September 12, 1900): 52.
9. Ibid.
10. "Cincinnati," *JCHR* (May 28, 1902): 60; "Declines to Surrender Desirable Leased Store to Permit New Building," *JCHR* (December 18, 1901): 21; "Cincinnati," *JCHR* (March 5, 1902): 54; "Cincinnati," *JCHR* (April 16, 1902): 64; "Victory Gained by Newstedt," *Cincinnati Enquirer*, April 25, 1902, 10; "Cincinnati," *JCHR* (April 30, 1902): 59; "Cincinnati," *JCHR* (May 7, 1902): 57; "Cincinnati," *JCHR* (May 21, 1902): 55; "Declares He Will Hold Fort," *Cincinnati Enquirer*, December 11, 1901, 12.
11. "Cincinnati," *JCHR* (August 9, 1905): 63.
12. "Cincinnati," *JCHR* (September 13, 1905): 73.
13. Newstedt dealt in cut glass between 1904 and 1908; "Cincinnati," *JCHR* (September 2, 1908): 88; "Cincinnati," *JCHR* (September 21, 1904): 76; Mention of his watch repairing department is found here: "Cincinnati," *JCHR* (April 3, 1907): 83; "Selecting a gold watch for Billy at Newstedt's," *Cincinnati Enquirer*, April 22, 1910, 14.
14. "Men and Matters," *Cincinnati Enquirer*, March 27, 1914, 11; George Newstedt, obituary, February 23, 1953.
15. George Newstedt, eBay listings and private collections, Cincinnati silver binders, Cincinnati Art Museum.
16. "Burglars," *Cincinnati Enquirer*, July 25, 1904, 5.
17. "Cincinnati," *JCHR* (March 6, 1901): 51; Marriage record, Hamilton County Probate Records, vol. 152, 237, http://www.probatect.org/CourtRecordsArchive/bukmarriages.aspx; "Mrs. Anna Tudor Dies," *Cincinnati Enquirer*, July 16, 1920, 5; Ann T. Newstedt, burial record, Spring Grove Cemetery.
18. Burial records, Spring Grove Cemetery; 1910, 1920, 1930 Federal Censuses, Cincinnati, Hamilton, Ohio; George Newstedt, obituary, February 23, 1953.
19. George Newstedt, obituary, February 23, 1953; "Preparations Complete for First Biennial Convention of the Retail Jewelers Information Association of Cincinnati, O.," *JCHR* (August 21, 1912): 73; "Cincinnati," *JCHR* (October 2, 1912): 119; "Cincinnati," *JCHR* (October 9, 1912): 110.
20. 1923 Cincinnati City Directory.
21. 1943–1956 Cincinnati City Directories.
22. 1953–1956 Cincinnati City Directories. There is no listing for the firm in the 1957 City Directory.
23. In addition to Elizabeth Hall, her sons Richard T. Hall, David N. Hall, and daughter Marjorie (Mrs. Edward Wagner) are also listed as proprietors. 1958–1965 Cincinnati City Directories.
24. 1965 Cincinnati City Directory.
25. "After 191 years, jeweler to close," *Cincinnati Post*, April 12, 1996; 1965–1992 Cincinnati City Directories.
26. "After 191 years, jeweler to close," April 12, 1996.
27. Ibid.; 2013 Cincinnati City Directory.

94. OSKAMP & BRO.

1856/57, 1859

The firm of Oskamp & Bro. was one of two concerns maintained by Lewis (b. 1828) and Augustus Oskamp (b. about 1836–1889), brothers of **Clemens** and **Theodore Oskamp**.[1] In 1853, they established their first retail firm, Oskamp & Co. (1853–1862), specializing in imported watches, jewelry, and clocks.[2] It was located at 16 Sycamore Street, near Pearl Street. In March 1856 they were reported to have owned some real estate, and to have invested $15,000 to $20,000 in Oskamp & Co.[3] Although they were said to be of excellent character, prudent, and regarded with general favor, they were not deemed to be in very comfortable circumstances.[4] At the end of 1856, or in the very early months of 1857, they formed the wholesale firm of Oskamp & Bro. at 72 Main Street.[5] Oskamp & Bro. advertised (fig. 94.1) · as "IMPORTERS AND WHOLESALE Dealers in Watches, Jewelry, Clocks, Watch Material Tools, Plated Ware &c."[6]

Between May 1857 and March 1859 Lewis partnered with Benjamin (Bernard) Schwegman (b. about 1822–1889) to form Oskamp & Schwegman, which maintained the same specialization as Oskamp & Bro. and continued business at the same Main Street location.[7] During this period, neither Augustus nor Oskamp & Bro. appeared in the city directories.[8]

On March 17, 1859, Oskamp & Bro. announced their relocation to 108 Main Street, above Third Street, "where they will still be happy to wait on their old friends and customers."[9] While Oskamp & Bro. was included in the 1860 Cincinnati City Directory, R.G. Dun & Co. reports that Lewis and Augustus had dissolved their partnership by January 1860.[10] As part of their dissolution agreement, Augustus took over the 120-acre farm that the brothers co-owned in Miamiville, Clermont Co., and no capital was taken out of the business. Lewis continued at their Main Street stand working under his own name until 1861 (fig. 94.2), when he ran into trouble with creditors.[11] Following Lewis' failure, the business was put in Augustus' name. While Augustus ran his farm and created a successful business in trading horses and cashmere goats, Lewis ran the store.[12] Much of the stock, according to credit reporters, came from Lewis' brother, Clemens, who paid Lewis a "liberal commission" on his sales.[13] The firm of Augustus Oskamp relocated to 36 West Fifth Street in 1865, and continued there until 1868.[14] In 1869, Augustus partnered with James Bindley, Jr.(1843–1896) to create Oskamp & Bindley, but withdrew from the firm less than a year later.[15] Augustus presumably retired from the business at this time and returned to his farm in Miamiville, where he died

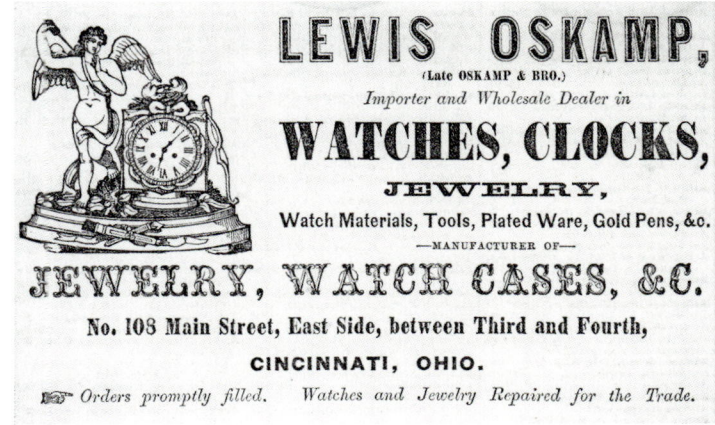

FIG. 94.1: Advertisement, *Cincinnati Enquirer*, March 3, 1859, 2

FIG. 94.2: Advertisement, *William's Cincinnati City Directory*, Cincinnati: C.S Williams, 1861, 42

in September 1889 after a long illness.[16] According to the 1869 and 1871 City Directories, Lewis was working at the northeast corner of Main and Pearl, the same address as **Clemens Hellebush**'s establishment.

Silver marked by Oskamp & Bro. is very rare. To date, only a small number of tablespoons with tipped, exaggerated fiddle handles and pointed shoulders have been documented with mark 94.1.[17] It is unlikely that Oskamp & Bro. produced any of the silver that bears the firm's mark. Silver marked by the other firms in which Lewis and Augustus were involved has not been found.

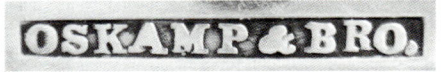

MARK 94.1

1. Ancestry.com, *New York Passenger Lists, 1820–1850* [online database], Provo, Utah: Ancestry.com Operations Inc., 2003; 1860 Federal Census, Cincinnati, Hamilton, Ohio; 1860, 1870, and 1880 Federal Censuses, Miami Township, Clermont, Ohio; 1900 Federal Census, Middletown, Butler, Ohio; Lewis' name is spelled Louis in some census and city directory listings, but his advertisements listed him as Lewis.

2. 1853–1862 Cincinnati City Directories; An 1856 report from R.G. Dun & Co. notes that the brothers had commenced "some 5 or 6 years ago in a very small way with limited means." Ohio, Vol. 2, p. 78, R.G. Dun & Co. Collection, Baker Library, Harvard Business School; Ohio, Vol. 1, p. 360, R.G. Dun & Co. Collection; According to information gleaned from the Cincinnati city directories, partners in Oskamp & Co. in 1858 were Lewis Oskamp and Henry Stagman, who was employed as a watch maker at Oskamp & Co. in 1857. In 1859, partners in the firm were L. Oskamp, Benjamin Schwegman, and H. Stagman. In 1860, partners were L. Oskamp and H. Stagman. In 1861, partners were Augustus Oskamp and H. Stagman.

3. Ohio, Vol. 2, p. 78, R.G. Dun & Co. Collection.

4. Ibid.

5. 1857 Cincinnati City Directory.

6. Advertisement, *Cincinnati Enquirer*, March 3, 1859, 2.

7. 1858, 1859 Cincinnati City Directories; Ohio, Vol. 2, p. 78, R.G. Dun & Co. Collection; Advertisement, *Cincinnati Enquirer*, June 7, 1857, 2; In city directories, Schwegman was listed as both Benjamin and Bernard. Prior to his involvement with Oskamp, he operated a wholesale fruit and candy store, coffee shop, and eating saloon. Following his partnership with Oskamp, he returned to dealing in food and beverage commodities. 1846–1869 Cincinnati City Directories; 1850, 1870, 1880 Federal Censuses, Cincinnati, Hamilton, Ohio; Bernard Schwegman, death record, Cincinnati Health Department, University of Cincinnati Archives and Rare Books Library, http://hdl.handle.net/2374.UC/520460

8. 1858, 1859 Cincinnati City Directories; The absence of a listing for Augustus Oskamp may be explained by his move to a farm in Clermont County by 1860 or earlier. 1860 Federal Census, Miami, Clermont, Ohio.

9. Advertisement, *Cincinnati Enquirer*, March 18, 1859, 2; "City Matters," *Cincinnati Enquirer*, March 17, 1859, 2.

10. Ohio, Vol. 2, p. 78, R.G. Dun & Co. Collection.

11. Ibid.

12. Ohio, Vol. 2, p. 91, R.G. Dun & Co. Collection.

13. Ohio, Vol. 2, p. 78, R.G. Dun & Co. Collection.

14. 1865–1868 Cincinnati City Directories.

15. Ohio, Vol. 7, p. 179, R.G. Dun & Co. Collection; 1869 Cincinnati City Directory; Bindley was the son of a master carpenter. He was active as an attorney as well as a jewelry merchant; Jas. Bindley, burial record, Spring Grove Cemetery, Cincinnati, Ohio; 1860, 1870, 1880 Federal Censuses, Cincinnati, Hamilton, Ohio; 1874–1880 Cincinnati City Directories.

16. Augustus Oskamp, death notice, *Cincinnati Enquirer*, September 18, 1889.

17. Oskamp & Bro., eBay listings and private collections, Cincinnati silver binders, Cincinnati Art Museum.

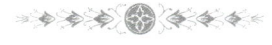

95. OSKAMP JEWELRY CO.

1904–1930

When **Oskamp, Nolting & Co.** discontinued their retail business to focus on the wholesale trade in February 1904, William S.P. Oskamp purchased **Charles A. Nolting**'s interest in their retail stock and Carew Building store. The new endeavour, named Oskamp Jewelry Co., was managed by Oskamp's son William Herbert Oskamp (1881–1931).[1] A 1906 advertisement for the firm describes a varied stock which included silver wares (fig. 95.1).[2] Most, if not all, of the firm's stock was likely purchased in the East and abroad.[3]

In September 1908 a newspaper report confirmed rumors of the firm's imminent closure, explaining that William Herbert Oskamp wished to devote his time to other interests, and auction sales were held in November.[4] However, in January 1909, these sales were discontinued and it was announced that the firm would not close, but continue in business until their lease in the Carew Building expired in February 1910.[5] William Herbert Oskamp resigned and transferred his interest in the jewelry firm to his father in February 1909, and the firm relocated to a new store at the northwest corner

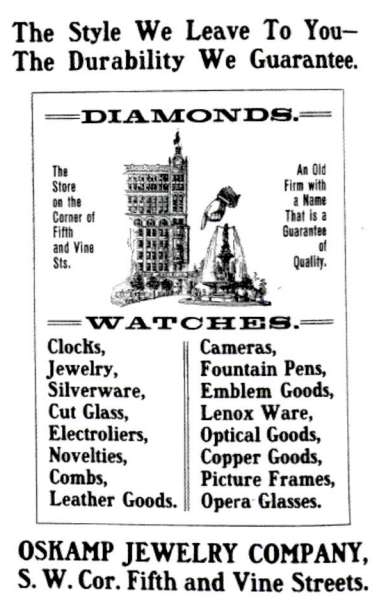

FIG. 95.1: Advertisement, *William's Cincinnati City Directory*, Cincinnati: Cincinnati Directory Office, 1906, 2064

of Seventh and Race Streets in March 1910 (fig. 95.2).[6] There, amid elaborate displays of diamonds, jewelry, and watches, was a "no less attractive" display of sterling silver ranging "from large tea sets and candelabra, through a complete line of tableware to the smallest pieces."[7] Additionally, "large chests of hardwood containing 150 to 300 pieces of table ware were much admired."[8] A new branch of the business, an auto and motor boat supply shop, was located in the building's basement.[9]

In 1921, Dixie Terminal, which was built for street-car transit, opened at Fourth and Walnut Streets. Oskamp Jewelry Co. moved there to the 10-story north building, which housed railroad ticket agencies, the Cincinnati Stock Exchange, administrative offices of the Cincinnati Street Railway Company, commercial offices, and shops. Upon the announcement of the firm's twenty-year lease of the space at Dixie Terminal, representatives from the Terminal Company proclaimed that it was their goal "to make Fourth Street what Fifth Avenue is to New York City," and therefore sought to attract the "most exclusive specialty shops in the Middle West."[10] A local reporter, window shopping at the Terminal in October 1921, noted a Colonial-style tea and coffee service in the window of Oskamp Jewelry Co. and published an engraving that depicts a partial view of the jewelry store's interior with his article (fig. 95.3).[11] Later directory listings indicate that the firm continued to deal primarily in diamonds, watches, silverware, and cut glass.[12] The last listing for the firm appeared in the 1930/31 City Directory.

Mark 95.1 has been observed on a sauceboat, and on a tray (fig. 95.4) with the Frank M. Whiting Co. (North Attleboro, Massachusetts) manufacturer's mark. Cincinnati souvenir spoons by Manchester Silver Co. (Providence, Rhode Island) and teaspoons by Towle Mfg. Co. (Newburyport, Massachusetts) in their "Old Colonial" (1895) pattern have been found with the incuse mark "OSKAMP JEWELRY CO."[13]

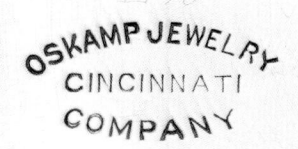

MARK 95.1

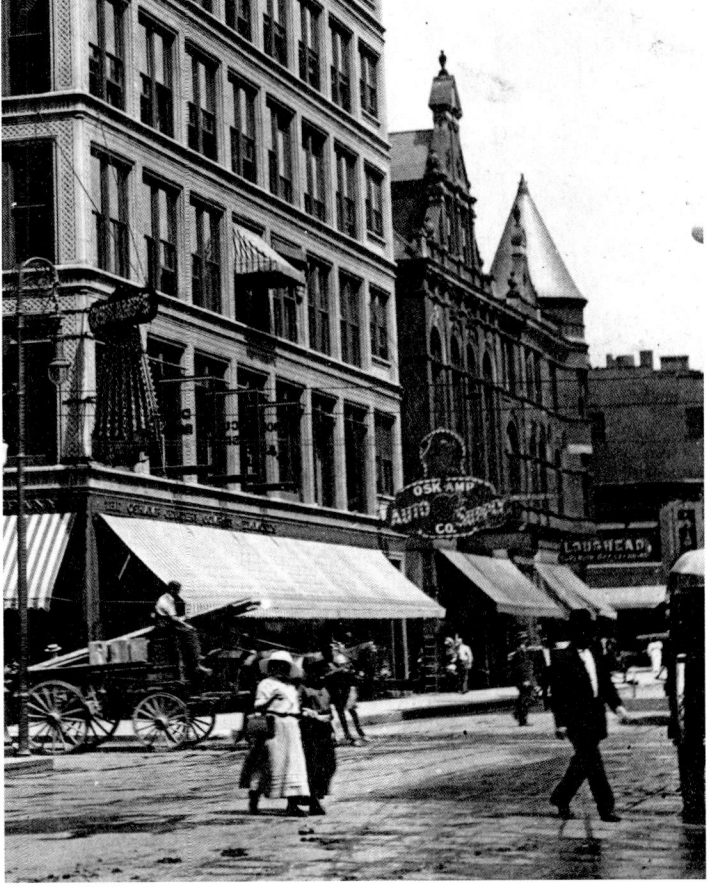

FIG. 95.2: Oskamp Jewelry Company and Oskamp Auto Supply Company, northwest corner, Seventh and Race Streets, Cincinnati Historical Society

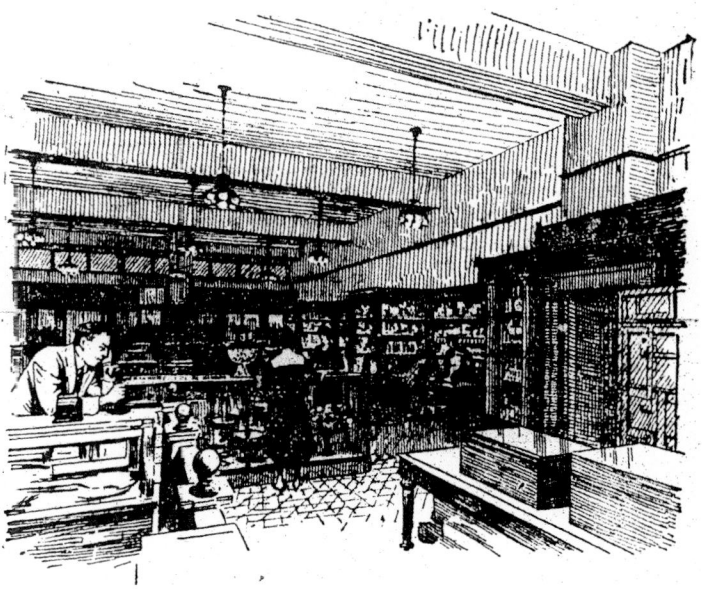

FIG. 95.3: Oskamp Jewelry Company, from Francis Clement Faulkner, "Cure For Blues is Found," *Cincinnati Enquirer*, October 30, 1921, G7

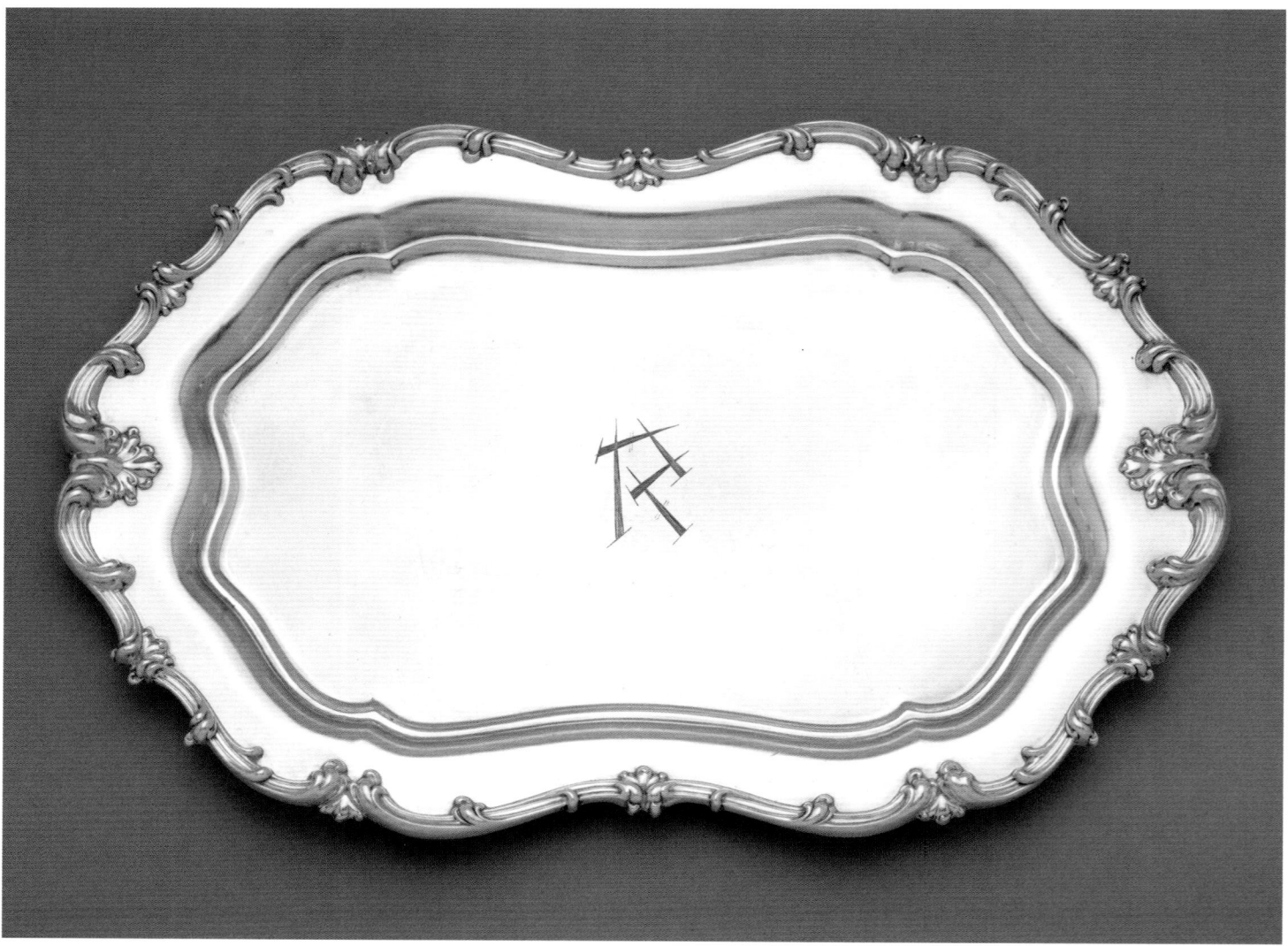

FIG. 95.4: Oskamp Jewelry Co., retailer, Frank M. Whiting Co., manufacturer, (estab. 1896, closed 1940), *Tray*, 1896–1930, 14 × 9⅛ in. (35.6 × 23.2 cm), CAM, Gift of James Randolph Hillard, M.D. and Aingeal Grehan, 2007.205

1. "Cincinnati," *Jewelers' Circular and Horological Review* (February 10, 1904): 61; "Cincinnati," *JCHR* (September 30, 1908): 95; The Carew Building was located at the southwest corner of Fifth and Vine Streets; William Herbert Oskamp, burial record, Spring Grove Cemetery, Cincinnati, Ohio.
2. 1906 Cincinnati City Directory, 2064. Similar advertisements in the city directories of 1907 and 1908 include "Bohemian Ware" in the list of available commodities, and the word "DESIGNERS" appears in bold

typeface at the bottom of the advertisement.
3. "Cincinnati," *JCHR* (July 20, 1904): n.p.; "Cincinnati," *JCHR* (October 11, 1905): 74.
4. "Cincinnati," *JCHR* (September 30, 1908): 95; "Interesting: History of an Interesting Corner," *Cincinnati Enquirer*, September 24, 1908, 7; "Cincinnati," *JCHR* (November 11, 1908): 95.
5. "Cincinnati," *JCHR* (January 6, 1909): 82.
6. "Cincinnati," *JCHR* (February 24, 1909): 83; "Gems Flashed Amid

Flowers At Opening of New Store of the Oskamp Jewelry Company on Race Street," *Cincinnati Enquirer*, March 16, 1910, 8.
7. Ibid.
8. Ibid.
9. "Auto and Motor Boat: Supplies Handled Over Large Territory By the Oskamp Auto Supply Company," *Cincinnati Enquirer*, August 21, 1910, D6; William S.P. Oskamp and his sons E. Gordon Oskamp (1884–1976) and William Werk Oskamp (1886–1976) were the principals of the Oskamp Auto Supply Co.; 1910

Cincinnati City Directory; E. Gordon Oskamp and William Werk Oskamp, burial records, Spring Grove Cemetery.
10. "Makes Twenty-Year Lease," *Cincinnati Enquirer*, April 20, 1917, 3.
11. Francis Clement Faulkner, "Cure For Blues is Found," *Cincinnati Enquirer*, October 30, 1921, G7.
12. 1926–1930 Cincinnati City Directories.
13. Oskamp Jewelry Co., eBay listings and private collections, Cincinnati silver binders, Cincinnati Art Museum.

96. CLEMENS OSKAMP

1822–1887, w. about 1850–1887

CLEMENS OSKAMP (THE FIRM)

1854–1902

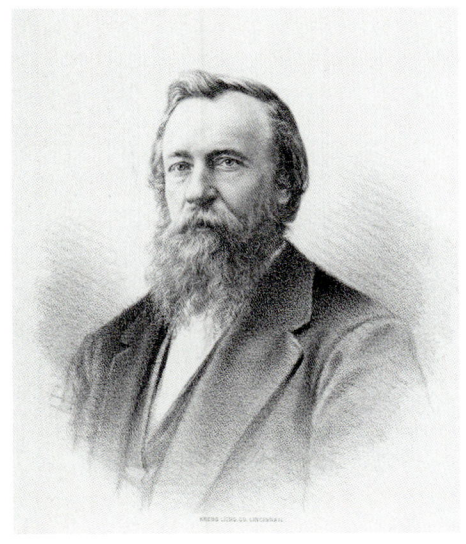

FIG. 96.1: Clemens Oskamp, from Van Armin Tenner, *Cincinnati Sonst Und Jetzt*, Cincinnati: Druck van Mecklenborg & Rosentahl, 1878, 64

Clemens Oskamp (fig. 96.1) was born in Westphalia, Prussia, on August 19, 1822, to Theresa (b. about 1794, d. after 1854) and Joseph Casper Oskamp (b. about 1777), a farrier.[1] The Oskamp family boarded the *Ship of New York* in Bremen, to avoid Prussian military service, and arrived in New York on June 19, 1838.[2] Clemens was one of at least seven children, and his brothers **Theodore**, Lewis, and Augustus (see **Oskamp & Bro.**), and Augustus' son **Joseph A. Oskamp** were also, at one time or another, involved in Cincinnati's silver, jewelry, watch, clock, and fancy goods trade. Clemens apprenticed with Anthony Harkness (b. about 1793–1858), who owned an iron foundry, and learned the trade of brass finishing.[3] In 1844 and 1846, Clemens was boarding and working as a finisher and is said to have played a part in the production of the first locomotive built in Cincinnati.[4] Following his apprenticeship, "in search of a field for his remarkable aptitude as a machinist," Clemens headed south and for a few years worked in the construction of machinery.[5] He is listed in the 1849/50 Cincinnati Directory as a finisher but around this time, he joined his brother Theodore Oskamp in his watch, clock, and jewelry busi-

ness at 62 Main Street.[6] Clemens "devoted all of his spare hours to acquiring a thorough knowledge of the watchmakers art, wherein he was greatly assisted by his knowledge of mechanics."[7] When Theodore died in 1854, Clemens took over the business.[8]

In addition to building up the business that now operated under his name, Clemens Oskamp began purchasing a number of properties in the city, which he rented for additional income. In 1859, credit reporters noted that financially, he was better off than all of his brothers. They estimated his worth to be between $50,000 and $60,000 in 1861, and by 1867, he was believed to be worth about $100,000, which included the $5,000 he drew each year in rent from his real estate.[9] In 1868, Oskamp built a five-story building (fig. 96.2) on the west side of Vine Street, between

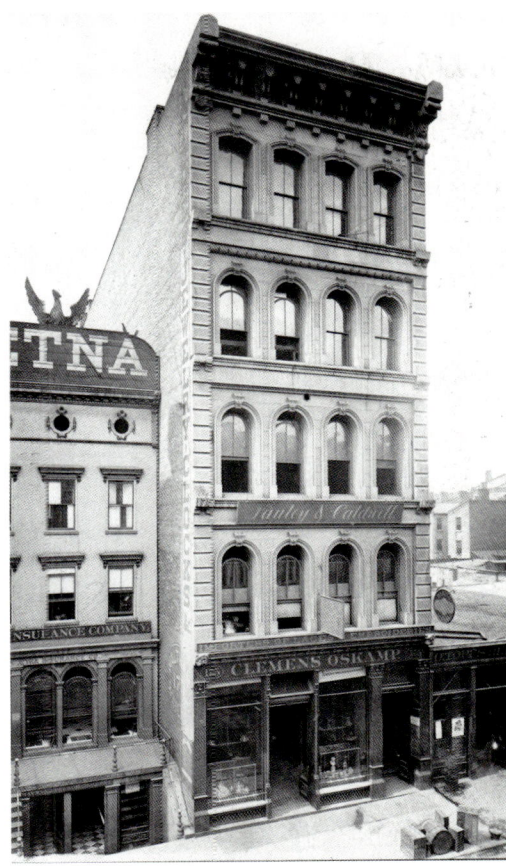

FIG. 96.2: Clemens Oskamp, 175 Vine Street, "Views of Cincinnati Business Houses 1873," Cincinnati Historical Society

Fourth and Fifth Streets (175 Vine Street).[10] He had relocated his wholesale business there by February 1869, and expanded into the retail business.[11] Considerable in scale, the frontage of his store measured 30 feet and its depth 100 feet, and his trade was said to have doubled.[12]

Oskamp's stock included watches, diamonds, solid silverware, plated ware, clocks, jewelry, bronzes, and other fancy goods.[13] He purchased directly from the diamond markets in Europe and employed "many of the best setters in the country."[14] A newspaper article in 1870 notes the store's stock of silver from the Gorham Mfg. Co. (Providence, Rhode Island) was "guaranteed to be of sterling quality." It goes on to say that "No spoons or forks are offered by Mr. Oskamp except [those] made of such fine metal."[15]

In September 1874 Oskamp announced the opening of his new silverware manufactory at the corner of Harrison and Culvert Streets (fig. 96.3).[16] The three-story building had a front of 25 feet and a depth of 100 feet (fig. 96.4).[17] Oskamp had purchased the complete silverware manufacturing business of silversmith Francis A. Bunnell (1830–1896) of Syracuse, New York.[18] Evidence for this exists in the fact that many of the silver patterns produced by Bunnell and marked by him were also found with the manufacturer marks of Clemens Oskamp. Bunnell's "Fox Head" pattern is one such example.[19] In 1875, Bunnell appears in the Cincinnati city directory as a foreman, boarding and working at Culvert and Harrison Streets. In the city for a year or less, most likely without his family, he was undoubtedly here to help Oskamp set up the manufactory. Oskamp advertised, "We are making everything in the Table-Ware line, from a Salt Spoon to a Soup Ladle. We guarantee our silver to be of the fineness of U.S. coin, and are finishing our Ware equal to the best."[20] The factory was said to contain "the newest and most perfect machinery and devices," which enabled the firm "to turn out patterns of workmanship of the most exquisite and beautiful finish."[21] Oskamp advertised "COMPLETE WEDDING OUTFITS made to order at short notice" that could be ready and cased in "elegant Morocco or Black Walnut Cases."[22] An 1875 advertisement designed with bold letters read, "ARE YOU AWARE that we are Headquarters for Silver Ware of all kinds, our own manufacture?"[23] In December of that year, another advertisement proclaimed, "WE HAVE CONTINUED manufacturing Solid Silver Ware during the whole of the past summer, and having accumulated an immense stock of no less than ONE THOUSAND DOZENS [sic] SILVER SPOONS AND FORKS, together with a large variety of Fancy Pieces, have determined to offer these goods at a very slight advance above the actual cost for production . . ."[24] In 1875, Oskamp's display at the Cincinnati Industrial Exposition included solid silverware for the first time.[25]

A fire at the manufactory on June 10, 1876, did not deter Oskamp.[26] He announced (fig. 96.5) that he was "IN THE FIELD AGAIN" on July 20, 1876, and "HAVING COMPLETELY REBUILT MY FACTORY recently damaged by fire, I am now better than ever prepared to fill all orders for the manufacture of Solid Silver and Gold Ware."[27] With examples of his wares on view in his salesroom, he invited the public to "see what Cincinnati is doing in the way of utilizing precious metals." He also called special attention to his solid silver spoons that "being made by the new process, besides being more durable, admit of a finer polish than those made the old way."[28] In December, Oskamp announced that "Notwithstanding the hard times, we have continued running our Factory full time during the whole summer, both in Jewelry as well as in the Silverware Departments. We have been able to do this by making concessions on our production in order to dispose of it . . . Silver Spoons are also reduced so that we are actually selling solid silver Teaspoons for $6 per set, which is but little more than the price of triple plate."[29] His teaspoons continued to sell at this price through 1879.[30]

Oskamp billed himself as a silversmith in many of his advertisements, but it is doubtful that he was so in the traditional sense. While he would have been quite familiar with the mechanics of his operations, he had a number of skilled hands working for him.[31] In the 1880 Products of Industry Census, he reported as a jeweler with $5,000 worth of capital, employing, at most, 33 hands at one

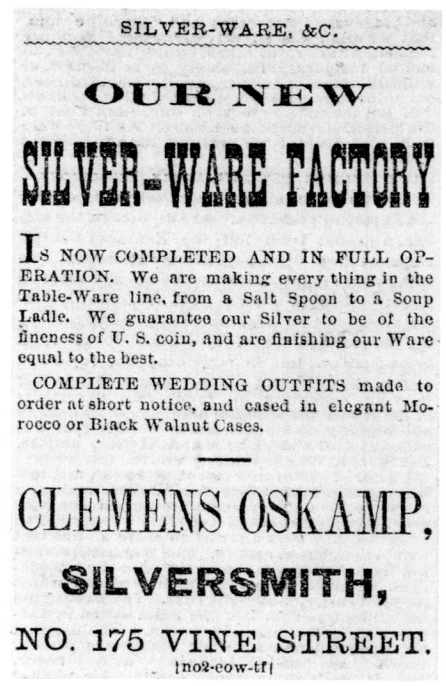

FIG. 96.3: Advertisement, *Cincinnati Enquirer*, September 2, 1874, 8

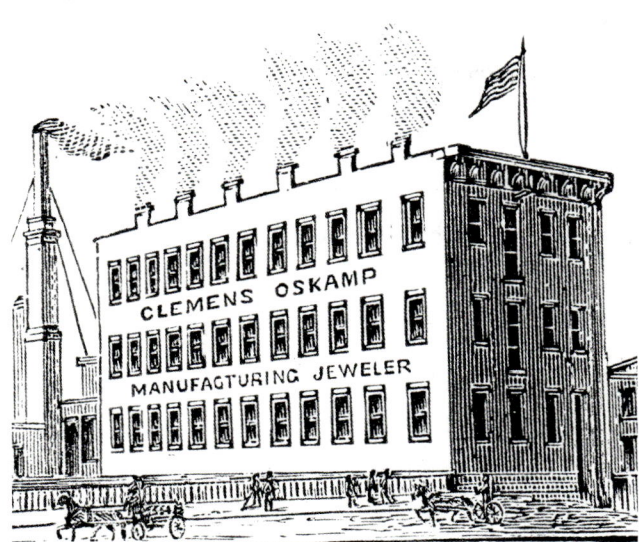

ABOVE: FIG. 96.4: Clemens Oskamp's manufactory, Daniel J. Kenny, *Illustrated Cincinnati: A Pictorial Handbook*, Cincinnati: G.E. Stevens, 1875, 211

RIGHT: FIG. 96.5: Advertisement, *Cincinnati Enquirer*, July 20, 1876, 8

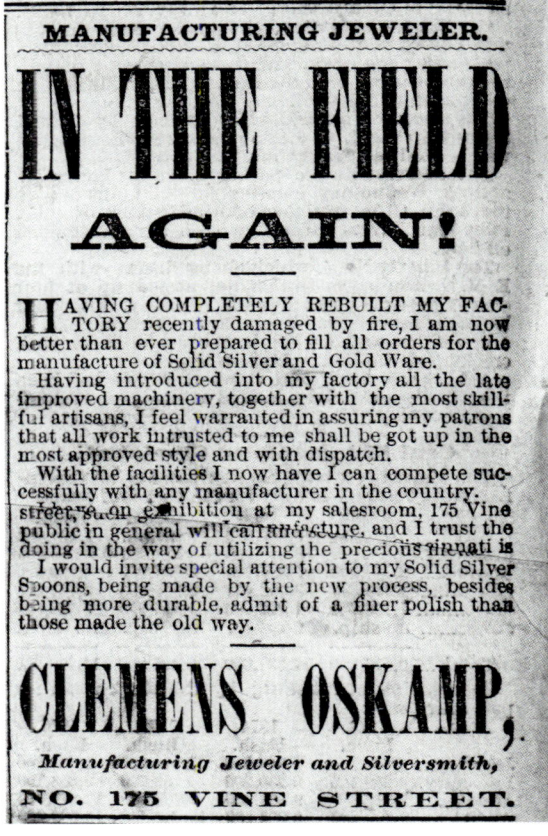

time (averaging twenty men, two women, and eight children), paying a total of $20,000 in annual wages and working ten hours a day. The business had operated full time for six months that year. Skilled mechanics were paid $3 an hour, while "ordinary laborers" were paid $2 an hour. Material worth $3,000 was utilized to create $30,000 worth of product.[32]

By and large, manufacturing and importing goods for the wholesale trade was the firm's principal business, and it was reported that, during the season, dealers from various parts of the country could be observed in Oskamp's wholesale department "laying in supplies." His wholesale department was reportedly so complete and his goods sold at such reasonable prices, that retailers could buy as cheaply at Oskamps as they could in the large cities of the East, and consequently save themselves the trouble of traveling long distances by simply purchasing at his store.[33] His traveling salesmen went far and wide at regular intervals with large stocks of goods, and the firm's trade was established in the states of Virginia, Iowa, Kansas, Illinois, Tennessee, Indiana, Kentucky, Michigan, and Arkansas.[34]

With reference to the range of silver wares offered by Oskamp, an 1881 advertisement reads, "If you want to see an elegant display of Silverware, such as Tea Sets, Ice Sets, Fruit Stands, Toilets,

Casters, Cake Baskets, Card Baskets, Vases, Scent Jugs and in fact everything that is desirable in the way of Silverware, then call at the old established Jewelry store of CLEMENS OSKAMP."[35] We also know from other advertisements and extant wares that he made silver combs, and flatware in a number of different patterns.[36] Oskamp retailed much of what was made at his manufactory, as well as works produced by other firms. Silver wares (mostly flatware) that bear his marks alongside the manufacturer marks of Joseph Seymour & Co. (Syracuse), Francis A. Bunnell & Co. (Syracuse), Frank M. Whiting Co. (North Attleboro, Massachusetts), Reed & Barton (Taunton, Massachusetts), and Towle Mfg. Co. (Newburyport, Massachusetts) have been documented.[37]

Mark 96.1 appears to have been Oskamp's manufacturer mark.[38] It has been documented on jewelry; spoons with exaggerated, tipped fiddle handles with pointed shoulders—one of which also bears the retailer mark of H. Terlau & Co. (Covington, Kentucky) and some that bear marks (probably of journeymen) in the shape of an anchor and a cross; spoons with tipped fiddle handles and pointed shoulders; a spoon with a tipped fiddle handle and minimal shoulders; flatware in the "Fox Head" pattern; spoons and forks with handles similar to **Duhme & Co.**'s "No. 1" (circa 1869) pattern, with straight and twist stems; and flatware in Oskamp's "Medallion" pattern.[39]

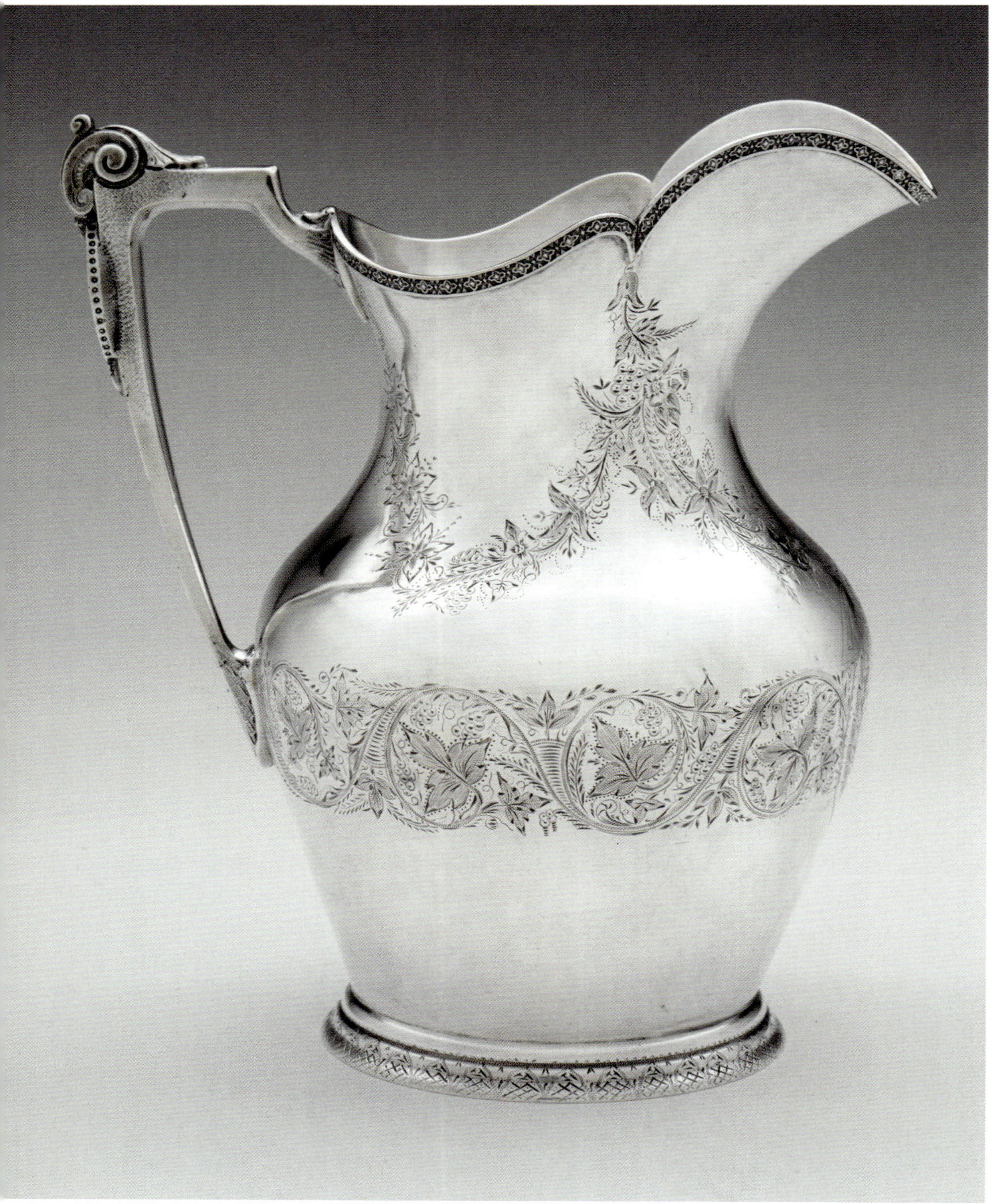

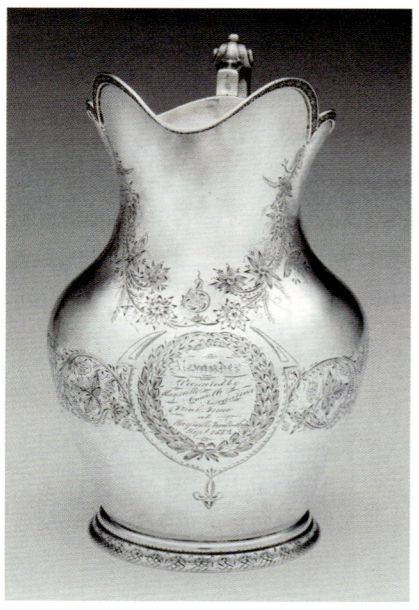

FIG. 96.6: Clemens Oskamp, *Pitcher*, c. 1882, 9½ × 8¾ in. (24.1 × 22.2 cm), CAM, Museum Purchase with funds provided by Mr. and Mrs. Charles Fleischmann III, 2005.33. Inscription: ALEXANDER Presented by Maysville A & M Association Trial Time at Maysville, Kentucky Sept. 1882

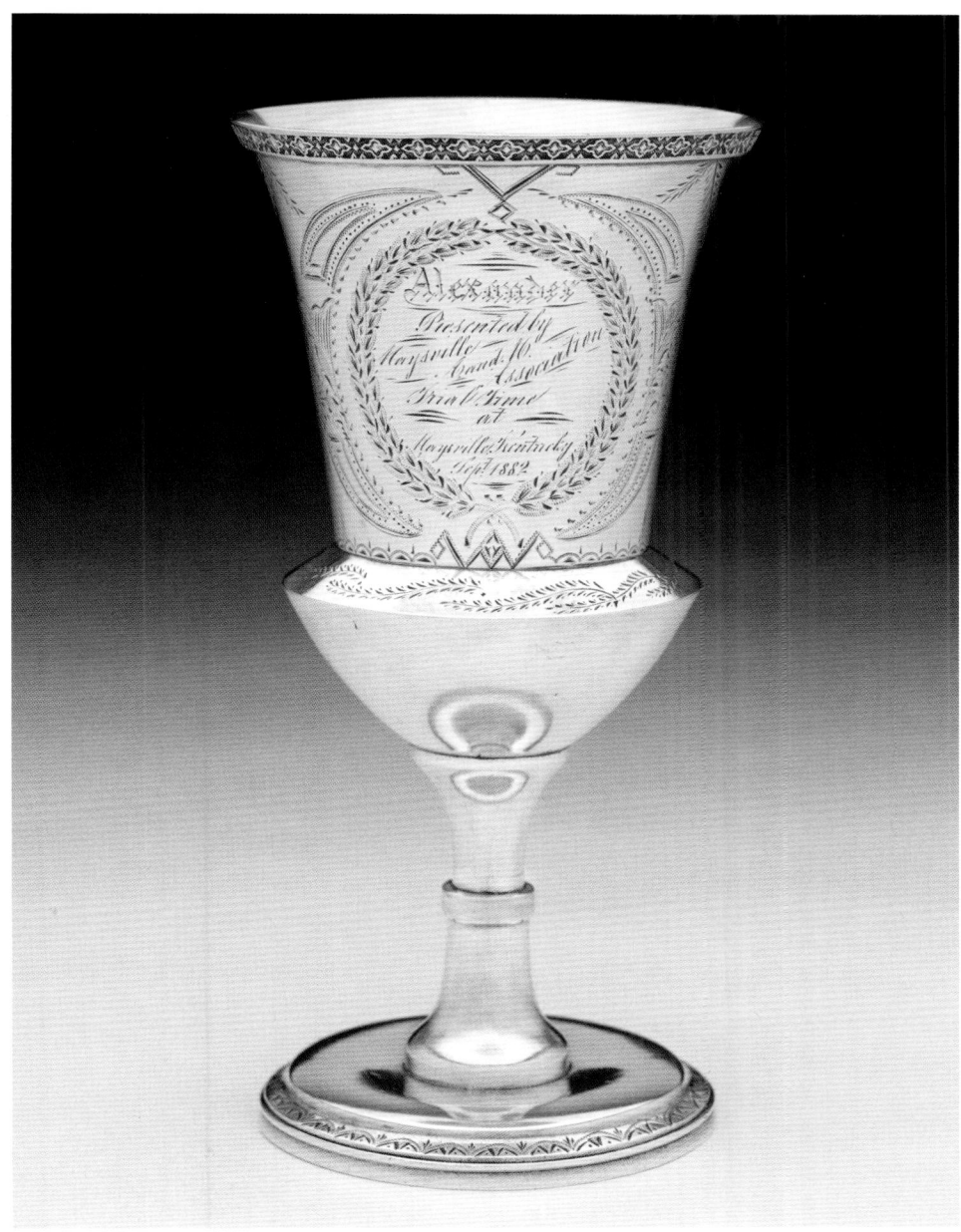

FIG. 96.7: Clemens Oskamp, *Goblet*, c. 1882, 6¾ × 3⅜ in. (17.1 × 8.6 cm), CAM, Museum Purchase with funds provided by Mr. and Mrs. Charles Fleischmann III, 2005.34. Inscription: ALEXANDER Presented by Maysville A & M Association Trial Time at Maysville, Kentucky Sept. 1882

The "Medallion" pattern features a bright-cut modified fiddle handle with nib terminal and an applied oval medallion with the profile of a woman.[40] An incuse "C.O." is also thought to be one of Oskamp's manufacturer marks. It appears on spoons with tipped, exaggerated fiddle handles and pointed shoulders (some of which are also struck with a journeyman's five-pointed star or eagle mark); flatware in Oskamp's "Medallion" pattern; spoons with handles similar to Duhme & Co.'s "No. 1" (circa 1869) pattern; and an unidentified die-pressed pattern with fiddle handle that features a flower at the tip and a border of leaves and pellets.[41] John R McGrew records instances where the incuse mark "C.O." is accom-panied by either a right-facing eagle or a much-deteriorated bust. It seems that these were journeyman marks and that these punches were first used in Connecticut before they were employed in Ohio.[42]

Mark 96.2 is believed to be a retail mark, as it appears in tandem with Oskamp's manufacturer marks as well as the manufacturer marks of other firms. It appears on die-pressed patterns by Whiting, Reed & Barton, and Towle, as well as spoons with tipped, exaggerated fiddle handles that bear the marks of Joseph Seymour.[43] Mark 96.2 appears on a pair of master salts and on the pitcher and goblet (figs. 96.6 and 96.7) presented as a prize in September 1882 by the Maysville A. & M. Association.[44]

Mark 96.3 is rarely seen. It has been found on a miniature beaker. An incuse mark, "CLEMENS OSKAMP" has been recorded on a berry spoon in an unidentified die-pressed pattern with fruit and foliage, patented October 11, 1887, with an illegible maker's mark.[45]

It is unclear how long Oskamp's silver manufactory operated. As late as 1887, advertisements noted him as a silversmith, but advertisements or notices that mention his manufactory do not appear after 1879.[46] This, combined with the knowledge that he was selling a lot of silver made by other makers between the 1880s and early 1900s suggests that the silver manufactory had closed sometime around 1880. In June 1897 the Hurlburt Tournament cup, purportedly designed by the firm, was declared "one of the finest specimens of silversmithing seen in Cincinnati for a long time."[47] It contained 30 ounces of sterling silver and was seven inches high and five inches in diameter. While it might have been designed and made by staff at Oskamp's as a special commission, it may well have been produced elsewhere.

On May 23, 1847, Oskamp wed Mary Fisher (b. Germany, 1824–1898) of Cincinnati.[48] They had eight children: Henry (1848–1927), who was working for his father by 1876, but eventually went into the furniture business; Amelia (about 1852–1917), who married Oskamp's longtime employee **John C. Daller** (1846–1919); Anna (b. about 1852); Clemens (1853–1937), who was in the cattle business in Wyoming Territory; William S.P. (1854–1933) and Alfred (1860–1941), who were both associated with their father's firm; Eleanor (b. about 1862), who married Fred Brunning; and Margaret Antoinette "Nettie" (b. about 1864) who married Starr Ford.[49] In addition to Clemens Oskamp's role as a leading businessman, he was a devout Catholic and served as president of the Catholic Institute. He was also a member of the Cincinnati Horticultural Society, Cincinnati's Board of Trade (1876–1881), the Acclimatization Society for the importation of song birds, the Cuvier Club, Mercer County Shooting Club, and president of the Zoological Garden (1877).[50]

Clemens Oskamp died of pneumonia and paralysis on April 7, 1887.[51] His estate, real and personal, was estimated to be worth $800,000. It was left to his wife, Mary, who also served as executrix of his will.[52] Her son Alfred and son-in-law John C. Daller bought her interest in the business and continued at the Vine Street location.[53] When Alfred left the business around 1893 to pursue the manufacture of mixed paints, his mother succeeded him as Daller's partner.[54] Daller had worked for Clemens Oskamp since 1860, and had married Amelia in 1872.[55] Mary Oskamp died in July 1898. The first codicil to her will gave Daller the right to purchase her remaining interest in the store at any time within the 20 year-period following her death. The second codicil named him sole

executor of the estate, and a handwritten statement, ostensibly executed by Mary Oskamp, absolved him of any debts he owed from the initial purchase of his partnership in the business.[56] The will, its codicils, and the note were contested by Mrs. Oskamp's heirs, but, ultimately, all were deemed valid by the courts.[57] Daller continued to run the store, and in 1900 bought the watch chain factory of George Herrmann to add to his existing jewelry manufacturing plant.[58] Alfred Oskamp "resumed his relations" with Daller and returned to the business in July 1899.[59] By the spring of 1902, following a careful appraisal of the company by **William Michie, Jr.** and **Albert Bros.**, and the finalizing of all the necessary payments from Daller and from the estate of Mary A. Oskamp to her heirs, Daller formed **The Clemens Oskamp Co.**[60]

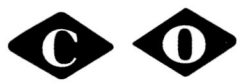

MARK 96.1

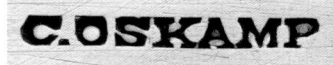

MARK 96.2

C.OSKAMP

MARK 96.3

1. Ancestry.com, *New York Passenger Lists, 1820–1957* [online database], Provo, Utah: Ancestry.com Operations Inc., 2010; 1850 Federal Census, Cincinnati, Hamilton, Ohio; Clemens Oskamp, burial record, Spring Grove Cemetery, Cincinnati, Ohio; "Clemens Oskamp," *Illustrated Graphic News* 7, no. 16 (April 16, 1887): 247; S.B. Nelson and J.M. Runk, *History of Cincinnati and Hamilton County, Ohio*, Cincinnati: S.B. Nelson & Co., 1894, 911; "Death's Victory: Mr. Clemens Oskamp, a Prominent Citizen, Passes Away," *Cincinnati Enquirer*, April 8, 1887, 4.

2. Ancestry.com, *New York Passenger Lists, 1820–1850* [online database], Provo, Utah: Ancestry.com Operations Inc., 2003; "Death's Victory: Mr. Clemens Oskamp, a Prominent Citizen, Passes Away," April 8, 1887.

3. 1839/40–1849/50 Cincinnati City Directories; Anthony Harkness, burial record, Spring Grove Cemetery; D.J. Kenny, "Clemens Oskamp," *Illustrated Cincinnati: A Pictorial Handbook*, Cincinnati: G.E. Stevens, 1875, 396; Nelson and Runk, *History of Cincinnati*, 911.

4. 1844, 1846 Cincinnati City Directories, "Death's Victory: Mr. Clemens Oskamp, a Prominent Citizen, Passes Away," April 8, 1887.

5. "Clemens Oskamp" (April 16, 1887).

6. Ibid.; Kenny, "Clemens Oskamp," 396; Ohio, Vol. 1, p. 247, R.G. Dun & Co. Collection, Baker Library, Harvard Business School.

7. Ibid

8. Theodore Oskamp, will dated September 3, 1854, proved September 25, 1854, vol. 17, p. 515, Hamilton County Registry of Probate, Cincinnati, Ohio.

9. Ohio, Vol. 1, pp. 247 and 259, R.G. Dun & Co. Collection; Ohio, Vol. 6, p. 198, R.G. Dun & Co. Collection.

10. Nelson and Runk, *History of Cincinnati*, 911; Advertisement, 1869 Cincinnati City Directory, 696; "Removal," *Cincinnati Enquirer*, February 10, 1869, 5; "The Holidays," *Cincinnati Daily Gazette*, December 2, 1870, 1; Kenny, "Clemens Oskamp," 396.

11. Ibid.

12. Ibid.; Nelson and Runk, *History of Cincinnati*, 911.

13. Ibid.; Kenny, "Clemens Oskamp," 396; Advertisement, *Cincinnati Enquirer*, December 23, 1869, 5.

14. "Christmas," *Cincinnati Daily Gazette*, December 21, 1872, 2.

15. "The Holidays," December 2, 1870.

16. Advertisement, *Cincinnati Enquirer*, September 2, 1874, 8.

17. Kenny, "Clemens Oskamp," 396.

18. R. David Ives, "Francis A. Bunnell and His Successor Clemens Oskamp," *Silver Magazine* (November/December 1991): 13.

19. Clemens Oskamp, eBay listings and private collections, Cincinnati silver binders, Cincinnati Art Museum; This pattern is sometimes also referred to as "Wolf's Head." It was a full line pattern. Single examples have been found to bear the incuse stamps of "C.O." and "C. OSKAMP" side by side.

20. Advertisement, *Cincinnati Enquirer*, September 9, 1874, 8.

21. Kenny, "Clemens Oskamp," 396.

22. Advertisement, *Cincinnati Enquirer*, September 2, 1874, 8.

23. Advertisement, *Cincinnati Commercial Tribune*, May 22, 1875, 12.

24. Advertisement, *Cincinnati Commercial Tribune*, December 21, 1875, 8.

25. In 1873, he exhibited clocks and watches; in 1874, plated wares; 1875, plated and solid silver wares; and in 1881, plated wares. He received a gold medal for his 1881 display. *Report of the Board of Commissioners of the Cincinnati Industrial Exposition held in Cincinnati, Ohio under the auspices of the Board of Trade, Chamber of Commerce and Ohio Mechanics' Institute, from September 8th to October 9th, 1875*, Cincinnati: Published by Order of the Board, 1875, 325; *Report of the Board of Commissioners of the Cincinnati Industrial Exposition held in Cincinnati, Ohio under the auspices of the Board of Trade, Chamber of Commerce and Ohio Mechanics' Institute, from September 3rd to October 4th, 1873*, Cincinnati: Published by Order of the Board, 1873, 187; *Report of the Board of Commissioners of the Cincinnati Industrial Exposition held in Cincinnati, Ohio under the auspices of the Board of Trade, Chamber of Commerce and Ohio Mechanics' Institute, from September 2nd to October 3rd, 1874*, Cincinnati: Published by Order of the Board, 1874, 253; D.J. Kenny, *Kenny's Cincinnati Exposition Guide and Catalogue of the Fine Arts Department . . . at the Fifth Cincinnati Industrial Exposition of 1874 . . .*, Cincinnati: Cincinnati Gazette Company, 1874, 75; *Report of the Board of Commissioners of the Cincinnati Industrial Exposition held in Cincinnati, Ohio under the auspices of the Board of Trade, Chamber of Commerce and Ohio Mechanics' Institute, from September 7th to October 8th, 1881*, Cincinnati: Published by Order of the Board, 1881, 177.

26. "Lively Times at Oskamp's," *Cincinnati Enquirer*, July 23, 1876, 8.

27. "Manufacturing Jeweler, In the Field Again," *Cincinnati Enquirer*, July 20, 1876, 8.

28. It is not known what this "new process" entailed. "Manufacturing Jeweler, In the Field Again," July 20, 1876, 9.

29. "Holiday Announcement of Clement[*sic*] Oskamp," *Cincinnati Daily Gazette*, December 16, 1876, 1

30. Advertisement, *Cincinnati Commercial Tribune*, December 11, 1879, 8.

31. "Manufacturing Jeweler, In the Field Again," July 20, 1876, 9.

32. 1880 Federal Non-Population Census Schedules, Products of Industry, Schedule 4, Hamilton County, Ohio.

33. Nelson and Runk, *History of Cincinnati*, 911; Kenny, "Clemens Oskamp," 396.

34. Kenny, "Clemens Oskamp," 396; Nelson and Runk, *History of Cincinnati*, 911.

35. Advertisement, *Cincinnati Commercial Tribune*, December 19, 1881, 8.

36. Advertisement, *Cincinnati Daily Gazette*, December 23, 1878, 1; D. Albert Soeffing, "A Medallion Pattern by Clemens Oskamp," *Silver Magazine* (November/December 1991): 16; Clemens Oskamp, eBay listings and private collections, Cincinnati Art Museum.

37. These double-marked flatware pieces are struck with an incuse "C. OSKAMP." Those patterns that could be identified are those that were patented between 1891 and 1902; Clemens Oskamp, eBay listings and private collections, Cincinnati Art Museum.

38. Mark 96.1 often appears in tandem with mark 96.2, which was probably Oskamp's retail mark.

39. Clemens Oskamp, eBay listings and private collections, Cincinnati Art Museum.

40. Soeffing, "A Medallion Pattern by Clemens Oskamp," (November/December 1991).

41. The unidentified pattern is stamped with mark 96.1 and mark 96.2 together, indicating that Oskamp manufactured and retailed it. Clemens Oskamp, eBay listings and private collections, Cincinnati Art Museum.

42. John R. McGrew, *Manufacturers' Marks on American Coin Silver*, Hanover, PA: Argyros Publications, 2004, 79, 96, 154.

43. Clemens Oskamp, eBay listings and private collections, Cincinnati Art Museum.

44. A. & M. Association probably refers to an Agricultural and Mechanical Association; *Pitcher* and *Goblet*, CAM, Museum Purchase with funds provided by Mr. and Mrs. Charles Fleischmann III, 2005.33, 2005.34; Clemens Oskamp, eBay listings and private collections, Cincinnati Art Museum.

45. Clemens Oskamp, eBay listings and private collections, Cincinnati Art Museum.

46. 1887 advertisement, sold on eBay, 2012, Clemens Oskamp, eBay listings and private collections, Cincinnati Art Museum.

47. "Cincinnati," *Jewelers' Circular and Horological Review* (June 16, 1897): 31; The current whereabouts of this cup are unknown.

48. "Clemens Oskamp" (April 16, 1887); Nelson and Runk, *History of Cincinnati*, 911; Mary A. Oskamp, burial record, Spring Grove Cemetery.

49. "Death's Victory: Mr. Clemens Oskamp, a Prominent Citizen, Passes Away." April 8, 1887; 1860, 1870, 1880 Federal Censuses, Cincinnati, Hamilton, Ohio; Burial records, Spring Grove Cemetery; Nelson and Runk, *History of Cincinnati*, 911; "Lively Times at Oskamp's," July 23, 1876; "Clemens Oskamp" (April 16, 1887); Mary A. Oskamp, will dated February 3, 1888, proved September 14, 1898, vol. 72, p. 393–414, Hamilton County Registry of Probate, Cincinnati, Ohio.

50. "Death's Victory: Mr. Clemens Oskamp, a Prominent Citizen, Passes Away," April 8, 1887; "Cincinnati Horticultural Society," *Cincinnati Enquirer*, May 15, 1871, 1; "Catholic Institute – Election Notice," *Cincinnati Enquirer*, December 15, 1871, 5; *Twelfth Annual and Thirteenth Statistical Report of the Cincinnati Board of Trade and Transportation*, Cincinnati: Bloch & Co., 1881, 24.

51. Clemens Oskamp, burial record; "Death's Victory: Mr. Clemens Oskamp, a Prominent Citizen, Passes Away," April 8, 1887.

52. "Death's Victory: Mr. Clemens Oskamp, a Prominent Citizen, Passes Away," April 8, 1887; "Obituary. Death of Clemens Oskamp," *JCHR* (May 1887): 137; Clemens Oskamp, will dated February 14, 1881, proved April 18, 1887, vol. 43, p. 548, Hamilton County Registry of Probate, Cincinnati, Ohio.

53. Rev. Charles Frederic Goss, "John C. Daller," *Cincinnati: The Queen City, 1788–1912*, Cincinnati: The S.J. Clarke Publishing Co., 1912, 142; "Fight of the Oskamp Estate," *Cincinnati Enquirer*, November 30, 1898, 5.

54. 1893, 1894 Cincinnati City Directories.

55. Goss, "John C. Daller," 142.

56. Mary A. Oskamp, will.

57. "Signature of Late Mrs. Oskamp To Paper Releasing Jos. [*sic*] Daller From Debt Is Said By an Expert to Have Been Forged," *Cincinnati Enquirer*, January 10, 1899, 12; "Sustained Is the Oskamp Will, but the Objectionable Codicil Is Set Aside," *Cincinnati Enquirer*, May 6, 1899, 16; "Daller Wins in the Oskamp Case," *Cincinnati Enquirer*, May 11, 1899, 12; "Last Decision in Mary A. Oskamp Will Case," *JCHR* (May 9, 1900): 19; "Cincinnati," *JCHR* (June 27, 1900): 37; "Cincinnati," *JCHR* (August 1, 1900): 45; "Cincinnati," *JCHR* (October 3, 1900): 44; "Cincinnati," *JCHR* (October 17, 1900): 55.

58. "Cincinnati," *JCHR* (April 25, 1900): 44.

59. 1900–1902 Cincinnati City Directories; "With the Old Firm," *Cincinnati Enquirer*, July 23, 1899, 20.

60. "Cincinnati," *JCHR* (May 14, 1902): 59; "Organization of the New Clemens Oskamp Co. Perfected," *JCHR* (June 4, 1902): 18.

97. OSKAMP, NOLTING & CO.
1886–1906

THE OSKAMP, NOLTING CO.
1906–1959

OSKAMP NOLTING INC.
1960–1980

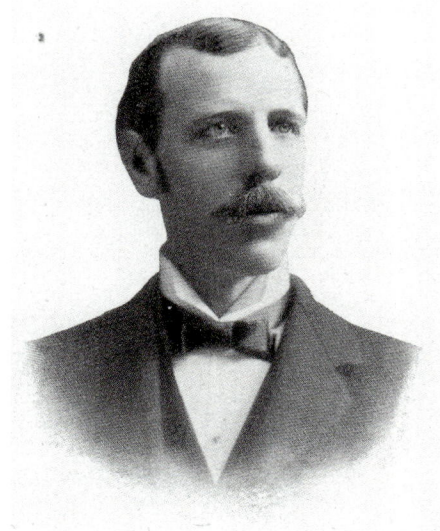

FIG. 97.1: William S.P. Oskamp,
from George W. Engelhardt,
Cincinnati: The Queen City,
Cincinnati: G.W. Engelhardt, 1901, 212

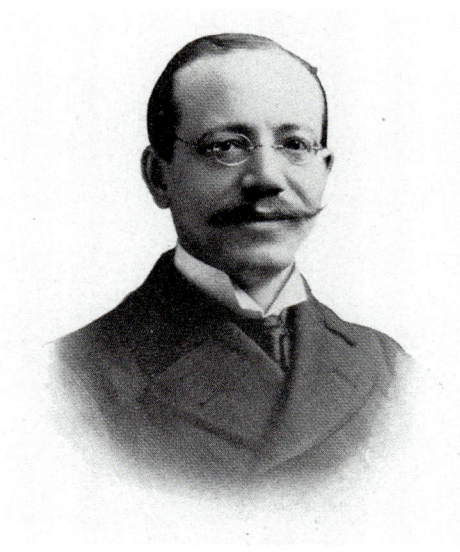

FIG. 97.2: Charles A. Nolting,
from George W. Engelhardt,
Cincinnati: The Queen City,
Cincinnati: G.W. Engelhardt, 1901, 212

The firm of Oskamp, Nolting & Co. was established by William S.P. Oskamp (1854–1953) and **Charles A. Nolting** (1850–1934).[1] Oskamp (fig. 97.1), born in Cincinnati, was the son of **Clemens Oskamp** and Mary Fisher.[2] He was educated at St. Xavier College in Cincinnati and learned the jeweler's trade in his father's store.[3] Nolting (fig. 97.2) was also born in Cincinnati, the son of Anna Barbara Jansen and Charles Philip Frederick Nolting, who was a maker of starch, and later a furniture manufacturer.[4] In 1864, when Nolting was thirteen, he went to work at **Duhme & Co.** as an errand boy, and over the following eighteen years served in all of Duhme's commercial departments, where he learned the trade.[5] Nolting had left Duhme by 1882, and established a partnership with Frank Lodwick (d. 1885), a co-worker at Duhme & Co.[6] The

wholesale jewelry firm of Lodwick & Nolting dissolved when Nolting bought Lodwick's interest in the business around July 1885.[7] Shortly after this time, Oskamp and Nolting became partners.[8] Oskamp, Nolting & Co. operated on the second floor of the Carlisle Building at the southwest corner of Fourth and Walnut Streets—the former site of Lodwick & Nolting, as well as the site of Duhme & Co.

Initially, Oskamp, Nolting & Co. was a wholesale firm only. They carried Swiss and American watches, jewelry and jewelers' findings, imported diamonds (loose or mounted), spectacles, clocks, and silverware.[9] They employed four traveling salesmen who canvassed the West and the South, and issued an annual catalogue, "the only one of its kind issued from Cincinnati," and purportedly "the

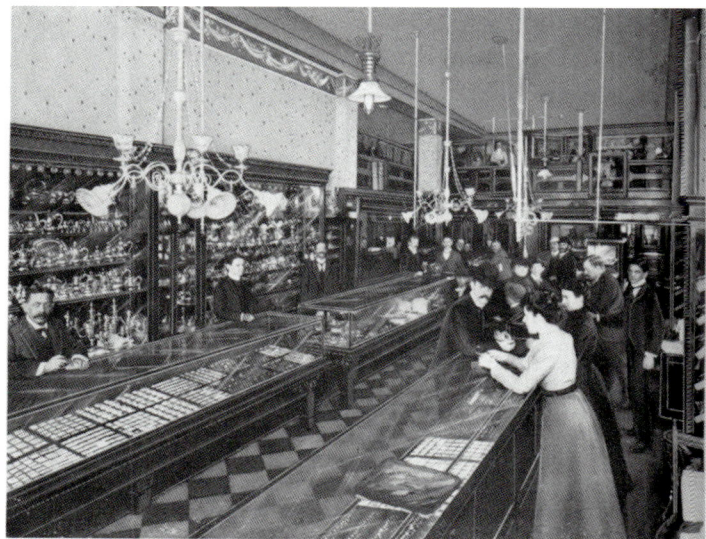

FIG. 97.3: Oskamp, Nolting & Co., from George W. Engelhardt, *Cincinnati: The Queen City*, Cincinnati: G.W. Engelhardt, 1901, 212

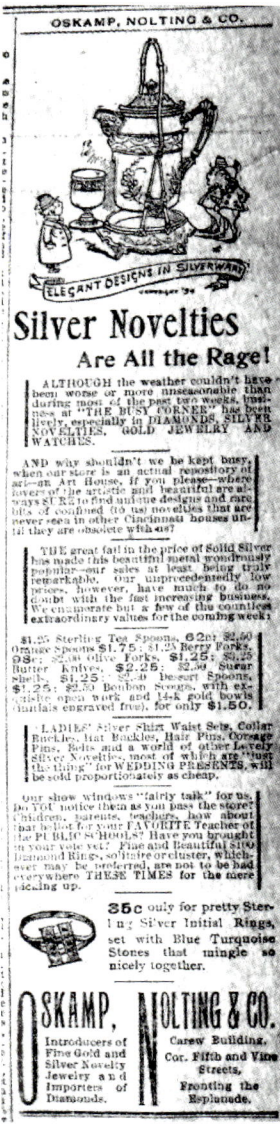

FIG. 97.4: Advertisement, *Cincinnati Enquirer*, May 27, 1894, 13, col. 9

largest published in America."[10] The firm often advertised as the "mammoth wholesale jewelers of America."[11] In 1891, the firm moved to the Carew Building at the southwest corner of Fifth and Vine, near Fountain Square.[12] Their new corner store was fitted with cases of San Domingo mahogany to "produce a magnificent effect" (fig. 97.3), and they also rented the entire basement on the Fifth Street side of the building allowing them "all the room they want."[13] With this move, the firm added a retail business to their Cincinnati operations. Meanwhile, their wholesale department continued to grow rapidly. In October, they had to rent two floors of a building at Race and Longworth Streets for the storage of duplicate stock and clocks. The space previously occupied by the clocks in the Carew Building was intended for their "increased stock of silverware."[14] They reported receiving 200 postal applications per day for their fall catalogue, "not including the applications from general store dealers which were thrown into the wastebasket."[15] In December 1895 they hired night staff to keep up with their increased trade.[16]

In May 1894 the firm advertised (fig. 97.4), at discounted prices, silver novelties that included sterling teaspoons, orange spoons, berry forks, olive forks, butter knives, sugar shells, dessert spoons, bonbon scoops "with exquisite openwork," ladies' silver shirt-waist sets, collar buckles, hat buckles, hair pins, corsage pins, and belts.[17] An invoice from October 1894 (fig. 97.5) indicates the sale and delivery by mail of a set of buttons to a customer in South Carolina. It was reported, "They make a special run on sterling novelties every Saturday, which has boomed them in the local

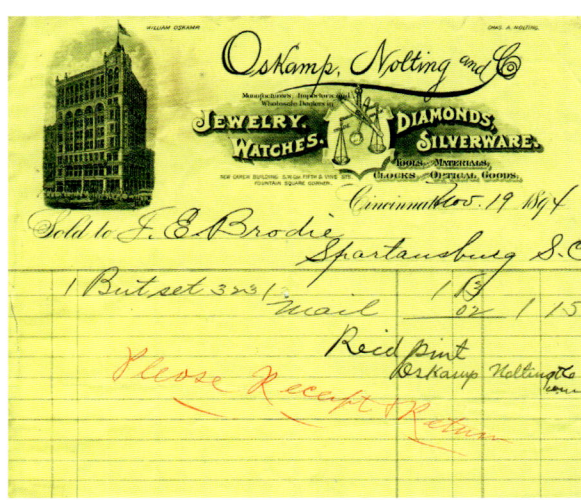

FIG. 97.5: Oskamp, Nolting & Co., *Billhead*, 1894

trade."[18] There is no documentation of Oskamp, Nolting & Co. manufacturing silver. However, like most jewelry stores, they did employ an engraver.[19] In 1896, they furnished a silver trowel to the Emanuel Baptist Church on Freeman Avenue that was auctioned off to raise funds for the church's ongoing construction, and in 1901, they provided a silver loving cup for the *Cincinnati Tribune* to present for amateur driving at the Oakley Races.[20]

In the later part of 1895, the firm opened an optical plant where they could "do all their own grinding and manufacture many optical novelties."[21] In the spring of 1897, they added a retail department for cameras and photographic supplies.[22] The growth and success of the firm's wholesale business led to its expansion, precipitating the firm's lease of a building on the west side of Elm between Fourth and Fifth Streets (413, 415, and 417 Elm Street) in 1902. There, they occupied two floors, providing them with a total of 4,000 square feet to establish "the finest jewelry department in the West."[23] Eventually, part of the fourth floor of the building was used for a clock and silverware room, where silver filled three wall cases along one end of the large room.[24] The success of the business is reflected in William S.P. Oskamp's purchase of an island in the Greenbrier River near Talcott, West Virginia in 1900. There, on "Oskamp Island" he built a lavish summer home.[25] By this time, the company claimed to maintain business "throughout the US, Mexico and South America."[26]

In February 1904 Oskamp, Nolting & Co. announced their retirement from the retail business "to devote all of their resources to the proper handling of their constantly expanding wholesale trade" at their Elm Street location. Their retail store in the Carew Building was bought by William S.P. Oskamp, and his son William Herbert Oskamp (1881-1931) ran the new venture, **Oskamp Jewelry Co.**[27] William S.P. Oskamp "practically retired from the business" around this time due to ill health. However, in 1905, it

was reported that he was instrumental in the organization of the Werk Realty Company, which had offices in the Carew Building. He was later involved again in the Oskamp Jewelry Co. and other family ventures.[28]

Oskamp, Nolting & Co.'s 1906 catalogue, *The Great American Jewelry Catalogue,* illustrates the extent of the firm's offerings, including Waltham watches, all types of watch cases, emblem charms, pins, medals, rings, brooches, toilet sets, lighting devices, eye glasses, bronze statuettes, record players, clocks, imported and American cut glass, as well as sterling and plated cups, trays, salt and pepper shakers, napkin rings, and dessert and chocolate sets.[29] In July 1906 the firm was granted charter as a stock company and became known as The Oskamp, Nolting Co. With a capital of $200,000, its incorporators were Charles A. Nolting; William Werk Oskamp (1886-1976), son of William S.P. Oskamp; Frederick Schaefer; Louis F. Twachtman (a traveling salesman for the firm); and Emil A. Bose.[30] The company purchased land at 26–30 West Seventh Street in 1911, on which it erected a six-story structure with a 68 foot front and 97 foot depth to house its wholesale business.[31] Nolting served as president until his retirement in 1922, when William Werk Oskamp assumed leadership.[32] By 1960, Alfred W. Katz had become president, and the firm was operating as Oskamp Nolting Inc.[33] On December 24, 1980, the firm officially closed its doors.[34]

Extant silver stamped with an incuse "O.N. & CO." or "OSKAMP, NOLTING & CO." stamp includes flatware in patterns by Howard Sterling Co. (Providence, Rhode Island) and Roger Williams Smith Silver Co. (Providence, Rhode Island); other die-pressed pattern spoons with unidentified or illegible manufacturer marks; souvenir spoons; and spoons, with and without twist stems, that feature fiddle handles embellished with bright cut decoration similar to that of the popular "Lily" pattern.[35]

1. William S.P. Oskamp, burial record, Spring Grove Cemetery, Cincinnati, Ohio; Charles A. Nolting, burial record, Spring Grove Cemetery.

2. William S.P. Oskamp, burial record.

3. S.B. Nelson and J.M Runk, *History of Cincinnati and Hamilton County, Ohio,* Cincinnati: S.B. Nelson & Co., 1894, 911.

4. Rev. Charles Frederic Goss, *Cincinnati: The Queen City, 1788–1912,* Cincinnati: The S.J. Clarke Publishing Co., 1912, 3: 389; Charles A. Nolting, burial record.

5. Goss, *Cincinnati: The Queen City,* 3:389; Nelson and Runk, *History of Cincinnati,* 911.

6. 1882–1886 Cincinnati City Directories; Frank O. Lodwick, death

notice, *Cincinnati Enquirer,* November 22, 1885, 5.

7. "Cincinnati," *Jewelers' Circular and Horlogical Review* (July 1886): 47.

8. Ibid.

9. "Cincinnati," *JCHR,* (July 1886); 1888 Cincinnati City Directory; Letterhead, Oskamp & Nolting, 1890, eBay listings and private collections, Cincinnati silver binders, Cincinnati Art Museum.

10. Records could be found for catalogues published in the years 1891, 1893, 1894, 1895, 1904, 1906, 1911, 1916, 1928, 1917, 1921, 1931, 1938, 1948, 1960, and 1968/69; "Trade Gossip," *JCHR* (May 27, 1891): 12; "Cincinnati" *JCHR* (March 14, 1893): 25; Nelson and Runk,

History of Cincinnati, 911; "Our Traveling Representatives," *JCHR* (June 26, 1895): 12.

11. Advertisement, *JCHR* (August 3, 1892): 18.

12. 1891 Cincinnati City Directory; "Cincinnati," *JCHR* (June 24, 1891): 1; "Cincinnati," *JCHR* (August 26, 1891): 33; "A Brilliant Debut," *Cincinnati Enquirer,* September 2, 1891, 8; "Cincinnati," *JCHR* (September 9, 1891): 25.

13. "Cincinnati," *JCHR* (August 26, 1891): 33.

14. "Cincinnati," *JCHR* (September 28, 1892): 10; "Cincinnati," *JCHR* (October 7, 1891): n.p.

15. "Cincinnati," *JCHR* (September 24, 1891): 34.

16. "Cincinnati," *JCHR* (December 4, 1895): 27.

17. Advertisement, *Cincinnati Enquirer,* May 27, 1894, 13.

18. "Cincinnati," *JCHR* (June 13, 1894): 24.

19. "Cincinnati," *JCHR* (September 9, 1896): 23.

20. "Cincinnati," *JCHR* (July 1, 1896): 26; "Cincinnati," *JCHR* (September 4, 1901): 59.

21. "Cincinnati," *JCHR* (November 13, 1895): 32.

22. "Cincinnati," *JCHR* (March 24, 1897): 25.

23. "Cincinnati," *JCHR* (June 18, 1902): 52; "Cincinnati," *JCHR* (June 25, 1902): 54; "Cincinnati," *JCHR* (February 10, 1904): 61.

24. "Cincinnati," *JCHR* (May 6, 1903): 64; "Cincinnati," *JCHR* (June 16, 1903): 60.

25. "Cincinnati," *JCHR* (September 12, 1900): 51; "Cincinnati," *JCHR* (November 28, 1900): 53; Oskamp is also noted as an incorporator of the Rich Hill Mining Co. in Missouri which sourced coal, lead, and zinc. *JCHR* (June 19, 1901): 51.

26. George W. Engelhardt, *Cincinnati: The Queen City*, Cincinnati: G.W. Engelhardt, 1901, 212.

27. "Cincinnati," *JCHR* (February 10, 1904): 61; "Cincinnati," *JCHR* (September 30, 1908): 95.

28. "Cincinnati," *JCHR* (May 10, 1905): 67; Cincinnati city directories; Oskamp's father-in-law was Michael Werk (d. 1893), the "great millionaire soap manufacturer." "Cincinnati," *JCHR* 20, no. 11 (December 1889): 104; "Cincinnati," *JCHR* (April 19, 1893): 31.

29. Oskamp, Nolting & Co., *The Great American Jewelry Catalogue*, Cincinnati, Ohio, 1905.

30. "Cincinnati," *JCHR* (July 25, 1906):

72; "Cincinnati," *JCHR* (March 26, 1907): 84.

31. "Cincinnati," *JCHR* (August 23, 1911): 95; "Cincinnati," *JCHR* (August 30, 1911): 106; "Cincinnati," *JCHR* (July 3, 1912): 93.

32. Conteur (Edwin Henderson), "Manufacture and Sale of Jewelry in Cincinnati During Preceding Century," *Cincinnati Enquirer*, October 23, 1923; Cincinnati city directories.

33. 1960 Cincinnati City Directory.

34. "Oskamp Nolting to Close Store

Christmas Eve," *Cincinnati Enquirer*, November 19, 1980, A1:2.

35. Oskamp, Nolting & Co., eBay listings and private collections, Cincinnati Art Museum; A souvenir spoon engraved with the "Lily" pattern in a private collection includes the mark "O. N. & CO." and an eagle mark that John R. McGrew associates with a journeyman possibly working for Clemens Oskamp. John R. McGrew, *Manufacturers' Marks on American Coin Silver*, Hanover, PA: Argyros Publications, 2004, 96.

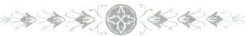

98. THE CLEMENS OSKAMP CO.

1902–1930

The Clemens Oskamp Co. was incorporated in May 1902 as the successor to the firm established by **Clemens Oskamp** (1822–1887). Its incorporators were **John C. Daller**, son-in-law and longtime employee of the late Clemens Oskamp; F.R. Williams; J.F. Usher; and George C. Kolb, Daller's son-in-law. Its officers were John C. Daller, president; F.R. Williams, vice president; and Clemens Oskamp Daller (John C. Daller's son), secretary and treasurer. Directors were John C. Daller; his sons Adrian O. and Clemens O.; F.R. Williams; George C. Kolb; and J.F. Usher.[1] The firm was established with $200,000 of common stock and $100,000 of preferred. Of the preferred stock, half was taken by the company, and the remaining half was offered for subscription and sold privately. Buyers were to yield a fixed, annual dividend of six percent each year.[2]

The Clemens Oskamp Co. (fig. 98.1) was a wholesale and retail firm that sold diamonds, watches, clocks, and jewelry. They also featured fancy goods that included sterling silver, silver plate, hand-painted china, and cut glass.[3] The breadth and variety of their line can be observed in two wholesale catalogues produced by the firm in 1912 and 1913.[4] The major trade journal reported that in addition to sales clerks and book keepers, they also employed several traveling salesmen, at least two watchmakers (Harry W. Devitt and C. Aune), and an engraver (A.C. Geiger), and maintained a repair shop.[5] In 1911, the firm employed about 25 men.[6] While it is possible that there were staff members capable of designing and making silver, it is unlikely that the firm produced much of what they sold, especially in silver wares. In January 1904 the firm dispensed of most, if not all, of their materials stock, selling it to

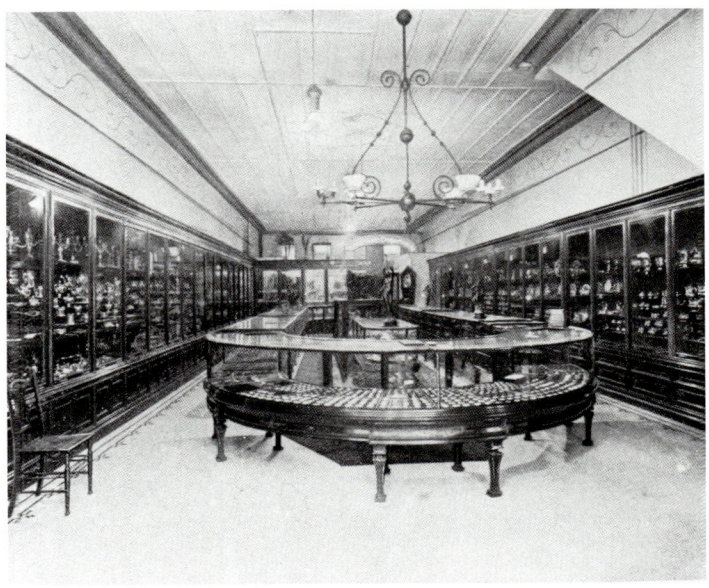

FIG. 98.1: The Clemens Oskamp Co., from Charles Gilbert Hall, *The Cincinnati Southern Railway: a History: a complete and concise history of the events attending the building and operation of the road*, Cincinnati: The McDonald Press, 1902

Joseph Hornback, a former employee of E. & J. Swigart and **Duhme & Co.**, who started his own watch makers and jewelry supply house.[7] To date, the only silver identified with this firm are examples of flatware in patterns patented by Reed & Barton (Taunton, Massachusetts) between 1900 and 1910. These examples are all marked with the incuse stamp, "THE C. OSKAMP CO."[8]

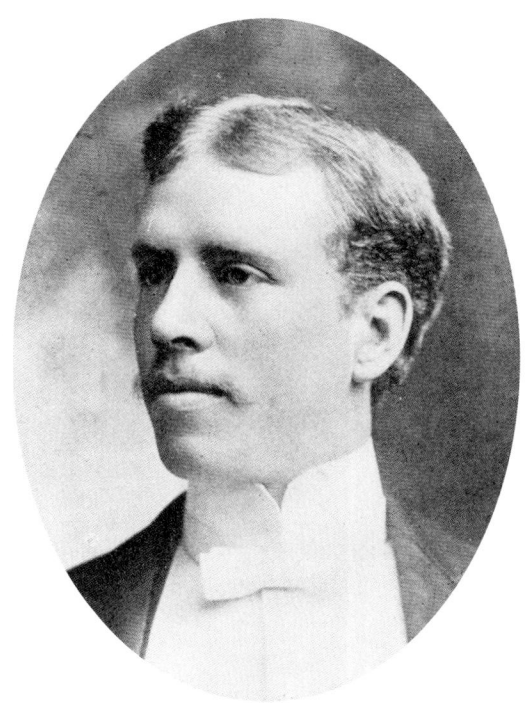

FIG. 98.2: Clemens Oskamp Daller (1873–1953), from Benjamin La Bree, *Notable Men of Cincinnati at the Beginning of the 20th Century*, Louisville, KY: Geo G. Fetter Co., 1904, 171

In 1907, the firm experienced an increase in its retail trade and added new cases to their showroom and a more extensive line of stock.[9] Their success was credited to Clemens Oskamp Daller (fig. 98.2) who had taken over as the store's retail manager.[10] But in June 1910, Clemens Oskamp Daller resigned, "owing to the pressure of outside business affairs in which he is interested and to which he will devote his entire time and energy in the future." He was succeeded as retail manager by his brother, John C. Daller, Jr.[11]

Until the end of 1910, the firm operated at the Vine Street location established by Clemens Oskamp in 1869.[12] But a dispute instigated by Marion D. Oskamp, a daughter-in-law of Clemens

Oskamp, who maintained an interest in the building with other Oskamp heirs, led to a sheriff's sale of the property in November 1909.[13] The Dallers, who had been renting space in the building, moved their concern at the end of 1910 to 520 Main Street, opposite the post office.[14] On October 4, 1911, The Clemens Oskamp Co. celebrated 68 years of continuous operation, and "a very large display of silver and diamonds was made on this occasion."[15] After John C. Daller's death in 1919, John C. Daller, Jr. became president of the firm.[16] Bernard S. Dickman (about 1861–1944) and George C. Kolb (1864–1944) managed the firm between about 1925 and 1930.[17] The Clemens Oskamp Co. did not appear in city directories after the publication of the 1929/30 edition.

1. "Cincinnati," *Jewelers' Circular and Horological Review* (May 14, 1902): 59; "Organization of the New Clemens Oskamp Co. Perfected," *JCHR* (June 4, 1902): 18; In May 1911 Charles D. Baker was elected treasurer and appointed as one of the directors; "Cincinnati," *JCHR* (May 10, 1911): 111.

2. "Organization of the New Clemens Oskamp Co. Perfected," (June 4, 1902).

3. 1902–1915 Cincinnati City Directories; "Cincinnati," *JCHR* (December 30, 1903): 55; "Cincinnati," *JCHR* (April 24, 1907): 83.

4. Partial facsimile of wholesale catalogues that were advertised on eBay, Cincinnati Art Museum, Decorative Arts & Design Department, The Clemens Oskamp Co. research file.

5. "Cincinnati," *JCHR* (April 3, 1907): 83; "Cincinnati," *JCHR* (November 17, 1909): 98; "Cincinnati," *JCHR* (May 8, 1907): 86; "Cincinnati," *JCHR* (August 18, 1909): 81; "Cincinnati," *JCHR* (February 15, 1911): 99; "Fire at Cincinnati Damages Quarters of Several Jewelry Concerns and Causes Much Excitement," *JCHR* (December 7, 1910): 73.

6. "Cincinnati," *JCHR* (January 18, 1911): 99.

7. "Cincinnati," *JCHR* (January 20, 1904): 64.

8. The Clemens Oskamp Co., eBay listings and private collections, Cincinnati silver binders, Cincinnati Art Museum.

9. "Cincinnati," *JCHR* (June 12, 1907): 89.

10. Advertisement, *JCHR* (August 12, 1908): 76; "Cincinnati," *JCHR* (October 7, 1908): 99.

11. "Cincinnati," *JCHR* (June 29, 1910): 92; "Cincinnati," *JCHR* (October 26, 1910): 111.

12. 1902–1915 Cincinnati City Directories; The address of the firm was 175 Vine, and after street renumbering in 1895, 417 Vine Street.

13. "Cincinnati," *JCHR* (December 1, 1909): 93.

14. "Cincinnati," *JCHR* (May 24, 1911): 97; "Fire at Cincinnati Damages Quarters of Several Jewelry Concerns and Causes Much Excitement" (December 7, 1910).

15. "Cincinnati," *JCHR* (October 4, 1911): 110.

16. 1920–1924 Cincinnati City Directories.

17. 1925–1930 Cincinnati City Directories; Bernard S. Dickman, burial record, Walnut Hills Cemetery, www.walnuthillscemetery.org; George C. Kolb was the husband of Gertrude Daller and is listed as the grandson-in-law of Clemens Oskamp in his burial record, Spring Grove Cemetery.

99. THEODORE OSKAMP

about 1825–1854, w. 1848–1854

Theodore Oskamp was born in Prussia in about 1825 to Theresa (b. about 1794, d. after 1854) and Joseph Casper Oskamp (b. about 1777), a farrier.[1] He was one of at least seven children: Wilhelm (b. about 1817); Lucille (b. about 1820); **Clemens** (1822–1887); Lewis (b. 1828); Amalie (b. about 1832); and Augustus (b. about. 1836–1889).[2] The Oskamp family boarded the *Ship of New York* in Bremen and arrived in New York on June 19, 1838.[3] They were in Ottawa, Putnam County, Ohio, in 1840.[4] Theodore appeared in the Cincinnati Business Directory of 1848/49 as a watch and clock maker working at 62 Main Street.[5] Nothing is known of his training. His older brother Clemens Oskamp reportedly lent him $300 which enabled him to start his business.[6] In 1850, he reported as a jeweler and watch maker with $2,000 capital, employing three hands, to whom he paid a total of $100 in annual wages. His firm utilized $2,000 of gold and silver to produce breastpins, rings, chains, and other jewelry valued at $25,000.[7] According to credit reports, his business continued to grow, and by January 1854 he was estimated to be worth between $10,000 and $15,000.[8] Eventually, Clemens joined him in business. Theodore became sick while in Attleboro, Massachusetts, and died in September 1854.[9] He left Clemens "the stock in trade and business of the firm of which he is a partner and the good will of the firm as the successor thereof, on condition of him paying the cost of said stock giving him ten years for the payment thereof with interest payable annual at six percent per annum."[10]

Theodore Oskamp's listings in city directories describe him as a watch maker. It is unlikely that he made any of the silver that bears his mark. Teaspoons and tablespoons, a cream ladle, and a sugar shovel with tipped, exaggerated fiddle handles and pointed shoulders, and a pair of tongs with shell terminals have been found with mark 99.1.[11]

Theodore's younger brothers, Lewis (also know as Louis) and Augustus, and his nephew Joseph were also involved in the Cincinnati silver, watch and clock, and jewelry trades, in the firms **Oskamp & Co.**, **Oskamp & Bro.**, and **Joseph A. Oskamp**. In the 1850 Federal Census, both Augustus and **Henry Korf**, watch makers, were living with Theodore Oskamp and his family.[12] Theodore and his wife, Magdalena Frey (1828–1896), daughter of Henry Frey, lived on Fifth Street and had one child, Louisa (b. 1849).[13]

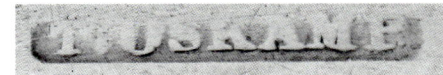

MARK 99.1

1. Ancestry.com, *New York Passenger Lists, 1820–1957* [online database], Provo, Utah: Ancestry.com Operations Inc., 2010; 1850 Federal Census, Cincinnati, Hamilton, Ohio.
2. Ancestry.com, *New York Passenger Lists, 1820–1850* [online database], Provo, Utah: Ancestry.com Operations Inc., 2003; 1860, 1870, and 1900 Federal Censuses, Cincinnati, Hamilton, Ohio.
3. Ancestry.com, *New York Passenger Lists, 1820–1850*.
4. 1840 Federal Census, Ottawa, Putnam, Ohio.
5. 1848/49 Cincinnati Business Directory; A later reminiscence suggests that this address was on the east side of Main Street, between Pearl and Second Streets. Conteur (Edwin Henderson), "Manufacture and Sale of Jewelry in Cincinnati During Preceding Century," *Cincinnati Enquirer*, October 23, 1923.
6. "Death's Victory: Mr. Clemens Oskamp, a Prominent Citizen, Passes Away," *Cincinnati Enquirer*, April 8, 1887, 4.
7. 1850 Federal Non-Population Census Schedules, Products of Industry, Schedule 4, Hamilton County, Ohio.
8. Ohio, Vol. 1, p. 53, R.G. Dun & Co. Collection, Baker Library, Harvard Business School
9. Ibid.
10. Theodore Oskamp, will; Ohio, Vol. 1, p. 53, R.G. Dun & Co. Collection.
11. Theodore Oskamp, eBay listings and private collections, Cincinnati silver binders, Cincinnati Art Museum.
12. 1850 Federal Census, Cincinnati, Hamilton, Ohio.
13. Theodore Oskamp, will dated September 3, 1854, proved September 25, 1854, vol. 17, p. 515, Hamilton County Registry of Probate, Cincinnati, Ohio; 1850 Federal Census, Cincinnati, Hamilton, Ohio; Marriage record, Hamilton County Probate Records, vol. A20, 397, http://www.probatect.org /CourtRecordsArchive /bukmarriages.aspx.

100. OWEN & CARLEY

1844–1846

Within weeks of the dissolution of **Owen & Read** in May 1844, **William Owen, Sr.** entered into a new partnership with **Samuel T. Carley**, who was primarily a manufacturer and retailer of jewelry.[1] Their shop, located on Main Street between Third and Fourth Streets, was probably the same space that had housed the firm of Owen & Read, and was later to house **Palmer & Owen**.

Because no period documents, notices, or advertisements for the firm have been found, little is known about the partnership of Owen & Carley. Although the 1846 Cincinnati City Directory lists them simply as "watchmakers," silver flatware with their mark has been documented, and it is likely that they also dealt in jewelry given Carley's long-standing identification as a manufacturing jeweler.[2] The mark of Owen & Carley (mark 100.1) has been found on silver spoons with tipped exaggerated fiddle handles (fig. 100.1).[3]

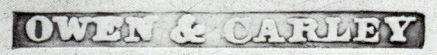

MARK 100.1

1. Ohio, Vol. 1, p. 91, R.G. Dun & Co. Collection, Baker Library, Harvard Business School.
2. Carley's occupation was given as a manufacturing jeweler (or jeweler) in every issue of the Cincinnati city directory between 1840 and 1863, except in 1846.
3. Owen & Carley, ebay listings and private collections, Cincinnati silver binders, Cincinnati Art Museum.

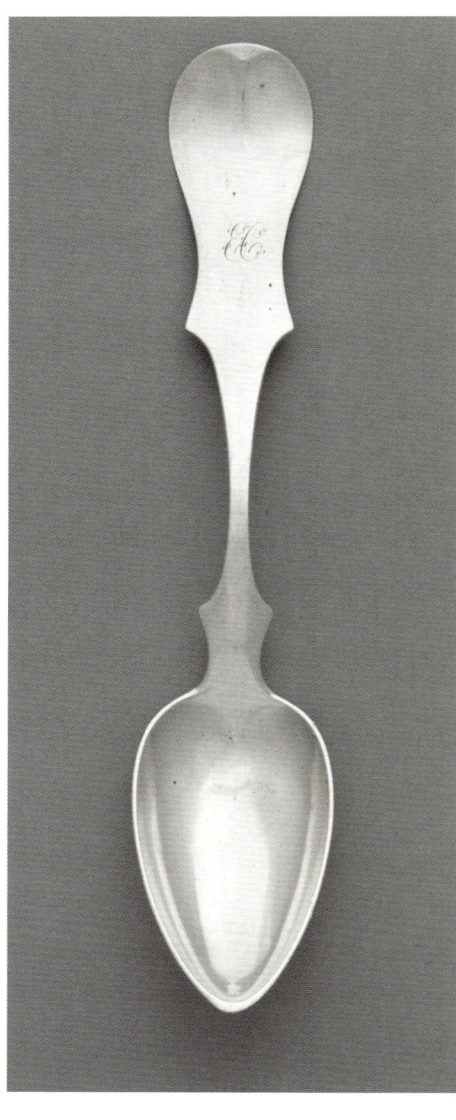

FIG. 100.1: Owen & Carley, *Tablespoon*, 1844–1846, L. 9 in. (22.9 cm), CAM, Museum Purchase: John S. Connor Fund, 2012.25

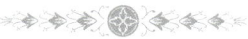

101. OWEN & READ

1837–1844

The partnership of **William Owen, Sr.** and James Read had been established by March 1837 when they advertised as watch makers, silversmiths and jewelers with a shop on Main Street, at 127 Main, "a little bit above Third."[1] The advertisement provides a list of items that they "have, and keep continually for sale," and enumerates a wide variety of fancy goods, spectacles, watches, and jewelry, as well as "Table, Dessert, Tea, Mustard and Salt SPOONS on hand or

manufactured to order—plated Tea and Table Spoons." It is also noted that "SILVER WORK and JEWELLRY [*sic*] of all kinds [would be] made and repaired at the *shortest notice*."[2] By 1840, they were located at 157 Main between Fifth and Sixth Streets, "nearly opposite the Commercial Bank," and had moved south on Main between Third and Fourth by 1842.[3] In 1842, the firm advertised their receipt of a new supply of goods "imported from England *by themselves.*"[4] The partnership dissolved in May 1844.[5] Documented silver marked by the firm includes flatware with early fiddle-shaped handles and a beaker.[6]

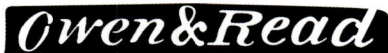

MARK 101.1

1. Advertisement, *Daily Evening Post*, March 27, 1837, reproduced in Beckman, 103.
2. Ibid.
3. 1839/40–1844 Cincinnati City Directories; Advertisement, 1839/40 Cincinnati City Directory, 41; Advertisement, *Cincinnati Enquirer*, February 8, 1842, 3. The 1839/40 advertisement indicates that they were at 155 Main, although the city directory lists 157 Main, probably a typographical error.
4. Advertisement, *Cincinnati Enquirer*, February 8, 1842, 3.
5. *Cincinnati Daily Gazette*, May 1, 1844, cited in Beckman, 103; Ohio, Vol. 1, p. 91, R.G. Dun & Co. Collection, Baker Library, Harvard Business School.
6. Owen & Read, ebay listings and private collections, Cincinnati silver binders, Cincinnati Art Museum.

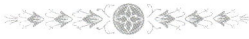

102. CHARLES OWEN

1824–1900, w. 1846–1891

Charles Owen was in Cincinnati by 1846, boarding with his older brother **William Owen, Sr.** and working as a watch maker.[1] Census listings give his occupation as "silversmith" in 1850, "jeweler" in 1870, and "jewelry store" in 1880.[2] From 1849 to 1860, Charles was listed as a watch maker or jeweler, working at the address of his brother's firms **William Owen** and **Palmer & Owen** located on Main Street between Third and Fourth, and later at the northwest corner of Fourth and Main Streets.[3] From 1861 to 1866, the business continued at the northwest corner of Fourth and Main Street but was conducted under the name of Charles Owen.[4] An 1865 advertisement for the firm describes their offerings as "Fine Watches, Magnificent Diamonds, Rich Jewelry and Elegant Silverware."[5] While the 1861 Directory listing describes the firm as "Manufacturers of Silver Ware & Jewelry & Dealer in Watches, Cutlery & Fancy Goods," the description had evolved to "Wholesale & Retail Dealer in Silver Ware & Jewelry" in the 1866 Directory.

On June 28, 1866, a "destructive" fire enveloped the whole block of the northwest corner of Fourth and Main Streets.[6] The businesses affected included **Herman Keck**, jeweler, **George A. Stinger**, silverware manufacturer, **Herman Franz Serodino**, jeweler, and (Charles) "Owen's extensive and magnificent jewelry store." Within a week, Owen, a "DEALER IN WATCHES, JEWELRY & SILVERWARE", was advertising that he had "temporarily removed to the store of W.H. Eveleth (Merchant Tailor) at 18 West Fourth Street."[7] The firm was still advertising under the name of Charles Owen in August 1866, but by October, the name had been changed to **William Owen & Co.** with Charles, William Owen, Sr.,

and William Owen, Jr. as principals of the firm.[8] After William Sr.'s death in 1886, Charles continued to work at the family firm until 1891, although his role was listed in the directories of this period as either clock maker or as a repairer (or inspector) of watches and clocks.[9]

Silver die-pressed flatware manufactured and marked by John Polhemus (New York City) or Wood & Hughes (New York City), as well as flatware bearing an exaggerated fiddle handle and marked **E. & D. Kinsey** have been found with the incuse mark "OWEN."[10] This mark can be attributed to the Charles Owen firm based on patent dates and stylistic characteristics, although an attribution to the William Owen, Sr. or William Owen & Co. firms cannot be ruled out.

Born in Dedham, Massachusetts in March 1824, Charles was the son of Elizabeth and William W. Owen.[11] After he married Mary Louisa Mariani (1834–1893) in 1852, the couple moved to Newport, Kentucky.[12] Charles died there in May 1900.[13] He and Mary Louisa were the parents of six children: Charles F. (Frank) (1854–1895), George W. (1856–1934), Emma M. (1860–1863), William J. (1861–1894), Harrison (Harry) R. (1868–1947), and Mary Emma (1870–1943).[14]

1. 1846 Cincinnati City Directory.
2. 1860, 1870, 1880 Federal Censuses, Newport, Campbell, Kentucky.
3. 1849/50–1860 Cincinnati City Directories; The 1855 City Directory indicates that he was working as a brush maker at Isaac Hickman's brush manufactory at 640 Western Row.
4. 1861–1866 Cincinnati City Directories; Ohio, Vol. 6, p. 139, R.G. Dun & Co. Collection, Baker Library, Harvard Business School.
5. Advertisement, *Cincinnati Enquirer*, December 26, 1865, 1.
6. "Destructive Fire Last Evening," *Cincinnati Enquirer*, June 29, 1866, 2.
7. Advertisement, *Cincinnati Enquirer*, July 7, 1866, 1.

8. "Charles Owen's" is included in a listing of venues for tickets to a concert benefitting widows and orphans, *Cincinnati Enquirer*, August 13, 1866, 2; "William Owens & Co." is included in a listing of venues for tickets to Handy Opera House, *Cincinnati Enquirer*, October 31, 1866, 2; 1867 Cincinnati City Directory; Ohio, Vol. 6, p. 139, R.G. Dun & Co. Collection.

9. 1886–1891 Cincinnati City Directories.
10. The Polhemus patterns are "Bead" (1850) and "Oriental" (1860) according to Noel D. Turner, *American Silver Flatware 1837–1910*, San Diego: A.S. Barnes & Company, 1972; Owen, eBay listings and private collections, Cincinnati silver binders, Cincinnati Art Museum.
11. Ancestry.com, *Massachusetts, Town*

Vital Collections, 1620–1988 [online database], Provo, Utah: Ancestry.com Operations Inc., 2011.
12. Marriage record, Hamilton County Probate Records, vol. B1, 336, http://www.probatect.org /CourtRecordsArchive /bukmarriages.aspx; Mary Louisa Owen, burial record, Spring Grove Cemetery, Cincinnati, Ohio; Notice of Mary Louisa Owen's death in

"Cincinnati," *Jewelers' Circular and Horological Review* (February 22, 1893).
13. Chas. Owen, burial record, Spring Grove Cemetery; "Death of Charles Owen," *JCHR* (May 16, 1900): 24.
14. Chas. F., George W., Harry, William, Mary Emma, and Emma M. Owen burial records, Spring Grove Cemetery.

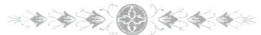

103. JOHN OWEN

b. about 1810, w. 1836–1853

John Owen, born in Pennsylvania (probably Philadelphia), is included in the 1836/37 Cincinnati City Directory as a silversmith boarding at Cyrus Coffin's.[1] His "Western Manufactory of Gold and Silver Spectacles" was located at 147 Main Street, opposite the Gazette Office.[2] An 1839 advertisement added jewelry and silver ware to the list of articles he produced.[3] In October 1841 he advertised as a partner of **James H. Martin** (Martin & Owen) in the manufacturing of spectacles and jewelry, but by the end of the year their partnership had dissolved.[4] By 1842, Owen had relocated his manufactory to Walnut Street, between Third and Baker Streets, "three doors above Third", its location until August 1844, when it moved to 27 Third Street, between Main and Walnut.[5] Eye glasses were Owen's specialty (fig. 103.1), but he also advertised "silver spoons on hand, and made to order."[6] According to the 1850 Products of Industry Census, he had $500 of capital invested in his business and employed two hands at $25 a month. His materials, $500 in gold and silver and $100 in glass, were used to produce $1,500 worth of spectacles.[7] Just a year later, it was reported that Owen employed four hands and used $6,750 worth of material to produce product valued at $9,000.[8] Owen disappears from records after 1853. In October 1860 guardianship of his wife, Isabella Murray (b. Ireland, about 1809, d. 1874), who had been declared insane, was granted to Owen's daughter, Isabel.[9] John Owen and Isabella had married in Cincinnati on February 6, 1838.[10] Owen had five children, for whom records were found, all born in Ohio: Bernard M. (b. about 1837, d. 1903), a baker; Frank (b. about 1840), also a baker; Isabel (b. about 1842); John (1846–1852); and Jesse W. (1848–1924), a dentist.[11]

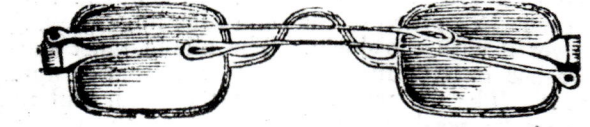

FIG. 103.1: Advertisement, *Cincinnati Enquirer*, June 21, 1843, 2

Spoons and a condiment ladle (fig. 103.2) with exaggerated fiddle handles and pointed shoulders have been found with mark 103.1.[12] Mark 103.2 has been documented on spoons and ladles with both exaggerated fiddle handles (typical of Cincinnati's post-1840 period) and straight-sided fiddle handles (typical to the period prior to 1840). Mark 103.3 has been noted on a coin silver coffee pot, circa 1820, which is also impressed with a six-pointed star, possibly a journeyman's mark; spectacles; and spoons with fiddle handles.[13] Marks 103.2 and 103.3 could be the mark of an earlier John Owen, working in Philadelphia from 1804 to 1831.[14] Isabella Owen's death notice was also published in Philadelphia and Iowa City newspapers, suggesting family ties in those areas.[15] While our subject's birthplace is only recorded as Pennsylvania, it is very likely that he was born in Philadelphia. However, a relationship between the John Owen working in Philadelphia, and the John Owen active in Cincinnati has not yet been established, nor has a relationship between our subject and **Charles** or **William Owen, Jr. and Sr.**

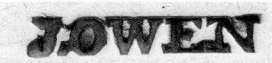

MARK 103.1

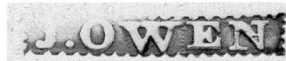

MARK 103.2

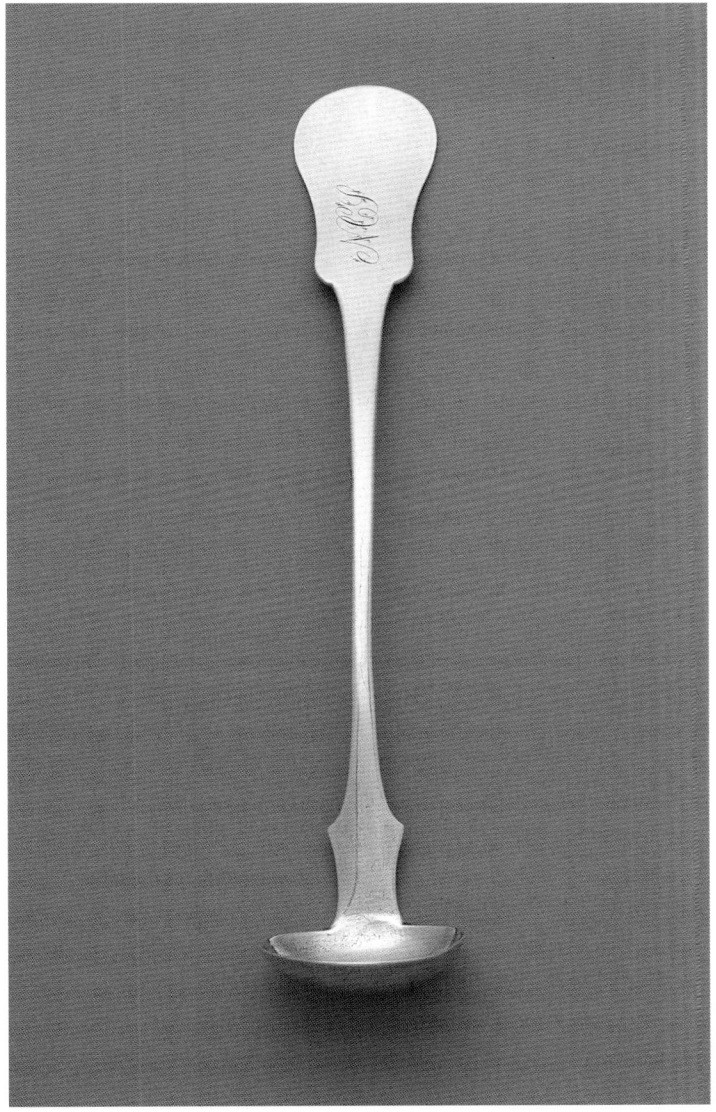

FIG. 103.2: John Owen, *Condiment Ladle*, c. 1840–1853, L. 5⁷⁄₁₆ in. (13.8 cm), CAM, Gift of John S. Conner, 1910.179

MARK 103.3

1. The 1839/40 Cincinnati City Directory gives Pennsylvania as Owen's place of nativity.
2. Advertisement, *Cincinnati Daily Gazette*, October 20, 1837, reproduced in Beckman, 102. This advertisement announces the Manufactory's move to 147 Main Street. Its previous location is unknown.
3. Advertisement, *Cincinnati Advertiser & Journal*, April 18, 1839, reproduced, Beckman, 102.
4. Advertisement, *Daily Times*, October 20, 1841, reproduced Beckman, 90; Their partnership was not listed in the 1842 Cincinnati City Directory.
5. 1842–1846 Cincinnati City Directories; Advertisement, *Cincinnati Enquirer*, June 21, 1843, 3; Advertisement, *Cincinnati Daily Gazette*, August 7, 1844, reproduced in Beckman 102.
6. Owen ran advertisements in the *Cincinnati Enquirer* often. The following were repeated a number of times: Advertisement, *Cincinnati Enquirer*, June 21, 1843, 3; Advertisement, *Cincinnati Enquirer*, January 11, 1850, 4; Advertisement, *Cincinnati Daily Gazette*, August 7, 1844, reproduced in Beckman 102.
7. 1850 Federal Non-Population Census Schedules, Products of Industry, Schedule 4, Hamilton County, Ohio.
8. Charles Cist, *Sketches and Statistics of Cincinnati in 1851*, Cincinnati: W.H. Moore & Co., 1851, 238.
9. Guardianship record, Hamilton County Probate Records, vol. 3, 515; 1850 Federal Census, Cincinnati, 6th Ward, Hamilton, Ohio; Death notice, *Cincinnati Enquirer*, September 25, 1874; Isabella Owen, death record, Cincinnati Health Department, University of Cincinnati Archives and Rare Books Library, http://hdl.handle.net/2374.UC /603090.
10. Marriage record, Hamilton County Probate Records, vol. A7, 203, http://www.probatect.org /CourtRecordsArchive /bukmarriages.aspx.
11. 1850 Federal Census, Cincinnati, 6th Ward, Hamilton, Ohio; Burial records, Spring Grove Cemetery, Cincinnati, Ohio; According to Bernard's burial record, he was 66 years old when he died in 1903, suggesting that he was born before Owen's marriage to Isabella; Reporter's Notebook, *Cincinnati Enquirer*, September 15, 1903, 2.
12. Beckman, xii; John Owen, eBay listings and private collections, Cincinnati silver binders, Cincinnati Art Museum.
13. John Owen, eBay listings and private collections, Cincinnati Art Museum; *Coffee Pot*, Fine Silver and Judaica, Skinner Inc., April 10, 2008, lot 189.
14. Stephen G.C. Ensko, *American Silversmiths and Their Marks*, New York: Dover Publications, 1983, 100.
15. Death notice, *Cincinnati Enquirer*, September 25, 1874.

104. WILLIAM OWEN & CO.

1866–1885

In October 1866 the firm of **Charles Owen** became William Owen & Co.[1] **William Owen, Sr.**, Charles Owen, and **William Owen, Jr.** were principals of the firm.[2] City directory listings between 1867 and 1885 variously described the firm as watch makers, jewelers, and dealers in silverware, or as importers (or dealers) of diamonds and watches, jewelry, and silverware. From 1883 to 1885, after the shop moved from the northwest corner of Fourth and Main Streets to 167 Vine Street, "dealers in watch materials and tools" was added to their listing. Watches, diamonds, jewelry, and silverware were included in all of their advertisements in local newspapers, while some of the advertisements also included fine cutlery, and "plated ware" such as tea sets, cake baskets, castors, and fruit dishes.[3]

Credit reports for the firm from 1867 to 1877 are positive, indicating that they enjoyed a good trade and kept a valuable stock; their credit was good and they were regarded as responsible, although they were reported to be slow to pay.[4] In 1873, they advertised, "Our stock has mostly been purchased since the Panic, and we can assure purchasers lower prices than any other house in the city."[5] The Panic of 1873 affected several Cincinnati firms. William Owen & Co. was one of three firms in the silver trade that applied for bankruptcy in 1878, and the credit reports during this time are not favorable.[6] But by 1880, credit reports become more encouraging and in 1882, it was reported that William Owen & Co. "were doing considerable bus[iness] and carrying a fair stock."[7] The firm was operating in the same location in 1886, but trading under the name of **M.C. Owen**, William Owen, Jr.'s wife.[8]

Although the firm's 1872 and 1874 City Directory listings and some of their advertisements from that time include "Manufacturers of Jewelry & Silver Ware," there is little evidence to support this claim.[9] The 1870 Products of Industry Census reports the firm's product as jobbing and repairing of jewelry.[10] The greatest number of hands employed by the firm that year was two, and the value of its product was $5,000.[11] Although silver flatware bearing the firm's mark is known, it was most likely produced elsewhere and merely retailed in the shop. There are two documented marks used by William Owen & Co.[12] Flatware similar to **Duhme & Co.**'s "No. 1" (circa 1869) pattern with twist stems and spoons with tipped, exaggerated fiddle handles have been noted with mark 104.1.[13] Mark 104.2 has been found on flatware in John Polhemus' "Oriental" (1855) and "Honeysuckle" (1867) patterns, and on a spoon that is also marked by Wood & Hughes (New York City).[14]

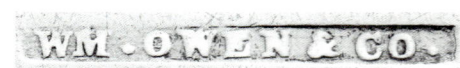

MARK 104.1

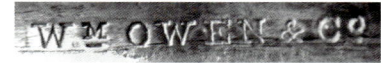

MARK 104.2

1. Ohio, Vol. 6, p. 139, R.G. Dun & Co. Collection, Baker Library, Harvard Business School. The credit report under William Owen & Co., recorded November 1866 reads, "the bus[iness] until a few weeks ago was carr'd on in the name of his [William's] bro[ther] Chas."
2. 1867 Cincinnati City Directory.
3. For a sample of the firm's advertisements in the *Cincinnati Enquirer*, see December 25, 1866, 2; November 18, 1867, 3; December 11, 1869; December 17, 1871, 5; December 19, 1873, 8; and July 15, 1874. In the *Commercial Tribune*, see December 17, 1876, 5; August 11, 1871, 6; January 10, 1874; For mention of plated ware and cutlery see the following advertisements: *Cincinnati Daily Gazette*, December 21, 1868, 2; *Cincinnati Enquirer*, June 16, 1873; and in the *Cincinnati Commercial Tribune*, December 19, 1873, 8; December 24, 1880, 8; December 22, 1881, 2; and December 14, 1882, 8.
4. Ohio, Vol. 6, p. 139, R.G. Dun & Co. Collection.
5. Advertisement, *Cincinnati Commercial Tribune*, December 19, 1873, 8; "The Panic" refers to the Panic of 1873, an international economic depression that lasted until 1879. Until the financial fall in 1930, it was referred to as "The Great Depression."
6. "Trade Gossip," *Jewelers' Circular and Horological Review* (May 1878): 80; *Jeweler, Silversmith and Watchmaker* (June 1878): 144; *JSW* (May 1878): 133; The other Cincinnati firms that filed for bankruptcy were **Julius Voss** and James C. Michie; Ohio, Vol. 6, p. 139, R.G. Dun & Co. Collection.
7. Ohio, Vol. 6, p. 430, R.G. Dun & Co. Collection.
8. 1886 Cincinnati City Directory.
9. Advertisement, *Cincinnati Enquirer*, August 11, 1871, 6.
10. 1870 Federal Non-Population Census Schedules, Products of Industry, Schedule 4, Hamilton County, Ohio.
11. Ibid.; In that same year, **David Kinsey**'s production of silverware was valued at $67,000 and **H. Keck & Co.**, manufacturers of jewelry produced $40,000.
12. A third mark, "W. Owen & CO.," was reported by Beckman, p. 104, but in seven years of intensive searching, we have not observed it.
13. William Owen & Co., eBay listings and private collections, Cincinnati silver binders, Cincinnati Art Museum.
14. Ibid.

105. WILLIAM OWEN, SR.

1809–1886, w. 1834–1885

The first Cincinnati record of William Owen, a watch and clock maker from Boston, is his listing as the partner of I.M. Stanley in Stanley & Owen, clock makers, in the 1836/37 City Directory.[1] The firm is also listed in the section "Foundries & Manufactories" at the end of the directory as "Stanley & Owen's Brass clock manufactory, east side Walnut between 3d & 4th."[2] By March 27, 1837, Owen was a partner in **Owen & Read**.[3]

After the dissolution of Owen & Read in 1844, Owen continued in business on Main Street between Third and Fourth Streets, first in a partnership with S.T. Carley (**Owen & Carley**), then from 1847 to 1850 under his own name.[4] His advertisements in 1849 carried the banner "JEWELRY! JEWELRY!" and trumpeted "The subscriber [William Owen] has just received a large and splendid assortment of Watches, Jewelry and Fancy Goods," followed by a detailed list of the goods.[5] Although the advertisement did not specify silverware, the 1850 Census gave Owen's occupation as silversmith.[6]

Early in 1850, Owen formed a partnership with **Abraham Palmer** (**Palmer & Owen**).[7] After the partnership was dissolved in March 1859, Owen continued in business on his own at their former address (the northwest corner of Fourth and Main Streets), advertising in December 1859 that he had just returned from New York with a "large and well-selected stock" consisting of watches, jewelry, fancy goods, and silver and plated ware.[8] Credit problems emanating from the Palmer & Owen years, which R.G. Dun & Co. reporters ascribed mainly to Palmer's actions, continued to plague Owen through 1860.[9] From 1861 to 1866 the business was carried on under the name of William Owen's brother, **Charles Owen**, although William continued to be associated with the firm as a jeweler or watch maker.[10] In late 1866, the name of the firm, still located at Fourth and Main Streets, was changed to **William Owen & Co.**[11] William Owen, Sr. continued to be one of the principals of the firm until 1885.[12]

William Owen was born in June 1809 in Dedham, Massachusetts, the son of Elizabeth and William W. Owen.[13] He died December 6, 1886, in Cincinnati.[14] In 1837, he married Keziah Abigail (Abby) Merry (1819–1852).[15] They were the parents of five children: Ann Elizabeth (Lizzie) (1837–1930); William Jr. (1842–1928); Matilda (Tillie) (1845–1935); John Merry (1848–1850); and Mary Keziah (1851–1852).[16] Following the death of Keziah, Owen married Sarah Jane Permar (1836–1891) in December 1852.[17] Together, they had four children: Mary Jane (May or Mamie) (1853–1928); John T.

(b.1856); Charles E.E. (Edward) (1859–1899); and Warren Colburn (1862–1934).[18]

Known silver struck with mark 105.1 includes teaspoons with early fiddle and exaggerated fiddle handles. Mark 105.2 has been observed on a small footed bowl.[19]

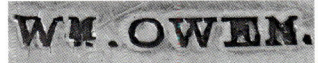

MARK 105.1

W.OWEN

MARK 105.2

1. The obituary cited in Beckman, page 103, could not be located. This obituary reportedly states that Owen practiced the watch-making trade in Boston where he took E. Howard on as an apprentice.
2. Advertisement, 1836/7 Cincinnati City Directory, 222.
3. Advertisement, *Daily Evening Post*, March 27, 1837, reproduced in Beckman, 103.
4. *Cincinnati Daily Gazette*, May 1, 1844, cited in Beckman, 103; Ohio, Vol. 1, p. 91, R.G. Dun & Co. Collection, Baker Library, Harvard Business School; 1848/49 Cincinnati Business Directory; 1849/50 Cincinnati City Directory.
5. Advertisement, *Cincinnati Enquirer*, September 30, 1849, 4; Advertisement, *Cincinnati Enquirer*, October 17, 1849, 4; Advertisement, *Cincinnati Enquirer*, December 19, 1849, 4.
6. 1850 Federal Census, Cincinnati, Hamilton, Ohio.
7. *Cincinnati Enquirer*, January 11, 1850, 2.
8. Ohio, Vol. 2, p. 169, R.G. Dun & Co. Collection; 1860 Cincinnati City Directory; Advertisement, *Cincinnati Enquirer*, December 23, 1859, 2.
9. Ohio, Vol. 2, p. 169, R.G. Dun & Co. Collection.
10. 1861–1866 Cincinnati City Directories; Ohio, Vol. 6, p. 139, R.G. Dun & Co. Collection says in November 1866: "the bus[iness] until a few weeks ago was carr[ie]d on in the name of his [William's] bro

Chas."; Charles Owen advertised in the *Cincinnati Enquirer*, July 7, 1866, 1; An October 13, 1866 advertisement in the *Cincinnati Enquirer*, p. 2, used William Owen & Co.
11. Advertisement, *Cincinnati Enquirer*, October 13, 1866, 1; 1867 Cincinnati City Directory.
12. 1867–1885 Cincinnati City Directories.
13. Ancestry.com, *Massachusetts, Town Vital Collections, 1620–1988* [online database], Provo, Utah: Ancestry.com Operations Inc., 2011; William Owen, Sr., burial record, Spring Grove Cemetery, Cincinnati, Ohio.
14. William Owen, Sr., burial record.
15. Marriage record, Hamilton County Probate Records, vol. A6, 402, http://www.probatect.org /CourtRecordsArchive /bukmarriages.aspx; Keziah Abby Owen, burial record, Spring Grove Cemetery.
16. Burial records, Spring Grove Cemetery.
17. Marriage record, Hamilton County Probate Records, vol. B3, 69, http://www.probatect.org /CourtRecordsArchive /bukmarriages.aspx; "Cincinnati," *Jewelers' Circular and Horological Review* (June 24, 1891): supplement 1.
18. Burial records, Spring Grove Cemetery.
19. William Owen, Sr., ebay listings and private collections, Cincinnati silver binders, Cincinnati Art Museum.

106. PALMER & HANKS

1839–1842

By June 12, 1839, **Abraham Palmer** and George Lucius Hanks (1813–1859) had created the firm Palmer & Hanks.[1] Hanks was from New York, the son of Alpheus and Zeniah Hanks.[2] He had arrived in Cincinnati by November 1835, when he advertised his new jewelry store which offered many types of jewelry and fancy goods, including "Silver and Plated Table and Tea Spoons."[3] The following year, he listed in the city directory as a watch maker.[4]

In 1835, both Palmer and Hanks had maintained locations on Main Street.[5] Their earliest notice as partners, submitted on June 12, 1839, indicates that they were still doing business on Main Street, at a location four doors above Third Street. In their advertisement, they promoted a newly arrived supply of surveyor instruments produced by a firm in West Troy, New York, for whom they were agents.[6] They listed as jewelers and silversmiths in the 1839/40 City Directory. Both **Dennis McHenry** and **Albert McMurphy**, who listed as silversmiths, were working at the firm in 1839.[7] The firm's tenure was brief, thus silver bearing their mark is rare. By 1842, perhaps even by 1841, Palmer and Hanks had gone their separate ways. Hanks was a partner in a bell and brass foundry in 1842, and Palmer continued in business alone.[8]

The mark of Palmer & Hanks (mark 106.1) has been found on a spoon with a fiddle handle and pointed shoulders.[9]

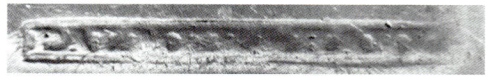

MARK 106.1

1. Advertisement, *Cincinnati Daily Gazette*, June 12, 1839, reproduced in Beckman, 106; 1839/40 Cincinnati City Directory.
2. Burial records, Spring Grove Cemetery, Cincinnati, Ohio; Hanks was married to Julia Bunce (1812–1896), born in Connecticut. They had two known children: George T.L. (1847–1913) and Louis D. (1841–1910). In 1860, after George Hanks, Sr.'s death, Julia was reported to own $18,000 in real estate and a personal estate valued at $12,000; 1860 Federal Census, Cincinnati, Hamilton, Ohio.
3. Advertisement, *Cincinnati Daily Gazette*, November 10, 1835, reproduced in Beckman, 62; No silver bearing the mark of George L. Hanks is known.
4. 1836/37 Cincinnati City Directory.
5. Advertisement, *Cincinnati Daily Gazette*, November 10, 1835, reproduced in Beckman, 62.
6. Advertisement, *Cincinnati Daily Gazette*, June 12, 1839, reproduced in Beckman, 106.
7. 1839/40 Cincinnati City Directory.
8. 1842 Cincinnati City Directory; 1850 Federal Census, Cincinnati, Hamilton, Ohio; A Cincinnati city directory was not published in 1841.
9. Palmer & Hanks, *Spoon*, private collection, Cincinnati silver binders, Cincinnati Art Museum.

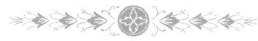

107. PALMER & OWEN

1850–1859

In January 1850 **William Owen, Sr.** and **Abraham Palmer** announced that they had "entered into a partnership for the purpose of carrying on a more extensive business in Jewelry, Silverware, Watches, &c."[1] Their shop was located on Main Street, between Third and Fourth Streets, at the address previously occupied by William Owen's shop, and located a short distance north of Palmer's former shop. Their partnership was an attempt at economic recovery for Palmer. Credit reports from 1849 indicate that Palmer, who had entered into some questionable real estate dealings was "bound to fail" and "borrows at high int[erest] & resorts to almost every means to sustain himself."[2]

Palmer & Owen advertised extensively throughout the following

months, offering a variety of fancy goods, gold and silver watches, jewelry, silverware, and plated goods.[3] Several of these advertisements noted that "The above Stock was selected with great care in the Eastern cities, and is now offered at prices which cannot fail to be satisfactory to the purchaser."[4] The silverware they sold included flatware designed by the well-known New York silversmith John Polhemus in the "Oriental" (1855) pattern.[5] In 1851, it was reported that Palmer & Owen "keep three hands engaged in the manufacture of silver ware, on a product yearly, of twelve thousand dollars."[6] Whether that silverware was flatware, hollowware, or both, has not been documented by any other period publications or extant records. The Palmer & Owen advertisements always included a reference to their repairs of watches and clocks carried out by "experienced workmen."[7]

Credit reports for the firm during the years 1850 to 1859 indicated that the business had its ups and downs, alternating between "d[oi]ng well" and "lost heavily the past y[ea]r."[8] By September 1858 the reports were mostly negative, noting that the firm was "In no sort of cr[edit] here, stock greatly reduced & not replenished lately."[9] Credit reporters' comments usually focused on problems attributed to Palmer such as "P. seems to be always getting into trouble."[10] The partnership was dissolved in March 1859.[11] Palmer became the proprietor and manager of The Great Western Museum while Owen continued the business on his own at the same location.[12] October 1859 credit reports concluded, "[Owen] has been better able of late to meet obligations, is econ[omical] & improved by being alone."[13]

The mark of Palmer & Owen has been found on a wide variety of flatware pieces in addition to the aforementioned examples produced by John Polhemus. Flatware with early tipped fiddle handles and pointed shoulders and those with later exaggerated fiddle handles and pointed shoulders (fig. 107.1) have also been documented with their mark.[14]

PALMER & OWEN

MARK 107.1

1. "New Firm," *Cincinnati Enquirer*, January 11, 1850, 2. This notice ran again on March 17, 1850, 4.
2. Ohio, Vol. 1, p. 91, R.G. Dun & Co. Collection, Baker Library, Harvard Business School.
3. Advertisement, *Cincinnati Enquirer*, January 8, 1850, 4. This advertisement ran again in the *Enquirer* on January 10, 1850, 4, on March 3, 1850, 4 and on October 8, 1850, 4. It also ran in the *Cincinnati Daily Times* on April 21, 1850, reproduced in Beckman, 107; Advertisement, *Cincinnati Enquirer*, October 8, 1850, 2. This advertisement also ran on October 11, 1850, 2.
4. Advertisement, *Cincinnati Enquirer*, January 8, 1850, 4.
5. Palmer & Owen eBay listings and private collections, Cincinnati silver binders, Cincinnati Art Museum; Noel D. Turner, *American Silver Flatware 1837–1910*, San Diego, CA: A.S. Barnes & Co., 1972, 105–106.
6. Charles Cist, *Sketches and Statistics of Cincinnati in 1851*, Cincinnati: William H. Moore & Co., 1851, 188.
7. Advertisement, *Cincinnati Enquirer*, January 8, 1850, 4; Watch makers known to be associated with the firm include **Charles G. Boerner** (1850–1856) and **Charles Owen** (1850–1859). 1850–1859 Cincinnati City Directories.
8. Ohio, Vol. 1, p. 91, Vol. 2, p. 169, R.G. Dun & Co. Collection.
9. Ibid.
10. Ibid.
11. Ibid.
12. "The Great Western Museum. Abraham Palmer, Proprietor," *Cincinnati Enquirer*, July 30, 1859, 1; 1860 Cincinnati City Directory.
13. Ohio, Vol. 2, p. 169, R.G. Dun & Co. Collection.
14. Palmer & Owen, eBay listings and private collections.

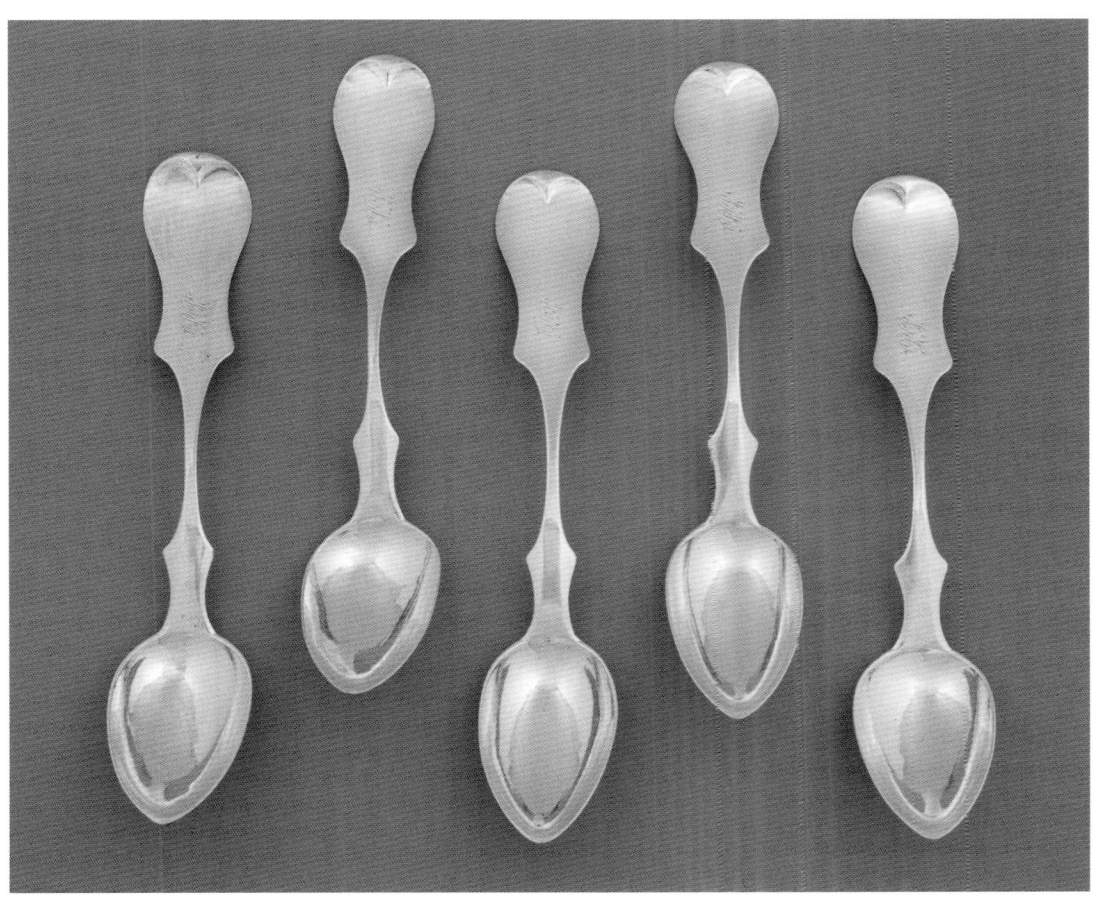

FIG. 107.1: Palmer & Owen, *Spoons*, 1850–1859, L. 7¼ in. (22.9 cm), CAM, Museum Purchase, 1962.74–78

108. PALMER & SMITH

1844–about 1847

Abraham Palmer and Harry R. Smith (see **Harry R. Smith & Co.**) were partners by late 1843, as they were listed in the 1844 Cincinnati City Directory as watch makers and silversmiths on Main Street. Their firm was included in the directory the following year, but by 1848, when the next directory was published, Palmer was working alone at the firm's old stand, and Smith had joined Joseph P. Beggs (see **J.P. Beggs & Co.**) in **Beggs & Smith**.[1] There are no known advertisements for this firm. There is mention of a "present" for a Mr. Davenport which was on display at their jewelry store on June 2, 1847, but details about the "present" are not disclosed.[2] Thus, little is known about their stock. Their mark (mark 108.1) has been observed on spoons and ladles with tipped, exaggerated fiddle handles and pointed shoulders. In at least one

case, their mark has been accompanied by two left-facing eagles in square cartouches.[3] These eagles (fig. 67.4) are likely the manufacturing marks of **Edward Kinsey** or **Pulaski Scovil**.[4]

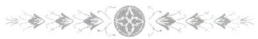

MARK 108.1

1. 1848/49 Cincinnati Business Directory; 1849/50 Cincinnati City Directory.
2. "Local Intelligence," *Cincinnati Enquirer*, June 2, 1847, 3.
3. Palmer & Smith, eBay listings and private collections, Cincinnati silver binders, Cincinnati Art Museum.
4. John R. McGrew, *Manufacturers' Marks on American Coin Silver*, Hanover, PA: Argyros Publications, 2004, 99.

109. ABRAHAM PALMER

1808–1880, w. 1833–1880

Abraham Palmer was born in Chester County, Pennsylvania, on August 16, 1808, the son of Quakers Ann Reeder (1783–1820) and Abraham Palmer (1771–1852).[1] The family moved to Baltimore in 1815, and to Frederick County, Maryland, in 1825.[2] In 1827, they moved to Richland County, Ohio.[3] Abraham's father was in the milling business in Chester County, and took up farming after he left Pennsylvania.[4]

The young Palmer remained in Baltimore where he entered into an apprenticeship with silversmith Samuel Kirk on June 1, 1825.[5] A mug (fig. 109.1), marked by Palmer and bearing an inscription indicating that it was presented in Cincinnati on January 1, 1833, provides the earliest documentation of Palmer's presence in Cincinnati. In the 1834 City Directory, he is listed as a silversmith on Fourth Street between Vine and Race Streets. In November 1835, he advertised as a "MANUFACTURER of Silver Ware, Spoons and Jewelry, WHOLESALE and RETAIL" at 151 Main Street, opposite the Branch Bank of the United States. Items could be made to order and it was promised that an assortment of silver spoons, watches, and jewelry were always on hand.[6] In 1838, he exhibited a set of silver castors at the first annual fair of the Ohio Mechanics' Institute, and

the following year, he joined forces with George L. Hanks (**Palmer & Hanks**).[7] This partnership had ended by 1842, when the two men were listed separately in the city directory. By 1844, Palmer had partnered with Harry R. Smith (**Palmer & Smith**).[8]

Palmer was working alone again in a shop at 119 Main Street by 1848.[9] The following year, he advertised watches, jewelry, music boxes, gold pens and pencil cases, and silverware and plated goods including "Britania [*sic*] Tea and Coffee Sets; Silver Forks, Table, Dessert, Tea and Cream Spoons; Silver Cups; Soup Ladles; Cream, Salt and Mustard Spoons, &c."[10] In January 1850 he ran the same advertisement, adding "I HAVE just received from the Eastern manufacturers a Splendid Silver Tea Sett [*sic*], which I should be pleased to have the public call to see. Silver Spoons, Forks and Cups kept constantly on hand and made to order."[11] All known advertisements related to Palmer indicate that he was making some wares in addition to retailing the wares of other manufacturers. The 1850 Federal Census indicates that his real estate was valued at $13,000, yet the records of R.G. Dun & Co. credit reporters indicate that his standing was uncertain, as he had entered into some questionable real estate dealings and "borrows at high interest and

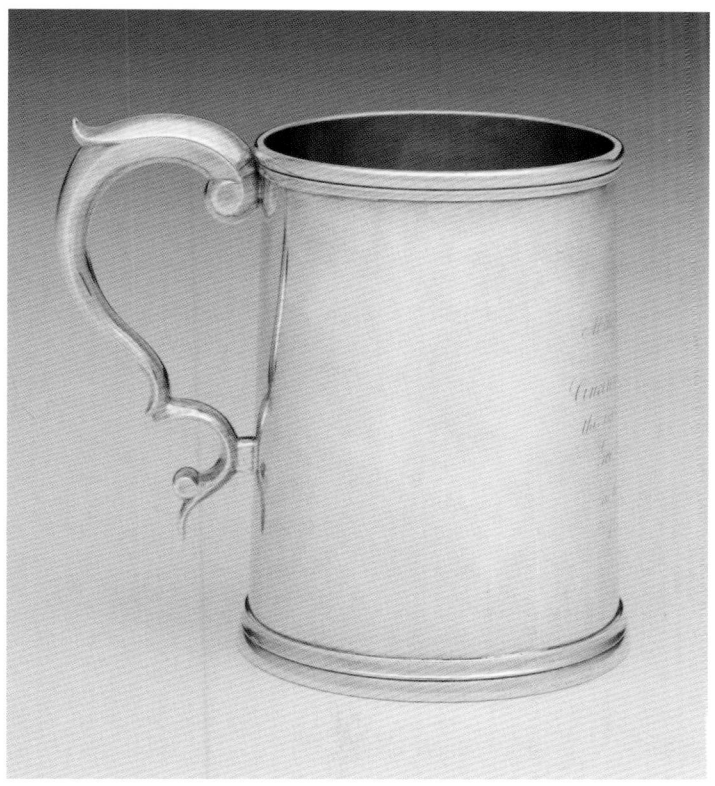

FIG. 109.1: Abraham Palmer, *Mug*, c. 1833, Beckman Collection, Cincinnati Museum Center. Inscription: At the first trial of skill by the Cincinnati Shooting Club this Cup was awarded to Geo. W. Neff Esq as the highest prize, 1st January 1833

resorts to almost every means to sustain himself."[12] His partnership with **William Owen, Sr.** (**Palmer & Owen**), established in 1850, was a failed attempt to recover. By October 1859 Palmer and Owen had dissolved their business.[13]

Palmer's personal estate was valued at $3,000 in the 1860 Federal Census.[14] That year, he had become proprietor of the Western Museum in Cincinnati, where he worked at least until 1861 when he ran unsuccessfully for county commissioner.[15] His occupation in the 1864 City Directory is given, again, as a jeweler, working on Vine Street and living in Walnut Hills. He listed in 1866 as a silversmith, and this is his final directory listing as such. Records show that in the late 1860s and early 1870s, he sold significant parcels of land in Walnut Hills.[16] In June 1880 he was recorded in the Federal Census as a member of the household of his son, Abraham Palmer, Jr., and it is indicated that despite suffering from an inflamed bladder, he still worked in a factory.[17] He died on December 9, 1880. The cause of death was given as diabetes, and he is buried in Spring Grove Cemetery.[18]

Abraham Palmer married Julietta McFarland (b. Baltimore) in 1832.[19] They had two sons: Eugene (b. 1833), who was working as a finisher for his father in 1850, and William (b. 1836). Julietta died in 1836, and Palmer married Maria Tratbas of Cincinnati in June 1337.[20] She died in 1842.[21] They had two children: **Robert H.** (b. 1838) and Josephine Maria (b. 1840). Palmer wed his third wife, Sarah Nehemiah of Cincinnati, in 1844.[22] They had six children before Sarah's death in 1868: Julietta (b. 1845), Sara Isabella (b. 1847), Abraham Jr. (b. 1850), Clara Elizabeth (b. 1852), Anna Reeder (b. 1855), and Ella L. (b. 1858).[23]

Palmer utilized three marks. Mark 109.1 has been documented on spoons with exaggerated fiddle handles and pointed shoulders; butter knives (also marked with a left-facing eagle with upturned wings and shielded breast (fig. 67.3), possibly the manufacturing mark of **Edward Kinsey**); beakers; and a sugar bowl. A tablespoon with an early fiddle handle and pointed shoulders bears mark 109.1, plus the aforementioned eagle (fig. 67.3) and Edward Kinsey's mark 67.1.[24] A spoon in a private collection features mark 109.1 overstruck with **Luke Kent**'s mark 61.2. The mug in fig. 109.1 bears mark 109.2, as well as the mark of **Shipp & Collins** (mark 128.2). Mark 109.3 has been documented on a spoon with a tipped, exaggerated fiddle handle and pointed shoulders.[25]

MARK 109.1

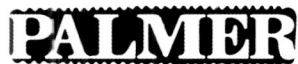

MARK 109.2

PALMER

MARK 109.3

1. Lewis Palmer, *A Genealogical Record of the Descendants of John and Mary Palmer*, Philadelphia: J.B Lippincott & Co., 1875, 56, 91; Burial records, Spring Grove Cemetery, Cincinnati, Ohio.
2. Palmer, *Descendants of John and Mary Palmer*, 56, 91; Abraham Palmer was

not listed in the 1822 or 1831 Baltimore City Directories.
3. Palmer, *Descendants of John and Mary Palmer*, 56; 1830 Federal Census, Jefferson, Richland, Ohio.
4. Palmer, *Descendants of John and Mary Palmer*, 56, 91; Burial records, Spring Grove Cemetery.

5. Jennifer Faulds Goldsborough, *Silver in Maryland*, Baltimore: Maryland Historical Society, 1983, 274.
6. Advertisement, *Daily Evening Post*, November 24, 1835, reproduced in Beckman, 104.
7. *Report of the First Annual Fair of the Ohio Mechanics' Institute*, Cincinnati: Ohio Mechanics' Institute, 1838, 24; 1840 Cincinnati City Directory; Advertisement, *Daily Gazette*, June 12, 1839, reproduced in Beckman, 106.
8. 1844 Cincinnati City Directory.
9. 1848/49 Cincinnati Business Directory.
10. Advertisement, *Daily Times*, October 27, 1849, reproduced in Beckman, 106.
11. Advertisement, *Cincinnati Enquirer*, January 1, 1850, 94.
12. Ohio, Vol. 1, p. 91, R.G. Dun & Co. Collection, Baker Library, Harvard Business School.
13. Ohio, Vol. 2, p. 169, R.G. Dun & Co. Collection.
14. 1860 Federal Census, Cincinnati, Hamilton, Ohio.
15. 1860, 1861 Cincinnati City Directories; "County Commissioner," *Cincinnati Enquirer*, September 18, 1861, 2.
16. 1866 Cincinnati City Directory; Real Estate Transfers, *Cincinnati Enquirer*, July 15, 1869, 7; Real Estate Transfers, *Cincinnati Enquirer*, February 2, 1872, 3; Real Estate Transfers, *Cincinnati Enquirer*, February 9, 1872, 3.
17. 1880 Federal Census, Cincinnati, Hamilton, Ohio.
18. Burial records, Spring Grove Cemetery.
19. Palmer, *Descendants of John and Mary Palmer*, 91.
20. 1850 Federal Census, Cincinnati, Hamilton, Ohio; Palmer, *Descendants of John and Mary Palmer*, 91, 168.
21. Palmer, *Descendants of John and Mary Palmer*, 91, 168.
22. Palmer, *Descendants of John and Mary Palmer*, 91.
23. Palmer, *Descendants of John and Mary Palmer*, 91, 168; 1860, 1880 Federal Censuses, Cincinnati, Hamilton, Ohio.
24. *Tablespoon*, Elizabeth Beckman Collection, Cincinnati Museum Center.
25. Abraham Palmer, eBay listings and private collections, Cincinnati silver binders, Cincinnati Art Museum; *Mug*, Elizabeth Beckman Collection, Cincinnati Museum Center.

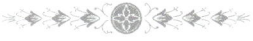

110. GEORGE D. PARKS

b. 1822, w. 1855–1868

Parks first appeared in Cincinnati city directories in 1855 with a shop on West Fifth Street, advertising as an importer and dealer of watches, clocks, jewelry, silverware, and fancy articles. His directory advertisements in 1857 and 1858 added "manufacturer" as well as "wholesale and retail" to his offerings.[1] R.G. Dun & Co. credit reports starting in 1855 recommended caution, noting that he had "failed once in New York and came here," and that while he was prudent and industrious, his means were "short" and he did not warrant a large credit.[2] Although R.G. Dun & Co. reported that he quit the business in April 1861, he continued to sell watches and jewelry at another location on Western Row (now Central Avenue) until 1868.[3] Census records give his occupation as a watch maker in 1860, and as a retired merchant in 1870.[4]

From 1870 to 1878, Parks was included in city directories either as a bookkeeper, or with no occupation given. Parks' wife, Margaret R., was listed as a widow in the 1879 and 1880 City Directories, although the 1880 Census listed George D. Parks as living with Margaret and their children at 31 Laurel Street; his occupation was given as traveling salesman.[5] George D. Parks was the owner of a lot in Spring Grove Cemetery and although his wife Margaret (1822–1889) and their six children are buried there, he is not.[6]

Silverware marked by George D. Parks is rare. A teaspoon struck with mark 110.1 has a tipped, exaggerated fiddle handle and pointed shoulders.[7]

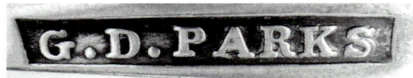

MARK 110.1

1. 1857, 1858 Cincinnati City Directories.
2. Ohio, Vol. 1, p. 184, R.G. Dun & Co. Collection, Baker Library, Harvard Business School; Further proof for his presence in New York prior to his arrival in Cincinnati can be found in Ancestry.com, *U.S. Civil War Draft Registrations Records, 1863–1865* [online database], Provo, Utah: Ancestry.com Operations Inc., 2010.
3. Ohio, Vol. 2, p 189, R.G. Dun & Co. Collection; 1861–1868 Cincinnati City Directories.
4. 1860, 1870 US Federal Censuses, Cincinnati, Hamilton, Ohio.
5. The same address is given in the 1879 and 1880 Cincinnati City Directories.
6. Burial records, Spring Grove Cemetery, Cincinnati, Ohio. Interment records include Sarah S. (1853–1911), George A. (1855–1913), Margaret Effie (1857–1928), Charles H. (1859–1952), Laura (1861–1924), and Infant (1864).
7. *Teaspoon*, Elizabeth Beckman Collection, Cincinnati Museum Center.

III. JOHN PICKERING

1788–1850, w. 1831 or earlier–1846

John Pickering, son of Samuel Pickering, was born in Castle Donnington, Leicestershire, England, on September 10, 1788.[1] He married Eliza (b. England 1791, d. Cincinnati 1866), daughter of George and Elizabeth Mastin, at Old St. Paul's Church in Philadelphia on January 19, 1812, and was probably the John Pickering working as a silver plater in that city between 1823 and 1824.[2] John's sons, George M. (1813–1893) and Joseph M. (1815–1894) were both born in New Jersey, suggesting that John was working there prior to his arrival in Cincinnati.[3]

Pickering was listed in the 1829 Cincinnati City Directory as a coach maker (likely a typographical error, since all subsequent occupation listings for John Pickering are clock maker) at Main between Sixth and Seventh Streets. In 1831, he listed as a clock maker at Seventh Street, between Main and Sycamore.[4] Absent from the city directories in 1834 and 1836, he reappears in the 1839/1840 City Directory, residing on the west side of John Street between Sixth and Longworth. He published a large advertisement that year for his clock repairing business located at the Ohio Mechanics' Institute on Third Street near Broadway (where he was also employed as an actuary and librarian through 1846).[5] The advertisement reads, "CLOCKS of all kinds, EITHER OF BRASS OR WOOD, CAREFULLY CLEANED, CORRECTLY REPAIRED and warranted BY JOHN PICKERING, CLOCK MAKER . . . all orders in his line of business will be thankfully received and promptly executed, either in the city or country."[6] In 1842, he was appointed a clock judge at the Fifth Annual Ohio Mechanics' Institute Fair.[7] Pickering, who is not included in city directory listings after 1846, died of cholera on July 16, 1850.[8]

The 1830 Federal Census indicates that John and Eliza were living in Cincinnati with three girls between the ages of newborn and nine, and three boys between the ages of ten and nineteen.[9] Ten years later, they reported living with one boy between the ages of 20 and 29, and four girls between the ages of five and twenty-nine.[10] Some of the boys reported may have been apprentices. In 1829, Harper Blakesley, clock maker, boarded at Pickering's, and in 1831, Alexander H. North, clock maker, also boarded there.[11]

Pickering was primarily a clock maker, but a fiddle-handled spoon with pointed shoulders with Pickering's mark (mark 111.1) is known.[12]

J.PICKERING

MARK III.I

1. John Pickering, burial record, Spring Grove Cemetery, Cincinnati, Ohio; Pickering's place of nativity is given as England in the 1840 Cincinnati City Directory; There is a record for the arrival of a John Pickering, possibly our subject, in Philadelphia from Bordeaux, France, on the *Ploughboy* on March 7, 1803. Ancestry.com, *Philadelphia Passenger Lists, 1800–1945* [online database], Provo, Utah: Ancestry.com Operations Inc., 2006.

2. Historic Pennsylvania Church and Town Records, Historical Society of Pennsylvania, reel 240; Eliza Pickering, burial record, Spring Grove Cemetery; Maurice Brix, *List of Philadelphia Silversmiths and Allied Artificers from 1682 to 1850*, Philadelphia: privately printed, 1920, 82; Ancestry.com, *Pennsylvania, Church and Town Records, 1708–1985* [online database], Provo, Utah: Ancestry.com Operations Inc., 2011.

3. George M. Pickering, burial record, Spring Grove Cemetery; Joseph M. Pickering, burial record, St. Paul's Lutheran Cemetery, Montgomery County, Pennsylvania; George

worked as a clock maker and repairer on Seventh Street in Cincinnati beginning in 1834 and into the 1860s. Joseph ran a fancy goods store, specializing in ladies' trims in Cincinnati between 1843 and 1866.

4. 1831 Cincinnati City Directory. There was no directory published for 1830.

5. Advertisement, 1839/1840 Cincinnati City Directory, 517, reproduced in Beckman, 110; 1842, 1843, 1844, 1846 Cincinnati City Directories.

6. Advertisement, 1839/1840 Cincinnati City Directory, 517, reproduced in Beckman.

7. "Ohio Mechanics' Institute," *Cincinnati Enquirer*, June 21, 1842, 3.

8. Obituary, *Cincinnati Daily Times*, July 16, 1850.

9. 1830 Federal Census, Cincinnati, Hamilton, Ohio.

10. 1840 Federal Census, Cincinnati, Hamilton, Ohio.

11. 1829, 1831 Cincinnati City Directories.

12. John Pickering, eBay listings and private collections, Cincinnati silver binders, Cincinnati Art Museum.

112. A. & J. PLAUT

1878–1933

Aaron (1844–1929) and Joseph M. Plaut (1852–1915) were half-brothers. Born in Germany, their father was Michael Jacob Plaut (1808–1876). Their mothers were Caroline Schlesinger (1816–1849) and Sophie Strauss (1822–1900) respectively.[1] The family emigrated, departing from Liverpool, England, in 1855.[2] They were in Cincinnati by 1858, when Michael was noted as the proprietor of a clothing store in the city directory.

The details of Aaron and Joseph's training are unknown. Between 1866 and 1868, Aaron was selling watches and jewelry at 255 Main Street.[3] In 1869, he is included in the city directory as a watch maker, and in 1877 he is noted as a jeweler, residing at 419 John Street. No working address is given.[4] He partnered with Leopold Strauss around 1877.[5] Their firm, Strauss & Plaut, advertised as wholesale jewelers, and remained in business for a year or less. Their shop was located in the popular Emery Arcade, a two-story, glass-roofed corridor that connected the Emery Hotel on Vine Street with Race Street, one block west. Built in 1877, it boasted stores, offices, a restaurant, and hotel.[6] Joseph was initially associated with his other brothers Jacob (1843–1882) and Abraham (1850–1912) in Fulton County, Kentucky, where they ran a general store and jewelry business.[7]

By July 15, 1878, Aaron and Joseph had combined their resources to establish A. & J. Plaut, a wholesale jewelry business located in the Emery Arcade.[8] Credit reporters noted that almost all of their purchases were made in the East and that they were highly spoken of by those who knew them and "said to be honest, reliable business men."[9] In January 1882 Ferdinand Phillips (1853–1915), brother-in-law of Aaron and Joseph, became a partner in the firm.[10] A. & J. Plaut advertised as the "WIDE AWAKE" jewelers.[11] They were jobbers (wholesale distributers providing supplies for the retail trade) of various American-made watches, "Meriden Silver Plate Co.'s Hollow Ware, Roger & Bro.'s Flat Ware," diamonds, and "the Latest Novelties in Jewelry."[12] An advertisement describing their line of sterling silver reads, "Our stock of Sterling Silver for table service and the toilet has been increased to such an extent as to enable us to offer the largest and best variety ever offered. All our goods are by the best makers, such as Gorham, Whiting, Reed & Barton. Every piece of goods we handle is guaranteed Sterling 925-1000 fine. The workmanship is such as to merit the approval of the most critical judges." Of their silver novelties, they added, "We can show the largest and best selected line of *Pungents, Toilet Bottles, Tablets, Match Safes, Bon-bonnieres,* [sic] Photo *Frames, Paper-Cutters and Book-Marks, Shoe- and Glove-Buttoners, Scissors* of every description, *Manicure Sets,* &c."[13] They also maintained a specialty in masonic emblems, precious and semi-precious stones, gold and silver jewelry, silver-plated tableware, cutlery, leather goods, clocks, bronzes and bric-a-brac, canes and umbrellas, and souvenir spoons.[14] In 1886, their firm was noted as "enterprising and active," with "a strong foothold among dealers in their section of the country."[15] They employed several traveling salesmen in the South and West, and their extensive, fully-illustrated catalogue of 1892 was deemed "a valuable reference book for the trade."[16]

By 1889, the firm had moved from the Emery Arcade to 131 Fourth Street.[17] At the end of 1896, with plans to move into new quarters, the firm announced that they were retiring from the retail business and would confine their activities to the wholesale business.[18] An auction sale of their stock began on December 1, 1896, and ran until January 1, 1897.[19] They leased a large store at 34 East Fourth Street—a very fashionable center that already boasted several other jewelry stores—and were engaged in business there by March 1897. But despite their previous announcement to give up their retail trade, they were "forced to keep up retailing, because of the stock on hand."[20] By 1900, the firm had moved to 14 East Fourth Street (Boylan Building) across from Pike's Opera House.[21]

In 1896, as members of the Cincinnati Wholesale Jewelers' Association, the Plauts proposed the formation of an association for fire insurance, as many of the jewelers in the city at that time felt discriminated against by insurance companies.[22] Whether or not such an association was formed is unclear. This proposal, combined with the fact that they sold bicycles during the summer, like many other jewelers did to supplement their income in the slow season, provides an interesting insight into the concerns of jewelers at the time.[23]

In October 1901 the firm announced that Joseph was leaving A. & J. Plaut. His share of the business was purchased by Aaron who would continue business under the existing name. Joseph planned to establish a jewelry clearing house and start a general commission business.[24] Joseph died on November 3, 1915, and was buried in Walnut Hills United Jewish Cemetery.[25] He and his wife, Bettie Waldham (1852–1932) had three known children: Hilda (1887–1953), Hortense (1890–1917), and Michael (1897–1992).[26]

Aaron continued to run A. & J. Plaut, and attended the World's Fair in St. Louis in 1904.[27] By 1909, Godfrey M. Braham (d. 1935), his son-in-law, and his son Michael Hoadly Plaut had joined the

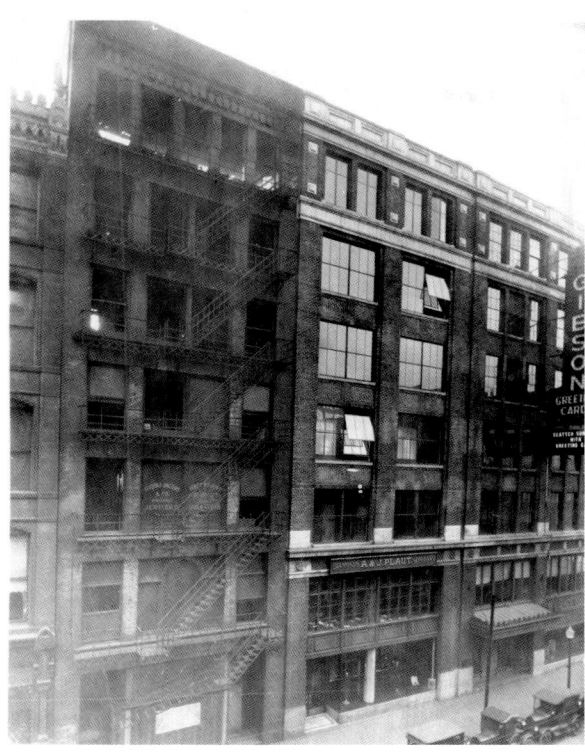

FIG. 112.1: **A. & J. Plaut, store exterior, photonegative, Cincinnati Historical Society**

firm as partners.[28] That year, when A. & J. Plaut's store space was leased to another party, they leased the entire third floor of the Schmidlapp Building at 128–130 East Fourth Street.[29] They held a close-out sale of their retail stock, beginning in October that year, and had resumed business, as wholesalers only, in their new location by January 1910.[30] Around 1917, the firm relocated to 811 Race Street, and in 1922, they moved to 231 West Fourth Street (fig. 112.1).[31] Aaron Plaut died in St. Petersburg, Florida, on January 26, 1929, and was buried in the Judah Touro Cemetery in Cincinnati.[32] He and his widow Jeanette Levi (1850–1941) had eight known children: Carrie (1871–1970, m. Godfrey Braham), Alicebelle (1873–1877), Miriam (1875–1955), Josie Leah (1876–1880), Hortense (1879–1975), Emma (1882–1960), Michael Hoadly (1883–1977), and Constance (1889–1964).[33] After Aaron's death, Godfrey M. Braham became president, Jeanette Plaut became vice president, and Michael Hoadly Plaut became secretary and treasurer of the firm.[34] They continued the business until 1933, when they formed Plaut Inc. and left the wholesale jewelry business to sell electrical appliances.[35]

The firm carried a large line of souvenir spoons, advertising 200 varieties.[36] They were especially known for their Cincinnati souvenir spoon, designed by **Charles F. Goettheim** (fig. 112.2).[37]

Goettheim was an engraver and designer who had previously worked at **Duhme & Co.** He applied for a patent for the spoon in May 1891, and Gorham produced the design.[38] By September 1891, it was noted that the firm had received the spoons and would have enough to supply the numerous orders already on their books.[39] The spoons were so popular that they sold out in six days.[40] The top of the spoon features the figure of the Roman soldier Cincinnatus, for whom Cincinnati is named, standing atop the seal of Ohio. The stem of the spoon represents the branch of the Ohio buckeye tree, attached to the bowl with two buckeyes, and the bowl boasts an

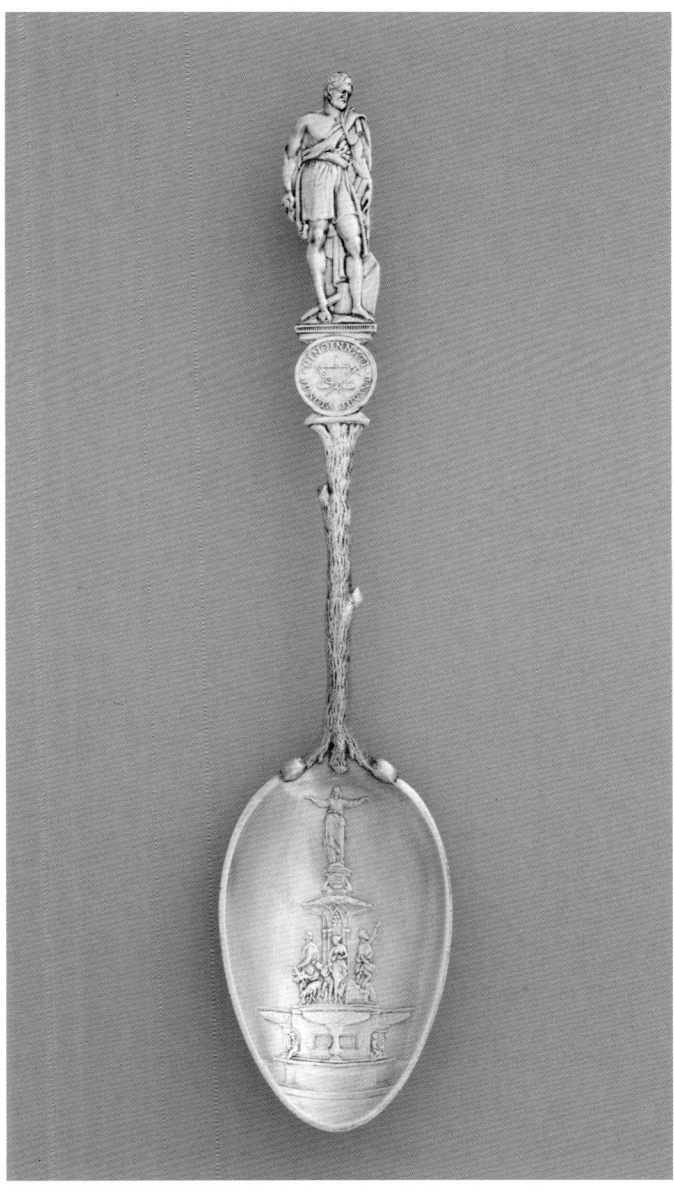

FIG. 112.2: **A. & J. Plaut, retailer, Charles F. Goettheim, designer, Gorham Mfg. Co., manufacturer, (estab. 1831), *Souvenir Spoon*, 1891–c. 1910, L. 5⅞ in. (14.9 cm), CAM, Gift of Michele Sandler, 2003.21**

engraving of the Tyler Davidson Fountain, a Cincinnati landmark since its dedication in 1871. This spoon design continued to be a popular seller, "with ready sales throughout the West as the representative Cincinnati spoon."[41]

During its 54 year tenure, A. & J. Plaut employed many skilled artisans and craftsmen. Most notable among these were Ferdinand Phillips (watch maker and partner), who would go on to establish **Richter & Phillips** in 1897, a wholesale jewelry firm that is still in operation today; and Joseph S. Voss (watch maker), who formed J.S. Voss and, later, **Joseph S. Voss & Son**.[42]

Silver was but one category of goods in A. & J. Plaut's line. They were not makers of silver. Evidence of their sources is found in extant pieces that are marked by both their firm (the wholesaler or retailer) and the maker. These pieces include flatware and small silver novelty items manufactured by Frank W. Smith Silver Co. (Gardner, Massachusetts), Ferdinand Fuchs & Brothers (New York), Reed & Barton (Taunton, Massachusetts), Whiting Mfg. Co. (New York City), and Gorham Mfg. Co. (Providence, Rhode Island). On occasion, the Plauts also bought from local manufacturers. A few examples bearing the Plaut mark (mark 112.1) are identical to shapes (spoons with tipped, exaggerated fiddle handles and pointed shoulders) and patterns (similar to Duhme & Co's "No. 1" [circa 1869]) associated with Cincinnati. A small percentage of these spoons associated with Cincinnati bear a stamped eagle mark. The maker associated with this eagle mark is not known at this time.[43]

MARK 112.1

1. Appel-Jones Family Tree, Ancestry.com, http://trees.ancestry .com/tree/4630635; "Michael Jacob Plaut," *Find A Grave*, www.finda-grave.com.

2. The immigration date used here is the one given in the 1900 Federal Census, Cincinnati, Hamilton, Ohio. A passport application submitted by Aaron and Joseph's brother Michael indicates that the family emigrated from Liverpool about July 1854. Ancestry.com, *U.S. Passport Applications, 1795–1925* [online database], Provo, Utah: Ancestry.com Operations Inc., 2007.

3. 1866, 1867, 1868 Cincinnati City Directories.

4. 1869 and 1877 Cincinnati City Directories. Aaron Plaut is not listed in the years between 1869 and 1877. The 1910 Federal Census indicates that his daughter Miriam was born in Tennessee in 1875.

5. 1878 Cincinnati City Directory.

6. The Arcade was demolished in 1929 for the construction of Carew Tower and its arcade which still exist today.

7. Boultinghouse, 333; Ohio, Vol. 11, p. 154, R.G. Dun & Co. Collection, Baker Library, Harvard Business School; Abraham Plaut later established Plaut Co., 6 West Pearl Street, Cincinnati, a wholesale notion dealership. He is not to be confused with Abraham M. Plaut (b. Kentucky, 1855, d. Cincinnati, 1932), who was known as A.M. Plaut. A.M. Plaut was also in the jewelry business in Cincinnati, beginning as early as 1883. He eventually managed the National Jewelry Company at the

Emery Arcade. A.M.'s brother, Bernard Plaut was also in the jewelry business in Cincinnati from as early as 1886 until about a year before his death in 1899. Their relation to Aaron and Joseph Plaut is likely, but yet to be confirmed; "Cincinnati," *Jewelers' Circular and Horlogiocal Review* (February 7, 1912): 189; "Abraham Plaut," *Find A Grave*, www.findagrave.com; Cincinnati city directories; Bernard Plaut and Abraham Plaut, burial records, www.jcemcin.org; "Plaut," death notice for Bernard Plaut, *Cincinnati Enquirer*, December 8, 1899, 7; Abraham Plaut, 1910 Federal Census, Cincinnati, Hamilton, Ohio; Abraham M. Plaut, will proved July 31, 1932, vol. 200, p. 123, Hamilton County Registry of Probate, Cincinnati, Ohio.

8. Ohio, Vol. 11, p. 154, R.G. Dun & Co. Collection.

9. Ibid.; An R.G. Dun & Co. report dated August 21, 1878, indicates that Aaron also had business in Brownsville, TN. The nature of this business is unknown.

10. Ferdinand Phillips married Sarah Plaut (1859–1932), sister of Aaron and Joseph; Ohio, Vol. 11, p. 154, R.G. Dun & Co. Collection; Sarah Plaut Phillips, burial record, United Jewish Cemetery of Price Hill, www.jcemcin.org

11. Advertisement, *JCHR* (July–August 1884): n.p.

12. Ibid.; Also see Advertisement, *Cincinnati Commercial Tribune*, December 21, 1889, 5; Later advertisements indicate that they

were special agents for Dueber, Hampden and Howard Watches. Advertisement, *Cincinnati Commercial Tribune*, September 16, 1890, 5.

13. Advertisement, *Cincinnati Commercial Tribune*, September 6, 1890, 5.

14. "Cincinnati," *JCHR* 14, no. 11 (December 1883): 370; "Trade Gossip," *JCHR* 15, no. 9 (October 1884): 299; Advertisement, *Cincinnati Commercial Tribune*, September 6, 1890, 5; "Cincinnati," *JCHR* (August 12, 1891): 34.

15. "Trade Gossip," *JCHR* 17, no. 7 (August 1886): 241.

16. "Cincinnati," *JCHR* 19, no 6 (July 1888): 17; "Cincinnati," *Late News Supplement to the JCHR* 25, no. 8 (September 21, 1892): 37; "Cincinnati," *JCHR* (August 18, 1897): 28; Copies of their catalogue could not be found at the time of this publication.

17. 1889 Cincinnati City Directory; When the streets of Cincinnati were renumbered in 1895, the address changed from 131 West Fourth Street to 105 West Fourth Street.

18. Ibid.; "Cincinnati," *JCHR* (December 2, 1896): 30.

19. "Cincinnati," *JCHR* (December 9, 1896): 28; "Cincinnati," *JCHR* (December 30, 1896): 22.

20. "Cincinnati," *JCHR* (February 17, 1897): 29; "Cincinnati," *JCHR* (March 10, 1897): 26; 1896–1899 Cincinnati City Directories.

21. 1900–1910 Cincinnati City Directories.

22. "The Forthcoming Interesting Dinner of the Cincinnati Wholesale Jewelers," *JCHR* (October 7, 1896):

10; "Cincinnati Wholesalers Dine and Discuss Various Matters," *JCHR* (October 14, 1896): 10.

23. "The Bicycle As a Jewelers' Side Line," *JCHR* (May 27, 1896): 6.

24. "Cincinnati," *JCHR* (October 2, 1901): 72.

25. 1913–1915 Cincinnati City Directories; Obituary, *Cincinnati Enquirer*, November 4, 1915, 4; "Joseph Plaut," *Find A Grave*, www.findagrave.com.

26. Appel-Jones Family Tree, Ancestry.com.

27. "Cincinnati," *JCHR* (November 2, 1904): 72.

28. 1909 Cincinnati City Directory; Godfrey Braham was the husband of Aaron Plaut's daughter, Carrie; Appel-Jones family tree, Ancestry.com.

29. "Cincinnati," *JCHR* (September 29, 1909): 87; "Cincinnati," *JCHR* (June 15, 1910): 93.

30. "Cincinnati," *JCHR* (July 6, 1910): 101; "Cincinnati," *JCHR* (October 5, 1910): 117; "Cincinnati," *JCHR* (January 4, 1911): 99.

31. 1910–1922 Cincinnati City Directories.

32. Death notice, *Cincinnati Enquirer*, January 27, 1929; "Aaron Plaut," *Find A Grave*, www.findagrave.com; Appel-Jones Family Tree, Ancestry.com.

33. Death notice, *Cincinnati Enquirer*, January 27, 1929; Appel-Jones Family Tree, Ancestry.com; 1910 Federal Census, Cincinnati, Hamilton, Ohio (Aaron Plaut indexed as Errand Plant).

34. 1930 Cincinnati City Directory; Marquis Boultinghouse notes a Jeanette Plaut who was listed as a

partner in J. Plaut & Mendel in the Louisville, KY city directory in 1858. This is not the same Jeanette Plaut (b. 1850) who was married to Aaron Plaut. Any relationship between the two women who share this name is unknown. Boultinghouse, 217.

35. 1933–34 Cincinnati City Directory; Godfrey Braham, obituary, *Cincinnati Times Star*, May 25, 1935, 31. Braham's obituary states that he

retired from active business a year and a half before his death when the firm of Plaut Inc. went out of business.

36. "Cincinnati," *JCHR* (August 12, 1891): 34.

37. Charles F. Goettheim. 1891. Design for a Spoon. US Patent 21,142, filed May 11, 1891, and issued Nov. 3, 1891; Robert Wilhelm, "Gorham's Cincinnatus Souvenir Spoon," *Silver*

Magazine (January/February 2012): 40–41.

38. "Cincinnati," *JCHR* (September 23, 1891): 31; "Cincinnati," *JCHR* (October 21, 1891): 31.

39. "Cincinnati," *JCHR* (September 23, 1891): 31.

40. "Cincinnati," *JCHR* (September 29, 1891): 33.

41. Ibid.

42. "Cincinnati," *JCHR* (February 17,

1897): 28; "Cincinnati," *JCHR* (March 29, 1905): 64.

43. A. & J. Plaut, eBay listings and private collections, Cincinnati silver binders, Cincinnati Art Museum. This eagle mark is not the same as those identified elsewhere in this book.

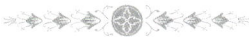

113. EDWARD PELL PRATT[1]

about 1792–1865, w. 1828–1830

Edward Pell Pratt was born in Montpelier, Vermont, around 1792.[2] He worked in New Hampshire for a time, where he trained John Tarlton (1795–1839) in the silversmith's trade, and then in Chillicothe, where he married Catherine Watson, daughter of John Watson on October 2, 1820.[3] They had one son, Edward Pell, Jr., who died of cholera on August 2, 1833.[4] In 1822, Pratt purchased land from his father-in-law on Water Street, and in 1830, he purchased lots on Paint Street, where he had maintained a shop since 1821.[5]

Pratt was active in Cincinnati by July 1828 while maintaining business interests in Chillicothe. On July 12, he submitted an advertisement in Cincinnati's *Saturday Evening Chronicle* as E.P. Pratt, the name he used most often in his business dealings.[6] The advertisement includes an illustration of spectacles and an announcement that he had opened shop in Cincinnati at 26 Main Street. A great assortment of available goods was listed, "Gold and Silver Lever and Plain Watches, Pearl, Filligree [sic], Jet, Paste and Berlin Jewellery [sic], Ladies' and Gentlemen's Chains, Seals and Keys, Cable Chains, Hearts and Crosses, Miniature Settings and Medallions, Gold, Silver, and Steel Spectacles, Gilt, Jet and Mohair Bracelets and Belts, Silver Plated Cake Baskets, Bottle Stands, Castors, Candlesticks, Snuffers and Trays, Silver Table, Tea, Salt and Mustard Spoons, Soup and Cream Ladles, and Sugar tongs, Ever Pointed Pencils, Gold and Silver Pens, Silver Thimbles, Plated Seals, Keys, Slides, and Rings, Britania [sic] Tea Setts [sic] and Coffee Pots, Fine Cutlery, and Military Goods; Eight Day Brass Clocks and Willard patent time pieces, together with a general assortment of

fancy articles." He also offered to buy or exchange old gold and silver, repair clocks and watches "in the best manner," and "manufacture silver plate to order at short notice."[7] From this we glean that in addition to offering a variety of goods for retail, he also had the ability to manufacture silver.

In September 1828 Pratt advertised that he had entered into a co-partnership with John E. Stretcher and Charles C. Beard to form Pratt, Stretcher & Beard.[8] Pratt and Beard were also partners in Chillicothe on Paint Street around this time.[9] Pratt, Stretcher and Beard of Cincinnati continued business at 26 Main Street and advertised a list of goods similar to those previously advertised by Pratt, as well as the ability to manufacture silver plate to order. However, no silver bearing the firm's name is known. The firm's tenure was short, as Beard withdrew in March 1829. Pratt & Stretcher continued on Main Street.[10] They listed as watch makers in the 1829 City Directory, but had dissolved by 1830 when Pratt returned to Chillicothe. There, he ran his own shop until partnering with **John J. Bangs** in 1839.[11] This partnership was dissolved by May 20, 1840, and Pratt continued on his own at the Paint Street location which served as both his shop and residence.[12] In 1852, a fire destroyed his building, but before the year was out, he had erected the building that still stands at 72 North Paint Street.[13]

On December 18, 1845, Pratt married Eliza Warren Stevens Ives (1804–1865).[14] Both were prominent members of St. Paul's Episcopal parish in Chillicothe.[15] Pratt continued to work in Chillicothe until his death from a skin infection on January 3, 1865.[16] Eliza died nineteen days later.[17] Edward Pell Pratt is buried in Cincinnati's Spring Grove Cemetery near his first wife, Catherine, and his daughter, Maria (1833–1867), who was married to daguerreotypist William Southgate Porter (1822–1889).[18] Pratt had two daughters with Catherine: Maria and Elizabeth.[19] Elizabeth married a Mr. Hunt who worked for Pratt and was purportedly the first to introduce the making of daguerreotypes to Chillicothe.[20]

Probate records for Pratt's estate enumerate a debt of $31.53 owed to C. & W.H. Allen (see **William Allen**), suggesting that the Allens supplied some of the goods sold at Pratt's Chillicothe store.[21] At the time of Pratt's death, his remaining stock, which included watches, jewelry, silver, other fancy goods, and store fittings were valued at $6,467.15. Charles F. Defeu took over Pratt's stand and presumably bought most of this stock.[22]

Silver found with mark 113.1 includes spoons with early fiddle handles, some with pointed shoulders, and others with rounded shoulders, and a pair of tongs with shell terminals. Mark 113.2 has been found on a spoon with a tipped, early fiddle handle and rounded shoulders; spoons with tipped, exaggerated fiddle handles and pointed shoulders; and a pair of tongs with claw terminals.[23]

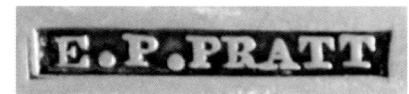

MARK 113.1

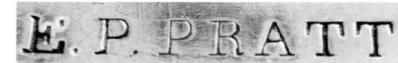

MARK 113.2

1. Previous sources have indicated that the E.P. Pratt working in Cincinnati was Ephraim P. Pratt. The smith working in Cincinnati and Chillicothe was Edward Pell Pratt. He should also not be confused with the Presbyterian Reverend E.P. Pratt (1816–1886), active in Portsmouth and Athens, Ohio; 1830 and 1840 Federal Censuses, Chillicothe, Ross, Ohio; M.P. Wheeler, *Evolution of Ella Wheeler Wilcox and Other Wheelers*, Madison, WI: M.P. Wheeler, 1921, 7–8; Charles William Tarleton, *The Tarleton Family*, Concord, NH: Ira C. Evans, 1900, 102; Eliza and Edward Pratt obituary, *Scioto Gazette*, January 24, 1865; Ross County Probate Records, http://www.rossprobate juvenile.com/Probate%20Index.pdf, case # 6145.

2. Burial records at Spring Grove Cemetery, Cincinnati, Ohio, give Pratt's birthplace as Massachusetts, but his obituary and the 1850 Federal Census give his birthplace as Vermont. Eliza and Edward Pratt obituary, January 24, 1865; Burial records, Spring Grove Cemetery.

3. Tarleton, *The Tarleton Family*, 102; In the 1850 Federal Census, an Albert Tarlton, clerk, is living with E.P. Pratt; "Ross County Ohio Marriages 1798–1845," *Ohio Genealogy Express*, http://www.ohiogenealogy express.com/ross/marriages

/rossco_marr_1798_1849_grm_p4 .htm, accessed August 15, 2012; The relationships, if any, between Edward Pell Pratt and Azariah Pratt and Elisha Pratt, silversmiths active in Marietta, Ohio, are unknown.

4. Pat Medert, Archivist, Ross County Historical Society to Maureen McLaughlin, email, January 3, 2012, Decorative Arts & Design Department, Cincinnati Art Museum, Edward Pell Pratt research file.

5. Ibid.

6. *Saturday Evening Chronicle*, July 19, 1828, reproduced in Beckman, 111.

7. Ibid.; At this time, the term "plate" was used to describe coin silver wares in general, not silver plated wares.

8. Advertisement, *The Western Tiller*, September 12, 1828, reproduced in Beckman, 112. Stretcher likely went on to Columbus and Hillsboro, Ohio. Elizabeth D. Beckman, "Silversmiths, Watch and Clock Makers, and Jewelers in Columbus, Ohio, before 1865," *The Magazine Antiques* (December 1978): 1300–1305.

9. Advertisement, *Scioto Gazette*, May 15, 1828.

10. Advertisement, *The Western Tiller*, March 11, 1829, reproduced in Beckman, 135.

11. 1830, 1840 Federal Censuses, Chillicothe, Ross, Ohio; *W.W. Reilly*

& Co.'s Ohio State Business Directory, Cincinnati: Morgan & Overend, 1834, 414; Beckman, 8; Advertisement, *Scioto Gazette*, May 23, 1839.

12. Advertisement, *Scioto Gazette*, May 20, 1840; "Sixty Explains," *The Chillicothe Leader* 4, no. 34 (January 8, 1887).

13. Pat Medert, Archivist, Ross County Historical Society to Maureen McLaughlin, email, January 3, 2012, Cincinnati Art Museum, Edward Pell Pratt research file.

14. Eliza was born in Massachusetts and married Shayler Ives (b. 1785 Bristol, CT, d. 1840) in 1821; "Ross County Ohio Marriages 1798–1845," *Ohio Genealogy Express*; Lyle S. Evans, *A Standard History of Ross County Ohio*, Chillicothe: Ross County Genealogical Society, 1987, 2:776; Eliza and Edward Pratt obituary, January 24, 1865. The obituary says that she was in her 63rd year, and calls into question the date of her birth (1804) given in Evans.

15. Eliza and Edward Pratt obituary, January 24, 1865.

16. Pratt is listed as a silversmith in the 1850 Federal Census, Chillicothe, Ross, Ohio; Eliza and Edward Pratt obituary, January 24, 1865; Death notice, *Daily Ohio State Journal*, February 2, 1865, 2.

17. Ibid.

18. The burial place of Eliza is unknown. The burial plots for Edward Pell Pratt and Catherine Pratt were owned by Pratt's son-in-law W.S. Porter. The burial record for Catherine Pratt indicates that she was removed from Chillicothe and interred on the same date as E.P. Pratt. The 1840 Federal Census indicates that there was a woman between the ages of 40 and 49 living with Pratt, making it likely that Catherine died between 1840 and 1845; Burial records, Spring Grove Cemetery; Eliza and Edward Pratt, obituary, January 24, 1865; 1850 Federal Census, Chillicothe, Ross, Ohio.

19. *The Chillicothe Leader* 4, no. 34 (January 8, 1887).

20. Ibid.

21. E.P. Pratt, estate inventory, dated February 11, 1865, Ross County Probate Court Archives, Chillicothe, Ohio.

22. Advertisement, *The Chillicothe Leader* (January 23, 1866).

23. E.P. Pratt, eBay listings and private collections, Cincinnati silver binders, Cincinnati Art Museum.

114. PHILIP P. PRICE

w. 1804–1836

Philip Price's first appearance in Cincinnati comes by way of an advertisement for his partnership with **Harmon Long** in September 1804 when the men commenced a clock and watch making business at the corner of Main and Front Streets.[1] Price's wife Mary, presumably his first wife, died in March of the following year.[2] Shortly thereafter, Long & Price ran an announcement that they had relocated to Main and Columbia Streets, "at the house formerly occupied by John Humes," where they sold all types of clocks, repaired and cleaned watches, and offered "all other kinds of gold and silver work done on the most reasonable terms and on the shortest notice."[3] In June 1806 the partnership dissolved and Price continued in the clock, watch, and jewelry business, seeking an apprentice of about 14 or 15 years of age to work with him in the house of Thomas Williams, "on Main Street opposite to that occupied by Long & Price."[4]

On June 26, 1806, he married Maria Malsbery (d. 1811), and in January 1807 he was part of the group that incorporated the Cincinnati University, an unrealized venture.[5] In September 1810 he advertised a two-story brick house for sale, the second door above the corner of Main and Market Streets. Presumably this is the house that he built on land purchased in 1806 from Francis Mennessier and his wife Mary (parents of **Peter Cazelles**' wife).[5] It is described as having "a good kitchen cellar, and out buildings . . . an excellent stand for any kind of business."[7] By December 1810 he had partnered with Alexander Simpson as **Simpson & Price**.[8] They set up their shop in the house of James C. Morris on Main Street, "near the Columbian Inn, and opposite A. Dunseth's Tin Manufactory," where they offered clocks, "watchworks," surveying instruments, "all kinds of gold and silver work," and constant employ to a journeyman who understood the business.[9] But, the partnership was very short-lived, ending by early January 1811 when Price advertised alone as a watch and clock maker, gold and silversmith.[10] In October, he submitted notice of a six-cent reward for the return of a runaway apprentice named Andrew Robb, "about 20 years of age, 5 feet 6 or 7 inches high."[11]

Price was an enlistment officer in the Middletown, Dayton, and Eaton areas, and a 2nd Lieutenant in the 14th Regiment Infantry in Ohio in 1812 and 1813.[12] Following action in the War of 1812, he announced in April 1815 that he had commenced in the clock and watch making, silversmith, and jewelry business at the location that he had listed for sale in 1810—"the second door above the corner of Main and Market Streets."[13]

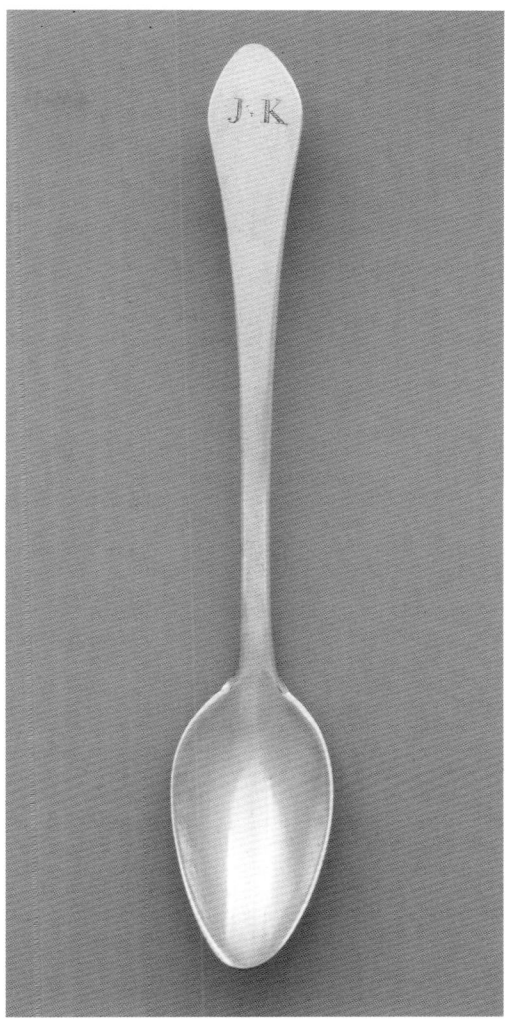

FIG 114.1: Philip Price, *Teaspoon*, 1804–1836, L. 5⅜ in. (13.7 cm), CAM, Gift of Mary Sering Kemper in memory of her Great-Grandfather, James Kemper, 1924.257

Price did not list in the first Cincinnati city directory published in 1819. In September 1823 he appeared in Lebanon, Ohio, advertising as a clock and watch maker "late from Cincinnati."[14] While in Lebanon, he married Mary R. Stites (circa 1791–1873), the daughter of Benjamin Stites II and Mary "Polly" Mills, on October 6, 1824.[15]

By 1829, Price had returned to Cincinnati, as he appeared in the city directory for that year, listing as a watch maker on Walnut, near Fifth Street. He continued to list at this location until 1834 when he was at Sixth Street between Elm and Plum. He is not included in directories after 1836, and it is likely that he died around this time.[16] There was at least one other Philip Price who worked in the Philadelphia/Chester County area as a watch and clock maker.[17] No relation between our subject and that Philip Price is known.

The spoon in fig. 114.1 is attributed to Philip Price and engraved with the initials of Rev. James Kemper (1753-1834).[18] Kemper was the first ordained Presbyterian minister in the Ohio Valley, arriving in Cincinnati in the early 1790s. He founded Cincinnati's Lane Seminary and several churches.[19] The spoon was given to the Cincinnati Art Museum by Kemper's great granddaughter.

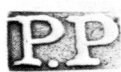

MARK 114.1

1. Advertisement, *Western Spy*, September 4, 1804, reproduced in Beckman, 90. Variants in historical records for the subject's given name are Philip and Phillip. Philip is used here, as it was used most frequently.
2. Death notice, *Liberty Hall*, March 1805, cited in Beckman, 113.
3. Advertisement, *Liberty Hall*, June 3, 1805, reproduced in Beckman, 113.
4. Advertisement, *Western Spy*, June 10, 1806, reproduced in Beckman, 113; Advertisement, *Western Spy*, October 7, 1806.
5. Marriage announcement, *Liberty Hall*, June 30, 1806, 3; Obituary, *Western Spy*, March 30, 1811; Ohio General Assembly, *Acts of the State of Ohio*, Chillicothe, Ohio: Joseph S. Collins & Co., 1807, 5:64–68; S.B. Nelson and J.M Runk, *History of Cincinnati and Hamilton County, Ohio*, Cincinnati: S.B. Nelson & Co., 1894, 98.
6. *Hamilton County Deed Book* D1,

recorded, April 5, 1806.
7. Advertisement, *Western Spy*, September 15, 1810.
8. Advertisement, *Liberty Hall*, December 5, 1810, reproduced in Beckman, 129.
9. Advertisement, *Liberty Hall*, December 5, 1810, reproduced in Beckman, 129.
10. Advertisement, *Western Spy*, January 5, 1811, reproduced in Beckman, 114.
11. Notice, *Western Spy*, November 16, 1811.
12. Advertisement, *Western Spy*, June 11, 1812; Advertisement, *Western Spy*, July 11, 1812; Notice, *Western Spy*, October 10, 1812; Notice, *Western Spy*, November 21, 1812; Notice, *Western Spy*, February 20, 1813; Notice, *Western Spy*, August 14, 1813, reproduced in Beckman, 114.
13. Advertisement, *Spirit of the Times*, April 8, 1815, reproduced in Beckman, 114.

14. Advertisement, *Western Star*, September 20, 1823.
15. *Cincinnati Pioneer Association Records and Minutes*, vol. 1, 331; Audrey Shields Hancock and Chuck Carey, "The Plight of Mary "Polly" Mills-Stites-Woodruff," http://cwcfamily.org/marymill.htm; Burial records, Spring Grove Cemetery, Cincinnati, Ohio; Death record, Cincinnati Health Department, University of Cincinnati, Archives and Rare Books Library, http://hdl.handle.net/2374.UC/598887; Death notice, *Cincinnati Commercial Tribune*, August 25, 1873, 5.
16. Philip Price does not appear in the 1840 Federal Census of Hamilton County, Ohio. Mary Price is listed alone that year, and in the 1850 Federal Census of Hamilton County, Ohio, she is listed as a widow. She eventually married Stephen Woodruff. It is not believed that he

was related to **Enos Woodruff**, the silversmith.
17. Brian Loomes, *Watchmakers and Clockmakers of the World*, vol. 2, London: N.A.G. Press, 1976; Maurice Brix, *List of Philadelphia Silversmiths and Allied Artificers from 1682 to 1850*, Philadelphia: privately printed, 1920; Advertisement, *General Advertiser* (Philadelphia), November 30, 1790, 4; Advertisement, *Poulson's American Daily Advertiser* (Philadelphia), January 3, 1818, 4; Advertisement, *Village Record* (West Chester, PA), April 1, 1818, 1; "Daring Robberies," *Charleston Courier*, June 13, 1826, 1; 1794–1841 Philadelphia City Directories.
18. James Kemper, death record, Spring Grove Cemetery.
19. Andrew Carr Kemper, *A Memorial of the Rev. James Kemper for the Centennial of Kentucky*, Louisville, KY: n.p., 1900.

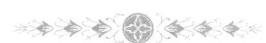

115. JOSEPH RAFEL[1]

1814–1885, w. 1836–circa 1840 or later

Born in Bonn, Germany, on January 28, 1814, Rafel arrived in New York around 1830, and worked there before going to Cincinnati around 1836.[2] In January 1837 he submitted a notice seeking the owner of a bundle of clothing left "on or about the 18th of November last" at his "store" on Front Street.[3] The nature of his trade was not given. In his only appearance in the Cincinnati city directories, he was listed in 1839/40 as a jeweler and silversmith on Main between Columbia and Front Streets. In September 1848 Rafel married Sarah Ruden (1823–1913) in New York City. Sarah was the daughter of Moses A. Ruden and Rebecca S. Gomperts, from Suriname.[4] Census data and other period documents confirm that he was working in New Orleans

from 1850 to 1861.[5] It is not clear when, between 1840 and 1848, Rafel left Cincinnati.

Listed as merchant in New Orleans in the 1850 Census, Rafel had a loan office and jewelry store under the St. Charles Hotel, which was destroyed by fire early in 1851.[6] He was back in business at the same location, advertising watches and jewelry as well as "sterling silver spoons, cups, forks &c." in 1853.[7] By 1857, he had moved his shop to Camp Street and was advertising a broad range of silver including flatware, cups, goblets, tea and breakfast sets, watches, clocks, jewelry, and other fancy goods.[8] Rafel remained in New Orleans until 1861. when he moved back to New York and worked as a broker until the end of the Civil War.[9]

Rafel returned to New Orleans and his shop on Camp Street at the end of the War. However, by November 1866 "JOSEPH RAFEL, GOLDSMITH, SILVERSMITH AND JEWELER, AND GENERAL DEALER IN FANCY MERCHANDISE" was advertising that he was "about to retire from business" and was offering his stock for sale at 25% below cost.[10] By 1870, Rafel was back in New York, working as a stockbroker on Wall Street until 1883, when he gave his occupation as "retired gentleman" in his application for U.S. naturalization.[11]

Joseph and Sarah Rafel were the parents of six children for whom records were found: Joseph (b. 1849); Frank (b. 1853); Florence (b. 1855); Henry (b. 1857); Viola (b. 1859); and William (b. 1862).[12] In 1900, Sarah reported that she was the mother of seven children, of whom five were living.[13] Joseph Rafel died suddenly at his residence in New York on September 18, 1885.[14]

Silver marked by Rafel probably dates to his years in New Orleans. His mark, "J. RAFEL" in rectangular cartouche, on a coin silver goblet includes "NEW ORLEANS" in a crescent-shaped cartouche, while examples of flatware with fiddle thread handles marked by Rafel are also often stamped "N.O."[15] Rafel does not seem to have been a practicing silversmith, as the wares bearing his marks appear to have been retailed, and not made, by him.

1   Rafel's surname is variously spelled Rafil, Rafele, and Rafael in period documents.
2. Malcolm H. Stern, *First Jewish Families: 600 Genealogies: 1654–1988*, Baltimore: Ottenheimer Publishers, 1991, 254; Although Rafel's 1880 application for naturalization gives his arrival as 1830, documentation of this was not found. It is probable that he was the Joseph Raffell, born 1815, who arrived in New York from London on May 31, 1834. Ancestry.com, *New York Passenger Lists, 1820–1957* [online database], Provo, Utah: Ancestry.com Operations Inc., 2010; *Crescent City Silver*, New Orleans The Historic New Orleans Collection, 1980, 100.
3. *Cincinnati Daily Gazette* 10, no. 2965, February 2, 1837, 3.
4. Joseph Rafel, death notice, *New York Herald*, September 20, 1885, 15; Stern, *First Jewish Families*, 254.
5. 1850 Federal Census, New Orleans, Orleans, Louisiana.
6. Ibid; Advertisement *Alexandria Gazette* (Alexandria, VA), August 25, 1851, 6.
7. Advertisement, *Le Courier de la Louisiane* (New Orleans), July 23, 1853, 4.
8. Advertisement, *The Daily True Delta* (New Orleans), January 8, 1857, 3.
9. *Cohen's New Orleans and Lafayette Directory 1861*, New Orleans Public Library, accessed online; 1860 Federal Census, New Orleans, Orleans, Louisiana; Ancestry.com, *U.S. IRS Tax Assessment Lists, 1862–1918* [online database], Provo, Utah: Ancestry.com Operations Inc., 2008; *Trow's New York City Directory 1865* and *1872–1884*, New York: John F. Trow.
10. Advertisement, *New Orleans Daily Delta*, November 20, 1866, reproduced in *Crescent City Silver*, Historic New Orleans, 100.
11. 1870 Federal Census, New York Ward 22, District 15, New York, New York; 1880 Federal Census, New York City, New York, New York; Ancestry.com, *U.S. Naturalization Record Indexes, 1791–1992* [online database], Provo, Utah: Ancestry.com Operations Inc., 2010.
12. 1850 Federal Census, Representative District 3, Orleans, Louisiana; 1870 Federal Census, New York City, New York, New York.
13. 1900 Federal Census New York City, New York, New York.
14. Joseph Rafel, death notice, September 20, 1885.
15. *Goblet*, Cowan's, March 15, 2008, lot 194; *Crescent City Silver*, Historic New Orleans, 100; Joseph Rafel, eBay listings and private collections, Cincinnati silver binders, Cincinnati Art Museum.

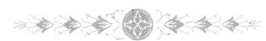

116. PHILIP LOUIS REESE

1837–1897, w. 1858–1859

Philip Louis Reese, son of German immigrants George Ries (1795–1877) and Wilhelmina Kaiser (1800–1854), was born in Kenton, Ohio, in September 1837.[1] His father was a blacksmith.[2] Philip had changed the spelling of his surname to Reese by 1858, when he was working as a watch maker at Weiler, Trost & Co. in Cincinnati.[3] In 1859, Reese moved to Mount Sterling, Kentucky, where his occupation was recorded as "jeweler" in the federal census records from 1860 to 1880, although when he registered for the Civil War draft, he gave his occupation as "silversmith."[4] A younger brother, William Henry Reese (1846–1935) joined Philip in 1862, working as a watch maker and jeweler in his shop.[5] The incuse stamp, "P.L. REESE & BRO." found on silverware reflects this association.[6] Other marks used by Reese include "P.L. REESE" in a rectangular

cartouche, and an incuse stamp "P.L. REESE."[7] Although anecdotal information includes three different references to "cups" with his mark which were premiums or trophies presented at local fairs and horse races, little else is known about these objects, of which Reese was probably the retailer and not the maker.[8]

Philip Reese started business in Mount Sterling as a jeweler selling "watches, clocks and jewelry."[9] An entrepreneur, his interests broadened to include sewing machines by 1876, a hotel by 1880, and bicycles in the 1890s.[10] His focus was increasingly on sewing machines by 1880, when it was reported that his sewing machine "business is one of gigantic proportions in our town," and that "Mr. Reese runs four wagons and a half-dozen hands constantly selling and delivering" sewing machines in eastern Kentucky.[11] By

1887, John W. Jones, who began working with Reese as an apprentice in about 1870, was advertising as a jeweler in Mount Sterling, apparently replacing Reese as the proprietor of the shop.[12]

Philip Reese married Frances Elizabeth Ragland (1842–1922) in 1859.[13] Their children were Fannie (1861–1950); Mattie (1864–1904); Lula (1866–1900); and Henry (1868–1904).[14] In 1868, William H. Reese married Mary Jane Ragland (1844–1921), the sister of Philip's wife Frances. Their children were Elizabeth "Lizzie" (b. 1869–1950); George (1871–1951); Harry (b. 1884); and Mattie (b. 1886).[15]

1. 1850 Federal Census, Kenton, Hardin, Ohio; Boultinghouse, 224; E. Elizabeth Johnson, unpublished manuscript, Cincinnati Art Museum, Decorative Arts & Design Department, Philip L. Reese research file; Philip L. Reese, *Find A Grave*, www.findagrave.com.
2. E. Elizabeth Johnson, unpublished manuscript.
3. 1858, 1859 Cincinnati City Directories.
4. 1860, 1870, 1880 Federal Censuses, Mount Sterling, Montgomery, Kentucky; Ancestry.com, *U.S. Civil War Draft Registration Records, 1863–1865* [online database], Provo, Utah: Ancestry.com Operations Inc., 2010.
5. 1870 Federal Census, Levee, Montgomery, Kentucky; 1880 Federal Census, Aarons Run, Montgomery, Kentucky; 1900 Federal Census, Magisterial District 3, Montgomery, Kentucky; William Reese, obituary, *Mount Sterling Advocate*, February 26, 1935, 1.
6. Boultinghouse, 305.
7. Photographs of these marks illustrate the entry on Philip L. Ries Reese, "Paulsen Family Tree," Ancestry.com.
8. "Riddles & Replies," *The Magazine Antiques* 42, no. 2 (August 1942): 97; Boultinghouse, 224.
9. Advertisement, *Hawes' Kentucky State Gazeteer and Business Directory for 1859–60*, cited in Boultinghouse, 224.
10. Reese was granted US Letters Patent No. 124,160 for an Improvement in the balance wheels of sewing machines in February 1872. See also "Reese's Headquarters," *Mount Sterling Advocate*, June 23, 1896, and *R.L. Polk's Kentucky State Gazetteer and Business Directory for 1876*, in which he is listed as "P.L. Reese, proprietor of a commercial room, dealing in jewelry and sewing machines," cited in Boultinghouse, 224.
11. Advertisement, *Mount Sterling Sentinel Democrat*, April 9, 1880.
12. Mrs. Charles C. Peters, daughter of P.L. Reese, to Lockwood Barr, letter, cited in Boultinghouse, 224; Advertisement, *R.L. Polk's Kentucky State Gazetteer & Business Directory for 1887–8*, cited in Boultinghouse, 173; John W. Jones of Mount Sterling was included in every Federal Census list from 1870–1930 and there is no evidence he was working elsewhere during those years. The 1870 Census for Kentucky includes ten different John W. Jones, all of whom were born 1850–60. Boultinghouse, 173, confused the Jones of Mount Sterling with the John W. Jones who worked in a jewelry store in Paris, KY in 1870 and 1880 and the John W. Jones who advertised as a jeweler in 1876–77 in Paris, KY.
13. Philip L. Ries Reese, "Paulsen Family Tree," Ancestry.com.
14. 1870, 1880 Federal Censuses, Mount Sterling, Montgomery, Kentucky; E. Elizabeth Johnson, unpublished manuscript.
15. 1880, 1900 Federal Censuses, Mount Sterling, Montgomery, Kentucky; E. Elizabeth Johnson, unpublished manuscript.

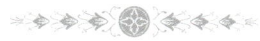

117. RHODES & ANTHONY

1836

The only known advertisement for this firm, composed of **Thomas F. Rhodes** and John Gould Anthony (fig. 117.1), appears in October 1836.[1] It announces that the firm, operating at 50 Main Street, has just received a fall supply of goods, including jewelry, silver spoons and spectacles, watches, clocks, and other fancy goods. It also notes that the firm will "make to order, Silver Spoons, Tumblers &c. and keep constantly on hand an assortment of Silver Ware of their own manufacture."[2] An addendum at the end of the advertisement indicates that it was also published in the *Dayton Journal*; *Richmond Palladium*; *Indianapolis Journal*; *Republic Banner* in Madison, Indiana; *Louisville Journal*; *Lexington Intelligencer*; *Maysville Eagle*; and *Missouri Republican* in St. Louis, providing a snapshot of their market area.

Rhodes and Anthony were both born in Rhode Island. Anthony was born in Providence on May 17, 1804.[3] He had arrived in Cincinnati by August 1834 when he joined **Allen, Rhodes & Co.**[4] He is not known to have been skilled in the silver, jewelry, or watch and clock making trades. Throughout his lifetime he had

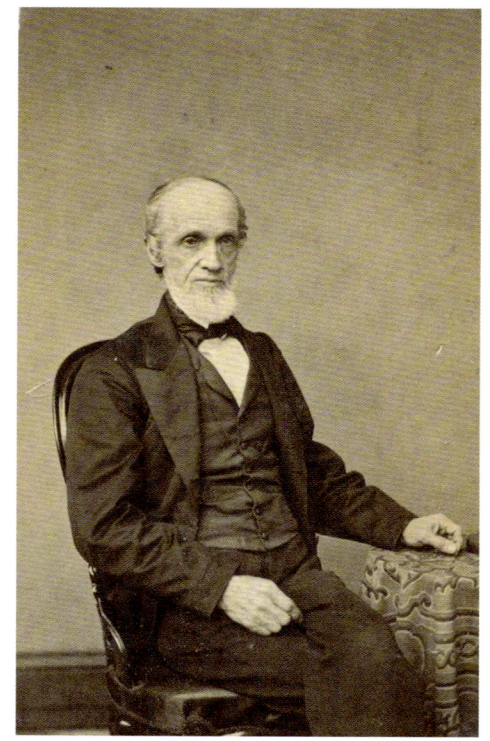

FIG. 117.1: John Gould Anthony, carte-de-visite, 1863, Increase A. Lapham papers, 1825–1930, Wisconsin Historical Society, 44738

numerous occupations. His chief interest was the study of shells and fossils, and he is remembered today for his achievements in the field of conchology.[5] He died in Cambridge, Massachusetts, on October 16, 1877.[6]

Rhodes & Anthony appears to have been very short-lived. **Samuel T. Carley** became a partner in the firm shortly after his arrival in Cincinnati, and the firm became Rhodes, Anthony & Carley (see **Rhodes, Anthony & Co.**). The new firm and partners appear in the 1837 *Western Address Directory*, for which information was likely collected for publication in late 1836.[7]

A rendering of the mark of Rhodes & Anthony, "Rhodes & Anthony" in a rectangular cartouche, was included in Elizabeth Beckman's study on Cincinnati silversmiths, but no silver bearing this mark has been documented in recent years.[8]

1　John Gould Anthony married Ann Whiting Rhodes on October 16, 1832. Ann Whiting Rhodes was the sister of Thomas Frederick Rhodes and James Fenner Rhodes. All were the children of Thomas and Lydia (Keene) Rhodes of Providence. Susan Rhodes, "Rhodes family tree," Ancestry.com, posted November 13, 1998; *Memorial Biographies of The New England Historical Genealogical Society, Towne Memorial Fund*, vol. 7, *1871–1880*, Boston: The New England Historical Genealogical Society, 1907, 265.

2　Notice, *Cincinnati Daily Gazette*, October 8, 1836, reproduced in Beckman, 6; A later advertisement for Rhodes, Anthony & Carley, appearing in the *Western Address Directory*, 1837, page 328, indicates that 50 Main was at the corner of Main and Columbia Streets.

3　*Memorial Biographies*, Historical Genealogical Society, 265.

4　Notice of new partnership, *Cincinnati Daily Gazette*, September 6, 1834, reproduced in Beckman, 117.

5　John Gould Anthony was a noted member of the Western Academy of Natural Sciences of Cincinnati. During his years in Cincinnati, he was a partner in the aforementioned firm, an independent and employed accountant, and a partner with a bookseller and publisher. In 1863, he moved to Cambridge, MA to work with Louis Agassiz at Harvard's Museum of Comparative Zoology. *Memorial Biographies*, Historical Genealogical Society, 265; 1870 Federal Census, Cambridge Ward 4, Middlesex, Massachusetts.

6　*Memorial Biographies*, Historical Genealogical Society, 265.

7　Advertisement, *Western Address Directory*, 1837, 328.

8　Beckman, 6.

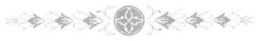

118. RHODES, ANTHONY & CO.

late 1836–1839 or earlier

This firm was composed of **Thomas F. Rhodes**, John Gould Anthony (see **Rhodes & Anthony**), and **Samuel T. Carley**. An advertisement for the firm of Rhodes, Anthony & Carley, "MANU-FACTURERS OF JEWELLERY [*sic*] & SILVER WARE," in business at the "Corner of Main (No. 50) and Columbia streets," appeared in the *Western Address Directory* in 1837. The information for this directory was likely collected in late 1836, not long after Carley arrived in Cincinnati and joined his new partners who had oper-ated previously as Rhodes & Anthony.[1] There were no Cincinnati city directories printed between the years of 1836 and 1839, and there are no additional known advertisements for Rhodes, Anthony & Carley or Rhodes, Anthony & Co., so piecing together information about these firms has been difficult. The firm name of Rhodes, Anthony & Carley has not been documented on any known extant silver. However, the firm name of Rhodes, Anthony & Co. (mark 118.1) has been observed on sugar tongs with claw terminals, and spoons and a cream ladle with fiddle handles and pointed shoulders.[2] Therefore, it is most probable that the partners advertised in the 1837 *Western Address Directory* under one name (Rhodes, Anthony & Carley) and marked their silver with another name (Rhodes, Anthony & Co.). The partners must have disbanded in or prior to 1839, as the next published directory lists Carley as an independent jewelry manufacturer, John G. Anthony with no occupation or business affiliation, and does not include Thomas F. Rhodes.[3]

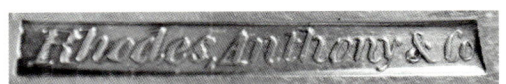

MARK 118.1

1.　Advertisement, *Western Address Directory*, 1837, 328.

2.　Beckman, 117; Rhodes, Anthony & Co., eBay listings and private collections, Cincinnati silver binders, Cincinnati Art Museum; *Tongs*, Elizabeth Beckman Collection, Cincinnati Museum Center.

3.　1839/40 Cincinnati City Directory.

119. JAMES F. RHODES

1822–1907, W. 1844–1855

James Fenner Rhodes was born in Providence, Rhode Island, on April 16, 1822, to Thomas F. Rhodes (1780–1834) and Lydia Keene (1780–1857).[1] He was the younger brother of **Thomas F. Rhodes**.[2] His grandparents were Elizabeth Fenner (1743–1824) and Captain William Rhodes (1742–1823), a wealthy commission merchant and landholder in Providence.[3] The details of James F. Rhodes' training as a silversmith are unknown. However, Providence was a burgeoning center for the jewelry trade, and it is possible that he may have trained with or under his older brother Thomas. James' father does not appear to have been involved in the trade.[4]

The first record of Rhodes in Cincinnati is found in the 1844 City Directory, where he is noted as a silversmith working on Main, between Third and Fourth Streets. In the next published directory (1846), he is listed as a watch maker boarding with John G. Anthony (see **Rhodes & Anthony**), the husband of Rhodes' sister, Ann Whiting Rhodes (1810–1898). During this year, from about February to October, Rhodes was in a partnership with **Francis Clark** that operated as Francis Clark & Co.[5] After their dissolution, Rhodes continued in business under his own name with fair success. Credit reporters estimated his worth to be between $3,000 and $5,000, and declared him safe for credit.[6] In the 1850/51 City Directory, he was listed as being in the jewelry and silverware business at 103 Main Street (three doors above Third Street)—the same address where Clark had been listed in 1848 and 1849.[7] It is presumed that Rhodes had taken over the business, because in 1850, he was employing Clark as a clerk.[8] Rhodes continued business at that address until his last Cincinnati city directory listing in 1856.[9] He was reported to have left the business that year, prior to the end of July, and relocated to Dubuque, Iowa.[10] However, he had returned to Cincinnati by June 1860, when he was recorded in the census as a farmer, living with the family of merchant George H. Hill, also born in Rhode Island.[11] In June 1863 he registered for the Civil War draft in Cincinnati, giving his occupation as merchant.[12] About 1865, Rhodes moved to Lancaster, Grant County, Wisconsin, where he worked as a farmer.[13] His occupation was stated as capitalist in the 1905 Wisconsin State Census.[14] It has been suggested that Rhodes left Cincinnati, and perhaps even the jewelry, watch, and silver business, due to health reasons, but this has not been documented.[15]

In 1853, Rhodes ran a wonderfully illustrated advertisement (fig. 119.1) as a "manufacturer and dealer in watches, jewelry and gold pens." The delightful "Colossus of Rhodes" features forks, spoons

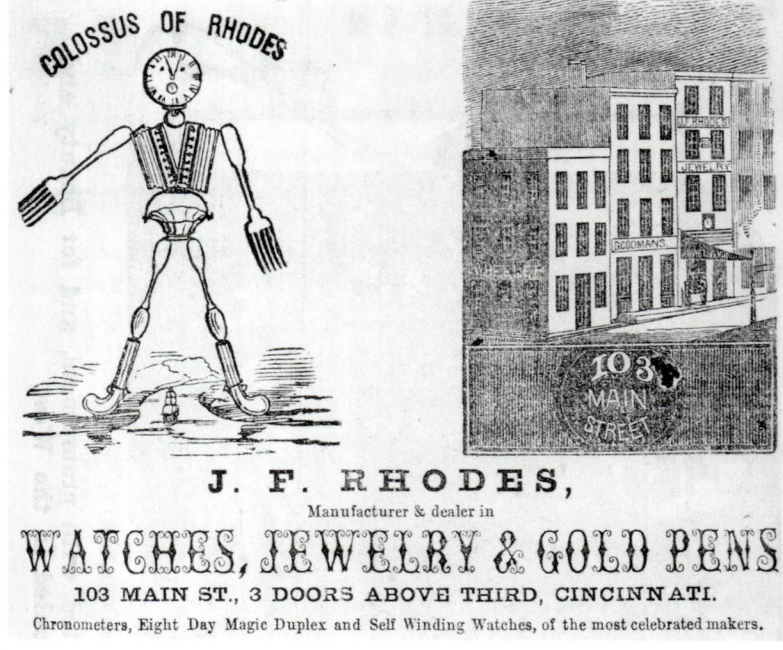

FIG. 119.1: Advertisement, *W.W. Reilly & Co.'s Ohio State Business Directory for 1853–4*, Cincinnati: Morgan & Overend, 1853, 1:97

and even a basket (perhaps of silver) among the variety of wares used in its construction. It is most likely that James Fenner Rhodes did not produce much, if any, of the silver that he sold.[16] Spoons with fiddle thread handles have been found with the incuse mark "RHODES."[17] A dessert spoon and teaspoon engraved "Rhodes" (fig. 119.2), and stamped with mark 119.1 reside in the Cincinnati Art Museum's collection. These marks, consisting of surname only, could have been used by either James F. or Thomas F. Rhodes. The dessert and teaspoon, given by James F. Rhodes' granddaughter, reportedly marked the occasion of the marriage of James F. Rhodes and Laura Lyons.[18]

On January 28, 1852, Rhodes married Sarah Anne Kingman (about 1832–1857) in Cincinnati.[19] They had two sons, James (1854–1883) and William (1856–1874).[20] On June 1, 1863, he married Laura Lyons (1831–1909) in Cincinnati.[21] They had four known children: Howard (1865–1951), Clara (1868–1938), Linda (1870), and Emma (b. about 1877).[22] James F. Rhodes died in Lancaster, Wisconsin, on August 17, 1907, and is buried at Hillside Cemetery.[23]

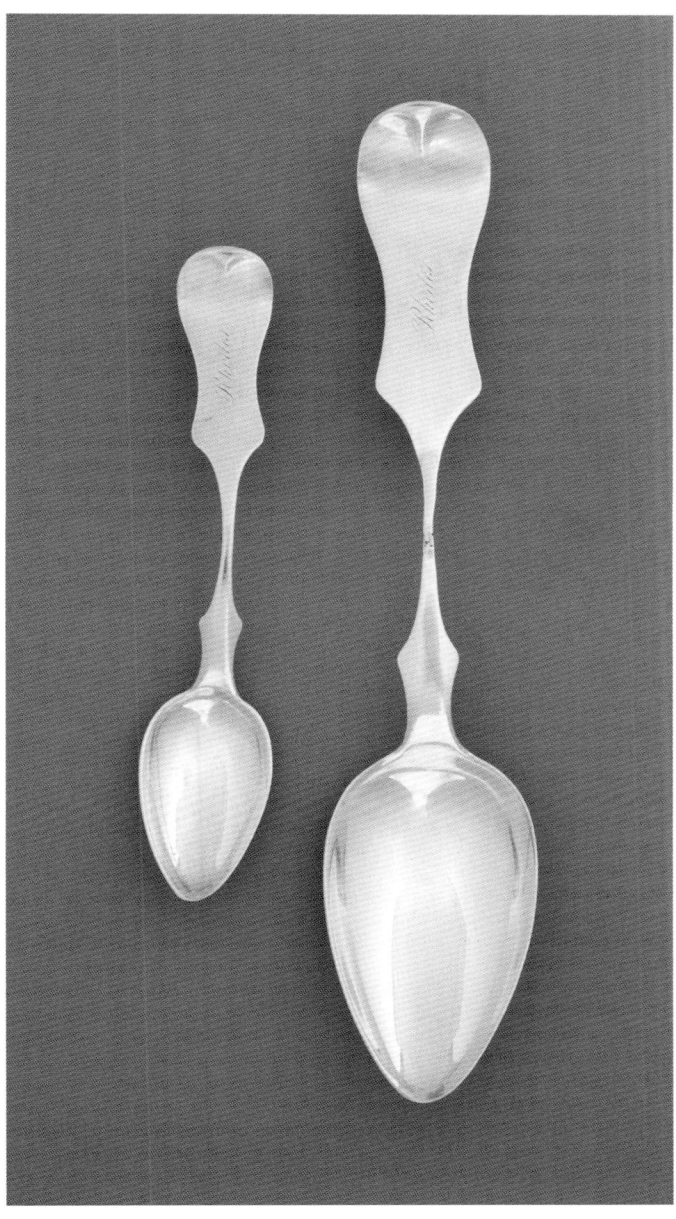

FIG. 119.2: James Rhodes or Thomas F. Rhodes, *Teaspoon* and *Dessert Spoon*, c. 1840, teaspoon: L. 5¾ in. (14.6 cm), dessert spoon: L. 8¾ in. (22.2 cm), CAM, Gift of Elizabeth Bushner Shepard, 1969.100, 1969.101

1. "Wisconsin, Deaths and Burials, 1835–1968," index, *FamilySearch*, https://familysearch.org/pal:/MM9.1.1/XLSX-TGK; Wm. Erik Voss, "James Fenner Rhodes," *American Silversmiths*, http://freepages.genealogy.rootsweb.ancestry.com/~silversmiths/makers/silversmiths/207942.htm.
2. Susan Rhodes, "Rhodes family tree," http://archiver.rootsweb.ancestry.com/th/read/RHODES/1998-11/0910997283.
3. Horace A. Keach, *Burrillville As It Was, And As It Is*, Providence: Knowles, Anthony & Co., 1856, 64.
4. Thomas F. Rhodes Sr. dealt in West Indian and dry goods; Advertisement, *Providence Gazette*, August 31, 1805, 1.
5. Ohio, Vol. 1, p. 141, R.G. Dun & Co. Collection, Baker Library, Harvard Business School.
6. Ibid.
7. 1848/49 Cincinnati Business Directory; 1849/50 Cincinnati City Directory.
8. R.G. Dun credit reporters note, "Jas F. Rhodes succeeds C. & R. [Clark & Rhodes]." However, there is no known documentation, to date, including marked wares, which support the notion that there was ever a firm active in Cincinnati under the name of Clark & Rhodes. Ohio, Vol. 1, p. 141, R.G. Dun & Co. Collection; 1850/1851 Cincinnati City Directory.
9. Edward H. Hill took over this address in 1857. 1857 Cincinnati City Directory.
10. Ohio, Vol. 1, p. 141, R.G. Dun & Co. Collection; James F. Rhodes' son, William, was born in Iowa on July 30, 1856. James Fenner Rhodes, "Pedigree Resource File," database, *FamilySearch*, https://familysearch.org/pal:/MM9.2.1/S1TD-23X.
11. 1860 Federal Census, Cincinnati, Hamilton, Ohio.
12. Ancestry.com, *U.S. Civil War Draft Registration Records, 1863–1865* [online database], Provo, Utah: Ancestry.com Operations Inc., 2010.
13. Rhodes' son Howard was born in Wisconsin, around 1865 according to the 1880 Federal Census. 1870 and 1880 Federal Censuses, Lancaster, Grant, Wisconsin.
14. Ancestry.com, *Wisconsin State Censuses, 1895 and 1905* [online database], Provo, Utah: Ancestry.com Operations Inc., 2007.
15. Beckman, 116.
16. Ohio, Vol. 1, p. 141, R.G. Dun & Co. Collection.
17. *Teaspoon*, Elizabeth Beckman Collection, Cincinnati Museum Center; Beckman, 116.
18. *Spoons*, Cincinnati Art Museum, 1969.100 and 1969.101, Registration Department, curatorial file.
19. Marriage record, Hamilton County Probate Records, vol. A 29, 106, Cincinnati, Ohio; Ancestry.com, *Iowa, State Census Collection, 1836–1925* [online database], Provo, Utah: Ancestry.com Operations Inc., 2007.
20. 1860 Federal Census, Cincinnati, Hamilton, Ohio; 1870 Federal Census, Lancaster, Grant, Wisconsin; James Fenner Rhodes, "Pedigree Resource File," database, *FamilySearch*.
21. Marriage record, Hamilton County Probate Records, vol. B 23, 2.
22. 1870, 1880, 1900 Federal Censuses, Lancaster, Grant, Wisconsin; James Fenner Rhodes, "Pedigree Resource File," database, *FamilySearch*.
23. "Wisconsin, Deaths and Burials, 1835–1968," index, *FamilySearch*; "James F. Rhodes," *Find A Grave*, www.findagrave.com; Death notice, *Cincinnati Enquirer*, August 19, 1907, 5.

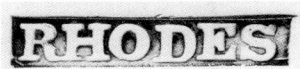

MARK 119.1

120. THOMAS F. RHODES

1808–1878, w. 1832–1836 or later

Thomas Frederick Rhodes was born in Providence, Rhode Island, in 1808. He was the older brother of **James F. Rhodes**.[1] The details of Thomas F. Rhodes' training as a silversmith are unknown, although Providence was known as a burgeoning center for the jewelry trade.

First notice of Thomas F. Rhodes' presence in Cincinnati appears in March 1832 when he advertises with Samuel P. Moore as Moore & Rhodes, having just arrived from the East "to establish themselves in the manufacture of jewelry."[2] Moore and Rhodes had been in business previously in Providence, where, at that time, there were 27 local jewelry firms employing 280 workers.[3] The partners must have seen Cincinnati as an opportunity to expand westward where there was less competition.[4] Following Moore's death in the summer of 1832, Thomas Rhodes continued the business at their stand on Lower Market Street.[5] By June 1833 he had joined **Caleb Allen** to form **Allen & Rhodes**, which became **Allen, Rhodes & Co.** when John G. Anthony, Rhodes' brother-in-law, joined the firm in August 1834.[6] It was not until after the establishment of Allen, Rhodes & Co. that there was an increased emphasis in advertising the partners' role as silver manufacturers. The firm dissolved by late 1836, and Rhodes does not appear in any subsequent Cincinnati directories.[7]

In 1850, Rhodes was living in Laughery, Dearborn County, Indiana, where he was working as a farmer.[8] It is probable that he had moved there by October 1840.[9] By 1857, the family had moved to Erie, Whiteside County, Illinois, where Rhodes continued to farm.[10] He died on August 13, 1878, and is buried in Havana, Mason County, Illinois.[11]

Rhodes married Eliza Billings Smith (1819–1896), daughter of John Smith and Mercy Ann Harris in 1839.[12] They had nine known children: John W. (d. infant 1840); John Waterman (b. about 1842); Thomas Brown (1843–1916); George F. (b. about 1844); Lydia Keene (1846–d. before 1850); William F. (b. about 1849); James Edward (b. about 1850); Katherine Billings (b. about 1854); and Walter Harris (b. 1857).[13]

Spoons marked "RHODES" have been documented (see James F. Rhodes, mark 119.1), but it is unclear which Rhodes brother, Thomas F. or James F., used this mark.[14]

1. Susan Rhodes, "Rhodes family tree," http://archiver.rootsweb.ancestry.com/th/read/RHODES/1998-11/0910997283; Wm. Erik Voss, http://freepages.genealogy.rootsweb.ancestry.com/~silversmiths/makers/silversmiths/207929.htm.
2. Advertisement, *Cincinnati Chronicle*, March 3, 1832, reproduced in Beckman, 117.
3. Advertisement, *Rhode Island American*, April 27, 1831, gives notice that the firm of S.P. Moore & Co. had dissolved on April 18, and that Moore was now partners with Thomas F. Rhodes (Moore & Rhodes); Advertisement, *Rhode Island American*, April 22, 1831, indicates that Moore & Rhodes were manufacturing jewelry at 43 Benefit Street, Rhode Island; *An Overview of the History of the Jewelry District*, http://www.jewelrydistrict.org/The District/History oftheJewelry District/tabid/65/Default.aspx.
4. Several members of the Rhodes family came to Cincinnati. Thomas F. Rhodes' brothers William (b. 1818), Charles (b.1807), and Edward (b. 1812) likely accompanied Thomas to Cincinnati, and later, his brother James Fenner came too. Charles and Edward established themselves as dry goods merchants and William as a clerk. Eventually his sister Ann (b. 1810) and her husband, John Gould Anthony arrived in the city; 1834–1856 Cincinnati City Directories; Susan Rhodes, "Rhodes family tree."
5. Notice, *Cincinnati Chronicle*, June 16, 1832, reproduced in Beckman, 117.
6. Advertisement, *Cincinnati Daily Gazette*, June 17, 1833, reproduced in Beckman, 1; Advertisement, *Cincinnati Daily Gazette*, September 6, 1834, reproduced in Beckman, 117; John Gould Anthony married Ann Whiting Rhodes on October 16, 1832. *Memorial Biographies of The New England Historical Genealogical Society, Towne Memorial Fund*, vol. 7, *1871–1880*, Boston: The New England Historical Genealogical Society, 1907, 266.
7. The last city directory listing for Allen, Rhodes & Co. appears in the 1836/37 City Directory. By 1837, the partners were listing in the *Western Address Directory* with new affiliations.
8. 1850 Federal Census, Laughery, Dearborn, Indiana.
9. John W., the infant son of Thomas F. and Eliza B. Rhodes, died in October 1840 in Wilmington, Dearborn County, Indiana. John W. Rhodes, death notice, *Cincinnati Daily Gazette*, October 28, 1840, 2.
10. Thomas' son, Walter was born in 1857 in Illinois, according to census information. 1870 Federal Census, Erie, Whiteside, Illinois.
11. Thomas Frederick Rhodes, *Find A Grave*, www.findagrave.com; Death notice, *Cincinnati Commerical Tribune*, August 29, 1878, 5.
12. Susan Rhodes, "Rhodes family tree." No marriage record could be found at the Hamilton County Probate Court. Susan Rhodes says they were married on July 2, 1839, but her source is not noted; Eliza Billing Smith's father, John Smith, and the metal smith John Smith (w. Cincinnati 1795–1802) are not believed to be the same person.
13. Susan Rhodes, "Rhodes family tree"; 1850 Federal Census, Laughery, Dearborn, Indiana; John W. Rhodes, death notice, October 28, 1840; 1870 Federal Census, Erie, Whiteside, Illinois.
14. *Dessert Spoon* and *Teaspoon*, Cincinnati Art Museum, Gifts of Elizabeth Bushner Shepard, 1969.100, 1969.101.

121. JOHN Q.A. SCHOOLFIELD

1812[1]–1892, w. 1836–1871 or later

John Q.A. Schoolfield was born in Baltimore, Maryland.[2] In 1836, he was listed in the Cincinnati City Directory as a silversmith boarding at William Borland's on Third Street between Walnut and Vine.[3] Nothing is known about Schoolfield's training.[4] In 1842, he was boarding with and possibly working for **Abraham Palmer**, also formerly of Baltimore.[5] In 1843 and 1844, he boarded at Main Street House and was listed in directories as a silversmith. In the 1850/51 City Directory he is listed as a silversmith working on the west side of Main Street, between Third and Fourth Streets, at the same address as C. & W.H. Allen (see **William Allen**). Schoolfield's appearances in city directories were irregular until his last listing in 1873. When his occupation is given, it is given as jeweler or silversmith, and his working address is never provided.[6]

The only information about Schoolfield's business and production comes to us through extant wares bearing his marks. A spoon with a transitional coffin/fiddle handle and pointed shoulders bears mark 121.1. This is the only mark that can be identified, with certainty, as our subject's. Mark 121.2 appears on spoons with tipped, exaggerated fiddle handles and pointed shoulders.[7] As this shape is a typical shape for Cincinnati, this mark also probably belongs to our John Schoolfield. There was another jeweler, John Schoolfield, who worked in Norwich, Connecticut, in the 1860s, 1870s, and 1880s.[8] A George G. Schoolfield (1824–1868), active in Columbia and St. Louis, Missouri, utilized a mark that included his first two initials, as well as the mark "SCHOOLFIELD" in a rectangular cartouche.[9] The incuse stamp "SCHOOLFIELD" has been documented on a spoon with a tipped, exaggerated fiddle handle with pointed shoulders, but as G.G. Schoolfield also marked spoons of this form, it is unclear whether this mark belongs to the Cincinnati or the Missouri Schoolfield.[10]

John Q.A. Schoolfield died on October 30, 1892, in the Cincinnati Old Men's Home.[11] His wife Honora Ann Sims (1822–1853), was the daughter of Elizabeth (1798–1865) and Robert Sims (1795–1883).[12] John and Honora married in 1845 and had one known child, Ella (b. about 1846).[13]

1. Schoolfield's birthdate was extrapolated from his burial and death records, and his obituary, which state that he was in his 80th year when he died. Federal census records give various years, from 1814 to 1820. Death notice, *Cincinnati Enquirer*, November 1, 1892, 5; John Schoolfield, burial record, Spring Grove Cemetery, Cincinnati, Ohio. Records from Spring Grove Cemetery are filed under John A. A. Schoolfield. This is a typographical error; John Q. Schoolfield, death record, Cincinnati Health Department, University of Cincinnati Archives and Rare Books Library, http://hdl.handle.net/2374.UC/661731.
2. 1850 Federal Census, Cincinnati, Hamilton, Ohio; John Schoolfield, burial record, Spring Grove Cemetery.
3. It is interesting to note that several other men active in the silver trade were boarding at Borland's boarding house at this time: William and Archibald Cooper (see **W. & A. Cooper**); **James Ryland**; **Ephraim Shepard**; and **George Stinger**.
4. Schoolfield did not appear in references relating to Baltimore silver, or in Baltimore city directories prior to his arrival in Cincinnati.
5. 1842 Cincinnati City Directory.
6. Schoolfield is absent from Cincinnati city directories periodically from 1849/50 to 1873. During these years, he was living with his in-laws, and Robert Sims, as head of household, was the only one listed at the address.
7. John Q.A. Schoolfield, eBay listings and private collections, Cincinnati silver binders, Cincinnati Art Museum; *Teaspoon*, Elizabeth Beckman Collection, Cincinnati Museum Center.
8. 1860, 1870, 1880 Federal Censuses, Norwich, New London, Connecticut.
9. "Schoolfield," SM Publications' Silver Salon Forums thread, active November 2004 through June 2008, www.smpub.com/ubb/Forum19/HTML/000470.html, accessed October 18, 2012; Engraved monograms referencing the Boone County Agricultural and Mechanical Association (Columbia, MO is in Boone County) appear on works marked "SCHOOLFIELD" in a rectangular cartouche, and on works marked "G. G. SCHOOLFIELD," linking both marks with George G. Schoolfield.
10. John Q.A. Schoolfield, eBay listings and private collections, Cincinnati Art Museum.
11. John Schoolfield, burial record; Death notice, *Cincinnati Enquirer*, November 1, 1892, 5.
12. The Sims family lived in Baltimore before coming to Cincinnati in about 1838. Elbert William R. Ewing, *Clan Ewing Scotland*, Ballston, VA: Cobden Publishing, 1922, 161–181; Robert and Elizabeth Sims, burial records, Spring Grove Cemetery.
13. Honora Ann Schoolfield, burial record, Spring Grove Cemetery; Marriage notice, *Cincinnati Daily Gazette*, December 24, 1845, cited by Beckman, 120; Marriage record, Hamilton County Probate Records, vol. 14, 401, http://www.probatect.org/CourtRecordsArchive/bukmarriages.aspx; The child of John and Honora Schoolfield is listed as Ella in the 1850 Federal Census, Cincinnati, Hamilton, Ohio, and as Mary in the 1860 Federal Census, Cincinnati, Hamilton, Ohio.

J.Q.A.SCHOOLFIELD

MARK 121.1

J.SCHOOLFIELD

MARK 121.2

122. SCOVIL & CO.

1830s

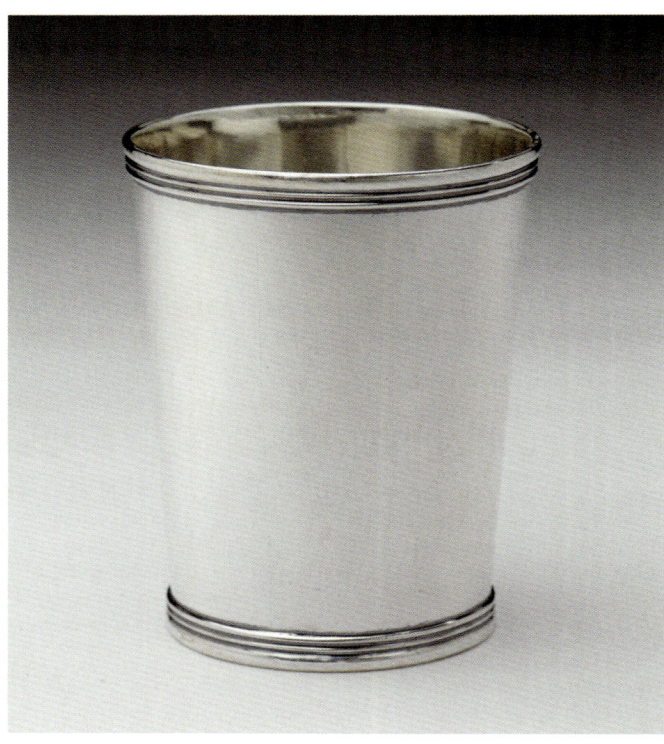

FIG. 122.1: Scovil & Co., *Beaker*, 1830s, 3⅝ × 3⅛ in. (9 × 7.9 cm), CAM, Museum Purchase: John S. Conner Fund, 2009.158

A beaker, in a private collection, bearing the mark of Scovil & Co. (mark 122.1) and a separate "Cincinnati" stamp in a rectangular cartouche confirms the firm's activities in this city.[1] While the principal of the firm was certainly **Pulaski Scovil**, his partner(s) are unknown. It is possible that the "& Co." represents Edward Kinsey before he was able to acquire equal interest in a business with Scovil (see **Scovil & Kinsey**, active about 1833–1836). Other beakers bearing the marks of both Scovil & Co. and **Edward Kinsey** suggest a relationship between the two.[2] Both men had experience in manufacturing silver. Scovil was manufacturing silver in the late 1820s/early 1830s, and Kinsey announced the opening of his own silver manufactory in 1836.

In addition to beakers, ladles and spoons with fiddle handles and pointed shoulders, and those with tipped, exaggerated fiddle handles and pointed shoulders have been found with the mark of Scovil & Co. One ladle with a tipped, exaggerated fiddle handle and pointed shoulders is also stamped with two shield-breasted eagles, facing left, with upturned wings, each inside a square cartouche (fig. 67.1).[3] These eagles are likely the manufacturing marks of Edward Kinsey.[4] Another beaker with mark 122.1 bears Edward Kinsey's mark 67.1, as well as a left-facing eagle without a shielded breast (fig. 67.4).[5] This eagle may be the manufacturing mark of either Edward Kinsey or Pulaski Scovil.[6]

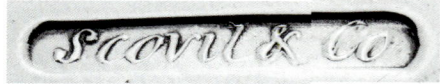

MARK 122.1

1. Scovil & Co., eBay listings and private collections, Cincinnati silver binders, Cincinnati Art Museum.
2. A beaker has been documented with Edward Kinsey's mark 67.1, a left-facing eagle (fig. 67.4, described by John R. McGrew as the "St. Louis Eagle"), and the mark of Scovil & Co.; Edward Kinsey, eBay listings and private collections, Cincinnati Art Museum.
3. Scovil & Co., eBay listings and private collections, Cincinnati Art Museum.
4. John R. McGrew, *Manufacturers' Marks on American Coin Silver*, Hanover, PA: Argyros Publications, 2004, 98.
5. Scovil & Co., eBay listings and private collections, Cincinnati Art Museum.
6. McGrew, *Manufacturers' Marks*, 99.

123. SCOVIL & KINSEY

about 1833–1836

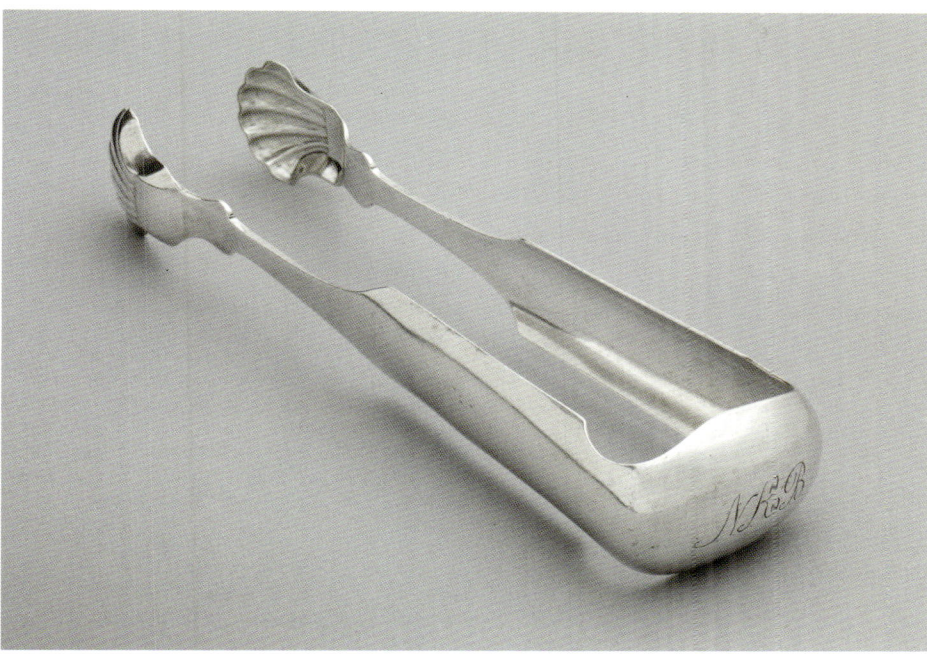

FIG. 123.1: Scovil & Kinsey, *Tongs*, about 1833–1836,
L. 5⅞ in. (14.9 cm), Private Collection

The exact dates of this partnership between **Pulaski Scovil** and **Edward Kinsey** are unknown.[1] The dates used here are based on the knowledge that Scovil had sold his interest in **C. Allen & Co.** in June 1833, and that Edward Kinsey had arrived in Cincinnati at about that time.[2] By 1836, Scovil had joined **Bushnell Willey** to form **Scovil, Willey & Co.** and Kinsey had opened his own silverware manufactory.[3] Both men had the means and knowledge to manufacture silver, as Scovil was purportedly doing so before his arrival in Cincinnati, and Kinsey went on to become one of the largest manufacturers in Cincinnati during the pre-Civil War era.

Mark 123.1 has been found on ladles and spoons with fiddle handles and rounded shoulders, tongs with shell terminals (fig. 123.1), and a pair of spectacles. A tablespoon with fiddle handle and rounded shoulders has been documented with the mark 123.2.[4]

1. It has been reported that Scovil & Kinsey operated on Front Street; this has not been substantiated. Rhea Mansfield Knittle, *Early Ohio Silversmiths and Pewterers, 1787–1847*, Cleveland: The Calvert-Hatch Co., 1943.
2. Notice, *Cincinnati Daily Gazette*, June 17, 1833, reproduced in Beckman, 121; Kinsey first appears in the 1834 Cincinnati City Directory as a resident of Newport; 1834, 1836/37 Cincinnati City Directories.
3. 1836/37 Cincinnati City Directory.
4. Scovil & Kinsey, eBay listings and private collections, Cincinnati silver binders, Cincinnati Art Museum; *Tablespoon*, Elizabeth Beckman Collection, Cincinnati Museum Center; Beckman, 121.

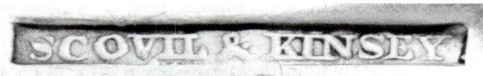

MARK 123.1

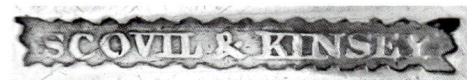

MARK 123.2

124. PULASKI SCOVIL

1808–1884, w. 1833–1838

Pulaski Scovil was the son of Anne Ames (d. 1871) and Roswell Scovil (1782-1865), born in Harwinton, Litchfield County, Connecticut, on January 28, 1808.[1] At the age of 18, he traveled to Livingston County, New York, and purchased 300 acres of timber and a saw mill, which he soon sold for a profit, and proceeded to Brockport in the company of a silversmith and jeweler of unknown identity, from whom he must have learned the trade.[2] He was purportedly soon owner of a business, manufacturing silverware and jewelry that he marketed through peddlers.[3] In 1831, he moved to Geneva, New York, where he continued that business, adding dry goods and notions.[4] In the fall of 1832, he took his goods to Buffalo and opened an auction store where he stayed for three months until his stock was depleted, and then traveled to Cincinnati.[5]

Upon arrival, Scovil established a partnership with **Caleb Allen, Jr.** to form **C. Allen & Co.**[6] In June 1833, he sold his interest in this business to **Thomas F. Rhodes**.[7] The establishment of the firm of **Scovil & Co.** may have followed. Scovil's partner(s) in this firm are unknown. It is likely that **Edward Kinsey**, a new arrival to the area, represented the "& Co.," and that the firm then evolved into **Scovil & Kinsey**.[8] This partnership was brief, as by 1836, Scovil had joined **Bushnell Willey** to create **Scovil, Willey & Co.** on Main Street between Third and Fourth Streets, and was possibly living part time in Illinois.[9] The partnership ended in 1838.[10] By the time the next city directory was published in 1840, both Willey and Scovil had moved on—Scovil to Havana, Illinois, and Willey to Kentucky.[11]

In Illinois, Scovil became active in the lumber-milling and grain business as well as farming, and land speculation.[12] He remained in Illinois until his death in 1884.[13] He had five wives: Sarah Jerome (1813–1840), who bore him six children; Olive Cross (d. 1844) who bore him two children; Anna Bordwine (b. 1829) who bore him two children before their divorce in 1852; Caroline Button (d. 1860), the widow of Pulaski's brother Julius, who brought two children into the marriage and bore him four more; and Hanna Jones (b. 1833) who had six children with Pulaski.[14]

Silver marked by Pulaski Scovil is exceedingly rare. A spoon with a fiddle handle and pointed shoulders that bears mark 124.1 is held in a private collection.[15]

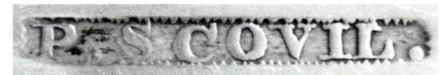

MARK 124.1

1. Ancestry.com, *Connecticut Town Birth Records, pre-1870 (Barbour Collection)* [online database], Provo, Utah: Ancestry.com Operations Inc., 2006; *History of Menard & Mason Counties, Illinois,* Chicago: O.L. Baskin & Co., 1879, 847; Homer Worthington Brainard, *A Survey of the Scovils or Scovills in England and America,* Hartford: privately printed, 1915, 505, 508, 512.
2. *History of Menard & Mason Counties,* Baskin, 847.
3. Ibid.
4. Ibid.
5. Ibid.
6. Notice, *Cincinnati Daily Gazette,* June 17, 1833, reproduced in Beckman, 121.
7. Ibid.
8. Ibid; Kinsey first appears in the 1834 Cincinnati City Directory as a resident of Newport. By 1836—the year that both Scovil and Kinsey first appear in Cincinnati directories with Cincinnati residential addresses around Fourth and Race—Kinsey had opened his own silverware manufactory. 1834, 1836/37 Cincinnati City Directories.
9. 1836 Cincinnati City Directory; Joseph Cochrane, *Centennial History of Mason County,* Springfield, IL: Rokker's Steam Printing House, 1876, 198. Cochrane records that Scovil was in Warren County by 1834 and in Mason County by 1836.
10. The *History of Menard & Mason Counties* indicates that Scovil relocated there in the spring of 1837.

However, the subscriber's record for the 1874 Illustrated Map of Mason County indicates that Scovil arrived in the county in 1838. Also, Scovil, Willey & Co. was dissolved in January 1838. *History of Menard & Mason Counties,* Baskin, 847; Subscriber's Record, "1847 Illustrated Map, Mason Co.," http://genealogy trails.com/ill/mason/1874/pg14.html; "Dissolution of Partnership," *Cincinnati Daily Gazette,* January 25, 1838, 2.
11. 1840 Federal Census, Tazewell, Indiana; Boultinghouse, 283.
12. Subscriber's Record, "1847 Illustrated Map, Mason Co."; Cochrane, *Centennial History of Mason County,* 198; *History of Menard & Mason Counties,* Baskin, 847.
13. *History of Menard & Mason Counties,* Baskin, 847; Cochrane, *Centennial History of Mason County,* 198; Michael J. Haase, "Haase-Meyers-Sauer Family History," http://ilrc.cas.muohio.edu/meyersde/genealogy/wc02/wc02_094.html.
14. 1850 Federal Census, Waterford, Fulton, Illinois; 1860 Federal Census, Township 20, Range 6, Mason, Illinois; 1870 and 1880 Federal Censuses, Salt Creek, Mason, Illinois; *History of Menard & Mason Counties,* Baskin, 847; Cochrane, *Centennial History of Mason County,* 198; Michael J. Haase, "Haase-Meyers-Sauer Family History."
15. Pulaski Scovil, eBay listings and private collections, Cincinnati silver binders, Cincinnati Art Museum.

125. SCOVIL, WILLEY & CO.

1836 or earlier–1838

Scovil, Willey & Co., described as a "fancy and comb store" in the 1836/37 City Directory, was located on Main Street between Third and Fourth Streets. Its proprietors were **Bushnell Willey**, **Pulaski Scovil**, and his cousin, Harvey Scovil (1810–1863).[1] While no advertisements or inventory lists exist from this firm, extant silver bearing their mark confirms that silver was part of their line of goods. Their mark (mark 125.1), which features a reversed ampersand, has been found on beakers (fig. 125.1); tongs with shell terminals; and spoons (fig. 125.2) and ladles with fiddle handles. These fiddle handled spoons and ladles have been observed with both round and pointed shoulders. Occasionally, a banner-shaped mark (mark 125.2) containing "CINCINNATI" accompanies mark

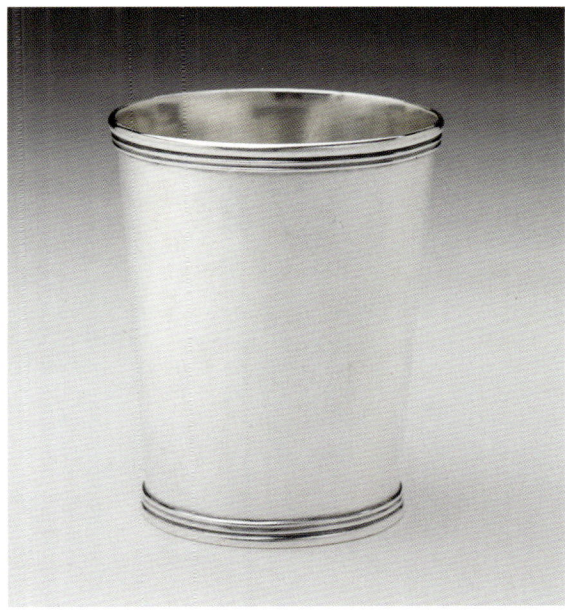

FIG. 125.1: Scovil, Willey & Co., *Beaker*, 1836–1838, 3⅝ × 3 in. (9.2 × 7.6 cm), CAM, Gift of Mr. and Mrs. Charles Fleischmann III, 2008.44

125.1. A left-facing eagle with down-turned wings, contained in a square cartouche (fig. 67.5), has been found alongside the firm's mark on a ladle and spoons.[2] This eagle may be the manufacturing mark of **Edward Kinsey** or Pulaski Scovil.[3] The firm of Scovil, Willey & Co. dissolved in January of 1838.[4]

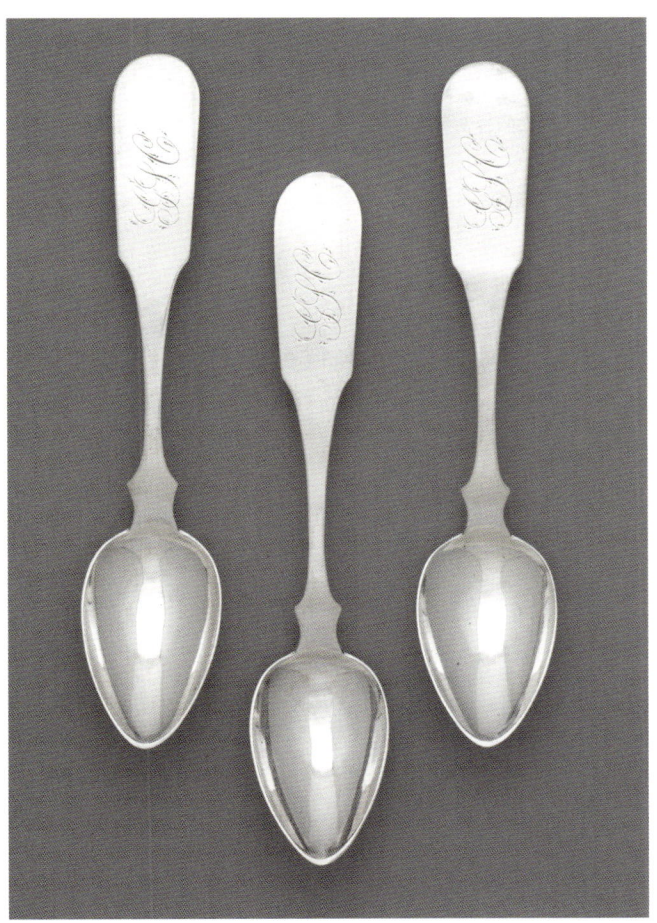

FIG. 125.2: Scovil, Willey & Co., *Teaspoons*, 1836–1838, L. 6 in. (15.2 cm), CAM, Given by Elizabeth M. and Annie W. Anderson in memory of their mother, Mrs. Buckner W. Anderson, 1969.746–748. Inscription: "GSC" for George and Sarah Carlisle, married 1828. George Carlisle (1797–1863) was one of Cincinnati's pioneer bankers and businessmen.

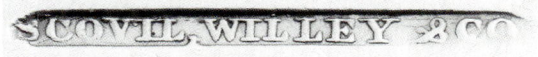

MARK 125.1

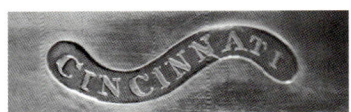

MARK 125.2

1. 1836/37 Cincinnati City Directory.
2. Scovil, Willey & Co., eBay listings and private collections, Cincinnati silver finders, Cincinnati Art Museum; John R. McGrew, *Manufacturers' Marks on American Coin Silver*, Hanover, PA: Argyros Publications, 2004, 98.
3. McGrew, *Manufacturers' Marks*, 99.
4. "Dissolution of Partnership," *Cincinnati Daily Gazette*, January 25, 1838, 2.

126. SEYMOUR & WILLISTON

1816–1820

Jeffrey Seymour (about 1793–1865) was born in Connecticut.[1] On September 21, 1818, he married Clarissa Bagg (1799–1873) in her native town, West Springfield, Massachusetts.[2] West Springfield was also the birthplace of Seymour's partner Othniel Horsford Williston (1792–after 1860), son of Captain John Williston, and the site of Othniel's marriage to Sally Ashley on January 27, 1816.[3]

Williston had arrived in Cincinnati by 1810.[4] The date of Seymour's arrival is unknown, as are details of the men's training. The first known advertisement of their partnership appeared in May 1816, announcing their arrival from Newark, New Jersey, and their commencement of "the Manufacturing of Jewelry . . . where they will make and supply the retailers of jewelry with all various kinds of work in their line, of the newest patterns, and of superior workmanship," adding "having had experience with some of the best workmen in the U.S. . . . they can furnish as cheap and as good work as can be obtained from N.Y. or Philadelphia."[5] Their shop was on Front Street, "two doors from Vine Street," and they advertised for two apprentices, "about 15 years of age."[6] An advertisement appearing in June announces that the firm would pay cash for human hair, "from 20 to 32 inches in length, dark brown and black will be preferred," suggesting that they were also producing hair jewelry.[7]

By late August 1819 the firm had expanded to include **Gabriel L. Benson**, formerly of New York, who listed as a silversmith at 148 Main Street in the city directory that year.[8] An advertisement for Seymour, Williston & Benson, "Watchmakers, Silversmiths, and Jewellers [sic]" announced that the firm had purchased the stock and stand of **Robert Best** and were now at 95 Main Street, "four doors below the U. States' Branch Bank" where they offered a variety of jewelry, "Silver and Plated Table and Tea Spoons . . . All kinds of Gold and Silver Ware manufactured on the shortest notice."[9] The firm must have investigated opportunities in the West, as **Jacob Deterly** records on December 24, 1819, "Jeffrey Seymour return'd from the West on Monday evening 22nd inst. Met with a poor market, —brought back the greater part of the goods he had,—it appears the St. Louis merchants can be better accommodated from the South—however on better terms."[10] Benson's involvement was short-lived. Evidence that the firm continued without him comes by way of Jacob Deterly's notation on March 2, 1820: "Not a Yanky trick, **A. [Abner] Sotcher** sold his thimble apparatus to Messrs. Seymour & Williston who have not yet obtain'd everything they feel inclined to think they are entitled

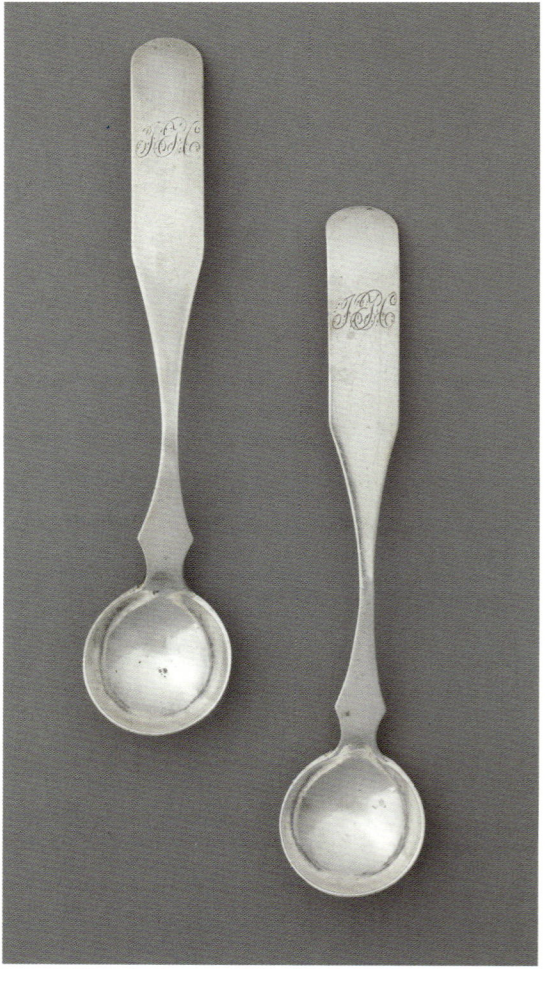

FIG. 126.1: Seymour & Williston, *Salt Spoons*, 1816–1820, L. 4¾ in. (12.1 cm), CAM, Gift of Mary Dandridge, 1928.38–39

to, have equivocated concerning said sale, and hesitate making any payment to said Sotcher."[11] Although Seymour & Williston are not included in city directories after 1819, they continued at least until August 1820, as they are noted in an advertisement as a venue for seal engraving executed by John C. Nuttman.[12]

Seymour remained in Cincinnati until his death in 1865.[13] He was a founding member of the Ohio Mechanics' Institute (est. 1828), and he built two fire engines for Fire Company No. 5 in 1829.[14] Later city directories list his occupation as printing-press maker, engine builder, city fire engineer, hose and belt manufacturer, and a dealer in gutta percha goods.[15]

Williston had relocated to Syracuse, New York by 1826, and by 1830, he was in New York City.[16] The 1850 Census indicates that his son John was a jeweler, living in New York City.[17] In 1850, Othniel Williston was living with his daughter, Charlotte A. Curtis, in New York, and, at the age of 67, was working as a policeman.[18]

A pair of salt spoons (fig. 126.1) bear mark 126.1. A set of spoons with fiddle handles and rounded shoulders feature the firm's mark alongside a suite of three marks—a lion, a bust, and a "G" each

contained in their own round cartouches.[19] John R. McGrew believes these marks to be manufacturer's marks belonging to an unidentified firm in Philadelphia.[20]

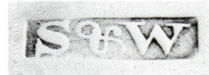

MARK 126.1

1. 1860 Federal Census, Cincinnati, Hamilton, Ohio; Burial records, Spring Grove Cemetery, Cincinnati, Ohio.
2. Announcement, *Western Spy*, October 10, 1818, reproduced in Beckman, 123.
3. New England Historical Society, *Massachusetts Town Birth Records* [online database], Provo, Utah: MyFamily.com Inc., 1999; Jordan Dodd, Liahona Research, comp., *Massachusetts Marriages, 1633–1850* [online database], Provo, Utah: MyFamily.com Inc., 2005.
4. 1810 Federal Census, Cincinnati, Hamilton, Ohio.
5. Advertisement, *Western Spy*, May 2, 1816, reproduced in Beckman, 123.
6. Ibid.
7. Advertisement, *Western Spy*, June 28, 1816, reproduced in Beckman, 148.
8. Announcement, *The Inquisitor and Cincinnati Advertiser*, August 31, 1819, reproduced in Beckman, 14; 1819 Cincinnati City Directory; Seymour listed as a jeweler living at 80 West Front, and Williston listed as a jewellery [sic] manufacturer at 79 West Front.
9. Advertisement, *Western Spy*, September 4, 1819, reproduced in Beckman, 148; The advertisement reproduced in Beckman, 123, cited as from *The Inquisitor and Cincinnati Advertiser*, June 22, 1819, could not be located in that issue.
10. Jacob Deterly, "*Remarks*" *of Jacob Deterly: diary from 1819 to 1848; life in southern Ohio: Cincinnati, Marietta, Athens* (transcribed and indexed by Madge Hubbard and Opal Saffell), Seattle: Northwest Lineage Researcher, 1972, 1:3.
11. Deterly, "Remarks," 1:6.
12. Advertisement, *Liberty Hall*, August 2, 1820, reproduced in Beckman, 99.
13. S.B Nelson and J.M. Runk, *History of Cincinnati and Hamilton County, Ohio*, Cincinnati: S.B. Nelson & Co., 1894, 124; Rev. Charles Frederic Goss, *Cincinnati: The Queen City, 1788–1912*, Cincinnati: The S.J. Clarke Publishing Co., 1912, 2:63.
14. Ibid.
15. 1831–1860 Cincinnati City Directories. He is absent from the 1834, 1842, and 1861–65 City Directories.
16. Dwight H. Bruce (ed.), *Onondaga's Centennial*, Boston: Boston History Co., 1896, 1:527; 1830 Federal Census, New York, New York. He may have arrived in New York as early as 1828, as the 1850 Census indicates that his daughter Mary J.
Williston was born in New York at that time.
17. 1850 Federal Census, New York, New York.
18. 1860 Federal Census, New York, New York.
19. Seymour & Williston, eBay listings and private collections, Cincinnati silver binders, Cincinnati Art Museum.
20. John R. McGrew, *Manufacturers' Marks on American Coin Silver*, Hanover, PA: Argyros Publications, 2004, 31.

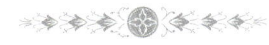

127. EPHRAIM E. SHEPARD

w. 1834–40

Ephraim Shepard first appears in the 1834 Cincinnati City Directory as a silversmith boarding at Lyman Rugg's in Newport, Kentucky, just across the river from Cincinnati.[1] A later directory listing indicates that he was from New York, yet nothing of his training or activities prior to his arrival in the Cincinnati area is known.[2] By 1836, he was boarding in Cincinnati at William Borland's on Third Street, between Walnut and Vine.[3] In 1839/40, he was listed as a silversmith employed at the firm of **Edward Kinsey** on the corner of Sixth and Walnut Streets.[4] Kinsey had also appeared in the area in 1834, boarding in Newport. In 1836, Kinsey set up his silver manufactory at the corner of Walnut and Third Streets, not far from where Shepard was boarding at the

time, thus it is possible that Shepard was working with Kinsey prior to 1839/40.

Elizabeth Beckman has noted a tablespoon dated 1831 and marked "E. E. SHEPARD" in a rectangular cartouche.[5] A letter written by Virginia Ruggs, which accompanied this tablespoon, explained that her father ran the first steam ferry across the Ohio River between Newport and Cincinnati, that her mother boarded hands on the ferry who paid her in silver, and that she used that silver to have this spoon and a few other table and teaspoons made.[6] Based on the date of this tablespoon, it is possible that Shepard was in the area by 1831. Unfortunately, the tablespoon referenced in Beckman could not be located at the time of this publication.[7] Another tablespoon with rounded shoulders and a fiddle handle bearing Shepard's mark is engraved "Robt. & Sarah Karr." The Karrs were reportedly married in Brown County on March 19, 1829.[8]

1. In the 1834 Directory, he is listed as Ephraim Shepherd. Subsequent directory listings and the spelling used on his hallmark punch indicate that the correct spelling was Shepard.
2. 1839/40 Cincinnati City Directory.
3. 1836/37 Cincinnati City Directory.
4. 1839/40 Cincinnati City Directory.
5. Beckman, 124.
6. Ibid.
7. This spoon could not be located in the Elizabeth Beckman Collection, Cincinnati Museum Center.
8. SM Publications' Silver Salon Forums, www.smpub.com/ubb /Forum/HTML/000243.html, posted November 21, 2002, accessed May 15, 2013.

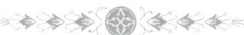

128. SHIPP & COLLINS

1829–1834

On February 3, 1829, **Jacob Deterly** records "S.A.M. Shipp and P. Collins watch makers inter'd [*sic*] into partnership."[1] Much of what we know about Samuel A.M. Shipp and **Peleg Collins**' business comes from the diary of Deterly. Shipp had worked for **Woodruff & Deterly**, and later partnered with Deterly in September 1826.[2] The latter arrangement came to an end in November 1828 when Deterly sold his interest in the shop's stock to Shipp, presumably to pay a debt incurred during his partnership with **Enos Woodruff**.[3] These goods were seemingly the seed stock for Shipp & Collins. Although Deterly was working primarily in Marietta, Ohio, at this time, he did occasionally return to work in the shop of Shipp & Collins.[4]

Shipp and Collins continued at 44 Main Street, Shipp and Deterly's former site. A portion of their stock was from the East. They described themselves as clock and watch makers who "keep constantly on hand a general assortment of Gold and Silver lever and plain watches. Also Fine Jewellery [*sic*], Military Goods, Silver Ware, Fancy Articles, &c. &c."[5] In directory listings, they are described as watch makers and jewelers.[6] They employed Elliot Foster, 1830; the silversmith James Read, 1830; the watch maker Horace Pitkin Woodridge (1802–1851), prior to March 1832; and the clock maker J. Jameson, 1832.[7] In 1831, the shop is listed at 53 Main, between Second and Front Streets.[8] That July, Shipp left for Philadelphia and New York, most probably to buy additional stock.[9] Hardship ensued when the shop flooded on February 15, 1832. Deterly writes, "Water rose so much and the rain together broke the levy. The backyard, cellar and shop filled instantly, about breakfast time." Three days later he penned, "Water rose very little last night. Depth at back door 5 feet 2 inches. 10 am water begins FALLING." And, on February 22, "Water fell below shop floor last night. We see terra firma again. Cold. A great cleaning up in the houses."[10] One

wonders if the flooding had anything to do with Deterly's May 8th entry, "the gable end wall of this building being pulled down," or if this was related to the establishment of a theatre on the second floor of the building, above the firm's watch shop.[11] In March 1833 Shipp traveled again to Philadelphia and New York, presumably to purchase stock.[12] By April 1834 Shipp and Collins' partnership had dissolved, as both men ran separate advertisements that month, Shipp at 53 Main Street and Collins at 117 Main Street.[13]

A spoon and a ladle with fiddle handles and pointed shoulders have been documented with mark 128.1.[14] Mark 128.2 has been identified on a surgical knife, also marked "Cincinnati"; a mug with an inscription dated 1833 that is also struck with the mark of **Abraham Palmer** (fig. 109.2); and a teaspoon with fiddle handle and pointed shoulders.[15]

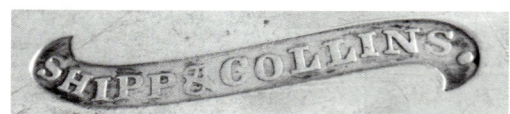

MARK 128.1

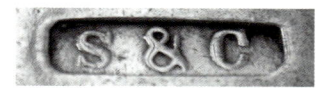

MARK 128.2

1. Jacob Deterly, *"Remarks" of Jacob Deterly: diary from 1819 to 1848; life in southern Ohio: Cincinnati, Marietta, Athens* (transcribed and indexed by Madge Hubbard and Opal Saffell), Seattle: Northwest Lineage Researcher, 1972, 2:37.
2. Deterly, *"Remarks,"* 1:39, 2:20.
3. Deterly, *"Remarks,"* 2:31–34.
4. Deterly, *"Remarks,"* 2:45, 47, 57, 62, 67.
5. Advertisement, reproduced in

Beckman, 126. Beckman cites the source for this advertisement as the 1828 Directory, but there was no directory published in that year. This advertisement could not be located in the 1829 City Directory, either.

6. 1829, 1831 Cincinnati City Directories.

7. Deterly, *"Remarks,"* 2:47, 67; Woodbridge would later partner with Shipp in St. Louis. Norman Mack,

Missouri's Silver Age: Silversmiths of the 1800s, Carbondale, IL: Southern Illinois University Press, 2005, 9; Deterly writes on March 17, 1832, "Mr. J. Jameson late of Springfield, Ohio got the back room on the second floor of Shipp & Collins' shop, fitted up for clock making. S.A.M. Shipp will have an interest in the time-piece manufacturing."

8. 1831 Cincinnati City Directory; The

change of address from 44 to 53 Main Street may not represent a move, as street numbers were not standardized until 1853, and prior to that were assigned and changed arbitrarily.

9. Deterly, *"Remarks,"* 2:59.
10. Deterly, *"Remarks,"* 2:66.
11. Deterly, *"Remarks,"* 2:67.
12. Deterly, *"Remarks,"* 2:78.
13. Advertisement, *Cincinnati Daily Gazette*, April 3, 1834, reproduced in

Beckman, 35.

14. Shipp & Collins, eBay listings and private collections, Cincinnati silver binders, Cincinnati Art Museum.

15. *Surgical Knife*, Cincinnati Museum Center; *Teaspoon*, Elizabeth Beckman Collection, Cincinnati Museum Center; *Mug*, Elizabeth Beckman Collection, Cincinnati Museum Center.

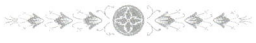

129. SIMPSON & PRICE

1810–1811

On December 5, 1810, **Alexander Simpson** advertised that he had moved from **Harmon Long**'s to the house of James C. Morris on Main Street, near the Columbian Inn, opposite A. Dunseth's Tin Manufactory.[1] He had partnered with **Philip Price**, announcing, "the business in future will be carried on under the firm of SIMPSON & PRICE."[2] The goods advertised by the firm include musical and chime clocks, surveying instruments, watch works, and "all kinds of gold and silver work made on the shortest notice and finished with elegance."[3] It is also noted that the highest price in cash would be given for old gold, silver, copper and brass, and that "a *Journeyman*, who understands his business, will meet with constant employ."[4] The firm was very short-lived, as notice that Price had dissolved the partnership was published in early January 1811.[5]

A teaspoon with tipped, fiddle handle and pointed shoulders has been found with the mark of Simpson & Price (mark 129.1). It also bears unidentified pseudo hallmarks.[6]

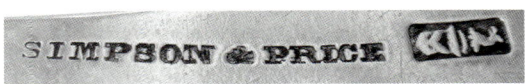

MARK 129.1

1. Advertisement, *Liberty Hall*, December 5, 1810, reproduced in Beckman, 129. Harmon Long's name is misspelled Herman in this advertisement.
2. Ibid.
3. Ibid.
4. Ibid.
5. *Western Spy*, January 5, 1811.
6. *Teaspoon*, Elizabeth Beckman Collection, Cincinnati Museum Center.

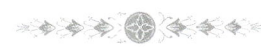

130. SMITH & BOERNER

1862–1864

This firm was established by Harry R. Smith (see **Harry R. Smith & Co.**) and Charles G. Boerner in March 1862, when **Jackson Slane** withdrew from **Beggs & Smith** (then managed by Smith, Slane and Boerner).[1] Boerner (1827–1900) was born in Artern, Germany, on April 14, 1827, and learned the trade of watch making from his father, Charles Boerner (1800–1852), who brought his

family to the United States in 1847.[2] The Boerners docked in New York and settled in Detroit, Michigan. Charles Jr. went first to Adrian, Michigan, and then established himself in Cincinnati in 1849.[3] He was employed as a watch maker at **Palmer & Owen** around 1850, and then had joined Beggs & Smith perhaps as early as 1854, but certainly by 1857.[4]

Smith & Boerner operated at the former stand of Beggs & Smith, located at 6 West Fourth Street, and advertised as "dealers in diamonds, watches, jewelry, and silver ware."[5] Prior to Smith & Boerner's establishment, the firm of Beggs & Smith struggled. It is noted in August 1862 that Smith & Boerner were "doing fairly for the times and will probably be until they are clear again."[6] Later, in 1863, it was reported that they were doing well, making money, and paying creditors, and even profiting from Beggs & Smith's failure.[7] On April 8, 1864, Boerner withdrew from the partnership because of his declining health. He moved to Vevay, Indiana, and set up shop with his brother F.A. Boerner, and continued to operate there until his death on January 26, 1900.[8]

A December 1863 advertisement for Smith & Boerner proclaims, "They have the Largest stock of Fancy Silver Goods! IN THE WEST," and their billhead mentions "silver tea sets, spoons, forks, etc." among the wares that they offered.[9] The firm bought most of their stock in the East.[10] Mark 130.1 has been found on spoons with tipped, exaggerated fiddle handles and pointed shoulders. The mark "SMITH & BOERNER," stamped incuse, has been observed on forks with die-pressed handles, including those in Whiting's "Le Cordon" (1850) pattern.[11]

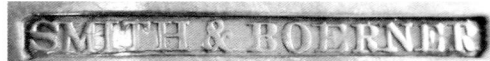

MARK 130.1

1. Ohio, Vol. 3, p. 12, R.G. Dun & Co. Collection, Baker Library, Harvard Business School.
2. *History of Switzerland County, Indiana, 1885*, Chicago: Weakley, Harraman & Co., 1885, accessed at http://myindianahome.net/gen/switz/records/bios/schb.html, November 4, 2006; Charles G. Boerner, obituary, *The Vevay Reveille*, February 1, 1900, 4.
3. Charles G. Boerner, obituary.
4. 1850/51–1857 Cincinnati City Directories; *History of Switzerland County, Indiana, 1885*, Weakley; 1860 Cincinnati City Directory.
5. 1862, 1863 Cincinnati City Directories.
6. Ohio, Vol. 5, p. 47, R.G. Dun & Co. Collection.
7. Ibid.
8. Ibid.; *History of Switzerland County, Indiana, 1885*, Weakley; Charles G. Boerner, obituary. Boerner is interred in Vevay Cemetery.
9. Advertisement, *Cincinnati Daily Enquirer*, December 25, 1863; Bill head, prices current files, Cincinnati Historical Society, box 1, folder 32.
10. Ohio, Vol. 5, p. 47, R.G. Dun & Co. Collection.
11. Smith & Boerner, eBay listings and private collections, Cincinnati silver binders, Cincinnati Art Museum.

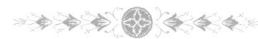

131. HARRY R. SMITH & CO.
1864–1901

Harry Rhodes Smith (1821–1903, active 1842–1901) was born in Columbus, Ohio, on July 18, 1821, the son of Ruth and John Smith, who had come to Ohio from Rhode Island in about 1815.[1] When Smith (fig. 131.1) was about five years old, his parents moved to Hebron, Ohio, a small town, east of Columbus, at the junction of the Ohio and Erie Canal with the National Road. There, his father established a country store and served as postmaster.[2]

Around 1837, the sixteen-year-old Smith made his way to Cincinnati, traveling down the Ohio and Erie Canal to Portsmouth and, from there, down the Ohio River to Cincinnati.[3] While his journey may have been undertaken only as an adventure, it is plausible that his end goal was to apprentice with **Peleg Collins**, a silversmith and watch maker from Rhode Island who had settled in Cincinnati by 1825.[4] Smith was not listed in the 1839/40 Cincinnati City Directory (the first published after 1837), possibly because he was still an apprentice. But he appears

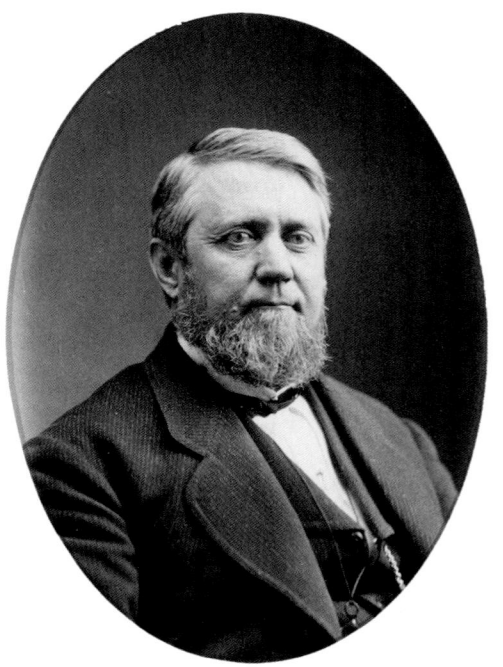

FIG. 131.1: Harry R. Smith, from M. Joblin, *Cincinnati Past and Present*, Cincinnati: Elm Street Printing Co., 1872, 262

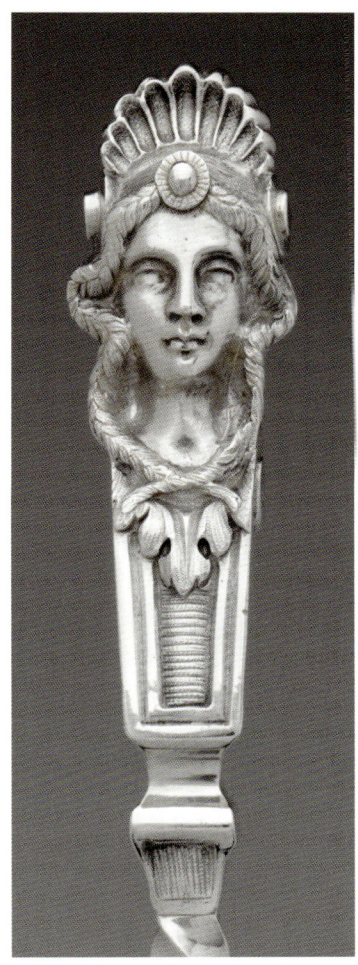

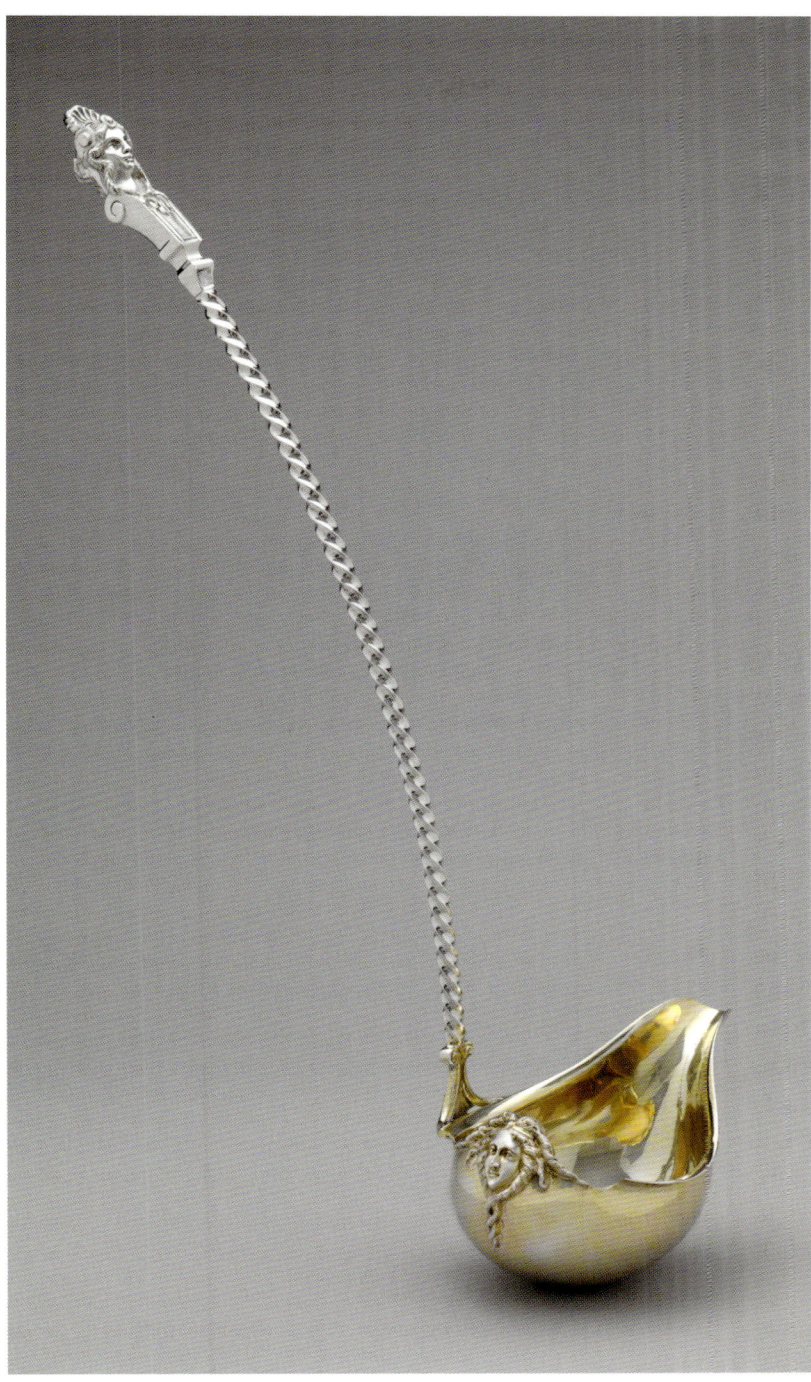

FIG. 131.2: Harry R. Smith, *Ladle*, c. 1870,
parcel gilt silver, L. 17 in. (43.2 cm), CAM,
Gift of Mr. and Mrs. Charles Fleischmann
III, 2005.18

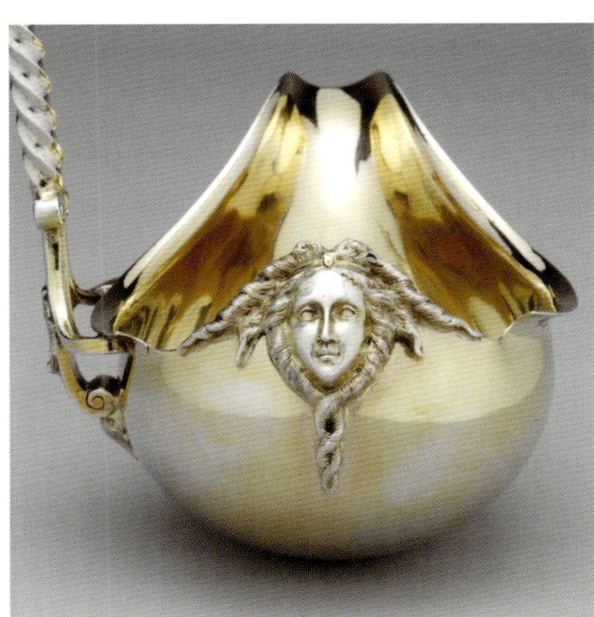

in the city directories in 1842, 1843, and 1844 as a watch maker boarding with Collins.

Smith partnered with **Abraham Palmer** to form **Palmer & Smith** (1843–about 1847); with Joseph P. Beggs to form **Beggs & Smith** (1848–1862); and with Charles G. Boerner to form **Smith & Boerner** (1862–1864). After Boerner withdrew from their partnership in April 1864, Smith continued as Harry R. Smith & Co., of which he was the sole proprietor, at Smith & Boerner's former West Fourth Street location.[5] An 1867 advertisement notes that his store opened at 7 o'clock in the morning, measured 90 feet deep, and featured a number of counters and cases, and walls adorned with pictures.[6]

Until 1882, the firm's advertisements focused on jewelry, watches and silver. Smith gave "jeweler" as his occupation for the federal censuses taken between 1850 and 1880.[7] But, he seems to have been particularly focused on the watch trade, as in 1871, 1872, and 1885, he was issued patents, with Rufus Folsom of Boston, for improvements relating to stem-winding watches.[8] In January 1870 it was reported that "Professor Abbe, from our own observatory, now furnishes the solar time to Mr. Harry R. Smith, jeweler, by whose time the fire department clock rings the hour at noon everyday. The time was previously telegraphed weekly from Philadelphia."[9] Smith also served as a railroad watch inspector.[10]

In 1864, Smith advertised "RICH FANCY SILVER GOODS" amongst his stock of diamonds, watches, and jewelry.[11] Advertisements like this, and extant silver bearing the mark of the firm confirm Smith's involvement in the silver trade. An 1869 newspaper article details a presentation of silver, procured from Smith's store, to the Rev. Dr. Oscar A. Hills, a local Presbyterian minister and his new wife. It notes that "a dozen silver table spoons, ditto dessert spoons, ditto teaspoons, two gold salt receivers with spoons, two large and elaborate silk flower stands, and one dozen silver knives and forks" were provided by Harry R. Smith & Co., and their "designs were all novel, chaste, and well selected, and engraved with "Hills" in German text."[12]

Although Palmer & Smith had advertised as "Manufacturers of Silver Ware and Jewelry" and Beggs & Smith boasted "Silverware, much of which is manufactured by themselves," it appears that, at this point in his career, Harry R. Smith was buying most of his wares in the East.[13] Several of his advertisements indicate that he was an agent for the Gorham Mfg. Co. (Providence, Rhode Island).[14] Flatware forms bearing the stamps of both Harry R. Smith & Co. and Gorham have been documented, as well as other flatware pieces, including table and teaspoons, ladles, and pie slices, stamped by both Harry R. Smith & Co. (retailer) and other manufacturers that include Peter L. Krider (Philadelphia), Wood &

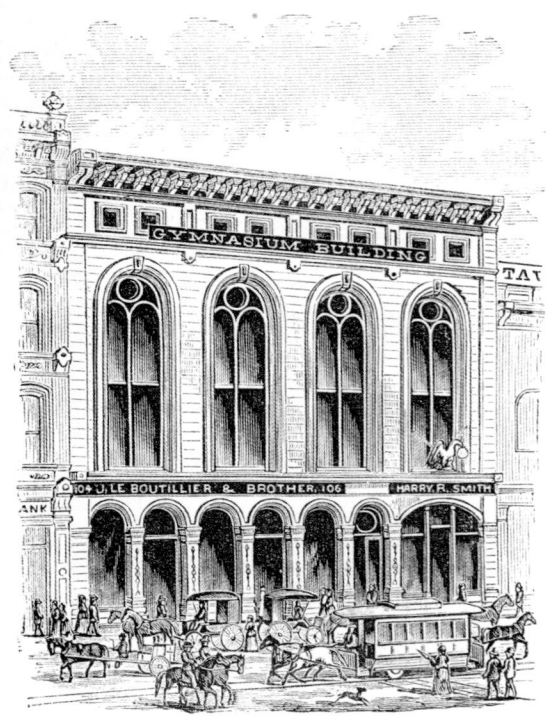

FIG. 131.3: Harry R. Smith & Co., from Daniel J Kenny, *Illustrated Cincinnati: A Pictorial Handbook,* Cincinnati: G.E. Stevens, 1875, 96

Hughes (New York City), and John R. Wendt & Co. (New York City).[15] The maker of the ladle illustrated in fig. 131.2 is unknown. In 1883, Smith began to advertise as an optician and dealer in spectacles, and this appears to have become his primary focus until the firm closed.

In 1860, prior to the failure of Beggs & Smith, Smith was reported to own real estate worth $8,000 and a personal estate worth $25,000.[16] At the time of Harry R. Smith & Co.'s establishment in 1864, credit reporters noted that Smith had a large stock and was doing a large business. They deemed him an "honorable, clever, good business man," estimating his total worth at between $80,000 and $100,000.[17] In 1870, he reported real estate worth $17,000, a personal estate worth $10,000, and credit reporters stated that he was making an average return on his stock of $33,000.[18] By 1872, he had fallen behind in his credit payments. Blame was placed on a sluggish market and overstocking; his loss of between $7,000 and $8,000 due to a dishonest employee, his former partner Joseph P. Beggs; and the fire that befell his Mount Auburn home, resulting in a loss of $6,000.[19] Smith still claimed to be worth over $50,000, but from this point on, he often asked for extensions in paying his creditors, and his business standing declined.[20] He had relocated his store to 102 West Fourth Street (fig. 131.3) by 1874.[21] In 1875, credit reporters remarked, "Smith's family lives extravagantly so that his prospects of accumulating anything are very slim."[22] In December 1876 he was reportedly closing out at auction. He held numerous auction sales between 1876 and 1878, but still continued in business, eventually settling with creditors.[23] In subsequent years, it was reported that he owned no property and that he was doing a very limited business.[24] In 1880, he reported capital worth $100; the employment of one hand in his shop, who was paid $936 a year in wages; $20 worth of material used for production; and a value of product worth $1,200.[25] There were no listings for Harry R. Smith & Co. in Cincinnati city directories after 1901, and no advertisements after this date are known.[26]

Smith died on December 19, 1903, at his Mount Auburn home from heart failure.[27] His widow, Anna McNaughton (1825–1908), was born in Schenectady, New York, to James and Sarah McNeil McNaughton. Anna and Harry had married in Dayton on November 13, 1851.[28] They had three children: McNaughton (b. about 1853); Rufus (b. about 1855), who became a judge of the Common Pleas Court of Hamilton County; and Sallie Rose (b. 1859).[29] Aside from Smith's activities in the jewelry, watch making, silver, and optometry trade, he was active in civic endeavors, including an appointment made by the Superior Court of Cincinnati as a trustee of the Cincinnati Southern Railway.[30]

Silver wares sold by Harry R. Smith & Co. bear mark 131.1 or an incuse "HARRY R. SMITH & Co."[31]

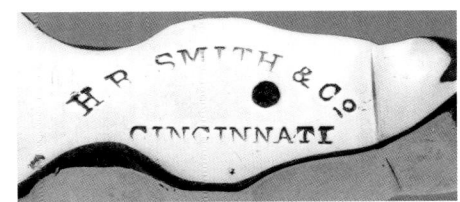

MARK. 131.1

1. Harry R. Smith, burial record, Spring Grove Cemetery, Cincinnati, Ohio; 1900 Federal Census, Cincinnati, Hamilton, Ohio; M. Joblin, *Cincinnati Past & Present, or Its Industrial History, As Exhibited in the Life-Labors of its Leading Men*, Cincinnati: Elm Street Printing Co., 1872, 263–266; Charles Greve, *Centennial History of Cincinnati and Its Representative Citizens*, Chicago: Biographical Publishing Co., 1904, 2:289–291; An article, likely a paid promotion, appearing in the *Cincinnati Enquirer*, December 13, 1867, states that Smith's great-grandparents had come to America with Christopher Columbus, and that he was a descendant of Tubal Cain, the metalworker mentioned in Genesis 4:22 of the Bible. These claims are unsubstantiated.
2. Joblin, *Cincinnati Past & Present*, 263.
3. Joblin, *Cincinnati Past & Present*, 264.
4. Beckman, 35; "Death of Harry R. Smith," *Jewelers' Circular and Horological Review* (December 30, 1903): 22; Greve, *Centennial History of Cincinnati*, 289; Joblin, *Cincinnati Past & Present*, 265.
5. Ohio, Vol. 5, p. 47, R.G. Dun & Co. Collection, Baker Library, Harvard Business School; 1864 and 1865 Cincinnati City Directories.
6. Advertisement, *Cincinnati Enquirer*, December 13, 1867, 2.
7. 1850, 1860, 1870, and 1880 Federal Censuses, Cincinnati, Hamilton, Ohio.
8. James W. Gibbs, *Buckeye Horology: A Review of Ohio Clock and Watch Makers*, Columbia, PA: The Art Crafters Printing Co., 1971, 95; Harry R. Smith and Rufus Folsom. 1871. Stem-Winding Watch. US Patent 119,880, filed Jun. 3, 1871, and issued Oct. 10, 1871.
9. *Cincinnati Enquirer*, January 1, 1870, 8.
10. "Death of Harry R. Smith" (December 30, 1903).
11. Advertisement, *Cincinnati Enquirer*, December 19, 1864, 2.
12. "Silver Service Presentation," *Cincinnati Enquirer*, November 5, 1869, 8.
13. Palmer & Smith advertisement, *Kimball and James' Business Directory for the Mississippi Valley*, Cincinnati: Kendall & Barnard, 1844, reproduced in Beckman, 130; Beggs & Smith advertisement, *Cincinnati Daily Times*, October 1, 1850, reproduced in Beckman, 130.
14. Advertisement, *Cincinnati Daily Gazette*, December 23, 1867, 2; Advertisement, *Cincinnati Daily Gazette*, May 19, 1868, 2; Advertisement, *Cincinnati Enquirer*, November 16, 1868, 5; Advertisement, *Cincinnati Daily Gazette*, December 21, 1868, 1.
15. Harry R. Smith & Co., eBay listings and private collections, Cincinnati silver binders. Cincinnati Art Museum.
16. 1860 Federal Census, Cincinnati, Hamilton, Ohio.
17. Ohio, Vol. 5, pp. 47, 122, R.G. Dun & Co. Collection.
18. 1870 Federal Census, Cincinnati, Hamilton, Ohio; Ohio, Vol. 8, p. 30, R.G. Dun & Co. Collection.
19. Ohio, Vol. 8, p. 30, R.G. Dun & Co. Collection; "Fire on Mount Auburn," *Cincinnati Enquirer*, March 24, 1872, 8; Fortunately, his losses sustained in the house fire were covered by insurance.
20. Ohio, Vol. 5, p. 122, R.G. Dun & Co. Collection.
21. 1874 Cincinnati City Directory.
22. Ohio, Vol. 10, p. 326, R.G. Dun & Co. Collection.
23. Ibid.; Advertisement for auction, *Cincinnati Daily Gazette*, April 7, 1877, 12; Notice of failure and assignment, *Jeweler, Silversmith and Watchmaker* 4, no. 6 (February 1878): 84; Advertisement for auction, *Cincinnati Commercial Tribune*, November 4, 1878, 5.
24. Ohio, Vol. 10, p. 417, R.G. Dun & Co. Collection.
25. 1880 Federal Non-Population Census Schedules, Products of Industry, Schedule 4, Hamilton County, Ohio.
26. 1901 Cincinnati City Directory.
27. "Death of Harry R. Smith" (December 30, 1903); Harry R. Smith, burial record; "Cincinnati Capitalist Dead," *Cleveland Plain Dealer*, December 20, 1903.
28. Anna McNaughton Smith, burial record, Spring Grove Cemetery; Joblin, *Cincinnati Past & Present*, 266.
29. Joblin, *Cincinnati Past & Present*, 266; 1860, 1870, 1880, 1900 Federal Censuses, Cincinnati, Hamilton, Ohio; Sallie's married name was Shaffer. Her husband had died by 1900, according to the federal census that year; An 1874 advertisement in Daniel J. Kenny's *Cincinnati Exposition Guide and Catalogue of the Fine Arts Department . . . at the Fifth Cincinnati Industrial Exposition of 1874 . . .*, Cincinnati: Cincinnati Gazette Company, 1874, n.p. indicates that Smith sold a gold watch, possibly of his own design, know as the "Sally Rose."
30. Greve, *Centennial History of Cincinnati*, 290–91.
31. Harry R. Smith & Co, eBay listings and private collections, Cincinnati silver binders, Cincinnati Art Museum.

132. GEORGE W. STALL

d. 1819, w. 1811–circa 1819

George W. Stall was born in Pennsylvania and probably worked in Philadelphia prior to his arrival in Cincinnati.[1] A transaction in the account books of Smith & Findlay places him in Cincinnati in April 1799.[2] He had served in the American Revolution, and by this time, was a lieutenant in the United States Army.[3] During his earliest years in Cincinnati, Stall lived in Mercersburg (now Newtown), east of the city center, where he farmed and ran an inn until 1808.[4] On May 6, 1806, he was married by Presbyterian Reverend Matthew G. Wallace to Maria Barbara Haiflaigh (1790–1870), daughter of Frederick Haiflaigh (d. 1809), formerly of Maryland.[5]

In 1810, George's brother John Stall died leaving him property on Front Street.[6] This is presumably where George opened up shop as a "Watch and Clock-Maker, GOLD & SILVER-SMITH" as per an elaborately illustrated newspaper announcement in July 1811.[7] The announcement advertises his shop on "FRONT-STREET, 3 doors below MAIN-STREET, opposite Dr. Cranmore's Drug-Store," where he offered "SILVER WORK, OF ALL KINDS."

Around or just after this time, he and Maria had two children: Edward G. and Frances Mary.[8] Stall fought in the War of 1812 battle at Brownstown, Michigan, on August 5, 1812, and sustained a severe wound in his left side from a musket ball, which broke three ribs. After the Surrender of Detroit in August 1812, Stall was taken prisoner, but returned to Cincinnati that fall.[9] Stall's name appears on an 1817 tax list in Cincinnati, and that winter he was on a military tour to "the lakes," during which he caught a "violent" cold which settled in his side. It was this malady that led to his death in the latter part of February 1819.[10] His widow Maria is listed as a grocer at the corner of Lodge Alley and Seventh Street in the 1834 City Directory. She raised her children independently in Cincinnati, collecting George's war pension until her death in August 1870.[11]

The hallmark "GS" in a square cartouche, possibly the mark of our subject, has been observed on early spoons in the private collections of Cincinnati families.[12] There were several other smiths besides George Stall who were working around this time in the region who also used, or could have used, a "GS" punch: George W. Snyder of Paris, Kentucky, w. 1803-13; George Shivery, an apprentice to Alexander Frazer, Lexington, Kentucky, in 1805; and George Smart of Lexington, Kentucky, w. 1794-1809.[13] Therefore, a clear attribution of George Stall's mark has not been made.

1. 1880 Federal Census, record for daughter Frances cites father born in Pennsylvania; William H. Powell records Stall as born in Germany in *List of Officers of the Army of the United States from 1799 to 1900, embracing a register of all appointments by the President of the United States in the volunteer service during the civil war, and of volunteer officers in the service of the United States*, New York: L.R. Hammersly & Co., 1900, 604. It is more likely that he was born in Pennsylvania. His brother John Stall came from Philadelphia and settled in Williamsburg, Ohio, then Cincinnati. John's family was very prominent in early Ohio. His daughter Elizabeth married General William Lytle, his daughter Mary Ann married Samuel Watts Davies, a mayor of Cincinnati, and his daughter Frances married Arthur St. Clair, Jr., a son of the governor of the Northwest Territory. John was listed as a china merchant in the 1791 Philadelphia City Directory; Virginius C. Hall, "Richard Allison: Surgeon to the Legion," *Bulletin of the Historical and Philosophical Society of Ohio* 9 (October 1951): 294; John Stull, Harry R. Stevens, "Samuel Watts Davies and The Industrial Revolution in Cincinnati," *Ohio Historical Quarterly* 70 (April 1961): 97–98; *Williamsburg and Its Founder; 1797–1947 Sesqui-Centennial of Williamsburg*, Williamsburg: Williamsburg Rotary Club, 1947, 5–6.

2. Smith and Findlay account book, Torrence papers, Cincinnati Historical Society, box 57, folder 4, reproduced in Beckman, 133.

3. William Powell, *List of Officers of the Army of the United States from 1779 to 1900*, 40; Ancestry.com, *The Official roster of the soldiers of the American Revolution buried in the state of Ohio* [online database], Provo, Utah: Ancestry.com Operations Inc., 2005.

4. Marie Dickore, "Newtown, First Named Mercersburg," *Bulletin of the Historical and Philosophical Society of Ohio* 8 (January 1950): 65; Advertisement [sale of wagon, five horses and farming utensils in Newtown], *Western Spy*, March 12, 1808.

5. Announcement, *Liberty Hall*, May 12, 1806; L.J. Critchfield, "Maria B. Stall et al. v. The City of Cincinnati et al.," *Reports of Cases Argued and Determined in the Supreme Court of Ohio*, 16:170–

178; 1850, 1870 Federal Censuses; Ancestry.com, *U.S. Pensioners, 1818–1872* [online database], Provo, Utah: Ancestry.com Operations Inc., 2007; Death notice, *Cincinnati Commercial Tribune*, August 4, 1870, 3.

6. Charles Hammond, "Lesse of F.M. Stall v. C. & E. Macalester," *Cases Decided in the Supreme Court of Ohio In Bank at December Term, 1839*, 9:19–25.

7. Advertisement, June 1811, reproduced (without citation) in Beckman, 134.

8. Hammond, *Cases Decided in the Supreme Court of Ohio*, 19–25; 1840, 1850 Federal Censuses, Cincinnati, Hamilton, Ohio; 1870, 1880 Federal Censuses, Columbia, Hamilton, Ohio.

9. United States Congress House Committee on Claims, *Maria B. Stall*, report no. 564, April 6, 1846 [electronic resource], Lexis Nexis U.S. Serial Set Digital Collection; Powell, *List of Officers of the Army of the United States from 1779 to 1900*, 604.

10. Ronald V. Jackson, Accelerated Indexing Systems, comp., *Ohio Census, 1790–1890* [online database], Provo, Utah: MyFamilies.com Inc., 1999; Hammond, *Cases Decided in the Supreme Court of Ohio*, 9:20–25; United States Congress House Committee, *Maria B. Stall*, report no. 564. Dates for Stall's death are given as 1816 in *Cases Decided in the Supreme Court*, and as 1818 or 1819 by deponents in *Maria B. Stall*. February 1819 was part of the testimony of Maria, Stall's widow, and is used here. No official death records could be located for George W. Stall.

11. 1834 Cincinnati City Directory; Ancestry.com, *U.S. Pensioners, 1818–1872* [online database], Provo, Utah: Ancestry.com Operations Inc., 2007.

12. Beckman, 134.

13. Boultinghouse, 247, 250, 254; Based on examples of **George Sullivan**'s silver found in Lynchburg, Virginia collections, Catherine B. Hollan was able to positively identify his initialed punch and differentiate between it and the mark described here. Hollan, *Virginia Silversmiths, Jewelers, Watch- and Clockmakers, 1607–1860, Their Lives and Marks*, McLean, VA: Hollan Press, 2010, 739.

133. GEORGE A. STINGER

about 1812–1891, w. 1836–1883

George Andrew Stinger was born in Washington, DC around 1812, and apprenticed with Samuel Kirk of Baltimore, Maryland, in 1827.[1] While in Baltimore, he married Elizabeth Ann Evans (b. Maryland, circa 1811) on November 3, 1833.[2] They had seven children for whom records were found: Frederick J.; Emma; Joseph P.; George A.; Virginia O.; Luilla C.; and Annie E.[3]

Stinger first appeared in Cincinnati in 1836, a silversmith boarding at William Borland's on Third Street between Walnut and Vine.[4] He listed as a silversmith and a silver manufacturer in directories until 1883 at various addresses.[5] The 1850 Products of Industry Census indicates that he had $700 in capital invested and five employees (four male and one female) in his jewelry, watch making, and silversmithing business. He paid total wages of $160 a month to his male laborers (about $40 a month per man) and $16 a month to his female employee. He reported the value of his raw material (silver) at $2,500 and the value of his product at $4,500.[6] By 1860, Stinger had moved his firm to the northwest corner of Fourth and Main Street—a multi-story building that housed members of the jewelry and silver trade as well as other trades.[7] In June 1866, a devastating fire erupted on the second floor of the building and eventually spread to the whole block.[8] However, Stinger, like others, rebuilt his business and continued in that location.

In 1869, he joined Joseph Noterman, formerly in the employ of Harry R. Smith (see **Harry R. Smith & Co.**), and **Joseph Jonas** to form Stinger, Noterman & Co.[9] The firm advertised as diamond cutters, and conducted business at the northwest corner of Fourth and Main Streets as well. This partnership lasted for only one year.[10] Noterman & Jonas (1870–1888) went on to run a large-scale jewelry manufacturing business, and it is assumed that Stinger, the principal partner in the previous, short-lived firm, and his long established reputation and clientele likely served as a springboard for Noterman and Jonas' later success.[11] Following the firm's dissolution, Stinger continued to list independently as a silversmith, but provided only a home address in city directories, indicating that he probably scaled back his activities. After 1884, his directory listings no longer include his occupation, suggesting that he had retired. He died on May 20, 1891.[12] Cause of death is given as softening of the brain.

Considering Stinger's long career in Cincinnati, it is odd that so little silver marked by him is known. Perhaps the rarity of marked pieces by Stinger is due to the fact that most of his wares bear the name of his retailers.[13] He is cited as the maker of a silver fire trumpet that was presented to the late president of the Independent Western Fire Engine Company in November 1846.[14] One side of the horn included the presentation inscription which incorporated "Made by G. A. Stinger," and the other side bore the figure of Hope and the inscription, "Hope leads the Conqueror to Victory." The current whereabouts of the horn are unknown. It may or may not be the same trumpet that Stinger entered in the 1851 Ohio Mechanics' Institute Fair.[15] A spoon with a tipped, exaggerated fiddle handle and pointed shoulders in a private collection bears his mark (mark 133.1).[16]

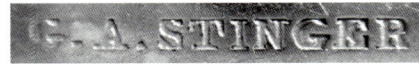

MARK 133.1

1. 1850–1880 Federal Censuses, Cincinnati, Hamilton, Ohio; George Stinger, death record, Cincinnati Health Department, University of Cincinnati Archives and Rare Books Library, http://hdl.handle.net/2374.UC/523919; Jennifer Faulds Goldsborough, *Silver in Maryland*, Baltimore: Maryland Historical Society, 1983, 284.
2. Jordan Dodd, Liahona Research, comp., *Maryland Marriages, 1655–1850* [online database], Provo, Utah: MyFamily.com Inc., 2004.
3. 1850, 1860 Federal Censuses, Cincinnati, Hamilton, Ohio; In the 1860 and 1880 Censuses, George A. Stinger, Jr. is listed as a machinist. Frederick J. Stinger is listed as a silversmith, age 15, in the 1850 Census, suggesting that he apprenticed and worked with his father. Frederick J. Stinger is most likely the person cited as S.J. Stinger in Rhea Mansfield Knittle, *Early Ohio Silversmiths and Pewterers 1787–1847*, Cleveland: The Calvert-Hatch Co., 1943.
4. 1836/37 Cincinnati City Directory.
5. 1839/40–1883 Cincinnati City Directories; Between 1839 and 1846, he was working on Western Row, between Fourth and Fifth Streets. Between 1848 and 1859, he was working on the east side of Bank Alley. Between 1860 and 1868, he was at 2 West Fourth Street (on the northwest corner of Main and Fourth), and between 1870 and 1883, he continued to list as a silversmith, but only provided a home address.
6. 1850 Federal Non-Population Census Schedules, Products of Industry, Schedule 4, Hamilton County, Ohio.

Stinger does not appear in the Federal Non-Population Census Schedules for 1870 or 1880. A Federal Non-Population Census is not known for 1860. His absences in 1870 and 1880 suggest that at this time, his business had become much smaller.
7. 1860 Cincinnati City Directory.
8. "Destructive Fire Last Evening," *Cincinnati Enquirer*, June 29, 1866, 2.
9. There were two men named **Joseph Jonas** active in the Cincinnati silver, jewelry, and watch and clock making trades. Reference is made here to Joseph Jonas (1844–1894, w. 1864–1894).
10. 1869 Cincinnati City Directory.
11. 1870, 1880 Federal Non-Population Census Schedules, Products of Industry, Schedule 4, Hamilton County, Ohio; Ohio, Vol. 8, pp. 109, 248, 331; R.G. Dun & Co. Collection, Baker Library, Harvard Business School.
12. George Stinger, death record.
13. There are no reports on Stinger in the reports of R.G. Dun & Co. This suggests that he bought little, if any, stock on credit and supports the notion that he was more of a maker than a retailer.
14. "Silver Horn Presentation," *Cincinnati Enquirer*, November 14, 1846, 3.
15. Beckman, 134.
16. George Stinger, eBay listings and private collections, Cincinnati silver binders, Cincinnati Art Museum.

134. ROBERT STURM

1874–1964, w. 1890–1932

Robert Sturm (fig. 134.1) was born in Cincinnati on September 16, 1874.[1] He was the son of German immigrants, Elizabeth Schmidt (1834–1909) and Philip Sturm (about 1830–1892).[2] In 1880, Sturm was six years old and living with his parents, three brothers and a sister (Frank, John, William, and Delia) on Harvey Avenue in the Cincinnati suburb of Avondale.[3] Another sister, Elizabeth had likely married and moved out by this time.[4] His father's occupation is given as gardener in the 1880 Census, but city directory listings, beginning in 1884, indicate that he was a huckster, or door-to-door salesman.[5] Robert's older brother John (1866–1917) was a blacksmith.[6] An unusual notice regarding his mother appeared in February 1890. It stated, "Mrs. Elizabeth Sturm left her husband and family, angry, and unknown to anyone where she went. Any money or notes she may [have] contracted will not be recognized by the undersigned. –Philip Sturm."[7] Eventually, she returned.[8]

The same year, at the age of sixteen, Robert Sturm is included in the city directory as a silversmith, residing at his parent's home on Elizabeth Street in Avondale.[9] It can be presumed that he apprenticed locally, but details of his education are unknown. He continued to appear in city directories as a silversmith until the 1896 edition, when his published occupation is conductor. The following year, he is noted as the manager of his brother's blacksmithing enterprise, John Sturm & Co.[10] This is short-lived, as in 1899, he is, again, working as a silversmith, and residing with his brother John and widowed mother at 3116 Lincoln Place in Avondale.[11]

By 1900, Sturm was a partner in the firm of Engbersen, Sturm & Co. (1900–1904) with **William J. Engbersen** and **Kenton C. Kunkle**. Advertising as silversmiths and aluminum workers, the firm was located at 230–232 Longworth Street from 1900 to 1901.[12] By 1902, Kunkle had left the firm and it had relocated to room 8 of the Lion Building on the southeast corner of Elm and Fifth Streets (434 Elm)—a location that housed numerous jewelry, watch, and metalworking businesses.[13] Wares bearing the mark of this firm have yet to be discovered.

While a partner of Engbersen, Sturm & Co., Robert married Cincinnati-born Catherine Hussey (1876–1903) on June 30, 1902.[14] Catherine bore him a son, Robert E. Sturm, Jr. (1903–1970), and died from complications during childbirth.[15] She is buried at the Catholic St. Joseph New Cemetery.

Following the dissolution of Engbersen, Sturm & Co., Robert lived west of downtown and listed independently as a silversmith at 512 Race Street, another building that housed several jewelry

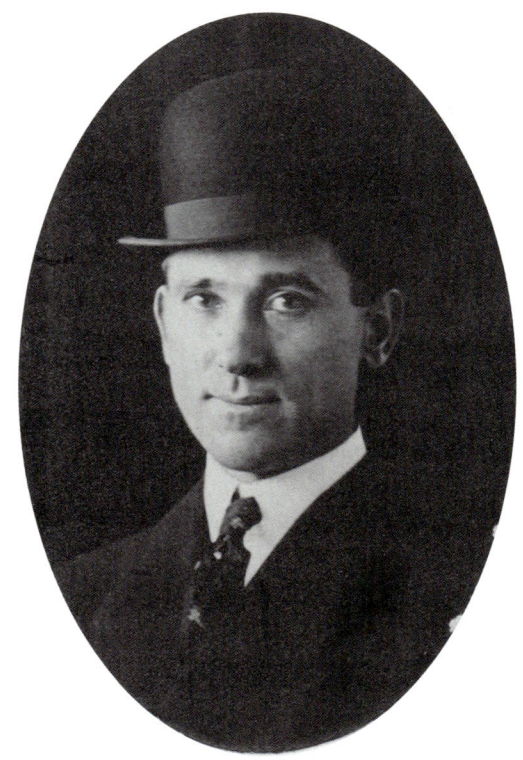

FIG. 134.1: Robert Sturm, c. 1905, CAM, Mary R. Schiff Library and Archives, Gift of Kathleen Puls

and watch making firms including Michaelson Bros. (1907–1920), Joseph Noterman & Co. (1895–1929), and the Cincinnati Watch Case Co. (1908–1921).[16] After the death of his mother in 1909, he returned to the family home on Lincoln Place.[17] The 1910 Federal Census reports that he was a silversmith with his own shop and that his home was owned free of a mortgage.[18] On August 24, 1911, he wed Bertha Mae Fuelling (1878–1959), daughter of Frederick W. Fuelling who owned a bakery in Avondale.[19] Following their marriage, the Sturms resided in the suburb of Norwood.[20]

By 1919, Sturm had returned to the shop in room 8 on the third floor of the Lion Building, and was listed as working there in city directories through 1931.[21] Data collected for the 1920 Federal Census states that he owned his home at 3940 Jefferson Avenue (Norwood) without mortgage, and that he was working as a silversmith in the jewelry industry.[22] Sixteen year-old Robert Jr. was working with him, and is not listed independently in city directories until 1923 when his enterprise, Monarch Stage Lighting Co., also operating in room 8 of the Lion Building, is included.[23]

There are no listings for Robert Sturm, Sr., in Cincinnati city directories after 1932. At this time, he had likely retired and moved to what his granddaughter describes as a "gentleman's farm" on Snider Road in Sycamore Township, where there were no crops, but a pony, chickens, and other small animals (fig. 134.2).[24] The 1940 Census indicates that he and Bertha had been there since at least 1935.[25] When the farm was divided by the construction of a highway in the early 1960s, he moved to 2803 Langdon Farm Road in the suburb of Pleasant Ridge. His granddaughter remembers that it was during this move that Sturm rid himself of a lot of his silver. Although his new home was smaller in size, it was, like his Snider Road home, decorated in the Arts and Crafts style.[26] Sturm died on September 25, 1964, after several bouts of cancer.[27] He is buried in Spring Grove Cemetery with his wife Bertha, in the lot owned by his father-in-law.[28] At the time of his death, Sturm's estate, which included over $196,000 in stocks and almost $20,000 in bonds and real estate alike, was appraised at $242,668.89[29] Beneficiaries of his will were his niece, Louise F. Bullock; Louise K. Schneider, his housekeeper and companion who received all of the silverware in Sturm's possession at the time of his death; his son Robert E. Sturm, Jr.; Roberta Sturm McWilliams and Kathleen Sturm Puls, his granddaughters; and the General Protestant Orphan Home and Shriner's Crippled Children's Hospital.[30]

Sturm worked in the Arts and Crafts tradition and style. For the majority of his career, he worked alone in a small shop, and all of his work was crafted by hand. His wares are comparable to the finest work of The Kalo Shop (Chicago, 1900–1970), The Dodge Silver Shop (Asheville, North Carolina, 1927–1942), and other well-recognized Arts and Crafts silver shops active at that time. They typically feature an all-over hand-hammered surface texture with applied monograms in Arts and Crafts-style lettering. Some examples feature applied medallions that are identical to those used by **Duhme & Co.** in the 1880s. It is possible that Sturm may have trained at Duhme & Co. or worked there early in his career, yet evidence of this has not been found.[31] Or, he may have acquired left-over medallions from his former business partner, Kenton C. Kunkle, who had worked for **Herman Keck**, an owner of **The Duhme Jewelry Co.** after the failure of **The Duhme Company**. The largest part of Sturm's income was likely made through his work for local jewelry and watch making firms, while his flatware and hollowware were rare, special commissions supported by a wealthy clientele which included Cincinnati mayor Murray Seasongood (1878–1983) who owned the sauceboat in fig. 134.7 and platter in figure 134.9. Pages from Sturm's sample books survive. These pages (figs. 134.3, 5, 8, 10, 13) include photographs, prices and other details for several of his designs. To date, five of Sturm's marks have been documented.

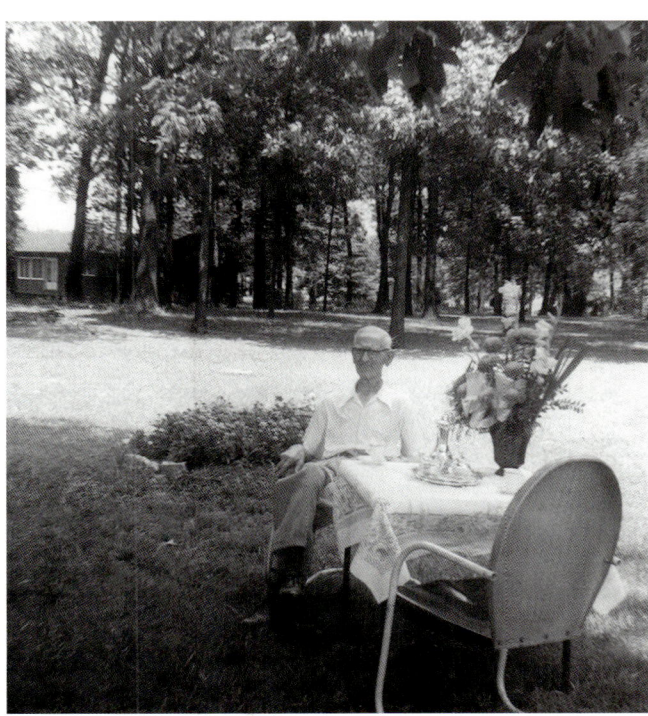

FIG. 134.2: Robert Sturm, 1962, CAM, Mary R. Schiff Library and Archives, Gift of Kathleen Puls

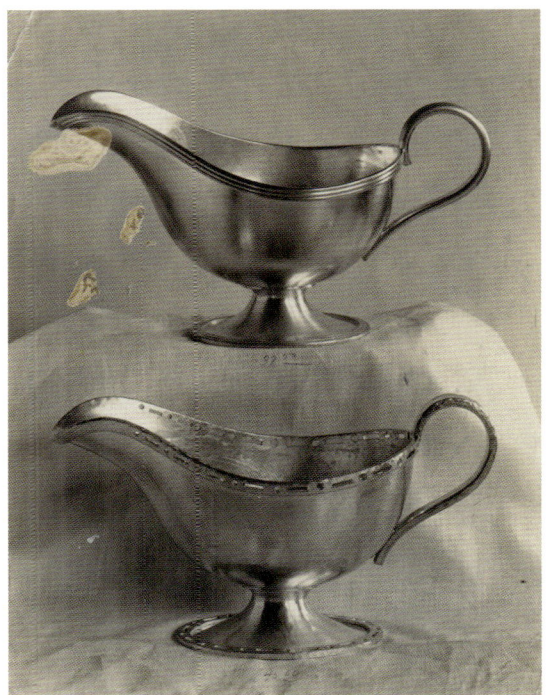

FIG. 134.3: Robert Sturm Sample Book: Sauce Boats, 1890–1930s, CAM, Mary R. Schiff Library and Archives, Gift of Kathleen Puls

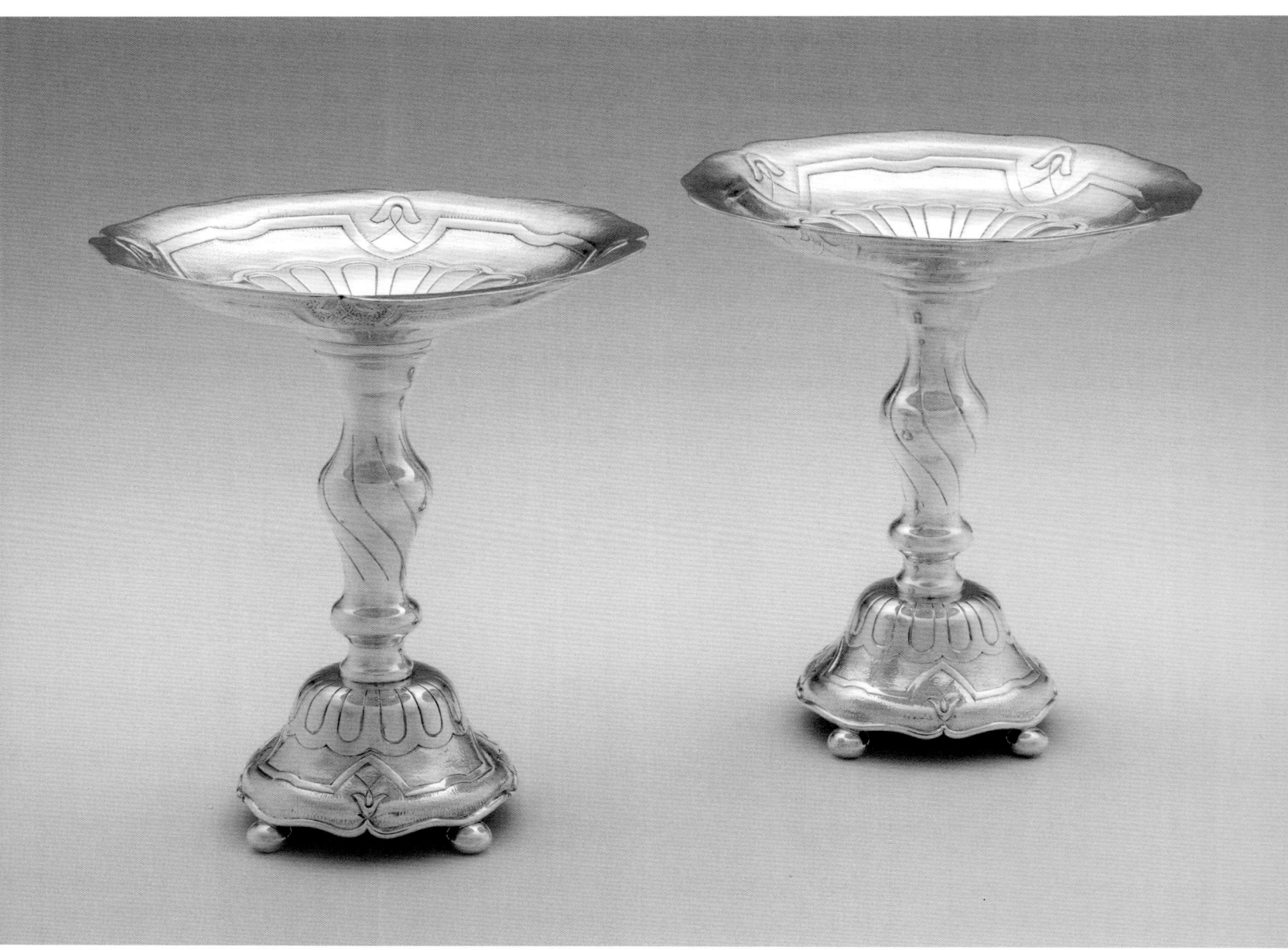

FIG. 134.4: Robert Sturm, *Pair of Tazzas*, 1890–1930s, 10 × 9¼ in.
(25.4 × 23.5 cm), CAM, Gift of Doctors James and Betty
Sutherland, 2001.152a–b

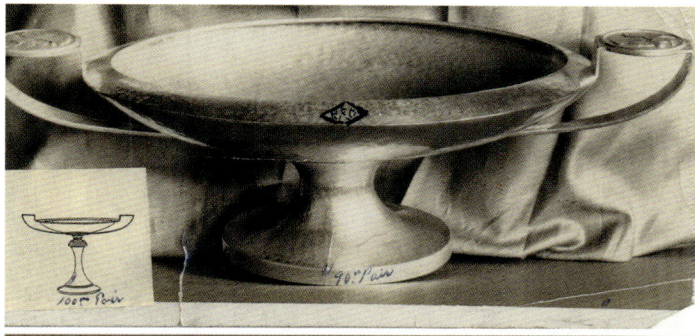

FIG. 134.5: Robert Sturm Sample Book: Footed Bowls, 1890–1930s, CAM, Mary R. Schiff Library and Archives, Gift of Kathleen Puls

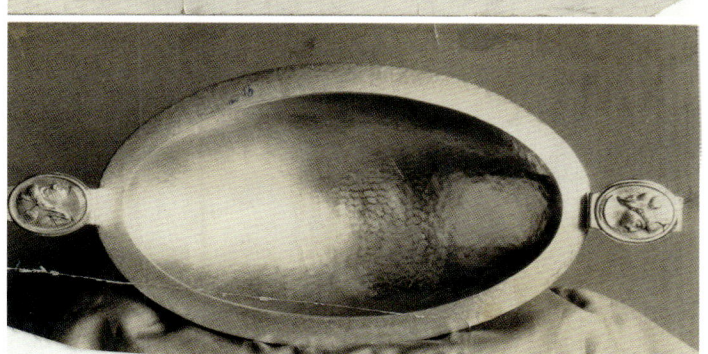

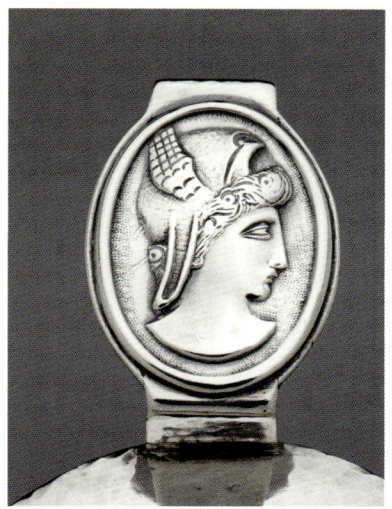

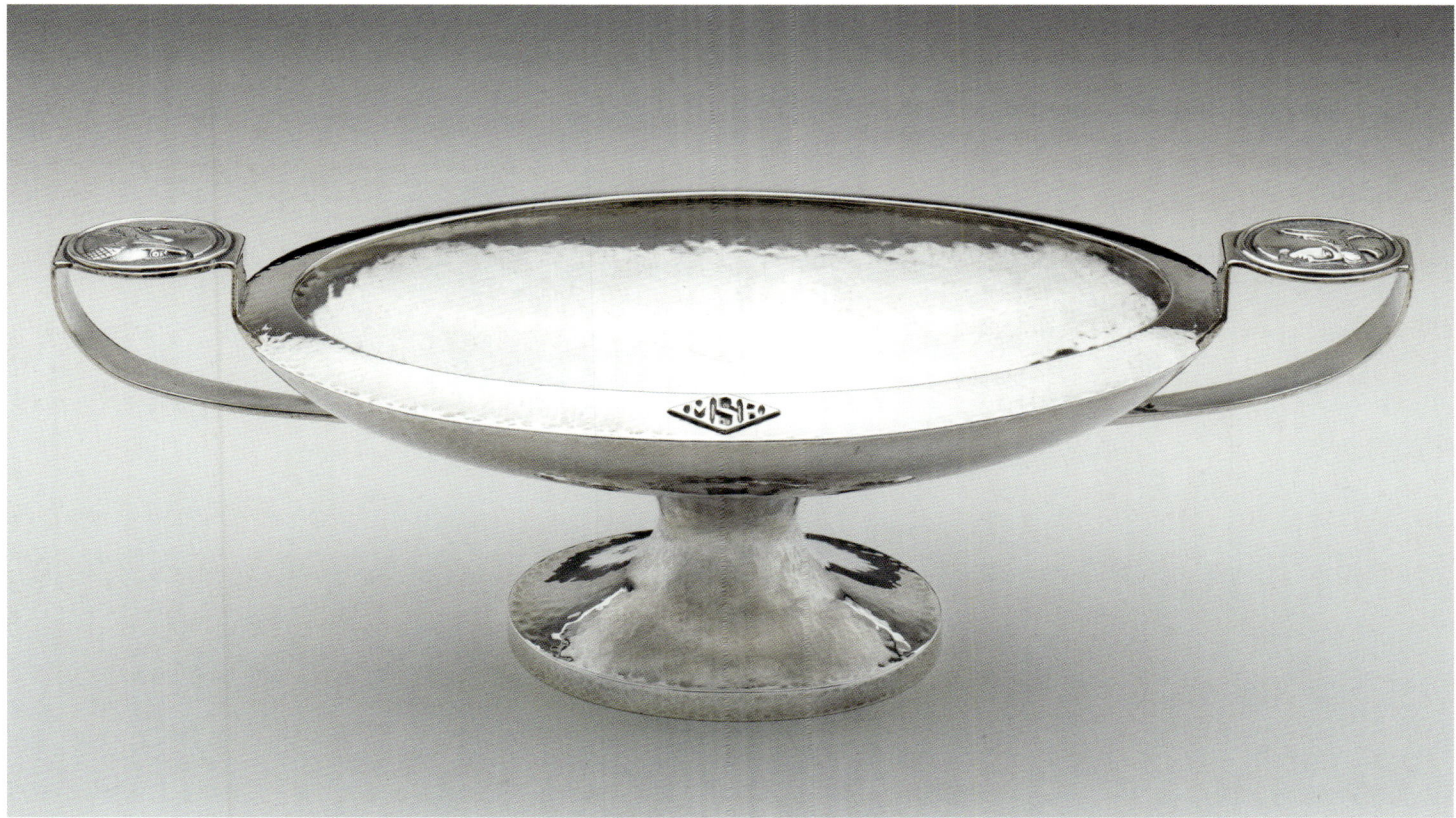

FIG. 134.6: Robert Sturm, *Footed Bowl* (from a pair), 1890–1930s, H. 3⅛ in. (7.9 cm) × W. 9⅛ in. (23.2 cm), CAM, Gift of James Randolph Hillard, M.D. and Aingeal Grehan, 2007.203a

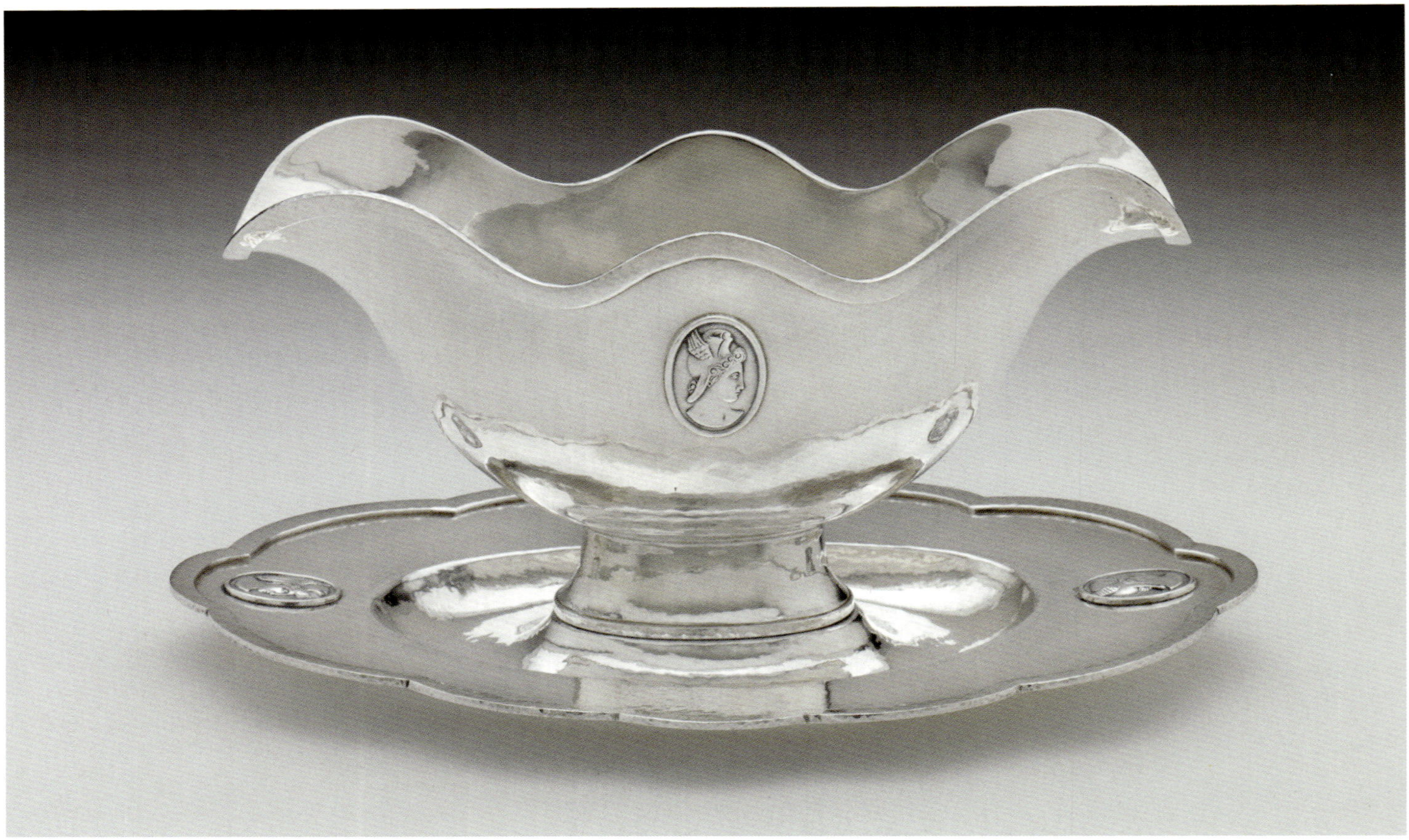

FIG. 134.7: Robert Sturm, *Sauce Boat*, 1890–1930s, 5⅛ × 10⅜ × 7¼ in. (13 × 26.4 × 18.4 cm), CAM, Museum Purchase with funds provided by Mr. and Mrs. Charles Fleischmann III, 2010.13

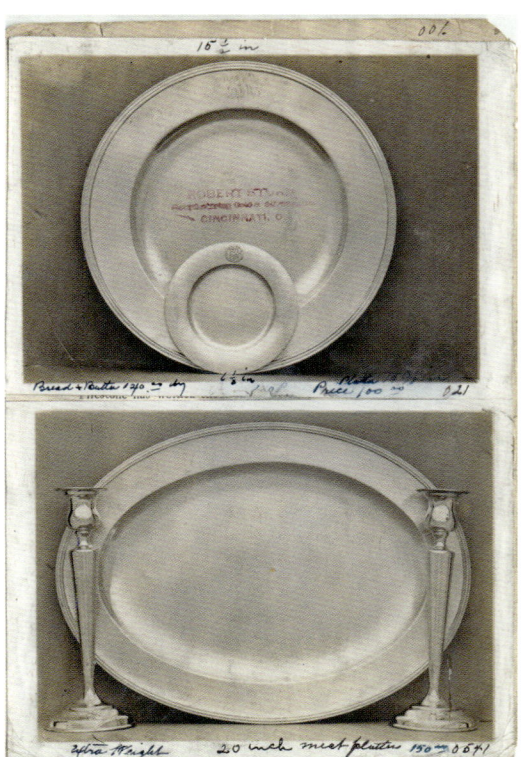

FIG. 134.8: Robert Sturm Sample Book: Plates, Platters, Candlesticks, 1890–1930s, CAM, Mary R. Schiff Library and Archives, Gift of Kathleen Puls

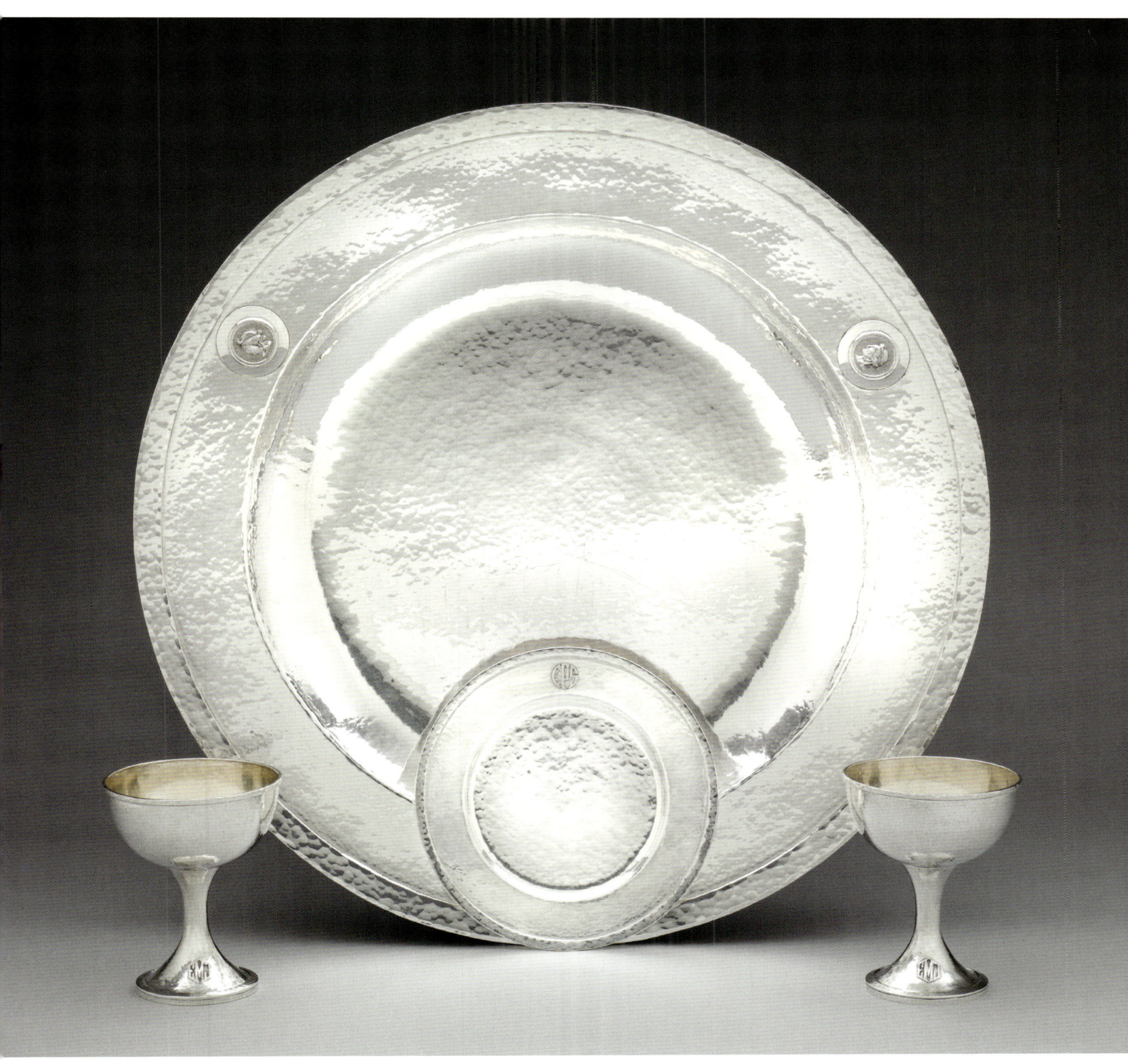

FIG. 134.9: Robert Sturm, *Platter*, 1890–1930s, 1¼ × 18 in. (3.2 × 45.7 cm), CAM, Museum Purchase with funds provided by Mr. and Mrs. Charles Fleischmann III, 2010.14; Robert Sturm, *Plate* (from a set of 12), 1890–1930s, D. 6½ in. (16.5 cm), CAM, Gift of James Randolph Hillard, M.D. and Aingeal Grehan, 2007.207a–l; Robert Sturm, *Pair of Goblets* (from a set of 12), 1890–1930s, 4½ × 3⅝ in. (11.4 × 9.2 cm), CAM, Gift of James Randolph Hillard, M.D. and Aingeal Grehan, 2007.208a–l

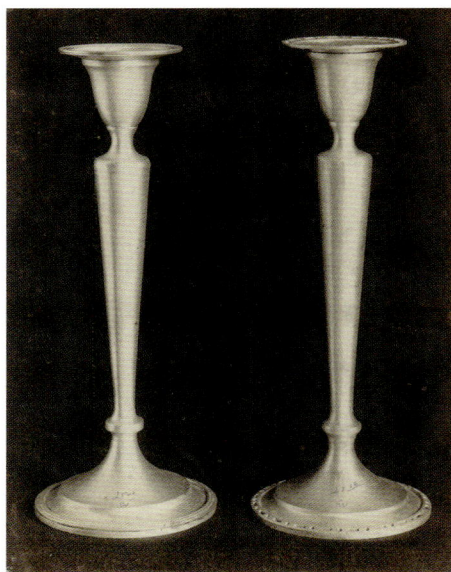

FIG. 134.10: Robert Sturm Sample Book: Candlesticks, 1890–1930s, CAM, Mary R. Schiff Library and Archives, Gift of Kathleen Puls

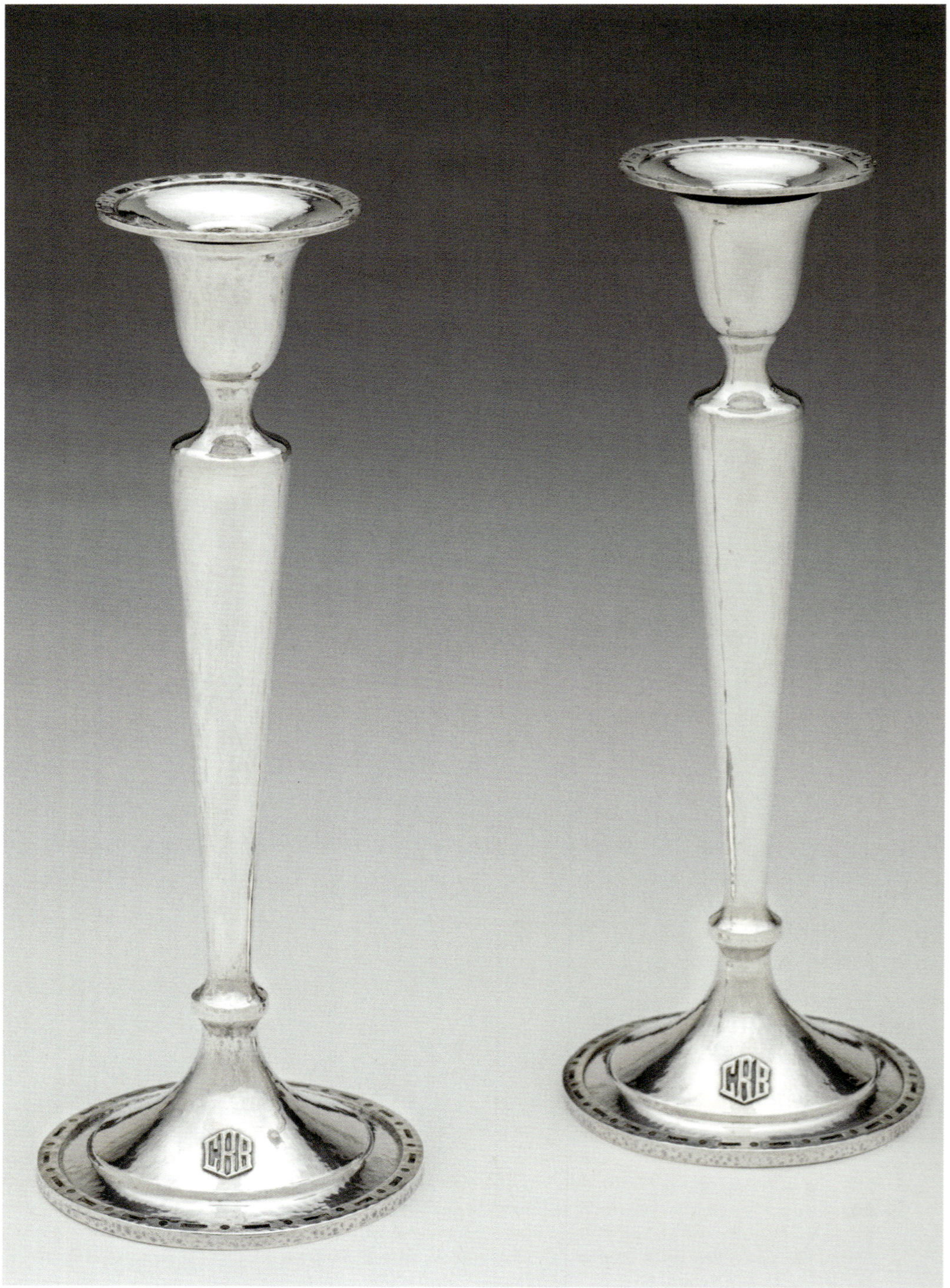

FIG. 134.11: Robert Sturm, *Pair of Candlesticks*, 1890–1930s, H. 11¾ in. (29.8 cm), W. base 4½ in. (11.4 cm), CAM, Museum Purchase: Decorative Arts Society Fund, 2012.16a–b

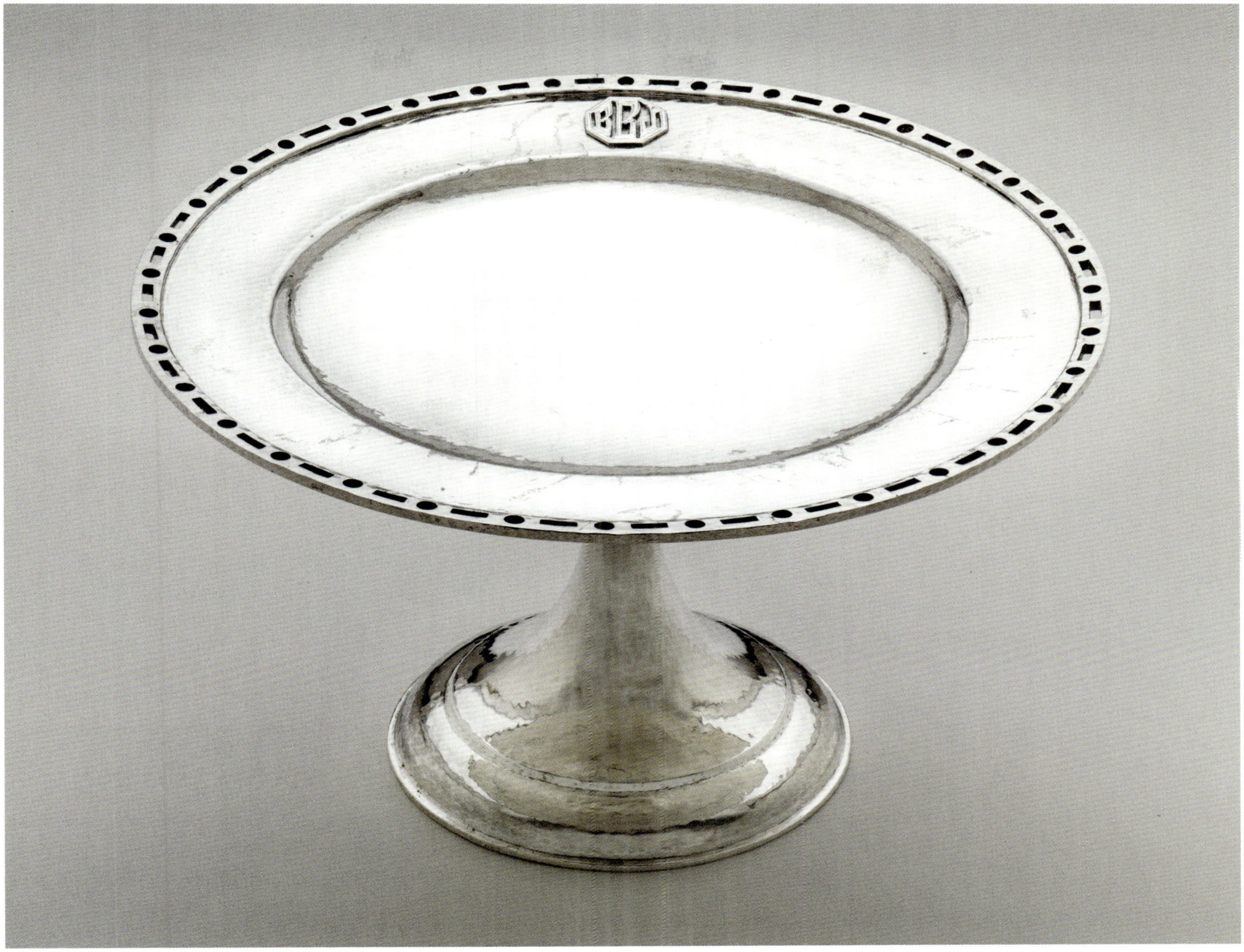

FIG. 134.12: Robert Sturm, *Footed Salver* (from a pair), 1890–1930s,
5 × 8½ in. (12.7 × 21.6 cm), CAM, Gift of James Randolph Hillard,
M.D. and Aingeal Grehan, 2007.210a

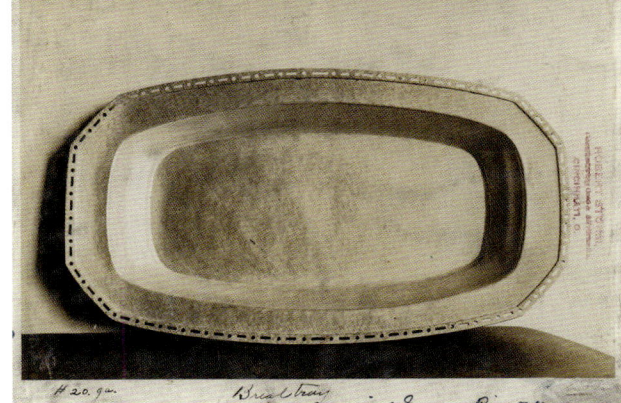

FIG. 134.13: Robert Sturm Sample
Book: Bread Tray, 1890–1930s,
CAM, Mary R. Schiff Library and
Archives, Gift of Kathleen Puls

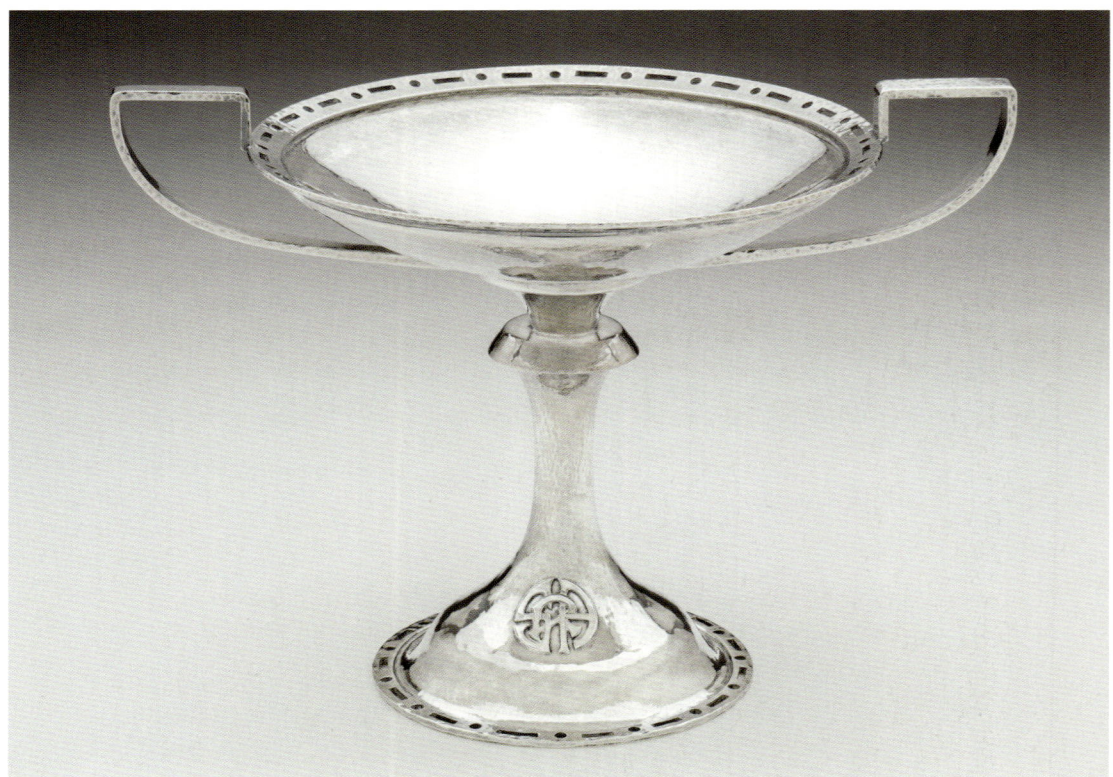

FIG. 134.14: Robert Sturm, *Tazza* (from a pair), 1890–1930s, 6¼ × 8⅞ in. (15.9 × 22.5 cm), CAM, Gift of James Randolph Hillard, M.D. and Aingeal Grehan, 2007.117b

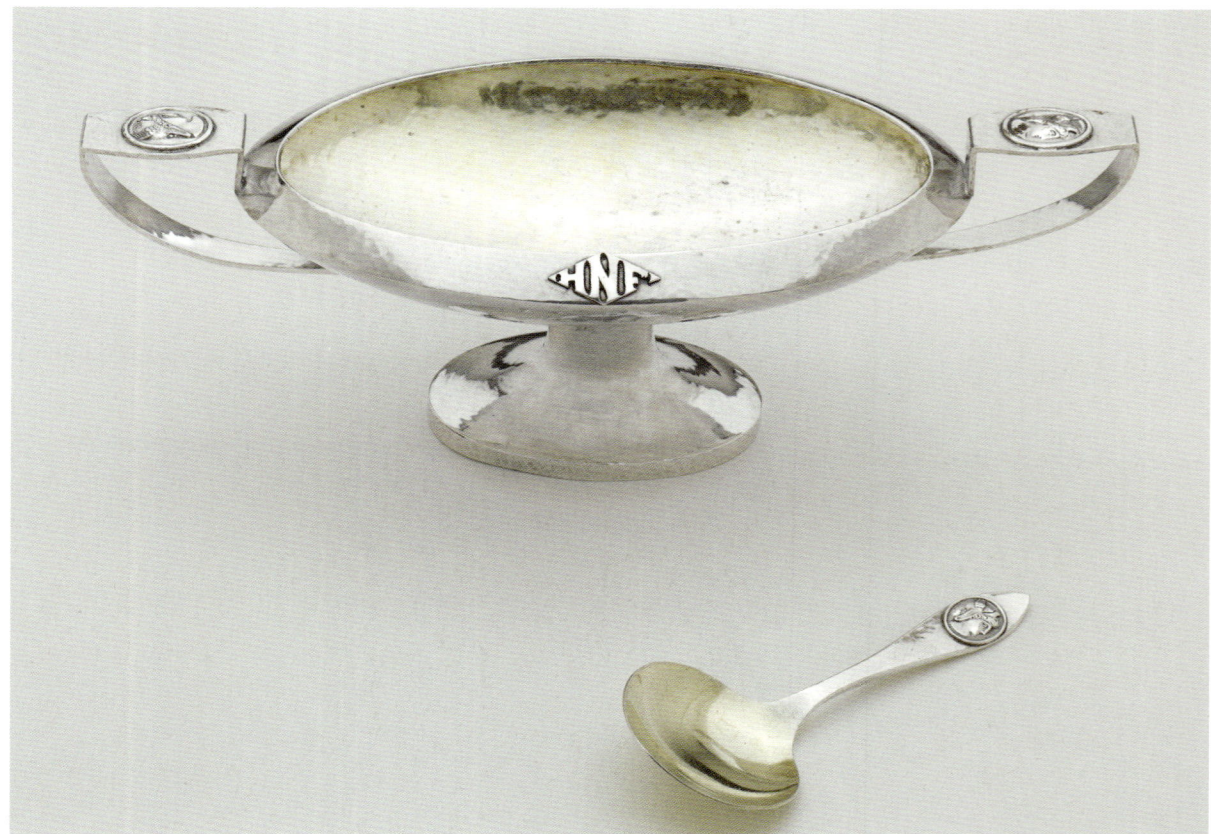

FIG. 134.15: Robert Sturm, *Footed Bowl and Spoon*, 1890s–1930s, bowl: 3¼ × 9½ × 4 in. (8.3 × 24.1 × 10.2 cm), spoon: L. 4⅝ in. (11.7 cm), Lent by Mr. and Mrs. Charles Fleischmann III, L25.2010a–b

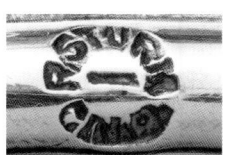

MARK 134.1

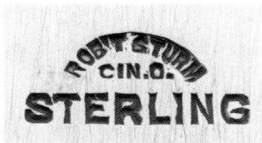

MARK 134.4

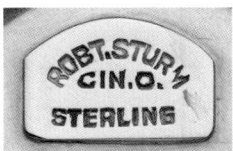

MARK 134.2

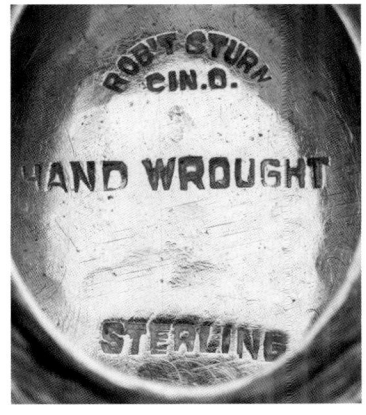

MARK 134.5

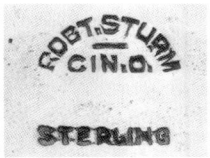

MARK 134.3

1. Ancestry.com, *World War I Draft Registration Cards, 1917–1918* [online database], Provo, Utah: Ancestry.com Operations Inc., 2005; Sturm was not a veteran, according to data collected in the 1930 Federal Census, Norwood, Hamilton, Ohio.

2. 1880 Federal Census, Avondale, Hamilton, Ohio; 1900 Federal Census, Cincinnati, Hamilton, Ohio; Marriage record, Hamilton County Probate Records, vol. 160, 255, http://www.probatect.org /CourtRecordsArchive /bukmarriages.aspx; Marriage record, Hamilton County Probate Records, vol. 234, 260; Philip Sturm, death record, Cincinnati Health Department, University of Cincinnati Archives and Rare Books Library, http://hdl.handle.net /2374.UC/3615599; Elizabeth Sturm, death notice, *Cincinnati Enquirer*, October 26, 1909, 7.

3. 1880 Federal Census, Avondale, Hamilton, Ohio; Elizabeth Sturm reported having given birth to twelve children. Six of them were living in 1900. 1900 Federal Census, Cincinnati, Hamilton, Ohio.

4. Elizabeth married Thomas Fleming. When Robert's brother John died in 1917, he left the majority of his $14,000 estate to Elizabeth. According to John's will, Robert received $25. He sued to set aside John's will; 1900 Federal Census,

Cincinnati, Hamilton, Ohio; John Sturm, will dated September 8, 1917, proved October 2, 1917, vol. 138, p 465, Hamilton County Registry of Probate, Cincinnati, Ohio; "Would Set Aside Sturm's Will," *Cincinnati Enquirer*, October 9, 1918, 11.

5. 1880 Federal Census, Avondale, Hamilton, Ohio; 1884–1890 Cincinnati City Directories.

6. 1884–1915 Cincinnati City Directories; "News of the Courts," *Cincinnati Enquirer*, October 9, 1918, 11.

7. Notice, *Cincinnati Enquirer*, February 17, 1890, 5.

8. In the 1893 Cincinnati City Directory she is enumerated as a widow, living on Elizabeth Street in Avondale with her son Robert.

9. 1890 Cincinnati City Directory.

10. 1897 Cincinnati City Directory; John Sturm's enterprise is listed as John Sturm & Co. for one year only, yet he continued to work as a blacksmith after this time.

11. 1899 Cincinnati City Directory. John's blacksmith shop was at 3112 Lincoln Place, next door to their home. By 1909, Lincoln Place had been renamed Durbin Place.

12. 1900, 1901 Cincinnati City Directories.

13. 1902–1904 Cincinnati City Directories.

14. Marriage record, Hamilton County Probate Records, vol. 160, 255;

Catherine was the daughter of Julia Scahill and Peter Hussey.

15. Ancestry.com, *Social Security Death Index* [online database], Provo, Utah: The Generations Network Inc., 2007; 1910 Federal Census, Cincinnati, Hamilton, Ohio; 1930 Federal Census, Norwood, Hamilton, Ohio; Katherine Sturm, death record, Cincinnati Health Department, University of Cincinnati Archives and Rare Books Library, http://hdl.handle.net/2347.UC/3911 59; "Cincinnati," *Jewelers' Circular and Horological Review* (May 6, 1903): 64.

16. 1904–1910 Cincinnati City Directories.

17. 1909 Cincinnati City Directory.

18. 1910 Federal Census, Cincinnati, Hamilton, Ohio.

19. Marriage record, Hamilton County Probate Records, vol. 234, 260; Bertha's surname appears in various places as Fulling or Fuelling. Initially, it may have been Fülling; Bertha Sturm, burial record, Spring Grove Cemetery, Cincinnati, Ohio.

20. 1888, 1913–1929 Cincinnati City Directories; 1900 Federal Census, Cincinnati, Hamilton, Ohio.

21. 1919–1931/32 Cincinnati City Directories.

22. 1920 Federal Census, Norwood, Hamilton, Ohio; In the 1930 Federal Census, Norwood, Hamilton, Ohio, Sturm's home was valued at $6,500.

23. 1923 Cincinnati City Directory;

Robert Sturm, Jr. was living in Los Angeles, CA by the time of his father's death.

24. Kathleen Sturm Puls, interview by Amy Dehan, October 22, 2009.

25. 1940 Federal Census, Sycamore, Hamilton, Ohio.

26. Kathleen Sturm Puls, interviews by Amy Dehan, October 22, 2009, and January 26, 2010.

27. Robert Sturm, codicil to will dated August 17, 1963, proved September 29, 1964, vol. 431, p. 142, Hamilton County Registry of Probate, Cincinnati, Ohio; Robert Sturm, burial record, Spring Grove Cemetery; Kathleen Sturm Puls, interviews by Amy Dehan.

28. Robert Sturm, burial record.

29. Inventory of Estate of Robert Sturm, Hamilton County Probate Court, estate no. 247449, filed October 24, 1964.

30. Robert Sturm, will; Kathleen Sturm Puls, interview by Amy Dehan, October 22, 2009.

31. It is possible that Sturm worked at Duhme & Co. when he was listed in the city directories as a silversmith with no working address given between 1890 and 1896. In 1893, Duhme reduced their manufacture of silver, but would still have been making jewelry.

135. GEORGE SULLIVAN

1775–1825, w. 1811–1815

George Sullivan, son of William Sullivant (1750–1790) and Sarah McDonald, was born in King George County, Virginia, in February 1775.[1] Following his father's death, George and his brother Enoch apprenticed with John Pittman of Falmouth, Virginia.[2] The boys were to serve until they were 21 years old and learn the gold and silversmith trade.[3] In 1795, Pittman moved to Fredericksburg, Virginia, and in the following year, he relocated to Alexandria, Virginia.[4] Both George and Enoch presumably accompanied him.[5] By 1802, George had relocated to Lynchburg, Virginia, where he joined the Methodist church that spring.[6] In November 1802 he insured his silversmith shop there, a single-story building on Second (now Main) Street, for $200.[7] George married Sally Cox, daughter of Valentine Cox, a fellow Methodist, on November 25, 1805.[8] In December of that year, they deeded a lot to the trustees of the Lynchburg Methodist Episcopal Church for the building of a church.[9]

By June 1808 Sullivan had moved to Lexington, Kentucky, where he advertised as a gold and silversmith, promising that his customers' "work shall be substantially done and after the neatest and most modern patterns," and that he kept "on hand a very handsome assortment of JEWELLERY [sic]."[10] In June 1810 Ichabod Woodruff, brother of **Enos Woodruff**, advertised as a silver plater in George Sullivan's shop. They were later joined by Ichabod and Enos' brother, Ezra.[11] This is presumably where Sullivan learned the technique of silver plating.

Sullivan had moved to Cincinnati by the spring of 1811, when he advertised that he had "COMMENCED THE Silver-Plating Business, NEXT door to Mr. Hafer's bake-house and nearly opposite the Columbian Inn."[12] In addition to carrying a variety of horse

and coach-related plated items, he also advertised that he would "keep on hand an assortment of SILVER WORK, such as *Table & Tea-spoons, Soup, Cream and Mustard Ladles, Sugar-tongs, Salt-shovels, Heads & Cantels, &c.*" and would "allow the full value for *cut silver* in any of the above articles, and will give the highest price for old Silver, Pewter, Brass and Copper." The advertisement concludes with a notice that Mrs. Sullivan has "an assortment of the most fashionable BONNETS, ARTIFICIAL FLOWERS & BAND-BOXES; all of which she will sell on very reasonable terms." While in Cincinnati, Sullivan was one of several citizens, including Nicholas Longworth, who worked to establish the Benevolent Society, and a poor house.[13] He moved to Dayton, Ohio, sometime after 1815, and died there in 1825.[14]

George Sullivan marked his silver with an initialed punch of "G S" in a rectangular cartouche. There is a pellet between the G and the S, and the serif of the G is slightly curved and angled.[15]

1. The surname Sullivant was simplified to Sullivan by William and Sarah's children. Catherine B. Hollan, *Virginia Silversmiths, Jewelers, Watch- and Clockmakers, 1607–1860: Their Lives and Marks*, McLean, VA: Hollan Press, 2010, 738.
2. Ibid.
3. Ibid.
4. Ibid.
5. Ibid.
6. George Barton Cutten, *The Silversmiths of Virginia*, Richmond, VA: The Dietz Press Inc., 1952, 66.
7. Hollan, *Virginia Silversmiths*, 738.
8. Jordan Dodd, *Virginia Marriages to 1800* [online database], Provo, Utah: Ancestry.com Operations Inc., 1997.
9. Hollan, *Virginia Silversmiths*, 738.
10. Advertisement, *The Reporter* (Lexington, KY), June 4, 1808, 3.
11. Hollan, *Virginia Silversmiths*, 739.
12. Advertisement, *Western Spy*, May 31, 1811, reproduced in Beckman, 136.
13. "Benevolent Society," *Western Spy*, February 25, 1815; *Western Spy*, December 8, 1815.
14. Hollan, *Virginia Silversmiths*, 739.
15. Based on examples of Sullivan's silver found in Lynchburg, Virginia, collections, Catherine B. Hollan was able to positively identify the initialed punch of George Sullivan and differentiate between it and the initialed punch used by George Snyder of Kentucky. Hollan, *Virginia Silversmiths*, 739.

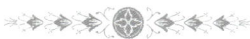

136. WILLIAM C. SWIFT

b. about 1815, w. 1842 or earlier–1865

The 1836/37 Cincinnati City Directory includes a silversmith named Swift (no first name given), boarding at Mrs. V. Laporte's on the northeast corner of Sycamore and Fifth Streets. In 1842, William C. Swift is listed as a watch maker boarding with **Abraham**

Palmer.[1] Swift, born in Connecticut around 1815, continues to appear in local directories between 1842 and 1865.[2] From 1849 to 1853, he is noted as a watch repairer and jeweler at the address of **Wilson McGrew**, and between 1856 and 1857, he was working as a watch maker and salesman in the shop of **S.T. Carley**. By July 1858 he had given **Henry Bliss** a $1,000 mortgage on a city lot of real estate in return for Bliss' stock and shop at 157 Main Street (just above Fourth Street).[3] At this time, credit reporters noted that Swift was "long employed in this business and understands it well, but drinks too much . . . cannot be safe for long."[4] True to their prediction, he appears to have failed by the end of 1860.[5] When Swift resurfaced in 1864, he was working as a watchman [*sic*], more likely, a watch maker, at the shop of **John B. Morris**.[6] The following year, he was employed by **Edward H. Hill** as a watch maker.[7] In 1870, Swift's personal estate was valued at $100, and he was working as a watch repairer in northern Brown County, Ohio.[8] The 1880 Federal Census documents his wife, Eleanor (b. 1829), as a widow, working in Chicago as a dress maker.[9] The Swifts had four children. Those on record include Laura (b. about 1847), George M. (b. 1849), and Alice (b. about 1859).[10]

Swift appears to have worked primarily as a watch maker and jeweler, although spoons with fiddle handles and rounded shoulders have been found with his marks.[11]

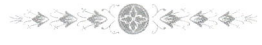

MARK 136.1   MARK 136.2

1. 1842 Cincinnati City Directory.
2. 1850 Federal Census, Cincinnati, Hamilton, Ohio; 1870 Federal Census, Perry, Brown, Ohio; 1842–1865 Cincinnati City Directories; Our subject may have been William Clark Swift, born June 19, 1815, in Mansfield Township, Tolland County, Connecticut, to Dan and Laura Swift. "Connecticut, Births and Christenings, 1649–1906," index, *FamilySearch*, https://familysearch.org/pal:/MM9.1.1/F74W-M8G.
3. Ohio, Vol. 3, p. 258, R.G. Dun & Co. Collection, Baker Library, Harvard Business School; Ohio, Vol. 4, p. 70, R.G. Dun & Co. Collection.
4. Ohio, Vol. 4, p. 70, R.G. Dun & Co. Collection.
5. 1860, 1861 Cincinnati City Directories. The last listing for Swift at 157 Main Street appears in the 1860 edition. In 1861, his occupation is given as joiner. He is not included in the 1862 or 1863 editions.
6. 1864 Cincinnati City Directory. Swift is enumerated at 36 Sycamore, the site of the shop of **Richard Clayton**, and later his successor, John B. Morris. This address was at the southeast corner of Second and Sycamore Streets.
7. 1865 Cincinnati City Directory.
8. 1870 Federal Census, Perry, Brown, Ohio.
9. 1880 Federal Census, Chicago, Cook, Illinois; 1900 Federal Census, Libertyville, Lake, Illinois.
10. Ibid.; 1850 Federal Census, Cincinnati, Hamilton, Ohio; 1870 Federal Census, Perry, Brown, Ohio.
11. William Swift, eBay listings and private collections, Cincinnati silver binders, Cincinnati Art Museum.

137. CELADON SYMMES

1770–1837, w. 1789–1790

Silver struck with the mark of Celadon Symmes has yet to be discovered. However, a pewter spoon mold (fig. 137. 1) and a set of jeweler's tools (fig. 137.2) said to have been used by Symmes are now in the collection of the Cincinnati Historical Society. They were presented by Symmes' grandson, William Symmes (b. 1851) in 1897.[1] These artifacts, in addition to the spoon molds itemized in Celadon Symmes' estate sale in 1837, suggest that he was involved in metalwork.[2] Nineteenth-century reminiscences tell us that he was possibly Cincinnati's first silversmith, predating **John Whitesides** who may have been working in the area by 1793.[3]

Symmes was born on May 30, 1770, in Sussex County, New Jersey.[4] He was the son of Timothy Symmes (b. 1744, Aquebogue, Long Island, New York, d. 1797) and Abigail Tutthill (d. 1776).[5] His father was, by all accounts, also a silversmith who apprenticed in New York or on Long Island, possibly with Elias Pelletreau of

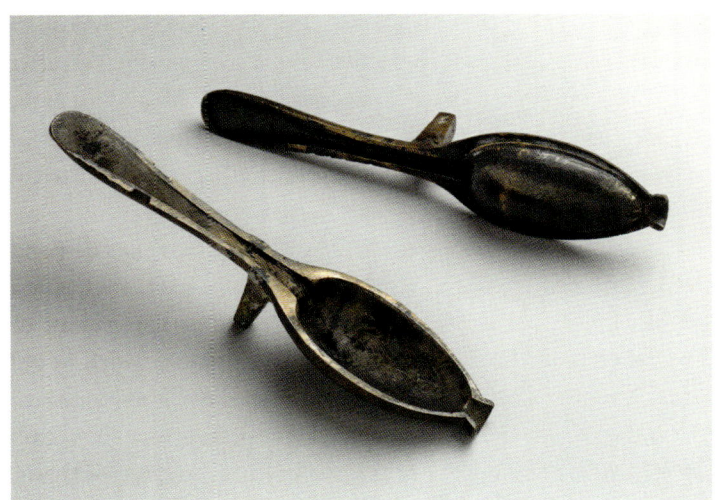

FIG. 137.1: Celadon Symmes, *Spoon Mold*, Cincinnati Museum Center

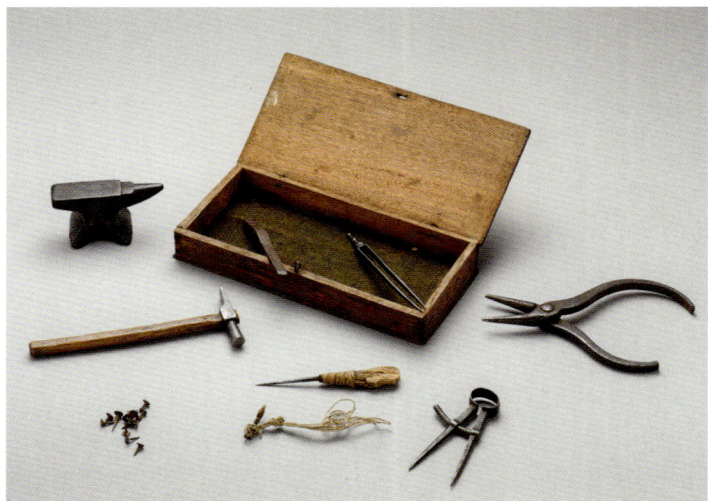

FIG. 137.2: Celadon Symmes, *Jeweler's Tool Box and Tools*, Cincinnati Museum Center

Southampton.[6] He was also a farmer, and is said to have maintained a silversmith shop on his farm in Newtown, Sussex County, New Jersey, where he moved around 1780.[7] Celadon and his brothers Daniel (1772–1827) and William (1774–1809) are believed to have apprenticed with their father.[8] Works marked by Timothy Symmes are unknown.

Timothy Symmes was the brother of John Cleves Symmes (1742–1814), the New Jersey Supreme Court Justice and Congressman, who with a number of other New Jerseyans created the Miami Company and negotiated with Congress the purchase of 330,000 acres of the Northwest Territory between the Great Miami and Little Miami Rivers, now known as the Miami Purchase or Symmes Purchase. This land included parts of present day Hamilton, Butler and Warren counties. Timothy and his family followed John Cleves Symmes to Ohio, arriving around 1789.[9] It was shortly thereafter that Celadon is said to have "bought a small lot of land for eight dollars [in Cincinnati]; built a shop eight × ten feet, and worked one year at his trade, that of a silversmith, which he had learned of his father. He then sold his shop for seventeen dollars."[10]

It is difficult to believe that there would have been any demand for silver this early in Cincinnati, as by this time there were only a handful of dwellings in Cincinnati proper and perhaps twenty or so more erected in outlying lots.[11] Fort Washington, which would become home to about 300 soldiers, was not completed until December 1789. If it is true that Symmes maintained a shop during this time, it is likely that he was crafting not silver, but basic, utilitarian forms out of other metals, such as pewter as the extant spoon mold suggests. His tool kit hints that he might also have

offered watch and jewelry repair services for those early settlers who had brought such items with them from the East.

In 1790, Celadon went to North Bend, Ohio, about 15 miles west of Cincinnati along the Ohio River, where he oversaw his uncle's farm and served in the militia.[12] His name appears in the account books of Cincinnati merchants Smith & Findlay between 1792 and 1800.[13] On October 14, 1794, Celadon wed Phebe Fitz Randolph in North Bend.[14] They had eleven children: twins William Cleves and a daughter (b. 1795, died in infancy); Daniel T. (b. November 5, 1798); John Cleves (1800–1837); Benjamin Randolph (b. 1802); a son (b. 1805, d. infancy); Celadon (b. 1807); Nancy H. (1810–1814); Esther Woodruff Hunter (b. 1811); Joseph Randolph (b. 1814); and Sarah Deborah Symmes Powers Danford (1817–1869).[15]

Celadon eventually bought a tract of land north of Cincinnati in what is now part of Butler County.[16] He spent the remainder of his life farming and served as justice of the peace, associate judge of the Court of Common pleas in Butler County, captain of a company of militia, and as a commissioner for leasing, as appointed by the Governor.[17] He died on July 11, 1837, and is buried in The Symmes Cemetery, a two-acre public burial ground which he had established on the southern side of his farm.[18] The appraisal of his estate and the sale of goods from it include listings for bellows, anvils, a set of tools, spoon molds, and seals and weights.[19]

1. "No Doubt it Was Pewter," *Piqua Daily Call*, May 29, 1897, 8. This is an account of the William Symmes' gift of the spoon mold to the Ohio Historical and Archaeological Society in 1897.
2. A set of tools, weights, and seals were purchased by Celadon's son (William's father), Joseph Randolph Symmes (b. 1814), from the Celadon Symmes estate. Spoon molds were purchased from the estate by John Hart; Celadon Symmes, estate packet 01684, Butler County Records Center and Archives, Hamilton, Butler County, Ohio.
3. John Adams Vinton, *The Symmes Memorial*, Boston: David Clapp & Son, 1873, 92.
4. Carl Mark Williams, *Silversmiths of New Jersey, 1700–1825*, Philadelphia: G.S. MacManus Co., 1949, 105; Vinton, *The Symmes Memorial*, 92; Ancestry.com, *Web: Ohio, Find A Grave Index, 1803–2011* [online database], Provo, Utah: Ancestry.com Operations Inc., 2012.
5. Vinton, *The Symmes Memorial*, 92; Williams, *Silversmiths of New Jersey*, 105; Henry A. and Mrs. Kate B. Ford, *History of Cincinnati, Ohio*, Cleveland: L.A. Williams, 1881, 295; Rev. Francis M. Symmes, "A Genealogical Tree of the Symmes Family," *History*

of Butler County, Cincinnnati: Biographical Publishing Co., 1882; Ancestry.com, *U.S. Sons of the American Revolution Membership Applications, 1889–1970* [online database], Provo, Utah: Ancestry.com Operations Inc., 2011.
6. Williams, *Silversmiths of New Jersey*, 105.
7. Timothy Symmes also fought in the Revolutionary War and served as a judge in the Common Pleas Court in Sussex County; Vinton, *The Symmes Memorial*, 65; Williams, *Silversmiths of New Jersey*, 105.
8. No marks are known for Daniel or William Symmes. David went on to become a lawyer. William gave up silversmithing for farming. Williams, *Silversmiths of New Jersey*, 105; Vinton, *The Symmes Memorial*, 95.
9. Daniel may have stayed behind in Newtown to continue in the silversmithing business, as suggested by Carl Mark Williams, but had settled in Cincinnati by 1802; Vinton, *The Symmes Memorial*, 92–95; Williams, *Silversmiths of New Jersey*, 105.
10. Vinton, *The Symmes Memorial*, 92; Rhea Mansfield Knittle, *Early Ohio Silversmiths and Pewterers 1787–1847*, Cleveland: The Calvert-Hatch Co., 1943, 26.
11. Beckman, 136–138; Vinton, *The*

Symmes Memorial, 92.

12. Vinton, *The Symmes Memorial*, 92; Beckman, 136–137.
13. Torrence papers, Cincinnati Historical Society, box 56, folder 4.
14. Wm. Erik Voss, "Celadon Symmes," American Silversmiths, http://freepages.genealogy.rootsweb. ancestry.com/~silversmiths/makers/ silversmiths/134669.htm; Edmund

West, comp., *Family Data Collection – Marriages* [online database], Provo, Utah: The Generations Network Inc., 2001; Vinton, *The Symmes Memorial*, 65; Yates Publishing, *U.S. and International Marriage Records, 1560–1900* [online database], Provo, Utah: Ancestry.com Operations Inc., 2004.
15. Vinton, *The Symmes Memorial*, 93–94;

Celadon Symmes, will dated March 13, 1835, proved September 2, 1837, Old Will Book 2:272, Butler County Records Center and Archives, Hamilton, Butler County, Ohio.
16. Celadon owned the area now known as Symmes Corner; Vinton, *The Symmes Memorial*, 93.
17. Vinton, *The Symmes Memorial*, 93; *Scioto Gazette and Chillicothe Advertiser*,

January 23, 1806; *Western Spy*, February 5, 1806.
18. Vinton, *The Symmes Memorial*, 93; Ancestry.com, *Web: Ohio, Find A Grave Index, 1803–2011*.
19. Celadon Symmes, estate packet 01684, Butler County Records Center and Archives.

138. FRANKLIN THORPE

1808–1900, w. 1834, 1842–1853

Franklin Thorpe was born in Washington, DC in February 1808.[1] His parents were born in Virginia.[2] Details of his training are unknown. He made his initial appearance in Cincinnati in 1834, when he appeared in the city directory that year as a watch maker on Sixth Street between Race and Elm. He then relocated to Lexington, Kentucky, where he advertised as a watch and clock maker, jeweler, and engraver in 1838, touting "CLOCKS, WATCHES, JEWELRY, SILVERWARE, FINE CUTTLERY [*sic*], FANCY GOODS, &c."[3] By 1842, he had returned to Cincinnati and had resumed his business on Main Street, between Court and Canal Streets.[4] His advertisement that year focused on watch making and watch and clock repair (fig. 138.1). By the time the following year's directory was published, he had relocated to the south side of Sixth Street, near Plum, and in addition to his watch and clock related skills, he advertised the making and repair of jewelry and the engraving of door plates.[5] He remained at this address until 1846, when he listed as a watch maker on the south side of Fifth, between Vine and Race Streets.[6] An advertisement published in August of that year (fig. 138.2) includes an engraving of his store front and notes that he keeps "a general assortment of CLOCKS, WATCHES, JEWELRY, SILVER WARE, SPECTACLES and FINE CUTLERY for sale."[7] There was no city directory published in 1847 or 1848, and Thorpe is not included in the 1849/50 edition.[8] But, by September 1849 he was advertising his return to the city and to his former stand "on Fifth Street, south side, near the corner of Elm."[9] In September 1850 he was recorded in the census as a watch maker, living in Cincinnati, and watch maker Henry Istmas, age 25, born in Maryland, was living with him and his wife.[10] A credit reporter noted in February of 1852 that Thorpe had failed in business some years ago (possibly while in Kentucky or during the period between late 1846 and September 1849) and never

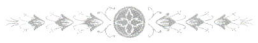

FIG. 138.1: Advertisement, from Charles Cist, comp., *Cincinnati City Directory for the year 1842*, Cincinnati: E. Morgan & Co., 359

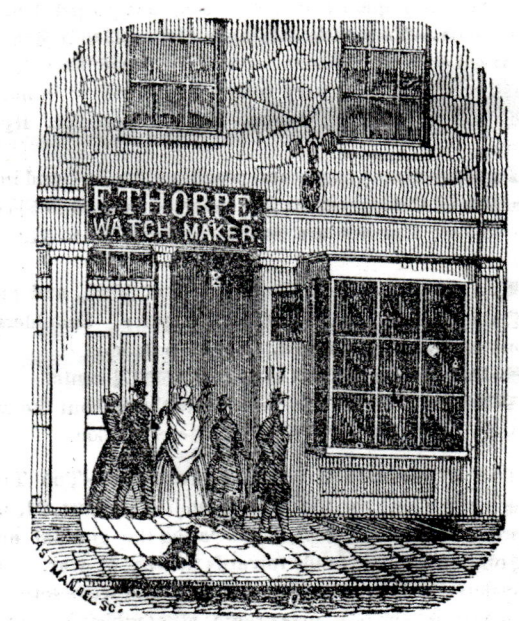

FIG. 138.2: Advertisement, *Weekly Advertiser*, August 31, 1846

recovered from it.[11] The R.G. Dun September 1853 report concluded that he was out of business.[12] Thorpe continued to work as a watch maker and dealer over the next several decades as he moved westward across the country. He was listed in Springfield, Illinois, city directories as a watch maker between 1860 and 1868.[13] In 1880, he was working in Sioux City, Iowa, and between 1885 and 1900, he was working in Denver, Colorado.[14]

Thorpe had married Ann (b. Kentucky, about 1814) by 1850 and in June 1862 he married Tamar Virginia Life (1846–1890) in Springfield, Illinois.[15] Tamar and Franklin had three known children: William, Minnie, and Mariam.[16] Franklin Thorpe died in 1900 and is buried in Riverside Cemetery, Denver, Colorado.[17]

Thorpe's focus was on the watch, clock, and jewelry trade, and it is unlikely that he produced any of the silver bearing his mark. Silver struck with his mark, an incuse "F. THORPE," is rarely seen. A set of tipped, exaggerated fiddle-handled forks with rounded shoulders have been documented.[18] It is possible, but not certain, that these were sold during his tenure in Cincinnati.

1. 1900 Federal Census, Denver, Arapahoe, Colorado; 1850 Federal Census, Cincinnati, Hamilton, Ohio.
2. 1880 Federal Census, Sioux City, Woodbury, Iowa; 1900 Federal Census, Denver, Arapahoe, Colorado.
3. Advertisement, 1838 Lexington, Kentucky City Directory, reproduced in Boultinghouse, 270.
4. 1842 Cincinnati City Directory.
5. 1843 Cincinnati City Directory, 350; This advertisement also appeared in the 1844 Cincinnati City Directory, 350, reproduced in Beckman, 139.
6. 1846 Cincinnati City Directory.
7. Advertisement, *Cincinnati Weekly Advertiser*, August 31, 1846.
8. There was a business directory published for 1848/49, but it did not include many of the silversmiths included in this book.
9. Advertisement, *Cincinnati Daily Commercial*, September 12, 1849, reproduced in Beckman, 139; Thorpe's whereabouts between late 1846 and September 1849 are, at this time, undocumented.
10. 1850 Federal Census, Cincinnati, Hamilton, Ohio.
11. Ohio, Vol. 1, pp. 91, 319, R.G. Dun & Co. Collection, Baker Library, Harvard Business School.
12. Ibid.
13. Ancestry.com. *U.S. City Directories, 1821–1989* [online database], Provo, Utah: Ancestry.com Operations, Inc., 2011.
14. 1880 Federal Census, Sioux City, Woodbury, Iowa; 1885–1900 Denver, Colorado City Directories; 1900 Federal Census, Denver, Arapahoe, Colorado.
15. 1850 Federal Census, Cincinnati, Hamilton, Ohio; Ann may have also been known as Fanny. Thorpe's wife is listed as Ann, b. KY in the 1850 Census, and as Fanny, b. KY in the 1860 Census. Jordan Dodd, Liahona Research, comp., *Illinois Marriages, 1851–1900* [online database], Provo, Utah: Ancestry.com Operations Inc., 2005; Tamar V. Thorpe, burial record, findagrave.com.
16. 1880 Federal Census, Sioux City, Woodbury, Iowa.
17. Franklin Thorpe, burial record, *Find A Grave*, findagrave.com.
18. Franklin Thorpe, eBay listings and private collections, Cincinnati silver binders, Cincinnati Art Museum.

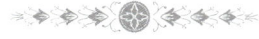

139. TICE & HUNTINGTON

1873[1]–1890

The firm of Tice & Huntington was composed of Charles L.F. Huntington (1841–1926) and Orceneth Fisher Tice (1834–1912)—who called himself O.F. Tice. Both men had been associated with Charles' uncle, John C. Huntington (1819–1887) in the firm of John C. Huntington & Co., a firm specializing in the sale of china, glass, Queensware, house furnishings, and by 1870, hotel and steamboat goods.[2] When John C. Huntington retired from the firm around 1872, Tice and Charles Huntington took over the firm, changing its name to Tice & Huntington.[3] The firm maintained John C. Huntington & Co.'s 119 Main Street store until relocating to 23 West Fourth Street around 1881.[4] It also continued to sell the same types of goods as those offered by its predecessor.[5] In 1886, their store was described as "handsomely fitted up," "one of the largest in the city," and "undoubtedly the most complete house furnishing establishment in the West."[6] With offices in Liverpool, England, and Paris, France, the firm imported some luxury goods such as art pottery, but also carried more mundane house furnishings such as iron, tin, wooden, and willow wares.[7]

Although the firm advertised silverware, including both silver plated ware and sterling flatware, it was evidently not a major component of their stock as extant wares with their mark are exceedingly rare. A silver punch ladle, in the fiddle thread pattern, with an incuse "TICE & HUNTINGTON" mark has been documented.[8] The stamped mark "T & H," in a rectangular cartouche that has been found on a teaspoon typical of those made earlier in the 19th century, can be reliably attributed to the silversmiths Thomas Trotter and John Huntington who were working in North Carolina in 1828.[9]

Tice & Huntington dissolved in 1890, with Charles Huntington continuing the business until 1898 at the Fourth Street location under his own name and advertising as "Successor to Tice and Huntington."[10] By 1891, Tice had partnered with H.F. West to form West & Tice Co., a firm located on West Fourth Street that also dealt in china, glass, earthenware, and fancy goods.[11]

1. 1873 Cincinnati City Directory.
2. 1865–1872 Cincinnati City Directories; Orceneth Fisher Tice, burial record, Spring Grove Cemetery, Cincinnati, Ohio; For more on the Huntington family and its involvement in the fancy goods trade in Cincinnati, see the biographies for **William C. Huntington**, **Huntington & LaBoyteaux** and **Huntington Brothers & Co.**; Advertisements in the 1870 Cincinnati City Directory, placed in the upper left

corner of all even numbered pages in the alphabetical listings read, "John C. Huntington & Co., / 119 Main St., Furnish / Hotels and Steamboats / See Page 1 for particulars." The list of wares advertised by the firm included silver plated wares; Charles L.F. Huntington and O.F. Tice were principals of John C. Huntington & Co. in 1870. 1870 Cincinnati City Directory.
3. Information provided in the 1870 Federal Census, Cincinnati, Hamilton,

Ohio indicates that John was a wealthy merchant whose assets included $60,000 in real estate and $37,000 in "personal estate." He retired from the firm about 1872; 1872–1873 Cincinnati City Directories.
4. 1871–1890 Cincinnati City Directories.
5. Ibid.
6. *Leading Manufacturers and Merchants of Cincinnati and Environs*, Cincinnati: International Publishing Co., 1886, 100.

7. Ibid.
8. Tice & Huntington, eBay listings and private collections, Cincinnati silver binders, Cincinnati Art Museum.
9. William Johnston Hogan, *Huntington Silversmiths 1763–1885*, Durham, NC: Sir Walter Press, 1977, 56–57.
10. 1891–1898 Cincinnati City Directories.
11. 1891 Cincinnati City Directory.

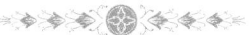

140. TRESSEL CO.

1925–1980s

Joseph Julius Tressel (fig. 140.1) was born in Cincinnati on August 12, 1875.[1] He was the son of German-born Mary (Martha) Schrieber and Julius Tressel.[2] In 1889, Joseph was apprenticed to Andrew Messmer (1851–1930), a gold and silver plater, and manufacturer of ornamental metalwork.[3] Joseph's father had been a bookkeeper for Messmer.[4] "I was farmed out to an old German with whom I lived and in whose shop I apprenticed," recalled Tressel. "I did household chores, worked in the shop 10 hours a day, and went to night school. He was a kind fellow, but a hard taskmaster. I didn't get paid for the first six months; then I got 25 cents a week. By the time I finished my apprenticeship I was earning—and I mean earning—$3.50 a week."[5] Between 1893 and 1895, Joseph also studied drawing and architecture at the Art Academy of Cincinnati, and, in 1919, he earned a certificate in chemistry at the Ohio Mechanics' Institute.[6]

Joseph Tressel's occupation is given as pattern maker in city directories between 1892 and 1899, as mold maker in 1900, and as plater in 1904 and 1905.[7] It is possible that he spent these years at Homan Manufacturing Company (1847–1941), where he is recorded as an employee from 1906 to 1922.[8] Homan specialized in the production of Britannia ware, pewter, German silver, and silver and gold electroplated ware, and by 1913, Tressel had become the firm's vice president.[9]

By 1923, Tressel was listing in city directories as a chemist, and by 1925, he had established The Tressel Plating Co. (later known as Tressel Inc. and Tressel Co.) in Cincinnati.[10] His firm specialized in plating and repair work, but extant silver and copper work marked by Tressel indicate that he also designed and manufactured his own

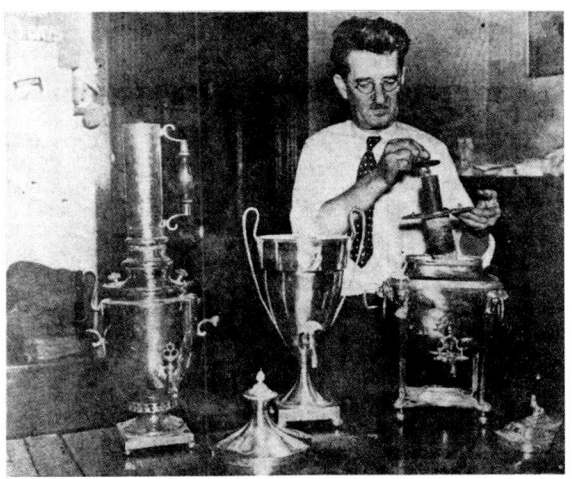

FIG. 140.1: Joseph J. Tressel in his workshop, from "Ancient Water Heaters Revealed on Work Bench of Repairman," *Cincinnati Times Star*, February 2, 1938, 4

pieces. These include an Arts and Crafts style copper pitcher (fig. 140.2, mark 140.1), and a silver menorah (fig. 140.3) presented to Benjamin S. Schwartz, President of B'nai Brith, in 1949.[11] Tressel was reportedly "nationally known as a chemist, molder, linguist, electrician, designer, silver and gold plater, and general repairman," and was in business until at least 1960.[12] He died on December 4, 1961, but the Tressel Co. continued in the business of polishing and repairing metalwork into the 1980s.[13] He and his wife Elsie E. LiBeau (1875–1951), daughter of William F. and Helen K. Callahan LiBeau, were married on December 15, 1898.[14]

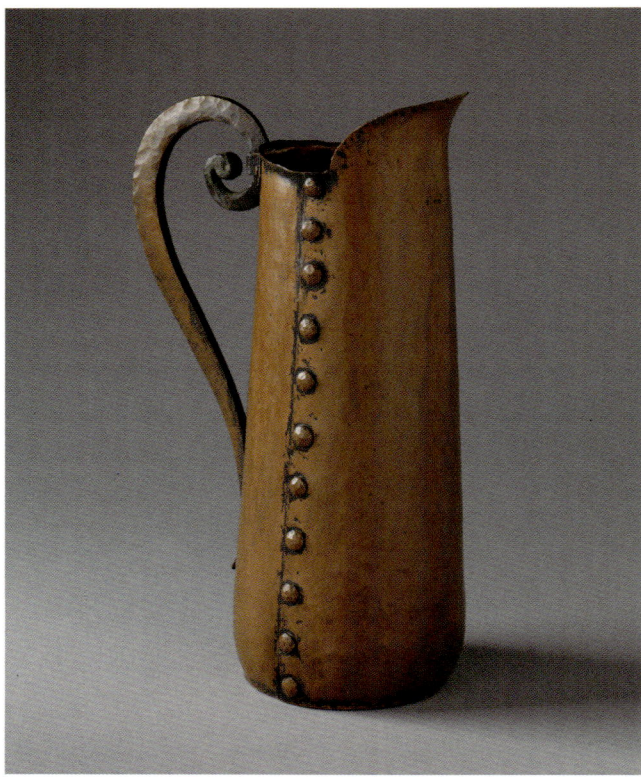

FIG. 140.2: Tressel Co., *Pitcher*, 1925–1960, copper, 11¾ × 7¼ in. (29.8 × 18.4 cm), CAM, Gift of Mr. and Mrs. Charles Fleischmann III, 2008.46

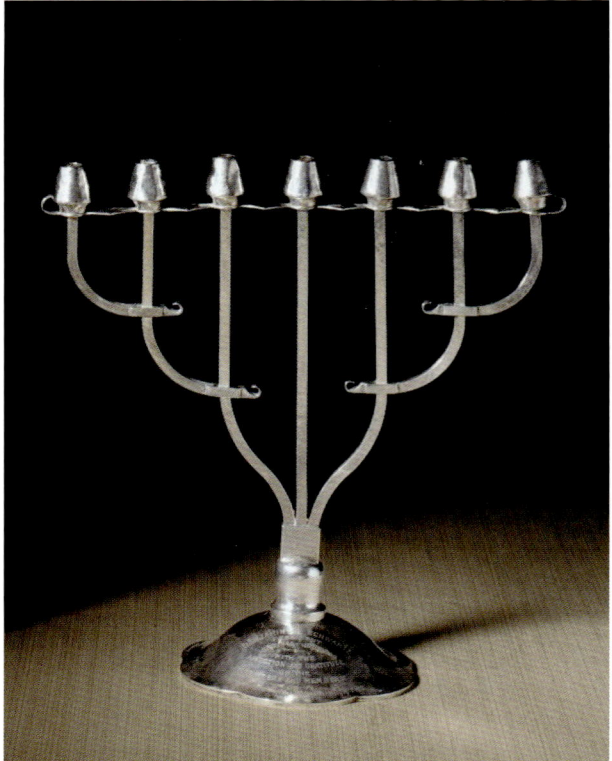

FIG. 140.3: Tressel Co., *Menorah*, c. 1949, H. 12¼ in. (31 cm). Inscription: To Benjamin S. Schwartz, President, June 1948–June 1949, with the affection and gratitude of the officers and members of District Grand Lodge Number Two, B'nai Brith. Photograph Courtesy of Sotheby's.

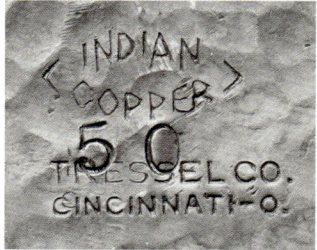

MARK 140.1

1. Ancestry.com, *World War I Draft Registration Cards, 1917–1918* [online database], Provo, Utah: The Generations Network Inc., 2005; Jos. Julius Tressel, birth record, Cincinnati Health Department, University of Cincinnati Archives and Rare Books Library, http://hdl.handle.net/2374.UC/164701.

2. "Ancient Water Heaters Revealed on Work Bench of Repairman," *Cincinnati Times Star*, February 2, 1938, 4, col. 4; 1880 Federal Census, Cincinnati, Hamilton, Ohio; Jack (Joseph) Tressel, burial record, Spring Grove Cemetery, Cincinnati, Ohio; Jos. Julius Tressel, birth record.

3. "Ancient Water Heaters Revealed on Work Bench of Repairman," February 2, 1938; *Leading Manufacturers and Merchants of Cincinnati and Environs*, Cincinnati: International Publishing Co., 1886, 108.

4. 1895 Cincinnati City Directory.

5. "Artist in Metal is 81: Recalls 25-Cent Weekly Pay," *Cincinnati Times Star*, February 24, 1956, 40, col. 6.

6. Ibid.; Cincinnati Art Academy card file, Mary R. Schiff Library and Archives, Cincinnati Art Museum.

7. A place of employment is not given for Tressel in these editions of the city directory.

8. 1892–1922 Cincinnati City Directories.

9. 1913 Cincinnati City Directory.

10. 1925 Cincinnati City Directory.

11. "Important Judaica," Sotheby's, New York, March 18, 2004, sale NO7969, lot 190; Benjamin S. Schwartz was well known for his civic involvement in Cincinnati, especially as a Juvenile Court judge, 1957–1974.

12. "Ancient Water Heaters Revealed on Work Bench of Repairman," February 2, 1938; 1960 Cincinnati City Directory.

13. Ancestry.com and Ohio Department of Health, *Ohio Deaths, 1908–1932, 1938–1944, 1958–2002* [online database], Provo, Utah: The Generations Network Inc., 2006; Obituary, *Cincinnati Enquirer*, December 6, 1961, 24, col. 8; Jack (Joseph) Tressel, burial record; Lois Rosenthal, *Living Better in Cincinnati: The Guide to the City's Best Kept Secrets*, Cincinnati: F & W Publications, 1987, 51; It is not clear who continued the business.

14. 1910, 1930, and 1940 Federal Censuses, Cincinnati, Hamilton, Ohio; Marriage record, Hamilton County Probate Records, vol. 139, 47, http://www.probatect.org/CourtRecordsArchive/bukmarriages.aspx; Elsie L. Tressel, burial record, Spring Grove Cemetery; Record of Joseph and Elsie's children could not be located. Joseph Tressel's obituary only mentions two living sisters, Mrs. Elizabeth King and Sister Mary Clara. Obituary, *Cincinnati Enquirer*, December 6, 1961, 24, col. 8.

141. ALBERT G. TUCKER

1821[1]–1858, w. 1842

Albert G. Tucker, silversmith, appears in Cincinnati city directories for one year, in 1842. That year, he married Eliza Jane Evans (1823–1906).[2] By 1850, Tucker had relocated to Lebanon, Ohio, and continued to work there as a silversmith.[3] Nathan Ingersoll, silversmith, age sixteen, was living with the family at this time.[4] Tucker died on November 5, 1858, and is buried in Claibourne Cemetery in Union County, Ohio.[5] He and his wife had at least five children: George (b. about 1845), John (b. about 1846), B.E. (born about 1848), Josephine (b. 1850), and Harry (1854–1855).[6]

Tucker's mark (mark 141.1) has been found on a sugar shovel and teaspoons with tipped, exaggerated fiddle handles and pointed shoulders.[7] Because so little is known about Tucker, it is difficult to say whether he made or retailed these wares. Their forms are typical of the Cincinnati area, and they could date from his time in Cincinnati, in Lebanon, or in Union County.

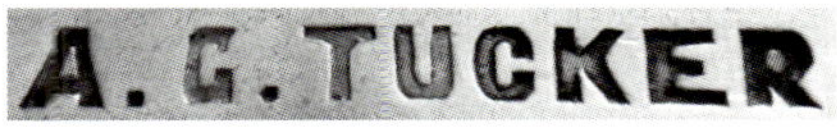

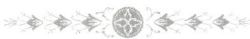

MARK 141.1

1. He was born June 3, 1821. A.G. Tucker, *Find A Grave*, www.findagrave.com.
2. Albert Tucker and Eliza Jane Evans, marriage record, Hamilton County Probate Records, vol. A10, 22, http://www.probatect.org/CourtRecordsArchive/bukmarriages.aspx.
3. 1850 Federal Census, Lebanon, Warren, Ohio.
4. Ibid.
5. A.G. Tucker, *Find A Grave*.
6. 1850 Federal Census, Lebanon, Warren, Ohio; 1860 Federal Census, Cincinnati, Hamilton, Ohio.
7. A.G. Tucker, eBay listings and private collections, Cincinnati silver binders, Cincinnati Art Museum.

142. ISAAC VAN NUYS[1]

1765–1848, w. 1795–circa 1807

Issac Van Nuys' ancestors emigrated from France to Holland at the time of the Massacre of St. Bartholomew in 1572 and then to New York and New Jersey in the early 18th century.[2] The silversmith Isaac Van Nuys was born on July 19, 1765, in Somerset County, near Millstone, New Jersey, the son of Cornelius Van Nuys (b. July 13, 1735, Millstone, New Jersey) and Neltie Amerman (b. 1735, New Jersey).[3] Two branches of the Van Nuys family went west in the early 1790s—Cornelius' family who may have settled briefly in Fayette County, Pennsylvania, before arriving in Cincinnati, and the family of his brother Isaac (1739–1804), who had settled in Mercer County, Kentucky, by 1791.[4]

The first record of the Van Nuys family in Cincinnati is the appearance of Isaac in records for the Cincinnati Court of Common Pleas in 1790.[5] Cornelius and his son Isaac purchased land in Cincinnati between 1790 and 1795 from John Cleves Symmes, also formerly of New Jersey, with government vouchers.[6] Isaac's lot was on Sycamore Street near Third Street.

The earliest documentation of Isaac's business in Cincinnati is a December 1795 advertisement (fig. 142.1) announcing his

FIG. 142.1: Adverisement, *Centinel of the North-Western Territory*, December 19, 1795

partnership with **John Smith**, his future brother-in-law, in a metal-smithing business, promising "*THE HIGHEST* price will be given for OLD COPPER, BRASS, &c. &c."[7] In the latter part of 1795, fellow New Jersey native **Isaac Paxton**, who would also become Van Nuys' brother-in-law, likely joined them.[8] The length of

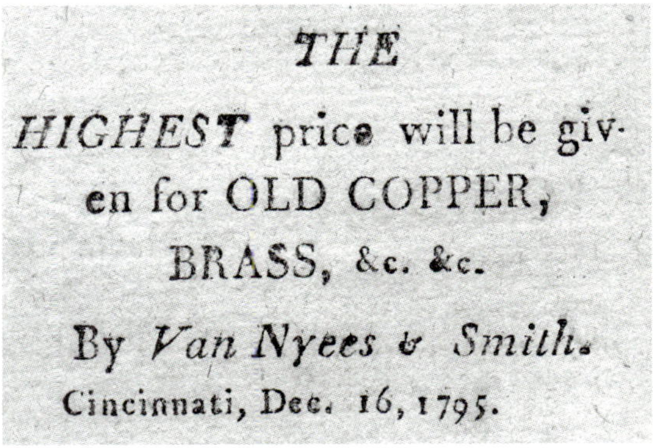

Van Nuys' partnership with Smith is unknown. Presumably, the partners had split before February 2, 1800, when General John S. Gano notes in his account book that he had paid Van Nuys $19.75 for six large silver tablespoons—a considerable and expensive commission for this time.[9]

Continuing in business alone, Van Nuys ran an advertisement in June 1805 for two apprentices "from 14 to 16 years of age—boys of the country will be preferred" to the "CLOCK & WATCH MAKING & TINNING" business.[10] In March of the following year, he bought a lot from Charles and Pamela Vattier on the north side of Market Street (later Pearl Street) with his "co-partner" **Thomas Best, Jr.** for $400.[11] Van Nuys and Best advertised for a "smart active LAD, about 14, or 15 years of age, as an apprentice to the Clock & Watch making, Silver-Smith and Jewelery bufinefs [*sic*]" on September 23, 1806.[12] Their partnership lasted about 9 months. It was dissolved by "mutual consent" by June 1807.[13]

Producing printing plates was not a far stretch for someone skilled in metal working, and Van Nuys, like **Samuel Best**, pursued this sideline in his business. In 1801, the first clerk of the city noted that Van Nuys had "printed historical certificates on the Treasury for Rice Bullock late auditor," and the following year, it was noted that the Northwest Territory was indebted to him for "striking bills."[14]

During his years in Cincinnati, Van Nuys was a leading figure in the community. He had purchased and sold numerous tracts of land, and by 1798 was paying over $3 in tax, one of the highest rates in Cincinnati.[15] In 1799, he and his father were each estimated to own property valued at $400.[16] In 1802, he was elected to be a trustee of the township of Cincinnati, and was a subscriber to the city's first library.[17]

Van Nuys had moved on to Rossville, Butler County, Ohio, by April 1810, and then to the Bethel-Greensfork Township area in Indiana around 1820.[18] Details of his later life are unknown. He died on November 25, 1848.[19] He and his wife, Elizabeth (Betsy) Broderick (d. 1850) had two children for whom records were found: Cornelius (1803–1880) and William (1810–1859).[20]

Wares marked by Van Nuys are exceedingly rare. A teaspoon (fig. 142.2) made in copper and plated with silver bears his mark. Other teaspoons from this set are known.

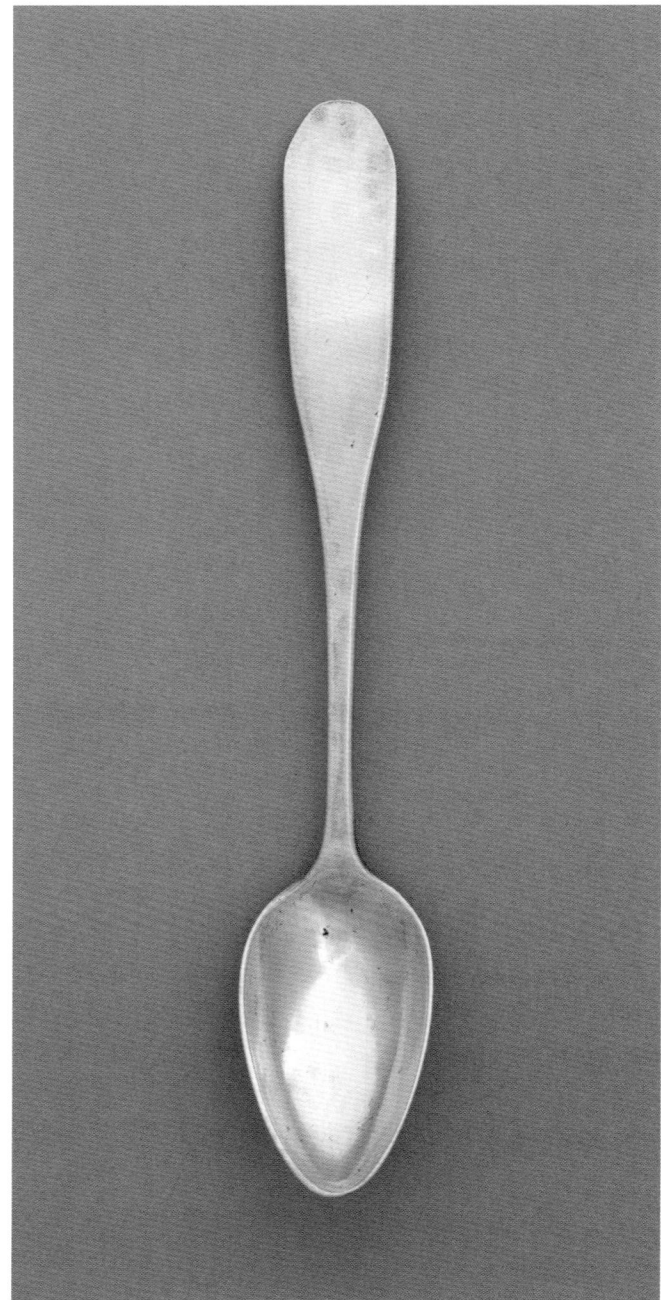

FIG. 142.2: Isaac Van Nuys, *Teaspoon*, 1795– c. 1807, silver on copper, L. 5½ in. (14 cm), CAM, Gift of Dr. and Mrs. James S. Widder, 2002.9

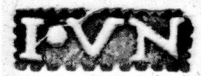

MARK 142.1

1. Van Nuys' surname appears in many variations in records. These variations include Vanice, VanNuys, Vannice, Vanhice, VanEys, Vannise, Vanise, Van Keys, Van Huys, and Van Nyees.

2. Carrie E. Allen, *A Record of the Family of Isaac Van Nuys (or Vannice) of Harrodsburg, Kentucky, son of Isaac Van Nuys of Millstone, New Jersey*, Chicago: Carrie E. Allen, 1916, 11.

3. Isaac was christened in Somerset County on August 4, 1765. Correspondence from Harold G. Miller to Marjorie Burress, Sikes papers, Mary R. Schiff Library and Archives, Cincinnati Art Museum, record group 14, series 1, box 6, folder 3; "Records of the Harlingen Reformed Dutch Church, Montgomery Township, Somerset County, Register of Baptisms," *The Genealogical Magazine of New Jersey* 19, no. 1 (January 1944), Newark, NJ: The Genealogical Society of New Jersey, 10–11; Yates Publishing, *U.S. and International Marriage Records, 1560–1900* [online database], Provo, Utah: Ancestry.com Operations Inc., 2004; Allen, *Family of Isaac Van Nuys*, 12–14.

4. 1790 Federal Census, Washington, Fayette, Pennsylvania; Allen, *Family of Isaac Van Nuys*, 31; Abraham (1780–1831), the son of Isaac (1739–1804), was a clock and watch maker and silversmith in Danville, Kentucky. Boultinghouse, 273. This information is included here as there has previously been confusion about these two branches of the family.

5. Jane Sikes, "Isaac Van Nyse," unpublished manuscript, Sikes papers, Mary R. Schiff Library and Archives, Cincinnati Art Museum, record group 14, series 1, box 9, folder 1; Cornelius Van Nuys would have been about 55 years old when he arrived in Cincinnati. We do not know anything of his occupation, only that he was active in support of the city's first Presbyterian Church, and that in 1801 he was appointed an Overseer of the Poor; Charles Cist, *Sketches & Statistics of Cincinnati in 1851*, Cincinnati: 1851, 138; William H. Moore & Co., Charles Greve, *Centennial History of Cincinnati and Its Representative Citizens*, Chicago: Biographical Publishing Co., 1904, 1:360–361; Announcement, *Western Star*, February 25, 1801.

6. Correspondence from Harold G. Miller to Marjorie Burress, Sikes papers, Mary R. Schiff Library and Archives; Greve, *Centennial History of Cincinnati*, 1:192; Henry A. and Mrs. Kate B. Ford, *History of Cincinnati, Ohio*, Cleveland: L.A. Williams, 1881, 35; S.B. Nelson and J.M Runk, *History of Hamilton County, Ohio*, Cincinnati: S.B. Nelson, 1894, 57.

7. Advertisement, *Centinel of the North-Western Territory*, December 19, 1795. John Smith married Isaac's sister Phebe in November, 1796. Charles Cist, *The Cincinnati Miscellany, or Antiquities of the West: And Pioneer History and General and Local Statistics*, Cincinnati: Caleb Clarke, 1845–1846, 2:71.

8. Paxton married Van Nuys' sister Magdalene Van Nuys Williams (1772–1826) in 1803. See **Isaac Paxton**.

9. John S. Gano manuscripts, Cincinnati Historical Society, box 2 ledger 1787–1802, 41.

10. Advertisement, *Western Spy*, June 12, 1805, reproduced in Beckman, 140.

11. Correspondence between Marjorie Burress and Harold G. Miller, September 30, 1989, Sikes papers, Mary R. Schiff Library and Archives, Cincinnati Art Museum; *Hamilton County Deed Book G1*, 10; This property was mortgaged to Vattier the same day, for the same amount, *Hamilton County Deed Book D1*, 206. Vattier, of Le Havre, moved west with General St. Clair's army. He amassed a fortune dealing in real estate. In 1813, Best and Van Nuys sold this property (bought in 1806) to Andrew Hopple for $700. *Hamilton County Deed Book L1*, 188. By this time Best was in Warren County (Lebanon) and Van Nuys was in Butler County, according to notarial examinations associated with the transfer.

12. Advertisement, *Western Spy*, September 23, 1806, reproduced in Beckman, 19.

13. "Dissolution of Partnership," *Western Spy*, June 5, 1807, reproduced in Beckman, 20. This notice was also published in the same newspaper on June 8, 1807.

14. John Reilly collection, Cincinnati Historical Society, box 1, 36; Notice, *Western Spy*, March 27, 1802; Salmon P. Chase (ed.), *The Statutes of Ohio and of the Northwestern Territory, adopted or enacted from 1788 to 1833 Inclusive . . .*, Cincinnati: Corey & Fairbank, 1833, 350.

15. Marjorie Byrnside Burress, *Early Rosters of Cincinnati and Hamilton County*, North Bend, Ohio: Burress, 1984, 23–25; In 1795, John Cleves Symmes and wife Susan sold Isaac Van Nuys half of lot 61 on Sycamore for $2 (*Hamilton County Deed Book A1*, 231); Van Nuys then sold half of this lot for $1,500 to John Whetstone of Anderson in 1807 (*Hamilton County Deed Book G1*, 354) and the other half to John Van Nuys in 1798. This and numerous other land transactions are detailed in correspondence between Marjorie Burress and Harold G. Miller, September 30, 1989, Sikes papers, Mary R. Schiff Library and Archives, Cincinnati Art Museum, record group 14, series 1, box 6, folder 3.

16. Burress, *Early Rosters*, 22–25.

17. James McBride, *Pioneer Biography: Sketches of the Lives of Some of the Early Settlers of Butler County, Ohio*, Cincinnati: Robert Clarke & Co., 1871, 1:104–105; Ford, *History of Cincinnati*, 258; Notice of elections, *Western Spy*, April 10, 1802.

18. Isaac's son William was born on April 8, 1810, in Rossville, Ohio; The obituary of Isaac's son Cornelius states that they were in Bethel, IN by 1820. Obituary, *Richmond Telegram* (Indiana), August 26, 1880; Allen, *Family of Isaac Van Nuys*, 184; 1830, 1840 Federal Censuses, Greensfork, Randolph, Indiana.

19. Allen, *Family of Isaac Van Nuys*, 184.

20. Isaac married Elizabeth Broderick on October 18, 1798, in Northbend, Ohio; Marjorie Byrnside Burress (ed.), *A Collection of Pioneer Marriage Records, Hamilton County, Ohio, 1789–1817*, Cincinnati: Burress, 1978, 1:72; Cornelius Van Nuys, obituary, August 26, 1880; Allen, *Family of Isaac Van Nuys*, 184.

143. C. & J. VANHOUTEN

1857–1862

Charles Vanhouten and his brother Joseph B. were born in New York about 1834 and 1829 respectively.[1] They first appeared in Cincinnati city directory listings in 1857. They advertised as silverware manufacturers, operating at 47 Richmond in 1857, and then at 114 George until their last directory listing in 1862.[2] The brothers listed their occupations as silversmith in the 1860 Census, and the silversmith **John Coe** is listed as working at the 47 Richmond address in the 1857 Cincinnati Directory, indicating that he may have been their employee.[3] The size and extent of the Vanhoutens' business is unknown. Charles Vanhouten enlisted in Company F of Ohio's 5th Infantry Regiment in April 1861. He did not survive the Civil War.[4] By 1870, Joseph had moved to Ramapo, New York (Rockland County), where he was managing a hotel until at least 1880.[5]

Their mark (mark 143.1) appears on a teaspoon with a tipped, exaggerated fiddle handle.[6]

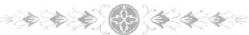

MARK 143.1

1. 1860 Federal Census, Cincinnati, Hamilton, Ohio.
2. 1857–1862 Cincinnati City Directories.
3. 1860 Federal Census, Cincinnati, Hamilton, Ohio; Coe appears in the 1853, 1857, and 1858 City Directories. His working address is only given in the 1857 edition.
4. Historical Data Systems, comp., *U.S. Civil War Soldier Records and Profiles* [online database], Provo, Utah: Ancestry.com Operations Inc., 2009.
5. 1870 and 1880 Federal Census, Rockland County, Ramapo.
6. C. & J. Vanhouten, eBay listings and private collections, Cincinnati silver binders, Cincinnati Art Museum.

---

144. JOSEPH S. VOSS & SON

1881–1899

Joseph Sixtus Voss (1832–1907) was born in Hanover, Germany.[1] His brothers William and **Julius Voss** were also active in Cincinnati's jewelry trade. Joseph (fig. 144.1) came to the United States in October 1850.[2] By 1851, he had joined his brother Julius in Cincinnati, and by 1853, they were advertising as J. Voss & Co. at 32 East Fifth Street. By 1855, the firm was located at 46 West Fifth, and both brothers were living at 54 West Fifth.[3] In 1855, Joseph married Maria Gertrude Specker (1834–1912).[4] They had eight children: John Henry (1858–1943); Marie Mollie (1858–1887); Edward Clemens (b. 1865); Emma (b. 1865); Louis A. (1866–1928); Frederick (b. 1867); Joseph Sixtus II (1870–1933); and Gertrude (b. 1873).[5]

In the 1860 Census, Joseph was enumerated as a jeweler with personal property worth $8,000, and was recorded as a neighbor of Herman "Henry" H. Duhme (see **Duhme & Co.**), who was also born in Hanover.[6] Joseph continued to work on Fifth Street, near Fountain Place, until 1875.[7] He purchased most of his stock locally and would "occasionally take stock from Eastern samplers."[8] In March 1859 credit reporters remarked that Joseph "is in better

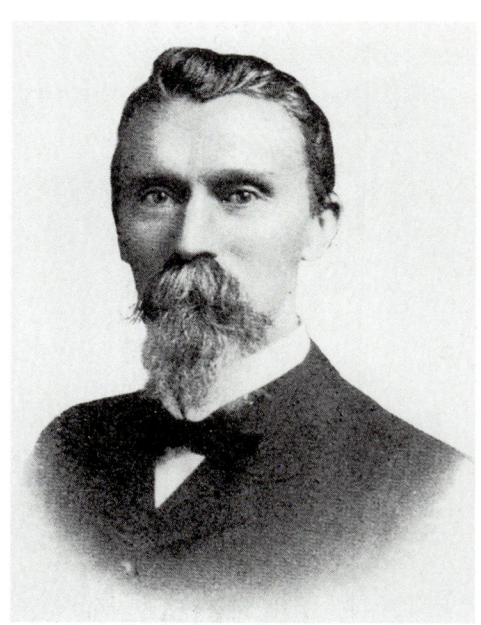

FIG. 144.1: Joseph S. Voss, from George W. Engelhardt, *Cincinnati: The Queen City*, Cincinnati: G.W. Engelhardt, 1901, 208

jewelry jobbing and repairing business to produce $3,600 worth of product.[13] He owned additional real estate in Covington, Kentucky, where he lived between 1862 and 1887, and by 1874, was estimated to be worth "fully $50,000, mostly real estate."[14] But in January 1876 he sold his stock to Manning, Robinson & Co.—about the same time as his brother Julius did the same—and went to work as a bookkeeper for **Clemens Hellebush**.[15] In 1880, Joseph was still listed in city directories as a bookkeeper at Hellebush's, but reported in the 1880 Federal Non-Population Census as a watch maker and clock repairer with $100 worth of capital, using $100 of material to produce $600 worth of product.[16]

By 1881, Joseph and his son John Henry had established themselves as Joseph S. Voss & Son, wholesale jewelers, working at the southeast corner of Fifth and Vine Street.[17] They had moved to 6 West Fourth Street by 1883, and remained there until 1893.[18] There, they occupied the main floor and basement of the four-story building (fig. 144.3), "25 × 100 feet in dimensions, . . . equipped

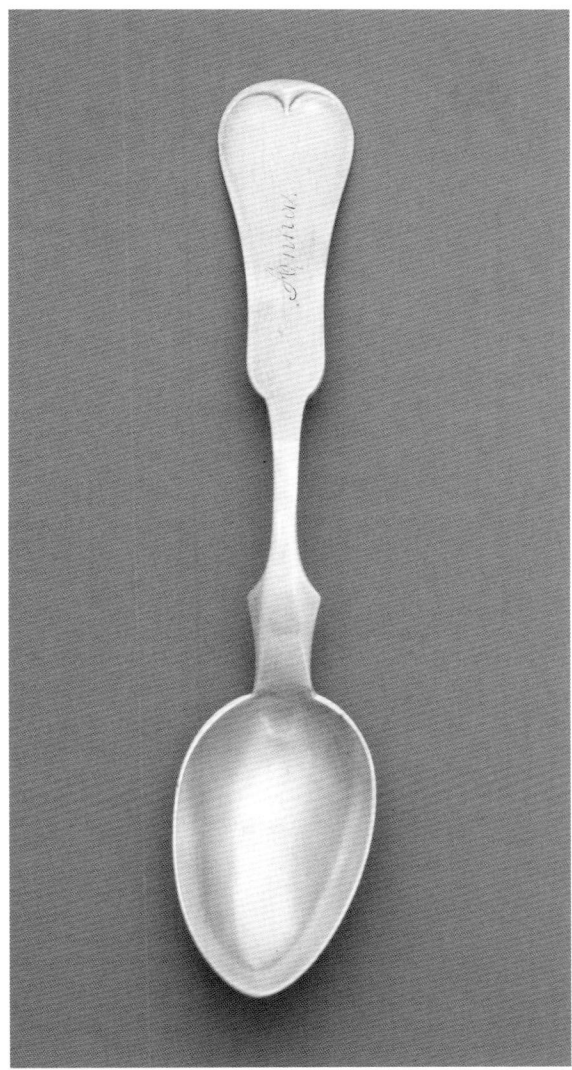

FIG. 144.2: Joseph S. Voss & Son, *Teaspoon*, 1881–1899, L. 5¾ in. (14.6 cm), CAM, Museum Purchase: John S. Conner Fund, 2012.12

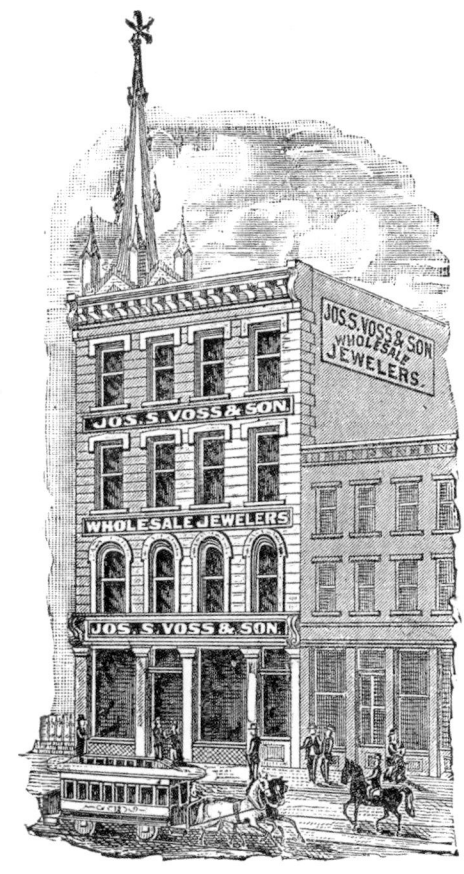

FIG. 144.3: Joseph S. Voss & Son, from John William Leonard, *The Centennial Review of Cincinnati: One Hundred Years of Progress . . .* , Cincinnati: J.M. Elstner, 1888, 67

credit than his brother Julius, but they are really one concern—this one buys for both."[9] It was also noted that a good deal of his stock came from **Clemens Oskamp**, "who lets him have all the goods he wants should matters go wrong, of course, [Oskamp] would be a preferred creditor."[10] In 1869, it was reported that Joseph was making money, and that, including property owned in Sedamsville (where Julius also owned property) and a capital of $5,000–$8,000 in his business, he was estimated to be worth $25,000.[11] The 1870 Federal Census indicates that he owned $40,000 of real estate and that the value of his personal estate was $5,000.[12] In business that year, he reported that he employed two hands and used $250 worth of silver, $100 worth of "springs &c." and $700 worth of gold in his

with every convenience and facility for their extensive business in Elgin, Waltham, Springfield, and all other favorite makes of American watches, as well as a superior line of the products of the best Swiss factories, watchcases of all makes in gold and silver, in connection with a full stock of jewelry of the oldest and most favorably known factories of the country."[19] In 1888, they employed three traveling salesmen who represented them in Ohio, Indiana, Illinois, Kentucky, Tennessee, Mississippi, Alabama, Georgia, and the South in general.[20] The firm is listed in the Neave Building at the northwest corner of Fourth and Race Streets in the 1894 Cincinnati City Directory. By 1900, they had become Jos. S. Voss & Sons, formally recognizing Joseph's sons Louis A., Edward

Clemens, and Joseph Jr., who had been working at the firm in various capacities since the mid-1890s.[21] Joseph Sr. died in November, 1907, and the business was continued by his sons, who relocated to 18 and 20 West Seventh Street, floor 5, by 1915.[22] The firm had closed its doors by 1925.[23]

The mark of Joseph S. Voss & Son has been documented on spoons with tipped, exaggerated fiddle handles (fig. 144.2).

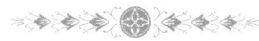

MARK 144.1

1. 1900 Federal Census, Cincinnati, Hamilton, Ohio; 1870 Federal Census, Covington, Kenton, Kentucky; Oliver Family Tree, http://trees.ancestry.com/ tree/15131622/person/241888520 ?pgNum=1, accessed October 30, 2012; Joseph's parents may have been Wilhelm V. Voss and Regina Doppmeier. *Emigrants from Grafschaft Bentheim*, www.dialogos-studies .com/BIS/subpages/emigrantlist .htm.

2. Ancestry.com, *New York Passenger and Immigration Lists, 1820–1850* [online database], Provo, Utah: Ancestry.com Operations Inc., 2003.

3. George W. Engelhardt, *Cincinnati, The Queen City*, Cincinnati: Geo. W. Engelhardt Co., 1901, 208; 1851/52,

1853, 1855, 1856 Cincinnati City Directories.

4. 1900 Federal Census, Cincinnati, Hamilton, Ohio; Joseph S. Voss, will dated August 26, 1898, proved January 9, 1908, vol. 104, p. 306, Hamilton County Registry of Probate, Cincinnati, Ohio.

5. 1860 and 1900 Federal Censuses, Cincinnati, Hamilton, Ohio; 1870 and 1880 Federal Censuses, Covington, Kenton, Kentucky; Julius Sixtus Voss family tree.

6. 1860 Federal Census, Cincinnati, Hamilton, Ohio.

7. Between 1862 and 1875, Joseph's working address is given as 54 West Fifth Street.

8. Ohio, Vol. 1, p. 193, R.G. Dun & Co. Collection, Baker Library, Harvard

Business School.

9. Ibid.

10. Ibid.

11. Ibid.

12. 1870 Federal Census, Covington, Kenton, Kentucky.

13. 1870 Federal Non-Population Census Schedules, Products of Industry, Schedule 4, Hamilton County, Ohio.

14. Ohio, Vol. 3, p. 25, R.G. Dun & Co. Collection; 1862–1887 Cincinnati City Directories.

15. Ohio, Vol. 3, p. 25, R.G. Dun & Co. Collection; 1879 Cincinnati City Directory.

16. 1880 Federal Non-Population Census Schedules, Products of Industry, Schedule 4, Hamilton County, Ohio.

17. 1881 Cincinnati City Directory; Their working address in 1881 was given as room 3, Wiggins Block.

18. 1883–1893 Cincinnati City Directories.

19. John William Leonard, *The Centennial Review of Cincinnati: one hundred years of progress in commerce, manufactures, the professions, and in social and municipal life*, Cincinnati: J.M. Elstner, 1888, 67.

20. Ibid.

21. 1894–1910 Cincinnati City Directories.

22. Julius Sixtus Voss family tree; Headstone, Calvary Cemetery, Cincinnati, Ohio; Joseph S. Voss, will; 1915 Cincinnati City Directory.

23. 1915–1930 Cincinnati City Directories.

---

145. JULIUS VOSS
1825–1887, w. 1849–1887

Julius Voss was born in Hanover, Germany, on April 1, 1825, and immigrated to America in 1848.[1] He and his brothers, William and Joseph (see **Joseph S. Voss & Son**), were all active in the Cincinnati jewelry business. Julius first appears in the 1849/50 Cincinnati City Directory as partner with Frederick Tappe in Tappe & Voss, watch makers working on the south side of Fifth Street between Smith and Park Streets.[2] By the time that the 1850/51 Directory was published, Julius was listed independently as a watch maker working on the north side of Fifth between Plum and Western Row. He continued business there until forming J. Voss & Company with

his brother Joseph.[3] Operating on Fifth Street, their firm appeared with the business listings for "Jewelry, Silver Ware, Watches &c." in the 1853 and 1855 editions of the city directory. By 1856, Julius and Joseph were maintaining separate shops, and by 1859, Julius and his brother William had established Julius Voss and Brother.[4] They advertised as jewelers at 54 West Fifth Street and bought most of their stock from **Clemens Oskamp**.[5] Julius was reportedly in Europe when the partnership failed in February 1860.[6] Having "inherited some means in Germany," he returned and paid off all the firm's debts.[7] In 1861, he listed independently as a dealer in watches, jewelry, etc. at 10 West Fifth Street.[8] In reports from November 1864, he was doing a fair business, but by March of 1867, he was no longer in business.[9] It was reported that he owned property in Sedamsville (seated on the Ohio River, five miles west of downtown Cincinnati), and that he was reportedly worth $18,000–$20,000, and clear of debts and encumbrances.[10] By 1868, he was back in business at 132 West Fourth Street, and from there moved to 94 West Fifth Street in 1874.[11] He remained on Fifth Street for the rest of his career.[12] While he continued to acquire property and wealth, several credit reports note that he was not well regarded in the trade. One reads, "Said to be very undesirable as a customer. Will beat down to the lowest price and then . . . [will] find fault and insist on reductions for imaginary imperfections."[13]

In October 1875 Voss announced that he was closing out and retiring. His stock of watches, clocks, and jewelry was offered for sale by Manning, Robinson & Co.[14] However, a year later, his close-out sale lingered and he was still in business. In 1878, he filed for bankruptcy and settled with creditors with the help of his brother Joseph S. Voss.[15] Julius Voss never fully recovered his business or wealth. He died on October 14, 1887, and is buried at the Old St. Joseph's Cemetery for German Catholics in Cincinnati.[16]

Voss and his wife Hermanna (b. about 1831) had at least seven children: George (b. about 1853); Anna (b. about 1857); Augusta (b. about 1859); Gussie (b. about 1861); Henry (b. about 1862); Clemens (b. about 1868); and Ida (b. about 1871).[17] In 1880, Hermanna and her youngest children were living with Anna and her husband George Gerke.[18] Hermanna and Julius had divorced, and the census that year lists her last name as Ashendorf.[19]

Julius S. Voss was a retail jeweler and did not produce any of the silver bearing his mark.[20]

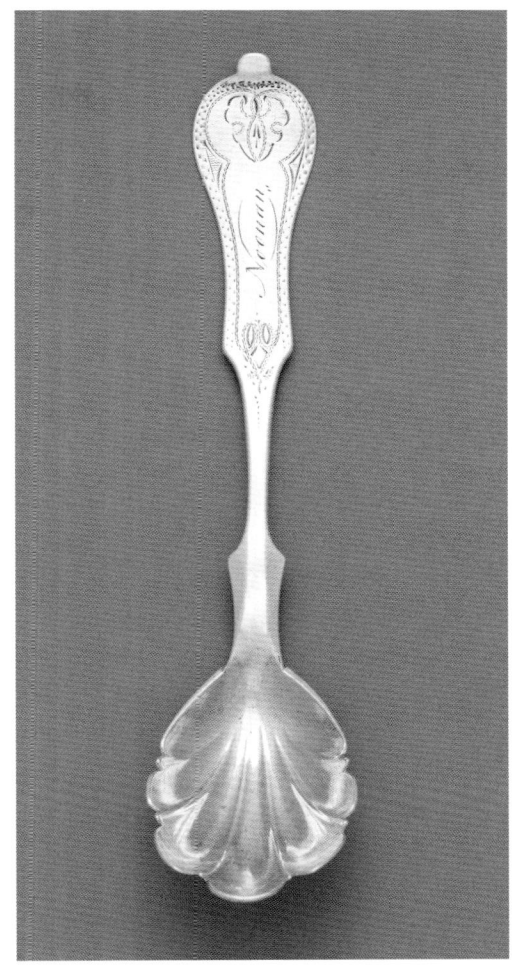

FIG. 145.1: Julius Voss, *Sugar Spoon*, 1860–1887, L. 6⅜ in. (16.2 cm), CAM, Gift of Mr. and Mrs. Charles Fleischmann III, 2005.17. Inscription: Noonan

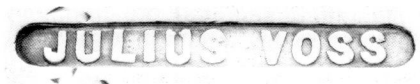

MARK 145.1

1. Clifford Neal Smith, *Early Nineteenth-Century German Settlers in Ohio (Mainly Cincinnati and Environs), Kentucky and Other States*, McNeal, AZ: Westland Publications, 1991, 66; Julius Voss' parents may have been Wilhelm V. Voss and Regina Doppmeier. *Emigrants from Grafschaft Bentheim*, www.dialogos-studies.com/BIS/subpages/emigrantlist.htm.

2. Tappe & Voss do not appear in subsequent city directories.

3. 1853 Cincinnati City Directory.

4. 1856, 1859 Cincinnati City Directories.

5. Ohio, Vol. 3, p. 146, R.G. Dun & Co. Collection, Baker Library, Harvard Business School.

6. Ibid.

7. Ibid.

8. 1861 Cincinnati City Directory.

9. Ohio, Vol. 3, p. 25, R.G. Dun & Co. Collection.

10. Ibid.

11. Ohio, Vol. 9, p. 115, R.G. Dun & Co. Collection; 1868–1874 Cincinnati City Directory.

12. 1874–1887 Cincinnati City Directories.

13. Ohio, Vol. 9, p. 115, R.G. Dun & Co. Collection.

14. "Jewelry &c.," *Cincinnati Commercial Tribune*, October 19, 1875, 5; Ohio, Vol. 9, p. 115, R.G. Dun & Co. Collection; "Closing-Out Sale," *Cincinnati Enquirer*, November 19, 1875, 5.

15. Ohio, Vol. 9, p. 115, R.G. Dun & Co. Collection; *Jeweler, Silversmith and Watchmaker* 4, no. 10 (June 1878): 144.

16. "Cincinnati," *Jewelers' Circular and Horological Review* 18, no. 2 (December 1887): 415; Julius Voss, death record, Cincinnati Health Department, University of Cincinnati Archives and Rare Books Library, http://hdl.handle.net/2374.UC/142082.

17. 1870, 1880 Federal Censuses, Cincinnati, Hamilton, Ohio.

18. 1880 Federal Census, Cincinnati, Hamilton, Ohio.

19. In the 1870 Federal Census, Hermanna's birthplace is given as Hanover, Germany. In the 1880 Federal Census, her and her parents' birthplace is given as Holland.

20. 1870 Federal Census, Cincinnati, Hamilton, Ohio; "Cincinnati," *JCHR* (December 1887).

146. WILLEY & BLAKSLEY

late 1830s/1840s

Several works marked by this firm have been documented, but there are no city directory listings, advertisements, or other known records for the partnership. Although Harper Blakesley has been cited as **Bushnell Willey**'s partner in this firm, further research is needed.

Harper Blakesley (b. about 1806 in Connecticut) was primarily involved in the clock business and advertised at various addresses between 1829 and 1836.[1] He later worked in Cincinnati as a machinist and a frame maker, and by 1860, he was in Jeffersonville, Indiana, employed as the superintendent at a pork house.[2] However, there were others with similar surnames, namely Edward and Garret Blakeslee, active in the Cincinnati and Kentucky clock trade at this time who could have partnered with Willey.[3]

The Willey & Blaksley stamp (mark 146.1), sometimes with "CINCINNATI" included in a separate rectangular cartouche, has been found on a creamer, beakers, and ladles (fig. 146.1) and spoons with either fiddle handles or tipped, exaggerated fiddle handles and pointed shoulders.[4] A creamer with Willey & Blaksley's mark (fig. 67.10) also bears the stamp of **Edward Kinsey**, who was likely the maker. In some instances, wares bearing the Willey & Blaksley stamp are also marked with a left-facing eagle with down-turned wings (fig. 67.5). This eagle may be the manufacturing mark of either Edward Kinsey or **Pulaski Scovil**.[5]

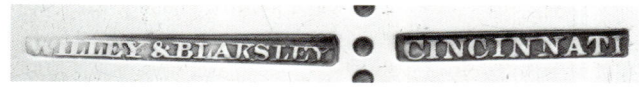

MARK 146.1

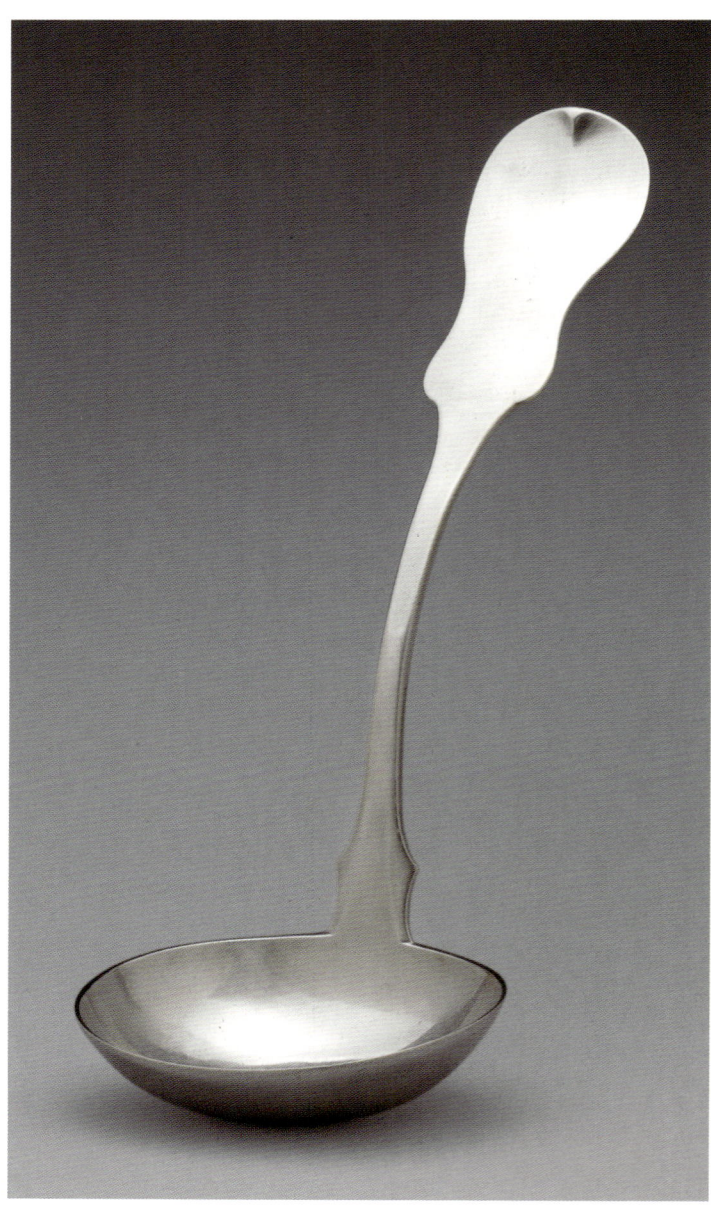

FIG. 146.1: Willey & Blaksley, *Ladle*, c. 1840, 12 × 4⅝ in. (33 × 11.7 cm), CAM, Gift of Dr. Michael Sze, 2002.80

1. Harper's surname is variously spelled Blackeslee, Blakesly and Blakeslee in period documents; Blakesley appears most often and is used here. 1860 and 1870 Federal Censuses, Jeffersonville, Clark, Indiana; 1829, 1831, 1834, and 1836 Cincinnati City Directories; Blaksley is listed among the 400 earliest settlers of Greene Township, Hamilton County, Ohio from between 1802 and 1850 in *Der Deutsche Pionier: Erinnerungen Aus Dem Pionierleben der Deutschen in Amerika*, Cincinnati: Deutschen Pionier-Verein von Cincinnati, 18:258.

2. 1843, 1844, 1849/1850 Cincinnati City Directories; 1860 and 1870 Federal Censuses, Jeffersonville, Clark, Indiana.

3. Beckman, 21–22; James W. Gibbs, *Buckeye Horology*, Columbia, PA: The Art Crafters Printing Co., 1971, 11.

4. Willey & Blaksley, eBay listings and private collections, Cincinnati silver binders, Cincinnati Art Museum.

5. Ibid.; John R. McGrew, *Manufacturers' Marks on American Coin Silver*, Hanover, PA: Argyros Publications, 2004, 98.

147. WILLEY & CO.

late 1830s

The mark of this firm has been documented on several beakers, as well as a sauce ladle with a fiddle handle and pointed shoulders.[1] While **Bushnell Willey** was clearly the principal, it is not clear who else was involved in the firm, or if the firm operated in Cincinnati, in Kentucky, or elsewhere. The punch mark used by this firm (mark 147.1) appears to be an altered version of the punch used by **Scovil, Willey & Co.** The letter style and spacing are identical and both punches feature a reversed ampersand. This suggests that Willey & Co. was active after the dissolution of Scovil, Willey & Co. in 1838.

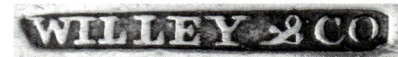

MARK 147.1

1. Willey & Co., eBay listings and private collections, Cincinnati silver binders, Cincinnati Art Museum.

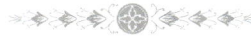

148. BUSHNELL WILLEY

1806–1850, w. about 1831–1838

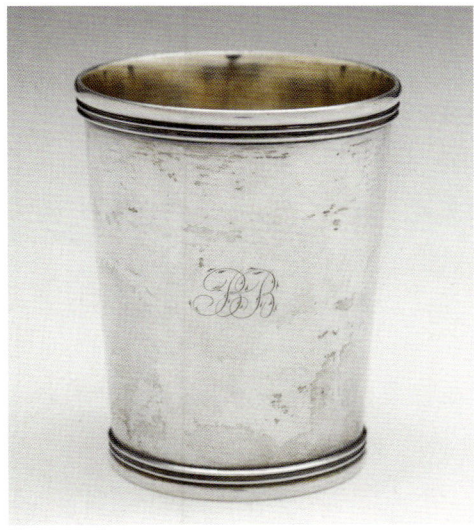

FIG. 148.1: Bushnell Willey, *Beaker*, 1831–1838, H. 3⁹⁄₁₆ in. (9 cm), Diam. 2¹⁵⁄₁₆ in. (7.5 cm), Courtesy of Samuel Baughman Craig, Jr.

Bushnell Willey was born in Vermont on April 3, 1806, to Phebe Warters (1780–1843) and Asa Willey (1770–1869).[1] His unusual first name came from his uncle, Captain Bushnell.[2] Willey's only listing in Cincinnati city directories occurred in 1836, when he listed as a partner at **Scovil, Willey & Co.**, which operated on Main Street. He was also a principal in **Willey & Co.** and **Willey & Blaksley.** In November 1838 he married Susannah Lail in Harrison County,

Kentucky.[3] In 1850, he was working as a peddler in Harrison County, and owned real estate valued at a sizeable $6,000.[4] Willey and his wife had two known children, Anna Bell (1844–1923) and John B. (b. about 1846).[5] Bushnell Willey died on July 20, 1850, in Middletown, Bourbon County, Kentucky, and was buried with his mother and father in Yaleville, Chenango County, New York.[6]

Willey's mark, along with the stamp of a shield-breasted eagle facing left (mark 148.1), has been documented on a beaker (fig. 148.1). This eagle is likely the manufacturing mark of **Edward Kinsey**.[7]

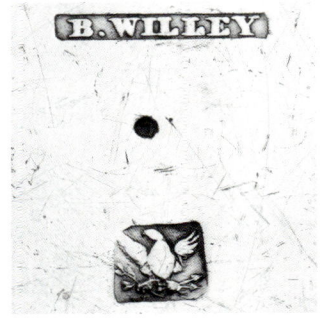

MARK 148.1

1. 1850 Federal Census, Harrison County, Kentucky; Yaleville Cemetery Records, Guilford, Chenango County, NY, http://www.newhorizons genealogicalservices.com/cem-ny-

chenango-guilford-yaleville-cemetery.htm, accessed August 15, 2012.
2. Beckman, 146.
3. "A Comprehensive Index of Marriage Records, Based on a Transcription of Harrison County, Kentucky's General Cross Index to Marriages 1 (1794–1893)," http://home.comcast.net /~harrisoncountykyus/records /marriage-records-index-no-1—la.htm, accessed August 15, 2012.
4. 1850 Federal Census, Harrison County, Kentucky.
5. Ibid.
6. Yaleville Cemetery Records, Guilford, Chenango County, NY, accessed August 15, 2012.
7. John R. McGrew, *Manufacturers' Marks on American Coin Silver*, Hanover, PA: Argyros Publications, 2004, 98.

149. J.C. WILMS, SR.

1827–1901, active 1855–1901

John Charles Wilms, son of Conrad and Wilhelmina Wilms, was born in Prussia in January 1827.[1] He came to the United States around 1848.[2] He first appears in Cincinnati in the 1855 City Directory as the partner of **Edmund Deppermann**. Their firm, Wilms & Deppermann (active 1855), advertised the sale of "jewelry, silverware, &c."[3] Some of their stock must have come from **Duhme & Co.**, who later sued the firm for $1,377.[4] After the dissolution of Wilms & Depperman, Wilms continued on his own and was listed in city directories under the business category of "watches, jewelry and silver ware" for the duration of his career.[5] He also advertised optometry.[6] In 1856, he reportedly employed five hands at $600 and his stock was valued at $450.[7] In 1864, credit reporters noted that he did "a small business, mostly repairing."[8] But his business grew over the years, and by 1876, he was believed to be worth between $13,000 and $15,000.[9] In 1858, he exhibited a "skeleton clock" at the Ohio Mechanics' Institute Fair, and in the 1886 Cincinnati Industrial Exhibition, he exhibited an assortment of goods classified as "clocks, jewelry, etc."[10]

Between 1856 and 1857, Wilms operated at 57 Sycamore Street.[11] He moved to the College Building on Walnut between Fourth and Fifth Streets (162 Walnut) in 1858, and remained there until 1879 (fig. 149.1), when he relocated to 178 West Fifth.[12] This move was surely precipitated by his difficulty in paying his debts. In 1880, credit reporters remarked, "Wilms is reported an honest man but has got in such shape that he is no longer safe to credit."[13] In February 1879 he gave a bill of sale to **Clemens Hellebush** for his remaining stock, valued at $509.[14]

By 1891, Wilms and his son, Frederick Wilms (1858–1933), had formed J.C. Wilms & Son (1891–1912).[15] They advertised as jewelers and maintained a shop at the northwest corner of Eighth and Vine Street (near Garfield Place). When J.C. Wilms, Sr. died on September 18, 1901, Frederick continued the business.[16]

J.C. Wilms, Sr. and his wife Elise Schultze (1835–1927) had ten known children: John C. (b. about 1855); Eliza (b. about 1857); Augusta (1860–1862); Edwin O. (b. about 1863), who was listed as a designer in the 1880 Federal Census; Frederick; Edward (b. about 1863, d. 1892); Dr. D.C. Wilms (b. about 1864, d. 1892); Matilda (b. about 1864); Emma (b. 1871); and Harvey (b. about 1873).[17]

The Jewelers' Circular and Horological Review reported in 1900 that J.C. Wilms "who has made himself conspicuous at times fighting spirit mediums, called on postal authorities and wanted them to stop the mail of certain palmists and fortune tellers, insisting such

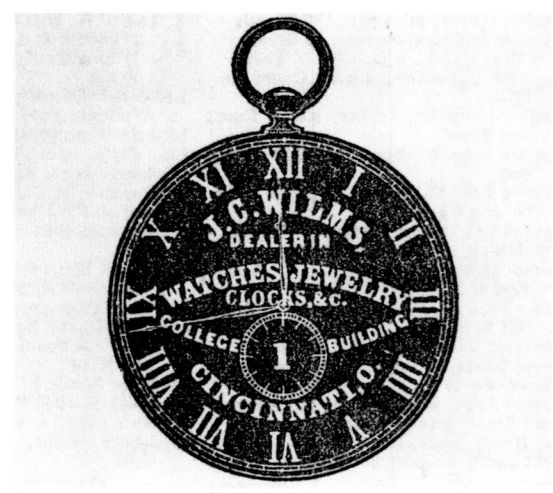

FIG. 149.1: Advertisement, *Williams' Cincinnati Directory, City Guide and Business Mirror*, Cincinnati: Williams & Co., 1862, 212

persons had no right to use the mails to further their enterprises." For this, he was sued for $25,000 by palmist Dr. Carl Perin.[18] Subsequently, it was noted that "he expended so much money exposing fraud that he left only a $5,000 estate."[19] His estate was later reported to be worth $2,500, and his store at Eighth and Vine Street was appraised at $1,839.92.[20]

Wilms Sr. was a dealer in jewelry, watches, and silverware. He was not a manufacturer. Credit reporters noted "buys most if not all of his stock here."[21] A set of six tablespoons with fancy fiddle-shaped handles and bright-cut decoration, similar to Duhme & Co.'s "No. 1" (circa 1869) pattern has been documented with mark 149.1.[22]

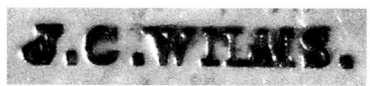

MARK 149.1

1. 1870, 1880, 1900 Federal Censuses, Cincinnati, Hamilton, Ohio; John C. Wilms, burial record, Spring Grove Cemetery, Cincinnati, Ohio.
2. 1900 Federal Census, Cincinnati, Hamilton, Ohio.
3. 1855 Cincinnati City Directory.
4. Ohio, Vol. 2, p. 262, R.G. Dun & Co. Collection, Baker Library, Harvard Business School.
5. 1856–1900 Cincinnati City Directories.
6. 1885, 1886 Cincinnati City Directories.
7. Ohio, Vol. 2, p. 262, R.G. Dun & Co. Collection.
8. Ibid.
9. Ibid.
10. *Report of the Sixteenth Exhibition of the Ohio Mechanics' Institute*, Cincinnati:

Ohio Mechanics' Institute, 1858, 84–85; *Jewelers' Circular and Horological Review* (October 1886): 333.

11. 1856, 1857 Cincinnati City Directories.

12. 1858–1890 Cincinnati City Directories; Wilms' address is given as 178 West Fifth Street in the 1880 edition of the city directory. Information for this edition was likely collected in the last half of 1879.

13. Ohio, Vol. 2, p. 307, R.G. Dun & Co. Collection.

14. Ibid.

15. 1891 Cincinnati City Directory; Frederick Wilms, Sr., burial record, Spring Grove Cemetery.

16. John C. Wilms, burial record; "Heart Disease Coupled with Kidney Trouble Causes Death of J.C. Wilms, a Well-Known Jeweler," *Cincinnati Enquirer*, September 19, 1901, 8; "Liberal Society Memorial Ceremonies For the Late J.C. Wilms," *Cincinnati Enquirer*, September 23, 1901, 5; G.G. Hubbell, "A Memorial Service," *The Free Thought Magazine* 19 (January–December 1901): 701–704.

17. Elise was born in Cologne, and died in Los Angeles. In other family burial records, her name is given as Eliza and as Elisabeth. Elise L. Wilms, Frederick Wilms, Sr., Augusta Wilms, Edwin I. Wilms, burial records, Spring Grove Cemetery; 1870, 1880, 1900 Federal Censuses, Cincinnati, Hamilton, Ohio; Dr. D.C. Wilms, "Despair Causes a Tragic Deed," *Cincinnati Enquirer*, April 30, 1892, 4; 'Heart Disease Coupled with Kidney Trouble Causes Death of J.C. Wilms, a Well-Known Jeweler," September 19, 1901.

18. "Cincinnati," *JCHR* (September 26, 1900): 56–57.

19. " Cincinnati," *JCHR* (October 2, 1901): 72.

20. "Cincinnati," *JCHR* (October 16, 1901): 66; "Cincinnati," *JCHR* (November 13, 1901): 71.

21. Ohio, Vol. 2, p. 262, R.G. Dun & Co. Collection.

22. J.C. Wilms, eBay listings and private collections, Cincinnati silver binders, Cincinnati Art Museum.

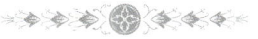

150. HARMON S. WINSLOW

about 1826–1887, w. 1856–1886

Harmon S. Winslow was born in Cincinnati.[1] From 1856 to 1862, he was listed in the city directory as a dentist, boarding on Sycamore Street.[2] However, in 1859, he was enumerated as both a dentist and as a silversmith working at the address of **E. & D. Kinsey**.[3] From 1863 onwards, his occupation was consistently given as silversmith.[4] It is presumed that although as a dentist Winslow may have been familiar with some aspects of the silver trade, he received much of his training under the tutelage of the Kinseys, with whom he worked until 1871.[5] In the 1870 Federal Census, he was enumerated as a 44 year-old journeyman silversmith with $2,300 in personal property.[6] In 1872 and 1873, he worked independently on Patterson Alley between Main and Walnut, and between 1874 and 1881 he was working at 135 Sycamore Street.[7] Of special note is his 1877 City Directory listing which describes him as "assayer and silver ware maker." This is the only known instance that any of the silversmiths included in this study advertised as an assayer. Cincinnati did not have an assay system, however most of the silversmiths by this time were working in sterling silver and would have tested their wares regularly to make sure that their materials met the sterling standard.[8]

Winslow's occupation is given as silverware manufacturer in 1883 and 1884, and he is working at the same address (6 West Fourth Street) as **Joseph S. Voss & Son**, and between 1885 and 1886, he shared an address with **H.T. Kent** (58 West Fifth Street).[9] It is not clear whether he worked for Joseph S. Voss & Son and H.T. Kent, or simply occupied the same multi-story buildings.

It is curious that although Winslow was an assayer and silverware maker, silver bearing his mark (mark 150.1) is very rare. Only a small number of spoons and a ladle with tipped, exaggerated fiddle handles and pointed shoulders have been documented through this project.[10] It is possible that much of his silver was marked and retailed by other firms.

Winslow died on September 28, 1887, of pneumonia.[11] He and his wife, Margaret "Kate" Bennett (1832–1874), had one daughter, Mary (b. about 1859).[12] After Margaret Winslow's death, he took a second wife, Mary.[13]

H.S. WINSLOW

MARK 150.1

1. Harmon S. Winslow, burial record, Spring Grove Cemetery, Cincinnati, Ohio.

2. 1856–1862 Cincinnati City Directories; He is also recorded as a dentist in the 1860 Federal Census, Cincinnati, Hamilton, Ohio.

3. 1859 Cincinnati City Directory.

4. 1863–1887 Cincinnati City Directories.

5. 1859–1871 Cincinnati City Directories; Winslow's working address is not given in directories published in 1862, 1863, or 1864. Based on his entries for 1859 and 1866–1871, it is most likely that he was working with the Kinseys during this time.

6. 1870 Federal Census, Cincinnati, Hamilton, Ohio.

7. 1872–1881 Cincinnati City Directories.

8. In 1896, Ohio passed legislation that declared that anyone selling anything marked as sterling, or in a box marked sterling, which did not prove to be sterling would be guilty of a misdemeanor. "The Circular's Sterling Silver Bill Now a Law in Ohio," *Jewelers' Circular and Horological Review* (March 4, 1896): 23.

9. 1883–1886 Cincinnati City Directories; The building at 6 West Fourth Street was four stories high. Joseph S. Voss & Son occupied the main floor and basement. H.T. Kent's location was described as an "elegant three-story brick building" with a more prominent location on Fountain Square. John W. Leonard, *Centennial Review of Cincinnati: one hundred years of progress in commerce,* *manufactures, the professions, and in social and municipal life*, Cincinnati: J.M. Elstner, 1888, 67, 69.

10. Harmon S. Winslow, eBay listings and private collections, Cincinnati silver binders, Cincinnati Art Museum.

11. Harmon S. Winslow, burial record.

12. Margaret was born in Piqua, Ohio to Joseph and Hannah Bennett. She married Harmon Winslow on June 17, 1852. According to descendant John Patterson, their daughter's name was Mary Edwina Winslow. She was known as "Winnie" and married George E. Bowman in Cincinnati in 1880; 1870 Federal Census, Cincinnati, Hamilton, Ohio; Mrs. Kate Winslow, burial record, Spring Grove Cemetery; John Patterson, descendant of Harmon Winslow, to Amy Dehan, email, December 10, 2012, Cincinnati Art Museum, Harmon Winslow research file.

13. 1880 Federal Census, Cincinnati, Hamilton, Ohio; According to John Patterson, Mary's maiden name was McCool. The surname of her first husband was Masters; John Patterson, descendant of Harmon Winslow, to Amy Dehan, Harmon Winslow research file.

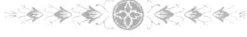

151. ADOLPH WITT

1832–1914, w. 1853–1914

Adolph Witt was born in Germany on July 29, 1832.[1] He arrived in America around 1850.[2] According to the 1853 Cincinnati City Directory, he was working as a watch maker at the address of **Richard Clayton**. When his co-worker Edward J. Hughes left Clayton's to establish his own firm (Hughes & O'Hara), Witt joined him.[3] When the firm became **Hughes & Dorland**, wholesalers and importers of watches and jewelry, in 1857, Witt stayed on as a watch maker, working with them until the partnership's dissolution in October 1860.[4] Witt then purchased much of Hughes & Dorland's old stock and took over their former stand at 19 Main Street.[5] He specialized in watches and jewelry, but also sold some silver. Around 1867, he moved to 173 West Fourth Street, a location that was not, according to R.G. Dun & Co. credit reporters, as profitable as his previous location.[6] There, they reported, "he lost everything he had previously made."[7] In 1870, he moved to 62 Main Street and, in the spring of 1872, to the northwest corner of Pearl and Main Streets.[8] In 1880, Witt reported as a jeweler with $1,000 worth of capital in his business.[9] He employed one hand, worked ten hours a day, and paid $250 in yearly wages.[10] That year, he utilized $125 worth of material to produce product worth $1,200.[11] In 1887, he was listed as a watch maker at 113 Sycamore, and in 1888, he was associated with George and Edward Simper, who advertised under the business heading of "Watches, Clocks & Jewelry."[12] By 1895, Witt was working for **Clemens Hellebush**, and by 1897, he was working at the address of Ben Schneider, a watch maker and jeweler on Vine Street.[13]

Witt died on December 22, 1914.[14] His death record notes that he was retired, but he had been listed as a watch maker in city directories up to and including the 1914 edition.[15] He and his wife

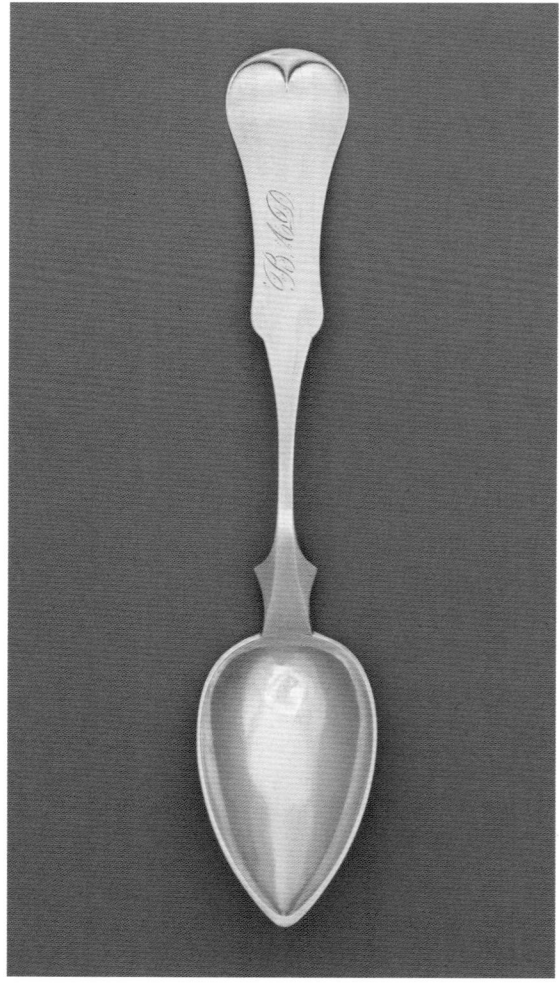

FIG. 151.1: Adolph Witt, *Tablespoon*, 1860–1887, 8⅜ × 1¾ in. (21.3 × 4.5 cm), CAM, Museum Purchase: John S. Conner Fund, 2013.10

Leopoldina Kuenzel (b. about 1835, Germany, d. 1913) had at least five children: Theodore (1854–1918); Bertha (1858–1915); Emma (1860–1928); Ida (1863–1913); and Clara (1876–1930).[16]

Silver bearing Witt's mark is very rare. Based on the shape of the spoon seen here, (fig. 151.1), he bought some, if not all, of his stock from local manufacturers.

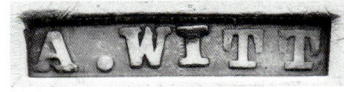

MARK 151.1

1. "Ohio, Deaths, 1908–1953," index and images, *FamilySearch*, https://familysearch.org/pal:/MM9.1.1/X8F4-VX8, accessed February 4, 2013, Adolph Witt, 22 Dec 1914, citing Norwood, Hamilton, Ohio, reference cn 66863, FHL microfilm 1983287; 1900 Federal Census, Columbia, Hamilton, Ohio.
2. Witt's immigration date is given as 1847 in the 1900 Federal Census, Columbia, Hamilton, Ohio. In the 1910 Federal Census, Norwood, Hamilton, Ohio, his arrival date is given as 1852, and his wife's as 1847. There is record of an Adolphus Witt, b. 1832, who arrived on July 30, 1850, on the *America*, departing Bremen, arriving in New York. This is likely our subject.
3. 1855 Cincinnati City Directory.
4. 1855–1860 Cincinnati City Directories.
5. Ohio, Vol. 2, p. 67, R.G. Dun & Co. Collection, Baker Library, Harvard Business School; Ohio, Vol. 4, p. 199, R.G. Dun & Co. Collection.
6. Ohio, Vol. 9, p. 194, R.G. Dun & Co. Collection; 1867–1868 Cincinnati City Directories; Also, in 1867, he applied for a patent for a watchman's register, Ancestry.com, *U.S. Patent and Trademark Office Patents, 1790–1909* [online database], Provo, Utah: Ancestry.com Operations Inc., 2008.
7. Ohio, Vol. 9, p. 194, R.G. Dun & Co. Collection.
8. Ibid.; 1872–1886 Cincinnati City Directories.
9. 1880 Federal Non-Population Census Schedules, Products of Industry, Schedule 4, Hamilton County, Ohio.
10. Ibid.
11. Ibid.
12. 1887, 1888 Cincinnati City Directories.
13. 1895–1901 Cincinnati City Directories; In the 1892 and 1896–1899 Cincinnati City Directories a second Adolph Witt, with the middle initial of "R," was listed as a watch maker. His working address is not given, but his home address differs from that of our subject. However, he was probably a relation.
14. Adolph Witt, burial record, Spring Grove Cemetery, Cincinnati, Ohio.
15. "Ohio, Deaths, 1908–1953," index and images, *FamilySearch*, Adolph Witt; 1914 Cincinnati City Directory.
16. The 1910 Federal Census, Norwood Ward 2, Hamilton, Ohio indicates that Leopoldina had six children and that five were living; The 1900 Federal Census, Columbia, Hamilton, Ohio indicates that Adolph and Leopoldina were married in 1852, whereas the 1910 Census indicates that they were married in 1854. No marriage records were found for them in Hamilton County, Ohio; Burial records, Spring Grove Cemetery; Theodore Witt, death record, Ancestry.com, *Kentucky, Death Records, 1852–1953* [online database], Provo, Utah: Ancestry.com Operations Inc., 2007.

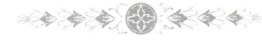

152. WOODRUFF & DETERLY

1817–1821

When **Robert Best** left the firm of **Robert Best & Co.** in the spring of 1817, the two remaining partners, **Enos Woodruff** and **Jacob Deterly** continued in business as Woodruff & Deterly on Main Street, in a house which they rented from Robert Best.[1] The men were active in the silver, watch, clock, and jewelry trade, and appear to have been making their own wares in addition to retailing the goods of others. An advertisement of November 1817 provides a sense of their business as they announce the receipt of gold and silver watches from England and "almost every article of SILVER WARE Used in this country, not inferior in quality or workmanship to any made here or bought from the Eastward [*sic*] . . . a large assortment of JEWELLERY [*sic*] . . . [and] a large quantity of PLATED BRIDLE BITS, STIRRUP IRONS, &c. &c."[2] Watch repair is also noted: "This branch is conducted by one of the firm, who, although he cannot boast of 'having learnt the Watch *Finishing* business in London,' nor even 'having learnt his business

in Europe,' yet can boast of having repaired [*not botched*] more watches in this town, within the last six years, than any other person—the humiliating fact of his having learnt his business in the back-woods to the contrary notwithstanding."[3] This pointed statement, which sheds light on the training of one of the partners, is surely meant as a jab towards the firm's competitors and past associates Samuel and Robert Best, whose advertisement six months earlier, underscored Samuel's experience "having learnt and followed the Watchmaking Business many years in Europe," and Robert's abilities to make and finish a patent lever watch.[4]

In 1819, Woodruff & Deterly were in business at 58 Main Street, and the silversmith **Abner Sotcher** appears to have been an employee.[5] In addition to their local concern, the firm maintained an interest in the Louisville-based firm of Elias Ayers (1791–1841), E. Ayers & Co. Deterly's diary entry, dated March 2, 1820, indicates that Woodruff left Cincinnati for Louisville on the steamboat *Gen'l*

Pike, "on business concerning the Establishment there, to take Inventory & etc."[6] Eleven days later, Deterly notes, "Enos Woodruff returned from Louisville in company with Elias Ayers." Presumably unhappy with their examination of the Ayers business, Deterly's entry on March 16, 1820, reads, "This day the firm of Elias Ayers & Co. at Louisville is considered dissolved and Woodruff & Deterly's dividend sold to Elias Ayers for $2500."[7]

A forewarning of Woodruff & Deterly's own dissolution can be read in Deterly's June 11, 1820 diary entry: "Enos Woodruff left here for Jersey at half past 10 a.m. Have wished since [that] the Devil had got him before he got back, he is one damned rascal."[8] Despite Deterly's wishes, Woodruff returned to Cincinnati on August 21 with his wife. They had, presumably, returned to

Woodruff's native New Jersey for stock, as on September 4, 1820, Deterly notes, "Our goods arrived last night, all in good order."[9] However, by February 2, 1821, Deterly and Woodruff were dividing their stock, tools and material. Their partnership was dissolved "by mutual consent" on February 1, 1821.[10] Subsequent entries in Deterly's diary refer to debts owed to various parties by Woodruff & Deterly, many of which lay the blame on Woodruff and on what Deterly caustically describes as his "honorable mode of adjusting accounts." A debt of $3,000 was owed to Philadelphia jeweler and watch maker Samuel Hildeburn (1787–1856).[11]

The mark (152.1) of Woodruff & Deterly has been found on a creamer (fig. 152.1), a beaker, and teaspoons with fiddle handles and pointed shoulders (fig. 152.2).[12]

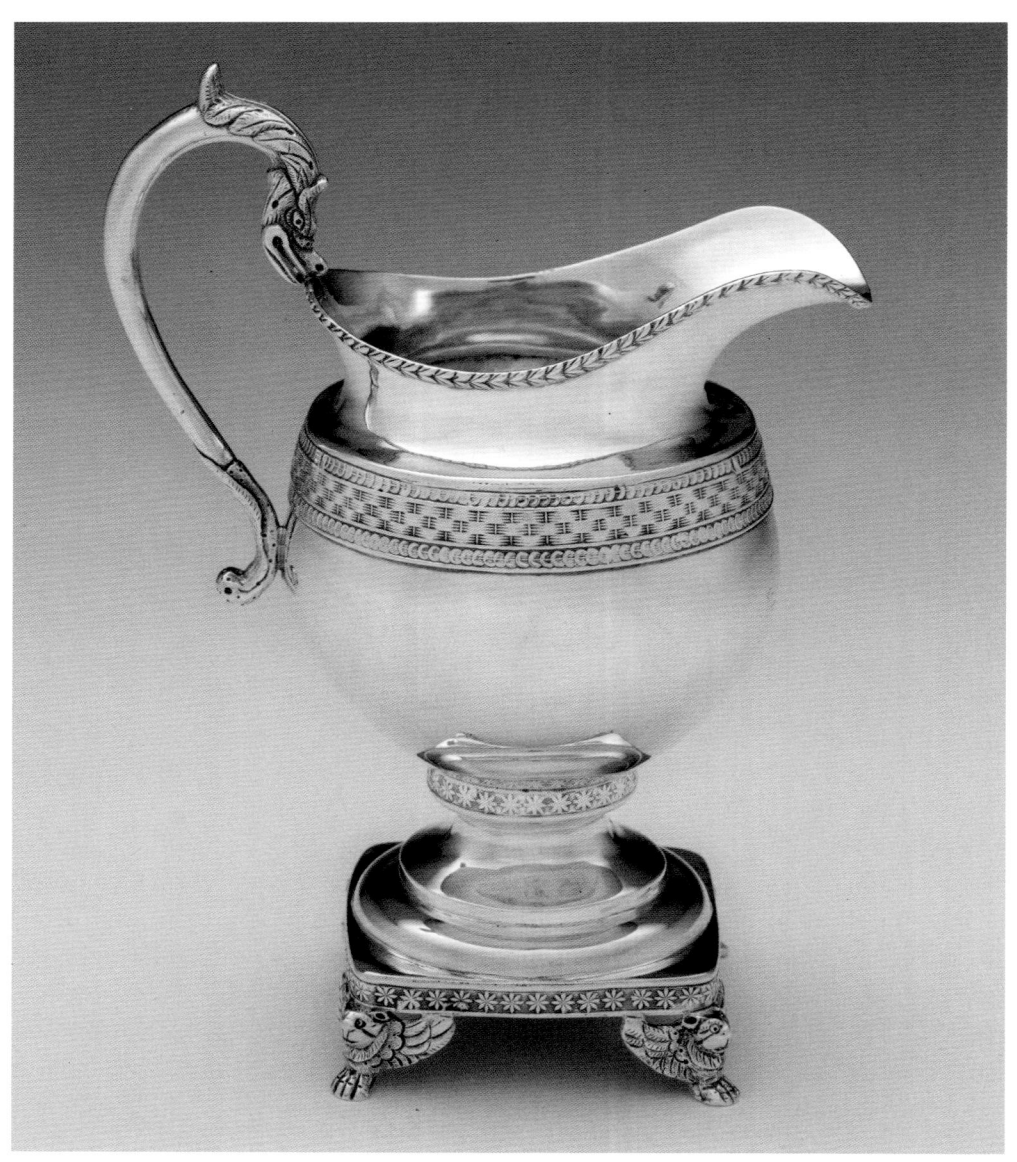

FIG. 152.1: Woodruff & Deterly, *Creamer,* 1817–1821, 7¾ × 6 in. (19.7 × 15.2 cm), CAM, Museum Purchase with funds provided by Mr. and Mrs. Charles Fleischmann III, 2005.48

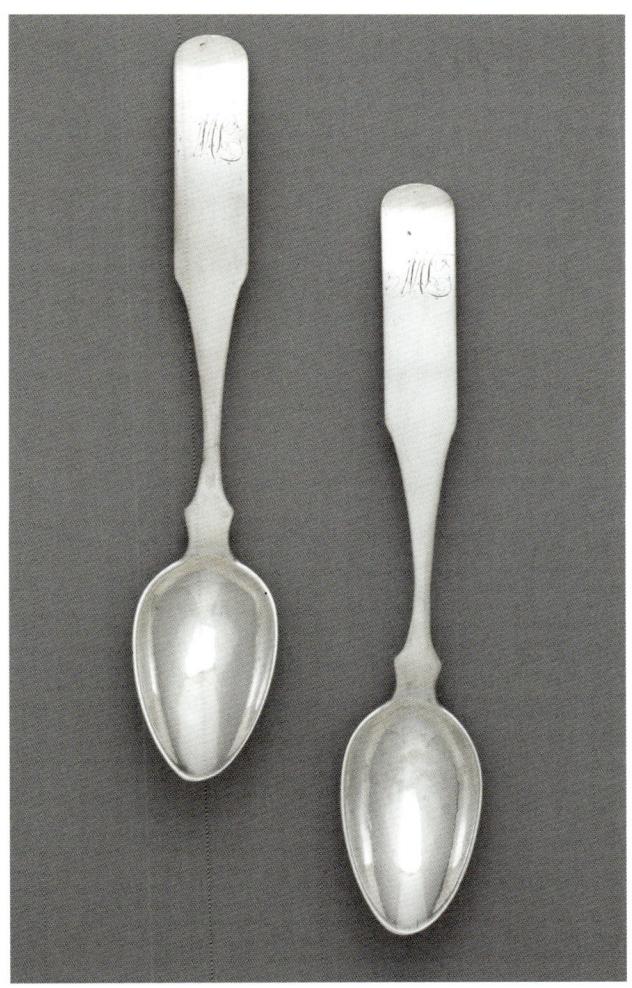

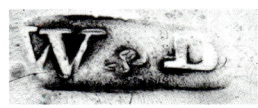

MARK 152.1

1. Advertisements, *Liberty Hall*, May 5, 1817, 3, cols. 2 & 4, reproduced in Beckman, 17.
2. Advertisement, *Liberty Hall*, November 24, 1817, reproduced in Beckman, 149.
3. Ibid.
4. Advertisement, *Liberty Hall*, May 5, 1817, reproduced in Beckman, 17.
5. 1819 Cincinnati City Directory.
6. Jacob Deterly, *"Remarks" of Jacob Deterly: diary from 1819 to 1848; life in southern Ohio: Cincinnati, Marietta, Athens* (transcribed and indexed by Madge Hubbard and Opal Saffell), Seattle: Northwest Lineage Researcher, 1972, 1:2, 8, 10.
7. Ibid.
8. Ibid.
9. Ibid.
10. Deterly, *"Remarks,"* 1:12, 13; Advertisement, *Western Spy*, April 7, 1821, reproduced in Beckman, 43.
11. Deterly, *"Remarks,"* 1:32, 34, 39 & 2:8.
12. *Creamer*, Museum Purchase with funds provided by Mr. and Mrs. Charles Fleischmann III, Cincinnati Art Museum, 2005.48; *Beaker*, Elizabeth Beckman Collection, Cincinnati Museum Center; *Spoons* (a pair), Given by Elizabeth M. and Annie W. Anderson in memory of their mother, Mrs. Buckner W. Anderson, Cincinnati Art Museum, 1969.737, 1969.738.

FIG. 152.2: Woodruff & Deterly, *Teaspoons*, 1817–1821, L. 5¾ in. (14.6 cm), CAM, Given by Elizabeth M. and Annie W. Anderson in memory of their mother, Mrs. Buckner W. Anderson, 1969.737–738

153. WOODRUFF & WHITE

1827– late 1833/early 1834

The firm of **Enos Woodruff** and George L. White operated at 58 Main Street, previously the site of Woodruff's shop.[1] The earliest known advertisement for the store appeared in 1827 (fig. 153.1), wherein the subscribers "beg leave to inform the Ladies and Gentlemen of Cincinnati, that they have just received from New-York and Philadelphia, an elegant assortment of fashionable JEWELLERY [*sic*], WATCHES, &c."[2] Among the lengthy list of articles featured are "Silver Spectacles . . . [and] Silver Table, Tea, Sugar & Soup Spoons." In 1829, the men listed as silversmiths in the city directory, and in 1831, an advertisement billed them as a military store (a continuation of Woodruff's endeavors since 1826) that also offered "Watches and Jewelry, Ladies and Gentlemen's Gold Patent Lever, Silver Lever, English capped, jeweled and plain Watches; chains, seals, keys, ear-rings, finger-rings &c. of all

NEW JEWELLERY AND WATCHES.
NO. 58, MAIN STREET.

WOODRUFF & WHITE, beg leave to inform the Ladies and Gentlemen of Cincinnati, that they have just received from New-York and Philadelphia, an elegant assortment of fashionable JEWELLERY, WATCHES, &c. which they offer for sale at reduced prices.

The following articles constitute part of their assortment:

Gold Patent Lever WATCHES,
Silver   do.   do.
English, Swiss, and French do.
Ladies' and Gentlemen's Gold Watch
    Chains, Seals and Keys,
Gold Cable Neck Chains,
Diamond, Pearl and Topaz, Amethyst,
    Coral, Jet and Paste Ear Rings,
Finger Rings and Breast Pins,
Bracelets, Clasps, and Coral Beads,
Medallions and Miniature Settings,
Silver Spectacles, Dirks,
Ever-point Pencils,
Silver Table, Tea, Sugar & Soup Spoons,
Steel Chains, Seals and Keys,
Gilt   do.   do.   do.
Cincinnati, Nov. 24.   43 6t

FIG. 153.1: Advertisement, *Saturday Evening Chronicle*, November 24, 1827

descriptions, Silver Ware, &c."[3] The last mention of the firm is found in the 1834 City Directory.[4] By February 1834 White had moved on to Madison, Indiana.[5] Woodruff remained in Cincinnati, at least until 1844.[6]

Silver marked by Woodruff & White is exceedingly rare (fig. 153.2). We do not know anything about White's training, but Woodruff was trained as a silversmith. The Woodruff & White firm never advertised as silver manufacturers. Rather, their advertisements emphasized their sale of goods procured elsewhere. It is uncertain whether they made any of the silver bearing their mark.

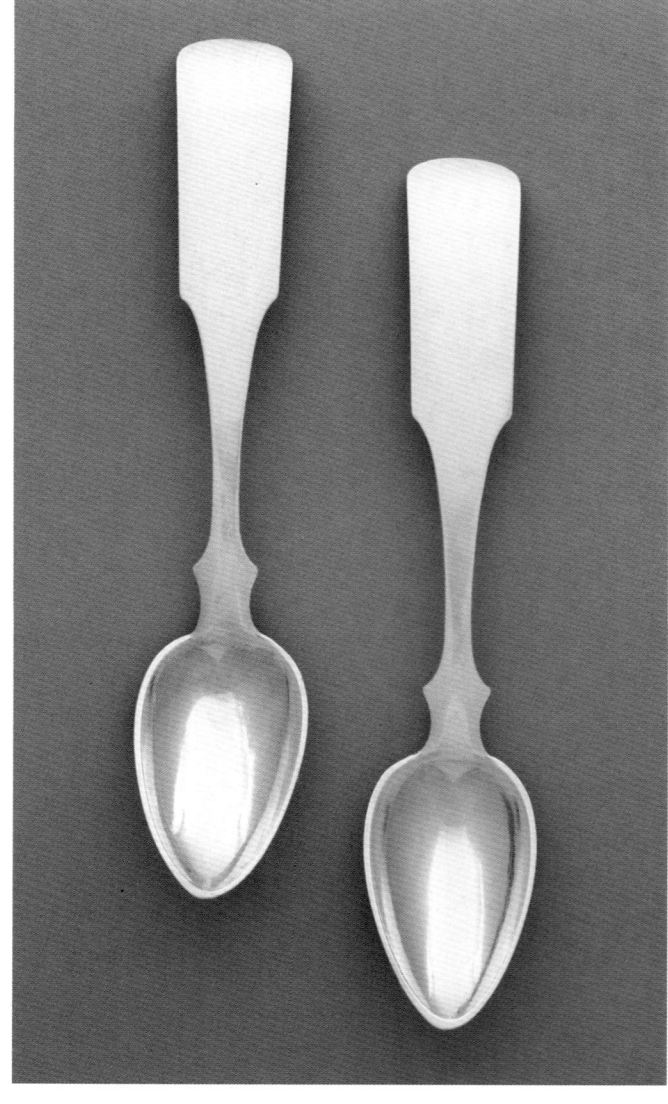

FIG. 153.2: Woodruff & White, *Spoons*, 1827–1834, L. 7⅛ in. (18.1 cm), CAM, Gift of John S. Conner, 1910.216, 1910.219

MARK 153.1

1. 1825, 1829, 1831 Cincinnati City Directories.
2. Advertisement, *Saturday Evening Chronicle*, November 24, 1827, 3, col. 3, reproduced in Beckman, 150.
3. Advertisement, 1829 Cincinnati City Directory, reproduced in Beckman, 144; Advertisement, *Cincinnati Commercial Register*, April 21, 1826.
4. White's personal listing does not indicate an association with the firm, however Woodruff's personal entry notes that he is with the firm of Woodruff & White. The firm of Woodruff & White does not have its own listing.
5. Beckman, 144, cites a February 27, 1834 notice of White's partnership with C.B. McCullough in the *Republican and Banner* (Madison, IN).
6. 1834, 1836/37, 1842, 1843, 1844 Cincinnati City Directories; Beckman, 144.

154. ENOS WOODRUFF

b. 1780, w. about 1810–1834 or later

Enos Woodruff came from a line of silversmiths, platers, and watch and clock makers active in Elizabethtown, New Jersey. Members of the Woodruff family had immigrated from England, and settled in New Jersey and New York as early as 1665.[1] Enos and his brothers, Ezra (b. 1787) and Ichabod (b. 1788), who were later active in Kentucky, learned the trade from their father, Enos Woodruff (1749–1821), a Revolutionary War veteran. The young Enos Woodruff (b. 1780) would have begun his apprenticeship around the age of 13. By the time he was 30 years old, he and his brothers had moved out West, presumably with the financial backing of their father.[2] Enos is documented in Cincinnati by 1810, and Ezra and Ichabod had established themselves in Lexington, Kentucky, by 1811.[3]

Enos presumably worked alone until 1813 when he purchased **Jacob Deterly**'s interest in **Best & Deterly** and joined **Robert Best** to form **Best & Woodruff**.[4] The partners advertised as silversmiths, clock and watch makers, jewelers and platers. They manufactured some goods while also retailing wares made in the East. By 1815, Deterly had joined Best & Woodruff, and the partners commenced business as **Robert Best & Co.**[5] This firm dissolved two years later when Robert Best left to join his brother **Samuel Best**, and Enos Woodruff and Jacob Deterly formed **Woodruff & Deterly**.[6]

After the dissolution of Woodruff & Deterly in February 1821, Woodruff continued in business on his own at 58 Main Street.[7] Advertisements suggest that while he was still active in the clock, watch making, jewelry and silver trade, he also dealt in military equipment. An April 1826 advertisement notes his receipt of a "general assortment of *MILITARY GOODS*," including "Silver plated and gilt mounted sabres; plated, gilt and steel mounted cut and thrusts; gold, silver, gilt and plated epaulettes and wings; gold and silver lace; plumes of all kinds; silk and worsted sashes; hat plates; worsted wings; abridgements of Scott's Military Discipline, &c. &c."[8]

By 1827, Woodruff had joined George L. White to form **Woodruff & White**, a partnership that lasted until late 1833 or early 1834.[9] Woodruff was elected and served as an associate judge for the Cincinnati Court of Common Pleas from 1827 to 1831.[10] He continued to appear in city directories, with no occupation listed, through 1844.[11] Spoons with coffin-shaped handles have been found with mark 154.1, which could be attributed to either Enos or Ezra Woodruff.[12]

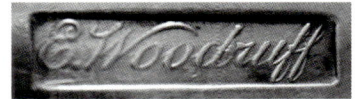

MARK 154.1

1. Boultinghouse, 287-291; Wm. Erik Voss, *American Silversmiths*, 2011, http://freepages.genealogy.rootsweb. ancestry.com/~silversmiths/makers/ silversmiths/102183.htm, accessed July 7, 2011; *The Family of John Woodruff of Elizabethtown and Westfield, NJ*, http://wc.rootsweb.ancestry.com /cgi-bin/igm.cgi?op=PED&db =elizawoodruffs&id=I3147, accessed July 8, 2011.

2. Boultinghouse, 290; The brothers may have traveled west in the company of Elias Ayers (1791–1841), who may also have apprenticed with Enos Woodruff in New Jersey; Boultinghouse, 35; Ayers established E. Ayers & Co. around 1813 in

Louisville, Kentucky, a company that both Enos Woodruff and Jacob Deterly appear to have subsequently had interest in. See Woodruff & Deterly entry.

3. Ronald V. Jackson, Accelerated Indexing Systems, comp., *Ohio Censuses, 1790–1890* (1810 tax list) [online database], Provo, Utah: Ancestry.com Operations Inc., 1999; Catherine B. Hollan, *Virginia Silversmiths, Jewelers, Watch- and Clockmakers, 1607–1860, Their Lives and Marks*, McLean, VA: Hollan Press, 2010, 739.

4. Advertisement, *Western Spy*, September 27, 1813, reproduced in Beckman, 13.

5. Advertisement, *Western Spy*, February 18, 1815, reproduced in Beckman, 13.

6. Advertisement, *Western Spy*, November 19, 1817, reproduced in Beckman, 41.

7. Deterly, "*Remarks*" of Jacob Deterly: diary from 1819 to 1848; life in southern Ohio: Cincinnati, Marietta, Athens (transcribed and indexed by Madge Hubbard and Opal Saffell), Seattle: Northwest Lineage Researcher, 1972, 1:12, 13; Advertisement, *Western Spy*, April 7, 1821, reproduced in Beckman, 43; 1825 Cincinnati City Directory.

8. Advertisement, *Cincinnati Commercial Register*, April 21, 1826, reproduced

in Beckman, 150.

9. Advertisement, *Saturday Evening Chronicle*, November 24, 1827, 3, col. 3, reproduced in Beckman, 150; 1834 Cincinnati City Directory.

10. Deterly, "*Remarks*," 2:23; Henry A. and Mrs. Kate B. Ford, *History of Cincinnati, Ohio*, Cleveland: L.A. Williams, 1881, 240.

11. 1836, 1842–1844 Cincinnati City Directories.

12. Enos Woodruff, eBay listings and private collections, Cincinnati silver binders, Cincinnati Art Museum; *Teaspoon*, Winterthur Museum, Gift of Mr. and Mrs. Alfred E. Bissel, 1962.0240.640.

APPENDIX A

CINCINNATI SILVERSMITHS AND FIRMS WITHOUT KNOWN WARES AND SENIOR MEMBERS OF MAJOR FIRMS

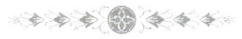

JANET C. HAARTZ

Working dates reflect those years the person or firm was involved in activities related to the silver trade in Cincinnati. The abbreviation CCD is used for Cincinnati City Directory.

ALBERT BROTHERS (1891–1922)[1] Louis H. Albert (1859–1948) worked as a clerk or salesman for the local jewelry firms **Duhme & Co.**, Lodwick & Nolting, and **Oskamp, Nolting & Co.** from 1881 to 1890.[2] In 1891, he and his brother Edward (1850–1918) opened a wholesale jewelry firm, Albert Brothers, in the Pike Building at Fourth and Plum.[3] Although the firm initially focused on watches, clocks, and jewelry, in 1895, they advertised, "In addition to our already large stock, we have added a line of Sterling Silver Ware."[4] By 1912, they were advertising as "wholesalers of everything in jewelry, watches, diamonds, cut glass, clocks, etc."[5] After Edward's death in 1918, Louis continued to head the firm until 1922. In 1923, Robert J. Seifert became the president and the firm's name was changed to The Albert & Seifert Co.

ALBERTSON, J.R. (w. 1861–1869) Jeweler and salesman for **Duhme & Co.** 1861, 1866–1869 CCDs. His "large acquaintance with the church congregations made him invaluable in their (Duhme's) trade" according to a later reminiscence.[6]

ALICH, ANDREW (1848–1918, w. 1868–1918) Son of German immigrants Catharine and Andrew Alich, Alich worked as a watch maker at an unidentified firm in Cincinnati between 1868 and 1872.[7] In 1873, he opened a retail store on Linn Street, advertising in the CCD business listings for "Watches, Clocks & Jewelry." Extant images of the store's exterior display advertising signs that include silverware, diamonds, and "fine repairing" as well as jewelry, watches, and clocks.[8] The firm continued to advertise in the CCD business listings after moving to Liberty Street in 1878. Images of the store's interior depict a large and varied assortment of jewelry, watches, clocks, and fancy goods, as well as a commodious area for the repair of clocks and watches.[9]

Elizabeth and Andrew Alich were married in April 1872 in Dearborn County, Indiana.[10] They had five children: Anna (b. 1873), Frances (b. 1877), Katherine (b. 1879), Edward (b. 1884), and William (b. 1888).[11] Edward appears in the 1903–1920 CCDs as a jeweler and William is listed as a jeweler in the 1904–1912 CCDs. Both were probably working in their father's shop. After Andrew's death in January 1918 Elizabeth continued the business through 1919, but by 1920, it no longer appeared in the CCD.[12]

ALLEN, CALEB JR. (1808–1873, w. 1834–1872) The son of Caleb (1773–1844) and Hannah Allen, Caleb Allen, Jr. was born in

Rhode Island in 1808.[13] He and his brother, **William Allen**, also a silversmith, presumably trained in the Northeast. Caleb Jr. established himself in Cincinnati prior to June 1833, when a newspaper advertisement announced that his first partner, **Pulaski Scovil**, had sold his interest in **C. Allen & Co.** to **Thomas F. Rhodes**, thereby dissolving the firm.[14] The venture of **Allen & Rhodes** ensued with an advertisement the same day indicating that they would "manufacture and keep for sale an extensive assortment of JEWELRY," some of which had been recently received from New York and Philadelphia, at 36 Lower Market Street.[15] In August 1834 John G. Anthony joined the firm, creating **Allen, Rhodes & Co.**, operating at the northeast corner of Main and Second Streets.[16] The firm continued, advertising as manufacturers of silver plate and jewelry as well as retailers of a broad variety of goods, until the establishment of a partnership between Caleb Allen and his brother William, known as **C. Allen & Co.** around 1836.[17] They offered a mix of their own manufactured goods and wares bought for retail. Caleb Allen was very successful. In 1850, he was reported to own property worth $11,500.[18] By 1860, his personal and real property was estimated at $60,000, and by 1870 at $165,000.[19] Allen died in Cincinnati on October 16, 1873.[20]

In August 1835 Caleb married Caroline Hastings (1813–1892), daughter of Nathan and Abigail Hastings.[21] They were the parents of ten children: Albert H. (1837–1869), Elizabeth D. (b. about 1839), Caroline H. (b. about 1841), Nathan Hastings (1843–1909), Sarah A. Allen James (1845–1918), Mary D. (b. about 1847), Frank C. (1849–51), Abbie H. (b. about 1851), Alice H. (b. about 1854), and Charles F. (b. about 1856).[22]

ALLEN, WILLIAM (1813–1889, w. 1836–1873) A younger brother of **Caleb Allen, Jr.**, William Allen was born in Massachusetts in 1813. The family moved to Providence, Rhode Island, when he was three years old.[23] Having apprenticed and learned the trade of a "high back comb maker," he worked in that trade in Rhode Island until 1835, when he decided to move to the West in search of better opportunities.[24] By 1836, he had reached Cincinnati via Cleveland, and joined his brother Caleb, an established silversmith and jewelry manufacturer, in the firm **C. Allen & Co.** An advertisement in 1840 highlighted their manufacture of jewelry, but also included their offerings as dealers in clocks, watches, and fancy goods.[25] From 1842–44, the shop operated under the name of William H. Allen, "Manufacturer of Jewelry," although William's occupation was given as silversmith in the alphabetical listings of the CCDs.[26] In the 1846 CCD, the firm's name had been changed to C. & W.H. Allen, and by 1853, the firm's business model had changed to "importers," or wholesalers only, and they continued to offer a broad variety of goods.[27] After the firm closed in 1872,

CCD listings do not include an occupation for William, although it was reported that he served as a director of "one or more" insurance companies.[28]

In March 1841 William married Mary Davis Mann (1820–1891), daughter of Mary and Anson Mann.[29] They had no children. At his death in 1889, William's will bequeathed "to my beloved wife all the residue of my estate real and personal (after the payments of my debts aforesaid) to hold and enjoy the same during the term of her natural life." After her death, the residue was bequeathed to eleven beneficiaries, in amounts varying from $2,000 to $30,000, with any remainder to go to the heirs of his brother Caleb.[30]

ALMS & DOEPKE (1865–1955)[31] William H. Alms (1842–1920), William F. Doepke (1838–1908), and Frederick H. Alms (1839–1898) opened a dry goods shop on Main Street north of the Miami and Erie Canal in 1865.[32] The shop prospered, and by 1903, had evolved into a large, general department store located at the intersection of the Miami and Erie Canal and Main Streets, offering dry goods, notions, carpets, house furnishing goods, fancy goods, clothing, and millinery. The household furnishings offered included silver wares as they advertised in the 1903–1908 CCD business listings for "Silver Ware."

ALMS, HENRY (w. 1870) Silversmith at **Duhme & Co.**, 1870 CCD.

ALMS, JOHN (w. 1866–1877) Silversmith at **Duhme & Co.**, 1870 CCD. Appears in various CCDs between 1866–1877 as a jeweler, chain maker, or porter at Duhme & Co. and at Dueber Watch Case Manufacturing Co.

ALMS, WILLIAM (w. 1869–1879) Silversmith at **Duhme & Co.**, 1872 CCD. Appears in various CCDs between 1869–1878 as a polisher or silver finisher at Duhme & Co.

AMERICAN JEWELRY CO. (1879–1890, 1895–1903, 1908–1965)[33] The American Jewelry Company was the successor to the various other firms owned or managed by **Abraham Steinau, Jr.** Located in the Emery Arcade, the firm was initially owned by **Selig Amberg** and managed by Steinau, who in 1881, bought Amberg's interest.[34] By 1884, the jewelry firm's offerings had expanded to include silverware.[35] An 1889 advertisement listed, in addition to jewelry and watches, a large assortment of silver articles made by Gorham, including "solid" silver flatware, silver flasks, card cases, and hair brushes and combs with silver handles.[36] Steinau moved the business to the corner of Fourth and Race in 1891, changing the firm's name to A. Steinau, Jr.[37]

From 1895–1903 and 1908–1928, the name was again being used by a firm in the Emery Arcade that advertised watches, clocks, and jewelry in the CCDs. There were frequent changes in managers and/or proprietors over the ensuing years until Abraham Rosenbaum became the proprietor in 1918. In 1928, Rosenbaum moved the shop to East Sixth Street.

ANDERSON, JOHN C. (w. 1877–79) Silversmith, 1879 CCD. Appears in 1877 CCD as watch maker.

ANDRICK, LOUIS (w. 1873) Silversmith, 1873 CCD.

ANGE, SOLOMON (1788–1861, w. 1836–1861) Born in Switzerland on December 15, 1788, Ange sailed from France on the *Aurora*, arriving in New York in December 1824.[38] He was working as a goldsmith in New York City from 1826–1828.[39] Ange was in Cincinnati by 1834, when he married Maria B. Damiael.[40] The 1836–1861 CCDs give his occupation variously as silversmith, jeweler, goldsmith, clock manufacturer, or watch maker. Although Ange advertised in the CCD business listings for "Jewelry, Silver Ware, Watches &c." from 1853 to 1861, silverware with his mark has not been documented to date.

It seems that Ange's wife Maria died, because in August 1837 he married Evelina (or Evalina) Mennet in Switzerland County, Indiana.[41] They were the parents of five children: Elizabeth J., Louisa, Theodore, Charles, and William. Solomon died in 1861 and is interred with Evelina (1808–1865) in Spring Grove Cemetery.[42]

ANKENY, EMMETT W. (1840–1874, w. 1864–1874) Ankeny was born in 1840, the son of Sabra and Peter B. Ankeny, a printer in Guernsey County, Ohio.[43] Emmett Ankeny's first exposure to the retail jewelry trade was likely with the jeweler Bethuel Borton, a close neighbor in his youth. He was in Cincinnati by 1862, working at **Duhme & Co.** as a clerk, the occupation given when he registered for the Civil War Draft in 1863.[44] By 1870, he was a manager and senior member of the Duhme firm. A reminiscence published in 1923 recalled him as a close friend of Herman Duhme who was "invaluable in the business."[45]

In 1870, Ankeny married Belle Hymeneal; no records were found of children born to them.[46] Ankeny died prematurely, of pneumonia, in March 1874 and was interred in Portsmouth, Ohio.[47]

ASPINWALL & EYSTER (1853) A short-lived partnership of **Chauncey B. Aspinwall** and Andrew A. Eyster (b. 1831), that was included in the 1853 CCD business listings under "jewelry, silver ware, watches, etc."[48] By 1855, Aspinwall was working alone as a jeweler and Eyster had his own shop, advertising "Watches & Jewelry."[49] Credit reports in 1856 for Eyster were positive: "married, fair character and habits, good business capacity."[50] However, in March 1867 the reports noted that he "buys stolen property & there are 2 indictments now *vs* him;" and in November 1869 added "Has been sent to the penitentiary for 6 years on a charge of receiving stolen goods."[51]

ASPINWALL, EDWARD G. (1829–1850) Son of **Chauncey B. Aspinwall**. Edward's occupation was given as watch maker and jeweler in 1850.[52]

ASPINWALL, THEODORE H. (1839–1864, w. 1859–60)[53] Son of **Chauncey B. Aspinwall.** Appears as watch maker or jeweler in 1859–1860 CCDs, working at 103 Main, the address of **Edward H. Hill**.

ASPINWALL, WILLIAM HENRY (1834–1869)[54] Son of **Chauncey B. Aspinwall**. Appears in 1859–1869 CCDs as engraver or jeweler; he was working for **C.B. Aspinwall & Co.** in 1868.

BARTH, FREDERICK (w. 1849–1881) Barth appeared in the 1849/50 CCD as "engine turner, watchcase engraver, and manufacturer of binders' tools." Over the next 31 years, his occupation was given as watch maker, engraver, jeweler, or gold and silver smith. As the proprietor of a jewelry store, he advertised in the CCD business listings from 1858 to 1878 for "jewelry, silver ware, watches &c." Credit reports for the firm were positive, deeming him honest and industrious, as well as good for modest bills.[55]

BECHT, LEWIS H. (1857–1941, w. 1879–1930)[56] Silversmith, 1879–1883 CCDs and 1880 Census. Appears in 1884–1910 CCDs as clerk or jewelry salesman at **Clemens Oskamp**'s, **The Duhme Jewelry Co.**, or **A. & J. Plaut**. His occupation is given as jewelry salesman in the Federal Census records for 1900–1930.

BECKER, JOHN (w. 1870–79) Silversmith, 1872 CCD. Appears in various CCDs between 1870–1879 as gilder or silver worker.

BENDER, WILLIAM (w. 1872–1914) Silversmith, 1872–74 CCDs. Appears in 1876–1914 CCDs as goldsmith or jeweler, working for the jewelry manufacturers **Herman Keck Manufacturing Co.** or Noterman & Jonas.

BENDORF, AUGUST (w. 1856–1861) Silversmith, 1857 CCD. Appears in various CCDs between 1856–1861 as plater or laborer.

BENSON, GABRIEL L. (b. 1796, w. 1819–1825)[57] Benson was included in the 1819 CCD as a silversmith at 148 Main. In June of that year, an advertisement in a Cincinnati newspaper for "G.L. Benson & Co., Watchmakers, Silversmiths & Jewellers [*sic*]" announced a wide variety of watches, jewelry, silver and plated table and tea spoons on hand as well as "All Kinds of Gold and Silver Ware manufactured on the shortest notice."[58] By late August of that year, Benson was in a partnership with Jeffrey Seymour and Othniel Williston (**Seymour & Williston**). They advertised that they had taken "the stand and stock lately occupied by **Robert Best**" at 95 Main.[59] The 1819 CCD includes listings for the partnership as well as for silversmith Benson, jewelry manufacturer Seymour and watch maker Williston.

In 1820, the notice "Married, At Cincinnati, Ohio on 13th ult. by the Rev. Mr. Wm. Burk, Mr. Gabriel L. Benson, formerly of this city, to Abigail Mills, daughter of Mr. Peter Mills of the former place," was carried in a New York City publication.[60] Benson appeared in the 1825 CCD as a watch maker, but no later record of him was found.

BERENS, FRED. (w. 1873–1874) Silversmith, 1874 CCD. Appears in 1873 CCD as machine hand.

BERNING, HENRY (w. 1874–1877) Silversmith, 1876 CCD. Appears in 1874, 1875, 1877 CCDs as watch case maker.

BERTLING, ERNST (1811–1866, w. 1842–1866)[61] Bertling's occupation was given as goldsmith or jeweler in the 1842–1867 CCDs. In 1853, he opened a jewelry store, advertising in the CCD business listings for "Jewelry, Silver Ware, Watches &c." until 1865, and in the listings for "Watches, Clocks & Jewelry" in 1866 and 1867. Credit reports noted that although the business was small, his credit was good for small amounts.[62] His widow Johanna (1814–1887) and son John (1854–1912) continued the business through 1879.[63]

BESWICK, WILLIAM (w. 1881–1885) Silversmith, 1883–84 CCDs. Appears in 1881/82, 1885 CCDs as polisher or nickel plater.

BEST & WOODRUFF (1813–1815) In September 1813 **Enos Woodruff** purchased **Jacob Deterly**'s interest in the partnership of **Best & Deterly**, and established a partnership with **Robert Best**.[64] Clues about the Best & Woodruff operation can be pieced together from their earliest advertisement: "The highest price in cash will be given for old Gold, Silver, Copper, Brass and Pewter," indicates that they were melting material to create new wares, while also purchasing some of their stock from the East as noted in the statement that they "have just received a large and elegant assort-

ment of the best Philadelphia *Jewelry* with an assortment of *Miniature Glasses."* In silver wares, they advertised "a general assortment of SILVER WARE . . . Soup and Milk Ladles, Cream or Jelly Spoons, Table, Desert [*sic*], Tea, Salt and Mustard ditto [spoons], Sugar Tongs, Tumblers, Saddle Mounting, &c., All of which they will sell as low as can be purchased in the western country."[65]

Best & Woodruff also advertised the addition of silver plating to their practice, offering "an assortment of *Bridle-bits, Stirrup-irons, . . . Saddle mountings,* and *Carriage moulding* [*sic*]," noting "Carriage mounting and other articles in their line will be plated on the shortest notice."[66] This activity in silver plating would continue when Deterly purchased an interest in the business and it became **Robert Best & Co.** in 1815.[67]

It appears that Best and Woodruff's partnership garnered a side business, established in August of 1815, not long after the formation of Robert Best & Co. Advertised with the heading, "Another Link in the Chain of Independence," Best and Woodruff announced their thimble manufactory, producing specimens that could be seen at their warehouse on Main Street. "Those *domestic* Thimbles can be afforded at the Eastern price, and at the same time are much neater and stronger. The patriotism of our Ladies will reward an establishment intended wholly for their benefit."[68]

BEYLAND, CHARLES F. (w. 1866–1877) Silversmith, 1866 CCD. Appears in 1868–1877 CCDs as a burnisher at **Duhme & Co.**

BILTZ, THEODORE (1841–1883, w. 1865–1883)[69] Silversmith, 1865–1883 CCDs and 1870, 1880 Federal Censuses. Worked at **Duhme & Co.**

BINLEY, JAMES (w. 1869) Silversmith, 1869 CCD.

BISBEE, ISAIAH (w. 1817) In 1817, Bisbee advertised in the *Western Spy* that he had taken a shop on Main Street where he offered a "good assortment" of "Watches, Rich Pearl Jewellery [*sic*], and Silver Spoons," adding that the silver table and tea spoons were "of the latest patterns from the Boston manufactory."[70] He left Cincinnati before 1819, as he is not listed in that or later CCDs. He may have been the Isaiah Bisbee recorded in the 1830 Federal Census, residing in southeastern Indiana (Caesar Creek Township, Dearborn County), not far from Cincinnati.

BOCCA, A. (w. 1869) Silversmith, 1869 CCD.

BODKER, JOHN H. (w. 1874–1882) Silversmith, 1874–1880, 1882 CCDs. Bodker's work address in the 1874, 1875 CCDs corresponds to that of silversmith **Harmon S. Winslow**. Appears as conductor, Cincinnati Street Railroad Co. in 1881 CCD. His surname was also spelled as Boedker in some CCDs.

BOEDKER, WILLIAM (w. 1874–1876) Silversmith, 1874 CCD. Appears as watchman in 1876 CCD.

BODLEY, THOMAS N. (w. 1872) Silversmith, 1872 CCD. Appears as bookkeeper in 1875 CCD and as grainer (operator of a machine for graining lithographic printing plates) in 1876 CCD.

BOHMANN, HENRY (w. 1877) Silversmith, 1877 CCD.

BOLLMAN FREDERICK (b. about 1820, w. 1850–1864)[71] Silversmith, 1850/51 CCD. Appears as goldsmith in the 1860 Federal Census and 1863 CCD, and as a jeweler or manufacturing jeweler in CCDs between 1855–1864.

BOLSTER, AUGUST (w. 1860) Silversmith, 1860 CCD.

BOLSTER, HENRY C. (w. 1853) Silversmith, 1853 CCD.

BORCHERS, ROBERT (w. 1879–1883) Silversmith, 1882–1883 CCDs. Appears as jeweler in 1879–1880 CCDs.

BOSSARD, JOHN (w. 1866–1880) Silversmith, 1867, 1872, 1876, 1877, 1879, 1880 CCDs. Appears as jeweler, music teacher, piano tuner, painter, or surgical instrument maker in CCDs between 1866–1880. His work address in the 1873–1880 CCDs corresponds to that of the dental and surgical instrument manufacturer William Autenrieth.

BRACKMEIER, ALBERT (w. 1877) Silversmith, 1877 CCD.

BRACKMEIER, EDWARD (w. 1876) Silversmith, 1876 CCD.

BRAMKAMP, HENRY (w. 1858–1882) Silversmith, 1858, 1870 CCDs. Appears as salesman, grocer, porter, or burnisher in CCDs between 1861–1882. Worked at **E. & D. Kinsey** and **Duhme & Co.**

BRAMKAMP, J. (w. 1857) Silver worker, 1857 CCD at **E. & D. Kinsey**.

BRANT, H. (w. 1855–1859) Silversmith, 1855–1859 CCDs. Worked at **E. & D. Kinsey.**

BRATHOLD, FRED. (w. 1857) Silver worker, 1857 CCD. Worked at **E. & D. Kinsey**.

BREITHOLL, HY (w. 1858) Silversmith, 1858 CCD. Worked at **E. & D. Kinsey**.

BROCKMEIER, EDWARD (w. 1873–1877) Silversmith, 1875–1876 CCDs. Appears as clerk or salesman in CCDs between 1873–1877.

BRODERSEN, EMIL (1833–1909, w. 1859–1909)[72] Born in Germany, Brodersen arrived in New York from Hamburg on the *Austria* in July 1858; the passenger manifest lists his occupation as watch maker.[73] The 1859 CCD listed him as a watch maker, working at 16 West Fourth, the address for the firms of **Joseph Draper** and **Henry Jenkins**. By 1866, he was working as a watch maker for **David Kinsey**. He continued working for the Kinsey firms until 1880, when he began working for **Clemens Oskamp**. From 1892–1901, he was a watch maker for **Harry R. Smith & Co.** and then worked as a watch maker for **The Duhme Jewelry Co.** until his death in 1909.[74]

BUCHHOLZ, HARRY (w. 1883) Silversmith, 1883 CCD. Appears as teamster or driver in 1884–1888 CCDs.

BUSCH, EDWARD (w. 1873) Silversmith, 1873 CCD. Appears as molder in 1875 CCD.

CADWALLADER, PHARES F. (w. 1875) Silversmith, 1875 CCD. Appears as grainer (operator of a machine for graining lithographic printing plates) in 1877–79 CCDs.

CALLAHAN, JOHN B. (1849–1921, w. 1866–1913)[75] The son of Irish immigrants George and Mary E. Callahan, John started working as a clerk for **David Kinsey** around 1865 and continued with the firm after David Kinsey's death in 1874.[76] Callahan and **Louis A. Kinsey** bought out **Edward W. Kinsey** in 1875, changing the firm's name to **David Kinsey & Co.**, "Manufacturer of Silver Ware & Jewelry."[77] According to credit reports, Callahan withdrew from the firm in 1877, although the CCDs indicate that he continued to work there through 1882, when the store was closed and the stock liquidated.[78] Callahan subsequently worked as a salesman for other jewelry and silverware firms, including **Clemens Hellebush** (1883–1894), **The Duhme Jewelry Co.** (1898–1909), and **The Clemens Oskamp Co.** (1910–1913). From 1914 until his death in 1921, Callahan was a broker for Albert W. Schell & Co., a general insurance agency.

Callahan married Elizabeth Mallory in 1875.[79] They were the parents of nine children: Alice (b. 1875), Anneta (b. 1876), George C.

(b. 1878), Charlotte (b. 1880), Florence (b. 1882), Marjory (b. 1885), William H. (b. 1887), Sarah (b. 1889), and Clara (b. 1893).[80]

CAMERON, JOSEPH (w. 1851) Silversmith, 1851 CCD.

CAMLER, DAVID (w. 1863) Silversmith, 1863 CCD.

CARLISLE-OSBORNE CO. (THE) (1894–1895, 1899–1900)[81] A wholesale firm that advertised in the CCD business listings for importers, manufacturers, and wholesale dealers of "watches, jewelry, etc." in 1894, and in the "silverware" category in 1899–1900. The 1900 CCD noted the factory was in Mansfield, Ohio. From 1896–1898, the firm operated under the name of **The Carlisle-Osborne Silver Co.**

CARLISLE-OSBORNE SILVER CO. (THE) (1896–1898) A wholesale firm that advertised silverware in the 1896–1898 CCD business listings. The address for the firm was the same as that of **The Carlisle–Osborne Co.**

CHANDLESS, GEORGE (w. 1875–1880) Silversmith, 1879–1880 CCDs. Appears as silver finisher or foreman in 1875–1878 CCDs. Worked at the corner of Harrison and Culvert, the address of **Clemens Oskamp**'s factory.

CHOATE, ROBERT W. (w. 1839/40) Silversmith from Delaware, 1839/40 CCD. Probably a brother of **Stephen D. Choate**, Robert was in Louisville, Kentucky, by 1850, living with the Stephen Choate family and working as a watch maker and jeweler.[82]

CLAUSSEN, GEORGE (w. 1871–1876) Silversmith, 1871–75 CCDs. Appears as jeweler in 1876 CCD.

CLOSE, HENRY (w. 1857–1859). Silversmith, 1859 CCD, working at the address of **E. & D. Kinsey**. Appears as jeweler in 1857 CCD.

CLOSS, FREDERICK (1830–1909, w. 1857–1891) Born in Goeppingen, Germany, Closs sailed to New York from Germany on the *Gondar* in May 1852.[83] He was in Cincinnati by 1854, when he married Regina Abele, also born in Germany.[84] In 1857, he was working as a silversmith for **E. & D. Kinsey**. His occupation is recorded as silversmith, watch maker, or jeweler in period documents.[85] The proprietor of a jewelry store from 1861 to 1879, he advertised in the CCD business listings under "jewelry, silver ware, watches, etc." or "watches, clocks and jewelry." From 1886–1891, Closs returned to working as a silversmith; his employer

could not be identified as only his residential address is listed in the CCDs.

Frederick and Regina Closs (1836–1887) were the parents of five children: Mary, Johanna, Frederick, Frank, and Laura.[86] Closs died on January 8, 1909, in Cincinnati.[87]

CLUSKER, CHARLES (w. 1850) Silversmith at **E. & D. Kinsey**, 1850 CCD.

COE, JOHN (w. 1857–1858) Silversmith, 1857–1858 CCDs. Worked at the address of **C. & J. Vanhouten** in 1857.

COLEMAN, HENRY (w. 1857) Silversmith, 1857 CCD. Appears as finisher in 1859 CCD.

CONWAY, THOMAS A. (1794–1871, w. 1825–1847)[88] Born in Maryland, Conway worked as a watch and clock maker in Baltimore, 1819–1824.[89] He was in Cincinnati by early 1825, when he appeared as a watch maker in the CCD published that year. In May 1832 Conway formed a partnership with the silversmith **Dennis McHenry**, establishing **Conway & McHenry**, which was "dissolved by mutual consent" in 1834.[90] Conway returned to working as a watch maker for other firms, including that of **Nathan L. Hazen**. From 1842 to early 1847, he was again in business by himself, advertising in the 1844 CCD business listings under watch makers and silversmiths; credit reports described him as very poor but honest.[91] After 1848, Conway appeared in CCDs intermittently with no occupation listed through 1865.[92] By 1870, Conway was living with his son Thomas Jr. in Milwaukee, Wisconsin, his occupation given as retired merchant.[93]

Conway married Catherine Rickard (1799–1849) in 1820, in Baltimore, MD.[94] They were the parents of six children: Wilton A. (b. 1822), Mason A. (b. 1827), Mary C. (b. 1834), Laura (b. 1836), Ella (b. 1838), and Thomas A. (b 1841).[95]

CONWAY & McHENRY (1832–1834) "Conway & McHenry, Jewelers, Watchmakers & Silversmiths" was a partnership between watch maker **Thomas A. Conway** and silversmith and jeweler **Dennis McHenry**, both of whom were originally from Baltimore, Maryland.[96] Their stock included "a splendid assortment of articles in their line" including "Silver Table, Tea, Desert [*sic*] and Cream Spoons and Sugar Tongs" as well as silver spectacles, thimbles, jewelry, fancy goods, and watches.[97] The firm continued until February 1834 when a notice of the dissolution of the partnership "by mutual consent" was published.[98]

COWARD, SAMUEL (w. 1836/37) Silversmith, 1836/37 CCD.

COX, RODOLPHO (1819–1854, w. 1839–1852)[99] Born in Virginia, Cox was working in Cincinnati as a silversmith for **Samuel Musgrove** in 1839. His occupation was given in the CCDs as a silversmith or jeweler through 1851.

CRANE, H. WALDO (w. 1860–61) Silversmith, 1860 CCD. Appears in 1861 CCD as silver plater.

DALLER, JOHN (1814–1886, w. 1839–1881)[100] Born in Germany in 1814, Daller arrived in New Orleans in early 1838, and shortly thereafter was in Cincinnati where he opened a jewelry shop on the east side of Vine Street, between the Miami and Erie Canal (now Central Parkway) and Twelfth Street.[101] His business prospered and, by 1842, he had moved across the street to larger quarters. He carried a varied stock, advertising in the CCD business listings for "Jewelry, Silver Ware, Watches, etc." as well as in the listings for clocks and watches. A watch and clock maker by training, Daller likely was only a retailer of the silverware he sold. Credit reports in 1860 described Daller as an "honest, hardworking German" of limited means, and noted that he paid creditors regularly.[102]

Daller's son **Joseph** was working at the shop by 1862, and in the 1868 CCD, the firm was listed as John Daller & Son. Joseph succeeded his father as the proprietor of the firm around 1867.[103] Although "retired," John continued to work at the shop as a watch maker for "a portion of his time."[104] John died at his home in Newport, Kentucky, in 1886. An obituary described him as an "industrious and competent business man" who "enjoyed the confidence of all who knew him," adding that he had accumulated "quite a fortune."[105]

John Daller married Theresa Kiehl (1821–1903) in 1840.[106] They were the parents of two children: Joseph (1843–1923) and Mary C. (1846–1932) who married her father's apprentice, **John C. Dueber**.[107]

DALLER, JOHN C. (1846–1919, w. 1865–1919)[108] The son of Francisca and Clement Daller, John was born in Germany and emigrated with his parents before 1850.[109] At the age of 14, he was apprenticed to his uncle, Hermann Daller, a jeweler in Ripley, Ohio.[110] By 1865, John had returned to the Cincinnati area and was working as a watch maker for **Clemens Oskamp**. Over the next 20 years, he worked as a clerk, salesman, and traveling agent for the firm, before becoming one of the principals in 1888, and then the president of **The Clemens Oskamp Co.** in 1903. In 1872, Daller married Amelia Oskamp, daughter of Clemens Oskamp. They were the parents of seven children: Clemens O. (1873–1953), Geneva (b. 1875), Gertrude (1878–1905), Adele (b. 1879), John C. Jr. (1882–

1924), Charles (b. 1883), and Adrian O. (b. 1889).[111] The family moved to the College Hill area in 1892.[112]

DALLER, JOSEPH (1843–1923, w. 1862–1895)[113] The son of German immigrants Theresa and **John Daller**, Joseph followed in the watch-making and jewelry trade. Initial credit reports were positive but cautious, noting that he was honest and reliable, "but of mod(est) means."[114] Located at a gateway to the booming area called Over-the-Rhine for its concentration of German immigrants, his firm thrived. In 1886, it was reported that Joseph Daller "has been obliged to increase his facilities" and, having torn down the original building on the site, erected "a handsome, five-story brownstone building" for the business where he employed several "skilled workmen."[115] His stock was large and varied and included "fine watches," clocks, "first-class jewelry," and "silverware of every description."[116] A watch maker and jeweler by training, Joseph Daller was likely a retailer of silver wares and not a manufacturer.

In 1895, Joseph Daller sold the business and the "good will" of the firm (but not the real estate) to John Bertling (1854–1912), the son of Johanna and **Ernst Bertling**. A watch maker and long-time employee at the firm, Bertling advertised his firm as the "Successor to Joseph Daller."[117] Daller retired from the jewelry business in 1895 and devoted his time to his real estate and other investments.[118] Never married, he died in 1923.

DALTON, JOHN (w. 1839/40) Silversmith, 1839/40 CCD. Appears as coach trimmer or carriage manufacturer in 1842–1849/50 CCDs.

DASSELL, FREDERICK ANTON (1830–1894, w. 1856–1894)[119] Born on October 21, 1830, in Germany, Dassell arrived in New York in December 1854 from Bremen, Germany, on the *Atlantic*; his destination was given as "Cinsennade" on the passenger manifest.[120] He was in Cincinnati by 1856, working as a jeweler at the address of the shops of **Richard Clayton** and **Henry Jenkins**. Dassell operated a retail jewelry store from 1860 to 1894, advertising in the CCD business listings for "Jewelry, Silver Ware, Watches &c.," or "Watches, Clocks & Jewelry." His longevity in the business was undoubtedly the result of his "careful and prudent" approach to the business.[121] Dassell's occupation was recorded as jeweler or goldsmith in census records, and as watch maker in military registration records.[122] In September 1856 Dassell married Johanna Hoch (b. Germany, 1836).[123] They were the parents of ten children: Mary, Frederick, Werner, Henry, Frank, Rudolph, Flora, Sophie Barbara, Edward, and Albert.[124] After Dassell's death in August 1894, the shop closed.

DAVIDSON, WILLIAM A. (1844–1910, w. 1862–1910)[125] Born in Scotland, Davidson appears as a silversmith in the 1860 Federal Census, living at the same address as James C. Michie (**see W. & J.C. Michie**), also a silversmith.[126] He worked as a watch maker in Cincinnati from 1862–1889, and then opened a jewelry store in the Emery Arcade, W.A. Davidson & Co.

He married Sarah J. Schofield in 1865; they were the parents of eight children: Alice (b. 1866), William (b. 1868), Edward (b. 1870), Nellie (b. 1873), Blanche (b. 1878), Margery (b. 1879), Charles (b. 1882), and Earl (b. 1889).[127]

DAY, WILLIAM (1845–1925, w. 1861–1879, 1915–1925)[128] Born in 1845 to German immigrants Louisa and Lambert Day, William was a goldsmith and jeweler who worked for other Cincinnati jewelers and silversmiths, including **William Wilson McGrew**, from 1861–1869.[129] In 1870, Day and another McGrew employee, **Jackson Slane**, formed a partnership (Slane and Day), and advertised as "Diamond Setters and Manufacturers of Fine Jewelry."[130] Credit reports for the business were initially favorable, but indicated problems by early 1876, and the business failed that year.[131]

By 1880, Day was working in Lexington, Kentucky, advertising in the Lexington city directories through 1898/99 as a jeweler, watch maker, and optician as well as a manufacturing jeweler.[132] From 1900–1910, he worked as a jeweler in Brooklyn, New York.[133] Day, his wife Mary (b. 1852), and son William C. (b. 1878) returned to Cincinnati around 1915, where he worked as a jeweler until his death in 1925.[134]

DEGARMO, GARRET S. (w. 1871) Silversmith, 1871 CCD. Appears in 1867–1870 CCDs as clerk.

DEPPERMANN, EDMUND (1828–1886, w. 1853–1886)[135] Born in Germany, Deppermann immigrated to the United States in 1848.[136] He was in Cincinnati by 1850, living with the **Joseph P. Serodino** family.[137] In the 1853 CCD, his occupation was given as a manufacturing jeweler; by 1855, he was a partner in a retail jewelry firm with **J.C. Wilms, Sr.**, and from 1869–1883, he was a partner of **Herman Keck, Sr.** in the firm **H. Keck & Co.**, diamond setters and manufacturing jewelers.[138] By November 1883 the partnership had been dissolved and Deppermann had formed a new firm, The Deppermann Jewelry Co. that advertised as manufacturers of watch cases and jewelry.[139] The firm continued under the leadership of Deppermann's son Paul for only one year after Deppermann's death in 1886. Period documents utilized various spellings for his surname; the passport issued in 1873 has the spelling used here.[140]

DE YOUNG, R. (w. 1836–1851) Silversmith and jeweler, 1836/37 CCD. Appears in 1839–1853 CCDs as watch maker, clock repairer, or barber. The spelling of his surname and given name varies in the directories: DeYoung, Young, or Deyoung and Raphael, Ralph, Richard, or Richard D. It has been suggested that these names may represent two different people, but an examination of the addresses at which these men lived supports the assumption that it was in fact just one man.[141]

DIEDERICH, CHARLES N. (1854–1943, w. 1870–1923)[142] Son of German immigrants Ferdinand and Mary Diederich, Charles was born in New York in September 1854.[143] The family had arrived in the Cincinnati area by 1857, when Ferdinand was listed as a tinner in the CCD. By the time Charles was 16, he was working as an "engraver in gold."[144] He appears as an engraver in the 1871–1923 CCDs, working first for **Duhme & Co.** and subsequently for **Duhme Bros. & Co.** until 1904. Although he continues be listed in the CCDs as an engraver until 1923, the listings after 1904 do not indicate where he was employed and provide only his home address.

Diederich married Rosa Fleischmann (1854–1925) in August 1877; they were the parents of three children for whom records were found: Bertha M., Albert E., and Clara H.[145]

DIETRICHS, CHARLES (1817–1883, w. 1856–1867)[146] Silversmith, goldsmith or jeweler, 1857–1865 CCDs. Appears in other CCDs as silver plater or gilder. Worked for **E. & D. Kinsey**.

DILLON, JOHN (w. 1877–1880) Silversmith, 1877–1880 CCDs.

DISE, FREDERICK (w. 1853) Silversmith, 1853 CCD.

DISERENS, ALBERT D. (w. 1861–1863) Silversmith, 1861, 1863 CCDs.

DISERENS, FRED. JR. (w. 1857–1863) Silversmith, 1859 CCD working at **E. & D. Kinsey**. Appears in various CCDs between 1857–1863 as clerk or jeweler at the Kinsey firms.

DONOHOE, RICHARD (w. 1861–1871) Silversmith, 1861, 1867 CCDs. Appears in CCDs between 1863–1871 as jeweler, brass finisher or as proprietor of Richard Donohoe & Co., which advertised in the 1869 CCD business listings for "Jewelry, Silver Ware, Watches &c." A partnership with Michael Fanning as "diamond setters" appears in the 1871 CCD.

DORAN, JOHN (w. 1829–1831) Silversmith, 1829, 1831 CCDs.

DORNSEIFER, HENRY A. (1811–1883, w. 1848–1883)[147] Born in Germany, Dornseifer's shop on Main Street was included in the 1848/49 business directory listings for "Watch and Clockmakers' Stores."[148] Through the 1850s, he advertised in CCD business listings for "Jewelry, Silver Ware, Watches &c." In 1863, he moved his shop to the Cumminsville area, at that time a suburb of Cincinnati. Federal census records list his occupation as silversmith (1850), clock and watch dealer (1860), deals in jewelry (1870), and keeps watch makers' shop (1880).[149] Credit reports in 1869 noted that the business was mostly repairing and that Dornseifer was an "Honest, sober, steady old man too concientous [sic] to ever get rich."[150] After Dornseifer's death in 1883, his son Louis (1862–1934) continued the business, changing the name to L.E. Dornseifer (1885–1899) and Dornseifer Jewelry Co. (1900–1922).[151]

Henry was in Cincinnati by 1847, when he married Charlotte A. White (1830–1900).[152] They were the parents of seven children: Sarah (b. 1853), John (b. 1857), William (b. 1859), Louis (b. 1862), Clara (b. 1865), Ida (b. 1870), and Frank (b. 1874).[153]

DUEBER, JOHN C. (1841–1907, w. 1860–1899)[154] Goldsmith, 1860 Census. In 1873, with the assistance of **John** and **Joseph Daller**, he formed the Dueber Watch Case Manufacturing Company, which grew to be one of the largest such firms in the United States by the late 19th century.[155] The firm started in Cincinnati in 1873, moved to Newport, Kentucky, in 1876, and then relocated to Canton, Ohio, in 1889.

DUNLEVY & RYLAND (1849–1850) A short-lived partnership of **William D. Dunlevy** and **William T. Ryland**, working as silversmiths on the north side of Sixth Street, 1849/50 CCD.

DUNLEVY, WILLIAM D. (1811–1880, w. 1839–1853)[156] Born in Pennsylvania in 1811, Dunlevy worked intermittently as a silversmith in Cincinnati. He worked for **J. Draper** in 1839, appeared in the 1843, 1846 CCDs as a barkeeper and then worked again as a silversmith from 1849–1853. He was possibly the silversmith recorded in Baltimore from 1858–1860 and in Philadelphia from 1870–1880.[157]

EBERHARDT, WILLIAM (w. 1881–1890) Silversmith, 1883 CCD. Appears as porter or watch case maker in CCDs between 1881–1890.

EHA, PAUL (w. 1850–1852) Silversmith, 1850/51 CCD. Appears in 1851/52 CCD as a watch maker.

EHMEN, JNO A. (w. 1873) Silversmith, 1873 CCD.

EINSTEIN, ALFRED (w. 1873–1877) Silversmith, 1873–1875 CCDs. Appears as foreman in 1877 CCD.

ELIAS, ELLIS H. (about 1838–1881, w. 1861–1863) The son of John and Elizabeth Elias who immigrated to the United States from Wales in 1836, Ellis was born around 1838 in Gallia County, Ohio.[158] The brother of **Henry P. Elias**, he appeared as a jeweler in Cincinnati in the 1860 Federal Census. In the 1861 CCD, Ellis Elias and James Horn were listed as the proprietors of a jewelry store, Horn & Co., although credit reports noted that Ellis Elias was "the real owner of this concern" and that he was a "sharp energetic man" and was making money.[159] By April 1861 Ellis Elias had "sold out and quit" the business.[160] However, he was soon back in the business as the proprietor of a jewelry firm, which advertised in the CCD business listings for "Watchmakers" in 1862 and for "Jewelry, Silver Ware, Watches &c." in 1863. His last appearance in the CCDs was in 1864.[161]

By 1872, Ellis H. Elias was in New York City, as were his brothers Henry P., John, **Richard**, and William M. "Moses."[162] William and Ellis were associated with a retail firm, The Geneva Watch Company, and were listed in New York City Directories from 1878–1881 as the proprietors of a shop selling watches and fancy goods, while Richard worked at a nearby address as a jeweler.[163] In the 1880 Census, Ellis' trade was recorded as "fancy goods."[164] Ellis H. Elias died in New York City on June 22, 1881.[165]

ELIAS, RICHARD H. (1843–1924, w. 1858–1870) The youngest son of Welsh immigrants John and Elizabeth Elias, Richard was born near Gallipolis, Ohio, in December 1843.[166] At the age of 15, he was working as a clerk in Cincinnati at the shop of his oldest brother, **Henry P. Elias**.[167] From 1859 through 1865, he appeared in the CCDs as a clerk, watch maker or jeweler.[168] Another brother, William M. "Moses" Elias, was also working in the H.P. Elias shop as a clerk or watch maker from 1859 through 1864.[169] By 1867, the shop's name was changed to H.P. Elias and Brothers with William M. "Moses" and Richard H. Elias in charge while H.P. Elias was devoting his efforts "exclusively to his new hotel."[170] Credit reports from August 1869 note that Richard had bought out his brothers' interests several months previously and the shop was doing business under the name of R.H. Elias.[171]

The first of a series of advertisements appeared in October 1869 announcing that "Mr. R.H. ELIAS has been advised by his physician to discontinue the Jewelry business that he has been pursuing for so many years on account of its being too confining and injurious to his health."[172] The advertisements also announced a most ingenious scheme to dispose of the merchandise and other assets of the store: 98,000 tickets were offered for sale at $1 each (with a quantity discount) entitling the buyer to a free concert and a chance at one of the prizes consisting of diamonds, watches, jewelry, silverware and store fixtures worth a total of $98,000. Apparently, the sale of tickets did not proceed as expeditiously as expected: the date for the prize drawing, originally slated for November 13, was postponed first to December 21, then to December 25 and finally to January 15. The first published accounts of the lottery winning numbers did not appear until March 1870; the firm was still listed in the 1870 CCD.[173] The 1870 Census, recorded in September 1870, included Richard H. Elias (occupation jeweler) and his family. By 1878, Richard Elias was working as a jeweler in New York City and continued to work there as a jeweler through 1910.[174] He died in Collins Center, New York, in 1924.[175]

Richard Elias married Jennie C. Menagar in Gallia County, Ohio, in October 1867.[176] They had four children: Etta (b. 1869, Ohio), Leon (b. 1873, New York), Lester (b. 1879, New York), and Harry (b. 1882, New York).[177]

ELLIOT, EDMUND G. (w. 1849/50) Silversmith, 1849/50 CCD.

ENGBERSEN, WILLIAM J. (1851–1926, w. 1869–1917)[178] The son of German immigrants Ana Catharina and Henry Engbersen, William was born in Butler County, Ohio. The family had moved to Cincinnati by 1860.[179] Where Engbersen received his training is not known; he was working as a silversmith for **Duhme & Co.** by 1869 and the 1870 Census listed his occupation as "journeyman silversmith."[180] He continued to work as a silversmith, probably for Duhme, through 1894.[181] From 1895–1899, he operated a dry goods store with his wife Mary, at the same address as their residence, while simultaneously being listed as a silversmith in the CCDs.

In 1900, Engbersen formed a partnership with silversmiths **Robert Sturm** and **Kenton Kunkle**. The firm of Engbersen, Sturm & Co., advertised in the "silversmiths" category of the business directory as silver and aluminum workers. Although Kunkle left the firm before the 1902 CCD was published, Engbersen and Sturm continued to operate through 1904, moving to the Lion Building on Elm Street in 1903. By 1905, Sturm also had left the firm but Engbersen continued the business as William Engbersen & Co. until 1915. It is not clear who comprised the "& Co." as only William's name was associated with the firm in the CCD listings. It is probable that Kunkle returned to work with Engbersen as his business address was the same as Engbersen's from 1906–1915.[182] The firm apparently closed in about 1915 as Engbersen is listed in the 1916 CCD as a silversmith working at the northwest corner of

Fourth and Race Streets, the location of **George H. Newstedt**'s jewelry store.[183] Information about the products of the Engbersen firms has not been found nor have wares bearing their mark been documented to date.

Engbersen married Mary Elizabeth Hüllman (1850–1923) in 1872.[184] They were the parents of six children: Mary (b. 1873), Anna (b. 1876), Joseph (b. 1878), Rosa (b. 1880), August (b. 1885), Frieda (b. 1893).[185]

FANNING, PATRICK F. (circa 1834–1875, w. 1850–1875)[186] An immigrant from Ireland, Fanning apprenticed with **Edward Kinsey** in 1850, and worked as a silversmith for the **E. & D. Kinsey** and **David Kinsey** firms until at least 1869.[187] Later documents record his occupation as silversmith, but do not indicate where he was employed.[188]

FEENEY, HARRY (w. 1872) Silversmith, 1872 CCD.

FELTMANN, WILLIAM H. (w. 1839–1861) Listed as a silversmith in the 1842, 1857 CCDs, Feltmann appears in other CCDs between 1839–1861 as a goldsmith, spectacle maker, or jeweler. He worked at the address of Francis Doll, a watch case maker, from 1859–1861.

FILES, AASSER (w. 1839–1846) Goldsmith, 1839/40 CCD. The CCD listing may be a second entry (alternate spelling) for Alexander Falize, a jeweler, who worked for **S.T. Carley** from 1839 to 1846.

FINN, GEORGE W. (w. 1872) Silversmith, 1872 CCD. Appears as plater in 1871, 1873 CCDs.

FISCHER, MARTIN (w. 1874–1879) Silversmith, 1878 CCD. Appears in various CCDs between 1874–1879 as a jeweler or watch case maker working for **Duhme & Co.**

FLETCHER, DAVID E. (1838–1921, w. 1870–1920)[189] The son of Sally and D.W. Fletcher, David was born in Massachusetts, but worked in Cincinnati for over 50 years as a watch maker.[190] For 30 of those years, he worked for Duhme firms, initially at **Duhme & Co.** (1874–1893), followed by **The Duhme Company**. (1894–1897), **The Duhme Jewelry Co.** (1898), and then **Duhme Bros. & Co.** (1899–1903).[191] That he was a valued Duhme employee can be inferred from a notation on the interment record for his father-in-law (David Bleaks) that the remains were delivered courtesy of Duhme & Co.[192] Fletcher opened his own shop in 1904, embellishing his listing in the 1904 CCD with "Watchmaker; over 30 years with Duhme & Co." He continued to work until he was 82 years old, advertising in the 1904–1920 CCD business listings for watches, clocks and jewelry, or retail jewelers. Fletcher married Clara Isabel Bleaks (1850–1932) in 1872. They were the parents of four daughters: Lois Agnes (b. 1874), Luella (b. 1876), Edna Belle (b. 1878), and Clarine (b. 1879).[193]

FURST, SIMON (b. Germany 1805, w. 1850) Furst was not listed in the CCDs but was listed as a silversmith in the 1850 Federal Census for Cincinnati, Hamilton, Ohio.

FURST, SOLOMON (w. 1853–1859) Furst advertised in the 1853–1859 CCDs business listings for "jewelry, silverware, watches, etc." Appears as peddler in 1849–1851 CCDs.

GABLER, CHARLES A.F. (1822–1885, w. 1853–1884)[194] Born in Germany, Gabler was in Cincinnati by 1851, when he married Barbara Diebler.[195] Listed in the CCDs as a silversmith from 1853 to 1884, Gabler worked for **E. & D. Kinsey** until 1862, when he left to work for **Duhme & Co.** Gabler's occupation was given as jeweler in the 1881 and 1882 CCDs.

GALBREATH, ROBERT HARVEY (1843–1915, w. 1861–1905)[196] Galbreath was the son of Nancy and James Galbreath (1809–1858), a successful Cincinnati manufacturer of axes and other tools.[197] He started working as a salesman at **Duhme & Co.** in 1861, but left in 1865 to manage his late father-in-law's photographic supply firm, Peter Smith & Co. Galbreath returned to Duhme & Co. in 1867, where he became a principal or partner in the firm around 1868.[198] He remained with the firm and its successors, **The Duhme Company**, **The Duhme Jewelry Co.**, and **Duhme Brothers & Co.** through 1905, serving in various leadership roles, including partner, president of The Duhme Company, and general manager of The Duhme Jewelry Co. In 1905, Galbreath left Cincinnati for New York City where, it was reported, he had taken a position with Tiffany & Co.[199] He returned to Cincinnati in March 1909 to work as a broker although he was all too soon involved in various activities related to the bankruptcy proceedings for The Duhme Jewelry Co.[200] He returned to New York City after 1910, and died there in 1915.[201]

During his years in Cincinnati, Galbreath was an active participant in various civic endeavors, serving as a trustee of the Cincinnati Museum Association and the Art Academy of Cincinnati. He was a member of the Board of Commissioners for the 1879 Cincinnati Industrial Exposition, and in 1881, president of the Industrial Exposition. He was also a member of the Cincinnati Board of Trade.

Galbreath married Emily J. Smith (1845–1910) in 1864.[202] They were the parents of one child, Nellie (1866–68) who died of bronchitis.[203]

GALLAGHER, MATTHEW (circa 1830–1895, w. 1857–1895)[204] Silversmith, 1858–1861, 1865, 1875 CCDs. Appears in other CCDs between 1857–1895 as silver burnisher. Census records list his occupation as silversmith (1860) or "burnisher silver" (1880). Gallagher worked for **E. & D. Kinsey** and **David Kinsey** from 1857–1869. Although he continued to be listed in the CCDs until 1895, the listings after 1869 only give his home address and do not indicate where he was employed.

GAOB, J. (w. 1869) Silversmith, 1869 CCD.

GARNER, JOHN (d. 1832, w. 1829–1832) In May 1809 Garner was working with Thomas Cain in Knoxville, Kentucky. By October of that year, the partnership had been dissolved "by mutual consent" but Garner continued at the same address as a watch and clock maker and gold and silversmith until April 1811, when he moved to another Knoxville address. In September 1811 Garner announced that he was leaving Knoxville, and by June 1812, was working in Nashville, Tennessee. He worked in Nashville until about 1815, and then moved to Bowling Green, Kentucky, a short distance north of Nashville.[205]

Garner was in Cincinnati by 1829, when he appeared in the 1829 CCD as a silversmith. In the 1831 CCD, his occupation was given as watch maker. A March 1832 entry in **Jacob Deterly**'s diary notes that "(Horace P.) Woodbridge leaves off work at **Shipp & Collins**, watchmaker shop and goes to work at (**Nathan L.**) **Hazen** & Garner's shop."[206] No other documentation of that partnership has been found; it must have been short-lived as Garner died in Cincinnati early in 1832.[207]

Silver wares that can be reliably attributed to John Garner have not been documented. Two "GARNER" (in a rectangular cartouche) marks found on silver flatware are illustrated in Caldwell who attributes them to either John Garner or Griffin Garner (w. Knoxville 1816–1821).[208] A third mark, "I. GARNER" (in a rectangular cartouche) found on a coin silver spoon is more probably the mark of John Garner and possibly dates to Garner's time in Cincinnati.[209] The spoon bears a close resemblance to a spoon marked by Robert Wynne which can be firmly dated to the years 1827–1830, when Wynne was working as a silversmith in Salisbury, NC.[210]

GAYLE, WILLIAM H. (1801–1897, w. 1855–1887)[211] Born in Virginia, Gayle married Louisa Woods in Iowa in 1848.[212] By 1853, they had relocated to Cincinnati where Gayle worked as a bookkeeper and salesman for **Richard Clayton** and **Henry Jenkins**.[213] In 1862, he joined **Duhme & Co.**, where he worked as a clerk and salesman through 1887. His obituary noted that he "was a jeweler by trade and was with Duhme & Co. for 50 years."[214] A reminiscence published in 1923 recalled him as "Pop Gail [*sic*], a famous diamond salesman, who lived to be 95."[215] Gayle's surname was variously spelled as Gale, Gaile, and Gayl in period documents.

GILMORE, ROBERT (w. 1834-1837) Listed as a silversmith in the 1834 CCD, Gilmore's occupation was given as a watch maker in the 1836/37 CCD. He was still in Cincinnati in 1837, when a notice published in a local newspaper offered a reward to the finder of a lost watch if it was left at Gilmore's shop.[216] No later records for Gilmore were found.

GLUSENKAMP, RUDOLPH (w. 1875-76) Silversmith, 1875, 1876 CCDs.

GOETTHEIM, CHARLES F. (1854-1929, w. 1872-1900)[217] The son of German immigrants Maria and Franz Goettheim, Charles was born in Cincinnati in 1854. An apprentice lithographer at the age of 16, he continued to work as a lithographer through 1872.[218] The 1873-1883 CCDs list his occupation as an engraver; he was working at **Duhme & Co.** when the 1881 CCD was published. From 1884-1889, his occupation was listed as designer or engraver (or both) at Duhme. A reminiscence published in 1923 recalled that he was the "chief designer" at Duhme, while a contemporary account called him "a well known [*sic*] engraver, who was for years connected with the Duhme firm and did all their designing."[219]

In 1890, Goettheim joined **A. & J. Plaut** as a salesman and manager of the retail department of the firm which was mainly a wholesale business.[220] He simultaneously continued design work and was granted a design patent for a "new & useful design" for a spoon in 1891.[221] The overall design, envisaged as "emblematic" of the city of Cincinnati, features a statuette of the Roman general Cincinnatus as the finial, a circular medallion with the official seal of the city of Cincinnati on the handle, and in the bowl, a chased image of the Tyler Davidson Fountain that had been a Cincinnati landmark since 1871. The spoon, manufactured by the Gorham Mfg. Co., carries the A. & J. Plaut retailer's mark on the reverse of the bowl.[222]

In 1895, Goettheim and Isaac Plaut left A. & J. Plaut and opened a retail jewelry, silverware, and fancy goods store on Race Street. They advertised in the CCD business listings for "Silver Ware," "Watches, Clocks & Jewelry," and "Fancy Goods (Retail)" from 1895-1897. Unfortunately, they started the business at the beginning of an economic depression and it failed in 1897.[223]

Goettheim returned to working for a Duhme firm, **The Duhme Jewelry Co.**, in 1898 and 1899, but left the silver and jewelry trades in 1900 to work as a salesman for the investment firm, Feder Holzman & Co. From 1906 through 1928, he continued working as an investment banker and securities broker with his own firm, Charles F. Goettheim & Co.[224]

GORDON, JONATHAN B. (1802-1874, w. 1824-1831)[225] Born in New Jersey in 1802, Gordon was living in Cincinnati by 1824 when he married Jane Haisher.[226] He advertised as a "Silversmith and Jeweller [*sic*]" in 1824, and was listed as a silversmith in the 1825 and 1831 CCDs.[227] After 1831, the CCDs list a variety of other occupations for Gordon, including laborer, engine finisher, news carrier, and railroad agent.[228]

Jonathan and Jane Gordon (1806-1879) were the parents of seven children for whom records were found: William L. (1825-1854), Ann Eliza (1834-1914), Margaret C. (1836-1916), Alice Gordon Jackson (1838-1910), Caroline Gordon Kohl (1831-1924), Henry (1844-1930), and Charles A. (1850-1924).[229]

GRAH, GEORGE (w. 1869-1873) Silversmith, 1872 CCD. Appears in various CCDs between 1869-1873 as jeweler.

GRAVES, THOMAS (w. 1829) Silversmith, 1829 CCD. No later records for Graves have been found. It seems unlikely that he was the Thomas H. Graves, a real estate and money broker in Cincinnati in the 1850s, who hailed from Kentucky.[230]

GRAY, WM. (w. 1853) Silversmith, 1853 CCD.

GRUB, JACOB (w. 1871-1874) Silversmith, 1874 CCD. Appears in 1871-1873 CCDs as show case maker.

GSCHWIND, ANTON (w. 1866-1879) Silversmith, 1868 CCD. Appears in various CCDs between 1866-1879 as porter, laborer, or silverware finisher. He worked at **Duhme & Co.** in 1879.

HAFFNER, FERDINAND (w. 1857-1868) Silversmith or goldsmith, 1857-1868 CCDs.

HAGEMAN, EDWARD (w. 1850/51) Silversmith, 1850/51 CCD.

HAGEMANN, JOHN (w. 1867-1900) Goldsmith, jeweler, and enameler, 1867-1884 CCDs, working for **Duhme & Co.** In 1885, he opened a retail jewelry store on Main Street, advertising in the 1885-1900 CCD business listings for "Jewelry, Silver Ware, Watches &c."

HAHN, A. (w. 1870–74) Silversmith, 1870 CCD. Appears as finisher, polisher or jeweler in 1871–1874 CCDs.

HAHN, HENRY (1848–1914, w. 1872–1904) Born in Germany in 1848, Hahn immigrated to the United States in 1866, and was in Cincinnati by 1870, working in a notion store.[231] He appeared in the 1872 CCD as a silversmith. By 1876, Hahn was working as a wholesale jeweler on the second floor of the Carlisle Building, which was the location of a large number of jewelers including **Duhme & Co.**[232] Beginning in 1878, Hahn advertised in the CCD business listings as a wholesale dealer in watches and jewelry. He relocated to the Wiggins Block at the southeast corner of Fifth and Vine in 1881, and by 1884, had changed the firm's name to Henry Hahn & Company (1884–1904).[233] The firm was a wholesale jobber that dealt in jewelry, watches, clocks, and silverware, advertising in the CCD business listings for silverware as well as for "watches, jewelry &c (importers, manufacturers and wholesale dealers in)."[234] The advertisements in the "Silver Ware" listings were dropped after 1896. Hahn's nephew Julius Hahn joined the firm as a traveling salesman around 1890. When Henry Hahn retired in May 1904 Julius Hahn and Isidor Oppenheimer took over the firm, changing the name to Hahn & Oppenheimer.[235] Henry Hahn died in September 1914 in Cincinnati.[236]

HANCKING, HENRY (w. 1857) Silversmith, 1857 CCD.

HANKINS, H. (w. 1864) Silversmith, 1864 CCD, working at **David Kinsey**'s shop.

HARRIS, CALEB K. (b. about 1816, w. 1839–1853)[237] Silversmith, 1839/40–1853 CCDs. In 1839, he was working at **Edward Kinsey**'s and in 1846 was boarding with **David Kinsey**, an indication that he was working at the Kinsey firms during those years. The 1839/40 CCD gives his nativity as "UC" (Upper Canada) while the 1850 Census lists it as New York.[238] In November 1846 Harris married Mary Ann Davis, a native of England.[239]

HARRIS, JAMES (w. 1856) Silversmith, 1856 CCD. Appears in 1857–1867 CCDs as finisher or machinist.

HARRIS, WILLIAM (w. 1839/40) A native of England, Harris was listed in the 1839/40 CCD as a silversmith and watch maker. In June 1839 he advertised "a good assortment of jewelry" and "Watch Cases and Jewelry of every description made to order or repaired" in a local newspaper.[240] No later records of him were found.

HARRIS, WILLIAM (b. circa 1823, w. 1849/50) Born in New York, William was recorded as a silversmith living with **Caleb K. Harris** in the 1850 Federal Census; his occupation was listed as finisher in the 1849/50 CCD. He would have been too young to have advertised his own business in 1839, and no evidence was found for a link between him and the earlier **William Harris** or between him and other men in the trade with the same name: a jewelry peddler in Louisville, an apprentice silversmith in Maryland, or a watch maker in New York City in 1830.[241]

HARVIGOTTE, HENRY (w. 1857) Silversmith, 1857 CCD.

HATCH, SAMUEL (1824–1894, w. 1853–1874) The earliest Cincinnati record for Samuel Hatch is the 1853 CCD, in which he is listed as a clerk at 124 Main, an address that could not be associated with any silver or jewelry firm in the city.[242] In the 1855–1861 CCDs, Hatch is listed as a clerk, jeweler or salesman at **Duhme & Co.** Although he was included as one of the principals of Duhme & Co. in the 1857 and 1858 CCDs, credit reports in January 1857 noted that the **L.P. Muller**, Samuel Hatch and **Albert Pratt** who "appear in the firm are not partners, having only an interest for services in lieu of salary."[243] A reminiscence published in 1923 recalled only that Hatch was one of the early associates in the jewelry business with Herman Duhme.[244] Hatch left Duhme & Co. when the Civil War broke out and obtained a "sutlership" for an Ohio regiment.[245] Hatch had returned to Cincinnati by October 1862, and established a partnership with Henry Jenkins, **Jenkins & Hatch**, that advertised as "Importers & Wholesale Dealers in Watches, Jewelry & Manufacturers of Silver Ware" and was located on the second floor of the Carlisle Building, upstairs from Duhme & Co.[246] The last Cincinnati record for Samuel Hatch was 1874 when he was still listed as a principal in the Jenkins & Hatch firm and resided on West Seventh Street. In the 1880 Federal Census, Hatch was a patient in the Massachusetts General Hospital in Boston; his "sickness or disability" was "paralysis."[247]

Samuel Hatch was born in Scituate, Plymouth County, Massachusetts, in 1824, the son of Mercy Turner and Samuel Hatch.[248] The 1850 Census lists him as a farmer in Scituate; subsequent censuses record his occupation as merchant or jeweler. In January 1848 Hatch married Cornelia M. Rodgers (b. 1825) in Scituate, Massachusetts.[249] They had four children for whom records were found: Josiah (b. 1848, NY), Willard R. (b. 1849, MA), Emily (b. 1856, OH), and Frank (b. 1869, OH).[250] Samuel Hatch died in May 1894 in Scituate; the cause of death, "locomotor ataxia for 10 years," provides confirmation of the 1880 census record.[251]

HAVEN, N.L. (w. 1834) Silversmith, 1834 CCD.

HAVERKOTTE, H. (w. 1858) Silversmith, 1858 CCD, working for **E. & D. Kinsey**.

HAWEKOTTE, GEORGE F. (w. 1859) Silversmith, 1859 CCD. Appears in CCDs between 1861–1872 as finisher, machinist or engineer.

HAWEKOTTE, HENRY JR. (w. 1857-9) Silversmith, 1857, 1859 CCDs. Worked at **E. & D. Kinsey**.

HAWEKOTTE, HENRY L. (w. 1853–1864) Silversmith, 1853, 1857-61, 1864 CCDs.

HAYNES, JOHN R. (w. 1848–1859) Haynes appeared in the 1848–1859 directories as a watch maker and jeweler.[252] In 1850, he advertised as a "Dealer in Watches, Clocks, Jewelry, etc.," adding "watches, clocks, &c. repaired."[253] His advertisements in local newspapers also included "silver ware" as well as watches, jewelry and fancy goods.[254] In 1851, Cist reported that Haynes "manufactures to order all kinds of jewelry and silver ware" and that the value of his product during the past year was $5,000.[255] Given the emphasis on silverware in period sources, it is remarkable that Haynes' mark has not been found to date on any silver.

In 1853, credit reports noted that Haynes was "hon(est) indust(rious) & stands fair" with a moderate business. However, by 1856, his business was a "small concern, quite weak" and by 1857, he was "hard pressed." In 1859, the business closed.[256] Haynes did not appear in any subsequent CCDs.

Beckman reports that Haynes was included in the "1850 Cincinnati Census," born around 1825 in New York and was married to Mary, born around 1826 in Pennsylvania.[257] This information could not be verified through local or online genealogy records

HAZEL, HENRY (w. 1863) Silversmith, 1863 CCD.

HEINZE, OSCAR A. (1852–1908, w. 1869–1908)[258] Silversmith, 1870-73 CCDs. Heinze appears as a silver chaser, engraver, mold maker, or jeweler from 1875–1908. He worked at **Duhme & Co.** in 1869. In other years, the CCD listings do not indicate a work address. The 1900 Census lists his occupation as "saloon keeper," which corresponds to the 1898, 1900, and 1901 CCD listings. However, since he was also listed as an engraver or mold maker in the CCDs between 1899 and 1909, he was probably operating a saloon as a supplementary source of income.

HELFRICH, ALBERT (w. 1874–1882) Silversmith, 1877 CCD. Appears in 1874-1882 CCDs as a gilder.

HENNKENS, HENRY (1833–1901, w. 1857–1894)[259] Silversmith or silver burnisher, 1857–1894 CCDs. Worked as a silversmith or burnisher for **E. & D. Kinsey** from 1857–1860, and as a burnisher at the address of **Jenkins & Hatch** in 1872. In other years, the CCD listings do not indicate a work address. His surname was also rendered as Henkin, Hankins, Henneken, Hennekens, Hennekins, Hennikins, Hennegan, or Henneckens in period documents. Born in Germany, Hennkens married Dorothea Lanfersick (1836–1923), also of Germany, in May 1857.[260] They had four children: George (b. 1858), Ella (b. 1860), William (b. 1863), and Charles (b. 1865).[261] Henry Hennkens died of typhoid fever early in 1901.

HENOCHSBERG, JOS. A. (about 1848–1921, w. 1867–1919)[262] Henochsberg worked as a silversmith, finisher, or polisher from 1867 to 1879. In 1875, he worked at **Duhme & Co.**; other 1867-1879 CCD listings give only his home and not work addresses. From 1880 to 1919, Henochsberg worked for various wholesale jewelry and watch firms, including **A.G. Schwab & Brother**, the Eclipse Jewelry Co., and Fox Brothers & Co. Henochsberg died in Cincinnati on February 23, 1921. His surname was also rendered as Hanochsburg, Honochsburg, Henocksberg, or Henuchsberg in period documents.

HENRICHSON, HERMAN (w. 1872–1880) Silversmith, 1877 CCD. Appears in various CCDs between 1872–1880 as watch case maker or jeweler.

KECK, HERMAN SR. (1832–1892, w. 1856–1892) and **THE HERMAN KECK MANUFACTURING CO.** (1887–1909)[263] Herman Keck, Sr. was in Cincinnati by 1856, working and advertising as a manufacturing jeweler.[264] In 1868, Keck and **Edmund Deppermann** entered into a partnership, H. Keck and Co., as manufacturing jewelers and diamond setters. When the partnership was dissolved in 1883, Keck continued the business alone at 175 Vine, which was also the address of the **Clemens Oskamp** firm.[265] Keck's oldest son, Herman Jr. joined the firm in 1884 as a jeweler, and another son, Oscar started working as the bookkeeper in 1886.[266] The name of the firm was changed to The Herman Keck Manufacturing Co. in 1887, with Herman Sr. as president and Herman Jr. promoted to the position of treasurer. By 1891, Oscar Keck had also become an officer (secretary) of the firm.

After the death of Herman Sr. in 1892, Herman Jr. became president and Oscar became secretary-treasurer.[267] They soon embarked upon ambitious expansion plans. In early 1895, they formed a partnership with a Belgian diamond merchant to start Coetermans, Henrichs & Keck Diamond Cutting Co. in Cincinnati.[268] The venture was not without problems. The U.S. Treasury Department filed suit in 1895, alleging Herman Keck had imported diamond cutters in violation of the Alien Contract Labor Law, and in 1896, he was indicted on a charge of smuggling diamonds.[269] After lengthy court proceedings, he was acquitted in both cases.[270] Although the diamond-cutting firm was not listed as a separate entity in the CCDs after 1899, the plant operations continued under the banner of **The Duhme Jewelry Co.** at least through 1903.[271]

In May 1897 the Kecks again expanded their operations by forming a new firm, The Duhme Jewelry Co., with members of the Duhme family.[272] Another joint venture between the Duhmes and Kecks, the **Duhme Manufacturing Co.**, followed in January 1898.[273] This venture also ran into difficulties. Dissension between the Duhme brothers and the Keck brothers led to the ousting of the Duhmes from the management of the store in May 1898.[274] By July, the Herman Keck Manufacturing Co. was consolidating the plant operations for both firms in the Carlisle Building, which had been occupied by Duhme firms since 1859.[275] Ensuing labor unrest over shop rules led to a strike by about 50 engravers, silversmiths, and polishers of the "H. Keck Jewelry Co." in October 1899.[276]

In late 1900, The Duhme Jewelry Co., now considered to be the "retail branch" of the Herman Keck Manufacturing firm, moved to new and "palatial" quarters on West Fourth Street and for the next few years, both firms seemed to prosper.[277] After the premature death of Herman Keck in December 1906 Oscar Keck assumed control of the firms, serving as both president and treasurer of the Herman Keck Manufacturing Co. and The Duhme Jewelry Co.

The economic turmoil that began in October 1907, known as "The Panic of 1907," led to financial distress across the country and the failure of even large manufacturing firms. Oscar Keck requested an extension of time from creditors in early 1908 and, unable to meet the payment due dates, requested an additional extension in October 1908. The major creditors agreed to an extension, with the proviso that if the creditor's committee investigating the affairs of the two companies found no improvements in the business, they could declare all debts payable immediately.[278] Keck attempted to stave off bankruptcy by holding an auction of stock from The Duhme Jewelry Co. to raise the needed funds, announcing that the business would reopen at the end of the sale.[279]

Since the sale proceeds were insufficient, large creditors of the Herman Keck Manufacturing Company filed involuntary bankruptcy proceedings in the U.S. Federal District Court in February 1909, charging that the president (Oscar Keck) of both companies was "wholly incompetent and unfit to control the company." The receivership was later extended to include The Duhme Jewelry Co. as the firms were too "interwoven" to be handled separately.[280] The court battles raged for more than a year. Clara Keck, the widow of Herman, also filed suit alleging fraud by Oscar Keck.[281] Oscar filed suit against the receiver, claiming he was selling articles at low prices that "would prove ruinous to the creditors," and creditors of The Duhme Jewelry Co. claimed priority over the creditors of the manufacturing company, stating they were separate and distinct corporations.[282] The court's decision, issued in May 1910, was that the assets of The Duhme Jewelry Co. could be applied to the debts of the manufacturing company as they were "in reality one concern" and the debts of one were therefore the debts of the other.[283] In the end, although The Duhme Jewelry Co. assets were more than sufficient to cover its debts, it was a casualty of the problems of the manufacturing company, and both firms ceased to exist.

Born in Germany, Herman Keck, Sr. married another German immigrant, Mary Epp (1840–1889) in 1859.[284] They were the parents of six children: Emma (1860–1943), Amanda (1863–1949), Herman Jr. (1865–1906), Oscar (1867–1928), Edward (1870–1901), and Willie (1875–1879).[285] In 1893, Herman Keck, Jr. married Clara Graser, the bookkeeper for the Herman Keck Manufacturing Co. They had one child, Herman (1898–1960).[286] Oscar Keck married Ursula Ann Moore in 1907. No records were found of children born to them.[287]

HILGEFORT, HENRY (w. 1850–1853) Silversmith, 1853 CCD. Appears in various CCDs between 1850–1859 as jeweler, salesman, or porter.

HOEFER, HENRY JR. (w. 1878–1880) Silversmith, 1879–1880 CCDs. Appears in various CCDs between 1878–1886 as watch case maker, or varnisher.

HOESE, CHARLES (w. 1879–1894) Silversmith, 1882 CCD. Appears in various CCDs between 1877–1895 as a clerk, jeweler watch maker, or watch case maker. In 1882, Hoese worked for **Duhme & Co.**; in other years, CCD listings give only his home and not work addresses.

HOESE, JACOB JR. (w. 1873–1878) Silversmith, 1873–1878 CCDs. Appears as a jeweler in 1877 CCD.

HOFFMANN, LOUIS (w. 1874–1879) Silversmith, 1874, 1879 CCDs. Appears as a show case maker in CCDs between 1873–1883.

HOFMANN, EDMUND (w. 1889–1893) Silversmith, 1890 CCD. Appears in various CCDs between 1889–1893 as goldsmith or engraver.

HOOKER, EVELYN R. (1881-1961, w. 1912)[288] The 1900 Census gives her occupation as "at school," and indicates that she is in Massachusetts, probably at Smith College. She had returned to Cincinnati by 1912, and was listed in the American Art Directory that year with "silverware" listed as her medium. She was listed in the 1917 American Art Directory as a painter.[289] Subsequent federal census records give her occupation as "none."[290]

HUMMEL, LOUIS F.E. (1858-1944, w. 1875-1941)[291] The son of German immigrants John and Elizabeth Hummel, Louis was born in Cincinnati. He first appeared in the 1875-1880 CCDs as a clerk at the jewelry firm **Jandorf & Mayer**, and then was a traveling salesman (1882-1884) for the manufacturing jeweler Noterman & Jonas.[292] In 1885, Hummel opened a shop in the Emery Arcade, selling a wide variety of jewelry and fancy goods, including "silverware of every description."[293] He advertised in the CCD business listings under "Watches, Clocks & Jewelry" from 1886-1896, as a "Dealer in Diamonds, Watches, & Jewelry" from 1888-1893, and as a "Dealer in Diamonds, Watches, Jewelry, Marble Clocks & Silverware" from 1894-1896.

The poor economy of the 1890s took its toll on 87 Cincinnati firms including that of Hummel.[294] His financial problems were first reported in September 1896, but by February 1897, he had made arrangements with his creditors and the firm was able to continue with the name changed to "Hummel's Jewelry Store."[295] From 1897-1905, Hummel's wife, Annie was listed as the proprietor and Louis as the manager of the jewelry store in the CCDs; the *Jewelers' Circular and Horological Review* referred to it as "Mrs. A.E. Hummel's store" in March 1905.[296] Louis regained the title of proprietor in 1906. When the Emery Arcade was demolished to make way for the construction of the Carew Tower Complex in 1929, Hummel moved his store to 435 Walnut, and in 1935, moved a final time to the southeast corner of Vine and Fourth. After Hummel's death, the firm continued with his son, Louis J. Hummel, as president until it closed in 1952.[297]

Hummel married Anne E. Scahill (1863-1941) in January 1884.[298] They were the parents of two children, Louis (b. 1899), and Anna (b. 1904).[299]

IRVING, JOHN (w. 1886-1892) Silversmith, 1886-1892 CCDs.

JENKINS & HATCH (1862-1874) In October 1862 Dun reported that **Henry Jenkins** and **Samuel Hatch**, both of whom had worked at various firms in the silver and jewelry trade in Cincinnati for many years, had entered into a partnership as wholesale dealers, Jenkins & Hatch.[300] The firm was located on the second floor of the Carlisle Building, above **Duhme & Co.** Jenkins & Hatch was first listed in the 1863 CCD, advertising as "Importers & Wholesale Dealers in Watches, Jewelry and Manufacturers of Silver Ware." In 1864 and subsequent years, the CCD descriptions included only "watches, jewelry, etc." but advertisements in the CCD business listings and local newspapers through 1871 clearly indicated that they were wholesale dealers of "solid" silver and silver-plated ware as well as of watches and jewelry.[301] Although the addresses in the CCDs for the firm varied (51 West Fourth, southwest corner of Walnut and Fourth, or Carlisle Building), these were alternative descriptions of the location of the Carlisle Building. Advertisements in local newspapers from 1868-1873 invariably gave the location of the firm as "Room No. 3 Carlisle Building."

Credit reports for the firm from 1864 through March 1870 were favorable—"doing a very fair business which is well managed and profitable" was a typical comment. Financial problems surfaced shortly thereafter, and in October 1870 the reports indicated that they were asking for extensions in payment to their creditors.[302] The October 1871 reports noted that the company "has been weakened much" although the business continued through 1873.[303] The report for July 1873 stated that "There will probably be a dissolution as J. wants to withdraw at the same time," and it was noted in October that the firm would "be closed out at an Assignees sale."[304]

The assignee was Alexander Starbuck, who had been associated with Jenkins & Hatch at the time of its 1871 financial problems.[305] Starbuck started wrapping up the business and selling the assets in July 1873.[306] Advertisements in the Cincinnati newspapers for the sales started with notices of "GREAT BARGAINS!" in September 1873, progressed to "HOLIDAY GOODS AT PANIC PRICES!" in December 1873, and finally ended in June 1874 with published notices for the auction of the remaining stock and fixtures of Jenkins & Hatch.[307]

JENKINS, HENRY (1820-1877, w. 1842-1874)[308] Born in Ireland, the son of William and Catherine Jenkins, Jenkins was working as a watch maker in Cincinnati in 1842, boarding at "Misses Jenkins."[309] He was not listed again until the 1850/51 CCD when he was listed as a jeweler. Credit reports in 1856 indicate that at that time he had been working with his brother-in-law **Richard Clayton** for eight or nine years. Around 1853, Richard Clayton transferred all interest in the jewelry department of his firm to Jenkins, while retaining the clock and watch trade that was located on the second floor of his shop. Although Jenkins focused on the jewelry trade, he was also the overall manager of Clayton's business.[310] By December of 1858 Jenkins and his partners **John B. Morris** and G.B. Harting, had bought out Clayton and were conducting the business under the name of H. Jenkins & Co. Jenkins was apparently the majority partner as he was entitled to half of the profits while Morris and Harting each would receive one quarter.[311] H. Jenkins & Co. advertised in the 1860 and 1861 CCD business listings under "Jewelry, Silverware and Watches, etc.," "Watch Makers," and "Watch Cases, Materials and Tools."

Silver teaspoons with a fiddle handle and rounded shoulders marked "H. Jenkins" in a rectangular cartouche with rounded corners or with serrated edges are known.[312] Since the form of these teaspoons is comparable to those manufactured at an earlier date, they were probably made by Harman Jenkins, who worked in Albany, NY from 1817–1823.[313]

In March 1861 Jenkins sold his interest in the firm to John B. Morris and George B. Harting, and the firm's name was changed to Morris & Harting.[314] Henry Jenkins briefly worked as a clerk for **Duhme & Co.** but by October 1862 he had formed a partnership with **Samuel Hatch** (**Jenkins & Hatch**), wholesale dealers in "watches, jewelry, etc."

Jenkins married Mary L. Butterfield (1825–1921) around 1849.[315] They lived in Cincinnati until 1855 and then moved to Ludlow, Kentucky, living next door to Richard Clayton.[316] Mary and Henry were the parents of seven children: Clara (b. 1849), William (1852–1884), Lizzie (1854–1875), Harry (Henry) (1857–1919), Louis (1859–1909), Mary P. (1861–1865), and Carlisle (1868–1936).[317] After Henry died of malarial fever in 1877, Mary continued to live in Kenton County, Kentucky until her own death in 1921.

JOHN, JOHN WESLEY (1840–1922, w. 1869–1915)[318] Silversmith, 1869–1870 CCDs and 1870 Federal Census. Appears in other CCDs as a watch maker, jeweler, or manager for John B. Bobe's jewelry store from 1874–1898 and as a watch maker at **Richter & Phillips** from 1901–1912. The 1910 Census lists his occupation as manufacturing jeweler. The son of Eleanor and Samuel John, John Wesley John married Mary L. Carman (1843–1925) on July 8, 1871.[319]

JOHNSON, JOSEPH (w. 1874) Silversmith, 1874 CCD.

JOHNSON, THOMAS (w. 1875) Silversmith, 1875 CCD, working at the address of **Clemens Oskamp**'s factory at Culvert and Harrison.

JOHNSON, WILLIAM M. (w. 1836–1840) A silversmith from Virginia, Johnson was listed in the 1836/37 and 1839/40 CCDs. He also appeared as a painter and glazier in the 1842–43 CCDs.[320] Johnson was the only silversmith identified as African-American in this study.[321] No other information about his work or life was found.

JOHNSTON, THOMAS (w. 1839/40) Silversmith, 1839/40 CCD, working at **E. Kinsey**'s.

JONAS, JOSEPH (1792–1869, w. 1817–1867) Born in England in 1792, Jonas arrived in New York in 1816 with the goal of settling in Cincinnati.[322] After a short stay in New York, he went to Philadelphia, and there completed his plans to continue on to Cincinnati, ignoring the admonishments of friends who tried to dissuade him from going to a place so far removed from civilization. Leaving Philadelphia on January 2, 1817, he arrived in Cincinnati in March 1817 and by May of that year was in a partnership with **Alexander McGrew** on Main Street, that advertised as "Clock and Watch Makers and Silversmiths and Jewellers [sic]."[323] In 1819, the partnership was dissolved "by mutual consent" and Jonas opened his own shop as a "Watch-Maker, Silversmith, & Jeweller [sic]."[324] In 1823, he returned to Philadelphia, where he married Rachel Seixas (1801–1827) on December 10.[325] They had returned to Cincinnati by March 1824, when he advertised that he had "again entered into business as a 'Watchmaker, Silversmith and Jeweller [sic]'" at 117 Main Street.[326]

Although he trained as a watch maker, Jonas always advertised as both a silversmith and watch maker, noting in 1819 that he "manufactures and keeps on hand SILVER-WARE, of all descriptions." To date, silverware marked by Jonas has not been documented. A clock signed "Jos. Jonas. Cincinnati." on the face is the only tangible record of his work found to date.[327]

Jonas returned to England in 1838, and while there married Martha Oppenheim (circa 1803–1867), returning to New York in May 1839.[328] By 1841, he had returned to Cincinnati and was engaged as a stock and exchange broker, undoubtedly an expansion of the "Exchange Office" referred to in his 1824 advertisement.[329] Census records for 1850 and 1860 report his occupation as "retired merchant."[330]

Published reports concerning Jonas' activities after he returned from London focus not on his commercial activities but on his involvement in civic affairs and the Jewish community. Jonas, called the "father of Democracy in this city," was an ardent supporter of the Democratic Party and, especially, General Andrew Jackson's campaign for the presidency in 1828.[331] From 1860 to 1862, Jonas served as a representative of Hamilton County in the Ohio House of Representatives.[332] His most enduring contributions, however, were to the establishment and development of a worship community for the Jewish inhabitants of Cincinnati. Jonas has been widely credited as the key person in organizing the first Jewish services in 1819, the first Jewish cemetery in 1821, the first congregation in 1824, the first synagogue in 1836, and in the formation of early religious schools and a benevolent association in Cincinnati.[333] He also served as an officer of the congregation on multiple occasions, and at his death, the congregation noted that he was "the founder of our holy congregation, the pioneer of Judaism in the west, and the truly conscientious, pious Jew."[334]

Jonas and his second wife, Martha, were the parents of four children: Annie (b. 1839), Rosette (b. 1841), Michael (b. 1844), and Sarah (b. 1846).[335] After Martha's death in 1867, Joseph Jonas left Cincinnati to live with his daughter, Annie Moses, in Mobile, Alabama and died there in May 1869.[336]

JONAS, JOSEPH (1844–1894, w. 1864–1894)[337] The son of Annie and Peter Jonas, an organ builder, Jonas was born in Germany in 1844, and came to the United States with his parents in 1849.[338] He worked as a jeweler or watch maker in Cincinnati from 1864 to 1868, becoming one of the principals in Stinger, Noterman & Co. diamond setters, in 1869.[339] After **George A. Stinger** left the firm, Jonas and Joseph Noterman continued as Noterman & Jonas manufacturing jewelers.[340] The partnership was dissolved around 1888, and Joseph Jonas formed another jewelry manufacturing firm, Jonas, Dorst & Co., with Jacob Dorst, who had been a traveling salesman for **Duhme & Co.**[341] After Jonas' death in October 1894, the firm continued through 1897 with his widow, Pauline and Jacob Dorst as the principals of the firm.[342]

KAUFMAN, BENJAMIN (w. 1861–1864) Silversmith, 1864 CCD. Appears in 1861 CCD as jeweler.

KELLY, CHARLES (1821–1890, w. 1842–1889)[343] Born in Ireland, Kelly was in Cincinnati by 1842, when he was listed as a silversmith in the CCD. From 1843 to 1889, the CCD listings give his occupation as spectacle maker or manufacturer in most years, although he is intermittently listed as a silversmith. In the 1860 CCD, his occupation was listed as "manufacturer of jewelry" although he advertised in the business listings for spectacles. From 1860 to 1889, Kelly advertised in the CCD business listings for spectacle manufacturing or spectacle frame maker. It is curious that spectacles marked by Kelly have not been identified to date, since spectacles marked by **John Owen** and **Joseph Draper**, who also worked in Cincinnati as spectacle makers and silversmiths, are known.[344]

In 1843, Kelly married Lydia Bloomfield.[345] They were the parents of five children for whom records were found: Helen (b. 1846), Andrew (b. 1849), Charles (b. 1851), Beverly (b. 1852), and Ella (b. 1855).[346]

KENK, FRED. (w. 1860) Silversmith, 1860 CCD.

KENNEY, EDWARD (w. 1844) Kenney appears in the 1844 CCD, advertising in the business listings under "Watchmakers and Silversmiths" with the same address as **Edward Kinsey**. Since Kenney does not appear in the alphabetical listings of the directory, it is probable that this entry is an erroneous spelling for Edward Kinsey.

KENT, HERBERT TOWNSEND (1856–1918, w. 1874–1905)[347] The son of Adeline and **Luke Kent, Jr.** and the third generation of his family in the trade, Kent started working as a clerk in his father's shop when he was eighteen.[348] Five years later the business was struggling, in part due to its location but also because Luke Kent had borrowed money to buy out his partner of many years, **William Michie, Jr.** On July 31, 1879, Luke Kent published a notice that he had sold all his stock and fixtures to Herbert Kent.[349] In early 1880, Herbert relocated the shop to an "elegant three-story brick building" on West Fifth Street, a more prominent location on Fountain Square.[350] The new location and frequent advertisements touting "Solid Silver and Silver Plated Ware of all kinds" as well as gold and silver watches and jewelry, seemed to resuscitate the business and it prospered through that decade.[351] Troubles were again evident in 1891; business was slow, as were collections and in August 1891 Herbert Kent "made an assignment" (i.e. filed for bankruptcy), listing liabilities of about $6,500 and assets of $4,000.[352] *The Jewelers' Circular and Horological Review* noted that the goods would be sold at auction, adding "The sympathy of the local trade are with him as he was popular with everybody."[353] For the next 14 years, Kent was associated with the various **Duhme** firms and then entered the real-estate business.[354]

Herbert Kent married Mary H. Suyden (1856–1894) in 1891.[355] They were the parents of two children: Dorothy (b. 1892) and a stillborn infant (b. 1894).[356] In 1899, five years after Mary's death, Kent married Alice M. Babbitt (1856–1928).[357] Kent died of pneumonia in Cincinnati in March 1918.

KENT, THOMAS (1815–1880, w. 1836–1846)[358] The son of Elizabeth and **Luke Kent, Sr.**, Thomas worked as a watch maker and jeweler in Cincinnati until 1846. He was working as a silversmith or jeweler in Nashville, Tennessee, in 1850.[359] By 1864, Kent had relocated to Virginia City, Nevada, and worked there as a watch maker and jeweler until at least 1870.[360] By 1880, he was in San Francisco, California, where he died of liver cancer early in 1880.[361] Kent had married Matilda Armitage, a native of Ireland, in 1836.[362]

KING, FRED. (w. 1858, 1860) Silversmith, 1858, 1860 CCDs, working at the address of **E. & D. Kinsey**.

KINNEY, JOHN (w. 1868–1875) Silversmith, 1873 CCD. Appears in various CCDs between 1868–1875 as a silver plater.

KINSEY, CHARLES STANLEY (1843-1897, w. 1865)[363] The oldest son of Julia and **David Kinsey**, Charles worked in his father's shop as a silversmith for only one year after returning from service in the Union Army during the Civil War. He subsequently worked as a surveyor or civil engineer in the Cincinnati area before moving to California where, in 1888, his youngest daughter was born and he registered to vote. Admitted to the U.S. National Home for Disabled Volunteer Soldiers in Sawtelle, California, in 1895, Charles died there of acute myelitis in 1897.[364]

Charles married Myra E. Gilbert (b. 1850) in 1868.[365] They were the parents of five children: Raphael (b. 1869), George (b. 1871), Bessie (b. 1874), Gilbert (b. 1881), and Eugenia V. (b. 1888).[366]

KINSEY, EDWARD WILLIAM (1851-1913, w. 1870-1875)[367] The son of Julia and **David Kinsey**, Edward began working as a clerk in his father's firm at the age of 19. At the time of his father's death in March 1874, he was the firm's bookkeeper and then served as the manager until early 1875, when he sold his interest in the firm to his brother, **Louis A. Kinsey** and **John Callahan**.[368] He remained in Cincinnati, where he operated a livery stable and worked for the U.S. Post Office, until about 1886. Edward was living in the Los Angeles, California, area by 1890 and he was joined there by the rest of his family before 1896.[369]

Edward married Esther A. Badley (b. 1853) in 1873. They were the parents of three sons: David (b. 1874), Edward P. (b. 1876), and William E. (b. 1877).[370]

KINSEY, THOMAS (1773-1865, w. 1850-1865)[371] A silversmith trained in Wales, Thomas was the father of **David** and **Edward Kinsey**. The family was in the Cincinnati area by 1834, when he was included on the tax lists for Campbell County, Kentucky. That same year, his son Edward Kinsey was listed as a silversmith in the Newport section of the Cincinnati city directory.[372] Census records list his occupation as a silversmith and jeweler.[373]

KINSLEY, JOHN R. (w. 1857-1867) Silversmith, 1860 CCD. Appears in various CCDs between 1857-1867 as a silver plater.

KLEINE, LOUIS (w. 1875-1877) Silversmith, 1876, 1877 CCDs, working for **Duhme & Co.** Appears as watch maker in 1875 CCD.

KOENING, FRED. (w. 1858) Silversmith, 1858 CCD.

KOHMAN, J.H. (w. 1866) Silversmith, 1866 CCD, working at address of **David Kinsey**.

KOPS, FRED. (w. 1870-1877) Silversmith, 1870-77 CCDs.

Appears in the 1875 CCD as jeweler. His surname was also rendered as Kaps, Kopps, or Kopf in the CCDs.

KORMORN, FRED. (w. 1857) Silver finisher, 1857 CCD working at the address of **E. & D. Kinsey**.

KRAMER, FRANK T. (w. 1882-1893) Per the 1882 CCD, Kramer was working as a clerk at **Duhme & Co.** From 1886 to 1893, CCDs list his occupation as silversmith or goldsmith. A foreman in Duhme's flatware manufacturing department in 1892, Kramer probably replaced **Justus Kruckemeyer**.[374]

KROGMANN, GEORGE (b. circa 1863, w. 1878-1882)[375] Silversmith, 1878, 1880, 1882 CCDs. Occupation given as apprentice silversmith in the 1880 Federal Census.

KRUCKEMEYER, JUSTUS (1841-1889, w. 1862-1889)[376] Born in Hanover, Germany, Kruckemeyer arrived in New Orleans with a younger brother, Louis, in February 1860 and came to Cincinnati shortly thereafter, traveling up the Mississippi and Ohio Rivers.[377] The 1862-1864 CCDs list his occupation as silversmith at **Duhme & Co.** In 1864, he and his brother Louis enlisted in the Union Army, serving as privates in the Company B, Ohio 65th Infantry Battalion.[378] Upon his return to Cincinnati, he was associated with a bakery, Bernard Jahr & Company.[379] Kruckemeyer was once again working as a silversmith at Duhme & Co. in 1867, and continued there until his death in 1889. A reminiscence published in 1923 recalled that he was "at the head of the silversmithing department" and that "Duhme's was in the lead of this line of work in the West those days; such stores as this were not to be seen in any other city west of the Alleghanies [sic] . . . The manufacture of sterling silverware included even great punch bowls and hollowware generally."[380] Kruckemeyer's occupation was listed as a journeyman silversmith in the 1870 Federal Census and as a silversmith in the 1880 Federal Census.

Kruckemeyer married Helena Jahr, also an immigrant from Germany. Census records indicate that they were the parents of six children: Johanna (b. 1866), Bernard (b. 1868), Dora (b. 1870), Gustave (b. 1874), Ella (b. 1875), and Erna (b. 1881).[381] Kruckemeyer's surname was rendered as Kauckemeier, Kruckmeyer, Krueckemeyer, and Kruckemeier and his given name as Justice or Justes in some period documents.

KUTZ, JOSEPH (w. 1875-1877) Silversmith, 1875-77 CCDs.

LABOYTEAUX, ISAAC NAPOLEON (1827-1894, w. 1850-1894)[382] LaBoyteaux was born in Mount Pleasant, Ohio, (now the Cincinnati suburbs of College Hill and Mount Healthy) to early settlers of that area, Phoebe and Peter J. LaBoiteaux, a soldier in the Revolutionary War.[383] Isaac was first listed in the 1849/50 CCD as a clerk at Katzenberger, Straus & Co., a clothing and dry goods merchant at 94 Main. In July 1850 he partnered with the watch maker and jeweler **William C. Huntington** in the firm **Huntington & LaBoyteaux**.[384] When the firm became **Huntington Brothers & Co.** in February 1856, LaBoyteaux's association with it ended. He apparently left Cincinnati from 1856 through 1866, but returned in 1867, working for **Duhme & Co.** as a jeweler, salesman, or advertising manager until at least 1894.[385] His residence during those years was described in a Cincinnati guidebook as "octagonal . . . probably the only house of its kind in the United States" and as "having superb views on all sides."[386]

LaBoyteaux married Margaret McLenan (1835–1909) in 1856.[387] Records of five children born to them have been found: Grace (1856–1949), R.R. (1858–1887), Edward (1863–1892), Isaac (1864–1912), and Charles Louis (1866–1947).[388] The LaBoyteaux name was also rendered in period documents as Laboyteaux, La Boyteaux and LaBoiteaux, which was used in the burial records of Spring Grove Cemetery.

LAIBLE, GEORGE (w. 1872-1883) Silversmith, 1872, 1882, 1883 CCDs. Appears in various CCDs between 1873-1886 as show case maker.

LANGON, EDWARD (w. 1876) Silversmith, 1876 CCD.

LARY, WILLIAM (w. 1831) Silversmith, 1831 CCD.

LAUBNER, JOHN (w. 1883) Silversmith, 1883 CCD. Appears in various CCDs between 1881-1884 as nickel or silver plater.

LAUCH, FRED. (w. 1873) Silversmith, 1873 CCD. Appears in various CCDs between1870-1888 as jeweler, silver plater, gilder, tanner, or laborer.

LEDE, ADOLPH (w. 1867) Silversmith, 1867 CCD.

LEEDS, ELY W. (w. 1873-1874) Silversmith, 1873 CCD. Occupation given as jeweler in 1874 CCD.

LEEFSON, JOHN (w. 1872) Silversmith, 1872 CCD.

LEESMAN, JOHN (w. 1881-1883) Silversmith, 1881, 1883 CCDs. Appears as laborer or printer in 1884-1887 CCDs.

LEMMON, JOHN (w. 1871-1872) Silversmith, 1871, 1872 CCDs.

LEVI, BARNET (w. 1822-about 1825) Barnet Levi, a native of Liverpool, England, arrived in Cincinnati in June 1819.[389] An 1822 advertisement for Barnit [*sic*] Levi & Co. included "a set of Watch Makers' Tools; also a good assortment of watch materials for sale" and "WATCHES repaired on reasonable terms."[390] In 1824 and 1825, a local newspaper's weekly directory of merchants listed Barnet Levi as a silversmith and watch maker at Main and Third.[391]

Joseph Jonas, with Barnet Levi, Lewis Cohen, **Joseph Levy**, and David Israel Johnson conducted the first Jewish services in the western portion of the United States in the autumn of 1819.[392] Levi apparently left Cincinnati before the efforts in 1824 to formally organize the congregation, since he is not mentioned in the reports about that proposed undertaking.[393]

LLOYD, THOMAS (w. 1861) Silversmith working at **E. & D. Kinsey**, 1861 CCD. Appears in 1857, 1858 CCDs as clerk or porter.

LOEWE, HENRY (w. 1870-1871) Silversmith, 1870, 1871 CCDs and 1870 Census. Appears in CCDs between 1868-1874 as grocer, finisher, or comb maker. His surname is spelled Loeve in the 1871 CCD.

LONG, HARMON (d. 1824, w. 1804-1824)[394] One of the earliest settlers in Cincinnati, Long engaged in numerous and varied business endeavors over the years. In 1804, the partnership of **Philip Price** and Long advertised that "they have commenced the Clock & Watchmaking business at the corner of main & front street" and added that "Harman Long carries on the Tinning business" at the same location.[395] The partnership was dissolved "by mutual consent" in June 1806.[396] In 1808, Long and John Mears advertised that they had resumed the "coppersmith business."[397] The partnership continued at least through 1811 when they advertised that "they still continue the above (Coppersmith & Tinning) business at their old stand, on Main-street, near the corner of Columbia street."[398] Long subsequently opened a carding machine operation and the "Cincinnati Dyeing Business," which was "located at Herman [*sic*] Long's place at the corner of Main and Columbia Streets."[399]

Little is known about Long's personal life. The marriage of his daughter, Nancy, to Martin Miller was reported in 1810.[400] In 1811, a report of the election of "Township and corporation officers" noted that Jonathan Pancost and Harmon Long were elected "Overseers of the Poor."[401] Long was listed in the 1819 CCD, living on Front Street, but no occupation was included.[402] His given name was also rendered as Herman [*sic*] or Harmon in some period documents.

LONG, JAS O. (w. 1874) Silversmith, 1874 CCD. Appears in 1875 CCD as blacksmith.

LOTON, GEORGE W. (w. 1839/40) Silversmith, 1839/40 CCD.

LOVENHARTH, BENJ. (w. 1860) Silversmith, 1860 CCD.

LOVING, __ [no given name] (w. 1875) Silversmith, 1875 CCD.

LYON, JOSEPH W. (w. 1872–1889) Silversmith, 1874, 1875, 1879–1881, 1883 CCDs. Appears in various CCDs between 1872–1889 as watch case maker, jeweler, or watch maker. Census records list him as a silversmith in 1880.[403] Lyon followed the Dueber Watch Case factory when it moved to Canton, Ohio, in 1889. Canton city directories list him as an employee of the Dueber firm in 1890 and 1891. Census data list his occupation as a watch engraver or watch worker in 1900 and 1910.[404]

LYONS MERCANTILE SUPPLY CO. (THE) (1898) Appears only in the 1898 CCD as a dealer in "wholesale silverware" at 216 West Fourth, H.H. Kingery, manager. The firm advertised in the business listings under silverware.

MAAG, FRED. (w. 1872–1880) Silversmith, 1872–78 CCDs, 1880 Census.

MAHLMAN, HENRY (w. 1858–1873) Silversmith, 1865–1873 CCDs. Also appears in 1858, 1859 CCDs as jeweler.

MARK, FRED. (w. 1870) Silversmith, 1870 CCD.

MARLMANN, CHARLES (1861–1926, w. 1878–1882)[405] The son of silversmith **Henry F. Marlmann**, Charles worked as a watch maker. After 1883, the CCDs give his occupation as a carpenter, cabinet maker, or "saloon."

MARLMANN, HENRY C. (1825–1880, w. 1862–1879)[406] Silversmith, 1870, 1872, 1876–1878 CCDs. Worked at the address of **Duhme & Co.** in 1865 as a silver plater. Appears in 1862–1879 CCDs as a plater, silver finisher, polisher, gilder or jeweler. Marlmann's given name was also rendered as Henry, H.C., and C. Henry. Residential addresses, census data and the name of the spouse (widow) were utilized to distinguish between Henry C. and Henry F. Marlmann.

MARLMANN, HENRY F. (1835–1914, w. 1856–1896)[407] Silversmith, 1858, 1861–1863, 1870–1872, 1874–1876, 1882, 1884, 1886, 1888–1890 CCDs. Born in Germany, Marlmann arrived in New Orleans with his parents and siblings in 1853.[408] He was in Cincinnati by 1856, when he was listed in the CCD as a polisher. He worked as a silversmith for **E. & D. Kinsey** and at the address of **Duhme & Co.** He appears in various CCDs between 1856–1896 as a silver finisher, goldsmith, gold and silver melter, smelter, or gold refiner. Marlmann's given name was also rendered as Henry, H.F., Henry R., or H.R.F. Residential addresses, census data and the spouse's name were utilized to distinguish between Henry C. and Henry F. Marlmann.

MAYLE, EBENEZER (circa 1818–1889, w. 1839/40)[409] Born in England, Mayle arrived in New York in 1831. By 1839, he was in Cincinnati, working as a silversmith at **E. Kinsey**'s.[410] He appears in subsequent CCDs and in census records as a news carrier, bookseller, or bookstore owner. He had moved to Columbus, Ohio by 1875, and died there in 1889.[411]

McCALLION, JAMES (w. 1870–1875) Silversmith, 1871 CCD. Appears in various CCDs between 1870–1875 as a clerk, silver plater or laborer.

McDONALD, ALEXANDER (w. 1839/40) Silversmith, 1839/40 CCD.

McGURK, JAMES F. (w. 1886–1893) Silversmith, 1890, 1891, 1893 CCDs. Appears in various CCDs between 1886–1893 as polisher or plater.

McMURPHY, ALBERT (w. 1839/40) Silversmith from Delaware, boarding at **Abraham Palmer**'s and probably working at the shop of **Palmer and Hanks**, per the 1839/40 CCD.

McQUARTERS, HUGH (w. 1817–1819) McQuarters appeared in the 1817 tax list for Cincinnati and in the 1819 CCD as a silversmith at 111 Main; his residence was on Sixth Street between Main and Walnut.[412] A reminiscence published in 1923 recalled that he was one of the first silversmiths in Cincinnati and was working on Main Street but includes no other information about him.[413]

MEHMERT, JOSEPH (1842–1922, w. 1863–1921)[414] Born in Germany, Mehmert was in Cincinnati by 1863 where he was selling "notions." By 1868, he was also offering watches and jewelry in a shop on Broadway. Initial credit reports were positive, noting that he was honest and industrious but that his business was small.[415]

By March 1870 he was out of business and working for **Clemens Oskamp**.[416] In 1877, he opened a jewelry shop on Freeman Avenue which prospered: in 1886, it was described as "One of the prominent houses engaged in the jewelry industry." His stock included watches, clocks, jewelry, solid silver and plated ware, and other fancy goods as well as watch makers' tools.[417]

Mehmert's firm increasingly focused on the trade in watch makers' tools and materials as well as jewelers' findings and supplies. His exhibit at the 1886 Cincinnati Industrial Exposition included clocks and jewelry as well as watch makers' tools and materials.[418] By 1901, the firm, described as the "Oldest established house in Cincinnati in this line," had a second location in the Glen Building on Race Street for its wholesale operations, in addition to the retail shop on Freeman.[419]

Mehmert married Elizabeth (Lisette) (1845–1897), in Germany around 1867.[420] They had two children: Joseph Jr. (b. 1877) and Otto (b. 1884). In 1898, Joseph married Margaret Jansen (b. 1869), with whom he had three more children: Johanna (b. 1900), Edwin (b. 1901), and Amelia (b. 1906).[421]

MERCANTILE SUPPLY CO. Appears only in 1897 CCD as a dealer in "wholesale silverware" at 214 West Fourth, Charles E. Ehler, manager. The firm advertised in the business listings under "silver ware."

METZGER, JACOB (1845–1882, w. 1871–1882)[422] Silversmith, 1874, 1875 CCDs, 1880 Federal Census. He appears in various CCDs between 1871–1882 as a jeweler or watch maker. A native of Bavaria, Jacob Metzger was the son of John Metzger, a jeweler and watch maker in Cincinnati from 1855 to 1878. Jacob Metzger was working as a silversmith in South Carrollton, Kentucky, a small town not far from Cincinnati in 1870, but had returned to Cincinnati in time to be included in the 1871 CCD.[423]

MEYER, LEOPOLD (w. 1849–1864) Meyer appeared in the 1849/50 CCD as a watch repairer, working at the address of **William Wilson McGrew**'s shop. He worked as a watch maker through 1858, when he opened his own shop at 189 Walnut, advertising in the CCD business listings under "Jewelry, Silver Ware, Watches, etc." Credit reports noted it was a profitable business with good stock and described Meyer as "honest, cautious, and not apt to buy more than he can pay for."[424] In 1864, Meyer closed the shop and became a partner in his father-in-law's firm, A. Kempfer's Sons, a manufacturer of "stomach bitters."

MEYER, WM. (w. 1868–1883) Silversmith, 1870, 1872 CCDs, working at **Duhme & Co.** Appears in various CCDs between 1868– 1883 as a watch case maker, polisher, finisher, or porter at Duhme & Co.

MIERENFELD, HERMAN J. (1852–1941, w. 1869–1923)[425] Silversmith, 1869–1887 CCDs. Mierenfeld worked as a silversmith or watch maker at **Duhme & Co.** Census records list his occupation as silversmith in 1870 and 1880.[426] Mierenfeld moved to Bellevue, Kentucky, in 1892, and in 1895, opened a shop there advertising "Watches, Clocks & Jewelry."[427] From 1901–1923, he worked as a watch maker or watch repairer for other firms, including **A. & J. Plaut** and Joseph E. Smith, a jeweler in Lockland, a suburb of Cincinnati. A younger brother, Albert J. (b. 1858), who worked as a watch maker or jeweler from 1874 through at least 1930, operated a jewelry store on Eastern Avenue, advertising in the 1889–1914 CCD business listings under "Watches, Clocks and Jewelry."

The son of German immigrants Anna Rosina and John Mierenfeld, Herman married Elizabeth Darpel (1855–1934) in 1877.[428] They were the parents of seven children for whom records were found: Rosa (b. 1878), Mary (b. 1879), Flora (b. 1883), Joseph (b. 1885), Herman A. (b. 1888), Raymond J. (or John R.) (b. 1893), and Elizabeth A. (Lily) (b. 1896).[429] Mierenfeld's surname was also rendered as Mirenfeld, Merinfield, Mernfeld, Mieranfield, or Minnifield, and his given name as Herman J., H. J., J. Herman, John H., or Hermon in period documents.

MILBIS, NATHAN (w. 1831) Listed as a silversmith in the 1831 CCD, Milbis lived on Main Street in the "Northern Liberties," an area north of the Cincinnati city limits. He appears in the 1819 and 1825 CCDs as a grocer.

MILLER, FRED. (w. 1881–1890) Silversmith, 1881 CCD. Appears in 1882–1890 CCDs as an engraver.

MILLER, JACOB (w. 1877–1880) Silversmith, 1880 CCD. Appears as jeweler in 1877 CCD.

MILLER, WILLIAM (w. 1873–1880) Silversmith, 1873 CCD. Appears in 1874–1880 CCDs as a watch case maker or gilder.

MITCHELL, JAMES (w. 1857–1870) Silversmith, 1857, 1870 CCDs, working at the address of the **E. & D. Kinsey** or **David Kinsey** shop. Appears in various CCDs between 1859–1866 as a finisher.

MOHLMANN, JOHN (w. 1872) Silversmith, 1872 CCD.

MORMAN, H. (w. 1857–1859) Silversmith or silver finisher 1857, 1859 CCDs, working at the **E. & D. Kinsey** shop.

MOREAU, FRANCIS (w. 1836–1846) Silversmith, 1846 CCD. Appears in 1836/37–1844 CCDs as a clock maker or watch maker. His surname was also rendered as Moro, Morrow, or Monroe in the CCDs.

MOWRY, JOHN (w. 1867) Silversmith, 1867 CCD.

MUDGE, CHARLES LEONARD (1844–1924, w. 1870–1919)[430] Born in Portsmouth, New Hampshire, Mudge was recorded as a jeweler there in the 1870 Federal Census but was also included in the 1870 CCD as a clerk at the address of **William Wilson McGrew**'s shop.[431] He was a clerk at **Duhme & Co.** by 1871, and he continued working there as a salesman through the 1894 reorganization and change of the firm's name to **The Duhme Company**. In 1898, he joined the **Frank Herschede** firm and continued there as a salesman until he retired in 1919. A reminiscence published in 1923 recalled him as one of the more memorable employees at **Duhme & Co.**, noting that "Charles Mudge, from Boston, was also a good salesman."[432]

In 1872, Mudge married the widow Emma Estep Lovell (1845–1915).[433] No records of children of this marriage were found. Emma's son, Edward H. Lovell (1860–1926), lived with them and followed in Mudge's footsteps as a clerk and salesman at **Duhme & Co.** and was later a manager at **George Newstedt**'s firm.[434]

MULLER, LOUIS PHILLIPUS (1814–1885, w. 1850–1883)[435] Louis Muller and his family arrived in New York City from Holland aboard the *Meldon* in August 1849 and proceeded to Cincinnati that same year.[436] Muller worked as a bookkeeper for **Duhme & Co.** from the time it was a small firm located on Main Street and was advertising as "importers & dealers in watches & fancy goods" through the 1880s. He was listed as one of the principals of Duhme & Co. from 1856–1858, although credit reports noted that he was not a partner, "having only an interest for services in lieu of salary."[437] A reminiscence published in 1923 recalled him as one of the more memorable employees at **Duhme & Co.**, noting that he "was long the bookkeeper—until his death."[438]

Muller was born on March 29, 1814, in the West Indies to Dutch parents.[439] He was in Amsterdam, Holland, when he married Elisa Wilhelmina C. Remme (1817–1892).[440] They were the parents of nine children, four of whom were born in Holland: Louis Jr., William C., Louisa, and Johanna. Born in Ohio were Henry, Anna Marie, Henrietta, James, and Mary Ann (or Anne Mary).[441] Muller's surname was also rendered as Miller, Mueller, or Moller and his given name as L.P. or Lewis in period documents.

NAGEL, MARTIN (w. 1882) Silversmith, 1882 CCD. Appears in various CCDs between 1877–1886 as a baker, polisher, varnisher, burnisher and show case maker.

NASH, COLEMAN (w. 1825) Silversmith and watch maker, 1825 CCD. He worked at 58 Main, also the address of **Enos Woodruff**, **Joseph Thornton** and **William Kimberly**. Nash did not appear in any other CCDs.

NEET, C. (w. 1857) Silversmith, 1857 CCD, working at **E. & D. Kinsey**.

NERNEY, ALFRED G. (w. 1863–1879) Silversmith, 1863, 1866 CCDs. Appears in 1867–1879 CCDs as a silver plater, working for Morrison & Corcoran, a silver plating firm.

NEUHAUS, THEODORE SR. (1837–1885, w. 1858–1885)[442] Born in Germany, Neuhaus arrived in New York in 1854, and was in Cincinnati by 1858, working as a silversmith at **E. & D. Kinsey**.[443] He worked for the Kinseys through 1865 and then at **Duhme & Co.** (1866–1885). His occupation was invariably given as silversmith in federal census records (1870, 1880) and CCD listings except in the 1860 Census, where he was listed as a jeweler.

Neuhaus married Elizabeth Landon (1835–1919), also a native of Germany.[444] They were the parents of seven children for whom records were found: Edward (1863–1893), Theodore Jr. (1865–1937), William (1869–1925), Pauline (b. 1871), Lillian (b. 1873), Louis (b. 1875), and Carl (1880–1887).[445] Edward and Theodore Jr. followed their father in the trade: Edward was a watch maker and jeweler while **Theodore Jr.**, also a silversmith, became the superintendent of the silver manufacturing department at **Duhme & Co.** before establishing his own firm, **Theodore Neuhaus & Co.** Pauline and Lillian worked at the Duhme firms as salesladies or a stockkeepers between 1890 and 1898.

In 1867, Neuhaus and **Theodore Biltz** purchased land in the new suburb Walnut Hills, and by 1868, had subdivided the plot. Neuhaus then built a home on Spring Street.[446] Theodore Sr. died of meningitis at the age of 48. His surname was also rendered as Newhouse, Newhause, Newhaus, Neihaus, Niehause, or Newhaus in period documents.

NITZE, ALBERT (w. 1881–1882) Silversmith, 1881, 1882 CCDs. Worked at **Duhme & Co.**

NOELCKE, LOUIS (1838–1902, w. 1865–1902)[447] Born in Germany in 1838, Noelcke arrived in New York in June 1862 from Hamburg on the *Bavaria*, his occupation listed as goldsmith on the ship's manifest.[448] By 1865, he was working in Cincinnati as a jeweler at **Duhme & Co.** where he became the foreman or superintendent of the jewelry department from 1880 through 1891. In 1893, Noelcke opened a jewelry store on East McMillan Street, advertising in the CCD business listings under "Watches, Clocks and Jewelry." After Noelcke's death in 1902, his widow, Anna, and son, August, operated the store until it closed in 1915.

Louis and Anna Noelcke (1840–1915) were married in 1854; they were the parents of three children for whom records were found: Louis A. (1865–1907), Edward (b. 1869), and August (b. 1871).[449] Noelcke's sons were also employed by **Duhme & Co.**—Louis A. as a jeweler (1882–1891), Edward as a watch maker (1886–1891), and August as an engraver (1887–1891).

NOLTING, CHARLES A. (1850–1934, w. 1868–1923)[450] The son of German immigrants Anna Barbara and Charles P.F. Nolting, Charles A. Nolting was born in Cincinnati. Orphaned at a young age, he began working at age 13 as an errand boy for **Duhme & Co.**, and with **Emmett W. Ankeny** as an early mentor, Nolting was gradually given increasing responsibilities in the business.[451] In 1882, Nolting formed a wholesale jewelry firm, Lodwick and Nolting, with Frank O. Lodwick, another long-term Duhme employee who had risen from a clerk's position to that of assistant bookkeeper for the firm.[452] Credit reports indicate that the new firm had a reasonable amount of capital and carried a "good stock" of silverware, watch cases and watch movements, and jewelry. Lodwick retired from the business in July 1885 due to ill health, and Nolting was left to carry on by himself.[453]

The business expanded greatly when **William S.P. Oskamp** (a son of **Clemens Oskamp**) joined forces with Nolting in 1887, and the firm became **Oskamp, Nolting & Co.** In 1892, a well-known trade publication opined that the resulting increase of capital had provided the "impetus that has made them known throughout the commercial world."[454] The firm's offerings, which included only "Watches, Diamonds, &c." in 1888, had expanded to "diamonds, watches, silverware, cut glass ware, optical goods, etc." by 1905.[455] In 1907, Nolting sold his interest in the retail operations to his partner and continued solely as a wholesale dealer trading as **The Oskamp, Nolting Co.** Nolting served as president of the new firm until his retirement in 1922, maintaining and enhancing its reputation as "one of the most successful jewelry concerns in America."[456]

In 1874, Nolting married Amelia Twachtman (1853–1924), the daughter of a prominent Cincinnati furniture manufacturer.[457] They were the parents of eight children: Alice (b. 1877), Lilly (b. 1879), Louis (b. 1880), Edwin (b. 1882), Florence (b. 1884), Myrtle (b. 1889), Wesley (b. 1892), and Mildred (b. 1894).[458] When Nolting died in 1934, *The New York Times* noted that "until his retirement, eleven years ago, he devoted his entire life to the jewelry business."[459]

O'BRIEN, JAMES (w. 1881–1883) Silversmith, 1881–1883 CCDs. Appears in CCDs as a marble polisher after 1884.

OSKAMP, JOSEPH A. (1854–1920, w. 1873–1878)[460] The son of Mary Frey and Augustus Oskamp and a nephew of **Clemens Oskamp**, Joseph worked as a watch maker for **John B. Morris** from 1870–1876.[461] In 1876, he opened his own shop on Main Street, advertising in the CCD business listings for watches, clocks, jewelry, silver and plated ware. Credit reports were initially favorable for the "young man of good char(acter) and industrious habits," but turned negative in late 1878, and Oskamp closed the business in December, auctioning the stock.[462] From 1879 to 1884, he worked in the wholesale grocery business of his father-in-law, B.G. Stall, but was in Kansas City, Missouri, before 1900, working as a jeweler. Oskamp remained in Missouri, working as a jeweler through at least 1910. By 1920, he had retired.[463]

Oskamp married Elizabeth Stall in 1878; records were found for one son, Joseph A. Jr. (b. 1888).[464] Widowed by 1899, Oskamp returned to Cincinnati to marry Henriette Gaither Bell (1856–1912).[465] Widowed again, Oskamp married his third wife, Theodosia M. Swain (1860–1946) in 1913.[466]

OTTEMER, JOHN (w. 1849/50) Silversmith, 1849/50 CCD.

OWEN, A. (w. 1857) Silversmith, 1857 CCD.

OWEN, M.C. (1886–1888) The firm "M.C. Owen," which was billed as the "Successor to Wm. Owen & Co" in the 1886 CCD, was at the same location, 167 Vine, and advertised the same variety of goods, "watches, clocks, jewelry, silverware, fine watch materials & tools" as its predecessor. **William Owen, Jr.** was listed as the manager of the shop; the person corresponding to "M.C." was not identified but it was undoubtedly Mary C. ("May") Booth Owen (1856–1914), the wife of William Owen, Jr.[467] Although William Jr. had worked in the family's jewelry firms since 1862, Mary Owen's role in the firm prior to the death of William Sr. in 1886 is unknown. Silverware with a mark that can be firmly attributed to this firm has not been documented to date. The mark "OWEN" (incuse Roman letters) that has been found on silver flatware was probably used by the earlier Owen firms of **William Owen, Sr.** or **Charles Owen**.

OWEN, WILLIAM JR. (1842–1928, w. 1862–1918)[468] The oldest son of Keziah Abigail and **William Owen, Sr.**, William Jr.

worked as a clerk and bookkeeper for his uncle **Charles Owen**'s firm from 1862–1866. When the firm name changed to **William Owen & Co.** in 1867, William Jr. was listed with his father and uncle as one of the principals of the firm. After his father's death in 1886, William Jr. continued with the firm, then called **M.C. Owen**, and in 1889 the firm's name became simply William Owen, with William Jr. as the principal. Over the next twelve years, the shop moved to new locations in 1890, in 1900, and finally, in 1902, to 425 Elm where it remained until it was closed in 1918. In July 1905 Owen was reported to have opened a retail branch of the firm in Ludlow, KY, but no other information about the shop was found.[469]

Although the firm advertised in the CCD business listings that the stock included silverware, jewelry, clocks and watches, silverware with a mark that can be firmly attributed to this firm has not been documented to date. The mark "OWEN" (incuse Roman letters) that has been documented on silver flatware was probably used by the earlier firms of William Owen Sr. or Charles Owen.[470]

Through the years, the shop was mainly a family operation. William's uncle, Charles Owen, was a watch maker until he retired in 1891, and brother Charles E. was the watch maker until his death in 1899. Sister Mary Jane ("Mamie") taught china decoration and sold artists materials at the shop, while sisters Lizzie and Tillie were salesladies.[471] When William Owen, Jr. retired, a national trade journal reported "One old business that closed during the summer of 1918, which had been one of the landmarks of the city, was that of William Owen, who had been in business for over 50 years. Mr. Owen, while he was still active and filled with energy, decided to retire from the mercantile world. With the exception of the small watch business, which he still maintains from his home, and the inspection of watches for a railroad, he remains quietly at home among his children and grandchildren."[472]

After his marriage to Mary C. ("May") Booth in 1876, the couple lived in Newport, Kentucky, until moving back to Cincinnati around 1886.[473] They were the parents of two children for whom records were found: Alfred (1876–1951) and Florence (b. 1882).[474]

PAHREN, CHARLES (1862–1919, w. 1878–1915)[475] Pahren worked as a silversmith at **Duhme & Co.** (1878–1893), and worked at the **Herman Keck Manufacturing Company** and **The Duhme Jewelry Co.** (1899–1904). He continued to work as a silversmith between 1905 and 1915, but only his residence was given in directories and his employer is not indicated. Pahren married Mary Vortkamp in June 1888.[476] They were the parents of four children: Josephine, Aloysius, Edwin, and Marie.[477] Pahren's surname is also rendered as Phrasen, Pahrew or Pah in period documents.

PALMER, ROBERT H. (1838–1908, w. 1866–1889)[478] The son of **Abraham Palmer** and his second wife, Maria Tratbas, Robert H. worked with his father at the Western Museum before his service in the Civil War.[479] Although he worked as a silversmith in Cincinnati for many years after the war, the directory listings give only his home address and do not indicate where he was employed. In January 1891 he was admitted to the U.S. National Home for Disabled Volunteer Soldiers in Dayton, Ohio and died there in October 1908.

PARKS, JOHN (w. 1864–1869) Silversmith, 1864–1869 CCDs, working at the address of **David Kinsey**.

PARTL, WENZEL (1837–1906, w. 1862–1906)[480] The son of Rose and John Partl, Wenzel was born in Austria and arrived in the United States in 1852.[481] He began working as a jeweler and diamond cutter for **Duhme & Co.** in 1862 and by 1877, was working as a jeweler at the address of the **William and J.C. Michie** firm. In 1891, Partl advertised in the CCD business listings as a manufacturing jeweler based at the Aetna Building on Vine Street. He continued working as a manufacturing jeweler until his death in 1906. A reminiscence published in 1923 recalled that William Partell [*sic*] was foreman of the gold factory at Duhme & Co.[482]

Partl married Catharina Bechyne (1840–1901) in 1864.[483] They were the parents of seven children for whom records were found: Frank (b. 1866), Louisa (b. 1867), Mary Helen (b. 1869), Otto (b. 1871), Joseph F. (b. 1874), Catherine (b. 1878), and Rosalia (b. 1879).[484]

PAXTON, ISAAC (1770–1861, w. 1795–1801)[485] The son of Annetje and Anthony Pickston (Paxton), Paxton was born in 1770 in Essex County, New Jersey, about 40 miles from the birthplace of another early Cincinnati silversmith, **Isaac Van Nuys**.[486] Trained as a silversmith, he worked in New Jersey until 1791, and then set out for Kentucky. Deterred by reports of Indian hostilities in the West, he stopped and worked as a silversmith in Staunton, Virginia for about a year and then, in the summer of 1792, enlisted in one of the army regiments activated under General Anthony Wayne for the purpose of securing the Northwest Territory against Indian attacks. He received an honorable discharge in July 1795 at Greenville, Ohio, but there were no funds to pay him for his three years of service. Without money, he walked the 90 miles to Cincinnati where he found work in a silversmith shop.[487] Upon learning in October that the soldiers in Greenville were being paid, he walked from Cincinnati to Greenville, where he collected his pay, and then walked back to Cincinnati.[488]

Paxton continued to work in Cincinnati as a silversmith until 1801, when he moved to Butler County, north of Cincinnati.[489] In

1807, Paxton purchased a farm in western Butler County but sold it in 1813, and moved to Hamilton, where he opened a shop at which he worked "at his trade until the infirmities of age compelled him to decline business."[490] In 1813, the silversmith Henry Wallace (1788–1818) left the employ of **Samuel Best** in Cincinnati and joined Paxton. They advertised that they were "commencing a clock- and watchmaking and silversmith business" where "the highest cash price would be given for old gold, silver, copper, brass, and pewter."[491] Although Paxton's occupation was reported as silversmith in census records and other period documents, no silverware bearing his mark has been documented to date.[492]

Paxton married the widow Magdalane (Van Nuys) Williams (1771–1826), a sister of Isaac Van Nuys, in 1803.[493] In 1831, he married Eliza Saunders Phares (1794–1869), a widow and mother of three children: William S. (b. 1815), Louisa (b. 1822), and Isaac (b. 1822).[494] Paxton and Eliza were the parents of one daughter, Eliza Ann (1832–1841).[495]

PEERS, HENRY (w. 1860–1861) Gold and silversmith, 1861 CCD. Appears in 1860 CCD as jeweler.

PERDNAUX, L. (w. 1866) Silversmith, 1866 CCD, working at the address of **David Kinsey**.

PERKMAN, F. (w. 1871) Silversmith, 1871 CCD.

PETERMAN, ADAM (w. 1870) Silversmith, 1870 CCD, working at **Duhme & Co.**

PHILLIPS, JAMES (w. 1827–1829) On May 14, 1827, Jacob Deterly recorded in his diary, "James Phillips returned to set in again to work with **Samuel Musgrove** to learn the silver smith business."[496] Since Samuel Musgrove was from Hardin County, Kentucky, it is likely that Musgrove's apprentice was the James Phillips from Elizabethtown in Hardin County. Phillips remained in Cincinnati through 1834, but by 1837, had returned to Elizabethtown, entering into a partnership with the silversmith Andrew Fairleigh, A. Fairleigh & Co.[497] It could not be determined if this James Phillips was related to other silversmiths of the same name.[498]

PICKER, EDWARD (w. 1873–1877) Silversmith, 1873–1875 CCDs. Appears as jeweler in 1876, 1877 CCDs. Surname also rendered as Pickel, Piecker or Pickert in period documents.

PIGMAN, JOHN (1820–1887, w. 1839–1872)[499] Born in Lawrence County, Virginia, Pigman was working as a silversmith

at **Edward Kinsey**'s shop in Cincinnati in 1839.[500] For the next 32 years, he continued to work as a silversmith at the Kinsey firms except for the years 1861–1865, when he served in the Ohio 5th Infantry Regiment during the Civil War.[501] In 1872, he was admitted to the U.S. National Home for Disabled Volunteer Soldiers in Dayton, Ohio and died there on April 25, 1887.

PRATT, ALBERT C. (1826–1909, w. 1850–1859)[502] An accountant in his native Rhode Island at the time of the 1850 Federal Census. Pratt was in Cincinnati, working for C. & W.H. Allen when the 1850/51 CCD was published.[503] He continued with the Allen firm until 1856, when he was working at the address of **Duhme & Co.** A reminiscence published in 1923 noted that Pratt, **L.P. Muller**, and **Samuel Hatch** were early associates of Herman Duhme in the jewelry business.[504] The 1857 and 1858 CCDs included them as principals, with Herman Duhme, of **Duhme & Co.** However, credit reports in January 1857 noted that "tho' their names appear in the firm, are not partners, having only an interest in lieu of salary."[505] In April 1859 Pratt left Cincinnati, moving to New York City where he initially worked for Schuyler, Hartley & Graham, a sporting goods company.[506] He apparently never returned to the jewelry and silver trade as subsequent census records give his occupation as an insurance or real estate agent.[507]

Pratt married Penelope Bidwell in May 1855.[508] They were the parents of eight children, only two of whom, Trevor (b. 1860) and Florence (b. 1868), survived beyond their first year.[509] The others were Gilbert L. (b. 1858), Margaret F. (b. 1861), A.C. (b. 1864), Harry R. (b. 1865), Effie L. (b. 1870), and Cora G. (b. 1871).

PUTNAM, EDMUND (w. 1831) Operated a "comb and fancy store" in 1831 on Main Street between Fourth and Fifth Streets. An advertisement in the 1831 CCD provided a long list of goods that were for sale, including "Silver and Plated Spoons, Ladles and Sugar Tongs" as well as a wide array of plated silver tableware, jewelry, and watches.[510] In 1834, Putnam was operating a boarding house at the corner of Symmes and Lawrence; he was not listed in subsequent CCDs.

REIS, EDWARD J. (w. 1839/40) Silversmith from Maryland working at **Joseph Draper**'s, 1839/40 CCD.

RENGERS, ANTHONY (1871–1927, w. 1889–1926)[511] Anthony was the son of German immigrants Elizabeth and Hubert Rengers, a watch maker by trade and the proprietor of a jewelry store in Cincinnati from 1866–1885.[512] Anthony was listed in CCDs as a jeweler in 1889, and as a silversmith or metal worker from 1890 to 1912, but since only his home address was included, it is not possible to identify the firm(s) at which he worked. He subsequently worked as a jeweler or salesman for the wholesale jewelry firm, **Albert Brothers**. Anthony Rengers and his wife Mary had two sons for whom records were found: Herbert (b. 1902) and Lawrence (b. 1906).[513] Rengers died of cardiac spasms at his home in Newport, Kentucky, in February 1927.

RICHTER, NORBERT (1802–1867, w. 1850–1867)[514] Richter and his family, immigrants from Germany, were in Cincinnati by 1850, when Norbert was listed in the CCD as a silversmith. From 1857 to 1859, he worked as a jeweler at the address of **E. & D. Kinsey**. Listed as a goldsmith in the 1860 Federal Census, Richter opened a jewelry and watch store, Norbert Richter & Co. in 1861.[515] The shop, on Vine between Fourteenth and Fifteenth Streets, was in the area known as Over-the-Rhine where many German immigrants lived and worked. In 1862, Richter's oldest son Frank joined the firm and its name was changed to Norbert Richter & Son. After Norbert's death in 1867, the shop continued under Frank Richter's name through 1872, when he closed the shop and moved to Texas.[516]

Norbert and his wife Barbara (1811–1888) were the parents of five children for whom records were found: Francis (Frank) (b. 1836), Albert (b. 1842), Charles (1844–1922), George (1851–1939), and Barbara (b. 1853).[517] All four sons engaged in the jewelry and/or watch making trades: Frank and Albert were watch makers, Charles an engraver at **Duhme & Co.**, and George a spectacle maker, jeweler and one of the founders of **Richter and Phillips**.

RICHTER & PHILLIPS (1897–present)[518] George Richter (1851–1939) and Ferdinand Phillips (1853–1915) founded the wholesale jewelry and retail mail order firm Richter & Phillips in 1897.[519] By 1910, the firm also included a retail store. Initially located at 417 Race between Fourth and Fifth Streets, the firm moved to the Sinton Building at Fifth and Main in 1903; to West Sixth in 1912; to the Temple Bar Building on East Court Street in 1926; and finally to its current location at Sixth and Main in 1976. Although the firm's advertisements indicate that its primary focus was diamonds, watches, and jewelry, by 1912, they were also dealing in cut glass, sterling silver, fancy goods, and art goods.[520] The report of a burglary at the firm in 1910 noted that the loss was "several hundred dollars' worth of goods, mostly silverware."[521] When George Richter left the firm in 1900, his nephew Charles Edward Richter became Phillips' partner.[522] Charles Richter continued with the firm until his death in 1936, when Fred Fehr, who had invested in the firm in 1930, became the proprietor of the firm.[523]

George Richter, the youngest son of **Norbert Richter**, was working as a spectacle maker in Cincinnati in 1871. He relocated

to Winchester, Kentucky, where he worked and advertised as a jeweler from 1879 through 1892.[524] In 1893, George returned to Cincinnati, working as a jeweler at a wholesale jewelry firm, probably **A. & J. Plaut**. George left Richter & Phillips in 1900 to start the Simplex Interior Telephone Co., with which he was associated until he retired in 1925. George and his wife Charlotte (1854–1939) were the parents of two children born while they lived in Kentucky: Norbert C. (b. 1875) and Estella (b. 1877).[525]

Ferdinand Phillips, the son of German immigrants Abraham and Caroline Phillips, started working as a salesman for A. & J. Plaut in 1878, and by 1882, was one of the partners in that firm.[526] Published reports indicate that he was primarily the buyer for the Richter & Phillips firm, traveling frequently.[527] Phillips married Sarah Plaut (1859–1932) around 1882; they had five children for whom records were found: Morris (b. 1883), Edna (b. 1886), Jesse (b. 1888), J. Harvey (Harry J.) (b. 1890), and Helen (b. 1893).[528] Morris and J. Harvey continued working at Richter & Phillips after Ferdinand Phillips' death in 1915.

Charles Edward Richter (1871–1936), grandson of Norbert Richter and son of Charles and Wilhelmina Richter, was a watch maker and jeweler from 1887–1897, and from 1898–1899, was the manager of the jewelry department of a large department store, The Fair.[529] He became one of the principals of Richter & Phillips in 1900, and was associated with that firm until his death. Charles Richter married Naomi Kaetker (1878–1943) in May 1899; no records of children were found.[530]

RIEDER, ADAM (1849–1883, w. 1869–1883)[531] The son of German immigrants Christina and Christopher Rieder, Adam worked as a silversmith at **Duhme & Co.** from 1869 until his death in 1883. Rieder and his wife, Kate, were the parents of two children for whom records were found: John (b. 1875) and George (1882–1883).[532] The Rieder surname was also rendered as Reader, Reider or Reeder in period documents.

RISE, FERD. (w. 1875) Silversmith, 1875 CCD.

ROHR, HENRY (w. 1839/40) Silversmith b. Germany, 1839/40 CCD.

ROLLISTON, T.C. (w. 1880) Silversmith, 1880 CCD.

RUF, JOHN (w. 1871) Silversmith, 1871 CCD.

RUPPILER, FEDOR (about 1827–about 1887, w. 1850–1868, 1877–1883)[533] Born in Prussia, Ruppiler arrived in New Orleans in February 1849 on the *Moselle* from London; his occupation was given as goldsmith on the passenger manifest.[534] By 1850, he was in Cincinnati, working as a jeweler at the address of **S.T. Carley**'s shop from 1853–1859. He left Cincinnati around 1868, worked as a manufacturing jeweler in Chicago, Illinois, and then returned in 1877, working as a jeweler at **Duhme & Co.**[535] Ruppiler's given name was also rendered as Feodor, Fidor, Theo, Theodore, Frank, Fred, and Frederick in period documents.

Ruppiler and his wife Antoinette (1835–1900) were the parents of two children for whom records were found, Ada (1866–1911) and Rudolph F. (1870–1908).[536] Fedor died around 1887. No death record was found but he appeared in the 1885 City Directory for Covington and his wife ("Antonia") was listed as "widow Fedor" in 1890.[537]

RYLAND, J. (w. 1843–1844) The only documentation found for the silversmith "J. Ryland" are his listings in the 1843–1844 CCDs. Beckman identifies him as either the James Ryland (1777–1855) who was born in England or his son, James William (1820–after 1890).[538] However, as both were listed with other occupations in CCDs between 1829–1860, this is unlikely.[539]

Boultinghouse suggests that the "__ (no first name) Ryland" who was an apprentice of the Lexington, Kentucky, silversmith Samuel Ayres in 1795, may have been the Ryland included in Beckman; confirmation was not found.[540]

A silver teaspoon in a private Cincinnati collection with a straight fiddle handle that is engraved with a basket of flowers, and marked "J.B.R" in a rectangular cartouche, might be attributable to James Ryland.[541] However, the early form makes it unlikely that it was made while J. Ryland worked in Cincinnati.

RYLAND, WILLIAM T. (1821–1863, w. 1844–1850)[542] Born in England, Ryland was in Cincinnati by 1844, when he was listed as a silversmith in the CCD. He appeared again as a silversmith in the 1846 CCD and in 1849, as a partner of **William D. Dunlevy** in the firm **Dunlevy & Ryland**. Ryland remained in Cincinnati through 1859, working as a bartender or keeper of a coffee house.[543] An Indiana resident in 1861, he volunteered for service in the Civil War and died in the Battle of Gettysburg in 1863. William Ryland, age 20, who was listed as a gold cutter in the 1841 Census for Birmingham, England, may have been the Ryland who worked as a silversmith in Cincinnati, but this could not be confirmed.[544]

SALAMON, GEORGE W. (w. 1857–1861) Silversmith, 1861 CCD. Appears in 1857 CCD as a watch maker, spelled Salomon.

SALMON, ALFRED (1799–1889, w. 1825–1844)[545] Born in England, Salmon came to the United States in 1821, and was well-established in Cincinnati by 1823, when he was one of three men serving on the concert committee for a local musical society.[546] A silversmith on Fourth Street, between Main and Walnut, he and Cincinnati grocer Josiah Warren, in 1825, joined 1,000 other Americans and Europeans gathered in New Harmony, Indiana, as members of an experimental Owenite community, a commune based on "principles of social-economic equality." When the community disbanded in 1827, Salmon and Warren returned to Cincinnati.[547] Salmon worked as a watch maker, first on Main near Seventh and subsequently on Elm, north of Ninth Street, between 1829 and 1844.

From 1849 to 1853, CCDs list his occupation as music teacher.[548] Around 1858, Salmon and his family moved to New York City where he taught music and also served as the organist and choir director for a Manhattan church.[549] While Salmon is remembered in the Midwest as a silversmith, he is remembered in New York as an "accomplished organist and music teacher." In September 1889 Salmon committed suicide by jumping into the North River at the tip of Manhattan. Under the headline "A well-to-do old man jumps into the North River," the *New York Herald-Tribune* reported that he was "much respected" in the neighborhood but had recently been worrying needlessly about perceived financial difficulties.[550]

In October 1825 while in New Harmony, Salmon married Elizabeth Palmer.[551] They were the parents of three daughters for whom records were found: Sarah (b. 1835), Mary Frances (b. before 1840), and Ellen (b. 1850).[552]

SALZER, JOSEPH M. (1844–1918, w. 1867–1868, 1880)[553] Born in Germany in 1844, Salzer arrived in New York in 1866, and was working in Cincinnati as a watch maker by 1867. Listed in the 1868 CCD as a watch maker and as a silversmith, he had moved to Carlisle, Kentucky, by 1870, where he advertised as a jeweler and optician.[554] He remained in Carlisle until 1879, although in 1876 he was also listed as a partner with his brother Edward in Salzer & Brother, a manufacturer of shirt fronts and a manufacturer's agent for cotton goods. Salzer returned to Cincinnati in 1879, and in 1880, was simultaneously working as a watch maker and in the manufacturing firm with his brother. After 1880, his occupation was recorded only as a manufacturer's agent.[555]

Salzer and his wife Charlotte were the parents of nine children for whom records were found: Gustave (b. 1876), Bertha (b. 1877), Samuel (b. 1879), Moses (b. 1881), Henry (b. 1883), Matilda (b. 1885), Max (b. 1889), Julius (b. 1890), and Clarence (b. 1893).[556] The Salzer surname was also rendered as Saltzer in period documents.

SANDFORD, R. (w. 1834) Silversmith, 1834 CCD.

SAXTON, CHARLES (w. 1856–1858) Silversmith, 1856–1858 CCDs.

SCHMALZ, JOHN H. (1857–1887, w. 1873–1882)[557] Born in Maryland to German immigrants Anna Maria and John Schmalz, John H. worked as a silversmith in Cincinnati from 1873–1882.[558] As only his home address was given in the CCDs, it was impossible to identify the firm(s) at which he apprenticed or worked. However, as his occupation was given as "spoonmaker" in 1880, it is probable that he was working for **Duhme & Co.** at that time.[559] He worked as a tinner between 1883 and 1887. Schmalz married the widow Louisa Asbury in 1882.[560] John H. died of pulmonary consumption in 1887, the disease to which his mother had succumbed in 1884.[561]

SCHNEIDER, BEN (1849–1911, w. 1869–1911)[562] and **BEN SCHNEIDER JEWELRY CO.** (1901–1958)[563] Ben Schneider came to the United States from Austria around 1856 with his parents, Magdalena and John B. Schneider.[564] Working with his father John, who was for many years (1857–1892) a jeweler in Cincinnati, Ben began learning the jewelry trade at the age of 15.[565] By 1869, Ben had opened a jewelry shop on Vine Street. He moved to Liberty, and then to 385 Vine Street in 1873, where the firm remained until it closed. Henry Rohs (1863–1915), an apprentice watch maker and jeweler, lived with the Schneider family in 1880 and subsequently married Schneider's daughter Josephine.[566] The firm's name was changed to Ben Schneider Jewelry Co. in 1901, when Ben Schneider's oldest son Frank and Henry Rohs became principals in the firm. After Ben's death in 1911, the firm continued under the management of Henry and Frank until Henry's death in 1915, when Josephine assumed an active role. By 1920, Ben's younger sons Ben B. and Oscar C. were also taking a more prominent role in the management of the firm.

Schneider's jewelry store initially carried only watches, clocks, and jewelry, but by 1884, the stock had expanded to include silverware, spectacles, and other fancy goods.[567] The firm continued to advertise silverware through 1930.[568] Although Elgin watches marked with the firm's name on the dial and the movement have been documented, silver marked with the firm's name has not been recorded to date.[569]

Schneider married Margaret Weiler (1850–1921) around 1869.[570] They were the parents of seven children: Josephine (1871–1952), Frank (1873–1939), Theresia (b. 1878), Flora (b. 1884), Benjamin B. (b. 1887), Oscar (1890–1932), and Rudolph (1894–1953).[571] Between 1869 and 1880, Schneider's given name was rendered as Benedict or Benjamin but later documents as well as advertisements for the firm invariably used the shortened "Ben."

SCHRODER, DAVID (1851–1903, w. 1875–1902) and **D. SCHRODER & CO.** (1881–1898) David Schroder opened a wholesale jewelry firm in August 1875 using savings from his employment as a clerk at a wholesale dry goods firm, Moses & Company and backing from his father, B. Schroder, a wealthy merchant and real estate investor.[572] Initial credit reports were cautious, stating that Schroder knew "nothing about this business," but he was an astute businessman and the business prospered, earning good credit reports by 1881. In 1876, Schroder hired Aaron Herman (1851–1920), an employee of another wholesale jewelry firm, **A. Steinau & Co.**[573] Aaron Herman became one of the principals of the firm in 1881, and the firm's name was changed to D. Schroder & Co. David Schroder's younger brother, Isidore Schroder (1861–1941) joined the firm in 1889.[574] D. Schroder & Co. was a wholesale firm that initially carried jewelry, watches, and watch cases, but by 1893, it was advertising as "JOBBERS AND AGENTS OF EVERYTHING PERTAINING TO THE JEWELRY LINE" including silverware and novelties.[575]

The firm appeared to have weathered the economic downturn of 1893, and in November of that year, Herman reported that there had been a "decided improvement in business the last few days."[576] However, like many other Cincinnati firms of that era, financial problems ensued and the business filed for bankruptcy in 1898, citing assets of $60,000 and liabilities of $65,000.[577] David Schroeder opened a clock shop on Main Street, which he continued to run until ill health forced him to close the business in 1902.[578] Aaron Herman joined the wholesale jewelry firm of Herman & Loeb as a traveling salesman; Isidore joined the wholesale jewelry firm of **A.G. Schwab & Brother** as a salesman.[579]

SCHROEDER, FRED. (w. 1870–1886) Silversmith, 1873–75 CCDs. Appears in various CCDs between 1870–1886 as a jeweler or watch chain maker.

SCHROEDER, JOSEPH (w. 1866–1877) Silversmith, 1867 CCD. Appears in various CCDs between 1866–1877 as a silver plater or jeweler.

SCHWAB, ABRAHAM G. (1848–1931, w. 1872–1920),[580] **A.G. SCHWAB & BRO.** (1878–1906)[581] and **A.G. SCHWAB & SONS** (1907–1963)[582] Born in Germany, Abraham G. Schwab arrived in the United States in 1866 and was in Cincinnati by 1870, living with his sister Bertha and brother-in-law, the jeweler Louis Gutmann (1839–1901).[583] Schwab worked for Gutmann until 1878, when he left to start a wholesale jewelry business. His brother, **Moses Schwab**, joined him in June of that year and the firm's name became A.G. Schwab and Bro. Strictly a wholesale operation, the firm advertised that they were "Wholesale Dealers in Fine & Cheap Jewelry & Importers of Watches, Spectacles & Fancy Goods."[584] Credit reports were favorable, noting that they were doing good business and meeting all bills promptly.[585] By 1886, it was reported that their trade "extends throughout all of the Southern and Western States."[586] Although the firm specialized in watches and diamonds, they carried a full line of goods, including silverware.[587]

Abraham Schwab's son, Julian, and son-in-law Louis Lange (1874–1954) joined the firm around 1900, and his younger son, Herbert, joined the firm in 1907.[588] Moses Schwab withdrew from the firm in 1907, and the firm's name was changed to A.G. Schwab & Sons.[589] The firm thrived: a catalogue published in 1920 ran to 498 pages with a wide variety of watches, diamonds, jewelry, sterling silver tableware, and fancy goods.[590] When Abraham Schwab retired around 1920, the firm continued through 1954 under the direction of Louis Lange, and Julian and Herbert Schwab. After Lange's death in 1954, Julian and Herbert Schwab were principals of the firm until it closed in 1963.

In 1878, Abraham Schwab married Annette Schroder (1855–1938), a sister of **David Schroder**.[591] They were the parents of four children: Estelle (b. 1878), Rubie (1880–1957), Julian (1882–1966), and Herbert (1885–1969).[592]

SCHWAB, MOSES (1853–1934, w. 1872–1934) and THE MOSES SCHWAB JEWELRY CO. (1907–1934)[593]

Born in Germany, Moses Schwab arrived in the United States around 1868 and was in Cincinnati by 1870, living with his sister Bertha and brother-in-law, the jeweler Louis Gutmann.[594] Moses worked as a clerk and salesman at Gutmann's firm from 1872–1878, then he joined his brother Abraham in the wholesale jewelry firm **A.G. Schwab & Bro.** In 1907, Moses withdrew from that firm to start another wholesale jewelry firm that was primarily a purveyor of jewelry, diamonds, and watches although silverware was included in the CCD advertisements.[595]

Moses Schwab married Rosa Long (1859–1920) in 1880.[596] They were the parents of three daughters: Essie (1881–1963), Gertie (b. 1882), and Florence (b. 1885).[597]

SCHWING, JOSEPH G. (1867–1939, w. 1885–1897)[598]

Born in Lawrenceburg, Indiana, the son of German immigrants Katherine and Franz (Frank) Schwing, Joseph worked as an engraver at **Duhme & Co.** from 1885 to 1893.[599] From 1894 to 1897, CCDs list his occupation as a watch maker or jeweler. After the Dueber Watch Case Manufacturing Co. moved to Canton, Ohio, Schwing also relocated, working there as an engraver from 1902–1906.[600] Schwing's occupation was given as "retired engraver" in the jewelry industry on his death certificate.

SEHLSTEDT, JOHN A. (1816–1905, w. 1865–1880)[601]

Born in Sweden, Sehlstedt moved to the United States in 1852. The Swedish emigration records list his occupation as "guldsmeges" or goldsmith.[602] By 1865, Sehlstedt was working as a silversmith in Cincinnati and his given name had been anglicized to John from Johan. It was not possible to identify the firm(s) at which Sehlstedt worked as only his home address was given in CCDs. By 1885, he was working as a silversmith in Baltimore.[603] Sehlstedt married Anna Maria Pflum (or Phlum) in Cincinnati in 1867. They were the parents of eight children, three of whom were still alive in 1900: Gustav (b. 1867), Albert (b. 1873), and Anna (b. 1878).[604] Sehlstedt's surname was also rendered as Sehlstaedt, Sehlstett, Schlstedt, Schelstedt, Schisfedt, Schlesledt, Seelstedt, or Schlstedt in period documents.

SERODINO, HERMAN FRANZ (1821–1879, w. 1851–1879)[605]

Born in Germany, the son of Emilie and **Joseph Pierre Serodino**, Herman worked as a jeweler for Keibel, the Crown Jeweler in St. Petersburg, Russia, before coming to the United States in August 1849.[606] He sailed from Kronstadt, Russia, to Boston on the *Lyman*; the passenger manifest lists his occupation as "goldsmith."[607] By 1850, Herman had joined his parents and brother Joseph in Cincinnati.[608] "Joseph and Hermann Serodino" are included in the 1853 CCD business listings for watches, jewelry, and silverware, but no address is given, nor is the firm listed in the CCD alphabetical section. Herman is listed in the alphabetical section of the 1853 CCD as a jeweler at 148 Walnut, the address of the jewelry manufacturer **S.T. Carley**. From 1856–1859, he worked as a jeweler at the southwest corner of Main and Fourth, the address of **William Wilson McGrew**. In 1864, Serodino was in a partnership with Patrick Lennon as diamond setters, at the same address as jeweler **Harry R. Smith**.[609] From 1865–1868, he worked as a jeweler in a multi-story building at the northwest corner of Main and Fourth which housed numerous businesses, including those of **Herman Keck**, **G.A. Stinger**, and **William Owen**. Serodino subsequently worked for **Duhme & Co.** as a foreman in the jewelry manufacturing department. An article describing the Duhme display at the 1871 Cincinnati Industrial Exposition noted that "one who was all-important in this [the Duhme] establishment" was "Mr. Serodino, the diamond setter and the foreman in the factory."[610] A reminiscence published in 1923 recalls him as "the great goldsmith" at Duhme & Co.[611]

Serodino married Bertha Heinemann (1832–1898), also an immigrant from Germany, in 1854.[612] They were the parents of six children: Henry (b. 1855), Charles (b. 1857), Herman (b. 1859), Oscar (b. 1861), Ella (b. 1864), and Frank (b. 1872).[613] Herman Franz Serodino died in 1879 of apoplexy.[614] The Serodino surname was also rendered as Serodine, Serodina, Sarodina, Sirodino, or Scrodina in period documents.

SERODINO, JOSEPH PIERRE (1792–1862, w. 1859)[615] **Joseph Serodino**, his wife Emilie (1795–1863) and their son Joseph (b. about 1823) arrived in Baltimore, Maryland, from Bremen, Germany, in November 1847, on the *Hermine* where Joseph's occupation was given as tinmaker on the passenger manifest.[616] By 1850, the Serodinos were living in Cincinnati where Joseph was listed as a boarding house keeper in the census and as a tavern keeper in the CCD.[617] The Serodinos' oldest son, **Herman Franz Serodino**, had joined them by 1850. According to family lore, Joseph Pierre trained as a goldsmith and jeweler, probably in his homeland, Alsace-Lorraine, and worked as a jeweler and goldsmith in St. Petersburg, Russia, before coming to the United States, but supporting documentation has not been found.[618] The 1859 CCD lists I.P. Serodina [*sic*] as a silversmith, the only evidence that he practiced the trade in Cincinnati. The Joseph Serodino who advertised with **Herman Serodino** in the 1853 CCD business listings for jewelry, silverware, and watches, was probably Joseph Pierre Serodino.[619] However, the Joseph Serodino listed in the 1855 to 1858 CCDs as a clerk could have been either Joseph Pierre or his son, Joseph.

In the 1860 Federal Census, no occupation is given for Joseph Pierre. He died two years later at the age of 70 and is buried in Walnut Hills Cemetery with his wife Emilie.

SHERIDAN, PATRICK (w. 1875) Silversmith, 1875 CCD, working at the address of **Clemens Oskamp**'s manufactory.

SHOTT, EZEKIEL (1845–1892, w. 1868–1892)[620] Born in Dillsboro, Indiana, to German immigrants Moses and Harriet Shott, Ezekiel enlisted in the U.S. Army in 1861 as a "musician" (bugler) during the Civil War.[621] Discharged in Arkansas, he worked as a grocer in Pine Bluff before returning to Cincinnati around 1867, where he worked in the family's jewelry and cigar shop on West Fifth Street.[622] In 1870, Shott purchased the stock of the family shop, continuing the business under his name at the same address. By 1879, he had expanded the shop's offerings, advertising as a "Dealer in Diamonds, Watches, Clocks and Jewelry, Silver Ware, Bronzes, Spectacles, &c."[623] The shop was relocated to the Emery Arcade in 1887 and the name was changed in 1891 to "The Jewelry and Novelty Bazaar." After Shott's death in 1892, his widow Fannie moved the business to a location on Central Avenue, closing it two years later.

A very successful businessman, Shott died in 1892 "leaving a fortune" that included a large amount of property and interests in other business enterprises.[624] His success was, at least in part, the result of his activities as a money lender.[625] In 1870, Shott married Fannie Simon (1849–1920).[626]

SHOURDS, SAMUEL (1810–1872, w. 1836–1844)[627] Born in New Jersey in 1810, Shourds worked as a silversmith in Cincinnati from 1836 to 1844, but as only his home address is given in the CCDs, it is not possible to identify the firm(s) for which he worked. In 1850, the Shourds family was living at a Shaker community in Turtle Creek Township near Lebanon, Ohio, where his occupation was given as silversmith.[628] The family left the Shaker community before 1855 and moved to New Jersey where Samuel worked as a jeweler until his death.[629] Shourds may have been a descendant of a clock maker of the same name who worked from about 1740 to 1760 in Bordentown, New Jersey. However, the Shourds surname was common in New Jersey in the 18th and 19th centuries and no documentation of a relationship has been found.[630]

Shourds and his wife Almira Addis (1814–1883), the daughter of John and Elizabeth Addis, were the parents of five children: Eliza (b. about 1834), Emily or Emma (b. about 1841), Charles (b. about 1844), Eugene (b. about 1849), and Oscar (b. 1855).[631] Shourds' surname was also rendered as Sourds or Shoards in period documents.

SHUMARD, SAMUEL (w. 1834) Silversmith, 1834 CCD.

SILVERSMITH & M'CARTY (w. 1850/51) The partners advertised as silverware manufacturers in the CCD, but nothing else could be learned about the firm. There were no individuals with those names in the CCD alphabetical listings.

SIMONSON, WILLIAM (w. 1876) Silversmith, 1876 CCD.

SIMPSON, ALEXANDER (w. 1809–1813) Newspaper advertisements provide the only documentation for Alexander Simpson's Cincinnati residence as he was not included in the tax lists for 1810 or 1817, nor was he listed in the 1819 CCD.[632] The first advertisement, in May 1809, announced that Simpson had "commenced business" as a clock, watch and "mathematical instrument maker" at the corner of Market and Sycamore Streets.[633] In 1810, he relocated to the house of Herman [*sic*] (**Harmon**) **Long** on Main Street, and in December of that year he moved to a different location on Main Street, announcing that "the business in future will be carried on under the firm of **SIMPSON & PRICE**" and noting that they offered musical and chime clocks, time pieces, surveying instruments, and "all kinds of gold and silver work made on the shortest notice and finished with elegance."[634] Simpson's partnership with the silversmith **Philip Price** was very short-lived. In January 1811 Price announced the dissolution of the partnership and Simpson simultaneously advertised that he had moved and was manufacturing survey instruments of various types.[635] Simpson continued to advertise in local newspapers through 1813, moving one final time to Main Street near the Market House.[636] It is clear from his advertisements that he sold clocks, repaired watches, and was engaged in the manufacture of surveying instruments. Only the advertisement announcing the partnership with Price includes a reference to gold and silver work, which was undoubtedly expected to be Price's major contribution to the firm.

It is possible that he was the Alexander Simpson who was granted a divorce in Ohio from his wife in 1804.[637] If so, he had remarried by 1813, as his advertisements in 1813 and 1814 included the notice that "MRS. SIMPSON Continues to instruct Ladies on the Piano Forte." It is more likely that he was the clock, watch, and mathematical instruments maker who worked in western Maryland (1799–1805) and Brownsville, Pennsylvania (1806).[638] Simpson's first advertisement in Cincinnati included a certificate of endorsement from five men, issued in Brownsville (Southwestern Pennsylvania), June 24, 1806: "We the subscribers have carefully examined an instrument made by A. Simpson . . . it is better calculated to make a true survey than any other we have ever seen."[639]

SLANE, JACKSON (1829–1890, w. 1855–1890)[640] Born in Virginia in 1829, the son of Barbara and Elias Slane, Jackson was working as a clerk in Tiffin, Ohio in 1850.[641] He moved to Cincinnati around 1855, where he worked as a bookkeeper for **Beggs & Smith**. When Beggs left the firm in 1859, Jackson Slane and **Charles Boerner** became partners with **Harry R. Smith**, retaining the firm's name of Beggs & Smith.[642] Slane withdrew from the firm in 1862, enlisting in the Union Army as a 2nd Lieutenant.[643] By 1864, he had returned to Cincinnati and was working as a jeweler and bookkeeper for **William Wilson McGrew**.[644] In July 1870 Slane and **William Day**, another McGrew employee, formed the firm Slane & Day. Directory advertisements touted the firm as "Diamond Setters & Manufacturers of Fine Jewelry"; the Federal Non-Population Census for that year recorded the business as a manufacturer of jewelry, employing five males and one female with a stock of materials (gold, silver, precious stones) worth about $9,000.[645] The business was described as "silverware and jewelry" in the membership list of the Cincinnati Board of Trade in 1870. Credit reports in the early years of the partnership were favorable and noted that the principal business of the firm was doing work for other jewelers.[646] However, reports in January 1876 noted that Slane & Day had mortgaged their fixtures and stock and the firm failed later that year.[647] Slane continued in the trade as a diamond broker until his death in 1890.

Slane married Esther (Hettie) W. Cameron (1836–1893) in 1859.[648] They had five children: Anna (b. 1860), George (b. 1863), Charles (b. 1868), Frank (b. 1870), and Clark (b. 1871).[649]

SMALTE, J.H. (w. 1873) Silversmith, 1873 CCD. Appears in 1874 CCD as a driver for the Cincinnati Omnibus Co.

SMITH, CHARLES S. (w. 1870–1889) Silversmith, 1882 CCD. Appears in various CCDs between 1870–1889 as a clerk, silver plater, burnisher, jeweler, or watch case maker at **Duhme & Co.**

SMITH, CONRAD (b. 1797, w. 1829–1852)[650] Born in Pennsylvania, Smith was working as a silversmith in Cincinnati by 1829, living at Lydia Tomlinson's boarding house.[651] He was next included in the 1839/40 CCD and was still boarding at the same address, suggesting that he had remained in Cincinnati but, like the names of other boarders of that era, his had not been reliably collected for the directories. From 1846 to 1852, Smith worked as a silversmith or jeweler on Bank Alley, probably as an independent craftsman. Bank Alley was at that time also the location of other jewelers and silversmiths, including **George Stinger**, **William Feltmann**, **Dennis McHenry**, **Charles Kelly**, and **Herman Keck**. Listed as a silversmith in the 1850 Federal Census, Smith's occupation was given as a goldsmith in the 1850 Industry Census, where he was credited with a capital of $400, one employee and a product, jewelry, valued at $1,500 for the year.[652] He was not found in the CCDs after 1852, although a shoemaker of the same name was listed in the 1856 CCD.[653]

SMITH, E.W. (w. 1885–1886) Advertised in the CCD business listings for watches, clocks and jewelry. He was listed in the 1885 alphabetical section as the proprietor of *The Cincinnati Sporting and Dramatic Journal* and an installment dealer in silverware and clocks, but was not included in the 1886 alphabetical listings.

SMITH, EDWARD (w. 1874) Silversmith, 1874 CCD.

SMITH, GEORGE (w. 1846) Silversmith, 1846 CCD.

SMITH, JOHN (w. 1795–1802) In December 1795 Smith and **Isaac Van Nuys** advertised their metal-smithing business in Cincinnati, promising the "HIGHEST price will be given for OLD COPPER, BRASS, &c. &c."[654] In July 1802 Smith advertised that he "has commenced the GOLD SMITH & WATCH MAKING business, in the house opposite Mr. Nathaniel Reeder's store on Main street [*sic*]," and added that he also repaired watches."[655] There were several John (no middle initial) Smiths who worked as silversmiths and watch makers in the late 18th and 19th centuries.[656] It is possible that the silversmith active in Cincinnati was the John Smith who worked in Virginia (1789–1792), or Baltimore, MD (1814–1825), or Philadelphia, PA (1818–1822) but no documentation to confirm this has been found. An early fiddle-handled spoon struck with "I (pellet) SMITH" in a rectangular cartouche exists in a Cincinnati collection; the mark is that of the John Smith who worked in Baltimore.[657] In November 1796 Smith married his partner's sister, Phebe Van Nuys.[658] Phebe died in 1815 and is buried with **Isaac Paxton** and his family in Hamilton, Ohio.[659] No death or burial records for John Smith were found.

SOHNGER, WILLIAM (w. 1879) Silversmith, 1879 CCD.

SOLMAN, EDWARD (w. 1836) Silversmith, 1836 CCD.

SOTCHER, ABNER (1790–1826, w. 1817–1826)[660] Born in New Jersey, Sotcher was in Cincinnati by 1810, when he was included in the 1810 tax list for Cincinnati Township, Ohio.[661] He served as a private during the War of 1812, returning to Cincinnati, where he was included in the 1817 tax list.[662] Listed as a silversmith in the 1819 CCD, he was working at the address of **Woodruff & Deterly**. By 1820, Sotcher had formed a partnership with another silversmith, **Samuel Musgrove**. **Jacob Deterly**'s diary noted on March 7, 1820, that they had "commenced plating" and that their partnership was dissolved on April 7, 1820.[663] Sotcher was not listed in the 1825 CCD, probably because he did not live within the city limits of Cincinnati. The published notice for settlement of his estate listed Sarah Sotcher, who lived in Cincinnati Township, as the administrator when he died in 1826.[664]

SPEIER, JULIUS (b. about 1838, w. 1857–1860) Silversmith, 1860 CCD. Speier advertised in the 1859 and 1860 CCD business listings under "Jewelry, Silver Ware, Watches &c." Appears as a watch maker in the 1857 CCD. Listed as a peddler in the 1860 Federal Census, he was in Lexington, Kentucky, working as a hide dealer in 1870, and as a "commission" [merchant] in 1880.[665]

SPENCE, SIDNEY D. (w. 1867–1875) Silversmith, 1871 CCD. Appears in various CCDs between 1867–1875 as a jeweler, pen or pencil case maker working for the gold pen manufacturer, John Holland & Co.

STACKMAN, ARNST (w. 1848–1850) Silversmith, 1849/50 CCD. He was included in the 1848/49 Cincinnati Business Directory listings under "Watch and Clock Maker's Stores."

STEINAU, ABRAHAM JR. (1844–1904, w. 1868–1894)[666] "Abe" Steinau was active in several firms that sold jewelry, watches, silver, and fancy goods. His first venture was A. Steinau & Co. (1868–1875) with W.H. Loewenstein who had been a partner of Steinau's father-in-law, Selig Amberg, in the hat and cap trade. After Loewenstein retired in 1869, Steinau's father Joseph joined the business and the firm's name was changed to J. and A. Steinau. It was a short-lived partnership. By August, Abe Steinau was working alone and the firm's name reverted to A. Steinau & Co. October 1870 credit reports noted that the firm sold "a large amount of cheap jewelry" and was making a "handsome profit," but by September 1872 it was in bankruptcy.[667] The firm reopened at a new location, 80 West Fourth, in November of that year. Aaron Herman, an experienced jeweler, joined the firm.[668] Business was reported to be good through January 1875, but by October, Steinau's firm was again in bankruptcy and it closed before the end of the year.[669]

With the backing of Selig Amberg, who was by that time also in the jewelry business as S. Amberg & Co., the Steinau Jewelry Co. (1876–1879) opened in the Emery Arcade with Abe Steinau as the manager or proprietor. Although the firm continued to be known as the purveyor of cheap jewelry, its success grew as a result of some shrewd marketing efforts. Steinau designed and patented the "Imperial Casket," a set of jewelry in a leather box, which sold for $1.00.[670] It was sent postpaid to the purchaser and accompanied by a catalogue which generated future sales. However, although financial difficulties had been left behind, the firm still retained a "poor reputation" in the trade due to the earlier bankruptcies.[671]

In June 1879 the firm name was changed to **American Jewelry Co.** (1879–1890). It operated at the same location with Abe Steinau as the manager. Steinau became the proprietor when he bought Amberg's interest in January 1881.[672] The prospects of the firm improved, as did the quality of the stock. By 1884, advertisements included sterling silverware made by the Gorham Mfg. Co.[673]

Steinau relocated once again in October 1891 to the corner of Fourth and Race, dropping the American Jewelry name and operating under his own name.[674] In January 1894 Steinau auctioned the stock and retired, "a wealthy man," from the jewelry business.[675]

Steinau married Pauline Amberg (1849–1871) around 1869.[676] In 1872, a widower, he married Pauline's younger sister, Jennie (1856–1933).[677] They were the parents of eight children: Emma (b. 1873), Mary (b. 1875), Infant (b. 1877), Stella (b. 1878), James Garfield (b. 1881), Edgar (b. 1883), Gilbert (b. 1885), and Irene (b. 1888).[678]

STEINHART, LOUIS (w. 1879) Silversmith, 1879 CCD. Appears in 1880–1883 CCDs as a clerk, salesman, or traveling agent for Albert Mayer & Brothers, "wholesale hats, gloves, etc."

STEWART, EDWARD (w. 1877) Silversmith, 1877 CCD. Appears in various CCDs between 1874–1882 as a silver plater or burnisher.

STINGER, JOSEPH (1844–1923, w. 1868–1877)[679] Born in Cincinnati, a son of the Cincinnati silversmith **George A. Stinger**, Joseph was in California working as a silversmith at the age of 16.[680] In August 1861 he was in San Francisco, where he enlisted in the Union Army, serving until his discharge in 1864.[681] He had returned to Cincinnati and was working as a silversmith or in a related trade from 1868–1877. In 1880, Stinger was working as a silver plater in St. Louis, MO.[682] Seemingly not one to put down roots, Stinger was working in Baltimore in 1900.[683] Between 1903 and 1922, he was repeatedly admitted to and then discharged from U.S. National Homes for Disabled Volunteer Soldiers in Danville, IL and Dayton, OH.[684] Military records during those years give his occupation as a die maker. The final entry is dated April 1923, after his death.

Stinger married Melinda Ledoux (1850–1922) around 1867 in Cincinnati. They were the parents of seven children: Clotilde (b. 1869), George (b. 1870), Josepha E. (b. 1873), Charles (b. 1875), Joseph E. (b. 1879), Melinda (b. 1881), and John (b. 1887). While Joseph wandered, Melinda remained in St. Louis from 1880 until her death in 1922.[685]

STORY, SAMUEL (w. 1883–1885) Silversmith, 1883–1885 CCDs. Appears in various CCDS between 1877–1889 as machinist, brass finisher, polisher, clerk, or car cleaner.

STRAVA, HARMON (w. 1853) Goldsmith, 1853 CCD.

STRIETBECK, CHARLES (about 1845–1895, w. 1868–1885)[686] Silversmith, silver chaser or engraver, 1868–1885 CCDs. His occupation was listed as "chaser and engraver" in the 1880 Federal Census. The directory listings give only his home address and do not indicate where he was employed. The 1885–1894 CCDs give his occupation as a grocer in the Fairmount area of Cincinnati. His surname was also rendered as "Stortbeck" or "Streitbeck" in period documents.

STRUNK, CHRISTIAN HENRY (1828–1911, w. 1857–1892)[687] Born in Germany, Christian H. Strunk arrived in the United States in 1850.[688] He worked as a silversmith at the address of the **Kinsey** firms from 1857 to 1865 and subsequently worked at **Duhme & Co.** as a silversmith or engraver. After 1878, he worked as a "watchman" for Duhme & Co. Strunk's surname was also rendered as Stronk or Strunck while his given name was

recorded as C.H., Christopher, Christ. H., or Henry in some period documents.

Strunk and his wife Wilhelmina (Mina, Minnie) (1824–1892) were the parents of two sons, Frederick (b. 1856) and Henry Jr. (b. 1861).[689] Frederick was a goldsmith and jeweler who worked for **Clemens Hellebush** until 1887, and then worked as a manufacturing jeweler in partnerships with Charles Gerlach and Rudolph Hug.[690] Henry Jr. was a watch maker.[691]

STUTTELBERG, ARNOLD (w. 1839–1844) Silversmith, 1842 CCD. A native of Germany, Stuttelberg arrived in Baltimore in 1836.[692] He appears in the 1839/40, 1843, and 1844 CCDs as a goldsmith. The only other period documentation found for him was the record of his marriage to Caroline Wessler in May 1839 and his appearance in the 1840 Federal Census for Cincinnati.[693]

SUMMERFIELD, GEORGE (w. 1858–1868) Silversmith, 1858, 1866–68 CCDs. Appears in various CCDs between 1859–1868 as painter or soldier.

SUNDERMAN, HENRY (w. 1857–1864) Silversmith, 1858, 1861, 1864 CCDs, working at 24 West Fifth Street, the address of the **Kinsey** firms. Appears in various CCDs between 1857–1864 as silver finisher or laborer.

SWIFT, ___ (w. 1836/37) Silversmith, 1836/37 CCD. Swift's given name was not included in the CCD. He may have been the watch maker and jeweler, **William C. Swift**, who first appeared in the 1839/40 CCD.

TAFEL, THEODORE (w. 1874–1878) Silversmith, 1875–1876 CCDs, working for a dental and surgical instrument manufacturer. Appears in 1874, 1878 CCDs as a surgical instrument maker.

TELTHESTER, JOHN H. (1852–1923, w. 1869–1907)[694] Telthester worked as a silversmith from 1869 to 1894 and from 1899 to 1907. He appears as a jeweler or conductor in the 1895–1898 CCDs. The CCDs list only his home address and do not indicate where he was employed.

THEUERKAUF, WILLIAM (w. 1877–1881) Silversmith, 1877–1881 CCDs, working at **Duhme & Co.**

THOMPSON, JOSEPH P. (w. 1871–1874) Silversmith, 1874 CCD. Appears in 1871–1873 CCDs as a Britannia worker.

THOMPSON, LORENZO D. (w. 1873–1896) Silversmith, 1878–1879 CCDs. Appears in various CCDs between 1873–1896 as a silver finisher, buffer, or silver plater.

THORNTON, JOSEPH (1801–1877, w. 1825)[695] Listed as a watch maker and silversmith in the 1825 CCD, Thornton was working at 58 Main, also the address of **Enos Woodruff**, **Coleman Nash**, and **William Kimberly**. In 1923, a reminiscence noted that "Two men who combined watchmaking and silversmithing were Joseph Thornton from the District of Columbia and **Enos Woodruff**, from New Jersey."[696] Thornton's career as a silversmith was apparently very short as subsequent CCDs give his occupation as a produce merchant in partnership with his older brother Benjamin (1795–1843), a mail agent, letter carrier, or a steamboat captain.[697]

Thornton was the son of Jane (1764–1842) and Joseph Thornton (1763–1821). Joseph Thornton (b. 1763) was one of the first settlers of Cincinnati, arriving with the Israel Ludlow party from Limestone (Maysville), Kentucky late in 1787.[698]

TODD, TRACY (w. 1839/40) A silversmith from Virginia, Todd appeared only in the 1839/40 CCD. The record of his marriage to Nancy Marshall in May of 1844 indicates that he was still living in the Cincinnati area, but apparently not within the city limits.[699]

TURRELL, JOHN (b. 1820, w. 1873–1887)[700] Silversmith, 1880 CCD. Appears in various CCDs between 1873–1887 as a spoon caster or maker, silver plater, or Britannia worker. Worked at the address of Homan & Co., a silver and nickel plated ware manufacturer.

ULRICH, GEORGE (w. 1888–1892) Silversmith, 1888–1891 CCDs. Appears as a silver plater in 1892 CCD.

VAUPEL, JOHN C. (w. 1874–1881) Silversmith, 1877 CCD. Appears in various CCDs between 1874–1881 as a watch case maker, assistant bookkeeper, or clerk at **Duhme & Co.**

VOGT, HENRY (w. 1864–1870) Silversmith, 1864 CCD. Appears as jeweler in 1867–1870 CCDs.

WAGENLAENDER, WILLIAM G., SR. (1838–1919, w. 1866–1919)[701] Born in Germany, Wagenlaender was in Cincinnati working as a silversmith by 1866; his occupation was listed as "journeyman silversmith" in the 1870 Federal Census. From 1876 to 1894, Wagenlaender worked as a jeweler or "ring turner" for **Duhme & Co.**[702] In 1895, he started a firm manufacturing rings,

employing two of his sons, William G. Jr. (1870–1952) and Emil J. (1878–1949).[703] In 1896, William Jr. was listed as a principal in the firm and the firm's name became William Wagenlaender & Son. When Emil became one of the principals of the firm in 1911, the name was changed to include "Sons." In 1913, William Sr. turned the firm over to his sons, and the name was changed to William Wagenlaender's Sons. After 1915, it became Wagenlaender Brothers until it closed in 1924. William Sr. continued to work there until his death in 1919.

William Sr. married Mary Eith (1837–1906) while still living in Germany. They were the parents of four children for whom records were found: Sophie (b. 1863), Fred (1868–1929), William G. Jr. (1870–1952), and Emil (1878–1949).[704] The surname was spelled Wagenlaender in the CCDs; census and death records utilized the spelling Wagenlander, while both were used in various publications.

WAGNER, EMIL (1841–1931, w. 1872–1922)[705] Born in Germany, Wagner arrived in New York in April 1871 on the *Europa*; his occupation was listed on the passenger manifest as goldsmith.[706] By October 1871 Wagner was in Cincinnati, working as a jeweler or silversmith. From 1876 to 1882, he advertised in the CCD business listings under watches, clocks, and jewelry. He was apparently working as a jeweler at another shop from 1883–1895, but in 1896, he was again advertising as a jeweler with a shop on Freeman Avenue. His son Frank, a watch maker, joined the firm in 1900. The name of the firm was changed to E. Wagner & Son in 1906, when Frank was listed as a principal in the firm. Frank's wife Alma Frida (1883–1979) worked in the shop with Emil after Frank's death and became the proprietor after Emil retired in 1923.[707]

Wagner married Christiana Sprule (1848–1918) in 1871.[708] They were the parents of six children for whom records were found: Gustave Adolph (b. 1873), Emilia (b. 1877), Frank (1881–1919), Christina (b. 1886), Caroline (b. 1887), Margaret (b. 1889).[709]

WAGNER, JOHN (w. 1868) Silversmith, 1868 CCD.

WALLENSTEIN, MAYER & CO. (1903–1952)[710] In December 1903 Albert C. Wallenstein (1881–1952) and Walter Mayer (1878–1947), both of whom had been traveling salesmen for the wholesale jewelry firm S. & H. Gilsey, formed another wholesale jewelry firm, Wallenstein, Mayer & Co.[711] The firm prospered and by 1906, they were enlarging their business, adding a "new and extensive line of solid silver."[712] In 1907, the firm added another room to be used for an "extensively" expanded selection of hollowware and clocks.[713] The firm's *1912 Annual Catalogue* included, in addition to jewelry, clocks, and watches, a large selection of flatware and hollowware as well as "toilet sets" for grooming purposes.[714] After the death of Albert Wallenstein in 1952, Harry Greenwold became president of the firm and the firm's name was changed to Harry Greenwold-Wallenstein-Mayer Co.

WALSH, THOMAS (w. 1880–1882) Silversmith, 1880 CCD. Appears in 1881, 1882 CCDs as silver plater or silver buffer.

WALTER, B. (w. 1869) Silversmith, 1869 CCD.

WALTER, LOUIS (w. 1869) Silversmith, 1869 CCD. Appears in 1871 CCD as show case maker.

WEIST, JULIUS J. (1857–1885, w. 1873–1885)[715] Born in Lancaster, New York to German immigrants Robert and Dorothy Weist, Julius was working as a watch maker in Cincinnati at the age of 16. With support from his father, a produce merchant and grocer, Weist opened a jewelry store in 1878 on Main Street in the Over-the-Rhine neighborhood.[716] He advertised in the CCDs as a "Dealer in Fine Watches, Clocks, Jewelry and Silverware." The silverware was probably plated, not sterling, as credit reports estimate the investment in his stock at a modest $600. Later reports indicate that he was doing a small business and carried a "fair" stock.[717] The firm closed when Weist died of pulmonary consumption in September 1885.

WELLS, LEMUEL T. (1809–1879, w. 1846)[718] Born in Connecticut, Lemuel was the son of Elizabeth and Oliver Wells (1794–1836).[719] Oliver Wells arrived in Cincinnati in 1817, and established the first type foundry west of the Alleghenies.[720] Lemuel initially worked in the family business, but by 1839, was a partner of James Foster, Jr. in Wells & Foster, a firm that made surveying instruments and town clocks.[721] The 1846 CCD lists Wells' occupation as "silversmith, boards **David Kinsey**" but does not indicate where he worked.

By 1849, Wells had returned to the family business, the Cincinnati Type Foundry. After the death of his older brother Horace (1797–1851), he managed the business while simultaneously developing improvements to the printing machinery, obtaining five patents related to printing presses or their components.[722] In 1861, Wells transferred the business to his nephew Charles Wells and started a new endeavor with George Foster to manufacture copper face type, which was at that time a very speculative and new use of that metal.[723] By 1870, Wells had moved to a suburb of St. Louis, MO, where he started another type foundry.[724] He remained there until his death in 1879.

In 1845, Lemuel Wells married Mary Frances Foster, daughter of the well-known Cincinnati businessman James F. Foster, Sr. and

sister of Wells' partner.[725] Lemuel and Mary were the parents of eight children: James, Lemuel, George, Frank, Harry, Clara, William, and James F.[726]

WENNING, WILLIAM H. (1822–1907, w. 1848–1893)[727] Born in Germany, Wenning arrived in New York from Bremen in 1846.[728] By 1848, he was in Cincinnati where the brothers Henry and William Wenning advertised in the listings for "Jewelry, Watches, Silverware Stores & Manufacturers" in the 1848/49 Cincinnati Business Directory. When the 1849/50 CCD was published, Henry was in the iron business and William was working alone as a silversmith. From 1850–1859, William operated a jewelry, silverware and watch shop on Main Street. During the Civil War, he operated a soap and candle manufactory, but returned to the jewelry trade in 1866, opening a shop on Linn Street. Credit reports over the years noted that he was "industrious and considered perfectly honorable" and that his business while small was profitable.[729] Wenning retired in about 1893, and the business continued until 1919 under his son Charles (1855–1941). Charles closed the shop and retired around 1919.[730]

William Wenning and his wife Elizabeth (1826–1917) were the parents of six children for whom records were found: William Jr., Henrietta, Charles, Gustav, Emma, and Louis.[731] Wenning's given name appeared as Henry W., and his brother as Henry N., in the 1849/50 CCD.

WERLING, AUGUST (w. 1879–1881) Silversmith, 1880 Federal Census. Appears in 1879–1881 CCDs as silver layer or gilder.

WHITE, EDWARD T. (w. 1842–1844) Silversmith, 1842 CCD. Appears in 1843, 1844 CCDs as watch maker.

WHITESIDE, SAMUEL H. (1780–1851, w. 1810–1824)[732] Born in Rockbridge County, Virginia, Whiteside was included in the 1810 tax list for Cincinnati, but was also listed in the 1810 Census for Mercersburg, Pennsylvania, a small town some 20 miles north of Hagerstown, Maryland.[733] He married Anna Stewart in Hagerstown in September 1811.[734] By 1813, Whiteside had returned to Cincinnati where he advertised as a "Watch & Clockmaker, Silversmith & Jeweller [*sic*]" who "carries on the above business in all its various branches, in the neatest manner, and on the shortest notice."[735] He remained in Cincinnati until at least 1820, appearing in the 1819 CCD as a silversmith and as "engaged in manufactures" in the 1820 Census.[736] Around 1824, the family moved to Millcreek Township, a largely rural area outside the Cincinnati city limits, and settled on a sizeable farm.[737] Although census data indicate he was "engaged in agriculture," his son later recalled that he was a "jeweler by trade," so he may have continued to ply the trade while also farming.[738]

Samuel and Anna Whiteside (1793–1865) were the parents of two children for whom records were found: Amanda (about 1815–about 1845) and Addison (1816–after 1893). Samuel died in 1851, leaving all of his personal property and real estate to his wife, stipulating that upon her death it was to be the inheritance of his son Addison.[739] He also made provision to give $3,000 and pay college tuition for Amandus Silsby, the son of his daughter, Amanda.[740] Although some period documents spell the surname as Whitesides, it is rendered as Whiteside in his will and marriage records.

WHITESIDES, JOHN (w. 1793) The only evidence found for the presence of "John Whitesides, silversmith" in Cincinnati is an entry in the account book of Cincinnati merchants Smith & Findlay which details his purchase of fabric, buttons, yarn and "sticks" (possibly knitting needles) for which he paid in cash.[741] He was not listed in the Ohio census or tax lists of 1790, 1810, or 1817, nor was he found in later census compilations for Ohio.

Hollan has identified him as the Whiteside born in Augusta (later Rockbridge) County in western Virginia, who was working as a silversmith in Winchester, Virginia in 1787.[742] However, the John Whiteside(s) in Cincinnati could also have been one of the other John Whitesides found in early census data for Pennsylvania, Virginia, Kentucky, Indiana, and Illinois.

WILLIS, WILLIAM HENRY (1827–1911, w. 1850–1893)[743] Born in Germany, Willis was in Cincinnati by August 1849, when he married Caroline Langhorst.[744] He worked as a silversmith from 1850 until 1893, except during the Civil War when he worked as a baker. Willis worked initially at the **E. & D. Kinsey** shop and subsequently was at **Duhme & Co.** In the 1880 Census, his occupation was listed as a silver spoon and fork maker.[745]

William and Caroline were the parents of four children for whom records were found: John (b. 1850), Amelia (b. 1854), William (b. 1856), and Charles (b. 1860).[746] Willis' surname was also rendered as Willies, Vilicus, or Willows and his given name as Wilhelm, H.W., or Henry W. in some period documents.

WINSLOW, JAMES (w. 1866) Silversmith, 1866 CCD.

WOLF, NICHOLAS (w. 1875) Silversmith, 1875 CCD. Appears in 1876–1883 CCDs as a gilder or picture frame maker.

WORTHINGTON, ELIZABETH (1885–1974, w. 1912)[747] Born in Cincinnati, the daughter of Susan C. and William

Worthington, Elizabeth was listed in the 1912 *American Art Directory*, her medium given as "silverware."[748] She undoubtedly picked up the craft during studies at the Art Academy of Cincinnati where she was enrolled in the curriculum for "Decorative Design, China Painting, Metal and Leather Work" in 1909 and 1910.[749] In 1913, Worthington married Achilles H. Pugh.[750] They were the parents of four children: Elizabeth (b. 1915), Henry (b. 1917), Louise (b. 1919), and William (b. 1922).[751]

YOST, HENRY (w. 1842) Silversmith and watch maker, 1842 CCD.

YOUNG, CHARLES (w. 1872) Silversmith, 1872 CCD.

ZIMMERLEY, T. (w. 1866–1871) Silversmith, 1871 CCD. Appears in 1866–1870 CCDs as a watch case maker or engraver.

ZIMMERMANN, GUSTAV ADOLPHUS (1858–1935, w. 1875–1934)[752] The son of Johanna and **Jacob Zimmermann**, Gustav arrived in New York with his parents in 1867.[753] He worked as a watch chain maker at **Duhme & Co.** before opening a shop in Dayton, Kentucky, in 1884.[754] Zimmermann, who advertised that he was a dealer in silverware, jewelry, watches, fancy goods, notions, Queensware, etc., relocated his shop to Cincinnati's Broadway Street in 1886, and continued there until it closed in 1934. Little is known about the extent of his stock—an article about a burglary in 1891 mentions only a gold watch, diamond studs, and a ring.[755]

Zimmermann married Carolyn Boehm (1859–1923) in 1878 in Newport, Kentucky.[756] They were the parents of one daughter, May Belle (b. 1892).[757] The surname was also rendered as Zimmerman, and his given name as Gus or Gust, in period documents.

ZIMMERMANN, JACOB (1816–1883, w. 1870–1883)[758] In 1867, Jacob Zimmermann and his family left their native Switzerland, arriving in New York in June on the *William Penn*.[759] A jeweler by trade, Jacob brought his brass jeweler's bench lathe with him. It is in the collection of the Cincinnati Museum Center, CMS1990.394. By 1870 the Zimmermanns were living in Cincinnati where Jacob worked as a silversmith or machinist for **Duhme & Co.** until his death. The family moved to Newport, Kentucky, around 1872. Jacob and Johanna Zimmermann (b. 1822, Germany) were the parents of nine children born in Germany: Carl, Emilia, Bertha, Mathilda, Gustav, Emma, Otto, Emil, Frida, and one born in Ohio, Clara.[760] The surname was also rendered as Zimmerman in period documents.

References

AVERDICK: Michael R. Averdick, *A Directory of Silversmiths, Jewelers, Watch and Clock Makers and Related Trades of Covington and Newport, Kentucky & Vicinity, 1833–1900,* Covington, KY: 829 Willard Street Press, 2002

BECKMAN: Elizabeth D. Beckman, *An In-Depth Study of the Cincinnati Silversmiths, Jewelers, Watch and Clockmakers Through 1850,* Cincinnati: B.B. & Co., 1975

BOULTINGHOUSE: Marquis Boultinghouse, *Silversmiths, Jewelers, Clock and Watch Makers of Kentucky, 1785–1900,* Lexington, KY: privately published, 1980

CALDWELL: Benjamin H. Caldwell, *Tennessee Silversmiths,* Winston-Salem, NC: Museum of Early Southern Decorative Arts, 1988

CATHOLIC CEMETERIES: Burial records, Cincinnati Catholic Cemetery Society [Baltimore Pike, St. John, St. Jospeh, St. Mary], www.cccsohio.org

CCD: Cincinnati City Directories, 1819–1941. http://virtuallibrary.cincinnatilibrary.org/virtuallibrary/vl_citydir.aspx

CHS: Cincinnati Historical Society

CIST 1841: Charles Cist, *Cincinnati in 1841: Its Early Annals and Future Prospects,* Cincinnati: E. Morgan, 1841

CIST 1851: Charles Cist, *Sketches and Statistics of Cincinnati in 1851,* Cincinnati: Wm. H. Moore & Co., 1851

CIST MISCELLANY: Charles Cist, *The Cincinnati Miscellany*, vol. 2, Cincinnati: Robinson & Jones, 1846

CIVIL WAR DRAFT: U.S. Civil War Draft Registrations Records, 1863–1865, https://familysearch.org

CONTEUR: Conteur (Edwin Henderson), "Manufacture and Sale of Jewelry in Cincinnati During Preceding Century," *Cincinnati Enquirer,* October 23, 1923

CUTTEN: George Barton Cutten, *The Silversmiths, Watchmakers and Jewelers of The State of New York Outside of New York City*, New York: privately printed, 1939

CUTTEN VIRGINIA: George Barton Cutten, *The Silversmiths of Virginia*, Richmond, Virginia: The Dietz Press Inc., 1952.

DARLING: The Darling Foundation, *New York State Silversmiths*, Eggertsville, New York: The Darling Foundation, 1964

DETERLY: Jacob Deterly, *"Remarks" of Jacob Deterly: diary from 1819 to 1848; life in southern Ohio: Cincinnati, Marietta, Athens,* transcribed and indexed by Madge Hubbard and Opal Saffell, Seattle: Northwest Lineage Researcher, 1972

DUN: Ohio volumes, R.G. Dun & Co. Collection, Baker Library, Harvard Business School

ENGELHARDT: George W. Engelhardt, *Cincinnati, The Queen City,* Cincinnati: Geo. W. Engelhardt Co., 1901

FEDERAL CENSUS: U.S. Federal Census, Cincinnati, Hamilton, Ohio

FORD: Henry A. Ford and Mrs. Kate B. Ford, *History of Cincinnati,* Cleveland: L.A. Williams & Co., 1881

GIBBS: James W. Gibbs, *Dixie Clockmakers*, Gretna, LA: Pelican Publishing Co., 1979

GOLDSBOROUGH: Jennifer Faulds Goldsborough, *Silver in Maryland*, Baltimore: Museum and Library of Maryland History, Maryland Historical Society, 1983

GOSS: Charles F. Goss, *Cincinnati, The Queen City, 1788–1912*, Cincinnati: S.J. Clarke Publishing Company, 1912

GREVE: Charles T. Greve, *Centennial History of Cincinnati and Its Representative Citizens*, Chicago: Biographical Publishing Co, 1904

GREENWOOD CEMETERY: Burial records, Greenwood Cemetery Association, Hamilton, Butler, Ohio, www.greenwoodcemeteryhamilton.com/Burials-on-the-Web

HCPC, MARRIAGES: Hamilton County Probate Court Archived Records, Marriages, www.probatect.org/CourtRecordsArchive/bukmarriages.aspx

HCPC, WILLS: Hamilton County Probate Court Archived Records, Wills, http://www.probatect.org/CourtRecordsArchive/bukwills.aspx

HOLLAN: Catherine B. Hollan, *Virginia Silversmiths, Jewelers, Watch- and Clockmakers, 1607–1860*, McLean, VA: Hollan Press, 2010.

JCHR: *Jewelers' Circular and Horological Review* (titled *Jewelers' Keystone,* 1869–1873, and later *The Jewelers' Circular and Horological Review,* 1873–1912, following the merger of the *American Horological Journal,* est. 1869, and *The Jewelers' Circular,* est. 1870)

JEWISH CEMETERIES: Burial records, Jewish Cemeteries of Greater Cincinnati [Chestnut Street, Clifton, Covedale, Hamilton, Montgomery, Walnut Hills], www.jcemcin.org/genealogy

JEWISH ENCYCLOPEDIA: *The Jewish Encyclopedia*, vol. 4, New York and London: Funk and Wagnalls Company, 1912

JOBLIN: M. Joblin, *Cincinnati Past and Present*, Cincinnati: Elm Street Printing Co., 1872.

KENNY: Daniel J. Kenny, *Kenny's Illustrated Cincinnati*, Cincinnati: Geo. E. Stevens & Co., 1875

LEADING MANUFACTURERS: *Leading Manufacturers and Merchants of Cincinnati and Environs*, New York: International Publishing Co., 1886

LEONARD: John W. Leonard, *The Centennial Review of Cincinnati: one hundred years of progress in commerce, manufactures, the professions, and in social and municipal life*, Cincinnati: J.M. Elstner, 1888

MACK: Norman Mack, *Missouri's Silver Age*, Carbondale, IL: Southern Illinois University Press, 2005

MARKENS: Isaac Markens, *The Hebrews in America: A Series of Historical & Biographical Sketches*, New York: Isaac Markens, 1888

MCBRIDE: James McBride, *Pioneer Biography: Sketches of the Lives of some of the Early Settlers of Butler County, Ohio*, vol. 2, Cincinnati: Robert Clarke & Co., 1871

MORSE: Edgar W. Morse, *Silver in the Golden State*, Oakland, CA: The Oakland Museum History Department, 1986.

NELSON: *History of Cincinnati and Hamilton County, Ohio*, Cincinnati: S.B. Nelson & Co., 1894

OHIO DEATHS: Ohio Deaths, 1908–1953, https://familysearch.org.

PHILLIPSON: David Phillipson, "The Jewish Pioneers of the Ohio Valley," *Publications of the American Jewish Historical Society* 8, Baltimore, MD: Lord Baltimore Press, 1900

PLEASANTS AND SILL: J. Hall Pleasants and Howard Sill, *Maryland Silversmiths, 1715–1830*, Baltimore: Lord Baltimore Press, 1930

ROBSON: Charles Robson, *Biographical Encyclopedia of Ohio*, Cincinnati: Galaxy Publishing Co.,1876

SHOTWELL: John B. Shotwell, *A History of the Schools of Cincinnati*, Cincinnati: The School Life Co., 1902

SPRING GROVE: Burial records, Spring Grove Cemetery, Cincinnati, Ohio, www.springgrove.org/genealogy

UC: Cincinnati Health Department, University of Cincinnati Archives and Rare Books Library, Cincinnati Birth and Death Records, 1865–1912, http://drc.libraries.uc.edu/handle/2374.UC/2032

VON KHRUM: Paul Von Khrum, *Silversmiths of New York City*, New York: Von Khrum, 1978

WALNUT HILLS: Burial records, Walnut Hills Cemetery, Cincinnati, Ohio, http://www.walnuthillscemetery.org/Genealogy.html

WIERNIK: Peter Wiernik, *History of the Jews in America*, New York: The Jewish Press Publishing Company, 1912

1. 1891–1922 CCDs.
2. Spring Grove; 1881–1890 CCDs.
3. Spring Grove.
4. *JCHR* (November 13, 1895): 35.
5. *JCHR* (August 11, 1912): 128.
6. Conteur.
7. 1850 Federal Census; 1868–1872 CCDs.
8. CHS, Photograph Files, "Shops & Stores," GA-6-014, GA-11-010.
9. CHS, Photograph Files, "Shops & Stores," GA-8-001, GA-6-002.
10. Indiana Marriages, 1900–1941, https://familysearch.org
11. 1900 Federal Census.
12. Catholic Cemeteries.
13. Spring Grove.
14. Advertisement, *Cincinnati Daily Gazette*, June 17, 1833, reproduced in Beckman, 121. It should be noted that there were two entities that went by the name of C. Allen & Co., the earlier firm comprised of Caleb Allen, Jr. and Pulaski Scovil, and a later firm comprised of Caleb and William Allen.
15. Advertisement, *Cincinnati Daily Gazette*, June 17, 1833, reproduced in Beckman, 1.
16. Advertisement, *Cincinnati Daily Gazette*, September 6, 1834, reproduced in Beckman, 117; 1836 CCD, advertising section (not paginated) at front.
17. Advertisement, *Western Address Directory*, 1837, cited in Beckman, 2.
18. 1850 Federal Census.
19. 1860, 1870 Federal Census.
20. Spring Grove.
21. HCPC, Marriages, vol. A-5, p. 190; Massachusetts Deaths, 1841–1915, https://familysearch.org.
22. Spring Grove; 1860, 1870 Federal Census; HCPC, Wills, vol. 30, p. 1–2.
23. Spring Grove; Robson, 20–21.
24. Such combs, used in the high, elaborate hair styles favored by fashionable women of the early 19th century, were primarily for decoration. Commonly made out of horn or tortoise-shell, they were intricately carved and/or cut and could be as high as 6". See Frances A. Breckenridge, *Recollections of a New England Town*, The Journal Publishing Co, Meriden CT: 1899, 129–30. John W. Sheppard (w. 1829–1872) was initially a comb maker in Cincinnati. When fashions changed and they were no longer in demand, he turned to retailing other "fancy goods."
25. Advertisement, 1839/40 CCD, 50.
26. Advertisement, 1842 CCD, 230; 1842–1844 CCDs.
27. Advertisement, 1853 CCD 272; 1855 CCD, 144; 1856 CCD, 128; Robson, 20.
28. Robson, 21.
29. Robson, 21; Spring Grove.
30. HCPC, Wills, vol. 50, p. 331–444.
31. 1866–1955 CCDs.
32. *Cincinnati Daily Gazette*, November 2, 1878, 12; Spring Grove.
33. 1879–1965 CCDs.
34. Dun, vol. 11, p. 274.
35. 1884–1888 CCDs.
36. Advertisement, *Cincinnati Commercial Tribune*, December 20, 1889, 5.
37. JCHR (October 14, 1891):28; 1391–1894 CCDs.
38. Spring Grove; Enyel dit Ange, age 36, goldsmith, New York Passenger Lists, 1820–1857, www.ancestry.com.
39. Von Khrum, 6; Darling, 19.
40. HCPC, Marriages, vol. A-4, p. 188.
41. Indiana Marriages, 1780–1992, https://familysearch.org.
42. Spring Grove; 1860 Federal Census.
43. 1850 Federal Census, Guernsey County, Ohio.
44. "The Late Emmett W. Ankeny," *Cincinnati Enquirer*, March 30, 1874, 8; Civil War Draft.
45. Conteur.
46. *Cincinnati Enquirer*, August 26, 1870, 8.
47. Emmit [sic] Ankeny, death notice, *Cincinnati Daily Gazette*, March 30, 1874, 5; Emmett Ankeny, death notice, *Cincinnati Commercial*, March 29, 1874, 7; Burial records, Greenlawn Cemetery, Portsmouth, Ohio.
48. 1860 Federal Census.
49. 1855 CCD.
50. Dun, vol. 2, p. 154.
51. Ibid.; 1870 Federal Census, Columbus, Ward 1, Ohio.
52. Spring Grove; 1850 Federal Census.
53. *US Veterans Gravesites*, circa 1775–2006, Knoxville National Cemetery, Ancestry.com.
54. 1850 Federal Census; Spring Grove.
55. Dun, vol. 4, p. 140.
56. Ohio Deaths; 1900 Federal Census.
57. Birth date published at http://genforum.genealogy.com/benson/messages/2767.html.
58. Advertisement, *The Inquisitor & Cincinnati Advertiser*, June 22, 1819, reproduced in Beckman, 11.
59. 1819 CCD; Advertisement, *Western Spy*, September 4, 1819. An identical advertisement is reproduced in Beckman, 123, who cites publication in *The Inquisitor and Cincinnati Advertiser*, June 22, 1819. However, it does not appear in this issue.
60. "Married," *Ladies' Literary Cabinet*, vol.2, no. 2 (Saturday May 20, 1820): 16.
61. UC.
62. Dun, vol. 2, p. 265.
63. Spring Grove; 1868–1879 CCDs.
64. Notice, *Liberty Hall*, October 19, 1813, 2.
65. Advertisement, *Western Spy*, September 27, 1813, reproduced in Beckman, 13.
66. Ibid.
67. Advertisement, *Western Spy*, February 18, 1815, reproduced in Beckman, 13.
68. Advertisement, *Western Spy*, August 25, 1815.
69. UC (Theo. Beltz).
70. Advertisement, *Western Spy*, August 21, 1817, reproduced in Beckman, 21.
71. 1860 Federal Census.
72. U.S. Passport Applications, 1795–1925, M. Emil Brodersen, Issue Date April 2, 1879, www.ancestry.com.
73. New York Passenger Lists 1820–1957, www.ancestry.com.
74. Ohio Deaths.
75. 1900 Federal Census; Ohio Deaths; 1866–1915 CCDs.
76. Dun, vol. 10, p. 342.
77. Dun, vol. 10, p. 239.
78. Dun, vol. 10, p. 289.
79. 1900 Federal Census.
80. 1880, 1900 Federal Censuses.
81. 1894–1900 CCDs.
82. 1850 Federal Census, Louisville, Jefferson, Kentucky; 1852 Louisville City Directory, cited in Boultinghouse, 87.
83. U.S. Passport Applications, 1795–1925, www.ancestry.com; New York Passenger Lists, 1820–1957, www.ancestry.com.
84. HCPC, Marriages, vol. B6, p. 329.
85. 1850, 1860, 1880 Federal Censuses; Civil War Draft; 1857–1891 CCDs.
86. 1860, 1870 Federal Censuses; 1880 Federal Census, Laurelton, Franklin, IN (Regina Close); Regina Closs, burial record, Conwell Cemetery, Laurel, IN, *findagrave.com*.
87. Death notice, *Cincinnati Freie Presse*, January 10, 1909, 8.
88. Spring Grove.
89. Pleasants and Sill, 284, 294; Goldsborough, 247; Pleasants and Sill report that he was one of the few Maryland watch and clock makers who did not also make or sell silver. Directory listings in Cincinnati invariably give his occupation as a watch maker.
90. Advertisement, *Cincinnati Daily Gazette*, May 1, 1832, reproduced in Beckman, 96; Advertisement, *Cincinnati Whig*, February 10, 1834, reproduced in Beckman, 97.
91. Dun, vol. 1, p. 90.
92. Thomas A. has been confused with another Thomas Conway, a carpenter and builder who worked in Cincinnati in the 1850s, see Beckman, 37. A careful comparison of CCDs, cemetery and census records supports a distinction between the two men.
93. 1870 Federal Census, Milwaukee, Milwaukee, Wisconsin.
94. Maryland Marriages 1666–1970, https://familysearch.org; Spring Grove. Beckman (p. 37) reports that Conway married Sara Light in 1835, again mixing together the two Thomas Conways. After Catherine's death in 1849, federal census data for Thomas A. Conway does not include a spouse.
95. 1850 Federal Census; Spring Grove.
96. Pleasants and Sill, 29, 161, 184, 284, 294, 299.
97. Advertisement, *Cincinnati Daily Gazette*, May 1, 1832, and September 18, 1832, reproduced in Beckman, 96, 37.
98. Advertisement, *Cincinnati Whig*, February 10, 1834, reproduced in Beckman, 97.
99. Spring Grove; 1839/40–1851/52 CCDs.
100. Obituary, *JCHR* 27, no. 6 (July 1886): 203; 1839/40–1881 CCDs.
101. Ford, 529. Other sources (Beckman, 40, Leonard, 67) record the year as 1837.
102. Dun, vol. 4, p. 811.
103. Ford, 529; *Leading Manufacturers*, 89; Leonard, 67.
104. Ford, 529; Dun, vol. 7, p. 406.
105. *JCHR* 27, no. 6 (July 1886): 203.
106. HCPC, Marriages, vol. A-8, p. 270; UC.
107. *JCHR* (November 20, 1918): 96; Gibbs, 155; Catholic Cemeteries.
108. Spring Grove; 1865–1915 CCDs.
109. 1850 Federal Census, Green Township, Hamilton, Ohio.
110. 1860 Federal Census, Ripley, Brown, Ohio; John C. was not related to John or Joseph Daller.
111. Spring Grove.
112. *JCHR* (February 1, 1903): 134.
113. 1900 Federal Census; Ohio Deaths; 1862–1895 CCDs.
114. Dun, vol. 7, p. 406.
115. *Leading Manufacturers*, 89.
116. Leonard, 67.
117. *Cincinnati Enquirer*, August 15, 1912, 11. It is likely that Bertling, listed in the 1870 Federal Census as "apprentice watchmaker," had been apprenticed to John Daller.
118. Daller had extensive real estate investments as well as a significant investment in the Dueber Watchcase Manufacturing Co.; Dun, vol. 4, p. 81; Gibbs, 157.
119. UC (Fred A. Dassel); 1856–1894 CCDs.
120. familysearch.org, Friedrich Anton Dassel; New York Passenger Lists, 1820–1857, Anton Dassel, www.ancestry.com.
121. Dun, vol. 8, p. 150.
122. 1860, 1870, 1880 Federal Censuses; Civil War Draft.
123. Ohio County Marriages, 1790–1950, https://familysearch.org; 1900 Federal Census.
124. 1880 Federal Census.
125. Spring Grove;1860 Federal Census, Xenia, Greene, Ohio; 1862–1910 CCDs.
126. 1860 Federal Census, Xenia, Greene, Ohio.
127. Kentucky Marriages; 1900 Federal Census; Spring Grove; 1861–1925 CCDs.
128. 1870 Federal Census, Newport, Campbell, Kentucky.

129. Dun, vol. 8, p. 187.
130. 1872–1876 CCDs.
131. Dun, vol. 8, pp. 187, 221.
132. 1880 Federal Census, Lexington, Fayette, KY; Advertisement, 1893 Lexington City Directory, reproduced in Boultinghouse, 95.
133. 1900, 1910 Federal Census, Brooklyn, Kings, NY.
134. Burial record, St. Stephens Cemetery, Ft. Thomas, KY; 1915–1925 CCDs; 1925 Federal Census.
135. Walnut Hills.
136. Clifford Neal Smith, *Early Nineteenth Century German Settlers in Ohio (Mainly Cincinnati and Environs), Kentucky, and Other States*, McNeal, AZ: Westland Publications, 1991, part 4A, 14.
137. 1850 Federal Census.
138. 1869–1883 CCDs; Dun, vol. 9, pp. 22, 23, 144, 145.
139. 1884 CCD.
140. U.S. Passport Applications, 1795–1925, www.ancestry.com.
141. Beckman, 44.
142. Walnut Hills; Ohio Deaths.
143. 1860 Federal Census.
144. 1870 Federal Census.
145. HCPC, Marriages, vol. 71, p. 124; Walnut Hills; 1900 Federal Census.
146. 1860 Federal Census; Indiana Death Index 1882-1920, familysearch.com.; 1856–1867 CCDs.
147. Spring Grove; 1849/50–1883 CCDs.
148. *Williams' Cincinnati Guide and General Business Directory for 1848/49*, Cincinnati: C.S. Williams & Son, 1848.
149. 1850, 1860, 1870, 1880 Federal Censuses.
150. Dun, vol. 8, p. 62.
151. Spring Grove; 1885-1922 CCDs.
152. HCPC, Marriages, vol A18, p. 438; Spring Grove.
153. Spring Grove.
154. Catholic Cemeteries; 1860–1899 CCDs.
155. Gibbs, 155-7.
156. 1850 Federal Census; Philadelphia, Pennsylvania Death Index, 1803–1915, https://familysearch.org; 1839/40–1853 CCDs.
157. Goldsborough, 250; 1870, 1880 Federal Censuses, Philadelphia, Philadelphia, Pennsylvania.
158. New York 1820–1850 Passenger and Immigration Lists, www.ancestry.com. The ship manifest lists the parents, Henry (age 4), Jane (age 2), and John (age 6 months). Four more children were born in Ohio: William Moses, Eli (Ellis H.), Richard H., and Ellen.; Recorded birth years for Ellis Elias vary between 1836 and 1840. The most probable year was 1838, the year given in the 1860 Federal Census and the Civil War Draft .
159. Dun, vol. 1, p. 156.
160. Ibid.
161. Another Ellis Elias appears in the CCDs from 1857 to 1904. At least one of his appearances (messenger in 1862) occurs when E.H. Elias was also listed. Elias (no middle initial) Ellis was listed with various occupations, including loan office, pawn broker, traveling salesman, and auctioneer. The 1900 Federal Census lists him as born in England, 1837.
162. *New York Herald–Tribune*, April 2, 1872.
163. New York City Directories.
164. 1880 Federal Census, New York City, New York, New York.
165. *Cincinnati Daily Gazette*, June 30, 1881, 3. The CDG article also gives details about the estate and claimants/heirs thereto: Richard H. Elias, William H. Elias, John W. Elias, Jane E. Byrnes (sister, of Gallipolis, OH), Elias H. Skees (nephew, of Charlestown, WV), and Maggie Elias (widow) as well as some unsavory comments about Elias' business methods.
166. 1900 Federal Census, Manhattan, New York, New York.
167. 1858 CCD.
168. The 1863 CCD indicates that he was a clerk at the shop of another brother, Ellis H. Elias.
169. 1859–1864 CCDs.
170. Dun, vol. 5, p. 51.
171. Ibid.
172. *Cincinnati Enquirer*, 1869: October 18, 5; November 1, 5; November 9, 5; December 13, 5; December 22, 5; December 30, 8.
173. Advertisement, *Cincinnati Enquirer*, March 1, 1870, 5.
174. 1878 New York City Directory; 1880, 1900, 1910 Federal Censuses, Manhattan, New York, New York
175. Elias is interred at Collins Center Cemetery, www.findagrave.com.
176. Ohio, County Marriages, 1789–1994, https://familysearch.org; 1869–1875 CCDs.
177. 1870 Federal Census; 1880 and 1900 Federal Censuses, Manhattan, New York, NY.
178. 1900 Federal Census; Ohio Department of Health, Ohio Deaths 1908–1932, 1938–2007; 1869–1917 CCDs.
179. 1860 Federal Census.
180. 1869 CCD; 1870 Federal Census.
181. Since the Engbersen residence was within the city limits after 1874, the CCDs list only his home address, not his employer.
182. Both worked in room 22 of the Lion Building in 1906–1907 and both were located in room 14 from 1908–1915.
183. According to family history, after 1914, Engbersen worked for local jewelry stores, repairing items. John J. Engbersen (grandson of William J. Engbersen) to Amy Dehan, May 12, 2005.
184. 1900 Federal Census; Ohio Deaths.
185. 1900 Federal Census.
186. Death notice, *Cincinnati Commercial*, June 22, 1875, 5; 1857–1875 CCDs.
187. 1850 Federal Census.
188. Civil War Draft; 1870 Federal Census, 1870–1875 CCDs.
189. Spring Grove.
190. 1870–1920 CCDs.
191. Advertisement, *Cincinnati Enquirer*, November 8, 1898, 12: "Notice: Mr. D.E. Fletcher, For thirty years in charge of the Watch Repairing Department of the former firm of Duhme & Co, can now be found with Duhme Brothers & Co."
192. Spring Grove.
193. 1900 Federal Census, Columbia Township, Hamilton, Ohio; Spring Grove.
194. Carl A.F. Gabler, Spring Grove.
195. HCPC, Marriages, vol. A27, p. 320.
196. Spring Grove; 1861–1905 CCDs.
197. Spring Grove, 1842–1858 CCDs.
198. 1867–1888 CCDs; Conteur; Newstedt and Knighton, *A Cincinnati Saga*, 47; Dun, vol. 3, p. 98.
199. *JCHR* (September 20, 1905): 81.
200. *JCHR* (March 24, 1909): 88; *JCHR* (December 15, 1909): 88.
201. 1910 Federal Census; Spring Grove.
202. 1900 Federal Census; Spring Grove.
203. Spring Grove.
204. UC.
205. Caldwell, 90.
206. Deterly 2:67.
207. Isaac Covalt, Cemetery Records of Methodist Episcopal Church, Cincinnati, m85, microfilm #59, roll #2, CHS.
208. Caldwell, 89.
209. Garner, eBay listings and private collections, Cincinnati silver binders, Cincinnati Art Museum.
210. Ibid.; William Johnston Hogan, *Huntington Silversmiths 1763–1885*, Durham, NC: Sir Walter Press, 1977, 55–56; 1855–1887 CCDs.
211. Spring Grove.
212. Iowa Marriages, 1809–1992, https://familysearch.org.
213. William Disney, *Reports of Cases Argued and Determined in The Superior Court of Cincinnati from 1858 to 1860*, Cincinnati: Robert Clarke & Co., 1871, 2:86–90.
214. *JCHR* 34 (May 19, 1897): 7.
215. Conteur.
216. Advertisement, *Cincinnati Daily Gazette*, April 29, 1837, reproduced in Beckman, 58.
217. Spring Grove; 1872–1900 CCDs.
218. 1870 Federal Census; 1872 CCD.
219. Conteur; *JCHR* 34 (May 19, 1897): 15.
220. Plaut was a wholesale and retail firm from 1879–1910. It was wholesale only after 1910.
221. United States Patent Office: Design No. 21,142, November 5, 1891.
222. Robert M. Wilhelm, "Gorham's Cincinnatus Souvenir Spoon," *Silver Magazine* 44, no. 1 (January/February 2012): 40; *Souvenir Spoon*, Cincinnati Art Museum, Gift of Michele Sandler, 2003.21.
223. *JCHR* 34 (May 19, 1897): 15.
224. *Investment News' Directory of Investment Bankers and Brokers of America*, Chicago, IL: Investment Service Company, 1922, 273; 1906–1928 CCDs.
225. Spring Grove.
226. HCPC, Marriages, vol. A2, p. 311. Jane's maiden name has been recorded with various spellings: as Harsha in Beckman (p 59) and in death records for her children Ann Eliza, Charles A., and Alice G.; as Henshaw in the record for daughter Margaret C.; and as Harsker in her own burial record. She was probably the daughter of the cooper, Thomas Harshe, who appeared in the 1819 CCD.
227. Advertisement, *Cincinnati Emporium*, December 2, 1824, reproduced in Beckman, 59.
228. The 1850, 1860, and 1870 Federal Censuses also list his occupation as a railroad agent; 1834–1874 CCDs.
229. Spring Grove.
230. 1850 Federal Census; 1849/50–1860 CCDs; Boultinghouse does not include a silversmith of the name Graves in Kentucky.
231. U.S. Passport Applications 1795–1925, www.ancestry.com; 1870, 1900 Federal Censuses; 1870 CCD.
232. 1876 CCD.
233. 1884 CCD. No information as to the persons who constituted the "and Company" was found.
234. *Leading Manufacturers*, 188.
235. *JCHR* (April 13, 1904): 63; Hahn's occupation is given as "own income" in the 1910 Federal Census.
236. Ohio Deaths.
237. 1850 Federal Census.
238. 1839/40 CCD, 484. The province of Upper Canada in British North America encompassed the present-day region of the province of Ontario.
239. HCPC, Marriages, vol. A16, p. 292.
240. Advertisement, *Cincinnati Advertiser & Journal*, June 27, 1839, reproduced in Beckman, 63.
241. Boultinghouse, 150; Goldsborough, 257; Von Khrum, 63.
242. A hardware firm, Jacob L. Wayne, was at 124 Main.
243. Dun, vol. 3, p. 5.
244. Conteur.
245. Dun, vol. 3, p. 240; A sutler was an army camp follower who peddled provisions to soldiers.
246. 1863 CCD.
247. 1880 Federal Census, Boston, Suffolk, Massachusetts.
248. Massachusetts, Town Vital Collections, 1620–1988, www.ancestry.com.
249. Ibid.

250. 1850 Federal Census, Scituate, Plymouth, Massachusetts: 1870 Federal Census.

251. Massachusetts, Town Vital Collections, 1620–1988, www.ancestry.com.

252. 1848/49 Cincinnati Business Directory; 1849/50–1859 CCDs.

253. Advertisement, 1850/51 CCD, 48.

254. Advertisements, *Cincinnati Enquirer*, June 28, 1851, 3 continuing through to June 16, 1853, 3.

255. Cist 1851, 238.

256. Dun, vol. 1, p. 379.

257. Beckman, 63.

258. UC.

259. Spring Grove.

260. HCPC, Marriages, vol. B14, p. 366.

261. Spring Grove.

262. 1920 Federal Census; Ohio Deaths.

263. 1887–1909 CCDs; Spring Grove.

264. 1856–1868 CCDs.

265. Dun, vol. 9, p. 145.

266. UC; 1884, 1886 CCDs.

267. The "Jr" was no longer employed in documents and publications.

268. *JCHR* (February 1895): 27.

269. *JCHR* (August 1895): 26; *JCHR* (May 6, 1896): 13.

270. *JCHR* (November 26, 1896): 32; *JCHR* (January 2, 1901): 34; *JCHR* (May 15, 1901): 21; *Cincinnati Enquirer*, January 10, 1899, 7; May 9, 1901, 8.

271. *JCHR* (July 8, 1903): 56.

272. *Cincinnati Enquirer*, May 5, 1897, 5. Incorporators were Mary Caroline Duhme (wife of Herman), Lucille Duhme (wife of Frank), Herman Keck, H.M. Caldwell, Rankin D. Jones, and Francis B. Jones.

273. *Cincinnati Enquirer*, January 22, 1898, 30. Incorporators were Herman and Frank Duhme, Herman and Oscar Keck, and Theodore Neuhaus, Jr.

274. *Cincinnati Enquirer*, May 3, 1898, 8; *JCHR* (May 25, 1898): 13; *JCHR* (September 19, 1900): 53.

275. *JCHR* (July 13, 1898): 30.

276. *Cincinnati Enquirer*, October 27, 1899, 7, October 30, 1899, 10, October 31, 1899, 5.

277. *Cincinnati Enquirer*, April 1, 1909, 11, December. 14, 1909, 5; *JCHR* (September 5, 1900): 48, 49, (September 12, 1900): 52; *Cincinnati Enquirer*, February 9, 1909, 12.

278. *Cincinnati Enquirer*, February 9, 1909, 12.

279. *JCHR* (October 7, 1908): 99, (November 4, 1908): 97, (January 13, 1909): 50.

280. *Cincinnati Enquirer*, February 9, 1909, 17; *JCHR* (February 10, 1909): 65, (February 17, 1909): 59.

281. *The New York Times*, March 7, 1909, 1.

282. *Cincinnati Enquirer*, April 1, 1909, 11, December 14, 1909, 5, May 27, 1910, 8; *JCHR* (February 9, 1910): 83, (April 27, 1910): 102.

283. *JCHR* (June 1, 1910): 65.

284. Spring Grove; HCPC, Marriages, vol. 22, p. 112, no. 277.

285. Spring Grove; California Death Index 1940–1997, Amanda Keck; UC: Herman Jr.; Oscar [whose birth date was erroneously recorded as 23 April 1880], Kentucky Death Records, 1852–1953, www.ancestry.com.

286. HCPC, Marriages, vol. 121, p. 177, no. 353; Ohio Soldiers WWI, www.ancestry.com; Ohio Deaths.

287. Kentucky Marriage Records, 1852–1914, www.ancestry.com; 1910, 1920 Federal Censuses, Cincinnati, Hamilton, Ohio and Newport, Campbell, Kentucky.

288. Spring Grove.

289. Florence N. Levy, (ed.), Craftsmen chapter, *American Art Directory*, New York: American Art Annual, 1912, 45; "Who's Who in American Art," *American Art Directory*, New York: American Art Annual, 1917, 516.

290. 1900 Federal Censuses, Cincinnati, Hamilton, Ohio and Northampton, Hampshire County, Massachusetts; 1910, 1920 Federal Censuses; 1930 Federal Census, Larchmont, Westchester, New York.

291. Spring Grove; 1875-1941 CCDs.

292. *Leading Manufacturers*, 107; 1882 CCD.

293. *Leading Manufacturers*, 107.

294. "Cincinnati," *JCHR* 33, no. 23 (January 6, 1897).

295. "Cincinnati," *JCHR* 33, no. 23 (February 21, 1897); 1897 CCD.

296. *JCHR* (March 22, 1905).

297. The firm's last CCD listing was in 1952.

298. HCPC, Marriages, vol. 89, p. 438; Spring Grove.

299. 1900, 1910 Federal Censuses.

300. Dun, vol. 3, p. 240.

301. Advertisements: *Cincinnati Enquirer*, December 17, 1868, 5; December 24, 1869, 4; *Cincinnati Commercial Tribune*, December 22, 1869, 5; and *Cincinnati Times Star*, December 21, 1871, 2.

302. Dun, vol. 3, p. 235.

303. Ibid.

304. Dun, vol. 3, p. 316.

305. 1871 CCD lists Starbuck as "at Jenkins & Hatch's, 51 W. 4th."

306. Dun, vol. 3, p. 316.

307. Advertisements: *Cincinnati Enquirer*, September 7, 1873, 8; December 15, 1873, 8; June 2, 1874, 8; June 8, 1874, 8.

308. Spring Grove.

309. 1842 CCD.

310. Dun, vol. 1, p. 433.

311. Dun, vol. 1, p. 132.

312. H. Jenkins, eBay listings and private collections, Cincinnati silver binders, Cincinnati Art Museum.

313. Cutten, 7.

314. Dun, vol. 1, p. 428.

315. Spring Grove. Reports exist (Beckman, 71, Boultinghouse, 171) that Henry's first wife died because

the 1850 Federal Census lists his spouse as Lucinda, born in Ireland, while subsequent census listings and burial records give his wife as Mary L. born in Vermont. However, the 1850 Federal Census lists her birthplace as Vermont and it is likely that Henry's wife, Mary Lucinda, used her full name for some records but was known as Lucinda.

316. 1850–1880, 1900–1920 CCDs.

317. Spring Grove.

318. Spring Grove.

319. HCPC, Marriages, vol. B27, indexed as Mary L. Cannary, p. 365; Spring Grove.

320. Beckman (p. 72) expressed reservations as to whether the silversmith and painter/glazier were the same person, as "William Johnson" was a fairly common name in the directories of that era. However, there was only one William M. Johnson listed in the CCDs between 1829 and 1850 and his home addresses are the same for all listings.

321. In the 1839/40 CCD, his name appears in both the "white" and "colored" listings. In the 1842, 1843 CCDs, his name appears in the "colored" listings.

322. Phillipson, 43–57. The report is based on Jonas' memoir, published in *Occident* 1 (1842/43): 547.

323. Advertisement, *Western Spy*, May 16, 1817, reproduced in Beckman, 72, with the date given as May 15.

324. Advertisements, *The Inquisitor & Cincinnati Advertiser*, May 17, 1819, *Liberty Hall*, June 19, 1819, reproduced in Beckman, 72, 92.

325. Barnett A. Elzas, *Jewish Marriage Notices from the Newspapers of Charleston, SC 1775–1906*, New York: Bloch & Co., 1917, 13; Jewish Cemeteries.

326. Advertisement, *Cincinnati Emporium*, March 11, 1824, reproduced in Beckman, 73.

327. Joseph Jonas, eBay listings and private collections, Cincinnati silver binders, Cincinnati Art Museum.

328. Gibbs, 146; New York Passenger Lists, 1820–1957, www.ancestry.com.

329. Cist 1841, advertisement in unnumbered pages at end.

330. 1850, 1860 Federal Censuses; Jewish Cemeteries.

331. Joblin, 15; "Hon. Joseph Jonas," *Citizens Memorial Association of Cincinnati: In Memoriam*, Cincinnati: A.E. Jones, 1881, 1:190; "In Memoriam of Joseph Jonas," *Cincinnati Enquirer*, April 5, 1867, 1.

332. Nelson, 249.

333. Phillipson, 43–47; Markens, 101; Wiernik, 137–141; *Jewish Encyclopedia*, 4:89–91.

334. Phillipson, 57.

335. 1850 Federal Census.

336. Phillipson, 56.

337. 1900 Federal Census, Covington, Kenton, Kentucky; Kentucky Death Records, 1852–1953, www.ancestry.com; Jonas was not related to the earlier silversmith and watch maker of the same name.

338. Averdick, 35.

339. 1864–1869 CCDs.

340. Dun, vol. 8, p. 109; 1870–1888 CCDs.

341. 1877–1888 CCDs.

342. 1897 CCD.

343. UC, indexed as Charles Kelley.

344. John Owen, Joseph Draper, eBay listings and private collections, Cincinnati silver binders, Cincinnati Art Museum.

345. HCPC, Marriages, vol. A12, p. 176.

346. 1860 Federal Census.

347. Spring Grove; 1874–1905 CCDs.

348. 1874 CCD.

349. "Business Change," *Cincinnati Enquirer*, July 31, 1879, 8.

350. Dun, vol. 4, p. 396; Leonard, 69.

351. Advertisements, *Cincinnati Daily Gazette*, December 14, 1880, 10; *Cincinnati Commercial Tribune* 24, December 24, 1880, 8; *Cincinnati Enquirer*, December 22, 1881, 5; *Cincinnati Commercial Tribune*, December 11, 1879, 8, December 24, 1880, 8, December 18, 1881, 12; *Cincinnati Daily Gazette*, December 6, 1879, 12, March 16, 1880, 8, April 13, 1880, 11, December 22, 1881, 1.

352. "Bedimmed Jewels," *Cincinnati Enquirer*, August 18, 1891, 8.

353. *JCHR* 23, no. 4 (August 26, 1891): 33.

354. Duhme & Co., 1892–3; The Duhme Company, 1894–7; The Duhme Jewelry Co., 1898; Duhme Brothers & Co., 1899–1904. See *JCHR* (October 21, 1891): 31; "Notice," *Cincinnati Enquirer*, November 8, 1898, 12; 1892-1904 CCDs; Goss, 3:96; *JCHR* (February 21, 1906): 68; *Cincinnati Enquirer*, November 6, 1911, 2, August 17, 1910, 12.

355. HCPC, Marriages, vol. 115, p. 162.

356. UC.

357. HCPC, Marriages, vol. 139B, p. 310; Spring Grove.

358. *Old Woodward, A Memorial Relating to Woodward High School, 1831–1836 and Woodward College, 1836–1851 in the City of Cincinnati*, Cincinnati: 'Old Woodward' Club, 1884.

359. 1850 Federal Census, Nashville, Davidson, Tennessee; 1853/4, *Nashville State of Tennessee and General Commercial Directory*, Nashville, TN.

360. 1864 *Mercantile Guide and Directory for Virginia City, Gold Hill and American City*, Nevada; 1870 Federal Census, Virginia City, Storey, Nevada.

361. Federal Census Mortality Schedules, California, 1850–1885, www.ancestry.com.

362. HCPC, Marriages, vol. 6A, p. 113.

363. U.S. Passport Applications, 1795–

1925, www.ancestry.com; U.S. National Homes for Disabled Volunteer Soldiers, 1866–1938, https://familysearch.org; 1865 CCD.

364. U.S. National Homes for Disabled Volunteer Soldiers, 1866–1938, https://familysearch.org.

365. HCPC, Marriages, vol. C7, pp. 54–55.

366. U.S. Passport Applications, 1795–1925, [Bessie, birthdate], www.ancestry.com; 1900 Federal Census, Los Angeles, Los Angeles, California.

367. 1900 Federal Census, Los Angeles, Los Angeles, California; death date published in *California Decisions: The Official Organ of the Supreme Court of the State of California*, vol. 55, *January–June, 1918*, San Francisco, CA: The Recorder Printing and Publishing Company, 1918, 647–650; 1870–1875 CCDs.

368. Dun, vol. 10, p. 342.

369. California, Voter Registers, 1866–1898, residence years: 1890, 1896.

370. 1880 Federal Census; 1900 Federal Census, Los Angeles, Los Angeles, California.

371. Spring Grove.

372. Averdick, 36.

373. 1850, 1860 Federal Censuses.

374. *JCHR* (January 18, 1893): 31.

375. 1880 Federal Census.

376. Spring Grove; 1880 Federal Census; U.S. Passport Applications, 1795–1925, application dated May 12, 1887, www.ancestry.com.

377. Goss, 3:288.

378. U.S. Civil War Soldier Records and Profiles, 1861–1865, www.ancestry.com.

379. 1866 CCD.

380. Conteur.

381. 1870, 1880, 1900 Federal Censuses; Spring Grove.

382. Spring Grove. The 1827 date corresponds to the date recorded in Federal Census records (1850, 1880) and Civil War Draft, Western District, Jefferson, Indiana. Beckman (p. 88) records the date as 1824.

383. Spring Grove; Nelson, 434.

384. Dun, vol. 1, p. 170.

385. During those years he was either living in College Hill (which was outside of the city limits) or in Madison, Indiana, where he registered in 1863 for the Civil War Draft, appeared in U.S. IRS Tax Assessment Lists and where four of his children were born. U.S. IRS Tax Assessment Lists, 1862–1918, www.ancestry.com; 1867–1894 CCDs.

386. Kenny, 327.

387. HCPC, Marriages, vol. B13, p. 78; Margaret Le Boiteaux, Spring Grove.

388. Spring Grove.

389. Markens, 101.

390. Advertisement, *Cincinnati Advertiser*,

March 12, 1822, reproduced in Beckman, 88. The spelling "Barnit" was probably a typesetter's error as all other sources spell the name as "Barnet."

391. *Cincinnati Advertiser*, cited in Beckman, 88.

392. Phillipson, 43–57; Greve, 1:940; Wiernik identifies the services as Rosh Ha-Shanna [sic] and Yom Kippur, p. 138.

393. Wiernik, 137–141; *Jewish Encyclopedia*, 90; Markens, 101; Greve, 940; Phillipson, 43–57.

394. Long's death was noted in Deterly, 2:1, October 25, 1824 (Mon.) "Herman [sic] Long is to be interred this afternoon he died yesterday, some time in the forenoon."

395. *Western Spy & Hamilton Gazette* 6 (October 1804): 3; A similar advertisement appeared in *Liberty Hall* on June 3, 1805, reproduced in Beckman, 113.

396. *Western Spy & Hamilton Gazette* 7, no. 358 (June 10, 1806).

397. *Western Spy & Hamilton Gazette* 10, no. 470 (August 13, 1808).

398. *Western Spy (Cincinnati)* 1, no. 48 (August 10, 1811), also 1 (November 2, 1811).

399. *Western Spy (Cincinnati)* 1, no. 34 (May 4, 1811); *Western Spy (Cincinnati)* 2, no. 78 (March 7, 1812); Harry R. Stevens, "Samuel Watts and the Industrial Revolution in Cincinnati," *The Ohio Historical Quarterly* (April 1961), vol. 70, no. 2, 95.

400. *Western Spy & Hamilton Gazette* 1, no. 9 (November 9, 1810).

401. *Western Spy (Cincinnati)* 1, no. 30 (April 6, 1811).

402. An earlier biography interprets a blank space between Long's name and address in the CCD as a "ditto" of the occupation on the line above his name and reports his occupation as a tailor. Beckman, 90.

403. 1880 Federal Census.

404. 1900, 1910 Federal Censuses, Canton, Stark, Ohio.

405. Charles Marlmann is interred at Vine Street Hill Cemetery, Cincinnati, Ohio, www.findagrave.com; 1878–1923 CCDs.

406. Henry C. Marlman [sic], UC.

407. H.F. Marlmann is interred at Vine Street Hill Cemetery, Cincinnati, Ohio, www.findagrave.com; Henry Marlmann, Ohio Deaths.

408. New Orleans Passenger Lists, 1838–1945, www.ancestry.com.

409. New York Passenger and Immigration Lists, 1820–1850, www.ancestry.com; "Deaths in Columbus," *Columbus City Directory for 1889–90*, R.L. Polk & Co., 28; 1839/40–1858 CCDs.

410. 1839/40 CCD.

411. *Columbus Directory for 1875*, R.C. Hellrigle & Co.; 1880 Federal

Census, Columbus, Franklin, Ohio.

412. Ohio Censuses, 1790–1890 [1817 Tax List, Cincinnati Township], www.ancestry.com.

413. Conteur.

414. U.S. Passport Applications, 1785–1925, www.ancestry.com; "Funeral to be Monday," *Cincinnati Enquirer*, February 18, 1922, 8; 1863–1921 CCDs.

415. Dun, vol. 7, p. 117.

416. Dun, vol. 11, p. 125.

417. *Leading Manufacturers*, 226.

418. *JCHR*, vol. 17, no. 9 (October 1886): 333.

419. Engelhardt, 211.

420. Baltimore Passenger Lists, 1829–1948 and 1954–1957, www.ancestry.com; UC.

421. HCPC, Marriages, vol. 136, p. 313, no. 625; UC; 1900, 1910 Federal Censuses.

422. UC.

423. 1870 Federal Census, South Carrollton, Muhlenberg, Kentucky; Boultinghouse, 203.

424. Dun, vol. 3, p. 121.

425. Kentucky Death Records 1852–1953, www.ancestry.com.

426. 1870, 1880 Federal Censuses.

427. 1897–1900 City Directories, Bellevue, Kentucky, cited in Averdick, 49; Boultinghouse, 330.

428. 1860 Federal Census; HCPC, Marriages, vol. 71, p. 281, no. 561; Kentucky Death Records, 1852–1953, www.ancestry.com.

429. 1880 Federal Census; 1900, 1910 Federal Censuses, Bellevue, Campbell, Kentucky.

430. Spring Grove.

431. 1870 Federal Census, Portsmouth, Rockingham, New Hampshire.

432. Conteur.

433. 1900, 1910 Federal Censuses; Spring Grove.

434. Spring Grove.

435. Walnut Hills; 1850/51–1884 CCDs.

436. New York Passenger Lists, 1820–1957, L.P. Muller, www.ancestry.com; 1850 Federal Census: Muller's son Henry was born in 1849 in Ohio.

437. Dun, vol. 3, p. 5.

438. Conteur.

439. 1860 Federal Census; Allen Family Tree, www.ancestry.com.

440. Walnut Hills.

441. Walnut Hills; Spring Grove; 1860, 1870 Federal Censuses.

442. UC; Tedor [sic] Neuhaus, Walnut Hills; 1858–1885 CCDs.

443. New York Passenger lists, 1820–1957, www.ancestry.com; 1860, 1880 Federal Censuses.

444. Walnut Hills.

445. Walnut Hills; 1880 Federal Census.

446. "Real Estate," *Cincinnati Enquirer*, March 14, 1867, 1. The street name was changed to Hemlock in 1890.

447. UC; 1865–1902 CCDs.

448. New York Passenger Lists, 1820–1957, www.ancestry.com.

449. 1900 Federal Census; UC; Walnut Hills.

450. Spring Grove.

451. Conteur; *JCHR* (August 24, 1892): 38; Nelson, 211–212; Goss, 3:389.

452. Dun, vol. 12, p. 230.

453. *Leading Manufacturers*, 101.

454. *JCHR* (August 24, 1892): 38.

455. 1888, 1905 CCDs.

456. 1907–1922 CCDs; Goss, 3:390; Conteur.

457. Spring Grove; Goss, 3:390; Nelson, 911.

458. 1900 Federal Census; Spring Grove.

459. Obituary, *The New York Times*, December 31, 1934, 13.

460. 1870 Federal Census, Miami Township, Clermont County, Ohio; Missouri Death Certificates 1910–1962, www.sos.mo.gov/archives.

461. Dun, vol. 10, p. 306.

462. Ibid.

463. 1900, 1910, 1920 Federal Censuses, Kansas City, Jackson County, Missouri; Marriage license issued in 1899 in Cincinnati records his residence as Kansas City.

464. Dun, vol. 10, p. 306; 1900 Federal Census, Kansas City, Jackson County, Missouri.

465. HCPC, Marriages, vol. 140, p. 56; Missouri Death Certificates 1910–1962, www.sos.mo.gov/archives.

466. Missouri Marriage Records, 1805–2002, www.ancestry.com; Missouri Death Certificates 1910–1962, www.sos.mo.gov/archives.

467. Spring Grove.

468. Ibid.; 1862–1918 CCDs.

469. *JCHR* (July 5, 1905): 63.

470. Owen, eBay listings and private collections, Cincinnati silver binders, Cincinnati Art Museum.

471. *JCHR* (August 26, 1903): 68, (January 28, 1903): 57, (February 25, 1903): 55; *Cincinnati Enquirer*, December 8, 1907, A12.

472. *JCHR* (February 5, 1919): 397.

473. Averdick, 60; 1886 CCD; 1910 Federal Census.

474. Spring Grove; 1900 Federal Census.

475. Ohio Deaths; 1878–1915 CCDs.

476. HCPC, Marriages, vol. 105, p. 448, no. 891.

477. 1900 Federal Census.

478. U.S. National Homes for Disabled Volunteer Soldiers, 1866–1938, https://familysearch.org; 1866–1889 CCDs.

479. 1860, 1861 CCDs.

480. Spring Grove; 1862–1906 CCDs.

481. 1900 Federal Census.

482. Conteur.

483. Spring Grove; HCPC, Marriages, vol. B24R, p. 265. Their surnames are spelled Parst and Bethyne in the marriage license.

484. 1880 Federal Census; Spring Grove.

485. Greenwood Cemetery; McBride, 140.

486. Frederic Ellsworth Kip and Margarita L. Hawley, *History of the Kip family in America*, Boston:

Hudson Printing Co., 1928, 151, http://openlibrary.org/books/OL67 29435M/History_of_the_Kip_family_in_America.

487. His employer was likely his future brother-in-law, Isaac van Nuys, but confirmation has not been found.

488. McBride, 103–140.

489. It is tempting to speculate that he joined Celadon Symmes, another early Cincinnati silversmith, who had moved to what is now southern Butler County by 1801, but this relationship has not been confirmed.

490. McBride, 140.

491. Advertisement, *Western Spy*, Cincinnati, December 25, 1813, quoted in Hollan, 590; Greenwood Cemetery. Wallace is buried in the Paxton plot where the inscription on the monument includes "partner of Isaac Paxton (silversmith)." Also buried there is Phebe, a sister of Isaac's first wife Magdalane and the wife of the Cincinnati silversmith John Smith. Burress/Miller correspondence in Sikes papers, Mary R. Schiff Library and Archives, Cincinnati Art Museum, record group 14, series 1, box 6, file 3.

492. 1850, 1860 Federal Censuses, Hamilton, Butler, Ohio.

493. McBride, 140; Greenwood Cemetery. Her given name was also spelled Madeline in some period documents. Magdalane is the name used in the burial record.

494. McBride, 140; Greenwood Cemetery; Powell Family Tree, www.ancestry.com.

495. Greenwood Cemetery.

496. Deterly.

497. G.D. Gardner, "A Glimmer from the Past: Art of the Silversmiths in Hardin County," *Bits and Pieces of Hardin County History* (Winter 2008), Elizabethtown, KY: Hardin County Historical Society; 1834 CCD.

498. The silversmith James D. Phillips was active in New York from 1826–1831, the years that James Phillips was training and working in Cincinnati. A James W. Phillips worked in West Virginia after 1836, and James L. Phillips worked in Baltimore, MD during the third quarter of the 19th century. Von Khrum, 102; Hollan, 609; Advertisement, *The Magazine of American History* (November 1888): 7.

499. U.S. National Homes for Disabled Volunteer Soldiers 1866–1938, https://familysearch.org; 1839–1872 CCDs.

500. Lawrence County is now in the State of West Virginia.

501. U.S. Civil War Records and Profiles, 1861–1865, www.ancestry.com.

502. Hill-Watt Family Tree, www.ancestry.com; 1850/51–1859 CCDs.

503. 1850 Federal Census, Providence, Providence County, Rhode Island.

504. Conteur.

505. Dun, vol. 3, p. 5.

506. Dun, vol. 3, p. 15.

507. 1870, 1880, 1900 Federal Censuses, New York City, New York County, New York.

508. HCPC, Marriages, vol. B9, p. 43, no. 155.

509. Spring Grove; 1870, 1880 Federal Censuses, New York City, New York County, New York.

510. Advertisement, 1831 CCD, unnumbered pages at front of directory.

511. Kentucky Death Records, 1852–1953, www.ancestry.com; 1889–1926/27 CCDs.

512. 1866–1885 CCDs.

513. 1910 Federal Census.

514. UC; 1850/51–1867 CCDs.

515. 1860 Federal Census.

516. Dun, vol. 8, p. 58.

517. UC; 1860 Census.

518. 1897–1965 CCDs.

519. Obituary, *Cincinnati Enquirer*, December 22, 1915, 5; Ohio Deaths; "Jeweler Fred Fehr celebrates 50 years Downtown," *Downtowner Pulse*, October 3, 2007, 8; 1897 CCD.

520. Advertisements, "Headquarters for Diamonds," *JCHR* (August 12, 1908): 76, (December 13, 1911): 96, (October 8, 1912): 100, (August 14, 1912): 130.

521. "Cincinnati," *JCHR* (August 10, 1910): 103.

522. 1900–1925 CCDs; In 1901, George Richter left to start the Simplex Telephone Co.

523. 1900–1935 CCDs; Fred Fehr's son, also named Fred, took over after his father's retirement. "Jeweler Fred Fehr celebrates 50 Years Downtown," October 3, 2007.

524. 1880 Federal Census, Winchester, Clark, Kentucky; *Kentucky State Gazetteer and Business Directory*, R.L. Polk & Co., cited in Boultinghouse, 334. George advertised as a jeweler in 1879-80 and 1887-8, and as George Richter & Co. in 1891-2. Boultinghouse, who was unaware of the Norbert Richter family of Cincinnati, suggests that George Richter may have been the brother of the Louisville, KY jeweler Eugene Richter. Based on Cincinnati directories, Census records, and Ohio Death Records, there is no apparent relationship.

525. 1880 Federal Census, Winchester, Clark, Kentucky.

526. Dun, vol. 11, p. 154.

527. *JCHR* (April 5, 1905): 64, (April 12, 1905): 60, (March 21, 1906): 67, (April 17, 1907): 81.

528. 1900 Federal Census.

529. He is interred at Vine Street Hill Cemetery, www.findagrave.com; 1887–1897 CCDs.

530. Naomi Kaetker Richter, Vine Street Hill Cemetery, www.findagrave.com; 1900 Federal Census; HCPC, Marriages, vol. 140, p. 273.

531. Kentucky Death Records, 1852–1953, www.ancestry.com; 1869–1883 CCDs.

532. 1880 Federal Census, Covington, Kenton, Kentucky.

533. 1850/51–1883 CCDs.

534. New Orleans Passenger Lists, 1820–1945, www.ancestry.com.

535. 1870, 1872, 1876 Chicago City Directories.

536. Kentucky Death Records, 1852–1953, www.ancestry.com; 1880 Federal Census, Covington, Kenton, Kentucky; Ada Ruppiler Mooar, R.F. Rupplier are interred at Linden Grove Cemetery, Covington, www.findagrave.com.

537. Averdick, 69.

538. Beckman, 118; Spring Grove; California, Voter Registers, 1890. James W. Ryland registered to vote in Los Angeles in 1890; a death date was not found.

539. James Ryland arrived in Philadelphia from Liverpool on the *William Penn* in April 1826, and by 1829, James and his wife Anne were in Cincinnati where they operated a young ladies' academy from 1829 through 1844. Their son, James William, was a student at Woodward High School from 1832–1835, graduated from the University of Cincinnati, College of Law in 1838, and was admitted to the Ohio Bar in 1842. James W. worked as an attorney from 1843-46 and subsequently as a merchant, dealing in hardware and cutlery. Philadelphia Passenger and Immigration Lists, 1800–1850, www.ancestry.com; 1829–1860 CCDs; *Old Woodward, A Memorial Relating to Woodward High School, 1831–1836 and Woodward College, 1836–1851 in the City of Cincinnati*, Cincinnati: 'Old Woodward' Club, 1884, 269; "List of the Graduates of The Cincinnati Law School 1833-1904," Law Department of the University of Cincinnati, 1905, 51; 'Roll of the Bar of Hamilton County," *Ohio Law Bulletin*, 1897, 37:408.

540. Boultinghouse, 231.

541. J. Ryland, eBay listings and private collections, Cincinnati silver binders, Cincinnati Art Museum.

542. 1850 Federal Census; U.S. Civil War Records and Profiles 1861–1865, www.ancestry.com. William T. Ryland, Decatur County, Indiana, enlisted 24 April, 1861, casualty of Battle of Gettysburg, 2 July, 1863.

543. 1850/51–1858 CCDs.

544. 1841 England Census, Birmingham, Warwickshire, England.

545. Death notice, *New York Herald-Tribune*, September 14, 1889, 7; New Jersey Deaths and Burials Index, 1798–1971.

546. Harry R. Stevens, "Further Adventures in Refinement: Early Concert Life in Cincinnati," *Bulletin of the Historical and Philosophical Society of Ohio* 5 no. 4 (December 1947): 22-32; 1825-1853 CCDs.

547. George B. Lockwood, "The New Harmony Communities," Marion, IN: The Chronicle Co., 1902, 14. Salmon was probably one of the two watch makers in the commune.

548. 1849–1853 CCDs; Harry R. Stevens, "The First Cincinnati Music Festival," *Bulletin of the Historical and Philosophical Society of Ohio* 20 (July 1962): 186-196.

549. *The American Musical Directory – 1861*, New York: Thomas Hutchison, 1861, 228; 1860, 1880 Federal Censuses, New York, New York, New York; 1868, 1872, 1884 NY City Directories.

550. Conteur; "Committed Suicide at Ninety" *New York Herald-Tribune*, September 14, 1889, 1.

551. Lockwood, "The New Harmony Communities," 117.

552. 1840 Federal Census; 1860 Federal Census, New York, New York, New York; Spring Grove. While an earlier biography (Beckman, 116) reports that Mary Frances died in 1866, that was the year the remains were relocated from the Catharine Street Grounds to Spring Grove.

553. U.S. Passport Applications, 1795–1925, www.ancestry.com; Ohio Deaths; 1867, 1868, 1880 CCDs.

554. 1870 Federal Census, Carlisle, Nicholas, Kentucky; Advertisement cited in Boultinghouse, 231. Boultinghouse gives his location as Cadiz, which is in western Kentucky while the census and city directories give Carlisle.

555. 1900, 1910 Federal Censuses; CCDs.

556. 1900 Federal Census.

557. UC; 1873–1882 CCDs.

558. Baltimore Passenger and Immigration Lists, 1820–1872, www.ancestry.com. John Schmalz, tailor, arrived in Baltimore in December 1852. The family was in Cincinnati by 1866.

559. 1880 Federal Census.

560. HCPC, Marriages, vol. B30, p. 427.

561. UC.

562. 1900 Federal Census, Madisonville, Hamilton, Ohio; UC; 1869–1910 CCDs.

563. 1901–1958 CCDs.

564. Obituary, *JCHR* (March 22, 1911): 76a.

565. 1857–1892 CCDs.

566. 1880, 1900 Federal Censuses; Ohio Deaths.

567. Advertisements, 1884–1890 CCDs.

568. 1890–1930 CCDs.

569. In 1904, Elgin produced watches marked on the movement "Made

expressly for the Ben Schneider Jewelry Co." and on the dial. "Ben Schneider Jewelry Co., Cincinnati, Ohio," www.Elginwatches.org.

570. 1900 Federal Census.

571. 1880, 1900 Federal Censuses; Spring Grove.

572. Dun, vol. 10, p. 253.

573. 1900, 1920 Federal Censuses; Obituary, *Cincinnati Enquirer*, August 21, 1920, 5.

574. Jewish Cemeteries.

575. Advertisement, *JCHR* (February 28, 1893): 11; Leonard, 69.

576. *JCHR* (November 8, 1893): 28.

577. *JCHR* 34 (May 19, 1897): 15.

578. Obituary, *JCHR* (August 26, 1903) 46.

579. 1899 CCD.

580. Jewish Cemeteries; 1872–1920 CCDs.

581. Dun, vol. 11, p. 139; 1879–1906 CCDs.

582. *JCHR* (April 3, 1907): 83; 1907–1963 CCDs.

583. U.S. Passport Applications, 1795–1925, www.ancestry.com; 1870 Federal Census; Louis Gutmann, obituary, *Cincinnati Enquirer*, February 2, 1901, 8.

584. 1879 CCD.

585. Dun, vol. 11, p. 139.

586. *Leading Manufacturers*, 92.

587. Leonard, 71.

588. 1900, 1907 CCDs; Lange, the son of another Cincinnati jeweler, Hermann Lange, married Rubie Schwab. Obituary, *Cincinnati Times Star*, May 27, 1957.

589. *JCHR* (April 3, 1907): 83.

590. A.G. Schwab & Sons, eBay listings and private collections, Cincinnati silver binders, Cincinnati Art Museum.

591. Jewish Cemeteries; *JCHR* (January 1903): 56.

592. 1880, 1900 Federal Censuses; Jewish Cemeteries.

593. Dun, vol. 11, p. 139; Jewish Cemeteries.

594. 1870, 1910 Federal Censuses.

595. *JCHR* (April 3, 1907): 83; *JCHR* (April 10, 1907): 76; Advertisement, *JCHR* (July 17, 1907): 74; 1907–1910 CCDs.

596. *JCHR* (June 7, 1905): 58, reports their 25th anniversary celebration; Jewish Cemeteries.

597. 1880, 1900 Federal Censuses; Jewish Cemeteries.

598. Kentucky Death Records, 1852–1953, www.ancestry.com; 1885–1897 CCDs.

599. 1880 Federal Census, Newport, Campbell, Kentucky; 1885–1893 CCDs.

600. 1902–1906 City Directories, Canton, Ohio.

601. 1900 Federal Census, Baltimore Ward 10, Baltimore, Independent City, Maryland; family tree, Swanson425, www.ancestry.com.

602. Johan Abraham Sehlstedt, *Emigranten Populär*, 1783–1951, www.ancestry.com.

603. 1885, 1887, 1890, 1891, 1895, 1899, 1900–1902 Baltimore City Directories.

604. 1900 Federal Census, Baltimore Ward 10, Baltimore, Independent City, Maryland.

605. Spring Grove; 1851/52–1879 CCDs.

606. "Diamonds, Jewelry, &C.," *Cincinnati Enquirer*, December 16, 1871, 4; A great-grandson of Herman Serodino has a business card with "Serodino / Jeweler" in French and "Serodino / Goldsmith" in Russian as well as the address "House of Thal, near The Red Bridge" thought to be Joseph Pierre Serodino's card. It is more likely to be that of Herman Serodino. Correspondence from V.P. Serodino to Charles Knighton, Decorative Arts Curatorial File, Cincinnati Art Museum.

607. Herman Serodins [*sic*], Boston Passenger and Crew Lists, 1820–1943, www.ancestry.com.

608. 1850 Federal Census, indexed as "Hennan Serodine." silversmith.

609. Civil War Draft, indexed as "Hurman Sirodino"; 1864 CCD.

610. "Art in the Exposition," *Cincinnati Enquirer*, October 7, 1871, 8.

611. Conteur.

612. HCPC, Marriages, vol B6, p. 113, no. 459; Spring Grove.

613. 1870, 1880 Federal Censuses.

614. UC; Spring Grove.

615. Walnut Hills; 1849/50–1860 CCDs.

616. Baltimore Passenger and Immigration Lists, 1820–1872, www.ancestry.com; Walnut Hills.

617. 1850 Federal Census.

618. Correspondence from V.P. Serodino to Charles Knighton, Decorative Arts Curatorial File, Cincinnati Art Museum.

619. No address was given for the firm, nor was it included in the alphabetical listings.

620. Jewish Cemeteries; 1868–1892 CCDs.

621. 1860 Federal Census, Clay, Dearborn, Indiana; U.S. Civil War Soldier Records and Profiles, 1861–1865, www.ancestry.com; Obituary, *Cincinnati Enquirer*, July 17, 1892, 11.

622. Although Shott's obituary says he purchased the shop from his father, the shop was listed in the 1868 and 1869 CCDs under the name of his brother, B.F (Ben) Shott.

623. Advertisement, 1879 CCD, 898.

624. Obituary, "Zeke Dead," *Cincinnati Enquirer*, July 17, 1892, 11.

625. *Cincinnati Enquirer*, September 15, 1881, 4, July 2, 1884, 6, Obituary, July 17, 1892, 11.

626. "A Pleasant Tin Wedding" (anniversary celebration), *Cincinnati Enquirer*, March 15, 1880, 4; Jewish Cemeteries.

627. New Jersey Deaths and Burials Index, 1798–1971, www.ancestry.com; 1836/7–1844 CCDs.

628. 1850 Federal Census, Turtle Creek, Warren, Ohio.

629. 1860, 1870 Federal Censuses, Newark, Essex, NJ; 1861–1896 Newark, NJ City Directories; The Shourds' youngest son was born in New Jersey in 1855.

630. William E. Drost, *Clocks and Watches of New Jersey*, Elizabeth, NJ: Engineering Publishers, 1966, 220.

631. New Jersey Deaths and Burials Index, 1798–1971.

632. Ohio Censuses 1790–1890 [1810, 1817 Tax Lists, Cincinnati Township], www.ancestry.com.

633. Advertisement, *Liberty Hall*, May 13, 1809, reproduced in Beckman, 123. Other local craftsmen who advertised mathematical instruments were Luke Kent, Jr., Joseph G. Joseph, and Lemuel Wells. Advertisement, 1839/40 CCD, 50.

634. Advertisement, *Liberty Hall*, December 5, 1810, reproduced in Beckman, 129.

635. Advertisement, *Western Spy* (Cincinnati), January 5, 1811, reproduced in Beckman, 114; Advertisement, *Liberty Hall*, January 1, 1811.

636. Advertisements, *Western Spy* (Cincinnati), February 6, 1813, March 10, 1813, April 17, 1813, May 8, 1813.

637. *Western Spy and Hamilton Gazette*, September 19, 1804, reproduced in Beckman, 128.

638. Pleasants and Sill, 241; James Biser Whisker, *Pennsylvania Silversmiths, Goldsmiths and Pewterers, 1684–1900*, Lewiston, New York: The Edwin Mellen Press, 1939, 25.

639. Advertisement, *Liberty Hall*, May 18, 1809, reproduced in Beckman, 128.

640. Spring Grove; 1855–1890 CCDs.

641. 1850 Federal Census, Tiffin, Seneca, Ohio.

642. Dun, vol. 3, p. 12.

643. U.S. Civil War Soldier Records and Profiles, www.ancestry.com.

644. Dun, vol. 8, p. 167.

645. 1870 Federal Non-Population Census Schedules, Products of Industry, Schedule 4, Hamilton County, Ohio.

646. Dun, vol. 8, p. 167.

647. Dun, vol. 8, p. 221.

648. U.S. and International Marriage Records, 1560–1980, www.ancestry.com.

649. Spring Grove.

650. 1850 Federal Census; 1829–1851/52 CCDs.

651. 1829 CCD; Beckman, 129, shortens the name to Thomson.

652. 1850 Federal Non-Population Census Schedules, Products of Industry, Schedule 4, Hamilton County, Ohio.

653. The occupation could have been a transcription error for silversmith, but the address, in what was then the northern part of the city, was distant from his previous addresses.

654. *Centinel of the North-Western Territory*, December 19, 1795.

655. *Western Spy and Hamilton Gazette*, July 31, 1802. Beckman, 131, cites a similar advertisement dated August 7, 1802, which was not found.

656. Ralph M. Kovel, *Kovel's American Silver Marks*, New York: Crown Publishers, 1989, 252; Hollan, 715; Cutten Virginia, 217; Pleasants and Sill, 183.

657. Pleasants and Sill, 183.

658. Cist Miscellany, 2:71.

659. "Phebe, wife of silversmith John Smith, Died Oct. 10, 1815, aged 42 years," Grave marker, Greenwood Cemetery [source].

660. *American Genealogical Biographical Index, Records of the officers and men of New Jersey in wars 1791–1815*, Trenton, NJ: 1909, 59.

661. Ohio Censuses, 1790–1890 [1810 Tax List, Cincinnati Township], www.ancestry.com; Beckman, 133, gives his birthplace as London, probably based on his address (London [street] between Western Row and John) in the 1819 CCD.

662. U.S. War of 1812 Service Records, 1812–1815, https://familysearch.org; Ohio Censuses, 1790–1890 [1817 Tax List, Cincinnati Township], www.ancestry.com.

663. Deterly, 1:6; 7. Beckman (p. 133) and Boultinghouse (p. 208) interpret the comment as indicating that the partnership was initiated in March.

664. Advertisement, *National Republican & Ohio Political Register*, September 7, 1826, reproduced in Beckman, 133.

665. 1870, 1880 Federal Censuses, Lexington, Fayette, Kentucky.

666. Jewish Cemeteries; 1869–1900 CCDs.

667. Dun, vol. 7, p. 214, vol. 9, p. 169.

668. Dun, vol. 9, p. 168.

669. Dun, vol. 9, pp. 362, 363.

670. Design for a Set of Jewelry, US Patent 10,648, issued April 23, 1878; Walter A. Bartlett, "Trademark #5667," *Digest of Trade Marks*, Washington, DC: Bigson Bros. Printers, 1893; Advertisement, New York Public Library Digital Gallery, Detail ID 831791, http://digitalgallery.nypl.org/.

671. Dun, vol. 4, p. 374, vol. 11, p. 85.

672. Dun, vol. 11, p. 274.

673. Advertisements: 1884–1888 CCDs, *Cincinnati Commercial Tribune* 49, no. 79, December 20, 1889, 5.

674. *JCHR* 8 (September 23, 1891): 31; *JCHR* 11 (October 14, 1891): 28.

675. *JCHR* (January 3, 1894): 22; *JCHR* (August 17, 1904): 18.

676. Jewish Cemeteries.

677. Jewish Cemeteries; 1900 Federal Census; Dun, vol. 8, pp. 167, 221.

678. 1900, 1910 Federal Censuses; UC; Spring Grove; Jewish Cemeteries.

679. 1850 Federal Census; Burial records, Mount Olive Cemetery, St Louis, MO; 1868–1877 CCDs.

680. 1860 Federal Census, Long Barn, Yuba, CA.

681. U.S. National Homes for Disabled Volunteer Soldiers, 1866–1938, https://familysearch.org.

682. 1880 Federal Census, St Louis, Independent City, MO.

683. 1900 Federal Census, Baltimore, Independent City, MD.

684. Records of U.S. National Homes for Disabled Volunteer Soldiers, 1866–1938.

685. Burial records, Mount Olive Cemetery, St Louis, MO, http://search.stlcathcem.org; 1880, 1900, 1910, 1920 Federal Censuses, St. Louis, Independent, MO.

686. Spring Grove; 1868–1885 CCDs.

687. 1900 Federal Census; UC; Obituary, Cincinnati Enquirer, October 28, 1911, 7; 1857–1910 CCDs.

688. 1900 Federal Census.

689. UC; 1870, 1880 Federal Census.

690. 1873–1913 CCDs.

691. 1878–1887 CCDs

692. Baltimore Passenger Lists 1820–1908 and 1954–7, www.ancestry.com.

693. HCPC, Marriages, vol. 8A, p. 66.

694. Ohio Deaths; Burial record, Vine St. Hill Cemetery, Cincinnati, Ohio; 1869–1910 CCDs.

695. Spring Grove.

696. Conteur.

697. Spring Grove; 1829–1876 CCDs.

698. Spring Grove; Greve, 1:184; Ohio Censuses, 1790–1890 [1810 and 1817 Tax Lists, Cincinnati Township], www.ancestry.com; An earlier biography of the younger Joseph identified him, instead of his father, as one of the first "Cincinnati pioneers"; Beckman, 138.

699. HCPC, Marriages, vol. A13, p. 59.

700. 1880 Federal Census.

701. Kentucky Death Records, 1852–1953, www.ancestry.com; 1866–1919 CCDs.

702. A ring turner operated a special lathe to make rings.

703. Kentucky Death Records, 1852–1953, www.ancestry.com.

704. 1880, 1900 Federal Censuses, Newport, Campbell, Kentucky; Kentucky Death Records, 1852–1953, www.ancestry.com.

705. U.S. Passport Applications, 1795–1925, www.ancestry.com; Walnut Hills; 1872–1924 CCDs.

706. New York Passenger Lists, 1820–1957, www.ancestry.com.

707. Ohio Deaths; Walnut Hills.

708. HCPC, Marriages, vol. B28, p. 151; Walnut Hills.

709. 1880, 1900 Federal Censuses; Walnut Hills.

710. 1904–1953/54 CCDs; JCHR (December 16, 1903).

711. Jewish Cemeteries.

712. JCHR (February 14, 1906): 67.

713. JCHR (May 27, 1909).

714. Wallenstein, Mayer & Co., eBay listings and private collections, Cincinnati silver binders, Cincinnati Art Museum.

715. UC; 1860 Federal Census, Lancaster, Erie, New York, indexed as "Weisback"; 1870, 1880 Federal Censuses; 1873–1885 CCDs.

716. Dun, vol. 11, p. 137.

717. Ibid.

718. Missouri Birth and Death Records, 1834–1910, www.sos.mo.org; 1834–1862 CCDs.

719. Spring Grove.

720. The Inland Printer 28, no. 1 (October 1901): 99; Albert Welles, History of the Welles Family in England and Normandy and Their Descendants in the USA, New York: Albert Welles, 1876, 176.

721. Advertisement, 1839/40 CCD, 50.

722. The Inland Printer 28, no. 1 (October 1901): 99; Improved Printing Press, US Patent 12,568, issued March 20, 1855; Tympans for Printing Press, US Patent 20179, issued May 4, 1858; Paper Feeder for Printing Press, US Patent 21859, issued Oct. 19, 1858; Printing Press, US Patent 25357, issued Sep. 6, 1859.

723. The Inland Printer 28, no. 1 (October 1901): 99.

724. 1870 Federal Census, Carondelet, St. Louis, MO.

725. HCPC, Marriages, vol. A14, p. 240.

726. 1860 Federal Census; 1870 Federal Census, Carondelet, St. Louis, MO.

727. U.S. Passport Applications, 1795–1925, www.ancestry.com; UC; 1849/50–1893 CCDs.

728. New York Passenger Lists, 1820–1957, www.ancestry.com.

729. Dun, vol. 1, p. 233; vol. 2, p. 68.

730. 1940 Federal Census; HCPC, Wills, vol. 259, p. 582; 1894–1919 CCDs.

731. Ohio Deaths; 1880 Federal Census.

732. "Addison H. Whiteside," Portrait and Biographical Record of Iroquois County, Illinois; Chicago: Lake City Publishing Co, 1893, 361; Hollan identifies him as Samuel Hayes, the youngest son of Moses and Margaret Whiteside and gives birthdates of circa 1756 (p. 804) and circa 1780 (p. 806). He may have been the Samuel (no middle initial) Whiteside cited in Cutten Virginia (p. 176) who was in Staunton, Virginia in 1802, advertising that he had commenced business and wanted to employ a journeyman clock maker.

733. 1810 Federal Census, Mercersburg, Franklin, Pennsylvania; Ohio Censuses, 1790–1890 [1813, 1817 Tax Lists, Cincinnati Township], www.ancestry.com; Period documents record numerous Samuel Whitesides, including one who was in Cincinnati by 1789, was one of the original purchasers of land in Cincinnati, and was listed in the 1790 Federal Census. Greve, 192, Ford, 35. The records for a Samuel H. Whiteside can all be associated with the present subject.

734. Maryland Marriages, 1655–1850, www.ancestry.com; Hollan (p. 806) cites advertisements regarding a lost watch published in January and April 1811 by Whiteside and John Springer in Hagerstown, and although there is no reference to their trade(s), it can be inferred that they were jewelers and/or watch makers.

735. Liberty Hall, June 22, 1813 (dated May 18), and December 21, 1813 (dated October 1813), reproduced in Beckman, 145, 146.

736. 1820 Federal Census.

737. 1830, 1840, 1860 Federal Censuses, Millcreek, Hamilton, Ohio; Selected U.S. Non Population Census Schedules, 1850–1880, Millcreek, Hamilton, Ohio, Enumeration date 1860 (Addison H. Whitesides).

738. "Addison H. Whiteside," Portrait and Biographical Record of Iroquois County, Illinois, Chicago: Lake City Publishing Co, 1893, 361.

739. HCPC, Wills, vol. 10, p. 198.

740. Amanda married John Silsby in 1844. HCPC, Marriages, vol. A12, p. 372.

741. Torrence papers, box 56, folder 3, 134, CHS.

742. Hollan, 804. Hollan's identification is based on inferences from dates Whiteside was known to be in Rockbridge County and Cincinnati.

743. Kentucky Death Records, 1852–1953, www.ancestry.com.; 1850 Federal Census; 1853–1893 CCDs.

744. HCPC, Marriages, vol. A22, p. 307, no. 1015.

745. 1880 Federal Census, Newport, Campbell, Kentucky.

746. 1870 Federal Census.

747. Spring Grove.

748. Florence N. Levy, (ed.), Craftsmen chapter, American Art Directory, New York: American Art Annual, 1912, 68.

749. Catalogue of Students 1903–1904, Art Academy of Cincinnati, 1904, 28; "Life Classes," Catalogue 1905, Art Academy of Cincinnati, 31; "Classes in Decorative Design, China Painting, Metal and Leather Work," Catalogue 1909, Art Academy of Cincinnati, 34; "Classes in Decorative Design, China Painting, Metal and Leather Work," Catalogue 1910, Art Academy of Cincinnati, 35.

750. W.P. Anderson, Anderson Family Records, Cincinnati: privately published, 1936, 160.

751. 1920, 1930 Federal Censuses.

752. 1900 Federal Census, Newport, Campbell, Kentucky; Savage Family Tree, Brown/Droste Family Tree, www.ancestry.com; 1875–1933/34 CCDs.

753. New York, Passenger Lists, 1820–1957, www.ancestry.com.

754. Averdick, 86.

755. JCHR 23, no. 13 (October 28, 1891): 16.

756. Kentucky Death Records, 1852–1953, www.ancestry.com; Marriages, St. Johns United Church of Christ, Newport, Kentucky.

757. 1910 Federal Census, Newport, Campbell, Kentucky.

758. Jacob Zimmerman, Evergreen Cemetery, Southgate, Campbell County, Kentucky, www.findagrave.com; 1870–1882 CCDs.

759. New York, Passenger Lists, 1820–1957, www.ancestry.com.

760. 1880 Federal Census, Newport, Campbell, Kentucky.

APPENDIX B

INVENTORY OF THE CINCINNATI ART MUSEUM'S
CINCINNATI SILVER COLLECTION

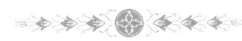

NORA KOHL

Maker/Retailer				
Maker (when Cincinnati individual/firm was the retailer) or Double Mark				
Object	Date	Credit Line	Accession no.	Fig. no.

Allen, Rhodes & Co. (estab. 1834, closed 1836)				
Beaker	1834–1836	Museum Purchase: John S. Conner Fund	2009.159	Fig. 2.1
Loring Andrews & Co. (estab. 1895, closed 1903)				
Jacobi & Jenkins (MD, estab. circa 1894, closed 1903)				
Covered Vegetable Dish	circa 1895–1903	From the Collection of Mrs. Frank L. Wright II	2001.1a–b	Fig. 4.3
Beggs & Smith (estab. 1848, closed 1862)				
Mug	circa 1855	Gift of James Randolph Hillard, M.D. and Aingeal Grehan	2007.184	Fig. 9.3
Tea and Coffee Service	circa 1850	Gift of Corinne Lawson Pennington Coler in honor of her great, great, great grandfather, Fenton Lawson (1808–1853)	2006.109a–e	Fig. 9.2
Grosjean & Woodward (NY, estab. 1840, closed 1862)				
Pitcher	circa 1859	Gift of Ellen G. Rionda	1959.88	Fig. 9.4
James Dixon & Sons (England, estab. 1806, closed 1976)				
Tray	1848–1862	Gift of Corinne Lawson Pennington Coler in honor of her great, great, great grandfather, Fenton Lawson (1808–1853)	2006.110	
J.P. Beggs & Co., (estab. 1842, closed 1843)				
Creamer	circa 1843	Gift of Mr. and Mrs. Charles Fleischmann III	2005.19	Fig. 10.2
Sugar	circa 1843	Gift of Mr. and Mrs. Charles Fleischmann III	2005.20a–b	Fig. 10.2
Tablespoon	1842–43	Bequest of Fanny Bryce Lehmer	1936.788	Fig. 10.1
Best & Deterly (estab. 1812, closed 1813)				
Beakers (4)	1812–1813	Gift of Doctors James and Betty Sutherland	2002.49a–d	Fig. 12.1
Tablespoon	1812–1813	Gift of John S. Conner	1910.210	Fig. 12.2
Robert Best (b. 1790, d. 1830)				
Salt Shovel	1812–1819	Gift of Mrs. Jane Sikes Hageman	2002.83	Fig. 14.4

* Multiple examples of this type of form by the same maker, and gifted by the same donor

Maker (when Cincinnati individual/firm was the retailer) or Double Mark				
Object	Date	Credit Line	Accession no.	Fig. no.

R. Best & Co. (estab. 1815, closed 1817)

Beaker	1815–1817	Museum Purchase: Gift of Harry G. Friedman, by exchange	2001.2	Fig. 15.2
Dessert Spoon	1815–1817	Gift of Dr. Suzanne A. Beutler	1983.202	Fig. 15.3
Serving Spoon	1815–1817	Anonymous Gift	2002.7	Fig. 15.3
Spectacles and Case	1815–1817	Anonymous Gift	2002.8a–b	Fig. 15.1

Samuel Best (b. 1776, d. 1859)

Sugar Tongs	1802–1818	Museum Purchase	1962.118	Fig. 16.7
Tablespoon	1804	Gift of Doris Dupraz	1969.537–538	Fig. 16.3
Tablespoon	1802–1818	Given by Elizabeth M. and Annie W. Anderson in memory of their mother, Mrs. Buckner W. Anderson	1969.734	Fig. 16.8
Tablespoon	1804	Gift of Doris Dupraz	1991.1	Fig. 16.3
Tall-Case Clock	1810–1815	Museum Purchase	1966.1175	

Henry Bliss (b. circa 1808, d. 1862)

Dessert Spoons (2)	circa 1860	Gift of Doris Dupraz	1991.3.1–2	Fig. 20.1

Francis Clark (b. circa 1800)

Teaspoon	1848–1850	Given by Elizabeth M. and Annie W. Anderson in memory of their mother, Mrs. Buckner W. Anderson	1969.739	Fig. 26.1

Richard Clayton (b. 1807, d. 1877)

Teaspoons (3)	circa 1850	Museum Purchase: John S. Conner Fund	2012.4a–c	Fig. 28.4
Teaspoons (6)	circa 1850	Museum Purchase: John S. Conner Fund	2013.75a–f	

Peleg Collins (b. 1798)

Tablespoon	circa 1840–1850	Given by Elizabeth M. and Annie W. Anderson in memory of their mother, Mrs. Buckner W. Anderson	1969.733	Fig. 29.1

W. & A. Cooper (estab. 1836, closed 1837)

Covered Pitcher	1836–1837	Museum Purchase with funds provided by Mr. and Mrs. Charles Fleischmann III	2005.43	Fig. 31.3

Garret T. Dorland (b. 1829, d. 1892)

Teaspoon	1853–1881	Museum Purchase: John S. Conner Fund	2012.13	Fig. 35.1

Duhme & Co. (estab. 1843, closed 1893)

Beaker	circa 1875–1893	Gift of James Randolph Hillard, M.D. and Aingeal Grehan	2007.182	
Berry Spoon	circa 1870	Gift of James Randolph Hillard, M.D. and Aingeal Grehan	2007.129	
Bonbon Spoon	1880s	Gift of James Randolph Hillard, M.D. and Aingeal Grehan	2007.151	Fig. 38.39
Bowl	1880–1893	Museum Purchase with funds provided by Mr. and Mrs. Charles Fleischmann III	2005.60	
Bowl	circa 1875–1893	Gift of James Randolph Hillard, M.D. and Aingeal Grehan	2007.200	
Butter Dish	1860s	Museum Purchase with funds provided by Mr. and Mrs. Charles Fleischmann III	2005.67a–b	Fig. 38.8
Candlesticks (2)	1890s	Gift of James Randolph Hillard, M.D. and Aingeal Grehan	2007.197a–b	
Clothes Brush with Tray	1860–1889	Gift of Dr. Suzanne A. Beutler	1983.209a–b	
Coffee Pot	1870s	Gift of Dr. and Mrs. James L. Hecht	1984.199	
Coffee Pot	circa 1892	Gift of James Randolph Hillard, M.D. and Aingeal Grehan	2007.118	Fig. 38.37
Compote	1860s	Gift of Joan S. Reis	1985.174	Fig. 38.7
Compote	1880–1893	Museum Purchase with funds provided by Mr. and Mrs. Charles Fleischmann III	2005.54	
Compote	circa 1869	Museum Purchase with funds provided by Mr. and Mrs. Charles Fleischmann III	2005.62	
Compote	1870s	Gift of James Randolph Hillard, M.D. and Aingeal Grehan	2007.119	Fig. 38.25
Compote	1870s	Gift of James Randolph Hillard, M.D. and Aingeal Grehan	2007.199	Fig. 38.26
Condiment Ladle	circa 1865	Gift of James Randolph Hillard, M.D. and Aingeal Grehan	2007.125	
Condiment Ladle	circa 1880	Gift of James Randolph Hillard, M.D. and Aingeal Grehan	2007.126	
Creamer	1870s	Gift of Dr. and Mrs. James L. Hecht	1984.200	
Creamer and Sugar	circa 1875–1893	Museum Purchase with funds provided by Mr. and Mrs. Charles Fleischmann III	2005.64a–b	
Creamer and Sugar	circa 1875–1893	Gift of James Randolph Hillard, M.D. and Aingeal Grehan	2007.190a–b	
Creamer and Sugar	circa 1875–1893	Gift of James Randolph Hillard, M.D. and Aingeal Grehan	2007.191a–b	
Creamer and Sugar	circa 1875–1893	Gift of James Randolph Hillard, M.D. and Aingeal Grehan	2007.192a–b	

* Multiple examples of this type of form by the same maker, and gifted by the same donor

Maker/Retailer					
Maker (when Cincinnati individual/firm was the retailer) or Double Mark					
Object	Date	Credit Line		Accession no.	Fig. no.

Duhme & Co. (continued)

Object	Date	Credit Line	Accession no.	Fig. no.
Cruet Stand	circa 1880	Museum Purchase with funds provided by Mr. and Mrs. Charles Fleischmann III	2005.68	Fig. 38.11
Cruet Stand	circa 1880	Gift of James Randolph Hillard, M.D. and Aingeal Grehan	2007.124a–h	Fig. 38.12
Cup	circa 1875	Gift of James Randolph Hillard, M.D. and Aingeal Grehan	2007.170	Fig. 38.5
Cup	circa 1865	Gift of James Randolph Hillard, M.D. and Aingeal Grehan	2007.172	Fig. 38.5
Cup	circa 1870	Gift of James Randolph Hillard, M.D. and Aingeal Grehan	2007.173	
Cup	circa 1875–1893	Gift of James Randolph Hillard, M.D. and Aingeal Grehan	2007.181	
Cup	circa 1890s	Gift of James Randolph Hillard, M.D. and Aingeal Grehan	2007.185	
Dinner Fork	1860s	Gift of Dr. Suzanne A. Beutler	1983.200	Fig. 38.19
Ewer	1860s	Museum Purchase with funds provided by Mr. and Mrs. Charles Fleischmann III	2005.69	Fig. 38.6
Fish Serving Knife	circa 1866	Gift of James Randolph Hillard, M.D. and Aingeal Grehan	2007.165	
Fish Serving Set with Case	circa 1887	Gift of Dorothy Krug Newstedt	1975.266a–c	Fig. 38.38
Fish Serving Set	circa 1865	Gift of James Randolph Hillard, M.D. and Aingeal Grehan	2007.158a–b	Fig. 38.14
Fish Serving Set	1860s	Gift of James Randolph Hillard, M.D. and Aingeal Grehan	2007.159a–b	Fig. 38.18
Fish Slice*	1860s	Museum Purchase with funds provided by Mr. and Mrs. Charles Fleischmann III	2005.70; 2005.73	Fig. 38.19
Flask	circa 1875–1893	Gift of James Randolph Hillard, M.D. and Aingeal Grehan	2007.196	
Footed Bowl	1880s	Museum Purchase	2000.156	Fig. 38.33
Footed Bowl	1880s	Museum Purchase with funds provided by Mr. and Mrs. Charles Fleischmann III	2005.57	Fig. 38.41
Footed Bowl*	circa 1890–1893	Gift of James Randolph Hillard, M.D. and Aingeal Grehan	2007.113; 2007.122	
Footed Bowl	late 19th century	Gift of James Randolph Hillard, M.D. and Aingeal Grehan	2007.188	
Fork	circa 1887	Gift of Dorothy Krug Newstedt	1975.266b	
Goblet	1860s	Museum Purchase with funds provided by Mr. and Mrs. Charles Fleischmann III	2005.49	Fig. E2.1
Goblet*	circa 1860	Gift of James Randolph Hillard, M.D. and Aingeal Grehan	2007.179; 2007.183	
Goblet*	circa 1870	Gift of James Randolph Hillard, M.D. and Aingeal Grehan	2007.176; 2007.177	
Goblet*	circa 1880	Gift of James Randolph Hillard, M.D. and Aingeal Grehan	2007.175; 2007.178a–d; 2007.180	
Ice Cream Server	1870s	Gift of James Randolph Hillard, M.D. and Aingeal Grehan	2007.145	Fig. 38.28
Ice Cream Spoons (2)	1870s	Gift of James Randolph Hillard, M.D. and Aingeal Grehan	2007.146a–b	Fig. 38.28
Jelly Server	circa 1885	Gift of James Randolph Hillard, M.D. and Aingeal Grehan	2007.148	
Knife	circa 1865	Gift of James Randolph Hillard, M.D. and Aingeal Grehan	2007.154	Fig. 38.19
Knife	1860s	Gift of James Randolph Hillard, M.D. and Aingeal Grehan	2007.157	Fig. 38.13
Knife	circa 1865	Gift of James Randolph Hillard, M.D. and Aingeal Grehan	2007.167	Fig. 38.15
Ladle	circa 1880s	Gift of Mrs. John L. Strubbe	1993.139	
Ladle	1880s	Gift of Edward J. Requardt	2003.268	Fig. 38.39
Ladle	1870s	Museum Purchase with funds provided by Mr. and Mrs. Charles Fleischmann III	2005.65	Fig. 38.23
Ladle	1860s	Gift of Mr. and Mrs. Charles Fleischmann III	2005.23	Fig. 38.16
Ladle*	circa 1885	Gift of James Randolph Hillard, M.D. and Aingeal Grehan	2007.127; 2007.130; 2007.138; 2007.141	
Ladle	1860s	Gift of James Randolph Hillard, M.D. and Aingeal Grehan	2007.131	Fig. 38.13
Ladle	1860s–1870s	Gift of James Randolph Hillard, M.D. and Aingeal Grehan	2007.132	
Ladle	circa 1870	Gift of James Randolph Hillard, M.D. and Aingeal Grehan	2007.133	Fig. 38.9
Ladle	circa 1870	Gift of James Randolph Hillard, M.D. and Aingeal Grehan	2007.134	
Ladle	circa 1870	Gift of James Randolph Hillard, M.D. and Aingeal Grehan	2007.135	Fig. 38.10
Ladle	circa 1865	Gift of James Randolph Hillard, M.D. and Aingeal Grehan	2007.136	Fig. 38.10
Ladle (Lily)	circa 1880s	Gift of James Randolph Hillard, M.D. and Aingeal Grehan	2007.139	Fig. 38.43
Ladle	circa 1880s	Gift of James Randolph Hillard, M.D. and Aingeal Grehan	2007.142	
Ladle	circa 1874	Gift of James Randolph Hillard, M.D. and Aingeal Grehan	2007.143	Fig. 38.23
Ladle	1860s	Gift of James Randolph Hillard, M.D. and Aingeal Grehan	2007.144	
Ladle (Duhme No. 3)	circa 1890	Gift in memory of Charles H. (Randy) Randolph, DDS, from his wife, children and grandchildren	2011.290	Fig. 38.44
Lettuce Fork	circa 1890	Gift of James Randolph Hillard, M.D. and Aingeal Grehan	2007.161	
Loving Cup	1889	Gift of James Randolph Hillard, M.D. and Aingeal Grehan	2007.214	
Mug	circa 1880	Gift of James Randolph Hillard, M.D. and Aingeal Grehan	2007.174	Fig. 38.5
Mug	circa 1887	Bequest of Edmund Kerper	1959.33	Fig. 38.5

* Multiple examples of this type of form by the same maker, and gifted by the same donor

Maker (when Cincinnati individual/firm was the retailer) or Double Mark				
Object	Date	Credit Line	Accession no.	Fig. no.

Duhme & Co. (continued)

Object	Date	Credit Line	Accession no.	Fig. no.
*Mug**	circa 1865	Museum Purchase with funds provided by Mr. and Mrs. Charles Fleischmann III	2005.55; 2005.71; 2005.72	
Mug	circa 1860	Gift of James Randolph Hillard, M.D. and Aingeal Grehan	2007.110	
Mug	circa 1881	Gift of James Randolph Hillard, M.D. and Aingeal Grehan	2007.111	Fig. 38.5
Mug	circa 1865	Gift of James Randolph Hillard, M.D. and Aingeal Grehan	2007.168	
Mug	1870s	Gift of James Randolph Hillard, M.D. and Aingeal Grehan	2007.171	Fig. 38.5
Oyster Serving Spoon	circa 1885	Gift of James Randolph Hillard, M.D. and Aingeal Grehan	2007.140	
Pastry Fork	1843–1893	Gift of John S. Conner	1910.358	
Pastry Server	1860s	Gift of James Randolph Hillard, M.D. and Aingeal Grehan	2007.155	Fig. 38.19
Pastry Server	circa 1875	Gift of James Randolph Hillard, M.D. and Aingeal Grehan	2007.166	Fig. 38.27
*Pastry Server**	circa 1885	Gift of James Randolph Hillard, M.D. and Aingeal Grehan	2007.152; 2007.153	
Pickle Caster	circa 1880	Gift of James Randolph Hillard, M.D. and Aingeal Grehan	2007.116a–c	
Pitcher	1860s	Museum Purchase with funds provided by Mr. and Mrs. Charles Fleischmann III	2005.50	
Pitcher	circa 1877	Gift of James Randolph Hillard, M.D. and Aingeal Grehan	2007.198	
Salad Fork	1843–1893	Given by Elizabeth M. and Annie W. Anderson in memory of their mother, Mrs. Buckner W. Anderson	1969.749	
Salad Spoon and Fork	circa 1880s	Gift of James Randolph Hillard, M.D. and Aingeal Grehan	2007.121a–b	Fig. 38.40
Salts (4)	circa 1875–1893	Museum Purchase with funds provided by Mr. and Mrs. Charles Fleischmann III	2005.58a–d	
Salts (2)	circa 1875–1893	Museum Purchase with funds provided by Mr. and Mrs. Charles Fleischmann III	2005.59a–b	
Salver	circa 1875–1893	Museum Purchase with funds provided by Mr. and Mrs. Charles Fleischmann III	2005.56	
Salver	circa 1875–1893	Gift of James Randolph Hillard, M.D. and Aingeal Grehan	2007.189	
Serving Fork	circa 1885	Gift of James Randolph Hillard, M.D. and Aingeal Grehan	2007.163	
Serving Knife	circa 1875	Gift of James Randolph Hillard, M.D. and Aingeal Grehan	2007.162	
Serving Spoon	1860s	Gift of Dorothy Krug Newstedt	1975.267	Fig. 38.13
*Serving Spoon**	1843–1893	Gift of Dr. Suzanne A. Beutler	1983.212; 1983.213	
Serving Spoon	circa 1870	Gift of Dr. Suzanne A. Beutler	1983.214	Fig. 38.9
Serving Spoon	1860s	Museum Purchase with funds provided by Mr. and Mrs. Charles Fleischmann III	2005.66	Fig. 38.16
Serving Spoon	circa 1885	Gift of James Randolph Hillard, M.D. and Aingeal Grehan	2007.128	
Serving Spoon	1860s	Gift of James Randolph Hillard, M.D. and Aingeal Grehan	2007.147	Fig. 38.13
Serving Spoon	1880s	Gift of James Randolph Hillard, M.D. and Aingeal Grehan	2007.150	Fig. 38.39
Serving Spoon	circa 1885	Gift of James Randolph Hillard, M.D. and Aingeal Grehan	2007.156	
Serving Spoon	circa 1885	Gift of James Randolph Hillard, M.D. and Aingeal Grehan	2007.160	
Snuff Box	circa 1882	Gift of the Estate of Margaret Mayberry Clark	1965.217	Fig. 38.35
Soup Spoon	circa 1870	Gift of Rose Wallace Kumler	1964.95	Fig. 38.9
Soup Spoons (6)*	1869–1893	Gift of Rose Wallace Kumler	1964.97; 1964.98; 1964.99; 1964.100	
Soup Spoons (5)	1843–1893	Gift of Mr. and Mrs. Charles Fleischmann III	2005.2a–e	
Souvenir Spoon	1892	Gift of Mrs. John H. Hall	1936.41	
Spike	1879–1880	Gift of the Trustees of the Southern Railroad	1884.309	
*Spoon**	1843–1893	Gift of Dr. Suzanne A. Beutler	1983.201; 1983.203; 1983.204; 1983.206	
Sugar Shaker	1880s	Musuem Purchase with funds provided by Mr. and Mrs. Charles Fleischmann III	2005.63a–b	Fig. 38.42
Tablespoons (3)	circa 1860	Gift of Doris Dupraz	1991.2.1–3	
Tea and Coffee Service	late 1870s–1880s	Gift of Dr. and Mrs. James L. Hecht	1984.198–202	Fig. 38.36
Tea and Coffee Service	circa 1890	Gift of James Randolph Hillard, M.D. and Aingeal Grehan	2007.123a–e	
Tea Cannister	circa 1890s	Gift of Alice Falck in memory of Dr. and Mrs. Samuel Rabkin	1986.1251	
Tea Pot	1870s	Gift of Dr. and Mrs. James L. Hecht	1984.198	
Tea Service	circa 1877	Gift of James Randolph Hillard, M.D. and Aingeal Grehan	2007.202a–g	
Tea Service with Presentation Case	1860s	Museum Purchase with funds provided by Mr. and Mrs. Charles Fleischmann III	2005.12a–d	Fig. 38.17
Teaspoon	1843–1893	Bequest of Fanny Bryce Lehmer	1936.784	
Teaspoon (Dresden)	circa 1890	Gift in memory of Charles H. (Randy) Randolph, DDS, from his wife, children and grandchildren	2011.289	Fig. 38.45
Teaspoons (6)	circa 1843–1893	Gift of Mr. and Mrs. Charles Fleischmann III	2005.1a–f	

* Multiple examples of this type of form by the same maker, and gifted by the same donor

Object	Date	Credit Line	Accession no.	Fig. no.
Duhme & Co. (continued)				
Tureen	1870s	Museum Purchase: John S. Connor Endowment, Mark P. Herschede Endowment, and Dwight J. Thomson Endowment	1999.207	Fig. 38.21
Tureen	1870s	Museum Purchase: Gloria W. Thomson Fund for the Decorative Arts	2013.74a–b	Fig. 38.22
Vanity Box	late 19th century	Gift of James Randolph Hillard, M.D. and Aingeal Grehan	2007.201	
Vase	1870s	Gift of James Randolph Hillard, M.D. and Aingeal Grehan	2007.120	Fig. 38.24
Waste Bowl	1870s	Gift of Dr. and Mrs. James L. Hecht	1984.201	
John Polhemus (NY, b. circa 1811, d. 1877)				
Ladle (Empire)	post 1857	Bequest of Charlotte H. Mackenzie	1936.507	
Whiting Mfg. Co. (MA, CT, RI, estab. 1866, closed 1926)				
Ladle (Hyperion)	circa 1888	Gift of James Randolph Hillard, M.D. and Aingeal Grehan	2007.137	
George W. Shiebler & Co. (NY, estab. 1876, closed 1915)				
Teaspoon (Flora)	circa 1889	Bequest of Fanny Bryce Lehmer	1936.777; 1936.779; 1936.780	
The Duhme Company (estab. 1893, closed 1897)				
Bowl	1893–1897	Museum Purchase with funds provided by Mr. and Mrs. Charles Fleischmann III	2005.61	
The Duhme Manufacturing Co. (estab. 1898, closed 1898)				
Funnel	1898	Gift of James Randolph Hillard, M.D. and Aingeal Grehan	2007.193	
Turkish Coffee Pot	1898	Museum Purchase	2000.157	Fig. 38.48
Henry H. Duhme (b. 1814, d. 1874)				
Knife	circa 1863	Museum Purchase: John S. Connor Fund	2011.8	Fig. 38.3
Nathan Hazen (b. 1809, d. 1851)				
Teaspoon	circa 1840–1851	Gift of Dr. Suzanne A. Beutler	1983.198	Fig. 46.1
Hazen & Collins (estab. 1843, closed 1847)				
Ewer	1843–1847	Museum Purchase with funds provided by Mr. and Mrs. Charles Fleischmann III	2005.74	Fig. 47.2
Spoon	1843–1847	Source Unknown	X1981.14	Fig. 47.1
The Frank Herschede Co. (estab. 1905, closed 1964)				
Beaker	circa 1906	Museum Purchase with funds provided by Mr. and Mrs. Charles Fleischmann III	2005.53	Fig. 49.3
George W. Shiebler & Co. (NY, estab. 1876, closed 1915)				
Loving Cup	1904	Gift of Phillip C. and Whitney Rowe Long	2002.118	Fig. 49.2
Edward H. Hill (b. 1812, d. 1878)				
Dessert Spoon	1840–1873	Given by Mimi Morgan in memory of her mother, Miriam Katherine Vandervort Morgan	2013.3	Fig. 50.2
Tablespoon	1840–1873	Given by Mimi Morgan in memory of her mother, Miriam Katherine Vandervort Morgan	2013.1	Fig. 50.2
Teaspoon	1840–1873	Given by Mimi Morgan in memory of her mother, Miriam Katherine Vandervort Morgan	2013.2	Fig. 50.2
Hughes & Dorland (estab. 1857, closed 1860)				
Teaspoon	1857–1860	Museum Purchase: John S. Conner Fund	2012.53	Fig. 53.1
E.E. Isbell & Co. (estab. 1875, closed circa 1895)				
Footed Bowl	1875–1895	Museum Purchase with funds provided by Mr. and Mrs. Charles Fleischmann III	2005.44	Fig. 57.3
Tablespoon	1875–1895	Gift of Louise Eastman Warrington	1975.75	Fig. 57.4
Teaspoon	circa 1888	Bequest of Fanny Bryce Lehmer	1936.781	
Teaspoon	1875–1895	Given by Elizabeth M. and Annie W. Anderson in memory of their mother, Mrs. Buckner W. Anderson	1969.751	Fig. 57.4
Gorham Mfg. Co. (RI, estab. 1831)				
Teaspoon	circa 1888	Bequest of Fanny Bryce Lehmer	1936.773	Fig. 57.4
Joseph G. Joseph (b. 1801, d. 1873)				
Chamberstick	1834–1846	Museum Purchase with funds provided by Mr. and Mrs. Charles Fleischmann III	2005.45	Fig. 59.1

* Multiple examples of this type of form by the same maker, and gifted by the same donor

Object	Date	Credit Line	Accession no.	Fig. no.
Luke Kent, Sr. (b. circa 1771, d. 1842), or Luke Kent, Jr. (b. 1812, d. 1895)				
Teaspoon	circa 1840–1860	Anonymous Gift	2011.29	Fig. 61.2
David Kinsey (b. 1819, d. 1874)				
Beaker	1861–1874	Gift of John S. Conner	1910.382	Fig. 64.4
Tea Service	1861–1874	Gift of Mr. and Mrs. Charles Fleischmann III	2009.143a–d	Fig. 64.3
Teaspoon	1861–1874	Museum Purchase: John. S. Conner Fund	2012.14	Fig. 64.5
E. & D. Kinsey (active 1844–1861)				
Dessert Fork	1844–1861	Given by Elizabeth M. and Annie W. Anderson in memory of their mother, Mrs. Buckner W. Anderson	1969.745	Fig. 66.15
Dessert Spoons (6)	1844–1861	Gift of Mr. C. Dudley Brown in memory of Lillian C. and Salmon Brown	1988.210.7–12	
Ladle	1844–1861	Given in memory of Virginia Mueller by the Altrusa Club Members, Her Sister and Friends	1976.322	
Ladle	1844–1861	Gift of Dr. Suzanne A. Beutler	1983.207	Fig. 66.7
Mug	1844–1861	Bequest of Virginia H. Irwin	1956.401	Fig. 66.5
Pitcher	circa 1856	Gift of James Randolph Hillard, M.D. and Aingeal Grehan	2007.194	
Salver	1849	Museum Purchase: Lee Cowan Group Art Purchase Fund	2003.158	Fig. 66.4
Salver	1844–1861	Museum Purchase with funds provided by Mr. and Mrs. Charles Fleischmann III	2005.46	
Sugar Shovel	1844–1861	Gift of John S. Conner	1910.192	Fig. 66.8
Tablespoons (6)	circa 1850s	Gift of Mr. C. Dudley Brown in memory of Lillian C. and Salmon Brown	1988.210.13–18	
Teapot	1844–1861	Gift of James Randolph Hillard, M.D. and Aingeal Grehan	2007.195	Fig. 66.12
Teaspoons (5)	1844–1861	Given by Elizabeth M. and Annie W. Anderson in memory of their mother, Mrs. Buckner W. Anderson	1969.740–744	Fig. 66.15
Teaspoons (6)	1844–1861	Gift of Mr. C. Dudley Brown in memory of Lillian C. and Salmon Brown	1988.210.1–6	
Teaspoon	1844–1861	Gift of Dr. Suzanne A. Beutler	1983.205	
Toast Rack	1844–1861	Gift of Mr. and Mrs. Charles Fleischmann III	2009.1	Fig. 66.13
George McDannold (KY, b. circa 1801)				
Beaker	circa 1845	Gift of Mr. and Mrs. Charles Fleischmann III	2005.24	
Grosjean & Woodward (NY, estab. 1840, closed 1862)				
Coffee Pot, Creamer, and Waste Bowl	1844–1861	Gift of Mr. and Mrs. Charles Fleischmann III	2007.5a–c	Fig. 66.11
"Good Samaritan" Pitcher	1844–1861	Museum Purchase	2000.158	Fig. 66.10
Sugar Bowl	1844–1861	Gift of Mr. and Mrs. Charles Fleischmann III	2005.22a–b	Fig. 66.11
Edward Kinsey (b. 1810, d. 1865)				
Beaker	1834–1844	Gift in memory of Mary Distler by her friends	1974.149	
Coffee Pot	1834–1844	Museum Purchase with funds provided by Mr. and Mrs. Charles Fleischmann III	2005.35	Fig. 67.8
Ewer	1834–1844	Museum Purchase	1907.194	Fig. 67.6
Sugar Bowl	1834–1844	Purchased with funds contributed by the Altrusa Club of Cincinnati in memory of Marcella Schwarb	1968.315	Fig. 67.9
Willey & Blaksley (late 1830s/1840s)				
Creamer	circa 1840	Museum Purchase with funds provided by Mr. and Mrs. Charles Fleischmann III	2005.47	Fig. 67.10
Kenton C. Kunkle (b. 1861, d. 1941)				
Compote	1937	Museum Purchase: John S. Connor Fund	2005.7	Fig. 70.1
McGrew & Beggs (estab. 1843, closed 1848)				
Tablespoon	1843–1848	Museum Purchase: John S. Conner Fund	2013.11	Fig. 77.1
Alexander McGrew (b. circa 1775, d. 1843)				
Teaspoons (9)	1817–1819	Museum Purchase	1962.109–117	Fig. 78.3
Teaspoon	1817–1819	Given by Elizabeth M. and Annie W. Anderson in memory of their mother, Mrs. Buckner W. Anderson	1969.750	
William Wilson McGrew (b. 1833, d. 1893)				
Cup	circa 1869	Gift of Jane Hageman	2000.159	Fig. 80.6
Pitcher	1860s	Museum Purchase	2000.160	Fig. 80.4
Tea and Coffee Service	circa 1856	Museum Purchase	2000.161a–f	Fig. 80.5

* Multiple examples of this type of form by the same maker, and gifted by the same donor

Maker/Retailer				
Maker (when Cincinnati individual/firm was the retailer) or Double Mark				
Object	Date	Credit Line	Accession no.	Fig. no.

William Wilson McGrew (continued)

Peter Krider (PA, b. 1821, d. 1895)				
Goblet	circa 1860	Gift of Mr. and Mrs. Charles Fleischmann III	2005.21	
Gorham Mfg. Co. (RI, estab. 1831)				
Salts (2)	1868	Museum Purchase with funds provided by Mr. and Mrs. Charles Fleischmann III	2005.52a–b	

Wilson McGrew (b. 1800, d. 1859)

Beaker	1836–1856	Museum Purchase with funds provided by Mr. and Mrs. Charles Fleischmann III	2005.51	Fig. 81.4
Butter Knives (2)	circa 1840–1856	Museum Purchase	1962.87–88	Fig. 81.1
Condiment Ladle	circa 1840–1856	Museum Purchase	1962.86	Fig. 81.1
Salt Spoon	1836–1856	Gift of John S. Conner	1910.178	
Salt Spoons (2)	circa 1840–1856	Museum Purchase	1962.84–85	Fig. 81.1
Tablespoons (5)	circa 1840–1856	Museum Purchase	1962.79–83	Fig. 81.1
Tablespoons (2)	1836–1856	Given by Elizabeth M. and Annie W. Anderson in memory of their mother, Mrs. Buckner W. Anderson	1969.735–736	Fig. 81.2
Teaspoon	1836–1856	Gift of John S. Conner	1910.145	
Teaspoons (20)	circa 1840–1856	Museum Purchase	1962.89–108	Fig. 81.1
John Polhemus (NY, b. circa 1811, d. 1877)				
Teaspoon (Honeysuckle)	1837–1856	Gift of Dr. Suzanne A. Beutler	1983.199	Fig. 81.3

Theodore McMurphey (b. 1814, d. 1848)

Teaspoon	1839–1842	Museum Purchase: John S. Conner Fund	2012.52	Fig. 83.1

W. & J.C. Michie (estab. 1867, closed 1875)

Teaspoon	1867–1875	Gift of Charles Cleves	2011.25	Fig. 87.2

Oskamp Jewelry Co. (estab. 1904, closed 1930)

Whiting Mfg. Co. (NY, estab. 1896, closed 1940)				
Tray	1896–1930	Gift of James Randolph Hillard, M.D. and Aingeal Grehan	2007.205	Fig. 95.4

Clemens Oskamp (b. 1822, d. 1887)

Goblet	circa 1882	Museum Purchase with funds provided by Mr. and Mrs. Charles Fleischmann III	2005.34	Fig. 96.7
Pitcher	circa 1882	Museum Purchase with funds provided by Mr. and Mrs. Charles Fleischmann III	2005.33	Fig. 96.6

Owen & Carley (estab. 1844, closed 1846)

Tablespoon	1844–1846	Museum Purchase: John S. Connor Fund	2012.25	Fig. 100.1

John Owen (active 1836–1853)

Condiment Ladle	circa 1840–1853	Gift of John S. Conner	1910.179	Fig. 103.2

Palmer & Owen (estab. 1850, closed 1859)

Spoons (5)	1850–1859	Museum Purchase	1962.74–78	Fig. 107.1

A. & J. Plaut (estab. 1878, closed circa 1933

Coffee Spoon	1878–circa 1910	Gift of John S. Conner	1910.212	
Gorham Mfg. Co. (RI, estab. 1831)				
Souvenir Spoon	1891–circa 1910	Gift of Michele Sandler	2003.21	Fig. 112.2

Philip Price (active 1804–1836)

Teaspoon	1804–1836	Gift of Mary Sering Kemper in memory of her Great-Grandfather, James Kemper	1924.257	Fig. 114.1

James F. Rhodes (b. 1822, d. 1907) or Thomas F. Rhodes (b. 1808, d. 1878)

Dessert Spoon	circa 1840	Gift of Elizabeth Bushner Shepard	1969.100	Fig. 119.2
Teaspoon	circa 1840	Gift of Elizabeth Bushner Shepard	1969.101	Fig. 119.2

Scovil & Co. (estab. 1832, closed 1837)

Beaker	1830s	Museum Purchase: John S. Conner Fund	2009.158	Fig. 122.1

Scovil, Willey & Co. (estab. by 1836, closed 1838)

Beaker	1836–1838	Gift of Mr. and Mrs. Charles Fleischmann III	2008.44	Fig. 125.1
Teaspoons (3)	1836–1838	Given by Elizabeth M. and Annie W. Anderson in memory of their mother, Mrs. Buckner W. Anderson	1969.746–748	Fig. 125.2

* Multiple examples of this type of form by the same maker, and gifted by the same donor

Maker (when Cincinnati individual/firm was the retailer) or Double Mark				
Object	Date	Credit Line	Accession no.	Fig. no.

Seymour & Williston (estab. 1816, closed 1820)

Salt Spoons (2)	1816–1820	Gift of Mary Dandridge	1928.38; 1928.39	Fig. 126.1

Harry R. Smith & Co. (estab. 1864, closed 1901)

Ladle	circa 1870	Gift of Mr. and Mrs. Charles Fleischmann III	2005.18	Fig. 131.2

Robert Sturm (b. 1874, d. 1964)

Candlesticks (2)	1890–1930s	Museum Purchase: Decorative Arts Society Fund	2012.16a–b	Fig. 134.11
Compotes (2)	circa 1925	Gift of James Randolph Hillard, M.D. and Aingeal Grehan	2007.212a–b	
Footed Bowl	1890–1930s	Gift of James Randolph Hillard, M.D. and Aingeal Grehan	2007.204	
Footed Bowls (2)	1890–1930s	Gift of James Randolph Hillard, M.D. and Aingeal Grehan	2007.203a–b	Fig. 134.6
Footed Bowls (2)	1890–1930s	Gift of James Randolph Hillard, M.D. and Aingeal Grehan	2007.209a–b	
Footed Salvers (2)	1890–1930s	Gift of James Randolph Hillard, M.D. and Aingeal Grehan	2007.210a–b	Fig. 134.12
Goblets (12)	1890–1930s	Gift of James Randolph Hillard, M.D. and Aingeal Grehan	2007.208a–l	Fig. 134.9
Plates (12)	1890–1930s	Gift of James Randolph Hillard, M.D. and Aingeal Grehan	2007.207a–l	Fig. 134.9
Platter	1890–1930s	Gift of James Randolph Hillard, M.D. and Aingeal Grehan	2007.206	
Platter	1890–1930s	Museum Purchase with funds provided by Mr. and Mrs. Charles Fleischmann III	2010.14	Fig. 134.9
Sauce Boat	1890–1930s	Museum Purchase with funds provided by Mr. and Mrs. Charles Fleischmann III	2010.13	Fig. 134.7
Tazza	1890–1930s	Gift of James Randolph Hillard, M.D. and Aingeal Grehan	2007.112	
Tazza	1890–1930s	Gift of James Randolph Hillard, M.D. and Aingeal Grehan	2007.213a	
Tazzas (2)	1890–1930s	Gift of James Randolph Hillard, M.D. and Aingeal Grehan	2007.117a–b	Fig. 134.14
Tazzas (2)	1890–1930s	Gift of Doctors James and Betty Sutherland	2001.152a–b	Fig. 134.4

Tressel Co. (estab. 1925, closed 1980s)

Pitcher (copper)	1925–1960	Gift of Mr. and Mrs. Charles Fleischmann III	2008.46	Fig. 140.2

Isaac Van Nuys (b. 1765, d. 1848)

Teaspoon	1795–circa 1807	Gift of Dr. and Mrs. James S. Widder	2002.9	Fig. 142.2

Joseph S. Voss & Son (estab. 1880, closed 1925)

Teaspoon	1881–1899	Museum Purchase: John S. Conner Fund	2012.12	Fig. 144.2

Julius Voss (b. 1825, d. 1887)

Sugar Spoon	1860–1887	Gift of Mr. and Mrs. Charles Fleischmann III	2005.17	Fig. 145.1

Willey & Blaksley (late 1830s/1840s)

Ladle	circa 1840	Gift of Dr. Michael Sze	2002.80	Fig. 146.1
Edward Kinsey (b. 1810, d. 1865)				
Creamer	circa 1840	Museum Purchase with funds provided by Mr. and Mrs. Charles Fleischmann III	2005.47	Fig. 67.10

Adolph Witt (b. 1832, d. 1914)

Tablespoon	1860–1887	Museum Purchase: John S. Conner Fund	2013.10	Fig. 151.1

Woodruff & Deterly (estab. 1817, closed 1821)

Creamer	1817–1821	Museum Purchase with funds provided by Mr. and Mrs. Charles Fleischmann III	2005.48	Fig. 152.1
Teaspoons (2)	1817–1821	Given by Elizabeth M. and Annie W. Anderson in memory of their mother, Mrs. Buckner W. Anderson	1969.737–738	Fig. 152.2

Woodruff & White (estab. 1827, closed 1834)

Spoons (2)	1827–1834	Gift of John S. Conner	1910.216; 1910.219	Fig. 153.2

---

* Multiple examples of this type of form by the same maker, and gifted by the same donor

SELECTED BIBLIOGRAPHY

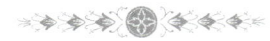

Manuscript Collections

Baker Library, Harvard Business School
    R.G. Dun & Company credit report volumes, 1840–1895
Cincinnati Historical Society
    Prices current files
    Torrence papers
    John J. Rowe Collection
Mary R. Schiff Library and Archives, Cincinnati Art Museum
    Jane Sikes Hageman papers
    Samuel Best, Diary
    Robert Sturm collection
University of Cincinnati Library, Special Collections
    Ohio Mechanics' Institute Collection

Newspapers

Centinel [*sic*] *of the North-Western Territory*, 1793–1796
Cincinnati Advertiser and Journal, 1818–1840
Cincinnati Commercial, 1865–1883, later the *Commercial Gazette*, 1883
Cist's Weekly Advertiser, 1847–1853
Daily Cincinnati Commercial, 1846–1854, later the *Cincinnati Commercial*, 1865–1883
Daily Cincinnati Gazette, 1827–1857, later the *Cincinnati Daily Gazette*, 1857–1883
Liberty Hall, 1804–1815, later *Liberty Hall and Cincinnati Gazette*, 1815–1857
The Cincinnati Enquirer, 1841– (also titled during its run as *The Daily Cincinnati Enquirer*, *The Cincinnati Daily Enquirer*)
The New York Times, 1851–
Times-Star, 1887–1893, later the *Cincinnati Times Star*, 1893–1958
Western Spy and Hamilton Gazette, 1799–1805, later *Western Spy and Miami Gazette*, 1805–1810

Journals and Periodical Articles

Bulletin of the Historical and Philosophical Society of Ohio, 1943–1963
    Lockett, Anne Hoge. "Cincinnati Clockmakers, 1800–1825." 9, no. 2 (April 1, 1953): 107.
Cincinnati Historical Society Bulletin, 1964–1982
Jewelers' Keystone, 1869–1873, later *The Jewelers' Circular and Horological Review*, 1873–1912 (following the merger of the *American Horological Journal*, est. 1869, and *The Jewelers' Circular*, est. 1870)
Jeweler, Silversmith and Watchmaker, 1876–1877
Ohio Valley History, 2001–2006
Queen City Heritage, 1983–1999
Quarterly Publication of the Historical and Philosophical Society of Ohio, 1906–1923
Scientific American
    "The Manufacture of Silverware." 36, no. 19 (12 May 1877): 290–91.
    "American Industries, No. 22. The Manufacture of Silver-Plated Ware." 41, no. 19 (8 November 1879): 296.
Silver Magazine
    Hillard, James Randolph, M.D., Benjamin Randolph, John Roger Newstedt, M.D., and Charles Knighton. "Duhme & Company of Cincinnati, Part I: New Insights into the Manufacturer and Its Flatware." (September/October 1997): 20.
    — "Duhme & Company of Cincinnati, Part II, New Insights into the Manufacturer and Its Hollowware." (November/December 1997): 52.
The Magazine Antiques
    Sikes, Jane. "The Best Family of Silversmiths." (July 1974).

Directories

Cincinnati City Directory. 1819, 1825, 1829, 1831, 1834, 1836/37, 1839/40, 1842, 1843, 1844, 1846, 1848/49, 1849/50, 1850/51, 1851/52, 1853, 1855 through 1940. (The city's directories were not published annually until after 1854. There was no 1854 edition. Titles and publishers of these directories often differed from year to year. Later directories were consulted as needed.)

Covington and Newport Directory, 1902 through 1920

W.W. Reilly & Co.'s Ohio State Business Directory . . . for 1853–1854. Cincinnati: Morgan & Overend, 1853.

Lyford, W.G. *Western Address Directory.* Baltimore: Printed by J. Robinson, 1837.

Government Publications and Other Records

Federal Census Records, 1820–1940

Federal Non-Population Census Schedules, 1850, 1870, 1880

Hamilton County Probate Records: Marriage Books; Will Books; Estate Records, and Guardianship Records

Records of the US Patents and Trademark Office

Spring Grove Cemetery Records

Jewish Cemeteries of Cincinnati Records

Cincinnati Birth and Death Records 1865–1912, University of Cincinnati

Annual Reports

Cincinnati Board of Trade and Transportation. *Annual and Statistical Report of the Cincinnati Board of Trade and Transportation,* 1870–1884.

Cincinnati Chamber of Commerce and Merchants' Exchange. *Annual Report of the Chamber of Commerce and Merchant's Exchange,* 1849–1917.

Cincinnati Industrial Exposition. *Annual Report of the General Committee of the Cincinnati Industrial Exposition,* 1870–1888.

Contemporary Published Works

A History of the Manufactures of Cincinnati. Cincinnati: J.D. Campbell, 1870.

Austerlitz, E.H. *Cincinnati, from 1800 to 1875, A Condensed History of Cincinnati Combined with Exposition Guide for 1875, Fully Illustrated, together with a description of pictures and works of art, exhibited at the Cincinnati Industrial Exposition, 1875.* Cincinnati: Bloch & Co., 1875.

Cist, Charles. *Cincinnati in 1841: Its Early Annals and Future Prospects.* Cincinnati: E. Morgan, 1841.

— *The Cincinnati Miscellany, or Antiquities of the West: And Pioneer History and General and Local Statistics.* 2 vols. Cincinnati: Caleb Clarke, 1845–1846.

— *Sketches and Statistics of Cincinnati in 1851.* Cincinnati: Wm. H. Moore & Co., 1851.

— *Sketches and Statistics of Cincinnati in 1859.* Cincinnati: Wm. H. Moore & Co., 1859.

Deterly, Jacob. *"Remarks" of Jacob Deterly: diary from 1819 to 1848; life in southern Ohio: Cincinnati, Marietta, Athens.* Transcribed and indexed by Madge Hubbard and Opal Saffell. Seattle: Northwest Lineage Researcher, 1972.

Drake, Benjamin and E.D. Mansfield. *Cincinnati in 1826.* Cincinnati: Morgan, Lodge and Fisher, 1827.

Drake, Daniel. *Natural and Statistical View, or Picture of Cincinnati and Miami Country.* Cincinnati: Looker & Wallace, 1815.

Engelhardt, George W. *Cincinnati, The Queen City.* Cincinnati: George W. Engelhardt Co., 1901.

Ford, Henry A., and Mrs. Kate B. Ford. *History of Cincinnati, Ohio.* Cleveland: L.A. Williams, 1881.

Goss, Reverend Charles F. *Cincinnati: The Queen City, 1788–1912.* 4 vols. Cincinnati: The S.J. Clarke Publishing Co., 1912.

Greve, Charles. *Centennial History of Cincinnati and Its Representative Citizens.* 2 vols. Chicago: Biographical Publishing Co., 1904.

History of Cincinnati and Hamilton County, Ohio. Cincinnati: S.B. Nelson & Co., 1894.

Joblin, M. *Cincinnati Past and Present. . . .* Cincinnati: Elm Street Printing Co., 1872.

Kenny, D.J. *Illustrated Cincinnati: A Pictorial Handbook.* Cincinnati: G.E. Stevens, 1875.

— *Cincinnati Illustrated: a Pictorial Guide to Cincinnati and the Suburbs.* Cincinnati: Robert Clarke & Co., 1879.

Leading Manufacturers and Merchants of Cincinnati and Environs. Cincinnati: International Publishing Company, 1886.

Leonard, John W. *The Centennial Review of Cincinnati: One Hundred Years of Progress in Commerce, Manufacturing, the Professions and in Social and Municipal Life.* Cincinnati: J.M. Elstner, 1888.

Marquis, Albert N., ed. *The Industries of Cincinnati. The advantages, resources, facilities and commercial relations of Cincinnati as a center of trade and manufacture; a brief review of the past and present conditions and a delineation of representative industrial and commercial establishments of the city.* Cincinnati: A.N. Marquis, 1883.

Maxwell, Sidney D. *The Suburbs of Cincinnati: Sketches.* Cincinnati: G.E. Stevens, 1870.

— *The Manufacturers of Cincinnati. . . .* Cincinnati: R. Clarke & Company, 1878.

Robson, Charles, comp. *Biographical Encyclopedia of Ohio of the Nineteenth Century.* Cincinnati: Galaxy Publishing Co., 1876.

Stevens, George E. *The Queen City in 1869.* Cincinnati: George S. Blanchard & Co., 1869.

Secondary Sources

Aaron, Daniel. *Cincinnati, Queen City of the West 1819–1838.* Columbus: Ohio State University Press, 1992.

Averdick, Michael R. *A Directory of Silversmiths, Jewelers, Watch and Clock Makers and Related Trades of Covington and Newport, Kentucky & Vicinity 1833–1900.* Covington, KY: 829 Willard Street Press, 2002.

Beckman, Elizabeth. *An In-depth Study of the Cincinnati Silversmiths, Jewelers, Watch and Clockmakers Through 1850 Also Listing the More Prominent Men in These Trades from 1851 until 1900.* Cincinnati: B.B. & Co., 1975.

Boultinghouse, Marquis. *Silversmiths, Jewelers, Watch and Clock Makers of Kentucky, 1785–1900.* Lexington, KY: M. Boultinghouse, 1980.

Carpenter, Charles H. *Gorham Silver, 1831–1981*. New York: Dodd, Mead & Co., 1982.

Carpenter, Charles H., with Mary Grace Carpenter. *Tiffany Silver*. New York: Dodd, Mead & Co., 1978.

Cummins, Virginia Raymond, comp. *Hamilton County, Ohio Court and other Records*. 3 vols. Cincinnati: General Printing Co., 1966-1969.

Cutten, George Barton. *The Silversmiths, Watchmakers and Jewelers of The State of New York Outside of New York City*. New York: privately printed, 1939.

— *The Silversmiths of Virginia*. Richmond, VA: The Dietz Press Inc., 1952.

Ensko, Stephen G.C. *American Silversmiths and their Marks*. New York: Dover Publications, 1983.

Fennimore, Donald. *Delaware Silver: The Col. Kenneth P. and Regina I. Brown Collection*. Dover, DE: Sewel C. Biggs Museum of American Art, 2008.

Gibbs, James W. *Buckeye Horology: A Review of Ohio Clock and Watch Makers*. Columbia, PA: The Art Crafters Printing Co., 1971.

Goldsborough, Jennifer Faulds. *Silver in Maryland*. Baltimore: Museum and Library of Maryland History, Maryland Historical Society, 1983.

Glazer, Walter Stix. *Cincinnati: 1840, The Social and Functional Organization of an Urban Community during the Pre-Civil War Period*. Columbus: Ohio State University Press, 1999.

Hagan, Tere. *Sterling Flatware: An Identification and Value Guide*. Gas City, IN: L-W Book Sales, 1999.

Hollan, Catherine B. *Virginia Silversmiths, Jewelers, Watch- and Clockmakers, 1607–1860: Their Lives and Marks*. McLean, VA: Hollan Press, 2010.

Kauffman, Henry J. *The Colonial Silversmith*. Mendham, NJ: Astragal Press, 1995.

Knittle, Rhea Mansfield. *Early Ohio Silversmiths and Pewterers 1787–1847*. Cleveland: The Calvert-Hatch Co., 1943.

Mack, Norman. *Missouri's Silver Age: Silversmiths of the 1800s*. Carbondale, IL: Southern Illinois University Press, 2005.

McGrew, John R. *Manufacturers' Marks on American Coin Silver*. Hanover, PA: Argyros Publications, 2004.

Ohio Federal Writers' Project. *They Built A City: 150 Years of Industrial Cincinnati*. Cincinnati: Cincinnati Post, 1938.

Rainwater, Dorothy T. *Encyclopedia of American Silver Manufacturers*. 3rd ed. West Chester, PA: Schiffer Publishing Ltd., 1986.

Redfearn, Jerome. *Indiana Silversmiths, Clock Makers, and Watchmakers, 1779–1900*. Georgetown, KY: Americana Publications, 1984.

Ross, Steven J. *Workers on the Edge: Work, Leisure, and Politics in Industrializing Cincinnati, 1788–1890*. New York: Columbia University Press, 1985.

Soeffing, D. Albert. *Silver Medallion Flatware*. New York: New Books Inc., 1988.

Von Khrum, Paul. *Silversmiths of New York City*. New York: Von Khrum, 1978.

Venable, Charles. *Silver in America 1840–1940: A Century of Splendor*. New York: Harry N. Abrams Inc., 1995.

Wade, Richard. *The Urban Frontier: The Rise of Western Cities, 1790–1830*. Urbana and Chicago: University of Illinois Press, 1996.

Ward, Barbara McLean, and Gerald W.R. Ward, eds. *Silver in American Life*. New York: American Federation of the Arts, 1979.

Ward, David, Katherine S. Howe, and Michael K. Brown. *Marks of Achievement: Four Centuries of American Presentation Silver*. New York: Harry N. Abrams for the Museum of Fine Arts, Houston, 1987.

Waters, Deborah Dependahl. "'The Workmanship of an American Artist': Philadelphia's Precious Metals Trades and Crafts, 1788-1832." PhD diss., University of Delaware, 1981.

Unpublished Manuscripts and Internet Sources

Newstedt, John Roger, and Charles von D. Knighton. "A Cincinnati Saga: The McNicoll-Duhme Connection." Unpublished manuscript, 1996. Located in Duhme & Co. research files, Cincinnati Art Museum.

Voss, Wm. Erik. *American Silversmiths*. http://freepages.genealogy.rootsweb.com/~silversmiths/makers/silversmiths

Ancestry.com online databases: census and voter records; birth, marriage, death records; public member family trees; military records; immigration and travel records.

Familysearch.org

www.findagrave.com

INDEX

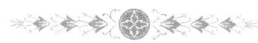